HALSBURY'S
Laws of England

FOURTH EDITION
1996 REISSUE

Volume 7(1)

HALSBURY'S

Laws of England

FOURTH EDITION
1996 REISSUE

LORD HAILSHAM OF ST. MARYLEBONE

Lord High Chancellor of Great Britain
1970–74 and 1979–87

Volume 7(1)

BUTTERWORTHS

LONDON   1996

UNITED KINGDOM	Butterworths, a Division of Reed Elsevier (UK) Ltd Halsbury House, 35 Chancery Lane, **London** WC2A 1EL and 4 Hill Street, **Edinburgh** EH2 3JZ
AUSTRALIA	Butterworths, **Sydney, Melbourne, Brisbane, Adelaide, Perth, Canberra** and **Hobart**
CANADA	Butterworths Canada Ltd, **Toronto** and **Vancouver**
HONG KONG	Butterworths Asia, **Hong Kong**
IRELAND	Butterworth (Ireland) Ltd, **Dublin**
MALAYSIA	Malayan Law Journal Sdn Bhd, **Kuala Lumpur**
NEW ZEALAND	Butterworths of New Zealand Ltd, **Wellington** and **Auckland**
SINGAPORE	Butterworths Asia, **Singapore**
SOUTH AFRICA	Butterworth Publishers (Pty) Ltd, **Durban**
USA	Michie, **Charlottesville**, Virginia

FIRST EDITION

Published in 31 volumes between 1907 and 1917 under the Editorship of the Rt. Hon. the Earl of Halsbury, Lord High Chancellor of Great Britain, 1885–86, 1886–92 and 1895–1905

SECOND EDITION

Published in 37 volumes between 1931 and 1942 under the Editorship of the Rt. Hon. the Viscount Hailsham, Lord High Chancellor of Great Britain, 1928–29 and 1935–38

THIRD EDITION

Published in 43 volumes between 1952 and 1964 under the Editorship of the Rt. Hon. the Viscount Simonds, Lord High Chancellor of Great Britain, 1951–54

FOURTH EDITION

Published in 56 volumes between 1973 and 1987 under the Editorship of the Rt. Hon. Lord Hailsham of St. Marylebone, Lord High Chancellor of Great Britain, 1970–74 and 1979–87

ISBN (complete set, standard binding) 0 406 03400 1
(this volume, standard binding) 0 406 04575 5

Typeset by Thomson Litho Ltd, East Kilbride, Scotland
Printed and bound in Great Britain by
Clays Ltd, St Ives plc

Editor

GORDON HOBBS, B.A.
A SOLICITOR OF THE SUPREME COURT

Managing Editor (Commissioning)

DEBORAH SAUNDERS, B.A.
OF GRAY'S INN, BARRISTER

Sub-editor

HELEN HALVEY, LL.B.

Administrative Manager

SARAH L. HORNSBY, Dip. Pub.

Indexer

B. BURKE, B.Sc.

Publisher

JAMES BOWMAN, LL.B.
A SOLICITOR OF THE SUPREME COURT

The Title Companies in Volume 7(I) has been contributed by:

T. PETER E. CURRY

of The Middle Temple and Lincoln's Inn,
one of Her Majesty's Counsel; a Bencher of The Middle Temple

BRENDA M. HANNIGAN, M.A., LL.M.,

a Solicitor of the Supreme Court of Ireland
Senior Lecturer in Law, University of Southampton

The law stated in this volume is in general that in force on 1 March 1996, although subsequent changes have been included wherever possible.

TABLE OF CONTENTS

REFERENCES AND ABBREVIATIONS

ACT	Australian Capital Territory
A-G	Attorney General
Adv-Gen	Advocate General
affd	affirmed
affg	affirming
Alta	Alberta
App	Appendix
art	article
Aust	Australia
B	Baron
BC	British Columbia
C	Command Paper (of a series published before 1900)
c	chapter number of an Act
CA	Court of Appeal
CAC	Central Arbitration Committee
CA in Ch	Court of Appeal in Chancery
CB	Chief Baron
CCA	Court of Criminal Appeal
CC Fees Order 1982	County Court Fees Order 1982 (SI 1982/1706) as subsequently amended (see the current County Court Practice)
CCR	County Court Rules 1981 (SI 1981/1687) as subsequently amended (see the current County Court Practice)
CCR	Court for Crown Cases Reserved
C-MAC	Courts-Martial Appeal Court
CO	Crown Office
COD	Crown Office Digest
Can	Canada
Cd	Command Paper (of the series published 1900–18)
Cf	compare
ch	chapter
cl	clause
Cm	Command Paper (of the series published 1986 to date)
Cmd	Command Paper (of the series published 1919–56)
Cmnd	Command Paper (of the series published 1956–86)
Comr	Commissioner
Corpn	Corporation
Court Forms (2nd Edn)	Atkin's Encyclopaedia of Court Forms in Civil Proceedings, 2nd Edn. See note 2, p 13 post

Court Funds Rules 1987	Court Funds Rules 1987 (SI 1987/821) as subsequently amended (see the current Supreme Court Practice and County Court Practice)
DC	Divisional Court
DPP	Director of Public Prosecutions
EAT	Employment Appeal Tribunal
EC	European Community
ECJ	Court of Justice of the European Community
ECSC	European Coal and Steel Community
EEC	European Economic Community
Edn	Edition
EFTA	European Free Trade Association
Euratom	European Atomic Energy Community
Ex Ch	Court of Exchequer Chamber
ex p	ex parte
Fed	Federal
Forms & Precedents (5th Edn)	Encyclopaedia of Forms and Precedents other than Court Forms, 5th Edn. See note 2, p *13* post
GLC	Greater London Council
HC	High Court
HL	House of Lords
H of C	House of Commons
IRC	Inland Revenue Commissioners
Ir	Ireland
J	Justice
JA	Judge of Appeal
JC	Justiciary Cases
Kan	Kansas
LA	Lord Advocate
LC	Lord Chancellor
LCC	London County Council
LCJ	Lord Chief Justice
LJ	Lord Justice of Appeal
LoN	League of Nations
MR	Master of the Rolls
Man	Manitoba
n	note
NB	New Brunswick
NI	Northern Ireland
NS	Nova Scotia
NSW	New South Wales
NZ	New Zealand
Nfld	Newfoundland
OJ	The Official Journal of the European Community published by the Office for Official Publications of the European Community
Ont	Ontario

P	President
PC	Judicial Committee of the Privy Council
PEI	Prince Edward Island
QBD	Queen's Bench Division of the High Court
Qld	Queensland
Que	Quebec
r	rule
RDC	Rural District Council
RPC	Restrictive Practices Court
RSC	Rules of the Supreme Court 1965 (SI 1965/1776) as subsequently amended (see the current Supreme Court Practice)
reg	regulation
Res	Resolution
revsd	reversed
Rly	Railway
s	section
SA	South Africa
S Aust	South Australia
SC	Supreme Court
SC Fees Order 1980	Supreme Court Fees Order 1980 (SI 1980/821) as subsequently amended (see the current Supreme Court Practice)
SI	Statutory Instruments published by authority
SR & O	Statutory Rules and Orders published by authority
SR & O Rev 1904	Revised Edition comprising all Public and General Statutory Rules and Orders in force on 31 December 1903
SR & O Rev 1948	Revised Edition comprising all Public and General Statutory Rules and Orders and Statutory Instruments in force on 31 December 1948
SRNI	Statutory Rules of Northern Ireland
Sask	Saskatchewan
Sch	Schedule
Sess	Session
TS	Treaty Series
Tas	Tasmania
UDC	Urban District Council
UN	United Nations
V-C	Vice-Chancellor
Vict	Victoria
W Aust	Western Australia

NOTE 1. A general list of the abbreviations of law reports and other sources used in this work can be found in vol 54 (Reissue) Consolidated Table of Cases at p *v* et seq.

NOTE 2. Where references are made to other publications, the volume number precedes and the page number follows the name of the publication; eg the reference '12 Forms & Precedents (5th Edn) 44' refers to volume 12 of the Encyclopaedia of Forms and Precedents, page 44.

NOTE 3. An English statute is cited by short title or, where there is no short title, by regnal year and chapter number together with the name by which it is commonly known or a description of its subject matter and date. In the case of a foreign statute, the mode of citation generally follows the style of citation in use in the country concerned with the addition, where necessary, of the name of the country in parentheses.

NOTE 4. A statutory instrument is cited by short title, if any, followed by the year and number, or, if unnumbered, the date.

TABLE OF STATUTES

This Table relates only to statutes cited in Volume 7(1). A consolidated Table for Volumes 7(1) and 7(2) appears in Volume 7(2); and a consolidated Table for Volumes 7(1), 7(2) and 7(3) appears in Volume 7(3).

TABLE OF STATUTORY INSTRUMENTS

This Table relates only to statutory instruments cited in Volume 7(1). A consolidated Table for Volumes 7(1) and 7(2) appears in Volume 7(2); and a consolidated Table for Volumes 7(1), 7(2) and 7(3) appears in Volume 7(3).

TABLE OF
EUROPEAN COMMUNITY
LEGISLATION

This Table relates only to legislation cited in volume 7(1). A consolidated Table for Volumes 7(1) and 7(2) appears in Volume (2); and a consolidated Table for volumes 7(1), 7(2) and 7(3) appears in Volume 7(3).

TABLE OF CASES

This Table relates only to cases cited in Volume 7(1). A consolidated Table for Volumes 7(1) and 7(2) appears in Volume 7(2); and a consolidated Table for Volumes 7(1), 7(2) and 7(3) appears in Volume 7(3).

PARA

A

PARA

B

PARA

C

PARA

G

PARA

H

K

PARA

L

PARA

S

COMPANIES

3. COMPANIES REGULATED BY THE COMPANIES CLAUSES ACTS

Volume 7(3)

6. CORPORATE INSOLVENCY

1. INTRODUCTION

(1) IN GENERAL

1. Nature of company. The word 'company' imports an association of a number of individuals[1] formed for some common purpose[2]. Such an association may be either incorporated (that is, a body corporate with perpetual succession[3]) or unincorporated[4]. An incorporated company is a legal person separate and distinct from the individual members of the company[5], whereas an unincorporated company has no such separate existence and it is not in law an entity distinguishable from its members[6].

There are many other bodies corporate which, although they may largely or partially engage in trading or comparable activities, are not commonly described as companies. These fall broadly into three categories:

(1) those incorporated pursuant to some general Act of Parliament permitting incorporation to be effected by any body of persons which fulfils certain specified conditions: of these the chief examples are building societies[7] and industrial and provident societies[8];

(2) those known as public corporations: these are each the creation of a royal charter or, more commonly, a special Act of Parliament which defines the objects, constitution and powers of the corporation; they are created to fulfil in each case some special social or economic purpose: examples include the British Broadcasting Corporation[9]; the Radio Authority[10]; the Independent Television Commission[11]; London Regional Transport[12]; the Coal Authority[13]; and the Port of London Authority[14]; and

(3) insurance companies, which, for this purpose, includes any person or body of persons (whether incorporated or not) carrying on insurance business[15], the conduct of whose business is regulated by the provisions of the Insurance Companies Act 1982[16].

1 The word usually involves two ideas: (1) that the members of the association are so numerous that it cannot aptly be described as a firm or partnership; and (2) that a member may transfer his interest in the association without the consent of all the other members: see *Re Stanley, Tennant v Stanley* [1906] 1 Ch 131 at 134 per Buckley J. See also *Smith v Anderson* (1880) 15 ChD 247 at 273, CA per James LJ.

A single individual may, if he wishes, carry on business under the style of 'Such and such Company', but he does not thereby become a 'company' in any sense of the word. However, a person who is not a public company may not use 'plc'; nor may a person trade or carry on business under a name or title of which 'limited' is the last word unless duly incorporated with limited liability: see para 162 post.

2 The purpose for which they have joined together must be of a more or less permanent character, though in common, as distinguished from legal, parlance the word 'company' is used to describe a number of individuals associated or assembled for a single occasion.

3 A company need no longer have a common seal: see the Companies Act 1985 s 36A(3) (as added) and para 1130 post.

4 *Re St James' Club* (1852) 2 De GM & G 383 at 389; *Re Griffith, Carr v Griffith* (1879) 12 ChD 655.

5 See para 92 post.

6 A company which is neither a corporation nor a partnership is a thing unknown to the common law: see Lindley's Law of Companies (6th Edn) 2; *Macintyre v Connell* (1851) 1 Sim NS 225 at 233.

7 See BUILDING SOCIETIES.

8 See INDUSTRIAL AND PROVIDENT SOCIETIES. Such societies are normally described as 'limited': see the Industrial and Provident Societies Act 1965 s 5(2) and INDUSTRIAL AND PROVIDENT SOCIETIES vol 24 (Reissue) para 43.

9 The British Broadcasting Corporation is a body incorporated by royal charter: see TELECOMMUNICATIONS vol 45 para 517.

10 See the Broadcasting Act 1990 s 83, Sch 8 and TELECOMMUNICATIONS.

11 See ibid s 1, Sch 1 and TELECOMMUNICATIONS.

12 See the London Regional Transport Act 1984 s 1, Sch 1 and LONDON GOVERNMENT.
13 See the Coal Industry Act 1994 s 1, Sch 1 and MINES.
14 See PORTS AND HARBOURS vol 36 para 457.
15 See the Insurance Companies Act 1982 s 96(1) and INSURANCE vol 25 (Reissue) para 15 note 3.
16 See INSURANCE vol 25 (Reissue) para 15.

2. Scope of the title. This title deals with the law relating to:
(1) companies regulated by the Companies Act 1985 and subsequent legislation[1];
(2) companies regulated by the Companies Clauses Acts[2];
(3) unregistered companies so far as they are affected by the provisions of the Companies Act 1985[3];
(4) companies formed outside England and Wales[4]; and
(5) corporate insolvency[5].

1 See para 7 et seq post. As to the subsequent legislation see para 20 post.
2 See para 1599 et seq post.
3 See para 1758 et seq post.
4 See para 1771 et seq post.
5 See para 2001 et seq post.

3. Arrangement of the title. Companies incorporated by registration under the Companies Act 1985 are governed by the provisions of that Act and subsequent legislation[1]; and so also are the companies which were incorporated by registration under the earlier Companies Acts, namely the Joint Stock Companies Acts[2], the Companies Act 1862, the Companies (Consolidation) Act 1908, the Companies Act 1929 and the Companies Acts 1948 to 1983[3]. Part 2 of this title deals with companies regulated by the Companies Act 1985[4].

The provisions of the Companies Clauses Acts[5] apply to companies incorporated by a special Act of Parliament; and Part 3 of this title covers companies regulated by those Acts[6].

Certain of the provisions of the Companies Act 1985 apply to companies which are not in general regulated by either of the foregoing codes; these provisions are dealt with in Part 4[7].

Part 5 deals with companies formed in Scotland, Northern Ireland, in parts of the Commonwealth and in foreign countries[8].

Part 6 deals with corporate insolvency[9].

1 See para 20 post.
2 For the Acts included in the expression 'the Joint Stock Companies Acts' see para 11 note 2 post.
3 See the Companies Act 1985 s 735(1) and para 11 post. The following Acts could be cited by the collective title 'the Companies Acts 1948 to 1983': the Companies Act 1948; the Companies Act 1967 Pt I (ss 1–57), Pt III (ss 109–118); the European Communities Act 1972 s 9; the Stock Exchange (Completion of Bargains) Act 1976 ss 1–4; the Insolvency Act 1976 s 9; the Companies Act 1976; the Companies Act 1980; the Companies Act 1981 (except ss 28, 29); and the Companies (Beneficial Interests) Act 1983 (all repealed): see the Companies Act 1981 s 119 (2) and the Companies (Beneficial Interests) Act 1983 s 7(2).
4 See para 7 et seq post.
5 For the Acts included in the expression 'the Companies Clauses Acts' see para 1599 post.
6 See para 1599 et seq post.
7 See para 1765 et seq post.

8 See para 1771 et seq post.
9 See para 2001 et seq post.

(2) EC LEGISLATION

4. EC Treaty requirements in general. Companies[1] formed in accordance with
the law of a member State of the European Community and having their registered
office, central administration or principal place of business within the Community
must, for the purpose of applying the provisions of the chapter of the EC Treaty
dealing with the right of establishment[2], be treated in the same way as natural persons
who are nationals of member States[3]. Member States of the European Community
must, in so far as necessary, engage in negotiations with each other with a view to
ensuring for the benefit of their nationals:
  (1) the mutual recognition of companies;
  (2) the retention of their legal personality in cases where their seat is transferred
      from one country to another; and
  (3) the possibility for companies governed by the laws of different countries to form
      mergers[4].
Member States of the European Community must treat nationals of other member
States in the same manner, as regards participation by such nationals in the capital of
companies, as they treat their own nationals[5].

  1 For these purposes, 'companies' means companies constituted under civil or commercial law, including
    co-operative societies and other legal persons governed by public or private law, save for those which
    are non-profit-making: EC Treaty (Treaty establishing the European Economic Community (Rome,
    25 March 1957; TS 1 (1973); Cmnd 5179)) art 58, 2nd para; Treaty on European Union (Maastricht,
    7 February 1992; Cm 1934) Title II art G para (1).
  2 Ie the EC Treaty arts 52–58: see EUROPEAN COMMUNITIES vol 52 para 16·01 et seq.
  3 Ibid art 58, 1st para.
  4 See ibid art 220. See also para 5 post.
  5 Ibid art 221. This is without prejudice to the application of the other provisions of the EC Treaty:
    art 221.

5. Freedom of establishment; EC Council Directives. Within the framework
of the relevant EC Treaty provisions[1], restrictions on the freedom of establishment of
nationals of a member State of the Community in the territory of another member
State were to be progressively abolished[2]. Such progressive abolition was also to apply
to restrictions on the setting up of agencies, branches or subsidiaries by nationals of any
member State established in the territory of any member State[2]. Freedom of establishment includes the right to take up and pursue activities as self-employed persons and to
set up and manage undertakings and, in particular, companies under the conditions laid
down by the law of the country of establishment for its own nationals and prohibits the
member State of origin from hindering the establishment in another member State of
one of its nationals or a company incorporated under its legislation and having its
registered office, central administration or principal place of business within the
Community[3].
The EC Council is required by the EC Treaty to issue Directives[4] in order to
implement the General Programme for the abolition of existing restrictions on
freedom of establishment[5], in particular by co-ordinating to the necessary extent the
safeguards which, for the protection of interests of members and others, are required by
member States of companies with a view to making such safeguards equivalent

throughout the Community[6]. Under this power, the Council has issued the following series of Directives:

(1) the First Directive of 9 March 1968[7], which governs the co-ordination of national provisions concerning disclosure of basic documents and other information, the validity of obligations entered into by limited liability companies and the 'nullity' of such companies[8];

(2) the Second Directive of 13 December 1976[9], which applies to public companies (including those limited by guarantee) having a share capital and governs the formation and capital of such companies[10]; a Directive of 23 November 1992[11] amending the Second Directive has also been adopted, extending the restrictions on companies purchasing their own shares to acquisitions by subsidiaries, something already prohibited by the Companies Act 1985[12];

(3) the Third Directive of 9 October 1978[13], relating to particular types of mergers of public limited liability companies[14];

(4) the Fourth Directive of 25 July 1978[15], relating to annual accounts[16];

(5) an amended proposal for a draft Fifth Directive[17] relating to the structure of public limited liability companies and the powers and obligations of their organs;

(6) the Sixth Directive of 17 December 1982[18], relating to the division of public limited liability companies[19];

(7) the Seventh Directive of 13 June 1983[20], relating to consolidated accounts[21];

(8) a Directive of 8 November 1990[22], amending the Fourth and Seventh Directives, relating to accounting exemptions for small and medium-sized companies and the publication of annual accounts in ECUs;

(9) a Directive of 8 November 1990[23], extending the scope of the Fourth and Seventh Directives to accounts of certain partnerships and unlimited companies;

(10) the Eighth Directive of 10 April 1984[24], relating to the status and qualification of auditors[25];

(11) a draft proposal for a Ninth Directive[26] on groups initially under discussion in 1984 was subsequently withdrawn and there has been little progress since then;

(12) a proposal for a draft Tenth Directive[27] on cross-border mergers of public limited companies was initially under discussion in 1985 but there has been little progress since then;

(13) the Eleventh Directive[28] of 21 December 1989, relating to the disclosure requirements of branches of certain types of company;

(14) the Twelfth Directive[29] of 30 December 1989, relating to single member private companies;

(15) a draft Thirteenth Directive[30] on the conduct of take-over bids has been under discussion for some time.

In addition to the numbered series of company law Directives, there are other significant Directives on the safeguarding of employees' rights in the event of transfers of undertakings or businesses or parts of them[31], the disclosure of major shareholdings in listed companies[32] and insider dealing[33], as well as a series of Directives on the regulation of admission to listing of securities and on securities regulation[34].

EC Council Regulations[35] have also made provision for a new form of entity for joint ventures called a European Economic Interest Grouping[36]; but little progress has been made on a proposal for a statute for a European company[37].

1 Ie the EC Treaty (Treaty establishing the European Economic Community (Rome, 25 March 1957; TS 1 (1973); Cmnd 5179)) arts 52–58; Treaty on European Union (Maastricht, 7 February 1992; Cm 1934) Title II art G para (1): see generally EUROPEAN COMMUNITIES vol 52 para 16·24 et seq.

2 EC Treaty art 52, 1st para. In addition to setting up agencies, branches, or subsidiaries, a company may also exercise its right of establishment by taking part in the incorporation of a company in another member State: see Case 81/87 *R v HM Treasury, ex p Daily Mail and General Trust plc* [1989] QB 446, [1989] 1 All ER 328, ECJ.

3 EC Treaty art 52, 2nd para; Case 81/87 *R v HM Treasury, ex p Daily Mail and General Trust plc* [1989] QB 446, [1989] 1 All ER 328, ECJ. However, the right of establishment could not be interpreted as conferring on companies incorporated under a law of a member State the right to transfer their central management and control and their central administration to another member State while retaining their status as companies incorporated under the legislation of the first member State: *R v HM Treasury, ex p Daily Mail and General Trust plc* supra.

4 A Directive is binding on a member State, although the member State has a discretion as to the manner of implementation: see generally EUROPEAN COMMUNITES vol 51 para 3·63 et seq. The European Court of Justice has consistently held that, in the absence of implementing legislation, wherever the provisions of a Directive appear, as far as their subject matter is concerned, to be unconditional and sufficiently precise, individuals are entitled to invoke them against all national legislation which does not conform with the Directive and may invoke such provisions as lay down rights which can be enforced against the State: Case 8/81 *Becker v Finanzamt Münster-Innenstadt* [1982] ECR 53, [1982] 1 CMLR 499, ECJ; Cases C-19-C20/90 *Karella and Karellas v Ministry of Industry, Energy and Technology* [1994] 1 BCLC 774, [1993] 2 CMLR 865, ECJ; Cases C-134-C-135/91 *Kerafina v Republic of Greece* [1993] 2 CMLR 277, ECJ. Even where the Directive does not have direct effect, a member State in some circumstances may be liable in damages to individuals for failure to implement a Directive: Cases C-6/90, C-9/90 *Francovich and Bonifaci v Italy* [1991] ECR I-5357, [1993] 2 CMLR 66, ECJ. In applying national law, whether the provisions in question were adopted before or after a Directive, the national courts called upon to interpret the law, are required to do so, as far as possible, in the light of the wording of the purpose of the Directive in order to achieve the result pursued by the latter: Case C-106/89 *Marleasing SA v La Comercial Internacional de Alimentación SA* [1990] ECR I-4135, [1992] 1 CMLR 305, ECJ. Moreover EC law requires that a national court which, in a case before it concerning EC law, considers that the sole obstacle which precludes it from granting interim relief is a rule of national law must set aside that rule: Case C-213/89 *R v Secretary of State for Transport, ex p Factortame Ltd (No 2)* [1991] 1 AC 603; sub nom *Factortame Ltd v Secretary of State for Transport (No 2)* [1991] 1 All ER 70, ECJ.

5 As to this General Programme see EUROPEAN COMMUNITIES vol 52 para 16·24.

6 EC Treaty art 54(1),(3)(g); and see EUROPEAN COMMUNITIES vol 51 para 11·06.

7 Ie EC Council Directive 68/151 (OJ L65, 13.3.68, p 8), implemented by the European Communities Act 1972 s 9 (repealed) (re-enacted in the Companies Act 1985).

8 See further EUROPEAN COMMUNITIES vol 51 para 11·07 et seq.

9 Ie EC Council Directive 77/91 (OJ L26, 31.1.77, p 1), implemented by the Companies Act 1980 Pts I-III (ss 1-45) (repealed) (re-enacted in the Companies Act 1985).

10 See further EUROPEAN COMMUNITIES vol 51 para 11·13 et seq.

11 Ie EC Council Directive 92/101 (OJ L347, 28.11.92, p 64).

12 See the Companies Act 1985 s 23 (as substituted) and para 363 post.

13 Ie EC Council Directive 78/855 (OJ L295, 20.10.78, p 36), implemented by the Companies (Mergers and Divisions) Regulations 1987, SI 1987/1991 (see paras 70, 1463 et seq post).

14 See further EUROPEAN COMMUNITIES vol 51 para 11·32 et seq.

15 Ie EC Council Directive 78/660 (OJ L222, 14.8.78, p 11) (amended by EC Council Directives 84/569 (OJ L314, 4.12.84, p 28); 90/604 (OJ L317, 16.11.90, p 57); 90/605 (OJ L317, 16.11.90, p 60)), implemented by the Companies Act 1981 Pt I (ss 1-21) (repealed: re-enacted in the Companies Act 1985). See also EUROPEAN COMMUNITIES vol 51 para 11·19 text and note 1.

16 See EUROPEAN COMMUNITIES vol 51 para 11·19 et seq.

17 A draft Fifth Directive was first proposed in 1972 (see OJ C131, 13.12.72, p 49) but no progress has been made in negotiating this Directive mainly because of the lack of agreement on its provisions on worker participation and representation: see EUROPEAN COMMUNITIES vol 51 para 11·62. An amended version was submitted on 19 August 1983 (see OJ C240, 9.9.83, p 2) and again on 20 December 1990 (see OJ C7, 11.1.91, p 4).

18 Ie EC Council Directive 82/891 (OJ L378, 31.12.82, p 47), implemented by the Companies (Mergers and Divisions) Regulations 1987.

19 See EUROPEAN COMMUNITIES vol 51 para 11·44 et seq.

20 Ie EC Council Directive 83/349 (OJ L193, 18.7.83, p 1) (amended by EC Council Directives 90/604, 90/605), implemented by the Companies Act 1989 Pt I (ss 1–23) (see para 801 et seq post).

21 See EUROPEAN COMMUNITIES vol 51 para 11·50 et seq.

22 Ie EC Council Directive 90/604, implemented by the Companies Act 1985 (Accounts of Small and Medium-sized Enterprises and Publication of Accounts in ECUs) Regulations 1992, SI 1992/2452 (see paras 820, 900 et seq post). A further amendment has been agreed raising the financial ceilings for small and medium-sized companies: see EC Council Directive 94/8 of 21 March 1994 (OJ L82, 25.3.94, p 33).

23 Ie EC Council Directive 90/605, implemented by the Partnerships and Unlimited Companies (Accounts) Regulations 1993, SI 1993/1820 (see para 930 et seq post).

24 Ie EC Council Directive 84/253 (OJ L126, 12.5.84, p 20), implemented by the Companies Act 1989 Pt II (ss 24–54) (see para 955 et seq post), the Company Auditors (Examinations) Regulations 1990, SI 1990/1146 (see para 984 post) and the Companies Act 1989 (Register of Auditors and Information about Audit Firms) Regulations 1991, SI 1991/1566 (see paras 992–994 post).

25 See EUROPEAN COMMUNITIES vol 51 paras 11·55–11·57.

26 See EUROPEAN COMMUNITIES vol 51 para 11·65.

27 See OJ C23, 25.1.85, p 11.

28 Ie EC Council Directive 89/666 (OJ L395, 30.12.89, p 36), implemented by the Companies Act 1985 (Disclosure of Branches and Bank Accounts) Regulations 1992, SI 1992/3178 (see paras 876, 928, 1073 post) and the Oversea Companies and Credit and Financial Institutions (Branch Disclosure) Regulations 1992, SI 1992/3179 (see para 1790 et seq post).

29 Ie EC Council Directive 89/667 (OJ L395, 30.12.89, p 40), implemented by the Companies (Single Member Private Limited Companies) Regulations 1992, SI 1992/1699 (see para 81 post).

30 For an amended proposal submitted on 14 September 1990 see OJ C 240, 26.9.90, p 7. It is understood that the EC Commission is preparing a revised draft of the Directive.

31 Ie EC Council Directive 77/187 of 14 February 1977 (OJ L61, 5.3.77, p 26), implemented by the Transfer of Undertaking (Protection of Employment) Regulations 1981, SI 1981/1794 (as amended) (see EMPLOYMENT vol 16 (Reissue) para 249 et seq). See also EUROPEAN COMMUNITIES vol 51 para 11·18. EC Council Directive 94/95 of 22 September 1994 (OJ L254, 30.9.94, p 64) on the establishment of a European Works Council or a procedure in Community scale undertakings and Community scale groups of undertakings for the purposes of informing and consulting employees has been adopted but under the Treaty on European Union (Maastricht, 7 February 1992) Protocol on Social Policy the United Kingdom has opted out of this provision.

32 Ie EC Council Directive 88/627 (OJ L348, 17.12.88, p 62), implemented by the Disclosure of Interests in Shares (Amendment) Regulations 1993, SI 1993/1819, and the Disclosure of Interests in Shares (Amendment) (No 2) Regulations 1993, SI 1993/2689 (see para 735 et seq post).

33 Ie EC Council Directive 89/592 (OJ L334, 11.11.89, p 30), implemented by the Criminal Justice Act 1993 Pt V (ss 52–64) (see para 1218 et seq post).

34 See EC Council Directive 79/279 (OJ L66, 16.3.79, p 21) (amended by EC Council Directives 82/148 (OJ L62, 5.3.82, p 22); 88/627 (OJ L348, 17.12.88, p 62)), co-ordinating the conditions for the admission of securities to official listing; EC Council Directive 80/390 (OJ L100, 17.4.80, p 1) (amended by EC Council Directives 87/345 (OJ L185, 4.7.87, p 81); 90/211 (OJ L112, 3.5.90, p 24); 94/18 (OJ L135, 31.5.94, p 1), co-ordinating the requirements for drawing up, scrutiny and distribution of listing particulars to be published for the admission of securities to official stock exchange listing; EC Council Directive 82/121 (OJ L48, 20.2.82, p 26), on information to be published on a regular basis by companies the shares of which have been admitted to official stock exchange listing, all of which were implemented by the Stock Exchange (Listing) Regulations 1984, SI 1984/716 (repealed and replaced by the Financial Services Act 1986 Pt IV (ss 142–156B) (as amended): see para 281 et seq post); EC Council Directive 89/298 (OJ L124, 5.5.89, p 8), co-ordinating the requirements for the drawing up, scrutiny and distribution of the prospectus to be published when transferable securities are offered to the public, implemented in part by the Companies Act 1985 (Mutual Recognition of Prospectuses) Regulations 1991, SI 1991/823 (revoked) and now by the Public Offers of Securities Regulations 1995, SI 1995/1537 (see para 300 et seq post).

35 As to the distinction between EC Council Directives and EC Council Regulations see EUROPEAN COMMUNITIES vol 51 para 3·61 et seq.

36 Ie EC Council Regulation 2137/85 (OJ L199, 31.7.85, p 1), implemented by the European Economic Interest Grouping Regulations 1989, SI 1989/638 (see para 1831 et seq post).

37 The first formal proposal by the EC Commission for a European Company Statute was in 1970. An amended proposal was submitted on 16 May 1991 (see OJ C176, 8.7.91, p 1) but there has been little progress since then.

6. EC mutual recognition of companies. The original member States of the European Community signed a Convention on the Mutual Recognition of Companies and Bodies Corporate on 29 February 1968[1]. The convention is not yet in force, not having been ratified by the Netherlands; and its future remains in question[1].

1 See EUROPEAN COMMUNITIES vol 51 para 11·05.

2. COMPANIES REGULATED BY THE COMPANIES ACT 1985

(1) IN GENERAL

(i) The Present Statute Law

7. Companies Act 1985. The Companies Act 1985[1], which is a consolidating Act[2], is the successor to various earlier statutes which from time to time made general provision for the incorporation of companies by means of registration at a public office, and without the necessity of obtaining a special Act of Parliament or a royal charter[3].

All companies formed or registered under any of these statutes, as well as companies formed and registered under the Companies Act 1985, are now regulated by that Act[4], the Companies Consolidation (Consequential Provisions) Act 1985 and Part V of the Criminal Justice Act 1993[5], all three of these Acts together being denominated 'the Companies Acts'[6].

1 For this citation see the Companies Act 1985 s 747.
2 The Companies Act 1985 was passed to consolidate the Companies Acts 1948, 1967, 1976, 1980, 1981 and 1983, other than the provisions dealing with business names (now contained in the Business Names Act 1985: see para 166 et seq post) and insider dealing (formerly contained in the Company Securities (Insider Dealing) Act 1985 but now contained in the Criminal Justice Act 1993 Pt V (ss 52–64): see para 1218 et seq post). In addition, the Companies Consolidation (Consequential Provisions) Act 1985 contains provision for certain transitional matters and savings.
3 The earlier Acts which require notice are: (1) An Act to Regulate Joint Stock Companies (1844); (2) An Act to Regulate Joint Stock Banks in England (1844); (3) the Limited Liability Act 1855; (4) the Joint Stock Companies Act 1856; (5) the Joint Stock Companies Act 1857; (6) the Joint Stock Banking Companies Act 1857; (7) the Joint Stock Companies Amendment Act 1858; (8) An Act to enable Joint Stock Banking Companies to be formed on the principle of Limited Liability (1858). These statutes (all repealed) were discussed in the first edition of this work. Subsequent Acts are mentioned at paras 15–18 post; and other statutes containing provisions generally applicable to companies incorporated by special statutes for public purposes are considered in para 1599 et seq post.
4 See the Companies Act 1985 ss 675, 676, 735(1). For savings see the Companies Consolidation (Consequential Provisions) Act 1985 s 31 and para 8 et seq post. As to the formation of companies under the Companies Act 1985 see para 80 et seq post.
5 Ie the Criminal Justice Act 1993 Pt V (ss 52–64) (insider dealing): see para 1218 et seq post.
6 Companies Act 1985 s 744 (amended by the Criminal Justice Act 1993 s 79(13), Sch 5 para 4(2)). The Companies Consolidation (Consequential Provisions) Act 1985 by itself is denominated 'the Consequential Provisions Act'; and the Criminal Justice Act 1993 Pt V (ss 52–64) is denominated 'the insider dealing legislation': Companies Act 1985 s 744 (amended by the Criminal Justice Act 1993 Sch 5 para 4(1)).

8. Re-enactment of former provisions. The Companies Act 1985 re-enacts the effect of the provisions of the earlier statutes which are repealed[1], including the effect of reforms introduced by the Companies Acts 1967, 1976, 1980, 1981 and 1983. Many of the provisions of the Companies Act 1985 apply to companies formed before it was passed, although they have not been registered under it[2]; and a reference in any enactment, instrument or document to any provision of the repealed statutes is to be construed as a reference to the corresponding provision of the Companies Act 1985, the Company Securities (Insider Dealing) Act 1985[3], the Business Names Act 1985[4], or the Companies Consolidation (Consequential Provisions) Act 1985, as appropriate[5]. The repeal does not affect the incorporation of any company registered or re-registered under any repealed enactment[6].

1 All the previous Companies Acts are repealed (save for so much of the Companies Act 1967 Pt II (ss 58-108) (insurance companies) as was still then unrepealed) as from 1 July 1985 by the Companies Consolidation (Consequential Provisions) Act 1985 s 29, Sch 1.
2 See para 11 post.
3 Ie the Company Securities (Insider Dealing) Act 1985 (repealed): see now the Criminal Justice Act 1993 Pt V (ss 52-64) and para 1218 et seq post.
4 See para 166 et seq post.
5 Companies Consolidation (Consequential Provisions) Act 1985 s 31(1)(a),(6). See further para 10 post. This is without prejudice to the operation of the Interpretation Act 1978 ss 16, 17 (construction of references to repealed enactments and savings: see STATUTES vol 44(1) (Reissue) paras 1303, 1306): Companies Consolidation (Consequential Provisions) Act 1985 s 31(11).
6 Ibid s 31(8)(a).

9. Continuance of former Table A etc. Nothing in the new Acts[1] affects the application of:
  (1) Table B in the Joint Stock Companies Act 1856[2]; or
  (2) Table A in the Companies Act 1862, the Companies (Consolidation) Act 1908, the Companies Act 1929 or the Companies Act 1948[3],
to any company existing immediately before 1 July 1985[4].

The current Table A[5] does not, therefore, replace these former provisions, except in relation to companies registered on or after 1 July 1985[6].

1 'The new Acts' means the Companies Act 1985, the Business Names Act 1985, the Companies Consolidation (Consequential Provisions) Act 1985 and the Company Securities (Insider Dealing) Act 1985 (repealed: see now the Criminal Justice Act 1993 Pt V (ss 52-64) and para 1218 et seq post): Companies Consolidation (Consequential Provisions) Act 1985 s 31(1)(a).
2 As to the preservation of such a company's power to make contracts in writing signed by its agents see *Prince v Prince* (1866) LR 1 Eq 490.
3 The Companies Act 1948 Sch 1, Table A was divided into two parts, Part II applying to private companies as then defined. Part II was repealed by the Companies Act 1980 s 88, Sch 4, which also made a few small changes in various articles in Table A Part 1. A new Table A intended to come into force 'on the day on which there comes into force an Act to consolidate the greater part of the Companies Acts' was proposed to be introduced by the Companies (Alteration of Table A etc) Regulations 1984, SI 1984/1717, but those regulations were revoked before they could come into effect by the Companies (Tables A to F) Regulations 1985, SI 1985/805, made on 23 May 1985. These latter regulations (which were subsequently amended by SI 1985/1052, coming into effect on 1 August 1985) themselves came into effect on 1 July 1985: reg 1. As they were made before 1 July 1985 (the date on which the Companies Act 1985 came into force (s 746)), they were made in exercise of the powers conferred on the Secretary of State by the Companies Act 1948 s 454(2) (repealed), as well as under the powers conferred by the Companies Act 1985 s 3 (see paras 102, 108, 115 post) and s 8 (see paras 529, 533 post). As to the effect of this see para 10 post.
4 Companies Consolidation (Consequential Provisions) Act 1985 s 31(1)(c),(8)(b).
5 See para 529 post.
6 See the Companies (Tables A to F) Regulations 1985 reg 1.

10. Continuity of the law. So far as anything done or treated as done under or for the purposes of any provision of the old Acts[1] could have been done under or for the purposes of the corresponding provision of the new Acts, it is not invalidated by the repeal of that provision but has effect as if done under or for the purposes of the corresponding provision of the new Acts[2]. Any order, regulation or other instrument made or having effect under any provision of the old Acts is, in so far as its effect is preserved by these provisions, to be treated for all purposes as made and having effect under the corresponding provision of the new Acts[2].

Where any period of time specified in a provision of the old Acts was current immediately before 1 July 1985, the new Acts have effect as if the corresponding provision had been in force when the period began to run[3]. Without prejudice to the above, any period of time so specified and current is deemed for the purposes of the new Acts to run from the date or event from which it was running immediately before 1 July 1985, and to expire (subject to any provision of the new Acts for its extension) whenever it would have expired if the new Acts had not been passed[3]. Any rights, priorities, liabilities, reliefs, obligations, requirements, powers, duties or exemptions dependent on the beginning, duration or end of such a period as above mentioned are to be under the new Acts as they were or would have been under the old Acts[3].

Where in any provision of the new Acts there is a reference to another provision of those Acts, and the first-mentioned provision operates, or is capable of operating, in relation to things done or omitted, or events occurring or not occurring, in the past (including in particular past acts of compliance with any enactment, failures of compliance, contraventions, offences and convictions of offences), the reference to that other provision is to be read as including a reference to the corresponding provision of the old Acts[4].

A contravention of any provision of the old Acts committed before 1 July 1985 may not be visited with any severer punishment under or by virtue of the new Acts than would have been applicable under that provision at the time of the contravention[5]. Where, however, an offence for the continuance of which a penalty was provided has been committed under any provision of the old Acts, proceedings may be taken under the new Acts in respect of the continuance of the offence after 1 July 1985 in the like manner as if the offence had been committed under the corresponding provisions of the new Acts[6]; and the repeal of any transitory provision of the old Acts (not replaced by any corresponding provision of the new Acts) requiring a thing to be done within a certain time does not affect a person's continued liability to be prosecuted and punished in respect of the failure, or continued failure, to do that thing[7].

A reference in any enactment, instrument or document (whether express or implied, and in whatever phraseology) to a provision (whether first in force before or after the Companies Act 1948 or contained in that Act) which is replaced by a corresponding provision of the new Acts is to be read, where necessary to retain for the enactment, instrument or document the same force and effect as it would have had but for the passing of the new Acts, as, or as including, a reference to that corresponding provision[8].

Nothing in the new Acts affects the registration or re-registration of any company under the former Companies Acts[9], or the continued existence of any company by virtue of such registration or re-registration[10]; or the operation of any enactment providing for any partnership, association or company being wound up, or being wound up as a company or as an unregistered company under any of the former Companies Acts[11].

Where any provision of the new Acts was, immediately before 1 July 1985, contained in or given effect by a statutory instrument (whether or not made under a power in any of the old Acts), then the above provisions have effect as if that provision was contained in the old Acts, and in so far as the provision was, immediately before 1 July 1985, subject to a power (whether or not under the old Acts) of variation or revocation, nothing in the new Acts is to be taken as prejudicing any future exercise of the power[12].

All the above provisions are without prejudice to the operation of the Interpretation Act 1978[13] which provides for savings from, and the effect of, repeals[14].

1 For these purposes, 'the old Acts' means the Companies Acts 1948 to 1983 and any other enactment which is repealed by the Companies Consolidation (Consequential Provisions) Act 1985 and replaced by a corresponding provision in the new Acts: Companies Consolidation (Consequential Provisions) Act 1985 s 31(1)(b). For the meaning of 'the new Acts' see para 9 note 1 ante. For the Acts which may be cited as 'the Companies Acts 1948 to 1983' see para 3 note 3 ante.
2 Companies Consolidation (Consequential Provisions) Act 1985 s 31(2).
3 Ibid s 31(1)(c),(3).
4 Ibid s 31(4).
5 Ibid s 31(1)(c),(5).
6 Ibid s 31(5)(a).
7 Ibid s 31(5)(b).
8 Ibid s 31(6). The generality of s 31(6) is not affected by any specific conversion of references made by the Companies Consolidation (Consequential Provisions) Act 1985, nor by the inclusion in any provision of the new Acts of a reference (whether express or implied, and in whatever phraseology) to the provision of the old Acts corresponding to that provision, or to a provision of the old Acts which is replaced by a corresponding provision of the new Acts: Companies Consolidation (Consequential Provisions) Act 1985 s 31(7).
9 For the meaning of 'the former Companies Acts' see (by virtue of the Companies Consolidation (Consequential Provisions) Act 1985 s 32) the Companies Act 1985 s 735(1)(c) and para 11 note 2 post.
10 Companies Consolidation (Consequential Provisions) Act 1985 s 31(8)(a).
11 Ibid s 31(8)(c). As to the continuation of former Table A provisions see para 9 ante.
12 Companies Consolidation (Consequential Provisions) Act 1985 s 31(1)(c),(10).
13 Ie the Interpretation Act 1978 ss 16, 17: see STATUTES vol 44(1) (Reissue) paras 1303, 1306. For the purposes of s 17(2) (construction of references to enactments repealed and replaced; continuity of powers preserved in repealing enactment), any provision of the old Acts which is replaced by a provision of the Companies Act 1985, the Company Securities (Insider Dealing) Act 1985 (repealed: see now the the Criminal Justice Act 1993 Pt V (ss 52–64) and para 1218 et seq post) or the Business Names Act 1985 (see para 166 et seq post) is deemed to have been repealed and re-enacted by that one of the new Acts and not by the Companies Consolidation (Consequential Provisions) Act 1985: s 31(11). Anything saved from repeal by the Companies Act 1948 s 459, and still in force immediately before 1 July 1985, remains in force notwithstanding the repeal of the whole of that Act: Companies Consolidation (Consequential Provisions) Act 1985 s 31(1)(c),(9).
14 Ibid s 31(11).

(ii) Application of the Present Statute Law

11. Application to companies formed and registered under previous Acts. The Companies Act 1985 applies not only to companies[1] formed and registered under that Act but also to 'existing companies', that is, companies formed and registered under the former Companies Acts[2]. In its application to existing companies the Companies Act 1985[3] applies in the same manner as if the company had been formed and registered under that Act[4].

One effect of this application is that no re-registration is necessary, even to enable the company to wind up voluntarily[5].

1 In the Companies Act 1985, unless the contrary intention appears, 'company' means a company formed and registered under that Act, or an existing company (see text and note 2 infra): s 735(1)(a),(4).
2 Ibid s 735(1)(b). 'The former Companies Acts' means the Joint Stock Companies Acts, the Companies Act 1862, the Companies (Consolidation) Act 1908, the Companies Act 1929 and the Companies Acts

1948 to 1983: Companies Act 1985 s 735(1)(c). 'Existing company' does not, however, include a company registered under the Joint Stock Companies Acts, the Companies Act 1862 or the Companies (Consolidation) Act 1908 in what was then Ireland: Companies Act 1985 s 735(1)(b). 'The Joint Stock Companies Acts' means the Joint Stock Companies Act 1856, the Joint Stock Companies Acts 1856, 1857, the Joint Stock Banking Companies Act 1857 and the Act to enable Joint Stock Banking Companies to be formed on the principle of limited liability, or any one or more of those Acts (as the case may require), but does not include the Joint Stock Companies Act 1844: Companies Act 1985 s 735(3).

3 For this purpose, the Companies Act 1985 is to be read as including certain provisions of the Insolvency Act 1986, and also the Company Directors Disqualification Act 1986: see para 20 text to note 12 and note 12 post.

4 Companies Act 1985 s 675(1). Reference, express or implied, to the date of registration is, however, to be read as the date at which the company was registered under the Joint Stock Companies Acts, the Companies Act 1862, the Companies (Consolidation) Act 1908, the Companies Act 1929 or the Companies Act 1948: Companies Act 1985 s 675(2). Nothing in s 675 applies to companies registered in Northern Ireland or the Republic of Ireland: s 679. As to companies formed in Northern Ireland or the Republic of Ireland see para 1779 et seq post.

5 *Re London Indiarubber Co* (1866) 1 Ch App 329.

12. Application to companies registered but not formed under previous Acts. The Companies Act 1985[1] applies to every company registered but not formed under the Joint Stock Companies Acts[2], the Companies Act 1862, the Companies (Consolidation) Act 1908, the Companies Act 1929 or the Companies Act 1948 in the same manner as it is declared[3] to apply to companies registered but not formed under the Companies Act 1985[4]. However, a company registered under the Joint Stock Companies Acts may cause its shares to be transferred in the manner previously in use, or in such other manner as the company may direct[5].

The provisions of the Companies Act 1985 apply, therefore, to companies which were formed before, but registered under, either the Joint Stock Companies Acts, the Companies Act 1862, the Companies (Consolidation) Act 1908, the Companies Act 1929 or the Companies Act 1948. The registration of such a company (other than a company registered under the Joint Stock Companies Acts) under the Companies Act 1985 is prohibited[6].

1 For this purpose, the Companies Act 1985 is to be read as including certain provisions of the Insolvency Act 1986, and also the Company Directors Disqualification Act 1986: see para 20 text to note 12 and note 12 post.

2 For the meaning of 'the Joint Stock Companies Acts' see para 11 note 2 ante.

3 Ie under the Companies Act 1985 Pt XXII Ch II (ss 680–690) (as amended): see para 24 et seq post.

4 Ibid s 676(1). Reference, express or implied, to the date of registration is, however, to be read as referring to the date at which the company was registered under the Joint Stock Companies Acts, the Companies Act 1862, the Companies (Consolidation) Act 1908, the Companies Act 1929 or the Companies Act 1948: Companies Act 1985 s 676(2). Nothing in s 676 applies to companies registered in Northern Ireland or the Republic of Ireland: s 679. As to companies formed in Northern Ireland or the Republic of Ireland see para 1779 et seq post.

5 Ibid s 678(1).

6 See ibid s 680(2) and para 23 head (3)(a) post.

13. Application to unlimited companies registered as limited. The Companies Act 1985[1] applies to every unlimited company registered or re-registered as limited in pursuance of the Companies Act 1879 or the corresponding provision of the Companies (Consolidation) Act 1908[2], the Companies Act 1929[3], the Companies Act 1948[4] or the Companies Act 1967[5] in the same manner as it applies to an unlimited company re-registered as limited in pursuance of the Companies Act 1985[6]. Reference, express or implied, to the date of registration or re-registration is, however, to be read as referring to the date at which the company was registered or re-registered as a limited company under the relevant enactment[7]. Therefore, where an unlimited company has registered under an earlier enactment, it need not re-register under the Companies Act 1985.

1 For this purpose, the Companies Act 1985 is to be read as including certain provisions of the Insolvency Act 1986, and also the Company Directors Disqualification Act 1986: see para 20 text to note 12 and note 12 post.
2 Ie the Companies (Consolidation) Act 1908 s 57 (repealed).
3 Ie the Companies Act 1929 s 16 (repealed).
4 Ie the Companies Act 1948 s 16 (repealed).
5 Ie the Companies Act 1967 s 44 (repealed).
6 Companies Act 1985 s 677(1). As to re-registration see paras 124, 126 post. Nothing in s 677 applies to companies registered in Northern Ireland or the Republic of Ireland: s 679. As to companies formed in Northern Ireland or the Republic of Ireland see para 1779 et seq post.
7 Ibid s 677(2).

14. Application to unregistered companies. Certain provisions of the Companies Act 1985 apply, subject to some limitations or modifications, to all bodies corporate incorporated in and having a principal place of business in Great Britain, with certain exceptions[1], as if those bodies corporate were companies registered under the Act[2].

These provisions apply similarly to any unincorporated body of persons entitled by virtue of letters patent to any of the privileges conferred by the (now repealed) Chartered Companies Act 1837[3] and not registered under any other public general Act of Parliament[4]. Notwithstanding the repeal of the Chartered Companies Act 1837 and the Chartered Companies Act 1884[5] the power of Her Majesty to grant a charter of incorporation of limited duration or to extend or renew such a charter or privileges of such a charter is not affected[6].

1 Ie except for any body incorporated by or registered under any public general Act of Parliament, any body not formed for the purpose of carrying on a business which has for its object the acquisition of gain by the body or by its individual members, and any body for the time being exempted by direction of the Secretary of State (or before him by the Board of Trade). As to the Board of Trade see TRADE AND INDUSTRY vol 47 (Reissue) para 2 note 1.
2 See ibid s 718(1),(2); the Companies (Unregistered Companies) Regulations 1985, SI 1985/680 (as amended); and para 1767 post.
3 The Chartered Companies Act 1837 and the Chartered Companies Act 1884 were repealed by the Statute Law (Repeals) Act 1993 s 1(1), Sch 1 Pt V. As to the Chartered Companies Act 1837 and the Chartered Companies Act 1884 see COMPANIES vol 7(2) (1988 Reissue) para 2379 et seq.
4 See the Companies Act 1985 s 718(4).
5 See note 3 supra.
6 Statute Law (Repeals) Act 1993 s 1(2), Sch 2 para 11.

(iii) Legislation before 1985

15. Companies Act 1862. Such of the earlier statutes as were then in force were repealed by the Companies Act 1862[1], but this repeal did not affect the incorporation of any company registered under any Act so repealed[2].

The Companies Act 1862 governed all companies registered after 2 November 1862[3], until 1 April 1909[4], and its provisions (except Table A) also applied to companies formed and registered, or registered but not formed, under the Joint Stock Companies

Acts[5], or any of them, as if they had been formed and registered under that Act (as companies limited by shares or unlimited as the case might be) with the necessary qualifications as to reference to the date of registration, and as to the power of altering Table B of the Joint Stock Companies Act 1856[6].

The Companies Act 1862 permitted registration under the Act of every then existing company (including those registered under the Joint Stock Companies Acts) consisting of seven or more members, and any company thereafter formed in pursuance of any Act (except the Companies Act 1862) or letters patent, or being a company working mines within and subject to the stannaries jurisdiction, or being otherwise duly constituted by law, and consisting of seven or more members[7]. The registration might be with unlimited liability, or with liability limited by shares or by guarantee; and the registration might take place with a view to the company being wound up[7]. This enactment was subject to certain exceptions and regulations[8] practically identical with the exceptions and regulations in regard to the power for existing companies to register under the Companies Act 1985[9].

Restrictions on the formation of new companies, associations or partnerships for the purpose of carrying on business for gain without being registered under the Act were imposed by the Companies Act 1862[10]; these were similar to those imposed by the Companies Act 1985[11].

1 Companies Act 1862 s 205, Sch 3 (repealed).
2 Ibid s 206 (repealed).
3 Ibid s 2 (repealed).
4 Companies (Consolidation) Act 1908 s 296 (repealed).
5 For the meaning of 'the Joint Stock Companies Acts' in the Companies Act 1862 see s 175 (repealed).
6 See ibid ss 176, 177 (repealed).
7 Ibid s 180 (repealed).
8 See ibid s 179 (repealed).
9 See paras 25 et seq, 75 et seq post.
10 See the Companies Act 1862 s 4 (repealed).
11 See the Companies Act 1985 ss 716, 717 (as amended) and para 21 et seq post.

16. Legislation between 1908 and 1929. The Companies Act 1862 was amended by subsequent statutes[1], and was, with those statutes, repealed by the Companies (Consolidation) Act 1908, which incorporated most of their provisions. That Act was amended by the Companies Act 1913, the Companies (Particulars as to Directors) Act 1917[1] and the Companies Act 1928, and on 1 November 1929 those Acts were in their turn repealed and consolidated, together with certain other enactments, by the Companies Act 1929.

1 These Acts, together with the Companies (Foreign Interests) Act 1917, were collectively known as the Companies Acts 1908 to 1917: Companies (Particulars as to Directors) Act 1917 s 4.

17. Legislation of 1947. The Companies Act 1929 was itself substantially amended by the Companies Act 1947[1], a few sections of which were brought into force on 1 December 1947[2]. The remainder of the Companies Act 1947 came into force on 1 July 1948[3], only to be almost wholly repealed and replaced by the Companies Act 1948[4], which came into operation on the same day[5]. The Companies Act 1948 consolidated the provisions of the Companies (Particulars as to Directors) Act 1929 and the Companies Act 1947.

1 This Act followed the Report of the Committee on Company Law Amendment 1945 (Cmd 6659), presided over by Lord Cohen (then Cohen J).

2 Companies Act 1947 s 123(2); Companies Act (Commencement) Order 1947, SR & O 1947/2503, art 1.
3 Companies Act 1947 (Commencement) Order 1948, SI 1948/439, art 1.
4 See the Companies Act 1948 s 459(1), Sch 17. Section 459(1) and Sch 17 Pt I were themselves repealed by the Statute Law Revision Act 1953 s 1, Sch 1.
5 Companies Act 1948 s 462(2).

18. Legislation between 1948 and 1985. The Companies Act 1948 was substantially amended by Part I of the Companies Act 1967[1], which came into force at various dates between 27 October 1967 and 27 July 1968[2]. Meanwhile, the concept of a floating charge was for the first time introduced into the law of Scotland by the Companies (Floating Charges) (Scotland) Act 1961[3]. The 1948 and 1961 Acts and Part I of and Schedules 1 to 4 to the 1967 Act were collectively referred to as the Companies Acts 1948 to 1967[4]. The Companies (Floating Charges) (Scotland) Act 1961 was repealed and replaced by the Companies (Floating Charges and Receivers) (Scotland) Act 1972. The European Communities Act 1972[5] contained provisions implementing the First EC Council Directive on company law[6]. The Stock Exchange (Completion of Bargains) Act 1976, which was passed mainly to facilitate the adoption of a computerised settlement and stock transfer system, affected the procedures relating to the issue of certificates and the maintenance of registers and other records. The Insolvency Act 1976[7] provided for the disqualification of directors in certain circumstances from the management of companies. The general law of companies was again amended, principally in relation to accounts, disclosure of interests in shares and disqualification orders, by the Companies Act 1976 which came into force at various dates between 24 January 1977 and 1 January 1985[8]. The Companies Act 1948, Parts I and III of the Companies Act 1967, the Companies (Floating Charges and Receivers) (Scotland) Act 1972, the European Communities Act 1972[9], the Stock Exchange (Completion of Bargains) Act 1976[10], the Insolvency Act 1976[11], and the Companies Act 1976 were collectively referred to as the Companies Acts 1948 to 1976[12].

The Companies Act 1980 mainly implemented the Second EC Council Directive on company law[13], in so far as not previously enacted. The 1980 Act regulated the formation of public companies, and provided for the maintenance of their capitals. It also dealt with the duties of directors and conflicts of interest and made insider dealing a criminal offence. It came into force at various dates between 23 June 1980 and 1 October 1983[14]. The Companies Acts 1948 to 1980 comprised the Acts cited as the Companies Acts 1948 to 1976 together with the 1980 Act[15].

The Companies Act 1981 mainly implemented the Fourth EC Council Directive on company law[16]. It dealt with the form and content of company accounts. It also dealt with company and business names, share capital and the disclosure of interests in voting shares in public companies. It came into force at various dates between 1 January 1984 and 1 January 1985[17]. The Companies Acts 1948 to 1981 comprised the Acts cited as the Companies Acts 1948 to 1980 together with[18] the 1981 Act[19].

The Stock Transfer Act 1982 contained minor amendments of the Companies Act 1948 relating to transfers[20]; and the Employment Act 1982 amended the Companies Act 1967[21] in relation to the contents of the directors' report concerning the involvement of employees in the affairs of the company[22].

The Companies (Beneficial Interests) Act 1983 dealt, as its name implies, with the beneficial interest of companies in shares. It came into force on 26 July 1983[23]. That Act, and the Companies Acts 1948 to 1981, were cited together as the Companies Acts 1948 to 1983[24].

1 The Companies Act 1967 followed the Report of the Committee on Company Law Amendment 1962 (Cmd 1749) presided over by Lord Jenkins.
2 The Companies Act 1967 ss 25-34 (both inclusive) came into force on 27 October 1967 (three months after the Act was passed); ss 2-16 (both inclusive) and ss 18-24 (both inclusive) and Schs 1 and 2 on 27 January 1968 (six months after the Act was passed); and s 27 on 27 July 1968 (12 months after the Act was passed): s 57(1).
3 As to floating charges generally see para 1260 et seq post.
4 Companies Act 1967 s 130(2) (repealed).
5 Ie the European Communities Act 1972 s 9 (repealed).
6 As to the First Directive see para 5 ante.
7 Ie the Insolvency Act 1976 s 9 (repealed).
8 See the Companies Act 1976 s 45(3) (repealed) and the various commencement orders made under it.
9 See note 5 supra.
10 Ie the Stock Exchange (Completion of Bargains) Act 1976 ss 1-4 (repealed).
11 See note 7 supra.
12 Companies Act 1976 s 45(2) (repealed).
13 As to the Second Directive see para 5 ante.
14 See the Companies Act 1980 s 90(3) (repealed) and the various commencement orders made under it.
15 Ibid s 90(2) (repealed).
16 As to the Fourth Directive see para 5 ante.
17 See the Companies Act 1981 s 119(3) (repealed) and the various commencement orders made under it.
18 Ie together with the Companies Act 1981 except ss 28, 29 (repealed).
19 Ibid s 119(2) (repealed).
20 See the Stock Transfer Act 1982 Sch 2.
21 Ie the Companies Act 1967 s 16 (repealed).
22 See the Employment Act 1982 s 1 (repealed).
23 Ie the date of the Royal Assent.
24 Companies (Beneficial Interests) Act 1983 s 7(2) (repealed).

(iv) Consolidating and Subsequent Legislation

19. The consolidating legislation of 1985. With a view to facilitating the consolidation of the Companies Acts, the Companies Act 1981[1] contained novel provisions enabling the normal parliamentary procedure applicable to consolidation bills[2] to be short-circuited. It was provided that Her Majesty might, by Order in Council, make such amendments of the Companies Acts[3] and of any other enactment relating to companies, whenever passed, as might be jointly recommended by the Law Commission and the Scottish Law Commission as desirable to enable a satisfactory consolidation of the whole or the greater part of the Companies Acts to be produced[4]. Such an Order in Council could not be made unless a draft of the Order had been laid before and approved by a resolution of each House of Parliament[5]; nor would it come into force unless there was passed either a single Act consolidating the whole or the greater part of the Companies Acts (with or without other enactments relating to companies) or a group of two or more Acts which between them consolidated the whole or the greater part of those Acts (with or without other enactments so relating)[6]. If such an Act or group of Acts was passed, the Order would come into force on the day on which that Act or group of Acts came into force[7].

Pursuant to these provisions, two Orders in Council[8] were made amending the Companies Acts, thus paving the way for the consolidation of those Acts. Advantage was taken of the alternative proffered in the above provisions, and there were in all four consolidating Acts:

(1) the Companies Act 1985, which consolidated all the main provisions of the Companies Acts;

(2) the Company Securities (Insider Dealing) Act 1985, the title of which was self-explanatory[9];

(3) the Business Names Act 1985, the title of which is also self-explanatory; and

(4) the Companies Consolidation (Consequential Provisions) Act 1985, which made provision for transitional matters and savings, repeals (including, in accordance with the recommendations of the Law Commission, the repeal of certain provisions of the Companies Act 1948 which were no longer of practical utility) and consequential amendment of other Acts.

All these Acts came into force on 1 July 1985[10]. It is in fact the last of these four Acts which repeals all the Acts and provisions so consolidated[11].

1 Ie the Companies Act 1981 s 116 (repealed).

2 See PARLIAMENT vol 34 paras 1314, 1315.

3 For these purposes, 'the Companies Acts' meant the Companies Acts 1948 to 1981 (see para 18 text to note 19 ante) and any enactments passed after the Companies Act 1981 for the citation of which together with those Acts provision was made by any enactment so passed: Companies Act 1981 s 116(4) (repealed).

4 Ibid s 116(1) (repealed).

5 Ibid s 116(2)(a) (repealed).

6 Ibid s 116(2)(b) (repealed).

7 Ibid s 116(2)(c) (repealed). The date is 1 July 1985: see the Companies Act 1985 s 746. No Order in Council might be made subsequently: Companies Act 1981 s 116(3) (repealed).

8 Ie the Companies Acts (Pre-Consolidation Amendments) Order 1984, SI 1984/134; and the Companies Acts (Pre-Consolidation Amendments) (No 2) Order 1984, SI 1984/1169.

9 The Company Securities (Insider Dealing) Act 1985 was repealed by the Criminal Justice Act 1993 s 79(14), Sch 6 Pt I and replaced by the provisions of Pt V (ss 52-64): see paras 20, 1218 et seq post.

10 Companies Act 1985 s 746; Company Securities (Insider Dealing) Act 1985 s 18 (repealed); Business Names Act 1985 s 10; Companies Consolidation (Consequential Provisions) Act 1985 s 34.

11 See the Companies Consolidation (Consequential Provisions) Act 1985 s 29, Sch 1. So much of the Companies Act 1967 Pt II (ss 58-108) (insurance companies) as was then unrepealed was left outstanding: Companies Consolidation (Consequential Provisions) Act 1985 Sch 1. As to replaced provisions and the Interpretation Act 1978 s 17(2) see para 10 note 13 ante.

20. Legislation subsequent to the 1985 consolidation. Subsequent to the consolidation of company law effected in 1985[1], there has been further legislation of major importance in company law.

The Insolvency Act 1985 was passed on 30 October 1985. Part II of that Act dealt with company insolvency, and substantially altered the provisions of the Companies Act 1985 in relation to winding up, besides introducing an entirely new procedure in the shape of the making of an administration order[2], and facilitating the making of voluntary arrangements[3]. It also altered the law relating to receivers, whether appointed in or out of court[4], and introduced the new concept of an 'administrative receiver'[5]. The Act was directed to be brought into force on such a day as the Secretary of State might, by order made by statutory instrument, appoint, with the power for different days to be so appointed for different purposes and for different provisions[6]. The Act was brought into effect piecemeal between 1 February and 29 December 1986[7]. It was itself largely repealed by the Insolvency Act 1986[8], which consolidated the winding-up provisions of the Companies Act 1985 and of the Insolvency Act 1985, and related subject matters. It was directed to come into force on the day appointed under the Insolvency Act 1985 for the coming into force of Part III of that Act immediately after that Part of that Act came into force for England and Wales, which proved to be 29 December 1986[9].

The remainder of the Insolvency Act 1985, in so far as it dealt with companies, was concerned with the disqualification of company directors, and the provisions for this were consolidated with the like provisions of the Companies Act 1985 by the Company Directors Disqualification Act 1986, which was directed to come into force simultaneously with the Insolvency Act 1986[10]: In certain provisions of the Companies Act 1985 references to that Act and the Companies Acts[11] include certain provisions of the Insolvency Act 1986 and the Company Directors Disqualification Act 1986[12].

The Financial Services Act 1986, whose main concern is indicated in its title[13], nevertheless had considerable effect in relation to prospectuses[14], take-over offers[15], and insider dealing[16]. It was provided that this Act should come into force on such day as the Secretary of State might by order appoint, and that different days might be appointed for different purposes or different provisions[17]. The Act has been brought into effect piecemeal from 15 November 1986[18]. In certain provisions of the Companies Act 1985 references to the Companies Acts include certain provisions of the Financial Services Act 1986[19].

The Companies Act 1989 was passed to amend (inter alia) the law relating to company accounts; to make new provision with respect to the persons eligible for appointment as company auditors; to amend the provisions of the Companies Act 1985 and certain other enactments with respect to investigations and powers to obtain information and to confer new powers exercisable to assist overseas regulatory authorities; and to make new provision with respect to the registration of company charges[20]. The Act is being brought into effect piecemeal from 16 November 1989[21].

The Foreign Corporations Act 1991 was passed to make provision about the status in the United Kingdom of bodies incorporated or formerly incorporated under the laws of certain territories outside the United Kingdom[22] and came into force on 25 September 1991[23]; and the Oversea Companies and Credit and Financial Institutions (Branch Disclosure) Regulations 1992[24] introduced new provisions relating to the disclosure requirements in respect of branches opened by certain companies in a member State and the publication of annual accounting documents by credit and financial institutions with effect from 1 January 1993[25].

Part V of the Criminal Justice Act 1993[26] repealed the Company Securities (Insider Dealing) Act 1985 and introduced new provisions relating to insider dealing with effect from 1 March 1994[27].

The Insolvency Act 1994 and the Insolvency (No 2) Act 1994 were passed respectively to amend the law relating to contracts of employment adopted by administrators, administrative receivers and certain other receivers[28] in respect of contracts of employment adopted on or after 15 March 1994[29] and to amend the law relating to corporate insolvency and winding up, so far as it concerns the adjustment of certain prior transactions[30], with effect from 26 July 1994[31].

The Deregulation and Contracting Out Act 1994 contains (inter alia) provisions to reduce certain of the burdens affecting the registrar of companies and the official receiver[32].

1 See para 19 ante.
2 See the Insolvency Act 1985 ss 27–44 (now the Insolvency Act 1986 ss 8–27 (as amended): see para 2080 et seq post).
3 See the Insolvency Act 1985 ss 20–26 (now the Insolvency Act 1986 ss 1–7: see para 2044 et seq post).
4 See the Insolvency Act 1985 ss 45–55 (now the Insolvency Act 1986 ss 28–49 (as amended): see paras 1347 et seq, 2147 et seq post).

5 See the Insolvency Act 1985 ss 48–54 (now the Insolvency Act 1986 ss 42–48 (as amended): see para 2147 et seq post).

6 Insolvency Act 1985 s 236(2).

7 See the various commencement orders made under ibid s 236(2), the last of which still left two provisions of the Insolvency Act 1985 not yet brought into force, namely Sch 6 para 45 (subsequently repealed by the Companies Act 1989 s 212, Sch 24) (extension of the period from two to 12 years from dissolution during which the court might declare such dissolution void), and the Insolvency Act 1985 Sch 10 (subsequently repealed by the Insolvency Act 1986 s 438, Sch 12) in so far as it provided for the repeal of the Companies Act 1985 s 467(3)–(5) (relating to the disqualifications for appointment of a person as a receiver in Scotland): Insolvency Act 1985 (Commencement No 5) Order 1986, SI 1986/1924, art 4.

8 See the Insolvency Act 1986 s 438, Sch 12.

9 See ibid s 443; the Insolvency Act 1985 (Commencement No 5) Order 1986.

10 Company Directors Disqualification Act 1986 s 25.

11 For the meaning of 'the Companies Acts' see para 60 note 1 post.

12 Unless the contrary intention appears, in the Companies Act 1985 'the Insolvency Act' means the Insolvency Act 1986; and in the Companies Act 1985 s 375(1)(b) (see para 678 post), s 425(6)(a) (see para 1447 post), s 460(2) (see para 1405 post), s 675 (see para 11 ante), s 676 (see para 12 ante), s 677 (see para 13 ante), s 699(1) (see para 1784 post), s 728 (see paras 2496, 2501 post), Sch 21 para 6(1) (see para 26 post) the words 'this Act' are to be read as including the Insolvency Act 1986 Pts I–VII (ss 1–251) (as amended), ss 411, 413 (as amended), 414, 416, 417 and the Company Directors Disqualification Act 1986: Companies Act 1985 s 735A(1),(3) (added by the Insolvency Act 1986 s 439(1), Sch 13 Pt II; amended by the Companies Act 1989 s 212, Sch 24).

In the Companies Act 1985 s 704(5),(7),(8) (as amended) (see para 60 post), s 706(1) (see para 64 post), s 707(1) (see para 65 post), s 707A(1) (as added) (see para 68 post), s 708(1)(a),(4) (see para 66 post), s 709(1),(3) (as substituted) (see para 67 post), s 710A (as added) (see para 67 post), s 713(1) (see para 69 post), s 729 (see para 1511 post), s 732(3) (see paras 1165, 1168 post) references to the Companies Acts include the Insolvency Act 1986 Pts I–VII (ss 1–251) (as amended), ss 411, 413 (as amended), 414, 416, 417 and the Company Directors Disqualification Act 1986: Companies Act 1985 s 735A(2),(3) (added by the Insolvency Act 1986 Sch 13 Pt II; amended by the Companies Act 1989 s 127(5); the Deregulation and Contracting Out Act 1994 s 76, Sch 16 para 9).

13 See the Financial Services Act 1986 preamble.

14 See ibid Pt IV (ss 142–156B) (as amended) (listed securities: see para 281 et seq post), Pt V (ss 158–171) (repealed) (unlisted securities: see now the Public Offers of Securities Regulations 1995, SI 1995/1537 and para 300 et seq post).

15 See the Financial Services Act 1986 Pt VI (s 172), Sch 12 and para 1202 post.

16 See ibid Pt VII (ss 173–178) (as amended) and para 1218 et seq post.

17 Ibid s 211(1).

18 See the various commencement orders made under ibid s 211(1).

19 In the Companies Act 1985 s 704(5),(7),(8) (see para 60 post), s 706(1) (see para 64 post), s 707(1) (see para 65 post), s 707A(1) (as added) (see para 68 post), s 708(1)(a),(4) (see para 66 post), s 709(1),(3) (see para 67 post), s 710A (as added) (see para 67 post) and s 713(1) (see para 69 post) references to the Companies Acts include references to the Financial Services Act 1986 Pt IV (ss 142–156B) (as amended) and the Public Offers of Securities Regulations 1995 reg 4(2) (see para 302 post) and reg 10(1) (see para 317 post): Companies Act 1985 s 735B (added by the Companies Act 1989 s 127(6); amended by the Deregulation and Contracting Out Act 1994 Sch 16 para 10); Public Offers of Securities Regulations 1995 reg 22.

20 See the Companies Act 1989 preamble.

21 See ibid s 215(1) and the various commencement orders made under s 215(2),(3).

22 See the Foreign Corporations Act 1991 preamble and para 1787 post.

23 See ibid s 2(3).

24 Ie the Oversea Companies and Credit and Financial Institutions (Branch Disclosure) Regulations 1992, SI 1992/3179: see para 1790 et seq post.

25 See ibid reg 1(3).

26 Ie the Criminal Justice Act 1993 Pt V (ss 52–64): see para 1218 et seq post.

27 See the Criminal Justice Act 1993 (Commencement No 5) Order 1994, SI 1994/242, art 2, Schedule.

28 See the Insolvency Act 1994 preamble.

29 See ibid s 1(7).

30 See the Insolvency (No 2) Act 1994 preamble.

31 See ibid s 6(2).

32 See the Deregulation and Contracting Out Act 1994 preamble.

(v) Companies which must Register

21. Partnerships of more than 20 persons. No company, association or partnership consisting of more than 20 persons may be formed for the purpose of carrying on any business[1] that has for its object the acquisition of gain[1] by the company, association or partnership, or by its individual members, unless it is registered as a company under the Companies Act 1985, or is formed in pursuance of some other Act of Parliament[2], or of letters patent[3]. This provision does not, however, prohibit the formation:

(1) for the purpose of carrying on practice as solicitors[4], of a partnership consisting of persons each of whom is a solicitor[5];

(2) for the purpose of carrying on practice as accountants, of a partnership which is eligible for appointment[6] as a company auditor[7];

(3) for the purpose of carrying on business as members of a recognised stock exchange[8], of a partnership consisting of persons each of whom is a member of that stock exchange[9];

(4) for any purpose prescribed by regulations, which may include a purpose mentioned above, of a partnership of a description so prescribed[10].

Even if the members of a company do not, at its inception, exceed 20, the company becomes illegal if they subsequently exceed that number[11]. Some associations, for example mutual assurance associations, consisting of more than 20 persons, could, however, be lawfully formed before 1862[12], and, if so formed, did not require registration; any such association, if formed before 1862 and consisting of a fluctuating number of members, some members leaving and new members joining from time to time, is not formed afresh whenever a new member joins it[13].

1 For the meaning of 'carrying on business' and 'gain' see para 22 post.
2 For the meaning of 'formed in pursuance of some other Act of Parliament' see *Re Ilfracombe Permanent Mutual Benefit Building Society* [1901] 1 Ch 102. A limited partnership is formed pursuant to another statute ie the Limited Partnerships Act 1907: see PARTNERSHIP vol 35 (Reissue) para 205 et seq. As to the restrictions on the size of limited partnerships see PARTNERSHIP vol 35 (Reissue) para 206.
3 Companies Act 1985 s 716(1). The expression 'formed in pursuance of letters patent' must be read in connection with the power of the Crown to incorporate companies: see CORPORATIONS vol 9 para 1201. Section 716(1) does not, however, apply in relation to any body of persons for the time being approved for the purposes of the Marine and Aviation Insurance (War Risks) Act 1952 by the Secretary of State, being a body the objects of which are or include the carrying on of business by way of the reinsurance of risks which may be reinsured under any agreement for the purpose mentioned in s 1(1)(b) (see INSURANCE vol 25 (Reissue) para 794): Companies Act 1985 s 716(5).
   Nothing in s 716 (as amended) is to be taken to prevent the formation of an employers' association which is neither registered as a company under the Companies Act 1985 nor otherwise incorporated (Trade Union and Labour Relations (Consolidation) Act 1992 s 127(3)); nor are the Companies Act 1985 s 716 (as amended) and any corresponding enactment previously in force deemed to have invalidated the formation of any insurance company which, immediately before 3 November 1966, was carrying on in Great Britain insurance business of any class relevant for the purposes of the Insurance Companies Act 1974 Pt I (ss 1–11) (repealed) and was carrying on business of that class on 25 July 1973 (Insurance Companies Act 1982 s 89(1),(2) (amended by the Companies Consolidation (Consequential Provisions) Act 1985 s 30, Sch 2)).
4 For these purposes, 'solicitor' means a solicitor of the Supreme Court (see SOLICITORS vol 44(1) (Reissue) para 5): Companies Act 1985 s 716(3)(a) (substituted by the Companies Act 1989 s 145, Sch 19 para 15(1),(3))..
5 Companies Act 1985 s 716(2)(a).
6 Ie under the Companies Act 1989 s 25: see para 956 post.
7 Companies Act 1985 s 716(2)(b) (amended by the Companies Act 1989 (Eligibility for Appointment as Company Auditor) (Consequential Amendments) Regulations 1991, SI 1991/1997, reg 2, Schedule para 53(1),(3)).
8 For these purposes, 'recognised stock exchange' means The International Stock Exchange of the United Kingdom and the Republic of Ireland Limited and any other stock exchange for the time being

recognised by the Secretary of State by order made by statutory instrument: Companies Act 1985 s 716(4) (substituted by the Companies Act 1989 Sch 19 para 15(1),(3)). As a consequence of the separation of the Irish Stock Exchange from the London Stock Exchange with effect from midnight on 8 December 1995 the registered name of The International Stock Exchange of the United Kingdom and the Republic of Ireland Limited is now 'London Stock Exchange Limited'. At the date at which this volume states the law no other stock exchange had been so recognised.

9 Companies Act 1985 s 716(2)(c).

10 Ibid s 716(2)(d) (added by the Companies Act 1989 Sch 19 para 15(1),(2)). The following professions have been so prescribed or, in the case of heads (1)-(3) infra, are treated as having been so prescribed, subject to the limitations imposed by the relevant regulations, by virtue of the Companies Consolidation (Consequential Provisions) Act 1985 s 31(2),(11) and the Interpretation Act 1978 s 17(2)(b):

   (1) surveyors, auctioneers, valuers, estate agents, land agents and estate managers (Partnerships (Unrestricted Size) No 1 Regulations 1968, SI 1968/1222 (amended by SI 1994/644));

   (2) building designers (Partnerships (Unrestricted Size) No 4 Regulations 1970, SI 1970/1319 (amended by SI 1992/1438));

   (3) loss adjusters (Partnerships (Unrestricted Size) No 5 Regulations 1982, SI 1982/530);

   (4) insurance brokers (Partnerships (Unrestricted Size) No 6 Regulations 1990, SI 1990/1581);

   (5) town planners (Partnerships (Unrestricted Size) No 7 Regulations 1990, SI 1990/1969);

   (6) multi-national partnerships of lawyers (Partnerships (Unrestricted Size) No 8 Regulations 1991, SI 1991/2729);

   (7) member firms of The International Stock Exchange of the United Kingdom and the Republic of Ireland Limited (Partnerships (Unrestricted Size) No 9 Regulations 1992, SI 1992/1028);

   (8) consulting engineers (Partnerships (Unrestricted Size) No 10 Regulations 1992, SI 1992/1439);

   (9) patent agents and registered trade mark agents (Partnerships (Unrestricted Size) No 11 Regulations 1994, SI 1994/644);

   (10) actuaries (Partnerships (Unrestricted Size) No 11 Regulations 1996, SI 1996/262).

11 *Re Thomas, ex p Poppleton* (1884) 14 QBD 379; and see para 1761 post. As to illegal companies see para 1758 et seq post.

12 *Bear v Bromley* (1852) 18 QB 271.

13 *Shaw v Simmons* (1883) 12 QBD 117.

22. Meaning of 'carrying on business' and 'gain'. Business is carried on only where there is a joint relation of persons for the common purpose of performing jointly a succession of acts, and not where the relation exists for a purpose which is to be completed by the performance of one act. If, therefore, more than 20 persons between whom no contractual relation exists subscribe to a fund to be invested in the shares of companies by trustees for the subscribers, the subscribers do not carry on a business, and probably the trustees, even if more than 20, do not do so either[1], even though the shares are acquired with the object of pooling them and promoting an amalgamation with another company[2].

'Business' is a wider term than 'trade', and may include hiring land and employing a manager to farm it[3]; but it does not include the activities of a mutual land society, composed of a number of persons who subscribe to form a fund to be used in buying land which is to be divided among the subscribers[4], nor the activities of an association of persons who contribute sums to be applied in relieving its members in the case of sickness, the balance being distributable at the end of each year[5].

'Gain' is not limited to pecuniary gain or confined to commercial profits only, and a company is formed for the acquisition of gain if it is formed to acquire something, as distinguished from a company formed for spending something[6].

Mutual insurance companies[7], mutual loan societies[8], and building societies[9] are within the prohibition[10] because their objects are the acquisition of gain by their individual members[11]. A voluntary superannuation scheme is not a business of mutual insurance carried on for gain[12].

1 *Smith v Anderson* (1880) 15 ChD 247, CA, overruling *Sykes v Beadon* (1879) 11 ChD 170.
2 *Dominion Iron and Steel Co Ltd v Invernaim* [1927] WN 277.
3 *Harris v Amery* (1965) LR 1 CP 148.
4 *Wigfield v Potter* (1881) 45 LT 612; *Crowther v Thorley* (1884) 50 LT 43, CA; *Re Siddall* (1885) 29 ChD 1, CA.
5 *Re One and All Sickness and Accident Assurance Association* (1909) 25 TLR 674. Cf the decisions on the meaning of 'business' as used in relation to leases: see LANDLORD AND TENANT vol 27(1) (Reissue) para 565.
6 *Re Arthur Average Association for British, Foreign and Colonial Ships, ex p Hargrove & Co* (1875) 10 Ch App 542 at 547n.
7 *Re Padstow Total Loss and Collision Assurance Association* (1882) 20 ChD 137, CA.
8 *Jennings v Hammond* (1882) 9 QBD 225; *Shaw v Benson* (1883) 11 QBD 563, CA; *Wilkinson v Levison* (1925) 42 TLR 97; *Greenberg v Cooperstein* [1926] Ch 657. See also *Dominion Iron and Steel Co Ltd v Invernaim* [1927] WN 277.
9 *Re Ilfracombe Permanent Mutual Benefit Building Society* [1901] 1 Ch 102.
10 Ie the prohibition mentioned in para 21 ante.
11 The Joint Stock Companies Act 1844 and the Joint Stock Companies Act 1856 did not prohibit a mutual association formed for the purpose of acquiring profit or gain for its individual members, and not for the association itself, and accordingly the 1844 Act did not apply to mutual associations: *Bear v Bromley* (1852) 18 QB 271 (mutual loan society); *R v Whitmarsh* (1850) 15 QB 600; *Moore v Rawlins* (1859) 6 CBNS 289 (mutual land societies).
12 *Armour v Liverpool Corpn* [1939] Ch 422, [1939] 1 All ER 363, distinguishing *Re Padstow Total Loss and Collision Assurance Association* (1882) 20 ChD 137, CA.

(vi) Companies which may not Register

23. Companies and associations incapable of registration. The companies or associations which may not be registered under the Companies Act 1985 are:

(1) trade unions and other organisations of workers[1];

(2) persons associated together for any unlawful purpose[2]; and

(3) companies prohibited in express terms by the 1985 Act from so registering, namely:

    (a) a company registered in any part of the United Kingdom[3] under the Companies Act 1862, the Companies (Consolidation) Act 1908, the Companies Act 1929 or the Companies Act 1948[4];

    (b) a company having the liability of its members limited by Act of Parliament or letters patent, and not being a joint stock company[5].

Registration after the commencement of a winding up[6] is a nullity[7].

1 A trade union, other than a special register body, may not be registered as a company under the Companies Act 1985; and any such registration of a trade union, whenever effected, is void: Trade Union and Labour Relations (Consolidation) Act 1992 ss 10(3)(a), 117(3)(a)(ii). 'Special register body' means an organisation whose name appeared immediately before 16 September 1974 in the special register maintained under the Industrial Relations Act 1971 s 84 (repealed), and which is a company registered under the Companies Act 1985 or is incorporated by charter or letters patent: Trade Union and Labour Relations (Consolidation) Act 1992 s 117(1). An employers' association may be either a body corporate or an unincorporated association (s 127(1)); but nothing in the Companies Act 1985 s 716 (as amended) (see para 21 ante) is to be taken to prevent the formation of an employers' association which is neither registered as a company under the Companies Act 1985 nor otherwise incorporated (see the Trade Union and Labour Relations (Consolidation) Act 1992 s 127(3) and para 21 note 3 ante).
2 Companies Act 1985 s 1(1). See paras 80, 1760 post.
3 'United Kingdom' means Great Britain and Northern Ireland: Interpretation Act 1978 s 5, Sch 1. 'Great Britain' means England, Scotland and Wales: Union with Scotland Act 1706 preamble art I; Interpretation Act 1978 s 22(1), Sch 2 para 5(a). Neither the Channel Islands nor the Isle of Man are within the United Kingdom.
4 Companies Act 1985 s 680(2). As to re-registration, however, see paras 124, 126 post. The definition of 'company' and 'existing company' in the Companies Act 1985 (see para 11 ante) excludes companies registered under the Joint Stock Companies Acts, the Companies Act 1862 or the Companies

(Consolidation) Act 1908 in what was then Ireland: see para 11 note 2 ante. Such companies may not, therefore, register under the Companies Act 1985 s 680(1) (see para 24 post).

5　Ibid s 680(3). For the meaning of 'joint stock company' see para 25 note 2 post.

6　As to the effect of commencement of winding up generally see paras 2249, 2250 post.

7　*Re Hercules Insurance Co* (1871) LR 11 Eq 321 at 323.

(vii) Companies not formed under the Companies Act 1985 but which may Register

A. IN GENERAL

24. Classes of companies. Subject to certain exceptions[1] and qualifications[2], any of the following companies may at any time, on making application in the prescribed form[3], register under the Companies Act 1985 as an unlimited company, or as a company limited by shares, or as a company limited by guarantee[4]:

(1) any company consisting of two or more members, which was in existence on 2 November 1862[5], including any company registered under the Joint Stock Companies Acts[6];

(2) any company formed after 2 November 1862, whether before or after 1 July 1985, in pursuance of any Act of Parliament (other than the Companies Act 1985)[7], or of letters patent, or being otherwise duly constituted according to law, and consisting of two or more members[8].

A company is not, however, prevented from registering under the Companies Act 1985 as a private company limited by shares or by guarantee solely because it has only one member[9].

A company duly constituted according to law is one which is constituted by registration under some Act of Parliament or in pursuance of an Act of Parliament or under letters patent or under some constitution ejusdem generis. It is doubtful whether a partnership of less than 20 persons constituted merely by the consensual agreement of the partners can be regarded as a company duly constituted according to law; if such a partnership is formed not for the purpose of carrying on a business but simply for the purpose of being registered with a view to winding up, it is not a company entitled to be registered[10] under the Companies Act 1985[11].

A company governed by a deed of settlement may register in this way with a view to going into voluntary liquidation, and then selling its assets to another company under the statutory provisions relating to winding up[12]. By registering, a company may, however, lose powers which it possessed under its former constitution[13].

1　As to the companies which may not be registered under the Companies Act 1985 see para 23 ante.

2　See infra and para 25 post.

3　For the prescribed form of application see the Companies (Forms) Regulations 1985, SI 1985/854, reg 4(1), Sch 3, Form 680a (joint stock company), Form 680b (company not a joint stock company). In the provisions of the Companies Act 1985, other than those relating to winding up, 'prescribed' means prescribed by statutory instrument made by the Secretary of State: s 744. In relation to any provision of the Companies Act 1985 conferring a function transferred to the Treasury by the Transfer of Functions (Financial Services) Order 1992, SI 1992/1315, the Companies Act 1985 s 744 has effect as if 'prescribed' meant prescribed by statutory instrument made by the Treasury: Transfer of Functions (Financial Services) Order 1992 art 10(1), Sch 4 para 2.

4　Companies Act 1985 s 680(1). The registration is not invalid by reason that it has taken place with a view to the company's being wound up: s 680(1). Industrial and provident societies and friendly societies are by other statutes empowered to register as companies under the Companies Act 1985: see FRIENDLY

SOCIETIES vol 19(1) (Reissue) paras 252, 425; INDUSTRIAL AND PROVIDENT SOCIETIES vol 24 (Reissue) para 164. The court may order the conversion of certain collecting societies into mutual companies under the Companies Act 1985: see INDUSTRIAL ASSURANCE vol 24 (Reissue) para 313.

5　Ie the date on which the Companies Act 1862 came into force.

6　Companies Act 1985 s 680(1)(a). For the meaning of 'the Joint Stock Companies Acts' see para 11 note 2 ante.

7　Eg a water company incorporated by a special Act.

8　Companies Act 1985 s 680(1)(b).

9　Ibid s 680(1A) (added by the Companies (Single Member Private Limited Companies) Regulations 1992, SI 1992/1699, reg 2(1)(b), Schedule para 7). As to single member private limited companies see para 81 post.

10　Ie under the Companies Act 1985 Pt XXII Ch II (ss 680–690) (as amended).

11　*R v Registrar of Joint Stock Companies, ex p Johnston* [1891] 2 QB 598, CA.

12　*Southall v British Mutual Life Assurance Society* (1871) 6 Ch App 614.

13　*Droitwich Patent Salt Co Ltd v Curzon* (1867) LR 3 Exch 35.

25. Restrictions on power to register. The general restrictions on the power to register under the Companies Act 1985 are:

(1) a company having the liability of its members limited by Act of Parliament or letters patent may not register as an unlimited company, or as a company limited by guarantee[1];

(2) a company which is not a joint stock company[2] may not register as a company limited by shares[3];

(3) a company may not register without the assent of a majority of such of its members as are present in person or by proxy (in cases where proxies are allowed) at a general meeting summoned for the purpose[4];

(4) a company whose members' liability is not limited by Act of Parliament or letters patent may not register as a limited company without the assent of a resolution passed by a three-fourths majority[5];

(5) when a company is registering as a company limited by guarantee, the assent to registration must be accompanied by a resolution declaring the liability of each member to contribute[6];

(6) certain documents have to be delivered to the registrar and duly verified[7].

1　Companies Act 1985 s 680(4).

2　For the purposes of ibid ss 680–690 (as amended), as far as relates to registration of companies as companies limited by shares, 'joint stock company' means a company (1) having a permanent paid-up or nominal share capital of fixed amount divided into shares, also of fixed amount, or held and transferable as stock, or divided and held partly in one way and partly in the other; and (2) formed on the principle of having for its members the holders of those shares or that stock, and no other persons: s 683(1). Such a company when registered with limited liability under the Companies Act 1985 is deemed a company limited by shares: s 683(2).

3　Ibid s 680(5).

4　Ibid s 681(1). In computing any majority under s 681 when a poll is demanded, regard is to be had to the number of votes to which each member is entitled according to the company's regulations: s 681(3).

5　See ibid s 681(2) and para 75 post. See also note 4 supra.

6　See ibid s 681(4) and para 75 post.

7　See ibid s 681(5),(6) and para 76 post. As to the requirements on registration see para 75 et seq post.

B.　EFFECT OF REGISTRATION

26. Application of the Companies Act 1985. Where a company not formed, but authorised to register, under the Companies Act 1985 has been registered[1], all the provisions of that Act[2] apply to the company, and to its members, contributories and creditors, in the same manner in all respects as if it had been formed under that Act[3], subject to certain qualifications[4]. Notwithstanding any provisions contained in an Act of Parliament, royal charter or other instrument[5] constituting or regulating the company, the provisions of the 1985 Act apply with respect to:

(1) the registration of an unlimited company as limited[6];

(2) the powers of an unlimited company on registration as a limited company to increase the nominal amount of its share capital and to provide that a portion of its share capital shall not be capable of being called up except in the event of winding up[7]; and

(3) the power of a limited company to determine that a portion of its share capital shall not be capable of being called up except in the event of winding up[8].

1 Ie under the Companies Act 1985 s 680 (as amended): see para 24 ante. As to the mode of registration see para 75 et seq post.
2 For the purposes of ibid s 689, Sch 21 para 6(1), the Companies Act 1985 is to be read as including certain provisions of the Insolvency Act 1986 and also the Company Directors Disqualification Act 1986: see para 20 text to note 12 and note 12 ante.
3 Companies Act 1985 Sch 21 para 6(1).
4 See ibid Sch 21 para 6(2)–(6) (as amended) and paras 27, 33 post.
5 For these purposes, 'instrument' includes deed of settlement, contract of copartnery and letters patent: ibid Sch 21 para 1.
6 Ibid Sch 21 para 7(a). See para 126 post.
7 Ibid Sch 21 para 7(b). See para 128 post.
8 Ibid Sch 21 para 7(c). See para 177 post.

27. Provisions which do not apply. Where a company not formed, but authorised to register, under the Companies Act 1985 has been registered[1], Table A[2] does not apply unless adopted by special resolution[3]. The provisions relating to the numbering of shares[4] do not apply to any joint stock company[5] whose shares are not numbered[6].

1 Ie under the Companies Act 1985 s 680 (as amended): see para 24 ante.
2 Ie the Companies (Tables A to F) Regulations 1985, SI 1985/805, Schedule, Table A (amended by SI 1985/1052). As to Table A generally see para 529 et seq post.
3 Companies Act 1985 s 689, Sch 21 para 6(2). As to special resolutions see para 683 post.
4 See para 438 post.
5 For the meaning of 'joint stock company' see para 25 note 2 ante.
6 Companies Act 1985 Sch 21 para 6(3).

28. Certificate of registration. On compliance with the requirements of the Companies Act 1985 with respect to registration[1] by a company not formed, but authorised to register, under that Act, the registrar of companies[2] must give a certificate (which may be signed by him, or authenticated by his official seal[3]) that the company applying for registration is incorporated as a company under that Act and, in the case of a limited company, that it is limited[4]. On the issue of the certificate, the company is to be so incorporated[5]; and the certificate is conclusive evidence that the requirements of the Companies Act 1985 in respect of registration, and of matters precedent and incidental to it, have been complied with[6].

Where, on an application by a joint stock company[7] to register as a public company[8] limited by shares, the registrar of companies is satisfied that the company may be so registered, the certificate of incorporation must state that the company is a public company; and that statement is conclusive evidence that the requirements of the Companies Act 1985 relating to registration as such[9] have been complied with and that the company is a public company so limited[10].

1 Ie the requirements of the Companies Act 1985 Pt XXII Ch I (ss 680-690) (as amended).
2 As to the registrar of companies see para 60 post.
3 For these purposes, 'official seal', in relation to the registrar of companies, means a seal prepared under
   the Companies Act 1985 s 704(4) (see para 60 post) for the authentication of documents required for or
   in connection with the registration of companies: s 744.
4 Ibid s 688(1).
5 Ibid s 688(2).
6 Ibid s 688(3).
7 For the meaning of 'joint stock company' see para 25 note 2 ante.
8 For the meaning of 'public company' see para 82 post.
9 Ie the Companies Act 1985 s 685: see para 77 post.
10 Ibid s 688(4).

29. Vesting of property. All property belonging to or vested in a company[1] not formed, but authorised to register, under the Companies Act 1985 at the date of its registration thereunder passes to and vests in the company on registration for all the estate and interest of the company in the property[2].

1 As to whether the property of partners so passes to the company where the partnership is wrongfully
   registered see *Re Cussons Ltd* (1904) 73 LJ Ch 296; *Hammond v Prentice Bros Ltd* [1920] 1 Ch 201.
2 Companies Act 1985 s 689, Sch 21 para 2.

30. Creditors. Registration of a company not formed, but authorised to register, under the Companies Act 1985 does not affect the rights or liabilities of the company in respect of any debt or obligation incurred, or any contract entered into, by, to, with or on behalf of the company before registration[1]. If an unregistered company registers with unlimited liability, the shareholders are, in a winding up, liable beyond the amount unpaid on their shares for the expenses of the winding up, but not beyond that amount for any breach of contract under the terms of which there was only a limited liability[2].

Where a member of an unregistered company who is personally liable to be sued for the debts of the company has parted with his shares before registration, and so has not become a member of the registered company, he is not, by reason only of the registration, released from his pre-existing liability[3].

1 Companies Act 1985 s 689, Sch 21 para 3. Under earlier Acts a similar provision has been held not to
   apply so that members of an unlimited company subsequently registered with limited liability were
   rendered liable to contribute sums beyond the limit of the amount due on the shares held by them in
   order to meet debts contracted before registration: see *Re Sheffield and Hallamshire etc Society Ltd,
   Fountain's Case, Swift's Case* (1865) 4 De GJ & Sm 699.
2 *Lethbridge v Adams, ex p Liquidator of the International Life Assurance Society* (1872) LR 13 Eq 547.
3 *Lanyon v Smith* (1863) 3 B & S 938; *Harvey v Clough* (1863) 8 LT 324.

31. Pending actions and execution. All actions and other legal proceedings which at the time of registration are pending by or against a company not formed, but authorised to register, under the Companies Act 1985, or the public officer or any member of it, may be continued in the same manner as if registration had not taken place[1]. Execution cannot, however, issue against the effects of any individual member of the company of any judgment, decree or order obtained in such an action or proceeding; but, in the event of the property and effects of the company being insufficient to satisfy the judgment, decree or order, an order may be obtained for winding up the company[2].

1 Companies Act 1985 s 689, Sch 21 para 4(1).
2 Ibid Sch 21 para 4(2).

32. Continuance of existing constitution. All provisions contained in any Act of Parliament or other instrument[1] constituting or regulating a company not formed, but authorised to register, under the Companies Act 1985, including, in the case of a company registered as limited by guarantee, the resolution declaring the amount of the guarantee[2], are deemed to be conditions and regulations of the company, in the same manner and with the same incidents[3] as if so much of them as would, if the company had been formed under the Companies Act 1985, have been required to be inserted in the memorandum, were contained in a registered memorandum, and the residue were contained in registered articles[4].

1 For the meaning of 'instrument' see para 26 note 5 ante.
2 This includes also the statement under the Companies Act 1985 s 681(5)(a), and any statement under s 684(2) (see paras 76, 78 post): s 689, Sch 21 para 5(2).
3 The power of alteration of the memorandum of a company (see para 99 post) is not an incident of the contents of it: *Re Salisbury Railway and Market House Co Ltd* [1969] 1 Ch 349, [1967] 1 All ER 813 (if the special Act obliges the company to construct and maintain something for the benefit of the public, it cannot without further statutory authority abandon its undertaking in reliance upon an alteration of its objects under what is now the Companies Act 1985 s 4 (as substituted) (see para 1184 post)).
4 Companies Act 1985 Sch 21 para 5(1),(2).

33. Power to alter constitution. On registration under the Companies Act 1985 a company not formed, but authorised to register, under the Companies Act 1985 retains any power of altering its constitution or regulations which is vested in it by virtue of its existing constitution[1], except in so far as the power is restricted by any order made by the court[2]; but in the absence of any such power the company cannot alter any provision contained in any Act of Parliament relating to it[3], nor without the sanction of the Secretary of State can it alter any provision contained in any letters patent relating to it[4]. It has no power to alter any provision contained in a royal charter or letters patent with respect to its objects[5]. Where a company does not have power[6] to alter a provision, it does not have power to ratify acts of the directors in contravention of the provision[7].

Further, the company cannot alter any such provisions of its existing constitution as would, if it had originally been formed under the Companies Act 1985, have been required to be contained in its memorandum of association and are not authorised to be altered by that Act[8].

1 Companies Act 1985 s 689, Sch 21 para 9; and see *Droitwich Patent Salt Co v Curzon* (1867) LR 3 Exch 35; *Holmes v Newcastle-upon-Tyne Freehold Abattoir Co* (1875) 1 ChD 682.
2 Ie under the Companies Act 1985 s 461(3): see para 1414 post.
3 Ibid Sch 21 para 6(4)(a). See *Re Salisbury Railway and Market House Co Ltd* [1969] 1 Ch 349, [1967] 1 All ER 813.
4 Companies Act 1985 Sch 21 para 6(4)(b).
5 Ibid Sch 21 para 6(5).
6 Ie by virtue of ibid Sch 21 para 6(4) or (5): see supra.
7 Ibid Sch 21 para 6(6) (added by the Companies Act 1989 s 108(2)).
8 Companies Act 1985 Sch 21 para 8. The provisions of the memorandum of association which may be altered are:
   (1) without the court's sanction: alteration of objects (see s 4 (as substituted) and para 1184 post); change of name (see s 28(1) and para 160 post); alteration of conditions which could have been contained in the articles (see s 17 and para 541 post); increase of capital (see s 121(2)(a) and para 201 post); cancellation of shares not issued or agreed to be issued (see s 121(2)(e) and para 218 post);

conversion of paid-up shares into stock and reconversion of that stock into shares (see s 121(2)(c) and para 209 post); consolidation and division of share capital into shares of larger amount (see s 121(2)(b) and para 205 post); sub-division of shares into shares of smaller amount (see s 121(2)(d) and para 207 post); rendering the liability of directors unlimited (see s 307 and para 627 post); and

(2) subject to confirmation by the court: reduction of share capital (see s 135 and para 241 post); and reorganisation of capital under a scheme of arrangement (see s 425 (as amended) and para 1447 et seq post).

34. Substitution of memorandum and articles for deed of settlement. A company which has been registered[1] but not formed under the Companies Act 1985 may by special resolution[2] alter the form of its constitution by substituting a memorandum and articles for a deed of settlement[3]. The provisions of that Act with respect to applications to the court for cancellation of alterations of the objects of a company, and matters consequential on the passing of resolutions for such alterations[4], then apply, so far as applicable, but with the following modifications:

(1) there is substituted for the printed copy of the altered memorandum required to be delivered to the registrar of companies a printed copy of the substituted memorandum and articles; and

(2) on the delivery to the registrar of the substituted memorandum and articles, or on the date when the alteration is no longer liable to be cancelled by order of the court, whichever is the later, the substituted memorandum and articles apply to the company as if it were a company registered under the 1985 Act[5] with that memorandum and those articles, and the company's deed of settlement ceases to apply to the company[6].

Such an alteration may be made either with or without any alteration of the objects of the company[7], but, although it is liable to cancellation by the court[8], it does not in either case require the prior confirmation of the court[9].

A company registered under the Joint Stock Companies Act 1856, the Companies Act 1862, the Companies (Consolidation) Act 1908, or the Companies Act 1929, may alter the objects contained in its memorandum or deed of settlement[10], or substitute a memorandum and articles for its deed of settlement, even though it has not re-registered or is debarred from re-registering under the Companies Act 1985[11], and therefore does not fall directly within the scope of the provisions[12] set out above[13].

1 Ie in pursuance of the Companies Act 1985 Pt XXII Ch II (ss 680–690) (as amended): see para 23 et seq ante.

2 As to special resolutions see para 683 post.

3 Companies Act 1985 s 690(1). For these purposes, 'deed of settlement' includes any contract of copartnery or other instrument constituting or regulating the company, not being an Act of Parliament, a royal charter or letters patent: s 690(4). As to alterations in articles which involve breach of contract see para 540 post.

4 Ie ibid ss 4–6 (as amended): see paras 1184–1187 post.

5 Ie under ibid Pt I (ss 1–42) (as amended).

6 Ibid s 690(2). The same principles apply as regards the alterations which can be made under s 690 as apply to alterations under s 4 (as substituted). For cases see paras 1184–1187 post. The application to the court to cancel an alteration is by petition (RSC Ord 102 r 4(1)(h)); and the procedure on application and the practice of the court in respect thereto are, with the exception of the modifications set out in the Companies Act 1985 s 690, the same as those on an application under s 4 (as substituted).

7 Ibid s 690(3).

8 Ie under ibid s 4 (as substituted).

9 If a company at the same time as it adopts a memorandum and articles of association proposes to convert itself from an unlimited to a limited company, it should first re-register itself as a limited company (see para 126 post): *Royal Exchange Buildings, Glasgow, Proprietors* 1911 SC 1337. The objects clause in a memorandum substituted for a deed of settlement must not merely set out the objects by referring to the old deed of settlement: *Royal Exchange Buildings, Glasgow, Proprietors* supra.

10 Under the Companies (Memorandum of Association) Act 1890 s 1(1) (repealed) express provision was made for an alteration of a deed of settlement: see *Re Reversionary Interest Society Ltd* [1892] 1 Ch 615. In the Companies Act 1985 s 4 (as substituted) (see para 1184 post), which contains corresponding provisions, there is no such express provision, but its absence does not alter the position. In the case of such a company the general power of altering objects conferred by s 4 (as substituted) applies by virtue of ss 675, 676 (see paras 11, 12 ante): see *Re Hewitt Bros Ltd* (1931) 75 Sol Jo 615 (where such an alteration was sanctioned in the case of a company registered under the Companies Act 1862). Sanction of the court is not now required to be obtained under the Companies Act 1985 s 4 (as substituted), unless application is made thereunder for the alteration to be cancelled.

11 As to companies which cannot register under the Companies Act 1985 see para 23 ante; and as to existing companies to which that Act applies see para 11 ante.

12 Ie ibid s 690: see supra.

13 In the case of such a company the power conferred by ibid s 690 applies by virtue of ss 675, 676 (see paras 11, 12 ante): see *Re Sherborne Gas and Coke Co Ltd* [1936] WN 20. Cf *Re Nitrophosphate and Odams Chemical Manure Co* [1893] WN 141; *Re Hong Kong and China Gas Co Ltd* [1898] WN 158; *Re Copiapo Mining Co* [1899] WN 25; *Re Euphrates and Tigris Steam Navigation Co Ltd* [1904] 1 Ch 360 (not following *Re General Credit Co* [1891] WN 153).

35. Liability of contributories of companies not formed, but authorised to register, under the Companies Act 1985. In the event of a company being wound up which has been registered[1] but not formed under the Companies Act 1985, every person is a contributory, in respect of the company's debts and liabilities contracted before registration, who is liable:

(1) to pay, or contribute to the payment of, any debt or liability so contracted; or

(2) to pay, or contribute to the payment of, any sum for the adjustment of the rights of the members among themselves in respect of any such debt or liability; or

(3) to pay, or contribute to the amount of, the expenses of winding up the company, so far as relates to the debts or liabilities mentioned above[2].

Every such contributory is liable to contribute to the assets of the company, in the course of the winding up, all sums due from him in respect of any such liability[3].

1 Ie under the Companies Act 1985 s 680 (as amended) or previous corresponding provisions in the Companies Act 1948 or earlier Acts: see para 24 ante.

2 Insolvency Act 1986 s 83(1),(2).

3 Ibid s 83(3). In the event of the death, bankruptcy or insolvency of any such contributory, the provisions of the Insolvency Act 1986 with respect to the personal representatives of deceased contributories (see para 2471 post) and to the trustees of bankrupt or insolvent contributories respectively (see para 2469 post) apply: s 83(4).

36. Winding up; stay of actions. The provisions of the Insolvency Act 1986 with respect to staying and restraining actions or proceedings against a company at any time after the presentation of a winding-up petition and before the making of a winding-up order[1], where the application to stay or restrain is by a creditor, extend to actions or proceedings against any contributory of a company registered under the Companies Act 1985[2] or the previous corresponding legislation[3].

When an order has been made for winding up a company registered[4] but not formed under the Companies Act 1985, no action or proceeding may be commenced or proceeded with against the company or its property or any contributory in respect of any debt of the company, except by leave of the court, and subject to such terms as the court may impose[5].

1 Ie the Insolvency Act 1986 s 126(1): see para 2646 post.

2 Ie under the Companies Act 1985 s 680 (as amended): see para 24 ante.

3 Insolvency Act 1986 s 126(2).

4 See note 2 supra.
5 Insolvency Act 1986 s 130(3).

(2) PROMOTION OF COMPANIES

(i) Nature of Promoters

37. Meaning of 'promoter'. The term 'promoter' is not now defined by statute[1]. The meaning of the term has, however, been dealt with in numerous cases[2].

The term 'promoter' is not a term of law, but of business[3]. It is a short and convenient way of designating those who set in motion the machinery by which the Companies Act 1985 enables them to create an incorporated company[4]. It involves the idea of exertion for the purpose of getting up and starting a company[5], and also the idea of some duty towards the company imposed by, or arising from, the position which the so-called promoter assumes towards it[6].

The question whether a person is or is not a promoter is a question of fact depending upon what the so-called promoter really did[7], and a judge in summing up to a jury is not bound to define the term[8].

A person who as principal procures or aids in procuring the incorporation of a company is generally a promoter of it, and he does not escape from liability by acting through agents[9]. Persons who act professionally only, such as counsel, solicitors, accountants, printers of offer documents, and the like, are not, however, promoters[10].

1 In the Joint Stock Companies Act 1844 s 3 (repealed) the term was defined as meaning 'every person acting by whatever name in the forming and establishing of a company at any period prior to the company obtaining complete registration'. 'Promoter' was formerly defined, in connection with liability for statements in a prospectus or offer for sale, to mean a promoter who was a party to the prospectus or offer for sale, or the portion of it containing the untrue statement, other than a person acting in a professional capacity: see the Companies Act 1948 s 43(5) (repealed); the Companies Act 1985 s 67(3) (repealed by the Financial Services Act 1986 s 212(3), Sch 17 Pt I).
2 See infra and para 38 et seq post.
3 *Whaley Bridge Calico Printing Co v Green* (1880) 5 QBD 109 at 111 per Bowen J.
4 *Erlanger v New Sombrero Phosphate Co* (1878) 3 App Cas 1218 at 1268, HL per Lord Blackburn; and see *Twycross v Grant* (1877) 2 CPD 469 at 541, CA. Persons working together to form a company are not necessarily to be regarded as partners: *Keith Spicer Ltd v Mansell* [1970] 1 All ER 462, [1970] 1 WLR 333, CA.
5 *Official Receiver and Liquidator of Jubilee Cotton Mills Ltd v Lewis* [1924] AC 958 at 968, HL.
6 *Emma Silver Mining Co v Lewis & Son* (1879) 4 CPD 396 at 407; *Re Great Wheal Polgooth Co Ltd* (1883) 53 LJ Ch 42.
7 *Lydney and Wigpool Iron Ore Co v Bird* (1886) 33 ChD 85 at 93, CA; *Twycross v Grant* (1877) 2 CPD 469 at 476, 541, CA; *Emma Silver Mining Co v Lewis & Son* (1879) 4 CPD 396.
8 *Emma Silver Mining Co v Lewis & Son* (1879) 4 CPD 396 at 407.
9 *Phosphate Sewage Co v Hartmont* (1877) 5 ChD 394, CA; *Official Receiver and Liquidator of Jubilee Cotton Mills Ltd v Lewis* [1924] AC 958, HL.
10 See *Re Great Wheal Polgooth Co Ltd* (1883) 53 LJ Ch 42 (solicitors).

38. Instances showing who are promoters. Instances of persons who are promoters are as follows. Where a person wishing to sell property agrees with others that they are to form a company, and that he is to sell the property to it, the others receiving part of the purchase money, then, when the agreement is performed, the others are promoters[1]; and the owner of the property is also a promoter[2]. A person who joins with other persons in agreeing to purchase property with the view of selling it to a company which they intend to form, and subsequently do form, is a promoter[3]. Where a person takes in hand the formation of a company to buy the property of a third person, he is a promoter; and he incurs the liabilities of a promoter, even though the company is substantially different in character from the one he had anticipated, if he stands by and allows his agent to alter the plan of promotion[4].

Where the owner of a concession agrees with a financial agent that the concession is to be sold to contractors with a view to its being sold by them to a company to be formed forthwith for the purpose, the contractors finding funds necessary for such formation, the owner, the agent and the contractors are all promoters[5]. Similarly, where the agent of a syndicate, or trustee for a company, purchases property and sells it to a new company formed forthwith by the syndicate or company for the purpose, the members of the syndicate, or the company, as the case may be, are promoters[6].

Where the owners of property agree with two persons that they are to form a company to purchase it, and one of such persons agrees with a third person to carry out the scheme, and all three take part in procuring a board for the company, and in the preparation and issue of a prospectus, all three are promoters[7]. Brokers who, in consideration of being paid part of the purchase money, assist a person in selling property to a proposed company and allow their names to appear on the company's prospectus as being ready to answer any inquiries relating to the property, and answer such inquiries, are promoters[8].

Where a person purchases property with the view of selling it to a company which he subsequently forms, and another person enters into a sham contract with him for the purchase of the property, to be used in negotiating the sale to the company, and the company subsequently buys on terms which give a profit, they are both promoters[9]. Where a person agrees with the owners of property to form a company to purchase it at cost price, the company agreeing to pay a commission to him, and he thereupon forms the company, and is a party to the preparation and issue of the prospectus and the procuring of a board of directors, he is a promoter[10].

Directors of a promoting company are promoters where the promoting company is an alias for themselves, they being the only directors and entitled to share all the profits[11].

1 *Hichens v Congreve* (1831) 4 Sim 420.
2 *Beck v Kantorowicz* (1857) 3 K & J 230; *Bagnall v Carlton* (1877) 6 ChD 371 at 382, CA.
3 *Lindsay Petroleum Co v Hurd* (1874) LR 5 PC 221; *Gluckstein v Barnes* [1900] AC 240, HL.
4 See *Official Receiver and Liquidator of Jubilee Cotton Mills Ltd v Lewis* [1924] AC 958 at 965, HL (where the defendant had intended the company to be a private company having as its shareholders only two others who knew the facts of the promotion).
5 *Twycross v Grant* (1877) 2 CPD 469, CA.
6 *Erlanger v New Sombrero Phosphate Co* (1878) 3 App Cas 1218, HL.
7 *Bagnall v Carlton* (1877) 6 ChD 371, CA; cf *Re Leeds and Hanley Theatres of Varieties Ltd* [1902] 2 Ch 809, CA (where a company was held to be a promoter).
8 *Emma Silver Mining Co v Lewis & Son* (1879) 4 CPD 396.
9 *Whaley Bridge Calico Printing Co v Green* (1880) 5 QBD 109.
10 *Emma Silver Mining Co v Grant* (1879) 11 ChD 918.
11 *Re Darby, ex p Brougham* [1911] 1 KB 95.

39. When persons are not promoters. Persons do not become promoters on purchasing a property and shortly afterwards selling it at a profit to a company subsequently formed to buy it, if at the time of the contract they have taken no step to form the company[1], and even though the price is agreed to be paid partly in shares of a company which the purchasers propose to form[2]. If, however, the whole essence of the scheme from the first is that a number of persons are to purchase property and form a company to purchase it from them, they must disclose to the company, when formed, the whole of the profits made by them on the transaction[3].

1 *Ladywell Mining Co v Brookes* (1887) 35 ChD 400 at 409, CA; *Re Cape Breton Co* (1885) 29 ChD 795, CA (affd sub nom *Cavendish Bentinck v Fenn* (1887) 12 App Cas 652, HL); *Gluckstein v Barnes* [1900] AC 240, HL; *Re Lady Forrest (Murchison) Gold Mine Ltd* [1901] 1 Ch 582.
2 *Re Coal Economising Gas Co, Gover's Case* (1875) 1 ChD 182, CA.
3 *Gluckstein v Barnes* [1900] AC 240, HL.

40. When promotion begins and ends. It is a question of fact in each case at what time a person begins[1] or ceases to be a promoter of a company.

A person may become a promoter of a company either before or after its incorporation[2]. A person, although not a director, may be a promoter of a company which is already incorporated but the capital of which has not been taken up, and which is not yet in a position to perform the obligations imposed upon it by its creators[3].

A promoter does not cease to be such by reason only of the formation of the company and the appointment of its directors, but only when the directors take into their own hands what remains to be done in the way of forming the company[4], and when there is no question open between the promoter and the company[5].

1 *Ladywell Mining Co v Brookes* (1887) 35 ChD 400, CA; *Re Olympia Ltd* [1898] 2 Ch 153 at 181, 182, CA (affd sub nom *Gluckstein v Barnes* [1900] AC 240, HL); *Tyrrell v Bank of London* (1862) 10 HL Cas 26 at 40; *Albion Steel and Wire Co v Martin* (1875) 1 ChD 580.
2 *Twycross v Grant* (1877) 2 CPD 469 at 503, CA; and see *Lagunas Nitrate Co v Lagunas Syndicate* [1899] 2 Ch 392 at 428, CA.
3 *Emma Silver Mining Co v Lewis & Son* (1879) 4 CPD 396 at 407.
4 *Twycross v Grant* (1877) 2 CPD 469 at 541, CA.
5 *Eden v Ridsdales Rly Lamp and Lighting Co Ltd* (1889) 23 QBD 368, CA.

(ii) Fiduciary Relation of Promoters to the Company

41. Promoter not trustee or agent of company. A promoter stands in a fiduciary position with respect to the company which he promotes from the time when he first becomes until he ceases to be a promoter of it[1]; but his relation to the company is not that of trustee and beneficiary, or agent and principal[2]. A promoter may acquire assets as a trustee for a company. Whether he does so or not is a question of fact, and, where the plan of promotion is that he should sell assets to an intended company at a profit, the presumption is that as regards those assets he is not a trustee in the ordinary sense, but may, as vendor or agent to the vendors, make a profit on the sale to the company, even if he is also its director or one of its directors, provided that he makes full disclosure to the company[3]. The onus, however, lies upon the promoter to prove that he has made full disclosure[4].

1 *Twycross v Grant* (1877) 2 CPD 469 at 538, CA; *Erlanger v New Sombrero Phosphate Co* (1878) 3 App Cas 1218 at 1236, 1269, HL; *Lagunas Nitrate Co v Lagunas Syndicate* [1899] 2 Ch 392 at 422, CA; *Gluckstein v Barnes* [1900] AC 240, HL.
2 *Lydney and Wigpool Iron Ore Co v Bird* (1886) 33 ChD 85, CA; *Lagunas Nitrate Co v Lagunas Syndicate* [1899] 2 Ch 392 at 426, CA. A promoter was not a 'trustee or person acting in a fiduciary capacity' within the meaning of the Debtors Act 1869 s 4(3): see *Phosphate Sewage Co v Hartmont* (1877) 25 WR 743.
3 *Erlanger v New Sombrero Phosphate Co* (1878) 3 App Cas 1218 at 1236, HL; *Salomon v A Salomon & Co Ltd* [1897] AC 22 at 33, HL; *Lagunas Nitrate Co v Lagunas Syndicate* [1899] 2 Ch 392 at 422, CA; *A-G for Canada v Standard Trust Co of New York* [1911] AC 498, PC; *Omnium Electric Palaces Ltd v Baines* [1914] 1 Ch 332 at 347, CA. See also *Jacobus Marler Estates Ltd v Marler* (1913) 85 LJPC 167n.

4 *Cavendish Bentinck v Fenn* (1887) 12 App Cas 652 at 661, HL; *Re Darby, ex p Brougham* [1911] 1 KB 95; *Re Jubilee Cotton Mills Ltd* [1922] 1 Ch 100 at 117 (revsd [1923] 1 Ch 1, CA; revsd sub nom *Official Receiver and Liquidator of Jubilee Cotton Mills Ltd v Lewis* [1924] AC 958, HL). See further paras 48, 49 post.

42. Account of secret profits. A promoter may not retain any profit made out of a transaction to which the company is a party without full disclosure[1]. Where disclosure has not been made, the company may affirm the contract and sue him for an account and payment of profits[2]. The claim of the company may also be enforced by a misfeasance summons in the winding up of the company[3], and is provable in bankruptcy[4].

Interest may be recovered as from the time when the promoter received the profits[5]. The burden of proving that profit has in fact been made by a promoter lies on the company[6].

If the vendors to a company are the same persons as its shareholders, and the consideration is shares of the company, the profit, if any, is not secret and the company cannot recover it[7].

1 See paras 48-50 post.
2 *Lydney and Wigpool Iron Ore Co v Bird* (1886) 33 ChD 85, CA; *Beck v Kantorowicz* (1857) 3 K & J 230; *Hitchens v Congreve* (1831) 4 Sim 420; *Fawcett v Whitehouse* (1829) 1 Russ & M 132; *Whaley Bridge Calico Printing Co v Green* (1880) 5 QBD 109; *Bagnall v Carlton* (1877) 6 ChD 371, CA; *Emma Silver Mining Co v Grant* (1879) 11 ChD 918; *Mann and Beattie v Edinburgh Northern Tramways Co* [1893] AC 69, HL; *Gluckstein v Barnes* [1900] AC 240, HL; and see *Re Sale Hotel and Botanical Gardens Co Ltd, ex p Hesketh* (1898) 78 LT 368, CA.
3 *Pearson's Case* (1877) 5 ChD 336, CA; *Nant-y-Glo and Blaina Ironworks Co v Grave* (1878) 12 ChD 738; *Official Receiver and Liquidator of Jubilee Cotton Mills Ltd v Lewis* [1924] AC 958, HL; *Gluckstein v Barnes* [1900] AC 240, HL. The promoters taking fully paid-up shares, although they may have to pay the nominal value of them, are not contributories in respect of them: *Carling, Hespeler, and Walsh's Cases* (1875) 1 ChD 115, CA; *De Ruvigne's Case* (1877) 5 ChD 306, CA; and see para 2492 post. As to misfeasance summonses see para 2448 et seq post.
4 See para 57 post and the cases cited in the notes thereto.
5 *Gluckstein v Barnes* [1900] AC 240 at 255, HL; *Nant-y-Glo and Blaina Ironworks Co v Grave* (1878) 12 ChD 738; and see TRUSTS vol 48 (Reissue) paras 964-966.
6 *Cavendish Bentinck v Fenn* (1887) 12 App Cas 652 at 659, HL.
7 *Re Ambrose Lake Tin and Copper Mining Co, ex p Taylor, ex p Moss* (1880) 14 ChD 390, CA.

43. Amount of profit. In estimating the amount of secret profit for which a promoter is liable, deductions are made for legitimate expenses incurred in forming and bringing out the company, such as fees for reports of surveyors, charges of solicitors and brokers, sums expended in good faith in securing the services of directors, and payments to officers of the company and the press in relation to the company[1]. Deductions cannot, however, be claimed for sums paid to the company by the vendors to compromise the company's proceedings against them to rescind the purchase[2], nor the difference (arranged under a compromise to which the company is not a party) between what was to be paid by the promoter to the agent of the company and what was actually paid[3], nor the value of the services in respect of which the profit is paid to him[4]. Deductions have been disallowed in the case of sums paid in obtaining from another person a guarantee for the taking of shares[5].

1 *Emma Silver Mining Co v Grant* (1879) 11 ChD 918; *Bagnall v Carlton* (1877) 6 ChD 371, CA; *Lydney and Wigpool Iron Ore Co v Bird* (1886) 33 ChD 85, CA; *Benson v Heathorn* (1842) 1 Y & C Ch Cas 326 at 340; *Re Darby, ex p Brougham* [1911] 1 KB 95 at 101; *Official Receiver and Liquidator of Jubilee Cotton Mills Ltd v Lewis* [1924] AC 958, HL.
2 *Bagnall v Carlton* (1877) 6 ChD 371, CA.

3 *Grant v Gold Exploration and Development Syndicate Ltd* [1900] 1 QB 233, CA.
4 *Re Sale Hotel and Botanical Gardens Co Ltd, Hesketh's Case* (1897) 77 LT 681 at 682; revsd on other grounds (1898) 78 LT 368, CA.
5 *Lydney and Wigpool Iron Ore Co v Bird* (1886) 33 ChD 85, CA. It would appear that the ground for the decision in that case was that the whole transaction was improper and not that the payment of such a sum would in itself have been illegal even if made by the company: see *Metropolitan Coal Consumers' Association v Scrimgeour* [1895] 2 QB 604 at 607, 608. The latter question cannot now arise: see para 194 et seq post.

44. Joint and several liability. Promoters are jointly and severally liable in respect of secret profits, and, if one pays the whole of the joint liability, he may recover the proper proportion from his co-promoters[1].

1 *Gluckstein v Barnes* [1900] AC 240 at 247, 255, HL; and see *Gerson v Simpson* [1903] 2 KB 197, CA.

45. Rescission of the contract. Instead of claiming an account of the secret profits, the company may bring an action for rescission of the contract for sale and return of the consideration and payment of dividends and interest paid on shares and debentures forming part of the consideration; and, if the shares have been sold, the company may claim payment of the proceeds with interest[1]. Where part of the consideration is exchanged for shares in another company, the amount repayable is the actual value of those shares and not the value for purposes of the exchange[2]. As a general rule, rescission of a voidable contract may be obtained against a vendor only where the property can be restored to him; but this rule has no application where the property has been reduced by his fault, and, moreover, if compensation can be made for any deterioration, rescission with compensation may be awarded[3]. A company cannot be deprived of its remedy of rescission or other remedies by any provisions in its articles[4].

The remedy by rescission may be the only remedy where the promoter has bought and paid for the property before he sells it to the company, and was not at the time of his purchase in a fiduciary relation to the company[5].

1 This is implied in the judgments in *Erlanger v New Sombrero Phosphate Co* (1878) 3 App Cas 1218, HL; *Phosphate Sewage Co v Hartmont* (1877) 5 ChD 394, CA; *Lagunas Nitrate Co v Lagunas Syndicate* [1899] 2 Ch 392, CA; *Official Receiver and Liquidator of Jubilee Cotton Mills Ltd v Lewis* [1924] AC 958, HL.
2 *Official Receiver and Liquidator of Jubilee Cotton Mills Ltd v Lewis* [1924] AC 958 at 967, HL.
3 *Lagunas Nitrate Co v Lagunas Syndicate* [1899] 2 Ch 392 at 456, CA per Rigby LJ. As to the remedy of rescission see MISREPRESENTATION vol 31 para 1114 et seq.
4 *Omnium Electric Palaces Ltd v Baines* [1914] 1 Ch 332 at 347, CA.
5 *Ladywell Mining Co v Brookes* (1887) 35 ChD 400, CA; *Re Cape Breton Co* (1885) 29 ChD 795, CA (affd sub nom *Cavendish Bentinck v Fenn* (1887) 12 App Cas 652, HL); *Burland v Earle* [1902] AC 83, PC.

46. Other remedies of company. If the remedy by rescission is not open, or if the company elects to affirm the contract, the company may have a good cause of action for deceit or fraud, negligent misrepresentation[1] or breach of duty[2]. Where there has been a breach of duty, nominal damages, or if the breach has resulted in loss to the funds and assets of the company, substantial damages, may be recovered[3]. The liability for breach of duty cannot be enforced by a contributory in a winding up by means of a misfeasance summons unless the breach of duty has resulted in a loss to the assets of the company[4]. Where a vendor has agreed to give to a promoter a profit undisclosed by the promoter, the company may recover from the vendor any part of such profit which has not been paid over[5].

1 Ie under the Misrepresentation Act 1967 s 2: see MISREPRESENTATION vol 31 para 1103.
2 See eg *Ellis v Colman, Bates and Husler* (1858) 25 Beav 662 (specific performance of ultra vires contract refused on the ground that the court could neither enforce the contract nor compel the defendants to make good their representations; the remedy of the plaintiffs lay in action at law for damages); and MISREPRESENTATION vol 31 para 1090 et seq; SPECIFIC PERFORMANCE vol 44(1) (Reissue) para 813 et seq.
3 *Cavendish Bentinck v Fenn* (1887) 12 App Cas 652 at 658, 662, 664, HL; *Re Leeds and Hanley Theatres of Varieties Ltd* [1902] 2 Ch 809 at 826, 830, CA; and see *Jacobus Marler Estates Ltd v Marler* (1913) 85 LJPC 167n.
4 *Cavendish Bentinck v Fenn* (1887) 12 App Cas 652, HL; affg *Re Cape Breton Co* (1885) 29 ChD 795, CA. As to misfeasance summonses see para 2448 et seq post.
5 *Whaley Bridge Calico Printing Co v Green* (1880) 5 QBD 109; cf *Grant v Gold Exploration and Development Syndicate* [1900] 1 QB 233, CA.

47. Remedies of shareholders and debenture holders. In an action by the shareholder or debenture or debenture stock holder who has been injured, a promoter may be liable in respect of a prospectus or listing particulars either for compensation under the statutory liability[1] or for damages for deceit[2].

1 See the Financial Services Act 1986 s 150 (as amended), the Public Offers of Securities Regulations 1995, SI 1995/1537, reg 14 and paras 345 et seq, 349 et seq respectively post.
2 See para 332 post. As to criminal liability see para 58 post.

(iii) Disclosure by Promoters

48. Duty of full disclosure. In order to be in a position to retain any profit made by him, or to resist an action for rescission or damages, a promoter, before completion of the transaction out of which the profit is made, must have made full disclosure to the company of the fact that he is interested in the transaction, of the nature of his interest, and of all other material facts[1].

Whether the exact amount of profit is required to be stated has not yet been settled[2].

1 *Re Darby, ex p Brougham* [1911] 1 KB 95; *A-G for Canada v Standard Trust Co of New York* [1911] AC 498, PC; and see the cases cited in para 43 note 1 ante.
2 See *Chesterfield and Boythorpe Colliery Co v Black* (1877) 37 LT 740; *Re Lady Forrest (Murchison) Gold Mine Ltd* [1901] 1 Ch 582; *Lagunas Nitrate Co v Lagunas Syndicate* [1899] 2 Ch 392, CA; *Gluckstein v Barnes* [1900] AC 240 at 258, HL. A person may buy a property at one price and sell it to a company at a higher price without disclosing even the fact that he is getting a profit, provided that he is not a promoter: *Re Coal Economising Gas Co, Gover's Case* (1875) 1 ChD 182, CA.

49. What amounts to disclosure. Disclosure may be made in any one of several ways, as, for example, by the memorandum or articles of association of the company[1], or by communication to such shareholders of the company as become such by applying for shares on the footing of a prospectus or an offer for sale which makes due disclosure[2], or by communication to a board of directors of the company which is independent of the promoters[3], or by communication in any way to the original shareholders, at any rate if no future shareholders are contemplated[4].

Even if disclosure is made to the original shareholders or if for other reasons they cannot complain of the want of it, there may, in some cases, exist a fiduciary relation between the promoters and future shareholders if the admission of the latter to membership of the company formed part of the plan of promotion[5].

1 *Re British Seamless Paper Box Co* (1881) 17 ChD 467 at 475, CA. Disclosure is made in this way because of the notice which every member and outsider dealing with the company has of the contents of the articles (*Re Bank of Hindustan, China and Japan, Campbell's Case, Hippesley's Case, Alison's Case* (1873) 9 Ch App 1 at 22; *Griffith v Paget* (1877) 6 ChD 511 at 517; *Mahony v East Holyford Mining Co* (1875) LR 7 HL 869 at 893; and see para 145 post), and possibly because of the statutory effect of the articles (see the Companies Act 1985 s 14(1) and para 140 post; *Lagunas Nitrate Co v Lagunas Syndicate* [1899] 2 Ch 392 at 424, CA). See, however, *Gluckstein v Barnes* [1900] AC 240, HL.
2 *Lagunas Nitrate Co v Lagunas Syndicate* [1899] 2 Ch 392 at 428, CA; *Gluckstein v Barnes* [1900] AC 240 at 249, HL; *Omnium Electric Palaces Ltd v Baines* [1914] 1 Ch 332 at 347, 351, CA.
3 *Erlanger v New Sombrero Phosphate Co* (1878) 3 App Cas 1218 at 1236, HL; *Re Fitzroy Bessemer Steel Co Ltd* (1884) 50 LT 144; *Gluckstein v Barnes* [1900] AC 240, HL. See further para 50 post.
4 *Salomon v A Salomon & Co Ltd* [1897] AC 22, HL; and see *Re Ambrose Lake Tin and Copper Mining Co, ex p Taylor, ex p Moss* (1880) 14 ChD 390, CA; *Re British Seamless Paper Box Co* (1881) 17 ChD 467, CA; *A-G for Canada v Standard Trust Co of New York* [1911] AC 498, PC.
5 See *Re British Seamless Paper Box Co* (1881) 17 ChD 467, CA; *Re Postage Stamp Automatic Delivery Co* [1892] 3 Ch 566; *Bland's Case* [1893] 2 Ch 612, CA; *Lagunas Nitrate Co v Lagunas Syndicate* [1899] 2 Ch 392 at 428, CA; *Re Leeds and Hanley Theatres of Varieties Ltd* [1902] 2 Ch 809 at 827, CA; *Re Darby, ex p Brougham* [1911] 1 KB 95.

50. What is an independent executive. A board of directors, whether provided by the promoters or otherwise, is an independent executive when its members are aware that the property which the company is asked to buy is the property of the promoters, and when they are competent and intelligent judges as to whether the purchase ought or ought not to be made, and capable of exercising an intelligent, independent and impartial judgment on the transaction[1]. Directors appointed by the vendors do not generally constitute an independent board; in such a case the only effective way of making disclosure is by the articles, and, if a prospectus is issued, in the prospectus also[2]. Where promoters appoint themselves, or some of their number, to be sole guardians and protectors of their creature, the company, they are not an independent board, and the fact that the articles purport to protect them from the liability to account as persons standing in a fiduciary relation to the company will not help them[3]. If a company is avowedly formed with a board of directors who are not independent, but who are stated to be the intended vendors of property to the company, or their agents, the company cannot set aside the purchase agreement merely on the ground that the directors are not independent[4].

Where a company is one which does not invite the public to subscribe for its shares (although it is not a private company within the meaning of the Companies Act 1985[5], and every shareholder is aware of all the circumstances attending the formation of the company), the absence of an independent board of directors is immaterial[6].

1 *Erlanger v New Sombrero Phosphate Co* (1878) 3 App Cas 1218, HL.
2 *Re Olympia Ltd* [1898] 2 Ch 153, CA; affd sub nom *Gluckstein v Barnes* [1900] AC 240, HL. See also *Selangor United Rubber Estates Ltd v Cradock (No 3)* [1968] 2 All ER 1073, [1968] 1 WLR 1555 (persons nominated as directors to do what they are told by an outsider are fixed with his knowledge).
3 *Gluckstein v Barnes* [1900] AC 240 at 248, HL; *Bland's Case* [1893] 2 Ch 612, CA.
4 *Lagunas Nitrate Co v Lagunas Syndicate* [1899] 2 Ch 392 at 425, CA; but cf *Re Olympia Ltd* [1898] 2 Ch 153 at 168, CA; affd sub nom *Gluckstein v Barnes* [1900] AC 240, HL (where a clause in the articles, declaring that the validity of the agreement for sale should not be impeached on the ground that the vendors as promoters or otherwise stood in a fiduciary relation to the company, was held nugatory).
5 See para 105 et seq post.
6 *Salomon v A Salomon & Co Ltd* [1897] AC 22 at 36, 57, HL; *Larocque v Beauchemin* [1897] AC 358 at 364, PC; *Felix Hadley & Co Ltd v Hadley* (1897) 77 LT 131; *Re Innes & Co* [1903] 2 Ch 254 at 260, CA.

(iv) Payment by Company of Promoter's Expenses

51. Liability of company. A promoter has no right of indemnity against the company which he promotes in respect of any obligation undertaken on its behalf before its incorporation[1], and may not sue it upon a contract, made by him with an agent or trustee on its behalf before its incorporation, stipulating that it shall pay the promoters a certain sum for preliminary expenses, even where the articles of association provide that the company shall defray the preliminary expenses[2]. Thus, in spite of such a provision, the solicitor who prepares the memorandum and articles cannot sue the company for his costs of doing so[3], and the promoter, or his solicitor, who has paid the fees on registering the company, cannot recover them from the company[3]; nor is the promoter, or a person employed by him, entitled to sue the company in respect of any payment for services rendered or expenses incurred before its incorporation in promoting it, unless after its incorporation it expressly agrees with him to make such payment, or, from other facts, the court can infer a new contract to reimburse him[4]. The company cannot ratify an agreement purporting to be made on its behalf before its incorporation[5]; and its acts cannot be evidence of a new agreement to reimburse the promoter if they can be shown to have been made with reference to the obligations of the company to indemnify a third person[6]. A company is not bound in equity to pay the preliminary expenses because it has adopted and derived benefit from services performed before its incorporation[7]. Where a promoter procures a company to be formed by fraudulent means and by fraud induces shareholders to join it, he cannot recover expenses which he otherwise might have recovered[8].

Whether there is a fresh contract between the company and the promoters after incorporation is a question of fact[9].

1 *Melhado v Porto Alegre Rly Co* (1874) LR 9 CP 503. See also para 1127 post.
2 *Melhado v Porto Alegre Rly Co* (1874) LR 9 CP 503. As to the personal liability of a person purporting to contract on behalf of a company at a time when the company is not formed see para 54 post.
3 See para 1126 note 1 post.
4 See the cases cited in para 1127 notes 1, 2 post.
5 See the cases cited in para 1126 note 2 post.
6 *Re Rotherham Alum and Chemical Co* (1883) 25 ChD 103, CA.
7 *Re English and Colonial Produce Co Ltd* [1906] 2 Ch 435, CA, overruling the dictum in *Re Hereford and South Wales Waggon and Engineering Co* (1876) 2 ChD 621 at 624, CA, and probably some similar observations in *Re Empress Engineering Co* (1880) 16 ChD 125, CA. See also *Re National Motor Mail-Coach Co Ltd, Clinton's Claim* [1908] 2 Ch 515, CA.
8 *Re Hereford and South Wales Waggon and Engineering Co* (1876) 2 ChD 621, CA.
9 *Browning v Great Central Mining Co* (1860) 5 H & N 856; *Howard v Patent Ivory Manufacturing Co, Re Patent Ivory Manufacturing Co* (1888) 38 ChD 156 at 165; cf *Re English and Colonial Produce Co Ltd* [1906] 2 Ch 435, CA.

52. Power of company to pay registration expenses. Generally, a company by its memorandum of association, and its directors by its articles, are expressly empowered to pay all expenses of and incidental to its incorporation and flotation. Table A merely provides that the directors may exercise all the powers of the company[1]. Even where there is express general power to pay preliminary expenses to a promoter, payment should not be made without vouchers or investigation[2]; but, if the memorandum of association empowers the directors without further authority to pay a specific sum for the costs and expenses of promoters, payment may be made without a bill of costs being required[3]. The expenses which may be properly paid include registration fees, a sum charged for a report on the value of property to be purchased by it, legal costs, advertisements, printing and brokers' fees[4]. Directors may be made personally liable for sums improperly paid to promoters[5]. Where the articles state the amounts to be paid to promoters for procuring concessions and for preliminary expenses, shareholders may not complain that the amounts are excessive[6] unless the promoter has acted fraudulently[7]. If, however, the money is paid and an action to recover it is compromised with knowledge of the facts, the money cannot afterwards be recovered[8].

1 See the Companies (Tables A to F) Regulations 1985, SI 1985/805, Schedule, Table A art 70. As to Table A generally see para 529 et seq post.
2 *Re Englefield Colliery Co* (1878) 8 ChD 388 at 401, CA (where directors' calls were paid out of payments to promoters).
3 *Croskey v Bank of Wales* (1863) 4 Giff 314 at 332.
4 *Lydney and Wigpool Iron Ore Co v Bird* (1886) 33 ChD 85,CA; and see para 43 ante. Reasonable sums may be paid to brokers for placing a company's shares: see *Metropolitan Coal Consumers' Association v Scrimgeour* [1895] 2 QB 604, CA, distinguishing *Re Faure Electric Accumulator Co* (1888) 40 ChD 141, and overruling that case in so far as it held that payment of brokerage by a company was in itself illegal. See also the Companies Act 1985 s 98(3) and para 200 post. As to underwriting see para 194 et seq post.
5 *Re Anglo-French Co-operative Society, ex p Pelly* (1882) 21 ChD 492, CA; *Re London and Provincial Starch Co* (1869) 20 LT 390; *Re Brighton Brewery Co, Hunt's Case* (1868) 37 LJ Ch 278.
6 *Re Anglo-Greek Steam Co* (1866) LR 2 Eq 1.
7 *Re Madrid Bank, ex p Williams* (1866) LR 2 Eq 216.
8 *Re General Exchange Bank, ex p Preston* (1868) 37 LJ Ch 618.

53. Acceptance of presents from promoters. Directors or other officers of the company or its agents at the time of promotion accepting gifts from promoters are liable to account to the company for the money or shares or other property received[1], and, in the case of fully-paid shares which have diminished in value, the nominal amount of the shares must be accounted for[2]. An article authorising a promoter to give shares to the directors has been rejected as fraudulent[3], but full disclosure may prevent liability[4]. Where several directors receive presents with mutual knowledge, they are jointly and severally liable for the whole amount[5].

The acceptance of gifts by an agent of the company is a ground for the company rescinding the purchase contract[6] if the transaction is not revealed to the company[6], whether or not the gift influences the conduct of the agent[7]. If the promised gift is not handed over, the agent cannot recover it[8].

1 *Pearson's Case* (1877) 5 ChD 336, CA; *De Ruvigne's Case* (1877) 5 ChD 306, CA; *Nant-y-Glo and Blaina Ironworks Co v Grave* (1878) 12 ChD 738; *Mitcalfe's Case* (1879) 13 ChD 169, CA; *Re Carriage Co-operative Supply Association* (1884) 27 ChD 322; *Eden v Ridsdales Rly Lamp and Lighting Co Ltd* (1889) 23 QBD 368, CA; *McKay's Case* (1875) 2 ChD 1, CA; *Re Howatson Patent Furnace Co* (1887) 4 TLR 152; *Archer's Case* [1892] 1 Ch 322, CA (agreement by promoters to buy directors' shares at par); *Re London and South Western Canal Ltd* [1911] 1 Ch 346 (directors had promoters' shares transferred to them as their qualification and held them on trust for the promoters). See further para 2454 post.
2 See the cases cited in note 1 supra and *Hay's Case* (1875) 10 Ch App 593; *Weston's Case* (1879) 10 ChD 579, CA; *Bland's Case* [1893] 2 Ch 612, CA (directors inaccurately stated in the contract with the company to be part vendors).
3 *Re Eskern Slate Slab Quarries Co Ltd, Clarke and Helden's Cases* (1877) 37 LT 222; cf *Miller's Case* (1877) 5 ChD 70, CA.
4 *Re Postage Stamp Automatic Delivery Co* [1892] 3 Ch 566 (disclosure in a contract registered with the registrar); *Re Olympia Ltd* [1898] 2 Ch 153 at 169, 174, CA (affd sub nom *Gluckstein v Barnes* [1900] AC 240, HL); *Re Innes & Co Ltd* [1903] 2 Ch 254 at 265, 266, CA; and as to the law relating to disclosure by promoters see paras 48–50 ante.
5 *Re Carriage Co-operative Supply Association* (1884) 27 ChD 322.
6 *Panama and South Pacific Telegraph Co v India Rubber, Gutta Percha, and Telegraph Works Co* (1875) 10 Ch App 515, CA; *Smith v Sorby* (1875) 3 QBD 552n.

7 *Industries and General Mortgage Co Ltd v Lewis* [1949] 2 All ER 573; and see AGENCY vol 1(2) (Reissue) para 151.

8 *Harrington v Victoria Graving Dock Co* (1878) 3 QBD 549.

(v) Promoter's Liability

54. Liability to outsiders. A contract which purports to be made by or on behalf of a company at a time when the company has not been formed[1] has effect, subject to any agreement to the contrary, as one made with the person purporting to act for the company or as agent for it[2], and he is personally liable[3] on the contract accordingly[4]. No exclusion of personal liability will be implied merely by the manner of signature of the contract[5]. Personal liability under the contract comes to an end once it has been performed, or rescinded by either party under some power in the contract, or by consent of all parties, or when the company has, with the consent of the other contracting party, undertaken the liability of the promoter under the contract[6]. Where, however, there is a contract to pay out of a specific fund, the personal liability exists only to the extent of the fund, if any[7].

1 This does not cover the situation where a company has been formed but changes its name; contracts made at that time are not pre-incorporation contracts since a change of name is not a re-formation or re-incorporation of the company (*Oshkosh B'Gosh Inc v Dan Marbel Inc Ltd* [1989] 1 CMLR 94, [1989] BCLC 507, CA); nor does it cover contracts entered into by a company which has been formed but which was trading under an incorrect name (*Badgerhill Properties Ltd v Cottrell* [1991] BCLC 805, CA).

2 For these purposes, a contract can purport to be made on behalf of a company or by a company even though that company is known by both parties not to be formed and that it is only about to be formed: *Phonogram Ltd v Lane* [1982] QB 938 at 943, [1981] 3 All ER 182 at 186, CA per Lord Denning MR. A contract cannot, however, purport to be made on behalf of a company not yet formed if no one had thought of the new company at the time of contracting: *Cotronic (UK) Ltd v Dezonie* [1991] BCLC 721, CA (parties contracted with first company which in fact had been struck off the register and dissolved and, when this was discovered years later, a second company was incorporated; it was impossible to say that the contract purported to be made by or on behalf of the second company).

3 It would seem that, on grounds of mutuality, the promoter is also entitled to enforce the contract: see *Newborne v Sensolid (Great Britain) Ltd* [1954] 1 QB 45, [1953] 1 All ER 708, CA.

4 Companies Act 1985 s 36C(1) (substituted by the Companies Act 1989 s 130(4)). The Companies Act 1985 s 36C(1) (as so substituted) applies to the making of a deed under the law of England and Wales as it applies to the making of a contract: s 36C(2)(a) (substituted by the Companies Act 1989 s 130(4)). The Companies Act 1985 s 36C(1) (as so substituted) re-enacts in substantially the same terms the Companies Act 1985 s 36(4) (itself re-enacting the European Communities Act 1972 s 9(2),(9) (repealed)), which negatived the decisions in *Hollman v Pullin* (1884) Cab & El 254 and *Newborne v Sensolid (Great Britain) Ltd* [1954] 1 QB 45, [1953] 1 All ER 708, CA. For the law prior to this provision see *Nockels v Crosby* (1825) 3 B & C 814; *Re Rotherham Alum and Chemical Co* (1883) 25 ChD 103, CA; *Mant v Smith* (1859) 4 H & N 324; *Lake v Duke of Argyll* (1844) 6 QB 477. See further para 1126 post.

    The Secretary of State may make provision by regulations applying the Companies Act 1985 s 36 (as substituted) (see para 1129 post), s 36A (as substituted) (see para 1130 post) and s 36C (as substituted) to companies incorporated outside Great Britain, subject to such exceptions, adaptations or modifications as may be specified in the regulations; and such regulations must be made by statutory instrument which is subject to annulment in pursuance of a resolution of either House of Parliament: Companies Act 1989 s 130(6). In exercise of the power so conferred the Secretary of State made the Foreign Companies (Execution of Documents) Regulations 1994, SI 1994/950 (amended by SI 1995/1729).

    The Companies Act 1985 s 36C (as substituted) applies to companies incorporated outside Great Britain; and references in s 36C (as substituted) to a company are to be construed as references to a company incorporated outside Great Britain: Foreign Companies (Execution of Documents) Regulations 1994 regs 2, 3 (amended by SI 1995/1729). This had not previously been the case: see *Rover International Ltd v Cannon Film Sales Ltd* [1987] BCLC 540; revsd on other grounds sub nom *Rover International Ltd v Cannon Film Sales Ltd (No 3)* [1989] 3 All ER 423, [1989] 1 WLR 912, CA.

The Companies Act 1985 s 36C (as substituted) also applies to any unregistered company: see the Companies (Unregistered Companies) Regulations 1985, SI 1985/680, reg 4, Sch 1 (as amended) and para 1767 post.

5 *Phonogram Ltd v Lane* [1982] QB 938, [1981] 3 All ER 182, CA. Much had seemed to turn in the older cases on the manner in which contracts had been signed, although they might more accurately have been stated as turning on issues of the parties' intentions: *Phonogram Ltd v Lane* supra at 945 and at 188 per Oliver LJ. It was argued in *Phonogram Ltd v Lane* supra that questions as to the manner of signature were still relevant to what is now the Companies Act 1985 s 36C (as substituted) in view of the words 'subject to any agreement to the contrary'. This view was rejected, since to interpret the statutory provision in that way would defeat the whole purpose of that provision: *Phonogram Ltd v Lane* supra at 946 and at 182 per Oliver LJ. Unless there is a clear exclusion of personal liability, the promoter is personally liable however he expresses his signature: *Phonogram Ltd v Lane* supra at 944 and at 187 per Lord Denning MR.

6 *Re English and Colonial Produce Co Ltd* [1906] 2 Ch 435, CA; *Kelner v Baxter* (1866) LR 2 CP 174; *Re Northumberland Avenue Hotel Co* (1866) 33 ChD 16, CA; *Scott v Lord Ebury* (1867) LR 2 CP 255. A company cannot adopt or ratify a pre-incorporation contract but must contract again on identical terms: *Natal Land and Colonization Co Ltd v Pauline Colliery and Development Syndicate Ltd* [1904] AC 120, PC; and see paras 1126, 1127 post. The issue is not addressed by the statutory provisions.

7 *Giles v Smith* (1847) 11 Jur 334; *Andrews v Ellison* (1821) 6 Moore CP 199; *Gurney v Rawlins* (1836) 2 M & W 87 at 90; *Re Athenaeum Society and Prince of Wales Society, Durham's Case* (1858) 4 K & J 517.

55. Promoters as partners.
Promoters associated only to form a company are not in partnership[1]. Where, however, they incur joint liability, each is liable to make contribution to the extent of his share[2]; and they may be partners if they join together in buying property in order to sell it at a profit to a company which they form to purchase it[3].

1 *Wood v Duke of Argyll* (1844) 6 Man & G 928; *Bright v Hutton, Hutton v Bright* (1852) 3 HL Cas 341 at 368; *Keith Spicer Ltd v Mansell* [1970] 1 All ER 462, [1970] 1 WLR 333, CA. For the essential characteristics of a partnership see PARTNERSHIP vol 35 (Reissue) para 1.

2 *Boulter v Peplow* (1850) 9 CB 493; *Batard v Hawes* (1853) 2 E & B 287 at 290 (provisional committee members of projected company are not partners, but liable to contribute as co-contractors); *Edger v Knapp* (1843) 5 Man & G 753 (joint contractors; one having paid debt was entitled to contribution from others; contractors had acted as directors of proposed company); *Mant v Smith* (1859) 4 H & N 324 (taxation by one partner of the bill of a solicitor employed by the partnership).

3 Ie if they carrry on the business of acquiring the property and reselling it with a view of profit: see the Partnership Act 1890 s 1 and PARTNERSHIP vol 35 (Reissue) para 1.

56. Liability to and for each other.
In the absence of an express contract, one of several promoters may not sue another for remuneration for services in connection with the promotion[1]; but a person assisting promoters may sue for remuneration for his services if there is a contract express or implied to pay for them[2].

Promoters are not as such agents for each other, or liable for the other's acts; but an authority to act for each other may be inferred from the terms of a public prospectus or from conduct[3].

1 *Holmes v Higgins* (1822) 1 B & C 74.

2 *Mant v Smith* (1859) 4 H & N 324; *Lucas v Beach* (1840) 1 Man & G 417.

3 *Reynell v Lewis, Wyld v Hopkins* (1846) 15 M & W 517; *McEwan v Campbell* (1857) 2 Macq 499, HL.

57. Circumstances in which liability terminated.
After the dissolution of the company no proceedings may be taken against the promoter on behalf of the company unless the dissolution is set aside[1].

Where a promoter is adjudged bankrupt, a company may prove in his bankruptcy for any secret profits obtained by him[2]. His order of discharge releases him from any debt or liability to the company which is provable in the bankruptcy, unless it was a debt he incurred in respect of, or forbearance in respect of which was secured by means of, any fraud or fraudulent breach of trust to which he was a party[3].

Where a promoter has received a secret profit, he cannot, in proceedings by the company or its liquidator to recover the profit, set up the provisions of the Limitation Act 1980 by way of defence[4].

In general, the liability of a promoter has always been enforceable against his estate after his death[5]; since 25 July 1934 all causes of action subsisting against a deceased at his death survive against his estate[6].

1 See *Coxon v Gorst* [1891] 2 Ch 73. See also para 2691 post.
2 *Re Darby, ex p Brougham* [1911] 1 KB 95. See further *Re Kent County Gas Light and Coke Co Ltd* [1913] 1 Ch 92 (where it was held that the liquidator of a company having proved in the bankruptcy of a promoter for a sum as damages for breach of trust in relation to the company could not, after so electing to prove against the promoter, prove against the joint estate of a firm of which that promoter and another promoter were the partners).
3 See the Insolvency Act 1986 s 281(3) and BANKRUPTCY vol 3(2) (Reissue) para 631.
4 See the Limitation Act 1980 s 32(1) (no period of limitation applies to an action by a beneficiary under a trust in respect of any fraud or fraudulent breach of trust to which the trustee was a party or privy or to recover from the trustee trust property or its proceeds in his possession or previously received by him and converted to his use); *Re Sale Hotel and Botanical Gardens Co Ltd, Hesketh's Case* (1897) 77 LT 681 (revsd on other grounds) (1898) 78 LT 368, CA); *Re Sharpe, Re Bennett, Masonic and General Life Assurance Co v Sharpe* [1892] 1 Ch 154 at 172, CA; cf *Tintin Exploration Syndicate Ltd v Sandys* (1947) 177 LT 412. Before the passing of the Trustee Act 1888 s 8 (replaced by the Limitation Act 1980 s 32), where a director had received money from a third party in such circumstances as to amount to a fraud on the company, the court applied the Statute of Limitations by analogy as from the date when the beneficiary knew the facts: *Metropolitan Bank v Heiron* (1880) 5 ExD 319, CA; and see *Re Sale Hotel and Botanical Gardens Co Ltd, Hesketh's Case* supra at 682. See further LIMITATION OF ACTIONS vol 28 para 833 et seq.
  As to defences founded on laches see *Lindsay Petroleum Co v Hurd* (1874) LR 5 PC 221 at 239; *Erlanger v New Sombrero Phosphate Co* (1878) 3 App Cas 1218, HL; *Re Sharpe, Re Bennett, Masonic and General Life Assurance Co v Sharpe* supra at 168, CA; *Concha v Murrieta* (1889) 40 ChD 543 at 553, CA (varied on the facts [1892] AC 670, HL).
5 For analogous cases against directors see para 617 notes 10–12 post.
6 See EXECUTORS vol 17 para 1564.

58. Criminal liability. Promoters of a company may incur criminal liability in connection with the publication of advertisements in connection with listing applications[1] or contravention of the statutory provisions governing offers of unlisted securities[2]. In certain cases promoters may be indicted for conspiracy[3].

1 See the Financial Services Act 1986 s 154 (as amended) and paras 294, 295 post.
2 See the Public Offers of Securities Regulations 1995, SI 1995/1537, reg 16 and para 320 post.
3 *R v Aspinall* (1876) 2 QBD 48, CA.

59. Suspension of promoters from managing companies. The court[1] may make a disqualification order[2] against a person where he is convicted of an indictable offence, whether on indictment or summarily, in connection with the promotion, formation, management, liquidation or striking off of a company[3], or with the receivership or management of a company's property[4].

The maximum period of disqualification which may be imposed under these provisions is, where the disqualification order is made by a court of summary jurisdiction, five years, and in any other case, 15 years[5].

An application for such an order may be made by the Secretary of State, the official receiver or the liquidator or any past or present member or creditor of the company in

relation to which the person in question has committed or is alleg
ted an offence or other default[6].

1   For these purposes, 'the court' means (1) any court having jurisdiction to w
relation to which the offence was committed; or (2) the court by or befc
convicted of the offence; or (3) in the case of a summary conviction in Englar
magistrates' court acting for the same petty sessions area: Company Directors E
s 2(2). As to the courts having winding-up jurisdiction see paras 2004, 2196 et seq post.
2   For the meaning of 'disqualification order' see para 1417 post.
3   For these purposes, 'company' includes any company which may be wound up under the Insolvency
Act 1986 Pt V (ss 220–229 (as amended): see para 2898 et seq post): Company Directors Disqualification
Act 1986 s 22(1),(2)(b).
4   Ibid s 2(1) (amended by the Deregulation and Contracting Out Act 1994 s 39, Sch 11 para 6). As to
disqualification for persistent breaches of the companies legislation see para 1419 post.
5   Company Directors Disqualification Act 1986 s 2(3). As to the application of s 2 (as amended) see para
1418 note 5 post.
6   See ibid s 16(2) and para 1433 post.

(3) FORMATION AND REGISTRATION

(i) Matters applying to all Companies

A. REGISTRATION OFFICES AND PRACTICE

60. Offices and officers. For the purposes of the registration of companies under
the Companies Acts[1], there are offices in England and Wales and in Scotland, at such
places as the Secretary of State thinks fit[2]. The Secretary of State may appoint such
registrars[3], assistant registrars, clerks and servants as he thinks necessary for that purpose,
make regulations with respect to their duties, and remove any persons so appointed[4].
With the concurrence of the Treasury, he may fix their salaries, which must be paid out
of money provided by Parliament[5], and may direct a seal or seals to be prepared for the
authentication of documents[6] required for or in connection with the registration of
companies[7]. Any seal so prepared is referred to in the Companies Act 1985 as the
registrar's official seal[7].

Wherever by the Companies Acts[8] any act is directed to be done to or by the
registrar of companies, it must, until the Secretary of State otherwise directs, be done in
England or Wales or Scotland, as the case may be, to or by the existing registrar of
companies, or to or by such person as the Secretary of State may for the time being
authorise[9]. In the event of the Secretary of State altering the constitution of the existing
registration offices or any of them, any such act must be done to or by such officer and
at such place with reference to the local situation of the registered offices of the
companies to be registered as the Secretary of State may appoint[10].

In so far as the registrar of companies does not already have power to do so, he may
authorise an officer of his to exercise any function of his which is conferred by or under
any enactment[11]. Anything done or omitted to be done by an officer so authorised in,
or in connection with, the exercise or purported exercise of the function is to be
treated for all purposes as done or omitted to be done by the registrar of companies in
his capacity as such[12]; but this provision does not apply for the purposes of any criminal
proceedings brought in respect of anything so done or omitted to be so done[13].

Where, by virtue of an order made under the Deregulation and Contracting Out
Act 1994[14], a person is authorised by the registrar of companies to accept delivery[15] of

.y class of documents which are under any provision of the Companies Acts to be delivered to the registrar, then, if:

(1) the registrar directs that documents of the class shall be delivered to a specified address of the authorised person; and

(2) the direction is printed and made available to the public, with or without payment,

any document of that class which is delivered to an address other than the specified address is treated for the purpose of those Acts as not having been delivered[16].

1 'The Companies Acts' means the Companies Act 1985, the Companies Consolidation (Consequential Provisions) Act 1985 and the Criminal Justice Act 1993 Pt V (ss 52-64) (see para 1218 et seq post): Companies Act 1985 s 744 (amended by the Criminal Justice Act 1993 s 79(13), Sch 5 para 4(1)).

2 Companies Act 1985 s 704(1).

3 Unless the contrary intention appears, 'the registrar of companies' and 'the registrar', in the Companies Act 1985, mean the registrar or other officer performing under that Act the duty of registration of companies in England and Wales or in Scotland, as the case may require: s 744. In the Insolvency Rules 1986, SI 1986/1925, 'registrar' has a different meaning: see para 2814 post.

4 Companies Act 1965 s 704(2). As to the delegation of the registrar's functions see para 61 post.

5 Ibid s 704(3).

6 For these purposes, 'document' includes information recorded in any form: ibid s 715A(1) (added by the Companies Act 1989 s 127(1)). As to the authentication of documents see para 67 post.

7 Companies Act 1985 s 704(4).

8 In ibid s 704(5),(7),(8) (as amended), references to the Companies Acts include certain provisions of the Insolvency Act 1986 and of the Financial Services Act 1986 and also the Company Directors Disqualification Act 1986: see para 20 text to notes 12, 19 and notes 12, 19 ante.

9 Companies Act 1985 s 704(5). See also note 8 supra.

10 Ibid s 704(6).

11 Deregulation and Contracting Out Act 1994 s 74(1),(4)(a).

12 Ibid s 74(2),(4)(a).

13 Ibid s 74(3),(4)(a).

14 Ie under ibid s 69: see para 61 post.

15 For these purposes, references to delivering a document include sending, forwarding, producing or, in the case of a notice, giving it: Companies Act 1985 s 715A(2) (added by the Companies Act 1989 s 127(1)).

16 Companies Act 1985 s 704(7),(8) (added by the Deregulation and Contracting Out Act 1994 s 76, Sch 16 para 8). See also note 8 supra.

61. Power to contract out the registrar of companies' functions. If the Secretary of State by order so provides, any function of the registrar of companies which is conferred by or under any enactment and which, by virtue of any enactment or rule of law, may be exercised by an officer of his and which is not otherwise excluded[1] may be exercised by, or by employees of, such person (if any) as may be authorised in that behalf by the registrar or the Secretary of State[2]. The Secretary of State may not, however, make such an order in relation to the registrar of companies without first consulting him[3].

An order so made may provide that any such function may be exercised, and an authorisation given by virtue of such an order may, subject to the provisions of the order, authorise the exercise of such a function:

(1) either wholly or to such extent as may be specified in the order or authorisation;

(2) either generally or in such cases or areas as may be so specified; and

(3) either unconditionally or subject to the fulfilment of such conditions as may be so specified[4].

An authorisation given by virtue of such an order:

(a) must be for such period, not exceeding ten years, as is specified in the authorisation;

(b) may be revoked at any time by the Secretary of State or the registrar; and
(c) must not prevent the Secretary of State or the registrar or any other person from exercising the function to which the authorisation relates[5].

Where by virtue of such an order a person is authorised to exercise any function of the Secretary of State or the registrar, anything done or omitted to be done by or in relation to the authorised person (or an employee of his) in, or in connection with, the exercise or purported exercise of the function is to be treated for all purposes as done or omitted to be done by or in relation to the Secretary of State or the registrar in his capacity as such[6]; but this provision does not apply for the purposes of so much of any contract made between an authorised person and the Secretary of State or the registrar as relates to the exercise of the function or for the purposes of any criminal proceedings brought in respect of anything done or omitted to be done by the authorised person (or any employee of his)[7].

Where by virtue of such an order a person is authorised to exercise any function of the Secretary of State or the registrar and the order or authorisation is revoked at a time when a relevant contract[8] is subsisting, the authorised person is entitled to treat the relevant contract as repudiated by the Secretary of State or the registrar (and not as frustrated by reason of the revocation)[9].

1 Ie by the Deregulation and Contracting Out Act 1994 s 71. A function is excluded from s 69 (see infra) if (1) its exercise would constitute the exercise of jurisdiction of any court or of any tribunal which exercises the judicial power of the State; or (2) its exercise, or a failure to exercise it, would necessarily interfere with or otherwise affect the liberty of any individual; or (3) it is a power or right of entry, search or seizure into or of any property; or (4) it is a power or duty to make subordinate legislation: s 71(1). Section 71(1)(b),(c) (see heads (2), (3) supra) does not exclude any function of the official receiver attached to any court: s 71(2). As to the official receiver see para 2263 et seq post.
2 Ibid ss 69(1),(2), 79. In exercise of the powers so conferred the Secretary of State, after consulting the registrar of companies, made the Contracting Out (Functions in relation to the Registration of Companies) Order 1995, SI 1995/1013, art 3, Sch 1: see para 62 post.
3 Deregulation and Contracting Out Act 1994 ss 69(3), 79.
4 Ibid s 69(4).
5 Ibid s 69(5).
6 Ibid ss 72(1),(2), 79.
7 Ibid ss 72(3), 79.
8 For these purposes, 'relevant contract' means so much of any contract made between the authorised person and the Secretary of State or the registrar of companies as relates to the exercise of the functions: ibid ss 73(3), 79.
9 Ibid ss 73(1),(2), 79.

62. Contracted out functions of the registrar of companies. Any function of the registrar of companies for England and Wales which is listed below may be exercised by, or by employees of, such person (if any) as may be authorised in that behalf by the registrar of companies for England and Wales[1]:

(1) any function of receiving any return, account or other document required to be filed with, delivered or sent, or notice of any matter required to be given, to the registrar which is conferred by or under any enactment[2];
(2) any functions in relation to:
    (a) the incorporation of companies and the change of name of companies[3];
    (b) the re-registration and change of status of companies[4], the registration of an order and minute of reduction of share capital[5] and the re-registration of public companies[6] on reduction of capital[7];
(3) functions conferred by or under the following provisions of the Companies Act 1985:

(a) those relating to companies' registered numbers[8] and registration of branches of oversea companies[9], except in so far as they relate respectively to the determination of the form of companies' registered numbers and branches' registered numbers;

(b) those relating to the delivery to the registrar of documents in legible form[10], except in so far as they relate to specification of requirements for the purpose of enabling the copying of documents delivered to the registrar;

(c) those relating to the delivery to the registrar of documents other than in legible form[11], except in so far as they relate to the approval of the non-legible form in which information may be conveyed to the registrar;

(d) those relating to inspection etc of records kept by the registrar[12], except in so far as they relate to the determination of the means of facilitating the exercise of the right of persons to inspect records kept by the registrar, or the form in which copies of the information contained in those records may be made available;

(e) those relating to certificates of incorporation[13];

(f) those relating to the provision and authentication by the registrar of documents in non-legible form[14], except in so far as they relate to the approval of the means of communication to the registrar of information in non-legible form[15];

(4) functions conferred by or under the Newspaper Libel and Registration Act 1881[16] relating to the registrar's duty to enter returns on the register[17];

(5) functions conferred by or under the Limited Partnerships Act 1907[18] relating to the inspection of documents registered[19];

(6) functions conferred by or under the Insurance Companies Act 1982[20] relating to the rescission, variation and publication of requirements and documents deposited with the Secretary of State[21];

(7) functions conferred by or under the European Economic Interest Grouping Regulations 1989[22] relating to the inspection of documents[23];

(8) functions conferred by or under any provision of the Companies Act 1985 listed in heads (2) and (3) above to the extent specified therein where any such provision is applied[24] to European Economic Interest Groupings[25].

1 Contracting Out (Functions in relation to the Registration of Companies) Order 1995, SI 1995/1013, art 3. As to the contracting out of functions of the registrar of companies for Scotland see art 4, Sch 2.

2 Ibid art 3, Sch 1 para 1.

3 Ie under the Companies Act 1985 Pt I Chs I, II (ss 1–34) (as amended): see paras 80 et seq, 154 et seq post.

4 Ie by or under ibid Pt II (ss 43–55) (as amended): see para 118 et seq post.

5 Ie ibid s 138: see paras 266–268 post.

6 Ie ibid ss 139, 147: see paras 269, 366 post.

7 Contracting Out (Functions in relation to the Registration of Companies) Order 1995 Sch 1 para 2.

8 Ie the Companies Act 1985 s 705 (as substituted): see para 63 post.

9 Ie ibid s 705A (as added): see para 1799 post.

10 Ie ibid s 706 (as substituted): see para 64 post.

11 Ie ibid s 707 (as substituted): see para 65 post.

12 Ie ibid s 709 (as substituted): see para 67 post.

13 Ie ibid s 710 (as substituted): see para 67 post.

14 Ie ibid s 710A (as substituted): see para 67 post.

15 Contracting Out (Functions in relation to the Registration of Companies) Order 1995 Sch 1 para 3.

16 Ie by or under the Newspaper Libel and Registration Act 1881 s 13: see LIBEL vol 28 para 218.

17 Contracting Out (Functions in relation to the Registration of Companies) Order 1995 Sch 1 para 4.

18 Ie by or under the Limited Partnerships Act 1907 s 16: see PARTNERSHIP vol 35 (Reissue) para 209.

19 Contracting Out (Functions in relation to the Registration of Companies) Order 1995 Sch 1 para 5.

20 Ie by or under the Insurance Companies Act 1982 s 47 or s 65: see INSURANCE vol 25 (Reissue) paras
    845, 846.
21 Contracting Out (Functions in relation to the Registration of Companies) Order 1995 Sch 1 para 6.
22 Ie by or under the European Economic Interest Grouping Regulations 1989, SI 1989/638, reg 14: see
    para 1842 post.
23 Contracting Out (Functions in relation to the Registration of Companies) Order 1995 art 2(1), Sch 1
    para 7.
24 Ie by the European Economic Interest Grouping Regulations 1989 reg 18: see para 1831 post.
25 Contracting Out (Functions in relation to the Registration of Companies) Order 1995 Sch 1 para 8. For
    these purposes, 'European Economic Interest Grouping' means a European Economic Interest
    Grouping as defined in the European Economic Interest Grouping Regulations 1989 reg 2(1) (see para
    1831 post): Contracting Out (Functions in relation to the Registration of Companies) Order 1995
    art 2(1).

63. Companies' registered numbers. The registrar of companies must allocate to
every company[1] a number, which is to be known as the company's registered number[2];
and companies' registered numbers must be in such form, consisting of one or more
sequences of figures or letters, as the registrar may from time to time determine[3]. Upon
adopting a new form of registered number, the registrar may make such changes of
existing registered numbers as appear to him to be necessary[4].

A change of a company's registered number has effect from the date on which the
company is notified by the registrar of the change; but for a period of three years
beginning with the date on which that notification is sent by the registrar the statutory
requirement[5] as to the use of the company's registered number on business letters and
order forms is satisfied by the use of either the old number or the new[6].

1 For these purposes, 'company' includes (1) any oversea company which has complied with the
   Companies Act 1985 s 690A(2), Sch 21A para 1 (see para 1792 post), other than a company which
   appears to the registrar not to have a branch in Great Britain; (2) any oversea company which has
   complied with s 691 (see paras 1804, 1805 post), other than a company which appears to the registrar not
   to have a place of business in Great Britain; and (3) any body to which any provision of the Companies
   Act 1985 applies by virtue of s 718 (see paras 1765-1768 post): s 705(5) (substituted by the Companies
   Act 1989 s 145, Sch 19 para 14; amended by the Oversea Companies and Credit and Financial
   Institutions (Branch Disclosure) Regulations 1992, SI 1992/3179, reg 4, Sch 3 paras 3, 5). 'Place of
   business' includes a share transfer or share registration office: Companies Act 1985 s 744.
2 Ibid s 705(1) (substituted by the Companies Act 1989 s 145, Sch 19 para 14). Any function of the
   registrar of companies for England and Wales conferred by or under the Companies Act 1985 s 705 (as
   substituted) may be exercised by, or by employees of, such person (if any) as may be authorised in that
   behalf by the registrar of companies for England and Wales, except in so far as it relates to the
   determination of the form of companies' registered numbers: Contracting Out (Functions in relation to
   the Registration of Companies) Order 1995, SI 1995/1013, art 3, Sch 1 para 3(a). As to the contracting
   out of the registrar of companies' functions generally see paras 61, 62 ante.
3 Companies Act 1985 s 705(2) (substituted by the Companies Act 1989 Sch 19 para 14). See also note 2
   supra.
4 Companies Act 1985 s 705(3) (substituted by the Companies Act 1989 Sch 19 para 14). See also note 2
   supra.
5 Ie the Companies Act 1985 s 351(1)(a): see para 1135 post.
6 Ibid s 705(4) (substituted by the Companies Act 1989 Sch 19 para 14). See also note 2 supra.

64. Delivery to the registrar of documents in legible form. The following
provisions apply to the delivery[1] to the registrar of companies under any provision of
the Companies Acts[2] of documents[3] in legible form[4].

The document must:

(1) state in a prominent position the registered number of the company to which it
     relates and in specified cases[5] the registered number of the branch to which it
     relates;

(2) satisfy any requirements prescribed by regulations for these purposes; and
(3) conform to such requirements as the registrar may specify for the purpose of enabling him to copy the document[6].

If a document is delivered to the registrar which does not comply with the requirements of these provisions, he may serve on the person by whom the document was delivered, or, if there are two or more such persons, on any of them, a notice indicating the respect in which the document does not comply[7]. Where the registrar serves such a notice, then, unless a replacement document is delivered to him within 14 days after the service of the notice and complies with the requirements of these provisions or the provisions relating to delivery to the registrar of documents otherwise than in legible form[8], or is not rejected by him for failure to comply with those requirements, the original document is deemed not to have been delivered to him[9].

1 For the meaning of references to delivering a document see para 60 note 15 ante.
2 For the meaning of 'the Companies Acts' see para 60 note 1 ante. In the Companies Act 1985 s 706(1) (as substituted), references to the Companies Acts include certain provisions of the Insolvency Act 1986 and of the Financial Services Act 1986 and also the Company Directors Disqualification Act 1986: see para 20 text to notes 12, 19 and notes 12, 19 ante.
3 For the meaning of 'document' see para 60 note 6 ante.
4 Companies Act 1985 s 706(1) (substituted by the Companies Act 1989 s 125(1)). For these purposes, 'legible', in the context of documents in legible or non-legible form, means capable of being read with the naked eye: Companies Act 1985 s 715A(1) (added by the Companies Act 1989 s 127(1)).
   Any function of the registrar of companies for England and Wales conferred by or under the Companies Act 1985 s 706 (as substituted) may be exercised by, or by employees of, such person (if any) as may be authorised in that behalf by the registrar of companies for England and Wales, except in so far as it relates to specification of requirements for the purpose of enabling the copying of documents delivered to the registrar: Contracting Out (Functions in relation to the Registration of Companies) Order 1995, SI 1995/1013, art 3, Sch 1 para 3(b). As to the contracting out of the registrar of companies' functions generally see paras 61, 62 ante.
5 Ie if the document is delivered by an oversea company under the Companies Act 1985 s 695A(3) (as added) (see para 1798 post), s 703P (as added) (see para 2912 post), s 703Q (as added) (see para 2913 post), s 690A(2), Sch 21A (as added) (see para 1791 et seq post) or s 699AA(2), Sch 21D (see paras 1819–1821 post).
6 Ibid s 706(2) (substituted by the Companies Act 1989 s 125(1); amended by the Oversea Companies and Credit and Financial Institutions (Branch Disclosure) Regulations 1992, SI 1992/3179, reg 4, Sch 3 paras 3, 6). Regulations made for the purposes of the Companies Act 1985 s 706 (as substituted) may make different provision with respect to different descriptions of document: s 706(5) (substituted by the Companies Act 1989 s 125(1)). At the date at which this volume states the law no regulations had been so made. See also note 4 supra.
7 Companies Act 1985 s 706(3) (substituted by the Companies Act 1989 s 125(1)). See also note 4 supra.
8 Ie the Companies Act 1985 s 707 (as substituted): see para 65 post.
9 Ibid s 706(4) (substituted by the Companies Act 1989 s 125(1)). For the purposes of any enactment imposing a penalty for failure to deliver, so far as it imposes a penalty for continued contravention, no account is to be taken of the period between the delivery of the original document and the end of the period of 14 days after service of the registrar's notice: Companies Act 1985 s 706(4) (as so substituted). See also note 4 supra.

65. Delivery to the registrar of documents otherwise than in legible form. The following provisions apply to the delivery[1] to the registrar of companies under any provision of the Companies Acts[2] of documents[3] otherwise than in legible form[4].

Any requirement to deliver a document to the registrar, or to deliver a document in the prescribed form, is satisfied by the communication to the registrar of the requisite information in any non-legible form prescribed for these purposes by regulations or approved by the registrar[5].

Where the document is required to be signed or sealed, it must instead be authenticated in such manner as may be prescribed by regulations or approved by the registrar[6].

The document must:

(1) contain in a prominent position the registered number of the company to which it relates and in specified cases[7] the registered number of the branch to which it relates;

(2) satisfy any requirements prescribed by regulations for these purposes; and

(3) be furnished in such manner, and conform to such requirements, as the registrar may specify for the purpose of enabling him to read and copy the document[8].

If a document is delivered to the registrar which does not comply with the requirements of these provisions, he may serve on the person by whom the document was delivered, or, if there are two or more such persons, on any of them, a notice indicating the respect in which the document does not comply[9]. Where the registrar serves such a notice, then, unless a replacement document is delivered to him within 14 days after the service of the notice and complies with the requirements of these provisions or the provisions relating to delivery to the registrar of documents in legible form[10], or is not rejected by him for failure to comply with those requirements, the original document is deemed not to have been delivered to him[11].

The Secretary of State may by regulations make further provision with respect to the application of these provisions in relation to instantaneous forms of communication[12].

1 For the meaning of references to delivering a document see para 60 note 15 ante.

2 For the meaning of 'the Companies Acts' see para 60 note 1 ante. In the Companies Act 1985 s 707(1) (as substituted), references to the Companies Acts include certain provisions of the Insolvency Act 1986 and of the Financial Services Act 1986 and also the Company Directors Disqualification Act 1986: see para 20 text to notes 12, 19 and notes 12, 19 ante.

3 For the meaning of 'document' see para 60 note 6 ante.

4 Companies Act 1985 s 707(1) (substituted by the Companies Act 1989 s 125(2)). For the meaning of 'legible' see para 64 note 4 ante.

    Any function of the registrar of companies for England and Wales conferred by or under the Companies Act 1985 s 707 (as substituted) may be exercised by, or by employees of, such person (if any) as may be authorised in that behalf by the registrar of companies for England and Wales, except in so far as it relates to the approval of the non-legible form in which information may be conveyed to the registrar: Contracting Out (Functions in relation to the Registration of Companies) Order 1995, SI 1995/1013, art 3, Sch 1 para 3(c). As to the contracting out of the registrar of companies' functions generally see paras 61, 62 ante.

5 Companies Act 1985 s 707(2) (substituted by the Companies Act 1989 s 125(2)). Regulations made for the purposes of the Companies Act 1985 s 707 (as substituted) may make different provision with respect to different descriptions of document and different forms of communication and as respects delivery to the registrar for England and Wales and delivery to the registrar for Scotland: s 707(8) (substituted by the Companies Act 1989 s 125(1)). At the date at which this volume states the law no such regulations had been made.

6 Companies Act 1985 s 707(3) (substituted by the Companies Act 1989 s 125(2)).

7 Ie if the document is delivered by an oversea company under the Companies Act 1985 s 695A(3) (as added) (see para 1798 post), s 703P (as added) (see para 2912 post), s 703Q (as added) (see para 2913 post), s 690A(2), Sch 21A (as added) (see para 1791 et seq post) or s 699AA(2), Sch 21D (see paras 1819–1821 post).

8 Ibid s 707(4) (substituted by the Companies Act 1989 s 125(1); amended by the Oversea Companies and Credit and Financial Institutions (Branch Disclosure) Regulations 1992, SI 1992/3179, reg 4, Sch 3 paras 3, 6).

9 Companies Act 1985 s 707(5) (substituted by the Companies Act 1989 s 125(1)).

10 Ie the Companies Act 1985 s 706 (as substituted): see para 64 ante.

11 Ibid s 707(6) (substituted by the Companies Act 1989 s 125(1)). For the purposes of any enactment imposing a penalty for failure to deliver, so far as it imposes a penalty for continued contravention, no

account is to be taken of the period between the delivery of the original document and the end of the period of 14 days after service of the registrar's notice: Companies Act 1985 s 707(6) (as so substituted).

12 Ibid s 707(7) (substituted by the Companies Act 1989 s 125(1)). At the date at which this volume states the law no such regulations had been made.

66. Fees payable to registrar. The Secretary of State may by regulations made by statutory instrument require the payment to the registrar of companies of such fees as may be specified in the regulations[1] in respect of:

(1) the performance by the registrar of such functions under the Companies Acts[2] as may be so specified, including the receipt by him of any document[3] which under those Acts is required to be delivered[4] to him[5];

(2) the inspection of documents kept by him under those Acts[6].

A statutory instrument containing any such regulations and requiring the payment of a fee in respect of a matter for which no fee was previously payable, or increasing a fee, must be laid before Parliament after being made and ceases to have effect at the end of the period of 28 days[7] beginning with the day on which the regulations were made (but without prejudice to anything previously done under the regulations or to the making of further regulations) unless in that period the regulations are approved by resolution of each House of Parliament[8]. A statutory instrument containing regulations otherwise than as above is subject to annulment in pursuance of a resolution of either House of Parliament[9].

The registrar may charge a fee for any services provided by him otherwise than in pursuance of an obligation imposed on him by law[10].

1 The regulations currently in force are the Companies (Fees) Regulations 1991, SI 1991/1206 (amended by SI 1992/2876; SI 1994/2217; SI 1995/1423).

2 For the meaning of 'the Companies Acts' see para 60 note 1 ante. In the Companies Act 1985 s 708(1)(a) and s 708(4) (see note 5 infra), references to the Companies Acts include certain provisions of the Insolvency Act 1986 and of the Financial Services Act 1986 and also the Company Directors Disqualification Act 1986: see para 20 text to notes 12, 19 and notes 12, 19 ante.

3 For the meaning of 'document' see para 60 note 6 ante.

4 For the meaning of references to delivering a document see para 60 note 15 ante.

5 Companies Act 1985 s 708(1)(a) (amended by the Companies Act 1989 s 127(2)(a)). Fees paid to the registrar under the Companies Acts must be paid into the Consolidated Fund: Companies Act 1985 s 708(4). As to registration fees in particular see para 73 post.

6 Ibid s 708(1)(b) (amended by the Companies Act 1989 ss 127(2)(b), 212, Sch 24).

7 In reckoning the period of 28 days no account is to be taken of any time during which Parliament is dissolved or prorogued or during which both Houses are adjourned for more than four days: Companies Act 1985 s 708(2).

8 Ibid s 708(2).

9 Ibid s 708(3).

10 Ibid s 708(5).

67. Inspection etc of records kept by the registrar. Any person may inspect any records kept by the registrar for the purposes of the Companies Acts[1] and may require:

(1) a copy, in such form as the registrar considers appropriate, of any information contained in those records; or

(2) a certified copy of, or extract from, any such record[2].

The right of inspection extends to the originals of documents[3] delivered[4] to the registrar in legible[5] form only where the record kept by the registrar of the contents of the document is illegible or unavailable[6].

A copy of, or extract from, a record kept at any of the offices for the registration of companies in England and Wales or Scotland, certified in writing by the registrar (whose official position it is unnecessary to prove) to be an accurate record of the contents of any document delivered to him under the Companies Acts[7], is in all legal proceedings admissible in evidence as of equal validity with the original document and as evidence of any fact stated therein of which direct oral evidence would be admissible[8].

Copies of or extracts from records furnished by the registrar may, instead of being certified by him in writing to be an accurate record, be sealed with his official seal[9].

No process for compelling the production of a record kept by the registrar may issue from any court except with the leave of the court; and any such process must bear on it a statement that it is issued with the leave of the court[10].

Any person may require a certificate of the incorporation of a company, signed by the registrar or authenticated by his official seal[11].

Any requirement of the Companies Acts[12] as to the supply by the registrar of a document may, if the registrar thinks fit, be satisfied by the communication by the registrar of the requisite information in any non-legible form prescribed for these purposes by regulations or approved by him[13]. Where the document is required to be signed by him or sealed with his official seal, it must instead be authenticated in such manner as may be prescribed by regulations or approved by the registrar[14].

1 For the meaning of 'the Companies Acts' see para 60 note 1 ante. In the Companies Act 1985 s 709(1),(3) (as substituted) (see infra) and in s 710A (as substituted) (see infra) references to the Companies Acts include certain provisions of the Insolvency Act 1986 and of the Financial Services Act 1986 and also the Company Directors Disqualification Act 1986: see para 20 text to notes 12, 19 and notes 12, 19 ante.

2 For the meaning of 'document' see para 60 note 6 ante.

3 Companies Act 1985 s 709(1) (substituted by the Companies Act 1989 s 126(2)). Any function of the registrar of companies for England and Wales conferred by or under the Companies Act 1985 s 709 (as substituted) may be exercised by, or by employees of, such person (if any) as may be authorised in that behalf by the registrar of companies for England and Wales, except in so far as it relates to the determination of the means of facilitating the exercise of the right of persons to inspect records kept by the registrar, or the form in which copies of the information contained in those records may be made available: Contracting Out (Functions in relation to the Registration of Companies) Order 1995, SI 1995/1013, art 3, Sch 1 para 3(d). As to the contracting out of the registrar of companies' functions generally see paras 61, 62 ante.

4 For the meaning of references to delivering a document see para 60 note 15 ante.

5 For the meaning of 'legible' see para 64 note 4 ante.

6 Companies Act 1985 s 709(2) (substituted by the Companies Act 1989 s 126(2)). See also note 3 supra.

7 See note 1 supra.

8 Companies Act 1985 s 709(3) (substituted by the Companies Act 1989 s 126(2)). In England and Wales this is subject to compliance with any applicable rules of court under the Civil Evidence Act 1968 s 5 (see EVIDENCE vol 17 para 59) or the Police and Criminal Evidence Act 1984 s 69(2) (see CRIMINAL LAW vol 11(2) (Reissue) para 1158): Companies Act 1985 s 709(3) (as so substituted). See also note 3 supra.

9 Ibid s 709(4) (substituted by the Companies Act 1989 s 126(2)). As to the registrar's official seal see paras 28 note 3, 60 ante. See also note 3 supra.

10 Companies Act 1985 s 709(5) (substituted by the Companies Act 1989 s 126(2)). See also note 3 supra.

11 Companies Act 1985 s 710 (substituted by the Companies Act 1989 s 126(2)). Any function of the registrar of companies for England and Wales conferred by or under the Companies Act 1985 s 710 (as so substituted) may be exercised by, or by employees of, such person (if any) as may be authorised in that behalf by the registrar of companies for England and Wales: Contracting Out (Functions in relation to the Registration of Companies) Order 1995 Sch 1 para 3(e).

12 See note 1 supra.

13 Companies Act 1985 s 710A(1) (substituted by the Companies Act 1989 s 126(2)). Any function of the registrar of companies for England and Wales conferred by or under the Companies Act 1985 s 710A (as substituted) may be exercised by, or by employees of, such person (if any) as may be authorised in that behalf by the registrar of companies for England and Wales, except in so far as it relates to the

determination of the form of companies' registered numbers: Contracting Out (Functions in relation to the Registration of Companies) Order 1995 Sch 1 para 3(f).

14 Companies Act 1985 s 710A(2) (substituted by the Companies Act 1989 s 126(2)). See also note 13 supra.

68. Keeping of company records by the registrar. The information contained in a document[1] delivered[2] to the registrar of companies under the Companies Acts[3] may be recorded and kept by him in any form he thinks fit, provided that it is possible to inspect the information and to produce a copy of it in legible form[4]. This is sufficient compliance with any duty of his to keep, file or register the document[4].

The originals of documents delivered to the registrar in legible form must be kept by him for ten years, after which they may be destroyed[5].

Where a company[6] has been dissolved, the registrar may, at any time after the expiration of two years from the date of the dissolution, direct that any records in his custody relating to the company may be removed to the Public Record Office[7]; and records in respect of which such a direction is given must be disposed of in accordance with the enactments relating to that Office and the rules made under them[8].

1 For the meaning of 'document' see para 60 note 6 ante.
2 For the meaning of references to delivering a document see para 60 note 15 ante.
3 For the meaning of 'the Companies Acts' see para 60 note 1 ante. In the Companies Act 1985 s 707A(1) (as added) references to the Companies Acts include certain provisions of the Insolvency Act 1986 and of the Financial Services Act 1986 and also the Company Directors Disqualification Act 1986: see para 20 text to notes 12, 19 and notes 12, 19 ante.
4 Companies Act 1985 s 707A(1) (added by the Companies Act 1989 s 126(1)). For the meaning of 'legible' see para 64 note 4 ante.
5 Companies Act 1985 s 707A(2) (added by the Companies Act 1989 s 126(1)).
6 For these purposes, 'company' includes a company provisionally or completely registered under the Joint Stock Companies Act 1844: Companies Act 1985 s 707A(4) (added by the Companies Act 1989 s 126(1)).
7 As to the Public Record Office see CONSTITUTIONAL LAW vol 8 para 1291 et seq.
8 Companies Act 1985 s 707A(3) (added by the Companies Act 1989 s 126(1)). The Companies Act 1985 s 707A(3) (as so added) does not extend to Scotland: s 707A(3) (as so added).

69. Enforcement of company's duty to make returns. If a company, having made default in complying with any provision of the Companies Acts[1] which requires it to deliver[2] a document[3] to the registrar of companies or to give notice to him of any matter, fails to make good the default within 14 days after the service of a notice on the company requiring it to do so, the court may, on an application made to the court by any member or creditor of the company or by the registrar of companies, make an order directing the company and any officer of it to make good the default within such time as may be specified in the order[4]. Any such order may provide that all costs of and incidental to the application shall be borne by the company or by any officers of the company responsible for the default[5]. Nothing in this provision prejudices the operation of any enactment imposing penalties on a company or its officers in respect of any such default[6].

The application is by originating summons in the general form[7], and should be made against the company, and in a proper case against any officer alleged to be responsible for the default. The officer may be made to pay the costs. The application may be made by any member or creditor of the company or by the registrar. Application must be made to the court having jurisdiction to wind up the company[8]. In the High Court of Justice the jurisdiction is assigned to the Chancery Division[9].

The originating summons and all affidavits, notices and other documents under it must be entitled in the matter of the company and in the matter of the Companies Act 1985[10]. A respondent to an originating summons issued in pursuance of the above provisions must acknowledge service[11].

The evidence must prove the default, service of the notice[12] and default in complying with it, and also, except where the applicant is the registrar, the status of the applicant as creditor or member.

1 For the meaning of 'the Companies Acts' see para 60 note 1 ante. In the Companies Act 1985 s 713(1) (as amended) references to the Companies Acts include certain provisions of the Insolvency Act 1986 and of the Financial Services Act 1986 and also the Company Directors Disqualification Act 1986: see para 20 text to notes 12, 19 and notes 12, 19 ante.
2 For the meaning of references to delivering a document see para 60 note 15 ante.
3 For the meaning of 'document' see para 60 note 6 ante.
4 Companies Act 1985 s 713(1) (amended by the Companies Act 1989 s 127(4)). For a successful application for attachment by the registrar based on failure to comply with an order made under these provisions see *Re George Dowman Ltd* (1960) Times, 26 July.
5 Companies Act 1985 s 713(2).
6 Ibid s 713(3).
7 See RSC Ord 102 r 2(1),(2)(b).
8 See the Companies Act 1985 s 744 (definition of 'the court'). As to the courts with winding-up jurisdiction see paras 2004, 2196 et seq post.
9 See RSC Ord 102 r 5(1).
10 RSC Ord 102 r 5(2).
11 See RSC Ord 102 r 2(1),(2), App A, Form 8.
12 Ie the notice referred to in the Companies Act 1985 s 713(1) (as amended): see supra.

70. Public notice by registrar of receipt and issue of documents. The registrar of companies must cause to be published in the Gazette[1] notice of the issue or receipt by him of documents of any of the following descriptions, stating in the notice the name of the company, the description of document and the date of issue or receipt:

(1) any certificate of incorporation of a company[2];
(2) any document making or evidencing an alteration in a company's memorandum or articles[3];
(3) any notification of a change among the directors of a company[4];
(4) any copy of a resolution of a public company which gives, varies, revokes or renews an authority for the allotment of relevant securities[5];
(5) any copy of a special resolution of a public company effecting the disapplication of pre-emption rights[6];
(6) any report as to the value of a non-cash asset[7];
(7) any statutory declaration delivered in connection with the share capital requirements of a public company[8];
(8) any notification of the redemption of shares[9];
(9) any statement or notice delivered by a public company in connection with the registration of particulars of special rights[10];
(10) any accounts and reports delivered by a company[11];
(11) a copy of any resolution or agreement which must be forwarded to the registrar within 15 days after it is passed or made[12] and which:
    (a) states the rights attached to any shares in a public company, other than shares which are in all respects uniform[13] with shares previously allotted; or
    (b) varies rights attached to any shares in a public company; or
    (c) assigns a name or other designation, or a new name or designation, to any class of shares in a public company[14];

(12) any return of allotments of a public company[15];

(13) any notice of a change in the situation of a company's registered office[16];

(14) any copy of a winding-up order in respect of a company[17];

(15) any order for the dissolution of a company on a winding up[18];

(16) any return by a liquidator of the final meeting of a company on a winding up[19];

(17) any copy of a draft of the terms of a scheme delivered to the registrar of companies[20] with regard to mergers and divisions of public companies[21];

(18) any copy of an order[22] in respect of a compromise or arrangement[23] with regard to mergers and divisions of public companies[24];

(19) any return delivered[25] in respect of branch registration[26];

(20) any document delivered[27] in respect of branch registration[28];

(21) any notice[29] of the closure of a branch of an oversea company[30];

(22) any document delivered[31] consisting of the accounts and reports of a foreign credit or financial institution[32];

(23) any document delivered[33] consisting of the accounts and reports of an oversea company subject to branch registration, other than a credit or financial institution[34];

(24) any return delivered[35] consisting of particulars of the winding up of an oversea company subject to branch registration[36].

1 For these purposes, 'the Gazette' means, as respects companies registered in England and Wales, the London Gazette and, as respects companies registered in Scotland, the Edinburgh Gazette: Companies Act 1985 s 744. In the case of an unregistered company (see para 1765 et seq post) notice of the receipt by the registrar of companies of (1) any instrument constituting or regulating the company; and (2) any notice of the situation of the company's principal office, must be included in the matters which the registrar is required to cause to be published in the Gazette by virtue of s 711 (as amended): Companies (Unregistered Companies) Regulations 1985, SI 1985/680, reg 6(g).

2 Companies Act 1985 s 711(1)(a).

3 Ibid s 711(1)(b).

4 Ibid s 711(1)(c).

5 Ibid s 711(1)(d). Such an authority is given under s 80 (as amended): see para 447 post.

6 Ibid s 711(1)(e). Such a resolution is passed under s 95(1), (2) or (3): see para 462 post.

7 Ibid s 711(1)(f). Such a report is made under s 103 (as amended) (see para 468 post) or s 104 (see para 469 post).

8 Ibid s 711(1)(g). Such a declaration is delivered under s 117: see para 652 post.

9 Ibid s 711(1)(h). Such notification is given under s 122: see paras 206, 208, 218 post.

10 Ibid s 711(1)(j). Such statement or notice is delivered under s 128: see para 185 post.

11 Ibid s 711(1)(k) (amended by the Companies Act 1989 s 23, Sch 10 para 14). Such documents are delivered under the Companies Act 1985 s 242(1) (as substituted): see para 817 post.

12 Ie a resolution or agreement to which ibid s 380 (as amended) applies: see para 691 post.

13 Ie for purposes of ibid s 128: see para 185 post.

14 Ibid s 711(1)(l).

15 Ibid s 711(1)(m).

16 Ibid s 711(1)(n).

17 Ibid s 711(1)(p).

18 Ibid s 711(1)(q).

19 Ibid s 711(1)(r).

20 Ie under ibid s 427A(1), Sch 15B para 2(1) (as added and renumbered): see para 1466 post.

21 Ibid s 711(1)(s) (added by the Companies (Mergers and Divisions) Regulations 1987, SI 1987/1991, reg 2(b)).

22 Ie under the Companies Act 1985 s 425(2) (see para 1447 post) or s 427 (see para 1460 et seq post).

23 Ie a compromise or arrangement to which ibid s 427A(1) (as added and amended) applies: see para 1463 post.

24 Ibid s 711(1)(t) (added by the Companies (Mergers and Divisions) Regulations 1987 reg 2(b)).

25 Ie under the Companies Act 1985 Sch 21A paras 1, 7 or 8 (as added): see paras 1792, 1797 post.

26 Ibid s 711(1)(u) (added by the Oversea Companies and Credit and Financial Institutions (Branch Disclosure) Regulations 1992, SI 1992/3179, reg 4, Sch 3 paras 3, 7).

27 Ie under the Companies Act 1985 Sch 21A paras 1 or 8 (as added): see paras 1792, 1797 post.
28 Ibid s 711(1)(v) (added by the Oversea Companies and Credit and Financial Institutions (Branch Disclosure) Regulations 1992 Sch 3 paras 3, 7).
29 Ie under the Companies Act 1985 s 695A(3) (as added): see para 1798 post.
30 Ibid s 711(1)(w) (added by the Oversea Companies and Credit and Financial Institutions (Branch Disclosure) Regulations 1992 Sch 3 paras 3, 7).
31 Ie under the Companies Act 1985 Sch 21C (as added): see paras 1816-1818 post.
32 Ibid s 711(1)(x) (added by the Oversea Companies and Credit and Financial Institutions (Branch Disclosure) Regulations 1992 Sch 3 paras 3, 7).
33 Ie under the Companies Act 1985 Sch 21D (as added): see paras 1819-1821 post.
34 Ibid s 711(1)(y) (added by the Oversea Companies and Credit and Financial Institutions (Branch Disclosure) Regulations 1992 Sch 3 paras 3, 7).
35 Ie under the Companies Act 1985 s 703P (as added): see para 2912 post.
36 Ibid s 711(1)(z) (added by the Oversea Companies and Credit and Financial Institutions (Branch Disclosure) Regulations 1992 Sch 3 paras 3, 7).

71. Effect of lack of official notification. The purpose of the statutory provisions as to public notice of documents by the registrar[1] is not to ensure constructive notice of the relevant events to persons dealing with the company[2], but rather to ensure that such persons have an opportunity, if they wish to avail themselves of it, to find out information about these events[3]. Further, a company is not entitled to rely against other persons on the happening of any of the following events:

(1) the making of a winding-up order in respect of the company, or the appointment of a liquidator in a voluntary winding up of the company[4]; or

(2) any alteration of the company's memorandum or articles of association[5]; or

(3) any change among the company's directors[6]; or

(4) (as regards service of any document on the company) any change in the situation of the company's registered office[7],

if the event has not been officially notified[8] at the material time and is not shown by the company to have been known at that time to the person concerned, or if the material time fell on or before the fifteenth day after the date of official notification (or, where the fifteenth day was a non-business day[9], on or before the next day that was not) and it is shown that the person concerned was unavoidably prevented from knowing of the event at that time[10].

1 Ie the Companies Act 1985 s 711 (as amended): see para 70 ante.
2 As to notice of the constitution of a company see para 1137 post.
3 *Official Custodian of Charities v Parway Estates Developments Ltd* [1985] Ch 151, [1984] 3 All ER 679, CA.
4 Companies Act 1985 s 42(1)(a). See *Re Peek, Winch and Tod Ltd* (1979) 130 NLJ 116, CA.
5 Companies Act 1985 s 42(1)(b).
6 Ibid s 42(1)(c).
7 Ibid s 42(1)(d).
8 For these purposes, 'official notification' means (1) in relation to anything stated in a document of any of the descriptions set out in ibid s 711(1) (as amended) (see para 70 ante), the notification of that document in the Gazette; and (2) in relation to the appointment of a liquidator in a voluntary winding up, the notification of it in the Gazette under the Insolvency Act 1986 s 109 (see para 2703 post); and 'officially notified' is to be construed accordingly: Companies Act 1985 ss 42(2)(a), 711(2) (amended by the Insolvency Act 1986 s 439(1), Sch 13 Pt I). For the meaning of 'the Gazette' see para 70 note 1 ante.
9 For these purposes, 'non-business day' means a Saturday or Sunday, Christmas Day, Good Friday and any other day which is a bank holiday in the part of Great Britain where the company is registered: Companies Act 1985 s 42(2)(b). 'Bank holiday' means a holiday under the Banking and Financial Dealings Act 1971 (see TIME vol 45 para 1119 et seq): Companies Act 1985 s 744.
10 Ibid s 42(1). As to the proposed abolition of the doctrine of deemed notice see s 711A (added by the Companies Act 1989 s 142(1)). However, at the date at which this volume states the law no order had been made bringing the Companies Act 1989 s 142 into force.

72. Registrar's index of company names. The registrar of companies must keep an index of the names of the following bodies:

(1) companies as defined by the Companies Act 1985[1];

(2) companies incorporated outside the United Kingdom and Gibraltar which have complied with their duty to register[2] and which do not appear to the registrar of companies not to have a branch in Great Britain[3];

(3) companies incorporated outside Great Britain which have complied with the obligation to deliver documents to the registrar[4] and which do not appear to the registrar of companies not to have a place of business[5] in Great Britain[6];

(4) incorporated and unincorporated bodies to which any provision of the Companies Act 1985 is made to apply[7];

(5) limited partnerships registered under the Limited Partnerships Act 1907[8];

(6) companies within the meaning of the Companies (Northern Ireland) Order 1986[9];

(7) companies incorporated outside Northern Ireland which have complied with the obligation to deliver documents to the registrar and which do not appear to the registrar not to have a place of business in Northern Ireland[10]; and

(8) societies registered under the Industrial and Provident Societies Act 1965 or the Industrial and Provident Societies Act (Northern Ireland) 1969[11].

The Secretary of State may by order in a statutory instrument vary the above heads by the addition or deletion of any class of body, except any within heads (1) or (3) above, whether incorporated or unincorporated; and any such statutory instrument is subject to annulment in pursuance of a resolution of either House of Parliament[12].

1 Companies Act 1985 s 714(1)(a). For the meaning of 'company' as so defined see para 11 note 1 ante.
2 Ie under ibid s 690A(2), Sch 21A para 1 (as added): see para 1792 post.
3 Ibid s 714(1)(aa) (added by the Oversea Companies and Credit and Financial Institutions (Branch Disclosure) Regulations 1992, SI 1992/3179, reg 4, Sch 3 paras 3, 8).
4 Ie the obligation under the Companies Act 1985 s 691 (as amended): see para 1804 post.
5 For the meaning of 'place of business' see para 63 note 1 ante.
6 Companies Act 1985 s 714(1)(b).
7 Ibid s 714(1)(c). As to such application see s 718 and para 1766 et seq post.
8 Ibid s 714(1)(d).
9 Ibid s 714(1)(e); Interpretation Act 1978 s 17(2)(a).
10 Companies Act 1985 s 714(1)(f).
11 Ibid s 714(1)(g).
12 Ibid s 714(2). At the date at which this volume states the law no order had been so made.

B. FEES AND STAMP DUTIES

73. Registration and re-registration fees. The Secretary of State may by regulations made by statutory instrument require the payment to the registrar of companies of fees in respect of the performance by the registrar of his functions under the Companies Acts[1].

The fee for registration of a company on its formation under the Companies Act 1985[2], for registration of a company not formed, but authorised to register, under the 1985 Act[3], and for the re-registration of a company under the 1985 Act[4] is £20[5].

1 See the Companies Act 1985 s 708(1)(a) (as amended) and para 66 ante.
2 See para 80 et seq post.
3 Ie pursuant to the Companies Act 1985 Pt XXII Ch II (ss 680–690) (as amended): see para 75 et seq post.
4 Ie pursuant to ibid Pt II (ss 43–55): see para 118 et seq post.
5 Companies (Fees) Regulations 1991, SI 1991/1206, reg 4, Schedule, Fee 1 (amended by SI 1994/2217).

74. Stamp duties. Stamp duty is no longer chargeable on any statement relating to the nominal share capital of a limited company on its incorporation[1]. Stamp duty may, however, be chargeable on the transfer of assets of a business to a company[2].

1 See the Finance Act 1973 s 49(1)(a). See also para 280 post.
2 See STAMP DUTIES vol 44(1) (Reissue) para 1027 et seq.

C. REGISTRATION OF COMPANIES NOT FORMED UNDER THE COMPANIES ACT 1985 BUT WHICH MAY REGISTER

75. Assent of members. A company not formed, but authorised to register, under the Companies Act 1985 may not so register[1] without the assent of a majority of such of its members as are present in person or by proxy (in cases where proxies are allowed) at a general meeting summoned for the purpose[2]. Where a company not having the liability of its members limited by Act of Parliament or letters patent is about to register as a limited company, the majority required so to assent consists of not less than three-fourths of the members present in person or by proxy at the meeting[3]. Where a company is about to register as a company limited by guarantee, the assent to its being so registered must be accompanied by a resolution declaring that each member undertakes to contribute to the company's assets, in the event of its being wound up while he is a member, or within one year after he ceases to be a member, for payment of the company's debts and liabilities contracted before he ceased to be a member, and of the costs and expenses of winding up, and for the adjustment of the rights of the contributories among themselves, such amount as may be required, not exceeding a specified amount[4].

In computing any majority when a poll is demanded, regard is to be had to the number of votes to which each member is entitled according to the company's regulations[5].

1 Ie under the Companies Act 1985 s 680 (as amended): see para 24 ante.
2 Ibid s 681(1).
3 Ibid s 681(2).
4 Ibid s 681(4).
5 Ibid s 681(3). As to voting at meetings see para 670 et seq post.

76. Documents to be delivered in case of joint stock company. Before the registration of a joint stock company[1] not formed, but authorised to register, under the Companies Act 1985[2] there must be delivered to the registrar:

(1) a statement in the prescribed form[3] that the registered office[4] of the company is to be situated in England and Wales, or in Wales, as the case may be[5];

(2) a statement in the prescribed form[6] specifying the intended situation of the company's registered office after registration[7];

(3) in an appropriate case, if the company wishes to be registered with the Welsh equivalent[8] of 'public limited company' , or, as the case may be, 'limited' as the last words or word of its name, a statement to that effect[9];

(4) a statement in the prescribed form[10] specifying the name with which the company is proposed to be registered[11];

(5) a list in the prescribed form[12] showing the names and addresses of all persons who on a day named in the list, not more than 28 clear days before the day of registration, were members of the company, with the addition of the shares or

stock held by them respectively (distinguishing, in cases where the shares are numbered, each share by its number)[13];

(6) a copy of any Act of Parliament, royal charter, letters patent, deed of settlement, contract of copartnery or other instrument constituting or regulating the company[14];

(7) if the company is intended to be registered as a limited company, a statement[15] specifying the following particulars:

  (a) the nominal share capital of the company and the number of shares into which it is divided, or the amount of stock of which it consists; and

  (b) the number of shares taken and the amount paid on each share[16].

1 For the meaning of 'joint stock company' see para 25 note 2 ante. The registrar may require such evidence as he thinks necessary for the purpose of satisfying himself whether a company proposing to be registered is or is not a joint stock company: Companies Act 1985 s 686(3).
2 Ie under ibid s 680 (as amended): see para 24 ante.
3 For the prescribed form of statement see the Companies (Forms) Regulations 1985, SI 1985/854, reg 4(1), Sch 3, Form 680a; and for the meaning of 'prescribed' see para 24 note 3 ante.
4 As to the registered office of a company see para 150 post.
5 Companies Act 1985 s 681(5)(a),(6).
6 See note 3 supra.
7 Companies Act 1985 s 681(5)(b),(6).
8 For the Welsh equivalents see para 156 post.
9 Companies Act 1985 s 681(5)(c),(6).
10 See note 3 supra.
11 Companies Act 1985 s 684(1)(a).
12 For the prescribed form of list see the Companies (Forms) Regulations 1985 Sch 3, Form 684.
13 Companies Act 1985 s 684(1)(b) (amended by the Companies Act 1985 s 145, Sch 19 para 12).
14 Companies Act 1985 s 684(1)(c).
15 See note 3 supra.
16 Companies Act 1985 s 684(2).

77. Registration of joint stock company as public company. A joint stock company[1] applying to be registered[2] as a company limited by shares may, subject to satisfying certain conditions[3] and making the application in the required manner[4], apply to be registered as a public company[5]. The resolution that the company be a public company may change the company's name by deleting the word 'company' or the words 'and company', or its or their equivalent in Welsh ('cwmni' , 'a'r cwmni'), including any abbreviation of them[6].

The joint stock company's application must be made in the form prescribed[7] for the purpose, and must be delivered to the registrar of companies together with the following documents, in addition to those already mentioned[8]:

(1) a copy of the resolution that the company be a public company[9];

(2) a copy of a written statement by an accountant with the appropriate qualifications[10] that in his opinion a relevant balance sheet[11] shows that at the balance sheet date[12] the amount of the company's net assets was not less than the aggregate of its called-up share capital and undistributable reserves[13];

(3) a copy of the relevant balance sheet, together with a copy of an unqualified report[14] (by an accountant with such qualifications) in relation to that balance sheet[15];

(4) a copy of any valuation report prepared[16] in a case where shares have been recently allotted[17]; and

(5) a statutory declaration in the prescribed form[18] by a director or secretary of the company:

(a) that the necessary conditions[19] have been satisfied; and

(b) that, between the balance sheet date referred to in head (2) above and the joint stock company's application, there has been no change in the company's financial position that has resulted in the amount of its net assets becoming less than the aggregate of its called-up share capital and undistributable reserves[20].

1 For the meaning of 'joint stock company' see para 25 note 2 ante.
2 Ie under the Companies Act 1985 s 680 (as amended): see para 24 ante.
3 Ie the conditions set out in ibid s 44(2)(a),(b) (where applicable) (see para 119 post) and s 45(2)-(4) (see para 120 post) as applied by s 685 (as amended).
4 Ie in accordance with ibid s 685(4): see infra.
5 Ibid s 685(1). Section 44 (see para 119 post) and s 45 (see para 120 post) apply for this purpose as in the case of a private company applying to be re-registered under s 43 (see para 118 post), but as if a reference to the special resolution required by s 43 were to the joint stock company's resolution that it be a public company: s 685(2).
6 Ibid s 685(3).
7 For the prescribed form of application see the Companies (Forms) Regulations 1985, SI 1985/854, reg 4(1), Sch 3, Form 680a.
8 Ie those required by the Companies Act 1985 s 684 (as amended): see para 76 ante.
9 Ibid s 685(4)(a).
10 For these purposes, 'accountant with the appropriate qualifications' means a person who would be eligible for appointment as the company's auditor, if it were a company registered under the Companies Act 1985: s 685(6) (amended by the Companies Act 1989 (Eligibility for Appointment as Company Auditor) (Consequential Amendments) Regulations 1991, SI 1991/1997, reg 2, Schedule para 53(1),(2)). As to eligibility for appointment as a company's auditor see para 955 et seq post.
11 For these purposes, 'relevant balance sheet' means a balance sheet prepared as at a date not more than seven months before the joint stock company's application to be registered as a public company limited by shares: Companies Act 1985 s 685(6).
12 For these purposes, 'balance sheet date' has the same meaning as in ibid Pt VII (ss 221-262A (as amended): see para 809 note 7 post): s 742(1) (substituted by the Companies Act 1989 s 23, Sch 10 para 15).
13 Companies Act 1985 s 685(4)(b). For these purposes, 'undistributable reserves' has the meaning given by s 264(3) (see para 702 note 5 post): s 685(6).
14 Ibid s 46 (see para 121 post) applies, with necessary modifications, for the interpretation of the reference to an unqualified report by the accountant: s 685(6).
15 Ibid s 685(4)(c).
16 Ie under ibid s 44(2)(b) as applied by s 685 (as amended).
17 Ibid s 685(4)(d).
18 For the prescribed form of statutory declaration see the Companies (Forms) Regulations 1985 Sch 3, Form 685.
19 Ie the conditions referred to in note 3 supra.
20 Companies Act 1985 s 685(4)(e). The registrar may accept a declaration under s 685(4)(e) as sufficient evidence that the conditions referred to in that provision have been satisfied: s 685(5).

78. Documents to be delivered by company not joint stock company. Before the registration of any company not formed, but authorised to register, under the Companies Act 1985[1] and not being a joint stock company[2], there must be delivered to the registrar of companies:

(1) a statement in the prescribed form[3] that the registered office[4] of the company is to be situated in England and Wales, or in Wales, as the case may be[5];

(2) a statement in the prescribed form[6] specifying the intended situation of the company's registered office after registration[7];

(3) in an appropriate case, if the company wishes to be registered with the Welsh equivalent[8] of 'public limited company' or, as the case may be, 'limited' as the last words or word of its name, a statement[9] to that effect[10];

(4) a statement in the prescribed form[11] specifying the name with which the company is proposed to be registered[12];

(5) a list showing with respect to each director or manager of the company:
    (a) in the case of an individual, his name[13], address, occupation and date of birth;
    (b) in the case of a corporation or Scottish firm, its corporate or firm name and registered or principal office[14];

(6) a copy of any Act of Parliament, letters patent, deed of settlement, contract of copartnery or other instrument constituting or regulating the company[15]; and

(7) in the case of a company intended to be registered as a company limited by guarantee, a copy of the resolution declaring the amount of the guarantee[16].

The lists of members and directors and any other particulars relating to the company which are required[17] to be delivered to the registrar must be verified by a statutory declaration in the prescribed form[18] made by any two or more directors or other principal officers of the company[19].

1 Ie under the Companies Act 1985 s 680 (as amended): see para 24 ante.
2 For the meaning of 'joint stock company' see para 25 note 2 ante. The registrar may require such evidence as he thinks necessary for the purpose of satisfying himself whether a company proposing to be registered is or is not a joint stock company: ibid s 686(3).
3 For the prescribed form of statement see the Companies (Forms) Regulations 1985, SI 1985/854, reg 4(1), Sch 3, Form 680b; and for the meaning of 'prescribed' see para 24 note 3 ante.
4 As to a company's registered office see para 150 post.
5 Companies Act 1985 s 681(5)(a),(6).
6 See note 3 supra.
7 Companies Act 1985 s 681(5)(b),(6).
8 For the Welsh equivalents see para 156 post.
9 See note 3 supra.
10 Companies Act 1985 s 681(5)(c),(6).
11 See note 3 supra.
12 Companies Act 1985 s 686(1)(a).
13 For these purposes, a person's 'name' means his Christian name (or other forename) and surname, except that, in the case of a peer, or an individual usually known by a title, the title may be stated instead of his Christian name (or other forename) and surname or in addition to either or both of them: ibid s 686(1A) (added by the Companies Act 1989 s 145, Sch 19 para 5(1),(3)).
14 Companies Act 1985 s 686(1)(b) (amended by the Companies Act 1989 Sch 19 para 5(1),(2)).
15 Companies Act 1985 s 686(1)(c).
16 Ibid s 686(1)(d).
17 Ie by ibid Pt XXII Ch II (ss 680-690) (as amended).
18 For the prescribed form of statutory declaration see the Companies (Forms) Regulations 1985 Sch 3, Form 686.
19 Companies Act 1985 s 686(2).

79. Name of company. Where a company (whether a joint stock company[1] or not) is to be registered[2] as a public company, its name must end with the words 'public limited company' or, if it is stated that the company's registered office is to be situated in Wales, with those words or their equivalent in Welsh ('cwmni cyfyngedig cyhoeddus'); and those words or that equivalent may not be preceded by the word 'limited' or its equivalent in Welsh ('cyfyngedig')[3].

In the case of a company limited by shares or by guarantee (not being a public company) the name must have 'limited' as its last word (or, if the company's registered office is to be situated in Wales, 'cyfyngedig') unless the company can satisfy the requirements for dispensing with the word 'limited' as part of its name[4].

If the company is registered with limited liability, any additions to the company's name set out in the statements delivered on registration[5] are to form and be registered as the last part of the company's name[6].

Where the name of a company seeking registration[7] is a name by which it is precluded from registration by the statutory prohibition on the registration of certain names[8], either absolutely or because the Secretary of State would not approve of it, the company may change its name with effect from the date on which it is so registered[9]. Such a change of name requires the like assent of the members as is required by the other procedural requirements[10] for registration[11].

1 For the meaning of 'joint stock company' see para 25 note 2 ante.
2 Ie under the Companies Act 1985 Pt XXII Ch II (ss 680–690) (as amended).
3 Ibid s 687(1),(2).
4 Ibid s 687(3). As to dispensing with the word 'limited' see para 112 et seq post.
5 Ie the statements delivered under ibid s 684(1)(a) (see para 76 ante) or s 686(1)(a) (see para 78 ante).
6 Ibid s 687(4).
7 Ie under ibid s 680 (as amended): see para 24 ante.
8 Ie ibid s 26: see para 156 post.
9 Ibid s 682(1). As to names and change of name generally see para 154 et seq post.
10 Ie by ibid s 681: see para 75 ante.
11 Ibid s 682(2).

D. GENERAL PROVISIONS AS TO NEW COMPANIES

80. Formation of new company. Any two or more persons[1] associated for a lawful purpose[2] may, by subscribing their names to a memorandum of association and otherwise complying with the statutory requirements in respect of registration, form an incorporated company, with or without limited liability[3]. A company so formed may be:

(1) a company having the liability of its members limited by the memorandum to the amount, if any, unpaid on the shares respectively held by them ('a company limited by shares')[4]; or

(2) a company having the liability of its members limited by the memorandum to such amount as the members may respectively thereby undertake to contribute to the assets of the company in the event of its being wound up ('a company limited by guarantee')[5]; or

(3) a company not having any limit on the liability of its members ('an unlimited company')[6].

Notwithstanding the above provisions[7], one person may, for a lawful purpose, by subscribing his name to a memorandum of association and otherwise complying with the requirements of the Companies Act 1985 in respect of registration, form an incorporated company being a private company limited by shares or by guarantee[8].

Any contract, so far as it relates to the formation of a company[9] or to its constitution, or the rights or obligations of its corporators or members, is exempt from the prohibitions on the exclusion of liability imposed by the Unfair Contract Terms Act 1977[10].

1 For the meaning of 'persons' see para 83 post.
2 The registrar of companies has a duty not to register an unlawful association: *R v Registrar of Companies, ex p Bowen* [1914] 3 KB 1161 at 1167. See also *R v Registrar of Companies, ex p A-G* [1991] BCLC 476 (where the registration of a company whose main object was the organising of the services of a prostitute was quashed as the purpose was contrary to public policy and unlawful). As to companies which are illegal see para 1758 et seq post.

3 Companies Act 1985 s 1(1).
4 Ibid s 1(2)(a).
5 Ibid s 1(2)(b). With effect from 22 December 1980, a company cannot be formed as, or become, a company limited by guarantee with a share capital: s 1(4).
6 Ibid s 1(2)(c).
7 Ie ibid s 1(1): see supra.
8 Ibid s 1(3A) (added by the Companies (Single Member Private Limited Companies) Regulations 1992, SI 1992/1699, reg 2(1)(b), Schedule para 1). As to single member private limited companies see para 81 post.
9 For these purposes, 'company' means any body corporate or unincorporated association and includes a partnership: Unfair Contract Terms Act 1977 s 1(2), Sch 1 para 1(d).
10 Ibid Sch 1 para 1(d). As to the Unfair Contract Terms Act 1977 generally see CONTRACT. Similarly the Unfair Terms in Consumer Contracts Regulations 1994, SI 1994/3159, do not apply to any contract relating to the incorporation or organisation of companies or partnerships: see reg 3(1), Sch 1 para (d) and CONTRACT.

81. Single member private companies limited by shares or by guarantee. Notwithstanding any enactment[1] or rule of law to the contrary, a private company limited by shares or by guarantee[2] may be formed by one person, in so far as permitted by the Companies Act 1985[3], and may have one member; and accordingly:

(1) any enactment or rule of law which applies in relation to a private company limited by shares or by guarantee applies, in the absence of any express provision to the contrary, with such modification as may be necessary in relation to such a company which is formed by one person or which has only one person as a member as it does in relation to such a company which is formed by two or more persons or which has two or more persons as members; and

(2) without prejudice to the generality of the foregoing, the Companies Act 1985 and the Insolvency Act 1986 have effect with the specified[4] amendments[5].

1 For these purposes, 'enactment' includes an enactment comprised in subordinate legislation; and 'subordinate legislation' has the same meaning as in the Interpretation Act 1978 s 21(1) (see STATUTES vol 44(1) (Reissue) para 1381): Companies (Single Member Private Limited Companies) Regulations 1992, SI 1992/1699, reg 2(2).
2 Ie within the meaning of the Companies Act 1985 s 1 (as amended): see para 80 ante and para 82 post.
3 Ie by ibid s 1 (as amended).
4 For the amendments so specified see paras 24, 80 ante and paras 380, 410, 543, 597, 667, 700, 2202 post.
5 Companies (Single Member Private Limited Companies) Regulations 1992 reg 2(1). A person who before 15 July 1992 is liable by virtue of the Companies Act 1985 s 24 (see para 410 post) for the payment of the debts of a private company limited by shares or by guarantee is not so liable for the payment of the company's debts contracted on or after that date: Companies (Single Member Private Limited Companies) Regulations 1992 reg 3.

82. Meaning of 'public company' and 'private company'. A public company is a company limited by shares or limited by guarantee and having a share capital, being a company:

(1) the memorandum of which states that it is to be a public company; and

(2) in relation to which the provisions of the Companies Act 1985 or the former Companies Acts[1] as to the registration or re-registration of a company as a public company have been complied with on or after 22 December 1980[2].

A private company is a company that is not a public company[3].

A company registered as a public company on its original registration may not do business or exercise any borrowing powers until the registrar of companies has issued a certificate to the effect that he is satisfied that the nominal value of the company's allotted share capital is not less than the authorised minimum[4].

1 For the meaning of 'the former Companies Acts' see para 11 note 2 ante.
2 Companies Act 1985 ss 1(3), 735(2). As to such requirements see para 118 et seq post; and as to the history of the term 'public company' see para 104 note 2 post.
3 Ibid ss 1(3), 735(2). As to the advantages of a private company see paras 106, 107 post.
4 See ibid s 117(1),(2) and para 652 post.

83. Meaning of 'persons'. For the purpose of subscribing to the memorandum of association, 'persons' includes aliens, although residing abroad[1], even when the company is formed to own a British ship, which cannot be owned by aliens[2], persons who are trustees for other subscribers[3], and persons who sign by agents, although only orally appointed[4]. It also includes corporations and limited companies[5], and it may perhaps also include minors[6].

If a firm name is, with the authority of the firm, subscribed to a memorandum, the partners are joint holders of the shares subscribed for[7]. If an individual subscribes in his own name as agent for a firm, and the firm takes up the shares subscribed for, he is absolved from liability[8].

1 *Princess Reuss v Bos* (1871) LR 5 HL 176.
2 *R v Arnaud* (1846) 9 QB 806; and see BRITISH NATIONALITY vol 4(2) (Reissue) para 66 note 9. For the meaning of 'British ship' see SHIPPING vol 43 para 119.
3 *Salomon v A Salomon & Co Ltd* [1897] AC 22 at 46, HL.
4 *Re Whitley Partners Ltd* (1886) 32 ChD 337, CA.
5 See the Interpretation Act 1978 ss 5, 22(1), 23(1), Sch 1, Sch 2 para 4(1)(a) (meaning of 'person') and STATUTES vol 44(1) (Reissue) para 1382. See also the Companies Act 1985 s 375 and para 678 post; *Re Barned's Banking Co, ex p Contract Corpn* (1867) 3 Ch App 105; *Pharmaceutical Society v London and Provincial Supply Association* (1880) 5 App Cas 857, HL; *Union SS Co of New Zealand Ltd v Melbourne Harbour Trust Comrs* (1884) 9 App Cas 365, PC.
6 See *Re Laxon & Co (No 2)* [1892] 3 Ch 555; *Re Nassau Phosphate Co* (1876) 2 ChD 610. On attaining full age a minor may repudiate the contract which arises on his signature (*Re Hertfordshire Brewery Co* (1874) 43 LJ Ch 358; *Re Laxon & Co (No 2)* supra at 561, 562 per Vaughan Williams J); but such repudiation does not invalidate the incorporation of the company (*Re Hertfordshire Brewery Co* supra). See also para 374 post.
7 *Weikersheim's Case* (1873) 8 Ch App 831; and see *Niemann v Niemann* (1889) 43 ChD 198, CA.
8 *Dunster's Case* [1894] 3 Ch 473, CA.

84. Contents of memorandum. The memorandum of every company must state:

(1) the name of the company[1];
(2) the objects of the company[2];
(3) whether the registered office[3] of the company is to be situated in England and Wales[4], or situated in Wales[5], or situated in Scotland[6].

If a company has a registered office which is situated in Wales, it may by special resolution[7] alter its memorandum so as to provide that its office is to be so situated[8].

The memorandum of a company limited by shares or by guarantee must also state that the liability of its members is limited[9].

The memorandum of a company limited by guarantee must also state that each member undertakes to contribute to the assets of the company if it should be wound up while he is a member, or within one year after he ceases to be a member, for payment of the debts and liabilities of the company contracted before he ceases to be a member, and of the costs, charges and expenses of winding up, and for adjustment of the rights of the contributories among themselves[10], such amount as may be required, not exceeding a specified amount[11].

In the case of a company having a share capital, the memorandum must also (unless it is an unlimited company) state the amount of the share capital with which the company proposes to be registered and the division of the share capital into shares of a fixed amount[12]. Subject to the necessity for a public company to have a sufficient nominal capital in pounds sterling to be able to allot shares to the extent of the authorised minimum[13], there is no necessity for the capital to be in pounds sterling, or for it to be all in one particular currency[14]. Each share must, however, be expressed solely in one particular currency[15]. No subscriber of the memorandum may take less than one share[16]; and there must be shown in the memorandum against the name of each subscriber the number of shares he takes[17].

A company may not alter the conditions contained in its memorandum except in the cases, in the mode and to the extent for which express provision is made by the Companies Act 1985[18].

The memorandum must be signed by each subscriber in the presence of at least one witness, who must attest the signature[19]. Since 1 August 1970 stamp duty has not been chargeable[20].

1 Companies Act 1985 s 2(1)(a). As to names see para 79 ante and para 154 et seq post.
2 Ibid s 2(1)(c). As to the objects see paras 86, 1094 post.
3 As to the registered office see para 150 post.
4 Companies Act 1985 s 2(1)(b).
5 Ibid s 2(2). The purpose of selecting Wales alone is to take advantage of the provisions of the Companies Act 1985 which permit the use of the Welsh equivalents for 'limited' and 'public limited company' in the name of the company: see para 79 ante. As to the submission of forms in Welsh to the registrar of companies see para 90 post.
6 Ibid s 2(1)(b).
7 As to special resolutions see para 683 post.
8 Companies Act 1985 s 2(2).
9 Ibid s 2(3).
10 See para 2463 et seq post.
11 Companies Act 1985 s 2(4).
12 Ibid s 2(5)(a).
13 For the meaning of 'authorised minimum' see para 652 note 6 post.
14 *Re Scandinavian Bank Group plc* [1988] Ch 87, [1987] 2 All ER 70.
15 *Re Scandinavian Bank Group plc* [1988] Ch 87 at 107, [1987] 2 All ER 70 at 79 per Harman J.
16 Companies Act 1985 s 2(5)(b).
17 Ibid s 2(5)(c).
18 Ibid s 2(7). As to such express provision see s 4 (as substituted) (see paras 1184, 1185 post) and s 17 (see para 541 post).
19 Ibid s 2(6). The only case in which the memorandum is not signed is where it and the articles are substituted for a deed of settlement: see s 690(2) and para 34 ante.
20 Finance Act 1970 s 32, Sch 7 para 1(2)(d).

85. Forms of memorandum. Subject to the general statutory requirements as to memoranda[1], the form of the memorandum of association of:

(1) a public company[2], being a company limited by shares;

(2) a public company, being a company limited by guarantee and having a share capital;

(3) a private company[3] limited by shares;

(4) a private company limited by guarantee and not having a share capital;

(5) a private company limited by guarantee and having a share capital[4]; and

(6) an unlimited company having a share capital,

is to be as specified respectively for such companies by regulations made by the Secretary of State, or as near to that form as circumstances admit[5].

1 Ie subject to the provisions of the Companies Act 1985 ss 1, 2: see paras 80, 82, 84 ante.
2 For the meaning of 'public company' see para 82 ante.

3 For the meaning of 'private company' see para 82 ante.
4 With effect from 22 December 1980, a company cannot be formed as, or become, a company limited by
  guarantee with a share capital: see the Companies Act 1985 s 1(4) and para 80 ante.
5 Companies Act 1985 s 3(1). Regulations under s 3 must be made by statutory instrument subject to
  annulment in pursuance of a resolution of either House of Parliament: s 3(2). In exercise of the power so
  conferred and of the power conferred by the Companies Act 1948 s 454(2) (repealed) (see para 9 ante)
  the Secretary of State made the Companies (Tables A to F) Regulations 1985, SI 1985/805 (amended by
  SI 1985/1052), which prescribe the following forms of memorandum for specified types of company:
  Table B–private company limited by shares; Table C–company limited by guarantee and not having a
  share capital; Table D–public company limited by guarantee and having a share capital; Table
  E–unlimited company having a share capital; Table F–public company limited by shares.

86. Statement of company's objects.

86. Statement of company's objects. The objects should be clearly defined, as the
company, whether limited or unlimited, may do only what is within or is incidental to
the objects stated in its memorandum[1]. The validity of an act done by a company may
not, however, be called into question on the ground of lack of capacity by reason of
anything in the company's memorandum[2].

The objects to be stated are those which the company during its corporate life is to
pursue, and by the fulfilment of which it is to earn profit, and have no relation to acts to
be done after the corporate life has come to an end. Thus, the distribution of the
corporate assets in liquidation cannot be defined by the memorandum so as to deprive
shareholders of the rights given them by statute[3].

Where the company's memorandum states that the object of the company is to carry
on business as a general commercial company:

(1) the object of the company is to carry on any trade or business whatsoever; and
(2) the company has power to do all such things as are incidental or conducive to
    the carrying on of any trade or business by it[4].

1 *Ashbury Railway Carriage and Iron Co Ltd v Riche* (1875) LR 7 HL 653; and see para 1094 post. Before the
  Companies Act 1948 (repealed) the question was raised whether the registrar could refuse to register a
  company whose objects clause set out a profusion of objects and it was suggested that, if the company
  were so registered, the Crown might commence proceedings to have the certificate of incorporation
  cancelled (*Re Anglo-Cuban Oil, Bitumen and Asphalt Co Ltd* [1917] 1 Ch 477, CA; affd sub nom *Cotman v
  Brougham* [1918] AC 514, HL); no such proceedings have ever been taken. See also para 91 post.
2 See the Companies Act 1985 s 35(1) (as substituted) and para 1107 post.
3 *Bisgood v Henderson's Transvaal Estates Ltd* [1908] 1 Ch 743 at 757, CA, overruling *Cotton v Imperial and
  Foreign Agency and Investment Corpn* [1892] 3 Ch 454, and *Fuller v White Feather Reward Ltd* [1906] 1 Ch
  823, and approving *Bisgood v Nile Valley Co Ltd* [1906] 1 Ch 747.
4 Companies Act 1985 s 3A (added by the Companies Act 1989 s 110(1)).

87. Requirements of articles of association.

87. Requirements of articles of association. In the case of a company limited by
shares there may, and in the case of a company limited by guarantee or unlimited there
must, be registered with the memorandum articles of association signed by the
subscribers to the memorandum[1] and prescribing regulations[2] for the company[3]. The
articles may adopt all or any of the regulations contained in Table A[4].

Where a company, not relying simply on Table A, has any articles of association, the
articles must be printed[5], be divided into paragraphs numbered consecutively[6], and be
signed by each subscriber of the memorandum in the presence of at least one witness
who must attest the signature[7]. Since 1 August 1970 stamp duty has not been
chargeable[8].

In the case of a company limited by shares, if articles are not registered, or, if articles
are registered, in so far as they do not exclude or modify Table A, that Table (so far as
applicable, and as in force at the date of the company's registration) constitutes the

company's articles, in the same manner and to the same extent as if articles in the form of that Table had been duly registered[9].

In the case of an unlimited company having a share capital, the articles must state the amount of share capital with which the company proposes to be registered[10].

Under EC law it may be that the articles should, in a case where the number of directors is only one, explicitly state, for the purpose of registration, that such one director may alone represent the company, even though this is in any event the position under the general law[11].

1 Articles duly registered and acted on for many years may be held binding, even though not signed: *Ho Tung v Man On Insurance Co* [1902] AC 232, PC.
2 Throughout the Companies Act 1985, a company's 'regulations' means its articles of association, either express or as contained in Table A, and not the provisions of its memorandum. The Act requires many powers of companies to be expressly taken by articles in contradistinction to their memoranda.
3 Companies Act 1985 s 7(1).
4 Ibid s 8(1). Table A is as prescribed by regulations made by the Secretary of State by statutory instrument subject to annulment in pursuance of a resolution of either House of Parliament: Companies Act 1985 s 8(1),(5). The current regulations are contained in the Companies (Tables A to F) Regulations 1985, SI 1985/805 (amended by SI 1985/1052). The articles of Table A are set out under the headings devoted to the matters to which they respectively relate: see further para 529 note 2 post. As to Table A generally see further para 529 et seq post. As to the Secretary of State's power to make regulations prescribing a new Table G containing articles of association appropriate for a partnership company see para 531 post.
5 Companies Act 1985 s 7(3)(a).
6 Ibid s 7(3)(b).
7 Ibid s 7(3)(c).
8 Finance Act 1970 s 32, Sch 7, para 1(2)(d).
9 Companies Act 1985 s 8(2). As to the importance of using words clearly excluding Table A see *Fisher v Black and White Publishing Co* [1901] 1 Ch 174, CA.
10 Companies Act 1985 s 7(2).
11 See Case 32/74 *Friedrich Haaga GmbH* [1974] ECR 1201, [1975] 1 CMLR 32, ECJ (interpreting the First Council Directive of 9 March 1968, art 2(1)(d), 2nd sentence). As to EC Directives see para 5 ante.

88. Registration of documents by registrar. The company's memorandum and articles, if any[1], must be delivered to the registrar of companies for England and Wales or to the registrar of companies for Scotland according to the situation of the registered office of the company as stated by the memorandum[2]. With the memorandum there must also be delivered a statement in the prescribed form[3] containing the names and requisite particulars[4] of the person who is, or the persons who are, to be the first director or directors of the company, and the person who is, or the persons who are, to be the first secretary or joint secretaries of the company[5]. The statement must be signed by or on behalf of the subscribers of the memorandum and must contain a consent signed by each of the persons named in it as a director, as secretary or as one of joint secretaries, to act in the relevant capacity[6]. Where a memorandum is delivered by a person as agent for the subscribers, the statement must specify that fact and the person's name and address[7]. The statement must also specify the intended situation of the company's registered office on incorporation[8].

Where the memorandum states that the association to be registered is to be a public company, the amount of the share capital stated in the memorandum to be that with which the company proposes to be registered must not be less than the authorised minimum[9] in pounds sterling or in whatever other currencies, if any, the remainder of the capital of the company may consist of[10].

The registrar of companies must not register a company's memorandum so delivered unless he is satisfied that all the requirements of the Companies Act 1985 in respect of registration and of matters precedent and incidental to it have been complied with[11]. Subject to this, the registrar must retain and register the memorandum and articles, if any, so delivered to him[12].

The duty of the registrar as to registration has never been purely ministerial[13]. He should consider whether the requirements of the Companies Act 1985 have been complied with and refuse registration if he conceives that they have not[14]. The court will not interfere by mandamus with the decision of the registrar unless it is shown either that the registrar had not in fact exercised his discretion, or that he had exercised it upon some wrong principle of law, or that he had been influenced by extraneous considerations which he ought not to have taken into account[15].

A statutory declaration in the prescribed form[16] by a solicitor engaged in the formation of the company, or by a person named as being one of the first directors or secretaries of the company in the statement delivered to the registrar of companies[17], that those requirements have been complied with must be delivered to the registrar, who may accept such a declaration as sufficient evidence of compliance[18].

1 As to the circumstances in which articles are to be registered see para 87 ante.
2 Companies Act 1985 s 10(1).
3 For the prescribed form of statement see the Companies (Forms) (Amendment) Regulations 1995, SI 1995/736, reg 3, Sch 2, Form 10. For the prescribed version of the form in Welsh see the Companies (Welsh Language Forms and Documents) (Amendment) Regulations 1995, SI 1995/734, reg 4, Schedule, Form 10CYM. For the meaning of 'prescribed' see para 24 note 3 ante.
4 For the requisite particulars see para 89 post.
5 Companies Act 1985 s 10(2). An appointment by any articles delivered with the memorandum of a person as director or secretary of the company is void unless he is named as a director or secretary in the statement: s 10(5).
6 Ibid s 10(3).
7 Ibid s 10(4).
8 Ibid s 10(6).
9 Ibid s 11. For the meaning of 'authorised minimum' see para 652 note 6 post.
10 As to the company's capital consisting of shares in a number of different currencies see para 84 text to notes 12-14 ante; and see generally *Re Scandinavian Bank Group plc* [1988] Ch 87 at 104, [1987] 2 All ER 70 at 77 per Harman J.
11 Companies Act 1985 s 12(1).
12 Ibid s 12(2).
13 *R v Registrar of Companies* [1912] 3 KB 23 at 34, DC per Avory J; *Bowman v Secular Society Ltd* [1917] AC 406 at 439, HL per Lord Parker of Waddington.
14 *Cotman v Brougham* [1918] AC 514 at 523, HL; *R v Registrar of Joint Stock Companies, ex p More* [1931] 2 KB 197, CA (refusal to register company with unlawful objects). As to the refusal of registration where the name of the company is undesirable see para 156 post.
15 *R v Registrar of Companies* [1912] 3 KB 23 at 34, DC per Avory J. See also *R v Registrar of Companies, ex p Bowen* [1914] 3 KB 1161; *R v Registrar of Companies, ex p A-G* [1991] BCLC 476; and the cases cited in para 91 note 7 post.
16 For the prescribed form of statutory declaration see the Companies (Forms) (Amendment) Regulations 1995 Sch 2, Form 12. For the prescribed version of the form in Welsh see the Companies (Welsh Language Forms and Documents) (Amendment) Regulations 1995 Schedule, Form 12CYM.
17 Ie under the Companies Act 1985 s 10(2): see supra.
18 Ibid s 12(3).

89. The requisite particulars of directors and secretaries. Subject as provided below, the statement to be delivered with the memorandum[1] must contain the following particulars with respect to each person named as director[2]:

(1) in the case of an individual, his present name[3], any former name[4], his usual residential address, his nationality, his business occupation (if any), particulars of any other directorships held by him, or which have been held by him, and his date of his birth[5];

(2) in the case of a corporation or Scottish firm, its corporate or firm name and registered or principal office[6].

It is not necessary for the statement to contain particulars of a directorship:

(a) which has not been held by a director at any time during the five years preceding the date on which the statement is delivered to the registrar[7];

(b) which is held by a director in a company[8] which is dormant[9] or grouped[10] with the company delivering the statement, and, if he also held that directorship for any period during those five years, was for the whole of that period either dormant or so grouped[11]; and

(c) which was held by a director for any period during those five years in a company which for the whole of that period was either dormant or grouped with the company delivering the statement[12].

The statement must contain the following particulars with respect to the person named as secretary or, where there are to be joint secretaries, with respect to each person named as one of them:

(i) in the case of an individual, his name, any former name and his usual residential address; and

(ii) in the case of a corporation or a Scottish firm, its corporate or firm name and registered or principal office[13].

If, however, all the partners in a firm are joint secretaries, the name and principal office of the firm may be stated instead of the particulars otherwise so required[14].

1 Ie the statement to be made under the Companies Act 1985 s 10(2): see para 88 ante.
2 Ibid s 10(2), Sch 1 para 1.
3 For these purposes, 'name' means a person's Christian name (or other forename) and surname, except that, in the case of a peer, or an individual usually known by a title, the title may be stated instead of his Christian name (or other forename) and surname or in addition to either or both of them: ibid Sch 1 para 4(a) (substituted by the Companies Act 1989 s 145, Sch 19 para 7(1),(5)).
4 For these purposes, the reference to a former name does not include (1) in the case of a peer, or an individual normally known by a British title, the name by which he was known previous to the adoption of or succession to the title; or (2) in the case of any person, a former name which was changed or disused before he attained the age of 18 years or which has been changed or disused for 20 years or more; or (3) in the case of a married woman, the name by which she was known previous to the marriage: Companies Act 1985 Sch 1 para 4(b) (substituted by the Companies Act 1989 Sch 19 para 7(1),(5)).
5 Companies Act 1985 Sch 1 para 1(a) (amended by the Companies Act 1989 Sch 19 para 7(1),(2)(a),(b)).
6 Companies Act 1985 Sch 1 para 1(b) (amended by the Companies Act 1989 Sch 19 para 7(1),(3)).
7 Companies Act 1985 Sch 1 para 2(1)(a).
8 For these purposes, 'company' includes any body corporate incorporated in Great Britain: ibid Sch 1 para 2(2). References in the Companies Act 1985 to a body corporate or to a corporation do not include a corporation sole, but include a company incorporated elsewhere than in Great Britain; such references to a body corporate do not include a Scottish firm: s 740.
9 Ibid s 250(3) (as substituted) (see para 1058 post) applies as regards whether and when a company is or has been 'dormant': Sch 1 para 2(2)(a) (amended by the Companies Act 1989 s 145, Sch 10 para 17).
10 For these purposes, a company is treated as being or having been at any time grouped with another company if at that time it is or was a company of which that other is or was a wholly-owned subsidiary, or if it is or was a wholly-owned subsidiary of the other or of another company of which that other is or was a wholly-owned subsidiary: Companies Act 1985 Sch 1 para 2(2)(b). For the meaning of 'wholly-owned subsidiary' see para 827 post.
11 Ibid Sch 1 para 2(1)(b).
12 Ibid Sch 1 para 2(1)(c).
13 Ibid Sch 1 para 3(1) (amended by the Companies Act 1989 Sch 19 para 7(1),(4)).
14 Companies Act 1985 Sch 1 para 3(2).

90. Documents relating to Welsh companies. The following provisions relate to any document[1] which:

(1) is delivered[2] to the registrar of companies under the Companies Act 1985 or the Insolvency Act 1986[3]; and

(2) relates to a company, whether already registered or to be registered, whose memorandum states that its registered office is to be situated in Wales[4].

A document to which these provisions apply may be in Welsh but must on delivery to the registrar be accompanied by a certified translation[5] into English[6]. The requirement for such a translation does not, however, apply to documents of such descriptions as may be prescribed for these purposes[7] or to documents in a form prescribed[8] in Welsh, or partly in Welsh and partly in English[9].

Where the registrar receives a document in Welsh without a certified translation into English, he must, if that document is to be available for inspection, himself obtain such a translation; and that translation is treated as delivered to him in accordance with the same provision as the original[10].

A company whose memorandum states that its registered office is to be situated in Wales may deliver to the registrar a certified translation into Welsh of any document in English which relates to the company and which is or has been delivered to the registrar[11].

1 For the meaning of 'document' see para 60 note 6 ante.
2 For the meaning of references to delivering a document see para 60 note 15 ante.
3 Companies Act 1985 s 710B(1)(a) (added by the Welsh Language Act 1993 s 30(1),(6)). As to delivery of documents to the registrar of companies see paras 64, 65 ante.
4 Companies Act 1985 s 710B(1)(b) (added by the Welsh Language Act 1993 s 30(1),(6)).
5 For these purposes, 'certified translation' means a translation certified in the prescribed manner to be a correct translation: Companies Act 1985 s 710B(8) (added by the Welsh Language Act 1993 s 30(1),(6)).
A translation of a document into English is certified to be a correct translation:
(1) if the translation was made in the United Kingdom, by:
  (a) a notary public in any part of the United Kingdom;
  (b) a solicitor (if the translation was made in Scotland), a solicitor of the Supreme Court of Judicature of England and Wales (if it was made in England or Wales), or a solicitor of the Supreme Court of Judicature of Northern Ireland (if it was made in Northern Ireland);
  (c) a person certified by a person mentioned in heads (1)(a) and (1)(b) supra to be known to him to be competent to translate the document into English; or
  (d) in the case of a translation obtained by the registrar pursuant to the Companies Act 1985 s 710B(4) (as added) (see infra), the person who has translated the document into English; or
(2) if the translation was made outside the United Kingdom, by:
  (a) a notary public;
  (b) a person authorised in the place where the translation was made to administer an oath;
  (c) any of the British officials mentioned in the Commissioners for Oaths Act 1889 s 6 (as amended); or
  (d) a person certified by a person mentioned in heads (2)(a)-(c) supra, to be known to him to be competent to translate the document into English:
Companies (Welsh Language Forms and Documents) Regulations 1994, SI 1994/117, regs 2, 5. The British officials mentioned in the Commissioners for Oaths Act 1889 s 6 are: every British ambassador, envoy, minister, chargé d'affaires, and secretary of embassy or legation exercising his functions in any foreign country, and every British consul-general, consul, vice-consul, acting consul, pro-consul, and consular agent, acting consul-general, acting vice-consul and acting consular agent exercising his functions in any foreign place: s 6(1) (amended by the Commissioners for Oaths Act 1891 s 2).
6 Companies Act 1985 s 710B(2) (added by the Welsh Language Act 1993 s 30(1),(6)). The provisions of the Companies Act 1985 s 228(2)(f) (as substituted and amended) (see para 876 post), s 242(1) second sentence (as substituted and amended) (see para 818 post), s 243(4) (as substituted and amended) (see para 821 post), s 272(5) (as amended) (see para 709 post) and s 273(7) (as amended) (see para 710 post) and Sch 9 Pt II para 7(3) (as substituted and amended) (consolidated accounts of banking groups; requirement to provide certified translations into English of certain documents delivered to the registrar) do not apply where a translation is required by s 710B(2) (as so added) or would be required but for s 710B(3) (as added) (see infra): s 710B(6),(7) (added by the Welsh Language Act 1993 s 30(1),(6)).

7 The documents so prescribed are: (1) a copy of the memorandum and articles of a relevant company as delivered for registration, or as altered; (2) a copy of the annual accounts of a relevant company; (3) a copy of the annual report (within the meaning of Pt VII (ss 221-226A) (as amended): see ss 234, 234A (as substituted) and para 876 note 9 post) of the directors of a relevant company; (4) a copy of the auditors' report (within the meaning of Pt VII (ss 221-226A) (as amended): see ss 235-237 (as substituted) and para 1059 post) on the accounts of a relevant company; and (5) any document appended, by virtue of s 243(2) (as substituted) (accounts of subsidiary undertakings to be appended in certain cases: see para 821 post) or Sch 9 Pt II para 7(2) (as added) (consolidated accounts of banking groups; information as to undertaking in which shares are held as a result of a financial assistance operation), to the annual accounts of a relevant company: Companies (Welsh Language Forms and Documents) Regulations 1994 reg 4(1),(2) (amended by SI 1995/734). For these purposes, a 'relevant company' is such a company as is mentioned in the Companies Act 1985 s 710B(1)(b) (as added) (see text head (2) supra), other than a public company whose shares or debentures, or any class of whose shares or debentures, are listed within the meaning of s 251(1) (see para 914 note 2 post): Companies (Welsh Language Forms and Documents) Regulations 1994 regs 2, 4(3) (substituted by SI 1994/727).

8 Ie by virtue of the Welsh Language Act 1993 s 26: see CONSTITUTIONAL LAW.

9 Companies Act 1985 s 710B(3) (added by the Welsh Language Act 1993 s 30(1),(6)). For the forms so prescribed in Welsh, or partly in Welsh and partly in English, see the Companies (Welsh Language Forms and Documents) (Amendment) Regulations 1995, SI 1995/734; the Companies (Welsh Language Forms and Documents) (No 2) Regulations 1995, SI 1995/1480; the Companies (Welsh Language Forms and Documents (No 3) Regulations 1995, SI 1995/1508; and the Companies (Welsh Language Forms and Documents) Regulations 1996, SI 1996/595.

10 Companies Act 1985 s 710B(4) (added by the Welsh Language Act 1993 s 30(1),(6)).

11 Companies Act 1985 s 710B(5) (added by the Welsh Language Act 1993 s 30(1),(6)).

91. Certificate of incorporation. On the registration of a company's memorandum, the registrar of companies must give a certificate that the company is incorporated and, in the case of a limited company, that it is limited[1]. The certificate may be signed by the registrar, or authenticated by his official seal[2].

Where the registrar registers an association's memorandum which states that the association is to be a public company[3], the certificate of incorporation must contain a statement to that effect[4]. The registrar's duty to certify may be enforced by an order of mandamus[5]. The registrar is also required to cause notice of the issue of the certificate to be published in the Gazette[6].

A certificate of incorporation given in respect of an association is conclusive evidence:

(1) that the requirements of the Companies Act 1985 in respect of registration and of matters precedent and incidental to it have been complied with, and that the association is a company authorised to be registered, and is duly registered, under that Act[7]; and

(2) if the certificate contains a statement that the company is a public company, that the company is such a company[8].

If a company is registered with illegal objects, the existence of a certificate precludes its corporate status being challenged without, however, making those objects legal[9], but the statutory provision[10] is not expressed to bind the Crown, and the Attorney General, on behalf of the Crown, may institute proceedings by way of certiorari to cancel a registration improperly or erroneously allowed[11].

A copy of the certificate certified in writing by the registrar is admissible in evidence in legal proceedings[12], and, as against the company itself, registration may be evidenced by other means, for example by producing its sealed share certificate[13].

1 Companies Act 1985 s 13(1).

2 Ibid s 13(2). As to the registrar's official seal see paras 28 note 3, 60 ante.

3 For the meaning of 'public company' see para 82 ante.

4 Companies Act 1985 s 13(6).

5 This was the procedure adopted in *R v Whitmarsh* (1850) 15 QB 600; *R v Registrar of Joint Stock Companies* (1847) 10 QB 839.

6 See the Companies Act 1985 s 711(1)(a) and para 70 ante.

7 Ibid s 13(7)(a). Before the Companies Act 1900 there was some doubt as to the meaning of 'conclusive': see *Re National Debenture and Assets Corpn* [1891] 2 Ch 505, CA. See also *Ladies' Dress Association Ltd v Pulbrook* [1900] 2 QB 376, CA. The extended wording of the Companies Act 1900 s 1 (now the Companies Act 1985 s 13) shows that 'conclusive' means what it says: *Hammond v Prentice Bros Ltd* [1920] 1 Ch 201. As to the possibility of a proceeding in the nature of a scire facias see *Salomon v A Salomon & Co Ltd* [1897] AC 22 at 30, HL; and as to scire facias see CORPORATIONS vol 9 para 1332 and CROWN PROCEEDINGS. Since the Companies Act 1985 is not expressed to bind the Crown, the issue of a certificate of incorporation may be challenged by the Attorney General (but by nobody else) by way of judicial review: see *R v Registrar of Companies, ex p Central Bank of India* [1986] QB 1114 at 1169-1171, [1986] 1 All ER 105 at 117, 118, CA per Lawton LJ, at 1175-1178 and at 122-124 per Slade LJ and at 1178-1180, 1182, 1183 and at 124, 125, 127, 128 per Dillon LJ; *R v Registrar of Companies, ex p A-G* [1991] BCLC 476.

8 Companies Act 1985 s 13(7)(b).

9 *Bowman v Secular Society Ltd* [1917] AC 406 at 438, 439, HL per Lord Parker of Waddington.

10 Ie the Companies Act 1985 s 13.

11 *Bowman v Secular Society Ltd* [1917] AC 406 at 439, 440, HL per Lord Parker of Waddington. See also *Cotman v Brougham* [1918] AC 514 at 519, HL. Cf *R v Registrar of Joint Stock Companies, ex p More* [1913] 2 KB 197, CA (refusal of the registrar to register a company formed to deal in tickets in the Irish Hospitals Sweepstake upheld). See also note 7 supra.

12 See the Companies Act 1985 s 709(3) (as substituted) and para 67 ante.

13 *Mostyn v Calcott Hall Mining Co* (1858) 1 F & F 334.

92. Effect of incorporation. From the date of incorporation[1], the subscribers of the memorandum, together with such other persons as may from time to time become members of the company, are a body corporate by the name contained in the memorandum[2], separate and distinct from the individual members of the company[3]. That body corporate is then capable forthwith of exercising all the functions of an incorporated company, but with such liability on the part of its members to contribute to its assets in the event of its being wound up as is provided by the Companies Act 1985 and the Insolvency Act 1986[4].

If, however, the company is registered as a public company[5], it may not do business or exercise any borrowing power unless the registrar has issued it with a further certificate to the effect that he is satisfied that its allotted share capital is not less than the authorised minimum[6], or the company is re-registered as a private company[7].

The persons named in the statement[8] as directors, secretary or joint secretaries are, on the company's incorporation, deemed to have been respectively appointed as its first directors, secretary or joint secretaries[9].

1 Ie the date mentioned in the certificate of incorporation: see para 91 ante. The company is incorporated from the beginning of the day so mentioned: *Official Receiver and Liquidator of Jubilee Cotton Mills Ltd v Lewis* [1924] AC 958, HL. The statute does not authorise the day to be ante-dated: *Official Receiver and Liquidator of Jubilee Cotton Mills Ltd v Lewis* supra at 974.

2 Companies Act 1985 s 13(3).

3 *John Foster & Sons v IRC* [1894] 1 QB 516 at 528, 530, CA; *Salomon v A Salomon & Co Ltd* [1897] AC 22 at 42, 51, HL; *Booth v Helliwell* [1914] 3 KB 252; *R v Grubb* [1915] 2 KB 683, CCA; *IRC v Sansom* [1921] 2 KB 492, CA; *Rainham Chemical Works Ltd v Belvedere Fish Guano Co* [1921] 2 AC 465 at 475, HL; *Re Fasey, ex p Trustees* [1923] 2 Ch 1 at 18, CA; *Gramophone and Typewriter Ltd v Stanley* [1908] 2 KB 89 at 99, CA per Fletcher Moulton LJ; *Ebbw Vale UDC v South Wales Traffic Area Licensing Authority* [1951] 2 KB 366 (sub nom *R v South Wales Traffic Licensing Authority, ex p Ebbw Vale UDC* [1951] 1 All ER 806); *Lee v Lee's Air Farming Ltd* [1961] AC 12, [1960] 3 All ER 420, PC; *Tunstall v Steigmann* [1962] 2 QB 593, [1962] 2 All ER 417, CA; *J H Rayner (Mincing Lane) Ltd v Department of Trade and Industry* [1990] 2 AC 418 at 482; sub nom *Maclaine Watson & Co Ltd v Department of Trade and Industry* [1989] 3 All ER 523 at

531, HL per Lord Templeman and at 505, 506 and at 549 per Lord Oliver of Aylmerton. As to the circumstances in which an individual or individuals may be considered the directing mind of the company see para 1157 post.

4 Companies Act 1985 s 13(4) (amended by the Insolvency Act 1986 s 439(1), Sch 13 Pt I).

5 For the meaning of 'public company' see para 82 ante.

6 For the meaning of 'authorised minimum' see para 652 note 6 post.

7 Companies Act 1985 ss 13(4), 117(1).

8 Ie the statement under ibid s 10: see para 88 ante.

9 Ibid s 13(5).

93. Piercing the corporate veil. A company is a legal entity separate and distinct from its members[1]. This is also the position within a group of companies where the fundamental principle is that each company in a group (a relatively modern concept) is a separate legal entity possessed of separate legal rights and liabilities[2]. There may, however, be cases where the wording of a particular statute[3] or contract justifies the treatment of parent and subsidiary as one company, at least for some purposes[4]; or where the court will 'pierce the corporate veil', not because it considers it just to do so[5] but because special circumstances exist indicating that it is a mere facade concealing the true facts[6]. In identifying what is a mere facade, the motive of those behind the company will be relevant[7]. The court will go behind the status of the company as a separate legal entity distinct from its shareholders, and will consider who are the persons, as shareholders or even as agents, directing and controlling the activities of the company[8]. The device of a corporate structure will often have been used to evade limitations imposed on conduct by law[9] and rights of relief which third parties already possess[10] against a defendant[11] so justifying the court's piercing the veil.

Where, however, this is not the position, even though an individual's connection with a company may cause a transaction with that company to be subjected to strict scrutiny, the corporate veil will not be pierced[12]. Nor is the court entitled to lift the veil as against a company which is a member of a corporate group merely because the corporate structure has been used so as to ensure that the legal liability, if any, in respect of particular future activities of the company will fall on another member of the group rather than the defendant company[13].

It may be that liabilities or obligations will arise without piercing the corporate veil because there is an agency relationship between a parent company and a subsidiary[14], or between a company and its shareholders[15], but this may not be inferred merely from control of the company or ownership of its shares[16]. It will depend on an investigation of all aspects of the relationship between the parties and there is no presumption of such agency[17].

For the purpose of taxation, there are numerous statutory provisions which in effect require the corporate veil to be pierced[18]; and the courts have in recent years shown an increasing tendency for such purposes to look at the economic consequences of transactions rather than their strict format, thus in effect bypassing the question of corporate identity[19].

1 See para 92 ante.

2 *Albacruz v Albazero, The Albazero* [1977] AC 774 at 807, [1975] 3 All ER 21 at 28, CA per Roskill LJ; *Bank of Tokyo Ltd v Karoon* [1987] AC 45n at 64n, [1986] 3 All ER 468 at 486, CA; *Adams v Cape Industries plc* [1990] Ch 433 at 532, [1991] 1 All ER 929 at 1016, CA per Slade LJ; *Acatos & Hutcheson plc v Watson* [1995] 1 BCLC 218. Dicta by Lord Denning MR in *Littlewoods Mail Order Stores Ltd v McGregor (Inspector of Taxes), Littlewoods Mail Order Stores Ltd v IRC* [1969] 3 All ER 855 at 860, [1969] 1 WLR 1241 at 1254, CA; *Wallersteiner v Moir* [1974] 3 All ER 217 at 238, [1974] 1 WLR 991 at 1013; *DHN Food Distributors Ltd v London Borough of Tower Hamlets* [1976] 3 All ER 462 (sub nom *DHN Food Distributors Ltd v Tower Hamlets London Borough Council* [1976] 1 WLR 852, CA) to the effect that the courts should

look at the whole group of companies as an economic entity have been disapproved subsequently: *Woolfson v Strathclyde Regional Council* 1978 SLT 159, HL; *Adams v Cape Industries plc* supra.

3 In *Dimbleby & Sons Ltd v National Union of Journalists* [1984] 1 All ER 751 at 758, [1984] 1 WLR 427 at 435, HL, Lord Diplock noted that, if the veil is to be pierced by a statutory provision, one would expect that parliamentary intention to be expressed in clear and unequivocal language. One example is the requirement of group accounts: see para 875 post.

4 *Adams v Cape Industries plc* [1990] Ch 433 at 536, [1991] 1 All ER 929 at 1019, CA where the Court of Appeal would have categorised the following cases in this way: *Harold Holdsworth & Co (Wakefield) Ltd v Caddies* [1955] 1 All ER 725, [1955] 1 WLR 352 (contract governing management obligations of director of parent company could make provision for management of subsidiary); *Scottish Co-operative Wholesale Society Ltd v Meyer* [1959] AC 324, [1958] 3 All ER 66, HL (parent company activities inseparable from those of subsidiary for the purposes of the Companies Act 1948 s 210 (repealed: minority remedy in case of oppression) (and see *Nicholas v Soundcraft Electronics Ltd* [1993] BCLC 360, CA on similar facts); *DHN Food Distributors Ltd v London Borough of Tower Hamlets* [1976] 3 All ER 462; sub nom *DHN Food Distributors Ltd v Tower Hamlets London Borough Council* [1976] 1 WLR 852, CA (companies without separate business activities treated as one for the purposes of a statute governing compensation payable for compulsory purchase order made by local council); *Revlon Inc v Cripps and Lee Ltd* [1980] FSR 85, CA (companies in a group treated as one for the purposes of the meaning of 'proprietor' of a trade mark in the Trade Marks Act 1938 (repealed)); Cases 6-7/73 *Instituto Chemioterapico Italiano SpA and Commercial Solvents Corpn v EC Commission* [1974] ECR 223, ECJ (parent and subsidiary to be treated as one undertaking for the purposes of EC Treaty arts 85, 86 regulating competition).

5 See *Adams v Cape Industries plc* [1990] Ch 433 at 537, [1991] 1 All ER 929 at 1020, CA per Slade LJ. See also *Taylor v Pace Developments Ltd* [1991] BCC 406, CA (court refused to order sole director and shareholder personally liable for costs where an insolvent company had unsuccessfully defended court proceedings although it may be possible so to order in certain cases as eg where the company's defence was not bona fide). Equally a company must pursue its litigation through legal advisers and may not be represented by its sole director and 99% shareholder (*Radford v Freeway Classics Ltd, Radford v Samuel* [1994] 1 BCLC 445, CA) save in exceptional circumstances (*Arbuthnot Leasing International Ltd v Havelet Leasing Ltd* [1991] 1 All ER 591 (sub nom *ALI Finance Ltd v Havelet Leasing Ltd* [1992] 1 WLR 455); *Re a company (No 001029 of 1990), ex p F Ltd* [1991] BCLC 567; and see para 1182 post).

6 *Woolfson v Strathclyde Regional Council* 1978 SLT 159, HL; *National Dock Labour Board v Pinn & Wheeler Ltd* [1989] BCLC 647; *Adams v Cape Industries plc* [1990] Ch 433 at 503, [1991] 1 All ER 929 at 987, CA; *Acatos & Hutcheson plc v Watson* [1995] 1 BCLC 218.

7 *Jones v Lipman* [1962] 1 All ER 442, [1962] 1 WLR 832; *Adams v Cape Industries plc* [1990] Ch 433 at 540, [1991] 1 All ER 929 at 1023, CA.

8 See *Merchandise Transport Ltd v British Transport Commission* [1962] 2 QB 173 at 206, 207, [1961] 3 All ER 495 at 517, 518, CA per Danckwerts LJ. Thus eg if a company is so under the unfettered control of one particular individual as to be in effect his alter ego, it may be concluded that documents belonging to the company are within the 'power' of the individual for the purpose of discovery: *Dallas v Dallas* (1960) 24 DLR (2d) 746 (BC CA). Cf *B v B* [1978] Fam 181, [1979] 1 All ER 801; cf *Re Tecnion Investments Ltd* [1985] BCLC 434, CA (where a contrary conclusion was reached).

9 *Re Darby, ex p Brougham* [1911] 1 KB 95 (company formed by fraudulent company promoters treated as a mere alias for them); *Daimler Co Ltd v Continental Tyre and Rubber Co (Great Britain) Ltd* [1916] 2 AC 307, HL (company formed in England but controlled by German shareholders regarded as an enemy alien); *Jones v Lipman* [1962] 1 All ER 442, [1962] 1 WLR 832 (specific performance ordered against company to which defendant had transferred property to avoid such an action against himself; the company was a device and a sham); *Gilford Motor Co Ltd v Horne* [1933] Ch 935 (company used deliberately as a vehicle for conduct of activities which it was unlawful for the defendant to conduct); *Re Bugle Press Ltd, Re Houses and Estates Ltd* [1961] Ch 270, [1960] 3 All ER 791, CA (company incorporated to facilitate the expropriation of minority shareholders in another company by majority); *Aveling Barford Ltd v Perion Ltd* [1989] BCLC 626 (sale of assets at gross undervalue by company to another controlled by the same shareholder in an attempt to disguise an unauthorised return of capital to that shareholder). There is a degree of overlap between this category and the cases cited in note 10 infra.

10 *Re a Company* [1985] BCLC 333, CA (chain of companies used to dispose of assets otherwise susceptible to a Mareva injunction treated in same way as owner would have been); *Creasey v Breachwood Motors Ltd* [1993] BCLC 480 (company transferred assets to another company to avoid contingent liabilities arising from claim for wrongful dismissal against the first company; claimant allowed to pursue the assets into the second company); *Bank of Credit and Commerce International SA v BRS Kumar Bros Ltd* [1994] 1 BCLC 211 (company shifted assets to another company to avoid reach of charges granted to creditors of first company; receiver appointed over assets of second company).

11 See *Adams v Cape Industries plc* [1990] Ch 433 at 544, [1991] 1 All ER 929 at 1026, CA.

12 See *Farrar v Farrars Ltd* (1888) 40 ChD 395 at 406, CA (sale by mortgagee to company in which he held shares). 'A sale by a person to a corporation of which he is a member is not, either in form or in substance, a sale by a person to himself' : *Farrar v Farrars Ltd* supra at 409 per Lindley LJ. See also *Salomon v A Salomon & Co Ltd* [1897] AC 22, HL; *Taylor v Pace Developments Ltd* [1991] BCC 406, CA (cited in note 5 supra).

13 *Adams v Cape Industries plc* [1990] Ch 433 at 544, [1991] 1 All ER 929 at 1026, CA.

14 *Firestone Tyre and Rubber Co Ltd v Lewellin (Inspector of Taxes)* [1957] 1 All ER 561, [1957] 1 WLR 464, HL (an assessment of tax upheld where the business of both the parent company and the subsidiary were carried on by the subsidiary as agent for the parent company); *Smith, Stone and Knight Ltd v Birmingham Corpn* [1939] 4 All ER 116 (compensation for compulsory purchase payable by local authority where subsidiary carried on business as agent for the parent company); *Re FG (Films) Ltd* [1953] 1 All ER 615, [1953] 1 WLR 483 (British subsidiary brought into existence for sole purpose of obtaining British classification for film made in reality by American parent company).

15 *Rainham Chemical Works Ltd (in liquidation) v Belvedere Fish Guano Co Ltd* [1921] 2 AC 465, HL.

16 *JH Rayner (Mincing Lane) Ltd v Department of Trade and Industry* [1989] Ch 72 at 188; sub nom *Maclaine Watson & Co Ltd v Department of Trade and Industry* [1988] 3 All ER 257 at 310, CA.

17 *Adams v Cape Industries plc* [1990] Ch 433 at 536, [1991] 1 All ER 929 at 1020, CA.

18 Eg the Finance Act 1986 ss 75-77 (see para 1491 et seq post); the Inheritance Tax Act 1984 s 94 (as amended) (see INHERITANCE TAXATION vol 24 (Reissue) para 433 et seq); the Income and Corporation Taxes Act 1988 Pt XI (ss 414-422 (as amended): see INCOME TAXATION vol 23 (Reissue) para 1292 et seq); and the Taxation of Chargeable Gains Act 1992 ss 29, 30 (see CAPITAL GAINS TAXATION vol 5(1) (Reissue) paras 172-177).

19 See eg *Furniss (Inspector of Taxes) v Dawson* [1984] AC 474 at 508, [1984] 1 All ER 530, HL; *Craven (Inspector of Taxes) v White* [1989] AC 398, [1988] 3 All ER 495, HL; *Fitzwilliam v IRC* [1993] 3 All ER 184, [1993] 1 WLR 1189, HL. The Inland Revenue will look at the real transaction carried out by the taxpayer: see INCOME TAXATION vol 23 (Reissue) para 25. As to tax avoidance see INCOME TAXATION vol 23 (Reissue) para 1533 et seq.

94. Nationality, domicile and residence. When incorporated, the company is a legal entity or persona distinct from its members[1], and its property is not the property of the members[2]. The nationality[3] and domicile[4] of a company is determined by its place of registration. A company incorporated in the United Kingdom will normally have both British nationality and English or Scottish domicile, depending upon its place of registration, and it will be unable to change that domicile[4]. A company incorporated in the United Kingdom will nevertheless be regarded as having an enemy character if the persons in de facto control of its affairs are resident in an enemy country, or, wherever resident, are adhering to the enemy or taking instructions from or acting under the control of enemies[5].

The residence of a company is of great importance in revenue law[6], and at common law the test of company residence is where its real business is carried on, that is to say where its central control and management is located[7]. A company which is incorporated in the United Kingdom is, however, regarded for the purposes of the Taxes Acts as resident there and accordingly, if a different place of residence is given by any rule of law, that place is no longer to be taken into account for those purposes[8]. A company incorporated outside the United Kingdom is resident in the United Kingdom if its central management and control is in the United Kingdom[9]. It follows that, if such central control is divided, the company, provided that it is not incorporated in the United Kingdom, may have more than one residence[10].

Issues as to title to shares in a company are to be decided by the law of the place where the shares are situated, the lex situs, which in the ordinary way will be the law of the place where the company is incorporated[11]. The head office of a company is not necessarily the registered office of the company, but is the place where the substantial business of the company is carried on and its negotiations conducted[12]. Like an individual or a firm, a company may, for the purposes of the Rules of the Supreme Court, carry on business in more places than one[13].

1 See para 92 ante.
2 *Re George Newman & Co* [1895] 1 Ch 674 at 685, CA.
3 *Janson v Driefontein Consolidated Mines Ltd* [1902] AC 484, HL.
4 *Gasque v IRC* [1940] 2 KB 80.
5 *Daimler Co Ltd v Continental Tyre Rubber Co (Great Britain) Ltd* [1916] 2 AC 307, HL. Such a company is still an English, or Scottish, company and subject to the common law prohibition against trading with the enemy: *Kuenigl v Donnersmarck* [1955] 1 QB 515, [1955] 1 All ER 46. For the meaning of 'enemy' see WAR vol 49 para 149.
6 As to residence for the purposes of corporation tax see INCOME TAXATION vol 23 (Reissue) para 1254; and as to the locality of assets for the purposes of inheritance tax see INHERITANCE TAXATION vol 24 (Reissue) para 599 et seq. As to service on foreign companies, for which purpose considerations of residence are relevant, see para 1773 post.
7 See *De Beers Consolidated Mines Ltd v Howe* [1906] AC 455, HL; *Egyptian Delta Land and Investment Co Ltd v Todd (Inspector of Taxes)* [1929] AC 1, 14 TC 119, HL; *Unit Construction Co Ltd v Bullock (Inspector of Taxes)* [1960] AC 351, [1959] 3 All ER 831, HL. In determining whether a company is ordinarily resident out of the jurisdiction for the purpose of making an order for security for costs against a company, the test is that applied in tax cases for assessing a company's place of residence ie where the central control and management of the company actually abides: *Re Little Olympian Each Ways Ltd (No 2)* [1995] 1 BCLC 48.
8 See the Finance Act 1988 s 66(1) and INCOME TAXATION vol 23 (Reissue) para 1254. A company which would otherwise be resident in the United Kingdom for these purposes may be treated as resident outside the United Kingdom as a result of an arrangement for double taxation relief: see INCOME TAXATION vol 23 (Reissue) para 1101.
9 See the cases cited in note 7 supra. See also *Swedish Central Rly Co Ltd v Thompson* [1925] AC 495, HL. Cf *The Polzeath* [1916] P 241, CA; *Re Hilton, Gibbes v Hale-Hinton* [1909] 2 Ch 548.
10 *Union Corpn Ltd v IRC* [1952] 1 All ER 646, CA; affd without reference to this point [1953] AC 482, [1953] 1 All ER 729, HL. See further CORPORATIONS vol 9 para 1225.
11 *Macmillan Inc v Bishopsgate Investment Trust plc (No 3)* [1996] 1 All ER 585, CA. The locality of the shares of a company is that of the register of shares which is usually, but not always, kept in the country of incorporation: *Baelz v Public Trustee* [1926] Ch 863; *A-G v Higgins* (1857) 2 H & N 339; *Brassard v Smith* [1925] AC 371, PC; *Erie Beach Co Ltd v A-G for Ontario* [1930] AC 161, PC; *International Credit and Investment Co (Overseas) Ltd v Adham* [1994] 1 BCLC 66.
12 *Keynsham Blue Lias Lime Co Ltd v Baker* (1863) 2 H & C 729; and see *Aberystwyth Promenade Pier Co Ltd v Cooper* (1865) 35 LJQB 44 (where the pier erected and maintained by the company was at Aberystwyth, and the registered office was at Westminster where the company's business was carried on and service should be effected).
13 *Davies v British Geon Ltd* [1957] 1 QB 1, [1956] 3 All ER 389, CA.

95. Change of residence. There is no longer any requirement for a company to obtain Treasury consent where that company wishes to transfer its residence from the United Kingdom[1]. All transactions of the following classes are, however, unlawful, unless carried out with the consent of the Treasury, that is to say:

(1) for a body corporate resident in the United Kingdom to cause or permit a body corporate not resident in the United Kingdom over which it has control to create or issue any shares or debentures;

(2) except for the purpose of enabling a person to be qualified to act as a director, for a body corporate so resident to transfer to any person, or cause or permit to be transferred to any person, any shares or debentures of a body corporate not so resident over which it has control, being shares or debentures which it owns or in which it has an interest[2].

1 See the Income and Corporation Taxes Act 1988 s 765(1)(a),(b) (repealed by the Finance Act 1988 ss 105(6),(7), 148, Sch 14 Pt IV with effect from 15 March 1988, although the repeal does not affect an

application for Treasury consent made before that date or a consent already granted). See also Case 81/87 *R v HM Treasury, ex p Dail Mail and General Trust plc* [1989] QB 446, [1989] 1 All ER 328, ECJ.

2 Income and Corporation Taxes Act 1988 s 765(1) (amended by the Finance Act 1988 s 105(6),(7), Sch 14 Pt IV; the Finance Act 1990 s 68(1)). The Income and Corporation Taxes Act 1988 s 765(1) (as so amended) does not apply, however, to a transaction which is a movement of capital to which EC Council Directive 88/361 (OJ L178, 8.7.88, p 5) art 1 applies: Income and Corporation Taxes Act 1988 s 765A(1) (added by the Finance Act 1990 s 68(2),(4)). See INCOME TAXATION vol 23 (Reissue) paras 1574, 1579.

96. Company trading in more than one state. The domicile of a trading company is not changed by its doing business in another country; but, if it carries on business in several states, it resides for the purposes of suit, and may be sued or sue, in as many places as it carries on business[1].

A company may have localised its obligation to a creditor by the course of its business[2], or by the terms of the contract as to where the debt should be recoverable[3].

1 *Carron Iron Co v Maclaren* (1855) 5 HL Cas 416 at 450; *New York Life Insurance Co v Public Trustee* [1924] 2 Ch 101 at 120, CA per Atkin LJ. Cf para 94 text to note 12 ante.

2 *R v Lovitt* [1912] AC 212, PC.

3 *New York Life Insurance Co v Public Trustee* [1924] 2 Ch 101, CA. See further CONFLICT OF LAWS vol 8(1) (Reissue) para 908.

97. Powers of the company. A company registered under the Companies Act 1985 is a statutory corporation[1], and therefore has not, as a corporation at common law has, prima facie the power to deal with its property and to bind itself by contract as freely as an ordinary individual[2]. The statute must not be taken to have created a corporation at common law and then scrutinised to see how far any of the incidents of a corporation at common law have been thereby excluded. The statute or the memorandum of the company is, as it were, its charter, and defines its powers[3]. The company has no powers other than those which are expressly conferred upon it by the statute or memorandum of association or are incidental to the objects therein defined or enumerated[4]; but this restriction is of less significance now in view of the statutory protection given to third parties dealing with a company against limitations arising under the company's constitution[5].

A company, unless it is a private company, cannot exercise all its functions on incorporation, inasmuch as it has to comply with certain statutory requirements before it can commence business or exercise its borrowing powers[6].

1 *Ashbury Railway Carriage and Iron Co v Riche* (1875) LR 7 HL 653 at 693.

2 *Baroness Wenlock v River Dee Co* (1883) 36 ChD 675n at 685n, CA (affd (1885) 10 App Cas 354, HL); and see CORPORATIONS vol 9 para 1333.

3 *Ashbury Railway Carriage and Iron Co v Riche* (1875) LR 7 HL 653 at 667, 668.

4 *Ashbury Railway Carriage and Iron Co v Riche* (1875) LR 7 HL 653; and see *Blackburn Building Society v Cunliffe, Brooks & Co* (1882) 22 ChD 61 at 70, CA (affd sub nom *Cunliffe, Brooks & Co v Blackburn and District Benefit Building Society* (1884) 9 App Cas 857, HL); *Cotman v Brougham* [1918] AC 514, HL.

5 See the Companies Act 1985 ss 35, 35A (as substituted) and paras 1107, 1108 post.

6 See para 652 post.

98. Company seal. A company which has a common seal[1] must have its name[2] engraved in legible characters on the seal; and, if the company fails to comply with this requirement, it is liable on summary conviction to a fine not exceeding one-fifth of the statutory maximum[3]. If an officer of a company or a person on its behalf uses or authorises the use of any seal purporting to be a seal of the company on which its name is not so engraved, he is liable on summary conviction to a fine not exceeding one-fifth of the statutory maximum[4].

1 A company need not have a common seal: see the Companies Act 1985 s 36A(3) (as added) and para 1130 post. As to the use of the company's seal see paras 1114, 1116, 1117, 1129, 1131 post.
2 As to the permitted contractions of the words 'limited' , 'public limited company' and their Welsh equivalents, which may be included as part of the ordinary name of the company, see para 154 post. Apart from these, it appears that 'company' may be abbreviated for present purposes to 'coy' and 'limited' to 'ltd'. As to whether 'and' may be replaced by '&' see para 1134 note 2 post. See also *F Stacey & Co Ltd v Wallis* (1912) 106 LT 544 ('ltd' for 'limited'); *Banque de l' Indochine et de Suez SA v Euroseas Group Finance Co Ltd* [1981] 3 All ER 198 ('Co' for 'Company').
3 Companies Act 1985 s 350(1) (substituted by the Companies Act 1989 s 130(7), Sch 17 para 7); Companies Act 1985 s 730, Sch 24. For the meaning of 'the statutory maximum' see para 1161 post.
4 Ibid ss 350(2), 730, Sch 24.

99. Alteration of memorandum and articles. The conditions contained in the memorandum of association, even though their insertion is not required by the Companies Act 1985[1], cannot be altered, except in the cases, in the mode and to the extent for which express provision is made in that Act[2].

The alterations which may be made in the memorandum without the confirmation of the court are change of name[3], alteration of objects[4], change of status[5], alteration of conditions in the memorandum which could have been contained in the articles[6], increase of capital[7], cancellation of capital not issued or agreed to be issued[8], conversion of fully-paid shares into stock[9], reconversion of stock into shares[9], consolidation of shares into shares of larger amount[10], sub-division of capital into shares of smaller amount[11], and the rendering of the liability of officers unlimited[12]. The alterations which may be made in the memorandum, subject to confirmation by the court, are reduction of paid or unpaid capital[13], reorganisation of capital[14] and any other alteration under a scheme of arrangement[15].

The articles of association may from time to time be altered by special resolution[16].

A company is not entitled to rely against other persons on any alteration of its memorandum or articles if the alteration has not been officially notified at the material time and is not shown by the company to have been known at that time to the person concerned, or if the material time fell on or before the fifteenth day after the date of official notification and it is shown that the person concerned was unavoidably prevented from knowing of the event at that time[17].

1 See *Ashbury v Watson* (1885) 30 ChD 376, CA.
2 Companies Act 1985 s 2(7).
3 See para 160 post.
4 See para 1184 post.
5 Ie from a public company to a private company (see para 129 et seq post) and vice versa (see para 118 et seq post), or from a limited company to an unlimited company (see para 124 post) and vice versa (see para 126 post).
6 See paras 541, 542 post.
7 See para 201 post.
8 See para 218 post.
9 See para 209 post.
10 See para 205 post.
11 See para 207 post.
12 See para 627 post.
13 See para 241 post.
14 The conversion of a company's capital into the equivalent in decimal currency does not involve any alteration of the memorandum: *Re Harris and Sheldon Group Ltd* [1971] 2 All ER 87n, [1971] 1 WLR 899.

15 As to schemes of arrangement see para 1447 et seq post.
16 See para 538 post.
17 See the Companies Act 1985 s 42(1)(b) and para 71 ante.

100. Notification of statutory changes in memorandum or articles. Where an alteration is made in a company's memorandum or articles of association by any statutory provision, whether contained in an Act of Parliament or in an instrument made under an Act, a printed copy of the Act or instrument must, not later than 15 days after that provision comes into force, be forwarded to the registrar of companies and recorded by him[1]. Where a company is required[2] to send to the registrar any document making or evidencing an alteration in the company's memorandum or articles of association[3], the company must send with it a printed copy of the memorandum or articles as altered[4].

If a company fails to comply with any of these provisions, the company, and any officer of the company who is in default, is liable on summary conviction to a fine not exceeding one-fifth of the statutory maximum and, on conviction after continued contravention, to a daily default fine not exceeding one-fiftieth of the statutory maximum[5].

1 Companies Act 1985 s 18(1). As to the official notification of the receipt of the document see para 70 ante. In the case of an unregistered company (see para 1765 et seq post): (1) for references to the memorandum or articles of association of a company there must be substituted references to any instrument constituting or regulating the company; (2) s 18 has effect as if (a) for the words 'by any statutory provision, whether contained in an Act of Parliament or in an instrument made under an Act, a printed copy of the Act or instrument' there were substituted the words 'a printed copy of the instrument effecting the alteration' and for the words 'that provision comes into force' there were substituted the words 'that instrument comes into effect'; and (b) in the case of a company incorporated on or after 5 January 1976 it required a printed copy of any instrument constituting or regulating the company to be forwarded to the registrar of companies not later than 15 days after the date of the incorporation of the company and recorded by him, notwithstanding that such instrument has not been the subject of any alteration: Companies (Unregistered Companies) Regulations 1985, SI 1985/680, reg 6(a),(b).
2 Ie by the Companies Act 1985 s 18 or otherwise.
3 Ie other than a special resolution under ibid s 4 (as substituted): see para 1184 post.
4 Ibid s 18(2).
5 Ibid ss 18(3), 730, Sch 24. For the meaning of 'officer who is in default' , 'the statutory maximum' and 'daily default fine' see para 1161 post.

101. Copies of memorandum and articles. On being so required by any member, a company must send to him a copy of the memorandum and of the articles (if any), and a copy of any Act of Parliament which alters the memorandum, subject to payment:

(1) in the case of a copy of the memorandum and of the articles, of five pence or such less sum as the company may prescribe; and

(2) in the case of a copy of an Act, of such sum not exceeding its published price as the company may require[1].

If a company makes default in complying with any of the above provisions, the company, and every officer of it who is in default, is liable for each offence on summary conviction to a fine not exceeding one-fifth of the statutory maximum[2].

Where an alteration is made in a company's memorandum, every copy of the memorandum issued after the date of the alteration must be in accordance with the alteration[3]. If, where any such alteration has been made, the company at any time after the date of the alteration issues any copies of the memorandum which are not in accordance with the alteration, the company, and every officer of the company who is in default, is liable on summary conviction to a fine not exceeding one-fifth of the statutory maximum[4].

1 Companies Act 1985 s 19(1).
2 Ibid ss 19(2), 730, Sch 24. For the meaning of 'officer who is in default' and 'the statutory maximum' see para 1161 post.
3 Ibid s 20(1).
4 Ibid ss 20(2), 730, Sch 24.

(ii) Company Limited by Shares

A. MEMORANDUM AND ARTICLES

102. Contents of memorandum. The memorandum of association of a company limited by shares[1] must state:
(1) the name of the company[2] with, if the company is to be a public company[3], 'public limited company' or, if the company is to be a private company[4], 'limited' as the last words or word in its name[5] (except where the word 'limited' is dispensed with)[6];
(2) whether the registered office of the company is to be situated in England and Wales, or Wales, or Scotland[7];
(3) the objects of the company[8];
(4) that the liability of its members is limited[9]; and
(5) the amount of the share capital with which the company proposes to be registered, and the division of the share capital into shares of a fixed amount[10].
There must also be shown in the memorandum against the name of each subscriber the number of shares he takes, being at least one share[11]. If no number is written after his name, a subscriber is liable to pay for one share at least[12].
The memorandum of a limited company may also provide that the liability of the directors or managers, or of the managing director, is to be unlimited[13].

1 The prescribed form of memorandum for a private company limited by shares is given in Table B, and for a public company limited by shares is given in Table F: see para 85 note 4 ante.
2 Companies Act 1985 s 2(1)(a).
3 For the meaning of 'public company' see para 82 ante.
4 For the meaning of 'private company' see para 82 ante.
5 See the Companies Act 1985 s 25 and para 154 post. If the company's registered office is to be situated in Wales, the corresponding Welsh words may be used: see para 154 post.
6 As to dispensing with the word 'limited' see paras 112, 113 post.
7 Companies Act 1985 s 2(1)(b),(2); and see para 82 ante.
8 Ibid s 2(1)(c). See para 86 ante.
9 Ibid s 2(3).
10 Ibid s 2(5)(a). See para 84 ante and para 173 post.
11 Ibid s 2(5)(b),(c).
12 *Portal v Emmens* (1876) 1 CPD 664 at 667, CA. As to subscribers see further para 358 et seq post.
13 See the Companies Act 1985 s 306(1) and para 627 post.

103. Contents of articles. Where articles of association are not registered[1], or, if articles are registered, in so far as they do not exclude or modify Table A, that Table (so far as applicable, and as in force at the date of the company's registration) constitutes the company's articles, in the same manner and to the same extent as if articles in the form of that Table had been duly registered[2].

If the company intends to issue share warrants to bearer, special authority for that purpose must be given by the articles[3].

The articles may authorise the issue of redeemable shares[4] and the purchase of the company's own shares[5], and may also authorise the company to increase its capital, to consolidate and divide its shares into shares of larger amount, to convert paid-up shares into stock and to reconvert stock into paid-up shares, to sub-divide its shares into shares of a smaller amount, and to cancel shares not taken or agreed to be taken and diminish the amount of the company's share capital by the amount of the shares so cancelled[6]; also to reduce its capital[7] and share premium account[8]. The articles may also authorise the company to alter its memorandum so as to impose unlimited liability on its directors or managers, or any managing director[9].

1 As to the registration of articles see para 87 ante.
2 Companies Act 1985 s 8(2). As to the importance of using words clearly excluding Table A see *Fisher v Black and White Publishing Co* [1901] 1 Ch 174, CA. As to Table A generally see para 529 et seq post.
3 See the Companies Act 1985 s 188(1) (as substituted) and para 493 post. In *Pilkington v United Railways of the Havana and Regla Warehouses Ltd* [1930] 2 Ch 108, it was unsuccessfully contended that the corresponding provision of the Companies Act 1929 had altered the law so as to preclude the issue of warrants in respect of stock.
4 See the Companies Act 1985 s 159(1) and para 219 post.
5 See ibid s 162(1) (purchase by public company out of distributable profits or proceeds of fresh issue of shares: see para 222 post), s 171(1) (purchase by private company out of capital: see para 232 post).
6 See ibid s 121(1),(2) and para 201 et seq post.
7 See ibid s 135(1) and paras 215, 241 post.
8 See ibid s 130(3) and para 188 post.
9 See ibid s 307(1) and para 627 post.

B. PUBLIC COMPANY

104. Nature and powers of public company. A public company is a company limited by shares or guarantee and having a share capital, being a company:

(1) the memorandum of which states that it is to be a public company; and
(2) in relation to which the provisions of the Companies Act 1985 or the former Companies Acts[1] as to the registration or re-registration of a company as a public company have been complied with on or after 22 December 1980[2].

The name of a public company must end with the words 'public limited company' or, if the memorandum states that the company's registered office is to be situated in Wales, those words or their equivalent in Welsh ('cwmni cyfyngedig cyhoeddus'); and those words or that equivalent may not be preceded by the word 'limited' or its Welsh equivalent ('cyfyngedig')[3].

A company registered as a public company on its original incorporation may not do business or exercise any borrowing powers unless the registrar of companies has issued it with a certificate that he is satisfied that the nominal value of the company's allotted share capital is not less than the authorised minimum[4]. Such a certificate is conclusive evidence that the company is entitled to do business and exercise any borrowing powers[5].

1 For the meaning of 'the former Companies Acts' see para 11 note 2 ante.
2 Companies Act 1985 ss 1(3), 735(2). See also para 82 ante. Before the Companies Act 1907 the term 'public company' was understood to mean a company which invited the public to subscribe for its shares, and companies which did not do so were often called private companies and are so described in many judgments (see *Re British Seamless Paper Box Co* (1881) 17 ChD 467 at 473, CA; *Re George Newman & Co* [1895] 1 Ch 674 at 685, CA; *Salomon v A Salomon & Co Ltd* [1897] AC 22 at 43, HL; *Re*

Wragg Ltd [1897] 1 Ch 796 at 807, CA), although the legal status of such a company is that of a public company (*Re Sharp, Rickett v Sharp* (1890) 45 ChD 286 at 290, CA; *Re Lysaght, Lysaght v Lysaght* [1898] 1 Ch 115 at 122, CA; *Trevor v Whitworth* (1887) 12 App Cas 409 at 434, HL). Thereafter the term 'public company' , which was not defined, was used in contradistinction to 'private company', which was defined as a company which by its articles restricted the right to transfer its shares, limited the number of its members (excluding persons in or formerly in the employment of the company) to 50, and prohibited any invitation to the public to subscribe for its shares and debentures: see the Companies Act 1948 ss 28, 455(1) (repealed). In other Acts the term 'public company', although not expressly defined, may include a private company: see eg *Re White, Theobald v White* [1913] 1 Ch 231 at 238 (decided under the Apportionment Act 1870).

3 Companies Act 1985 s 25(1).
4 Ibid s 117(1),(2). For the meaning of 'authorised minimum' see para 652 note 6 post.
5 Ibid s 117(6).

C. PRIVATE COMPANY

105. Restrictions on powers of private company. A private company within the meaning of the Companies Act 1985 is a company that is not a public company[1]. A private limited company, other than a company limited by guarantee and not having a share capital, commits an offence if it:

(1) offers to the public, whether for cash or otherwise, any shares in or debentures of the company; or

(2) allots or agrees to allot, whether for cash or otherwise, any shares in or debentures of the company with a view to all or any of those shares or debentures being offered for sale to the public[2].

A company guilty of such an offence, and any officer of it who is in default, is liable on conviction on indictment to a fine or on summary conviction to a fine not exceeding the statutory maximum[3].

Nothing in the above provisions affects the validity of any allotment or sale of shares or debentures, or of any agreement to allot or sell shares or debentures[4].

1 Companies Act 1985 s 1(3). For the meaning of 'public company' see para 82 ante.
2 Ibid s 81(1). For these purposes, 'offer for sale to the public' has the meaning given by ss 58–60: s 81(1). Sections 58–60 are repealed for all purposes by the Financial Services Act 1986 s 212(3), Sch 17 Pt I, except in so far as they are necessary for the purposes of defining terms in the Companies Act 1985 s 81 and s 83 (see para 451 post): see the Financial Services Act 1986 (Commencement) (No 13) Order 1995, SI 1995/1538, art 2(a)(i).
    For purposes of the Companies Act 1985, it is evidence, unless the contrary is proved, that an allotment of, or an agreement to allot, shares or debentures was made with a view to their being offered for sale to the public if it is shown that an offer of the shares or debentures, or of any of them, for sale to the public was made within six months after the allotment or agreement to allot or that, at the date when the offer was made, the whole consideration to be received by the company in respect of the shares or debentures had not been so received: s 58(3).
    Subject to s 60 (see infra), any reference in the Companies Act 1985 to offering shares or debentures to the public is to be read, subject to any provision to the contrary, as including a reference to offering them to any section of the public, whether selected as members or debenture holders of the company concerned, or as clients of the person issuing the prospectus, or in any other manner: s 59(1). The same applies to any reference in the Companies Act 1985, or in a company's articles, to an invitation to the public to subscribe for shares or debentures: s 59(2). For these purposes, 'prospectus' means any prospectus, notice, circular, advertisement, or other invitation, offering to the public for subscription or purchase any shares in or debentures of a company: s 744.
    Section 59 does not require an offer or invitation to be treated as made to the public if it can properly be regarded, in all the circumstances, as not being calculated to result, directly or indirectly, in the shares or debentures becoming available for subscription or purchase by persons other than those receiving the offer or invitation, or otherwise as being a domestic concern of the persons receiving and making it: s 60(1). In particular, a provision in a company's articles prohibiting invitations to the public to

subscribe for shares or debentures is not to be taken as prohibiting the making to members or debenture holders of an invitation which can properly be regarded as falling within s 60(1): s 60(2). For the purposes of s 60(1), an offer of shares in or debentures of a private company, or an invitation to subscribe for such shares or debentures, is to be regarded (unless the contrary is proved) as being a domestic concern of the persons making and receiving the offer or invitation if it falls within any of the following descriptions: s 60(3). It is to be so regarded if it is made to an existing member of the company making the offer or invitation, an existing employee of that company, a member of the family of such a member or employee or an existing debenture holder: s 60(4). The members of a person's family are the person's husband or wife, widow or widower and children (including stepchildren) and their descendants and any trustee (acting in his capacity as such) of a trust the principal beneficiary of which is the person himself or herself, or any of those relatives: s 60(5). The offer or invitation is also to be so regarded if it is to subscribe for shares or debentures to be held under an employees' share scheme: s 60(6). The offer or invitation is also to be so regarded if it falls within s 60(4) or (6) (see supra) and it is made on terms which permit the person to whom it is made to renounce his right to the allotment of shares or issue of debentures, but only in favour of such a person as is mentioned in s 60(4) (see supra) or, where there is an employees' share scheme, of a person entitled to hold shares or debentures under the scheme: s 60(7). Where application has been made to the competent authority for the purposes of the Financial Services Act 1986 Pt IV (ss 142-156B) (as amended): see para 281 et seq post), for admission of any securities to the Official List, then an offer of those securities for subscription or sale to a person whose ordinary business it is to buy or sell shares or debentures, whether as principal or agent, is not deemed an offer to the public for purposes of the Companies Act 1985 Pt III (ss 56-79): s 60(8) (amended by the Official Listing of Securities (Change of Competent Authority) Regulations 1991, SI 1991/2000, reg 5(1)). For the meaning of 'employees' share scheme' see para 120 note 8 post.

The Companies Act 1985 s 81 is repealed by the Financial Services Act 1986 Sch 17 Pt I to the following extent:

(1) in so far as it applies in relation to any investment which is listed or the subject of an application for listing under Pt IV (ss 142-156B) (as amended) (Financial Services Act 1986 (Commencement No 3) Order 1986, SI 1986/2246, art 5, Sch 4);

(2) in so far as it applies to a prospectus offering for subscription, or to any form of application for, units in a body corporate which is a recognised scheme (Financial Services Act 1986 (Commencement) (No 8) Order 1988, SI 1988/740, art 2, Schedule).

A private company may not apply for listing on the Stock Exchange: see the *Listing Rules* r 3.2.

3 Companies Act 1985 ss 81(2), 730, Sch 24. See also note 2 supra. For the meaning of 'officer who is in default' and 'the statutory maximum' see para 1161 post.

4 Ibid s 81(3).

106. Advantages of private company. The advantages of a private company as compared with a company which is not a private company are:

(1) the statutory provisions relating to the offer of equity securities[1] to existing shareholders on a pre-emptive basis[2] may be excluded by a provision contained in a private company's memorandum or articles[3];

(2) a private company may allot shares as fully or partly paid up otherwise than in cash without first obtaining a valuation of such consideration[4];

(3) a private company is free from the restrictions on transfers of non-cash assets in the initial period[5];

(4) a private company is free from the restrictions regarding its initial and any reduced capital being equal to or above the authorised minimum[6];

(5) there is no necessity for a private company to call an extraordinary general meeting on a serious loss of capital[7];

(6) a private company is not obliged to deal with shares in the company held by or for it in the same way as a public company[8];

(7) a private company is not subject to the special restriction on giving financial assistance only if the company has net assets which are not thereby reduced, or, to the extent to which those assets are reduced, out of distributable profits[9];

(8) the restrictions on the provision of financial assistance in connection with the acquisition of shares in a private company or its holding company are relaxed[10];

(9) on making the return required by a company which has purchased its own shares, a private company is not required to state the aggregate amount paid by the company for the shares and the maximum and minimum prices paid in respect of each class purchased[11];

(10) a private company may redeem or purchase its own shares out of capital[12];

(11) there is no obligation upon shareholders to disclose substantial interests in shares in a private company[13];

(12) the period for the laying and delivery of a private company's accounts is ten months after the end of the relevant accounting reference period, as opposed to seven months in the case of a public company[14];

(13) the penalty for failure to deliver accounts to the registrar of companies is lower for a private company[15];

(14) a private company may, if it satisfies the statutory conditions, claim the exemptions for small and medium-sized companies[16] and, where it is a parent company of a group headed by that company which qualifies as a small or medium-sized group and is not an ineligible group, it need not prepare group accounts[17];

(15) a private company need keep its accounting records for a period of only three, as opposed to six, years[18];

(16) a private company may, if it satisfies the statutory conditions, be exempt from audit[19] and from the obligation to appoint auditors[20];

(17) a private company may, if it is a dormant company, make itself exempt from the statutory provisions relating to the audit of accounts[21];

(18) a private company may pass elective resolutions[22];

(19) a private company is not subject to the restriction on distribution of assets by reference to its called-up share capital and undistributable reserves[23];

(20) a private company need not have more than one director[24];

(21) a private company limited by shares or by guarantee may be formed[25] and may carry on business with only one member[26];

(22) two or more persons may be appointed directors by the company in general meeting by a single resolution[27];

(23) there is no automatic age limit in respect of the directors of a private company unless it is a subsidiary of a public company or of a body corporate registered under the law relating to companies for the time being in force in Northern Ireland as a public company[28];

(24) a proxy appointed by a member to attend and vote at a general meeting or class meeting has the same right as the member to speak at the meeting[29];

(25) a private company may apply to the registrar of companies to have the company's name struck off the register[30].

1 For the meaning of 'equity security' see para 457 note 2 post.
2 As to the pre-emptive basis see the Companies Act 1985 ss 89-96 and para 457 et seq post.
3 See ibid s 91 and para 459 post.
4 See ibid s 103(1) and para 468 post.
5 See ibid s 104(1) and para 469 post. For the meaning of 'the initial period' see para 469 post.
6 See ibid ss 117(1), 139(1) and paras 652, 269 respectively post. For the meaning of 'authorised minimum' see para 652 note 6 post.
7 See ibid s 142(1) and para 213 post.
8 See ibid s 146 and para 366 post.
9 See ibid s 154 and para 275 post.
10 See ibid ss 155-158 and paras 276-278 post.
11 See ibid s 169(2) and para 229 post.

12　See ibid ss 171–176 (as amended) and paras 232–237 post. This is subject to the right of a single member of the company who did not consent to, or vote in favour of, the necessary resolution to apply to the court for its cancellation: see s 176 and para 237 post.

13　See ibid s 198(1) and para 735 post. Consequently there is no requirement to keep a register of interests in such shares (see s 211(1) and para 747 post) or power to demand such information (see s 212(1) and para 748 post); but as to disclosure by directors see ss 324–329 (as amended) and para 564 et seq post.

14　See ibid s 244 (as substituted) and para 822 post.

15　See ibid s 242A(2) (as added) and para 819 post.

16　See ibid s 246 (as substituted and amended) and para 900 post.

17　See ibid s 248 (as substituted) and para 902 post.

18　See ibid s 222(5) (as substituted) and para 802 post.

19　See ibid ss 249A–249E (as added) and para 1054 et seq post.

20　See ibid s 388A (as added and substituted) and para 1033 post.

21　See ibid s 250 (as substituted and amended) and para 1058 post.

22　See ibid s 379A (as added) and para 686 post.

23　See ibid s 264(1),(4) and para 702 post.

24　See ibid s 282(3) and para 543 post.

25　See ibid s 1(3A) (as added) and para 80 ante.

26　See ibid s 24 (as amended) and para 410 post.

27　See ibid s 292(1) and para 546 post.

28　See ibid s 293(1) and para 637 post.

29　See ibid s 372(1) and para 674 post.

30　See ibid ss 652A–652F (as added) and paras 1500–1503 post.

107. Advantages over limited partnership. The principal advantage of a private company, as compared with a limited partnership, is that shareholding directors may have in their hands the management of the business without incurring the risk of being under unlimited liability for the debts incurred[1].

1　See the Limited Partnerships Act 1907 s 6(1) and PARTNERSHIP vol 35 (Reissue) para 214.

(iii) Company Limited by Guarantee

108. Contents and form of memorandum. In the case of a company limited by guarantee[1] the memorandum of association must state:

(1) the name of the company[2], with 'limited' (or, if the registered office of the company is situated in Wales, 'limited' or the Welsh equivalent 'cyfyngedig') or, if the memorandum states that the company is to be a public company, with 'public limited company' (or the Welsh equivalent 'cwmni cyfyngedig cyhoeddus') as the last word or words in its name[3] (except where the statutory requirements for dispensing with this necessity are satisfied)[4];

(2) whether the registered office of the company is to be situated in England and Wales, or Wales, or Scotland[5];

(3) the objects of the company[6];

(4) that the liability of the members is limited[7]; and

(5) that each member undertakes to contribute to the assets of the company in the event of its being wound up while he is a member, or within one year after he ceases to be a member, for payment of the debts and liabilities of the company contracted before he ceases to be a member, and of the costs, charges and expenses of winding up, and for adjustment of the rights of the contributories, among themselves, such amount as may be required, not exceeding a specified amount[8].

With effect from 22 December 1980, a company cannot be formed as, or become, a company limited by guarantee with a share capital[9].

The memorandum may provide that the liability of the directors or managers, or of the managing director, is to be unlimited[10].

There are statutory forms of the memoranda of association of companies limited by guarantee without or with a share capital[11].

The memorandum must be signed, attested, and delivered for registration in accordance with the general provisions previously stated[12].

1 For the meaning of 'company limited by guarantee' see para 80 ante.
2 Companies Act 1985 s 2(1)(a).
3 See ibid s 25 and para 154 post.
4 As to dispensing with the word 'limited' see paras 112, 113 post.
5 See the Companies Act 1985 s 2(1)(b),(2) and para 84 ante.
6 Ibid s 2(1)(c).
7 Ibid s 2(3).
8 Ibid s 2(4).
9 Ibid s 1(4). Previously, if the company had a share capital, the memorandum had also to state the amount of the share capital with which the company proposed to be registered and the division thereof into shares of a fixed amount, and each subscriber had to write opposite his name the number of shares he took, not being less than one share: Companies Act 1948 s 2(4) (repealed).
10 See the Companies Act 1985 s 306(1) and para 627 post.
11 Ie the Companies (Tables A to F) Regulations 1985, SI 1985/805, reg 2, Schedule, Tables C, D: see para 85 ante and para 530 post.
12 See paras 84, 88 ante.

109. Effect of division of undertaking into shares. For the purpose of the provisions of the Companies Act 1985 relating to the memorandum of a company limited by guarantee[1] and those prohibiting the formation of a company limited by guarantee with a share capital[2], every provision in the memorandum or articles, or in any resolution, of a company limited by guarantee registered on or after 1 January 1901 purporting to divide the undertaking of the company into shares or interests is to be treated as a provision for a share capital, notwithstanding that the nominal amount or number of the shares or interests is not specified by the provision[3].

1 Ie including the Companies Act 1985 s 15.
2 Ie ibid s 1(4): see para 108 ante.
3 Ibid s 15(2); Companies Consolidation (Consequential Provisions) Act 1985 s 10. A company limited by guarantee and not having a share capital, registered before 1 January 1901, could, by special resolution, divide its undertaking into a specified number of shares or interests of no defined or fixed monetary amount, each share or interest being merely a certain proportion of the whole undertaking: *Malleson v General Mineral Patents Syndicate Ltd* [1894] 3 Ch 538.

110. Void provisions. If a company limited by guarantee has no share capital, and is registered on or after 1 January 1901, every provision in the memorandum or articles or in any resolution of the company purporting to give any person a right to participate in the divisible profits of the company, otherwise than as a member, is void[1].

1 Companies Act 1985 s 15(1); Companies Consolidation (Consequential Provisions) Act 1985 s 10. This provision prevents a person from sharing in the profits of a guarantee company registered on or after 1 January 1901, unless he is a member, and as such is under a liability to contribute to the assets of the company in the event of its being wound up.

111. Articles of association. In the case of a company limited by guarantee, there must be registered with the memorandum of association, articles of association prescribing regulations for the company, which may adopt all or any of the articles of Table A[1]; but none of the articles of Table A applies except such of them as are expressly adopted. If so desired, the articles of association may give the company power to alter its memorandum so as to impose unlimited liability upon its directors or managers or any managing director[2].

The articles of a company limited by guarantee with a share capital may authorise the company to alter its share capital[3].

There are statutory forms of articles of companies limited by guarantee without or with a share capital[4]. The articles must be signed by the subscribers to the memorandum[5], and must be printed, divided into numbered paragraphs, attested and delivered for registration pursuant to the general provisions previously stated[6].

1 Companies Act 1985 ss 7(1), 8(1). As to Table A see para 87 note 4 ante and para 529 et seq post.
2 See the Companies Act 1985 s 307(1) and para 627 post.
3 See ibid ss 121, 135 and para 201 et seq post.
4 Ibid s 8(4)(a),(b). The form, in the case of a company limited by guarantee and not having a share capital, is that contained in Table C, and, in the case of a company limited by guarantee and having a share capital, is that contained in Table D as, in each case, prescribed by regulations made by the Secretary of State, or as near to that form as circumstances admit: Companies Act 1985 s 8(4). For the current Tables C, D see the Companies (Tables A to F) Regulations 1985, SI 1985/805, reg 2, Schedule. Provided that he follows the general form of the relevant Table, the draftsman is free to add, subtract or vary the articles as circumstances require: *Gaiman v National Association for Mental Health* [1971] Ch 317, [1970] 2 All ER 362.
5 Companies Act 1985 s 7(3)(c).
6 See paras 87, 88 ante.

(iv) Limited Company without the Word 'Limited'

112. Exemption from requirement of 'limited' as part of name. Certain companies are exempt from the requirements of the Companies Act 1985 relating to the use of 'limited'[1] as part of the company name[2].

A private company[3] limited by guarantee is exempt from those requirements, and so too is a company which on 25 February 1982[4] was a private company limited by shares with a name which, by virtue of a licence under previous legislation[5], did not include 'limited'; but in either case, to have the exemption, the company must comply with the following requirements[6]:

(1) the objects of the company are (or, in the case of a company about to be registered, are to be) the promotion of commerce, art, science[7], education, religion, charity[8] or any profession, and anything incidental or conducive to any of those objects[9]; and

(2) the company's memorandum or articles:

(a) require its profits (if any) or other income to be applied in promoting its objects;

(b) prohibit the payment of dividends to its members; and

(c) require all the assets which would otherwise be available to its members generally to be transferred on its winding up either to another body with objects similar to its own or to another body the objects of which are the promotion of charity and anything incidental or conducive thereto (whether or not the body is a member of the company)[10].

A statutory declaration that a company complies with the above requirements may be delivered to the registrar of companies, who may accept the declaration as sufficient evidence of the matters stated in it; and the registrar may refuse to register a company by a name which does not include the word 'limited' unless such a declaration has been delivered to him[11]. Such a declaration must be in the prescribed form[12] and be made:

   (i) in the case of a company to be formed, by a solicitor engaged in its formation or by a person named as director or secretary in the statement required to accompany the memorandum[13];

   (ii) in the case of a company not formed under companies legislation but authorised to register under the Companies Act 1985[14], by two or more directors or other principal officers of the company; and

   (iii) in the case of a company proposing to change its name so that it ceases to have the word 'limited' as part of its name, by a director or secretary of the company[15].

A company which is exempt from the requirements relating to the use of 'limited' and does not include that word as part of its name is also exempt from the statutory requirements relating to the publication of its name[16] and the sending of lists of members[17] to the registrar of companies[18].

1 As to the use of the word 'limited' see para 154 post. In these provisions, references to the word 'limited' include (in an appropriate case) its Welsh equivalent ('cyfyngedig'), and the appropriate alternative ('ltd' or 'cyf', as the case may be): Companies Act 1985 s 30(6).

2 Ibid s 30(1).

3 For the meaning of 'private company' see para 82 ante.

4 Ie the day before the coming into force of the predecessor of the Companies Act 1985 s 30 ie the Companies Act 1981 s 25 (repealed).

5 Ie under the Companies Act 1948 s 19 (repealed).

6 Companies Act 1985 s 30(2).

7 'Science' is not confined to pure or speculative science, or science generally, but includes various branches of science, such as mechanical or engineering science: *IRC v Forrest* (1890) 15 App Cas 334, HL.

8 For the meaning of 'charity' see *Income Tax Special Purposes Comrs v Pemsel* [1891] AC 531, HL and CHARITIES vol 5(2) (Reissue) para 1 et seq.

9 Companies Act 1985 s 30(3)(a).

10 Ibid s 30(3)(b).

11 Ibid s 30(4).

12 For the prescribed forms of statutory declaration see the Companies (Forms) (Amendment) Regulations 1995, SI 1995/736, reg 3, Sch 2, Forms 30(5)(a), 30(5)(b) and 30(5)(c). For the prescribed version of the forms in Welsh see the Companies (Welsh Language Forms and Documents) (No 3) Regulations 1995, SI 1995/1508, reg 2, Schedule, Forms 30(5)(a)CYM, 30(5)(b)CYM and 30(5)(c)CYM.

13 Ie the statement to be delivered under the Companies Act 1985 s 10(2): see para 88 ante.

14 Ie under ibid s 680 (as amended): see para 24 ante.

15 Ibid s 30(5).

16 See para 152 post.

17 See para 1064 post.

18 Companies Act 1985 s 30(7).

113. Designated agencies. A company is exempt from the requirements of the Companies Act 1985 relating to the use of 'limited' as part of the company name[1] if:

   (1) it is a designated agency[2]; and

   (2) its memorandum and articles comply with the general statutory requirements[3] as to such exemption[4].

1 As to these requirements see para 154 et seq post.

2 For these purposes, a 'designated agency' is a body to which functions are transferred by the Secretary of State by an order under the Financial Services Act 1986 s 114(1): s 114(3). The body to which functions are, subject to certain conditions, transferred by the first order under s 114(1) is the Securities and Investments Board Limited: see s 114(2). As to the functions transferred see s 114(4),(5) and MONEY.

3 Ie the requirements specified in the Companies Act 1985 s 30(3)(b): see para 112 head (2) ante.

4 Financial Services Act 1986 s 116, Sch 9 para 2(1). In the Companies Act 1985 s 30(4) (statutory declaration of compliance with requirements: see para 112 ante), the reference to the requirements of s 30(3) includes a reference to the requirements of the Financial Services Act 1986 Sch 9 para 2(1): Sch 9 para 2(2).

114. Prohibition on alteration of memorandum or articles. A company which is exempt[1] from the statutory requirements relating to the use of 'limited'[2] as part of its name, and whose name does not include 'limited', must not alter its memorandum or articles of association so that it ceases to comply with those requirements[3]. A company which contravenes that provision, and any officer of it who is in default, is liable on summary conviction to a fine not exceeding the statutory maximum and, on conviction after continued contravention, to a daily default fine not exceeding one-tenth of the statutory maximum[4].

If it appears to the Secretary of State that such a company has:

(1) carried on any business other than the promotion of any of the permitted objects[5]; or

(2) applied any of its profits or other income otherwise than in promoting such objects; or

(3) paid a dividend to any of its members,

or that the company, being a designated agency[6], has ceased to be such, he may, in writing, direct the company to change its name by resolution of the directors within such period as may be specified in the direction, so that its name ends with 'limited'[7]. A company which fails to comply with such a direction, and any officer of the company who is in default, is liable on summary conviction to a fine not exceeding one-fifth of the statutory maximum, and, on conviction after continued contravention, to a daily default fine not exceeding one-fiftieth of the statutory maximum[8].

A copy of any such resolution must be forwarded to the registrar of companies within 15 days[9].

A company which has received such a direction may not thereafter be registered by a name which does not include 'limited', without the approval of the Secretary of State[10].

1 Ie under the Companies Act 1985 s 30 (see para 112 ante) or the Financial Services Act 1986 s 116, Sch 9 para 2 (see para 113 ante).
2 For these purposes, references to the word 'limited' include (in an appropriate case) its Welsh equivalent ('cyfyngedig'), and the appropriate alternative ('ltd' or 'cyf', as the case may be): Companies Act 1985 s 31(4).
3 Ibid s 31(1). The requirements referred to are those of s 31(3) (see para 112 ante): s 31(1).
4 Ibid ss 31(5), 730, Sch 24. For the meaning of 'officer who is in default', 'the statutory maximum' and 'daily default fine' see para 1161 post.
5 Ie the objects mentioned in ibid s 30(3): see para 112 ante.
6 For the meaning of 'designated agency' see para 113 note 2 ante.
7 Companies Act 1985 s 31(2); Financial Services Act 1986 Sch 9 para 2(3).
8 Companies Act 1985 ss 31(6), 730, Sch 24.
9 Ibid ss 31(2), 380(1). See further para 691 post.
10 Ibid s 31(3).

(v) Unlimited Company

115. Contents of memorandum. In the case of an unlimited company, the memorandum of association must state:

(1) the name of the company;

(2) whether the registered office of the company is to be situated in England and Wales, or Wales, or Scotland; and

(3) the objects of the company[1].

If the company has a share capital, the memorandum need not state the amount or its division into shares[2], but each subscriber of the memorandum must write opposite to his name the number of shares he takes, not being less than one[3].

There is a statutory form of memorandum of an unlimited company with a share capital[4]; and, whether the company has or has not a share capital, the memorandum must be signed, attested and delivered for registration in accordance with the general provisions previously mentioned[5].

1 Companies Act 1985 s 2(1), (2). See generally para 84 ante.
2 See ibid s 2(5)(a).
3 Ibid s 2(5)(b),(c).
4 Ie the Companies (Tables A to F) Regulations 1985, SI 1985/805, reg 2, Schedule, Table E: see para 85 ante and para 530 post.
5 See paras 84, 88 ante.

116. Articles. In the case of an unlimited company, there must be registered with the memorandum, articles of association which may adopt all or any of the provisions of Table A[1]; but none of those provisions applies except those which are expressly adopted[2].

If the company has a share capital, the articles must state the amount of share capital with which the company proposes to be registered[2]. There is a statutory form of articles of an unlimited company with a share capital[3].

The articles must be printed, divided into numbered paragraphs, signed, attested and delivered for registration in accordance with the general provisions previously mentioned[4].

A company registered as unlimited may re-register itself as a limited company[5].

1 Companies Act 1985 ss 7(1), 8(1). As to Table A generally see para 529 et seq post.
2 Companies Act 1985 s 7(2). As to the duty of an unlimited company to notify the registrar of increases in membership see para 361 post.
3 Ibid s 8(4)(c). The form is to be in accordance with Table E prescribed by regulations made by the Secretary of State, or as near to that form as circumstances admit: Companies Act 1985 s 8(4). The current Table E is set out in the Companies (Tables A to F) Regulations 1985, SI 1985/805, Schedule, and states what the capital is and into what shares it is divided, and it gives the company power by special resolution to alter its share capital to the extent allowed by the Act. It also adopts certain of the provisions of Table A: see para 530 post.
4 See paras 87, 88 ante.
5 See para 126 post.

117. Advantages of an unlimited company. The directors of an unlimited company are not required[1] to deliver to the registrar of companies accounts and reports in respect of a financial year[2] if the following conditions are met[3]. The conditions are that at no time during the relevant accounting reference period[4]:

(1) has the company been, to its knowledge, a subsidiary undertaking[5] of an undertaking which was then limited;

(2) have there been, to its knowledge, exercisable, by or on behalf of two or more undertakings which were then limited, rights which, if exercisable by one of them, would have made the company a subsidiary undertaking of it; or

(3) has the company been a parent company[6] of an undertaking which was then limited[7].

The references to an undertaking being limited at a particular time are to an undertaking, under whatever law established, the liability of whose members is at that time limited[7].

The exemption conferred by the above provisions does not apply if the company is a banking[8] or insurance[9] company or the parent company of a banking[10] or insurance[11] group, or the company is a qualifying company[12] or at any time during the relevant accounting period the company carried on business as the promoter of a trading stamp scheme within the Trading Stamps Act 1964[13].

1 Ie by the Companies Act 1985 s 242 (as substituted and amended): see para 818 post.
2 For the meaning of 'financial year' see para 806 post.
3 Companies Act 1985 s 254(1) (substituted by the Companies Act 1989 s 17). Where a company is so exempt from the obligation to deliver accounts, the Companies Act 1985 s 240 (as substituted) (see para 938 post) has effect with the following modifications: (1) in s 240(3)(b) for the words from 'whether statutory accounts' to 'have been delivered to the registrar' the words 'that the company is exempt from the requirement to deliver statutory accounts' must be substituted; and (2) in s 240(5) for the words 'as required to be delivered to the registrar under section 242' the words 'as prepared in accordance with this Part and approved by the board of directors' must be substituted: s 254(4) (substituted by the Companies Act 1989 s 17).
4 For the meaning of 'accounting reference period' see para 807 post.
5 For the meaning of 'subsidiary undertaking' see para 828 post; and for the meaning of 'undertaking' see para 806 note 5 post.
6 For the meaning of 'parent company' see para 828 post.
7 Companies Act 1985 s 254(2) (substituted by the Companies Act 1989 s 17).
8 For these purposes, 'banking company' means a company which is authorised under the Banking Act 1987 (see BANKING vol 3(1) (Reissue) para 17 note 4): Companies Act 1985 s 744 (amended by the Companies Act 1989 s 23, Sch 10 para 16).
9 For these purposes, 'insurance company' means the same as in the Insurance Companies Act 1982 (see INSURANCE vol 25 (Reissue) para 15 note 3): Companies Act 1985 s 744.
10 For the meaning of 'banking group' see para 927 note 2 post.
11 For the meaning of 'insurance group' see para 927 note 5 post.
12 For these purposes, an unlimited company incorporated in Great Britain is a qualifying company if each of its members is a limited company or another unlimited company, or a Scottish firm, each of whose members is a limited company: Partnerships and Unlimited Companies (Accounts) Regulations 1993, SI 1993/1820, reg 9(1). Any reference in reg 9(1) to a limited company, another unlimited company or a Scottish firm includes a reference to any comparable undertaking incorporated in or formed under the law of any country or territory outside Great Britain: reg 9(2).
13 Companies Act 1985 s 254(3) (substituted by the Companies Act 1989 s 17; amended by the Companies Act 1985 (Bank Accounts) Regulations 1991, SI 1991/2705, reg 6, Sch 2 para 1; the Partnerships and Unlimited Companies (Accounts) Regulations 1993 reg 10; the Companies Act 1985 (Insurance Companies Accounts) Regulations 1993, SI 1993/3246, regs 5(1), 7, Sch 2 para 2). As to trading stamp schemes see SALE OF GOODS vol 41 para 899.

(4) RE-REGISTRATION

(i) Re-registration of Private Company as Public

118. Procedure on re-registration. Subject to the following provisions[1], a private company[2] (other than a company not having a share capital) may be re-registered as a public company[3] if a special resolution[4] that it should be so re-registered is passed, and an application for re-registration is delivered to the registrar of companies, together with the necessary documents[5]. A company cannot be so re-registered[6] if it has previously been re-registered as unlimited[7].

The special resolution must:

(1) alter the company's memorandum so that it states that the company is to be a public company; and

(2) make such other alterations in the memorandum as are necessary to bring it (in substance and in form) into conformity with the requirements of the Companies Act 1985 with respect to the memorandum of a public company[8]; and

(3) make such alterations in the company's articles as are requisite in the circumstances[9].

The application must be in the prescribed form[10] and be signed by a director or the secretary of the company; and the documents to be delivered with it are:

(a) a printed copy of the memorandum and articles as altered in pursuance of the resolution;

(b) a copy of a written statement by the company's auditors that in their opinion the relevant balance sheet[11] shows that at the balance sheet date[12] the amount of the company's net assets[13] was not less than the aggregate of its called-up share capital and undistributable reserves[14];

(c) a copy of the relevant balance sheet, together with a copy of an unqualified report[15] by the company's auditors in relation to that balance sheet;

(d) if shares have been allotted by the company between the date as at which the relevant balance sheet was prepared and the passing of the above specified resolution otherwise than for cash[16], a copy of the valuation report required in such a case[17];

(e) a statutory declaration in the prescribed form[18] by a director or secretary of the company that the necessary special resolution has been passed and that the relevant conditions[19] (so far as applicable) have been satisfied, and that between the balance sheet date and the application for re-registration there has been no change in the company's financial position that has resulted in the amount of its net assets becoming less than the aggregate of its called-up share capital and undistributable reserves[20].

A resolution that a company be re-registered as a public company may change the company name by deleting the word 'company' or the words 'and company', or its or their equivalent in Welsh ('cwmni', 'a'r cwmni'), including any abbreviation of them[21].

1 Ie the Companies Act 1985 ss 43-48 (as amended): see infra and para 119 et seq post.
2 For the meaning of 'private company' see para 82 ante.
3 For the meaning of 'public company' see para 82 ante.
4 As to special resolutions see para 683 post.
5 Companies Act 1985 s 43(1). As to the necessary documentation see infra.
6 Ie re-registered under ibid s 43.
7 Ibid s 43(1).
8 As to such requirements, which include compliance with the provisions as to the company's name, see para 102 ante and para 154 et seq post.
9 Companies Act 1985 s 43(2).
10 For the prescribed form of application see the Companies (Forms) (Amendment) Regulations 1995, SI 1995/736, reg 3, Sch 2, Form 43(3).
11 For these purposes, 'relevant balance sheet' means a balance sheet prepared as at a date not more than seven months before the company's application to be re-registered: Companies Act 1985 s 43(4).
12 For these purposes, 'balance sheet date' has the same meaning as in Pt VII (ss 221-262A (as amended): see para 809 note 7 post): ibid s 742(1) (substituted by the Companies Act 1989 s 23, Sch 10 para 15).
13 For the meaning of 'net assets' see para 702 note 3 post.
14 For the meaning of 'called-up share capital' see para 174 post; and for the meaning of 'undistributable reserves' see para 702 note 5 post.
15 For the meaning of 'unqualified report' see para 121 post.
16 As to the consequences of such an allotment see para 119 post.

17 As to such valuation report see para 119 post.
18 For the prescribed form of statutory declaration see the Companies (Forms) (Amendment) Regulations 1995 Sch 2, Form 43(3)(e).
19 Ie the conditions of the Companies Act 1985 s 44 (as amended) (see para 119 post) and s 45 (see para 120 post).
20 Ibid s 43(3).
21 Ibid s 43(5).

119. Consideration for shares recently allotted to be valued. If shares have been allotted by the company between the date as at which the relevant balance sheet[1] was prepared and the passing of the special resolution to re-register[2], and those shares were allotted as fully or partly paid up as to their nominal value or any premium on them otherwise than in cash, then, subject to the following provisions, the registrar of companies must not entertain an application by the company for re-registration unless beforehand the consideration for the allotment has been valued in accordance with the standard procedure in the case of public companies[3], and a report with respect to the value of the consideration has been made to the company (in accordance with such procedure) during the six months immediately preceding the allotment of the shares[4].

Where an amount standing to the credit of any of the company's reserve accounts, or of its profit and loss account, has been applied in paying up (to any extent) any of the shares allotted or any premium on those shares, the amount applied does not count as consideration for the allotment, and accordingly the above restriction[5] does not apply to it[6]. Nor does that restriction apply if the allotment is in connection with an arrangement[7] providing for it to be on terms that the whole or part of the consideration for the shares allotted is to be provided by the transfer to the company or the cancellation of all or some of the shares, or of all or some of the shares of a particular class, in another company[8] (with or without the issue to the company applying for re-registration of shares, or of shares of any particular class, in that other company)[9]. This last provision does not, however, exclude the application of the above restriction[10] unless under the arrangement it is open to all the holders of the shares of the other company in question (or, where the arrangement applies only to shares of a particular class, all the holders of the other company's shares of that class) to take part in the arrangement[11]. In determining whether that is the case, shares held by or by a nominee of the company allotting shares in connection with the arrangement, or by or by a nominee of a company which is that company's holding company[12] or subsidiary[13] or a company which is a subsidiary of its holding company, are to be disregarded[14].

Nor does the above restriction[15] apply to preclude an application for re-registration, if the allotment of the company's shares is in connection with its proposed merger with another company, that is, where one of the companies concerned proposes to acquire all the assets and liabilities of the other in exchange for the issue of shares or other securities of that one to shareholders of the other, with or without any cash payment to shareholders[16].

1 For the meaning of 'relevant balance sheet' see para 118 note 11 ante.
2 As to the special resolution see para 118 ante.
3 Ie in accordance with the Companies Act 1985 s 108: see para 471 post.
4 Ibid s 44(1),(2).
5 Ie ibid s 44(2): see supra.
6 Ibid s 44(3).
7 For these purposes, 'arrangement' means any agreement, scheme or arrangement, including an arrangement sanctioned in accordance with ibid s 425 (as amended) (company compromise with

creditors and members: see para 1447 et seq post), or the Insolvency Act 1986 s 110 (liquidator in voluntary winding up accepting shares as consideration for sale of company's property: see paras 1480, 2722 post): Companies Act 1985 s 44(7) (amended by the Insolvency Act 1986 s 439(1), Sch 13 Pt I).

8 For these purposes, 'another company' includes any body corporate and any body to which letters patent have been issued under the Chartered Companies Act 1837 (repealed): Companies Act 1985 s 44(7)(b). As to the repeal of the Chartered Companies Act 1837 see para 14 ante.
9 Companies Act 1985 s 44(4).
10 See note 5 supra.
11 Companies Act 1985 s 44(5).
12 For the meaning of 'holding company' see para 827 post.
13 For the meaning of 'subsidiary' see para 827 post.
14 Companies Act 1985 s 44(5).
15 Ie ibid s 44(2).
16 Ibid s 44(6).

120. Additional requirements relating to share capital. For a private company to be re-registered as a public company[1], the following conditions with respect to its share capital must be satisfied at the time the relevant special resolution[2] is passed[3]:

(1) the nominal value of the company's allotted share capital must be not less than the authorised minimum[4];

(2) each of the company's allotted shares must be paid up at least as to one-quarter of the nominal value of that share and the whole of any premium on it[5];

(3) if any shares in the company or any premium on them have been fully or partly paid up by an undertaking given by any person that he or another should do work or perform services (whether for the company or any other person), the undertaking must have been performed or otherwise discharged[6];

(4) if shares have been allotted as fully or partly paid up as to their nominal value or any premium on them otherwise than in cash, and the consideration for the allotment consists of or includes an undertaking to the company (other than one to which the condition in head (3) above applies), then either the undertaking must have been performed or otherwise discharged, or there must be a contract between the company and some person pursuant to which the undertaking is to be performed within five years from the time the resolution for re-registration is passed[7].

For the purpose of determining whether the conditions in heads (2), (3) and (4) above are complied with, the following shares in the company may be disregarded:

(a) any share which was allotted in pursuance of an employees' share scheme[8] and by reason of which the company would, but for this provision, be precluded by the condition in head (2) above (but not otherwise) from being re-registered as a public company[9]; and

(b) any share which was allotted before 22 June 1982[10],

but a share is not to be so disregarded if the aggregate in nominal value of that share and other shares proposed to be so disregarded is more than one-tenth of the nominal value of the company's allotted share capital[11]. Any shares so disregarded are to be treated as not forming part of the allotted share capital for the purposes of the condition in head (1) above[12].

1 As to the re-registration of a private company as a public company see para 118 ante.
2 Ie the special resolution required by the Companies Act 1985 s 43: see para 118 ante.
3 Ibid s 45(1).
4 Ibid s 45(2)(a). Section 45(2)(a) is subject to s 45(5)-(7) (see infra): s 45(2). For the meaning of 'authorised minimum' see para 652 note 6 post. Provided that this requirement is satisfied, there is no reason why the company should not additionally have other capital expressed in one or more currencies other than sterling: *Re Scandinavian Bank Group plc* [1988] Ch 87, [1987] 2 All ER 70.

5 Companies Act 1985 s 45(2)(b). Section 45(2)(b) is subject to s 45(5)-(7) (see infra): s 45(2).
6 Ibid s 45(3) Section 45(3) is subject to s 45(5) (see infra): s 45(3).
7 Ibid s 45(4). Section 45(4) is subject to s 45(5) (see infra): s 45(4).
8 For these purposes, 'employees' share scheme' means a scheme for encouraging or facilitating the holding of shares or debentures in a company by or for the benefit of the bona fide employees or former employees of the company, the company's subsidiary or holding company, or a subsidiary of the company's holding company or the wives, husbands, widows, widowers or children or stepchildren under the age of 18 of such employees or former employees: ibid s 743. As to such schemes see para 1517 et seq post. For the purposes of s 743, a company which immediately before the commencement of the Companies Act 1989 s 144(1) (ie 1 November 1990) (meaning of 'subsidiary' and 'holding company') was a subsidiary of another company is not to be treated as ceasing to be such a subsidiary by reason of s 144(1) coming into force: s 144(4), Sch 18 para 37.
9 Companies Act 1985 s 45(5)(b).
10 Ibid s 45(5)(a). 22 June 1982 was the end of the transitional period for which provision was made by the Companies Act 1980.
11 Companies Act 1985 s 45(6). However, for this purpose the allotted share capital is to be treated as not including any shares disregarded under s 45(5)(b) (see text head (a) supra): s 45(6).
12 Ibid s 45(7).

121. Meaning of 'unqualified report'. The following provisions explain the reference in the re-registration requirements[1] to an unqualified report of the company's auditors on the relevant balance sheet[2].

If the balance sheet was prepared for a financial year[3] of the company, the reference is to an auditors' report stating without material qualification the auditors' opinion that the balance sheet has been properly prepared in accordance with the Companies Act 1985[4].

If the balance sheet was not prepared for a financial year of the company, the reference is to an auditors' report stating without material qualification the auditors' opinion that the balance sheet has been properly prepared in accordance with the provisions of the Companies Act 1985 which would have applied if it had been so prepared[5].

A qualification is regarded as material unless the auditors state in their report that the matter giving rise to the qualification is not material for the purpose of determining, by reference to the company's balance sheet, whether at the balance sheet date[6] the amount of the company's net assets[7] was not less than the aggregate of its called up share capital[8] and undistributable reserves[9].

1 Ie in the Companies Act 1985 s 43(3)(c): see para 118 head (c) ante.
2 Ibid s 46(1). For the meaning of 'relevant balance sheet' see para 118 note 11 ante.
3 For the meaning of 'financial year' see para 806 post.
4 Companies Act 1985 s 46(2) (substituted by the Companies Act 1989 s 23, Sch 10 para 1).
5 Companies Act 1985 s 46(3) (substituted by the Companies Act 1989 Sch 10 para 1). For the purposes of an auditors' report under the Companies Act 1985 s 46(3) (as so substituted), the provisions of the Companies Act 1985 are deemed to apply with such modifications as are necessary by reason of the fact that the balance sheet is not prepared for a financial year of the company: s 46(3) (as so substituted).
6 For the meaning of 'balance sheet date' see para 809 note 7 post.
7 For these purposes, 'net assets' has the meaning given by the Companies Act 1985 s 264(2) (see para 702 note 3 post): s 46(4) (substituted by the Companies Act 1989 Sch 10 para 1).
8 For the meaning of 'called up share capital' see para 174 post.
9 Companies Act 1985 s 46(4) (as substituted: see note 7 supra). For these purposes, 'undistributable reserves' has the meaning given by s 264(3) (see para 702 note 5 post): s 46(4) (as so substituted).

122. Certificate of re-registration. If the registrar of companies is satisfied, on an application for re-registration[1], that a company may be re-registered as a public company, he must retain the application and other documents delivered to him[2], and issue the company with a certificate of incorporation stating that the company is a public company[3]. The registrar may accept the requisite statutory declaration[4] as sufficient evidence that the necessary special resolution[5] has been passed and the other conditions of re-registration satisfied[6].

The registrar must not issue the certificate if it appears to him that the court has made an order confirming a reduction of the company's capital which has the effect of bringing the nominal value of the company's allotted share capital below the authorised minimum[7].

Upon the issue to a company of such a certificate of incorporation the company, by virtue of the issue of that certificate, becomes a public company[8], and any alterations in the memorandum and articles set out in the resolution take effect accordingly[9]. The certificate is conclusive evidence that the requirements of the Companies Act 1985 in respect of re-registration[10] and of matters precedent and incidental to it have been complied with, and that the company is a public company[11].

1 Ie under the Companies Act 1985 s 43: see para 118 ante.
2 As to such documents see ibid s 43(3) and para 118 ante.
3 Ibid s 47(1).
4 Ie the declaration under ibid s 43(3)(e): see para 118 ante.
5 Ie the special resolution required by ibid s 43(1): see para 118 ante.
6 Ibid s 47(2).
7 Ibid s 47(3). For the meaning of 'authorised minimum' see para 652 note 6 post.
8 As to the nature and powers of a public company see para 104 ante.
9 Companies Act 1985 s 47(4). As to such alterations see para 118 heads (2), (3) ante.
10 For such requirements see para 118 ante.
11 Companies Act 1985 s 47(5).

123. Modification for unlimited company re-registering. In relation to unlimited companies[1], the above provisions as to re-registration[2] are modified[3].

The necessary special resolution[4] must, in addition to the matters already mentioned[5]:

(1) state that the liability of the members is to be limited by shares, and what the company's share capital is to be; and

(2) make such alterations in the company's memorandum as are necessary to bring it in substance and in form into conformity with the requirements of the Companies Act 1985 with respect to the memorandum of a company limited by shares[6].

The certificate of incorporation[7], in addition to containing the statement that the company is a public company[8], must state that the company has been incorporated as a company limited by shares; and, by virtue of the issue of the certificate, the company will become a public company so limited, and the certificate will be conclusive evidence of the fact that it is such a company[9].

An unlimited company having a share capital may, by its resolution for re-registration as a public company[10], do either or both of the following:

(a) increase the nominal amount of its share capital by increasing the nominal amount of each of its shares (but subject to the condition that no part of the increased capital is to be capable of being called up except in the event and for the purpose of the company being wound up);

(b) provide that a specified portion of its uncalled share capital[11] is not to be capable of being called up except in that event and for that purpose[12].

1 For the meaning of 'unlimited company' see para 80 ante.
2 Ie the Companies Act 1985 ss 43–47 (as amended): see paras 118–122 ante.
3 Ibid s 48(1).
4 Ie the special resolution required by ibid s 43(1): see para 118 ante.
5 Ie mentioned in ibid s 43(2): see para 118 ante.
6 Ibid s 48(2). As to the requirements with respect to the memorandum of a company limited by shares see para 102 ante.
7 Ie the certificate of incorporation issued under ibid s 47(1): see para 122 ante.
8 Ie the statement required by ibid s 47(1)(b): see para 122 ante.
9 Ibid s 48(3).
10 Ie under ibid s 43: see para 118 ante.
11 For the meaning of 'uncalled share capital' see para 174 note 14 post.
12 Companies Act 1985 s 124.

(ii) Re-registration of Limited Company as Unlimited

124. Procedure on re-registration. A company which is registered as limited, other than an unlimited company which has been re-registered as limited[1], may be re-registered as unlimited in pursuance of an application in that behalf complying with the following requirements[2]. However, a public company[3] cannot be re-registered under these provisions; nor can a company which has previously been re-registered as unlimited[4].

An application must be in the prescribed form[5] and be signed by a director or the secretary of the company, and be lodged with the registrar of companies, together with the documents mentioned below[6]. The application must set out such alterations in the company's memorandum as, if it is to have a share capital, are requisite to bring it (in substance and in form) into conformity with the requirements of the Companies Act 1985 with respect to the memorandum of a company to be formed as an unlimited company having a share capital[7], or, if it is not to have a share capital, are requisite in the circumstances[8].

If articles have been registered, the application must set out such alterations in them as, if the company is to have a share capital, are requisite to bring the articles (in substance and in form) into conformity with the requirements of the Companies Act 1985 with respect to the articles of a company to be formed as an unlimited company having a share capital[9], or, if the company is not to have a share capital, are requisite in the circumstances[10]. If articles have not been registered, the application must have annexed to it, and request the registration of, printed articles; and these must, if the company is to have a share capital, comply with the requirements mentioned above, and, if not, be articles appropriate to the circumstances[11].

The documents to be lodged with the registrar are:

(1) the prescribed form[12] of assent to the company's being registered as unlimited, subscribed[13] by or on behalf of all the members[14] of the company;

(2) a statutory declaration made by the directors of the company:

    (a) that the persons by whom or on whose behalf the form of assent is subscribed constitute the whole membership of the company; and

    (b) if any of the members have not subscribed that form themselves, that the directors have taken all reasonable steps to satisfy themselves that each person who subscribed it on behalf of a member was lawfully empowered to do so;

(3) a printed copy of the memorandum incorporating the alterations in it set out in the application; and

(4) if articles have been registered, a printed copy of them incorporating the alterations set out in the application[15].

1 Ie under the Companies Act 1967 s 44 (repealed) or the Companies Act 1985 s 51 (see para 125 post).
2 Ibid s 49(1),(2).
3 For the meaning of 'public company' see para 82 ante.
4 Companies Act 1985 s 49(3).
5 For the prescribed form of application see the Companies (Forms) (Amendment) Regulations 1995, SI 1995/736, reg 3, Sch 2, Form 49(1).
6 Companies Act 1985 s 49(4).
7 As to these requirements see para 115 ante.
8 Companies Act 1985 s 49(5).
9 As to these requirements see para 116 ante.
10 Companies Act 1985 s 49(6).
11 Ibid s 49(7).
12 For the prescribed form of assent see the Companies (Forms) (Amendment) Regulations 1995 Sch 2, Form 49(8)(a).
13 Subscription to a form of assent by the legal personal representative of a deceased member of a company is deemed subscription by him: Companies Act 1985 s 49(9)(a).
14 A trustee in bankruptcy of a member of a company is, to the exclusion of the latter, deemed a member of the company: ibid s 49(9)(b).
15 Ibid s 49(8).

125. Certificate of re-registration. The registrar of companies must retain the application and other documents lodged with him[1] and, if articles are annexed to the application, must register them[2]. He must also issue to the company a certificate of incorporation appropriate to the status to be assumed by it[3]. On the issue of the certificate, the company's status, by virtue of the issue, is changed from limited to unlimited[4], and the alterations in the memorandum set out in the application and, if articles have been previously registered, any alterations to the articles so set out take effect as if duly made by resolution of the company[5]. The certificate is conclusive evidence that the statutory requirements in respect of re-registration[6] and of matters precedent and incidental to it have been complied with, and that the company was authorised to be re-registered under the Companies Act 1985 and was duly so re-registered[7].

1 Ie under the Companies Act 1985 s 49: see para 124 ante.
2 Ibid s 50(1)(a).
3 Ibid s 50(1)(b).
4 Ibid s 50(2)(a).
5 Ibid s 50(2)(b). Accordingly, the provisions of the Companies Act 1985 apply to the memorandum and articles as altered: s 50(2)(c).
6 Ie the requirements of ibid s 49.
7 Ibid s 50(3).

(iii) Re-registration of Unlimited Company as Limited

126. Procedure on re-registration. A company which is registered as unlimited may be re-registered as limited if a special resolution[1] that it should be so re-registered is passed, and the following requirements are complied with in respect of the resolution and otherwise[2].

A company cannot be so re-registered as a public company[3]; and a company is excluded from so re-registering if it is unlimited by virtue of re-registration as such pursuant to the provisions of the Companies Act 1967[4] or the Companies Act 1985[5].

The special resolution must state whether the company is to be limited by shares or guarantee and:

(1) if it is to be limited by shares, must state what the share capital is to be and provide for the making of such alterations in the memorandum as are necessary to bring it (in substance and in form) into conformity with the requirements of the Companies Act 1985 with respect to the memorandum of a company so limited[6], and such alterations in the articles as are requisite in the circumstances[7];

(2) if it is to be limited by guarantee, must provide for the making of such alterations in its memorandum and articles as are necessary to bring them (in substance and in form) into conformity with the requirements of the Companies Act 1985 with respect to the memorandum and articles of a company so limited[8].

A copy of the special resolution must be forwarded to the registrar of companies within 15 days after it is passed[9]; and an application for the company to be re-registered as limited, framed in the prescribed form[10] and signed by a director or by the secretary of the company, must be lodged with the registrar, together with the necessary documents, not earlier than the day on which the copy of the resolution so forwarded is received by him[11].

The documents to be lodged with the registrar are:

(a) a printed copy of the memorandum as altered in pursuance of the resolution; and

(b) a printed copy of the articles as so altered[12].

1 As to special resolutions see para 683 post.
2 Companies Act 1985 s 51(1).
3 Ibid s 51(2). However (unless it has previously been re-registered as unlimited) it may be re-registered as a public company under s 43 (see para 118 ante): s 51(6).
4 Ie pursuant to the Companies Act 1967 s 53 (repealed).
5 Companies Act 1985 s 51(2). Such re-registration would have been effected under s 49: see para 124 ante.
6 For such requirements see ibid ss 2, 3 and paras 84, 85 ante.
7 Ibid s 51(3)(a).
8 Ibid s 51(3)(b).
9 Ibid ss 51(4), 380(1). See further para 691 post.
10 For the prescribed form of application see the Companies (Forms) (Amendment) Regulations 1995, SI 1995/736, reg 3, Sch 2, Form 51.
11 Companies Act 1985 s 51(4).
12 Ibid s 51(5).

127. Certificate of re-registration. The registrar of companies must retain the application and other documents lodged with him[1], and must issue to the company a certificate of incorporation appropriate to the status to be assumed by the company[2]. On the issue of the certificate, the status of the company, by virtue of the issue, is changed from unlimited to limited, and the alterations in the memorandum specified in the resolution and the alterations in, and additions to, the articles so specified take effect[3]. The certificate is conclusive evidence that the statutory requirements in respect of re-registration[4] and of matters precedent and incidental to it have been complied with, and that the company was authorised to be re-registered under the Companies Act 1985 and was duly so re-registered[5].

1 Ie under the Companies Act 1985 s 51: see para 126 ante.
2 Ibid s 52(1).
3 Ibid s 52(2).
4 Ie the requirements of ibid s 51.
5 Ibid s 52(3).

128. Alteration of share capital. An unlimited company having a share capital may, by its resolution for re-registration as a limited company[1], do either or both of the following:

    (1) increase the nominal amount of its share capital by increasing the nominal amount of each of its shares, but subject to the condition that no part of the increased capital is to be capable of being called up except in the event and for the purpose of the company being wound up;

    (2) provide that a specified portion of its uncalled share capital[2] is not to be capable of being called up except in that event and for that purpose[3].

1 Ie under the Companies Act 1985 s 51: see para 126 ante.
2 For the meaning of 'uncalled share capital' see para 174 note 14 post.
3 Companies Act 1985 s 124. As to calls on reserved uncalled capital see para 416 post; as to calls for the purpose of winding up see para 2493 et seq post; and as to the charging of uncalled capital see para 1245 post.

(iv) Re-registration of Public Company as Private

129. Procedure on re-registration. A public company[1] may be re-registered as a private company[2] if:

    (1) a special resolution complying with the statutory requirements[3] that it should be so re-registered is passed and has not been cancelled by the court[4];

    (2) an application for the purpose in the prescribed form[5] and signed by a director or the secretary of the company is delivered to the registrar of companies, together with a printed copy of the memorandum and articles of the company as altered by the resolution; and

    (3) the period during which an application to the court for the cancellation of the resolution may be made[6] has expired without any such application having been made; or

    (4) where such an application has been made, the application has been withdrawn or an order has been made[7] confirming the resolution and a copy of that order has been delivered to the registrar[8].

The special resolution must alter the company's memorandum so that it no longer states that the company is to be a public company and must make such other alterations in the company's memorandum and articles as are requisite in the circumstances[9].

Under these provisions[10] a company cannot be re-registered otherwise than as a company limited by shares or by guarantee[11].

1 For the meaning of 'public company' see para 82 ante.
2 For the meaning of 'private company' see para 82 ante.
3 Ie complying with the Companies Act 1985 s 53(2): see infra. As to special resolutions generally see para 683 post.
4 Ie cancelled under ibid s 54: see para 130 post.
5 For the prescribed form of application see the Companies (Forms) (Amendment) Regulations 1995, SI 1995/736, reg 3, Sch 2, Form 53.
6 As to this period see para 130 post.
7 Ie under the Companies Act 1985 s 54(5): see para 130 post.
8 Ibid s 53(1).
9 Ibid s 53(2). As to the memorandum and articles of a private company see paras 102, 103, 108 ante and para 529 post.
10 Ie under ibid s 53.

11 Ibid s 53(3). This means that it cannot be re-registered as an unlimited company under s 53. As to the re-registration of a limited company as unlimited see para 124 ante.

130. Litigated objection to resolution to re-register as private company. Where a special resolution by a public company to be re-registered as a private company[1] has been passed, an application may be made to the court for the cancellation of that resolution[2]. The application may be made:

(1) by the holders of not less in the aggregate than 5% in nominal value of the company's issued share capital or any class thereof;

(2) if the company is not limited by shares, by not less than 5% of its members; or

(3) by not less than 50 of the company's members;

but not by a person who has consented to or voted in favour of the resolution[3].

The application must be made within 28 days after the passing of the resolution and may be made on behalf of the persons entitled to make the application by such one or more of their number as they may appoint in writing for the purpose[4]. If such an application is made, the company must forthwith give notice in the prescribed form[5] of that fact to the registrar of companies[6]. A company which fails to comply with this requirement, and any officer of it who is in default, is liable on summary conviction to a fine not exceeding one-fifth of the statutory maximum and, on conviction after continued contravention, to a daily default fine not exceeding one-fiftieth of the statutory maximum[7].

On the hearing of the application, the court must make an order either cancelling[8] or confirming[9] the resolution and may:

(a) make that order on such terms and conditions as it thinks fit, and may, if it thinks fit, adjourn the proceedings in order that an arrangement may be made to the satisfaction of the court for the purchase of the interests of dissentient members; and

(b) give such directions and make such orders as it thinks expedient for facilitating or carrying into effect any such arrangement[10].

The court's order may, if the court thinks fit, provide for the purchase by the company of the shares of any of its members[11] and for the reduction accordingly of the company's capital, and may make such alterations in the company's memorandum and articles as may be required in consequence of that provision[12]. Within 15 days from the making of the court's order, or within such longer period as the court may at any time by order direct, the company must deliver to the registrar of companies an office copy of the order[13]. A company which fails to comply with this requirement, and any officer of it who is in default, is liable on summary conviction to a fine not exceeding one-fifth of the statutory maximum and, on conviction after continued contravention, to a daily default fine not exceeding one-fiftieth of the statutory maximum[14].

If the court's order requires the company not to make any, or any specified, alteration in its memorandum or articles, the company has not then power without the leave of the court to make any such alteration in breach of the requirement[15].

An alteration in the memorandum or articles made by virtue of an order under the above provisions, if not made by resolution of the company, is of the same effect as if duly made by resolution; and the Companies Act 1985 applies accordingly to the memorandum or articles as so altered[16].

1 Ie the special resolution under the Companies Act 1985 s 53: see para 129 ante.
2 Ibid s 54(1). The application is made by petition: RSC Ord 102 r 4(1)(j). The petition should state why the special resolution is being challenged: *Re a company (No 005685 of 1988), ex p Schwarcz (No 2)* [1989]

BCLC 427. The petition may be struck out where no proper grounds for complaint have been disclosed by the petitioner and the court can, on an application for striking out, consider the appropriateness of the remedy sought and the reasonableness of the conduct of the petitioner in the light of offers made to the petitioner to purchase his shares: *Re a company (No 005685 of 1988), ex p Schwarcz (No 2)* supra. It is not necessary to take out a summons for directions: RSC Ord 102 r 6(2)(c).
3 Companies Act 1985 s 54(2).
4 Ibid s 54(3).
5 For the prescribed form of notice see the Companies (Forms) (Amendment) Regulations 1995, SI 1995/736, reg 3, Sch 2, Form 54.
6 Companies Act 1985 s 54(4).
7 Ibid ss 54(10), 730, Sch 24. For the meaning of 'officer who is in default', 'the statutory maximum' and 'daily default fine' see para 1161 post.
8 The court may be disinclined to cancel the resolution where a very large majority of the shareholders have voted in favour of the resolution: see *Re a company (No 005685 of 1988), ex p Schwarcz (No 2)* [1989] BCLC 427 (94.5% of the shareholders voted in favour).
9 Little guidance is given to the court as to the exercise of its discretion. It would appear from the Companies Act 1985 s 54(5)(a),(6) (see infra) with its reference to the sale of the dissentient's shares that it was envisaged that it might be appropriate to invoke the court's jurisdiction where a dissentient shareholder finds himself locked into a company whereas previously, when the company was a public limited company, he had been able to transfer his shares more freely: see *Re a company (No 005685 of 1988), ex p Schwarcz (No 2)* [1989] BCLC 427 at 437.
10 Companies Act 1985 s 54(5).
11 The court may be disinclined to do this if a fair offer to purchase the petitioner's shares has been available but not taken up by the petitioner: *Re a company (No 005685 of 1988), ex p Schwarcz (No 2)* [1989] BCLC 427.
12 Companies Act 1985 s 54(6).
13 Ibid s 54(7).
14 Ibid ss 54(10), 730, Sch 24.
15 Ibid s 54(8).
16 Ibid s 54(9). As to the effect of changes in the memorandum or articles of association made by resolutions see paras 538, 1184, 1185 post.

131. Certificate of re-registration as private company. If the registrar of companies is satisfied that a company may be re-registered as a private company[1], he must retain the application and other documents[2] delivered to him and issue the company with a certificate of incorporation appropriate to a private company[3]. On the issue of the certificate the company, by virtue of the issue, becomes a private company and the alterations in the memorandum and articles set out in the requisite resolution[4] take effect accordingly[5]. The certificate is conclusive evidence that the statutory requirements[6] in respect of re-registration and of matters precedent and incidental to it have been complied with, and that the company is a private company[7].

1 Ie under the Companies Act 1985 s 53: see para 129 ante.
2 As to these documents see para 129 ante.
3 Companies Act 1985 s 55(1).
4 Ie the resolution required by ibid s 53.
5 Ibid s 55(2).
6 Ie the requirements of ibid s 53.
7 Ibid s 55(3).

(v) Old Public Companies

132. Meaning and classification of 'old public company'. An 'old public company' is a company limited by shares or by guarantee and having a share capital in respect of which the following conditions are satisfied:

(1) the company either existed on 22 December 1980[1] or was incorporated after that date pursuant to an application made before that date;

(2) on that date or, on the day of the company's incorporation, the company was not or (as the case may be) would not have been a private company within the Companies Act 1948[2]; and

(3) the company has not since that date or the day of the company's incorporation (as the case may be) either been re-registered as a public company[3] or become[4] a private company[5].

With some exceptions[6], references in the Companies Act 1985 to a public company, or a company other than a private company, are to be read as including, unless the context otherwise requires, references to an old public company, and references to a private company are to be read accordingly[7].

1 Ie the date of the coming into force of the corresponding provisions of the Companies Act 1980 (ie s 8 (repealed)).

2 Ie within the Companies Act 1948 s 28 (repealed), which defined a private company as one which by its articles restricted the right to transfer its shares, limited the number of its members (with certain exceptions) to 50, and prohibited any invitation to the public to subscribe for any shares or debentures of the company.

3 Ie under the Companies Consolidation (Consequential Provisions) Act 1985 s 2 (see para 133 post) or the corresponding preceding provisions of the Companies Act 1980 (ie s 8(3) (repealed)).

4 Ie under the Companies Consolidation (Consequential Provisions) Act 1985 s 4 (see para 135 post) or the corresponding preceding provisions of the Companies Act 1980 (ie s 8(8) (repealed)).

5 Companies Consolidation (Consequential Provisions) Act 1985 s 1(1).

6 Ie so much of the Companies Act 1985 as is derived from the Companies Act 1980 Pt I (ss 1-13) (repealed), namely the Companies Act 1985 s 1(1),(3) (see paras 80, 82 ante), s 3(1) (see para 85 ante), s 11 (see para 88 ante), s 12 (see para 88 ante), s 13(6),(7) (see para 91 ante), s 15(2) (see para 109 ante), s 25(1) (see para 154 post), s 33 (see para 162 post), ss 43-48 (as amended) (see paras 118-123 ante), s 51(6) (see para 126 note 3 ante), ss 53-55 (see paras 129-131 ante), s 117 (see para 652 post), s 124 (see para 123 ante), s 139 (see para 269 post), s 685 (see para 77 ante) and s 688(3),(4) (see para 28 ante).

7 Companies Consolidation (Consequential Provisions) Act 1985 s 1(2).

133. Re-registration as public company. An old public company[1] may be re-registered as a public company[2] if:

(1) the directors pass a resolution[3] that it should be so re-registered; and

(2) an application for the purpose in the prescribed form[4] and signed by a director or secretary of the company is delivered to the registrar of companies together with the documents mentioned below; and

(3) at the time of the resolution, certain conditions[5] are satisfied[6].

The resolution must alter the company's memorandum so that it states that the company is to be a public company and make such other alterations in it as are necessary to bring it in substance and in form into conformity with the requirements of the Companies Act 1985 with respect to the memorandum of a public company[7].

The documents referred to above are:

(a) a printed copy of the memorandum as altered in pursuance of the resolution; and

(b) a statutory declaration in the prescribed form[8] by a director or secretary of the company that the resolution has been passed and that the statutory conditions[9] were satisfied at the time of the resolution[10].

The registrar may accept such a declaration as sufficient evidence that the resolution has been passed and the necessary conditions were satisfied[11].

1 For the meaning of 'old public company' see para 132 ante.
2 For the meaning of 'public company' see para 82 ante.
3 Such a resolution is subject to the Companies Act 1985 s 380 (as amended) (see para 691 post), under which a copy of the resolution must be forwarded to the registrar within 15 days after it has been passed: Companies Consolidation (Consequential Provisions) Act 1985 s 2(3); Companies Act 1985 s 380(4)(k).
4 For the prescribed form of application see the Companies (Forms) Regulations 1985, SI 1985/854, reg 4(1), Sch 3, Form R7.
5 Ie the conditions specified in the Companies Consolidation (Consequential Provisions) Act 1985 s 3: see para 134 post.
6 Ibid s 2(1).
7 Ibid s 2(2). As to those requirements see paras 102, 108 ante.
8 For the prescribed form of statutory declaration see the Companies (Forms) Regulations 1985 Sch 3, Form R8.
9 See note 5 supra.
10 Companies Consolidation (Consequential Provisions) Act 1985 s 2(4).
11 Ibid s 2(5). The Companies Act 1985 s 47(1),(3)-(5) (procedure on and the effect of the issue of a certificate of re-registration: see para 122 ante) applies as it applies on an application under s 43 (see para 118 ante): Companies Consolidation (Consequential Provisions) Act 1985 s 2(6).

134. Conditions for re-registering. The following conditions must be satisfied at the time of a resolution[1] that an old public company be re-registered as a public company[2]:

(1) at the time concerned, the nominal value of the company's allotted share capital must not be less than the authorised minimum[3];

(2) in the case of all the shares of the company, or of all those of its shares which are comprised in a portion of the share capital which satisfies the condition in head (1) above:

(a) each share must be paid up at least as to one-quarter of the nominal value of that share and the whole of any premium on it;

(b) where any of the shares in question or any premium payable on them has been fully or partly paid up by an undertaking given by any person that he or another should do work or perform services for the company or another, the undertaking must have been performed or otherwise discharged; and

(c) where any of the shares in question has been allotted as fully or partly paid up as to its nominal value or any premium payable on it otherwise than in cash, and the consideration for the allotment consists of or includes an undertaking (other than one to which head (b) above applies) to the company, then either that undertaking must have been either performed or otherwise discharged, or there must be a contract between the company and some person pursuant to which the undertaking is to be performed within five years from the time of the resolution[4].

1 Ie a resolution under the Companies Consolidation (Consequential Provisions) Act 1985 s 2: see para 133 ante.
2 Ibid s 3(1).
3 Ibid s 3(2). For the meaning of 'authorised minimum' see para 652 note 6 post.
4 Ibid s 3(3).

135. Old public company becoming private. An old public company[1] may pass a special resolution not to be re-registered[2] as a public company; and the provisions of the Companies Act 1985 relating to the right of a shareholder to apply to the court for cancellation of a resolution[3] apply to the resolution as they would apply to a special resolution by a public company to be re-registered as private[4]. If either 28 days from the passing of the resolution elapse without such an application being made, or such an application is made and proceedings are concluded[5] on the application without the court making an order for the cancellation of the resolution, the registrar of companies must issue the company with a certificate stating that it is a private company; and the company then becomes a private company by virtue of the issue of the certificate[6].

If an old public company delivers to the registrar a statutory declaration in the prescribed form[7] by a director or secretary of the company that the company does not at the time of the declaration satisfy the specified conditions[8] for the company to be re-registered as public, the registrar must issue the company with a certificate stating that it is a private company; and the company then becomes a private company by virtue of the issue of the certificate[9].

A certificate so issued to a company is conclusive evidence that the requirements of the relevant provision have been complied with and that the company is a private company[10].

1 For the meaning of 'old public company' see para 132 ante.
2 Ie under the Companies Consolidation (Consequential Provisions) Act 1985 s 2: see para 133 ante.
3 Ie the Companies Act 1985 s 54: see para 130 ante.
4 Companies Consolidation (Consequential Provisions) Act 1985 s 4(1). For the prescribed form of notice to the registrar of companies of an application made to the court for the cancellation of such a special resolution see the Companies (Forms) Regulations 1985, SI 1985/854, reg 4(1), Sch 3, Form R7a (amended by SI 1987/752).
5 For these purposes, proceedings on the application are concluded (1) when the company has been notified that the application has been withdrawn; or (2) if not withdrawn, when the period mentioned in the Companies Act 1985 s 54(7) (as applied) for delivering an office copy of the court's order under s 54 (see para 130 ante) to the registrar (ie 15 days from the making of the order or such longer period as the court may direct) has expired: Companies Consolidation (Consequential Provisions) Act 1985 s 4(3)(a),(b).
6 Ibid s 4(2).
7 For the prescribed form of statutory declaration see the Companies (Forms) Regulations 1985 Sch 3, Form R9.
8 Ie the conditions specified in the Companies Consolidation (Consequential Provisions) Act 1985 s 3: see para 134 ante.
9 Ibid s 4(4).
10 Ibid s 4(5).

136. Failure by old public company to obtain new classification. If at any time a company which is an old public company[1] has not delivered to the registrar of companies a declaration that the company does not satisfy the specified conditions for re-registration as a public company[2], the company, and any officer of it who is in default, is guilty of an offence unless at that time the company has applied to be re-registered as a public company[3] and the application has not been refused or withdrawn, or has passed a special resolution not to be so re-registered, and the resolution has not been revoked, and has not been cancelled[4] by a court order[5].

A person guilty of an offence under this provision is liable on summary conviction to a fine not exceeding one-fifth of the statutory maximum and, on conviction after continued contravention, to a daily default fine not exceeding one-fiftieth of the statutory maximum for every day on which the provision is contravened[6].

1 For the meaning of 'old public company' see para 132 ante.
2 Ie a declaration under the Companies Consolidation (Consequential Provisions) Act 1985 s 4(4): see para 135 ante.
3 Ie under ibid s 2: see para 133 ante.
4 Ie under the Companies Act 1985 s 54 (see para 135 ante) (applied by the Companies Consolidation (Consequential Provisions) Act 1985 s 4(1)).

5 Companies Consolidation (Consequential Provisions) Act 1985 s 5(1). For the meaning of 'officer who is in default' see para 1161 post.
6 Ibid s 5(2). For the meaning of 'the statutory maximum' and 'daily default fine' see para 1161 post.

137. Shares of old public company held by or charged to itself. Notwithstanding the general provision[1] that references in the Companies Act 1985 to a public company or a company other than a private company are to be read as including an old public company[2], references to a public company in those provisions of the Companies Act 1985 which relate to the treatment of a company's shares when acquired by itself[3] do not include an old public company; and references in those provisions to a private company are to be read accordingly[4].

In the case of a company which after 22 March 1982[5] remained an old public company and did not before that date apply to be re-registered under the then statutory provisions[6] as a public company, any charge on its own shares which was in existence on or immediately before that date is a permitted charge for the purposes of those provisions of the Companies Act 1985[7] dealing with the maintenance of capital, and accordingly not void under the general provisions[8] to that effect[9].

1 Ie the Companies Consolidation (Consequential Provisions) Act 1985 s 1(2): see para 132 ante.
2 For the meaning of 'old public company' see para 132 ante.
3 Ie the Companies Act 1985 ss 146-149: see para 366 et seq post.
4 Companies Consolidation (Consequential Provisions) Act 1985 s 6(1),(2).
5 Ie the final date of the re-registration period for the purposes of the Companies Act 1980 s 9 (repealed).
6 Ie ibid s 8 (repealed).
7 Ie the Companies Act 1985 Pt V Ch V (ss 142-150).
8 Ie ibid s 150: see para 214 post.
9 Companies Consolidation (Consequential Provisions) Act 1985 s 6(3). See also the Companies Act 1985 s 150(4) (cited in para 214 post).

138. Trading under misleading name. An old public company[1] is guilty of an offence if it carries on any trade, profession or business under a name which includes, as its last part, the words 'public limited company' or 'cwmni cyfyngedig cyhoeddus'[2]. A company guilty of an offence under this provision, and any officer of the company who is in default, is liable on summary conviction to a fine not exceeding one-fifth of the statutory maximum and, on conviction after continued contravention, to a daily default fine not exceeding one-fiftieth of the statutory maximum[3].

1 For the meaning of 'old public company' see para 132 ante.
2 Companies Consolidation (Consequential Provisions) Act 1985 s 8(1).
3 Ibid s 8(2); Companies Act 1985 ss 33(3), 730, Sch 24. For the meaning of 'officer who is in default', 'the statutory maximum' and 'daily default fine' see para 1161 post.

139. Payment for share capital. Certain provisions of the Companies Act 1985 relating to the allotment of shares and debentures[1] apply to a company whose directors have passed and not revoked a resolution to be re-registered as a public company[2], as those provisions apply to a public company[3]. Some of those provisions[4] do not, however, apply to the allotment of shares by a company, other than a public company registered as such on its original incorporation, where the contract for the allotment was entered into:

    (1) except in a case falling within head (2) below, on or before 22 June 1982[5];

(2) in the case of a company re-registered or registered as a public company in pursuance of a resolution by a private company to be re-registered as a public company[6], or a resolution to be re-registered as a public company under the special provisions applying to old public companies[7], or a resolution by a joint stock company that the company be a public company[8], being (in each case) a resolution that was passed on or before 22 June 1982, before the date on which the resolution was passed[9].

1 Ie the Companies Act 1985 ss 99, 101-103 (as amended), 106, 108, 110-115 (as amended): see para 360 post (s 106) and para 464 et seq post (s 99 et seq).
2 Ie under the Companies Consolidation (Consequential Provisions) Act 1985 s 2: see para 133 ante.
3 Ibid s 9(1).
4 Ie the Companies Act 1985 ss 99, 101-103 (as amended), 108 and 112.
5 Ie the final date of the transitional period for the purposes of the Companies Act 1980 ss 31(2), 87(1) (repealed).
6 Ie under the Companies Act 1985 s 43: see para 118 ante.
7 Ie the Companies Consolidation (Consequential Provisions) Act 1985 s 2: see para 133 ante.
8 Ie under the Companies Act 1985 s 685: see para 77 ante.
9 Companies Consolidation (Consequential Provisions) Act 1985 s 9(2).

(5) EFFECT OF MEMORANDUM AND ARTICLES

140. Binding as if under seal. Subject to the provisions of the Companies Act 1985, the memorandum[1] and articles[2], when registered, bind the company and its members to the same extent as if they respectively had been signed and sealed by each member and contained covenants on the part of each member to observe all the provisions of the memorandum and of the articles[3]. By virtue of this, the memorandum and articles of association become a contract between the company and its members; it is a statutory contract of a special nature with its own distinctive features[4].

Once the articles are registered, the court has no power to rectify them even if they do not accord with what is proved to be the concurrent intention of the members[5]. The articles should, however, be regarded as a business document and should be construed so as to give them reasonable business efficacy, where a construction tending to that result is admissible on the language of the articles, in preference to a result which would or might prove unworkable[6]. A purely constructional implication is not precluded but the court will not imply a term from extrinsic circumstances[7].

Money payable by a member to the company under the memorandum or articles is a debt due from him to the company, and is of the nature of a specialty debt[8].

1 For these purposes, unless the contrary intention appears, 'memorandum', in relation to a company, means its memorandum of association, as originally framed or as altered in pursuance of any enactment: Companies Act 1985 s 744.
2 For these purposes, unless the contrary intention appears, 'articles' means, in relation to a company, its articles of association, as originally framed or as altered by resolution, including (so far as applicable to the company) regulations contained in or annexed to any enactment relating to companies passed before the Companies Act 1985, as altered by or under any such enactment: s 744.
3 Ibid s 14(1).
4 *Scott v Frank F Scott (London) Ltd* [1940] Ch 794, [1940] 3 All ER 508, CA; *Bratton Seymour Service Co Ltd v Oxborough* [1992] BCLC 693 at 698, CA per Steyn LJ.
5 *Scott v Frank F Scott (London) Ltd* [1940] Ch 794, [1940] 3 All ER 508, CA.
6 *Holmes v Lord Keyes* [1959] Ch 199 at 215, [1958] 2 All ER 129 at 318, CA per Jenkins LJ; *Robert Batcheller & Sons Ltd v Batcheller* [1945] Ch 169 at 177, [1945] 1 All ER 522 at 531 per Romer J.Cf *Grundt v Great Boulder Pty Gold Mines Ltd* [1948] Ch 145, [1948] 1 All ER 21, CA (where the preceding case was disapproved and the court refused to find any absurdity).

7 *Bratton Seymour Service Co Ltd v Oxborough* [1992] BCLC 693, CA.
8 Companies Act 1985 s 14(2). See also *St Johnstone Football Club Ltd v Scottish Football Association Ltd* 1965 SLT 171 (fines imposed pursuant to powers in articles). As to the relative force of the memorandum and articles see para 146 post.

141. How far articles constitute a contract. The question how far the memorandum and articles constitute a binding contract between a company and its members on the one hand and between its members inter se on the other hand, is one of great .difficulty and is not altogether clear[1]. It has, however, been held that the contractual force given to the articles of association is limited to those provisions which apply to the relationship of members in their capacity as members and does not extend to those provisions which govern the relationship of a company and its directors as such[2].

1 For a general discussion of this question see *Hickman v Kent or Romney Marsh Sheep Breeders' Association* [1915] 1 Ch 881.
2 *Beattie v E & F Beattie Ltd* [1938] Ch 708 at 721, [1938] 3 All ER 214 at 218, following *Hickman v Kent or Romney Marsh Sheep Breeders' Association* [1915] 1 Ch 881. As to arbitration clauses in articles constituting written agreements for submission to arbitration see ARBITRATION vol 2 (Reissue) para 609.

142. Contract between company and member. The articles constitute a contract between the company and a member in respect of his rights[1] and liabilities as a shareholder; and a company may sue a member and a member may sue a company to enforce and restrain breaches of the regulations contained in the articles dealing with such matters[2]. The purpose of the articles is to define the position of the shareholder as a shareholder, not to bind him in his capacity as an individual[3]. The articles do not constitute a contract between the company and a member in respect of rights and liabilities which he has in a capacity other than that of member, whether he becomes a member originally or subsequently[4]; and, where such rights and liabilities are the subject of a written agreement, the articles will not be imported unless they are referred to[5].

Where the articles provide that the company on incorporation is to enter into an agreement for the purchase of property and for the appointment of the vendor as a director, the vendor who becomes a shareholder cannot sue nor can any person claiming through the vendor sue or rely on the articles as constituting a contract[6]; and, where the articles provide that a solicitor who subsequently becomes a shareholder is to be the solicitor of the company, he cannot sue the company on the articles[7]. Similarly, where the articles provide that a director is to hold a certain number of shares, the provision does not constitute an agreement on his part to take the shares, even though he is already a member of the company[8].

The articles may be evidence of the terms upon which services are rendered to the company[9]; thus an agreement on the part of a director to act on the terms as to qualification contained in the articles[10], or on the part of the company to remunerate its directors on the terms of the articles[11], may be inferred from the subsequent action of the parties.

Any contract, so far as it relates to the constitution of the company, or the rights or obligations of its corporators or members, is exempt from the prohibitions on exclusion of liability imposed by the Unfair Contract Terms Act 1977[12].

1 A member may have legitimate expectations and interests not set out in the articles which the courts will be prepared to recognise in some circumstances: *Ebrahimi v Westbourne Galleries Ltd* [1973] AC 360, [1972] 2 All ER 492, HL (cited in para 2208 post). This is of particular importance in the context of

petitions by members under the Companies Act 1985 s 459 (as amended) alleging that the company's affairs are being or have been conducted in a manner which is unfairly prejudicial to their interests: see para 1405 post.

2 *Johnson v Lyttle's Iron Agency* (1877) 5 ChD 687, CA; *Pender v Lushington* (1877) 6 ChD 70; *Re Imperial Hydropathic Hotel Co, Blackpool v Hampson* (1882) 23 ChD 1, CA; *Bradford Banking Co Ltd v Briggs, Son & Co Ltd* (1886) 12 App Cas 29 at 33, HL; *Wood v Odessa Waterworks Co* (1889) 42 ChD 636; *Welton v Saffery* [1897] AC 299 at 315, HL; *Hickman v Kent or Romney Marsh Sheep Breeders' Association* [1915] 1 Ch 881; *Re Greene, Greene v Greene* [1949] Ch 333 at 340, [1949] 1 All ER 167 at 170 (no contract where article invalid); but see contra *Pritchard's Case* (1873) 8 Ch App 956 at 960; *Eley v Positive Government Security Life Assurance Co Ltd* (1875) 1 ExD 20 at 26 (on appeal (1876) 1 ExD 88 at 89, CA); *Baring-Gould v Sharpington Combined Pick and Shovel Syndicate* [1899] 2 Ch 80 at 89, CA; and see *Quin & Axtens Ltd v Salmon* [1909] AC 442 at 443, HL. As to actions by a shareholder against the company see paras 1110 et seq, 1169 et seq post.

3 *Bisgood v Henderson's Transvaal Estates Ltd* [1908] 1 Ch 743 at 759, CA per Buckley LJ.

4 *Pritchard's Case* (1873) 8 Ch App 956; *Eley v Positive Government Security Life Assurance Co* (1876) 1 ExD 88, CA; *Browne v La Trinidad* (1887) 37 ChD 1, CA; *Re Dale and Plant Ltd* (1889) 61 LT 206; *Re Famatina Development Corpn* [1914] 2 Ch 271 at 279; *Hickman v Kent or Rommey Marsh Sheep Breeders' Association* [1915] 1 Ch 881; *McEllistrim v Ballymacelligott Co-operative Agricultural and Dairy Society* [1919] AC 548 at 575, HL; *Beattie v E & F Beattie Ltd* [1938] Ch 708, [1938] 3 All ER 214.

5 *Re Alexander's Timber Co* (1901) 70 LJ Ch 767; *Boston Deep Sea Fishing and Ice Co v Ansell* (1888) 39 ChD 339, CA; *Re City Equitable Fire Insurance Co Ltd* [1925] Ch 407 at 521, CA.

6 *Pritchard's Case* (1873) 8 Ch App 956; *Browne v La Trinidad* (1887) 37 ChD 1, CA.

7 *Eley v Positive Government Security Life Assurance Co* (1876) 1 ExD 88, CA.

8 *Re Wheal Buller Consols* (1888) 38 ChD 42, CA; *Re Printing Telegraph and Construction Co of the Agence Havas, ex p Cammell* [1894] 2 Ch 392, CA; *Salisbury-Jones and Dale's Case* [1894] 3 Ch 356, CA.

9 See *Re City Equitable Fire Insurance Co Ltd* [1925] Ch 407 at 520, 521, CA and the cases cited in notes 10, 11 infra.

10 *Isaacs' Case* [1892] 2 Ch 158, CA; *Re Hercynia Copper Co* [1894] 2 Ch 403, CA; *Salton v New Beeston Cycle Co* [1899] 1 Ch 775; *Molineux v London, Birmingham and Manchester Insurance Co Ltd* [1902] 2 KB 589, CA; cf *Re International Cable Co Ltd, ex p Official Liquidator* (1892) 66 LT 253.

11 *Salton v New Beeston Cycle Co* [1899] 1 Ch 775; *Swabey v Port Darwin Gold Mining Co* (1889) 1 Meg 385, CA; *Re London and Scottish Bank, ex p Logan* (1870) LR 9 Eq 149; *Boston Deep Sea Fishing and Ice Co v Ansell* (1888) 39 ChD 339 at 366, CA; *Re New British Iron Co, ex p Beckwith* [1898] 1 Ch 324; cf *Re T N Farrer Ltd* [1937] Ch 352, [1937] 2 All ER 505.

12 Unfair Contract Terms Act 1977 s 1(2), Sch 1 para 1(d)(ii). As to the Unfair Contract Terms Act 1977 generally see CONTRACT. Similarly, the Unfair Terms in Consumer Contracts Regulations 1994, SI 1994/3159, do not apply to any contract relating to the incorporation or organisation of companies or partnerships: see reg 3(1), Sch 1 para (d) and CONTRACT.

143. Contract between members inter se. While the articles regulate the rights of the members inter se, they do not, it would seem, constitute a contract between the members inter se, but only a contract between the company and its members[1]; and, therefore, the rights and liabilities of members as members under the articles may be enforced by or against the members only through the company[2].

1 *Welton v Saffery* [1897] AC 299 at 315, HL per Lord Herschell; *Re Greene, Greene v Greene* [1949] Ch 333 at 340, [1949] 1 All ER 167 at 170; contra *Pritchard's Case* (1873) 8 Ch App 956; *Eley v Positive Government Security Life Assurance Co Ltd* (1876) 1 ExD 88 at 89, CA; *Browne v La Trinidad* (1887) 37 ChD 1, CA; *Borland's Trustee v Steel Bros & Co Ltd* [1901] 1 Ch 279 at 288; *Re Famatina Development Corpn Ltd* [1914] 2 Ch 271 at 279; and see *Salmon v Quin & Axtens Ltd* [1909] 1 Ch 311 at 318, CA per Farwell LJ (affd sub nom *Quin & Axtens Ltd v Salmon* [1909] AC 442, HL), qualifying dicta of Stirling J in *Wood v Odessa Waterworks Co* (1889) 42 ChD 636 at 642; *Rayfield v Hands* [1960] Ch 1, [1958] 2 All ER 194 (directors bound by provision in the articles that they would take at a fair value shares offered to them by the members).

Doubt as to whether an arbitration clause in the articles constitutes a written agreement for submission to arbitration within the Arbitration Act 1950 s 4(1), as between the parties concerned, justifies the court in refusing to stay an action: see *London Sack and Bag Co Ltd v Dixon and Lugton Ltd* [1943] 2 All ER 763 at 765, CA per Scott LJ, who cited the passages in the text. See further ARBITRATION vol 2 (Reissue) para 609.

2 See cases cited in para 142 note 2 ante and *MacDougall v Gardiner* (1875) 1 ChD 13, CA. Cf *Rayfield v Hands* [1960] Ch 1, [1958] 2 All ER 194 (where it was held to be unnecessary to join the company in the action).

144. Contract between company and outsider. As between the company and a person who is not a member, the articles do not in any circumstances constitute a contract of which that person may take advantage[1], as, for example, where they provide that the preliminary expenses of forming the company are to be paid out of the assets of the company[2] or that a solicitor is to be the solicitor of the company[3].

1 See *Hickman v Kent or Romney Marsh Sheep Breeders' Association* [1915] 1 Ch 881 at 897, 900; *Beattie v E & F Beattie Ltd* [1938] Ch 708 at 721, [1938] 3 All ER 214 at 218.
2 *Melhado v Porto Alegre Rly Co* (1874) LR 9 CP 503; *Re Rotherham Alum and Chemical Co* (1883) 25 ChD 103 at 110, CA; and see para 52 ante.
3 *Re Rhodesian Properties Ltd* (1901) 45 Sol Jo 580.

145. Notice of memorandum and articles. Members of a company are deemed to be aware of the contents of the memorandum and articles[1], and to understand their meaning[2]. Notice is not, however, to be imputed to persons who have been induced by fraudulent misrepresentations to take shares, since they are entitled to repudiate the contract of membership[3].

In favour of a person dealing with a company in good faith, the power of the board of directors to bind the company, or authorise others to do so, is deemed to be free of any limitation under the company's constitution[4]; and a party to a transaction with a company is not bound to inquire as to whether it is permitted by the company's memorandum or as to any limitation on the powers of the board of directors to bind the company or authorise others to do so[5].

1 *Peel's Case* (1867) 2 Ch App 674 at 684; *Sewell's Case* (1868) 3 Ch App 131 at 140; *Griffith v Paget* (1877) 6 ChD 511 at 517.
2 *Oakbank Oil Co v Crum* (1882) 8 App Cas 65 at 71, HL.
3 *Central Rly Co of Venezuela (Directors etc) v Kisch* (1867) LR 2 HL 99 at 123, as explained in *Oakes v Turquand and Harding* (1867) LR 2 HL 325 at 345, 346 per Lord Chelmsford; cf *Downes v Ship* (1868) LR 3 HL 343.
4 See the Companies Act 1985 s 35A (as substituted) and paras 583, 1108 post.
5 See ibid s 35B (as substituted) and paras 1109, 1137 et seq post.

146. Inconsistency between memorandum and articles. The articles are subordinate to the memorandum; any clause in them, if and so far as it is at variance with the memorandum, is to that extent overruled by it and inoperative[1], the memorandum being the charter of the company and defining its powers, while the articles of association play a subsidiary part, and define the duties, rights and powers of the governing body as between themselves and the company at large, and the mode and form in which the business of the company is to be carried on and in which changes in its internal regulations may from time to time be made[2]. The memorandum and articles may, however, in certain circumstances be read together, at all events so far as may be necessary to explain any ambiguity appearing in the terms of the memorandum or to supplement it upon any matter as to which it is silent[3].

1 *Guinness v Land Corpn of Ireland Ltd* (1882) 22 ChD 349 at 376; *Angostura Bitters (Dr J G B Siegert & Sons) Ltd v Kerr* [1933] AC 550 at 554, PC; *Re Duncan Gilmour & Co Ltd, Duncan Gilmour & Co Ltd v Inman* [1952] 2 All ER 871 at 874. Where the memorandum set out the division of capital into classes of shares

and the articles defined rights, it was held that there was no inconsistency and that the various rights of the classes of shares were defined properly by the articles, it having been suggested that under the memorandum the classes of shares were to have equal rights: *Humboldt Redwood Co Ltd (Liquidator) v Coats* 1908 SC 751.

2 *Ashbury v Watson* (1885) 30 ChD 376, CA.

3 *Angostura Bitters (Dr J G B Siegert & Sons) Ltd v Kerr* [1933] AC 550 at 554, PC; *Re Duncan Gilmour & Co Ltd, Duncan Gilmour & Co Ltd v Inman* [1952] 2 All ER 871. See also *Harrison v Mexican Rly Co* (1875) LR 19 Eq 358 and *Ashbury v Watson* (1885) 30 ChD 376, CA, as explained in *Re Marshall, Fleming & Co* 1938 SC 873 at 877, 878.

147. Articles at variance with statute. Any provision in the articles at variance with the provisions of the Companies Act 1985 is void, as, for example, an article purporting to authorise a company to extend its objects by a resolution of its directors[1]; to forfeit, instead of selling, shares for debts due from a member otherwise than as a contributory[2]; to pay dividends out of capital or allot shares at a discount[3]; to limit the right of a member to present a winding-up petition[4]; to shut dissentient shareholders out of their statutory rights on a reconstruction of the company[5]; to fetter the power of the company to alter its articles[6], or to increase its share capital[7], or to register a director's widow on his death as transferee of shares without a proper instrument of transfer having been delivered[8]. A provision in any article which is in accordance with Table A (as in existence from time to time[9]) is valid (subject to any subsequent legislation), as the Table has statutory authority[10].

1 As to the manner and circumstances in which a company may alter its objects see para 1184 post.
2 *Hopkinson v Mortimer, Harley & Co Ltd* [1917] 1 Ch 646.
3 *Welton v Saffery* [1897] AC 299, HL. As to the allotment of shares at a discount and the consequences of so allotting shares in contravention of the statutory prohibition see para 187 post.
4 *Re Peveril Gold Mines Ltd* [1898] 1 Ch 122, CA.
5 *Baring-Gould v Sharpington Combined Pick and Shovel Syndicate* [1899] 2 Ch 80, CA.
6 *Malleson v National Insurance and Guarantee Corpn* [1894] 1 Ch 200; *Russell v Northern Bank Development Corpn Ltd* [1992] 3 All ER 161, [1992] 1 WLR 588, HL. An agreement outside the articles between shareholders as to how they would exercise their voting rights on a resolution to alter the articles would, however, not necessarily be invalid: see para 149 post.
7 *Russell v Northern Bank Development Corpn Ltd* [1992] 3 All ER 161, [1992] 1 WLR 588, HL. See also note 6 supra.
8 *Re Greene, Greene v Greene* [1949] Ch 333, [1949] 1 All ER 167.
9 See paras 9, 140 note 2 ante.
10 *Lock v Queensland Investment and Land Mortgage Co* [1896] AC 461, HL.

148. Statutory construction of, and restrictions on, articles. In certain cases the Companies Act 1985 directs how articles are to be construed. Thus a provision in a company's articles which provides for payment of remuneration to a director free of tax has effect as if it provided for payment, as a gross sum subject to income tax, of the net sum for which it actually provides[1].

In other cases, the Companies Act 1985 provides that certain provisions contained in the articles are to be void. Thus the production to a company of any document which is by law sufficient evidence of probate of the will, or letters of administration of the estate, or confirmation as executor of a deceased person having been granted to some person must be accepted by the company as sufficient evidence of the grant, notwithstanding anything in its articles[2]. A provision of the articles is void in so far as it provides for the calling of a meeting of the company (other than an adjourned meeting) by a shorter notice than that prescribed by the Act itself[3]. A provision of the articles is void in so far as it would have the effect of requiring an instrument appointing a proxy, or any other document necessary to show the validity of, or otherwise relating to, the appointment of a proxy, to be received by the company or any other person more than 48 hours before a meeting or adjourned meeting in order that the appointment may be effective[4]. A provision of the articles is also void in so far as it would have the effect either:

(1) of excluding the right to demand a poll at a general meeting on any question other than the election of the chairman of the meeting or the adjournment of the meeting; or

(2) of making ineffective a demand for a poll on any such question which is made by certain categories of members[5].

1 See the Companies Act 1985 s 311(2) and para 578 post.
2 See ibid s 187 and para 518 post.
3 See ibid s 369(1) and para 660 post.
4 See ibid s 372(5) and para 675 post.
5 See ibid s 373(1) and para 672 post.

149. Shareholders' agreements. Individual shareholders may deal with their own interests by contract in such way as they may think fit; but such contracts, whether made by all or some only of the shareholders, create personal obligations, or an exceptio personalis against themselves only, and do not become a regulation of the company or binding on the transferees of the parties to it or upon new or non-assenting shareholders[1].

Thus, although a provision in a company's articles of association which restricts the company's statutory power to alter the articles, or a formal undertaking by the company to that effect, would be invalid[2], an agreement dehors the articles between shareholders as to how they are to exercise their voting rights on a resolution to alter the articles would not necessarily be so[3].

1 *Welton v Saffery* [1897] AC 299 at 331, HL per Lord Davey; applied in *Russell v Northern Bank Development Corpn Ltd* [1992] 3 All ER 161, [1992] 1 WLR 588, HL.
2 See para 147 ante.
3 *Russell v Northern Bank Development Corpn Ltd* [1992] 3 All ER 161, [1992] 1 WLR 588, HL. See also *Greenwell v Porter* [1902] 1 Ch 530; *Puddephatt v Leith* [1916] 1 Ch 200; *Bushell v Faith* [1969] 2 Ch 438, [1969] 1 All ER 1002, CA (affd [1970] AC 1099, [1970] 1 All ER 53, HL).

(6) REGISTERED OFFICE; SERVICE OF DOCUMENTS

150. Registered office. A company must at all times have a registered office to which all communications and notices may be addressed[1].

On incorporation the situation of the company's registered office is that specified in the statement sent[2] to the registrar of companies[3]. The company may, however, change the situation of its registered office from time to time by giving notice in the prescribed form[4] to the registrar[5]. The change takes effect upon the notice being registered by the registrar[6]; but, until the end of the period of 14 days beginning with the date on which it is registered, a person may validly serve any document on the company at its previous registered office[7].

For the purpose of any duty of a company:

(1) to keep at its registered office, or make available for public inspection there, any register, index or other document; or

(2) to mention the address of its registered office in any document,

a company which has given notice to the registrar of a change in the situation of its registered office may act on the change as from such date, not more than 14 days after the notice is given, as it may determine[8].

Where a company unavoidably ceases to perform at its registered office any such duty as is mentioned in head (1) above in circumstances in which it was not practicable to give prior notice to the registrar of a change in the situation of its registered office, but:

(a) resumes performance of that duty at other premises as soon as practicable; and

(b) gives notice accordingly to the registrar of a change in the situation of its registered office within 14 days of doing so,

it is not to be treated as having failed to comply with that duty[9].

In proceedings for an offence of failing to comply with any such duty as is mentioned in heads (1) and (2) above, it is for the person charged to show that, by reason of the matters referred to above[10], no offence was committed[11].

The memorandum of every company must state whether the registered office of the company is to be situated in England and Wales, or situated in Wales[12], or situated in Scotland[13]. This fixes the country in which the company is to be registered; and, since in this respect the provisions of the memorandum are unalterable[14], the situation of the registered office cannot be changed from England and Wales, or Wales, to Scotland or vice versa.

The situation of the registered office fixes the domicile of the company[15], and is important as regards the court which has the jurisdiction to wind up the company[16].

1 Companies Act 1985 s 287(1) (substituted by the Companies Act 1989 s 136).

2 Ie under the Companies Act 1985 s 10: see para 88 ante.

3 Ibid s 287(2) (substituted by the Companies Act 1989 s 136).

4 For the prescribed form of notice see the Companies (Forms) (Amendment) Regulations 1995, SI 1995/736, reg 3, Sch 2, Form 287. For the prescribed version of the form in Welsh see the Companies (Welsh Language Forms and Documents) (Amendment) Regulations 1995, SI 1995/734, reg 4, Schedule, Form 287CYM.

5 Companies Act 1985 s 287(3) (substituted by the Companies Act 1989 s 136). The registrar must cause notice of his receipt of the document to be published in the Gazette: Companies Act 1985 s 711(1)(n). As to official notification see paras 70, 71 ante. For the meaning of 'the Gazette' see para 70 note 1 ante.

6 This ensures that the situation of the registered office is always as indicated by the registrar of companies and resolves earlier confusion as to the date on which the change of situation takes effect: see eg *Re Garton (Western) Ltd* [1989] BCLC 304 (where the date of the passing of the resolution to change the registered office was suggested as the effective date).

7 Companies Act 1985 s 287(4) (substituted by the Companies Act 1989 s 136).

8 Companies Act 1985 s 287(5) (substituted by the Companies Act 1989 s 136).

9 Companies Act 1985 s 287(6) (substituted by the Companies Act 1989 s 136).

10 Ie the matters referred to in the Companies Act 1985 s 287(5) (as substituted) (see supra) or s 287(6) (as substituted) (see supra).

11 Ibid s 287(7) (substituted by the Companies Act 1989 s 136).

12 As to the possible effect on the company's name if the registered office is situated in Wales see para 154 post; and as to documents relating to Welsh companies see para 90 ante.

13 See the Companies Act 1985 s 2(1)(b) and para 84 ante. A company registered in England and Wales ought never to have a registered office in Scotland: *Re Baby Moon (UK) Ltd* (1985) 1 BCC 99, 298.

14 See para 99 ante.

15 *Gasque v IRC* [1940] 2 KB 80; and see para 94 ante.

16 See paras 2004, 2196 et seq post. As to service in winding up see para 2221 et seq post.

151. Service of documents on a company. A document may be served on a company by leaving it at or sending it by post, whether ordinary, registered[1] or recorded delivery[2], to the company's registered office[3]. 'Document' includes summons[4], notice, order and other legal process, and registers[5]. A summons to appear before a magistrate must be served at the registered office, and appearance by a solicitor to contest the validity of the service is not a waiver of the objection[6]. Service need not be by post; the document may be left with a director, or the secretary, at the registered office[7]. Service on the solicitor of the company is sufficient only where the company agrees to accept it and acknowledges service[8]. The secretary may waive service on him at the registered office by requesting that it may be served on him elsewhere[9].

Where there is no registered office, service at the office in fact used by the company will be sufficient[10]. Where there is no office, the company having ceased to carry on business, service on some of the former officers may be allowed[11].

1 *T O Supplies (London) Ltd v Jerry Creighton Ltd* [1952] 1 KB 42, [1951] 2 All ER 992.
2 Recorded Delivery Service Act 1962 s 1 read in the light of the case cited in note 1 supra.
3 Companies Act 1985 s 725(1); *Vignes v Stephen Smith & Co Ltd* (1909) 53 Sol Jo 716. This practice remains unaffected by the subsequent revisions of the Rules of the Supreme Court (see now RSC Ord 65 r 3): *Addis Ltd v Berkeley Supplies Ltd* [1964] 2 All ER 753, [1964] 1 WLR 943 (writ). Non-compliance with the Companies Act 1985 s 725(1) does not, however, necessarily constitute such an irregularity in the proceedings as to render them a nullity and entitle the defendant to have them set aside ex debito justitiae; instead non-compliance with s 725(1) may be a mere irregularity within RSC Ord 2 r 1(1) and as such does not nullify the proceedings: *Singh v Atombrook Ltd* [1989] 1 All ER 385, [1989] 1 WLR 810, CA, distinguishing *Vignes v Stephen Smith & Co Ltd* (1909) 53 Sol Jo 716 in so far as it was to be taken as an authority requiring service only at the registered office.
     As to service on a Scottish company in England see para 1778 post; as to service out of the jurisdiction see para 1773 post; and as to service on an oversea company see paras 1813, 1814 post.
4 'Summons' includes a default summons: *National Gas Engine Co Ltd v Estate Engineering Co Ltd* [1913] 2 IR 474. A writ of summons must be served on a company in the manner provided by the Companies Act 1985: *Wood v Anderston Foundry Co* (1888) 36 WR 918. See also PRACTICE AND PROCEDURE vol 37 para 159.
5 Companies Act 1985 s 744.
6 *Pearks, Gunston and Tee Ltd v Richardson* [1902] 1 KB 91, DC (summons served on an assistant at one of the company's shops); *Bridge v Adams* (1899) 63 JP 394.
7 *Watson v Sheather, Sons & Co Ltd* (1886) 2 TLR 473.
8 *Re Denver United Breweries Ltd* (1890) 63 LT 96.
9 *Re Taylor, Re Williams, ex p Railway Steel and Plant Co* (1878) 8 ChD 183 at 189, 190.
10 See *Re Fortune Copper Mining Co* (1870) LR 10 Eq 390 (building containing registered office demolished and business being carried on at another address).
11 *Gaskell v Chambers* (1858) 26 Beav 252.

152. Affixing company's name. Every company (except a limited company which is exempted from including the word 'limited' as part of its name[1]) must paint or affix, and keep painted or affixed, its name on the outside of every office or place in which its business is carried on, in a conspicuous position, in letters easily legible[2]. If a company does not so paint or affix its name or fails to keep its name so painted or affixed, the company, and every officer of the company who is in default, is liable on summary conviction to a fine not exceeding one-fifth of the statutory maximum and, on conviction after continued contravention, in the case of failure to keep the name painted or affixed, to a daily default fine not exceeding one-fiftieth of the statutory maximum[3].

1 See the Companies Act 1985 s 30(7) and para 112 ante.
2 Ibid s 348(1). As to permitted abbreviations see para 155 post. Although the abbreviated 'Ltd' in place of

'limited' is sufficient, 'Li' or 'L' is not: *F Stacey & Co Ltd v Wallis* (1912) 106 LT 544. As to a company carrying on business under a business name which does not consist of its corporate name without any addition see para 158 post.

3 Companies Act 1985 ss 348(2), 730, Sch 24. For the meaning of 'officer who is in default', 'the statutory maximum' and 'daily default fine' see para 1161 post.

153. Registers etc to be kept at registered office. The register of members[1] and the register of debenture holders[2] must be kept at the registered office, unless the work of making up the registers is done at another office of the company or is undertaken by some other person on behalf of the company, in which cases the registers may be kept at that other office or at the office of that other person[3]. The index of the names of members[4] and duplicates of overseas branch registers[5] must be kept at the place where the register of members is kept[6]. The register of directors and secretaries[7], the register of charges of a limited company[8] and a copy of every instrument creating a charge requiring registration must be kept at the registered office[9], but in the case of a series of uniform debentures a copy of one debenture of the series is sufficient[10]. The register of directors' service contracts or memoranda thereof[11] must be kept either at the registered office, the place where its register of members is kept, or its principal place of business[12], provided this is situated in that part of Great Britain in which the company is registered[13]. The register of directors' interests in shares in or debentures of the company or associated companies[14] must, if the register of members is kept at the registered office, be kept there, or, if not, either at the registered office or at the place where the register of members is kept[15]. The register of substantial individual interests in share capital of a public company[16] must be kept at the same place as the register of directors' interests[17]. The duty of a company to keep its registers at the registered office ceases when the company is in liquidation and possession of the registers has been taken by the liquidator[18].

The books containing the minutes of proceedings of any general meeting of a company must be kept at the company's registered office[19].

1 The register of members must not be kept, in the case of a company registered in England and Wales, at any place elsewhere than in England and Wales or, in the case of a company registered in Scotland, at any place elsewhere than in Scotland: s 353(1). As to the register of members see para 378 post; as to custody of the register of members see para 389 post; and as to the provisions applicable where the entries are not recorded in legible form see paras 656, 1295 post.
2 Ie unless, as appears to be contemplated, it is kept solely outside the United Kingdom: see ibid s 190 and para 1293 post.
3 Ibid ss 190(3), 353(1).
4 See para 381 post.
5 See para 399 post.
6 Companies Act 1985 ss 354(3), 362(3), Sch 14 Pt II para 4(1).
7 See paras 560, 649 post.
8 See para 1297 post.
9 Companies Act 1985 ss 288(1), 406(1), 407(1).
10 Ibid s 406(2).
11 See para 562 post.
12 For the meaning of 'place of business' see para 63 note 1 ante.
13 Companies Act 1985 s 318(3).
14 See para 571 post.
15 Companies Act 1985 s 325(5), Sch 13 Pt IV para 25(a), (b).
16 See para 747 post.
17 See the Companies Act 1985 s 211(8) and para 747 post.
18 *Re Kent Coalfields Syndicate* [1898] 1 QB 754, CA; and see para 2435 post.
19 See the Companies Act 1985 s 383(1) (as amended) and para 695 post.

(7) NAME, CHANGE OF NAME AND BUSINESS NAMES

(i) Name and Change of Name

154. Name to be stated in memorandum. Every company, whether limited by shares or by guarantee, or unlimited, must, in its memorandum of association, state the name of the company[1]. The name of a public company[2] must end with the words 'public limited company' or, if the memorandum states that the company's registered office is to be situated in Wales, those words or their equivalent in Welsh ('cwmni cyfyngedig cyhoeddus'); and those words or that equivalent may not be preceded by the word 'limited' or its equivalent in Welsh ('cyfyngedig')[3].

In the case of a company limited by shares or by guarantee (not being a public company), the name must have 'limited' as its last word, unless the company is entitled[4] to dispense with that word as part of its name[5]. If the company is to be registered with a memorandum stating that its registered office is to be situated in Wales, the name may have 'cyfyngedig' as its last word[6].

1 Companies Act 1985 s 2(1)(a). As to disclosure of a company's name on business documents see paras 1134, 1135 post; and as to disclosure of a company's name on the company's premises see para 152 ante.
2 As to the nature of a public company see para 104 ante.
3 Companies Act 1985 s 25(1).
4 Ie under ibid s 30: see para 112 ante.
5 Ibid s 25(2)(a).
6 Ibid s 25(2)(b).

155. Alternatives of statutory designations. A company which by any provision of the Companies Act 1985 is either required or entitled to include in its name, as its last part, any of the words specified below may, instead of those words, include as the last part of the name a specified abbreviation as follows[1]:

(1) 'limited' may be abbreviated to 'ltd.';
(2) 'public limited company' may be abbreviated to 'p.l.c.';
(3) 'cyfyngedig' may be abbreviated to 'cyf.'; and
(4) 'cwmni cyfyngedig cyhoeddus' may be abbreviated to 'c.c.c.'[2].

A reference in the Companies Act 1985 to the name of a company or to the inclusion of any of those words in a company's name includes a reference to the name including (in place of any of the words so specified) the appropriate alternative, or to the inclusion of the appropriate alternative, as the case may be[3]. A provision of that Act requiring a company not to include any of those words in its name also requires it not to include the specified abbreviated alternative[4].

1 Companies Act 1985 s 27(1).
2 Ibid s 27(4).
3 Ibid s 27(2).
4 Ibid s 27(3).

156. Prohibition on registration of certain names. A company may not be registered under the Companies Act 1985 by a name:

(1) which includes, otherwise than at the end of the name, any of the following words or expressions, that is to say, 'limited', 'unlimited', or 'public limited company' or their Welsh equivalents ('cyfyngedig', 'anghyfyngedig' and 'cwmni cyfyngedig cyhoeddus' respectively)[1];

(2) which includes, otherwise than at the end of the name, an abbreviation of any of those words or expressions[2];

(3) which is the same as a name appearing in the registrar's index of company names[3];

(4) the use of which by the company would in the opinion of the Secretary of State constitute a criminal offence[4]; or

(5) which in the opinion of the Secretary of State is offensive[5].

Except with the approval of the Secretary of State, a company may not be registered by a name which in the opinion of the Secretary of State would be likely to give the impression that the company is connected in any way with Her Majesty's government or with any local authority[6]; or by a name which includes any word or expression for the time being specified in the appropriate regulations[7].

1 Companies Act 1985 s 26(1)(a). As to these expressions see para 154 ante.
2 Ibid s 26(1)(b).
3 Ibid s 26(1)(c). In determining for this purpose whether one name is the same as another, there are to be disregarded:
  (1) the definite article, where it is the first word of the name;
  (2) the following words and expressions where they appear at the end of the name:
    'company' or its Welsh equivalent ('cwmni'),
    'and company' or its Welsh equivalent ('a'r cwmni'),
    'company limited' or its Welsh equivalent ('cwmni cyfyngedig'),
    'and company limited' or its Welsh equivalent ('a'r cwmni cyfyngedig'),
    'limited' or its Welsh equivalent ('cyfyngedig'),
    'unlimited' or its Welsh equivalent ('anghyfyngedig'), and
    'public limited company' or its Welsh equivalent ('cwmni cyfyngedig cyhoeddus');
  (3) abbreviations of any of those words or expressions where they appear at the end of the name; and
  (4) type and case of letters, accents, spaces between letters and punctuation marks;
  and 'and' and '&' are to be taken as the same: s 26(3).
4 Ibid s 26(1)(d). For names in respect of which a criminal offence might be committed by misuse see 8 Halsbury's Statutes (4th Edn) (1991 Reissue) 144–146.
5 Companies Act 1985 s 26(1)(e).
6 Ibid s 26(2)(a). For these purposes, 'local authority' means any local authority within the meaning of the Local Government Act 1972 (see LOCAL GOVERNMENT vol 28 para 1010 note 5) or the Local Government (Scotland) Act 1973, the Common Council of the City of London or the Council of the Isles of Scilly: Companies Act 1985 s 26(2). As to the Common Council of the City of London see LONDON GOVERNMENT vol 29 para 44 et seq; and as to the Council of the Isles of Scilly see LOCAL GOVERNMENT vol 28 para 1045. The functions conferred on the Secretary of State by s 26(2) may be exercised by, or by employees of, such person (if any) as may be authorised in that behalf by the Secretary of State: Contracting Out (Functions in relation to the Registration of Companies) Order 1995, SI 1995/1013, art 5, Sch 3 para 1(a). As to the contracting out of functions of the Secretary of State generally see paras 1508, 1509 post.
7 Companies Act 1985 s 26(2)(b). As to the appropriate regulations see para 157 post. See also note 6 supra.

157. Regulations about names. The Secretary of State may by regulations[1]:

(1) specify words or expressions for the registration of which as or as part of a company's corporate name his approval is required[2]; and

(2) in relation to any such word or expression, specify a government department or other body as the relevant body[3].

Where a company proposes to have as, or as part of, its corporate name any such word or expression and a government department or other body is specified as the relevant body in relation to that word or expression, a request must be made (in writing) to the relevant body to indicate whether (and if so why) it has any objections to the proposal[4]. The person who has made that request to the relevant body must submit to the registrar of companies a statement that it has been made and a copy of any response received from that body, together with the requisite statutory declaration[5], or copy of the special resolution changing the company's name, according as the case is one or other of those mentioned[6] above[7].

1 The regulations may contain such transitional provisions and savings as the Secretary of State thinks appropriate and may make different provision for different cases or classes of case: Companies Act 1985 s 29(5). The regulations must be made by statutory instrument, to be laid before Parliament after it is made; and the regulations cease to have effect at the end of 28 days beginning with the day on which the regulations were made (but without prejudice to anything previously done by virtue of them or to the making of new regulations), unless during that period they are approved by resolution of each House; in reckoning that period, no account is to be taken of any time during which Parliament is dissolved or prorogued or during which both Houses are adjourned for more than four days: s 29(6). As to the current regulations see note 2 infra.
2 Ibid s 29(1)(a). The approval of the Secretary of State may be required under s 26(2)(b): see para 156 ante. For the words or expressions so specified see the Company and Business Names Regulations 1981, SI 1981/1685 (amended by SI 1982/1653; SI 1992/1196; SI 1995/3022), which continue to have effect by virtue of the Companies Consolidation (Consequential Provisions) Act 1985 s 31(2) (see para 10 ante), and para 168 note 3 post.
3 Companies Act 1985 s 29(1)(b). For the relevant bodies so specified see the Company and Business Names Regulations 1981 (amended by SI 1982/1653; SI 1992/1196; SI 1995/3022) and para 168 note 4 post.
4 Companies Act 1985 s 29(2). The person to make the request is (1) in the case of a company seeking to be registered under Pt I (ss 1–42) (as amended), the person making the statutory declaration required by s 12(3) (see para 88 ante); (2) in the case of a company seeking to be registered under s 680 (as amended), the persons making the statutory declaration required by s 686(2) (see para 78 ante); and (3) in any other case, a director or secretary of the company concerned: s 29(2).
5 See note 4 supra.
6 Ie mentioned in the Companies Act 1985 s 29(2): see supra.
7 Ibid s 29(3). Sections 709, 710 (as substituted) (public rights of inspection of documents kept by registrar: see para 67 ante) do not apply to documents sent under s 29(3): s 29(4).

158. Other restrictions on names. A company may not carry on business with a name containing the words 'Red Cross', 'Geneva Cross', 'Red Crescent' or 'Red Lion and Sun' without the authority of the Defence Council[1]; nor a name closely resembling the name of an association incorporated by royal charter, which has its name protected[2] by Order in Council, without the authority of the association[3]; nor a name containing the word 'Anzac' or any word closely resembling that word without the authority of the Secretary of State given on the request of the government of the Commonwealth of Australia or of the Dominion of New Zealand[4]. In all these cases the registrar of companies will refuse to register a company unless the relevant authority is produced.

If a company carries on business under a business name which does not consist of its corporate name without any addition, it must comply with the requirements of the Business Names Act 1985[5].

The words 'limited' or 'cyfyngedig' may be lawfully used as the last word of a trading name only by a company incorporated with limited liability[6]. However, there is on the one hand no necessity to use the word 'company' as part of the company's name, nor on the other is there any restriction on its use. Subject to the restrictions already mentioned[7], the subscribers of the memorandum may choose any name they please[8].

In certain circumstances a director or shadow director[9] may be personally debarred from using the name of that company if it has gone into insolvent liquidation on or after 29 December 1986, or any name so similar as to suggest an association with that company[10].

1 See the Geneva Conventions Act 1957 s 6 (as amended) and TRADE MARKS vol 48 (Reissue) para 356.
2 Ie under the Chartered Associations (Protection of Names and Uniforms) Act 1926 s 1(1).
3 Ibid s 1(3). See further CORPORATIONS vol 9 para 1216.
4 See the 'Anzac' (Restriction on Trade Use of Word) Act 1916 s 1(1) and TRADE MARKS vol 48 (Reissue) para 357.
5 See para 166 et seq post.
6 See para 162 post. The inclusion of the word 'limited' in a corporate name is not, however, restricted to bodies incorporated under the Companies Act 1985; cf the Industrial and Provident Societies Act 1965 s 5(2), (5) (see INDUSTRIAL AND PROVIDENT SOCIETIES vol 24 (Reissue) para 43).
7 See para 155 et seq ante.
8 A company cannot, however, monopolise a word in ordinary use in the English language: *Aerators Ltd v Tollitt* [1902] 2 Ch 319. As to liability for passing-off see TRADE MARKS vol 48 (Reissue) para 165 et seq.
9 For the meaning of 'shadow director' see para 2664 note 1 post.
10 See the Insolvency Act 1986 s 216 and para 2675 post.

159. Registration with deceptive name. Where a company has been registered by a name which is the same as or, in the opinion of the Secretary of State, too like[1] a name appearing at the time of registration in the registrar's index of company names, or is the same as or, in the opinion of the Secretary of State, too like a name which should have appeared in that index at that time, the Secretary of State may, within 12 months of that time, in writing, direct the company to change its name within such period as he may specify[2].

If it appears to the Secretary of State that misleading information has been given for the purpose of a company's registration with a particular name, or that undertakings or assurances have been given for that purpose and have not been fulfilled, he may within five years of the date of its registration with that name in writing direct the company to change its name within such period as he may specify[3].

Where such a direction has been given[4], the Secretary of State may by a further direction in writing extend the period within which the company is to change its name, at any time before the end of that period[5].

A company which fails to comply with a direction under these provisions, and any officer of it who is in default, is liable on summary conviction to a fine not exceeding one-fifth of the statutory maximum and, on conviction after continued contravention, to a daily default fine not exceeding one-fiftieth of the statutory maximum[6].

Where a company so changes its name, the registrar of companies must (subject to the general restrictions already mentioned[7]) enter the new name on the register in place of the former name, and must issue a certificate of incorporation altered to meet the circumstances of the case; and the change of name has effect from the date on which the altered certificate is issued[8].

Except in the circumstances mentioned above, a company registered under the Companies Act 1985 is not entitled to carry on its business in such a way, or under such a name, as to represent that its business is the business of any other company or firm or person; and the absence of fraud is immaterial[9]. In such cases the old company or firm may apply to the court for an injunction, and the principles then apply which apply to individuals trading under identical or similar names[10]. This remedy is equally available to companies registered under the 1985 Act.

In some cases the court will grant an injunction before the new company has been registered[11], and will protect a foreign trader who has a market in England from having the benefit of his name annexed by a trader in England through registration under the 1985 Act of a company which assumes the name without justification[12].

1 The Companies Act 1985 s 26(3) (see para 156 ante) applies in determining whether a name is the same as or too like another: s 28(2).

2 Ibid s 28(2).
3 Ibid s 28(3).
4 Ie a direction under ibid s 26(2) or (3): see para 156 ante.
5 Ibid s 28(4).
6 Ibid ss 28(5), 730, Sch 24. For the meaning of 'officer who is in default', 'the statutory maximum' and 'daily default fine' see para 1161 post.
7 Ie subject to ibid s 26: see para 156 ante.
8 Ibid s 28(6); *Shackleford, Ford & Co Ltd v Dangerfield, Shackleford, Ford & Co Ltd v Owen* (1868) LR 3 CP 407; *Oshkosh B'Gosh Inc v Dan Marbel Inc Ltd* [1989] 1 CMLR 94, [1989] BCLC 507, CA.
9 *North Cheshire and Manchester Brewery Co v Manchester Brewery Co* [1899] AC 83, HL (injunction granted as businesses competing and appellant adopted name suggesting amalgamation); *Ewing v Buttercup Margarine Co Ltd* [1917] 2 Ch 1, CA (injunction granted as businesses competing and name adopted by defendants similar to that of Buttercup Dairy Co used by plaintiff); *Society of Motor Manufacturers and Traders Ltd v Motor Manufacturer's and Trader's Mutual Insurance Co Ltd* [1925] Ch 675, CA (injunction refused as businesses different and names consisted of words in ordinary use). See further TRADE MARKS vol 48 (Reissue) para 165 et seq.
10 See TRADE MARKS vol 48 (Reissue) para 267 et seq.
11 *Hendriks v Montagu* (1881) 17 ChD 638, CA; *Tussaud v Tussaud* (1890) 44 ChD 678.
12 *Anciens Etablissements Panhard et Levassor SA v Panhard Levassor Motor Co Ltd* [1901] 2 Ch 513.

160. Change of name. Any company may, by special resolution[1], change its name[2]. Where a company changes its name, and on payment of a fee[3], the registrar of companies must enter the new name on the register in place of the former name, and issue a certificate of incorporation altered to meet the circumstances of the case[4]. The change of name is not complete until it has been made upon the register and the new certificate has been issued; and, until the certificate is obtained, the company exists under its original name, although notice of a call stating the new name which is sent before the certificate is obtained is sufficient[5]. The change of name has effect from the date on which the altered certificate is issued[6].

The effect of the issue of the certificate of incorporation on change of name is not to re-form or reincorporate the company as a new entity but to recognise the continued existence of the company under its new name[7].

The change of name does not affect any rights or obligations of the company, or render defective any legal proceedings by or against it, and any legal proceedings that might have been continued or commenced against it by its former name may be continued or commenced against it by its new name[8].

If, after the issue of the certificate, it is found that the special resolution was not duly passed, application may be made to the registrar to vacate the registration[9].

In the case of a company proposing to change its name so that it ceases to have the word 'limited' (or its Welsh equivalent) as part of its name, the company must deliver to the registrar a statutory declaration in the prescribed form to the effect that the company complies with the statutory requirements relating to the exemption from the use of the word 'limited' as part of its name[10].

1 As to special resolutions see para 683 post.
2 Companies Act 1985 s 28(1). This is subject to s 31 (see para 114 ante) in the case of a company which has received a direction under s 31(2) from the Secretary of State: s 28(1). As to official notification of a change in the memorandum and its effect see paras 70, 71 ante.
3 The fee is £20: Companies (Fees) Regulations 1991, SI 1991/1206, reg 4, Schedule, Fee 3 (amended by SI 1994/2217).
4 Companies Act 1985 s 28(6).
5 *Shackleford, Ford & Co Ltd v Dangerfield, Shackleford, Ford & Co Ltd v Owen* (1868) LR 3 CP 407 at 411.
6 Companies Act 1985 s 28(6).
7 *Oshkosh B'Gosh Inc v Dan Marbel Inc Ltd* [1989] 1 CMLR 94, [1989] BCLC 507, CA.
8 Companies Act 1985 s 28(7).

9 See *Re Australasian Mining Co* [1893] WN 74 (where the court expressed the opinion that it had no jurisdiction to order the registrar to vacate the registration).
10 See the Companies Act 1985 s 30(5)(c) and para 112 ante.

161. Power to require company to abandon misleading name. If, in the Secretary of State's opinion, the name by which a company is registered gives so misleading an indication of the nature of its activities as to be likely to cause harm to the public, he may direct it to change its name[1]. If not duly made the subject of an application to the court, the direction must be complied with within a period of six weeks from the date of the direction or such longer period as the Secretary of State may think fit to allow[2]. If a company makes default in complying with such a direction, it is liable on summary conviction to a fine not exceeding one-fifth of the statutory maximum and, on conviction after continued contravention, to a daily default fine not exceeding one-fiftieth of the statutory maximum[3]. The company may, within a period of three weeks from the date of the direction, apply to the court[4] to set it aside; and the court may set the direction aside or confirm it and, if it confirms the direction, the court must specify a period within which it must be complied with[5].

Where a company so changes its name, the registrar of companies must enter the new name on the register in place of the former name[6], and must issue a certificate of incorporation altered to meet the circumstances of the case; and the change of name has effect from the date on which the altered certificate is issued[7]. Such a change of name by a company does not affect any of the rights or obligations of the company, or render defective any legal proceedings by or against it; and any legal proceedings that might have been continued or commenced against it by its former name may be continued or commenced against it by its new name[8].

1 Companies Act 1985 s 32(1).
2 Ibid s 32(2). The change of name must be effected by special resolution: see s 28(1) and para 160 ante.
3 Ibid ss 32(4), 730, Sch 24. For the meaning of 'the statutory maximum' and 'daily default fine' see para 1161 post.
4 'The court', in relation to a company, means the court having jurisdiction to wind up the company: ibid s 744. As to the courts having winding-up jurisdiction see paras 2004, 2196 post.
5 Ibid s 32(3).
6 Ie subject to ibid s 26: see para 156 et seq ante.
7 Ibid s 32(5). See also para 160 ante.
8 Ibid s 32(6).

162. Prohibition on trading under misleading name. A person who is not a public company[1] is guilty of an offence if he carries on any trade, profession or business under a name which includes, as its last part, the words, 'public limited company' or their equivalent in Welsh, 'cwmni cyfyngedig cyhoeddus'[2]. A public company is guilty of an offence if, in circumstances in which the fact that it is a public company is likely to be material to any person, it uses a name which may reasonably be expected to give the impression that it is a private company[3].

A person guilty of an offence under either of the above provisions, and, if that person is a company, any officer of the company who is in default, is liable on summary conviction to a fine not exceeding one-fifth of the statutory maximum and, on conviction after continued contravention, to a daily default fine not exceeding one-fiftieth of the statutory maximum[4].

If any person trades or carries on business under a name or title of which 'limited' or 'cyfyngedig', or any contraction or imitation of either of those words, is the last word, that person, unless duly incorporated with limited liability, is liable on summary conviction to a fine not exceeding one-fifth of the statutory maximum and, on conviction after continued contravention, to a daily default fine not exceeding one-fiftieth of the statutory maximum[5].

1 For the meaning of 'public company' see para 82 ante.
2 Companies Act 1985 s 33(1).
3 Ibid s 33(2).
4 Ibid ss 33(3), 730, Sch 24. For the meaning of 'officer who is in default', 'the statutory maximum' and 'daily default fine' see para 1161 post.
5 Ibid ss 34, 730, Sch 24. The penalty so imposed is the only penalty for the improper use of the word 'limited'; and a breach of the statutory prohibition does not have the effect of preventing a person from enforcing contracts or recovering moneys for work done: *Cotronic (UK) Ltd v Dezonie* [1991] BCLC 721, CA.

163. Indication of reduction of capital. Where a company is in the course of reducing its capital, and the reduction requires confirmation by the court, the court, on confirming the reduction, may order the company to add to its name as the last words 'and reduced' for such period as is specified in the order[1], and those words are during that period deemed to be part of the name of the company[2].

1 Companies Act 1985 s 137(2)(a). This is not, however, usual in practice. See further para 265 post.
2 Ibid s 137(3).

164. Alteration of objects. If an application is made to the court to cancel an alteration of a company's objects, and such alteration makes the existing name misleading, it is open to the court to confirm the alteration only upon the condition that the company changes its name[1].

1 See para 1185 post.

165. Name consisting of trade mark. Where a registered trade mark contains, or consists of, the name of a company, and the name of the company is subsequently changed, application should be made to the Registrar of Trade Marks to enter the change of name in the register of trade marks[1].

Where the registered proprietors of a mark transfer their business to a company under the same name with the addition of the word 'limited', that word will be allowed to be added to the mark[2], but the word 'limited' must not be abbreviated[3].

A company which has carried on business under another name is entitled to protection for the latter as a trade name, although it has not complied with the statutory requirements[4] as to the use of its name[5].

1 See the Trade Marks Act 1994 s 44 and TRADE MARKS vol 48 (Reisue) para 111; *Ex p New Ormonde Cycle Co Ltd* [1896] 2 Ch 520.
2 *Re Guinness & Co's Trade Mark* (1888) 5 RPC 316.
3 *Re Richard Hayward & Sons' Ltd's Trade Marks* (1896) 13 RPC 729; *Re Holbrooks Ltd's Registered Trade Marks* (1901) 18 RPC 447. See also TRADE MARKS vol 48 (Reissue) para 111.

4 See para 154 ante and para 1134 post.
5 *H E Randall Ltd v British and American Shoe Co Ltd* [1902] 2 Ch 354; *Pearks, Gunston and Tee Ltd v Thompson, Talmey & Co* (1901) 18 RPC 185, CA; and see *Employers' Liability Assurance Corpn v Sedgwick, Collins & Co* [1927] AC 95 at 119, 120, HL per Lord Blanesburgh.

(ii) Business Names

166. Persons subject to the Business Names Act 1985. The Business Names Act 1985 applies to any person who has a place of business[1] in Great Britain and who carries on business in Great Britain under a name which:

(1) in the case of a partnership[2], does not consist of the surnames[3] of all partners who are individuals and the corporate names of all partners who are bodies corporate[4] without any addition other than one permitted by that Act; or

(2) in the case of an individual, does not consist of his surname without any addition other than one so permitted; or

(3) in the case of a company[5], being a company which is capable of being wound up under the Insolvency Act 1986[6], does not consist of its corporate name without any addition other than one so permitted[7].

The following are permitted additions for the above purposes:

(a) in the case of a partnership, the forenames of individual partners or the initials[8] of those forenames or, where two or more individual partners have the same surname, the addition of 's' at the end of that surname; or

(b) in the case of an individual, his forename or its initial;

(c) in any case, any addition merely indicating that the business is carried on in succession to a former owner of the business[9].

1 For these purposes, 'business' includes a profession: Business Names Act 1985 s 8(1). 'Place of business' includes a share transfer or share registration office: Companies Act 1985 s 744 (applied by the Business Names Act 1985 s 8(2)).
2 For these purposes, 'partnership' includes a foreign partnership: Business Names Act 1985 s 8(1).
3 For these purposes, 'surname', in relation to a peer or person usually known by a British title different from his surname, means the title by which he is known: ibid s 8(1).
4 For these purposes, references to a body corporate do not include a corporation sole but include a company incorporated elsewhere than in Great Britain; but such references do not include a Scottish firm: Companies Act 1985 s 740 (applied by the Business Names Act 1985 s 8(2)).
5 For these purposes, 'company' means a company formed and registered under the Companies Act 1985 or an existing company: s 735(1) (applied by the Business Names Act 1985 s 8(2)). For the meaning of 'existing company' see para 11 ante.
6 See para 2193 post. For these purposes, the reference to a company capable of being wound up includes a reference to a company which would be so capable but for the Water Industry Act 1991 s 25 (power to make special administration order on winding-up petition: see WATER): Water Consolidation (Consequential Provisions) Act 1991 s 2(1), Sch 1 para 41.
7 Business Names Act 1985 s 1(1); Interpretation Act 1978 s 17(2)(a).
8 For these purposes, 'initial' includes any recognised abbreviation of a name: Business Names Act 1985 s 8(1).
9 Ibid s 1(2).

167. Prohibition of use of certain business names. Subject to the following provisions, a person to whom the Business Names Act 1985 applies[1] may not, without the written approval of the Secretary of State[2], carry on business[3] in Great Britain under a name which:

(1) would be likely to give the impression that the business is connected with Her Majesty's government or with any local authority[4]; or

(2) which includes any word or expression for the time being specified in regulations made under that Act[5].

This prohibition does not apply to the carrying on of a business by a person to whom the business has been transferred on or after 26 February 1982[6], and who carries on the business under the name which was its lawful business name[7] immediately before that transfer, during the period of 12 months beginning with the date of that transfer[8]. Nor does the prohibition apply to the carrying on of a business by a person who carried on that business immediately before 26 February 1982 and continues to carry it on under the name which immediately before that date was its lawful business name[9].

A person who contravenes the above provisions is guilty of an offence[10].

1 As to such persons see para 166 ante.
2 Ie one of Her Majesty's Principal Secretaries of State: Interpretation Act 1978 ss 5, 22(1), Sch 1, Sch 2 para 4(1)(b). In practice the functions under the Business Names Act 1985 are exercised by the Secretary of State for Trade and Industry: see TRADE AND INDUSTRY vol 47 (Reissue) para 2. Since 1992 the Secretary of State for Trade and Industry has, however, used the title President of the Board of Trade: see TRADE AND INDUSTRY vol 47 (Reissue) para 2.
3 For the meaning of 'business' see para 166 note 1 ante.
4 For these purposes, 'local authority' means any local authority within the meaning of the Local Government Act 1972 (see LOCAL GOVERNMENT vol 28 para 1010 note 5) or the Common Council of the City of London or the Council of the Isles of Scilly: Business Names Act 1985 s 8(1). As to the Common Council of the City of London see LONDON GOVERNMENT vol 29 para 44 et seq; and as to the Council of the Isles of Scilly see LOCAL GOVERNMENT vol 28 para 1045.
5 Ibid s 2(1). As to such regulations see para 168 note 3 post. Section 2 and s 3 (see para 168 post) do not prohibit a person from carrying on any business under a name which includes any word or expression specified for the purposes of ss 2, 3 by virtue of the amendments made by the Company and Business Names (Amendment) Regulations 1992, SI 1992/1196, reg 2(2), (3) (see para 168 notes 3, 4 post) to the Company and Business Names Regulations 1981, SI 1981/1685 (as amended) if (1) he carried on that business immediately before 12 June 1992; and (2) he continues to carry it on under the name which immediately before that day was its lawful business name: Company and Business Names (Amendment) Regulations 1992 reg 3(1). Nor do the Business Names Act 1985 ss 2, 3 prohibit a person to whom a business has been transferred on or after 12 June 1992 from carrying on that business during the period of 12 months beginning with the date of transfer so long as he continues to carry it on under the name which was its lawful business name immediately before that date: Business Names (Amendment) Regulations 1992 reg 3(2). The Business Names Act 1985 ss 2, 3 do not prohibit a person from carrying on any business under a name which includes any word or expression specified for the purposes of ss 2, 3 by virtue of the amendment made by the Company and Business Names (Amendment) Regulations 1995, SI 1995/3022, reg 3(a) (insertion after the words 'Chamber of Commerce' of the words 'Chamber of Commerce, Training and Enterprise') if (a) he carried on that business immediately before 1 January 1996; and (b) he continues to carry it on under the name which immediately before that day was its lawful business name: reg 4(1). Nor do the Business Names Act 1985 ss 2, 3 prohibit a person to whom a business has been transferred on or after 1 January 1996 from carrying on that business during the period of 12 months beginning with the date of transfer so long as he continues to carry it on under the name which was its lawful business name immediately before the date of the transfer: Company and Business Names (Amendment) Regulations 1995 reg 4(2).
    The functions conferred on the Secretary of State by the Business Names Act 1985 s 2 may be exercised by, or by employees of, such person (if any) as may be authorised in that behalf by the Secretary of State: Contracting Out (Functions in relation to the Registration of Companies) Order 1995, SI 1995/1013, art 5, Sch 3 para 2. As to the contracting out of functions of the Secretary of State generally see paras 1508, 1509 post.
6 Ie the day on which the Companies Act 1981 s 28 (repealed) came into force.
7 For these purposes, 'lawful business name', in relation to a business, means a name under which the business was carried on without contravening the Business Names Act 1985 s 2(1) or the Registration of Business Names Act 1916 s 2 (repealed): Business Names Act 1985 s 8(1).
8 Ibid s 2(2). See also note 5 supra.
9 Ibid s 2(3). See also note 5 supra.
10 Ibid s 2(4). As to offences see para 172 post. See also note 5 supra.

168. Words and expressions requiring the Secretary of State's approval. The Secretary of State[1] may by regulations[2]:

(1) specify words or expressions for the use of which as or as part of a business name his approval is required[3]; and

(2) in relation to any such word or expression, specify a government department or other body as the relevant body[4].

Where a person to whom the Business Names Act 1985 applies[5] proposes to carry on a business[6] under a name which is or includes any such word or expression, and a government department or other body is so specified in relation to that word or expression, that person must request (in writing) the relevant body to indicate whether (and if so why) it has any objections to the proposal, and must submit to the Secretary of State a statement that such a request has been made and a copy of any response received from the relevant body[7].

1 As to the Secretary of State see para 167 note 2 ante.
2 As to the procedure on the making of regulations see para 171 post.
3 Ie required under the Business Names Act 1985 s 2(1)(b): see para 167 head (2) ante. The Company and Business Names Regulations 1981, SI 1981/1685, reg 3, Sch 2 col 1 (amended by SI 1982/1653; SI 1992/1196; SI 1995/3022), which continues to have effect by virtue of the Companies Consolidation (Consequential Provisions) Act 1985 s 31(2) (see para 10 ante), specifies the following words and expressions (together with the plural and the possessive forms of those words and expressions): Abortion, Apothecary, Association, Assurance, Assurer, Authority, Benevolent, Board, British, Chamber of Commerce, Chamber of Commerce Training and Enterprise, Chamber of Industry, Chamber of Trade, Charitable, Charity, Charter, Chartered, Chemist, Chemistry, Contact Lens, Co-operative, Council, Dental, Dentistry, District Nurse, Duke, England, English, European, Federation, Friendly Society, Foundation, Fund, Giro, Great Britain, Group, Health Centre, Health Service, Health Visitor, Her Majesty, His Majesty, Holding, Industrial and Provident Society, Institute, Institution, Insurance, Insurer, International, Ireland, Irish, King, Midwife, Midwifery, National, Nurse, Nursing, Patent, Patentee, Police, Polytechnic, Post Office, Pregnancy Termination, Prince, Princess, Queen, Reassurance, Reassurer, Register, Registered, Reinsurance, Reinsurer, Royal, Royale, Royalty, Scotland, Scottish, Sheffield, Society, Special School, Stock Exchange, Trade Union, Trust, United Kingdom, University, Wales, Welsh and Windsor. See also para 167 note 5 ante.
  As to restrictions on the use of the words 'building society' see the Building Societies Act 1986 s 107 (as amended) and BUILDING SOCIETIES vol 4(2) (Reissue) para 960; and as to the restrictions on the use of banking names and descriptions, and as to the power to object to names of overseas institutions, see the Banking Act 1987 Pt III (ss 67–73), ss 76, 77 and BANKING vol 3(1) (Reissue) paras 123 et seq, 131, 132.
4 Business Names Act 1985 s 3(1). The Company and Business Names Regulations 1981 reg 4, Sch 2 col 2 (amended by SI 1982/1653; SI 1992/1196; SI 1995/3022), which continues to have effect by virtue of the Companies Consolidation (Consequential Provisions) Act 1985 s 31(2), specifies the following as the relevant bodies in relation to the words or expressions (and the plural and the possessive forms of those words or expressions) indicated in parentheses: the Central Midwives Board or the Central Midwives Board for Scotland (Midwife, Midwifery); the Charity Commission or the Scottish Home and Health Department (Charitable, Charity); the Council for the Education and Training of Health Visitors (Health Visitor); the Department for Education and Employment (Polytechnic, Special School); the Department of Health (Abortion, Health Centre, Health Service, Pregnancy Termination); the General Dental Council (Dental, Dentistry); the General Nursing Council for England and Wales or the General Nursing Council for Scotland (Nurse, Nursing); the General Optical Council (Contact Lens); the Home Office or the Scottish Home and Health Department (Duke, Her Majesty, His Majesty, King, Police, Prince, Princess, Queen, Royal, Royale, Royalty, Windsor); the Panel of Assessors in District Nurse Training (District Nurse); the Privy Council (University); and the Worshipful Society of Apothecaries of London or the Pharmaceutical Society of Great Britain (Apothecary).
5 As to such persons see para 166 ante.
6 For the meaning of 'business' see para 166 note 1 ante.
7 Business Names Act 1985 s 3(2).

169. Disclosure required of persons using business names. A person to whom the Business Names Act 1985 applies[1] must state in legible characters on all business[2] letters, written orders for goods or services to be supplied to the business, invoices and receipts issued in the course of the business and written demands for payment of debts arising in the course of the business:

    (1) in the case of a partnership[3], the name of each partner;

    (2) in the case of an individual, his name;

    (3) in the case of a company[4], its corporate name; and

    (4) in relation to each person so named, an address in Great Britain at which service of any document relating in any way to the business will be effective[5].

This requirement does not, however, apply in relation to any document issued by a partnership of more than 20 persons[6] which maintains at its principal place of business[7] a list of the names of all the partners, if none of the names of the partners appears in the document otherwise than in the text or as a signatory, and if the document states in legible characters the address of the partnership's principal place of business and that list of the partners' names is open to inspection at that place[8].

A person to whom the Business Names Act 1985 applies must, in any premises where the business is carried on and to which the customers of the business or suppliers of any goods or services to the business have access, display in a prominent position so that it may easily be read by such customers or suppliers a notice containing such names and addresses[9].

A person to whom the Business Names Act 1985 applies must also secure that the names and addresses required to be stated on his business letters, or which would have been so required but for the above exemption[10], are immediately given, by written notice, to any person with whom anything is done or discussed in the course of the business and who asks for such names and addresses[11].

The Secretary of State[12] may by regulations[13] require notices under either of the above provisions[14] to be displayed or given in a specified form[15].

A person who without reasonable excuse contravenes the above requirements[16], or any such regulations[17], is guilty of an offence[18].

1 As to such persons see para 166 ante.

2 For the meaning of 'business' see para 166 note 1 ante.

3 For the meaning of 'partnership' see para 166 note 2 ante.

4 For the meaning of 'company' see para 166 note 5 ante.

5 Business Names Act 1985 s 4(1)(a). As to civil remedies for breach of s 4 see para 170 post.

6 In general partnerships with more than 20 partners are prohibited: see para 21 ante and PARTNERSHIP vol 35 (Reissue) para 26.

7 For the meaning of 'place of business' see para 166 note 1 ante.

8 Business Names Act 1985 s 4(3). Where a partnership maintains such a list of the partners' names, any person may inspect the list during office hours: s 4(4). Where an inspection required by a person in accordance with s 4(4) is refused, any partner of the partnership concerned who without reasonable excuse refused that inspection, or permitted it to be refused, is guilty of an offence: s 4(7). As to the punishment of offences see para 172 post.

9 Ibid s 4(1)(b).

10 Ie but for ibid s 4(3): see supra.

11 Ibid s 4(2).

12 As to the Secretary of State see para 167 note 2 ante.

13 As to the making of regulations see para 171 post. At the date at which this volume states the law no regulations had been so made and no regulations have effect as if so made.

14 Ie under the Business Names Act 1985 s 4(1)(b) or (2): see supra.

15 Ibid s 4(5).

16 Ie ibid s 4(1) or (2): see supra.

17 Ie any regulations made under ibid s 4(5): see supra.

18 Ibid s 4(6). As to the punishment of offences see para 172 post.

170. Civil remedies for breach of provisions relating to disclosure. Any legal proceedings brought by a person to whom the Business Names Act 1985 applies[1] to enforce a right arising out of a contract made in the course of a business[2] in respect of which he was, at the time the contract was made, in breach of the statutory requirements as to disclosure[3] must be dismissed if the defendant to the proceedings shows:

(1) that he has a claim against the plaintiff arising out of that contract which he has been unable to pursue by reason of the latter's breach of such requirements; or

(2) that he has suffered some financial loss in connection with the contract by reason of the plaintiff's breach of those requirements,

unless the court[4] before which the proceedings are brought is satisfied that it is just and equitable to permit the proceedings to continue[5].

The above provisions are without prejudice to the right of any person to enforce such rights as he may have against another person in any proceedings brought by that person[6].

1 As to such persons see para 166 ante.
2 For the meaning of 'business' see para 166 note 1 ante.
3 Ie the Business Names Act 1985 s 4(1) or (2): see para 169 ante.
4 For these purposes, 'the court', in relation to a company, means the court having jurisdiction to wind up the company: Companies Act 1985 s 744 (applied by the Business Names Act 1985 s 8(2)). As to the courts having winding-up jurisdiction see paras 2004, 2196 post.
5 Business Names Act 1985 s 5(1).
6 Ibid s 5(2).

171. Regulations. Regulations under the Business Names Act 1985 must be made by statutory instrument and may contain such transitional provisions and savings as the Secretary of State[1] thinks appropriate, and may make different provision for different cases or classes of case[2].

In the case of regulations relating to words and expressions requiring his approval[3], the statutory instrument containing them must be laid before Parliament after the regulations are made and cease to have effect at the end of the period of 28 days[4] beginning with the day on which they were made (but without prejudice to anything previously done by virtue of them or to the making of new regulations) unless during that period they are approved by a resolution of each House of Parliament[5].

In the case of regulations made in relation to the forms of notice[6], the statutory instrument containing them is subject to annulment in pursuance of a resolution of either House of Parliament[7].

1 As to the Secretary of State see para 167 note 2 ante.
2 Business Names Act 1985 s 6(1).
3 Ie regulations made under ibid s 3: see para 168 ante.
4 In reckoning this period of 28 days, no account is to be taken of any time during which Parliament is dissolved or prorogued, or during which both Houses are adjourned for more than four days: ibid s 6(2).
5 Ibid s 6(2).
6 Ie under ibid s 4: see para 169 ante.
7 Ibid s 6(3).

172. Offences. Offences under the Business Names Act 1985 are punishable on summary conviction[1], a person guilty of such an offence being liable to a fine not exceeding one-fifth of the statutory maximum[2].

If, after a person has been convicted summarily of an offence in connection with the use of business names[3] or the disclosure of information[4], the original contravention is continued, he is liable on a second or subsequent summary conviction of the offence to a fine not exceeding one-fiftieth of the statutory maximum for each day on which the contravention is continued (instead of to the penalty which may be imposed on the first conviction of the offence)[5].

Where an offence[6] committed by a body corporate[7] is proved to have been committed with the consent or connivance of, or to be attributable to any neglect on the part of, any director, manager, secretary or other similar officer of the body corporate, or any person who was purporting to act in any such capacity, he as well as the body corporate is guilty of the offence and liable to be proceeded against and punished accordingly[8]. Where the affairs of a body corporate are managed by its members, this provision applies in relation to the acts and defaults of a member in connection with his functions of management as if he were a director of the body corporate[9].

1 Business Names Act 1985 s 7(1).
2 Ibid s 7(2). The Business Names Act 1985 is to be treated as included in the Companies Acts for the purposes of the Companies Act 1985 s 731 (summary proceedings: see para 1168 post) and s 732(3) (legal professional privilege: see para 1168 post): Business Names Act 1985 s 7(6). For the meaning of 'the statutory maximum' see para 1161 post.
3 Ie an offence under ibid s 2: see para 167 ante.
4 Ie an offence under ibid s 4(6): see para 169 ante.
5 Ibid s 7(3).
6 Ie an offence under ibid s 2 (see para 167 ante) or s 4(6) or (7) (see para 169 ante).
7 For the meaning of 'body corporate' see para 166 note 4 ante.
8 Business Names Act 1985 s 7(4).
9 Ibid s 7(5).

(8) CAPITAL

(i) In general

173. Meaning of 'capital'. The word 'capital', as used in the Companies Act 1985 and the statutes which it replaces, if unqualified, always means share capital as distinct, for example, from borrowed money, which is sometimes referred to as loan capital[1]. The word 'capital' sometimes means the 'nominal' capital of the company, namely that which is stated in the memorandum of association of any company limited by shares or by guarantee with a share capital, or in the articles of an unlimited company which has a capital divided into shares[2], and any increase of that nominal capital which has been made in the manner required by statute[3]. This 'nominal' capital does not at the outset, or necessarily at any time, represent money in the possession or ownership of the company, or assets of any kind, but the amount of nominal capital at any given time limits the power of the company to issue shares[4].

Subject to the requirement that a public company must have a sufficient share capital expressed in pounds sterling for it to be able to allot shares to the extent of the authorised minimum[5], there is no necessity for the entire capital to be expressed in pounds sterling, or for it to be all in one particular currency[6]. Each share must, however, be expressed solely in one particular currency[7].

1 The company is not a debtor to capital; the capital is not a debt of the company even to the shareholders: *Lee v Neuchatel Asphalte Co* (1889) 41 ChD 1 at 23, CA; *Verner v General and Commercial Investment Trust* [1894] 2 Ch 239 at 264, CA.

2 See paras 102, 108, 115 ante.

3 See paras 201–204 post.

4 Persons who conspire to issue shares beyond the number into which the nominal amount of the capital is divided may be indicted for conspiracy: *R v Mott* (1827) 2 C & P 521.

5 For the meaning of 'authorised minimum' see para 652 note 6 post.

6 *Re Scandinavian Bank Group plc* [1988] Ch 87, [1987] 2 All ER 70. See also *Re Anglo American Insurance Co Ltd* [1991] BCLC 564.

7 *Re Scandinavian Bank Group plc* [1988] Ch 87 at 107, [1987] 2 All ER 70 at 79 per Harman J.

174. Issued and unissued capital. The nominal capital stated in the memorandum or articles, as the case may be, or in the resolution of the company for increase[1], is at first, and may for the most part always be, 'unpaid' capital; but some of it, namely the shares subscribed for by the signatories to the memorandum of association, is at once 'issued' capital[2]. Shares registered in any person's name[3], or in respect of which a share certificate has been issued[4], are part of the 'issued' capital[5]. A matter of some difficulty is the distinction between when shares are allotted and when shares are issued[6]. The term 'issue' in relation to shares means something distinct from allotment and imports that some subsequent act has been done whereby the title of the allottee has been completed[7]. The allotment creates an enforceable contract for the issue of the shares[8]. The shares are issued when an application to the company has been followed by allotment and notification to the purchaser and completed by entry on the register of members[9]. The residue of the 'nominal' capital, or at any rate such of it as has not been agreed to be taken by any person, is 'unissued' capital[10]. Even when capital has been 'issued', the result is not always a contribution to the company's assets. In the absence of special regulations requiring the signatories of the memorandum to pay for their shares, they are not liable to do so until a call has been regularly made upon them[11].

Companies which invite the public to subscribe for their shares invariably require something on account of their nominal amount to be paid on application, and some other sum to be paid on allotment. The sums so paid represent 'partly paid' capital. Calls may be made for the difference between what has been paid and the nominal amount of shares[12]; when the difference has been paid, the share is 'fully paid', and the aggregate amount of such payments of application moneys, allotment moneys, and calls (if paid) represents 'paid-up' capital[13]. Contributions, voluntary or enforced, of any person becoming a member render the shares which he takes 'partly paid' or 'paid-up' capital, as the case may be. For the purposes of the Companies Act 1985, 'called-up share capital', in relation to a company, means so much of its share capital as equals the aggregate amount of the calls made on its shares, whether or not those calls have been paid, together with any share capital paid up without being called and any share capital to be paid on a specified future date under the articles, the terms of allotment of the relevant shares or any other arrangements for payment of those shares[14].

1 See the Companies Act 1985 s 121(1), (2)(a) and para 201 post.

2 *Dalton Time Lock Co v Dalton* (1892) 66 LT 704, CA; *Re Whitehead & Bros Ltd* [1900] 1 Ch 804; *Re Ebenezer Timmins & Sons Ltd* [1902] 1 Ch 238; *Re F W Jarvis & Co Ltd* [1899] 1 Ch 193; *Re Archibald D Dawnay Ltd* [1900] WN 152.

3 *Blyth's Case* (1876) 4 ChD 140, CA; *Re Ambrose Lake Tin and Copper Co, Clarke's Case* (1878) 8 ChD 635 at 641, CA. See also para 446 post.

4 *Bush's Case* (1874) 9 Ch App 554. As to the effect of a share certificate see para 487 post.

5 The cases cited in notes 2–4 supra were decided on the construction of the Companies Act 1867 s 25 (repealed and not re-enacted) in which the word 'issued' occurred.

6 It would seem that the meaning of 'issue' depends on the context of the enactment in which the word occurs: see para 446 text and note 4 post. See also *National Westminster Bank plc v IRC, Barclays Bank plc v IRC* [1995] 1 AC 119, [1994] 3 All ER 1, HL.

7 *National Westminster Bank plc v IRC, Barclays Bank plc v IRC* [1995] 1 AC 119, [1994] 3 All ER 1, HL; *Re Ambrose Lake Tin and Copper Co, Clarke's Case* (1878) 8 ChD 635 at 638, CA.
8 *National Westminster Bank plc v IRC, Barclays Bank plc v IRC* [1995] 1 AC 119 at 126, [1994] 3 All ER 1 at 6, HL per Lord Templeman.
9 *National Westminster Bank plc v IRC, Barclays Bank plc v IRC* [1995] 1 AC 119, [1994] 3 All ER 1, HL (tax relief to investors in shares in companies set up under the business expansion scheme was altered in respect of shares 'issued' after 16 March 1993; shares had been allotted before, but registration took place after, that date; shares were held to have been 'issued' after that date).
10 See the Companies Act 1985 s 121(2)(e) and para 218 post.
11 *Alexander v Automatic Telephone Co* [1900] 2 Ch 56, CA.
12 As to calls see para 416 et seq post.
13 Where shares are issued at a premium, the sums paid up will partly represent the premium, and the shares will not be 'fully paid' until the full nominal amount has been paid in addition to the premium.
14 Companies Act 1985 s 737(1). 'Uncalled share capital' is to be construed accordingly: s 737(2). These definitions apply unless a contrary intention appears: s 737(3).

175. Paid-up capital. The Companies Act 1985 limits the liability of the members of a company limited by shares to the amount, if any, unpaid on the shares respectively held by them[1]. This means that the liability continues so long as anything remains unpaid on a share, and may only be ended by payment in full[2]. When that payment in full is made, the amount paid represents 'paid-up' capital.

A share may be fully paid without any cash passing from the shareholder to the company. The circuitous process of paying up the nominal amount of the share and then taking back the money in satisfaction of the company's indebtedness for goods or other property sold to it is unnecessary. Thus, shares may be lawfully issued as 'fully paid' for considerations which the company has agreed to accept as representing in money's worth the nominal value of the shares[3], provided that the statutory conditions as to delivery for registration of a contract in writing or particulars relating to the shares and a return of the allotment are complied with[4]. Whilst the transaction is unimpeached, the court will not inquire into the value of the consideration[5], and it will not rescind a transaction which is not impeached as dishonest merely because the company may have paid an extravagant price for the property[6]. Thus, a specialty debt resulting from a call on shares may be discharged by accord and satisfaction, but the consideration must not be a mere blind or clearly colourable or illusory[7].

1 See the Companies Act 1985 s 1(2)(a) and para 80 ante. As to the means of payment generally see para 464 et seq post; and as to members' liability see para 2475 post and *Edmonton Country Club Ltd v Case* [1974] 4 WWR 626 (Can SC) (amendments to the articles purporting to require shareholders to pay an annual assessment on pain of forfeiture of their shares held ultra vires and void ab initio).
2 *Ooregum Gold Mining Co of India v Roper* [1892] AC 125 at 145, HL. As to the allotment of shares at a discount see para 187 post.
3 *Ooregum Gold Mining Co of India v Roper* [1892] AC 125 at 136, HL; *Chapman's Case* [1895] 1 Ch 771; *Pellatt's Case* (1867) 2 Ch App 527; *Gardner v Iredale* [1912] 1 Ch 700. As to delivery for registration of a contract in such a case see para 478 post.
4 See para 478 post. Public companies must comply with additional statutory constraints on the acceptance of non-cash consideration: see para 467 et seq post.
5 *Pell's Case* (1896) 5 Ch App 11; *Re Wragg Ltd* [1897] 1 Ch 796, CA; *Chapman's Case* [1895] 1 Ch 771. It is otherwise where the consideration is illusory or capable of obvious money measure (*Chapman's Case* supra; *Re Wragg Ltd* supra at 836; *Famatina Development Corpn Ltd v Bury* [1910] AC 439, HL; *Park Business Interiors Ltd v Park* [1992] BCLC 1034, Ct of Sess) or where from the terms of the contract it is obvious that the property acquired is not equivalent to the amount of capital which is treated as paid up (*Hong Kong and China Gas Co Ltd v Glen* [1914] 1 Ch 527). See also *Re Leinster Contract Corpn* [1902] 1 IR 349; *Brownlie, Petitioner, Scottish Heritages Co* (1899) 6 SLT 326.
6 *Ooregum Gold Mining Co of India v Roper* [1892] AC 125 at 143, HL; *Re Innes & Co Ltd* [1903] 2 Ch 254, CA.
7 *Re White Star Line Ltd* [1938] Ch 458, [1938] 1 All ER 607, CA; and see *Park Business Interiors Ltd v Park* [1992] BCLC 1034, Ct of Sess.

176. Other meanings of 'capital'. The word 'capital' is also used to mean such of the assets of a company, as, for example, its land, works, book debts and stock in trade, as represent the money subscribed or deemed to have been paid on its issued share capital[1]. Profits do not cease to be such (in the sense of their being distributable among the shareholders) by having been used for a length of time in the company's business[2]. The terms 'fixed capital' and 'circulating capital' have also been used, principally with reference to the subject of paying dividends out of capital, in relation to which they are no longer material.

1 *Verner v General and Commercial Investment Trust* [1894] 2 Ch 239 at 265, CA.
2 *Bouch v Sproule* (1887) 12 App Cas 385, HL; *Re Bridgewater Navigation Co* [1891] 2 Ch 317, CA; *Re Hoare & Co Ltd and Reduced* [1904] 2 Ch 208 at 214, CA.

177. Reserve capital. 'Reserve' capital is the capital which is not capable of being called up except in the event and for the purposes of the company being wound up[1]. The postponed liability may be created:
  (1) by an unlimited company on re-registering as a limited company either in respect of an increase of nominal capital on such re-registration, or in respect of any portion of its existing uncalled capital[2]; or
  (2) by a limited company in respect of any portion of its share capital which has not been already called up[3].
In the latter case the reserve liability must be determined by special resolution[3]. In either case the reserve capital cannot be mortgaged or charged by the company[4].

1 Reserve capital should be distinguished from the reserves created out of profits by most companies: see para 728 post.
2 See the Companies Act 1985 s 124 and para 128 ante.
3 See ibid s 120 and para 416 post.
4 See para 1245 post.

178. Statements as to capital in memorandum or articles. The amount of share capital of a company, whether limited by shares or guarantee, or unlimited, must be stated in the memorandum of association in the case of a company limited by shares, or limited by guarantee and having a share capital[1], and in the articles in the case of an unlimited company which has a share capital[2]. The number and fixed amount of shares must also be stated in the memorandum of a company limited by shares or by guarantee[3], and each share in a company having a share capital must, for the purpose of identification, be distinguished[4] by an appropriate number; but, if at any time all the issued shares in a company, or all the issued shares of a particular class, are fully paid up and rank pari passu for all purposes, none of them need thereafter have a distinguishing number so long as it remains fully paid up and ranks pari passu for all purposes with all shares of the same class for the time being issued and fully paid up[5]. The fixed amount of a share must be a monetary amount, but it is not necessary for the shares to be all of the same amount. The change into decimal currency was merely a change of label, involving no formalities[6].

1 See the Companies Act 1985 s 2(5)(a) and paras 102, 108, 115 ante. With effect from 22 December 1980 a company cannot be formed as, or become, a company limited by guarantee with a share capital: see s 1(4) and para 108 ante.
2 See ibid s 7(2) and paras 115, 116 ante. As to a share capital expressed otherwise than in pounds sterling see para 173 ante.
3 See ibid s 2(5)(a) and para 115 ante.

4 Ie when it is issued. As to a joint stock company, registered under ibid Pt XXII Ch II (ss 680–690) (as amended), whose shares are not numbered see para 27 ante.
5 Ibid s 182(2). See also para 438 post.
6 *Re Harris and Sheldon Group Ltd* [1971] 2 All ER 87n, [1971] 1 WLR 899.

179. Alterations to capital. In the case of a company limited by shares or by guarantee[1] and having a share capital, the fixed amount of a company's capital cannot be altered except by an alteration of the memorandum of association in one of the methods authorised by the Companies Act 1985[2].

1 With effect from 22 December 1980 a company cannot be formed as, or become, a company limited by guarantee with a share capital: see the Companies Act 1985 s 1(4) and para 108 ante.
2 See ibid ss 2(7), 121, 135; para 84 ante; and para 201 et seq post.

180. Preference shares. It is not necessary that equal rights and privileges should be attached to all shares; some may be preferential either as to capital or as to dividend, or as to both, or may have peculiar privileges in the matter of voting, or in other respects[1].

If there are no provisions in the memorandum as to preferential rights being attached to any shares, the company may by its articles of association attach to certain of its shares such preferential rights as it pleases; for there is no implied condition in the memorandum that equal rights shall be attached to all the shares[2]. Where the memorandum merely gives express power to issue preference shares as part of the original capital, the exercise of that power is governed by the articles[3].

Where a preferential dividend of a specified amount is attached to shares, the holders of the shares are (unless the articles or the terms of issue contain clear indications to the contrary) limited to the fixed dividend and not entitled to participate in profits to any greater extent[4].

If preference shares confer a preferential right in respect of dividend, the dividend is prima facie cumulative, that is to say, if the moneys applicable to dividend in one year are not sufficient to pay the preference dividend, the deficiency, including arrears, must be made good out of moneys so applicable in future years, before anything is paid as dividend to the holders of other shares ranking after such preference shares[5]. This dividend belongs to the holders of the shares when it is declared, not to the holders of the shares when the arrears accrued due, and no lapse of time will bar the right to payment of arrears in full before payment of any dividends on junior ranking shares[6]. The dividend may, however, be non-cumulative if the articles or terms of issue upon their true construction so provide[7].

Prima facie a preference share gives only a right to a preferential dividend and not a right to a preferential payment of the amount of the share out of capital in case of a winding up[8]. A preference as to repayment of capital may, however, be given[9].

Preference shares may be created having a priority over other preference shares, unless there is any provision in the memorandum or articles to prevent it, either on the original issue of both classes of shares or by an increase of capital[10].

1 These are generally called 'preference' shares, as distinguished from those which are not so privileged, generally called 'ordinary' shares. A company may also have 'deferred' shares, deferred in priority to the ordinary shares. There may be preference, ordinary and deferred shares, or shares of more classes than three, each of which has particular rights and conditions attached to it. Founders' shares were sometimes issued to recompense 'founders' or promoters of the company. They were usually shares of small nominal amount, which, although deferred in priority as to dividends, entitled the holders to the whole or a large percentage of the surplus profits remaining after payment of fixed dividends on the shares having priority to the founders' shares. As to voting rights generally see para 670 et seq post.

2 *Andrews v Gas Meter Co* [1897] 1 Ch 361, CA, overruling *Hutton v Scarborough Cliff Hotel Co Ltd* (1865) 2 Drew & Sm 521; *Sime v Coats* 1908 SC 751; and see *British and American Trustee and Finance Corpn v Couper* [1894] AC 399 at 417, HL; *Harrison v Mexican Rly Co* (1875) LR 19 Eq 358; *Guinness v Land Corpn of Ireland* (1882) 22 ChD 349 at 377, CA; *Re South Durham Brewery Co* (1885) 31 ChD 261 at 270, CA; *Humboldt Redwood Co Ltd (Liquidator) v Coats* 1908 SC 751; *Galloway v Hallé Concerts Society* [1915] 2 Ch 233 at 239.

3 *Campbell v Rofe* [1933] AC 91, PC. The Companies (Tables A to F) Regulations 1985, SI 1985/805, Schedule, Table A art 2 provides that, subject to the provisions of the Companies Act 1985, and without prejudice to any rights attached to any existing shares, any share may be issued with such rights or restrictions as the company may by ordinary resolution determine. As to Table A generally see para 529 et seq post.

4 *Will v United Lankat Plantations Co Ltd* [1914] AC 11, HL; cf *Steel Co of Canada Ltd v Ramsay* [1931] AC 270, PC.

5 *Henry v Great Northern Rly Co* (1857) 1 De G & J 606; *Webb v Earle* (1875) LR 20 Eq 556; *Miln v Arizona Copper Co* (1899) 36 SLR 741; *Patrick, Hillhead and Maryhill Gas Co Ltd v Taylor* (1888) 15 R 711; *Foster v Coles and M B Foster & Sons Ltd* (1906) 22 TLR 555; *Ferguson and Forester Ltd v Buchanan* 1920 SC 154.

6 *Godfrey Phillips Ltd v Investment Trust Corpn Ltd* [1953] Ch 449, [1953] 1 All ER 7. As to the priority of dividends on preference shares see para 725 post; and as to the taxation of company distributions see paras 733, 734 post.

7 *Staples v Eastman Photographic Materials Co* [1896] 2 Ch 303, CA; *Adair v Old Bushmills Distillery Co* [1908] WN 24; *J I Thornycroft & Co Ltd v Thornycroft* (1927) 44 TLR 9.

8 *Re London Indiarubber Co* (1868) LR 5 Eq 519.

9 See para 2592 post.

10 *Underwood v London Music Hall Ltd* [1901] 2 Ch 309.

181. Redeemable shares. Subject to certain conditions, a company limited by shares, or limited by guarantee and having a share capital, may, if so authorised by its articles, issue shares which are to be, or are liable to be, redeemed at the option of the company or the shareholder[1]. Since the conditions surrounding the exercise of this power are intimately bound up with the exercise by the company of its power to purchase its own shares which have not been issued as redeemable shares, both powers are considered together subsequently[2].

1 Companies Act 1985 s 159(1). Prior to the coming into force of the Companies Act 1981 s 34 (repealed) on 15 June 1982, only redeemable preference shares could be issued: see the Companies Act 1948 s 58(1) (repealed). It is not possible to convert existing shares into redeemable shares other than where the conversion is part of a properly authorised reduction of capital under the Companies Act 1985 s 135 (see para 241 post): see *Re St James' Court Estate Ltd* [1944] Ch 6; cf *Forth Wines Ltd, Petitioner* [1991] BCC 638, Ct of Sess.

2 See para 219 et seq post.

(ii) Class Rights

182. Variation of class rights. The following provisions govern the variation of the rights attached to any class of shares[1] in a company whose share capital is divided into shares of different classes[2].

Where the rights are attached to a class of shares otherwise than by the company's memorandum, and the company's articles do not contain provision with respect to the variation of the rights, those rights may be varied if, but only if:

(1) the holders of three-quarters in nominal value of the issued shares of that class consent in writing to the variation; or

(2) an extraordinary resolution passed at a separate general meeting of the holders of that class sanctions the variation[3];

and any requirement (howsoever imposed) in relation to the variation of those rights is complied with to the extent that it is not comprised in heads (1) and (2) above[4].

Where:

(a) the rights are attached to a class of shares by the memorandum or otherwise;

(b) the memorandum or articles contain provision for the variation of those rights; and

(c) the variation of those rights is connected with the giving, variation, revocation or renewal of an authority for allotment by the directors[5] or with a reduction of the company's share capital[6],

those rights may not be varied unless the condition mentioned in heads (1) or (2) above is satisfied and any requirement of the memorandum or articles in relation to the variation of rights of that class is complied with to the extent that it is not comprised in that condition[7].

If the rights are attached to a class of shares in the company by the memorandum or otherwise and:

(i) where they are so attached by the memorandum, the articles contain provision with respect to their variation which had been included in the articles at the time of the company's original incorporation; or

(ii) where they are so attached otherwise, the articles contain such provision (whenever first so included),

and in either case the variation is not connected as mentioned in head (c) above, those rights may only be varied in accordance with that provision of the articles[8].

If the rights are attached to a class of shares by the memorandum, and the memorandum and articles do not contain provision with respect to the variation of those rights, those rights may be varied if all the members of the company agree to the variation[9].

Any alteration of a provision contained in a company's articles for the variation of the rights attached to a class of shares, or the insertion of any such provision into the articles, is itself to be treated as a variation of those rights[10].

In the above provisions and (except where the context otherwise requires) in any provision for the variation of the rights attached to a class of shares contained in a company's memorandum or articles, references to the variation of those rights are to be read as including references to their abrogation[11].

The above provisions[12] apply only where the rights attached to a class of shares have been varied or abrogated and a distinction must be drawn between the rights of shareholders on the one hand and the results of exercising them or the enjoyment of the rights on the other hand[13].

The enjoyment of rights of preference shareholders is affected as a matter of business by the issue of additional preference shares with the same voting rights per share as those already existing, since the votes of the existing preference shareholders are diminished in power, but the voting rights as such are not varied[14]; nor are the rights of preference stockholders affected by the issue of additional ordinary shares, although the position of ordinary shareholders is thereby strengthened as against the preference stockholders[15]. Similarly, there is no variation of the rights of the holders of existing sub-divided shares where the company, in accordance with its articles, sub-divides shares, all sub-divided shares having the same voting rights, with the result that the holders of the existing sub-divided shares lose their power of enforcing control[16].

The repayment of capital on a reduction of capital[17] in accordance with the priorities as to the return of capital on a winding up does not constitute a variation or abrogation of the rights of preference shareholders but their fulfilment[18]; nor does such prior repayment of capital modify, commute, affect or deal with the rights of preference shareholders so as to require the consent of the class under the articles[19]. Preference shareholders may protect themselves by a provision in the articles providing that a repayment of capital on a reduction of capital shall be deemed to be a variation of the rights attached to the affected shares[20].

The company may validly make a payment to the shareholders whose rights are adversely varied to secure their acquiescence[21].

1   Rights or benefits which, although not attached to any particular shares, are conferred on the person concerned in his capacity as a member or shareholder of the company are for this purpose rights attached to a class of shares: *Cumbrian Newspapers Group Ltd v Cumberland & Westmorland Herald Newspaper and Printing Co Ltd* [1987] Ch 1, [1986] 2 All ER 816. A right conferred on an individual unrelated to any shareholding cannot be described as a class right: *Re Blue Arrow plc* [1987] BCLC 585 at 590. A right granted to a holder of particular shares imposed by a shareholders' agreement for the protection of a minority shareholder was a class right and had the same effect as if the right had been set out as class rights in the articles: *Harman v BML Group Ltd* [1994] 1 WLR 893, [1994] 2 BCLC 674, CA (a shareholders' meeting was not quorate without the presence of the holder of 'B' shares or his proxy).
2   Companies Act 1985 s 125(1).
3   The provisions of ibid s 369 (as amended) (length of notice for calling company meetings: see para 660 post), s 370 (general provisions as to meetings and votes: see para 660 et seq post) and ss 376, 377 (circulation of members' resolutions: see para 688 post), and the provisions of the company's articles relating to general meetings, apply, so far as applicable, in relation to any meeting of shareholders required by s 125 or otherwise to take place in connection with the variation of the rights attached to a class of shares, and so apply with the necessary modifications and subject to the following provisions, namely (1) the necessary quorum at any such meeting other than an adjourned meeting is to be two persons holding or representing by proxy at least one-third in nominal value of the issued shares of the class in question and at an adjourned meeting one person holding shares of the class in question or his proxy; (2) any holder of shares of the class in question present in person or by proxy may demand a poll: s 125(6).
4   Ibid s 125(2). Nothing in s 125(2) and s 125(3)–(5) (see infra) derogates from the powers of the court under ss 4–6 (as amended) (company's resolution to alter objects: see paras 1184–1187 post), s 54 (litigated objection to public company becoming private by re-registration: see para 130 ante), s 425 (as amended) (court control of company compromising with members and creditors: see paras 1447, 1448 post), s 427 (company reconstruction or amalgamation: see para 1460 post) and ss 459–461 (as amended) (protection of minorities: see paras 1405–1416 post): s 126.
5   Ie under ibid s 80: see para 447 post.
6   Ie under ibid s 135: see para 241 post.
7   Ibid s 125(3). See also note 4 supra.
8   Ibid s 125(4). See also note 4 supra.
9   Ibid s 125(5). See also note 4 supra.
10 Ibid s 125(7).
11 Ibid s 125(8). As to the distinction between variation and abrogation of rights see the guidance in *Re House of Fraser plc* [1987] BCLC 293 at 301, Ct of Sess. The variation of a right presupposes the existence of the right, the variation of the right, and the subsequent continued existence of the right as varied; abrogation presupposes the termination of rights without satisfaction or fulfilment: *Re House of Fraser plc* supra at 301.
12 Ie the Companies Act 1985 s 125: see supra.
13 *White v Bristol Aeroplane Co Ltd* [1953] Ch 65 at 74, [1953] 1 All ER 40 at 44, CA per Evershed MR and at 82 and at 49 per Romer LJ.
14 *White v Bristol Aeroplane Co Ltd* [1953] Ch 65, [1953] 1 All ER 40, CA, applying *Re Mackenzie & Co Ltd* [1916] 2 Ch 450 (rateable reduction on all shares, preference and ordinary, in pursuance of clause in articles authorising reduction of capital; not an alteration of the rights of preference shareholders although diminishing the actual preferential dividend).
15 *White v Bristol Aeroplane Co Ltd* [1953] Ch 65, [1953] 1 All ER 40, CA; *Re John Smith's Tadcaster Brewery Co Ltd* [1953] Ch 308, [1953] 1 All ER 518, CA.
16 *Greenhalgh v Arderne Cinemas Ltd* [1946] 1 All ER 512, CA.
17 As to reduction of capital see para 241 post.
18 *Re House of Fraser plc* [1987] BCLC 293, Ct of Sess; *Re Saltdean Estate Co Ltd* [1968] 3 All ER 829, [1968] 1 WLR 1844; and see para 244 post.
19 *House of Fraser plc v ACGE Investments Ltd* [1987] AC 387, [1987] 2 WLR 1083, HL; *Re Saltdean Estate Co Ltd* [1968] 3 All ER 829, [1968] 1 WLR 1844; and see para 244 post. The words 'modify, commute, affect or deal with' contemplate that after the relevant transaction the shareholders in question will

continue to possess some rights albeit of a different nature from those which they possessed before the transaction and do not cover the situation where there is a complete cancellation of the shares: *House of Fraser v ACGE Investments Ltd* supra.
20 See *Re Northern Engineering Industries plc* [1994] 2 BCLC 704, CA (reduction of capital so specified as a variation). In a protective provision of this type 'reduction' encompasses both piecemeal reduction of capital and repayment of an entire class on a reduction to zero.
21 *Caledonian Insurance Co v Scottish-American Investment Co Ltd* 1951 SLT 23.

183. Cancellation of variation of rights attached to classes of shares. If, in the case of a company whose share capital is divided into different classes of shares:

(1) provision is made by the memorandum or articles for authorising the variation[1] of the rights attached to any class of shares in a company subject to the consent of any specified proportion of the holders of the issued shares of that class, or the sanction of a resolution passed at a separate meeting of the holders of those shares, and, in pursuance of the provision, the rights attached to any class of shares are at any time varied; or

(2) the rights attached to any class of shares in a company are varied[2],

the holders of not less in the aggregate than 15% of the issued shares of that class, being persons who did not consent to or vote in favour of the resolution for the variation, may apply to the court to have the variation cancelled, and, if such an application is made, the variation has no effect unless and until it is confirmed by the court[3].

1 For these purposes, 'variation' includes abrogation; and 'varied' is to be construed accordingly: Companies Act 1985 s 127(6).
2 Ie under ibid s 125(2): see para 182 ante.
3 Ibid s 127(1), (2).

184. Procedure for cancellation. An application to the court for cancellation of a variation of rights must be made within 21 days after the date on which the consent was given or the resolution was passed (as the case may be), and may be made on behalf of the shareholders entitled to make the application by such one or more of their number as they may appoint in writing for the purpose[1].

The application is made by way of petition[2]. It is made to the court having jurisdiction to wind up the company[3]. Unless otherwise ordered, it must be supported by affidavit[4]. After the presentation of the petition the petitioner must take out a summons[5] for directions[6].

After hearing the applicant and any other persons who apply to the court to be heard and who appear to the court to be interested in the application, the court may disallow the variation if it is satisfied, having regard to all the circumstances of the case, that the variation would unfairly prejudice the shareholders of the class represented by the applicant; otherwise the court must confirm the variation[7]. Its decision on any such application is final[7].

Within 15 days after the making of an order by the court, the company must forward a copy of the order to the registrar of companies, and, if default is made in complying with that requirement, the company, and every officer of it who is in default, is liable on summary conviction to a fine not exceeding one-fifth of the statutory maximum and, on conviction after continued contravention, to a daily default fine not exceeding one-fiftieth of the statutory maximum[8].

1 Companies Act 1985 s 127(3). See *Re Suburban and Provincial Stores Ltd* [1943] Ch 156, [1943] 1 All ER 342, CA (the applicant must show on the face of his petition his title to sue and, if he does not himself

hold the necessary 15% of the shares, the petition must show that he has been appointed in writing by the necessary percentage of dissentient members; a later appointment is invalid); *Re Sound City (Films) Ltd* [1947] Ch 169, [1946] 2 All ER 521 (the authority must have been communicated to the applicant before the presentation of the petition).

2 RSC Ord 102 r 4(1)(e).
3 Companies Act 1985 s 744. As to the jurisdiction of the High Court see para 2197 post; and as to the jurisdiction of county courts see para 2198 post. As to the exercise of jurisdiction in the High Court and the title of proceedings see para 252 post.
4 RSC Ord 38 r 2(3).
5 See para 253 post.
6 RSC Ord 102 r 6(1).
7 Companies Act 1985 s 127(4).
8 Ibid ss 127(5), 730, Sch 24. For the meaning of 'officer who is in default', 'the statutory maximum' and 'daily default fine' see para 1161 post.

185. Registration of particulars of special rights. If a company allots shares with rights which are not stated in its memorandum or articles, or in any resolution or agreement which is required[1] to be sent to the registrar of companies, the company must deliver to the registrar of companies, within one month from allotting the shares, a statement in the prescribed form[2] containing particulars of those rights[3]. This does not apply if the shares are in all respects uniform with shares previously allotted; and shares are not for this purpose to be treated as different from shares previously allotted by reason only that the former do not carry the same rights to dividends as the latter during the 12 months immediately following the former's allotment[4]. Where the rights attached to any shares of a company are varied otherwise than by an amendment of the company's memorandum or articles or by a resolution or agreement which is required[5] to be sent to the registrar of companies, the company must within one month from the date on which the variation is made deliver to the registrar of companies a statement in the prescribed form[6] containing particulars of the variation[7].

Where a company, otherwise than by any such amendment, resolution or agreement, assigns a name or other designation, or a new name or other designation, to any class of its shares, it must within one month from doing so deliver to the registrar of companies a notice in the prescribed form[8] giving particulars of the name or designation so assigned[9].

If a company fails to comply with the above provisions, the company, and every officer of it who is in default, is liable on summary conviction to a fine not exceeding one-fifth of the statutory maximum and, on conviction after continued contravention, to a daily default fine not exceeding one-fiftieth of the statutory maximum[10].

1 Ie by the Companies Act 1985 s 380 (as amended): see para 691 post.
2 For the prescribed form of statement see the Companies (Forms) Regulations 1985, SI 1985/854, reg 4(1), Sch 3, Form 128(1) (amended by SI 1987/752).
3 Companies Act 1985 s 128(1).
4 Ibid s 128(2).
5 See note 1 supra.
6 For the prescribed form of statement see the Companies (Forms) Regulations 1985 Sch 3, Form 128(3) (amended by SI 1987/752).
7 Companies Act 1985 s 128(3).
8 For the prescribed form of notice see the Companies (Forms) Regulations 1985 Sch 3, Form 128(4) (amended by SI 1987/752).
9 Companies Act 1985 s 128(4).
10 Ibid ss 128(5), 730, Sch 24. For the meaning of 'officer who is in default', 'the statutory maximum' and 'daily default fine' see para 1161 post.

186. Registration of newly created class rights. If a company not having a share capital creates a class of members with rights which are not stated in its memorandum or articles or in a resolution or agreement which is required[1] to be sent to the registrar of companies, the company must deliver to the registrar within one month from the date on which the new class is created a statement in the prescribed form[2] containing particulars of the rights attached to that class[3]. If the rights of any class of members of the company are varied otherwise than by an amendment of the memorandum or articles or by such a resolution or agreement, the company must within one month from the date on which the variation is made deliver to the registrar a statement in the prescribed form[4] containing particulars of the variation[5]. If a company, otherwise than by such an amendment, resolution or agreement, assigns a name or other designation, or a new name or other designation, to any class of its members, it must within one month from doing so deliver to the registrar a notice in the prescribed form[6] giving particulars of the name or designation so assigned[7].

If a company fails to comply with the above provisions, the company, and every officer of it who is in default, is liable on summary conviction to a fine not exceeding one-fifth of the statutory maximum and, on conviction after continued contravention, to a daily default fine not exceeding one-fiftieth of the statutory maximum[8].

1 Ie under the Companies Act 1985 s 380 (as amended): see para 691 post.
2 For the prescribed form of statement see the Companies (Forms) Regulations 1985, SI 1985/854, reg 4(1), Sch 3, Form 129(1) (amended by SI 1987/752).
3 Companies Act 1985 s 129(1).
4 For the prescribed form of statement see the Companies (Forms) Regulations 1985 Sch 3, Form 129(2) (amended by SI 1987/752).
5 Companies Act 1985 s 129(2).
6 For the prescribed form of notice see the Companies (Forms) Regulations 1985 Sch 3, Form 129(3) (amended by SI 1987/752).
7 Companies Act 1985 s 129(3).
8 Ibid ss 129(4), 730, Sch 24. For the meaning of 'officer who is in default', 'the statutory maximum' and 'daily default fine' see para 1161 post.

(iii) Allotment of Shares at a Discount

187. Allotting shares at a discount. Since 23 June 1980[1] it has been unlawful for a company even with the sanction of the court to allot shares at a discount[2]. If shares are so allotted, the allottee is liable to pay the company an amount equal to the amount of the discount, with interest at the appropriate rate[3].

1 Ie the date on which the Companies Act 1980 s 2 (repealed) came into force. Previously, ie since 1 November 1929, the allotment of shares at a discount was permissible with the sanction of the court (see the Companies Act 1948 s 57 (repealed)), and the alteration in the law in 1980 contained a saving in respect of any application for such sanction which had been made to the court before 23 June 1980 and had not yet been disposed of (see the Companies Act 1980 s 21(4) (repealed)). Before 1 November 1929, apart from the statutory provision as to paying commissions for underwriting and brokerage (see para 194 post), a company limited by shares could not allot shares at a discount, ie allot shares at their nominal value with a liability to pay only a sum smaller than their nominal value either in money or money's worth: see *Ooregum Gold Mining Co of India v Roper* [1892] AC 125, HL; *Re Eddystone Marine Insurance Co* [1893] 3 Ch 9, CA (where bonus shares were issued as fully paid); *Hirsche v Sims* [1894] AC 654, PC; *Re Addlestone Linoleum Co* (1887) 37 ChD 191, CA; *Re Almada and Tirito Co* (1888) 38 ChD 415, CA; *Re New Chile Gold Mining Co* (1888) 38 ChD 475; *Keatinge v Paringa Consolidated Mines Ltd* (1902) 18 TLR 266; overruling *Re Plaskynaston Tube Co* (1883) 23 ChD 542; and *Re Ince Hall Rolling Mills Co* (1882) 23 ChD 545n; *Chapman v Great Central Freehold Mines Ltd* (1905) 22 TLR 90, PC; *Famatina Development Corpn Ltd v Bury* [1910] AC 439, HL (where a company proposed to issue shares as fully paid in satisfaction of a bonus on debentures payable only out of profits but profits had not been

earned; ultra vires); and *Hong Kong and China Gas Co Ltd v Glen* [1914] 1 Ch 527 (agreement to allot one-fifth of every increase of capital as consideration for property acquired; ultra vires). A contract to issue shares at a discount was void: *Welton v Saffery* [1897] AC 299 at 321, HL per Lord Macnaghten.
2 Companies Act 1985 s 100(1).
3 Ibid s 100(2). As to contravention of s 100 see para 465 post. For these purposes, 'the appropriate rate', in relation to interest, means 5% per annum or such other rate as may be specified by order made by the Secretary of State by statutory instrument subject to annulment in pursuance of a resolution of either House of Parliament: s 107. At the date at which this volume states the law no such order had been made.

(iv) Issue of Shares at a Premium

188. Share premium account. There are no statutory or other restrictions on the issue of shares at a premium; indeed, if the directors can obtain a premium on the issue, it is their duty to do so[1]. Subject to relief from these provisions in cases of merger[2] or group reconstruction[3], and to retrospective relief[4] and the powers of the Secretary of State[5], where shares are so issued, whether for cash or otherwise[6], a sum equal to the aggregate amount or value[6] of the premiums on those shares must be transferred to an account, called 'the share premium account', and the provisions of the Companies Act 1985 relating to the reduction of the share capital of a company[7] will, except as mentioned below, apply as if the share premium account were paid-up share capital of the company[8]. Thus, if the assets of the share premium account are to be distributed among shareholders, the transaction is to be regarded as if the company were reducing its paid-up share capital and the money distributed is capital and not income in the hands of the payee[9].

Notwithstanding the above, the share premium account may be applied by the company in paying up unissued shares of the company to be allotted to members as fully paid bonus shares, or in writing off:
(1) the preliminary expenses of the company[10]; or
(2) the expenses of, or the commission paid[11] or discount allowed on[12], any issue of shares or debentures of the company;
or in providing for the premium payable on redemption of debentures of the company[13].

If the company redeems any redeemable shares[14] which were issued at a premium, any premium payable on their redemption may be paid out of the proceeds of a fresh issue of shares made for the purpose of the redemption, up to an amount equal to:
(a) the aggregate of the premiums received by the company on the issue of the shares redeemed; or
(b) the current amount of the company's share premium account, including any sum transferred to that account in respect of premiums on the new shares,
whichever is the less[15]; and, in that case, the amount of the company's share premium account must be reduced by a sum corresponding, or by sums in the aggregate corresponding, to the amount of any payment made by virtue of this provision out of the proceeds of the issue of the new shares[15].

Where a private company exercises its power to redeem or purchase its own shares out of capital and the permissible capital payment is greater than the nominal amount of the shares purchased or redeemed, the share premium account may be reduced by a sum not exceeding the amount by which the permissible capital payment exceeds the nominal amount of the shares[16].

1 See *Lowry (Inspector of Taxes) v Consolidated African Selection Trust Ltd* [1940] AC 648 at 679, [1940] 2 All ER 545 at 565, HL per Lord Wright.

2 Ie under the Companies Act 1985 s 131 (as amended): see para 189 post.
3 Ie under ibid s 132: see para 190 post.
4 Ie under the Companies Consolidation (Consequential Provisions) Act 1985 s 12: see para 191 post.
5 Ie under the Companies Act 1985 s 134(1) or the Companies Consolidation (Consequential Provisions) Act 1985 s 12(6): see para 193 post.
6 Shares issued for a consideration other than cash are issued at a premium if the value of the assets in consideration of which they are issued is more than the nominal value of the shares: see *Henry Head & Co Ltd v Ropner Holdings Ltd* [1952] Ch 124 at 128, [1951] 2 All ER 994 at 997 per Harman J (where a holding company, formed for the purpose of amalgamating two existing companies, acquired assets of a greater value than the nominal value of the shares issued by it in exchange for the existing shares of the amalgamated companies; it was required to transfer the excess value of the assets acquired to its share premium account); *Shearer (Inspector of Taxes) v Bercain Ltd* [1980] 3 All ER 295.
7 See para 241 et seq post.
8 Companies Act 1985 s 130(1),(3),(4). Before the coming into operation of the Companies Act 1948 (repealed) any such premiums could also be distributed by way of dividend: *Drown v Gaumont-British Picture Corpn Ltd* [1937] Ch 402, [1937] 2 All ER 609.
9 *Re Duff's Settlement, National Provincial Bank Ltd v Gregson* [1951] Ch 923, [1951] 2 All ER 534, CA; and see further SETTLEMENTS vol 42 paras 956–958. See also *Quayle Munro Ltd, Petitioners* [1994] 1 BCLC 410, Ct of Sess (funds which were released from the share premium account following its cancellation in accordance with the statutory procedures and transferred to special reserve were available to be distributed as profits distributable by way of dividend). The procedure for reduction is the same as that for reduction of capital: RSC Ord 102 r 4(1)(c). See paras 191, 192 post.
10 See para 52 ante.
11 See para 194 post.
12 As to shares see para 187 ante (allotment at a discount is no longer possible); and as to debentures see para 1271 post.
13 Companies Act 1985 s 130(2).
14 See para 219 et seq post.
15 See the Companies Act 1985 s 160(2) and para 220 post. Section 160 (as amended) applies to the purchase by a company under s 162 (as amended) (see para 222 post) of its own shares as it applies to the redemption of redeemable shares: s 162(2) (substituted by the Companies Act 1989 s 133(1), (4)).
16 See the Companies Act 1985 s 171(5) and para 232 post.

189. Merger relief. Except where relief is given in respect of group reconstruction[1], the following provisions apply where the issuing company[2] has secured at least a 90% equity holding in another company[3] in pursuance of an arrangement[4] providing for the allotment of equity shares in the issuing company on terms that the consideration for the shares allotted is to be provided by the issue or transfer to the issuing company of equity shares[5] in the other company, or by the cancellation of any such shares not held by the issuing company[6].

If the equity shares in the issuing company allotted in pursuance of the arrangement in consideration for the acquisition or cancellation of equity shares in the other company are issued at a premium, the obligation to establish a share premium account[7] does not apply to the premiums on those shares[8]. Where the arrangement also provides for the allotment of any shares in the issuing company on terms that the consideration for those shares is to be provided by the issue or transfer to the issuing company of non-equity shares[9] in the other company or by the cancellation of any such shares in that company not held by the issuing company, such relief extends to any shares in the issuing company allotted on those terms in pursuance of the arrangement[10].

The issuing company is to be regarded for the purposes of these provisions as having secured at least a 90% equity holding in another company in pursuance of such an arrangement[11] if, in consequence of an acquisition or cancellation of equity shares in that company (in pursuance of that arrangement), it holds equity shares in that company (whether all or any of those shares were acquired in pursuance of that arrangement, or not) of an aggregate nominal value equal to 90% or more of the nominal value of that company's equity share capital[12]; but, where the equity share capital of the other company is divided into different classes of shares, these provisions do not apply unless the issuing company has secured at least a 90% holding in each of those classes of shares taken separately[13].

Shares held by a company which is the issuing company's holding company[14] or subsidiary[15], or a subsidiary of the issuing company's holding company, or by its or their nominees, are to be regarded for these purposes as held by the issuing company[16].

The relief given by the above provisions does not apply if the issue of shares took place before 4 February 1981[17].

1 Ie under the Companies Act 1985 s 132(8): see para 190 post.
2 References to the issuing company are to the company issuing the shares as mentioned in ibid s 130(1) (see para 188 ante): s 130(4).
3 For these purposes, 'company', except in references to the issuing company, includes any body corporate: ibid s 133(4). For the meaning of 'body corporate' see para 89 note 8 ante.
4 For these purposes, 'arrangement' means any agreement, scheme or arrangement (including an arrangement sanctioned under the Companies Act 1985 s 425 (as amended) (see para 1447 post) or the Insolvency Act 1986 s 110 (see para 1480 post): Companies Act 1985 s 131(7) (amended by the Insolvency Act 1986 s 439(1), Sch 13 Pt I).
5 For these purposes, 'equity shares' means shares comprised in the company's equity share capital (Companies Act 1985 s 131(7)(a)); and 'equity share capital' means, in relation to a company, issued share capital excluding any part of that capital which, neither as respects dividends nor as respects capital, carries any right to participate beyond a specified amount in a distribution (s 744).
6 Ibid s 131(1) (amended by the Companies Act 1989 s 145, Sch 19 para 1). The amendment so made is deemed always to have had effect: Companies Act 1989 Sch 19 para 1. For the meaning of the acquisition, issue, allotment and transfer of shares in connection with these provisions see para 192 post. Provisions relating to merger relief and relief in respect of group reconstruction (see para 190 post) were originally enacted by the Companies Act 1981 in order to relieve companies of the consequences of the decisions in *Henry Head & Co Ltd v Ropner Holdings Ltd* [1952] Ch 124, [1951] 2 All ER 994 and *Shearer (Inspector of Taxes) v Bercain Ltd* [1980] 3 All ER 295 (both cited in para 188 note 6 ante).
7 Ie under the Companies Act 1985 s 130: see para 188 ante.
8 Ibid s 131(2). See also note 6 supra.
9 For these purposes, 'non-equity shares' means any shares not comprised in the company's equity share capital: ibid s 131(7)(b).
10 Ibid s 131(3). See also note 6 supra.
11 Ie such an arrangement as is mentioned in ibid s 131(1) (as amended): see supra.
12 Ibid s 131(4). See also note 6 supra.
13 Ibid s 131(5).
14 For the meaning of 'holding company' see para 827 post.
15 For the meaning of 'subsidiary' see para 827 post.
16 Companies Act 1985 s 131(6).
17 Ibid s 131(8).

190. Relief in respect of group reconstructions. The following provisions apply where the issuing company[1]:

(1) is a wholly-owned subsidiary[2] of another company[3] ('the holding company')[4]; and

(2) allots[5] shares to the holding company, or to another wholly-owned subsidiary of the holding company, in consideration for the transfer to the issuing company of assets other than cash, being assets of any company ('the transferor company') which is a member of the group of companies which comprises the holding company and all its wholly-owned subsidiaries[6].

Where the shares in the issuing company allotted in consideration for the transfer are issued at a premium, the issuing company is not required[7] to transfer any amount in excess of the minimum premium value to the share premium account[8]. For these purposes, 'the minimum premium value' means the amount, if any, by which the base value of the consideration for the shares allotted exceeds the aggregate nominal value of those shares[9]; and the base value of the consideration for the shares allotted is the amount by which the base value of the assets transferred exceeds the base value of any liabilities of the transferor company assumed by the issuing company as part of the consideration for the assets transferred[10]. The base value of the assets transferred is to be taken as:

(a) the cost of those assets to the transferor company; or

(b) the amount at which those assets are stated in the transferor company's accounting records immediately before the transfer,

whichever is the less[11]. The base value of the liabilities assumed is to be taken as the amount at which they are stated in the transferor company's accounting records immediately before the transfer[12].

The relief afforded by the above provisions does not apply if the issue of shares took place before 21 December 1984[13]. However, to the extent that the relief allowed by these provisions would have been allowed pursuant to the Companies Act 1981, as originally enacted[14], the relief applies where the issue of shares took place between 4 February 1981 and 21 December 1984[15].

The provisions relating to merger relief[16] do not apply in a case falling within the above provisions[17].

1 For the meaning of references to the issuing company see para 189 note 2 ante.
2 For the meaning of 'wholly-owned subsidiary' see para 827 post.
3 For the meaning of 'company' see para 189 note 3 ante.
4 For the meaning of 'holding company' see para 827 post.
5 For the meaning of 'allots' for these purposes see para 192 post.
6 Companies Act 1985 s 132(1). See also para 189 note 6 ante.
7 Ie by ibid s 130: see para 188 ante.
8 Ibid s 132(2).
9 Ibid s 132(3).
10 Ibid s 132(4).
11 Ibid s 132(5)(a).
12 Ibid s 132(5)(b).
13 Ibid s 132(6). 21 December 1984 was the date of the coming into force of the Companies (Share Premium Account) Regulations 1984, SI 1984/2007, made under the Companies Act 1981 s 41, substituting a new s 38 for the existing s 38 of the Companies Act 1981.
14 Ie under ibid s 38 which as originally enacted is set out in the Companies Act 1985 s 132(7), Sch 25 as follows:

      38(1) This section applies where the issuing company:

        (a) is a wholly-owned subsidiary of another company ('the holding company'), and

        (b) allots shares to the holding company or to another wholly-owned subsidiary of the holding company in consideration for the transfer to it of shares in another subsidiary (whether wholly-owned or not) of the holding company.

      (2) Where the shares in the issuing company allotted in consideration for the transfer are issued at a premium, the issuing company shall not be required by section 56 of the 1948 Act to transfer any amount in excess of the minimum premium value to the share premium account.

      (3) In subsection (2) above 'the minimum premium value' means the amount (if any) by which the base value of the shares transferred exceeds the aggregate nominal value of the shares allotted in consideration for the transfer.

      (4) For the purposes of subsection (3) above, the base value of the shares transferred shall be taken as:

        (a) the cost of those shares to the company transferring them; or

        (b) the amount at which those shares are stated in that company's accounting records immediately before the transfer;

        whichever is the less.

      (5) Section 37 of this Act shall not apply in a case to which this section applies.

In the Companies Act 1985 Sch 25 'subsidiary' has the meaning given by s 736 (as originally enacted): Companies Act 1989 s 144(4), Sch 18 para 38. For the purposes of the Companies Act 1985, but subject to s 736(4) (as originally enacted) (see infra), a company is deemed to be a subsidiary of another if, but only if (1) that other either is a member of it and controls the composition of its board of directors, or holds more than half in nominal value of its equity share capital; or (2) the first-mentioned company is a subsidiary of any company which is that other's subsidiary: s 736(1) (as originally enacted). For these purposes, the composition of a company's board of directors is deemed to be controlled by another company if, but only if, by the exercise of some power exercisable by it without the consent or concurrence of any other person, that other company can appoint or remove the holders of all or a majority of the directorships: s 736(2) (as originally enacted). For the purposes of s 736(2) (as originally enacted), the other company is deemed to have power to appoint to a directorship with respect to which any of the following conditions is satisfied: (a) that a person cannot be appointed to it without the exercise in his favour by the other company of such a power as is mentioned supra; or (b) that a person's appointment to the directorship follows necessarily from his appointment as director of the other company; or (c) that the directorship is held by the other company itself or by a subsidiary of it: s 736(3) (as originally enacted).

In determining whether one company is a subsidiary of another (i) any shares held or power exercisable by the other in a fiduciary capacity are to be treated as not held or exercisable by it; (ii) subject to heads (iii), (iv) infra, any shares held or power exercisable by any person as a nominee for the other (except where the other is concerned only in a fiduciary capacity) or by, or by a nominee for, a subsidiary of the other, not being a subsidiary which is concerned only in a fiduciary capacity, are to be treated as held or exercisable by that other; (iii) any shares held or power exercisable by any person by virtue of the provisions of any debentures of the first-mentioned company or of a trust deed for securing any issue of such debentures are to be disregarded; and (iv) any shares held or power exercisable by, or by a nominee for, the other or its subsidiary (not being held or exercisable as mentioned in head (iii) supra) are to be treated as not held or exercisable by the other if the ordinary business of the other or its subsidiary, as the case may be, includes the lending of money, and the shares are so held or the power is so exercisable by way of security only for the purposes of a transaction entered into in the ordinary course of that business: s 736(4) (as originally enacted).

15 Ibid s 132(7). For possible relief where the shares were issued before 4 February 1981 see para 191 post.
16 See para 189 ante.
17 Companies Act 1985 s 132(8).

191. Retrospective relief. The relief given by the following provisions applies only where a company has issued shares, in circumstances to which the provisions apply, before 4 February 1981[1]. Subject as follows, they apply where the issuing company[2] has issued at a premium shares which were allotted in pursuance of any arrangement[3] providing for the allotment of shares in the issuing company on terms that the consideration for the shares allotted was to be provided by the issue or transfer to the issuing company of shares in another company[4] or by the cancellation of any shares in that other company not held by the issuing company[5]. The other company in question must either have been at the time of the arrangement a subsidiary[6] of the issuing company or of any company which was then the issuing company's holding company[7] or have become such a subsidiary on the acquisition or cancellation of its shares in pursuance of the arrangement[8].

Any part of the premiums on the shares so issued which was not transferred to the company's share premium account in accordance with the previous statutory provisions[9] must be treated as if they had never applied to those premiums, and may accordingly be disregarded in determining the sum to be included in the company's share premium account[10].

1 Companies Consolidation (Consequential Provisions) Act 1985 s 12(1). 4 February 1981 was the date of the publication of the Bill which became the Companies Act 1981, which contained in s 39 the precursor of these provisions. The Companies Consolidation (Consequential Provisions) Act 1985 s 12 is deemed included in the Companies Act 1985 Pt V Ch III (ss 130–134) (as amended) for the purposes of the Secretary of State's power under s 134 (see para 193 post) to make regulations in respect of relief from the requirements of s 130 (see para 188 ante): Companies Consolidation (Consequential Provisions) Act 1985 s 12(6).

2 Ie the company issuing shares as referred to in the Companies Act 1985 s 130(1): see para 188 ante.
3 For these purposes, 'arrangement' bears the same meaning as in ibid s 131(7) (see para 189 note 4 ante): Companies Consolidation (Consequential Provisions) Act 1985 s 12(5)(b).
4 For these purposes, 'company', except in references to the issuing company, includes any body corporate: ibid s 12(5)(a). For the meaning of 'body corporate' see para 89 note 8 ante.
5 Ibid s 12(2).
6 For the meaning of 'subsidiary' see para 827 post.
7 For the meaning of 'holding company' see para 827 post.
8 Companies Consolidation (Consequential Provisions) Act 1985 s 12(3).
9 Ie the Companies Act 1948 s 56 (repealed).
10 Companies Consolidation (Consequential Provisions) Act 1985 s 12(4).

192. Supplementary provisions. An amount corresponding to one representing the premiums or part of the premiums on shares issued by a company[1] which by virtue of any of the relevant statutory relief provisions[2] is not included in the company's share premium account[3] may also be disregarded in determining the amount at which any shares or other consideration provided for the shares issued is to be included in the company's balance sheet[4].

References in those provisions, however expressed, to the acquisition by a company of shares in another company, and the issue or allotment of shares to, or the transfer of shares to or by, a company, include respectively the acquisition of any of those shares by, and the issue or allotment or, as the case may be, the transfer of any of those shares to or by, nominees of that company[5].

References in those provisions to the transfer of shares in a company include the transfer of a right to be included in the company's register of members in respect of those shares[6].

1 For the meaning of 'company' see para 189 note 3 ante.
2 Ie the Companies Act 1985 s 131 (as amended) (merger relief: see para 189 ante) or s 132 (group reconstruction relief: see para 190 ante) or the Companies Consolidation (Consequential Provisions) Act 1985 s 12 (retrospective relief: see para 191 ante).
3 As to the share premium account see para 188 ante.
4 Companies Act 1985 s 133(1).
5 Ibid s 133(2); Companies Consolidation (Consequential Provisions) Act 1985 s 12(5). The reference in the Companies Act 1985 s 132 to the company transferring the shares is to be construed accordingly: s 133(2).
6 Ibid s 133(3).

193. Provision for extending or restricting relief. The Secretary of State may by regulations in a statutory instrument make such provision as appears to him to be appropriate:

    (1) for relieving companies from the statutory requirement to establish a share premium account[1] in relation to premiums other than cash premiums; or

    (2) for restricting or otherwise modifying any statutory reliefs from that requirement[2].

The regulations may make different provision for different cases or classes of case and may contain such incidental and supplementary provisions as the Secretary of State thinks fit[3]. No such regulations may be made unless a draft of the instrument containing them has been laid before Parliament and approved by a resolution of each House[4].

1 Ie as prescribed by the Companies Act 1985 s 130: see para 188 ante.
2 Ibid s 134(1). As to such reliefs see paras 189–191 ante.

3 Ibid s 134(2).
4 Ibid s 134(3). At the date at which this volume states the law no such regulations had been made.

(v) Underwriting and Brokerage

194. Statutory requirements. 'Underwriting' usually means agreeing to take the number of shares specified in an underwriting letter or agreement to the extent that the public or other persons do not subscribe for them before a fixed date[1].

It is lawful for a company to pay a commission to any person in consideration of his subscribing[2] or agreeing to subscribe, whether absolutely or conditionally, for any shares in the company, or procuring or agreeing to procure subscriptions, whether absolute or conditional, for any shares in the company if the following conditions are satisfied[3].

The payment of the commission must be authorised by the company's articles[4]; and

(1) the commission paid or agreed to be paid must not exceed 10% of the price at which the shares are issued or the amount or rate authorised by the articles, whichever is the less[5]; and

(2) the amount or rate per cent of commission paid or agreed to be paid, and the number of shares which persons have agreed for a commission to subscribe absolutely, must be disclosed in the manner required by the following provisions[6].

Those matters must, in the case of shares offered to the public for subscription, be disclosed in the prospectus[7]; and in the case of shares not so offered:

(a) they must be disclosed in a statement in the prescribed form[8] signed by every director of the company or by his agent authorised in writing, and delivered (before payment of the commission) to the registrar of companies for registration[9]; and

(b) where a circular or notice (not being a prospectus) inviting subscription for the shares is issued, they must also be disclosed in that circular or notice[10].

If default is made in complying with head (a) above as regards delivery to the registrar of the statement in prescribed form, the company, and every officer of it who is in default, is liable on summary conviction to a fine not exceeding one-fifth of the statutory maximum[11].

Unless the above conditions are complied with, no company may apply any of its shares or capital money, either directly or indirectly, in payment of any commission, discount[12] or allowance to any person in consideration of his subscribing or agreeing to subscribe, whether absolutely or conditionally, for any shares of the company, or procuring or agreeing to procure subscriptions, whether absolute or conditional, for any shares in the company[13]. This is so whether the shares or money are so applied by being added to the purchase money of any property acquired by the company or to the contract price of any work to be executed for the company, or whether the money is paid out of the nominal purchase money or contract price, or otherwise[14].

A vendor to, or promoter of, or other person who receives payment in money or shares from, a company has, and is deemed always to have had, power to apply any part of the money or shares so received in payment of any commission, the payment of which, if made directly by the company, would have been lawful under the above provisions[15].

1 *Re Licensed Victuallers' Mutual Trading Association, ex p Audain* (1889) 42 ChD 1 at 7, CA; *Re London-Paris Financial Mining Corpn Ltd* (1897) 13 TLR 569, CA.

2 'Subscribing' probably means entering into an agreement to take shares by means of a formal application or otherwise, under which there is a liability to pay: see *Arnison v Smith* (1889) 41 ChD 348 at 357, CA.

3 Companies Act 1985 s 97(1).

4 Authority in the memorandum but not in the articles is insufficient: *Re Bolivia Republic Exploration Syndicate Ltd* [1914] 1 Ch 139. As to the liability of auditors in respect of an improper payment of commission see *Re Bolivia Republic Exploration Syndicate Ltd* supra. A company cannot lawfully pay commission to a director for placing shares unless the director has thereby performed such special services as are authorised by the articles to be the subject of remuneration: *Ural Caspian Oil Corpn Ltd v Hume-Schweder* (1913) Times, 31 July. For a clause in articles authorising the payment of commissions see the Companies (Tables A to F) Regulations 1985, SI 1985/805, Schedule, Table A art 4 (amended by SI 1985/1052). As to Table A generally see para 529 et seq post.

5 Companies Act 1985 s 97(2)(a). Before the Companies Act 1900 s 8(1) (repealed) it was doubtful whether payment of underwriting commission was legal: see *Hilder v Dexter* [1902] AC 474 at 478, HL; and see para 43 note 5 ante. As to payment of brokerage before that Act see *Hilder v Dexter* supra at 478, 479, HL and para 52 note 4 ante.

6 Companies Act 1985 s 97(2)(b). Section 97(2)(b) and s 97(3),(4) (see infra) repealed by the Financial Services Act 1986 s 212(3), Sch 17 Pt I to the following extent:
   (1) in so far as they apply in relation to any investment which is listed or the subject of an application for listing under Pt IV (ss 142–156B (as amended): see para 281 et seq post) (Financial Services Act 1986 (Commencement No 3) Order 1986, SI 1986/2246, art 5, Sch 4);
   (2) in so far they apply to a prospectus offering for subscription, or to any form of application for, units in a body corporate which is a recognised scheme (Financial Services Act 1986 (Commencement) (No 8) Order 1988, SI 1988/740, art 2, Schedule).

7 For the meaning of 'prospectus' see para 105 note 2 ante.

8 For the prescribed form of statement see the Companies (Forms) Regulations 1985, SI 1985/854, reg 4(1), Sch 3, Form 97.

9 Companies Act 1985 s 97(3)(a). See also note 6 supra.

10 Ibid s 97(3)(b). See also note 6 supra.

11 Ibid ss 97(4), 730, Sch 24. See also note 6 supra. For the meaning of 'officer who is in default' and 'the statutory maximum' see para 1161 post.

12 Shares may not be allotted at a discount: see para 187 ante.

13 Companies Act 1985 s 98(1); and see *Banking Service Corpn Ltd v Toronto Finance Corpn Ltd* [1928] AC 333, PC.

14 Companies Act 1985 s 98(2).

15 Ibid s 98(4).

195. Option to take shares at par. In consideration of a person's taking or procuring subscriptions for shares, the company may give him an option to take further shares within a limited period at par without complying with the statutory provisions as to commissions and discounts[1], as such an option does not amount to an application of shares or capital money within those provisions[2].

1 See para 194 ante.
2 *Hilder v Dexter* [1902] AC 474, HL, overruling on this point *Burrows v Matabele Gold Reefs and Estates Co Ltd* [1901] 2 Ch 23, CA.

196. Reconstruction. On a sale of a company's undertaking to persons who agree to form a new company for the repurchase of the undertaking in consideration of shares to be allotted to the members of the selling company, any additional consideration paid by the new company apart from that for the shares is a commission or discount and is accordingly illegal unless the statutory conditions as to commissions are complied with[1].

1 *Booth v New Afrikander Gold Mining Co Ltd* [1903] 1 Ch 295, CA. This was a decision on the Companies Act 1900 s 8 (repealed), under which payment of a commission was authorised only upon an offer of

shares to the public. The provisions of s 8 (repealed) were, however, extended to authorise payment of commission on shares not offered to the public by the Companies Act 1907 s 8(2) (repealed). See also *Barrow v Paringa Mines (1909) Ltd* [1909] 2 Ch 658.

197. Commission to allot at discount. Transactions amounting to the illegal allotment of shares at a discount under colour of compliance with the statutory requirements as to commissions are not allowed[1].

1 *Keatinge v Paringa Consolidated Mines Ltd* (1902) 18 TLR 266. As to the allotment of shares at a discount see para 187 ante.

198. Underwriting letters. The construction of each underwriting letter depends upon its individual terms and differs widely in different cases[1]. The underwriting letter is usually signed on the terms of draft offer documents, and it is the practice to provide that the contract to underwrite will hold good notwithstanding variations between the draft offer documents and the offer documents as finally published. An alteration in the terms of the offer documents which substantially alters the risk is not such a variation[2]. Generally, the letter is not in itself a contract, but a mere offer[3], which, like other offers, requires acceptance before a contract comes into existence[4]; but the offer, if accepted within a reasonable time, need not be accepted before the result of the proposed issue of shares is known[5]. There may be acceptance without writing[6], and notice of acceptance may be inferred[7], or the writer of the letter may be estopped from setting up want of acceptance[8]. An underwriting letter authorising some other person to apply for shares, for a valuable consideration, if the offer is accepted by him, constitutes an authority coupled with an interest and is irrevocable[9]. If the underwriting letter requires the writer to subscribe if and when called upon, the request for him to subscribe is a condition precedent to his liability[10]. The contract is not personal[11], and the legal personal representatives of the underwriter may be sued on it[12].

1 *Re Consort Deep Level Gold Mines, ex p Stark* [1897] 1 Ch 575 at 593, CA.
2 *Warner International and Overseas Engineering Co Ltd v Kilburn, Brown & Co* (1914) 84 LJKB 365, CA; but see *Re Greater Britain Insurance Corpn Ltd, ex p Brockdorff* (1920) 124 LT 194, CA.
3 As eg in *Re Consort Deep Level Gold Mines Ltd, ex p Stark* [1897] 1 Ch 575, CA.
4 See CONTRACT vol 9 para 245 et seq.
5 *Hindley's Case* [1896] 2 Ch 121 at 135, CA; *Re Consort Deep Level Gold Mines Ltd, ex p Stark* [1897] 1 Ch 575 at 592, CA.
6 *North Charterland Exploration Co Ltd v Riordan* (1897) 13 TLR 281, CA. As to the withdrawal of an offer to take shares before acceptance see para 442 post and CONTRACT vol 9 para 239.
7 *Re Bultfontein Sun Diamond Mine Ltd* (1897) 75 LT 669, CA; *Premier Briquette Co v Gray* 1922 SC 329; but see *Re Consort Deep Level Gold Mines Ltd, ex p Stark* [1897] 1 Ch 575 at 593, CA.
8 *Re Henry Bentley & Co and Yorkshire Breweries Ltd, ex p Harrison* (1893) 69 LT 204, CA; *Re Consort Deep Level Gold Mines Ltd, ex p Stark* [1897] 1 Ch 575 at 592, CA.
9 *Re Hannan's Empress Gold Mining and Development Co, Carmichael's Case* [1896] 2 Ch 643, CA; cf *Re Henry Bentley & Co and Yorkshire Breweries Ltd, ex p Harrison* (1893) 69 LT 204, CA; explained in *Re Consort Deep Level Gold Mines Ltd, ex p Stark* [1897] 1 Ch 575, CA.
10 *Re Harvey's Oyster Co, Ormerod's Case* [1894] 2 Ch 474; *Re Bultfontein Sun Diamond Mine Ltd* (1897) 75 LT 669, CA; *Brussels Palace of Varieties Ltd v Prockter* (1893) 10 TLR 72, CA. A condition precedent to the writer's liability requiring a specified number of shares to be irrevocably applied for by the public is not fulfilled by the allotment of that number to another underwriter: *Boyer Ltd v Edwardes* (1901) 18 TLR 3, CA. The liability of an underwriter under an agreement providing for liability diminishing in accordance with the amount of public subscription for shares may be reduced by 'firm' agreements by other underwriters to take shares: see *Sydney Harbour Collieries Ltd v Earl Grey* (1898) 14 TLR 373, HL.
11 *Re Worthington, ex p Pathé Frères* [1914] 2 KB 299, CA.
12 *Warner Engineering Co Ltd v Brennan* (1913) 30 TLR 191.

199. Sub-underwriting. It is the usual practice for underwriters to enter into contracts with sub-underwriters, under which the latter agree to sub-underwrite a part of the shares for which the underwriters have subscribed and they sign a sub-underwriting letter. A sub-underwriting letter authorising an underwriter to apply for shares, for a valuable consideration, if the offer is accepted by him, constitutes, as in the case of an underwriting letter[1], an authority coupled with an interest, and is irrevocable[2].

1 See para 198 ante.
2 *Re Olympic Fire and General Reinsurance Co Ltd* [1902] 2 Ch 341, CA. It has been held in Scotland that, where the sub-underwriter signs an application form, he cannot repudiate his agreement, after receiving notice of allotment, on the ground that the underwriter did not communicate to him any acceptance of the offer contained in the sub-underwriting letter: *Premier Briquette Co v Gray* 1922 SC 329. As to the right of a sub-underwriter to obtain rescission of his contract to take shares see para 325 post.

200. Brokerage. A company may pay to brokers a reasonable sum by way of brokerage for placing shares[1]. 'Brokers' includes stockbrokers, bankers and the like who exhibit offer documents and send them to their customers, and by whose mediation the customers are induced to subscribe. It does not include anyone who does not carry on a business of this character[2].

1 See the Companies Act 1985 s 98(3) (cited in para 194 ante), saving the power of companies to pay such brokerage as was lawful before the 1985 Act.
2 *Metropolitan Coal Consumers' Association v Scrimgeour* [1895] 2 QB 604, CA (where the articles of association expressly authorised the payment of all brokerages payable in respect of the placing of any shares, and the commission paid to the stockbrokers for placing the shares was only 2.5% on their nominal amount). In this instance, the memorandum of association also expressly authorised the payment of brokerages, but the authority (if necessary at all) is none the better for being in the memorandum: *Metropolitan Coal Consumers' Association v Scrimgeour* supra at 607. Only ordinary brokerage in the regular way of business can be paid: *Metropolitan Coal Consumers' Association v Scrimgeour* supra at 610. Cf *Andreae v Zinc Mines of Great Britain Ltd* [1918] 2 KB 454.

(vi) Increase of Capital

201. Power to increase capital. A company limited by shares or limited by guarantee and having a share capital, if so authorised by its articles, may alter the conditions of its memorandum by increasing its share capital by new shares of such amount as it thinks expedient[1]. Any provision in the articles purporting to fetter the company's power to increase its share capital is void[2], although an agreement outside the articles between shareholders[3] as to how they would exercise voting rights on a resolution to increase the capital would not necessarily be invalid[4].

The power to increase share capital must be exercised by the company in general meeting[5]. On any such increase, there is no reason why the increased capital need be expressed in the same currency as the existing capital, or why the increased capital should be all in the same specific currency[6].

If the company is governed by Table A[7], the increase is made by an ordinary resolution[8] prescribing the amount of increase, and the shares into which it is divided[9]. If there is no authority under the articles to increase capital, the articles may be altered by special resolution[10] so as to give the power[11]. The increased capital may consist of preference shares, provided that this is not inconsistent with rights given by the memorandum of association[12]. The notice convening the meeting to pass the resolution for increase must specify the amount of the proposed increase[13].

1 Companies Act 1985 s 121(1), (2)(a). As to issuing copies of the memorandum embodying alterations see para 101 ante.
2 *Russell v Northern Bank Development Corpn Ltd* [1992] 3 All ER 161, [1992] 1 WLR 588, HL.
3 The company may not be a party to the agreement: *Russell v Northern Bank Development Corpn Ltd* [1992] 3 All ER 161, [1992] 1 WLR 588, HL.
4 *Russell v Northern Bank Development Corpn Ltd* [1992] 3 All ER 161, [1992] 1 WLR 588, HL. See also *Welton v Saffery* [1897] AC 299, HL. As to shareholders' agreements see para 149 ante.
5 Companies Act 1985 s 121(4) (derived from EC Council Directive 77/91 (OJ L26, 31.1.77, p 1) art 25). The provision is capable of being invoked directly by an individual against the State: Cases C-19–C-20/90 *Karella and Karellas v Ministry of Industry, Energy and Technology* [1994] 1 BCLC 774, [1993] 2 CMLR 865, ECJ (the Directive precluded national rules which, in order to ensure the survival and continued operation of particular undertakings, provided for an increase of a company's capital by an administrative act rather than a vote of the shareholders). See also Cases C-134–135/91 *Kerafina v Republic of Greece* [1993] 2 CMLR 277, ECJ. Where the provisions of a Directive appear, as far as their subject matter is concerned, to be unconditional and sufficiently precise, individuals are entitled to invoke them against the State: Case 8/81 *Becker v Finanzamt Münster-Innenstadt* [1982] ECR 53, [1982] 1 CMLR 499, ECJ (cited in para 5 note 4 ante). As to EC Directives generally see para 5 ante.
  The consents of class meetings will not normally be requisite, as such increase does not 'vary' or 'affect' class rights: see *White v Bristol Aeroplane Co Ltd* [1953] Ch 65, [1953] 1 All ER 40, CA; *Re John Smith's Tadcaster Brewery Co Ltd* [1953] Ch 308, [1953] 1 All ER 518, CA. See further para 183 ante.
6 *Re Scandinavian Bank Group plc* [1988] Ch 87, [1987] 2 All ER 70.
7 Ie by the Companies (Tables A to F) Regulations 1985, SI 1985/805, Schedule, Table A (amended by SI 1985/1052). As to Table A generally see para 529 et seq post.
8 As to ordinary resolutions see para 681 post.
9 Companies (Tables A to F) Regulations 1985 Schedule, Table A art 32(a). In other cases the power depends on the articles, which sometimes require the power to be exercised by a special or extraordinary resolution. Before the Companies Act 1929 there was no statutory provision as to the mode in which an increase of capital was to be effected, and in the case of companies governed by the Companies Act 1862 Sch 1, Table A which provided that the directors could effect an increase with the sanction of an extraordinary resolution of the company, it was held that, if the capital was increased without first obtaining the sanction, the irregularity was cured by the passing of subsequent resolutions: see *Sewell's Case* (1868) 3 Ch App 131; *Re London and New York Investment Corpn* [1895] 2 Ch 860. Under the Companies Act 1862 it was held that a company could delegate the power of increasing its capital to its directors: see *Mosely v Koffyfontein Mines Ltd* [1910] 2 Ch 382; revsd on another point sub nom *Koffyfontein Mines Ltd v Mosely* [1911] AC 409, HL. See also note 5 supra.
10 See paras 538, 687 post. For the meaning of 'articles' see para 140 note 2 ante. If the power to increase, consolidate and divide, sub-divide, convert or reconvert is absent from the articles, a single special resolution authorising the particular operation is effective without a previous resolution altering the articles: *Re Bank of Hindustan, China and Japan, Campbell's Case, Hippisley's Case, Alison's Case* (1873) 9 Ch App 1 at 21; *Taylor v Pilsen, Joel and Electric Light Co* (1884) 27 ChD 268; *Re North Cheshire Brewery Co Ltd* (1920) 64 Sol Jo 463. See, however, *Re Metropolitan Cemetery Co* 1934 SC 65 (where the company passed special resolutions to reduce and also to increase its capital and the court, while confirming the former, refused to include a reference to the latter as the company was not authorised by its articles to increase its capital and strict compliance with the Act was necessary).
11 As to alteration of articles see para 538 post.
12 *Andrews v Gas Meter Co* [1897] 1 Ch 361, CA.
13 *MacConnell v E Prill & Co Ltd* [1916] 2 Ch 57.

202. Compliance with articles. Any provisions contained in the articles[1] regulating the offer of the new shares must be complied with and an issue of shares in breach of such provisions will be restrained by the court[2]. Where the articles provide that new shares are to be offered to members[3], and the shares are created in the lifetime of a member of the company who dies before any offer is made, his legal personal representative stands in his shoes as regards the right to an allotment in proportion to his holding[4].

1 The Companies Act 1929 Sch 1, Table A art 35 provided that, subject to any direction to the contrary that might be given by the company in general meeting, all new shares should, before issue, be offered to such persons as at the date of the offer were entitled to receive notices from the company of general

meetings in proportion, as nearly as the circumstances admitted, to the amount of the existing shares to which they were entitled. No comparable provision was included in the Companies Act 1948 Table A, nor, having regard to the Companies Act 1985 s 89, under which in general offers to shareholders must be made on a pre-emptive basis (see para 457 post), is any such provision contained in the Companies (Tables A to F) Regulations 1985, SI 1985/805, Schedule, Table A. A private company may, however, make other provisions: see the Companies Act 1985 s 91(1) and para 459 post.

2 *Gas Meter Co Ltd v Diaphragm and General Leather Co Ltd* (1925) 41 TLR 342.
3 Ie as in the original Table A in the Companies Act 1862 (Sch 1, Table A art 27); but see note 1 supra.
4 *James v Buena Ventura Nitrate Grounds Syndicate Ltd* [1896] 1 Ch 456, CA. Cf the Companies Act 1985 s 90(4): see para 458 post. It is doubtful whether a different mode of allotment from that prescribed by the articles may be sanctioned by a special resolution as to allotment without first altering the articles: *James v Buena Ventura Nitrate Grounds Syndicate Ltd* supra; *Allen v Gold Reefs of West Africa Ltd* [1900] 1 Ch 656 at 677, CA.

203. Notice to registrar. If a company having a share capital, whether or not its shares have been converted into stock[1], increases its share capital beyond the registered capital, it must give the registrar of companies notice of the increase of capital within 15 days after the passing of the resolution authorising the increase and the registrar must record the increase[2]. The notice must include such particulars as may be prescribed[3] with respect to the classes of shares affected and the conditions subject to which the new shares have been or are to be issued[4]. There must be forwarded to the registrar together with the notice a printed copy of the resolution authorising the increase, or a copy of the resolution in some other form approved by the registrar[5]. If default is made in complying with these requirements, the company, and every officer of it who is in default, is liable on summary conviction to a fine not exceeding one-fifth of the statutory maximum and, on conviction after continued contravention, to a daily default fine not exceeding one-fiftieth of the statutory maximum[6].

1 As to the conversion of shares into stock see para 209 post; and as to the official notification of documents making or evidencing alterations in a company's memorandum or articles see para 70 ante.
2 Companies Act 1985 s 123(1). As from 8 December 1973 no fee has been payable.
3 For the prescribed particulars see the Companies (Forms) Regulations 1985, SI 1985/854, reg 4, Sch 3, Form 123 (amended by SI 1987/752) and Sch 4 Pt 1 (amended by SI 1986/2097).
4 Companies Act 1985 s 123(2).
5 Ibid s 123(3).
6 Ibid ss 123(4), 730, Sch 24. For the meaning of 'officer who is in default', 'the statutory maximum' and 'daily default fine' see para 1161 post.

204. Increase by unlimited company. An unlimited company having a share capital need not state the amount of it in its memorandum of association, but must state it in its articles[1], and may increase its share capital by special resolution[2]. An unlimited company having a share capital may, by its resolution for re-registration as a public company[3] or as a limited company[4], increase the nominal amount of its share capital by increasing the nominal amount of each of its shares, but subject to the condition that no part of the increased capital is to be capable of being called up except in the event and for the purpose of the company being wound up[5].

1 See the Companies Act 1985 ss 2(5)(a), 7(2).
2 See the Companies (Tables A to F) Regulations 1985, SI 1985/805, Schedule, Table E art 4(a). As to Table E generally see para 116 note 3 ante and para 530 post.

3 See para 118 ante.
4 See para 126 ante.
5 Companies Act 1985 s 124(a).

(vii) Consolidation of Capital and Sub-division of Shares

205. Power to consolidate capital. A company limited by shares, or a company limited by guarantee and having a share capital, if so authorised by its articles[1], may alter the conditions of its memorandum by consolidating and dividing all or any of its share capital into shares of larger amount than its existing shares[2]. The power must be exercised by the company in general meeting[3]. Consolidation and sub-division[4] may be effected by the same resolution, provided that the result does not involve fractional holdings[5]. If a company is governed by Table A, an ordinary resolution is required[6]. An unlimited company with a share capital may alter the capital clause in its articles by special resolution by consolidating its share capital into shares of a larger amount than its existing shares[7].

1 See para 201 note 9 ante.
2 Companies Act 1985 s 121(1), (2)(b). As to issuing copies of the memorandum embodying alterations see para 101 ante; and as to the consolidation of shares of different classes see para 1456 post.
3 Ibid s 121(4).
4 As to sub-division see para 207 post.
5 *Re North Cheshire Brewery Co Ltd* (1920) 64 Sol Jo 463.
6 See the Companies (Tables A to F) Regulations 1985, SI 1985/805, Schedule, Table A art 32. As to Table A generally see para 529 et seq post.
7 See ibid Schedule, Table E art 4(b). As to Table E generally see para 116 note 3 ante and para 530 post.

206. Notice to registrar of consolidation. If a company having a share capital has consolidated and divided its share capital into shares of larger amount than its existing shares, it must within one month after so doing give notice in the prescribed form[1] to the registrar of companies specifying the shares consolidated and divided[2]. If default is made in complying with this requirement, the company, and every officer of the company who is in default, is liable on summary conviction to a fine not exceeding one-fifth of the statutory maximum and, on conviction after continued contravention, to a daily default fine not exceeding one-fiftieth of the statutory maximum[3].

1 For the prescribed form of notice see the Companies (Forms) Regulations 1985, SI 1985/854, reg 4(1), Sch 3, Form 122 (amended by SI 1987/752).
2 Companies Act 1985 s 122(1)(a). As to the official notification of any document making or evidencing an alteration in a company's memorandum or articles see para 70 ante.
3 Ibid ss 122(2), 730, Sch 24. For the meaning of 'officer who is in default', 'the statutory maximum' and 'daily default fine' see para 1161 post.

207. Sub-division of shares. A company limited by shares, or a company limited by guarantee and having a share capital, may, if so authorised by its articles[1], alter the conditions of its memorandum by sub-dividing its shares, or any of them, into shares of smaller amount than is fixed by the memorandum, provided that in the sub-division the proportion between the amount paid and the amount, if any, unpaid on each reduced share is the same as it was in the case of the share from which the reduced share is derived[2]. The power must be exercised by the company in general meeting[3]. If a company is governed by Table A, an ordinary resolution is required[4]. An unlimited company with a share capital may by special resolution alter the capital clause in its articles by sub-dividing its shares into shares of smaller amounts than its existing ones[5].

The power to sub-divide cannot be given by the memorandum of association; but, where the company purports to sub-divide without having the power, a transfer of sub-divided shares, if they can be identified, is effectual to pass the original shares[6].

1 See para 201 note 9 ante.
2 Companies Act 1985 s 121(1), (2)(d), (3). As to the issue of copies of the memorandum embodying alterations see para 101 ante.
3 Ibid s 121(4). The consent of class meetings may also be required: see para 183 ante.
4 See the Companies (Tables A to F) Regulations 1985, SI 1985/805, Schedule, Table A art 32(c). As to dealing with fractions of shares which may result see art 33. As to Table A generally see para 529 et seq post.
5 See ibid Schedule, Table E art 4(c). As to Table E generally see para 116 note 3 ante and para 530 post.
6 *Re Financial Corpn, Feiling's and Rimington's Case, King's Case, Holmes's, Pritchard's, and Adams's Cases* (1867) 2 Ch App 714.

208. Notice to registrar of sub-division. If a company having a share capital has sub-divided its shares or any of them, it must within one month after so doing give notice in the prescribed form[1] to the registrar of companies specifying the shares sub-divided[2]. If default is made in complying with this requirement, the company, and every officer of the company who is in default, is liable on summary conviction to a fine not exceeding one-fifth of the statutory maximum and, on conviction after continued contravention, to a daily default fine not exceeding one-fiftieth of the statutory maximum[3].

1 For the prescribed form of notice see the Companies (Forms) Regulations 1985, SI 1985/854, reg 4(1), Sch 3, Form 122 (amended by SI 1987/752).
2 Companies Act 1985 s 122(1)(d). As to the official notification of any document making or evidencing an alteration in a company's memorandum or articles see para 70 ante.
3 Ibid ss 122(2), 730, Sch 24. For the meaning of 'officer who is in default', 'the statutory maximum' and 'daily default fine' see para 1161 post.

(viii) Conversion of Shares into Stock and Reconversion

209. Power of conversion and reconversion. A company limited by shares, or a company limited by guarantee and having a share capital[1], may, if so authorised by its articles, alter the conditions of its memorandum by converting all or any of its paid-up shares[2] into stock and, if so desired, subsequently reconverting that stock into paid-up shares of any denomination[3]. Stock cannot properly be created anew, but comes into existence by conversion of paid-up shares[4]. The power must be exercised in general meeting[5].

If a company having a share capital has converted any shares into stock or reconverted stock into shares, it must within one month after so doing give notice in the prescribed form[6] to the registrar of companies specifying the shares converted or stock reconverted, as the case may be[7]. If default is made in complying with this provision, the company, and every officer of the company who is in default, is liable on summary conviction to a fine not exceeding one-fifth of the statutory maximum and, on conviction after continued contravention, to a daily default fine not exceeding one-fiftieth of the statutory maximum[8].

1 See para 201 note 9 ante.
2 For these purposes, 'share' means share in the capital of a company and includes stock except where a distinction between stock and shares is express or implied: Companies Act 1985 s 744. For the meaning of 'stock' see para 210 post.
3 Ibid s 121(1), (2)(c).
4 *Re Home and Foreign Investment and Agency Co Ltd* [1912] 1 Ch 72. Where, however, a company which had power to convert its shares into stock issued stock direct without first issuing shares and converting them, it was held that this was irregular, but as a considerable time had elapsed since the issue, the irregularity was cured by lapse of time: *Re Home and Foreign Investment and Agency Co Ltd* supra.
5 Companies Act 1985 s 121(4).
6 For the prescribed form of notice see the Companies (Forms) Regulations 1985, SI 1985/854, reg 4(1), Sch 3, Form 122 (amended by SI 1987/752).
7 Companies Act 1985 s 122(1)(b),(c). As to the official notification of any document making or evidencing an alteration in a company's memorandum or articles see para 70 ante.
8 Ibid ss 122(2), 730, Sch 24. For the meaning of 'officer who is in default', 'the statutory maximum' and 'daily default fine' see para 1161 post.

210. Meaning of 'stock'. Stock is the aggregate of fully paid shares legally consolidated, portions of which aggregate may be transferred or split up into fractions of any amount, without regard to the original nominal amount of the shares[1]. Where the amount of stock standing in the name of the holder on 15 February 1971 was not a whole number of pounds, so much of the amount as was in shillings or pence was then treated as the corresponding amount[2] in decimal currency[3].

1 *Morrice v Aylmer* (1875) LR 7 HL 717 at 724.
2 Ie the corresponding amount calculated in accordance with the Decimal Currency Act 1969 Sch 1.
3 Ibid ss 8(3), 16(1). If previously transferable in multiples of one penny, after 15 February 1971 such stock is transferable in multiples of one new penny, and any prospectus or other document is to be read as so referring: s 8(1), (2).

211. Effect of conversion. The normal provision contained in articles in relation to stock is that the holders of stock are to have, according to the amount of the stock held by them, the same rights, privileges and advantages as regards dividends, voting at meetings and other matters as if they held the shares from which the stock arose, but no such privilege or advantage (except participation in the dividends and profits of the company and in the assets on winding up) is conferred by an amount of stock which would not, if existing in shares, have conferred that privilege or advantage.

Where the company has converted any of its shares into stock and given notice of the conversion of shares into stock to the registrar of companies, the register of members must show the amount and class of stock held by each member, instead of the amount of shares and the particulars relating to shares required by the Companies Act 1985[1].

1 Companies Act 1985 s 352(3)(b). Similarly, the list of members to be forwarded to the registrar under s 364A (as substituted) (see para 1064 post) must state the amount of stock held by each of the existing members instead of the number or nominal value of shares: see s 364A(8) (as substituted) and para 1064 post.

212. Stock warrants to bearer. Warrants to bearer may be issued in respect of stock[1].

1 *Pilkington v United Railways of the Havana and Regla Warehouses Ltd* [1930] 2 Ch 108. For the provisions as to share warrants which apply equally to stock warrants see further para 493 post. There are now no exchange control restrictions on the issue of such warrants, the Exchange Control Act 1947 having been repealed by the Finance Act 1987 s 72(7), Sch 16 Pt XI.

(ix) Maintenance of Capital

213. Duty of directors on serious loss of capital. Where the net assets of a public company[1] are half or less of its called-up share capital[2], the directors must, not later than 28 days from the earliest day on which that fact is known to a director of the company, duly convene an extraordinary general meeting[3] of the company for a date not later than 56 days from that day for the purpose of considering whether any, and if so what, steps should be taken to deal with the situation[4]. If there is a failure to convene such an extraordinary general meeting, each of the directors of the company who knowingly and wilfully authorises or permits the failure, or, after the expiry of the period during which that meeting should have been convened, knowingly and wilfully authorises or permits the failure to continue, is liable on conviction on indictment to a fine, or on summary conviction to a fine not exceeding the statutory maximum[5].

Nothing in these provisions authorises the consideration, at a meeting so convened, of any matter which could not have been considered at that meeting apart from these provisions[6].

1 For the meaning of 'public company' see para 82 ante.
2 For the meaning of 'called-up share capital' see para 174 ante.
3 For the meaning of 'extraordinary general meeting' see para 657 post.
4 Companies Act 1985 s 142(1).
5 Ibid ss 142(2), 730, Sch 24. For the meaning of 'the statutory maximum' see para 1161 post.
6 Ibid s 142(3).

214. Charges of public companies on own shares. A lien or other charge of a public company[1] on its own shares, whether taken expressly or otherwise, except a charge permitted by any of the following provisions, is void[2].

In the case of any description of company, a charge on its own shares is permitted if the shares are not fully paid and the charge is for any amount payable in respect of the shares[3]. In the case of a company whose ordinary business includes the lending of money, or consists of the provision of credit or the bailment (in Scotland, hiring) of goods under a hire purchase agreement[4], or both, a charge of the company on its own shares is permitted, whether the shares are fully paid or not, if it arises in connection with a transaction entered into by the company in the ordinary course of its business[5]. In the case of a company which is re-registered[6] or, having been formed otherwise than under companies legislation, is registered[7] under the Companies Act 1985 as a public company, a charge on its own shares is permitted if the charge was in existence immediately before the company's application for re-registration or, as the case may be, registration[8].

1 For the meaning of 'public company' see para 82 ante.
2 Companies Act 1985 s 150(1). As to shares of an old public company held by or charged to itself see the Companies Consolidation (Consequential Provisions) Act 1985 s 6(3) and para 137 ante. For the meaning of 'old public company' see para 132 ante.
3 Companies Act 1985 s 150(2).
4 For these purposes, 'hire-purchase agreement' has the same meaning as in the Consumer Credit Act 1974 (see HIRE PURCHASE vol 22 para 37): Companies Act 1985 s 744.
5 Ibid s 150(3).
6 As to re-registration as a public company see para 118 et seq ante.
7 Ie under the Companies Act 1985 s 680 (as amended): see paras 24, 25 ante.
8 Ibid s 150(4). Section 150(4) does not apply in the case of such a company as is referred to in the Companies Consolidation (Consequential Provisions) Act 1985 s 6(3) (see para 137 ante): Companies Act 1985 s 150(4).

(x) Reduction of Capital

A. IN GENERAL

215. Reduction of capital. In speaking of reduction of capital the word 'capital' includes nominal share capital, whether issued or unissued, and, if issued, whether fully paid or not[1]. A reduction of unissued capital may be combined with a reduction of issued capital, and issued capital may be reduced, whether fully paid or not[2].

> 1 For the meaning of 'share' see para 209 note 2 ante. A company may reduce its stock: see *Re Allsopp & Sons Ltd* (1903) 51 WR 644, CA. For a form of minute see *Re House Property and Investment Co Ltd* (1912) 106 LT 949. The redemption of redeemable shares in accordance with the Companies Act 1985 s 160 (see para 220 post) does not reduce the amount of the company's authorised share capital: s 160(4). A reduction of capital will normally amount to a disposal of an interest in the shares affected for the purpose of capital gains tax: see the Taxation of Chargeable Gains Act 1992 ss 122, 126–129 and CAPITAL GAINS TAXATION vol 5(1) (Reissue) paras 243, 252.
>
> 2 *Re Anglo-French Exploration Co* [1902] 2 Ch 845 at 852; *Re Ormiston Coal Co* 1949 SC 516. The Companies Act 1862 (repealed) did not expressly provide for any reduction of capital, but Sch 1, Table A arts 17–22 enabled the directors of companies regulated by the Table to forfeit shares on non-payment of calls. This forfeiture worked a reduction of capital not provided for in the body of that Act, but, as it had legislative sanction, it was undoubtedly legal, and similar provisions in the articles of association of companies which had not adopted Table A were also lawful and effective: *Trevor v Whitworth* (1887) 12 App Cas 409 at 417, HL; *Lock v Queensland Investment and Land Mortgage Co* [1896] AC 461, HL. As to forfeiture see para 522 et seq post.

216. How far sanction of court necessary. Reductions of capital are of two kinds: those which may be effected without the confirmation of the court; and those which may be effected only with such confirmation. Capital may in effect be reduced by forfeiture of shares for non-payment of calls, or by a surrender of shares made in circumstances which would justify a forfeiture[1]; and a company limited by shares may cancel nominal capital which has not been taken or agreed to be taken by any person[2]. With these exceptions, reduction always requires the sanction of the court in the case of a company limited by shares or by guarantee.

> 1 See para 522 et seq post. Capital may also be reduced in effect by the exercise by a private company of its power to purchase or redeem its shares out of capital (see para 232 post) but this scheme is subject to stringent statutory controls and provision is made for objections by members and creditors to the court (see para 237 post).
>
> 2 See para 218 post.

217. Unlimited companies. There is nothing to prevent an unlimited company, whenever registered, from providing by its memorandum and articles for a return of capital to its members[1]; and it may alter the capital clause in its articles by a special resolution reducing its share capital in any way[2].

> 1 *Re Borough Commercial and Building Society* [1893] 2 Ch 242 at 252. If the company has a share capital, the memorandum need not state the amount of it, although the articles must: Companies Act 1985 ss 2(5)(a), 7(2).
>
> 2 See the Companies (Tables A to F) Regulations 1985, SI 1985/805, Schedule, Table E art 4(e). As to Table E generally see para 116 note 3 ante and para 530 post.

218. Cancellation of unissued shares. A company limited by shares, or a company limited by guarantee and having a share capital, if so authorised by its articles[1], may alter the conditions of its memorandum by cancelling shares[2] which, at the date of the passing of the resolution to cancel them, have not been taken or agreed to be taken[3] by any person, and diminishing the amount of its share capital by the amount of the shares so cancelled[4]. The power must be exercised by the company in general meeting[5]. If the company is governed by Table A, an ordinary resolution is required[6].

A cancellation in pursuance of this power does not constitute a reduction of share capital for the purposes of the Companies Act 1985[7], and, therefore, does not require the confirmation of the court[8]. The existence of this power of cancellation does not, however, limit the methods of reducing capital with the confirmation of the court[9], and unissued capital may be so reduced as well as issued capital[10].

If a company having a share capital has cancelled any shares, otherwise than in connection with a reduction with the confirmation of the court[11], it must within one month after so doing give notice in the prescribed form[12] to the registrar of companies specifying the shares cancelled[13]. If default is made in complying with this requirement, the company, and every officer of the company who is in default, is liable on summary conviction to a fine not exceeding one-fifth of the statutory maximum and, on conviction after continued contravention, to a daily default fine not exceeding one-fiftieth of the statutory maximum[14].

1 For the meaning of 'articles' see para 140 note 2 ante. The Companies (Tables A to F) Regulations 1985, SI 1985/805, Schedule, Table A art 32(d) gives power to cancel unissued shares. As to Table A generally see para 529 et seq post.
2 See para 215 note 1 ante.
3 A company would only be prevented from cancelling shares where a person has entered into a contract to take the shares in question. Where a person has unilaterally consented to taking shares, the shares have not been 'agreed to be taken' for these purposes: *Re Swindon Town Football Co Ltd* [1990] BCLC 467 at 470.
4 Companies Act 1985 s 121(2)(e).
5 Ibid s 121(4).
6 Companies (Tables A to F) Regulations 1985 Schedule, Table A art 32.
7 Companies Act 1985 s 121(5).
8 *Re Anglo-French Exploration Co* [1902] 2 Ch 845 at 852. If, in addition to a reduction, unissued shares are to be sub-divided and cancelled, the cancellation should be effected as part of the process of reduction rather than separately under the Companies Act 1985 s 121: *Re Castiglione, Erskine & Co Ltd* [1958] 2 All ER 455, [1958] 1 WLR 688.
9 Ie under the Companies Act 1985 s 135: see para 241 post.
10 *Re Ormiston Coal Co* 1949 SC 516.
11 See para 241 post.
12 For the prescribed form of notice see the Companies (Forms) Regulations 1985, SI 1985/854, reg 4(1), Sch 3, Form 122 (amended by SI 1987/752).
13 Companies Act 1985 s 122(1)(f). As to the official notification of any documents making or evidencing an alteration in a company's memorandum or articles see para 70 ante.
14 Ibid ss 122(2), 730, Sch 24. For the meaning of 'officer who is in default', 'the statutory maximum' and 'daily default fine' see para 1161 post.

B. REDEEMABLE SHARES; PURCHASE BY A COMPANY OF ITS OWN SHARES

(A) *Redemption or Purchase in general*

219. Power to issue redeemable shares. A company limited by shares or limited by guarantee and having a share capital may[1], if authorised to do so by its articles[2], issue shares which are to be redeemed or are liable to be redeemed at the option of the company or the shareholder[3].

The prohibition on a company's acquiring its own shares[4] does not apply to the redemption or purchase of its own shares in accordance with the statutory provisions[5] relating to the purchase and redemption of shares[6]. Non-compliance with these statutory requirements will not be treated as a mere procedural irregularity capable of being waived or dispensed with or validated by unanimous agreement of all members entitled to vote at meetings of the company[7]. Where a scheme is not in accordance with the Companies Act 1985 and so in breach of the prohibition on a company's acquiring its own shares, the purported acquisition will be void and the company will be liable to a fine and every officer of the company who is in default will be liable to imprisonment or a fine[8].

No redeemable shares may be issued at a time when there are no issued shares of the company which are not redeemable[9]. Redeemable shares may not be redeemed unless they are fully paid; and the terms of redemption must provide for payment on redemption[10].

1 Ie subject to the Companies Act 1985 Pt V Ch VII (ss 159–181) (as amended): see para 220 et seq post.
2 Authority is given by the Companies (Tables A to F) Regulations 1985, SI 1985/805, Schedule, Table A art 3. As to Table A generally see para 529 et seq post.
3 Companies Act 1985 s 159(1).
4 Ie ibid s 143(1): see para 362 post.
5 Ie ibid Pt V Ch VII (ss 159–181) (as amended).
6 See ibid s 143(3)(a) and para 362 post.
7 See *Re SH & Co (Realisations) 1990 Ltd* [1993] BCLC 1309 at 1316 (where the court considered the statutory scheme relating to the giving of financial assistance by a company for the purchase of its own shares which is very similar to the scheme governing redemption and purchase of shares); *Precision Dippings Ltd v Precision Dippings Marketing Ltd* [1986] Ch 447 at 456, 457, [1985] 3 WLR 812 at 816, 817, CA (failure to comply with the statutory procedures governing auditors' reports when the company proposed to make a distribution on the basis of qualified accounts). An error which is so insignificant that no one could be thought to be prejudiced by its correction will not, however, invalidate the whole scheme: *Re Willaire Systems plc* [1987] BCLC 67, CA.
8 See the Companies Act 1985 s 143(2) and para 362 post.
9 Ibid s 159(2).
10 Ibid s 159(3). As to the proposed conditions to be satisfied as regards the terms and manner of redemption before redeemable shares may be issued see s 159A (added by the Companies Act 1989 s 133(1), (2)). However, at the date at which this volume states the law no order had been made bringing the Companies Act 1989 s 133(1), (2) into force.

220. Financing etc of redemption. Subject to the provisions set out below[1], and to those relating to private companies redeeming or purchasing their own shares out of capital[2] and to the terms of redemption or purchase enforceable in a winding up[3], redeemable shares may be redeemed only out of distributable profits[4] of the company or out of the proceeds of a fresh issue of shares made for the purposes of the redemption, and any premium payable on redemption must be paid out of distributable profits of the company[5].

If the company redeems any redeemable shares[6] which were issued at a premium, any premium payable on their redemption may be paid out of the proceeds of a fresh issue of shares made for the purpose of the redemption, up to an amount equal to:

(1) the aggregate of the premiums received by the company on the issue of the shares redeemed; or
(2) the current amount of the company's share premium account, including any sum transferred to that account in respect of premiums on the new shares,

whichever is the less; and, in that case, the amount of the company's share premium account[7] must be reduced by a sum corresponding, or by sums in the aggregate corresponding, to the amount of any payment made by virtue of this provision out of the proceeds of the issue of the new shares[8].

Redemption of shares may be effected[9] on such terms and in such manner as may be provided for by the company's articles[10].

Shares redeemed under these provisions are to be treated as cancelled on redemption, and the amount of the company's issued share capital is to be diminished by the nominal value of those shares accordingly; but the redemption of shares by a company is not to be taken as reducing the amount of the company's authorised share capital[11]. Without prejudice to this, where a company is about to redeem shares, it has power to issue shares up to the nominal value of the shares to be redeemed as if those shares had never been issued[12].

On redemption, the company must, within one month after so doing, give notice in the prescribed form[13] to the registrar of companies, specifying the shares redeemed[14]. If default is made in complying with this obligation, the company, and every officer of it who is in default, is liable on summary conviction to a fine not exceeding one-fifth of the statutory maximum and, on conviction after continued contravention, to a daily default fine not exceeding one-fiftieth of the statutory maximum[15].

1 Ie subject to the Companies Act 1985 s 160(2): see infra.
2 Ie subject to ibid s 171: see para 232 post.
3 Ie subject to ibid s 178(4): see para 239 post.
4 For these purposes, 'distributable profits', in relation to the making of any payment by a company, means those profits out of which it could lawfully make a distribution (within the meaning given by ibid s 263(2): see para 701 post) equal in value to the payment: s 181(a). See also *Quayle Munro Ltd, Petitioners* [1994] 1 BCLC 410, Ct of Sess (a special reserve arising from a properly authorised cancellation of a share premium account was a sum available for distribution under the Companies Act 1985 s 263(3) and therefore equally available under s 160(1)(a), even though a share premium account itself could not be so utilised).
5 Ibid s 160(1).
6 See para 241 et seq post.
7 As to the share premium account see para 188 et seq ante.
8 Companies Act 1985 s 160(2). This is one of the limited ways in which the share premium account may be reduced other than under a statutory scheme of reduction under s 135: see para 241 post.
9 Ie subject to ibid ss 162–181 (as amended): see para 221 et seq post.
10 Ibid s 160(3). Section 160(3) is repealed by the Companies Act 1989 s 133(1),(3)(a), and superseded by the Companies Act 1985 s 159A (added by the Companies Act 1989 s 133(1),(2)) (see para 219 note 10 ante), from a day to be appointed. However, at the date at which this volume states the law no order had been made bringing the Companies Act 1989 s 133(1),(2),(3)(a) into force.
11 Companies Act 1985 s 160(4).
12 Ibid s 160(5).
13 For the prescribed form of notice see the Companies (Forms) Regulations 1985, SI 1985/854, reg 4(1), Sch 3, Form 122 (amended by SI 1987/752).
14 Companies Act 1985 s 122(1)(e).
15 Ibid ss 122(2), 730, Sch 24. For the meaning of 'officer who is in default', 'the statutory maximum' and 'daily default fine' see para 1161 post.

221. Transitional cases and savings. Any preference shares issued by a company before 15 June 1982[1] which could but for the repeal by the Companies Act 1981 of the earlier law[2] have been redeemed under that law are subject to redemption in accordance with the current statutory provisions[3].

In a case to which the redeemable share provisions[4] so apply, any premium payable on redemption may, notwithstanding the repeal by the Companies Act 1981 of the earlier law, be paid out of the share premium account instead of out of profits, or partly out of that account and partly out of profits[5].

Any capital redemption reserve fund established before 15 June 1982 by a company for the purposes of the earlier law is to be known as the company's capital redemption reserve and is to be treated as if it had been established as required by the Companies Act 1985[6]; and, accordingly, a reference in any enactment or in the articles of any company, or in any other instrument, to a company's capital redemption reserve fund is to be construed as a reference to the company's capital redemption reserve[7].

1 Ie the date of the coming into force of the Companies Act 1981 s 45 (repealed).
2 Ie the Companies Act 1948 s 58 (repealed): see para 181 note 1 ante.
3 Companies Act 1985 s 180(1). The provisions referred to are Pt V Ch VII (ss 159–181) (as amended).
4 Ie ibid ss 159, 160: see paras 219, 220 ante.
5 Ibid s 180(2). Such payments are, however, subject to Pt V Ch VII (ss 159–181) (as amended) so far as payment is out of profits: s 180(2).
6 Ie by ibid s 170: see para 231 post.
7 Ibid s 180(3).

222. Power of company to purchase own shares. A company limited by shares or limited by guarantee and having a share capital may[1], if authorised to do so by its articles[2], purchase its own shares, including any redeemable shares[3].

A company may not so purchase its shares if as a result of the purchase there would no longer be any member of the company holding shares other than redeemable shares[4].

1 Ie subject to the Companies Act 1985 ss 163–181 (as amended): see para 223 et seq post. As to the need for strict compliance with the statutory requirements see para 219 text and notes 4–8 ante.
2 Authority is given by the Companies (Tables A to F) Regulations 1985, SI 1985/805, Schedule, Table A art 35. As to Table A generally see para 529 et seq post.
3 Companies Act 1985 s 162(1). Section 159 (see para 219 ante), s 160 (see para 220 ante) and s 161 (repealed) apply to the purchase by a company of its own shares under s 162 of its own shares as they apply to the redemption of redeemable shares, save that the terms and manner of purchase need not be determined by the articles as required by s 160(3): s 162(2).
4 Ibid s 162(3).

223. Meaning of 'off-market' and 'market' purchase. A purchase by a company of its own shares is 'off-market' if the shares either:
(1) are purchased otherwise than on a recognised investment exchange[1]; or
(2) are purchased on a recognised investment exchange but are not subject to a marketing arrangement on that investment exchange[2].
For this purpose, a company's shares are subject to a marketing arrangement on a recognised investment exchange if either:
(a) they are listed under Part IV of the Financial Services Act 1986[3]; or
(b) the company has been afforded facilities for dealings in those shares to take place on that investment exchange without prior permission for individual transactions from the authority governing that investment exchange and without limit as to the time during which those facilities are to be available[4].
A purchase by a company of its own shares is a 'market purchase' if it is a purchase made on a recognised investment exchange, other than a purchase which is an off-market purchase by virtue of head (2) above[5].

1 For these purposes, 'recognised investment exchange' means a body (other than an overseas investment exchange) declared by an order of the Secretary of State for the time being in force to be a recognised investment exchange for the purposes of the Financial Services Act 1986 (see MONEY): Companies Act 1985 s 163(4) (added by the Financial Services Act 1986 s 212(2), Sch 16 para 17(d)); Financial Services

Act 1986 s 207(1). 'Overseas investment exchange' means a recognised investment exchange in the case of which the recognition order was made by virtue of s 40 (see MONEY): s 207(1).

2 Companies Act 1985 s 163(1) (amended by the Financial Services Act 1986 Sch 16 para 17(a), (b)).

3 Ie the Financial Services Act 1986 Pt IV (ss 142–156B) (as amended) (official listing of securities: see para 281 et seq post).

4 Companies Act 1985 s 163(2) (amended by the Financial Services Act 1986 Sch 16 para 17(c)).

5 Companies Act 1985 s 163(3) (amended by the Financial Services Act 1986 Sch 16 para 17(a)).

224. Authority for off-market purchase. A company may only make an off-market purchase[1] of its own shares in pursuance of a contract approved in advance in accordance with the relevant statutory provisions[2].

The terms of the proposed contract must be authorised by a special resolution of the company before the contract is entered into[3]. In the case of a public company, the authority conferred by the resolution must specify a date on which the authority is to expire; and in a resolution conferring or renewing authority that date must not be later than 18 months after that on which the resolution is passed[4].

Subject to the above provision[5], the authority may be varied, revoked, or from time to time renewed, by special resolution of the company[6]. A special resolution to confer, vary, revoke or renew authority is, however, not effective if any member of the company holding shares to which the resolution relates exercises the voting rights carried by any of those shares in voting on the resolution and the resolution would not have been passed if he had not done so[7]. Such a resolution is not effective unless (if the proposed contract is in writing) a copy of the contract or (if not) a written memorandum of its terms[8] is available for inspection by members of the company both at the company's registered office for not less than 15 days ending with the date of the meeting at which the resolution is passed, and at the meeting itself[9].

A company may agree to a variation of an existing contract so approved, but only if the variation is authorised by a special resolution of the company before it is agreed to; and the above provisions[10] apply to the authority for a proposed variation as they apply to the authority for a proposed contract, save that a copy of the original contract or (as the case may require) a memorandum of its terms, together with any variations previously made, must also be so available for inspection[11].

1 For the meaning of 'off-market purchase' see para 223 ante.

2 Companies Act 1985 s 164(1). The relevant statutory provisions are s 164 (see infra) or s 165 (see para 225 post).

3 Ibid s 164(2). A written resolution is not effective if any of the requirements of s 381A(7), Sch 15A para 5 (as added) is not complied with: Sch 15A para 2(2) (added by the Companies Act 1989 s 114(1)). For these purposes, a 'written resolution' means a resolution agreed to, or proposed to be agreed to, in accordance with the Companies Act 1985 s 381A (as added): Sch 15A para 2(1)(a) (added by the Companies Act 1989 s 114(1)).

The following adaptations have effect in relation to a written resolution (1) conferring authority to make an off-market purchase of the company's own shares under the Companies Act 1985 s 164(2); (2) conferring authority to vary a contract for an off-market purchase of the company's own shares under s 164(7) (see infra); or (3) varying, revoking or renewing any such authority under s 164(3) (see infra): Sch 15A para 5(1) (added by the Companies Act 1989 s 114(1)). The Companies Act 1985 s 164(5) (see infra) does not apply; but, for the purposes of s 381A(1) (as added) (see para 697 post), a member holding shares to which the resolution relates is not regarded as a member who would be entitled to attend and vote: Sch 15A para 5(2) (added by the Companies Act 1989 s 114(1)). The Companies Act 1985 s 164(6) (see infra) does not apply, but the documents referred to therein and, where s 164(6) applies by virtue of s 164(7) (see infra), the further documents referred to therein must be supplied to each relevant member at or before the time at which the resolution is supplied to him for signature: Sch 15A para 5(3) (added by the Companies Act 1989 s 114(1)). The above adaptations also have effect in relation to a written resolution in relation to which the provisions of the Companies Act 1985 s 164(3)–(7) apply by virtue of s 165(2) (see para 225 post) or s 167(2) (see para 227 post): Sch 15A para 5(4) (added by the Companies

Act 1989 s 114(1)). A 'relevant member' means a member by whom, or on whose behalf, the resolution is required to be signed in accordance with the Companies Act 1985 s 381A (as added): Sch 15A para 2(1)(b) (added by the Companies Act 1989 s 114(1)).

4 Companies Act 1985 s 164(2), (4).

5 Ie subject to ibid s 164(4): see supra.

6 Ibid s 164(2), (3). See also note 3 supra.

7 Ibid s 164(2), (5). For this purpose: (1) a member who holds shares to which the resolution relates is regarded as exercising the voting rights carried by those shares not only if he votes in respect of them on a poll on the question whether the resolution shall be passed, but also if he votes on the resolution otherwise than on a poll; (2) notwithstanding anything in the company's articles, any member of the company may demand a poll on that question; and (3) a vote and a demand for a poll by a person as proxy for a member are the same respectively as a vote and a demand by the member: s 164(2), (5).

8 A memorandum of contract terms so made available must include the names of any members holding shares to which the contract relates; and a copy of the contract so made available must have annexed to it a written memorandum specifying any such names which do not appear in the contract itself: ibid s 164(2), (6).

9 Ibid s 164(2), (6).

10 Ie ibid s 164(3)–(6): see supra.

11 Ibid s 164(2), (7). See also note 3 supra.

225. Authority for contingent purchase contract. A contingent purchase contract is a contract entered into by a company and relating to any of its shares which does not amount to a contract to purchase those shares, but under which the company may (subject to any conditions) become entitled or obliged to purchase those shares[1]. A company may only make a purchase of its own shares in pursuance of a contingent purchase contract if the contract is approved in advance by a special resolution of the company before the contract is entered into[2].

1 Companies Act 1985 s 165(1).

2 Ibid s 165(2). Section 164(3)–(7) (see para 224 ante) applies to the contract and its terms: s 165(2). As to written resolutions of private companies see para 224 note 3 ante.

226. Authority for market purchase. A company may not make a market purchase[1] of its own shares unless the purchase has first been authorised by the company in general meeting[2]. That authority may be general for that purpose, or limited to the purchase of shares of any particular class or description, and may be unconditional or subject to conditions[3]. The authority must:

(1) specify the maximum number of shares authorised to be acquired;

(2) determine both the maximum and the minimum prices which may be paid for the shares; and

(3) specify a date on which it is to expire[4].

The authority may be varied, revoked or from time to time renewed by the company in general meeting[5]; and, in a resolution to confer or renew authority, the date on which the authority is to expire must not be later than 18 months after that on which the resolution is passed[6].

A company may under these provisions make a purchase of its own shares after the expiry of the time limit imposed to comply with head (3) above, if the contract of purchase was concluded before the authority expired and the terms of the authority permitted the company to make a contract of purchase which would or might be executed wholly or partly after its expiration[7].

A resolution so to confer or vary authority may determine either or both the maximum and minimum prices for purchase by specifying a particular sum, or providing a basis or formula for calculating the amount of the price in question without reference to any person's discretion or opinion[8].

A resolution of a company so conferring, varying, revoking or renewing authority must, within 15 days after it is passed, be forwarded to the registrar of companies[9], and a copy of such resolution must be embodied in or annexed to every copy of the articles issued after the passing of the resolution[10].

1 For the meaning of 'market purchase' see para 223 ante.
2 Companies Act 1985 s 166(1).
3 Ibid s 166(2).
4 Ibid s 166(3).
5 Ie subject to ibid s 166(3): see supra.
6 Ibid s 166(4).
7 Ibid s 166(5).
8 Ibid s 166(6).
9 Ibid ss 166(7), 380(1). As to the penalties for default see para 691 post.
10 Ibid ss 166(7), 380(2). As to the penalties for default see para 692 post.

227. Assignment or release of company's right to purchase own shares. The rights of a company under a contract duly approved[1], or under a contract for a purchase duly authorised[2], are not capable of being assigned[3]. An agreement by a company to release its rights under a contract so approved is void unless the terms of the release agreement are approved in advance by a special resolution[4] of the company before the agreement is entered into[5].

1 Ie under the Companies Act 1985 s 164 (see para 224 ante) or s 165 (see para 225 ante).
2 Ie under ibid s 166: see para 226 ante.
3 Ibid s 167(1).
4 As to special resolutions see para 683 post.
5 Companies Act 1985 s 167(2). Section 164(3)–(7) (see para 224 ante) applies to approval for a proposed release agreement as it applies to authority for a proposed variation of an existing contract: s 167(2). As to written resolutions of private companies see para 224 note 3 ante.

228. Payments apart from purchase price to be made out of distributable profits. A payment made by a company in consideration of:

(1) acquiring any right with respect to the purchase of its own shares in pursuance of an approved contingent purchase contract[1]; or

(2) the variation of an approved contract for off-market purchase[2] or an approved contingent purchase contract; or

(3) the release of any of the company's obligations with respect to the purchase of any of its own shares under either type of contract so approved or under an authorised contract for a market purchase[3],

must be made out of the company's distributable profits[4].

If the above requirements are not satisfied in relation to a contract, then:

(a) in a case within head (1) above, no purchase by the company of its own shares in pursuance of that contract is lawful;

(b) in a case within head (2) above, no such purchase following the variation is lawful[5]; and

(c) in a case within head (3) above, the purported release is void[6].

1 Ie a contract approved under the Companies Act 1985 s 165: see para 225 ante.
2 Ie a contract approved under ibid s 164: see para 224 ante.
3 Ie a contract for a purchase authorised under ibid s 166: see para 226 ante.
4 Ibid s 168(1). For the meaning of 'distributable profits' see para 220 note 4 ante.
5 Ie under ibid Pt V Ch VII (ss 159–181) (as amended).
6 Ibid s 168(2).

229. Disclosure by company of purchase of own shares. Within the period of 28 days beginning with the date on which any of its own shares purchased[1] by a company are delivered to it, the company must deliver to the registrar of companies for registration a return in the prescribed form[2] stating with respect to shares of each class purchased the number and nominal value of those shares and the date on which they were delivered to the company[3]. If default is made in delivering to the registrar any such return, every officer of the company who is in default is liable on conviction on indictment to a fine, or on summary conviction to a fine not exceeding the statutory maximum and, on conviction after continued contravention, to a daily default fine not exceeding one-tenth of the statutory maximum[4].

In the case of a public company[5], the return must also state:

(1) the aggregate amount paid by the company for the shares; and

(2) the maximum and minimum prices paid in respect of shares of each class purchased[6].

Where a company enters into an approved contract for an off-market purchase[7] or an approved contingent purchase contract[8], or an authorised contract for a market purchase[9], the company must keep at its registered office:

(a) if the contract is in writing, a copy of it; and

(b) if not, a memorandum of its terms,

from the conclusion of the contract until the end of the period of ten years beginning with the date on which the purchase of all the shares in pursuance of the contract is completed or, as the case may be, the date on which the contract otherwise determines[10]. If default is made in complying with this obligation, the company, and every officer of it who is in default, is liable on summary conviction to a fine not exceeding one-fifth of the statutory maximum and, on conviction after continued contravention, to a daily default fine not exceeding one-fiftieth of the statutory maximum[11]. The obligation to keep a copy of any contract or, as the case may be, a memorandum of its terms applies to any variation of the contract so long as it applies to the contract[12].

Every copy and memorandum so required to be kept must be open to inspection without charge by any member of the company and, if it is a public company, by any other person[13]. The company[14] must make every copy and memorandum available for such inspection for not less than two hours during the period between 9 am and 5 pm on each business day[15]; and it must permit a person inspecting those documents to copy any information made available for inspection by means of the taking of notes or the transcription of the information[16]. If such an inspection is refused, the company, and every officer of it who is in default, is liable on summary conviction to a fine not exceeding one-fifth of the statutory maximum and, on conviction after continued contravention, to a daily default fine not exceeding one-fiftieth of the statutory maximum[17]; and the court may by order compel an immediate inspection of it[18].

1 Ie under the Companies Act 1985 Pt V Ch VII (ss 159–181) (as amended): see para 219 et seq ante.

2 For the prescribed form of return see the Companies (Forms) Regulations 1985, SI 1985/854, reg 4(1), Sch 3, Form 169 (substituted by SI 1987/752). This return (save in any case in which the shares to which it relates were purchased under a contract entered into before 27 October 1986) is chargeable to stamp duty (see para 513 post): see the Finance Act 1986 s 66(2), (4), (5) (repealed by the Finance Act 1990 s 132, Sch 19 Pt VI from a day to be appointed).

3 Companies Act 1985 s 169(1).

4 Ibid ss 169(6), 730, Sch 24. For the meaning of 'officer who is in default', 'the statutory maximum' and 'daily default fine' see para 1161 post.

5 For the meaning of 'public company' see para 82 ante.

6 Companies Act 1985 s 169(2). Particulars of shares delivered to the company on different dates and under different contracts may be included in a single return to the registrar; and in such a case the amount required to be stated under s 169(2)(a) (see text head (2) supra) is the aggregate amount paid by the company for all the shares to which the return relates: s 169(3).

7 Ie under ibid s 164: see para 224 ante.

8 Ie under ibid s 165: see para 225 ante.

9 Ie under ibid s 166: see para 226 ante.

10 Ibid s 169(4).

11 Ibid ss 169(7), 730, Sch 24.

12 Ibid s 169(9).

13 Ibid s 169(5) (amended by the Companies Act 1989 ss 143(2), 212, Sch 24).

14 For these purposes, 'company' includes a body corporate to which the Companies Act 1985 s 723A (as added) (see para 230 post) is applied by any enactment: Companies (Inspection and Copying of Registers, Indices and Documents) Regulations 1991, SI 1991/1998, reg 2. As to the power to make regulations see para 230 post.

15 Ibid reg 3(1), (2)(a). For these purposes, 'business day' means, in relation to a company subject to any provision of the Companies (Inspection and Copying of Registers, Indices and Documents) Regulations 1991, any day except a Saturday or Sunday, Christmas Day, Good Friday and any other day which is a bank holiday in the part of Great Britain where that company is registered (or, in the case of a company that is a body corporate to which the Companies Act 1985 s 723A (as added) is applied by s 718 (see para 1765 post), the part of Great Britain where its principal office was situated on 5 January 1976 or, if it was incorporated after that date, the part of Great Britain where its principal office was situated immediately after incorporation): Companies (Inspection and Copying of Registers, Indices and Documents) Regulations 1991 reg 2.

16 Ibid reg 3(1), (2)(b). Regulation 3(2)(b) is not, however, to be construed as obliging a company to provide any facilities additional to those provided for the purposes of facilitating inspection: reg 3(3).

17 Companies Act 1985 ss 169(7), 730, Sch 24.

18 Ibid s 169(8).

230. Inspection of contracts, memoranda etc.

The Secretary of State may make provision by regulations as to the obligations of a company which is required by any provision of the Companies Act 1985 to make available for inspection any register, index or document or to provide copies of any such register, index or document, or part of it; and a company which fails to comply with the regulations is deemed to have refused inspection or, as the case may be, to have failed to provide a copy[1].

The regulations may make provision as to the time, duration and manner of inspection, including the circumstances in which and extent to which the copying of information is permitted in the course of inspection[2].

The regulations may define what may be required of the company as regards the nature, extent and manner of extracting or presenting any information for the purposes of inspection or the provision of copies[3].

Where there is power to charge a fee, the regulations may make provision as to the amount of the fee and the basis of its calculation[4].

Such regulations may make different provision for different classes of case[5].

Nothing in any provision of the Companies Act 1985 or in the regulations is to be construed as preventing a company from affording more extensive facilities than are required by the regulations or, where a fee may be charged, from charging a lesser fee than that prescribed or no fee at all[6].

Such regulations must be made by statutory instrument which is subject to annulment in pursuance of a resolution of either House of Parliament[7].

1 Companies Act 1985 s 723A(1) (added by the Companies Act 1989 s 143(1)). In exercise of the power so conferred the Secretary of State made the Companies (Inspection and Copying of Registers, Indices and Documents) Regulations 1991, SI 1991/1998 (see para 229 ante and paras 236, 390, 391, 560, 562, 574, 695, 755, 1294 post) which came into force on 1 November 1991: reg 1.

2 Companies Act 1985 s 723A(2) (added by the Companies Act 1989 s 143(1)).

3 Companies Act 1985 s 723A(3) (added by the Companies Act 1989 s 143(1)).
4 Companies Act 1985 s 723A(4) (added by the Companies Act 1989 s 143(1)).
5 Companies Act 1985 s 723A(5) (added by the Companies Act 1989 s 143(1)).
6 Companies Act 1985 s 723A(6) (added by the Companies Act 1989 s 143(1)).
7 Companies Act 1985 s 723A(7) (added by the Companies Act 1989 s 143(1)).

231. The capital redemption reserve. Where shares of a company are redeemed or purchased wholly out of the company's profits[1], the amount by which the company's issued share capital is diminished[2] on cancellation of the shares redeemed or purchased must be transferred to a reserve, called 'the capital redemption reserve'[3]. If the shares are redeemed or purchased wholly or partly out of the proceeds of a fresh issue and the aggregate amount of those proceeds is less than the aggregate nominal value of the shares redeemed or purchased, the amount of the difference must be transferred to the capital redemption reserve[4]; but this does not apply if the proceeds of the fresh issue are applied by the company in making a redemption or purchase of its own shares in addition to a payment[5] out of capital[6].

The provisions of the Companies Act 1985[7] relating to the reduction of a company's share capital apply as if the capital redemption reserve were paid-up share capital of the company, except that the reserve may be applied by the company in paying up its unissued shares to be allotted to members of the company as fully paid bonus shares[8].

1 Ie under the Companies Act 1985 Pt V Ch VII (ss 159–181) (as amended): see para 219 et seq ante.
2 Ie in accordance with ibid s 160(4): see para 220 ante.
3 Ibid s 170(1).
4 Ibid s 170(2).
5 Ie under ibid s 171: see para 232 post.
6 Ibid s 170(3).
7 Ie ibid Pt V Ch IV (ss 135–141) (as amended): see para 241 et seq post. As to the procedure see para 252 et seq post.
8 Ibid s 170(4). As to bonus shares see para 732 post.

(B) *Redemption or Purchase; Private Companies*

232. Power of private companies to redeem or purchase own shares out of capital. A private company[1] limited by shares or limited by guarantee and having a share capital may[2], if so authorised by its articles, make a payment in respect of the redemption[3] or purchase[4] of its own shares otherwise than out of its distributable profits[5] or the proceeds of a fresh issue of shares[6].

The payment which, if authorised[7], may be made by a company out of capital in respect of the redemption or purchase of its own shares is such an amount as, taken together with any available profits[8] of the company and the proceeds of any fresh issue of shares made for the purposes of the redemption or purchase, is equal to the price of redemption or purchase[9].

If the permissible capital payment for shares redeemed or purchased is less than their nominal amount, the amount of the difference must be transferred to the company's capital redemption reserve[10]; and, if the permissible capital payment is greater than the nominal amount of the shares redeemed or purchased, the amount of any capital redemption reserve, share premium account or fully paid share capital of the company, and any amount representing unrealised profits of the company for the time being standing to the credit of any revaluation reserve[11], may be reduced by a sum not exceeding, or by sums not in the aggregate exceeding, the amount by which the permissible capital payment exceeds the nominal amount of the shares[12]. Where, however, the proceeds of a fresh issue are applied by a company in making any redemption or purchase of its own shares in addition to a payment out of capital under these provisions, the references[13] to the permissible capital payment are to be read as referring to the aggregate of that payment and those proceeds[14].

1 For the meaning of 'private company' see para 82 ante.
2 Ie subject to the Companies Act 1985 ss 171–181 (as amended): see infra and para 233 et seq post. As to the need for strict compliance with the statutory requirements see para 219 text and notes 4–8 ante.
3 Ie under ibid s 160: see para 220 ante.
4 Ie under ibid s 162: see para 222 ante.
5 For the meaning of 'distributable profits' see para 220 note 4 ante.
6 Companies Act 1985 s 171(1). For these purposes, references to payment out of capital are, subject to s 171(6) (see infra), to any payment so made, whether or not it would be regarded apart from s 171 as a payment out of capital: ss 171(2), 181. As to the potential liability to refund the redemption or purchase price if the company is wound up within a year of payment see para 414 post.
7 Ie in accordance with ibid ss 171–181 (as amended).
8 As to available profits see para 233 post.
9 Companies Act 1985 s 171(3). The payment permissible under s 171(3) is referred to in ss 171–181 (as amended) as the permissible capital payment for the shares: ss 171(3), 181.
10 Ibid s 171(4). As to the capital redemption reserve see para 231 ante.
11 Ie a reserve maintained under ibid s 226(3), Sch 4 para 34 (as amended): see para 815 post.
12 Ibid s 171(5).
13 Ie in ibid s 171(4), (5): see supra.
14 Ibid s 171(6).

233. Availability of profits for purpose of redemption or purchase of own shares out of capital. The reference[1] to available profits of a private company is to the company's profits which are available for distribution[2]; but the question whether a company has any profits so available and the amount of any such profits are to be determined for this purpose in accordance with the following provisions, instead of the general provisions[3] normally applicable[4].

That question is to be determined by reference to:

(1) profits, losses, assets and liabilities;
(2) provisions for depreciation or diminution in value of assets or for retentions to meet liabilities or charges[5]; and
(3) share capital and reserves (including undistributable reserves), as stated in the relevant accounts for determining the permissible capital payment[6] for shares[7].

The relevant accounts for this purpose are such accounts, prepared as at any date within the period for determining the amount of the permissible capital payment[8], as are necessary to enable a reasonable judgment to be made as to the amounts of any of the items mentioned in heads (1), (2) and (3) above[9].

For purposes of determining the amount of the permissible capital payment for shares, the amount of the company's available profits, if any, determined in accordance with the above provisions is to be treated as reduced by the amount of any distributions lawfully made[10] by the company after the date of the relevant accounts and before the end of the period for determining the amount of that payment[11].

1 Ie in the Companies Act 1985 s 171(3)(a): see para 232 ante.
2 Ie within the meaning of ibid ss 263–281 (as amended): see para 701 et seq post.
3 Ie ibid ss 270–275 (as amended): see para 707 et seq post.
4 Ibid s 172(1).
5 Ie provisions of any of the kinds mentioned in ibid s 226(3), Sch 4 paras 88, 89: see paras 810 note 4, 832 note 24 respectively post.
6 For the meaning of 'permissible capital payment' see para 232 note 9 ante.

7 Companies Act 1985 s 172(2).
8 For these purposes, references to the period for determining the amount of the permissible capital payment for shares are to the period of three months ending with the date on which the statutory declaration of the directors purporting to specify the amount of that payment is made in accordance with ibid s 173(3) (see para 234 post): s 172(6).
9 Ibid s 172(3).
10 For these purposes, the reference to distributions lawfully made by the company includes (1) financial assistance lawfully given out of distributable profits in a case falling within ibid s 154 (see para 275 post) or s 155 (see para 276 post); (2) any payment lawfully made by the company in respect of the purchase by it of any shares in the company, except a payment lawfully made otherwise than out of distributable profits; and (3) a payment of any description specified in s 168(1) (see para 228 ante) lawfully made by the company: s 172(5). For the meaning of 'distributable profits' see para 220 note 4 ante.
11 Ibid s 172(4).

234. Conditions for payment out of capital. A payment out of capital by a private company for the redemption or purchase of its own shares is not lawful unless certain requirements[1] are satisfied[2]. The payment out of capital must be approved by a special resolution of the company[3].

The company's directors must make a statutory declaration specifying the amount of the permissible capital payment[4] for the shares in question and stating that, having made full inquiry into the affairs and prospects of the company, they have formed the opinion:

(1) as regards its initial situation immediately following the date on which the payment out of capital is proposed to be made, that there will be no grounds on which the company could then be found unable to pay its debts[5]; and

(2) as regards its prospects for the year immediately following that date, that, having regard to their intentions with respect to the management of the company's business during that year and to the amount and character of the financial resources which will in their view be available to the company during that year, the company will be able to continue to carry on business as a going concern (and will accordingly be able to pay its debts as they fall due) throughout that year[6].

The directors' statutory declaration must be in the prescribed form[7] and contain such information with respect to the nature of the company's business as may be prescribed, and must in addition have annexed to it a report addressed to the directors by the company's auditors stating that:

(a) they have inquired into the company's state of affairs; and

(b) the amount specified in the declaration as the permissible capital payment for the shares in question is in their view properly determined in accordance with the relevant statutory provisions[8]; and

(c) they are not aware of anything to indicate that the opinion expressed by the directors in the declaration as to any of the matters mentioned in heads (1) and (2) above is unreasonable in all the circumstances[9].

A director who makes a declaration under these provisions without having reasonable grounds for the opinion expressed in it is liable on conviction on indictment to imprisonment for a term not exceeding two years or a fine, or to both, or on summary conviction to imprisonment for a term not exceeding six months or a fine not exceeding the statutory maximum, or to both[10].

1 Ie the requirements of the Companies Act 1985 ss 173–175 (as amended): see infra and paras 235, 236 post.

2 Ibid s 173(1). Section 173(1) is subject to any order of the court under s 177 (see para 238 post): s 173(1). As to the need for strict compliance with the statutory requirements see para 219 text and notes 4–8 ante.

3 Ibid s 173(2). As to the special procedure necessary for passing such resolutions see para 235 post. A written resolution is not effective if any of the requirements of s 381A(7), Sch 15A para 6 (as added) is not complied with: Sch 15A para 2(2) (added by the Companies Act 1989 s 114(1)). The following adaptations have effect in relation to a written resolution giving approval under the Companies Act 1985 s 173(2): Sch 15A para 6(1) (added by the Companies Act 1989 s 114(1)). The Companies Act 1985 s 174(2) (see para 235 post) does not apply; but, for the purposes of s 381A(1) (as added) (see para 697 post), a member holding shares to which the resolution relates as a member who would be entitled to attend and vote: Sch 15A para 6(2) (added by the Companies Act 1989 s 114(1)). The Companies Act 1985 s 174(4) (see para 235 post) does not apply, but the documents referred to therein must be supplied to each relevant member at or before the time at which the resolution is supplied to him for signature: Sch 15A para 6(3) (added by the Companies Act 1989 s 114(1)). For the meaning of 'written resolution' and 'relevant member' see para 224 note 3 ante.

4 For the meaning of 'permissible capital payment' see para 232 note 9 ante.

5 Companies Act 1985 s 173(3)(a). In forming their opinion for the purposes of s 173(3)(a), the directors must take into account the same liabilities (including prospective and contingent liabilities) as would be relevant under the Insolvency Act 1986 s 122 (winding up by the court: see para 2206 post) to the question whether a company is unable to pay its debts: Companies Act 1985 s 173(4) (amended by the Insolvency Act 1986 s 439(1), Sch 13 Pt I).

6 Companies Act 1985 s 173(3)(b). As to the potential liability of a director who has no reasonable grounds for forming such opinion in the event of the company being wound up within a year from the date of payment see para 414 post.

7 For the prescribed form of statutory declaration see the Companies (Forms) Regulations 1985, SI 1985/854, reg 4(1), Sch 3, Form 173.

8 Ie the Companies Act 1985 ss 171, 172: see paras 232, 233 respectively ante.

9 Ibid s 173(5).

10 Ibid ss 173(6), 730, Sch 24. For the meaning of 'the statutory maximum' see para 1161 post.

235. Procedure for special resolution sanctioning payment out of capital.

The resolution required[1] to sanction payment out of a company's capital for the purchase of its own shares must be passed on, or within the week immediately following, the date on which the directors make the required statutory declaration[2]; and the payment out of capital must be made no earlier than five nor more than seven weeks after the date of the resolution[3].

The resolution is ineffective if any member of the company holding shares to which the resolution relates exercises the voting rights carried by any of those shares in voting on the resolution and the resolution would not have been passed if he had not done so[4]. For these purposes, a member who holds such shares is to be regarded as exercising the voting rights carried by them in voting on the resolution not only if he votes in respect of them on a poll on the question whether the resolution shall be passed, but also if he votes on the resolution otherwise than on a poll; and, notwithstanding anything in a company's articles, any member of the company may demand a poll on that question[5]. The resolution is also ineffective unless the required statutory declaration and auditors' report[6] are available for inspection by members of the company at the meeting at which the resolution is passed[7].

1 Ie by the Companies Act 1985 s 173 (as amended): see para 234 ante.

2 Ie under ibid s 173(3): see para 234 ante.

3 Ibid s 174(1).

4 Ibid s 174(2). As to written resolutions of private companies see para 234 note 3 ante.

5 Ibid s 174(3). As to the right to demand a poll generally see para 672 post. For these purposes, a vote and demand for a poll by a person as proxy for a member are the same (respectively) as a vote and demand by the member: s 174(5).

6 Ie required by ibid s 173 (as amended): see para 234 ante.

7 Ibid s 174(4). As to written resolutions of private companies see para 234 note 3 ante.

236. Publicity for proposed payment out of capital. Within the week immediately following the date of the resolution for payment out of capital[1] the company must cause to be published in the Gazette[2] a notice:

(1) stating that the company has approved a payment out of capital for the purpose of acquiring its own shares by redemption or purchase or both (as the case may be);

(2) specifying the amount of the permissible capital payment[3] for the shares in question and the date of the special resolution[4];

(3) stating that the required statutory declaration of the directors and the auditors' report[5] are available for inspection at the company's registered office; and

(4) stating that any creditor of the company may at any time within the five weeks immediately following the date of the resolution for payment out of capital apply to the court[6] for an order prohibiting the payment[7].

Within the week immediately following the date of the resolution the company must also either cause a notice to the same effect to be published in an appropriate national newspaper[8] or give notice in writing to that effect to each of its creditors[9].

Not later than the first notice date[10] the company must deliver to the registrar of companies a copy of the required statutory declaration of the directors and of the auditors' report[11]. The statutory declaration and auditors' report must be kept at the company's registered office throughout the period beginning with the first notice date and ending five weeks after the date of the resolution for payment out of capital, and must be open to the inspection of any member or creditor of the company without charge[12]. The company[13] must make the statutory declaration and auditors' report available for such inspection for not less than two hours during the period between 9 am and 5 pm on each business day[14]; and it must permit a person inspecting those documents to copy any information made available for inspection by means of the taking of notes or the transcription of the information[15]. If an inspection so required is refused, the company, and every officer of it who is in default, is liable on summary conviction to a fine not exceeding one-fifth of the statutory maximum and, on conviction after continued contravention, to a daily default fine not exceeding one-fiftieth of the statutory maximum[16]; and the court may by order compel an immediate inspection of the declaration or report in question[17].

1 Ie the resolution required by the Companies Act 1985 s 173 (as amended): see para 234 ante.

2 For the meaning of 'the Gazette' see para 70 note 1 ante.

3 For the meaning of 'permissible capital payment' see para 232 note 9 ante.

4 Ie under the Companies Act 1985 s 173 (as amended).

5 Ie required by ibid s 173 (as amended).

6 Ie under ibid s 176: see para 237 post.

7 Ibid s 175(1).

8 For these purposes, 'an appropriate national newspaper' means a newspaper circulating throughout England and Wales in the case of a company registered in England and Wales (or throughout Scotland, in the case of a company registered in Scotland): ibid s 175(3).

9 Ibid s 175(2).

10 For these purposes, references to the first notice date are to the day on which the company first publishes the notice required by ibid s 175(1) (see supra) or first publishes or gives the notice required by s 175(2), whichever is the earlier: s 175(4).

11 Ibid s 175(5).

12 Ibid s 175(6) (amended by the Companies Act 1989 ss 143(3), 212, Sch 24).

13 For the meaning of 'company' see para 229 note 14 ante.
14 Companies (Inspection and Copying of Registers, Indices and Documents) Regulations 1991, SI 1991/1998, reg 3(1), (2)(a). For the meaning of 'business day' see para 229 note 15 ante. As to the power to make regulations see para 230 ante.
15 Ibid reg 3(1), (2)(b). Regulation 3(2)(b) is not, however, to be construed as obliging a company to provide any facilities additional to those provided for the purposes of facilitating inspection: reg 3(3).
16 Companies Act 1985 ss 175(7), 730, Sch 24. For the meaning of 'officer who is in default', 'the statutory maximum' and 'daily default fine' see para 1161 post.
17 Ibid s 175(8).

237. Objections by company's members or creditors. Where a private company passes a special resolution[1] approving[2] any payment out of capital for the redemption or purchase of any of its shares, any member of the company other than one who consented to or voted in favour of the resolution, and any creditor of the company, may within five weeks of the date on which the resolution was passed apply to the court for cancellation of the resolution[3]. The application may be made on behalf of the persons entitled to make it by such one or more of their number as they may appoint in writing for the purpose[4].

If such an application is made, the company must forthwith give notice in the prescribed form[5] of that fact to the registrar of companies; and, within 15 days from the making of any order of the court on the hearing of the application, or such longer period as the court may by order direct, the company must deliver an office copy of the order to the registrar[6]. A company which fails to comply with this obligation, and any officer of it who is in default, is liable on summary conviction to a fine not exceeding one-fifth of the statutory maximum and, on conviction after continued contravention, to a daily default fine not exceeding one-fiftieth of the statutory maximum[7].

1 Ie under the Companies Act 1985 s 173 (as amended): see para 234 ante.
2 Ie for the purposes of ibid Pt V Ch VII (ss 159–181) (as amended).
3 Ibid s 176(1). Such an application is made by petition: RSC Ord 102 r 4(1)(k).
4 Companies Act 1985 s 176(2).
5 For the prescribed form of notice see the Companies (Forms) Regulations 1985, SI 1985/854, reg 4(1), Sch 3, Form 176 (amended by SI 1987/752).
6 Companies Act 1985 s 176(3).
7 Ibid ss 176(4), 730, Sch 24. For the meaning of 'officer who is in default', 'the statutory maximum' and 'daily default fine' see para 1161 post.

238. Powers of court on application. On the hearing of an application for cancellation of a resolution approving a private company's purchase of its own shares[1], the court may, if it thinks fit, adjourn the proceedings in order that an arrangement may be made to the court's satisfaction for the purchase of the interests of dissentient members or for the protection of dissentient creditors, as the case may be; and the court may give such directions and make such orders as it thinks expedient for facilitating or carrying into effect any such arrangement[2]. Without prejudice to such powers, the court must make an order on such terms and conditions as it thinks fit either confirming or cancelling the resolution; and, if the court confirms the resolution, it may in particular by order alter or extend any date or period of time specified in the resolution or in any relevant statutory provision[3] which applies to the redemption or purchase of shares to which the resolution refers[4].

The court's order may, if the court thinks fit, provide for the purchase by the company of the shares of any of its members and for the reduction accordingly of the company's capital, and may make such alterations in the company's memorandum and articles as may be required in consequence of that provision[5]. If the court's order requires the company not to make any, or any specified, alteration in its memorandum or articles, the company has not then power without leave of the court to make any such alteration in breach of the requirement[6]. An alteration in the memorandum or articles made by virtue of such an order, if not made by resolution of the company, is of the same effect as if duly made by resolution; and the Companies Act 1985 applies accordingly to the memorandum or articles as so altered[7].

1 Ie an application under the Companies Act 1985 s 176: see para 237 ante.
2 Ibid s 177(1).
3 Ie any provision of ibid Pt V Ch VII (ss 159–181) (as amended).
4 Ibid s 177(2).
5 Ibid s 177(3).
6 Ibid s 177(4). As to the power to alter the memorandum and articles generally see para 99 ante.
7 Ibid s 177(5).

239. Effect of company's failure to redeem or purchase. Where a company has, on or after 15 June 1982[1], issued shares on terms that they are or are liable to be redeemed, or has agreed to purchase any of its own shares, the company is not liable in damages in respect of[2] any failure on its part to redeem or purchase any of the shares[3]. The above provision is without prejudice to any right of the holder of the shares other than his right to sue the company for damages in respect of its failure; but the court must not grant an order for specific performance of the terms of redemption or purchase if the company shows that it is unable to meet the costs of redeeming or purchasing the shares in question out of distributable profits[4].

If the company is wound up and at the commencement of the winding up any of the shares have not been redeemed or purchased, the terms of redemption or purchase may be enforced against the company; and, when shares are so redeemed or purchased, they are treated as cancelled[5]. There are to be paid in priority to any amount which the company is so liable to pay in respect of any shares:

(1) all other debts and liabilities of the company, other than any due to members in their character as such;

(2) if other shares carry rights, whether as to capital or as to income, which are preferred to the rights as to capital attaching to the first-mentioned shares, any amount due in satisfaction of those preferred rights;

but, subject to that, any such amount is to be paid in priority to any amounts due to members in satisfaction of their rights, whether as to capital or income, as members[6].

1 Ie the date of the coming into force of the relevant provisions of the Companies Act 1981 (repealed).
2 This precludes the recovery, by the counterparty to the transaction, of damages directly flowing from the failure to redeem or purchase but not the recovery of damages by a third party for breach of contract, though the measure of damages for that breach may well be the failure to redeem or purchase: *British and Commonwealth Holdings plc v Barclays Bank plc* [1996] 1 All ER 381, [1996] 1 WLR 1, CA. This prohibition on damages was consistent with the rule in *Houldsworth v City of Glasgow Bank* (1880) 5 App Cas 317, HL but that rule has since been amended by the Companies Act 1985 s 111A (as added) (see para 332 post).
3 Ibid s 178(1), (2).
4 Ibid s 178(3). For the meaning of 'distributable profits' see para 220 note 4 ante.
5 Ibid s 178(4). Section 178(4) does not, however, apply if (1) the terms provided for the redemption or purchase to take place at a date later than that of the commencement of the winding up; or (2) during the period beginning with the date on which the redemption or purchase was to have taken place and ending with the commencement of the winding up the company could not at any time have lawfully made a distribution equal in value to the price at which the shares were to have been redeemed or purchased: s 178(5).
6 Ibid s 178(6).

240. Power of Secretary of State to modify the statutory provisions. The Secretary of State may by regulations made by statutory instrument modify the statutory provisions relating to redeemable shares and the purchase by a company of its own shares[1] with respect to any of the following matters[2]:

    (1) the authority required for a purchase by a company of its own shares;

    (2) the authority required for the release by a company of its rights under a contract for the purchase of its own shares or a contract under which the company may (subject to any conditions) become entitled or obliged to purchase its own shares;

    (3) the information to be included in a return required[3] to be delivered by a company to the registrar of companies;

    (4) the matters to be dealt with in the statutory declaration of the directors[4] with a view to indicating their opinion of their company's ability to make a proposed payment out of capital with due regard to its financial situation and prospects; and

    (5) the contents of the auditors' report required[5] to be annexed to that declaration[6].

The Secretary of State may also by regulations so made make such provision, including modification of the statutory provisions relating to redeemable shares and the purchase by a company of its own shares, as appears to him to be appropriate:

    (a) for wholly or partly relieving companies from the requirement[7] that any available profits must be taken into account in determining the amount of the permissible capital payment for shares; or

    (b) for permitting a company's share premium account to be applied, to any extent appearing to the Secretary of State to be appropriate, in providing for the premiums payable on redemption or purchase by the company of any of its own shares[8].

Regulations under these provisions may:

    (i) make such further modification of any of the statutory provisions relating to redeemable shares and the purchase by a company of its own shares as appears to the Secretary of State to be reasonably necessary in consequence of any provision made by him under such regulations[9];

    (ii) make different provision for different cases or classes of case; and

    (iii) contain such further consequential provisions, and such incidental and supplementary provisions, as he thinks fit[10].

---

1 Ie the Companies Act 1985 Pt V Ch VII (ss 159–181) (as amended): see para 219 et seq ante.

2 Ibid s 179(1). No regulations may be made under s 179 unless a draft of the instrument containing them has been laid before Parliament and approved by resolution of each House: s 179(4). At the date at which this volume states the law no such regulations had been made and none had effect as if so made.

3 Ie under ibid s 169(1): see para 229 ante.

4 Ie under ibid s 173: see para 234 ante.

5 Ie by ibid s 173: see para 234 ante.

6 Ibid s 179(1).

7 Ie the requirement of ibid s 171(3)(a): see para 232 ante.

8 Ibid s 179(2). For the meaning of 'permissible capital payment' see para 232 note 9 ante.

9 Ie by virtue of ibid s 179(1) or (2): see supra.

10 Ibid s 179(3). See also the Insolvency Act 1986 s 124(3) and para 2214 note 12 post.

C. CONFIRMATION OF REDUCTION BY THE COURT

241. Forms of reduction. A reduction of capital may be effected only in accordance with the Companies Act 1985[1]. Subject to confirmation by the court[2], a company limited by shares or a company limited by guarantee and having a share capital may, if so authorised by its articles, by special resolution[3] reduce its share capital[4] in any way[5]. In particular, and without prejudice to the above power, the company may:

(1) extinguish or reduce the liability on any of its shares in respect of share capital not paid up[6]; or

(2) either with or without extinguishing or reducing liability on any of its shares, cancel any paid-up share capital which is lost or unrepresented by available assets; or

(3) either with or without extinguishing or reducing liability on any of its shares, pay off any paid-up share capital which is in excess of the company's wants[7];

and the company may, if and so far as is necessary, alter its memorandum by reducing the amount of its share capital and of its shares accordingly[8].

The special resolution to reduce is in the Companies Act 1985 referred to as 'a resolution for reducing share capital'[9].

The provisions of the Companies Act 1985 relating to the reduction of a company's share capital apply as if the share premium account were part of its paid-up share capital[10] and as if the capital redemption reserve were paid-up share capital of the company[11].

---

1 *Hope v International Financial Society* (1876) 4 ChD 327, CA; *Trevor v Whitworth* (1887) 12 App Cas 409, HL; *Holmes v Newcastle-upon-Tyne Freehold Abattoir Co* (1875) 1 ChD 682; and see *Bannatyne v Direct Spanish Telegraph Co* (1886) 34 ChD 287, CA. A transaction which upon examination can be seen to involve a return of capital (other than one properly sanctioned by the court), in whatever form, under whatever label, and whether directly or indirectly, to a member is void: *British and Commonwealth Holdings plc v Barclays Bank plc* [1996] 1 All ER 381, [1996] 1 WLR 1, CA; *Aveling Barford Ltd v Perion Ltd* [1989] BCLC 626. A company cannot bind itself not to exercise its statutory power to reduce its capital, although an agreement outside the articles between shareholders as to how they would exercise their voting rights on a resolution to reduce the capital would not necessarily be invalid: see *Russell v Northern Bank Development Corpn Ltd* [1992] 3 All ER 161, [1992] 1 WLR 588, HL (cited in para 149 ante).

2 Where the necessary special resolution has been passed and the appropriate procedures have been observed (see para 242 et seq post), the courts habitually sanction reductions.

3 As to special resolutions see para 683 post. A written resolution may be used in the case of a private company: see the Companies Act 1985 s 381A (as added) and para 697 post. This removes the doubts expressed in *Re Barry Artist Ltd* [1985] 1 WLR 1305, [1985] BCLC 283 as to whether written resolutions are acceptable for the purposes of a reduction of capital.

4 See para 215 note 1 ante. The resolution to reduce capital can refer to the share capital as it will be when the court's confirmation is sought and not as it stands at the date of the resolution: *Re Tip-Europe Ltd* [1988] BCLC 231 (resolution for a reduction of share premium account made conditional on allotment of shares at a premium; court may confirm reduction provided that the condition is fulfilled by the time the court confirms the reduction). Cf *Re Transfesa Terminals Ltd* (1987) 3 BCC 647, distinguished in *Re Tip-Europe Ltd* supra.

5 Companies Act 1985 s 135(1). See *Forth Wines Ltd, Petitioners* [1991] BCC 638, Ct of Sess (conversion of issued ordinary shares into redeemable deferred shares redeemable on specified date two years later was a scheme for the reduction of capital in a particular but unusual way within the Companies Act 1985 s 135(1) where the purpose of conversion was to pay off the capital, the date of redemption being deferred in the interests of creditors). A cancellation of unissued shares under s 121 does not constitute a reduction of capital: see s 121(5) and para 218 ante. As to the circumstances in which a surrender of shares amounts to an illegal reduction of capital unless sanctioned as such see para 520 et seq post.

6 In *Re Doloswella Rubber and Tea Estates Ltd, and Reduced* [1917] 1 Ch 213, the court confirmed a reduction under which partly paid shares were sub-divided and the amount paid appropriated to some of the shares resulting, so making them fully paid, while the remainder of the shares which were wholly

unpaid were surrendered for reissue. In that case *Re Walker Steam Trawl Fishing Co Ltd, Petitioners* 1908 SC 123 (where the Scottish court refused to confirm a similar reduction) was not referred to.
7 For a case where there was a simultaneous reduction of capital and capitalisation of reserves so as to leave the shares after both operations had been concluded as still paid up in full see *Doloi Tea Co Ltd, Petitioners* 1961 SLT 168.
8 Companies Act 1985 s 135(2).
9 Ibid s 135(3).
10 See ibid s 130(3) and para 188 ante. See also *Re Tip-Europe Ltd* [1988] BCLC 231; *Re Ratners Group plc* [1988] BCLC 685; *Re Thorn EMI plc* [1989] BCLC 612; *Quayle Munro Ltd, Petitioners* [1994] 1 BCLC 410, Ct of Sess.
11 See the Companies Act 1985 s 170(4) and para 231 ante.

242. Reduction when company is winding up. The power of a limited company to reduce continues even after it has gone into liquidation[1]. If the reduction is part of a scheme of arrangement[2], the requirements of the Companies Act 1985 as regards reduction of capital must still be complied with[3].

1 *Re Cooper, Cooper and Johnson Ltd* [1902] WN 199; *Re Stephen Walters & Sons Ltd* [1926] WN 236.
2 Ie under the Companies Act 1985 s 425 (as amended): see para 1455 post.
3 *Re Cooper, Cooper and Johnson Ltd* [1902] WN 199. See further para 1456 post.

243. Reserve or returned capital. Capital which cannot be called up except in the event of, and for the purpose of, winding up[1] may be cancelled with the confirmation of the court[2].

Capital issued by a company registered under the Companies Act 1844[3] on the terms that it should be returned to the shareholders, and which had been so returned, was cancelled with the confirmation of the court, where the company had subsequently been registered with limited liability and had under its articles power to reduce capital[4].

1 As to reserve capital see para 177 ante.
2 *Re Midland Railway Carriage and Wagon Co* (1907) 23 TLR 661.
3 7 & 8 Vict c 110 (repealed).
4 *Re Midland Railway Carriage and Wagon Co* (1907) 23 TLR 661. Companies which under their deeds of settlement had power to reduce capital lost that power by registering as limited companies under the Companies Act 1862 (repealed): *Droitwich Patent Salt Co Ltd v Curzon* (1867) LR 3 Exch 35.

244. Confirmation by the court. A reduction of capital must be confirmed by the court[1] which has a discretion whether to do so[2]. Where the reduction does not involve the diminution of liability on any shares or the return of paid-up capital to any shareholder, the only question for the court is whether the proposed reduction is fair and equitable as between the different classes of shareholders[2]. The fairness of a proposed reduction is a matter to be decided by the court on the evidence before it[3].

Speaking generally, a reduction of capital need not be spread equally or rateably over all the shares of the company[4]. If there is nothing unfair or inequitable in the transaction, the shares of one or more shareholders may be extinguished without affecting other shares of the same or a different class[5], although a reduction which does not provide for uniform treatment of shareholders whose rights are similar is narrowly scrutinised[6].

The court can confirm a reduction even if there is a factual error in the resolution for reducing capital, provided that it is so insignificant that no one could be thought to be prejudiced by its correction[7].

1 See the Companies Act 1985 s 135(1) and para 241 ante.
2 *British and American Trustee and Finance Corpn v Couper* [1894] AC 399, HL; *Re Thomas de la Rue & Co Ltd and Reduced* [1911] 2 Ch 361; and see generally the cases cited in note 3 infra. As to the position of creditors see paras 246, 255 et seq post.
3 *Poole v National Bank of China Ltd* [1907] AC 229 at 239, HL. See generally *British and American Trustee and Finance Corpn v Couper* [1894] AC 399, HL; *Re Floating Dock Co of St Thomas Ltd* [1895] 1 Ch 691; *Re Thomas de la Rue & Co Ltd and Reduced* [1911] 2 Ch 361; *Carruth v Imperial Chemical Industries Ltd* [1937] AC 707, [1937] 2 All ER 422, HL; *Prudential Assurance Co Ltd v Chatterley-Whitfield Collieries Ltd* [1949] AC 512, [1949] 1 All ER 1094, HL; *Wilsons and Clyde Coal Co Ltd v Scottish Insurance Corpn Ltd* 1948 SC 360, CA (affd sub nom *Scottish Insurance Corpn Ltd v Wilsons & Clyde Coal Co Ltd* [1949] AC 462, [1949] 1 All ER 1068, HL); *Ex p Westburn Sugar Refineries Ltd* [1951] AC 625, [1951] 1 All ER 881, HL; *Re Saltdean Estate Co Ltd* [1968] 3 All ER 829, [1968] 1 WLR 1844; *Re William Jones & Sons Ltd* [1969] 1 All ER 913, [1969] 1 WLR 146; *House of Fraser plc v ACGE Investments Ltd* [1987] AC 387, [1987] 2 WLR 1083, HL; *Re Northern Engineering Industries plc* [1994] 2 BCLC 704, CA. Earlier cases had also considered whether confirmation should be refused out of regard to the interest of those members of the public who may be induced to take shares (see *Poole v National Bank of China Ltd* [1907] AC 229 at 239, HL; *Caldwell & Co Ltd v Caldwell* 1916 SC 120 at 121, HL; *Ex p Westburn Sugar Refineries Ltd* supra at 630 and at 884) but the court seems to give little weight to such considerations now (see *Re Grosvenor Press plc* [1985] 1 WLR 980, [1985] BCLC 286 (in the absence of special circumstances creditors and future shareholders adequately protected by statutory safeguards)).
4 *Re Quebrada Rly, Land and Copper Co* (1889) 40 ChD 363; *Re American Pastoral Co* (1890) 62 LT 625; *Re Gatling Gun Ltd* (1890) 43 ChD 628; *Re Agricultural Hotel Co* [1891] 1 Ch 396; *Re Dicido Pier Co* [1891] 2 Ch 354; *Re Pinkney & Sons SS Co* [1892] 3 Ch 125; *Re Newbery-Vautin (Patents) Gold Extraction Co Ltd* [1892] 3 Ch 127n; *Re Floating Dock Co of St Thomas Ltd* [1895] 1 Ch 691; *Re London and New York Investment Corpn* [1895] 2 Ch 860; *Re Hyderabad (Deccan) Co Ltd* (1896) 75 LT 23. A rateable reduction may work injustice: see *Re Credit Assurance and Guarantee Corpn Ltd* [1902] 2 Ch 601, CA.
5 *British and American Trustee and Finance Corpn v Couper* [1894] AC 399 at 406, 415, 417, HL; *Re National Dwellings Society Ltd* (1898) 78 LT 144; *Bannatyne v Direct Spanish Telegraph Co* (1886) 34 ChD 287, CA; *Re Direct Spanish Telegraph Co* (1886) 34 ChD 307; *Re Thomas de la Rue & Co Ltd and Reduced* [1911] 2 Ch 361; *Re Showell's Brewery Co Ltd and Reduced* (1914) 30 TLR 428; cf *Re Australian Estates and Mortgage Co Ltd* [1910] 1 Ch 414; *Re Hoare & Co Ltd and Reduced* [1910] WN 87.
   The decision that the power to confirm a reduction of capital by affecting only some of the shares is legal (*Re Gatling Gun Ltd* (1890) 43 ChD 628) has been approved by the House of Lords in *British and American Trustee and Finance Corpn v Couper* [1894] AC 399 (where the reduction involved the cancellation of the shares of all the American shareholders, who were to take over the American investments of the company in consideration for which the company, which would then consist only of English shareholders, was to retain the English assets). More recently in *Re Robert Stephen Holdings Ltd* [1968] 1 All ER 195n, [1968] 1 WLR 522, it was stated that the better practice in such cases where one part of a class is to be treated differently from another part of the same class (unless all the shareholders consent) is to proceed by way of a scheme of arrangement under what is now the Companies Act 1985 s 425 (as amended) (see para 1447 post), as this affords better protection to a non-assenting minority. In that case the court did confirm the reduction despite its affecting shareholders of the same class in different ways but no shareholder appeared to oppose the confirmation.
   As to a reduction which amounts to a variation of class rights see para 249 post.
6 *Poole v National Bank of China Ltd* [1907] AC 229, HL; and see the cases cited in note 5 supra.
7 *Re Willaire Systems plc* [1987] BCLC 67, CA. See also *Re European Home Products plc* [1988] BCLC 690 (where a more significant error occurred in the circulars sent to the shareholders setting out the proposed reduction but the court reluctantly confirmed the reduction as creditors were not affected and no shareholder regarded the mistake as being of such importance as to seek the court's refusal).

245. Reduction where shares of different classes. In the case of a reduction of capital lost or unrepresented by available assets[1], the reduction should prima facie, as between preference shares having a priority as to return of capital in winding up, and shares deferred in this respect, be effected at the expense of the latter[2]. A reduction is not, however, necessarily made on this basis where the preference shareholders under a power in the articles consent, as part of the scheme, to a modification of their rights as to capital[3]. All-round reductions are also confirmed where the preference shares confer only a priority as to dividends[4].

The fact that losses are, in case of winding up, to be borne by members in proportion to the amount paid up on their shares does not require the court to apply the same principle on a reduction as between shares of the same class with different amounts paid up on them[5].

Where surplus capital is being returned, the repayment should prima facie, as between preference shares having a priority as to the return of capital in winding up, and shares deferred in this respect, be effected at the expense of the former[6].

1 Capital properly expended in preliminary expenses is not such capital: *Re Abstainers and General Insurance Co* [1891] 2 Ch 124.

2 *Re Floating Dock Co of St Thomas Ltd* [1895] 1 Ch 691; *Re Agricultural Hotel Co* [1891] 1 Ch 396; *Re London and New York Investment Corpn* [1895] 2 Ch 860.

3 *Re Welsbach Incandescent Gas Light Co Ltd* [1904] 1 Ch 87, CA.

4 *Bannatyne v Direct Spanish Telegraph Co* (1886) 34 ChD 287, CA; *Re Barrow Haematite Steel Co* (1888) 39 ChD 582; *Re Mackenzie & Co Ltd* [1916] 2 Ch 450. See also *Re Quebrada Rly, Land and Copper Co* (1889) 40 ChD 363; *Re Union Plate Glass Co* (1889) 42 ChD 513.

5 *Re Credit Assurance and Guarantee Corpn Ltd* [1902] 2 Ch 601, CA.

6 *Re Chatterley-Whitfield Collieries Ltd* [1948] 2 All ER 593, CA (affd sub nom *Prudential Assurance Co Ltd v Chatterley-Whitfield Collieries Ltd* [1949] AC 512, [1949] 1 All ER 1094, HL); *Wilsons and Clyde Coal Co Ltd v Scottish Insurance Corpn Ltd* 1948 SC 360, CA (affd sub nom *Scottish Insurance Corpn Ltd v Wilsons & Clyde Coal Co Ltd* [1949] AC 462, [1949] 1 All ER 1068, HL); *Re Fowlers Vacola Manufacturing Co Ltd* [1966] VR 97; *Re Saltdean Estate Co Ltd* [1968] 3 All ER 829, [1968] 1 WLR 1844; *House of Fraser plc v ACGE Investments Ltd* [1987] AC 387, [1987] 2 WLR 1083, HL. See also paras 248, 249 post.

246. Proving loss of capital. Where the sole reason for reduction is the fact that capital is lost or unrepresented by available assets, the court requires evidence of such loss[1] and that it is permanent[2]. If, however, there are other valid reasons for reduction, it is immaterial that the reduction is not exactly commensurate with the loss or deficiency of assets, a reduction beyond the loss by the company being within the general words of the Companies Act 1985[3].

1 If reliance is placed upon a valuation to prove the value of a particular asset, the court will as a general rule require an affidavit by the valuer to the effect that the value shown by his valuation (which should be exhibited) is in his opinion fair and proper: *Practice Direction* [1947] WN 116.

2 *Re Jupiter House Investments (Cambridge) Ltd* [1985] BCLC 222 (reduction sanctioned even though no permanent loss shown, on faith of undertaking to place any moneys recovered to capital reserve); cf *Re Grosvenor Press plc* [1985] BCLC 286 (reduction similarly sanctioned on undertaking limited to protection of existing creditors).

3 *Poole v National Bank of China Ltd* [1907] AC 229, HL, with which cf, as to applying reserve funds in or towards wiping out losses of capital, *Re Hoare & Co Ltd and Reduced* [1904] 2 Ch 208, CA; *Re Rowland and Marwood's SS Co Ltd and Reduced* (1906) 51 Sol Jo 131; and see *Re Barrow Haematite Steel Co* [1901] 2 Ch 746, CA, observed upon in *Poole v National Bank of China Ltd* supra at 238. If the amount of capital to be written off as lost is more than the amount of proved loss, the court may, and probably will, direct an inquiry as to creditors. It has been held that it is unnecessary to prove that capital has been lost, or is unrepresented by available assets: *Re Louisiana and Southern States Real Estate and Mortgage Co* [1909] 2 Ch 552. The real effect of *Poole v National Bank of China Ltd* supra is probably that the courts need not be so strict as formerly in requiring evidence that the capital is lost or unrepresented by available assets; in *Caldwell v Caldwell & Co (Papermakers) Ltd* [1916] WN 70, HL, Lord Parker of Waddington, referring to this case, stated that he still thought that, where the reduction of capital was based on the ground that capital had been lost or was unrepresented by available assets, it was, though not necessary, at any rate wise and prudent to insist on some evidence of the fact.

247. Reductions which the court will not confirm. The court has refused to confirm a reduction by the surrender of paid-up deferred shares the holders of which were to receive a larger amount in paid-up ordinary shares, by which amount the capital was to be increased[1]; and a reduction scheme to wipe out the deficiency caused by an illegal allotment of shares at a discount[2]. The court may well refuse to confirm any reduction where the resolution for reducing the share capital is not for any discernible purpose but is simply an act in a vacuum[3].

1 *Re Development Co of Central and West Africa* [1902] 1 Ch 547.
2 *Re New Chile Gold Mining Co* (1888) 38 ChD 475.
3 See *Re Ratners Group plc* [1988] BCLC 685; *Re Thorn EMI plc* [1989] BCLC 612.

248. Return of capital. Where the reduction involves the diminution of liability on any shares or the return of paid-up capital, the court must see that the interests of creditors are safeguarded, but, subject thereto, the questions for consideration are the same as if there were no such diminution or return[1]. The fact that the reduction may have an ulterior motive is irrelevant[2], unless it is simply a device to avoid the payment of tax[3].

The court has sanctioned a return of capital in excess of the needs of the company even though a part of the portion returned was to be borrowed immediately by the company from the shareholders on the security of debentures[4]; a return of capital to be satisfied by the issue of debenture stock[5]; and a return made upon the footing that it may be called up again[6]. The actual return of the excess capital should not be made until after the order confirming the reduction and approving the minute has been made[7]. If the capital is not returned, the right of the shareholders to claim it will be barred after 12 years from the date of the notice of the order confirming the reduction[8]. It is not necessary that on a return of capital the shareholders should receive cash[9].

1 *Ex p Westburn Sugar Refineries Ltd* [1951] AC 625, [1951] 1 All ER 881, HL (transfer of company's assets, in consideration of reduction of capital, to holding company whose shares were held by same shareholders, held to be permissible although value of assets exceeded amount of reduction). See further para 244 ante.
2 *Ex p Westburn Sugar Refineries Ltd* [1951] AC 625, [1951] 1 All ER 881, HL.
3 *Re A and D Fraser Ltd* 1951 SC 394. Cf *Re David Bell Ltd* 1954 SC 33 (no objection that company could pay dividend equal to proposed return of capital).
4 *Re Nixon's Navigation Co* [1897] 1 Ch 872; *Re Lamson Store Service Co Ltd* [1897] 1 Ch 875n.
5 *Re Thomas de la Rue & Co Ltd and Reduced* [1911] 2 Ch 361 (scheme sanctioned on the condition that the debenture stock should be redeemed within 40 years).
6 *Re Fore-Street Warehouse Co Ltd* (1888) 59 LT 214; *Re Watson, Walker and Quickfall Ltd* [1898] WN 69; *Re Brown, Sons & Co* 1931 SC 701; *Re Stevenson, Anderson & Co Ltd* 1951 SC 346.
7 *Re Lees Brook Spinning Co* [1906] 2 Ch 394; *Re Anglo-Italian Bank Ltd and Reduced* (1906) 51 Sol Jo 48; *General Industrials Development Syndicate Ltd* [1907] WN 23, not following *Re Calgary and Edmonton Land Co* [1906] 1 Ch 141.
8 Limitation Act 1980 s 8(1); *Re Artisans' Land and Mortgage Corpn* [1904] 1 Ch 796 at 802. See also *Re Phoebe Gold Mining Co* [1900] WN 182.
9 *Ex p Westburn Sugar Refineries Ltd* [1951] AC 625, [1951] 1 All ER 881, HL; *Re Thomas de la Rue & Co Ltd and Reduced* [1911] 2 Ch 361. In that case there need not be an exact correlation between the capital reduced and the value of the assets transferred but, if what is offered to the shareholder is illusory, the court will refuse to confirm the reduction.

249. Reduction and variation of class rights. The cancellation of a particular class of shares and the return of the capital paid up thereon does not require the separate consent of the holders of the shares of that class unless it involves a variation of the rights attaching to those shares; and such cancellation and return of capital while the company is a going concern does not constitute a variation of the rights attached to the shares if the return of capital is made strictly in accordance with those rights on a winding up[1]. Shareholders may be protected against the risk of reduction in this way without their consent by a provision in the articles of association[2].

If a scheme of reduction does vary or abrogate class rights, despite the generality of the court's power to confirm[3] (and some suggestions to the contrary in older cases[4]), it is unlikely that the court would now confirm a reduction without the appropriate class consent having been obtained[5].

1　Re Northern Engineering Industries plc [1994] 2 BCLC 704 at 706, CA; Re Chatterley-Whitfield Colleries Ltd [1948] 2 All ER 593 (affd sub nom Prudential Assurance Co Ltd v Chatterley-Whitfield Colleries Ltd [1949] AC 512, [1949] 1 All ER 1094, HL); Re Saltdean Estate Co Ltd [1968] 3 All ER 829, [1968] 1 WLR 1844; House of Fraser plc v ACGE Investments Ltd [1987] AC 387, [1987] 2 WLR 1083, HL. This is so even if the preference shareholders also have further rights of participation as regards dividend: Re Saltdean Estate Co Ltd supra. It is not clear whether preference shares which are participating as to surplus on a winding up could be dealt with in this way although Re William Jones & Sons Ltd [1969] 1 All ER 913, [1969] 1 WLR 146 suggests that they can. In that instance, however, the preference shareholders raised no objection to being paid off, probably because they were to be paid off in full, although the shares stood at less than par. Moreover, there was no present prospect of the company being wound up so any enjoyment of surplus on a winding off would not occur for many years.

2　See Re Northern Engineering Industries plc [1994] 2 BCLC 704, CA (articles provided that the rights attached to the preference shares were deemed to be varied by a reduction of the capital paid up on the shares). Such a protective provision encompasses both piecemeal reduction of capital and repayment of an entire class on a reduction to zero: Re Northern Engineering Industries plc supra.

3　See para 244 ante and the cases there cited.

4　See eg Re William Jones & Sons Ltd [1969] 1 All ER 913, [1969] 1 WLR 146.

5　Re Northern Engineering Industries plc [1994] 2 BCLC 704 at 713, CA. In such a case shareholders voting at the class meeting must have regard to the interests of the class: Re Holders Investment Trust Ltd [1971] 2 All ER 289, [1971] 1 WLR 583.

250. Alteration of members' rights.　The court may confirm a reduction even if the voting powers of the members or their priorities are affected by it, or the scheme involves the extinction of liability in respect of arrears of preference dividends[1].

1　Re James Colmer Ltd [1897] 1 Ch 524: Re Allsopp & Sons Ltd (1903) 51 WR 644, CA; Re National Dwellings Society Ltd (1898) 78 LT 144; Re Oban and Aultmore-Glenlivet Distilleries Ltd (1903) 5 F 1140; and see Re Continental Union Gas Co Ltd (1891) 7 TLR 476; Re Hoare & Co Ltd and Reduced [1910] WN 87 (where a scheme under what is now the Companies Act 1985 s 425 (as amended) was at the same time approved). In the case of colliery companies affected by the provisions of the Coal Industry Nationalisation Act 1946, provision was made by s 25 for the adjustment inter se of the rights of different classes of shareholders in the assets of the company, as affected by the substitution of the compensation to be awarded under that Act, in order to preserve their relative pre-nationalisation interests in the company. It was argued that, until such compensation had been finally ascertained and any consequent adjustment in the rights of the shareholders made, no reduction of capital which involved the extinguishment of any class of shareholders should be confirmed by the court unless the rights of the class so paid off under s 25 were preserved; but this argument was rejected in Prudential Assurance Co Ltd v Chatterley-Whitfield Collieries Ltd [1949] AC 512, [1949] 1 All ER 1094, HL and Scottish Insurance Corpn Ltd v Wilsons & Clyde Coal Co Ltd [1949] AC 462, [1949] 1 All ER 1068, HL; cf Re Old Silkstone Collieries Ltd [1954] Ch 169, [1954] 1 All ER 68, CA (where two previous reductions had expressly safeguarded rights under the Coal Industry Nationalisation Act 1946 s 25); cf also Re Fife Coal Co Ltd 1948 SC 505; Re William Dixon Ltd 1948 SC 511; Re Saltdean Estate Co Ltd [1968] 3 All ER 829, [1968] 1 WLR 1844.

251. Power to reduce must be given in articles.　No reduction may take place unless authority to reduce is given by the articles[1], and an authority to do so which is given by the memorandum of association does not suffice[2]. The power may be given by the articles as originally framed or as altered by special resolution[3]. If the company is governed by Table A[4], the provisions of that Table authorise the company by special resolution to reduce its capital[5]. If the company has no power under its articles, whether by Table. A or otherwise, to reduce its capital, a special resolution must be passed altering them so as to authorise reduction of capital, and subsequently another special resolution must be passed for reduction[6].

1 See *Re MB Group plc* [1989] BCLC 672 (articles authorised reduction provided that it did not have the effect of reducing the share capital below the authorised minimum for public companies; provision not infringed by reduction below minimum for an instant of time followed by an increase of capital above minimum).
2 *Re Dexine Patent Packing and Rubber Co* (1903) 88 LT 791.
3 See the Companies Act 1985 s 744 (meaning of 'articles') and para 140 note 2 ante.
4 Ie the Companies (Tables A to F) Regulations 1985, SI 1985/805, Schedule, Table A (amended by SI 1985/1052). As to Table A generally see para 529 et seq post.
5 See ibid Schedule, Table A art 34.
6 There would appear to be no objection to the passing of both special resolutions at the same meeting. See also para 201 note 10 ante.

D. APPLICATION TO THE COURT FOR CONFIRMATION OF REDUCTION

252. Procedure. Where a company has passed a special resolution for reducing share capital, it may apply by petition to the court for an order confirming the reduction[1]. This procedure applies equally to the reduction of the share premium account[2] and to the reduction of the capital redemption reserve[3]. Application must be made to the court having jurisdiction to wind up the company[4]. In cases in the High Court, the jurisdiction is assigned to the Chancery Division[5].

The petition and all affidavits, notices and other documents in the proceedings must be entitled in the matter of the company in question, and in the matter of the Companies Act 1985[6].

The petition should state the incorporation, registered office, objects and capital of the company and set out the article giving it power to reduce its capital, the reasons for reduction and the special resolution. It need not state that the company is still carrying on business[7]. Where there is more than one class of shares, the petition should state whether any and which class has priority as to capital[8].

The petition must be supported by affidavit[9], and the certificate of registration, the memorandum and articles of association and the original of the current minute book of the proceedings at general meetings of the company must be exhibited[10]. An affidavit is also required proving the due convening and holding of the meetings which passed the special resolution for reduction and the register of members must be exhibited[11].

1 Companies Act 1985 s 136(1); RSC Ord 102 r 4(1)(d).
2 Companies Act 1985 s 130(3) (cited in para 188 ante); RSC Ord 102 r 4(1)(c).
3 Companies Act 1985 s 170(4) (cited in para 231 ante); RSC Ord 102 r 4(1)(l).
4 Companies Act 1985 s 744. As to the jurisdiction of the High Court see para 2197 post; and as to the jurisdiction of county courts see para 2198 post.
5 RSC Ord 102 r 5(1).
6 RSC Ord 102 r 5(2). When the petition is presented to the winding-up judge, it is not a 'winding-up matter' and should not be entitled 'Companies Court', unless the company is in liquidation.
7 *Re Great Universal Stores Ltd* [1960] 1 All ER 252n, [1960] 1 WLR 78.
8 *Re Mackenzie & Co Ltd* [1916] 2 Ch 450.
9 The evidence in support of a petition to confirm a reduction of capital need not show as regards any issue of shares made since 1900 for a consideration other than cash that the statutory requirements as to registration were complied with; it is sufficient to state in the petition the extent to which any issued shares, other than shares issued otherwise than for cash before 1901, are or are deemed to be paid up.

The existing practice will, however, remain unaltered in respect of issues of shares otherwise than for cash made before 1901 whilst the Companies Act 1867 s 25 (repealed) remained in operation: Chancery Practice Direction (6)D(i).

10 *Re Omnium Investment Co* [1895] 2 Ch 127.
11 *Re Uppingham Gas and Coke Co Ltd* (1901) 45 Sol Jo 483, altering the practice laid down on this point in *Re Omnium Investment Co* [1895] 2 Ch 127, and in *Re Leicester Mortgage Co Ltd* [1894] WN 108 at 116.

253. Summons for directions. After presentation of a petition for the confirmation of a reduction of capital, the petitioner must take out a summons for directions[1]. On the hearing, the court[2] may by order give such directions as to the proceedings to be taken before the hearing of the petition as it thinks fit including, in particular, directions for the publication of notices and the making of any inquiry[3]. The court may give directions for an inquiry to be made as to the debts of, and claims against, the company or as to any class or classes of such debts or claims; or as to the proceedings to be taken for settling the list of creditors entitled to object to the reduction and fixing the date by reference to which the list is to be made[4]. The power of the court under the Companies Act 1985[5] to direct that the statutory provisions relating to the settlement of a list of creditors[6] shall not apply as regards any class or classes of creditors may, however, be exercised on the hearing of the summons[7].

1 RSC Ord 102 r 6(1).
2 For these purposes, 'court' includes any judge of the Chancery Division whether sitting in court or in chambers and also the companies court registrar: RSC Ord 1 r 4(2); RSC Ord 102 r 1. In practice the application is made in the first instance to the registrar.
3 RSC Ord 102 r 6(3).
4 RSC Ord 102 r 6(4).
5 Ie under the Companies Act 1985 s 136(6): see para 256 post.
6 Ie under ibid s 136(3)–(5): see paras 255, 256, 261 post.
7 RSC Ord 102 r 6(4). As to the procedure where an inquiry as to creditors is not dispensed with see para 255 et seq post.

254. Setting down and advertising petition. Where there is no diminution of liability of, or payment of capital to, shareholders, there is usually no inquiry as to creditors and the petition is ordered to be set down as for an early date and advertised[1]. Prima facie, even in such cases the petition ought to be advertised[2]; but the court has a discretion to dispense with advertisement, if it is satisfied that the interests of creditors cannot be affected by what is proposed[3].

Notice of the presentation of the petition must be published at such times and in such newspapers as the court directs[4].

1 *Re Dicido Pier Co* [1891] 2 Ch 354.
2 *Re Consolidated Telephone Co Ltd* (1885) 54 LJ Ch 795.
3 Discretion was exercised in the following cases: *Re Plaskynaston Tube Co* (1883) 23 ChD 542; *Re Tambracherry Estates Co* (1885) 29 ChD 683, CA; *Re London and City Land and Building Co* [1885] WN 137; *Re People's Café Co* (1885) 55 LJ Ch 312; and also in *G Mackay & Co Ltd and Reduced* (1914) 52 SLR 64 (although the company was a private company). This discretion has but rarely been exercised in recent years.
4 See RSC Ord 102 r 10(a) and para 259 head (1) post.

E. CONSENT OF CREDITORS TO REDUCTION

255. Where creditors may object. If the proposed reduction of share capital involves either diminution of liability in respect of unpaid share capital or the payment of any paid-up share capital to a shareholder[1], and in any other case[2] if the court so directs, every creditor of the company who at the date fixed by the court is entitled to any debt or claim which, if that date were the commencement of the winding up of the company, would be admissible in proof against the company is entitled to object to the reduction[3].

1 Cancelling paid-up shares on the terms of the amount of paid-up capital being paid out of a sinking fund created for the purpose out of profits under special provisions in the articles is not payment of any paid-up share capital: see *Re Dicido Pier Co* [1891] 2 Ch 354.

2 The court will so direct only where a strong case is made out (*Re Meux's Brewery Co Ltd* [1919] 1 Ch 28); and the petition should not insert a prayer for an inquiry in such cases (*Cranston's Tea Rooms Ltd and Reduced, Petitioners* (1919) 46 SLR 208).

3 Companies Act 1985 s 136(2), (3); and see *Re Eastern and Australian SS Co Ltd and Reduced* (1893) 68 LT 321. As to creditors entitled to prove in winding up see para 2509 et seq post; and as to the treatment of creditors generally see para 256 post.

256. Settling list of creditors. If there are creditors so entitled to object, the court must settle a list of those creditors[1]. If a proposed reduction of share capital involves either the diminution of any liability in respect of unpaid share capital or the payment to any shareholder of any paid-up share capital, the court may, if having regard to any special circumstances of the case[2] it thinks proper to do so, direct that the statutory provisions relating to the creditors' right to object and the settling of a list of creditors[3] shall not to apply to any class or classes of creditors[4]. It is common practice for the company to offer certain undertakings[5] to secure the consent of creditors, thereby obviating the necessity of settling a list.

For the purpose of settling a list of creditors, the court must ascertain, as far as possible without requiring an application from any creditor, the names of the creditors and the nature and amount of their debts or claims, and may publish notices fixing a day or days within which creditors not entered on the list are to claim to be so entered, or are to be excluded from the right of objecting to the reduction[6].

Where, on the hearing of the summons for directions, the court has ordered an inquiry as to debts, then, subject to any directions given by the court[7], the company must, within seven days after the making of the order, file in the office of the registrar of the companies court an affidavit by an officer of the company competent to make it, verifying a list containing:

(1) the name and address of every creditor entitled to any debt or claim to which the inquiry extends;

(2) the amount due to each creditor in respect of such debt or claim or, in the case of a debt or claim which is subject to any contingency or sounds only in damages or for some other reason does not bear a certain value, a just estimate of its value; and

(3) the total of those amounts and values[8].

The deponent must state in the affidavit his belief that at the date fixed by the court as the date by reference to which the list is to be made there is no debt or claim which, if that date were the commencement of the winding up of the company, would be admissible in proof against the company, other than the debts or claims set out in the list and any debts or claims to which the inquiry does not extend, and must also state his means of knowledge of the matters deposed to[9]. The list must be left at the office of the registrar not later than one day after the affidavit is filed[10].

If an officer of the company wilfully conceals the name of any creditor entitled to object to the reduction, or wilfully misrepresents the nature or amount of the debt or claim of any creditor, or aids or abets or is privy to any such concealment or misrepresentation, he is guilty of an offence and liable on conviction on indictment to a fine, or on summary conviction to a fine not exceeding the statutory maximum[11].

1 Companies Act 1985 s 136(4).
2 Solvency is not a special circumstance: *Practice Note* [1930] WN 78; and see *Re Unifruitco SS Co* 1930 SC 1104; *Re Cadzow Coal Co Ltd* 1931 SC 272. The special circumstances must be such that the court is satisfied that the creditors will not be adversely affected by the proposed reduction: *Re Lucania Temperance Billiard Halls (London) Ltd* [1966] Ch 98, [1965] 3 All ER 879; *Anderson Brown & Co Ltd, Petitioners* 1965 SLT 99. In considering whether to dispense with the list of creditors, the court will consider whether a company holds sufficient cash and gilt-edged securities to cover all provable liabilities with a reasonable margin of safety as well as the amount which it is proposed to be returned to the shareholders, although its consideration is not limited to cash and gilt-edged securities; it may also take into account sums due to a company by its sundry debtors provided that such sums have been written down so as to exclude bad debts: *Re House of Fraser plc* [1987] BCLC 293, Ct of Sess; *Anderson Brown & Co Ltd, Petitioners* 1965 SC 81; *Re Lucania Temperance Billiard Halls (London) Ltd* supra.
3 Ie the Companies Act 1985 s 136(3)–(5): see para 255 ante; infra; and para 261 post.
4 Ibid s 136(6)
5 See *Re Antwerp Waterworks Co Ltd* [1931] WN 186 (court dispensed with an inquiry on the undertaking of the company to keep on deposit a sum considerably in excess of the liabilities as proved in evidence); *Quayle Munro Ltd, Petitioners* [1994] 1 BCLC 410, Ct of Sess (court dispensed with an inquiry on the giving of undertakings as to the manner in which the special reserve created on a reduction of the share premium account would be utilised). Before 1929 the court did not possess this power and it was held that the list had to be settled even if there was evidence that there were no creditors: see *Re Lamson Store Service Co Ltd, Re National Reversionary Investment Co Ltd* [1895] 2 Ch 726.
6 Companies Act 1985 s 136(4).
7 RSC Ord 102 r 6(5). RSC Ord 102 rr 7–12 (see infra and para 257 et seq post) all have effect subject to any directions given by the court under r 6: RSC Ord 102 r 6(5).
8 RSC Ord 102 r 7(1).
9 RSC Ord 102 r 7(2).
10 RSC Ord 102 r 7(3).
11 Companies Act 1985 ss 141, 730, Sch 24. For the meaning of 'the statutory maximum' see para 1161 post.

257. Inspection of list. Copies of the list of creditors with the omission, unless the court otherwise directs, of the amount due to each creditor and the estimated value of any debt or claim to which any creditor is entitled, must be kept at the registered office of the company and at the office of that company's solicitor and of that solicitor's London agent, if any[1]. Any person is entitled during ordinary business hours, on payment of a fee of five pence, to inspect the list at any such office and to take extracts from it[2].

1 RSC Ord 102 r 8(1). See also para 256 note 7 ante.
2 RSC Ord 102 r 8(2).

258. Notices to creditors. Within seven days[1] after filing the affidavit, the company must send by post to each creditor named in the list exhibited to the affidavit, at his last known address, a notice stating:

(1) the amount of the reduction of capital sought to be confirmed[2];
(2) the effect of the order directing an inquiry as to debts and claims[3];
(3) the amount or value specified in the list as due or estimated to be due to him[4]; and
(4) the time fixed by the court within which, if he claims to be entitled to a larger amount, he must send particulars of his debt or claim, and the name and address of his solicitor, if any, to the company's solicitor[5].

1 This period is to be reckoned exclusively of the day of filing and inclusively of the seventh day: see RSC Ord 3 r 2(2).

2 RSC Ord 102 r 9(a). See also para 256 note 7 ante.
3 RSC Ord 102 r 9(b).
4 RSC Ord 102 r 9(c).
5 RSC Ord 102 r 9(d).

259. Advertisement of petition and list. After filing the affidavit[1], the company must insert, in such newspapers and at such times as the court directs, a notice stating:

(1) the date of presentation of the petition and the amount of the reduction of capital thereby sought to be confirmed[2];

(2) the inquiry ordered[3] by the court[4];

(3) the places where the list of creditors may[5] be inspected[6]; and

(4) the time within which any creditor not named in the list who claims to be entitled to any debt or claim to which the inquiry extends must send his name and address, the name and address of his solicitor, if any, and particulars of his debt or claim to the company's solicitor[7].

1 See para 256 ante.
2 RSC Ord 102 r 10(a). See also para 256 note 7 ante.
3 Ie under RSC Ord 102 r 6: see para 253 ante.
4 RSC Ord 102 r 10(b).
5 Ie in accordance with RSC Ord 102 r 8: see para 257 ante.
6 RSC Ord 102 r 10(c).
7 RSC Ord 102 r 10(d).

260. Affidavit as to claims made by creditors. Within such time as the court directs, the company must file in the office of the registrar of the companies court an affidavit, made by the company's solicitor and an officer of the company competent to make it:

(1) proving service of the notices to creditors[1] and the advertisement[2] of the petition[3];

(2) verifying a list containing the names and addresses of the persons, if any, who in pursuance of such notices sent in particulars of debts or claims, specifying the amount of each debt or claim[4];

(3) distinguishing in such list those debts or claims which are wholly, or as to any and what part of them, admitted by the company, disputed by the company or alleged by the company to be outside the scope of the inquiry[5]; and

(4) stating which of the persons named in the list of creditors and which of the persons named in the list included in the affidavit have been paid or consent to the reduction sought to be confirmed[6].

1 Ie the notices mentioned in RSC Ord 102 r 9: see para 258 ante.
2 Ie the advertisement of the notice mentioned in RSC Ord 102 r 10: see para 259 ante.
3 RSC Ord 102 r 11(a). See also para 256 note 7 ante.
4 RSC Ord 102 r 11(b).
5 RSC Ord 102 r 11(c).
6 RSC Ord 102 r 11(d).

261. Proceedings where claim not admitted. If the company contends that a person is not entitled to be entered in the list of creditors in respect of any debt or claim or in respect of the full amount claimed by him in respect of any debt or claim, then, unless the company is willing to secure payment of that debt or claim by appropriating the full amount of the debt or claim, the company must, if the court so directs, send to that person by post at his last known address a notice requiring him within such time as may be specified in the notice, being not less than four clear days[1] after service of the notice, to file an affidavit proving his debt or claim, or, as the case may be, so much of it as is not admitted by the company, and to attend the adjudication of his debt or claim at the place and time specified in the notice, being the time appointed by the court for the adjudication of debts and claims[2].

If a creditor entered on the list, whose debt or claim is not discharged or has not determined, does not consent[3] to the reduction, the court may, if it thinks fit, dispense with his consent, on the company securing payment of his debt or claim by appropriating (as the court may direct) the following amount:

(1) if the company admits the full amount of the debt or claim, or, though not admitting it, is willing to provide for it, then the full amount;

(2) if the company does not admit, and is not willing to provide for, the full amount of the debt or claim, or if the amount is contingent or not ascertained, then an amount fixed by the court after the like inquiry and adjudication as if the company were being wound up by the court[4].

Any creditor who comes in to prove his title, debt or claim in pursuance of the notice requiring him to do so, is entitled, if his claim succeeds, to his costs incurred in establishing it, and, if his claim or any part of it fails, he may be ordered to pay the costs of any person incurred in opposing it[5].

1 At least four days must intervene between service of the notice and the date on which the affidavit must be filed: see RSC Ord 3 r 2(4) and PRACTICE AND PROCEDURE vol 37 para 26.

2 RSC Ord 102 r 12. See also para 256 note 7 ante. The notice states that, in default of his complying with the instructions, the creditor will be precluded from objecting to the proposed reduction, or, as the case may be, that he will, in all proceedings relative to the proposed reduction, be treated as a creditor for such amount only as is set against his name in the list. For the mode in which the notice is to be sent see para 258 ante.

3 The consent of a creditor may be proved in such manner as the court thinks sufficient: RSC Ord 102 r 14. Some evidence of consent is necessary: *Re Patent Ventilating Granary Co* (1879) 12 ChD 254; cf *Re Crédit Foncier of England* (1871) LR 11 Eq 356. In *Re Hydraulic Power and Smelting Co* [1914] 2 Ch 187, the court accepted as evidence of the consent of the holders of bearer debentures of the company an extraordinary resolution passed, pursuant to the trust deed securing the issue, by 87% of such holders.

4 Companies Act 1985 s 136(5). By maintaining a separate dividend account in which unclaimed dividends are duly entered, a company appropriates in such a way as the court would be justified in requiring: see *Arizona Copper Co Ltd, Petitioners* 1926 SC 315. The landlord of a company is entitled to security for future rent, the balance of the amount of the rent being brought into court with liberty to either party to apply to be paid what is due thereout: *Re Telegraph Construction Co* (1870) LR 10 Eq 384; *Palace Billiard Rooms Ltd and Reduced, Petitioners* 1912 SC 5; *Re Lucania Temperance Billiard Halls (London) Ltd* [1966] Ch 98, [1965] 3 All ER 879 (ten years' rent normally sufficient security for landlord's claims under long lease). As to proof of debts in winding up by the court see para 2509 et seq post.

5 RSC Ord 62 r 6(3).

262. Certificate as to creditors. The list of creditors entitled to object to the reduction of capital, as settled by the court in accordance with the above procedure[1], must be certified and filed by the registrar of the companies court[2]. The certificate must:

(1) specify the debts or claims, if any, disallowed by the court[3];

(2) distinguish the debts or claims, if any, the full amount of which is admitted by the company, the debts or claims, if any, the full amount of which, though not admitted by the company, the company is willing to appropriate, the debts or claims, if any, the amount of which has been fixed by adjudication[4] and other debts or claims[5];

(3) specify the total amount of the debts or claims payment of which has been secured[6] by appropriation[7];

(4) show which creditors consent to the reduction and the total amount of their debts or claims[8]; and

(5) specify the creditors who sought to prove their debts or claims[9] and state which of such debts or claims were allowed[10].

1 See para 255 et seq ante.
2 RSC Ord 102 r 13.
3 RSC Ord 102 r 13(a).
4 Ie under the Companies Act 1985 s 136(4): see para 256 ante.
5 RSC Ord 102 r 13(b).
6 See note 4 supra.
7 RSC Ord 102 r 13(c).
8 RSC Ord 102 r 13(d).
9 Ie under RSC Ord 102 r 12: see para 261 ante.
10 RSC Ord 102 r 13(e).

263. Hearing of petition. In any case in which the court has directed an inquiry as to creditors, the petition is not to be heard before the expiration of at least eight clear days[1] after the filing of the certificate as to creditors[2].

Before the hearing of the petition, a notice specifying the day appointed for the hearing must be published at such times and in such newspapers as the court may direct[3].

Any unsatisfied or unsecured creditor on the list who has not consented may appear to oppose the petition[4].

1 See RSC Ord 3 r 2(4) and PRACTICE AND PROCEDURE vol 37 para 26.
2 RSC Ord 102 r 15(1).
3 RSC Ord 102 r 15(2).
4 See the Companies Act 1985 s 136(3).

F. ORDER CONFIRMING REDUCTION

264. Order confirming reduction. The court may make an order confirming the reduction on such terms and conditions as it thinks fit, if it is satisfied, in cases where there are creditors entitled to object to the reduction[1], with respect to every such creditor, that either his consent[2] to the reduction has been obtained or his debt or claim has been discharged or has determined, or has been secured[3]; and in other cases, without regard to creditors, unless they can show a strong case[4]. Either in exercise of this power, or of its inherent jurisdiction, the court may correct immaterial errors in the resolution[5].

1 See para 255 ante.
2 As to evidence of consent see para 261 note 3 ante.
3 Companies Act 1985 s 137(1).
4 Thus in *Re Meux's Brewery Co Ltd* [1919] 1 Ch 28, debenture holders unsuccessfully objected that the proposed reduction would be prejudicial to their security by enabling the company to pay dividends out of profits instead of such profits being applied in making good the lost capital. No evidence was adduced, however, to show what part of the lost capital was attributable to circulating capital.

5 *Re Willaire Systems plc* [1987] BCLC 67, CA; *Re European Home Products plc* [1988] BCLC 690. See also para 244 text and note 7 ante.

265. Imposition of terms. The court's power to confirm is discretionary[1], and conditions may be imposed[2]. Thus, the court may require an alteration in the voting powers of different classes of shareholders[3], or evidence that the company's financial position has not altered since the registrar's certificate was made[4], or that there are no fresh creditors[5], or it may require money to be set aside to pay future rent[6]. The court may, if for any special reason it thinks proper to do so, make an order directing the company to add to its name as its last words the words 'and reduced' during such period commencing on or at any time after the date of the order as is specified in the order and those words are, until the expiration of the period specified in the order, deemed to be part of the name of the company[7]. The court may also make an order requiring the company to publish (as the court directs) the reasons for reduction, or such other information in regard to it as the court thinks expedient with a view to giving proper information to the public, and, if thought fit, the causes which led to the reduction[8]. The court will also provide for the costs of a dissentient shareholder in a proper case, and as far as possible encourages helpful criticism by such a shareholder[9].

1 *British and American Trustee and Finance Corpn v Couper* [1894] AC 399, HL; *Re Fore-Street Warehouse Co Ltd* (1888) 59 LT 214; *Re Watson, Walker and Quickfall Ltd* [1898] WN 69; *Re Thomas de la Rue & Co Ltd and Reduced* [1911] 2 Ch 361; cf *Poole v National Bank of China Ltd* [1907] AC 229 at 240, HL. For schemes of reduction which the court has confirmed or refused to confirm see para 241 et seq ante.
2 See the Companies Act 1985 s 137(1) and para 264 ante. See also *Re Jupiter House Investments (Cambridge) Ltd* [1985] 1 WLR 975, [1985] BCLC 222 and *Re Grosvenor Press plc* [1985] 1 WLR 980, [1985] BCLC 286 (possibility of capital being recovered; undertakings to protect creditors).
3 *Re Newbery-Vautin (Patents) Gold Extraction Co Ltd* [1892] 3 Ch 127n; *Re Pinkney & Sons SS Co* [1892] 3 Ch 125.
4 *Re Safety Oil Co Ltd* (1892) 36 Sol Jo 699 (under the practice then in force the certificate could be made either by the master or by the registrar).
5 *Re Safety Oil Co Ltd* (1892) 36 Sol Jo 699; *Re Watson, Walker and Quickfall Ltd* [1898] WN 69.
6 *Re Telegraph Construction Co* (1870) LR 10 Eq 384.
7 Companies Act 1985 s 137(2)(a), (3). In practice the court rarely makes such a direction.
8 Ibid s 137(2)(b); *Re Llynvi, Tondu and Ogmore Coal and Iron Co* (1877) 37 LT 373; *Re Truman, Hanbury, Buxton & Co Ltd* [1910] 2 Ch 498.
9 *Re Thomas de la Rue & Co Ltd and Reduced* [1911] 2 Ch 361.

266. Approval of minute. The court must approve a minute showing, with respect to the share capital of the company as altered by the order of the court confirming the reduction, the amount of such share capital, the number of shares into which it is to be divided, and the amount of each share, and the amount, if any, at the date of the registration of the minute deemed to be paid up on each share[1]. Embodying the minute in the confirmatory order is a sufficient approval[2].

1 Companies Act 1985 s 138(1). It is the practice for the minute to state amounts from and to which capital is reduced, and (where appropriate) the arithmetical numbering of shares remaining after the reduction. For forms of minutes see *Re West Cumberland Iron and Steel Co* (1888) 58 LT 152; *Re Britannia Mills Co, Huddersfield* [1888] WN 103; *Re International Conversion Trust Ltd* [1892] WN 100; *Re Chelmsford Land Co Ltd* [1904] WN 106 (where the court sanctioned a reduction by way of repayment of capital, and, on a subsequent application after the repayment had been effected, approved a minute showing the position of the capital as it was after repayment); *Re Solway SS Co* (1889) 61 LT 659. For a form of minute where shares have been forfeited see *Re Oceana Development Co Ltd* (1912) 56 Sol Jo 537; *Re Thomas Wolf & Son (1907) Ltd and Reduced* (1912) 57 Sol Jo 146; and see *Re North Pole Ice Co Ltd and Reduced* [1924] WN 131 (where it was decided that, when the reduction was followed by consolidation

and other alterations, the form of minute should state that the capital had been reduced 'by a special resolution confirmed by an order of the High Court of Justice'), explained in *Re Dampney & Co Ltd and Reduced* (1924) 68 Sol Jo 718. For a form of minute where the capital was increased forthwith on the reduction see *Re D Simpson Ltd* 1929 SC 65; *Re Anglo American Insurance Co Ltd* [1991] BCLC 564 (minute showing reduction of capital to nil without referring to immediate increase to $US 50 million would be positively misleading and not in accordance with the purpose of the statutory provision). See also *Re Harrods (Buenos Aires) Ltd* [1936] 2 All ER 1651 (reduction, increase, sub-division and consolidation); *Re Holland and Webb Ltd* [1936] 3 All ER 944 (reduction and consolidation); *Re Doloi Tea Co Ltd, Petitioners* 1961 SLT 168 (reduction followed by capitalisation leaving original shares fully paid up). Any cancellation or reduction of the share premium account which forms part of the reduction should not be referred to in the minute: *Re Paringa Mining and Exploration Co Ltd* [1957] 3 All ER 424, [1957] 1 WLR 1143.

2 *Re Sharp, Stewart & Co* (1867) LR 5 Eq 155 at 159. This is now the usual practice.

267. Registration of order and minute. The registrar of companies, on production to him of the order confirming the reduction of a company's share capital and delivery to him of a copy of the order and of the minute approved by the court, must register the order and minute[1]. On such registration, and not before, the resolution for reduction as confirmed by the registered order takes effect[2].

The registrar must certify the registration of the order and minute, and the certificate may be either signed by him or authenticated by his official seal[3]. His certificate is conclusive evidence that all the statutory requirements with respect to the reduction have been complied with, and that the company's share capital is as stated in the minute[4].

Where the special resolution has not been properly passed[5], or the company has no power under its articles to reduce its capital, the defect is cured by the certificate[6].

Notice of the registration of the court's order and the minute of reduction must be published in such manner as the court may direct[7]. Publication of the notice of registration cannot be dispensed with[8], but it is necessary to advertise only the registration, and the complete minute need not be set out[9]. The court usually directs that the registration is to be advertised in the same newspapers as those in which the hearing of the petition was advertised.

1 Companies Act 1985 s 138(1). This is subject to the provisions of s 139 (reduction of public company's capital below the authorised minimum: see para 269 post): s 138(1). As to the approval of the minute by the court see para 266 ante.
2 Ibid s 138(2). See *Re Castiglione, Erskine & Co Ltd* [1958] 2 All ER 455, [1958] 1 WLR 688.
3 Companies Act 1985 s 138(4)(a). As to the registrar's official seal see paras 28 note 3, 60 ante.
4 Ibid s 138(4)(b).
5 *Ladies' Dress Association Ltd v Pulbrook* [1900] 2 QB 376, CA.
6 *Re Walker and Smith Ltd* (1903) 72 LJ Ch 572. The conclusiveness of the minute renders it unnecessary to produce evidence, on future reductions, as to the history of the company's capital before the previous reduction.
7 Companies Act 1985 s 138(3).
8 *Re London Steamboat Co Ltd* (1883) 31 WR 781; *Re West African Telegraph Co Ltd* (1886) 55 LJ Ch 436; but see *Re Canada North-Western Land Co* [1885] WN 61.
9 *Re Oceana Development Co Ltd* (1912) 56 Sol Jo 537; *Re North Pole Ice Co Ltd and Reduced* [1924] WN 131.

268. Effect of registered minute. The minute, when registered, is deemed to be substituted for the corresponding part of the company's memorandum of association, and is valid and alterable as if it had been originally contained therein[1]. The substitution of such a minute for part of the company's memorandum is, for the purposes of the statutory provisions requiring copies of the memorandum to embody alterations made to it[2], deemed to be an alteration of the memorandum[3]; and every copy of the memorandum issued after the date of the registration of the order confirming the reduction must, therefore, be in accordance with the order[4]. If this is not done, the company, and every officer of the company who is in default, is liable on summary conviction to a fine not exceeding one-fifth of the statutory maximum for each occasion on which copies are so issued after the date of the alteration[5].

1 Companies Act 1985 s 138(5).
2 Ie ibid s 20: see para 101 ante.
3 Ibid s 138(6).
4 Ibid s 20(1).
5 Ibid ss 20(2), 730, Sch 24. For the meaning of 'officer who is in default' and 'the statutory maximum' see para 1161 post.

269. Public company reducing capital below authorised minimum. Where the court makes an order confirming a reduction of a public company's capital[1] which has the effect of bringing the nominal value of its allotted share capital below the authorised minimum[2], the registrar of companies must not register the order[3] unless the court otherwise directs, or the company is first re-registered as a private company[4]. The court may authorise the company to be so re-registered without its having passed the special resolution normally required[5]; and, where that authority is given, the court must specify in the order the alterations in the company's memorandum and articles to be made in connection with that re-registration[6]. The company may then be re-registered as a private company, if an application in the prescribed form[7] and signed by a director or secretary of the company is delivered to the registrar, together with a printed copy of the memorandum and articles as altered by the court's order[8]. On receipt of such an application, the registrar must retain it and the other documents delivered with it and issue the company with a certificate of incorporation appropriate to a company that is not a public company; and the company by virtue of the issue of the certificate becomes a private company, and the alterations in the memorandum and articles set out in the court's order take effect; and the certificate is conclusive evidence that the requirements of these provisions in respect of re-registration and of matters precedent and incidental to it have been complied with, and that the company is a private company[9].

1 See para 241 et seq ante.
2 For the meaning of 'authorised minimum' see para 652 note 6 post.
3 Ie under the Companies Act 1985 s 138: see para 264 et seq ante.
4 Ibid s 139(1), (2). As to the re-registration of a public company as a private company see para 129 et seq ante.
5 Ie required by ibid s 53: see para 129 ante.
6 Ibid s 139(3).
7 For the prescribed form of application see the Companies (Forms) Regulations 1985, SI 1985/854, reg 4(1), Sch 3, Form 139.
8 Companies Act 1985 s 139(4).
9 Ibid s 139(5).

270. Liability of members after reduction of capital. Where a company's share capital is reduced, a member of the company (past or present) is not liable in respect of any share to any call or contribution exceeding in amount the difference, if any, between the amount of the share as fixed by the minute and the amount paid, or (as the case may be) the reduced amount, if any, which is deemed to have been paid, on the share[1]. If, however, a creditor, entitled in respect of a debt or claim to object to the reduction[2], is, by reason of his ignorance of the proceedings for reduction, or of their nature and effect with respect to his claim, not entered on the list of creditors, and, after the reduction, the company is unable[3] to pay the amount of his debt or claim[4], then:

(1) every person who was a member of the company at the date of the registration of the order for reduction and minute is liable to contribute for the payment of the debt or claim in question an amount not exceeding that which he would have been liable to contribute if the company had commenced to be wound up on the day before that date[5]; and

(2) if the company is wound up, the court, on the application of the creditor in question and proof of his ignorance, may, if it thinks fit, settle accordingly a list of persons so liable to contribute, and make and enforce calls and orders on the contributories settled on the list, as if they were ordinary contributories in a winding up[6].

Nothing in the above provisions affects the rights of the contributories among themselves[7].

1 Companies Act 1985 s 140(1).
2 As to the creditors entitled to object see para 255 ante.
3 Ie within the meaning of the Insolvency Act 1986 s 123: see para 2206 post.
4 Companies Act 1985 s 140(2) (amended by the Insolvency Act 1986 s 439(1), Sch 13 Pt I).
5 Companies Act 1985 s 140(3).
6 Ibid s 140(4).
7 Ibid s 140(5).

(xi) Application of Capital

271. Payment of interest on advances. A company, if so authorised by its articles, may accept from any member the whole or a part of the amount remaining unpaid on any shares held by him, although no part of that amount has been called up[1]. The articles may provide that the company may pay interest on money so advanced, until the same would, but for such advance, become presently payable[2]. In such a case the interest may be paid out of capital[3].

1 Companies Act 1985 s 119(b). As to the exercise of this power see para 417 post.
2 See para 417 note 3 post.
3 *Lock v Queensland Investment and Land Mortgage Co* [1896] AC 461, HL (the articles permitted interest to be paid and the directors made the payment in good faith and in the honest exercise of their discretion). The interest is due to the shareholder in the character of a creditor: *Lock v Queensland Investment and Land Mortgage Co* supra, approving *Dale v Martin* (1883) 11 LR Ir 371. Cf *Re A M Wood's Ships' Woodite Protection Co Ltd* (1890) 62 LT 760.

272. Limits on company's power to deal with its assets. A company incorporated under the Companies Act 1985 or the Acts which it replaces, has not, as corporations at common law have, the power to do with its property all such acts as an ordinary person may do[1]. Thus, a company cannot otherwise than under the statutory provisions[2] make use of its assets to purchase or traffic in its own shares[3], and, subject to certain exceptions, a company may not provide financial assistance for the purchase or subscription of its own shares or the shares of its holding company[4].

1 See para 97 ante.
2 See para 222 et seq ante.

3 *Trevor v Whitworth* (1887) 12 App Cas 409, HL.
4 See para 273 post.

273. Financial assistance by a company for acquisition of its own shares generally prohibited. Subject to the exceptions mentioned below[1], where a person is acquiring, or is proposing to acquire, shares in a company, whether public or private[2], it is not lawful for the company or any of its subsidiaries[3] to give financial assistance[4] directly or indirectly for the purpose of that acquisition before or at the same time as the acquisition takes place[5].

Where a person has acquired shares in a company and any liability has been incurred[6], by that or any other person, for the purpose of that acquisition, it is not lawful for the company or any of its subsidiaries[7] to give financial assistance directly or indirectly for the purpose of reducing or discharging the liability so incurred[8].

For these purposes, 'financial assistance'[9] means financial assistance given:

(1) by way of gift;

(2) by way of guarantee, security or indemnity, other than an indemnity in respect of the indemnifier's own neglect or default, or by way of release or waiver[10];

(3) by way of a loan or any other agreement under which any of the obligations of the person giving the assistance are to be fulfilled at a time when, in accordance with the agreement, any obligation of another party to the agreement remains unfulfilled, or by way of the novation of, or the assignment of rights arising under, a loan or such other agreement; or

(4) in any other manner by a company the net assets[11] of which are thereby reduced to a material extent or which has no net assets[12].

Among the forms which financial assistance might take is the purchase of an asset at an overvalue; there can be no doubt but that this can constitute prohibited assistance[13]. However, even the purchase of an asset at a proper valuation will constitute financial assistance if it is effected with the sole purpose of putting the vendor into funds with which to purchase shares of the company and not in the sole commercial interests of the company itself[14]. Similarly, the payment of a debt owed by the company itself cannot be financial assistance[15], but the payment off of a parent company's debt by a subsidiary will constitute such assistance[16]. The payment of a dividend is not, however, financial assistance[17].

Where an agreement between the parties is capable of being performed in alternative ways, one lawful and one in breach of the provisions relating to financial assistance, it is to be presumed that the parties intend to carry out the agreement in a lawful and not in an unlawful manner[18].

If a company acts in contravention of these provisions, it is liable on conviction on indictment to a fine, or on summary conviction to a fine not exceeding the statutory maximum[19]. Every officer of the company who is in default is liable on conviction on indictment to imprisonment for a term not exceeding two years or a fine, or to both, or on summary conviction to imprisonment for a term not exceeding six months or a fine not exceeding the statutory maximum, or to both[19].

1 See paras 274–276 post.
2 As to the distinction see paras 104, 105 ante.
3 For the meaning of 'subsidiary' see para 827 post. The prohibition applies only to subsidiaries registered under the Companies Act 1985 and therefore a foreign subsidiary of an English parent company can give financial assistance for the acquisition of the latter's shares: *Arab Bank plc v Merchantile Holdings Ltd* [1994] Ch 71, [1994] 2 All ER 74. Any other interpretation would give the Companies Act 1985 s 151 an extra-territorial effect contrary to the general principles of private international law: *Arab Bank plc v*

Merchantile Holdings Ltd supra. The giving of financial assistance by a subsidiary is not ipso facto financial assistance by the parent company but it may involve unlawful conduct by the parent company either by procuring a breach of the prohibition or by constituting indirect financial assistance: *Arab Bank plc v Merchantile Holdings Ltd* supra at 80 and at 80.

4　It was held under the Companies Act 1948 s 54(1) (repealed) by which the 'provision of security' was prohibited that it was thereby implied that a company gave financial assistance to the purchaser of shares whether the security was valid or not; all that was required was that the lender should believe the security to be valid and on the strength of it make the loan: *Heald v O'Connor* [1971] 2 All ER 1105, [1971] 1 WLR 497. It mattered not if the giving of the security was ultra vires or not (*Heald v O'Connor* supra) since statute rendered the prohibition illegal in either case (*Heald v O'Connor* supra; *Selangor United Rubber Estates Ltd v Cradock (a bankrupt) (No 3)* [1968] 2 All ER 1073 at 1152–1154, [1968] 1 WLR 1555 at 1656–1659; *Dressy Frocks Pty Ltd v Bock* (1951) 51 SRNSW 390 (NSW FC); *Shearer Transport Co Pty Ltd v McGrath* [1956] VLR 316; *E H Dey Pty Ltd v Dey* [1966] VR 464; not following *Victor Battery Co Ltd v Curry's Ltd* [1946] Ch 242, [1946] 1 All ER 519). The company was held to be a person for whose benefit the illegality had been created so that, it could eg recover property transferred by the security, or recover damages it suffered as a result of giving financial assistance: *Wallersteiner v Moir* [1974] 3 All ER 217, [1974] 1 WLR 991, CA (not following dictum of Harman LJ in *Essex Aero Ltd v Cross* [1961] CA Transcript 388; *Victor Battery Co Ltd v Curry's Ltd* supra); *Belmont Finance Corpn Ltd v Williams Furniture Ltd (No 2)* [1980] 1 All ER 393, CA (where the company recovered the entire loss sustained through the purchase of the shares which it bought solely to facilitate the transaction). In addition there might be a claim based on breach of fiduciary duty owed to the company eg by directors or by a constructive trustee for it: *Selangor United Rubber Estates Ltd v Cradock (a bankrupt) (No 3)* supra. Illegality of this nature is readily severable in a contract containing other valid provisions: *Herbert Spink (Bournemouth) Ltd v Spink* [1936] Ch 544, [1936] 1 All ER 597; *South Western Mineral Water Co Ltd v Ashmore* [1967] 2 All ER 953, [1967] 1 WLR 1110; *Carney v Herbert* [1985] AC 301, [1985] 1 All ER 438, PC; *Neilson v Stewart* [1991] BCC 713, HL.

5　Companies Act 1985 s 151(1). There is no contravention of this provision where, considered as a whole, the balance of financial advantage is with the company: *Charterhouse Investment Trust Ltd v Tempest Diesels Ltd* [1986] BCLC 1. It is immaterial that the giving of the assistance (eg by means of a debenture) might otherwise be ultra vires the company (and hence void) in any event: *Heald v O'Connor* [1971] 2 All ER 1105, [1971] 1 WLR 497; *Selangor United Rubber Estates Ltd v Cradock (a bankrupt) (No 3)* [1968] 2 All ER 1073 at 1152–1154, [1968] 1 WLR 1555 at 1656–1659; *Dressy Frocks Pty Ltd v Bock* (1951) 51 SRNSW 390; *Shearer Transport Co Pty Ltd v McGrath* [1956] VLR 316; *E H Dey Pty Ltd v Dey* [1966] VR 464; not following *Victor Battery Co Ltd v Curry's Ltd* [1946] Ch 242, [1946] 1 All ER 519. See also *Parlett v Guppys (Bridport) Ltd* (1996) Times, 8 February, CA (the Companies Act 1985 s 151 did not apply to an agreement whereby four private companies together assumed liability for making future payments of salary bonus and pension, subject to there being sufficient profits, to one of its shareholders in return for that shareholder transferring shares in one of those companies; taking into account only that part of the salary which was immediately payable at the time the agreement was executed, there was held to be no material reduction in the net assets of the relevant company).

6　For these purposes, a reference to a person incurring a liability includes his changing his financial position by making an agreement or arrangement (whether enforceable or not and whether made on his own account, or with any other person) or by any other means: Companies Act 1985 s 152(3)(a).

7　See note 3 supra.

8　Companies Act 1985 s 151(2). For these purposes, a reference to a company giving financial assistance for the purpose of reducing or discharging a liability incurred by a person for the purpose of the acquisition of shares includes its giving such assistance for the purpose of wholly or partially restoring his financial position to what it was before the acquisition took place: s 152(3)(b).

9　The phrase 'financial assistance' has to be interpreted in the light of the language of ordinary commerce: *Charterhouse Investment Trust Ltd v Tempest Diesels Ltd* [1986] BCLC 1 at 10 et seq per Hoffman J (the surrender of tax losses by the company whose shares were being acquired to its holding company not shown to amount to company giving financial assistance for the purchase of its own shares). Quaere whether it could ever amount to such. As a penal provision the Companies Act 1985 s 151 should not be strained to cover transactions not fairly within it: *Charterhouse Investment Trust Ltd v Tempest Diesels Ltd* supra; *British and Commonwealth Holdings plc v Barclays Bank plc* [1996] 1 BCLC 1 at 25 (affd [1996] 1 All ER 381, [1996] 1 WLR 1, CA).

10　Each of the terms so used (guarantee, security, indemnity, release, waiver) can properly be described as a legal term of art: *British and Commonwealth Holdings plc v Barclays Bank plc* [1996] 1 BCLC 1 at 25 (affd [1996] 1 All ER 381, [1996] 1 WLR 1, CA ('indemnity' meaning a contract by one party to keep the other harmless from loss; on the facts no indemnity in this sense and therefore no financial assistance)).

11 For these purposes, 'net assets' means the aggregate of the company's assets, less the aggregate of its liabilities, which liabilities include any provision for liabilities or charges within the Companies Act 1985 s 226(3), Sch 4 para 89 (see para 832 note 24 post): s 152(2). See *Parlett v Guppys (Bridport) Ltd* (1996) Times, 8 February, CA.

12 Companies Act 1985 s 152(1)(a).

13 See *Belmont Finance Corpn Ltd v Williams Furniture Ltd* [1979] Ch 250, [1979] 1 All ER 118, CA (where a conspiracy to effect a breach of these provisions was alleged; it was held that the company was not a party to such conspiracy, so as to be debarred from suing; the guilty knowledge of its directors would not be imputed to the company).

14 *Belmont Finance Corpn Ltd v Williams Furniture Ltd (No 2)* [1980] 1 All ER 393, CA. It was queried whether there would have been a breach if the company had legitimately entered into the transaction in pursuit of its own commercial interests and not solely as a means of assisting the purchaser to acquire its shares, but nevertheless partly with the object of putting the purchaser in funds for this purpose, or with knowledge that the purchaser intended to use the proceeds of sale in this manner: *Belmont Finance Corpn Ltd v Williams Furniture Ltd (No 2)* supra at 402 per Buckley LJ. As to the possible effect of such knowledge cf *Steen v Law* [1964] AC 287 at 301, [1963] 3 All ER 770 at 776, PC per Lord Radcliffe. See now the Companies Act 1985 s 153(1), (2) and para 274 post. In *Brady v Brady* [1989] AC 755 at 778, [1988] 2 All ER 617 at 632, HL, Lord Oliver of Aylmerton noted that the Companies Act 1985 s 153(1),(2) was introduced to address the concerns arising from *Belmont Finance Corpn Ltd v Williams Furniture Ltd (No 2)* supra. The interpretation of those provisions adopted by the House of Lords in *Brady v Brady* supra may itself restrict their scope. See para 274 post.

15 *Spink (Bournemouth) Ltd v Spink* [1936] Ch 544, [1936] 1 All ER 597; *Burton v Palmer* [1980] 2 NSWLR 878 (NSW CA). The criticism of *Armour Hick Northern Ltd v Armour Trust Ltd* [1980] 3 All ER 833 at 837, 838; sub nom *Armour Hick Northern Ltd v Whitehouse* [1980] 1 WLR 1520 at 1525, 1526 per Mahoney JA in this latter case is based upon an incomplete newspaper report. It does not in any way conflict with the principle stated in the text.

16 *Armour Hick Northern Ltd v Armour Trust Ltd* [1980] 3 All ER 833; sub nom *Armour Hick Northern Ltd v Whitehouse* [1980] 1 WLR 1520.

17 *Re Wellington Publishing Co Ltd* [1973] 1 NZLR 133. See also the Companies Act 1985 s 153(3)(a) and para 274 head (1) post.

18 *Neilson v Stewart* [1991] BCC 713, HL (preferred construction of document reasonably susceptible of two meanings was one which did not render the agreement in breach of the financial assistance provisions). See also *Brady v Brady* [1989] AC 755, [1988] 2 All ER 617, HL (private company which had failed to utilise the relaxation provisions in favour of private companies (see para 276 post) and had entered into an agreement in breach of the Companies Act 1985 s 151 could obtain specific performance of the agreement subject to an undertaking to utilise the statutory provisions rendering the agreement lawful). This is only possible where there is no need for any departure from the agreed terms: *Brady v Brady* supra; and see *Plaut v Steiner* (1989) 5 BCC 352 (agreement did not permit of any performance which would be lawful and could not be enforced).

19 Companies Act 1985 ss 151(3), 730, Sch 24. For the meaning of 'officer who is in default' and 'the statutory maximum' see para 1161 post.

274. Transactions not prohibited in relation to acquisition of shares. The prohibition against providing financial assistance for the acquisition of shares in a company[1] does not prohibit a company from giving such assistance for the purpose of an acquisition of shares in it or its holding company[2] if the company's principal purpose[3] in giving that assistance is not to give it for the purpose of any such acquisition, or the giving of the assistance for that purpose is but an incidental part of some larger purpose of the company, and the assistance is given in good faith in the interests of the company[4].

Similarly, the prohibition against providing financial assistance directly or indirectly for the purpose of reducing or discharging a liability which has been incurred in the acquisition of shares in the company[5] does not prohibit the company from giving such assistance if its principal purpose[6] in giving the assistance is not to reduce or discharge any liability incurred by a person for the purpose of the acquisition of shares in the company or its holding company, or the reduction or discharge of any such liability is but an incidental part of some larger purpose of the company, and the assistance is given in good faith in the interests of the company[7].

Neither prohibition applies to:

(1) a distribution of a company's assets by way of dividend lawfully made[8] or a distribution made in the course of the company's winding up[9];

(2) the allotment of bonus shares[10];

(3) a reduction of capital duly confirmed by the court[11];

(4) a redemption or purchase of shares made in accordance with the statutory provisions[12];

(5) anything done in pursuance of an order of the court under the provisions dealing with compromises and arrangements with creditors and members[13];

(6) anything done under an arrangement made in pursuance of the statutory provisions enabling liquidators in winding up to accept shares as consideration for the sale of property[14]; or

(7) anything done under an arrangement[15] made between a company and its creditors which is binding on the creditors by virtue of the statutory provisions relating to such arrangements when made by a company about to be or in the course of being wound up[16].

Similarly neither prohibition applies:

(a) where the lending of money is part of the ordinary business of the company, to the lending of money by the company in the ordinary course of its business[17];

(b) to the provision by a company, in good faith in the interests of the company, of financial assistance for the purposes of an employees' share scheme[18];

(c) without prejudice to head (b) above, to the provision of financial assistance by a company or any of its subsidiaries[19] for the purpose of or in connection with anything done by the company, or a company in the same group[20], for the purpose of enabling or facilitating transactions in shares in the first-mentioned company between, and involving the acquisition of beneficial ownership of those shares by, any of the following persons:

  (i) the bona fide employees or former employees of that company, or of another company in the same group[20]; or

  (ii) the wives, husbands, widows, widowers, children or stepchildren under the age of 18 of any such employees or former employees;

(d) the making by a company of loans to persons (other than directors) employed in good faith by the company with a view to enabling those persons to acquire fully paid shares in the company or its holding company to be held by them by way of beneficial ownership[21].

1 Ie under the Companies Act 1985 s 151(1): see para 273 ante.

2 For the meaning of 'holding company' see para 827 post.

3 The focus of the Companies Act 1985 s 153 (as amended) is on the purpose of the financial assistance; and, in construing the word 'purpose' for these purposes, the court will bear in mind the mischief against which the statutory provisions are aimed and will distinguish between a purpose and the reason why a purpose is formed: *Brady v Brady* [1989] AC 755 at 779, [1988] 2 All ER 617 at 633, HL. Where reliance is placed on the fact that the company's principal purpose in giving the assistance is not to give it for the purpose of any such acquisition or, as the case may be, is not to reduce or discharge any liability incurred by a person for the purpose of the acquisition of shares in the company or its holding company, this envisages a principal and, by implication, a subsidiary purpose for the assistance: *Brady v Brady* supra at 778 and at 632. For example, the assistance may be given principally to acquire from the purchaser of shares in the company an asset which the company requires for its business: *Brady v Brady* supra at 778 and at 632. Where reliance is placed on the fact that the financial assistance is but an incidental part of some larger purpose of the company, it is necessary to find some larger overall corporate purpose of the company in which the giving of the financial assistance or the resultant reduction or discharge of

liability is merely incidental: *Brady v Brady* supra at 779 and at 633. The existence of reasons such as the commercial advantages flowing from the transaction do not amount to a larger purpose of which the assistance can properly be considered to be an incident: *Brady v Brady* supra at 779 and at 633. In *Brady v Brady* supra the purpose of the financial assistance was to assist in the financing of the acquisition of shares, although the reason for the financial assistance was to facilitate the break up of a business. That reason did not amount to the larger purpose required by the Companies Act 1985 s 153 (as amended) and therefore the financial assistance was not within s 153(2) (see infra). See also *Plaut v Steiner* (1989) 5 BCC 352.

4   Companies Act 1985 s 153(1). The words 'in good faith in the interests of the company' form a single composite expression and postulate a requirement that those responsible for procuring the company to provide the assistance act in the genuine belief that it is being done in the company's interest: *Brady v Brady* [1989] AC 755 at 777, [1988] 2 All ER 617 at 632, HL. The time at which this is to be considered is the time at which the assistance is given: *Brady v Brady* supra. If the company was insolvent at that time, the assistance could not be given in good faith in the interests of the company (*Plaut v Steiner* (1989) 5 BCC 352); nor would it be so given where the company giving the assistance had no interest in the transaction (*Plaut v Steiner* supra).
5   Ie under the Companies Act 1985 s 151(2): see para 273 ante.
6   See note 3 supra.
7   Companies Act 1985 s 153(2). See also note 4 supra.
8   See para 701 et seq post.
9   See para 2590 et seq post.
10   See para 732 post.
11   Ie under the Companies Act 1985 s 137: see para 215 et seq ante.
12   Ie under ibid Pt V Ch VII (ss 159–181) (as amended): see para 219 et seq ante.
13   Ie under ibid s 425 (as amended): see para 1447 et seq post.
14   Ie under the Insolvency Act 1986 s 110: see para 1480 et seq post.
15   Ie under ibid Pt I (ss 1–7): see para 2044 et seq post.
16   Companies Act 1985 s 153(3) (amended by the Insolvency Act 1986 s 439(1), Sch 13 Pt I).
17   This exemption does not apply, however, to a loan made for the specific purpose of the acquisition of shares in the company or its holding company: *Steen v Law* [1963] AC 287, [1963] 3 All ER 770, PC; *Fowlie v Slater* (23 March 1979, unreported).
18   For the meaning of 'employees' share scheme' see para 120 note 8 ante.
19   For the meaning of 'subsidiary' see para 827 post.
20   For these purposes, a company is in the same group as another company if it is a holding company or subsidiary of that company, or a subsidiary of a holding company of that company: Companies Act 1985 s 153(5) (added by the Financial Services Act 1986 s 196(1), (3); substituted by the Companies Act 1989 s 144(4), Sch 18 para 33(1), (3)).
21   Companies Act 1985 s 153(4) (amended by the Financial Services Act 1986 s 196(1), (2); the Companies Act 1989 s 132, Sch 18 para 33(1), (2)).

275. Special restriction for public companies.   In the case of a public company[1], the relaxations as to the giving of financial assistance[2] authorise the giving of such assistance only if the company has net assets[3] which are not thereby reduced, or, to the extent that those assets are thereby reduced, if the assistance is provided out of distributable profits[4].

1   For the meaning of 'public company' see para 82 ante.
2   Ie those contained in the Companies Act 1985 s 153(4): see para 274 heads (a)–(d) ante. For the meaning of 'financial assistance' see para 273 ante.
3   For these purposes, 'net assets' means the amount by which the aggregate of the company's assets exceeds the aggregate of its liabilities, taking the amount of both assets and liabilities to be as stated in the company's accounting records (see para 801 et seq post) immediately before the financial assistance is given (ibid s 154(2)(a)); and 'liabilities' includes any amount retained as reasonably necessary for the purpose of providing for any liability or loss which is either likely to be incurred or certain to be incurred but uncertain as to amount or as to the date on which it will arise (s 154(2)(b)).
4   Ibid s 154(1). For these purposes, 'distributable profits', in relation to the giving of any financial assistance, means those profits out of which the company could lawfully make a distribution equal in value to that assistance, and includes, in a case where the financial assistance is or includes a non-cash asset, any profit which, if the company were to make a distribution of that asset, would under s 276 (as

amended) (see para 713 post) be available for that purpose: s 152(1)(b). 'Distribution' has the meaning given by s 263(2) (see para 701 post): s 152(1)(c).

276. Relaxation of prohibitions for private companies. The above restrictions[1] do not prohibit a private company[2] from giving financial assistance in a case where the acquisition of shares in question is or was an acquisition of shares in the company, or, if it is a subsidiary[3] of another private company, in that other company, if the following provisions[4] are complied with as respects the giving of that assistance[5].

The financial assistance may be given only if the company has net assets[6] which are not thereby reduced, or, to the extent that they are reduced, if the assistance is provided out of distributable profits[7].

Financial assistance may not be given by a subsidiary in a case where the acquisition of shares in question is or was an acquisition of shares in its holding company[8], if it is also a subsidiary of a public company[9] which is itself a subsidiary of that holding company[10].

Unless the company proposing to give the financial assistance is a wholly-owned subsidiary[11], the giving of assistance must be approved by special resolution[12] of the company in general meeting[13]; and, where the financial assistance is to be given by the company in a case where the acquisition of shares in question is or was an acquisition of shares in its holding company, that holding company and any other company which is both the company's holding company and a subsidiary of that other holding company (except, in any case, a company which is a wholly-owned subsidiary) must also approve the giving of the financial assistance by special resolution in general meeting[14].

Any such special resolution must be passed on the date on which the directors of that company make the statutory declaration referred to below, or within the week immediately following that date[15].

The directors of the company proposing to give the financial assistance, and, where the shares acquired or to be acquired are shares in its holding company, the directors of that company and of any other company which is both the company's holding company and a subsidiary of that other holding company must before the financial assistance is given make a statutory declaration in the prescribed[16] form[17]. It must:

(1) contain such particulars of the financial assistance to be given, and of the business of the company of which they are directors, as may be prescribed[18] and must identify the person to whom the assistance is to be given[19]; and

(2) state that the directors have formed the opinion, as regards the company's initial situation immediately following the date on which the assistance is proposed to be given, that there will be no ground on which it could then be found to be unable to pay its debts, and either:

(a) if it is intended to commence the winding up of the company within 12 months of that date, that the company will be able to pay its debts in full within 12 months of the commencement of the winding up; or

(b) in any other case, that the company will be able to pay its debts as they fall due during the year immediately following that date[20].

In so forming their opinion, the directors must take into account the same liabilities (including contingent and prospective liabilities) as would be relevant[21] for the purpose of considering whether a company was unable to pay its debts for the purposes of a winding-up petition[22].

The directors' statutory declaration must have annexed to it a report addressed to them by their company's auditors stating that they have inquired into the state of affairs of the company and that they are not aware of anything to indicate that the opinion expressed by the directors in the declaration as to any of the matters of opinion contained in it is unreasonable in all the circumstances[23].

The statutory declaration and auditors' report must be delivered[24] to the registrar of companies together with a copy of any special resolution so passed by the company and delivered to the registrar in compliance with the statutory requirement in that behalf[25], or, where no such resolution is required to be passed, within 15 days after the making of the declaration[26].

If a company fails so to deliver the statutory declaration and auditors' report, the company, and every officer of it who is in default, is liable on summary conviction to a fine not exceeding the statutory maximum and, on conviction after continued contravention, to a daily default fine not exceeding one-fiftieth of the statutory maximum[27].

A director of a company who so makes a statutory declaration without having reasonable grounds for the opinion expressed in it is liable on conviction on indictment to imprisonment for a term not exceeding two years or a fine, or to both, or on summary conviction to imprisonment for a term not exceeding six months or a fine not exceeding the statutory maximum, or to both[28].

1 Ie those contained in the Companies Act 1985 s 151: see para 273 ante.
2 For the meaning of 'private company' see para 82 ante.
3 For the meaning of 'subsidiary' see para 827 post.
4 Ie the Companies Act 1985 s 155(2)–(6) (see infra), s 156 (see infra), s 157 (see infra and 277 post) and s 158 (see para 278 post).
5 Ibid s 155(1). Non-compliance with the statutory requirements will not be treated as a mere procedural irregularity capable of being waived or dispensed with or validated by unanimous agreement of all members entitled to vote at meetings of the company: *Re SH & Co (Realisations) 1990 Ltd* [1993] BCLC 1309 at 1316; and see *Precision Dippings Ltd v Precision Dippings Marketing Ltd* [1986] Ch 447 at 455–457, [1985] 3 WLR 812 at 815–817, CA. The consequence of non-compliance is that the relaxation provisions will not apply and there will be a breach of the statutory prohibition on the giving of financial assistance with all the consequences of unenforceability and liability to penal sanctions: *Re SH & Co (Realisations) 1990 Ltd* supra at 1317. The very severity of the consequences of non-compliance may encourage some leniency on the part of the court towards errors in compliance: see *Re SH & Co (Realisations) 1990 Ltd* supra at 1319. See also *Re Willaire Systems plc* [1987] BCLC 67, CA.
6 For these purposes, the Companies Act 1985 s 154(2) (meaning of 'net assets': see para 275 note 3 ante) applies for the interpretation of s 155(2): s 155(2).
7 Ibid s 155(2).
8 For the meaning of 'holding company' see para 827 post.
9 For the meaning of 'public company' see para 82 ante.
10 Companies Act 1985 s 155(3).
11 For the meaning of 'wholly-owned subsidiary' see para 827 post.
12 As to special resolutions see para 683 post.
13 Companies Act 1985 s 155(4). A written resolution is not effective if any of the requirements of s 381A(7), Sch 15A para 4 (as added) is not complied with: Sch 15A para 2(2) (added by the Companies Act 1989 s 114(1)). In relation to a written resolution giving approval under the Companies Act 1985 s 155(4) or s 155(5) (see infra), s 157(4)(a) (see para 277 head (1) post) does not apply, but the documents referred to therein must be supplied to each relevant member at or before the time at which the resolution is supplied to him for signature: Sch 15A para 4 (added by the Companies Act 1989 s 114(1)). For the meaning of 'written resolution' and 'relevant member' see para 224 note 3 ante.
14 Companies Act 1985 s 155(5). See also note 13 supra.
15 Ibid s 157(1).
16 For the prescribed form of statutory declaration see the Companies (Forms) Regulations 1985, SI 1985/854, reg 4(1), Sch 3, Form 155(6)(a) (declaration by directors of company), Form 155(6)(b) (declaration by directors of holding company). The requirement is that the statutory declaration be *in* the prescribed form and not *on* the prescribed form. If all the required particulars are delivered to the registrar, the fact that a particular piece of paper was not used does not mean that there has been non-compliance with the statutory obligation to deliver the prescribed particulars: *Re NL Electrical Ltd, Ghosh v 3i plc* [1994] 1 BCLC 22 (accurate and complete particulars delivered on form which had been

in use under the Companies Acts 1948–1981 were in the prescribed form although the form had been replaced by that in the Companies (Forms) Regulations 1985; there was no difference in content between the two versions).

17 Companies Act 1985 s 155(6).
18 The statutory provisions do not state how detailed the particulars must be but the prescribed form of statutory declaration (see note 16 supra) refers to the form of assistance and the principal terms on which it is given. If information sufficient to address those requirements is included in the statutory declaration, the fact that other matters are omitted does not prevent the particulars from being reasonably and fairly described as particulars of the form and principal terms of financial assistance: *Re SH & Co (Realisations) 1990 Ltd* [1993] BCLC 1309 (on the facts there had been compliance though it was a case close to the borderline). Solicitors responsible for completing such a statutory declaration should err on the side of caution and include a fuller form of particulars so as to remove any possible doubt as to whether there has been compliance: *Re SH & Co (Realisations) 1990 Ltd* supra at 1318.
19 Companies Act 1985 s 156(1).
20 Ibid s 156(2).
21 Ie under the Insolvency Act 1986 s 122 (as amended): see para 2206 post.
22 Companies Act 1985 s 156(3) (amended by the Insolvency Act 1986 s 439(1), Sch 13 Pt I).
23 Companies Act 1985 s 156(4).
24 The requirement is simply for delivery of the statutory declaration to the registrar; there is no requirement for its registration by the registrar: *Re SH & Co (Realisations) 1990 Ltd* [1993] BCLC 1309 at 1319; *Re NL Electrical Ltd, Ghosh v 3i plc* [1994] 1 BCLC 22 at 26.
25 Ie under the Companies Act 1985 s 380(4)(a): see para 691 post.
26 Ibid s 156(5). Failure to deliver the statutory declaration and auditors' report within the specified period does not result in the financial assistance being improperly provided: *Re NL Electrical Ltd, Ghosh v 3i plc* [1994] 1 BCLC 22. It does not render compliance with the relaxation provisions nugatory.
27 Companies Act 1985 ss 156(6), 730, Sch 24. See also *Re NL Electrical Ltd, Ghosh v 3i plc* [1994] 1 BCLC 22. For the meaning of 'officer who is in default', 'the statutory maximum' and 'daily default fine' see para 1161 post.
28 Companies Act 1985 ss 156(7), 730, Sch 24.

277. Cancellation or ineffectiveness of special resolution for the giving of financial assistance.

Where such a special resolution has been passed[1], an application may be made to the court for the cancellation of the resolution by the holders of not less in the aggregate than 10% in nominal value of the company's issued share capital or any class of it, or, if the company is not limited by shares, by not less than 10% of the company's members; but the application may not be made by a person who consented to or voted in favour of the resolution[2].

Save as to the number of applicants necessary to enable the application to be made[3], all the statutory provisions[4] relating to an application to the court to cancel a special resolution by a public company to be re-registered as a private company apply[5].

A special resolution for the giving of financial assistance[6] is not effective[7]:

(1) unless the statutory declaration made by the directors, together with the auditors' report annexed to it, is available for inspection by members of the company at the meeting at which the resolution is passed[8]; or

(2) if it is cancelled by the court on an application made in accordance with the above procedure[9].

1 Ie a special resolution required by the Companies Act 1985 s 155: see para 276 ante.
2 Ibid s 157(2). The application is made by petition: RSC Ord 102 r 4(1)(k). It is not necessary to take out a summons for directions: RSC Ord 102 r 6(1), (2)(d).
3 Ie save for the Companies Act 1985 s 54(2): see para 130 ante.
4 Ie ibid s 54(3)–(10): see para 130 ante.
5 Ibid s 157(3). For the prescribed notice of any such application made to the court see the Companies (Forms) Regulations 1985, SI 1985/854, reg 4(1), Sch 3, Form 157 (amended by SI 1987/752).
6 See note 1 supra.
7 Ie for purposes of the Companies Act 1985 s 155.
8 Ibid s 157(4)(a). As to written resolutions of private companies see para 276 note 13 ante.
9 Ibid s 157(4)(b).

278. Time for giving financial assistance by private company. The following provisions apply as to the time before and after which financial assistance may not be so given by a private company[1].

Where a special resolution is required to be passed approving the giving of assistance[2], the assistance must not be given before the expiry of the period of four weeks beginning with the date on which the special resolution is passed or, where more than one such resolution is passed, the date on which the last of them is passed, unless, as respects that resolution, or, if more than one, each of them, every member of the company which passed the resolution who is entitled to vote at general meetings of the company voted in favour of the resolution[3].

If an application for the cancellation of any such resolution is duly made[4], the financial assistance must not be given before the final determination of the application unless the court otherwise orders[5].

The assistance must not be given after the expiry of the period of eight weeks beginning with:

(1) the date on which the directors of the company proposing to give the assistance made their statutory declaration[6]; or

(2) where that company is a subsidiary[7] and both its directors and the directors of any of its holding companies[8] made such a declaration, the date on which the earliest of the declarations is made,

unless the court, on an application to cancel the special resolution[9], otherwise orders[10].

1 Companies Act 1985 s 158(1).
2 Ie by ibid s 155: see para 276 ante.
3 Ibid s 158(2).
4 Ie under ibid s 157: see para 277 ante.
5 Ibid s 158(3).
6 Ie under ibid s 155.
7 For the meaning of 'subsidiary' see para 827 post.
8 For the meaning of 'holding company' see para 827 post.
9 Ie under the Companies Act 1985 s 157: see para 277 ante.
10 Ibid s 158(4).

279. Loans to directors. Subject to certain limited exceptions, it is unlawful for a company to make a loan to any person who is its director or a director of its holding company, or to enter into any guarantee or provide any security in connection with a loan made to such a director by any other person[1].

1 See the Companies Act 1985 s 330 and para 598 et seq post.

(9) CAPITAL DUTY

280. Stamp duty in respect of chargeable transactions. The stamp duties chargeable on documents relating to chargeable transactions of capital companies[1] have been abolished in relation to any transaction occuring on or after 22 March 1988[2].

1 Ie by virtue of the Finance Act 1973 s 47 (repealed). 'Chargeable transactions' included the formation of a capital company and certain increases in the assets of a capital company: see Sch 19 para 1(a), (b). For the meaning of 'capital company' see s 48 (repealed).
2 Finance Act 1988 s 141(1), (2)(a). For transitional provisions see s 141(2)(b)–(d).

(10) OFFERS OF SHARES FOR SUBSCRIPTION OR PURCHASE

(i) Offers of Listed Securities

A. LISTING OF SECURITIES

281. Official listing of securities. The provisions of Part IV of the Financial Services Act 1986[1] govern the admission of securities[2] to the Official List[3]. The competent authority[4], that is to say London Stock Exchange Limited[5], may make rules ('listing rules') for the purposes of that Act[6].

Listing rules may make different provision for different cases[7]; and they may authorise the competent authority to dispense with or modify the application of the rules in particular cases and by reference to any circumstances[8].

Listing rules must be made by an instrument in writing[9]. Immediately after an instrument containing listing rules is made, it must be printed and made available to the public with or without payment[10]. A person is not to be taken to have contravened any listing rule if he shows that at the time of the alleged contravention the instrument containing the rule had not been made available as so required[11].

The production of a printed copy of an instrument purporting to be made by the competent authority on which is indorsed a certificate signed by an officer of the authority authorised by it for that purpose stating:

(1) that the instrument was made by the authority;

(2) that the copy is a true copy of the instrument; and

(3) that on a specified date the instrument was made available to the public as required under the above provisions[12],

is prima facie evidence of the facts stated in the certificate[13]. Any certificate purporting to be so signed is deemed to have been duly signed unless the contrary is shown[14]. Any person wishing to cite an instrument made by the competent authority may require the authority to cause a copy of it to be indorsed with such a certificate[15].

Listing rules may require the payment of fees to the competent authority in respect of applications for listing and the retention of securities in the Official List[16].

1 Ie the Financial Services Act 1986 Pt IV (ss 142–156B) (as amended): see infra and para 283 et seq post. These provisions provide for the carrying into effect of EC Council Directives 79/279 (OJ L66, 16.3.79, p 21), 80/390 (OJ L100, 17.4.80, p 1), 82/121 (OJ L48, 20.2.82, p 26) and 89/298 (OJ L124, 5.5.89, p 8) relating to Stock Exchange listings. See further para 5 ante and EUROPEAN COMMUNITIES vol 51 para 11·61. As to Stock Exchange listing generally see STOCK EXCHANGE vol 45 paras 5, 11, 79–82.

2 For the meaning of 'securities' see para 283 post.

3 For these purposes, 'the Official List' means the list maintained by the competent authority for the purposes of the Financial Services Act 1986 Pt IV (ss 142–156B) (as amended); and references to listing are references to inclusion in the Official List in pursuance of Pt IV (ss 142–156B) (as amended): s 142(7) (amended by the Official Listing of Securities (Change of Competent Authority) Regulations 1991, SI 1991/2000, reg 3(1)(c)). See further STOCK EXCHANGE vol 45 para 5.

4 Any functions of the competent authority under the Financial Services Act 1986 Pt IV (ss 142–156B) (as amended) may be exercised by its governing body or by any committee or sub-committee of that body or by any officer or servant of the authority except that listing rules (1) must be made only by the governing body of the authority or by a committee or sub-committee of that body; and (2) if made by a committee or sub-committee, cease to have effect at the end of the period of 28 days beginning with the

day on which they are made (but without prejudice to anything done under them) unless before the end of that period they are confirmed by the governing body of the authority: s 142(8) (substituted by the Official Listing of Securities (Change of Competent Authority) Regulations 1991 reg 3(1)(d)).
  5 As to the change of name of The International Stock Exchange of the United Kingdom and the Republic of Ireland Limited to London Stock Exchange Limited following the separation of the Irish Stock Exchange from the London Stock Exchange see para 21 note 8 ante. Irish companies are now treated as overseas companies for the purpose of listing charges and the *Listing Rules*. As to the *Listing Rules* see para 282 post.
  6 Financial Services Act 1986 s 142(6) (amended by the Official Listing of Securities (Change of Competent Authority) Regulations 1991 reg 3(1)(b)).
  7 Financial Services Act 1986 s 156(1).
  8 Ibid s 156(2).
  9 Ibid s 156(3).
10 Ibid s 156(4).
11 Ibid s 156(5).
12 Ie by ibid s 156(4): see supra.
13 Ibid s 156(6).
14 Ibid s 156(7).
15 Ibid s 156(8).
16 Ibid s 155.

282. The Listing Rules. The listing rules made by the Stock Exchange[1] govern admission to listing, the continuing obligations of issuers, the enforcement of those obligations and suspension and cancellation of listing[2]. They reflect:
  (1) requirements that are mandatory under EC Council Directives[3];
  (2) additional requirements of the Stock Exchange under its powers as competent authority in relation to securities covered by Part IV of the Financial Services Act 1986[4]; and
  (3) corresponding requirements in relation to other securities admitted to listing[5].
The listing rules deal with the following matters[6]:
  (a) compliance with and enforcement of the listing rules[7];
  (b) sponsors and listing agents[8];
  (c) conditions for listing[9];
  (d) methods of bringing securities to listing[10];
  (e) listing particulars[11];
  (f) contents of listing particulars[12];
  (g) listing application procedures[13];
  (h) publication and circulation of listing particulars[14];
  (i) continuing obligations[15];
  (j) transactions[16];
  (k) transactions with related parties[17];
  (l) financial information[18];
  (m) documents not requiring prior approval[19];
  (n) circulars[20];
  (o) purchase of own securities[21];
  (p) directors[22];
  (q) overseas companies[23];
  (r) property companies[24];
  (s) mineral companies[25];
  (t) scientific research based companies[26];
  (u) investment entities[27];
  (v) public sector issuers[28];
  (w) specialist securities (including eurobonds)[29];

(x)   miscellaneous securities[30];

(y)   companies undertaking major capital projects[31];

(z)   venture capital trusts[32].

1 As to the making of listing rules see para 281 ante.

2 See the Introduction to the *Listing Rules* ('the Yellow Book') published by London Stock Exchange Limited.

3 As to EC Council Directives see paras 5, 281 note 1 ante.

4 Ie the Financial Services Act 1986 Pt IV (ss 142–156B) (as amended): see para 281 ante and para 283 et seq post.

5 See the Introduction to the *Listing Rules*.

6 In addition to the matters listed below the *Listing Rules* also contain: definitions; rules for approval of prospectuses where no application for listing is made (see rr 1–18, Appendix); sponsor's undertaking (see Sch 1); sponsor's declaration of interests (see Sch 2); shareholder statement (see Sch 3); pricing statement (see Sch 2A); application for admission of securities to listing – shares and debt securities (see Sch 3A); application for admission of securities to listing – specialist and miscellaneous securities (see Sch 3B); declaration by sponsor (see Sch 4A); declaration by listing agent (see Sch 4B); block listing quarterly return (see Sch 5); declaration by issuer (see Sch 6); declaration of a director's business activities (see Sch 7); specimen preamble to a valuation certificate (see Sch 8); certificate from public sector issuer (see Sch 9); notification of major interests in shares (see Sch 10); notification of interests of directors and connected persons (see Sch 11); best practice provisions: directors' remuneration; charges for listing.

7 See ibid Ch 1 (rr 1.1–1.22).

8 See ibid Ch 2 (rr 2.1–2.27), Appendix.

9 See ibid Ch 3 (rr 3.1–3.37).

10 See ibid Ch 4 (rr 4.1–4.38).

11 See ibid Ch 5 (rr 5.1–5.34), Appendices 1, 2.

12 See ibid Ch 6 (rr 6.A–6.P.10).

13 See ibid Ch 7 (rr 7.1–7.13).

14 See ibid Ch 8 (rr 8.1–8.26).

15 See ibid Ch 9 (rr 9.1–9.49).

16 See ibid Ch 10 (rr 10.1–10.50), Appendix.

17 See ibid Ch 11 (rr 11.1–11.10).

18 See ibid Ch 12 (rr 12.1–12.59).

19 See ibid Ch 13 (rr 13.1–13.29), Appendices 1, 2.

20 See ibid Ch 14 (rr 14.1–14.26).

21 See ibid Ch 15 (rr 15.1–15.18).

22 See ibid Ch 16 (rr 16.1–16.18), Appendix.

23 See ibid Ch 17 (rr 17.1–17.78).

24 See ibid Ch 18 (rr 18.1–18.28).

25 See ibid Ch 19 (rr 19.1–19.17).

26 See ibid Ch 20 (rr 20.1–20.13).

27 See ibid Ch 21 (rr 21.1–21.25), Appendix.

28 See ibid Ch 22 (rr 22.1–22.32), Appendix.

29 See ibid Ch 23 (rr 23.1–23.88), Appendix.

30 See ibid Ch 24 (rr 24.1–24.67), Appendix.

31 See ibid Ch 25 (rr 25.1–25.4).

32 See ibid Ch 26 (rr 26.1–26.14).

283. Meaning of 'securities'. 'Securities' means[1] any of the following investments:

(1)   shares[2] and stock in the share capital of a company[3];

(2)   debentures, including debenture stock, loan stock, bonds, certificates of deposit and other instruments creating or acknowledging indebtedness issued otherwise than by the government of a member State or a local authority in a member State but excluding:

(a)   any instrument acknowledging or creating indebtedness for, or for money borrowed to defray, the consideration payable under a contract for the supply of goods or services;

   (b) a cheque or other bill of exchange[4], a banker's draft or a letter of credit;

   (c) a banknote, a statement showing a balance in a current, deposit or savings account or (by reason of any financial obligation contained in it) a lease or other disposition of property, a heritable security or an insurance policy;

(3) warrants or other instruments entitling the holder to subscribe for investments falling within head (1) above, whether or not such investments are for the time being in existence or identifiable; and

(4) certificates or other instruments which confer:

   (a) property rights in respect of any investments falling within head (1) above;

   (b) any right to acquire, dispose of, underwrite or convert an investment falling within head (1) above, being a right to which the holder would be entitled if he held any such investment to which the certificate or instrument relates; or

   (c) a contractual right (other than an option) to acquire any such investment falling within head (1) above otherwise than by subscription;

but this head does not apply to any instrument which confers rights in respect of two or more investments issued by different persons[5].

1 Ie for the purposes of the Financial Services Act 1986 Pt IV (ss 142–156B) (as amended): see para 281 ante; infra; and para 284 et seq post.

2 Ibid s 142 (as amended) has effect as if transferable shares in a body incorporated under the law of, or of any part of, the United Kingdom relating to industrial and provident societies were not investments to which s 142 (as amended) applies: Investment Services Regulations 1995, SI 1995/3275, reg 32, Sch 7 para 35(a).

3 For these purposes, 'company' includes any body corporate and any unincorporated body constituted under the law of a country or territory outside the United Kingdom, excluding an open-ended investment company but including a building society incorporated under the law of, or of any part of, the United Kingdom and any body incorporated under the law of, or of any part of, the United Kingdom relating to industrial and provident societies and credit unions: Financial Services Act 1986 Sch 1 para 1, note (amended by the Financial Services Act 1986 (Extension of Scope of Act) Order 1991, SI 1991/1104, art 2).

4 The Financial Services Act 1986 s 142 (as amended) has effect as if bills of exchange accepted by a banker were not investments to which s 142 (as amended) applies: Investment Services Regulations 1995 Sch 7 para 35(b).

5 See the Financial Services Act 1986 s 142(2), (3), (7), Sch 1 paras 1, 2, 4, 5 (as amended). The Secretary of State may by order direct that s 142 (as amended) shall apply also to investments falling within Sch 1 para 6 (units in a collective investment scheme) or to such investments of any class or description: s 142(4). An order under s 142(4) is subject to annulment in pursuance of a resolution of either House of Parliament: s 142(5). At the date at which this volume states the law no such order had been made.

   Nothing in Pt IV (ss 142–156B) (as amended) affects the powers of the competent authority in respect of investments to which s 142 (as amended) does not apply and such investments may be admitted to the Official List otherwise than in accordance with Pt IV (ss 142–156B) (as amended): s 142(9) (amended by the Official Listing of Securities (Change of Competent Authority) Regulations 1991, SI 1991/2000, reg 3(1)(e)). For the meaning of 'the competent authority' see para 281 ante; and for the meaning of 'the Official List' see para 281 note 3 ante.

284. Applications for listing.

An application for listing must be made to the competent authority[1] in such manner as the listing rules[2] may require[3].

No application may be made except by or with the consent of the issuer[4] of the securities[5]; and no application for listing may be made in respect of securities to be issued by a private company[6] or an old public company[7].

1 For the meaning of 'the competent authority' see para 281 ante.

2 For the meaning of 'listing rules' see para 281 ante. As to the *Listing Rules* see para 282 ante.

3 Financial Services Act 1986 s 143(1).

4 For these purposes, 'issuer', in relation to any securities, means the person by whom they have been or are to be issued, except that in relation to a certificate or other instrument falling within ibid s 1, Sch 1 para 5 (see para 283 head (4) ante), it means the person who issued or is to issue the securities to which the certificate or instrument relates: s 142(7). For the meaning of 'securities' see para 283 ante.

5 Ibid s 143(2).

6 For these purposes, 'private company' has the meaning given in the Companies Act 1985 s 1(3) (see para 82 ante): Financial Services Act 1986 s 207(1).

7 Ibid s 143(3). For these purposes, 'old public company' has the same meaning as in the Companies Consolidation (Consequential Provisions) Act 1985 s 1 (see para 132 ante): Financial Services Act 1986 s 143(3).

285. Admission to list. The competent authority[1] may not admit any securities[2] to the Official List[3] except on an application duly made[4] and unless satisfied that:

(1) the requirements of the listing rules[5] made by the authority for these purposes and in force when the application is made; and

(2) any other requirements imposed by the authority in relation to that application, are complied with[6].

Listing rules must require as a condition of admission to the Official List of any securities for which application for admission has been made and which are to be offered to the public in the United Kingdom[7] for the first time before admission:

(a) the submission to, and approval by, the authority of a prospectus in such form and containing such information as may be specified in the rules; and

(b) the publication of that prospectus[8].

Listing rules may require as a condition of the admission to the Official List of any other securities:

(i) the submission to, and approval by, the authority of a document ('listing particulars') in such form and containing such information as may be specified in the rules; and

(ii) the publication of that document;

or, in such cases as may be specified by the rules, the publication of a document other than listing particulars or a prospectus[9].

The competent authority may refuse an application:

(A) if it considers that by reason of any matter relating to the issuer[10] the admission of the securities would be detrimental to the interests of investors; or

(B) in the case of securities already officially listed in another member State, if the issuer has failed to comply with any obligations to which he is subject by virtue of that listing[11].

The competent authority must notify the applicant of its decision on the application within six months from the date on which the application is received or, if within that period the authority has required the applicant to furnish further information in connection with the application, from the date on which that information is furnished[12]. If the competent authority does not notify the applicant of its decision within the time so required, it is taken to have refused the application[13].

Where any securities have been admitted to the Official List, their admission may not be called into question on the ground that any requirement or condition for their admission has not been complied with[14].

1 For the meaning of 'the competent authority' see para 281 ante.

2 For the meaning of 'securities' see para 283 ante.

3 For the meaning of 'the Official List' see para 281 note 3 ante.

4 Ie in accordance with the Financial Services Act 1986 s 143: see para 284 ante.

5 For the meaning of 'listing rules' see para 281 ante. As to the *Listing Rules* see para 282 ante.

6 Financial Services Act 1986 s 144(1).
7 For the meaning of 'offer securities' see para 286 post; and for the meaning of 'offer to the public in the United Kingdom' see para 287 post.
8 Financial Services Act 1986's 144(2) (substituted by the Public Offers of Securities Regulations 1995, SI 1995/1537, reg 17, Sch 2 para 2(1)). The Financial Services Act 1986 s 144(2) (as so substituted) has effect without prejudice to the generality of the powers of the competent authority to make listing rules for the purposes of s 144 (as amended): s 144(2B) (added by the Public Offers of Securities Regulations 1995 Sch 2 para 2(1)).
9 Financial Services Act 1986 s 144(2A) (added by the Public Offers of Securities Regulations 1995 Sch 2 para 2(1)). The Financial Services Act 1986 s 144(2A) (as so added) has effect without prejudice to the generality of the powers of the competent authority to make listing rules for the purposes of s 144 (as amended): s 144(2B) (as added: see note 8 supra).
10 For the meaning of 'issuer' see para 284 note 4 ante.
11 Financial Services Act 1986 s 144(3).
12 Ibid s 144(4).
13 Ibid s 144(5).
14 Ibid s 144(6).

286. Offers of securities. A person offers securities[1] if, as principal:

(1) he makes an offer which, if accepted, would give rise to a contract for their issue or sale (which for this purpose includes any disposal for valuable consideration) by him or by another person with whom he has made arrangements for their issue or sale; or

(2) he invites a person to make such an offer, but not otherwise;

and, except where the context otherwise requires, 'offer' and 'offeror' are to be construed accordingly[2].

1 For the meaning of 'securities' see para 283 ante.
2 Financial Services Act 1986 s 142(7A)(a) (added by the Public Offers of Securities Regulations 1995, SI 1995/1537, reg 17, Sch 2 para 1(1), (3)). Whether a person offers securities to the public in the United Kingdom is to be determined in accordance with the Financial Services Act 1986 s 142(7A)(b), Sch 11A (as added) (see para 287 post): s 142(7A)(b) (added by the Public Offers of Securities Regulations 1995 Sch 2 para 1(1), (3)).

287. Offers of securities to the public in the United Kingdom. A person offers securities[1] to the public in the United Kingdom if, to the extent that the offer[2] is made to persons in the United Kingdom, it is made to the public and it is not an offer of securities where, to the extent that the offer is made to persons in the United Kingdom:

(1) the condition specified in any of heads (a) to (v) below is satisfied in relation to the offer; or

(2) where, in relation to an offer, the condition specified in one of heads (a) to (f), (j) to (m), (o), (p) and (s) below is satisfied in relation to part, but not the whole, of the offer and, in relation to each other part of the offer, the condition specified in a different head so specified is satisfied;

and, for these purposes, an offer which is made to any section of the public, whether selected as members or debenture holders of a body corporate[3], or as clients of the person making the offer, or in any other manner, is to be regarded as made to the public[4].

The following are the conditions so specified:

(a) the securities are offered to persons whose ordinary activities involve them in acquiring, holding, managing or disposing of investments (as principal or agent) for the purposes of their businesses or who it is reasonable to expect will acquire, hold, manage or dispose of investments (as principal or agent) for the purposes of their businesses, or are otherwise offered to persons in the context of their trades, professions or occupations[5];

(b) the securities are offered to no more than 50 persons[6];

(c) the securities are offered to the members of a club or association, whether or not incorporated, and the members can reasonably be regarded as having a common interest with each other and with the club or association in the affairs of the club or association and in what is to be done with the proceeds of the offer[7];

(d) the securities are offered to a restricted circle of persons whom the offeror reasonably believes to be sufficiently knowledgeable to understand the risks involved in accepting the offer[8];

(e) the securities are offered in connection with a bona fide invitation to enter into an underwriting agreement[9] with respect to them[10];

(f) the securities are offered to a government, local authority or public authority[11];

(g) the total consideration payable for the securities cannot exceed ecu[12] 40,000 (or an equivalent amount)[13];

(h) the minimum consideration which may be paid for securities acquired pursuant to the offer is at least ecu 40,000 (or an equivalent amount)[14];

(i) the securities are denominated in amounts of at least ecu 40,000 (or an equivalent amount)[15];

(j) the securities are offered in connection with a take-over offer[16];

(k) the securities are offered in connection with a merger[17];

(l) the securities are shares[18] and are offered free of charge to any or all of the holders of shares[19] in the issuer[20];

(m) the securities are shares, or specified investments[21] relating to shares, in a body corporate and are offered in exchange for shares in the same body corporate, and the offer cannot result in any increase in the issued share capital of the body corporate[22];

(n) the securities are issued by a body corporate and offered by the issuer, only to qualifying persons, and on terms that a contract to acquire any such securities may be entered into only by the qualifying person to whom they were offered or, if the terms of the offer so permit, any qualifying person[23];

(o) the securities result from the conversion of convertible securities[24] and listing particulars or a prospectus relating to the convertible securities were or was published[25] in the United Kingdom[26];

(p) the securities are issued by a charity[27], a housing association[28], an industrial or provident society[29] or a non-profit making association or body, recognised by the country or territory in which it is established, with objectives similar to those of a charity, a housing association, or an industrial or provident society, and the proceeds of the offer will be used for the purposes of the issuer's objectives[30];

(q) the securities offered are shares which are issued by, or ownership of which entitles the holder to membership of or to obtain the benefit of services provided by a building society[31], any body incorporated under the law of, or of any part of, the United Kingdom relating to industrial and provident societies or credit unions, or a body of a similar nature established in a member State[32];

(r) the securities offered are Euro-securities[33] and are not the subject of advertising likely to come to the attention of persons who are not professionally experienced in matters relating to investment[34];

(s) the securities are of the same class, and were issued at the same time, as securities in respect of which a prospectus has been duly[35] published[36];

(t)   the securities are debentures[37] with a maturity of less than one year from their date of issue[38];

(u)   the securities are[39] government or public securities[40];

(v)   the securities are not transferable[41].

1   For the meaning of 'securities' see para 283 ante.
2   For the meaning of 'offer' and cognate expressions see para 286 ante.
3   For these purposes, 'body corporate' includes a body corporate constituted under the law of a country or territory outside the United Kingdom: Financial Services Act 1986 s 207(1).
4   Ibid s 142(7A)(b), Sch 11A paras 1, 2, 4(1), (2) (added by the Public Offers of Securities Regulations 1995, SI 1995/1537, reg 17, Sch 2 para 2(2), Sch 3).
5   Financial Services Act 1986 Sch 11A para 3(1)(a) (added by the Public Offers of Securities Regulations 1995 Sch 3).
6   Financial Services Act 1986 Sch 11A para 3(1)(b) (added by the Public Offers of Securities Regulations 1995 Sch 3). For the purposes of determining whether the condition specified in the Financial Services Act 1986 Sch 11A para 3(1)(b) (as so added) or Sch 11A para 3(1)(g) (as added) (see text head (7) infra) is satisfied in relation to an offer, the offer is to be taken together with any other offer of the same securities which was (1) made by the same person; (2) open at any time within the period of 12 months ending with the date on which the offer is first made; and (3) not an offer to the public in the United Kingdom by virtue of that condition being satisfied: Sch 11A para 3(3) (added by the Public Offers of Securities Regulations 1995 Sch 3).
7   Financial Services Act 1986 Sch 11A para 3(1)(c) (added by the Public Offers of Securities Regulations 1995 Sch 3).
8   Financial Services Act 1986 Sch 11A para 3(1)(d) (added by the Public Offers of Securities Regulations 1995 Sch 3). In determining for the purposes of the Financial Services Act 1986 Sch 11A para 3(1)(d) (as so added) whether a person is sufficiently knowledgeable to understand the risks involved in accepting an offer of securities, any information supplied by the person making the offer is to be disregarded, apart from information about the issuer of the securities or, if the securities confer the right to acquire other securities, the issuer of those other securities: Sch 11A para 3(4) (added by the Public Offers of Securities Regulations 1995 Sch 3).
9   As to underwriting agreements see para 194 ante.
10   Financial Services Act 1986 Sch 11A para 3(1)(e) (added by the Public Offers of Securities Regulations 1995 Sch 3).
11   Financial Services Act 1986 Sch 11A para 3(1)(f) (added by the Public Offers of Securities Regulations 1995 Sch 3). For these purposes, 'government, local authority or public authority' means (1) the government of the United Kingdom, of Northern Ireland, or of any country or territory outside the United Kingdom; (2) a local authority in the United Kingdom or elsewhere; (3) any international organisation the members of which include the United Kingdom or another member State: Financial Services Act 1986 Sch 1 para 3, note (1) (applied by Sch 11A para 3(1)(f) (as so added)).
12   For these purposes, 'ecu' means the European currency unit as defined in EC Council Regulation 3320/94 (OJ L350, 31.12.94, p 27) (see EUROPEAN COMMUNITIES vol 51 para 5·18) or any Council regulation replacing the same, in either case as amended from time to time: Financial Services Act 1986 Sch 11A para 3(2) (added by the Public Offers of Securities Regulations 1995 Sch 3).
13   Financial Services Act 1986 Sch 11A para 3(1)(g) (added by the Public Offers of Securities Regulations 1995 Sch 3). See also note 6 supra. For the purposes of determining whether the condition specified in the Financial Services Act 1986 Sch 11A para 3(1)(g) (as so added), Sch 11A para 3(1)(h) (as added) (see text head (8) infra) or Sch 11A para 3(1)(i) (as added) (see text head (9) infra) is satisfied in relation to an offer, an amount, in relation to an amount denominated in ecu, is an 'equivalent amount' if it is an amount of equal value, calculated at the latest practicable date before (but in any event not more than three days before) the date on which the offer is first made, denominated wholly or partly in another currency or unit of account: Sch 11A para 3(5) (added by the Public Offers of Securities Regulations 1995 Sch 3).
14   Financial Services Act 1986 Sch 11A para 3(1)(h) (added by the Public Offers of Securities Regulations 1995 Sch 3). See also note 13 supra.
15   Financial Services Act 1986 Sch 11A para 3(1)(i) (added by the Public Offers of Securities Regulations 1995 Sch 3). See also note 13 supra.
16   Financial Services Act 1986 Sch 11A para 3(1)(j) (added by the Public Offers of Securities Regulations 1995 Sch 3). For these purposes, 'take-over offer' means (1) an offer which is a take-over offer within the meaning of the Companies Act 1985 Pt XIIIA (ss 428–430F (as amended): see para 1202 post) (or would be such an offer if Pt XIIIA (ss 428–430F) (as amended) applied in relation to any body

corporate); or (2) an offer made to all the holders of shares, or of shares of a particular class, in a body corporate to acquire a specified proportion of those shares ('holders' and 'shares' being construed in accordance with Pt XIIIA (ss 428–430F (as amended): see para 1202 post); but in determining for the purposes of head (2) supra whether an offer is made to all the holders of shares, or of shares of any class, the offeror, any associate of his (within the meaning of s 430E (as added): see para 1209 post) and any person whose shares the offeror or any such associate has contracted to acquire are not to be regarded as holders of the shares: Financial Services Act 1986 Sch 11A para 3(6) (added by the Public Offers of Securities Regulations 1995 Sch 3).

17 Financial Services Act 1986 Sch 11A para 3(1)(k) (added by the Public Offers of Securities Regulations 1995 Sch 3). For these purposes, 'merger' means a merger within the meaning of EC Council Directive 78/855 (OJ L295, 20.10.78, p 36) (see EUROPEAN COMMUNITIES vol 51 para 11·33): Financial Services Act 1986 Sch 11A para 3(1)(k) (as so added).

18 For these purposes, 'shares', except in relation to a take-over offer, means investments which are securities by virtue of falling within ibid Sch 1 para 1 (as applied for the purposes of s 142(3): see para 283 head (1) ante): Sch 11A para 3(2) (as added: see note 12 supra).

19 For these purposes, 'holders of shares' means the persons who, at the close of business on a date specified in the offer and falling within the period of 28 days ending with the date on which the offer is first made, were the holders of such shares: ibid Sch 11A para 3(7) (added by the Public Offers of Securities Regulations 1995 Sch 3).

20 Financial Services Act 1986 Sch 11A para 3(1)(l) (added by the Public Offers of Securities Regulations 1995 Sch 3).

21 Ie investments falling within the Financial Services Act 1986 Sch 1 paras 4 or 5: see para 283 heads (3), (4) ante.

22 Ibid Sch 11A para 3(1)(m) (added by the Public Offers of Securities Regulations 1995 Sch 3).

23 Financial Services Act 1986 Sch 11A para 3(1)(n) (added by the Public Offers of Securities Regulations 1995 Sch 3). For these purposes (1) a person is a 'qualifying person', in relation to an issuer, if he is a bona fide employee or former employee of the issuer or of another body corporate in the same group or the wife, husband, widow, widower or child or stepchild under the age of 18 of such an employee or former employee; and (2) the definition of 'issuer' in the Financial Services Act 1986 s 142(7) (as amended) (see para 284 note 4 ante) applies with the omission of the words from 'except that' to the end of the definition: Sch 11A para 3(8) (added by the Public Offers of Securities Regulations 1995 Sch 3). 'Group', in relation to a body corporate, means that body corporate, any other body corporate which is its holding company or subsidiary and any other body corporate which is a subsidiary of that holding company: Financial Services Act 1986 s 207(1).

24 For these purposes, 'convertible securities' means (1) securities falling within ibid Sch 1 para 2 (see para 283 head (2) ante) which can be converted into, or exchanged for, or which confer rights to acquire, securities; or (2) securities falling within Sch 1 paras 4 or 5 (as applied for the purposes of s 142(2): see para 283 heads (3), (4) ante); and 'conversion', in relation to convertible securities, means their conversion into or exchange for, or the exercise of rights conferred by them to acquire, other securities: Sch 11A para 3(2) (as added: see note 12 supra).

25 Ie under or by virtue of ibid Pt IV (ss 142–156B) (as amended), the Companies Act 1985 Pt III (ss 56–79) or the Public Offers of Securities Regulations 1995 (see para 300 et seq post). The Companies Act 1985 Pt III (ss 56–79), except ss 58–60 (see para 105 note 2 ante), in so far as they are necessary for the purposes of s 81 (see para 105 ante), s 83 (see para 451 post), and s 62, in so far as it is necessary for purposes of s 744, is repealed for all purposes by the Financial Services Act 1986 s 212(3), Sch 17 Pt I: Financial Services Act 1986 (Commencement) (No 13) Order 1995, SI 1995/1538, art 2(a)(i), (iii).

26 Financial Services Act 1986 Sch 11A para 3(1)(o) (added by the Public Offers of Securities Regulations 1995 Sch 3).

27 Ie a charity within the meaning of the Charities Act 1993 s 96(1): see CHARITIES vol 5(2) (Reissue) para 1.

28 Ie a housing association within the meaning of the Housing Act 1985 s 5(1): see HOUSING vol 22 para 445.

29 Ie an industrial or provident society registered in accordance with the Industrial and Provident Societies Act 1965 s 1(2)(b): see INDUSTRIAL AND PROVIDENT SOCIETIES vol 24 (Reissue) para 8.

30 Financial Services Act 1986 Sch 11A para 3(1)(p) (added by the Public Offers of Securities Regulations 1995 Sch 3).

31 Ie a building society incorporated under the law of, or of any part of, the United Kingdom: see BUILDING SOCIETIES.

32 Financial Services Act 1986 Sch 11A para 3(1)(q) (added by the Public Offers of Securities Regulations 1995 Sch 3).

33 For these purposes, 'Euro-securities' means investments which (1) are to be underwritten and distributed by a syndicate at least two of the members of which have their registered offices in different countries or territories; (2) are to be offered on a significant scale in one or more countries or territories other than the country or territory in which the issuer has its registered office; and (3) may be acquired pursuant to the offer only through a credit institution or other financial institution: Financial Services Act 1986 Sch 11A para 3(2) (as added: see note 12 supra). 'Credit institution' means a credit institution as defined in EC Council Directive 77/780 (OJ L322, 17.12.77, p 30) art 1; and 'financial institution' means a financial institution as defined in EC Council Directive 89/646 (OJ L386, 31.12.89, p 1) art 1: Financial Services Act 1986 Sch 11A para 3(2) (as so added).

34 Ibid Sch 11A para 3(1)(r) (added by the Public Offers of Securities Regulations 1995 Sch 3).

35 Ie under or by virtue of the Financial Services Act 1986 Pt IV (ss 142–156B) (as amended), the Companies Act 1985 Pt III (ss 56–79) or the Public Offers of Securities Regulations 1995. See also note 25 supra.

36 Financial Services Act 1986 Sch 11A para 3(1)(s) (added by the Public Offers of Securities Regulations 1995 Sch 3).

37 Ie investments falling within the Financial Services Act 1986 Sch 1 para 2.

38 Ibid Sch 11A para 3(1)(t) (added by the Public Offers of Securities Regulations 1995 Sch 3).

39 Ie are investments falling within the Financial Services Act 1986 Sch 1 para 3.

40 Ibid Sch 11A para 3(1)(u) (added by the Public Offers of Securities Regulations 1995 Sch 3).

41 Financial Services Act 1986 Sch 11A para 3(1)(v) (added by the Public Offers of Securities Regulations 1995 Sch 3).

288. Discontinuance and suspension of listing. The competent authority[1] may, in accordance with the listing rules[2], discontinue the listing of any securities[3] if satisfied that there are special circumstances which preclude normal regular dealings in the securities[4].

The competent authority may in accordance with the listing rules suspend the listing of any securities[5]. Securities the listing of which is so suspended are nevertheless regarded as listed for the purposes of the provisions relating to the obligations of issuers of listed securities[6] and fees[7] payable[8].

1 For the meaning of 'the competent authority' see para 281 ante.

2 For the meaning of 'listing rules' see para 281 ante. As to the *Listing Rules* see para 282 ante.

3 For the meaning of 'securities' see para 283 ante.

4 Financial Services Act 1986 s 145(1).

5 Ibid s 145(2).

6 Ie ibid s 153: see para 293 post.

7 Ie ibid s 155: see para 281 ante.

8 Ibid s 145(3).

289. General duty of disclosure in listing particulars. In addition to the information specified by listing rules[1] or required by the competent authority[2] as a condition of the admission of any securities[3] to the Official List[4], any listing particulars submitted to the competent authority[5] must contain all such information as investors and their professional advisers would reasonably require, and reasonably expect to find there, for the purpose of making an informed assessment of the assets and liabilities, financial position, profits and losses and prospects of the issuer[6] of the securities, and the rights attaching to those securities[7]. The information to be so included is such as is within the knowledge of any person responsible for the listing particulars[8] or which it would be reasonable for him to obtain by making inquiries[9]. In determining what information is required to be included, regard must be had:

(1) to the nature of the securities and of the issuer of the securities;
(2) to the nature of the persons likely to consider their acquisition;
(3) to the fact that certain matters may reasonably be expected to be within the knowledge of professional advisers of any kind which those persons may reasonably be expected to consult; and
(4) to certain information statutorily available[10] to investors or their professional advisers[11].

1 For the meaning of 'listing rules' see para 281 ante. As to the *Listing Rules* see para 282 ante.
2 For the meaning of 'the competent authority' see para 281 ante.
3 For the meaning of 'securities' see para 283 ante.
4 For the meaning of 'the Official List' see para 281 note 3 ante.
5 Ie under the Financial Services Act 1986 s 144 (as amended): see para 285 ante.
6 For the meaning of 'issuer' see para 284 note 4 ante.
7 Financial Services Act 1986 s 146(1). As to the application of s 146 to prospectuses see para 296 post.
8 For the meaning of 'person responsible for the listing particulars' see para 346 post.
9 Financial Services Act 1986 s 146(2).
10 Ie information available by virtue of requirements imposed under ibid s 153 (see para 293 post) or by or under any other enactment or by virtue of requirements imposed by a recognised investment exchange for the purpose of complying with Sch 4 para 2(2)(b) (persons dealing in investments to be afforded proper information for determining their current value). For the meaning of 'recognised investment exchange' see para 223 note 1 ante.
11 Ibid s 146(3).

290. Supplementary listing particulars. If at any time after the preparation of listing particulars[1] for submission to the competent authority[2] and before the commencement of dealings in the securities[3] following their admission to the Official List[4]:

(1) there is a significant[5] change affecting any matter contained in those particulars whose inclusion was required by statute[6] or by listing rules[7] or by the competent authority; or
(2) a significant new matter arises the inclusion of information in respect of which would have been so required if it had arisen when the particulars were prepared,

the issuer[8] of the securities must, in accordance with listing rules made for this purpose, submit to the competent authority for its approval and, if approved, publish supplementary listing particulars of the change or new matter[9].

Where the issuer of the securities is not aware of the change or new matter in question, he is not under any duty to comply with the above provisions unless he is notified of it by a person responsible for the listing particulars[10]; but it is the duty of any person responsible for those particulars who is aware of such a matter to give notice of it to the issuer[11].

1 For the meaning of 'listing particulars' see para 285 ante.
2 For the meaning of 'the competent authority' see para 281 ante.
3 For the meaning of 'securities' see para 283 ante.
4 For the meaning of 'the Official List' see para 281 note 3 ante.
5 For these purposes, 'significant' means significant for the purpose of making an informed assessment of the matters mentioned in the Financial Services Act 1986 s 146(1) (see para 289 ante): s 147(2).
6 Ie by ibid s 146: see para 289 ante.
7 For the meaning of 'listing rules' see para 281 ante. As to the *Listing Rules* see para 282 ante.
8 For the meaning of 'issuer' see para 284 note 4 ante.
9 Financial Services Act 1986 s 147(1). Section 147(1) applies also as respects matters contained in any supplementary listing particulars previously published under s 147 in respect of the securities in question: s 147(4). As to the application of s 147 to prospectuses see para 296 post.
10 For the meaning of 'person responsible for the listing particulars' see para 346 post.
11 Financial Services Act 1986 s 147(3).

291. Exemptions from disclosure. The competent authority[1] may authorise the omission from listing particulars[2] or supplementary listing particulars[3] of any information the inclusion of which would otherwise be required by statute[4] or by listing rules[5]:

(1) on the ground that its disclosure would be contrary to the public interest;

(2) on the ground that its disclosure would be seriously detrimental to the issuer[6] of the securities[7]; or

(3) in the case of debenture securities[8] of any class specified by listing rules, on the ground that its disclosure is unnecessary for persons of the kind who may be expected normally to buy or deal in the securities[9].

The Secretary of State or the Treasury[10] may issue a certificate to the effect that the disclosure of any information, including information that would otherwise have to be included in particulars for which they are themselves responsible, would be contrary to the public interest and the competent authority is entitled to act on any such certificate in exercising its powers under head (1) above[11].

These provisions are without prejudice to any powers of the competent authority under listing rules conferring upon it power to dispense with or modify the application of the listing rules in particular cases and by reference to any circumstances[12].

1 For the meaning of 'the competent authority' see para 281 ante.
2 For the meaning of 'listing particulars' see para 285 ante.
3 As to supplementary listing particulars see para 290 ante.
4 Ie by the Financial Services Act 1986 s 146: see para 289 ante.
5 For the meaning of 'listing rules' see para 281 ante. As to the *Listing Rules* see para 282 ante.
6 For the meaning of 'issuer' see para 284 note 4 ante.
7 No such authority may be granted in respect of, and no such authority is to be regarded as extending to, information the non-disclosure of which would be likely to mislead a person considering the acquisition of the securities as to any facts the knowledge of which it is essential for him to have in order to make an informed assessment: Financial Services Act 1986 s 148(2). For the meaning of 'securities' see para 283 ante.
8 Ie securities falling within ibid Sch 1 para 2 as modified by s 142(3)(b): see para 283 head (2) ante.
9 Ibid s 148(1). As to the application of s 148 to prospectuses see para 296 post.
10 The functions of the Secretary of State in ibid s 148(3) are not transferred to the Treasury; but this is without prejudice to the existing concurrent power of the Treasury under s 148(3): Transfer of Functions (Financial Services) Order 1992, SI 1992/1315, art 3, Sch 1 para 20.
11 Financial Services Act 1986 s 148(3).
12 Ibid ss 148(4), 156(2).

292. Registration of listing particulars. On or before the date on which listing particulars[1] or supplementary listing particulars[2] are published as required by listing rules[3], a copy of the particulars must be delivered for registration to the registrar of companies[4] and a statement that a copy has been so delivered must be included in the particulars[5].

If any particulars are published without a copy of them having been delivered as required by these provisions, the issuer[6] of the securities[7] in question and any person who is knowingly a party to the publication is guilty of an offence and is liable on conviction on indictment to a fine, or on summary conviction to a fine not exceeding the statutory maximum[8].

1 For the meaning of 'listing particulars 'see para 285 ante.
2 As to supplementary listing particulars see para 290 ante.
3 For the meaning of 'listing rules' see para 281 ante. As to the *Listing Rules* see para 282 ante.
4 For these purposes, 'the registrar of companies' means: (1) if the securities in question are or are to be issued by a company incorporated in Great Britain, the registrar of companies in England and Wales or

the registrar of companies in Scotland according to whether the company's registered office is in England and Wales or in Scotland; (2) if the securities in question are or are to be issued by a company incorporated in Northern Ireland, the registrar of companies for Northern Ireland; (3) in any other case, any of those registrars: Financial Services Act 1986 s 149(2).

5 Ibid s 149(1). As to the application of s 149 to prospectuses see para 296 post.
6 For the meaning of 'issuer' see para 284 note 4 ante.
7 For the meaning of 'securities' see para 283 ante.
8 Financial Services Act 1986 s 149(3). For the meaning of 'the statutory maximum' see para 1161 post.

293. Obligations of issuers of listed securities. Listing rules[1] may specify requirements to be complied with by issuers[2] of listed securities[3] and may make provision with respect to the action that may be taken by the competent authority[4] in the event of non-compliance, including provision:

(1) authorising the authority to publish the fact that an issuer has contravened any provision of the rules; and
(2) if the rules require an issuer to publish any information, authorising the authority to publish it in the event of his failure to do so[5].

These provisions apply to the issuer of securities included in the Official List[6] on 16 February 1987[7] as it applies to the issuer of securities included[8] by virtue of the Financial Services Act 1986[9].

1 For the meaning of 'listing rules' see para 281 ante. As to the *Listing Rules* see para 282 ante.
2 For the meaning of 'issuer' see para 284 note 4 ante.
3 For the meaning of 'securities' see para 283 ante.
4 For the meaning of 'the competent authority' see para 281 ante.
5 Financial Services Act 1986 s 153(1).
6 For the meaning of 'the Official List' see para 281 note 3 ante.
7 Ie the date of the coming into force of the Financial Services Act 1986 Pt IV (ss 142–156B) (as amended): see the Financial Services Act 1986 (Commencement No 3) Order 1986, SI 1986/2246, art 5(b).
8 Ie by virtue of the Financial Services Act 1986 Pt IV (ss 142–156B) (as amended): see para 281 et seq ante and para 294 et seq post..
9 Ibid s 153(2).

294. Advertisements and information in connection with listing applications. Where listing particulars[1] are, or are to be, published in connection with an application for the listing of any securities[2], no advertisement or other information of a kind specified by listing rules[3] may be issued in the United Kingdom[4] unless the contents of the advertisement or other information have been submitted to the competent authority[5] and that authority has either approved those contents or authorised the issue of the advertisement or information without such approval[6].

An authorised person[7] who contravenes this provision is treated as having contravened the conduct of business rules[8] or, in the case of a person who is an authorised person by virtue of his membership of a recognised self-regulating organisation[9] or certification by a recognised professional body[10], the rules of that organisation or body[11].

Subject to the qualification mentioned below[12], a person, other than an authorised person, who contravenes this provision is guilty of an offence and liable on conviction on indictment to imprisonment for a term not exceeding two years or a fine, or to both, or on summary conviction to a fine not exceeding the statutory maximum[13].

A person who in the ordinary course of a business other than investment business issues an advertisement or other information to the order of another person is, however, not guilty of an offence under this provision if he proves that he believed on reasonable grounds that the advertisement or information had been approved or its issue authorised by the competent authority[14]. Where information has been approved, or its issue has been so authorised, neither the person issuing it nor any person responsible for, or for any part of, the listing particulars[15] incurs any civil liability[16] by reason of any statement in or omission from the information if that information and the listing particulars, taken together, would not be likely to mislead persons of the kind likely to consider the acquisition of the securities in question[17].

1 For the meaning of 'listing particulars' see para 285 ante.
2 For the meaning of 'securities' see para 283 ante.
3 For the meaning of 'listing rules' see para 281 ante. As to the *Listing Rules* see para 282 ante. For these purposes, 'advertisement' includes every form of advertising, whether in a publication, by the display of notices, signs, labels or showcards, by means of circulars, catalogues, price lists or other documents, by an exhibition of pictures or photographic or cinematographic films, by way of sound broadcasting or television or by inclusion in any programme service (within the meaning of the Broadcasting Act 1990: see TELECOMMUNICATIONS), other than a sound or television broadcasting service, by the distribution of recordings, or in any other manner; and references to the issue of an advertisement are to be construed accordingly: Financial Services Act 1986 s 207(2) (amended by the Broadcasting Act 1990 s 203(1), Sch 20 para 45(1)(a)). As to the control of broadcast advertisements see TELECOMMUNICATIONS vol 45 paras 545, 546.
4 For these purposes, an advertisement or other information issued outside the United Kingdom is to be treated as issued in the United Kingdom if it is directed to persons in the United Kingdom or is made available to them otherwise than in a newspaper, journal, magazine or other periodical publication published and circulating principally outside the United Kingdom or in a sound or television broadcast transmitted principally for reception outside the United Kingdom: Financial Services Act 1986 s 207(3).
5 For the meaning of 'the competent authority' see para 281 ante.
6 Financial Services Act 1986 s 154(1). Section 154 (as amended) has effect (1) as if it included provision that, where a European institution carrying on home-regulated investment business in the United Kingdom contravenes s 154 (as amended), it is treated as having contravened rules made under Pt I Ch V (ss 47–63C (as amended): see MONEY) or in the case of an institution which is a member of a recognised self-regulating organisation, the rules of that organisation; and (2) as if the reference in s 154(3) (see infra) to a person other than an authorised person did not include a reference to a European institution carrying on home-regulated investment business in the United Kingdom: Banking Co-ordination (Second Council Directive) Regulations 1992, SI 1992/3218, reg 55, Sch 9 para 37.
   The Financial Services Act 1986 s 154 (as amended) also has effect as if (a) it included provision that, where a European investment firm carrying on home-regulated investment business in the United Kingdom contravenes s 154 (as amended), it is to be treated as having contravened rules made under Pt I Ch V (ss 47–63C) (as amended), or in the case of a firm which is a member of a recognised self-regulating organisation, the rules of that organisation; and (b) the reference in s 154(3) (see infra) to a person other than an authorised person did not include a reference to such a firm: Investment Services Regulations 1995, SI 1995/3275, reg 32, Sch 7 para 36. For the meaning of 'recognised self-regulating organisation' see note 9 infra.
   As to the application of the Financial Services Act 1986 s 154 (as amended) to prospectuses see para 296 post.
7 For these purposes, 'authorised person' means a person authorised to carry on investment business under ibid Pt I Ch III (ss 7–34) (as amended): s 207(1).
8 Ie rules made under ibid Pt I Ch V (ss 47–63C) (as amended).
9 For these purposes, 'recognised self-regulating organisation' means a body declared by an order of the Secretary of State for the time being in force to be a recognised self-regulating organisation for the purposes of the Financial Services Act 1986: s 207(1). See MONEY.
10 For these purposes, 'recognised professional body' means a body declared by an order of the Secretary of State for the time being in force to be a recognised professional body for the purposes of the Financial Services Act 1986: s 207(1). See MONEY.
11 Ibid s 154(2).
12 Ie subject to ibid s 154(4): see infra.
13 Ibid s 154(3). For the meaning of 'the statutory maximum' see para 1161 post. See also note 6 supra.
14 Ibid s 154(4).
15 For the meaning of 'person responsible for the listing particulars' see para 346 post.

16 For these purposes, the reference to a person incurring civil liability includes a reference to any other person being entitled as against that person to be granted any civil remedy or to rescind or repudiate any agreement: Financial Services Act 1986 s 154(5) (amended by the Companies Act 1989 s 197(2)).

17 Financial Services Act 1986 s 154(5) (as amended: see note 15 supra).

295. Approval or authorisation by the competent authority. The documents to be submitted to the competent authority[1] for approval of their contents before issue[2] are formal notices[3] and offer notices[4].

The following documents:

(1) a mini-prospectus[5];

(2) summary particulars[6]; and

(3) where listing particulars are, or are to be, published, any other document or advertisement, excluding listing particulars, which is to be issued in the United Kingdom and which is to be issued by or on behalf of an issuer for the purpose of announcing the admission to listing or issued for the purpose of announcing a public offer where a prospectus is required by the listing rules[7],

must also be submitted for authorisation, without approval of their contents[8], by the Stock Exchange before their issue[9]. Any other advertisement or document within head (3) above must contain:

(a) a statement that its issue has been authorised by the Stock Exchange without approval of its contents;

(b) a statement that listing particulars or a prospectus, as the case may be, have been or will be published; and

(c) the addresses and times at which copies of the listing particulars are or will be available to the public[10].

1 For the meaning of 'the competent authority' see para 281 ante.

2 Ie pursuant to the Financial Services Act 1986 s 154(1)(a): see para 294 ante.

3 A formal notice is an advertisement, not constituting listing particulars, containing certain specified information as required by the *Listing Rules* r 8.10: r 8.10. For the meaning of 'listing rules' see para 281 ante. As to the *Listing Rules* see para 282 ante.

4 An offer notice is a document, not constituting listing particulars, which has attached to it or which contains an application form; the notice must include all the items of information required for a formal notice (see note 3 supra) and a statement to the effect that listing particulars or a prospectus, as the case may be, have been published which alone contain full details of the issuer and of the securities being offered: *Listing Rules* r 8.11.

5 A mini-prospectus is a document, not constituting listing particulars, which has attached to it or which contains an application form and includes information drawn from listing particulars together with such additional information about the issuer and the securities as the issuer, subject to r 8.13, may decide: *Listing Rules* r 8.12. A mini-prospectus must include only information drawn from listing particulars, together with items in r 8.13(a)–(e): r 8.13.

6 In certain situations the listing rules permit summary particulars (instead of listing particulars) to be used provided that they contain sufficient information drawn from the listing particulars about the transaction in question to enable a shareholder to decide what action to take: see the *Listing Rules* r 5.32, 5.33.

7 Ie pursuant to the Financial Services Act 1986 s 144(2): see para 285 ante.

8 Ie pursuant to ibid s 154(1)(b): see para 294 ante.

9 See the *Listing Rules* r 8.24.

10 *Listing Rules* r 8.25.

B. PROSPECTUSES

296. Application of the statutory provisions to prospectuses. Certain of the provisions relating to the official listing of securities[1] apply in relation to a prospectus required by listing rules[2] as they apply in relation to listing particulars[3], but as if:

(1) any reference to listing particulars were a reference to a prospectus and any reference to supplementary listing particulars were a reference to a supplementary prospectus;

(2) any reference in the provisions relating to the persons responsible for particulars[4] to the issuer of securities included[5] a reference to the person offering or proposing to offer[6] them[7].

1 Ie the Financial Services Act 1986 s 146 (see para 289 ante), s 147 (see para 290 ante), s 148 (see para 291 ante), s 149 (see para 292 ante), s 150 (as amended) (see para 347 post), s 151 (see para 348 post), s 152 (as amended) (see para 346 post) and s 154 (as amended) (see para 294 ante and para 345 post).
2 Ie in accordance with ibid s 144(2) (as substituted): see para 285 ante.
3 For the meaning of 'listing particulars' see para 285 ante.
4 Ie the Financial Services Act 1986 s 152 (as amended), other than s 152(1)(b): see para 346 post.
5 Ie notwithstanding ibid s 142(7) (as amended) (definitions).
6 For the meaning of 'offer securities' see para 286 ante.
7 Financial Services Act 1986 s 154A (added by the Public Offers of Securities Regulations 1995, SI 1995/1537, reg 17, Sch 2 para 2(3)).

297. Approval of prospectus where no application for listing. Listing rules[1] may also provide for a prospectus to be submitted to and approved by the competent authority[2] where:

(1) securities[3] are to be offered to the public in the United Kingdom[4] for the first time;

(2) no application for listing of the securities has been made[5]; and

(3) the prospectus is submitted by or with the consent of the issuer[6] of the securities[7].

Listing rules so made may make provision:

(a) as to the information to be contained in, and the form of, a prospectus submitted under any such rules; and

(b) subject to the provisions of the Public Offers of Securities Regulations 1995[8], as to the timing and manner of publication of such a prospectus[9].

Listing rules so made may require the payment of fees to the competent authority in respect of a prospectus submitted for approval under the rules[10].

1 For the meaning of 'listing rules' see para 281 ante. As to the *Listing Rules* see para 282 ante.
2 For the meaning of 'the competent authority' see para 281 ante.
3 For the meaning of 'securities' see para 283 ante.
4 For the meaning of 'offer to the public in the United Kingdom' see para 287 ante.
5 Ie under the Financial Services Act 1986 Pt IV (ss 142–156B) (as amended): see para 281 et seq ante.
6 For the meaning of 'issuer' see para 284 note 4 ante.
7 Financial Services Act 1986 s 156A(1) (added by the Public Offers of Securities Regulations 1995, SI 1995/1537, reg 17, Sch 2 para 2(4)). The Financial Services Act 1986 s 146 (see para 289 ante), s 147 (see para 290 ante), s 148 (see para 291 ante), s 149 (see para 292 ante), s 150 (as amended) (see para 347 post), s 151 (see para 348 post), s 152 (as amended) (see para 346 post) and s 154 (as amended) (see para 294 ante) apply in relation to such a prospectus as they apply in relation to listing particulars but as if:
(1) any reference to listing particulars were a reference to a prospectus and any reference to supplementary listing particulars were a reference to a supplementary prospectus;
(2) in s 146(1) (see para 289 ante) the words 'as a condition of the admission of any securities to the Official List' were omitted and for the words 'section 144 above' there were substituted 'section 156A(1) below';
(3) in s 147(1) (see para 290 ante) for the words 'under section 144 above and before the commencement of dealings in the securities following their admission to the Official List' there were substituted 'under section 156A(1) below and before the end of the period during which the offer to which the prospectus relates remains open';
(4) in s 151(1)(d), (2)(d) (see para 348 post) the words 'that he continued in that belief until after the commencement of dealings in the securities following their admission to the Official List and' were

omitted and the words 'and, if the securities are dealt in on an approved exchange, that he continued in that belief until after the commencement of dealings in the securities on that exchange' were added at the end;

(5) notwithstanding s 142(7) (as amended), any reference in s 152 (as amended) (see para 346 post), other than in s 152(1)(b), to the issuer of securities included a reference to the person offering or proposing to offer them; and

(6) in s 154(1) (see para 294 ante) for the words 'Where listing particulars are or are to be published in connection with an application for the listing of any securities' there were substituted 'Where a prospectus is or is to be published in connection with an application for approval, then, until the end of the period during which the offer to which the prospectus relates remains open':

s 156A(3) (added by the Public Offers of Securities Regulations 1995 Sch 2 para 2(4)). For these purposes, 'approved exchange' means, in relation to dealings in securities, a recognised investment exchange approved by the Treasury for the purposes of the Public Offers of Securities Regulations 1995 (see para 300 et seq post) either generally or in relation to such dealings: Financial Services Act 1986 s 142(7) (amended by the Public Offers of Securities Regulations 1995 Sch 2 para 1(1), (2)).

8 Public Offers of Securities Regulations 1995 reg 4(2) (see para 302 post), reg 5 (see para 304 post), reg 6 (see para 305 post), reg 8 (see para 306 post), reg 9 (see para 316 post), reg 10 (see para 317 post), reg 11 (see para 318 post), reg 12 (see para 319 post), reg 13 (see para 349 post), reg 14 (see para 350 post) and reg 15 (see para 351 post) do not apply to a prospectus submitted for approval in accordance with listing rules made under the Financial Services Act 1986 s 156A (as added): Public Offers of Securities Regulations 1995 reg 4(3).

9 Financial Services Act 1986 s 156A(2) (added by the Public Offers of Securities Regulations 1995 Sch 2 para 2(4)).

10 Financial Services Act 1986 s 156A(4) (added by the Public Offers of Securities Regulations 1995 Sch 2 para 2(4)).

298. Publication of prospectus.

Where listing rules[1] require the publication of a prospectus, it is not lawful, before the time of publication of the prospectus, to offer the securities[2] in question to the public in the United Kingdom[3].

An authorised person[4] who contravenes the above provisions is treated as contravening the conduct of investment business rules[5] or, in the case of a person who is an authorised person by virtue of his membership of a recognised self-regulating organisation[6] or certification by a recognised professional body[7], the rules of that organisation or body[8].

A person, other than an authorised person, who contravenes the above provisions is guilty of an offence and liable on conviction on indictment to imprisonment for a term not exceeding two years or a fine, or to both, or on summary conviction to imprisonment for a term not exceeding three months or a fine not exceeding level 5 on the standard scale[9].

A person is not regarded[10] as contravening the above provisions by reason only of a prospectus not having fully complied with the requirements of listing rules as to its form or content[11].

Any contravention of the above provisions is actionable at the suit of a person who suffers loss as a result of the contravention subject to the defences and other incidents applying to actions for breach of statutory duty[12].

1 Ie listing rules made under the Financial Services Act 1986 s 144(2) (as substituted): see para 285 ante. As to the timing of publication see the *Listing Rules* rr 5.1, 8.8; and as to the *Listing Rules* generally see para 282 ante.

2 For the meaning of 'securities' see para 283 ante.

3 Financial Services Act 1986 s 156B(1) (added by the Public Offers of Securities Regulations 1995, SI 1995/1537, reg 17, Sch 2 para 2(4)). For the meaning of 'offer to the public in the United Kingdom' see para 287 ante.

4 For the meaning of 'authorised person' see para 294 note 7 ante.

5 Ie rules made under the Financial Services Act 1986 Pt I Ch V (ss 47–63C) (as amended): see MONEY.

6 For the meaning of 'recognised self-regulating organisation' see para 294 note 9 ante.

7 For the meaning of 'recognised professional body' see para 294 note 10 ante.
8 Financial Services Act 1986 s 156B(2) (added by the Public Offers of Securities Regulations 1995 Sch 2 para 2(4)).
9 Financial Services Act 1986 s 156B(3) (added by the Public Offers of Securities Regulations 1995 Sch 2 para 2(4)). For the meaning of 'the standard scale' see CRIMINAL LAW vol 11(2) (Reissue) para 808. The Financial Services Act 1986 s 156B(3) (as so added) does not apply to a European institution carrying on home-regulated investment business in the United Kingdom which contravenes s 156B(1) (as added) (see supra) but it is treated for all purposes (1) if it is not a member of a recognised self-regulating organisation, as having contravened rules made under Pt I Ch V (ss 47–63C) (as amended); or (2) if it is a member of a recognised self-regulating organisation, as having contravened the rules of that organisation: Public Offers of Securities Regulations 1995 Sch 2 para 3.
10 Ie without prejudice to any liability under the Financial Services Act 1986 s 150 (as amended): see para 347 post.
11 Ibid s 156B(4) (added by the Public Offers of Securities Regulations 1995 Sch 2 para 2(4)).
12 Financial Services Act 1986 s 156B(5) (added by the Public Offers of Securities Regulations 1995 Sch 2 para 2(4)).

C. MUTUAL RECOGNITION

299. Mutual recognition of listing particulars and prospectuses approved in other member States. Part IV of the Financial Services Act 1986[1] applies to a recognised European document[2]:

(1) as it applies in relation to listing particulars[3] or, as the case may be, to[4] a prospectus[5];

(2) subject to specified modifications[6].

The above provisions do not apply to listing particulars or a prospectus approved in another member State prior to 19 June 1995[7].

1 Ie the Financial Services Act 1986 Pt IV (ss 142–156B) (as amended): see para 281 et seq ante.
2 For these purposes, 'recognised European document' means a document consisting of a European document submitted to the UK authority pursuant to an application for listing under ibid s 143 (see para 284 ante) and, if information is required to be added to it in accordance with listing rules, including that information: Public Offers of Securities Regulations 1995, SI 1995/1537, reg 20, Sch 4 para 2. 'European document' means (1) listing particulars which have been approved by the competent authority in another member State and which EC Council Directive 80/390 (OJ L100, 17.4.80, p 1) art 24a requires or art 24a, 5th para permits to be recognised as listing particulars; (2) a prospectus which has been approved by the competent authority in another member State and which EC Council Directive 80/390 art 24b requires or which art 24b, 2nd para, in referring to art 24A, 5th para, permits to be recognised as listing particulars; or (3) a prospectus which has been approved by the competent authority in another member State, which EC Council Directive 89/298 (OJ L124, 5.5.89, p 8) art 21 requires or which art 21, 4th para permits to be recognised and which relates to securities which are the subject of an application for listing in the United Kingdom and which are to be offered in the United Kingdom prior to admission to listing in the United Kingdom by means of the prospectus; including in each case any supplement to listing particulars or a prospectus which, before the completion of the preparation of the recognised document for submission to the UK authority pursuant to an application for listing, has been approved pursuant to EC Council Directive 80/390 art 23 or EC Council Directive 89/298 art 18 by the competent authorities which approved the listing particulars or prospectus: Public Offers of Securities Regulations 1995 Sch 4 para 1(c). Where the European document submitted to the UK authority is a translation into English of the document approved by the competent authorities in another member State, then, unless the context otherwise requires, the document as translated is to be regarded as the European document rather than the document as approved: Sch 4 para 1(c).
    The term 'competent authority' includes a body designated by a member State pursuant to EC Council Directive 89/298 art 12; and 'the UK authority' means the competent authority for the purposes of the Financial Services Act 1986 Pt IV (ss 142–156B (as amended): see para 281 ante): Public Offers of Securities Regulations 1995 Sch 4 para 1(a), (b). 'Member State' means a State which is a Contracting Party to the Agreement on the European Economic Area signed at Oporto on 2 May 1992 (OJ L1, 3.1.94, p 3; CM 2073) as adjusted by the Protocol signed at Brussels on 17 March 1993 (OJ L1, 3.1.94, p 572): Public Offers of Securities Regulations 1995 reg 2(1). The Agreement on the European

Economic Area was made between the European Community and its member States and the states of the European Free Trade Association, namely Austria, Finland, Iceland, Liechtenstein, Norway, Switzerland and Sweden, and is intended to create an area of 19 countries throughout which the 'four freedoms' of the European Community (the free movement of goods, capital, services and people) will apply. As to the aims and provisions of the Agreement see 539 HL Official Report (5th series) col 1315 et seq. The Protocol adjusting that Agreement signed at Brussels on 17 March 1993 has the effect of excluding from the European Economic Area Agreement Switzerland, which chose on 1 December 1992 not to participate, and Liechtenstein; enables the Agreement to enter into force without being ratified by those two countries; and allows for Liechtenstein to join the Agreement at a future date: see 230 HC Official Report (6th series) cols 414, 463. Austria, Finland and Sweden, who were formerly member states of the European Economic Area, became full members of the European Community on 1 January 1995.

3 Ie within the meaning of the Financial Services Act 1986 s 144(2) (see para 285 ante) (in a case where the securities to which it relates will not be offered in the United Kingdom prior to admission to listing in the United Kingdom).

4 Ie to a prospectus to which ibid s 144 (see para 285 ante) applies (in a case where the recognised European document is a prospectus and the securities to which it relates are to be offered in the United Kingdom prior to admission to listing in the United Kingdom).

5 Public Offers of Securities Regulations 1995 Sch 4 para 3. Schedule 4 para 3 is subject to Sch 4 para 4 (see infra): Sch 4 para 3.

6 Ibid Sch 4 para 4. The modifications are as follows: (1) nothing in the Financial Services Act 1986 Pt IV (ss 142–156B) (as amended) requires the approval by the UK authority of a recognised European document which has been approved as described in the Public Offers of Securities Regulations 1995 Sch 4 para 1(c) (see note 2 supra); (2) in the Financial Services Act 1986 s 146 (see para 289 ante), s 147(1)(a) (see para 290 head (1) ante) and s 150(2) (see para 347 post) any reference to information specified or required by listing rules or required by the competent authority or to matter whose inclusion was required by listing rules or by the competent authority applies as if it were a reference to information required by or to matter whose inclusion was required by the legislation relating to the contents of prospectuses and listing particulars, or by the competent authorities, of the member State where the European document forming part of that recognised European document was approved; (2) nothing in s 147 (see para 290 ante) requires the approval by the UK authority of supplementary listing particulars or a supplementary prospectus which is, or is a translation into English of, a supplement which has been approved pursuant to EC Council Directive 80/390 art 23 or EC Council Directive 89/298 art 18 by the competent authority which approved the listing particulars or prospectus to which the supplement relates: Public Offers of Securities Regulations 1995 Sch 4 para 4. Subject to Sch 4 paras 1, 3 (see supra), references in the Financial Services Act 1986 Pt IV (ss 142–156B) (as amended) are to be taken to include references to supplementary prospectuses: Public Offers of Securities Regulations 1995 Sch 4 para 5.

7 Ibid Sch 4 para 6.

(ii) Offers of Unlisted Securities

A. IN GENERAL

300. Application of statutory provisions. Offers of unlisted securities were regulated by Part V of the Financial Services Act 1986[1] but that Part was only partly brought into force and the provisions of Part III of the Companies Act 1985[2] continued to apply. Part V of the Financial Services Act 1986[3] and Part III of the Companies Act 1985[4] have now been repealed and public offers of unlisted securities are regulated by the Public Offers of Securities Regulations 1995[5].

1 Ie the Financial Services Act 1986 Pt V (ss 158–171) (as amended).
2 Ie the Companies Act 1985 Pt III (ss 56–79).
3 Ie by the Public Offers of Securities Regulations 1995, SI 1995/1537, reg 17, Sch 2 para 4.
4 As to the repeal of the Companies Act 1985 Pt III (ss 56–79) see para 287 note 25 ante.
5 Ie the Public Offers of Securities Regulations 1995: see para 301 et seq post.

301. Investments to which the provisions apply. The following provisions[1] apply to any investment which is not admitted to official listing, nor the subject of an application for listing[2] and is either:

(1) shares[3] and stock in the share capital of a company[4];

(2) debentures[5], including debenture stock, loan stock, bonds, certificates of deposit and other instruments creating or acknowledging indebtedness, not being loan stock, bonds or other instruments creating or acknowledging indebtedness issued by or on behalf of a government, local authority or public authority[6] but excluding:

   (a) any instrument acknowledging or creating indebtedness for, or for money borrowed to defray, the consideration payable under a contract for the supply of goods or services;

   (b) a cheque or other bill of exchange[7], a banker's draft or a letter of credit;

   (c) a banknote, a statement showing a balance in a current, deposit or savings account or (by reason of any financial obligation contained in it) a lease or other disposition of property, a heritable security or an insurance policy[8];

(3) warrants or other instruments entitling the holder to subscribe for or acquire investments falling within heads (1) or (2) above[9]; or

(4) certificates or other instruments which confer:

   (a) property rights in respect of any investments falling within heads (1) or (2) above;

   (b) any right to acquire, dispose of, underwrite or convert an investment, being a right to which the holder would be entitled if he held any such investment to which the certificate or instrument relates; or

   (c) a contractual right, other than an option, to acquire any such investment otherwise than by subscription[10].

1 Ie the Public Offers of Securities Regulations 1995, SI 1995/1537, Pt II (regs 3–16): see infra and para 302 et seq post.

2 Ie in accordance with the Financial Services Act 1986 Pt IV (ss 142–156B) (as amended): see para 281 et seq ante. As to listing generally see STOCK EXCHANGE vol 45 para 5.

3 For these purposes, the Public Offers of Securities Regulations 1995 reg 3 has effect as if transferable shares in a body incorporated under the law of, or of any part of, the United Kingdom relating to industrial and provident societies were not investments to which Pt II (regs 3–16) is applied: Investment Services Regulations 1995, SI 1995/3275, reg 57, Sch 10 para 22(a).

4 Public Offers of Securities Regulations 1995 reg 3(1)(b); Financial Services Act 1986 Sch 1 para 1. For these purposes, 'company' includes any body corporate and also any unincorporated body constituted under the law of a country or territory outside the United Kingdom, but does not include a building society incorporated under the law of, or of any part of, the United Kingdom; nor does it include an open-ended investment company or any body incorporated under the law of, or of any part of, the United Kingdom relating to industrial and provident societies or credit unions: Sch 1 para 1, note (amended by the Financial Services Act 1986 (Extension of Scope of Act) Order 1991, SI 1991/1104, art 2; the Public Offers of Securities Regulations 1995 reg 3(2)(b)).

5 For these purposes, debentures having a maturity of less than one year from their date of issue are deemed to be excluded: Public Offers of Securities Regulations 1995 reg 3(2)(a).

6 For these purposes, 'government, local authority or public authority' means (1) the government of the United Kingdom, of Northern Ireland, or of any country or territory outside the United Kingdom; (2) a local authority in the United Kingdom or elsewhere; (3) any international organisation the members of which include the United Kingdom or another member State: Financial Services Act 1986 Sch 1 para 3, note (1). For the meaning of 'member State' see para 299 note 2 ante.

7 For these purposes, the Public Offers of Securities Regulations 1995 reg 3 has effect as if bills of exchange accepted by a banker were not investments to which Pt II (regs 3–16) are applied: Investment Services Regulations 1995 Sch 10 para 22(b).

8 Public Offers of Securities Regulations 1995 reg 3(1)(b); Financial Services Act 1986 Sch 1 para 2.

9 Public Offers of Securities Regulations 1995 reg 3(1)(b), (2)(c), (d); Financial Services Act 1986 Sch 1 para 4. It is immaterial whether the investments are for the time being in existence or identifiable: Sch 1 para 4, note (1).

10 Public Offers of Securities Regulations 1995 reg 3(1)(b), (2)(c); Financial Services Act 1986 Sch 1 para 5. Schedule 1 para 5 does not, however, include any instrument which confers rights in respect of two or more investments issued by different persons: Sch 1 para 5, note.

302. Registration and publication of prospectus. When securities[1] are offered to the public in the United Kingdom[2] for the first time, the offeror[3] must publish a prospectus by making it available to the public, free of charge, at an address in the United Kingdom, from the time he first offers the securities until the end of the period during which the offer remains open[4].

The offeror must, before the time of publication of the prospectus, deliver a copy of it to the registrar of companies[5] for registration[6].

1 For these purposes, 'securities' means investments to which the Public Offers of Securities Regulations 1995, SI 1995/1537, Pt II (regs 3–16) (see para 301 ante and para 304 et seq post) applies: reg 2(1).

2 For the meaning of 'offer securities' see para 304 post; and for the meaning of 'offer securities to the public in the United Kingdom' see para 305 post.

3 For the meaning of 'offeror' see para 304 post.

4 Public Offers of Securities Regulations 1995 reg 4(1). As to contraventions see para 320 post.

5 For these purposes, 'the registrar of companies', in relation to a prospectus relating to any securities, means (1) if the securities are or are to be issued by a company incorporated in Great Britain, the registrar of companies in England and Wales or the registrar of companies in Scotland according to whether the company's registered office is in England and Wales or in Scotland; (2) if the securities are or are to be issued by a company incorporated in Northern Ireland, the registrar of companies for Northern Ireland; (3) in any other case, any of those registrars: ibid reg 2(1).

6 Ibid reg 4(2). Regulation 4(2) does not apply to a prospectus submitted for approval in accordance with listing rules made under the Financial Services Act 1986 s 156A (as added) (see para 297 ante): Public Offers of Securities Regulations 1995 reg 4(3). For the purposes of the provisions mentioned in the Companies Act 1985 s 735B (as added) (see para 20 text to note 19 and note 19 ante), the Public Offers of Securities Regulations 1995 reg 4(2) is to be regarded as a provision of the Companies Acts: Public Offers of Securities Regulations 1995 reg 22. As to contraventions see para 320 post.

303. Mutual recognition of prospectuses approved in other member States. Where a prospectus[1] has been approved[2] in another member State, it is deemed[3] to comply with the provisions relating to the form and content of[4], and the general duty of disclosure in[5], a prospectus, provided that:

(1) where the prospectus as approved in the other member State was written in a language other than English, the prospectus has been translated into English and the translation has been certified to be a correct translation in the prescribed manner[6];

(2) the offer of securities to which the prospectus relates is made in the United Kingdom simultaneously with the making of the offer in the member State where the prospectus was approved or within three months after the making of that offer;

(3) there is added to the information contained in the prospectus as approved in the other member State such of the following information as is not included in the prospectus as so approved:

(a) a summary of the tax treatment relevant to United Kingdom resident holders of the securities;

(b) the names and addresses of the paying agents for the securities in the United Kingdom, if any;

    (c) a statement of how notice of meetings and other notices from the issuer of the securities will be given to United Kingdom resident holders of the securities; and

(4) where a partial exemption or partial derogation has been granted in the other member State[7]:

    (a) the partial exemption or partial derogation in question is of a type for which a corresponding partial exemption or partial derogation is made in the United Kingdom regulations[8]; and

    (b) the circumstances that justify the partial exemption or partial derogation also exist in the United Kingdom[9].

1 Where, prior to the delivery for registration to the registrar of companies of a prospectus which has been approved in another member State, a supplement to the prospectus has been approved pursuant to EC Council Directive 80/390 (OJ L100, 17.4.80, p 1) art 23 or EC Council Directive 89/298 (OJ L124, 5.5.89, p 8) art 18 in the member State where the prospectus was approved, the references in the Public Offers of Securities Regulations 1995, SI 1995/1537, reg 20, Sch 4 para 7 (see infra) and in Sch 4 para 8(1) are to be taken to be references to the prospectus taken together with the supplement: Sch 4 para 8(2). For the meaning of 'member State' see para 299 note 2 ante.

    Subject to Sch 4 para 8(2) (see supra), Pt II (regs 3–16) applies in relation to a recognised prospectus as it applies in relation to a prospectus to which Pt II (regs 3–16) (see paras 301, 302 ante and para 304 et seq post) would apply apart from this provision, except that in reg 9(1) (see para 316 post), reg 10(1)(a) (see para 317 post) and reg 14(2) (see para 350 post) the references to information or any matter required to be included in a prospectus by the Public Offers of Securities Regulations 1995 are to be taken to be references to information or any matter required to be included by virtue of the legislation relating to the contents of prospectuses of the member State where the recognised prospectus was approved and by virtue of Sch 4 para 8(1)(c) (see text head (3) infra): Sch 4 para 9. For these purposes, 'recognised prospectus' means a prospectus which has been approved in accordance with EC Council Directive 89/298 art 20 in another member State and satisfies the requirements of the Public Offers of Securities Regulations 1995 Sch 4 para 8(1)(a)–(c) (see text heads (1)–(3) infra); and, where the prospectus has been translated into English, the English version is the recognised prospectus: Sch 4 para 7.

2 Ie in accordance with EC Council Directive 89/298 art 20.

3 Ie for the purposes of the Public Offers of Securities Regulations 1995 reg 4(1): see para 302 ante.

4 Ie ibid reg 8: see para 306 post.

5 Ie ibid reg 9: see para 316 post.

6 Ie in the manner prescribed in the Companies (Forms) Regulations 1985, SI 1985/854, reg 6. A translation of a document into English is to be certified to be a correct translation:

  (1) if the translation was made in the United Kingdom, by:

    (a) a notary public in any part of the United Kingdom;

    (b) a solicitor (if the translation was made in Scotland), a solicitor of the Supreme Court of Judicature of England and Wales (if it was made in England or Wales), or a solicitor of the Supreme Court of Judicature of Northern Ireland (if it was made in Northern Ireland); or

    (c) a person certified by a person mentioned above to be known to him to be competent to translate the document into English (reg 6(a)); or

  (2) if the translation was made outside the United Kingdom, by:

    (a) a notary public;

    (b) a person authorised in the place where the translation was made to administer an oath;

    (c) any of the British officials mentioned in the Commissioners for Oaths Act 1889 s 6;

    (d) a person certified by a person mentioned in heads (2)(a), (b) or (c) supra to be known to him to be competent to translate the document into English (Companies (Forms) Regulations 1985 reg 6(b)).

    As to the British officials mentioned in the Commissioners for Oaths Act 1889 s 6 see para 90 note 5 ante. The Companies (Forms) Regulations 1985 reg 6 applies also for the purposes of the Companies Act 1985 s 272(5) (as amended) (see para 709 post), s 273(7) (as amended) (see para 710 post), s 691(1)(a) (see para 1804 post) and s 698 (meaning of 'certified'): Companies (Forms) Regulations 1985 reg 6.

7 Ie pursuant to EC Council Directive 89/298.

8 Ie the Public Offers of Securities Regulations 1995: see para 301 ante and para 304 et seq post.

9 Ibid Sch 4 para 8(1).

304. Offers of securities. A person is to be regarded as offering securities[1] if, as principal:

(1) he makes an offer which, if accepted, would give rise to a contract for the issue or sale[2] of the securities by him or by another person with whom he has made arrangements for the issue or sale of the securities; or

(2) he invites a person to make such an offer;

but not otherwise; and, except where the context otherwise requires, 'offer' and 'offeror' are to be construed[3] accordingly[4].

1 For the meaning of 'securities' see para 302 note 1 ante.
2 For these purposes, 'sale' includes any disposal for valuable consideration: Public Offers of Securities Regulations 1995, SI 1995/1537, reg 2(1).
3 Ie in ibid Pt II (regs 3–16): see paras 301, 302 ante and para 305 et seq post.
4 Ibid reg 5. Regulation 5 does not apply to a prospectus submitted for approval in accordance with listing rules made under the Financial Services Act 1986 s 156A (as added) (see para 297 ante): Public Offers of Securities Regulations 1995 reg 4(3).

305. Offers of securities to the public in the United Kingdom. A person offers securities[1] to the public in the United Kingdom if, to the extent that the offer[2] is made to persons in the United Kingdom, it is made to the public; and, for these purposes, an offer which is made to any section of the public, whether selected as members or debenture holders of a body corporate[3], or as clients of the person making the offer, or in any other manner, is to be regarded as made to the public[4].

An offer of securities is deemed not to be an offer to the public in the United Kingdom if, to the extent that the offer is made to persons in the United Kingdom:

(1) the condition specified in any of heads (a) to (u) below is satisfied in relation to the offer; or

(2) where, in relation to an offer, the condition specified in one of heads (a) to (g), (k) to (n), (p), (q) and (t) below is satisfied in relation to part, but not the whole, of the offer and, in relation to each other part of the offer, the condition specified in a different head so specified is satisfied[5].

The following are the conditions so specified:

(a) the securities are offered to persons whose ordinary activities involve them in acquiring, holding, managing or disposing of investments (as principal or agent) for the purposes of their businesses or who it is reasonable to expect will acquire, hold, manage or dispose of investments (as principal or agent) for the purposes of their businesses, or are otherwise offered to persons in the context of their trades, professions or occupations[6];

(b) the securities are offered to no more than 50 persons[7];

(c) the securities are offered to the members of a club or association, whether or not incorporated, and the members can reasonably be regarded as having a common interest with each other and with the club or association in the affairs of the club or association and in what is to be done with the proceeds of the offer[8];

(d) the securities are offered to a restricted circle of persons whom the offeror reasonably believes to be sufficiently knowledgeable to understand the risks involved in accepting the offer[9];

(e) the securities are offered in connection with a bona fide invitation to enter into an underwriting agreement[10] with respect to them[11];

(f) the securities are the securities of a private company[12] and are offered by that company to members or employees of the company, members of the families[13] of any such members or employees or holders of specified securities[14] issued by the company[15];

(g)   the securities are offered to a government, local authority or public authority[16];

(h)   the total consideration payable for the securities cannot exceed ecu[17] 40,000 (or an equivalent amount)[18];

(i)   the minimum consideration which may be paid for securities acquired pursuant to the offer is at least ecu 40,000 (or an equivalent amount)[19];

(j)   the securities are denominated in amounts of at least ecu 40,000 (or an equivalent amount)[20];

(k)   the securities are offered in connection with a take-over offer[21];

(l)   the securities are offered in connection with a merger[22];

(m)   the securities are shares[23] and are offered free of charge to any or all of the holders of shares[24] in the issuer[25];

(n)   the securities are shares, or specified investments[26] relating to shares, in a body corporate and are offered in exchange for shares in the same body corporate, and the offer cannot result in any increase in the issued share capital of the body corporate[27];

(o)   the securities are issued by a body corporate and offered by the issuer, only to qualifying persons[28] and on terms that a contract to acquire any such securities may be entered into only by the qualifying person to whom they were offered or, if the terms of the offer so permit, any qualifying person[29];

(p)   the securities result from the conversion of convertible securities[30] and listing particulars or a prospectus relating to the convertible securities were or was published[31] in the United Kingdom[32];

(q)   the securities are issued by a charity[33], a housing association[34], an industrial or provident society[35] or a non-profit making association or body, recognised by the country or territory in which it is established, with objectives similar to those of a charity, a housing association or an industrial or provident society, and the proceeds of the offer will be used for the purposes of the issuer's objectives[36];

(r)   the securities offered are shares and ownership of the securities entitles the holder to obtain the benefit of services provided by a building society[37], an industrial or provident society[38] or a body of a like nature established in a member State[39] or to membership of such a body[40];

(s)   the securities offered are Euro-securities[41] and are not the subject of advertising likely to come to the attention of persons who are not professionally experienced in matters relating to investment[42];

(t)   the securities are of the same class, and were issued at the same time, as securities in respect of which a prospectus has been duly[43] published[44];

(u)   the securities are not transferable[45].

1   For the meaning of 'securities' see para 302 note 1 ante.

2   For the meaning of 'offer' and cognate expressions see para 304 ante.

3   For these purposes, 'body corporate' is to be construed in accordance with the Financial Services Act 1986 s 207(1) (see para 287 note 3 ante): Public Offers of Securities Regulations 1995, SI 1995/1537, reg 2(1)

4   Ibid reg 6. Regulation 6 does not apply to a prospectus submitted for approval in accordance with listing rules made under the Financial Services Act 1986 s 156A (as added) (see para 297 ante): Public Offers of Securities Regulations 1995 reg 4(3).

5   Ibid reg 7(1), (3), (4).

6   Ibid reg 7(2)(a).

7　Ibid reg 7(2)(b). For the purposes of determining whether the condition specified in reg 7(2)(b) or reg 7(2)(h) (see text head (h) infra) is satisfied in relation to an offer, the offer is to be taken together with any other offer of securities of the same class which was (1) made by the same person; (2) open at any time within the period of 12 months ending with the date on which the offer is first made; and (3) deemed not to be an offer to the public in the United Kingdom by virtue of that condition being satisfied: reg 7(6).

8　Ibid reg 7(2)(c).

9　Ibid reg 7(2)(d). In determining for the purposes of reg 7(2)(d) whether a person is sufficiently knowledgeable to understand the risks involved in accepting an offer of securities, any information supplied by the offeror is to be disregarded, apart from information about the issuer of the securities or, if the securities confer the right to acquire other securities, the issuer of those other securities: reg 7(7).

10　As to underwriting agreements see para 194 ante.

11　Public Offers of Securities Regulations 1995 reg 7(2)(e).

12　For these purposes, 'private company' has the meaning given in the Companies Act 1985 s 1(3) (see para 82 ante): Public Offers of Securities Regulations 1995 reg 2(1).

13　For these purposes, the members of a person's family are the person's husband or wife, widow or widower and children (including stepchildren) and their descendants, and any trustee (acting in his capacity as such) of a trust the principal beneficiary of which is the person himself or herself, or any of those relatives: ibid reg 7(8)(a).

14　Ie securities falling within the Financial Services Act 1986 s 1, Sch 1 para 2 (see para 302 head (2) ante), including debentures having a maturity of less than one year from their date of issue.

15　Public Offers of Securities Regulations 1995 reg 7(2)(f), (8)(b).

16　Ibid reg 7(2)(g). For these purposes, 'government, local authority or public authority' has the same meaning as in the Financial Services Act 1986 Sch 1 para 3 (see para 287 note 11 ante): Public Offers of Securities Regulations 1995 reg 7(2)(g).

17　For these purposes, 'ecu' has the same meaning as it has for the purposes of the Financial Services Act 1986 Sch 11A para 3 (as added) (see para 287 note 12 ante): Public Offers of Securities Regulations 1995 reg 2(1).

18　Ibid reg 7(2)(h). See also note 7 supra. For the purposes of determining whether the condition specified in reg 7(2)(h), reg 7(2)(i) (see text head (i) infra) or reg 7(2)(j) (see text head (j) infra) is satisfied in relation to an offer, an amount, in relation to an amount denominated in ecu, is an 'equivalent amount' if it is an amount of equal value, calculated at the latest practicable date before (but in any event not more than three days before) the date on which the offer is first made, denominated wholly or partly in another currency or unit of account: reg 7(9).

19　Ibid reg 7(2)(i). See also note 18 supra.

20　Ibid reg 7(2)(j). See also note 18 supra.

21　Ibid reg 7(2)(k). For these purposes, 'take-over offer' means (1) an offer which is a take-over offer within the meaning of the Companies Act 1985 Pt XIIIA (ss 428–430F (as amended): see para 1202 post) (or would be such an offer if Pt XIIIA (ss 428–430F) (as amended) applied in relation to any body corporate); or (2) an offer made to all the holders of shares, or of shares of a particular class, in a body corporate to acquire a specified proportion of those shares ('holders' and 'shares' being construed in accordance with Pt XIIIA (ss 428–430F (as amended): see para 1202 post); but in determining for the purposes of head (2) supra whether an offer is made to all the holders of shares, or of shares of any class, the offeror, any associate of his (within the meaning of s 430E (as added): see para 1209 post) and any person whose shares the offeror or any such associate has contracted to acquire are not to be regarded as holders of the shares: Public Offers of Securities Regulations 1995 reg 7(10).

22　Ibid reg 7(2)(l). For these purposes, 'merger' means a merger within the meaning of EC Council Directive 78/855 (OJ L295, 20.10.78, p 36) (see EUROPEAN COMMUNITIES vol 51 para 11.33): Public Offers of Securities Regulations 1995 reg 7(2)(l).

23　For these purposes, 'shares', except in relation to a take-over offer, means investments falling within the Financial Services Act 1986 Sch 1 para 1 (see para 302 head (1) ante): Public Offers of Securities Regulations 1995 reg 7(5).

24　For these purposes, 'holders of shares' means the persons who, at the close of business on a date specified in the offer and falling within the period of 28 days ending with the date on which the offer is first made, were the holders of such shares: ibid reg 7(2), (11).

25　Ibid reg 7(2)(m). For these purposes, 'issuer', in relation to any securities, means the person by whom they have been or are to be issued: ibid reg 2(1).

26　Ie investments falling within the Financial Services Act 1986 Sch 1 paras 4 or 5: see para 302 heads (3), (4) ante.

27　Public Offers of Securities Regulations 1995 reg 7(2)(n).

28 For these purposes, a person is a 'qualifying person', in relation to an issuer, if he is a bona fide employee or former employee of the issuer or of another body corporate in the same group or the wife, husband, widow, widower or child or stepchild under the age of 18 of such an employee or former employee: ibid reg 7(12). 'Group' has the meaning given in the Financial Services Act 1986 s 207(1) (see para 287 note 23 ante): Public Offers of Securities Regulations reg 2(1).
29 Ibid reg 7(2)(o).
30 For these purposes, 'convertible securities' means (1) securities falling within the Financial Services Act 1986 Sch 1 para 2 (see para 302 head (2) ante) which can be converted into, or exchanged for, or which confer rights to acquire, securities; or (2) securities falling within Sch 1 paras 4 or 5; and 'conversion', in relation to convertible securities, means their conversion into or exchange for, or the exercise of rights conferred by them to acquire, other securities ('underlying securities'): Public Offers of Securities Regulations 1995 reg 2(1).
31 Ie under or by virtue of the Financial Services Act 1986 Pt IV (ss 142–156B (as amended): see para 281 et seq ante), the Companies Act 1985 Pt III (ss 56–79) or the Public Offers of Securities Regulations 1995.
32 Ibid reg 7(2)(p). As to the repeal of the Companies Act 1985 Pt III (ss 56–79) see para 287 note 25 ante.
33 Ie a charity within the meaning of the Charities Act 1993 s 96(1): see CHARITIES vol 5(2) (Reissue) para 1.
34 Ie a housing association within the meaning of the Housing Act 1985 s 5(1): see HOUSING vol 22 para 445.
35 Ie an industrial or provident society registered in accordance with the Industrial and Provident Societies Act 1965 s 1(2)(b): see INDUSTRIAL AND PROVIDENT SOCIETIES vol 24 (Reissue) para 8.
36 Public Offers of Securities Regulations 1995 reg 7(2)(q).
37 Ie a building society within the meaning of the Building Societies Act 1986 s 119(1): see BUILDING SOCIETIES vol 4(2) (Reissue) para 701.
38 Ie an industrial or provident society registered in accordance with the Industrial and Provident Societies Act 1965 s 1(2).
39 For the meaning of 'member State' see para 299 note 2 ante.
40 Public Offers of Securities Regulations 1995 reg 7(2)(r).
41 For these purposes, 'Euro-securities' has the same meaning as it has for the purposes of the Financial Services Act 1986 Sch 11A para 3 (as added) (see para 287 note 33 ante): Public Offers of Securities Regulations 1995 reg 2(1).
42 Ibid reg 7(2)(s).
43 Ie under or by virtue of the Financial Services Act 1986 Pt IV (ss 142–156B) (as amended), the Companies Act 1985 Pt III (ss 56–79) or the Public Offers of Securities Regulations 1995.
44 Ibid reg 7(2)(t).
45 Ibid reg 7(2)(u).

B. FORM AND CONTENT OF PROSPECTUS

306. In general. A prospectus must contain[1] the specified[2] information[3].

Where the requirement to include in a prospectus any information (the 'required information') is inappropriate to the issuer's[4] sphere of activity or to its legal form or to the securities[5] to which the prospectus relates, the requirement has effect as a requirement that the prospectus contain information equivalent to the required information but, if there is no such equivalent information, does not apply[6].

The information in a prospectus must be presented in as easily analysable and comprehensible a form as possible[7].

Where, on the occasion of their admission to dealings on an approved exchange[8], shares and stock in the share capital of a company[9] are offered on a pre-emptive basis to some or all of the existing holders of such securities, a body or person designated for these purposes by the Treasury has power to authorise the omission from a prospectus subject to these provisions of specified information[10], provided that up-to-date information equivalent to that which would otherwise be required by these provisions is available as a result of the requirements of that approved exchange[11].

Where a class of securities, being shares or stock in the share capital of a company[12], has been admitted to dealings on an approved exchange, a body or person designated for these purposes by the Treasury has power to authorise the making of an offer without a prospectus, provided that:

(1) the number or estimated market value or the nominal value or, in the absence of a nominal value, the accounting par value of the securities offered amounts to less than 10% of the number or of the corresponding value of securities of the same class already admitted to dealings; and

(2) up-to-date information equivalent to that required by these provisions is available as a result of the requirements of that approved exchange[13].

Where a person:

(a) makes an offer to the public in the United Kingdom[14] of securities which he proposes to issue; and

(b) has, within the 12 months preceding the date on which the offer is first made, published a full prospectus[15] relating to a different class of securities which he has issued, or to an earlier issue of the same class of securities,

he may publish, instead of a full prospectus, a prospectus which contains only the differences which have arisen since the publication of the full prospectus mentioned in head (b) above and any supplementary prospectus and which are likely to influence the value of the securities, provided that the prospectus is accompanied by that full prospectus and any supplementary prospectus or contains a reference to it or them[16].

1 Ie subject to the Public Offers of Securities Regulations 1995, SI 1995/1537, reg 8(2), (4)–(6) (see infra) and reg 11 (see para 318 post).

2 Ie the information specified in ibid reg 8(1), Sch 1 Pts II–X (paras 2–51): see para 307 et seq post. Schedule 1 is to be construed in accordance with Sch 1 Pt I (para 1): reg 8(1).

3 Ibid reg 8(1). Regulation 8 does not apply to a prospectus submitted for approval in accordance with listing rules made under the Financial Services Act 1986 s 156A (as added) (see para 297 ante): Public Offers of Securities Regulations 1995 reg 4(3).

4 For the meaning of 'issuer' see para 305 note 25 ante.

5 For the meaning of 'securities' see para 302 note 1 ante.

6 Public Offers of Securities Regulations 1995 reg 8(2). See also note 3 supra.

7 Ibid reg 8(3). See also note 3 supra.

8 For these purposes, 'approved exchange' means, in relation to dealings in securities, a recognised investment exchange approved by the Treasury for the purposes of the Public Offers of Securities Regulations 1995 either generally or in relation to such dealings; and the Treasury must give notice in such manner as it thinks appropriate of the exchanges which are for the time being approved: reg 2(1). 'Recognised investment exchange' has the meaning given in the Financial Services Act 1986 s 207(1) (see para 223 note 1 ante): Public Offers of Securities Regulations 1995 reg 2(1).

9 Ie securities falling within the Financial Services Act 1986 Sch 1 para 1: see para 301 head (1) ante.

10 For these purposes, 'specified information' means information specified in the Public Offers of Securities Regulations 1995 Sch 1 paras 41–47 (see paras 311–313 post): reg 8(4).

11 Ibid reg 8(4). See also note 3 supra.

12 See note 9 supra.

13 Public Offers of Securities Regulations 1995 reg 8(5). See also note 3 supra.

14 For the meaning of 'offer to the public in the United Kingdom' see para 305 ante.

15 For these purposes, a full prospectus is one which contains the information specified in the Public Offers of Securities Regulations 1995 Sch 1 Pts II–X (paras 2–51), other than any information whose omission is authorised by or under reg 11(2) or (4) (see para 318 post): reg 8(6).

16 Ibid reg 8(6). See also note 3 supra.

307. General requirements. The prospectus must contain:

(1) the name of the issuer[1] and the address of its registered office[2];

(2) if different, the name and address of the person offering the securities[3];

(3) the names and functions of the directors[4] of the issuer[5];

(4) the date of publication of the prospectus[6];

(5) a statement that a copy of the prospectus has been delivered for registration to the registrar of companies[7], indicating to which registrar of companies it has been delivered[8];

(6) a statement that the prospectus has been duly drawn up[9];

(7) the following words, 'If you are in any doubt about the contents of this document, you should consult a person authorised under the Financial Services Act 1986 who specialises in advising on the acquisition of shares and other securities', or words to the like effect[10].

1 For the meaning of 'issuer' see para 305 note 25 ante.
2 Public Offers of Securities Regulations 1995, SI 1995/1537, reg 8(1), Sch 1 para 2.
3 Ibid Sch 1 para 3. For the meaning of 'securities' see para 302 note 1 ante.
4 For these purposes, 'director', in relation to a body corporate, includes a person occupying in relation to it the position of director (by whatever named called) and any person in accordance with whose directions or instructions (not being advice given in a professional capacity) the directors of that body are accustomed to act: Financial Services Act 1986 s 207(1) (applied by the Public Offers of Securities Regulations 1995 reg 2(1)).
5 Public Offers of Securities Regulations 1995 Sch 1 para 4.
6 Ibid Sch 1 para 5.
7 Ie in accordance with ibid reg 4(2): see para 302 ante. For the meaning of 'the registrar of companies' see para 302 note 5 ante.
8 Ibid Sch 1 para 6.
9 Ibid Sch 1 para 7.
10 Ibid Sch 1 para 8.

308. Persons responsible for the prospectus and advisers. The prospectus must contain:

(1) the names, addresses (home or business) and functions of those persons responsible for the prospectus[1] or any part of the prospectus, specifying such part[2];

(2) a declaration by the directors[3] of the issuer[4] (or, if the offeror is not the issuer, by the directors of the offeror) that to the best of their knowledge the information contained in the prospectus is in accordance with the facts and that the prospectus makes no omission likely to affect the import of such information[5];

(3) a statement by any person who accepts responsibility for the prospectus, or any part of it, that he does so[6].

1 For these purposes, 'person responsible for the prospectus' has the same meaning as in the Public Offers of Securities Regulations 1995, SI 1995/1537, reg 13 (see para 349 post): reg 8(1), Sch 1 para 9.
2 Ibid Sch 1 para 9.
3 For the meaning of 'director' see para 307 note 4 ante.
4 For the meaning of 'issuer' see para 305 note 25 ante.
5 Public Offers of Securities Regulations 1995 Sch 1 para 10(1).
6 Ibid Sch 1 para 10(2). Schedule 1 para 10(2) is without prejudice to Sch 1 para 45 (see para 312 post): Sch 1 para 10(2).

309. The securities to which the prospectus relates and the offer. The prospectus must contain:

(1) a description of the securities[1] being offered, including the class to which they belong and a description of the rights attaching to them including (where applicable):

(a) if the securities are shares, rights as regards voting, dividends, return of capital on the winding up of the issuer[2] and redemption, and a summary of the consents necessary for the variation of any of those rights;

    (b) if the securities are debentures[3], rights as regards interest payable and repayment of principal;

    (c) if the securities are convertible securities[4], the terms and dates on which the holder of the convertible securities is entitled to acquire the related underlying securities[5], the procedures for exercising the entitlement to the underlying securities and such information relating to the underlying securities as would have been required under heads (a) or (b) above if the securities being offered had been the underlying securities[6];

(2) the date or dates, if any, on which entitlement to dividends or interest arises[7];

(3) particulars of tax on income from the securities withheld at source, including tax credits[8];

(4) the procedure for the exercise of any right of pre-emption attaching to the securities[9];

(5) any restrictions on the free transferability of the securities being offered[10];

(6) a statement as to whether the securities being offered have been admitted to dealings on a recognised investment exchange[11] or an application for such admission has been made; where no such application for dealings has been made, or such an application has been made and refused, a statement as to whether or not there are, or are intended to be, any other arrangements for there to be dealings in the securities and, if there are, a brief description of such arrangements[12];

(7) the purpose for which the securities are being issued[13];

(8) the number of securities being issued[14];

(9) the number of securities being offered[15];

(10) the total proceeds which it is expected will be raised by the offer and the expected net proceeds, after deduction of the expenses, of the offer[16];

(11) where the prospectus relates to shares which are offered for subscription, particulars as to:

    (a) the minimum amount which, in the opinion of the directors[17] of the issuer, must be raised by the issue of those shares in order to provide the sums (or, if any part of them is to be defrayed in any other manner, the balance of the sums) required to be provided in respect of each of the following, that is to say, the purchase price of any property purchased, or to be purchased, which is to be defrayed in whole or in part out of the proceeds of the issue, any preliminary expenses payable by the issuer and any commission so payable to any person in consideration of his agreeing to subscribe for, or of his procuring or agreeing to procure subscriptions for, any shares in the issuer, the repayment of any money borrowed by the issuer in respect of any of the foregoing matters and working capital; and

    (b) the amounts to be provided in respect of the matters mentioned otherwise than out of the proceeds of the issue and the sources out of which those amounts are to be provided[18];

(12) the names of any persons underwriting or guaranteeing the offer[19];

(13) the amount or the estimated amount of the expenses of the offer and by whom they are payable, including[20] a statement as to any commission payable by the issuer to any person in consideration of his agreeing to subscribe for securities to which the prospectus relates or of his procuring or agreeing to procure subscriptions for such securities[21];

(14) the names and addresses of the paying agents, if any[22];

(15) the period during which the offer of the securities is open[23];

(16) the price at which the securities are offered or, if appropriate, the procedure, method and timetable for fixing the price[24];

(17) the arrangements for payment for the securities being offered and the arrangements and timetable for their delivery[25];

(18) the arrangements during the period prior to the delivery of the securities being offered relating to the moneys received from applicants including arrangements for the return of moneys to applicants where their applications are not accepted in whole or in part and the timetable for the return of such moneys[26].

1 For the meaning of 'securities' see para 302 note 1 ante.
2 For the meaning of 'issuer' see para 305 note 25 ante.
3 For these purposes, 'debentures' means securities falling within the Financial Services Act 1986 s 1, Sch 1 para 2 (see para 301 head (2) ante): Public Offers of Securities Regulations 1995, SI 1995/1537, reg 8(1), Sch 1 para 1.
4 For the meaning of 'convertible securities' see para 305 note 30 ante.
5 For the meaning of 'underlying securities' see para 305 note 30 ante.
6 Public Offers of Securities Regulations 1995 Sch 1 para 11.
7 Ibid Sch 1 para 12.
8 Ibid Sch 1 para 13.
9 Ibid Sch 1 para 14.
10 Ibid Sch 1 para 15.
11 For the meaning of 'recognised investment exchange' see para 306 note 8 ante.
12 Public Offers of Securities Regulations 1995 Sch 1 para 16(1), (2).
13 Ibid Sch 1 para 17.
14 Ibid Sch 1 para 18.
15 Ibid Sch 1 para 19.
16 Ibid Sch 1 para 20.
17 For the meaning of 'director' see para 307 note 4 ante.
18 Public Offers of Securities Regulations 1995 Sch 1 para 21.
19 Ibid Sch 1 para 22.
20 Ie except in so far as information is required to be included in the prospectus by the Companies Act 1985 s 97(3): see para 194 ante.
21 Public Offers of Securities Regulations 1995 Sch 1 para 23.
22 Ibid Sch 1 para 24.
23 Ibid Sch 1 para 25.
24 Ibid Sch 1 para 26.
25 Ibid Sch 1 para 27.
26 Ibid Sch 1 para 28.

310. General information about the issuer and its capital. The prospectus must contain:

(1) the date and place of incorporation of the issuer[1] and, in the case of an issuer not incorporated in the United Kingdom, the address of its principal place of business in the United Kingdom, if any[2];

(2) the place of registration of the issuer and the number with which it is registered[3];

(3) the legal form of the issuer, the legislation under which it was formed and, if different, the legislation now applicable to it[4];

(4) a summary of the provisions in the issuer's memorandum of association determining its objects[5];

(5) if the liability of the members of the issuer is limited, a statement of that fact[6];

(6) the amount of the issuer's authorised share capital and any limit on the duration of the authorisation to issue such share capital[7];

(7) the amount of the issuer's issued share capital[8];

(8) the number and particulars of any listed and unlisted securities[9] issued by the issuer not representing share capital[10];

(9) the number of shares of each class making up each of the authorised and issued share capital, the nominal value of such shares and, in the case of the issued share capital, the amount paid up on the shares[11];

(10) the amount of any outstanding listed and unlisted convertible securities[12] issued by the issuer, the conditions and procedures for their conversion and the number of shares which would be issued as a result of their conversion[13];

(11) if the issuer is a member of a group[14], a brief description of the group and of the issuer's position in it, stating, where the issuer is a subsidiary[15], the name of its holding company[16];

(12) in so far as the offeror has the information, an indication of the persons, who, directly or indirectly, jointly or severally, exercise or could exercise control[17] over the issuer and particulars of the proportion of the issuer's voting capital held by such persons[18].

1 For the meaning of 'issuer' see para 305 note 25 ante.
2 Public Offers of Securities Regulations 1995, SI 1995/1537, reg 8(1), Sch 1 para 29.
3 Ibid Sch 1 para 30.
4 Ibid Sch 1 para 31.
5 Ibid Sch 1 para 32.
6 Ibid Sch 1 para 33.
7 Ibid Sch 1 para 34.
8 Ibid Sch 1 para 35.
9 For the meaning of 'securities' see para 302 note 1 ante.
10 Public Offers of Securities Regulations 1995 Sch 1 para 36.
11 Ibid Sch 1 para 37.
12 For the meaning of 'convertible securities' see para 305 note 30 ante.
13 Public Offers of Securities Regulations 1995 Sch 1 para 38.
14 For the meaning of 'group' see para 305 note 28 ante.
15 For these purposes, 'subsidiary' has the same meaning as in the Companies Act 1985 ss 736, 736A (as substituted) (see para 827 post): Public Offers of Securities Regulations 1995 Sch 1 para 1.
16 Ibid Sch 1 para 39. For these purposes, 'holding company' has the same meaning as in the Companies Act 1985 ss 736, 736A (as substituted) (see para 827 post): Public Offers of Securities Regulations 1995 Sch 1 para 1.
17 For these purposes, 'control' means the ability, in practice, to determine the actions of the issuer; and 'joint control' means control exercised by two or more persons who have an agreement or understanding, whether formal or informal, which may lead to their adopting a common policy in respect of the issuer: ibid Sch 1 para 1.
18 Ibid Sch 1 para 40.

311. The issuer's principal activities. The prospectus must contain:

(1) a description of the issuer's[1] principal activities and of any exceptional factors which have influenced its activities[2];

(2) a statement of any dependence of the issuer on patents or other intellectual property rights, licences or particular contracts, where any of these are of fundamental importance to the issuer's business[3];

(3) information regarding investments in progress where they are significant[4];

(4) information on any legal or arbitration proceedings, active, pending or threatened against, or being brought by, the issuer or any member of its group[5] which are having or may have a significant effect on the issuer's financial position[6].

1 For the meaning of 'issuer' see para 305 note 25 ante.
2 Public Offers of Securities Regulations 1995, SI 1995/1537, reg 8(1), Sch 1 para 41.

3 Ibid Sch 1 para 42.
4 Ibid Sch 1 para 43.
5 For the meaning of 'group' see para 305 note 28 ante.
6 Public Offers of Securities Regulations 1995 Sch 1 para 44.

312. The issuer's assets and liabilities, financial position and profits and losses. If the issuer[1] is a company to which the statutory provisions relating to accounts[2] apply otherwise than by virtue of the provisions relating to oversea companies[3], the prospectus must contain:

(1) the issuer's annual accounts[4] for the last three years[5] together with:
   - (a) a statement by the directors[6] of the issuer that the accounts have been prepared in accordance with the law, and that they accept responsibility for them, or a statement why they are unable to make such a statement;
   - (b) the names and addresses of the auditors of the accounts;
   - (c) a copy of the auditors' reports on the accounts[7]; and
   - (d) a statement by the auditors that they consent to the inclusion of their reports in the prospectus and accept responsibility for them, and have not become aware, since the date of any report, of any matter affecting the validity of that report at that date; or a statement why they are unable to make such a statement; or

(2) a report by a person qualified to act as an auditor[8] with respect to the state of affairs[9] and profit or loss shown by the issuer's annual accounts for the last three years[10] together with:
   - (a) the name and address of the person responsible for the report;
   - (b) if different, the name and address of the person who audited the accounts on which the report is based; and
   - (c) a statement by the person responsible for the report that in his opinion the report gives a true and fair view of the state of affairs and profit or loss of the issuer and its subsidiary undertakings[11], and that he consents to the inclusion of his report in the prospectus and accepts responsibility for it; or a statement why he is unable to make such a statement[12].

If the issuer is not a company to which the statutory provisions relating to accounts[13] apply or is a company to which those provisions apply by virtue of the provisions relating to oversea companies[14], the prospectus must contain:

(i) the issuer's accounts (and, if it is a parent undertaking[15], its subsidiary undertakings' accounts) for the last three years[16], prepared in accordance with the applicable law, together with:
   - (A) the name and address of the person responsible for the accounts;
   - (B) a statement by the person responsible for the accounts that they have been properly prepared in accordance with the applicable law, and that he accepts responsibility for them, or a statement why he is unable to make such a statement;
   - (C) the names and addresses of the auditors of the accounts and their reports; and
   - (D) a statement by the auditors that they consent to the inclusion of their reports in the prospectus and accept responsibility for them, and have not become aware, since the date of any report, of any matter affecting the validity of that report at that date; or a statement why they are unable to make such a statement; or

(ii) a report by a person qualified to act as an auditor with respect to the state of affairs and profit or loss shown by the issuer's accounts (and, if the issuer is a parent undertaking, by its subsidiary undertakings' accounts) for the last three years[17], such report to be drawn up in accordance with the applicable law, or as if the provisions of the Companies Act 1985 relating to annual accounts applied to the issuer, together with:

(A) the name and address of the person responsible for the report;

(B) if different, the name and address of the person who audited the accounts on which the report is based; and

(C) a statement by the person responsible for the report that in his opinion the report gives a true and fair view of the state of affairs and profit or loss of the issuer and its subsidiary undertakings and that he consents to the inclusion of his report in the prospectus and accepts responsibility for it; or a statement why he is unable to make such a statement[18].

Where more than nine months have elapsed at the date on which the offer is first made since the end of the last financial year[19] in respect of which accounts or a report are required to be included in the prospectus, there must also be included in the prospectus interim accounts of the undertaking concerned (which need not be audited but which must otherwise be prepared to the standard applicable to accounts required for each financial year) covering the period beginning at the end of the last financial year in respect of which accounts or a report are required to be included in the prospectus, and ending on the latest practicable date before (but not in any event more than three months before) the date on which the offer is first made, together with the name and address of the person responsible for the interim accounts and a statement by him that the interim accounts have been properly prepared in accordance with the law applicable to the undertaking, and that he consents to the inclusion of the accounts and statement in the prospectus and accepts responsibility for them; or a statement why he is unable to make such a statement; or a report by a person qualified to act as an auditor covering the same period with respect to the state of affairs and profit or loss of the undertaking concerned, prepared in accordance with the law applicable to the undertaking, together with the name and address of the person responsible for preparing the report, and a statement by him that he consents to the inclusion of the report in the prospectus and accepts responsibility for it; or a statement why he is unable to make such a statement[20].

If any interim accounts of the issuer have been published since the end of the last financial year of the issuer in respect of which accounts or a report are required to be included in the prospectus, other than interim accounts included in a prospectus[21], they must be included in the prospectus together with an explanation of the purpose for which the accounts were prepared, a reference to the legislation in accordance with which they were prepared and the name and address of the person responsible for them, and a statement from him that he consents to the inclusion of the accounts in the prospectus and accepts reponsibility for them[22].

1 For the meaning of 'issuer' see para 305 note 25 ante.

2 Ie the Companies Act 1985 Pt VII (ss 221–262A) (as amended): see para 801 et seq post.

3 Ie ibid s 700 (as substituted): see para 1823 post.

4 For these purposes, 'annual accounts' has the same meaning as in the Companies Act 1985 Pt VII (ss 221–262A (as amended): see para 817 note 2 post): Public Offers of Securities Regulations 1995, SI 1995/1537, reg 8(1), Sch 1 para 1.

5 For these purposes, 'the last three years', in relation to an undertaking whose accounts are required to be dealt with in a prospectus, means three completed financial years which immediately precede the date on which the offer is first made and which cover a continuous period of at least 35 months, disregarding

a financial year which ends less than three months before the date on which the offer is first made and for which accounts have not been prepared by that date: ibid Sch 1 para 1.

In so far as the issuer has not been in existence for the whole of the last three years, the requirement in Sch 1 para 45(1)(a) and Sch 1 para 45(2)(a) (see infra) that the prospectus contain accounts for the last three years is to be construed as a requirement that the prospectus contain the accounts which the undertaking concerned was required (by its constitution or by the law under which it is established) to prepare for financial years during its existence, disregarding a financial year which ends less than three months before the date on which the offer is first made and for which accounts have not been prepared by that date: Sch 1 para 45(6), (7)(a).

In so far as an issuer has not been in existence for the whole of the last three years, if an undertaking has not been required (by its constitution or by the law under which it is established) to prepare any accounts for financial years, the requirement in Sch 1 para 45(1) and Sch 1 para 45(2) (see infra) that the prospectus contain accounts for, or a report with respect to, the last three years is to be construed as a requirement that the prospectus contain a report by a person qualified to act as an auditor which includes (1) details of the profit or loss of the undertaking in respect of the period beginning with the date of its formation and ending on the latest practicable date before (but not in any event more than three months before) the date on which the offer is first made, and of its state of affairs at that latest practicable date; and (2) a statement by the person responsible for the report that in his opinion it gives a true and fair view of the state of affairs and profit or loss of the undertaking and that he consents to the inclusion of his report in the prospectus and accepts responsibility for it, or a statement why he is unable to make such a statement: Sch 1 para 45(6), (8). For the meaning of 'financial year' see note 19 infra.

6 For the meaning of 'director' see para 307 note 4 ante.
7 Ie within the meaning of the Companies Act 1985 s 235 (as substituted): see para 1059 post.
8 As to the persons qualified to act as auditors see para 955 et seq post.
9 For these purposes, 'state of affairs' means the state of affairs of the undertaking, in relation to its balance sheet, at the end of a financial year: Public Offers of Securities Regulations 1995 Sch 1 para 1.
10 In so far as the issuer has not been in existence for the whole of the last three years, the requirement in ibid Sch 1 para 45(1)(b) and Sch 1 para 45(2)(b) (see infra) that the prospectus contain a report with respect to the state of affairs and profit or loss for the last three years is to be construed as a requirement that the prospectus contain a report with respect to the accounts which the undertaking concerned was required (by its constitution or by the law under which it is established) to prepare for financial years during its existence, disregarding a financial year which ends less than three months before the date on which the offer is first made and for which accounts have not been prepared by that date: Sch 1 para 45(6), (7)(b). See also note 5 supra.
11 For these purposes, 'subsidiary undertaking' and 'undertaking' have the same meanings as in the Companies Act 1985 Pt VII (ss 221–262A (as amended): see paras 828, 806 note 5 respectively post): Public Offers of Securities Regulations 1995 Sch 1 para 1.
12 Ibid Sch 1 para 45(1). If, in the case of an issuer falling within Sch 1 para 45(1) or Sch 1 para 45(2) (see infra), the prospectus would otherwise include both separate accounts for the issuer and its subsidiary undertakings and consolidated accounts, either the separate accounts or the consolidated accounts may be omitted from the prospectus if their inclusion would not provide any significant additional information: Sch 1 para 45(4).

   If the issuer is a parent undertaking, the requirements of Sch 1 para 45(1) or, as the case may be, Sch 1 para 45(2) (see infra) apply to each subsidiary undertaking in respect of any part of the last three years for which information is not otherwise required by Sch 1 para 45(1) or (2): Sch 1 para 45(9). For the meaning of 'parent undertaking' see note 15 infra.
13 See note 2 supra.
14 See note 3 supra.
15 For these purposes, 'parent undertaking' has the same meaning as in the Companies Act 1985 Pt VII (ss 221–262A (as amended): see para 828 post): Public Offers of Securities Regulations 1995 Sch 1 para 1.
16 See note 5 supra.
17 See notes 5, 10 supra.
18 Public Offers of Securities Regulations 1995 reg 45(2). See also note 10 supra. If, in accordance with the law applicable to it, the accounts of an issuer falling within Sch 1 para 45(2) consist only of consolidated accounts with respect to itself and its subsidiary undertakings, the prospectus is not required by virtue of Sch 1 para 45(2) to include separate accounts for each undertaking, or to include a report which deals with the accounts of each undertaking separately: Sch 1 para 45(3).

   If an issuer falling within Sch 1 para 45(2) is not required by the law applicable to it to have its accounts audited: (1) if the accounts have not been audited, the prospectus must contain a statement to that effect and Sch 1 para 45(2)(a)(iii), (iv) or, as the case may be, Sch 1 para 45(2)(b)(ii) does not apply to the issuer; and (2) if the accounts have nonetheless been audited, the prospectus must contain a statement to that effect: Sch 1 para 45(5).

19 For these purposes, 'financial year' has the same meaning as in the Companies Act 1985 Pt VII (ss 221–262A (as amended): see para 806 post): Public Offers of Securities Regulations 1995 Sch 1 para 1.

20 Ibid Sch 1 para 45(10).

21 Ie in accordance with ibid Sch 1 para 45(10): see supra.

22 Ibid Sch 1 para 45(11).

313. The issuer's administration, management and supervision. The prospectus must contain:

(1) a concise description of the directors'[1] existing or proposed service contracts with the issuer[2] or any subsidiary[3] of the issuer, excluding contracts expiring, or determinable by the employing company without payment of compensation within one year, or an appropriate negative statement[4];

(2) the aggregate remuneration paid and benefits in kind granted to the directors of the issuer during the last completed financial year[5] of the issuer, together with an estimate of the aggregate amount payable and benefits in kind to be granted to the directors, and proposed directors, for the current financial year under the arrangements in force at the date on which the offer is first made[6];

(3) the interests of each director of the issuer in the share capital of the issuer, distinguishing between beneficial and non-beneficial interests, or an appropriate negative statement[7].

1 For the meaning of 'director' see para 307 note 4 ante.
2 For the meaning of 'issuer' see para 305 note 25 ante.
3 For the meaning of 'subsidiary' see para 310 note 15 ante.
4 Public Offers of Securities Regulations 1995, SI 1995/1537, reg 8(1), Sch 1 para 46.
5 For the meaning of 'financial year' see para 312 note 19 ante.
6 Public Offers of Securities Regulations 1995 Sch 1 para 47(1).
7 Ibid reg 47(2).

314. Recent developments in the issuer's business and prospects. The prospectus must contain:

(1) the significant recent trends concerning the development of the issuer's[1] business since the end of the last completed financial year[2] of the issuer[3];

(2) information on the issuer's prospects for at least the current financial year of the issuer[4].

1 For the meaning of 'issuer' see para 305 note 25 ante.
2 For the meaning of 'financial year' see para 312 note 19 ante.
3 Public Offers of Securities Regulations 1995, SI 1995/1537, reg 8(1), Sch 1 para 48.
4 Ibid Sch 1 para 49.

315. Convertible securities and guaranteed debentures. Where the prospectus relates to convertible securities[1], and the issuer[2] of the related underlying securities[3] is not the same as the issuer of the convertible securities, all the information to be contained in a prospectus[4] must be given in respect of the issuer of the convertible securities and specified information[5] must be given in respect of the issuer of the underlying securities[6].

Where the prospectus relates to debentures[7] which are guaranteed by one or more persons, the name and address and specified information[8] must also be given in respect of any guarantor who is not an individual[9].

1   For the meaning of 'convertible securities' see para 305 note 30 ante.
2   For the meaning of 'issuer' see para 305 note 25 ante.
3   For the meaning of 'underlying securities' see para 305 note 30 ante.
4   Ie the information specified in the Public Offers of Securities Regulations 1995, SI 1995/1537, reg 8(1), Sch 1: see para 307 et seq ante.
5   Ie the information specified in ibid Sch 1 para 2 (see para 307 ante) and Pt V (paras 29–40) (see para 310 ante), Pt VI (paras 41–44) (see para 311 ante), Pt VII (para 45) (see para 312 ante), Pt VIII (paras 46, 47) (see para 313 ante) and Pt IX (paras 48, 49) (see para 314 ante).
6   Ibid Sch 1 para 50.
7   For the meaning of 'debentures' see para 309 note 3 ante.
8   Ie the Public Offers of Securities Regulations 1995 Pt V (paras 29–40), Pt VI (paras 41–44), Pt VII (para 45), Pt VIII (paras 46, 47) and Pt IX (paras 48, 49).
9   Ibid Sch 1 para 51.

C. DUTY OF DISCLOSURE

316. General duty of disclosure. In addition to the information otherwise required to be included in a prospectus[1], a prospectus must contain[2] all such information as investors would reasonably require, and reasonably expect to find there, for the purpose of making an informed assessment of:

(1)   the assets and liabilities, financial position, profits and losses, and prospects of the issuer[3] of the securities[4]; and

(2)   the rights attaching to those securities[5].

The information to be so included is such information as is mentioned above which is within the knowledge of any person responsible for the prospectus[6] or which it would be reasonable for him to obtain by making inquiries[7].

In determining what information is required to be included in a prospectus by virtue of the above provisions regard must be had to the nature of the securities and of the issuer of the securities[8].

1   Ie by virtue of the Public Offers of Securities Regulations 1995, SI 1995/1537, reg 8: see para 306 ante.
2   Ie subject to the Public Offers of Securities Regulations 1995.
3   For these purposes, 'issuer', in relation to a certificate or other instrument falling within the Financial Services Act 1986 s 1, Sch 1 para 5 (see para 301 head (4) ante), means the person who issued or is to issue the securities to which the certificate or instrument relates: Public Offers of Securities Regulations 1995 reg 9(4). For the meaning of 'issuer' generally see para 305 note 25 ante.
4   For the meaning of 'securities' see para 302 note 1 ante.
5   Public Offers of Securities Regulations 1995 reg 9(1). Regulation 9 does not apply to a prospectus submitted for approval in accordance with listing rules made under the Financial Services Act 1986 s 156A (as added) (see para 297 ante): Public Offers of Securities Regulations 1995 reg 4(3).
6   For the meaning of 'person responsible for the prospectus' see para 308 note 1 ante.
7   Public Offers of Securities Regulations 1995 reg 9(2). See also note 5 supra.
8   Ibid reg 9(3). See also note 5 supra.

317. Supplementary prospectus. Where a prospectus has been registered[1] in respect of an offer of securities[2] and at any time while an agreement in respect of those securities can be entered into in pursuance of that offer:

(1)   there is a significant[3] change affecting any matter contained in the prospectus whose inclusion was required[4];

(2)   a significant new matter arises the inclusion of information in respect of which would have been so required if it had arisen when the prospectus was prepared; or

(3)   there is a significant inaccuracy in the prospectus,

the offeror[5] must deliver to the registrar of companies[6] for registration, and duly publish[7], a supplementary prospectus containing particulars of the change or new matter or, in the case of an inaccuracy, correcting it[8].

The provisions relating to the publication of a prospectus[9] apply to supplementary prospectus delivered for registration to the registrar of companies in the same way as they apply to a prospectus except that the obligation to publish the supplemetary prospectus begins with the time it is delivered for registration to the registrar of companies[10].

Where the offeror is not aware of the change, new matter or inaccuracy in question, he is not under any duty to comply with the above provisions[11] unless he is notified of it by a person responsible for the prospectus[12]; but any person responsible for the prospectus who is aware of such a matter is under a duty to give him notice of it[13].

1 Ie under the Public Offers of Securities Regulations 1995, SI 1995/1537, Pt II (regs 3–16): see para 301 et seq ante and paras 318, 319, 349–351 post.
2 For the meaning of 'securities' see para 302 note 1 ante.
3 For these purposes, 'significant' means significant for the purpose of making an informed assessment of the matters mentioned in the Public Offers of Securities Regulations 1995 reg 9(1)(a), (b) (see para 316 heads (1), (2) ante): reg 10(2).
4 Ie by ibid reg 8 (see para 315 ante) or reg 9 (see para 316 ante).
5 For the meaning of 'offeror' see para 304 ante.
6 For the meaning of 'the registrar of companies' see para 302 note 5 ante.
7 Ie in accordance with the Public Offers of Securities Regulations 1995 reg 10(3): see infra.
8 Ibid reg 10(1). Regulation 10 does not apply to a prospectus submitted for approval in accordance with listing rules made under the Financial Services Act 1986 s 156A (as added) (see para 297 ante): Public Offers of Securities Regulations 1995 reg 4(3). For the purposes of the provisions mentioned in the Companies Act 1985 s 735B (as added) (see para 20 text to note 19 and note 19 ante), the Public Offers of Securities Regulations 1995 reg 10(1) is to be regarded as a provision of the Companies Acts: Public Offers of Securities Regulations 1995 reg 22. As to contraventions see para 320 post.
   Where a supplementary prospectus has been so registered in respect of an offer, reg 10(1)–(4) has effect as if any reference to a prospectus were a reference to the prospectus originally registered and that supplementary prospectus, taken together: reg 10(5).
9 Ie ibid reg 4(1): see para 302 ante.
10 Ibid reg 10(3).
11 Ie ibid reg 10(1), (3): see supra.
12 For the meaning of 'person responsible for the prospectus' see para 308 note 1 ante.
13 Public Offers of Securities Regulations 1995 reg 10(4).

318. Exemptions from disclosure. The Treasury or the Secretary of State may authorise the omission from a prospectus[1] or supplementary prospectus[2] of information whose inclusion would otherwise be required[3] if it or he considers that disclosure of that information would be contrary to the public interest[4].

An offeror[5] may omit from a prospectus or supplementary prospectus information with respect to an issuer[6] whose inclusion would otherwise be required[7] if:

(1) he is not that issuer, nor acting in pursuance of an agreement with that issuer;

(2) the information is not available to him because he is not that issuer; and

(3) he has been unable, despite making such efforts, if any, as are reasonable, to obtain the information[8].

The competent authority[9] may authorise the omission from a prospectus or supplementary prospectus of information whose inclusion would otherwise be required[10] if:

(a) the information is of minor importance only, and is not likely to influence assessment of the issuer's assets and liabilities, financial position, profits and losses and prospects; or

    (b)   disclosure of that information would be seriously detrimental to the issuer and its omission would not be likely to mislead investors with regard to facts and circumstances necessary for an informed assessment of the securities[11].

1 As to the prospectus see para 306 et seq ante.
2 As to the supplementary prospectus see para 317 ante.
3 Ie by the Public Offers of Securities Regulations 1995, SI 1995/1537: see para 300 et seq ante.
4 Ibid reg 11(1). Regulation 11 does not apply to a prospectus submitted for approval in accordance with listing rules made under the Financial Services Act 1986 s 156A (as added) (see para 297 ante): Public Offers of Securities Regulations 1995 reg 4(3). The Financial Services Act 1986 s 188 (as substituted) (jurisdiction of High Court: see STOCK EXCHANGE) applies to proceedings arising out of any act or omission, or proposed act or omission, of the competent authority in the discharge or purported discharge of any function under the Public Offers of Securities Regulations 1995 reg 11 as it applies to the proceedings mentioned in the Financial Services Act 1986 s 188: Public Offers of Securities Regulations 1995 reg 23(2).
5 For the meaning of 'offeror' see para 304 ante.
6 For the meaning of 'issuer' see para 305 note 25 ante.
7 See note 3 supra.
8 Public Offers of Securities Regulations 1995 reg 11(2). See also note 4 supra.
9 Ie the competent authority for the purposes of the Financial Services Act 1986 Pt IV (ss 142–156B) (as amended): see para 281 ante.
10 See note 3 supra.
11 Public Offers of Securities Regulations 1995 reg 11(3). Regulation 9(4) (see para 316 ante) applies for the purposes of reg 11(3) as it applies for the purposes of reg 9: reg 11(4). The competent authority may make rules providing for the payment of fees to it for the discharge of its functions under reg 11(3): reg 11(5). The Financial Services Act 1986 s 156 (see para 281 ante) applies to rules made under the Public Offers of Securities Regulations 1995 reg 11(5) as it applies to listing rules: reg 11(6). For the meaning of 'securities' see para 302 note 1 ante. See also note 4 supra.

319. Advertisements etc in connection with offer of securities. An advertisement, notice, poster or document (other than a prospectus) announcing a public offer of securities[1] for which a prospectus is or will be required[2] must not be issued to or caused to be issued to the public in the United Kingdom by the person proposing to make the offer unless it states that a prospectus is or will be published, as the case may be, and gives an address in the United Kingdom from which it can be obtained or will be obtainable[3].

The general restriction on the issue of investment advertisements[4] does not apply to an investment advertisement which:

    (1)   is a prospectus, or supplementary prospectus, issued in accordance with the statutory provisions[5] relating to public offers of unlisted securities[6];

    (2)   relates to a prospectus or supplementary prospectus published or to be published in accordance with the statutory provisions relating to public offers of unlisted securities, and which contains no invitation or information which would make it an investment advertisement other than:

       (a)   the name and address of the person by whom the investments to which the prospectus or supplementary prospectus relates are to be offered[7], or other particulars for communicating with him;

       (b)   the nature and the nominal value of the investments to which the prospectus or supplementary prospectus relates, the number offered and the price at which they are offered;

       (c)   a statement that a prospectus or supplementary prospectus issued in accordance with the statutory provisions relating to public offers of unlisted securities is or will be available and, if it is not yet available, when it is expected to be; and

(d) instructions for obtaining a copy of the prospectus or supplementary prospectus[8]; or

(3) is required by a relevant EEA market[9] for admission of an investment to trading on that market which:

(a) contains the information which would be required by the statutory provisions relating to public offers of unlisted securities if it were a prospectus; and

(b) does not contain any information other than that required or permitted to be published by the rules of the relevant EEA market[10].

1 For the meaning of 'securities' see para 302 note 1 ante.
2 Ie under the Public Offers of Securities Regulations 1995, SI 1995/1537, Pt II (regs 3–16) see para 301 et seq ante and paras 349–351 post.
3 Ibid reg 12. As to contraventions see para 320 post. Regulation 12 does not apply to a prospectus submitted for approval in accordance with listing rules made under the Financial Services Act 1986 s 156A (as added) (see para 297 ante): Public Offers of Securities Regulations 1995 reg 4(3).
4 Ie the Financial Services Act 1986 s 57. No person other than an authorised person may issue or cause to be issued an investment advertisement in the United Kingdom unless its contents have been approved by an authorised person: s 57(1). 'An investment advertisement' means any advertisement inviting persons to enter or offer to enter into an investment agreement or to exercise any rights conferred by an investment to acquire, dispose of, underwrite or convert an investment or containing information calculated to lead directly or indirectly to persons doing so: s 57(2). As to the civil consequences and criminal penalties if a person issues or causes to be issued an investment advertisement in breach of s 57 see s 57(3), (5)–(9) and STOCK EXCHANGE. For the meaning of 'authorised person' see para 294 note 7 ante.
5 Ie the Public Offers of Securities Regulations 1995 Pt II (regs 3–16).
6 Financial Services Act 1986 (Investment Advertisements) (Exemptions) (No 2) Order 1995, SI 1995/1536, art 14(a).
7 Ie within the meaning of the Public Offers of Securities Regulations 1995: see para 304 ante.
8 Financial Services Act 1986 (Investment Advertisements) (Exemptions) (No 2) Order 1995 art 14(b).
9 For these purposes, 'relevant EEA market' means a market in an EEA State which is established under the rules of an investment exchange specified in ibid art 2, Sch 1 Pt I or which meets the criteria specified in Sch 1 Pt II: art 2. See STOCK EXCHANGE. 'EEA State' means a State which is a Contracting Party to the Agreement on the European Economic Area signed at Oporto on 2 May 1992 (OJ L1, 3.1.94, p 3) as adjusted by the Protocol signed at Brussels on 17 March 1993 (OJ L1, 3.1.94, p 572), but until that Agreement comes into force in relation to Liechtenstein does not include the State of Liechtenstein: Financial Services Act 1986 (Investment Advertisements) (Exemptions) (No 2) Order 1995 art 2. As to the European Economic Area see para 299 note 2 ante.
10 Ibid art 14(c).

D. CONTRAVENTIONS

320. In general. An authorised person[1] who:

(1) contravenes the provisions requiring the publication of a prospectus when securities are offered to the public in the United Kingdom for the first time[2]; or

(2) contravenes, where it applies, any requirement to deliver a copy of the prospectus to the registrar of companies for registration before the time of publication of the prospectus[3]; or

(3) issues, or causes to be issued by the person proposing to make the offer, an advertisement, notice, poster or document (other than a prospectus) announcing a public offer of securities without stating that a prospectus is or will be published and giving an address within the United Kingdom from where it can be obtained or will be obtainable[4]; or

(4) assists another person to contravene any of the above provisions,
is treated as having contravened the conduct of investment business rules[5] or, in the case of a person who is an authorised person by virtue of his membership of a recognised self-regulating organisation[6] or certification by a recognised professional body[7], the rules of that organisation or body[8].

A person other than an authorised person who contravenes the provisions relating to the registration and publication of a prospectus[9] or the provisions relating to advertisements etc in connection with an offer of securities[10], or who assists another person to contravene any of those provisions is guilty of an offence and liable on conviction on indictment to imprisonment for a term not exceeding two years or a fine, or to both, or on summary conviction to imprisonment for a term not exceeding three months or a fine not exceeding level 5 on the standard scale[11].

A person is not to be regarded[12] as having contravened the provisions relating to the registration and publication of a prospectus[13] by reason only of a prospectus not having fully complied with the requirements[14] as to its form or content[15].

Any contravention to which these provisions apply is actionable at the suit of a person who suffers loss as a result of the contravention subject to the defences and other incidents applying to actions for breach of statutory duty[16].

A European institution[17] carrying on home-regulated investment business[18] in the United Kingdom which contravenes the provisions relating to the registration and publication of a prospectus[19] or the provisions relating to advertisements etc in connection with an offer of securities[20], or which assists another person to contravene any of those provisions, is treated for all purposes:

    (a) if it is not a member of a recognised self-regulating organisation, as having contravened the conduct of investment business rules; or

    (b) if it is a member of a recognised self-regulating organisation, as having contravened the rules of that organisation[21].

1 For these purposes, 'authorised person' means a person authorised under the Financial Services Act 1986 Pt I Ch III (ss 7–34 (as amended): see MONEY): Public Offers of Securities Regulations 1995, SI 1995/1537 reg 16(5).
2 Ie ibid reg 4(1): see para 302 ante.
3 Ie ibid reg 4(2): see para 302 ante.
4 Ie ibid reg 12: see para 319 ante.
5 Ie rules made under the Financial Services Act 1986 Pt I Ch V (ss 47–63C) (as amended): see MONEY.
6 For these purposes, 'recognised self-regulating organisation' has the meaning given in ibid s 207(1) (see para 294 note 9 ante): Public Offers of Securities Regulations 1995 reg 16(5).
7 For these purposes, 'recognised professional body' has the meaning given in the Financial Services Act 1986 s 207(1) (see para 294 note 10 ante): Public Offers of Securities Regulations 1995 reg 16(5).
8 Ibid reg 16(1). The Financial Services Act 1986 s 201(1) (prosecution of offences), s 202 (offences by bodies corporate, partnerships and unincorporated associations) and s 203 (jurisdiction and procedure in respect of offences) apply to offences under the Public Offers of Securities Regulations 1995 as they apply to offences under the Financial Services Act 1986: Public Offers of Securities Regulations 1995 reg 23(6). See STOCK EXCHANGE.
9 Ie ibid reg 4(1) or, where it applies, reg 4(2).
10 See note 4 supra.
11 Public Offer of Securities Regulations 1995 reg 16(2). For the meaning of 'the standard scale' see CRIMINAL LAW vol 11(2) (Reissue) para 808.
12 Ie without prejudice to any liability under ibid reg 14: see para 350 post.
13 Ie ibid reg 4: see para 302 ante.
14 Ie the requirements of the Public Offers of Securities Regulations 1995.
15 Ibid reg 16(3).
16 Ibid reg 16(4).

17 For these purposes, 'European institution' has the same meaning as in the Banking Co-ordination (Second Council Directive) Regulations 1992, SI 1992/3218 (see BANKING): Public Offers of Securities Regulations 1995 reg 2(1).

18 For these purposes, 'home-regulated investment business' has the same meaning as in the Banking Co-ordination (Second Council Directive) Regulations 1992 (see BANKING): Public Offers of Securities Regulations 1995 reg 2(1).

19 See note 9 supra.

20 See note 4 supra.

21 Public Offers of Securities Regulations 1995 reg 16(6). The reference in reg 16(2) (see supra) to a person other than an authorised person is to be treated as not including a reference to such an institution: reg 16(6).

(iii) Misrepresentation in Offer Documents

A. IN GENERAL

321. Remedies for misrepresentation. The statutory liability[1] as to misstatements in listing particulars or a prospectus does not affect any liability which any person may incur under the general law apart from that liability[2]. In respect of the liability so incurred, the remedies for misrepresentation open to an allottee of shares, but not necessarily to a transferee of his shares[3], or to a person in whose favour an allotment of shares is renounced[4], are:

(1) rectification of the register of members and consequent relief;

(2) rescission of the contract[5];

(3) damages in an action of deceit[6] or negligent misrepresentation[7] or negligent misstatement[8];

(4) compensation or damages under the statutory provisions[9]; and

(5) criminal proceedings[10].

1 Ie the liability under the Financial Services Act 1986 s 150 (as amended) and s 154A (as added) (listed securities) and the Public Offers of Securities Regulations 1995, SI 1995/1537, reg 14 (unlisted securities): see para 339 et seq post.

2 Financial Services Act 1986 s 150(4); Public Offers of Securities Regulations 1995 reg 14(4). As to the exemptions from liability for non-compliance see paras 348, 351 post.

3 *Hyslop v Morel* (1891) 7 TLR 263; *Andrews v Mockford* [1896] 1 QB 372, CA. As to sub-underwriters see para 199 ante.

4 *Collins v Associated Greyhound Racecourses Ltd* [1930] 1 Ch 1 at 14, CA.

5 See para 324 post.

6 See para 332 post.

7 See the Misrepresentation Act 1967 s 2 and para 338 post.

8 See para 338 post.

9 See para 347 post (listed securities) and para 350 post (unlisted securities).

10 See para 354 post.

B. RECTIFICATION OF THE REGISTER AND CONSEQUENT RELIEF

322. Rectifying register on ground of misrepresentation. A person who has been induced to take shares by misrepresentation in an offer document relating to the subscription of shares may, if he can show repudiation, and that he has not so acted after discovering the misrepresentation as to have claimed or recognised any rights or liabilities as a shareholder[1], obtain relief on an application to rectify the register of members by removing his name from it and for the return to him of what he has paid with interest[2].

1 *First National Reinsurance Co Ltd v Greenfield* [1921] 2 KB 260; and see *Bwlch-y-Plwm Lead Mining Co v Baynes* (1867) LR 2 Exch 324; *Bentley & Co v Black* (1893) 9 TLR 580, CA; *Deposit Life Assurance v Ayscough* (1856) 6 E & B 761. Where an action for calls is commenced by a specially indorsed writ, leave to defend under RSC Ord 14 r 4 will not be granted, except on payment into court of the amount of calls: *Consolidated Finance Corpn Ltd v Rowntree* (1911) 46 LJo 458.
2 See the Companies Act 1985 s 359 and para 393 post; *Stewart's Case* (1866) 1 Ch App 574; *Wilkinson's Case* (1867) 2 Ch App 536; *Peel's Case* (1867) 2 Ch App 674; *Anderson's Case* (1881) 17 ChD 373; *Re London and Staffordshire Fire Insurance Co* (1883) 24 ChD 149; *Re Christineville Rubber Estates Ltd* (1911) 81 LJ Ch 63.

323. Defence to action for calls or specific performance. A person who has been induced to take shares by misrepresentation in an offer document relating to the subscription of shares[1] may set up the defence of misrepresentation to an action for calls on shares registered in his name, if he has commenced proceedings for rectification[2] or given some undertaking to commence them within a reasonable time after he has discovered the misrepresentation or if the shares have been forfeited[3]. To an action for specific performance of an agreement to take shares or debentures the usual defences in such an action are available[4].

1 Ie a person referred to in para 322 ante.
2 See para 393 post.
3 *Aaron's Reefs v Twiss* [1896] AC 273, HL.
4 See *Odessa Tramways Co v Mendel* (1878) 8 ChD 235, CA and para 1267 post. As to specific performance generally see SPECIFIC PERFORMANCE vol 44(1) (Reissue) para 801 et seq.

C. ACTION FOR RESCISSION

324. Grounds for action for rescission. If a subscription for shares, not being those which are subscribed for by a signatory to the memorandum of association[1], or debentures, is obtained by a material misrepresentation of fact, the contract is voidable at the election of the person deceived[2], and the court will in an action by the subscriber rescind the contract to take the shares or debentures and order restitution of the money paid under the contract with interest[3]. To obtain rescission the untrue statement need not be fraudulent or made with intent to deceive[4].

The contract may be rescinded on the ground of misrepresentation by the company's directors or other general agents, or special agents acting within the scope of their authority[5], but not by unauthorised persons making promises purporting to be made on its behalf[6]. The company will be liable where the offer documents, on the faith of which[7] subscriptions have to the knowledge of the company been made, were issued by promoters without the authority of and before the incorporation of the company, and even if the contents are not known to the directors[8]. The company will also be liable where, before the contract to take the shares is completed, the company becomes affected with knowledge that it has been induced by misrepresentation, even though made without authority[9].

In offer documents no misstatement, or concealment of any material facts or circumstances, is permitted. The public, invited thereby to join in any new adventure, ought to have the same opportunity of judging everything materially bearing on its true character as the promoters themselves possess; and the utmost honesty and candour ought to characterise the statements in the offer documents[10].

1 *Lord Lurgan's Case* [1902] 1 Ch 707. The contract of a signatory to the memorandum is of a very special kind; it is a contract whose existence is the basis of the creation of the corporation: *Lord Lurgan's Case* supra at 710 per Buckley J.

2   *Western Bank of Scotland v Addie* (1867) LR 1 Sc & Div 145, HL.

3   *Central Rly Co of Venezuela (Directors etc) v Kisch* (1867) LR 2 HL 99; *Gover's Case* (1875) 1 ChD 182 at 198, 199, CA.

4   *Smith's Case* (1867) 2 Ch App 604 (affd sub nom *Reese River Silver Mining Co Ltd v Smith* (1869) LR 4 HL 64 at 79); *Re London and Staffordshire Fire Insurance Co* (1883) 24 ChD 149; *Mathias v Yetts* (1882) 46 LT 497 at 506, CA; cf *Jackson v Turquand* (1869) LR 4 HL 305. See, however, para 328 text to note 18 post.

5   *Gover's Case* (1875) 1 ChD 182, CA; *New Brunswick and Canada Rly and Land Co v Conybeare* (1862) 9 HL Cas 711; *Lynde v Anglo-Italian Hemp Spinning Co* [1896] 1 Ch 178; and see *Lagunas Nitrate Co v Lagunas Syndicate* [1899] 2 Ch 392, CA; *Re Royal British Bank, Nicol's Case* (1859) 3 De G & J 387 at 430; *Re Royal British Bank, Mixer's Case* (1859) 4 De G & J 575; *Henderson v Lacon* (1867) LR 5 Eq 249 at 261.

6   *Re United Kingdom Shipowners' Co, Felgate's Case* (1865) 11 LT 613, CA. The company's secretary has no general authority to make representations: *Newlands v National Employers' Accident Association Ltd* (1885) 54 LJQB 428, CA; *Barnett v South London Tramways Co* (1887) 18 QBD 815 at 817, CA.

7   The misrepresentation must be an inducing cause to the contract: *Arnison v Smith* (1889) 41 ChD 348 at 369, CA per Lord Halsbury LC; *Drincqbier v Wood* [1899] 1 Ch 393 at 404.

8   *Hilo Manufacturing Co Ltd v Williamson* (1911) 28 TLR 164, CA; *Stewart's Case* (1866) 1 Ch App 574; *Downes v Ship* (1868) LR 3 HL 343; *Karberg's Case* [1892] 3 Ch 1, CA; *Re Canadian Direct Meat Co* (1892) 9 TLR 7, CA; *Lynde v Anglo-Italian Hemp Spinning Co* [1896] 1 Ch 178 at 183; *Collins v Associated Greyhound Racecourses Ltd* [1930] 1 Ch 1 at 14, CA, explaining the last two cases. There is no doubt that *Re Canadian Direct Meat Co* supra creates a difficulty, as in the Court of Appeal there was no finding that the company knew that the subscriptions had been made on the faith of the prospectus complained of, but relief was granted.

9   *Lynde v Anglo-Italian Hemp Spinning Co* [1896] 1 Ch 178.

10   *Central Rly Co of Venezuela (Directors etc) v Kisch* (1867) LR 2 HL 99 at 113; *New Brunswick and Canada Rly etc Co v Muggeridge* (1860) 1 Drew & Sm 363; *Henderson v Lacon* (1867) LR 5 Eq 249; *Denton v Macneil* (1866) LR 2 Eq 352; and see *Aaron's Reefs Ltd v Twiss* [1896] AC 273, HL. As to statements deemed to be untrue see para 334 post; and as to the effect of the omission of matters required by statute to be included in the offer documents see paras 347, 350 post.

325. Sub-underwriters. A sub-underwriter may not obtain rescission of his contract to take shares where he is an undisclosed principal, although he has relied on misrepresentations, unless he establishes that the underwriter who is his agent relied on the misrepresentations; and the entry of the name of the sub-underwriter in the register of members, pursuant to an authority contained in a letter of renunciation signed by the underwriters, cannot of itself be treated as a contract entered into on the basis of the offer documents[1].

1   *Collins v Associated Greyhound Racecourses Ltd* [1930] 1 Ch 1, CA.

326. Misrepresentation must be of fact. To afford ground for relief the misrepresentation must be one of fact and not of law[1], although a statement of facts which involves a conclusion of law is a statement of fact[2]. A representation as to the state of a person's mind, for example, as to his belief, although difficult of proof, is a statement of fact[3] and language expressed in the form of hope and expectation may be a representation of fact[4], although statements as to what will occur in the future are not usually statements of fact[5]. Although a statement may be true when made, if it becomes untrue before it is acted on, the action will be sustainable if the statement was intended to be then acted on[6]. Conversely, if a representation which was false when made becomes, by virtue of supervening facts, true when acted upon, the person acting thereon is not deceived thereby and no action is maintainable[7].

If a company does not intend that a report, set out in an offer document, should form the basis of the contract to take shares, it must dissociate itself from it in the clearest terms and make it clear that it does not vouch for the accuracy of the statements made in the report; thus, where a director or an agent makes a report which is published by the company and that report whether fraudulently or innocently contains untrue statements, the mere fact that the company states that it will not act on the report until verified is not a sufficiently clear statement that the company does not vouch for the accuracy of the report[8].

1 *Beattie v Lord Ebury* (1874) LR 7 HL 102.
2 *Eaglesfield v Marquis of Londonderry* (1876) 4 ChD 693 at 703, CA; *New Brunswick and Canada Rly and Land Co v Conybeare* (1862) 9 HL Cas 711; *West London Commercial Bank Ltd v Kitson* (1884) 13 QBD 360, CA; *Derry v Peek* (1889) 14 App Cas 337, HL.
3 *Edgington v Fitzmaurice* (1885) 29 ChD 459 at 483, CA.
4 *Aaron's Reefs Ltd v Twiss* [1896] AC 273, HL; cf *Jorden v Money* (1854) 5 HL Cas 185; *Citizens' Bank of Louisiana v First National Bank of New Orleans* (1873) LR 6 HL 352; *Maddison v Alderson* (1883) 8 App Cas 467, HL.
5 *Hallows v Fernie* (1868) 3 Ch App 467; *Beattie v Lord Ebury* (1874) LR 7 HL 102; *Bellairs v Tucker* (1884) 13 QBD 562; *Maddison v Alderson* (1883) 8 App Cas 467, HL; *Knox v Hayman* (1892) 67 LT 137, CA; *Bentley & Co v Black* (1893) 9 TLR 580, CA; cf *Jorden v Money* (1854) 5 HL Cas 185; *Citizens' Bank of Louisiana v First National Bank of New Orleans* (1873) LR 6 HL 352; and *Collins v Associated Greyhound Racecourses Ltd* [1930] 1 Ch 1 per Luxmoore J (approved on another point by the Court of Appeal when this point was not discussed [1930] 1 Ch 1 at 28).
6 *Anderson's Case* (1881) 17 ChD 373; *Re Scottish Petroleum Co* (1883) 23 ChD 413, CA; *With v O'Flanagan* [1936] Ch 575, [1936] 1 All ER 727, CA; cf *Hallows v Fernie* (1868) 3 Ch App 467.
7 *Ship v Crosskill* (1870) LR 10 Eq 73 at 85, 86.
8 *Mair v Rio Grande Rubber Estates Ltd* [1913] AC 853, HL; *Re Pacaya Rubber and Produce Co Ltd, Burns' Application* [1914] 1 Ch 542. As to the consent required from an expert to the issue of an offer document containing a statement by him see paras 348, 351 post.

327. Materiality of statements. Any statement will be construed in the natural and reasonable sense in which other persons are likely to read it[1]. The untrue statement must be material[2], that is to say of some importance[3], and the subscriber must be materially influenced by it, although it need not be the only inducement to subscribe[4].

If a person is induced to subscribe by a material misstatement, it is no defence to an action for rescission that he had the means of discovering and might with reasonable diligence have discovered that the statement was untrue[5].

The omission of facts is not a ground for rescission unless it is of such a nature as to make what is actually stated misleading[6].

1 *Arkwright v Newbold* (1881) 17 ChD 301, CA; *Arnison v Smith* (1889) 41 ChD 348, CA; *Smith v Chadwick* (1884) 9 App Cas 187, HL.
2 *Gover's Case* (1875) 1 ChD 182, CA; and see the cases cited infra.
    The following cases are referred to as showing what are material statements: (1) as to shares alleged to be subscribed see *Ross v Estates Investment Co* (1868) 3 Ch App 682; *Henderson v Lacon* (1867) LR 5 Eq 249; *Croydon v Prudential Loan and Discount Co Ltd* (1886) 2 TLR 535, CA; *Arnison v Smith* (1889) 41 ChD 348, CA; *Taylor v Oil and Ozokerite Co Ltd* (1913) 29 TLR 515; (2) as to contracts to purchase property see *Ross v Estates Investment Co* supra; *Central Rly Co of Venezuela (Directors etc) v Kisch* (1867) LR 2 HL 99; (3) as to property really non-existent see *Scott v Snyder Dynamite Projectile Co Ltd* (1829) 67 LT 104, CA; (4) as to property subject to a town planning resolution registered as a land charge see *Coles v White City (Manchester) Greyhound Association Ltd* (1929) 45 TLR 230, CA; (5) as to the amount of purchase money paid see *Capel & Co v Sim's Ships Compositions Co Ltd* (1888) 57 LJ Ch 713; (6) as to the value of property see *Reese River Silver Mining Co v Smith* (1869) LR 4 HL 64; *Re British Burmah Land Co Ltd* (1888) 4 TLR 631; (7) as to the persons by whom valuers of property have been employed see *Angus v Clifford* [1891] 2 Ch 449 at 456–458, 469, CA; (8) as to the object of issuing debentures offered for subscription see *Edgington v Fitzmaurice* (1885) 29 ChD 459, CA; (9) as to the amount of net profits of a business see *Glasier v Rolls* (1889) 42 ChD 436, CA; (10) as to the existence of parliamentary powers see *Peek v Derry* (1887) 37 ChD 541; revsd without reference to this point sub nom *Derry v Peek* (1889) 14 App Cas 337, HL; (11) as to the non-payment of promotion money see *Lodwick v Earl of Perth* (1884) 1 TLR 76; (12) as to the names of directors and others connected or to be connected with the company see *Re Metropolitan Coal Consumers' Association, Wainwright's Case* (1890) 63 LT 429, CA; *Karberg's Case*

[1892] 3 Ch 1, CA; (13) as to the company having obtained contracts or orders see *Snook v Self-Acting Sewing Machine Co* (1887) 3 TLR 612; *Greenwood v Leather Shod Wheel Co* [1900] 1 Ch 421, CA; and (14) as to the guarantee of dividends see *Kent v Freehold Land and Brickmaking Co* (1867) LR 4 Eq 588 (revsd on another point (1868) 3 Ch App 493); *Knox v Hayman* (1892) 67 LT 137, CA.

Statements as to certain persons being directors may or may not be material: see *Re Life Association of England, Blake's Case* (1865) 34 Beav 639; *Re Land Credit Co of Ireland, Munster's Case* (1866) 14 WR 957; *Hallows v Fernie* (1868) 3 Ch App 467; *Anderson's Case* (1881) 17 ChD 373; *Smith v Chadwick* (1882) 20 ChD 27, CA; *Re Scottish Petroleum Co* (1883) 23 ChD 413, CA; *Re Kent County Gas Light and Coke Co, ex p Brown* (1906) 95 LT 756.

3 *Smith v Chadwick* (1882) 20 ChD 27, CA.

4 *Edgington v Fitzmaurice* (1885) 29 ChD 459, CA; *Re London and Leeds Bank, ex p Carling, Carling v London and Leeds Bank* (1887) 56 LJ Ch 321; *Robson v Earl of Devon* (1857) 4 Jur NS 245.

5 *Redgrave v Hurd* (1881) 20 ChD 1, CA; cf *Aaron's Reefs Ltd v Twiss* [1896] AC 273, HL.

6 *Peek v Gurney* (1873) LR 6 HL 377 at 403; *Re Christineville Rubber Estates* (1911) 81 LJ Ch 63; *McKeown v Boudard-Peveril Gear Co* (1896) 65 LJ Ch 735, CA; *Aaron's Reefs Ltd v Twiss* [1896] AC 273, HL; *Components' Tube Co v Naylor* [1900] 2 IR 1; *New Brunswick and Canada Rly and Land Co v Conybeare* (1862) 9 HL Cas 711; *New Brunswick and Canada Rly and Land Co v Muggeridge* (1860) 1 Drew & Sm 363; *Oakes v Turquand and Harding, Peek v Same, Re Overend, Gurney & Co* (1867) LR 2 HL 325 at 341–345, 368; *Arkwright v Newbold* (1881) 17 ChD 301 at 311, CA; *Jury v Stoker and Jackson* (1882) 9 LR Ir 385; *Edgington v Fitzmaurice* (1885) 29 ChD 459 at 472, CA per Denman J; *Re Mount Morgan (West) Gold Mine Ltd, ex p West* (1887) 56 LT 622 at 623 per Kay J; *Derry v Peek* (1889) 14 App Cas 337, HL; *Scott v Snyder Dynamite Projectile Co Ltd* (1892) 67 LT 104, CA; *Re Dunlop-Truffault Cycle and Tube Manufacturing Co, ex p Shearman* (1896) 66 LJ Ch 25; *Cackett v Keswick* [1902] 2 Ch 456 at 476, CA; and see para 334 post.

As to the effect of the omission of matters required by statute to be included in the offer documents see paras 347, 350 post.

328. Loss of right to rescind.

The right of a shareholder to rescission is lost by his doing anything inconsistent with the right to repudiate after notice[1] of the misrepresentation, such as attempting to sell the shares[2], receiving dividends on them[3], or making further payments in respect of them[4]. Any such acts done before the notice of the misrepresentation will not affect his right to rescind[5], and the right is not affected by his attending a meeting of the company or opposing a winding-up petition as a shareholder after he has taken proceedings for rectification[6]. A person who has been induced to subscribe for shares by misrepresentations, and whose shares have, before he discovered the true facts, been forfeited for non-payment of calls, is not prejudiced by any subsequent delay in repudiating the contract[7].

The right to rescind is lost if the parties cannot be restored to their original positions[8].

The right to rescind is also lost by the commencement of the winding up of the company[9], whether the winding up is voluntary or not[10], or by the company becoming insolvent and stopping payment[11], unless in either case the shareholder has previously repudiated the shares, and has commenced proceedings for rescission or agreed with the company to be bound by such proceedings brought by some other person[12], or has taken other appropriate steps to have his name removed from the register[13].

The right is also lost on the failure of the shareholder to repudiate his shares within a reasonable time after he receives notice of the misrepresentation[14]. What is a reasonable time is a question of fact but delay in repudiating which is caused by reasonable negotiations with the company is excusable[15]. If there are several misrepresentations, the fact that the shareholder is precluded by delay as regards one is not a ground for refusing relief in respect of others subsequently discovered if proceedings as to these are commenced without undue delay[16].

The circumstances already mentioned in which the right to rescind is lost are applicable in the case of a voidable contract, and not where the contract to take shares is not merely voidable but void[17].

As an alternative to granting rescission, the court, if it is of opinion that it would be equitable to do so, having regard to the nature of the misrepresentation and the loss that would be caused by it if the contract were upheld, as well as to the loss that rescission would cause to the company, may declare the contract subsisting and award damages in lieu of rescission[18].

If on the facts it appears that a shareholder has a right, of which he was ignorant, to claim rescission, the cancellation of an allotment to him, though on invalid grounds, will stand[19].

1 In some cases the notice of the misrepresentation is given in a circular sent out by the company; but such a notice will not destroy the right of rescission unless it is proved to have been received by the shareholder: *Re London and Staffordshire Fire Insurance Co* (1883) 24 ChD 149. Cf *Arnison v Smith* (1889) 41 ChD 348, CA (where the circular was held not to have explained the misrepresentation).

2 *Re Hop and Malt Exchange and Warehouse Co, ex p Briggs* (1866) LR 1 Eq 483. As to a sale of shares in another company included in the same contract see *Maturin v Tredinnick* (1864) 4 New Rep 15.

3 *Scholey v Venezuela Central Rly Co* (1868) LR 9 Eq 266n.

4 *Re Dunlop-Truffault Cycle etc Manufacturing Co, ex p Shearman* (1896) 66 LJ Ch 25.

5 *Re Mount-Morgan (West) Gold Mine Ltd, ex p West* (1887) 56 LT 622.

6 *Re Metropolitan Coal Consumers' Association, ex p Edwards* (1891) 64 LT 561; *Foulkes v Quartz Hill Consolidated Gold Mining Co* (1883) Cab & El 156, CA; *Re Thomas Edward Brinsmead & Sons, Tomlin's Case* [1898] 1 Ch 104.

7 *Aaron's Reefs Ltd v Twiss* [1896] AC 273, HL. As to restraining forfeiture after proceedings for rescission see para 330 post.

8 See eg *Houldsworth v City of Glasgow Bank* (1880) 5 App Cas 317 at 331, HL per Lord Hatherley; and see generally MISREPRESENTATION vol 31 paras 1133, 1134. The requirement that the plaintiff in an action should be able to make substantial restitution in specie of the property which he has received can give rise to considerable problems in cases of assets such as quoted shares: see *Smith New Court Securities Ltd v Scrimgeour Vickers (Asset Management) Ltd* [1994] 4 All ER 225 at 234, 237, [1994] 1 WLR 1271 at 1280, 1283, CA (rescission was not available as the quoted shares, the subject of the misrepresentation, had been sold by the purchaser and, on the facts, damages proved an inadequate remedy as they could not reflect a subsequent market fall in share value). As to damages see para 337 post.

9 *Oakes v Turquand and Harding, Peek v Turquand and Harding, Re Overend, Gurney & Co* (1867) LR 2 HL 325; *Kent v Freehold Land and Brickmaking Co* (1868) 3 Ch App 493; *Hare's Case* (1869) 4 Ch App 503 at 512, 513; *Re Hull and County Bank, Burgess's Case* (1880) 15 ChD 507 (where there were assets in excess of the amount required to satisfy the creditors); *Re Lennox Publishing Co, ex p Storey* (1890) 6 TLR 357; *Re Scottish Petroleum Co* (1883) 23 ChD 413 at 436, CA; *Reese River Silver Mining Co v Smith* (1869) LR 4 HL 64; *Thomson's Case* (1898) 5 Mans 282. After the winding up has commenced, a shareholder suing for rescission may not amend his statement of claim in order to allege further misrepresentation discovered after the winding up commenced: see *Cocksedge v Metropolitan Coal Consumers' Association* [1891] WN 148, CA.

10 *Stone v City and County Bank* (1877) 3 CPD 282 at 295, CA.

11 *Tennent v City of Glasgow Bank* (1879) 4 App Cas 615, HL (where notice was given a day before the winding up commenced); cf *Re London and Leeds Bank, ex p Carling, Carling v London and Leeds Bank* (1887) 56 LJ Ch 321.

12 *Pawle's Case* (1869) 4 Ch App 497; *Re Scottish Petroleum Co* (1883) 23 ChD 413 at 436, CA; and see *Ashley's Case* (1870) LR 9 Eq 263; *McNiell's Case* (1870) LR 10 Eq 503; *First National Reinsurance Co Ltd v Greenfield* [1921] 2 KB 260.

13 *Whiteley's Case* [1900] 1 Ch 365 at 369, CA (where the defendant had obtained leave to defend prior to the winding up on an affidavit setting up misrepresentation); cf *Re Cleveland Iron Co, ex p Stevenson* (1867) 16 WR 95; *Re Etna Insurance Co Ltd* (1873) 6 IR Eq 298, CA.

14 *Bwlch-y-Plwm Lead Mining Co v Baynes* (1867) LR 2 Exch 324; *Pentelow's Case* (1869) 4 Ch App 178; *Taite's Case* (1867) LR 3 Eq 795; *Whitehouse's Case* (1867) LR 3 Eq 790; *Lawrence's Case* (1867) 2 Ch App 412; *Heymann v European Central Rly Co* (1868) LR 7 Eq 154; *Scholey v Venezuela Central Rly Co* (1868) LR 9 Eq 266n; *Pawle's Case* (1869) 4 Ch App 497; *Ashley's Case* (1870) LR 9 Eq 263; *Sharpley v Louth and East Coast Rly Co* (1876) 2 ChD 663, CA; *Cargill v Bower* (1878) 10 ChD 502; *Re London and Staffordshire Fire Insurance Co* (1883) 24 ChD 149; *Re London and Provincial Electric Lighting and Power Generating Co Ltd, ex p Hale* (1886) 55 LT 670; *Taylor v Oil and Ozokerite Co Ltd* (1913) 29 TLR 515; *First National Reinsurance Co Ltd v Greenfield* [1921] 2 KB 260; *Central Rly Co of Venezuela (Directors etc) v Kisch* (1867) LR 2 HL 99 at 125; cf *South London Greyhound Racecourses Ltd v Wake* [1931] 1 Ch 496 at 510.

15 *Neill's Case* (1867) 15 WR 894; *Heymann v European Central Rly Co* (1868) LR 7 Eq 154 at 168; *Ogilvie v Currie* (1868) 37 LJ Ch 541.

16 *Re London and Provincial Electric Lighting etc Co, ex p Hale* (1886) 55 LT 670; cf *Whitehouse's Case* (1867) LR 3 Eq 790.

17 *Alabaster's Case* (1868) LR 7 Eq 273; *Dougan's Case* (1873) 8 Ch App 540; *Wynne's Case* (1873) 8 Ch App 1002 at 1016; *Gorrissen's Case* (1873) 8 Ch App 507 at 519; *Beck's Case* (1874) 9 Ch App 392; *Baillie's Case* [1898] 1 Ch 110; *Re United Ports and General Insurance Co, Nelson's Case* [1874] WN 197.

18 Misrepresentation Act 1967 s 2(2). Damages may be awarded against the company under this head as well as for negligent misrepresentation (see para 338 post) but any award under this head must be taken into account in assessing its liability under the other: s 2(3). As to how this discretion might be exercised and as to the measure of damages under s 2(2) see *William Sindall plc v Cambridgeshire County Council* [1994] 3 All ER 932, [1994] 1 WLR 1016, CA.

19 *Re London and Mediterranean Bank Ltd, Wright's Case* (1871) 7 Ch App 55.

329. Compromise by surrender of shares. A surrender of shares, as a compromise of proceedings commenced in good faith for rescission on the ground of misrepresentation, is valid[1].

1 *Re Life Association of England, Blake's Case* (1865) 34 Beav 639; *Fox's Case* (1868) LR 5 Eq 118; *Re London and Mediterranean Bank Ltd, Wright's Case* (1871) 7 Ch App 55.

330. Restraining forfeiture of shares. After proceedings for rescission have been commenced, forfeiture of the shares for non-payment of calls will be restrained until the trial, on the plaintiff's giving an undertaking as to damages and paying the amount of the calls with interest thereon into court[1].

1 *Jones v Pacaya Rubber and Produce Co Ltd* [1911] 1 KB 455, CA, following *Lamb v Sambas Rubber and Gutta Percha Co Ltd* [1908] 1 Ch 845; and *Charran Ltd v Indian Motor Taxi Cab Co* (1910) unreported, CA (cited in *Jones v Pacaya Rubber and Produce Co Ltd* supra at 456, 458), and disapproving *Ripley v Paper Bottle Co* (1887) 57 LJ Ch 327.

331. Joinder of other causes of action. A person who has been induced to subscribe by misrepresentation may combine in the same action his claims for rescission against the company and for damages for deceit, for negligent misrepresentation or negligent misstatement, or for statutory compensation[1] against the directors or others[2].

1 Ie under the Financial Services Act 1986 s 150 (as amended) or s 154A (as added) (listed securities) or the Public Offers of Securities Regulations 1995, SI 1995/1537, reg 14 (unlisted securities): see para 339 et seq post.

2 See para 332 notes 7, 8 post.

D. ACTION OF DECEIT

332. Who may be sued. Although a company is liable to an action of deceit in respect of an act of its agent which is within the scope of his authority[1], actions of deceit in respect of misrepresentations in an offer document are generally brought against one or more of the directors or other persons responsible for such document; for the liability of the director remains. The right to rescission or damages as against the company[2] may, however, be barred by the fact that the company has gone into liquidation or otherwise[3].

Formerly a shareholder could not both retain his shares and bring an action against a company for deceit inducing him to buy from the company its shares or, by analogy, to take up shares of the company[4]. A person is, however, no longer debarred from obtaining damages or other compensation from a company by reason only of his holding or having held shares in the company or any right to apply or subscribe for shares or to be included in the company's register in respect of shares[5].

The shareholder may combine in the same action a claim for damages against directors for deceit in respect of statements in an offer document with a claim against them for the statutory relief[6] and a claim against the company for rescission[7]; and any number of shareholders may sue directors in one action of deceit[8].

1 See para 1119 et seq post.
2 *Houldsworth v City of Glasgow Bank* (1880) 5 App Cas 317, HL; *Re Hull and County Bank, Burgess's Case* (1880) 15 ChD 507; *Re Addlestone Linoleum Co* (1887) 37 ChD 191, CA, overruling *Re Government Security Fire Insurance Co, Mudford's Claim* (1880) 14 ChD 634 and *Great Australian Gold Mining Co, ex p Appleyard* (1881) 18 ChD 587. The effect of *Houldsworth v City of Glasgow Bank* supra has been reversed in so far as it relates to claims for damages and compensation: see infra.
3 See para 328 ante.
4 *Houldsworth v City of Glasgow Bank* (1880) 5 App Cas 317, HL; *Re Addlestone Linoleum Co* (1887) 37 ChD 191, CA. In principle it was thought that such a claim was inconsistent with the contract into which the plaintiff had entered and the plaintiff had, therefore, to have severed his connection with the company by agreement or judgment for rescission before he could sue the company for misrepresentation: see *Houldsworth v City of Glasgow Bank* supra at 324, 325 per Lord Cairns LC. This principle did not prevent proceedings being maintained for rescission in a proper case: see *Western Bank of Scotland v Addie* (1867) LR 1 Sc & Div 145 at 163, 164, HL.
5 Companies Act 1985 s 111A (added by the Companies Act 1989 s 131(1)).
6 Ie under the Financial Services Act 1986 s 150 (as amended) or s 154A (as added) (listed securities) or the Public Offers of Securities Regulations 1995, SI 1995/1537, reg 14 (unlisted securities): see para 339 et seq post. See also *Re a Company* [1986] BCLC 376 (where unusually the aggrieved purchasers sought to bring what was in substance a claim for damages for deceit by way of a petition under the Companies Act 1985 s 459 (see para 1405 post)).
7 *Frankenburg v Great Horseless Carriage Co* [1900] 1 QB 504, CA (where the defendants included the executors of a deceased director); and see *Greenwood v Humber & Co (Portugal) Ltd* (1898) 6 Mans 42; *Kent Coal Exploration Co v Martin* (1900) 16 TLR 486, CA. See also RSC Ord 15 rr 1, 4; and PLEADING vol 36 para 40; PRACTICE AND PROCEDURE vol 37 paras 246, 247. As to ordering an unsuccessful defendant to pay the costs of a successful defendant see *Bullock v London General Omnibus Co* [1907] 1 KB 264, CA; *Sanderson v Blyth Theatre Co* [1903] 2 KB 533, CA; *Rudow v Great Britain Mutual Life Assurance Society* (1881) 17 ChD 600 at 610, CA; and PRACTICE AND PROCEDURE vol 37 para 219.
8 *Arnison v Smith* (1889) 41 ChD 98 at 102, CA. One subscriber cannot maintain the action on behalf of himself and the others who have been misled: see *Hallows v Fernie* (1868) 3 Ch App 467; *Croskey v Bank of Wales* (1863) 4 Giff 314.

333. Grounds for action of deceit. Where an offer document contains a false and fraudulent[1] representation[2] as to a matter of fact, made in order to induce a person to act thereon, and he acts thereon relying on the representation and thereby sustains damage, he may recover damages therefor from the directors or other persons who were responsible for the issue thereof[3].

The false statement must be as to a matter of fact, not of law[4], and the fact must be ascertained at the time when the statement is made, in the sense that a statement as to something expected to happen in the future is generally only a matter of opinion[5].

The statement complained of must be a material representation[6], and, if it is not obviously material, the onus of showing materiality is on the plaintiff[7]. The plaintiff must also prove that the defendant was responsible for the offer document[8].

1 See para 334 post.
2 As to what amounts in law to a representation see MISREPRESENTATION vol 31 para 1005 et seq.

3 *Gerhard v Bates* (1853) 2 E & B 476; *Scott v Dixon* (1859) 29 LJ Ex 62n; *Burnes v Pennell* (1849) 2 HL Cas 497; *Richardson v Silvester* (1873) LR 9 QB 34; *Cullen v Thomson's Trustees* (1862) 4 Macq 424, HL; *Peek v Gurney* (1873) LR 6 HL 377; and see *Denton v Great Northern Rly Co* (1856) 5 E & B 860; *Williams v Swansea Harbour Trustees* (1863) 14 CBNS 845; *Arnison v Smith* (1889) 41 ChD 98, CA; *Edgington v Fitzmaurice* (1885) 29 ChD 459, CA.

4 *Eaglesfield v Marquis of Londonderry* (1876) 4 ChD 693, CA.

5 *Beattie v Lord Ebury* (1872) 7 Ch App 777 at 804; *Denton v Macneil* (1866) LR 2 Eq 352; and see the cases cited in para 326 note 5 ante.

6 *Smith v Chadwick* (1884) 9 App Cas 187, HL. As to the materiality of a representation see para 327 ante.

7 *Smith v Chadwick* (1882) 20 ChD 27 at 45, CA (affd (1884) 9 App Cas 187, HL); *Capel & Co v Sim's Ships Compositions Co Ltd* (1888) 57 LJ Ch 713 at 714.

8 *Henderson v Lacon* (1867) LR 5 Eq 249; *Ship v Crosskill* (1870) LR 10 Eq 73 at 82; *Watts v Atkinson* (1892) 8 TLR 235, CA.

334. Fraud must be proved. The plaintiff must further prove that the false representation contained in the offer document was fraudulent in the sense that it was made knowingly, or without belief in its truth, or recklessly, without caring whether it was true or false. The fact that a statement was made through carelessness, and without reasonable ground for believing it to be true, may be, but is not necessarily, evidence of fraud. If the false statement is made in the honest belief that it is true, it is not fraudulent, and does not give ground for an action of deceit[1]. Where a statement is ambiguous and capable of more than one meaning, the onus is on the plaintiff to show first that he has interpreted the words in the sense in which they were false, and has been deceived by them as so interpreted[2] and secondly, that this was the sense in which the defendant intended the words to be understood[3]. A true statement of fact may, by withholding other facts, be itself absolutely false[4].

1 *Derry v Peek* (1889) 14 App Cas 337, HL; and see *Arkwright v Newbold* (1881) 17 ChD 301, CA; *Glasier v Rolls* (1889) 42 ChD 436, CA; *Angus v Clifford* [1891] 2 Ch 449, CA; *Jackson v Turquand* (1869) LR 4 HL 305; *Watts v Atkinson* (1892) 8 TLR 235, CA. Different considerations apply to the statutory remedies given by the Financial Services Act 1986 s 150 (as amended) or s 154A (as added) (listed securities) or the Public Offers of Securities Regulations 1995, SI 1995/1537, reg 14 (unlisted securities): see para 339 et seq post. The directors may be made liable for negligence in an action by the company if they issued the offer documents without proper care, and if loss resulted, as the directors owe duties to the company: *Lagunas Nitrate Co v Lagunas Syndicate* [1899] 2 Ch 392 at 436, CA per Lindley MR.

2 *Smith v Chadwick* (1884) 9 App Cas 187, HL.

3 *Akerhielm v De Mare* [1959] AC 789, [1959] 3 All ER 485, PC, preferring *Derry v Peek* (1889) 14 App Cas 337, HL, *Angus v Clifford* [1891] 2 Ch 449, CA and *Lees v Tod* (1882) 9 R 807 at 854 to *Arnison v Smith* (1889) 41 ChD 348, CA.

4 *Peek v Gurney* (1873) LR 6 HL 377; *Gluckstein v Barnes* [1900] AC 240, HL; *R v Lord Kylsant* [1932] 1 KB 442, CCA; *R v Bishirgian* [1936] 1 All ER 586, CCA; cf the cases in para 327 notes 2, 6 ante.

335. Inducement to subscribe. A false statement need not be the only inducement to subscribe; it is sufficient to show that it was a material inducement[1]. A plaintiff cannot succeed unless he was directly induced to subscribe by the false statement, even if it was made with the intention that it should be acted on[2].

The function of the offer document is, as a rule, exhausted when the shares are issued and a person who is only a subsequent purchaser of shares in the market is not so connected with the prospectus as to render those who have issued it liable to indemnify him against the losses which he has suffered in consequence of his purchase[3]; but, if it contains a material false statement, and is intended to be acted on by a person other than the original allottees of the shares, that person, if deceived and injured, may maintain an action of deceit[4].

1 *Peek v Derry* (1887) 37 ChD 541, CA (revsd without affecting the point sub nom *Derry v Peek* (1889) 14 App Cas 337, HL); *Western Bank of Scotland v Addie* (1867) LR 1 Sc & Div 145, HL; *Re Royal British*

Bank, Nicol's Case (1859) 3 De G & J 387; Cleveland Iron Co v Stephenson (1865) 4 F & F 428; Clarke v Dickson (1859) 6 CBNS 453; Edgington v Fitzmaurice (1885) 29 ChD 459, CA; Moore v Burke (1865) 4 F & F 258; Arnison v Smith (1889) 41 ChD 348 at 369, CA; cf Re London and Leeds Bank, ex p Carling (1887) 56 LT 115.

2 Peek v Derry (1887) 37 Ch 541, CA; revsd sub nom Derry v Peek (1889) 14 App Cas 337, HL.

3 Peek v Gurney (1873) LR 6 HL 377 at 396–400, 410, overruling Bagshaw v Seymour (1858) 18 CB 903 and Bedford v Bagshaw (1859) 4 H & N 538; Barry v Croskey (1861) 2 John & H 1 at 23; Barrett's Case (1865) 3 De GJ & Sm 30. See further para 338 post.

4 Where the offer document is part of a scheme of fraud, continued after the issue by other devices, intended to induce the purchase of shares in the market, there is a good cause of action: Andrews v Mockford [1896] 1 QB 372 at 381, CA; Peek v Gurney (1873) LR 6 HL 377; Barry v Croskey (1861) 2 John & H 1; Levy v Langridge (1838) 4 M & W 337; Cullen v Thomson's Trustees (1862) 4 Macq 424 at 441, HL; Stainbank v Fernley (1839) 9 Sim 556.

336. Director's liability for acts of others. The fact that a director has joined in an authority to brokers to obtain subscriptions does not apparently render him liable in an action for deceit for misstatements of facts in an offer document issued by the brokers, not known of or authorised by him[1]. Nor is he so liable in respect of false representations in an offer document issued by his co-director or by any other agent of the company unless he has expressly authorised or tacitly permitted its issue[2].

A promoter is liable in respect of a misrepresentation made with his consent or by his agent within the scope of his actual or ostensible authority[3].

1 Weir v Bell (1878) 3 Ex D 238, CA. As to ratification see note 2 infra. As to the liability of a principal for misrepresentation by his agent see AGENCY vol 1(2) (Reissue) para 147.

2 Cargill v Bower (1878) 10 ChD 502; and see Re Denham & Co (1883) 25 ChD 752 at 765; Peek v Gurney (1873) LR 6 HL 377 at 392; Glasier v Rolls (1889) 42 ChD 436, CA; Mamham v Weaver (1899) 80 LT 412 at 413. The dicta of Kekewich J in Hoole v Speak [1904] 2 Ch 732 at 736 that a principal cannot ratify a tort committed by his agent is contrary to authority: see Hull v Pickersgill (1819) 1 Brod & Bing 282 at 286; Wilson v Barker (1833) 4 B & Ad 614; Wilson v Tumman (1843) 6 Man & G 236 at 242; Keighley, Maxsted & Co v Durant [1901] AC 240 at 246, 247, HL; Carter v St Mary Abbotts, Kensington Vestry (1900) 64 JP 548, CA.

3 Glasier v Rolls (1889) 42 ChD 436 at 441, CA; Dunnett v Mitchell (1885) 12 R 400; Arnison v Smith (1889) 41 ChD 348, CA.

337. Proceedings and damages. Mere delay in instituting an action of deceit does not debar the plaintiff from relief, as it may in an action for rescission; but an action for damages for deceit is barred after six years from the time the plaintiff acted on the fraudulent misrepresentation or, if the existence of the fraud has been concealed, from the date when the fraud was or might with reasonable diligence have been discovered[1].

The plaintiff must prove actual damage to himself[2], and the measure of damages in an action by a purchaser of shares is the difference between what he paid for the shares and their value on the date of acquisition[3]. In determining what was the true or real value of the shares at the date of acquisition[4], it is to be assumed that the market knew everything it actually did know but was not influenced by the misrepresentation itself[5]. It is not, however, to be assumed that the market is omniscient, that is to say that it knows everything relevant to the price of the shares which was in fact the case[6].

On death a right of action for deceit survives for or against the personal representatives of the deceased[7]. Discharge from bankruptcy does not, however, release a bankrupt from any bankruptcy debt which he incurred in respect of, or forbearance in respect of which was secured by means of, any fraud or fraudulent breach of trust to which he was a party[8].

1 See the Limitation Act 1980 ss 2, 32 and LIMITATION OF ACTIONS.
2 *Hyde v Bulmer* (1868) 18 LT 293.
3 *Arkwright v Newbold* (1881) 17 ChD 301 at 312, CA; *Peek v Derry* (1887) 37 ChD 541 at 593, 594, CA (revsd but without affecting this point sub nom *Derry v Peek* (1889) 14 App Cas 337, HL); *Arnison v Smith* (1889) 41 ChD 348 at 363, 364; *Clark v Urquhart* [1930] AC 28, HL. The person making the misrepresentation may also have to pay additional damages for consequential loss suffered by the person to whom the representation was made on account of his having entered into the contract: *Doyle v Olby (Ironmongers) Ltd* [1969] 2 QB 158, [1969] 2 All ER 119, CA (the defendant is bound to make reparation for all the actual damage flowing from the fraudulent inducement). See further MISREPRESENTATION vol 31 para 1092 et seq.
4 *Waddell v Blockey* (1879) 4 QBD 678, CA; cf *Naughton v O' Callaghan* [1990] 3 All ER 191.
5 *Smith New Court Securities Ltd v Scrimgeour Vickers (Asset Management) Ltd (Roberts, third party)* [1994] 4 All ER 225 at 235, [1994] 1 WLR 1271 at 1281, CA. This is a rational principle upon which to calculate the loss which directly flowed from the representation on the relevant date: *Smith New Court Securities Ltd v Scrimgeour Vickers (Asset Management) Ltd (Roberts, third party)* supra at 235 and at 1281 per Nourse LJ.
6 *Smith New Court Securities Ltd v Scrimgeour Vickers (Asset Management) Ltd (Roberts, third party)* [1994] 4 All ER 225 at 235, [1994] 1 WLR 1271 at 1281, CA. Market omniscience as a principle was entirely arbitrary and would allow damages to be increased or diminished by any fact or event which, unknown to anyone, actually existed or occurred before the relevant date, provided that it had emerged from the womb of time before the trial: *Smith New Court Securities Ltd v Scrimgeour Vickers (Asset Management) Ltd (Roberts, third party)* supra at 235 and at 1281 per Nourse LJ. The measure in this case was the difference between the price paid for a block of shares and the value of the shares in the market on the date in question ignoring the misrepresentations at issue which were as to the presence of other bidders for the shares. The measure would not take into account the fact that the company at that date was the victim of a massive fraud (only subsequently discovered) and the market value on that date was therefore an inflated one.
7 Law Reform (Miscellaneous Provisions) Act 1934 s 1(1); and see generally EXECUTORS vol 17 para 1564 et seq.
8 Insolvency Act 1986 s 281(3). See further BANKRUPTCY vol 3(2) (Reissue) para 631.

E. ACTION FOR NEGLIGENT MISREPRESENTATION OR NEGLIGENT MISSTATEMENT

338. Damages for negligent misrepresentation or negligent misstatement.
As an alternative to an action for deceit against the company[1], the shareholder may bring an action against it for negligent misrepresentation[2]. The company's liability for damages will be precisely the same as if the misrepresentation had been made fraudulently, save that it will be a defence to show that it had reasonable ground for believing, and did believe up to the time the contract was made, that the facts represented were true[3].

Such an action lies only against the other party to the contract[4], here the company, and thus not against the directors responsible; but directors may owe a duty of care to persons who subscribe for shares in reliance on a prospectus[5]. Such a duty is not owed, however, to a shareholder or anyone else who relies on the prospectus for the purpose of deciding whether to purchase shares in the company through the stock market because the prospectus is addressed to shareholders for the particular purpose of inviting a subscription for shares and, if it is used for the different purpose of buying shares in the stock market, there is not a sufficiently proximate relationship between the directors and the shareholder for a duty of care to arise on the part of the directors[6].

1 See para 332 ante.
2 Misrepresentation Act 1967 s 2. A claim made by an open-market purchaser of shares in a company (as opposed to an original subscriber or allottee) and based on alleged negligent misrepresentation by the company as to its assets, though necessarily conditional upon membership of the company, was not sufficiently closely related to the corporate nexus to be characteristically a member's claim and therefore such a claim did not amount to a claim 'in his character as a member' within the Insolvency Act 1986 s 74(2)(f) (see para 2479 post): *Soden v British and Commonwealth Holdings plc* [1995] 1 BCLC 686.

3 Misrepresentastion Act 1967 s 2(1). As to quantum of damages see *Royscot Trust Ltd v Rogerson* [1991] 2 QB 297, [1991] 3 All ER 294, CA; *Cemp Properties (UK) Ltd v Dentsply Research & Development Corpn (Denton, Hall & Burgin, third party)* [1991] 2 EGLR 197, CA; *William Sindall plc v Cambridgeshire County Council* [1994] 3 All ER 932, [1994] 1 WLR 1016, CA; and MISREPRESENTATION vol 31 para 1131.

4 See the Misrepresentation Act 1967 s 2(1) and MISREPRESENTATION vol 31 para 1103.

5 Ie they may be made liable under the doctrine of *Hedley Byrne & Co Ltd v Heller & Partners Ltd* [1964] AC 465, [1963] 2 All ER 575, HL (person in a special position who takes it upon himself to give information liable if information negligently given if the necessary requirements are met as to foreseeability of damage, proximity of relationship and the reasonableness or otherwise of imposing the duty): *Caparo Industries plc v Dickman* [1990] 2 AC 605, [1990] 1 All ER 568, HL; *Al-Nakib Investments (Jersey) Ltd v Longcroft* [1990] 3 All ER 321, [1990] 1 WLR 1390. See also *Morgan Crucible Co plc v Hill Samuel & Co Ltd* [1991] Ch 295; sub nom *Morgan Crucible Co Ltd v Hill Samuel Bank Ltd* [1991] 1 All ER 148, CA. See further NEGLIGENCE vol 34 para 53.

6 *Al-Nakib Investments (Jersey) Ltd v Longcroft* [1990] 3 All ER 321, [1990] 1 WLR 1390.

F. LIABILITY FOR MISSTATEMENTS UNDER THE FINANCIAL SERVICES ACT 1986

(A) *In general*

339. General conditions for liability. The basic condition for statutory compensation[1] is that statements contained in the offer documents[2] are untrue or misleading[3], or that there has been an omission of any matter required to be included[4] in them[5]. The person claiming compensation must have relied on the untrue statement or omission[6]. An untrue statement is one which is in fact false, and not one false in the belief of the person making it[7]. It is immaterial that the statement was not fraudulent[8]. The meaning which is important is that which the offer documents convey to those who read them; and the statutory liability is not affected by the consideration whether the statement is false in the sense in which it was used by those who made it[9].

1 As to statutory compensation see para 347 post (listed securities) and para 350 post (unlisted securities). The 'compensation' must be estimated and awarded with reference to the loss sustained, and does not resemble 'a penalty, damages, or a sum of money' imposed by statute as a punishment: *Thomson v Lord Clanmorris* [1900] 1 Ch 718 at 726, CA.

2 See paras 281, 294 ante (listed securities) and para 302 ante (unlisted securities).

3 See the Financial Services Act 1986 ss 150(1), 154A (as added) (listed securities: see para 347 post) and the Public Offers of Securities Regulations 1995, SI 1995/1537, reg 14 (unlisted securities: see para 350 post). Statements are untrue if they were misleading through the omission of material facts: see *Drincqbier v Wood* [1899] 1 Ch 393 at 407; approved in *Greenwood v Leather Shod Wheel Co* [1900] 1 Ch 421 at 434, CA. If, as regards contracts or otherwise, there is such an omission that the matter withheld would, if disclosed reasonably, have deterred or tended to deter an ordinarily provident investor from subscribing, he is entitled to relief: *Broome v Speak* [1903] 1 Ch 586 at 604, CA.

4 As to the matters required to be included see para 281 et seq ante (listed securities) and paras 316 et seq ante (unlisted securities).

5 The plaintiff must prove damage occasioned by the untrue statement: *Macleay v Tait* [1906] AC 24 at 31, HL; *Shepheard v Broome* [1904] AC 342, HL; *Nash v Calthorpe* [1905] 2 Ch 237, CA. At the trial he need show only that he has suffered damage, the amount of which can afterwards be ascertained by inquiry; and the measure of damages is the difference between the price paid for the shares or debentures and their fair value at the date of allotment in the same measure as in the case of an action for deceit (see para 337 ante): *Broome v Speak* [1903] 1 Ch 586, CA (on appeal sub nom *Shepheard v Broome* supra); *McConnel v Wright* [1903] 1 Ch 546, CA; *Stevens v Hoare* (1904) 20 TLR 407. In *Clark v Urquhart* [1930] AC 28, HL it was laid down that the measure of damages is the same as in an action for deceit, but Lord Atkin at 68 expressly reserved the right to consider whether the formula as to the measure of damages laid down in *McConnel v Wright* supra was correct or expressed in too rigid terms.

6 He will fail if he has merely relied on the names of the directors: *Baty v Keswick* (1901) 85 LT 18. Where there is an omission from the offer documents eg the non-disclosure of contracts, the person seeking

compensation must prove that, if he had been told of the matter omitted, he would not have subscribed for the shares or debentures: *Cackett v Keswick* [1902] 2 Ch 456 at 463, CA; *Nash v Calthorpe* [1905] 2 Ch 237, CA; *Macleay v Tait* [1906] AC 24 at 30, 31, HL. The following cases were decided under the Companies Act 1867 s 38 (repealed), to which the Directors' Liability Act 1890 was held applicable where the person issuing the offer document knew of the contracts: *Broome v Speak* [1903] 1 Ch 586, CA (affd sub nom *Shepheard v Broome* [1904] AC 342 at 346, HL); *J and P Coats Ltd v Crossland* (1904) 20 TLR 800.

7 *Broome v Speak* [1903] 1 Ch 586, CA; affd sub nom *Shepheard v Broome* [1904] AC 342, HL.
8 *Shepheard v Broome* [1904] AC 342, HL; *Clark v Urquhart* [1930] AC 28 at 56, 57, HL.
9 *Greenwood v Leather Shod Wheel Co* [1900] 1 Ch 421 at 434, CA; *Drincqbier v Wood* [1899] 1 Ch 393 at 402, 403.

340. Grounds of defence. The main ground of defence is reasonable belief, having made such inquiries (if any) as were reasonable, that the statement was true and not misleading, or that the matter whose omission caused the loss was properly omitted[1]. Liability may be avoided only by proving a reasonable ground of belief, and belief in fact[2]. Only reasonable, not sufficient, ground for belief is required, and reliance may to some extent be placed upon the advice and assistance of other persons[3]. Honest belief that the law does not require something material to be stated is no excuse[4]. The fact that other directors, whose honesty there is no reason to doubt, have authorised the offer documents is not a reasonable ground, nor should a director rely upon the statements of a promoter of the company[5]. In any action, particulars of the alleged grounds of reasonable belief may be ordered to be given[6].

1 See the Financial Services Act 1986 ss 151(1), (2), 154A (as added) (listed securities: see para 348 post) or the Public Offers of Securities Regulations 1995, SI 1995/1537, reg 15 (unlisted securities: see para 351 post).
2 *Greenwood v Leather Shod Wheel Co* [1900] 1 Ch 421, CA.
3 *Stevens v Hoare* (1904) 20 TLR 407 at 409.
4 *Shepheard v Broome* [1904] AC 342 at 347, HL.
5 *Adams v Thrift* [1915] 2 Ch 21, CA.
6 *Alman v Oppert* [1901] 2 KB 576, CA.

341. Right to contribution. Any person who becomes liable to make any payment by way of compensation for loss or damage sustained through untrue statements in offer documents[1] may recover contribution from any other person who is, or would, if sued, have been, liable in respect of the same damage[2].

1 See paras 345–348 post (listed securities) and paras 349–353 post (unlisted securities).
2 See the Civil Liability (Contribution) Act 1978 ss 1, 2 and TORT vol 45 para 1237 et seq.

342. Costs. If the defendant to an action for statutory compensation[1] establishes any of the defences open to him[2], he is entitled to the costs of the whole action, notwithstanding that the statements complained of were untrue or misleading, or the omission complained of is established[3].

1 As to such actions see paras 345–348 post (listed securities) and paras 349–353 post (unlisted securities).
2 As to such defences see para 348 post (listed securities) and para 351 post (unlisted securities).
3 See *Bird v Standard Oil Co of Canada* (1915) 85 LJKB 935, CA.

343. Period of limitation. Actions to recover any sum recoverable by virtue of any enactment must be brought within six years from the date on which the cause of action accrued[1].

1 Limitation Act 1980 s 9(1). In *Thomson v Lord Clanmorris* [1900] 1 Ch 718, CA it was held that an action for compensation under the Directors' Liability Act 1890 s 3 (repealed) was not an action 'for a penalty, damages or a sum of money' within the Civil Procedure Act 1833 s 3, and Lindley MR expressed the view that the cause of action accrues and time begins to run from the dates when the shares or debentures were subscribed for: see *Thomson v Lord Clanmorris* supra at 726 and LIMITATION OF ACTIONS vol 28 para 704.

The above period of limitation does not affect the special time limit for claiming contribution prescribed by the Limitation Act 1980 s 10: s 9(2).

344. Death of parties. An action for statutory compensation[1] is founded on a liability in tort[2] and on the death of a person entitled to maintain such an action or liable to pay compensation in respect of it, the cause of action survives for the benefit of or, as the case may be, against his estate[3].

1 Ie under either the Financial Services Act 1986 s 150 (as amended), s 154A (as added) (listed securities: see para 347 post) or the Public Offers of Securities Regulations 1995, SI 1995/1537, reg 14 (unlisted securities: see para 350 post).
2 *Geipel v Peach* [1917] 2 Ch 108 at 114, where Sargant J stated that the effect of the Companies (Consolidation) Act 1908 s 84 (repealed) was not to alter the tortious nature of the acts in respect of which there is to be a liability, but, speaking generally, to render it easier to establish liability against directors than in a common law action of deceit by raising certain legal presumptions against them. As to bankruptcy see *Greenwood v Humber & Co (Portugal) Ltd* (1896) 6 Mans 42 (where the question whether a claim under the Directors' Liability Act 1890 s 3 (repealed) was provable on the bankruptcy of a director or not was discussed but left undecided); and see para 337 ante and BANKRUPTCY.
3 Law Reform (Miscellaneous Provisions) Act 1934 s 1(1); and see EXECUTORS vol 17 para 1564 et seq.

(B) *Offers of Listed Securities*

345. In general. The offer documents in relation to listed securities will normally comprise listing particulars[1] or a prospectus[2] and an advertisement[3]. Where information has been approved, or its issue has been authorised under the statutory provision in that behalf[4], neither the person issuing it nor any person responsible for, or for any part of, the listing particulars or prospectus, will incur any civil liability[5] by reason of any statement in or omission from the information if that information and the listing particulars or prospectus, taken together, would not be likely to mislead persons of the kind likely to consider the acquisition of the securities[6] in question[7]. Subject to this qualification, the person or persons responsible for any listing particulars[8] or supplementary listing particulars[9] or prospectus[10] or supplementary prospectus[11] are liable to pay compensation to any person who has acquired any of the securities in question and thereby suffered loss[12].

1 See para 285 ante.
2 See paras 296–298 ante.
3 See para 294 ante.
4 Ie pursuant to the Financial Services Act 1986 s 154 (as amended) and s 154A (as added): see paras 294, 296 ante.
5 For these purposes, the reference to a person incurring civil liability includes a reference to any other person being entitled as against that person to be granted any civil remedy or to rescind or repudiate any agreement: ibid s 154(5) (amended by the Companies Act 1989 s 197(2)).
6 For the meaning of 'securities' see para 283 ante.
7 Financial Services Act 1986 s 154(5) (as amended: see note 5 supra).
8 As to the person responsible for listing particulars see para 346 post.
9 As to supplementary listing particulars see para 290 ante.
10 As to the person responsible for the prospectus see para 346 post.
11 As to the supplementary prospectus see paras 290, 296 ante.
12 See the Financial Services Act 1986 s 150 (as amended), s 154A (as added) and para 346 et seq post.

346. Persons responsible for particulars or prospectus. For the purposes of these provisions[1], the persons responsible for listing particulars[2] or supplementary listing particulars[3] or a prospectus[4] or a supplementary prospectus[5] are:

(1) the issuer[6] of the securities[7] to which the particulars or prospectus relate or relates;

(2) where the issuer is a body corporate[8], each person who is a director[9] of that body at the time when the particulars or prospectus are or is submitted to the competent authority[10];

(3) where the issuer is a body corporate, each person who has authorised himself to be named, and is named, in the particulars or prospectus as a director or as having agreed to become a director of that body either immediately or at a future time;

(4) each person who accepts, and is stated in the particulars or prospectus as accepting, responsibility for, or for any part of, the particulars or prospectus;

(5) each person not falling within any of heads (1) to (4) above who has authorised the contents of, or any part of, the particulars or prospectus[11].

A person is not responsible for any particulars or prospectus by virtue of head (2) above if they are or it is published without his knowledge or consent and, on becoming aware of their publication, he forthwith gives reasonable public notice that they were or it was published without his knowledge or consent[12]. Where a person has accepted responsibility for, or authorised, only part of the contents of any particulars or prospectus, he is responsible under heads (4) or (5) above for only that part and only if it is included in (or substantially in) the form and context to which he has agreed[13].

The following provisions apply where the particulars or prospectus relate or relates to securities which are to be issued in connection with an offer by, or by a wholly-owned subsidiary[14] of, the issuer for, or an agreement for the acquisition by (or by a wholly-owned subsidiary of) the issuer of, securities issued by another person or in connection with any arrangement whereby the whole of the undertaking of another person is to become the undertaking of the issuer, of a wholly-owned subsidiary of the issuer or of a body corporate which will become such a subsidiary by virtue of the arrangement[15]. In this case, if that other person, and where that other person is a body corporate, each person who is a director of that body at the time when the particulars or prospectus are or is submitted to the competent authority and each other person who has authorised himself to be named, and is named, in the particulars or prospectus as a director of that body, is responsible by virtue of head (4) above for any part of the particulars or prospectus relating to that other person or to the securities or undertaking to which the offer, agreement or arrangement relates, then no person is responsible for that part under heads (1), (2) or (3) above but without prejudice to his being responsible under head (4) above[15].

Neither head (2) nor head (3) above applies in the case of an issuer of international securities[16] of a class specified by listing rules[17] as being exempt from full disclosure[18] in listing particulars or supplementary listing particulars or a prospectus or supplementary prospectus[19]; nor does head (2) or head (3) or the proviso relating to directors mentioned above[20] apply in the case of any director certified by the competent authority as a person to whom such provision should not apply by reason of his having an interest, or of any other circumstances, making it inappropriate for him to be responsible by virtue of such provision[21].

Nothing in these provisions is to be construed as making a person responsible for any particulars or prospectus by reason of giving advice as to their contents in a professional capacity[22].

Where, by virtue of these provisions, the issuer of any shares pays or is liable to pay statutory compensation[23] for loss suffered in respect of shares for which a person has subscribed, no account is to be taken of that liability or payment in determining any question as to the amount paid on subscription for those shares or as to the amount paid up or deemed to be paid up on them[24].

1   Ie those contained in the Financial Services Act 1986 Pt IV (ss 142–156B) (as amended): see para 281 et seq ante.
2   As to listing particulars see para 285 ante.
3   As to supplementary listing particulars see para 290 ante.
4   As to the prospectus see paras 296–298 ante.
5   As to the supplementary prospectus see paras 290, 296 ante.
6   For the meaning of 'issuer' see paras 284 note 4, 296 head (2) ante.
7   For the meaning of 'securities' see para 283 ante.
8   For the meaning of 'body corporate' see para 287 note 3 ante.
9   For the meaning of 'director' see para 307 note 4 ante.
10 For the meaning of 'the competent authority' see para 281 ante. As to the submission to the competent authority see paras 285 ante.
11 Financial Services Act 1986 ss 152(1), 154A (added by the Public Offers of Securities Regulations 1995, SI 1995/1537, reg 17, Sch 2 para 2(3)). As to the application of the Financial Services Act 1986 s 152 to prospectuses generally see para 296 ante.
12 Ibid ss 152(2), 154A (as added: see note 11 supra). A director who knows that particulars are being published and does not ask to see them cannot be heard to say that they were published without his knowledge or consent: see *Drincqbier v Wood* [1899] 1 Ch 393 at 405, 406; *Watts v Bucknall* [1902] 2 Ch 628 (affd [1903] 1 Ch 766, CA); *J and P Coats Ltd v Crossland* (1904) 20 TLR 800. In such a case he cannot repudiate the particulars after an action has been brought, and repudiation by his statement of defence is not 'reasonable public notice': *Drincqbier v Wood* supra.
13 Financial Services Act 1986 ss 152(3), 154A (as added: see note 11 supra).
14 The Companies Act 1985 s 736 (as substituted) (meaning of 'subsidiary' and 'holding company': see para 827 post) applies for this purpose: Financial Services Act 1986 s 207(8). For these purposes, 'wholly-owned subsidiary' in relation to a person other than a body corporate, means any body corporate that would be his wholly-owned subsidiary if he were a body corporate: s 152(7).
15 Ibid ss 152(4), 154A (as added: see note 11 supra). Where (1) the same document contains particulars relating to the securities of two or more successor companies within the meaning of the Electricity (Northern Ireland) Order 1992, SI 1992/231, Pt III; and (2) any person's responsibility for any information included in the document is stated in the document to be confined to its inclusion as part of the particulars relating to the securities of any one of those companies, that person is not treated as responsible for that information in so far as it is stated in the document to form part of the particulars relating to the securities of any other of those companies: Financial Services Act 1986 s 152(4A) (added by the Electricity (Northern Ireland Consequential Amendments) Order 1992, SI 1992/232, art 3).
16 For these purposes, 'international securities' means any investment falling within the Financial Services Act 1986 Sch 1 para 2 (debentures) (as modified by s 142(3)(b): see para 283 head (2) ante) which is of a kind likely to be dealt in by bodies incorporated in or persons resident in a country or territory outside the United Kingdom, is denominated in a currency other than sterling or is otherwise connected with such a country or territory: s 152(6).
17 For the meaning of 'listing rules' see para 281 ante. As to the *Listing Rules* see para 282 ante.
18 Ie as required by the Financial Services Act 1986 ss 146, 154A (as added: see note 11 supra): see paras 289, 296 ante.
19 Ie under ibid ss 148(1)(c), 154A (as added: see note 11 supra): see paras 291, 296 ante.
20 Ie ibid s 152(4): see supra.
21 Ibid ss 152(5), 154A (as added: see note 11 supra).
22 Ibid ss 152(8), 154A (as added: see note 11 supra).
23 Ie under ibid s 150 (as amended) and s 154A (as added: see note 11 supra): see para 347 post.
24 Ibid ss 152(9), 154A (as added: see note 11 supra).

347. Compensation for false or misleading particulars or prospectus. Subject to statutory exemptions[1], the person or persons responsible for any listing particulars[2] or supplementary listing particulars[3] or prospectus[4] or supplementary prospectus[5] are liable to pay compensation to any person who has acquired[6] any of the securities in question and suffered loss in respect of them as a result of any untrue or misleading statement in the particulars or prospectus or the omission from them or it of any matter required to be included by the statutory provisions[7] relating to the general duty of disclosure in listing particulars and supplementary listing particulars or a prospectus and a supplementary prospectus[8].

Where listing rules[9] require listing particulars or a prospectus to include information as to any particular matter on the basis that the particulars must include a statement either as to that matter or, if such is the case, that there is no such matter, the omission from the particulars or a prospectus of the information is treated for the above purposes as a statement that there is no such matter[10]. Subject to statutory exemptions[11], a person who fails to comply with the requirement to deliver supplementary listing particulars or a supplementary prospectus[12] is liable to pay compensation to any person who has acquired any of the securities in question and suffered loss in respect of them as a result of the failure[13].

These provisions do not affect any liability which any person may incur apart therefrom[14].

No person, by reason of being a promoter[15] of a company or otherwise, incurs any liability[16] for failing to disclose any information which he would not be required to disclose in listing particulars or a prospectus in respect of a company's securities if he were responsible for those particulars or prospectus or, if he is responsible for them or it, which he is entitled to omit by virtue of the statutory exemptions[17] from disclosure[18].

1 Ie the exemptions from liability to pay compensation contained in the Financial Services Act 1986 ss 151, 154A (as added): see para 348 post.
2 For the meaning of 'listing particulars' see para 285 ante. As to the person or persons responsible for listing particulars see para 346 ante.
3 As to supplementary listing particulars see para 290 ante.
4 As to the prospectus see paras 296–298 ante; and as to the person or persons responsible for the prospectus see para 346 ante.
5 As to the supplementary prospectus see paras 290, 296 ante.
6 For these purposes, references to the acquisition by any person of securities include references to his contracting to acquire them or an interest in them: Financial Services Act 1986 ss 150(5), 154A (added by the Public Offers of Securities Regulations 1995, SI 1995/1537, reg 17, Sch 2 para 2(3)). For the meaning of 'securities' see para 283 ante.
7 Ie those contained in the Financial Services Act 1986 ss 146, 147, 154A (as added): see paras 289, 290, 296 ante.
8 Ibid ss 150(1), 154A (as added: see note 6 supra). As to the application of s 150 to prospectuses generally see para 296 ante.
9 For the meaning of 'listing rules' see para 281 ante. As to the *Listing Rules* see para 282 ante.
10 Financial Services Act 1986 ss 150(2), 154A (as added: see note 6 supra).
11 See note 1 supra.
12 Ie pursuant to the Financial Services Act 1986 ss 147, 154A (as added): see paras 290, 296 ante.
13 Ibid ss 150(3), 154A (as added: see note 6 supra).
14 Ibid ss 150(4), 154A (as added: see note 6 supra). As to such liability see paras 321–338 ante.
15 For the meaning of 'promoter' see para 37 ante.
16 For these purposes, the reference to a person incurring liability includes a reference to any other person being entitled as against that person to be granted any civil remedy or to rescind or repudiate any agreement: Financial Services Act 1986 s 150(6) (amended by the Companies Act 1986 s 197(1)).
17 Ie the exemptions from disclosure contained in the Financial Services Act 1986 ss 148, 154A (as added): see paras 291, 296 ante.
18 Ibid s 150(6) (as amended: see note 16 supra), s 154A (as added: see note 6 supra).

348. Exemption from liability to pay compensation. A person does not incur any statutory liability[1] for any loss in respect of securities caused by any such statement or omission as is there mentioned if he satisfies the court that at the time when the particulars[2] or prospectus[3] were or was submitted to the competent authority[4] he reasonably believed, having made such inquiries (if any) as were reasonable, that the statement was true and not misleading or that the matter whose omission caused the loss was properly omitted and:

(1) that he continued in that belief until the time when the securities were acquired[5]; or

(2) that they were acquired before it was reasonably practicable to bring a correction to the attention of persons likely to acquire the securities in question; or

(3) that, before the securities were acquired, he had taken all such steps as it was reasonable for him to have taken to secure that a correction was brought to the attention of those persons; or

(4) that he continued in that belief until after the commencement of dealings in the securities following their admission to the Official List[6] and that the securities were acquired after such a lapse of time that he ought in the circumstances to be reasonably excused[7].

A person does not incur any statutory liability for any loss in respect of securities caused by a statement purporting to be made by or on the authority of another person as an expert[8] which is, and is stated to be, included in the particulars or prospectus with that other person's consent if he satisfies the court that, at the time when the particulars or prospectus were or was submitted to the competent authority, he believed on reasonable grounds that the other person was competent to make or authorise the statement and had consented to its inclusion in the form and context in which it was included and:

(a) that he continued in that belief until the time when the securities were acquired; or

(b) that they were acquired before it was reasonably practicable to bring the fact that the expert was not competent or had not consented to the attention of persons likely to acquire the securities in question; or

(c) that, before the securities were acquired, he had taken all such steps as it was reasonable for him to have taken to secure that that fact was forthwith brought to the attention of those persons; or

(d) that he continued in that belief until after the commencement of dealings in the securities following their admission to the Official List and that the securities were acquired after such a lapse of time that he ought in the circumstances to be reasonably excused[9].

Without prejudice to the above provisions, a person does not incur any statutory liability for any loss in respect of any securities caused by any such statement or omission as is there mentioned if he satisfies the court:

(i) that, before the securities were acquired, a correction, or where the statement was one purporting to be made by or on the authority of an expert with his consent[10], the fact that the expert was not competent or had not consented, had been published in a manner calculated to bring it to the attention of persons likely to acquire the securities in question; or

(ii) that he took all such steps as it was reasonable for him to take to secure such publication and reasonably believed that it had taken place before the securities were acquired[11].

A person does not incur any statutory liability for any loss resulting from a statement made by an official person or contained in a public official document which is included in the particulars or prospectus if he satisfies the court that the statement is accurately and fairly reproduced[12]; nor does he incur any statutory liability whether in respect of untrue or misleading statements or omissions or failure to submit supplemental listing particulars or a supplementary prospectus[13] if he satisfies the court that the person suffering the loss acquired the securities in question with knowledge that the statement was false or misleading, of the omitted matter or of the change or new matter, as the case may be[14].

A person does not incur any statutory liability based on failure to submit supplementary listing particulars or a supplemenatry prospectus if he satisfies the court that he reasonably believed that the change or new matter in question was not such as to call for supplementary listing particulars or a supplementary prospectus[15].

1 Ie under the Financial Services Act 1986 ss 150(1), 154A (as added) (untrue or misleading statement or omission from listing particulars, supplemental listing particulars, prospectus or supplementary prospectus): see para 347 ante.
2 For the meaning of 'listing particulars' see para 285 ante. As to supplementary listing particulars see para 290 ante.
3 As to the prospectus and supplementary prospectus see paras 285, 290, 296 ante.
4 For the meaning of 'the competent authority' see para 281 ante. As to the necessity for submission to the competent authority see para 285 ante.
5 For these purposes, references to the acquisition of securities include references to contracting to acquire them or an interest in them: Financial Services Act 1986 ss 151(7), 154A (added by the Public Offers of Securities Regulations 1995, SI 1995/1537, reg 17, Sch 2 para 2(3)). For the meaning of 'securities' see para 283 ante.
6 For the meaning of 'the Official List' see para 281 note 3 ante.
7 Financial Services Act 1986 ss 151(1), 154A (as added: see note 5 supra). As to the application of s 151 to prospectuses generally see para 296 ante.
8 For these purposes, 'expert' includes any engineer, valuer, accountant or other person whose profession, qualifications or experience give authority to a statement made by him: ibid ss 151(7), 154A (as added: see note 5 supra).
9 Ibid ss 151(2), 154A (as added: see note 5 supra).
10 Ie a statement such as is mentioned in ibid s 151(2): see supra.
11 Ibid ss 151(3), 154A (as added: see note 5 supra).
12 Ibid ss 151(4), 154A (as added: see note 5 supra).
13 Ie under ibid ss 150(1) or (3), 154A (as added): see para 347 ante.
14 Ibid ss 151(5), 154A (as added: see note 5 supra).
15 Ibid ss 151(6), 154A (as added: see note 5 supra).

(C) *Offers of Unlisted Securities*

349. Persons responsible for prospectus. The persons responsible[1] for a prospectus[2] or supplementary prospectus[3] are:
(1) the issuer[4] of the securities[5] to which the prospectus or supplementary prospectus relates;
(2) where the issuer is a body corporate[6], each person who is a director[7] of that body corporate at the time when the prospectus or supplementary prospectus is published[8];
(3) where the issuer is a body corporate, each person who has authorised himself to be named, and is named, in the prospectus or supplementary prospectus as a

director or as having agreed to become a director of that body either immediately or at a future time;

(4) each person who accepts, and is stated in the prospectus or supplementary prospectus as accepting, responsibility for, or for any part of, the prospectus or supplementary prospectus;

(5) the offeror[9] of the securities, where he is not the issuer;

(6) where the offeror is a body corporate, but is not the issuer and is not making the offer in association with the issuer, each person who is a director of that body corporate at the time when the prospectus or supplementary prospectus is published; and

(7) each person not falling within any of heads (1) to (6) above who has authorised the contents of, or of any part of, the prospectus or supplementary prospectus[10].

A person is not responsible under heads (1), (2) or (3) above unless the issuer has made or authorised the offer in relation to which the prospectus or supplementary prospectus was published; and a person is not responsible for a prospectus or supplementary prospectus by virtue of head (2) above if it is published without his knowledge or consent and, on becoming aware of its publication, he forthwith gives reasonable public notice that it was published without his knowledge or consent[11].

Where a person has accepted responsibility for, or authorised, only part of the contents of any prospectus or supplementary prospectus, he is responsible under heads (4) or (7) above only for that part and only if it is included in (or substantially in) the form and context to which he has agreed[12].

Nothing in the above provisions is to be construed as making a person responsible for any prospectus or supplementary prospectus by reason only of giving advice as to its contents in a professional capacity[13].

Where, by virtue of the above provisions, the issuer of any shares pays or is liable to pay statutory compensation[14] for loss suffered in respect of shares for which a person has subscribed, no account is to be taken of that liability or payment in determining any question as to the amount paid on subscription for those shares or as to the amount paid up or deemed to be paid up on them[15].

1　Ie for the purposes of the Public Offers of Securities Regulations 1995, SI 1995/1537, Pt II (regs 3–16): see para 300 et seq ante.

2　As to the prospectus see para 306 et seq ante.

3　As to the supplementary prospectus see para 317 ante.

4　For the meaning of 'issuer' see para 305 note 25 ante.

5　For the meaning of 'securities' see para 302 note 1 ante.

6　For the meaning of 'body corporate' see para 305 note 3 ante.

7　For the meaning of 'director' see para 307 note 4 ante.

8　As to the requirement for publication see para 302 ante.

9　For the meaning of 'offeror' see para 304 ante.

10　Public Offers of Securities Regulations 1995 reg 13(1). Regulation 13 does not apply to a prospectus submitted for approval in accordance with listing rules made under the Financial Services Act 1986 s 156A (as added) (see para 297 ante): Public Offers of Securities Regulations 1995 reg 4(3).

11　Ibid reg 13(2). See also note 10 supra. A director who knows that a prospectus is being published and does not ask to see it cannot be heard to say that it was published without his knowledge or consent: see *Drincqbier v Wood* [1899] 1 Ch 393 at 404, 406; *Watts v Bucknall* [1902] 2 Ch 628 (affd [1903] 1 Ch 766, CA); *J and P Coats Ltd v Crossland* (1904) 20 TLR 800. In such a case he cannot repudiate the prospectus after an action has been brought; and repudiation by his statement of defence is not 'reasonable public notice': *Drincqbier v Wood* supra.

12　Public Offers of Securities Regulations 1995 reg 13(3). See also note 10 supra.

13　Ibid reg 13(4). See also note 10 supra.

14　Ie under ibid reg 14: see para 350 post.

15　Ibid reg 13(5). See also note 10 supra.

350. Compensation for false or misleading prospectus. The person or persons responsible for a prospectus[1] or supplementary prospectus is or are liable[2] to pay compensation to any person who has acquired[3] the securities to which the prospectus relates and suffered loss in respect of them as a result of any untrue or misleading statement in the prospectus or supplementary prospectus or the omission from it of any matter required[4] to be included[5].

Where a prospectus is required[6] to include information as to any particular matter on the basis that the prospectus must include a statement either as to that matter or, if such is the case, that there is no such matter, the omission from the prospectus of the information is to be treated[7] as a statement that there is no such matter[8].

A person who fails to comply with the provisions relating to a supplementary prospectus[9] is liable[10] to pay compensation to any person who has acquired any of the securities in question and suffered loss in respect of them as a result of the failure[11].

The above provisions do not affect any liability which any person may incur apart therefrom[12].

1　As to the persons responsible for a prospectus or supplementary prospectus see para 349 ante.
2　Ie subject to the Public Offers of Securities Regulations 1995, SI 1995/1537, reg 15: see para 351 post.
3　For these purposes, references to the acquisition by any person of securities include references to his contracting to acquire them or an interest in them: ibid reg 14(5). For the meaning of 'securities' see para 302 note 1 ante.
4　Ie by ibid reg 9 (see para 316 ante) or reg 10 (see para 317 ante).
5　Ibid reg 14(1). Regulation 14 does not apply to a prospectus submitted for approval in accordance with listing rules made under the Financial Services Act 1986 s 156A (as added) (see para 297 ante): Public Offers of Securities Regulations 1995 reg 4(3).
6　Ie by ibid reg 8: see para 315 ante.
7　Ie for the purposes of ibid reg 14(1): see supra.
8　Ibid reg 14(2). See also note 5 supra.
9　Ie ibid reg 10: see para 317 ante.
10　See note 2 supra.
11　Public Offers of Securities Regulations 1995 reg 14(3). See also note 5 supra.
12　Ibid reg 14(4). As to such liability see paras 321–338 ante. See also note 5 supra.

351. Exemption from liability to pay compensation. A person does not incur any statutory liability to pay compensation[1] for any loss in respect of securities[2] caused as a result of any untrue or misleading statement in the prospectus or supplementary prospectus or the omission from it of any matter required to be included[3] if he satisfies the court that, at the time when the prospectus or supplementary prospectus was delivered for registration[4], he reasonably believed, having made such inquiries, if any, as were reasonable, that the statement was true and not misleading or that the matter whose omission caused the loss was properly omitted and:

(1) that he continued in that belief until the time when the securities were acquired[5]; or

(2) that they were acquired before it was reasonably practicable to bring a correction to the attention of persons likely to acquire the securities in question; or

(3) that, before the securities were acquired, he had taken all such steps as it was reasonable for him to have taken to secure that a correction was forthwith brought to the attention of those persons; or

(4) that the securities were acquired after such a lapse of time that he ought in the circumstances to be reasonably excused, and, if the securities are dealt in on an approved exchange[6], that he continued in that belief until after the commencement of dealings in the securities on that exchange[7].

A person does not incur any statutory liability to pay compensation[8] for any loss in respect of securities caused by a statement purporting to be made by or on the authority of another person as an expert[9] which is, and is stated to be, included in the prospectus or supplementary prospectus with that other person's consent if he satisfies the court that at the time when the prospectus or supplementary prospectus was delivered for registration he believed on reasonable grounds that the other person was competent to make or authorise the statement and had consented to its inclusion in the form and context in which it was included and:

(a) that he continued in that belief until the time when the securities were acquired; or

(b) that they were acquired before it was reasonably practicable to bring the fact that the expert was not competent or had not consented to the attention of persons likely to acquire the securities in question; or

(c) that, before the securities were acquired, he had taken all such steps as it was reasonable for him to have taken to secure that that fact was forthwith brought to the attention of those persons; or

(d) that the securities were acquired after such a lapse of time that he ought in the circumstances to be reasonably excused and, if the securities are dealt in on an approved exchange, that he continued in that belief until after the commencement of dealings in the securities on that exchange[10].

Without prejudice to the above provisions, a person does not incur any statutory liability to pay compensation[11] for any loss in respect of any securities caused by any statement or omission if he satisfies the court:

(i) that, before the securities were acquired, a correction or, where the statement was one purporting to be made by or on the authority of an expert with his consent[12], the fact that the expert was not competent or had not consented had been published in a manner calculated to bring it to the attention of persons likely to acquire the securities in question; or

(ii) that he took all such steps as it was reasonable for him to take to secure such publication and reasonably believed that it had taken place before the securities were acquired[13].

A person does not incur any statutory liability to pay compensation[14] for any loss resulting from a statement made by an official person or contained in a public official document which is included in the prospectus or supplementary prospectus if he satisfies the court that the statement is accurately and fairly reproduced[15].

A person does not incur any liability to pay compensation, whether in respect of untrue or misleading statements or omissions or failure to deliver and publish a supplementary prospectus[16], if he satisfies the court that the person suffering the loss acquired the securities in question with knowledge that the statement was false or misleading, of the omitted matter or of the change, new matter or inaccuracy, as the case may be[17].

A person does not incur any liability to pay compensation for failure to deliver and publish a supplementary prospectus[18] if he satisfies the court that he reasonably believed that the change, new matter or inaccuracy in question was not such as to call for a supplementary prospectus[19].

1 Ie under the Public Offers of Securities Regulations 1995, SI 1995/1537, reg 14(1): see para 350 ante.
2 For the meaning of 'securities' see para 302 note 1 ante.
3 Ie any such statement or omission as is mentioned in the Public Offers of Securities Regulations 1995 reg 14(1). As to the prospectus see para 306 et seq ante; and as to the supplementary prospectus see para 317 ante.

4 As to delivery for registration see para 302 ante.
5 For these purposes, references to the acquisition of securities include references to contracting to acquire them or an interest in them: Public Offers of Securities Regulations 1995 reg 15(7).
6 For the meaning of 'approved exchange' see para 306 note 8 ante.
7 Public Offers of Securities Regulations 1995 reg 15(1). Regulation 15 does not apply to a prospectus submitted for approval in accordance with listing rules made under the Financial Services Act 1986 s 156A (as added) (see para 297 ante): Public Offers of Securities Regulations 1995 reg 4(3).
8 See note 1 supra.
9 For these purposes, 'expert' includes any engineer, valuer, accountant or other person whose profession, qualifications or experience give authority to a statement made by him: Public Offers of Securities Regulations 1995 reg 15(7).
10 Ibid reg 15(2). See also note 7 supra.
11 See note 1 supra.
12 Ie any such statement or omission as is mentioned in the Public Offers of Securities Regulations 1995 reg 15(2): see supra.
13 Ibid reg 15(3). See also note 7 supra.
14 See note 1 supra.
15 Public Offers of Securities Regulations 1995 reg 15(4).
16 Ie under ibid reg 14(1) or (3): see para 350 ante.
17 Ibid reg 15(5). See also note 7 supra.
18 Ie under ibid reg 14(3).
19 Ibid reg 15(6). See also note 7 supra.

352. Compensation for loss caused by contravention of statutory provisions. Any contravention by authorised persons and others of certain provisions relating to the offer of unlisted securities[1] is actionable at the suit of a person who suffers loss as a result of the contraventions subject to the defences and other incidents applying to actions for breach of statutory duty[2].

1 Ie any contravention to which the Public Offers of Securities Regulations 1995, SI 1995/1537, reg 16 applies: see para 320 ante.
2 Ibid reg 16(4).

353. Application of statutory provisions. A person who has subscribed for shares on the faith of a prospectus issued before the company's incorporation may be entitled to relief, apart from the statutory provisions, by way of rescission on the grounds of misrepresentation[1]. The effect of the prospectus will, however, normally be spent soon after its issue, and persons who subsequently apply for shares in the company, or take transfers from the holder of such shares, will be unable to rescind the transaction by virtue of anything contained in the prospectus[2].

1 *Lagunas Nitrate Co v Lagunas Syndicate* [1899] 2 Ch 392 at 427, CA per Sir N Lindley MR; *Hilo Manufacturing Co Ltd v Williamson* (1911) 28 TLR 164, CA. See further para 324 et seq ante.
2 *Collins v Associated Greyhound Racecourses Ltd* [1930] 1 Ch 1, CA; cf *Edinburgh United Breweries Ltd v Molleson* [1894] AC 96, HL (right to rescind does not run with the property); *Peek v Gurney* (1873) LR 6 HL 377 (same point). The office of the prospectus is fulfilled when the original allottee has got his shares. See also para 335 ante.

(iv) Criminal Offences

354. Publishing fraudulent statements. Where an officer of a body corporate[1] (or person purporting to act as such), with intent to deceive members or creditors[2] of the body corporate about its affairs, publishes or concurs in publishing a written statement or account which to his knowledge is or may be misleading, false or deceptive in a material particular, he is liable on conviction on indictment to imprisonment for a term not exceeding seven years, or on summary conviction to imprisonment for a term not exceeding six months or a fine not exceeding the prescribed sum, or to both[3].

Where the affairs of the body corporate are managed by its members, these provisions apply to any statement which a member publishes or concurs in publishing in connection with his functions of management as if he were an officer of the body corporate[4].

1 The provisions of the Theft Act 1968 s 19 apply to an unincorporated association as they apply to a body corporate: see s 19(1)–(3).
2 For these purposes, a person who has entered into a security for the benefit of a body corporate is to be treated as a creditor of it: ibid s 19(2).
3 Ibid s 19(1); Magistrates' Courts Act 1980 ss 17, 32(1), Sch 1 para 28. For the meaning of 'the prescribed sum' see CRIMINAL LAW vol 11(2) (Reissue) para 807. As to the imposition of a fine in lieu of or in addition to the sentence see the Powers of Criminal Courts Act 1973 s 30(1) (as amended) and CRIMINAL LAW vol 11(2) (Reissue) para 1232.
4 Theft Act 1968 s 19(3).

355. False and misleading statements. A person commits an offence if, for the purposes of or in connection with any application under the Financial Services Act 1986 or in purported compliance with any requirement imposed on him by or under that Act, he furnishes information which he knows to be false or misleading in a material particular or recklessly furnishes information which is false or misleading in a material particular[1]. A person guilty of such an offence is liable on conviction on indictment to imprisonment for a term not exceeding two years or a fine, or to both, or on summary conviction to imprisonment for a term not exceeding six months or a fine not exceeding the statutory maximum, or to both[2].

The above provisions apply to applications under the Public Offers of Securities Regulations 1995[3] as they apply to applications under the Financial Services Act 1986, and to requirements imposed on a person by or under the 1995 Regulations as they apply to requirements imposed on a person by or under the Financial Services Act 1986[4].

1 Financial Services Act 1986 s 200(1).
2 Ibid s 200(5). For the meaning of 'the statutory maximum' see para 1161 post.
3 Ie the Public Offers of Securities Regulations 1995, SI 1995/1537: see para 300 et seq ante.
4 Ibid reg 23(5). The Financial Services Act 1986 s 201(1) (prosecution of offences), s 202 (offences by bodies corporate, partnerships and unincorporated associations) and s 203 (jurisdiction and procedure in respect of offences) apply to offences under the Public Offers of Securities Regulations 1995 as they apply to offences under the Financial Services Act 1986: Public Offers of Securities Regulations 1995 reg 23(6). The Financial Services Act 1986 s 199 (as amended) (powers of entry) applies in relation to an offence under the Public Offers of Securities Regulations 1995 as it applies in relation to the offences mentioned in the Financial Services Act 1986 s 199 (as amended): Public Offers of Securities Regulations 1995 reg 23(4).

356. Misleading statements and practices. Any person who:

(1) makes a statement, promise or forecast which he knows to be misleading, false or deceptive or dishonestly conceals any material facts; or

(2) recklessly makes (dishonestly or otherwise) a statement, promise or forecast which is misleading, false or deceptive,

is guilty of an offence, if he makes the statement, promise or forecast or conceals the facts for the purpose of inducing, or is reckless as to whether it may induce, another person (whether or not the person to whom the statement, promise or forecast is made or from whom the facts are concealed) to enter or offer to enter into, or to refrain from entering or offering to enter into, an investment agreement[1] or to exercise, or refrain from exercising, any rights conferred by an investment[2].

Any person who does any act or engages in any course of conduct which creates a false or misleading impression as to the market in or the price or value of any investments is guilty of an offence if he does so for the purpose of creating that impression and of thereby inducing another person to acquire, dispose of, subscribe for or underwrite those investments or to refrain from doing so or to exercise, or refrain from exercising, any rights conferred by those investments[3]. In proceedings brought against any person for such an offence it is a defence for him to prove that he reasonably believed that his act or conduct would not create an impression that was false or misleading as to the matters so mentioned[4].

A person guilty of an offence under the above provisions is liable on conviction on indictment to imprisonment for a term not exceeding seven years or a fine, or to both, or on summary conviction to imprisonment for a term not exceeding six months or a fine not exceeding the statutory maximum, or to both[5].

1　For these purposes, 'investment agreement' means any agreement the making or performance of which by either party constitutes an activity which falls within any of the Financial Services Act 1986 Sch 1 Pt II (paras 12–16) (as amended) (activities constituting investment business: see MONEY) or would do so apart from Sch 1 Pt III (paras 17–25) (excluded activities) and Sch 1 Pt IV (paras 26, 27) (additional exclusions for persons without permanent place of business in the United Kingdom: see MONEY): s 44(9).

2　Ibid s 47(1). Section 47(1) does not, however, apply unless (1) the statement, promise or forecast is made in or from, or the facts are concealed in or from, the United Kingdom; (2) the person on whom the inducement is intended to or may have effect is in the United Kingdom; or (3) the agreement is or would be entered into or the rights are or would be exercised in the United Kingdom: s 47(4). In the Financial Services Act 1986, unless the context otherwise requires, 'investment' means any asset, right or interest falling within any of Sch 1 Pt I (paras 1–11) (as amended): s 1(1). As to the investments to which Pt IV (ss 142–156B (as amended): see para 281 et seq ante) applies see para 283 ante; and as to the investments to which the Public Offers of Securities Regulations 1995, SI 1995/1537 (see para 300 et seq ante) apply see para 301 ante.

3　Financial Services Act 1986 s 47(2). Section 47(2) does not apply unless (1) the act is done or the course of conduct is engaged in in the United Kingdom; or (2) the false or misleading impression is created there: s 47(5).

4　Ibid s 47(3).

5　Ibid s 47(6).

(11) TREASURY CONTROL OF CAPITAL RAISING

357. Requirement of Treasury consent. Treasury consent for the raising of money by companies by the issuing of shares[1] has not been required on and after 11 February 1991[2].

1　Ie under the Borrowing (Control and Guarantees) Act 1946 and the subordinate instruments made thereunder.

2　See the Government Trading Act 1990 s 4(1), (2), Sch 2 Pt I; the Government Trading Act 1990 (Appointed Day) Order 1991, SI 1991/132, art 2.

(12) MEMBERSHIP

(i) In general

358. Who are members. The members of a company are those persons (including corporations[1], if any) who collectively constitute the company, or, in other words, are its corporators. A member is not necessarily a shareholder, for an unlimited company or a company limited by guarantee may exist without a share capital[2].

1 *Re Barned's Banking Co, ex p Contract Corpn* (1867) 3 Ch App 105 at 113 per Lord Cairns LC; and see CORPORATIONS vol 9 para 1249 et seq. Cf the Companies Act 1985 s 375(1)(a) (representation of corporations at meetings of companies of which they are members: see para 678 post).
2 *Re South London Fish Market Co* (1888) 39 ChD 324, CA. See paras 108, 115 ante. As to warrant bearers being deemed members by provisions in articles see para 494 post. With effect from 22 December 1980 a company cannot be formed as, or become, a company limited by guarantee with a share capital: Companies Act 1985 s 1(4).

359. Subscribers of the memorandum. Whether the company is limited by shares, or by guarantee, or is unlimited, the subscribers of the memorandum of association become the first members of the company as from the date of incorporation mentioned in the registrar of companies' certificate of incorporation[1]. They are deemed to have agreed to become members of the company, and on its registration must be entered as such in its register of members[2], but neither this entry nor any allotment of shares is a condition precedent to their becoming members[3].

1 See paras 91, 92 ante.
2 Companies Act 1985 s 22(1).
3 *Nicol's Case, Tufnell and Ponsonby's Case* (1885) 29 ChD 421 at 445, CA; *Evans's Case* (1867) 2 Ch App 427; *Hall's Case* (1870) 5 Ch App 707; *Sidney's Case* (1871) LR 13 Eq 228; *Re London and Provincial Consolidated Coal Co* (1877) 5 ChD 525; *Re Argyle Coal and Cannell Co Ltd, ex p Watson* (1885) 54 LT 233.

360. Subscribers' liability. By subscribing, each subscriber at once irrevocably agrees to take from the company the number of shares placed opposite his signature[1], unless all its share capital has been duly allotted to other persons[2]. The fact that no shares are allotted to him and that he has ceased to be treated as a member for a considerable time does not relieve him from liability[3], though a valid surrender will do so[4]. A subscriber who is a director is bound to see that the allotment is made[5].

The subscriber's obligation to take shares is not satisfied by a transfer to him, or by an allotment to him of shares, credited as fully paid up, to which a third person is entitled[6]. The obligation of a person who subscribes in his own name, but in fact as an agent, is satisfied by his principal taking the number of shares subscribed for[7].

If a subscriber of the memorandum subsequently applies for and obtains an allotment of shares, the allotment, unless otherwise agreed, will include the shares subscribed for[8].

Shares taken by a subscriber of the memorandum of a public company[9] in pursuance of an undertaking of his in the memorandum, and any premium on the shares, must be paid up in cash[10]; and, if the company contravenes this provision, it, and any officer of it, who is in default is liable on conviction on indictment to a fine, or on summary conviction to a fine not exceeding the statutory maximum[11]. Otherwise the shares so subscribed for may be paid for either in cash or in money's worth[12]. The shares paid for in money's worth must, however, be identified with the shares subscribed for[13].

A subscriber for preference shares may take the like amount of ordinary shares instead[14]. If a person subscribes for shares, some of which are to be allotted as fully paid up, he is liable only as contributory in respect of the others; but, if he subscribes for fully paid-up shares only, he is liable for them as unpaid[15], except in so far as he has actually paid for them.

1 *Alexander v Automatic Telephone Co* [1900] 2 Ch 56, CA. Unless otherwise agreed, by the articles or otherwise, the subscriber is bound to pay only when calls are made: *Alexander v Automatic Telephone Co* supra.
2 *Mackley's Case* (1875) 1 ChD 247; and see *Evans's Case* (1867) 2 Ch App 427; *Re China SS and Labuan Coal Co Ltd, Drummond's Case* (1869) 4 Ch App 772 at 780.
3 *Re Imperial Land Co of Marseilles Ltd, Levick's Case* (1870) 40 LJ Ch 180; *Ex p London and Colonial Co Ltd, Tooth's Case* (1868) 19 LT 599; *Sidney's Case* (1871) LR 13 Eq 228.
4 *Re Freen & Co Ltd* (1866) 15 LT 406; *Snell's Case* (1869) 5 Ch App 22; *Hall's Case* (1870) 5 Ch App 707; *Re London and Provincial Consolidated Coal Co* (1877) 5 ChD 525.
5 *Evans's Case* (1867) 2 Ch App 427; *Hall's Case* (1870) 5 Ch App 707 at 711.
6 *Migotti's Case* (1867) LR 4 Eq 238; *Forbes and Judd's Case* (1870) 5 Ch App 270; *Dent's Case, Forbes' Case* (1873) 8 Ch App 768; cf *Re Pen'Allt Silver Lead Mining Co Ltd, Fraser's Case* (1873) 42 LJ Ch 358.
7 *Dunster's Case* [1894] 3 Ch 473, CA.
8 *Re Freen & Co Ltd* (1866) 15 LT 406; *Gilman's Case* (1886) 31 ChD 420; *Re China SS and Labuan Coal Co Ltd, Drummond's Case* (1869) 4 Ch App 772; *Dunster's Case* [1894] 3 Ch 473, CA.
9 For an extension of the scope of this provision see the Companies Act 1985 s 116 (as amended) and para 464 note 3 post.
10 Ibid s 106.
11 Ibid ss 114, 730, Sch 24. For the meaning of 'officer who is in default' and 'the statutory maximum' see para 1161 post.
12 *Re China SS and Labuan Coal Ltd, Drummond's Case* (1869) 4 Ch App 772; *Pell's Case* (1869) 5 Ch App 11; *Re Baglan Hall Colliery Co* (1870) 5 Ch App 346; *Jones' Case* (1870) 6 Ch App 48; *Maynard's Case* (1873) 9 Ch App 60; and see para 479 post. Directors cannot pay for the shares out of fees paid to themselves ultra vires (*Re Great Northern and Midland Coal Co Ltd, Currie's Case* (1863) 3 De G J & Sm 367 at 371), or out of money of the company paid to other persons ultra vires (*Hay's Case* (1875) 10 Ch App 593; cf *Re Canadian Oil Works Corpn, Eastwick's Case* (1876) 45 LJ Ch 225, CA).
13 *Fothergill's Case* (1873) 8 Ch App 270.
14 *Duke's Case* (1876) 1 ChD 620.
15 *Baron De Beville's Case* (1868) LR 7 Eq 11.

361. Members forming the corporation. The subscribers of the memorandum, together with such other persons as from time to time become members of the company, are a body corporate[1]. Each of those other persons becomes a member by agreeing[2] to become a member of the company and by his name being entered in its register of members[3].

1 See para 92 ante.
2 As to the nature of the agreement required see para 369 post.
3 Companies Act 1985 s 22(2).

362. General rule against company acquiring own shares. A company limited by shares or limited by guarantee and having a share capital must not acquire[1] its own shares, whether by purchase, subscription, or otherwise[2]. If a company purports to act in contravention of these provisions, the company, and every officer of the company who is in default, is liable on conviction on indictment to, in the case of the company, a fine, and, in the case of an officer of the company who is in default, imprisonment for a term not exceeding two years or a fine, or to both; on summary conviction, the company is liable to a fine not exceeding the statutory maximum, and an officer of it who is in default to imprisonment for a term not exceeding six months or a fine not exceeding the statutory maximum, or to both[3]. The purported acquisition is void[4].

A company limited by shares may, however, acquire any of its own fully paid shares otherwise than for valuable consideration[5]; and the above provisions[6] do not apply in relation to:

(1) the redemption or purchase of shares in accordance with the provisions[7] of the Companies Act 1985[8];

(2) the acquisition of shares in a reduction of capital duly made[9];

(3) the purchase of shares in pursuance of an order of the court pursuant to proceedings objecting to a proposed alteration of the company's objects[10], or to a proposed resolution for the company to be re-registered as private[11], or seeking relief[12] on the grounds of unfair prejudice to members[13]; or

(4) the forfeiture of shares, or the acceptance of shares surrendered in lieu, in pursuance of the articles[14], for failure to pay any sum payable in respect of the shares[15].

1 Ie subject to the Companies Act 1985 s 143(2), (3): see infra.
2 Ibid s 143(1), giving statutory force to *Trevor v Whitworth* (1887) 12 App Cas 409, HL; *Kirby v Wilkins* [1929] 2 Ch 444; *Vision Express (UK) Ltd v Wilson* [1995] 2 BCLC 419. This does not prohibit a company from acquiring the shares of another company ('the acquired company') in circumstances where the sole asset of the acquired company is shares in the acquiring company: *Acatos & Hutcheson plc v Watson* [1995] 1 BCLC 218 (in view of the potential for abuse, the court will, however, look carefully at the transaction to ensure that the directors have fulfilled their fiduciary duties to safeguard the interests of shareholders and creditors alike). See also *British and Commonwealth Holdings plc v Barclays Bank plc* [1996] 1 All ER 381, [1996] 1 WLR 1, CA.
  As to the prohibition on a body corporate being a member of a company which is its holding company see para 363 post.
3 Companies Act 1985 ss 143(2), 730, Sch 24. For the meaning of 'officer who is in default' and 'the statutory maximum' see para 1161 post.
4 Ibid s 143(2).
5 Ibid s 143(3). See eg *Re Castiglione's Will Trusts, Hunter v Mackenzie* [1958] Ch 549, [1958] 1 All ER 480.
6 Ie the Companies Act 1985 s 143(1): see supra.
7 Ie the provisions of ibid Pt V Ch VII (ss 159–181) (as amended): see para 219 et seq ante.
8 Ibid s 143(3)(a).
9 Ibid s 143(3)(b). As to a reduction of capital see para 241 ante.
10 Ie under ibid s 5: see para 1185 post.
11 Ie under ibid s 54: see para 130 ante.
12 Ie under ibid Pt XVII (ss 459–461) (as amended): see para 1405 et seq post.
13 Ibid s 143(3)(c).
14 See eg the Companies (Tables A to F) Regulations 1985, SI 1985/805, Schedule, Table A arts 18–22. As to Table A generally see para 529 et seq post.
15 Companies Act 1985 s 143(3)(d).

363. Membership of holding company. A body corporate[1] cannot[2] be a member of a company which is its holding company[3]; and any allotment or transfer of shares[4] in a company to its subsidiary[5] is void[6]. The prohibition does not, however, apply:

(1) where the subsidiary is concerned only as personal representative or trustee unless, in the latter case, the holding company or a subsidiary of it is beneficially interested under the trust[7];

(2) where the subsidiary is concerned only as a market maker[8].

Where a body corporate became a holder of shares in a company before 1 July 1948 or on or after that date and before 1 November 1990 in circumstances in which these provisions as they then had effect did not apply, but at any time on or after 1 November 1990 falls within the above prohibition[9] in respect of those shares, it may continue to be a member of that company; but, for so long as that prohibition would otherwise apply, it has no right to vote in respect of those shares at meetings of the company or of any class of its members[10].

Where a body corporate becomes a holder of shares in a company on or after 1 November 1990 in circumstances in which the above prohibition[11] does not apply, but subsequently falls within that prohibition in respect of those shares, it may continue to be a member of that company; but, for so long as that prohibition would otherwise apply, it has no right to vote in respect of those shares at meetings of the company or of any class of its members[12].

Where a body corporate is so permitted[13] to continue as a member of a company, an allotment to it of fully paid shares in the company may be validly made by way of capitalisation of reserves of the company; but, for so long as the above prohibition[14] would otherwise apply, it has no right to vote in respect of those shares at meetings of the company or of any class of its members[15].

1 For the meaning of 'body corporate' see para 89 note 8 ante.

2 Ie except as mentioned in the Companies Act 1985 s 23 (as substituted): see infra.

3 For the meaning of 'holding company' see para 827 post. See also note 6 infra.

4 For these purposes, in relation to a company other than a company limited by shares, the references to shares are to be construed as references to the interest of its members as such, whatever the form of that interest: Companies Act 1985 s 23(8) (substituted by the Companies Act 1989 s 129(1)).

5 For the meaning of 'subsidiary' see para 827 post. See also note 6 infra. The provisions of the Companies Act 1985 s 23 (as substituted and amended) apply to a nominee acting on behalf of a subsidiary as to the subsidiary itself: s 23(7) (substituted by the Companies Act 1989 s 129(1)).

6 Companies Act 1985 s 23(1) (substituted by the Companies Act 1989 s 129(1)). The following provisions have effect with respect to the operation of the Companies Act 1985 s 23 (as substituted): Companies Act 1989 s 144(4), Sch 18 para 32(1). In relation to times, circumstances and purposes before the commencement of s 144(1) (ie 1 November 1990), the references in the Companies Act 1985 s 23 (as substituted) to a subsidiary or holding company are to be construed in accordance with s 736 as originally enacted: Companies Act 1989 Sch 18 para 32(2). Where a body corporate becomes or ceases to be a subsidiary of a holding company by reason of s 144(1) coming into force, the prohibition in the Companies Act 1985 s 23 (as substituted) applies (in the absence of exempting circumstances), or ceases to apply, accordingly: Companies Act 1989 Sch 18 para 32(3). For the meaning of 'subsidiary' as originally enacted see para 190 note 14 ante. For the purposes of the Companies Act 1985 (as originally enacted), a company is deemed to be another's holding company if, but only if, the other is its subsidiary: s 736(5)(a) (as originally enacted).

7 Ibid s 23(2) (substituted by the Companies Act 1989 s 129(1)). For the purpose of ascertaining whether the holding company or a subsidiary is so interested, there must be disregarded (1) any interest held only by way of security for the purposes of a transaction entered into by the holding company or subsidiary in the ordinary course of a business which includes the lending of money; (2) any such interest as is mentioned in the Companies Act 1985 Sch 2 Pt I (paras 1–5) (as amended) (see para 364 post): s 23(2) (as so substituted).

8 Ibid s 23(3) (substituted by the Companies Act 1989 s 129(1)). For these purposes, a person is a market maker if (1) he holds himself out at all normal times in compliance with the rules of a recognised investment exchange other than an overseas investment exchange (within the meaning of the Financial Services Act 1986) as willing to buy and sell securities at prices specified by him; and (2) he is recognised as so doing by that investment exchange: Companies Act 1985 s 23(3) (as so substituted). For the meaning of 'recognised investment exchange' and 'overseas investment exchange' see para 223 note 1 ante.

9 Ie the prohibition in ibid s 23(1) (as substituted): see supra.

10 Ibid s 23(4) (substituted by the Companies Act 1989 s 129(1); amended by the Companies Act 1989 (Commencement No 6 and Transitional and Saving Provisions) Order 1990, SI 1990/1392, art 8; the Companies Act 1989 (Commencement No 7 and Transitional and Saving Provisions) Order 1990, SI 1990/1707, art 8).

11 See note 9 supra.

12 Companies Act 1985 s 23(5) (substituted by the Companies Act 1989 s 129(1); amended by the Companies Act 1989 (Commencement No 6 and Transitional and Saving Provisions) Order 1990 art 8;

the Companies Act 1989 (Commencement No 7 and Transitional and Saving Provisions) Order 1990 art 8).
13 Ie by virtue of the Companies Act 1985 s 23(4) or (5) (as substituted and amended): see supra.
14 See note 9 supra.
15 Companies Act 1985 s 23(6) (substituted by the Companies Act 1989 s 129(1)).

364. Meaning of 'beneficial interest'. There are three special cases which fall for consideration:

(1) a company's residual interests under pension and employees' share schemes;
(2) employer's charges and other rights of recovery; and
(3) a trustee's right to expenses, remuneration and indemnity.

Where shares in a company are held on trust for the purposes of a pension scheme[1] or an employees' share scheme[2], there is to be disregarded any residual interest which has not vested in possession, being an interest of the company or[3] of any subsidiary[4] of the company[5].

For these purposes, 'a residual interest' means a right[6] of the company or subsidiary in question ('the residual beneficiary') to receive any of the trust property in the event of:

(a) all the liabilities[6] arising under the scheme having been satisfied or provided for; or
(b) the residual beneficiary ceasing to participate in the scheme; or
(c) the trust property at any time exceeding what is necessary for satisfying the liabilities arising or expected to arise under the scheme[7].

A residual interest vests in possession, in a case within head (a) above, on the occurrence of the event there mentioned, whether or not the amount of the property receivable pursuant to the right mentioned under that head is then ascertained; and, in a case within heads (b) or (c) above, when the residual beneficiary becomes entitled to require the trustee to transfer to the beneficiary any of the property receivable pursuant to that right[8].

The following provisions have effect as regards the operation of those matters to which it is made to apply[9] in cases where a residual interest vests in possession[10]. Where any shares are exempt, by reason of the fact that a residual interest has not vested in possession[11], from the provision relating to the acquisition of shares by a nominee of the company[12] at the time when they are issued or acquired but the residual interest in question vests in possession before they are disposed of or fully paid up, those provisions apply to the shares as if the shares had been issued or acquired on the date on which that interest vests in possession[13]. Where for the same reason any shares are exempt from the provisions relating to the treatment of shares held by or for a public company[14] at the time when they are acquired but the residual interest in question vests in possession before they are disposed of, those provisions apply to the shares as if they had been acquired on the date on which that interest vests in possession[15]. The above provisions apply irrespective of the date on which the residual interest vests or vested in possession; but, where the date on which it vested was before 26 July 1983[16], they have effect as if the vesting had occurred on that date[17].

Where shares in a company are held on trust, there are to be disregarded, if the trust is for the purposes of a pension scheme, any such rights as are mentioned in heads (i) and (ii) below, and, if the trust is for the purposes of an employees' share scheme, any such rights as are mentioned in head (i) below being rights of the company or, as respects certain provisions[18], of any subsidiary of the company[19]. The rights referred to are:

(i) any charge or lien on, or set-off against, any benefit or other right or interest under the scheme for the purpose of enabling the employer[20] or former employer of a member of the scheme to obtain the discharge of a monetary obligation due to him from the member; and

(ii) any right to receive from the trustee of the scheme, or as trustee of the scheme to retain, an amount that can be recovered or retained under the provisions of the Pensions Schemes Act 1993 relating to the deduction of premium from refund of contributions[21] or otherwise as reimbursement or partial reimbursement for any contributions equivalent premium paid[22] in connection with the scheme under that Act[23].

Where a company is a trustee, there are to be disregarded any rights which the company has in its capacity as trustee including, in particular, any right to recover its expenses or be remunerated out of the trust property and any right to be indemnified out of that property for any liability incurred by reason of any act or omission of the company in the performance of its duties as trustee[24].

1 For these purposes, 'pension scheme' means any scheme for the provision of benefits consisting of or including relevant benefits for or in respect of employees or former employees; 'relevant benefits' means any pension, lump sum, gratuity or other like benefit given or to be given on retirement or on death or in anticipation of retirement or, in connection with past service, after retirement or death; and 'employee' is to be read as if a director of a company were employed by it: Companies Act 1985 Sch 2 Pt I para 5(1)–(3) (amended by the Companies Act 1989 s 23, Sch 10 para 18(1), (2), (6)).

2 For the meaning of 'employees' share scheme' see para 120 note 8 ante.

3 Ie as the Companies Act 1985 Sch 2 Pt I para 1 (as amended) applies for the purposes of s 23(2) (as substituted) (see para 363 ante).

4 For the meaning of 'subsidiary' see para 827 post.

5 Companies Act 1985 Sch 2 Pt I para 1(1) (amended by the Companies Act 1989 ss 129(2), 212, Sch 10 para 18(1)–(3), Sch 24).

6 For these purposes, references to a right include a right dependent on the exercise of a discretion vested by the scheme in the trustee or any other person; and references to liabilities arising under a scheme include liabilities that have resulted or may result from the exercise of any such discretion: Companies Act 1985 Sch 2 Pt I para 1(3).

7 Ibid Sch 2 Pt I para 1(2).

8 Ibid Sch 2 Pt I para 1(4).

9 Ie as regards ibid ss 144, 145 (see para 365 post) and ss 146–149 (see paras 366–368 post).

10 Ibid Sch 2 Pt I para 2(1) (amended by the Companies Act 1989 Sch 10 para 18(1), (2), Sch 24).

11 Ie by virtue of the Companies Act 1985 Sch 2 para 1(1) (as amended): see supra.

12 Ie ibid ss 144 145: see para 365 post.

13 Ibid Sch 2 Pt I para 2(3).

14 Ie ibid ss 146–149: see paras 366–368 post.

15 Ibid Sch 2 Pt I para 2(4).

16 Ie the date of the passing of the Companies (Beneficial Interests) Act 1983.

17 Companies Act 1985 Sch 2 Pt I para 2(5).

18 Ie as ibid Sch 2 Pt I para 3 (as amended) applies for the purpose of s 23(2) (as substituted).

19 Ibid Sch 2 Pt I para 3(1) (amended by the Companies Act 1989 s 129(2), Sch 10 para 18(1), (2), (4), Sch 24).

20 For these purposes, the word 'employer' is to be read as if a director of the company were employed by it: Companies Act 1985 Sch 2 Pt I para 5(3).

21 Ie the Pensions Schemes Act 1993 s 61: see SOCIAL SECURITY AND PENSIONS.

22 Ie under ibid Pt III Ch III (ss 50–68): see SOCIAL SECURITY AND PENSIONS.

23 Companies Act 1985 Sch 2 Pt I para 3(2) (amended by the Pension Schemes Act 1993 s 190, Sch 8 para 16(a); the Pensions Act 1995 s 151, Sch 5 para 11); Interpretation Act 1978 s 17(2)(a).

24 Companies Act 1985 Sch 2 Pt I para 4(1) (amended by the Companies Act 1989 Sch 10 para 18(1), (2), (5)(a), Sch 24). As the Companies Act 1985 Sch 2 Pt I para 4 (as amended) applies for the purposes of s 23(2) (as substituted), Sch 2 Pt I para 4(1) (as so amended) has effect as if references to a company included any body corporate which is a subsidiary of a company: Sch 2 para 4(2) (amended by the Companies Act 1989 s 129(2), Sch 10 para 18(1), (2), (5)(b), Sch 24). As respects the Companies Act 1985 ss 145, 146 and 148, Sch 2 Pt I para 4(1) (as so amended) applies where a company is a personal

representative as it applies where a company is a trustee: Sch 2 Pt I para 4(3) (added by the Companies Act 1989 Sch 10 para 18(1), (2), (5)).

365. Acquisition of shares by company's nominee. Where shares are issued to a nominee of a company limited by shares or limited by guarantee and having a share capital, or are acquired by a nominee of such a company from a third person as partly paid up, then, for all purposes, the shares are to be treated as held by the nominee on his own account, and the company is to be regarded as having no beneficial interest in them[1].

If a person is called on to pay any amount for the purpose of paying up, or paying any premium on, any shares in such a company which were issued to him, or which he otherwise acquired, as the company's nominee and he fails to pay that amount within 21 days from being called on to do so, then:

(1) if the shares were issued to him as subscriber to the memorandum by virtue of an undertaking of his in the memorandum, the other subscribers to the memorandum; or

(2) if the shares were otherwise issued to or acquired by him, the directors of the company at the time of the issue or acquisition, are jointly and severally liable with him to pay that amount[2].

If in proceedings[3] for the recovery of any such amount from any such subscriber or director it appears to the court that he is or may be liable to pay that amount, but that he has acted honestly and reasonably and, having regard to all the circumstances of the case, he ought fairly to be excused from liability, the court may relieve him, either wholly or partly, from his liability on such terms as the court thinks fit[4]. Where any such subscriber or director has reason to apprehend that a claim will or might be made for the recovery of any such amount from him, he may apply[5] to the court[6] for relief; and the court has the same power to relieve him as it would have had in proceedings for the recovery of that amount[7].

1 Companies Act 1985 ss 143(1), 144(1). Section 144(1) does not, however, apply to shares acquired otherwise than by subscription by a nominee of a public company, where a person acquires shares in the company with financial assistance given to him directly or indirectly by the company for the purpose of or in connection with the acquisition, and the company has a beneficial interest in the shares (s 145(1)); nor do s 144(1) and s 144(2) (see infra) apply to shares acquired by a nominee of a company when the company has no beneficial interest in those shares, or to shares issued in consequence of an application made before 22 December 1980 (the date when the Companies Act 1980 s 36 (repealed) came into force), or transferred in pursuance of an agreement to acquire them made before that date (Companies Act 1985 s 145(2)). For these purposes, Sch 2 (as amended) (see para 364 ante) has effect for the interpretation of references to a company having, or not having, a beneficial interest in shares: s 145(3).
2 Ibid s 144(2). See also note 1 supra.
3 Ie proceedings under ibid s 144.
4 Ibid s 144(3). See also para 624 post.
5 In the High Court the application is by originating summons in the expedited form: RSC Ord 102 r 2(1), (2).
6 For the meaning of 'the court' see para 161 note 4 ante.
7 Companies Act 1985 s 144(4).

366. Treatment of shares held by or for public company. Except as expressly otherwise provided[1], the following provisions apply to a public company[2]:

(1) where shares in the company are forfeited[3], or surrendered to the company in lieu[4], in pursuance of the articles, for failure to pay any sum payable in respect of the shares;

(2) where shares in the company are acquired by it otherwise than in relation to[5]:
   (a) the redemption or purchase of shares in accordance with the provisions of the Companies Act 1985;
   (b) the acquisition of shares in a reduction of capital duly made;
   (c) the purchase of shares in pursuance of an order of the court pursuant to proceedings objecting to a proposed alteration of the company's objects, or to a proposed resolution for the company to be re-registered as private, or seeking relief on the grounds of unfair prejudice to members; or
   (d) the forfeiture of shares, or the acceptance of shares surrendered in lieu, in pursuance of the articles, for failure to pay any sum payable in respect of the shares,
   and the company has a beneficial interest[6] in the shares;
(3) where the nominee of the company acquires shares in the company from a third person without financial assistance being given directly or indirectly by the company and the company has a beneficial interest in the shares; or
(4) where a person acquires shares in the company with financial assistance given to him directly or indirectly by the company for the purpose of or in connection with the acquisition, and the company has a beneficial interest in the shares[7].

Unless the shares or any interest of the company in them are previously disposed of, the company must not later than the end of the relevant period[8] from their forfeiture or surrender or, in a case within heads (2), (3) or (4) above, their acquisition, cancel them and diminish the amount of the share capital by the nominal value of the shares cancelled, and, where the effect of cancelling the shares will be that the nominal value of the company's allotted share capital is brought below the authorised minimum, apply for re-registration as a private company[9], stating the effect of the cancellation[10]. The company and, in a case within heads (3) or (4) above, the company's nominee or (as the case may be) the other shareholder must not exercise any voting rights in respect of the shares; and any purported exercise of those rights is void[11].

The directors may take such steps as are requisite to enable the company to carry out the above obligations[12] without complying with the normal statutory requirements[13] applicable in the case of a reduction of capital[14].

The steps taken may include the passing of a resolution[15] to alter the company's memorandum so that it no longer states that the company is to be a public company; and the resolution may make such other alterations in the memorandum as are requisite in the circumstances[16].

If the registrar is satisfied that the company may be re-registered under these provisions, he must retain the application and other documents delivered with it and issue the company with a certificate of incorporation appropriate to a company that is not a public company; and the company by virtue of the issue of the certificate becomes a private company, and the alterations in the memorandum and articles set out in the resolution take effect accordingly; and the certificate is conclusive evidence that the statutory requirements[17] in respect of re-registration and of matters precedent and incidental to it have been complied with, and that the company is a private company[18].

1 Ie by the Companies Act 1985 s 148: see para 367 post.
2 For the meaning of 'public company' see para 82 ante.
3 See para 522 et seq post.
4 See para 520 post.
5 Ie otherwise than by any of the methods mentioned in the Companies Act 1985 s 143(3)(a)–(d): see para 362 heads (1)–(4) ante.

6 For these purposes, ibid Sch 2 (as amended) (see para 364 ante) has effect for the interpretation of references to a company having, or not having, a beneficial interest in shares: s 146(1).

7 Ibid s 146(1).

8 For these purposes, 'the relevant period' is (1) three years in the case of shares forfeited or surrendered to the company in lieu of forfeiture or acquired as mentioned in ibid s 146(1)(b) or (c) (see text heads (2), (3) supra); (2) one year in the case of shares acquired as mentioned in s 146(1)(d) (see text head (4) supra): s 146(3).

9 As to the re-registration of a public company as a private company see para 129 et seq ante. For the meaning of 'authorised minimum' see para 652 note 6 post.

10 Companies Act 1985 s 146(2). As to sanctions for non-compliance see para 368 post. The application for re-registration must be in the prescribed form, must be signed by a director or secretary of the company, and must be delivered to the registrar of companies together with a printed copy of the memorandum and articles of the company as altered by the resolution: s 147(3). For the prescribed form of application see the Companies (Forms) Regulations 1985, SI 1985/854, reg 4(1), Sch 3, Form 147.

11 Companies Act 1985 s 146(4).

12 Ie under ibid s 146(2): see supra.

13 Ie under ibid s 135 (special resolution) and s 136 (confirmation by the court) (see para 252 et seq ante).

14 Ibid s 147(1).

15 Such a resolution is subject to the provisions of ibid s 380 (as amended) (see para 691 post), so that a copy must be forwarded to the registrar within 15 days: s 147(2).

16 Ibid s 147(2).

17 Ie those contained in ibid ss 146–148.

18 Ibid s 147(4).

367. Supplementary provisions. Where, after shares in a private company[1]:

(1) are forfeited in pursuance of the company's articles or are surrendered to the company in lieu of forfeiture[2]; or

(2) are acquired by the company otherwise than by such surrender or forfeiture, and otherwise than in relation to[3]:

   (a) the redemption or purchase of shares in accordance with the provisions of the Companies Act 1985;

   (b) the acquisition of shares in a reduction of capital duly made; or

   (c) the purchase of shares in pursuance of an order of the court pursuant to proceedings objecting to a proposed alteration of the company's objects, or to a proposed resolution for the company to be re-registered as private, or seeking relief on the grounds of unfair prejudice to members,

the company having a beneficial interest[4] in the shares; or

(3) are acquired by a nominee of the company from a third person without financial assistance being given directly or indirectly by the company[5], the company having a beneficial interest in the shares; or

(4) are acquired by any person with financial assistance given to him directly or indirectly by the company for the purpose of or in connection with the acquisition[6], the company having a beneficial interest in the shares,

the company is re-registered as a public company[7], the relevant statutory provisions[8] apply to the company as if it had been a public company at the time of the forfeiture, surrender or acquisition, but with the modification that any reference to the relevant period from the forfeiture, surrender or acquisition is to be treated as referring to the relevant period[9] from the re-registration of the company as a public company[10].

Where a public company or a nominee of a public company acquires shares in the company or an interest in such shares, and those shares are (or that interest is) shown in a balance sheet of the company as an asset, an amount equal to the value of the shares or (as the case may be) the value to the company of its interest in them must be transferred out of profits available for dividend to a reserve fund and is not then available for distribution[11].

1 For the meaning of 'private company' see para 82 ante.
2 See paras 520, 522 et seq post.
3 Ie otherwise than by any of the methods mentioned in the Companies Act 1985 s 143(3): see para 362 ante.
4 For these purposes, ibid Sch 2 (as amended) (see para 364 ante) has effect for the interpretation of references to a company having, or not having, a beneficial interest in shares: s 148(3).
5 Ie in the circumstances mentioned in ibid s 146(1)(c): see para 366 head (3) ante.
6 Ie in the circumstances mentioned in ibid s 146(1)(d): see para 366 head (4) ante.
7 As to the re-registration of a private company as a public company see para 118 et seq ante.
8 Ie those contained in the Companies Act 1985 ss 146, 147, 149: see para 366 ante and para 368 post.
9 For the meaning of 'the relevant period' see para 366 note 8 ante.
10 Companies Act 1985 s 148(1), (2).
11 Ibid s 148(4).

368. Sanctions for non-compliance. If a public company[1] required[2] to apply to be re-registered as a private company fails to do so before the end of the relevant period[3], the statutory restriction on public offers[4] applies to it as if it were a private company[5]; but, subject to this, the company continues to be treated for the purpose of the Companies Act 1985 as a public company until it is so re-registered[6]. If a company, when required to do so[7], fails to cancel any shares[8] or to make an application for re-registration, the company, and every officer of it who is in default, is liable on summary conviction to a fine not exceeding one-fifth of the statutory maximum and, on conviction after continued contravention, to a daily default fine not exceeding one-fiftieth of the statutory maximum[9].

1 For the meaning of 'public company' see para 82 ante.
2 Ie by the Companies Act 1985 s 146(2): see para 366 ante.
3 For the meaning of 'the relevant period' see para 366 note 8 ante.
4 Ie under the Companies Act 1985 s 81: see para 449 post.
5 Ie such as is mentioned in ibid s 146(2).
6 Ibid s 149(1).
7 Ie by ibid s 146(2), including s 146(2) as applied by s 148(1) (see para 367 ante).
8 As to the cancellation of shares generally see para 218 ante.
9 Companies Act 1985 ss 149(2), 730, Sch 24. For the meaning of 'officer who is in default', 'the statutory maximum' and 'daily default fine' see para 1161 post.

(ii) Agreement to become a Member

369. Requirement of an agreement. Except in the case of the subscribers to the memorandum of association[1], the Companies Act 1985 requires an agreement to become a member[2] and entry in the register of members in order to constitute membership[3]. No particular form of agreement is required[4] and it may be express or implied, written or oral[5].

By agreement is meant that a person assents to become a member and it does not require that there should be a binding contract between the person and the company[6]. Accordingly, where the name of a person is entered on the register of members with his consent, he is a member of the company, subject to the power vested in the court to rectify the register in cases of error[7].

1 See paras 359, 360 ante.
2 Any contract, so far as it relates to the constitution of a company or the rights or obligations of its
   corporators or members, is exempt from 'the prohibitions on exclusion of liability imposed by the
   Unfair Contract Terms Act 1977: see s 1(2), Sch 1 para 1(d) and CONTRACT. Similarly, the Unfair
   Terms in Consumer Contracts Regulations 1994, SI 1994/3159, do not apply to any contract relating
   to the incorporation or organisation of companies or partnerships: see reg 3(1), Sch 1 para (d) and
   CONTRACT.
        For cases where it was held that there was no agreement to become a member of a company limited
   by guarantee see *Re Premier Underwriting Association Ltd (No 2), Cory's Case* [1913] 2 Ch 81; *W R Corfield
   & Co v Buchanan* (1913) 29 TLR 258, HL.
3 See the Companies Act 1985 s 22(2) and para 358 ante. As to share warrant bearers being deemed
   members by provisions in the articles see para 494 post; and as to entries in the register of members in
   case of share warrants see para 384 post.
4 *Ritso's Case* (1877) 4 ChD 774, CA.
5 *Re New Theatre Co Ltd, Bloxam's Case* (1864) 33 LJ Ch 574, which shows that contracts to take shares
   were not within the Statute of Frauds (1677) s 17 (repealed).
6 *Re Nuneaton Borough Association Football Club Ltd* [1989] BCLC 454 at 456, 459, CA. See also *Re Railway
   Time Tables Publishing Co, ex p Sandys* (1889) 42 ChD 98, CA.
7 See the cases cited in note 6 supra. As to the power to rectify the register in cases of error see para 392 et
   seq post. See *POW Services Ltd v Clare* [1995] 2 BCLC 435 (entry of individuals with their consent on
   register of company limited by guarantee did not confer membership when this was in breach of an
   express provision on membership in the articles).

370. Express contract. While there is no requirement that there should be a
binding contract between a person and the company in order for a person to agree to
become a member[1], in most instances there will be a contractual relationship[2] governed by the ordinary law of contract.

To constitute an express agreement to take shares, there must be an absolute and
unqualified acceptance of a proposal to take or allot them and a communication of the
acceptance to the proposer; but, in the case of a qualified acceptance, there is a contract
if the qualification is agreed to, or if the applicant pays for the shares within the
specified time[3]. Where an application for shares is subject to a condition precedent, the
condition must be performed to create a liability to take them[4]. Where, however, the
application is subject to a condition subsequent, the liability arises although the
condition is never complied with[5]. An application for shares, being a mere offer, may
be withdrawn before it is accepted[6].

1 See para 369 text to notes 6, 7 ante.
2 It may be a contract between the shareholder and the company or one between the shareholder and the
   transferor of shares to him. In *Re Nuneaton Borough Association Football Club Ltd* [1989] BCLC 454, CA
   (see para 369 text to note 6 ante) there would have been a contract had there been a properly constituted
   board of directors of the company.
3 *Re Adelphi Hotel Co Ltd, Best's Case* (1865) 2 De GJ & Sm 650; *Addinell's Case* (1865) LR 1 Eq 225;
   Jackson v Turquand (1869) LR 4 HL 305; *Oriental Steam Navigation Co, ex p Briggs* (1861) 4 De GF & J 191;
   Pentelow's Case (1869) 4 Ch App 178; *Ex p Capper* (1850) 1 Sim NS 178; *Gustard's Case* (1869) LR 8 Eq
   438; *Beck's Case* (1874) 9 Ch App 392; *Re Leeds Banking Co, ex p Barrett* (1865) 2 Drew & Sm 415; and see
   paras 442–444 post.
4 *Roger's Case, Harrison's Case* (1868) 3 Ch App 633; cf *Wood's Case* (1873) LR 15 Eq 236; *Re London and
   Provincial Provident Association Ltd, Re Mogridge* (1888) 57 LJ Ch 932; *Simpson's Case* (1869) 4 Ch App
   184; *Gorrissen's Case* (1873) 8 Ch App 507; *Humphrey and Denman Ltd v Kavanagh* (1925) 41 TLR 378,
   CA.
5 *Elkington's Case* (1867) 2 Ch App 511; *Re Matlock Old Bath Hydropathic Co Ltd, Wheatcroft's Case* (1873)
   42 LJ Ch 853; *Bridger's Case* (1870) 5 Ch App 305; *Black & Co's Case* (1872) 8 Ch App 254; *Gore and
   Durant's Case* (1866) LR 2 Eq 349; *Re Alexandra Park Co, Sharon's Claim* (1866) 12 Jur NS 482; *Re Life
   Association of England, Thomson's Case* (1865) 4 De GJ & Sm 749; *Re Southport and West Lancashire
   Banking Co, Fisher's Case, Sherrington's Case* (1885) 31 ChD 120, CA; *Mare, Holmwood & Co v
   Anglo-Indian SS Co Ltd* (1886) 3 TLR 142, CA.

6 *Ramsgate Victoria Co v Montefiore, Ramsgate Victoria Hotel Co v Goldsmid* (1866) LR 1 Exch 109; *Re Bowron, Baily & Co, ex p Baily* (1868) 3 Ch App 592. See further CONTRACT vol 9 para 239. As to acceptance by allotment see para 442 post.

371. Implied contract. An agreement to take shares may be implied from conduct[1]. Although a person's name is entered in the register as the holder of shares allotted to him, no agreement will be implied, by reason only of his receiving notice of the allotment, if he forthwith repudiates them[2], or if he has not acted as the holder of the shares or otherwise accepted them[3]. In such a case, even when a winding up has supervened, he may have his name removed from the register in respect of the shares[4].

Where the articles of association of a company require a director to have a share qualification[5], the fact of a person becoming a director does not in itself constitute an agreement to take the required qualification shares from the company[6]. The memorandum and articles may, however, constitute a contract to take shares, as where they require every original holder of a founders' share to apply for and take a specified number of ordinary shares[7]. A statement in a prospectus that the directors will take all the ordinary shares not taken by the vendors does not constitute a contract by them to take such shares[8].

A person may be estopped by his conduct from denying that he agreed to accept shares, as, for example, where, being the registered holder of shares forming part of an irregular or invalid issue of capital, he deals with them as his own, by paying calls or receiving dividends, or by attempting to transfer them[9], or where he has held himself out as having in fact subscribed[10].

1 See para 442 et seq post.
2 *Austin's Case* (1866) LR 2 Eq 435; *Re Imperial Land Credit Corpn Ltd, ex p Eve* (1868) 37 LJ Ch 844. As to the necessity of assent on the part of the member see *Re Nuneaton Borough Association Football Club Ltd* [1989] BCLC 454 at 456, 459, CA and para 369 ante.
3 *Chapman and Barker's Case* (1867) LR 3 Eq 361 at 365; *Oakes v Turquand and Harding* (1867) LR 2 HL 325 at 350, 351; *Re Empire Assurance Corpn, Challis's Case, Somerville's Case* (1871) 6 Ch App 266; *Wynne's Case* (1873) 8 Ch App 1002; *Baillie's Case* [1898] 1 Ch 110.
4 *Arnot's Case* (1887) 36 ChD 702, CA.
5 See para 544 post.
6 *Brown's Case* (1873) 9 Ch App 102; and see para 557 post.
7 *General Phosphate Corpn v Horrocks* (1892) 8 TLR 350.
8 *Re Moore Bros & Co Ltd* [1899] 1 Ch 627, CA; *Todd v Millen* 1910 SC 868.
9 *Re Bank of Hindustan, China and Japan, Campbell's Case, Hippisley's Case* (1873) 9 Ch App 1 at 15.
10 *New Brunswick and Canada Rly and Land Co Ltd v Boore* (1858) 3 H & N 249; *Re Oola Lead and Copper Mining Co, Palmer's Case* (1868) 2 IR Eq 573; and see *Re Llanharry Hematite Iron Ore Co Ltd, Roney's Case* (1864) 33 LJ Ch 731; *Tothill's Case* (1865) 1 Ch App 85; *Re Patent File Co Ltd, ex p White* (1867) 16 LT 276.

372. Agent's contract. A person who agrees, on behalf of another, to take shares, without disclosing the agency, is personally liable to take them[1]. Where he purports to agree to take shares on behalf of another, but is without authority[2], he is liable, unless the other person ratifies the act[3], to pay damages for breach of warranty of authority, the measure of damages being the amount which the company has lost by losing the contract to take shares[4].

A person purporting to contract to take shares on behalf of a fictitious or non-existent person is himself bound to take them[5].

If an application is made for shares on behalf of a person who is ignorant of the matter, and he is registered as the holder, and the directors know that the person applying does not intend to take the shares himself, neither the person registered nor the applicant is liable as a shareholder; but the applicant is liable to those who are deceived for breach of an implied warranty of authority[6].

1   *Re Southampton, Isle of Wight and Portsmouth Improved Steam Boat Co Ltd, Bird's Case* (1864) 4 De GJ & Sm 200.
2   A person applying for shares in the name of a minor is himself liable: *Richardson's Case* (1875) LR 19 Eq 588; *Re North of England Joint Stock Banking Co, ex p Reavely* (1849) 1 H & Tw 118; *Re Electric Telegraph Co of Ireland, Maxwell's Case* (1857) 24 Beav 321.
3   *Levita's Case* (1870) 5 Ch App 489.
4   *Re National Coffee Palace Co, ex p Panmure* (1883) 24 ChD 367, CA (where, the alleged applicant being solvent, and the shares having become unsaleable, the loss was equivalent to the nominal value of the shares). As to the liabilities of agents on breach of warranty of authority see generally AGENCY vol 1(2) (Reissue) para 172.
5   *Re Wheal Emily Mining Co, Cox's Case* (1863) 4 De GJ & Sm 53; *Pugh and Sharman's Case* (1872) LR 13 Eq 566; *Savigny's Case* (1898) 5 Mans 336.
6   *Coventry's Case* [1891] 1 Ch 202 at 203, 211, CA; *Collen v Wright* (1857) 8 E & B 647; cf *Re London, Bombay, and Mediterranean Bank* (1881) 18 ChD 581.

373. Company taking shares. A contract by a company to take shares in another company is binding[1] even if the former company lacks the capacity to purchase such shares[2].

1   Ie provided that it is not a subsidiary of the latter: see the Companies Act 1985 s 23 (as substituted) and para 362 ante.
2   This is the effect of ibid s 35(1) (as substituted): see para 1107 post. As to a company's capacity and the effect of s 35 (as substituted) generally see para 1107 post.

374. Minors. A minor[1] may repudiate his membership and his holding in the company, either during his minority or upon attaining full age, because his agreement to take shares is voidable[2]; but he cannot recover money paid by him for shares unless there has been a total failure of consideration[3]. If, however, he does not repudiate[4] within a reasonable time after attaining full age, he will thenceforth be subject to all the liabilities of membership[5].

Where shares are transferred into the name of a minor, the transferor remains liable for calls in respect of the shares[6], whether at the time of the transfer he was aware that the transferee was a minor or not[7]; but, if he was ignorant of that fact, he may claim to have his liability transferred to the person who effected the transaction[8]. If, however, a company or the liquidator of a company, knowing the transferee to be a minor, is guilty of laches in making a claim against the transferor, the transferor is relieved from his liability[9]. He is also relieved by a subsequent transfer by the minor to an adult[10].

1   As to the attainment of majority at the age of 18 see the Family Law Reform Act 1969 s 1 and CHILDREN vol 5(2) (Reissue) para 601.
2   *Newry and Enniskillen Rly Co v Coombe* (1849) 3 Exch 565; *North Western Rly Co v M'Michael, Birkenhead, Lancashire and Cheshire Junction Rly Co v Pilcher* (1850) 5 Exch 114; *Re Alexandra Park Co, Hart's Case* (1868) LR 6 Eq 512; *Re Financial Corpn, Sassoon's Case* (1869) 20 LT 161 (affd 20 LT 424); *Hamilton v Vaughan-Sherrin Electrical Engineering Co* [1894] 3 Ch 589; Minors' Contracts Act 1987; and see CHILDREN vol 5(2) (Reissue) paras 612, 693. As to subscription of the memorandum of association by a minor see para 83 ante.
3   *Steinberg v Scala (Leeds) Ltd* [1923] 2 Ch 452, CA. If and in so far as *Hamilton v Vaughan-Sherrin Electrical Engineering Co* [1894] 3 Ch 589 decides the contrary, it must be treated as having been overruled: *Steinberg v Scala (Leeds) Ltd* supra at 457, 461, 462, 465.
4   As to confirmation see *Baker's Case* (1871) 7 Ch App 115; *Wilson's Case* (1869) LR 8 Eq 240; *Castello's Case* (1869) LR 8 Eq 504; *Mitchell's Case* (1870) LR 9 Eq 363; *Symons' Case* (1870) 5 Ch App 298; *Re Ottoman Financial Association, Cheetham's Case* [1869] WN 201; Minors' Contracts Act 1987.

5 *Cork and Bandon Rly Co v Cazenove* (1847) 10 QB 935; *Leeds and Thirsk Rly Co v Fearnley* (1849) 4 Exch
   26; *North Western Rly Co v M'Michael, Birkenhead, Lancashire and Cheshire Junction Rly Co v Pilcher* (1850)
   5 Exch 114; *Dublin and Wicklow Rly Co v Black* (1852) 8 Exch 181; *Lumsden's Case* (1868) 4 Ch App 31;
   Mitchell's Case (1870) LR 9 Eq 363; *Ebbetts' Case* (1870) 5 Ch App 302; *Re Yeoland Consols Ltd (No 2)*
   (1888) 58 LT 922. A director knowingly allotting shares to a minor is liable to the company for any loss
   thereby occasioned: *Re Crenver and Wheal Abraham United Mining Co, ex p Wilson* (1872) 8 Ch App 45.
6 *Re St George's Steam Packet Co, Litchfield's Case* (1850) 3 De G & Sm 141; *Re Electric Telegraph Co of
   Ireland, Reid's Case* (1857) 24 Beav 318; *Curtis's Case* (1868) LR 6 Eq 455; *Castello's Case* (1869) LR 8 Eq
   504; *Re Imperial Mercantile Credit Association, Edwards' Case* [1869] WN 211; *Weston's Case* (1870) 5 Ch
   App 614; *Re Crenver and Wheal Abraham United Mining Co, ex p Wilson* (1872) 8 Ch App 45. As to
   transfer of shares by a minor see para 504 post.
7 *Re Joint Stock Discount Co, Mann's Case* (1867) 3 Ch App 459n; *Capper's Case* (1868) 3 Ch App 458.
8 *Nickalls v Furneaux* [1869] WN 118; *Re National Provincial Marine Insurance Co, Maitland's Case* (1869) 38
   LJ Ch 554; *Brown v Black* (1873) 8 Ch App 939; *Richardson's Case* (1875) LR 19 Eq 588; *Watson v Miller*
   [1876] WN 18.
9 *Capper's Case* (1868) 3 Ch App 458 at 461 per Page Wood LJ; *Parson's Case* (1869) LR 8 Eq 656; *Re
   National Bank of Wales Ltd, Massey and Giffin's Case* [1907] 1 Ch 582.
10 *Gooch's Case* (1872) 8 Ch App 266.

375. Married women. The contractual liability of a married woman is the same as
the contractual liability of a single woman[1].

1 Law Reform (Married Women and Tortfeasors) Act 1935 s 1.

376. Enforcement of contract. Specific performance of an agreement to take and
pay for shares[1] or to allot shares[2] may be obtained[3].

In addition to obtaining a decree for the specific performance of a contract to allot
shares the disappointed allottee may obtain damages equal to the dividends at the rates
declared by the company between the date when the shares should have been allotted
and the date of actual allotment, together with interest on the dividends until
payment[4].

When a contract to take shares is disclaimed by a trustee in bankruptcy, the contract
is at an end and the company's remedy is a claim for damages against the bankrupt's
estate[5].

An agreement with a company to take shares proposed to be issued at a discount
cannot be enforced and an allottee of shares pursuant to such an agreement may have
the register rectified. He may, however, lose his remedy if he has assented to the
registration or has not sought the remedy promptly[6].

1 *Odessa Tramways Co v Mendel* (1878) 8 ChD 235, CA; and see *New Brunswick and Canada Rly and Land
   Co v Muggeridge* (1859) 4 Drew 686; *Oriental Inland Steam Co v Briggs* (1861) 2 John & H 625 (on appeal
   sub nom *Oriental Steam Navigation Co, ex p Briggs* (1861) 4 De GF & J 191); and see SPECIFIC
   PERFORMANCE vol 44(1) (Reissue) para 825 et seq.
2 *Sri Lanka Omnibus Co Ltd v Perera* [1952] AC 76, PC.
3 A distinction must, however, be drawn between cases where shares are readily available in the market
   (*Re Schwabacher* (1908) 98 LT 127) and where they are not (*Jobson v Johnson* [1989] 1 All ER 621, [1989] 1
   WLR 1026, CA; *Harvela Investments Ltd v Royal Trust Co of Canada (CI) Ltd* [1986] AC 207, [1985] 2 All
   ER 966, HL); and see SPECIFIC PERFORMANCE vol 44(1) (Reissue) para 825 et seq.
4 *Sri Lanka Omnibus Co Ltd v Perera* [1952] AC 76, PC.
5 *Re Hooley, ex p United Ordnance and Engineering Co Ltd* [1899] 2 QB 579. As to disclaimer generally see
   BANKRUPTCY vol 3(2) (Reissue) para 460 et seq.
6 See *Re Railway Time Tables Publishing Co, ex p Sandys* (1889) 42 ChD 98, CA; *Re Nuneaton Borough
   Association Football Club Ltd* [1989] BCLC 454, CA.

377. Option to take shares. A company may agree, for value, to give an option to
any one to take all or any of its shares[1]. If it does so, then whether the terms of the

option are to be varied in the event of a reconstruction of the company's capital depends solely upon the provisions of the option agreement itself[2]. The exercised after the commencement of winding up, in which case the liquidator may issue the shares and receive the money payable in respect of them, and place the name of the person exercising the option on the register of members and the list of contributories[3]. If the liquidator refuses to issue the shares, the measure of damages is the excess, if any, of the amount which the person would have received as his share of the assets as the holder of fully paid shares over the amount which he was to pay for them[4].

1 Full details of the contents of any outstanding option must be included in the company's balance sheet or documents circulated with it: see the Companies Act 1985 s 226(3), Sch 4 Pt III para 40 and para 841 post. As to share option schemes see para 1517 et seq post.
2 *Forsayth Oil and Gas NL v Livia Pty Ltd* [1985] BCLC 378, PC.
3 *Hirsch & Co v Burns* (1897) 77 LT 377, HL. As to granting an option to take further shares in the future at par in consideration for subscribing and procuring subscriptions for shares see para 195 ante.
4 *Hirsch & Co v Burns* (1897) 77 LT 377, HL.

(iii) Register of Members

A. CONTENTS

378. Maintenance of register. Every company must maintain a register of its members[1], which may be done either by making entries in bound books, or by recording the relevant particulars in any other manner[2]. Where, however, that register is not kept by making entries in a bound book, but by some other means, adequate precautions must be taken against falsification and for facilitating discovery[3]. If default is made in taking those precautions, the company, and every officer of it who is in default, is liable on summary conviction to a fine not exceeding one-fifth of the statutory maximum and, on conviction after continued contravention, to a daily default fine not exceeding one-fiftieth of the statutory maximum[4].

1 Companies Act 1985 s 352(1).
2 Ibid s 722(1). This provision was introduced in 1948. It has been held under previous Acts that rough memoranda on sheets of paper intended as materials from which a register might be prepared are not a register (*Re Printing, Telegraph and Construction Co of Agence Havas, ex p Cammell* [1894] 2 Ch 392, CA), and this is presumably still good law in spite of the relaxations as to the form of the register noted supra. This provision applies to all registers under the Companies Act 1985: see s 722(1). As to the provisions applicable to a register maintained otherwise than by recording the entries in a legible form see para 656 post.
3 Ibid s 722(2).
4 Ibid ss 722(3), 730, Sch 24. For the meaning of 'officer who is in default', 'the statutory maximum' and 'daily default fine' see para 1161 post.

379. Entries to be made in register. The company must enter in the register of members the following particulars:
(1) the names and addresses of members;
(2) the date on which each person was registered as a member; and
(3) the date at which any person ceased to be a member[1].
A company which has issued securities, title to which is permitted to be transferred by means of a relevant system, that is to say a computer-based system and procedures which enable title to units of a security to be evidenced and transferred without a written instrument, must enter on its register of members (not including an overseas

branch register), in respect of any class of shares which is a participating security, how many shares each member holds in uncertificated form and certificated form respectively[2].

In the case of a company having a share capital:

(a) with the names and addresses of the members there must be entered a statement of the shares held by each member, distinguishing each share by its number (so long as the share has a number[3]), and, where the company has more than one class of issued shares, by its class, and of the amount paid or agreed to be considered as paid on the shares of each member;

(b) where the company has converted any of its shares into stock and given notice of the conversion to the registrar of companies, the register must show the amount and class of stock held by each member, instead of the amount of shares and the particulars relating to shares specified in head (a) above[4].

The subscribers of the memorandum, as well as other persons agreeing to become members, must be entered in the register[5].

In the case of a company which does not have a share capital, but has more than one class of members, there must be entered in the register, with the names and addresses of the members, the class to which each member belongs[6].

If a company makes default in complying with the above provisions, the company, and every officer of it who is in default, is liable on summary conviction to a fine not exceeding one-fifth of the statutory maximum and, on conviction after continued contravention, to a daily default fine not exceeding one-fiftieth of the statutory maximum[7].

An entry relating to a former member of the company may be removed from the register after the expiration of 20 years from the date on which he ceased to be a member[8].

Liability incurred by a company from the making or deletion of an entry in its register of members, or from a failure to make or delete any such entry, is not enforceable more than 20 years after the date on which the entry was made or deleted or, in the case of any such failure, the failure first occurred[9].

The company must not enter in the register a statement that it has a lien on the shares of a member[10], and cannot insist on putting on the register anything except what is required by statute to be inserted in it[11].

1 Companies Act 1985 s 352(1), (2). As to the entries required where a private company has only one member see para 380 post.

2 See the Uncertificated Securities Regulations 1995, SI 1995/3272, regs 2(1), 3(1), 19(1), (6) and MONEY.

3 See para 438 post.

4 Companies Act 1985 s 352(1), (3).

5 See ibid s 22(1) and paras 358, 359 ante.

6 Ibid s 352(4), nullifying the decision in *Re Performing Rights Society Ltd, Lyttleton v Performing Rights Society Ltd* [1978] 3 All ER 972, [1978] 1 WLR 1197, CA.

7 Companies Act 1985 ss 352(5), 730, Sch 24; Uncertificated Securities Regulations 1995 reg 19(4). In reg 19(4) an officer of a participating issuer is in default in complying with the provision mentioned in reg 19(4) if, and only if, he knowingly and wilfully authorised or permitted the default: see reg 38 and MONEY. For the meaning of 'officer who is in default', 'the statutory maximum' and 'daily default fine' see para 1161 post. As to the provisions applicable to a register maintained otherwise than by recording the entries in legible form see para 656 post.

8 Companies Act 1985 s 352(6).

9 Ibid s 352(7). This is without prejudice to any lesser period of limitation: s 352(7); Uncertificated Securities Regulations 1995 reg 19(5).

10 *Re W Key & Son Ltd* [1902] 1 Ch 467.

11 *Re T H Saunders & Co Ltd* [1908] 1 Ch 415.

380. Statement that private company has only one member. If the number of members of a private company[1] limited by shares or by guarantee falls to one, there must, upon the occurrence of that event, be entered in the company's register of members[2] with the name and address of the sole member:

(1) a statement that the company has only one member; and

(2) the date on which the company became a company having only one member[3].

If the membership of a private company limited by shares or by guarantee increases from one to two or more members, there must, upon the occurrence of that event, be entered in the company's register of members, with the name and address of the person who was formerly the sole member, a statement that the company has ceased to have only one member together with the date on which that event occurred[4].

If a company makes default in complying with the above provisions, the company, and every officer of it who is in default, is liable on summary conviction to a fine not exceeding level 2 on the standard scale and, on conviction after continued contravention, to a daily default fine not exceeding one-tenth of level 2 on the standard scale[5].

1 For the meaning of 'private company' see para 82 ante.
2 As to the register of members see paras 378, 379 ante.
3 Companies Act 1985 s 352A(1) (added by the Companies (Single Member Private Limited Companies) Regulations 1992, SI 1992/1699, reg 2(1)(b), Schedule para 4(1)). As to single member private limited companies see para 81 ante.
4 Companies Act 1985 s 352A(2) (added by the Companies (Single Member Private Limited Companies) Regulations 1992 Schedule para 4(1)).
5 Companies Act 1985 s 352A(3) (added by the Companies (Single Member Private Limited Companies) Regulations 1992 Schedule para 4(1)); Companies Act 1985 s 730, Sch 24 (amended by the Companies (Single Member Private Limited Companies) Regulations 1992 Schedule para 4(2)). For the meaning of 'officer who is in default' and 'daily default fine' see para 1161 post; and for the meaning of 'the standard scale' see CRIMINAL LAW vol 11(2) (Reissue) para 808.

381. Index of names of members. Every company having more than 50 members must keep an index of the names of the members of the company, unless the register of members is in such a form as to constitute in itself an index, and must, within 14 days after the date on which any alteration is made in the register of members, make any necessary alteration in the index[1]. The index must contain in respect of each member a sufficient indication to enable the account of that member in the register to be readily found[2]; and it must at all times be kept at the same place as the register of members[3].

If default is made in complying with the above provisions, the company, and every officer of it who is in default, and, where the index is kept at the office of some person other than the company, that person, if himself in default, is liable on summary conviction to a fine not exceeding one-fifth of the statutory maximum and, on conviction after continued contravention, to a daily default fine not exceeding one-fiftieth of the statutory maximum[4].

The index must be kept either by making entries in bound books, or by recording the relevant particulars in any other manner[5]. Where, however, that index is not kept by making entries in a bound book, but by some other means, adequate precautions must be taken against falsification and for facilitating discovery[6]. If default is made in taking those precautions, the company, and every officer of it who is in default, is liable on summary conviction to a fine not exceeding one-fifth of the statutory maximum and, on conviction after continued contravention, to a daily default fine not exceeding one-fiftieth of the statutory maximum[7].

1 Companies Act 1985 s 354(1).
2 Ibid s 354(2).
3 Ibid s 354(3). As to the location of the register see para 389 post.
4 Ibid ss 354(4), 357, 730, Sch 24. For the meaning of 'officer who is in default', 'the statutory maximum' and 'daily default fine' see para 1161 post.
5 Ibid s 722(1). See also para 378 note 2 ante. This provision applies to all indexes under the Companies Act 1985: see s 722(1). As to the provisions applicable to an index maintained otherwise than by recording the entries in legible form see para 656 post.
6 Ibid s 722(2).
7 Ibid ss 722(3), 730, Sch 24.

382. How far entry necessary for membership. In order to constitute membership, entry on the register is necessary[1], except in the case of signatories or persons deemed to be signatories to the memorandum of association[2].

1 *Nicol's Case, Tufnell and Ponsonby's Case* (1885) 29 ChD 421, CA; *Re Macdonald, Sons & Co* [1894] 1 Ch 89, CA.
2 See para 359 ante.

383. Entry in case of firms and joint holders. Where the name of a firm is entered in the register as the holder of shares, the members of the firm are jointly liable for the shares[1]. A firm is not entitled to be registered in the name of the firm, but only in the names of its partners[2]. Where two or more persons hold a share or shares jointly, they may insist on having their names registered in such order as they choose, or to have their holding split into several joint holdings with their names in different orders[3].

1 *Weikersheim's Case* (1873) 8 Ch App 831; and see *Dunster's Case* [1894] 3 Ch 473, CA.
2 *Re Vagliano Anthracite Collieries Ltd* (1910) 79 LJ Ch 769.
3 *Re T H Saunders & Co Ltd* [1908] 1 Ch 415; *Burns v Siemens Bros Dynamo Works Ltd* [1919] 1 Ch 225.

384. Where there are share warrants. On the issue of a share warrant[1] the company must strike out of its register of members the name of the member then entered in it as holding the shares specified in the warrant as if he had ceased to be a member, and must enter in the register the following particulars:
(1) the fact of the issue of the warrant;
(2) a statement of the shares included in the warrant, distinguishing each share by its number so long as it has a number[2]; and
(3) the date of the issue of the warrant[3].
The bearer of a share warrant is, subject to the company's articles of association, entitled, on surrendering it for cancellation, to have his name entered as a member in the register of members[4]; and the company is responsible for any loss incurred by any person by reason of the company entering in the register the name of a bearer of a share warrant in respect of the shares specified in it without the warrant being surrendered and cancelled[5]. Until the warrant is surrendered, the above particulars[6] are deemed to be the particulars required by the Companies Act 1985 to be entered in the register of members; and, on the surrender, the date of the surrender must be entered in the register[7].
Except for the purpose of qualifying a director who requires share qualification[8], the bearer of a share warrant may, if the articles of the company so provide, be deemed a member of the company within the meaning of the Companies Act 1985, either to the full extent or for any purposes defined in the articles[9].

1 As to share warrants see para 493 post.
2 See para 438 post.
3 Companies Act 1985 s 355(1).
4 Ibid s 355(2). As to articles providing that share warrant bearers be deemed members see para 494 post.
5 Ibid s 355(3).
6 Ie the particulars specified in ibid s 355(1): see supra.
7 Ibid s 355(4).
8 Ie as provided by ibid s 291(2): see para 556 post.
9 Ibid s 355(5).

385. Trusts and equitable interests. No notice of any trust, expressed, implied or constructive, is to be entered on the register, or to be receivable by the registrar in the case of companies registered in England and Wales[1].

The entry of the Public Trustee by that name in the books of a company does not constitute notice of a trust, and a company is not entitled to object to enter the name of the Public Trustee on its books by reason only that the Public Trustee is a corporation, and in dealings with property the fact that the person or one of the persons dealt with is the Public Trustee does not of itself constitute notice of a trust[2].

Similarly, the company will not, by virtue of anything done for the purpose of keeping the register of directors' interests[3] or for complying with the provisions in relation thereto[4], be affected with notice of, or put upon inquiry as to, the rights of any person in relation to any shares or debentures[5].

Although a member, to the knowledge of the company, is merely a trustee (or legal mortgagee)[6] of shares registered in his name, he is liable to the company for calls and other obligations of membership[7], and this liability is not limited to the amount of the trust estate[8]. He is, however, entitled to be indemnified against all such liabilities by the beneficiary[9]; but he cannot maintain an action to enforce this right, unless the liability has been or is about to be enforced against him[10]. The right of indemnity may be assigned to the liquidator of the company, and enforced by him[11].

Where the articles of association supplement the statutory provision by expressly providing that the company is entitled to treat a shareholder as the absolute owner of his registered shares, and shall not be bound to recognise any equitable interest in shares, the company is not bound to accept or preserve notices of equitable interests, and such notices do not affect the company or its officers or agents with any trust[12]; but, where the company in which the shares are held claims to have a lien or charge on the shares for its own benefit, the company is liable to be affected with notice of the interests of third parties, and the provisions of the articles will not protect the company if, in the face of notice that the shareholder is not the beneficial owner of the shares, it makes advances or gives credit to the shareholder[13].

Notice to the company does not give any priority as between two persons claiming title to shares registered in the name of a third[14].

1 Companies Act 1985 s 360. See also the Companies (Tables A to F) Regulations 1985, SI 1985/805, Schedule, Table A art 5. As to Table A generally see para 529 et seq post. As to the position in Scotland see *Muir v City of Glasgow Bank* (1879) 4 App Cas 337 at 360, HL. As to executors see para 429 post.
2 Public Trustee Act 1906 s 11(5). See also TRUSTS vol 48 (Reissue) para 676.
3 Ie under the Companies Act 1985 s 325: see para 571 post.
4 Ie those contained in ibid s 325(1), Sch 13 (as amended).
5 See ibid Sch 13 para 24 and para 571 post.
6 *Royal Bank of India's Case* (1869) 4 Ch App 252; *Weikersheim's Case* (1873) 8 Ch App 831.
7 *Chapman and Barker's Case* (1867) LR 3 Eq 361; *Muir v City of Glasgow Bank* (1879) 4 App Cas 337, HL; cf *Re Moseley Green Coal and Coke Co Ltd, Barrett's Case* (1864) 4 De GJ & Sm 416; *Re Phoenix Life Assurance Co, Hoare's Case* (1862) 2 John & H 229; *Gray's Case* (1876) 1 ChD 664; *Re Electric Telegraph Co of Ireland, Bunn's Case* (1860) 2 De GF & J 275; *Re East of England Banking Co, ex p Bugg* (1865) 2

Drew & Sm 452. As to trust shares being sufficient to qualify a director see para 544 post; and as to lien on trust shares see para 431 post.

8 *Leifchild's Case* (1865) LR 1 Eq 231 at 235, 236; *Muir v City of Glasgow Bank* (1879) 4 App Cas 337, HL.

9 *Hardoon v Belilios* [1901] AC 118, PC; *Hemming v Maddick* (1872) 7 Ch App 395; *Hughes-Hallett v Indian Mammoth Gold Mines Co* (1882) 22 ChD 561; *Butler v Cumpston* (1868) LR 7 Eq 16; *James v May* (1873) LR 6 HL 328; *Cruse v Paine* (1869) 4 Ch App 441; *Chapman and Barker's Case* (1867) LR 3 Eq 361 (trusts for the company); and see *Re European Society Arbitration Acts, ex p Liquidators of the British Nation Life Assurance Association* (1878) 8 ChD 679 at 708, CA (enforcement against the beneficiary through and in name of trustee). A person holding shares as a trustee is accountable to the beneficiary: *Rooney v Stanton* (1900) 17 TLR 28, CA. As to his right of indemnity generally see TRUSTS vol 48 (Reissue) para 785.

10 *Hughes-Hallett v Indian Mammoth Gold Mines Co* (1882) 22 ChD 561; *Hobbs v Wayet* (1887) 36 ChD 256; and see *Re National Financial Co, ex p Oriental Commercial Bank* (1868) 3 Ch App 791.

11 *Hemming v Maddick* (1872) 7 Ch App 395; *Massey v Allen* (1878) 9 ChD 164; *Heritage v Paine* (1876) 2 ChD 594.

12 *Société Générale de Paris v Walker* (1885) 11 App Cas 20 at 30, HL; *Simpson v Molson's Bank* [1895] AC 270, PC. Probably, even where the articles contain no such provision (cf note 1 supra), the company is not bound to accept notices of equitable interests, but may treat a registered shareholder as the absolute owner of shares registered in his name. Such provisions do not operate to prevent an equitable owner of shares obtaining a court order to protect his equitable interests: *McGrattan v McGrattan* [1985] NI 28, CA.

13 *Rearden v Provincial Bank of Ireland* [1896] 1 IR 532; *Mackereth v Wigan Coal and Iron Co Ltd* [1916] 2 Ch 293; *Bradford Banking Co v Briggs, Son & Co Ltd* (1886) 12 App Cas 29, HL, applying the principle of *Hopkinson v Rolt* (1861) 9 HL Cas 514; and see *Bank of Africa v Salisbury Gold Mining Co* [1892] AC 281, PC. As to the equitable claims where shares have been transferred by an assignment for the benefit of creditors see *Peat v Clayton* [1906] 1 Ch 659.

14 *Roots v Williamson* (1888) 38 ChD 485; *Moore v North Western Bank* [1891] 2 Ch 599. The principle of *Dearle v Hall* (1828) 3 Russ 1 does not apply: *Société Générale de Paris v Walker* (1885) 11 App Cas 20 at 30, HL.

386. Stop notice and charging order. A person who has an equitable claim to shares may prevent his claim from being prejudiced by the registered holder dealing with them, by serving upon the company a stop notice[1], after which the company cannot permit the shares claimed to be dealt with by the registered holder, except after proper notice to the claimant[2].

A charging order cannot be made on shares for a debt due from the registered shareholder, if he is a trustee of the shares; for they are not stock (including shares, debentures and debenture stock) in which the judgment debtor has a beneficial interest[3].

A charging order may, however, be made in respect of a judgment debt due from a debtor who holds any beneficial interest in any shares, debentures or securities of any company incorporated in England and Wales, or incorporated outside England and Wales, or of any state or territory outside the United Kingdom if registered in a register kept at any place within England and Wales in relation to that interest[4].

1 See RSC Ord 50 rr 11–13 and EXECUTION vol 17 para 572.

2 *Société Générale de Paris v Tramways Union Co* (1884) 14 QBD 424 at 453, CA; affd sub nom *Société Générale de Paris v Walker* (1885) 11 App Cas 20, HL. As to equitable claims see further MORTGAGE vol 32 para 558; STOCK EXCHANGE.

3 See RSC Ord 50. The charge affects the beneficial interest: *Cragg v Taylor* (1867) LR 2 Exch 131; *South Western Loan Co v Robertson* (1881) 8 QBD 17; *Dixon v Wrench* (1869) LR 4 Exch 154; *Bolland v Young* [1904] 2 KB 824, CA; *Ideal Bedding Co Ltd v Holland* [1907] 2 Ch 157; *Hawks v McArthur* [1951] 1 All ER 22. As to charging orders on stocks and shares generally see EXECUTION vol 17 para 555 et seq.

4 Charging Orders Act 1979 ss 2(1)(a)(i), (2)(b)(ii), (iii), 6(1).

387. Exchange control restrictions. There are no exchange control restrictions affecting the register of members of a company[1].

1 The restrictions formerly contained in the Exchange Control Act 1947 s 13 were repealed by the Finance Act 1987 s 72(7), Sch 16 Pt XI.

388. Register as evidence. The register of members is prima facie evidence of any matters directed or authorised to be inserted in it by the Companies Act 1985[1] and in a winding up it is, as between the contributories of the company, prima facie evidence of the truth of all matters purporting to be recorded in it[2]. The register is not conclusive evidence, although the courts endeavour to make it as conclusive as they can consistently with the provisions of the Act[3].

Inaccuracies or omissions do not necessarily prevent the register from being evidence[4]. As, however, it is only prima facie evidence, a person whose name is registered, or omitted from the register, may adduce evidence to show that he ought not or ought to have been registered[5].

A book or document, intended to be a register of members[5], may be admitted in evidence as such, although the statutory requirements as to how it should be kept have not been regularly complied with[6].

1 Companies Act 1985 s 361. An entry on such a register as is mentioned in the Uncertificated Securities Regulations 1995, SI 1995/3272, reg 19(1) or (2) which records a person as holding units of a security in uncertificated form is evidence of such title to the units as would be evidenced if the entry on the register related to units of that security held in certificated form: reg 20(1). Regulation 20(1) is subject to reg 23(7): reg 20(1). See MONEY.

2 See the Insolvency Act 1986 s 191 and para 2834 post.

3 See *Reese River Silver Mining Co v Smith* (1869) LR 4 HL 64 at 80 per Lord Cairns; *Re Briton Medical and General Life Association* (1888) 39 ChD 61 at 71 per Stirling J.

4 *Wills v Murray* (1850) 4 Exch 843; *Bain v Whitehaven and Furness Junction Rly Co* (1850) 3 HL Cas 1; *Southampton Dock Co v Richards* (1840) 1 Man & G 448; *London and Brighton Rly Co v Fairclough* (1841) 2 Man & G 674.

5 *Carmarthen Rly Co v Wright* (1858) 1 F & F 282; *Portal v Emmens* (1876) 1 CPD 201 at 212 (affd (1876) 1 CPD 664, CA); *Hallmark's Case* (1878) 9 ChD 329, CA. As to rectification of the register see para 392 et seq post.

6 *Re Printing, Telegraph and Construction Co of the Agence Havas, ex p Cammell* [1894] 2 Ch 392, CA.

B. CUSTODY AND INSPECTION

389. Custody of register and index. A company's register of members must be kept at its registered office[1]. If, however, the work of making it up is done at another office of the company, it may be kept there; and, if the company arranges with some other person for the making up of the register to be undertaken on its behalf by that other, it may be kept at the office of the other at which the work is done[2]. In either case, if the company is registered in England and Wales, it must not be kept at any place elsewhere than in England and Wales, or, in the case of a company registered in Scotland, elsewhere than in Scotland[3]. Every company must send notice in the prescribed form[4] to the registrar of companies of the place where its register of members is kept, and of any change in that place[5]. If the company makes default for 14 days in so sending notice, the company, and every officer of it who is in default, and, where the register is kept at the office of some person other than the company, that person, if himself in default, is liable on summary conviction to a fine not exceeding one-fifth of the statutory maximum and, on conviction after continued contravention, to a daily default fine not exceeding one-fiftieth of the statutory maximum[6]. The notice need not be sent if the register has, at all times since it came into existence (or, in the case of a register in existence on 1 July 1948, at all times since then) been kept at the company's registered office[7].

The index of the names of members must at all times be kept at the same place as the register of members[8].

Neither the register nor the index may be dealt with by way of charge or otherwise in such a way as to interfere with the purposes for which they must be kept[9].

1 Companies Act 1985 s 353(1). As to the provisions applicable where the entries are recorded otherwise than in legible form see para 656 post.
2 Ibid s 353(1)(a), (b). Shares in a company are choses in action which are situate at the place where the existence of the choses in action is recorded. The situs of shares in a company is, therefore, at the registered office, or some other office, at which the register of members should be kept, which place must be within England and Wales or Scotland, as the case may be: *International Credit and Investment Co (Overseas) Ltd v Adham* [1994] 1 BCLC 66 at 72 per Harman J. See also para 94 text and note 11 ante.
3 Companies Act 1985 s 353(1).
4 For the prescribed form of notice see the Companies (Forms) (Amendment) Regulations 1995, SI 1995/736, reg 3, Sch 2, Form 353.
5 Companies Act 1985 s 353(2).
6 Ibid ss 353(4), 357, 730, Sch 24. For the meaning of 'officer who is in default', 'the statutory maximum' and 'daily default fine' see para 1161 post.
7 Ibid s 353(3).
8 Ibid s 354(3). As to the index of members see para 381 ante; and as to the penalty for non-compliance see para 381 ante.
9 *Re Capital Fire Insurance Association* (1883) 24 ChD 408 at 418, CA (where it was held that a solicitor had not acquired a lien as against the liquidator).

390. Inspection of register and index. On giving notice by advertisement in a newspaper circulating in the district in which its registered office is situated, a company may close the register of members for any time or times not exceeding in the whole 30 days in each calendar year[1].

Except when so closed, the register and the index of members' names must be open to the inspection of any member without charge, and of any other person on payment of such fee as may be prescribed[2]. The company[3] must make the register and index available for such inspection for not less than two hours during the period between 9 am and 5 pm on each business day[4]; and it must permit a person inspecting the register and index to copy any information made available for inspection by means of the taking of notes or the transcription of the information[5]. A company is not, however, obliged to present for inspection its register of members or an index of members' names in a manner which groups together entries by reference to whether a member has given an address in a particular geographical location, is of a particular nationality, has a holding of a certain size, is a natural person or not or is of a particular gender[6]. The right of inspection ceases when the company is being wound up[7]. The inspection may be made, under proper restrictions, by an agent of the member desiring inspection[8].

If an inspection so required is refused, the company, and every officer of it who is in default, and, where the register is kept at the office of some person other than the company, that person, if himself in default, is liable on summary conviction in respect of each offence to a fine not exceeding one-fifth of the statutory maximum[9]. In the case of any such refusal, the court may by order compel an immediate inspection of the register and index[10].

Where the register is kept at the office of some person other than the company, the power of the court[11] extends to the making of orders against that other and his officers and servants[12].

1 Companies Act 1985 s 358; and see *Gibson v Barton* (1875) LR 10 QB 329. Notwithstanding the Companies Act 1985 s 358 or any other enactment, a participating issuer must not close a register of securities relating to a participating security without the consent of the Operator: see the Uncertificated Securities Regulations 1995, SI 1995/3272, reg 22 and MONEY.

2 Companies Act 1985 s 356(1) (amended by the Companies Act 1989 ss 143(8)(a), 212, Sch 24). The fee so prescribed is £2.50 for each hour or part thereof during which the right of inspection is exercised: Companies (Inspection and Copying of Registers, Indices and Documents) Regulations 1991, SI 1991/1998, reg 5, Sch 2 para 1(d). As to taking copies of the register of members see para 391 post; and as to the power to make regulations see para 230 ante.

The object of giving non-members a right of inspection is to enable them to ascertain what assets they may rely on (*Oakes v Turquand and Harding, Peek v Turquand and Harding, Re Overend, Gurney & Co* (1867) LR 2 HL 325 at 366); cf the provision under the Companies Clauses Consolidation Act 1845 (see para 1634 post).

3 For the meaning of 'company' see para 229 note 14 ante.

4 Companies (Inspection and Copying of Registers, Indices and Documents) Regulations 1991 reg 3(1), (2)(a). For the meaning of 'business day' see para 229 note 15 ante.

5 Ibid reg 3(1), (2)(b). Regulation 3(2)(b) is not, however, to be construed as obliging a company to provide any facilities additional to those provided for the purposes of facilitating inspection: reg 3(3).

6 Ibid reg 4(1), (2).

7 *Re Kent Coalfields Syndicate* [1898] 1 QB 754, CA; *Re Yorkshire Fibre Co* (1870) LR 9 Eq 650.

8 *Re Joint-Stock Discount Co, Buchanan's Case* (1866) 15 LT 261; *Bevan v Webb* [1901] 2 Ch 59, CA; *Norey v Keep* [1909] 1 Ch 561.

9 Companies Act 1985 ss 356(5), 730, Sch 24. For the meaning of 'officer who is in default' and 'the statutory maximum' see para 1161 post.

10 Ibid ss 356(6), 357. The application for an order is by way of originating summons in the expedited form: RSC Ord 102 r 2(1), (2). For procedure on a summons under that order see para 69 ante. The affidavit in support of the summons must state that application was made at the proper time, and, if the application is not made by a member, must state the tender of the proper sum. In cases where copies are demanded, an offer to pay the proper fee for the copies must also be stated, and the order should provide for payment in the case of copies.

11 Ie under the Companies Act 1985 s 356(6): see supra.

12 Ibid s 357.

391. Copies of register of members. Any member of the company or other person may require a copy of the register, or of any part of it, on payment of such fee as may be prescribed[1]; but he is not entitled to take copies on his own account[2]. The company must cause any copy so required by any person to be sent to that person within ten days, beginning with the day next following that on which the requirement is received by the company[3]. A company[4] is not, however, obliged, in providing a copy of a part of its register of members, to extract entries from the register by reference to whether a member has given an address in a particular geographical location, is of a particular nationality, has a holding of a certain size, is a natural person or not or is of a particular gender[5].

If a copy is not so sent within the proper period, the same persons are liable to the same penalties as in the case of a refusal to inspect the register[6].

In the case of such default, the court may by order direct that the copies required be sent to the persons requiring them[7].

1 Companies Act 1985 s 356(3) (amended by the Companies Act 1989 ss 143(8)(c), 212, Sch 24). The fee so prescribed is, for the first 100 entries or part thereof copied, £2.50; for the next 1,000 entries or part thereof copied, £20.00; and, for every subsequent 1,000 entries or part thereof copied, £15.00: Companies (Inspection and Copying of Registers, Indices and Documents) Regulations 1991, SI 1991/1998, reg 5, Sch 2 para 2(d). As to the power to make regulations see para 230 ante.

2 *Re Balaghat Gold Mining Co* [1901] 2 KB 665, CA, overruling *Boord v African Consolidated Land and Trading Co* [1898] 1 Ch 596; cf the similar provisions relating to the register of debenture holders: see para 1294 post.

3 Companies Act 1985 s 356(3) (as amended: see note 1 supra).

4 For the meaning of 'company' see para 229 note 14 ante.
5 Companies (Inspection and Copying of Registers, Indices and Documents) Regulations 1991 reg 4(1), (3).
6 See the Companies Act 1985 ss 356(6), 357 and para 390 ante.
7 Ibid s 356(6).

C. RECTIFICATION OF REGISTER

392. Rectification by directors. The directors of a company may rectify the register of members without any application to the court, if there is no dispute, and the circumstances are such that the court would order rectification[1]; but ordinarily the protection of the court's order is essential to any rectification by the removal of the name of a registered holder of shares[2].

A participating issuer must not rectify a register of securities in relation to uncertificated units of a security held by a system-member except with the consent of the Operator or by order of a court in the United Kingdom[3]. A participating issuer who rectifies or otherwise changes an entry on a register of securities in relation to uncertificated units of a security (except in response to an Operator-instruction) must immediately notify the Operator and inform the system-members concerned of the change to the entry[4].

1 *Re London and Mediterranean Bank, Wright's Case* (1871) 7 Ch App 55; *Reese River Silver Mining Co v Smith* (1869) LR 4 HL 64 at 74; *Hartley's Case* (1875) 10 Ch App 157; *Smith v Brown* [1896] AC 614 at 622, PC; *First National Reinsurance Co Ltd v Greenfield* [1921] 2 KB 260 at 279.
2 *Re Derham and Allen Ltd* [1946] Ch 31 at 36.
3 See the Uncertificated Securities Regulations 1995, SI 1995/3272, reg 21(1) and MONEY. As to the penalties for breach of reg 21(1) or reg 21(2) (see infra) see reg 37(1), (2) and MONEY.
4 See ibid reg 21(2) and MONEY.

393. Rectification by court. On the application of the person aggrieved, or any member[1] of the company, or the company itself, the register of members may be rectified by the court[2]:

(1) if the name of any person is, without sufficient cause, entered in or omitted from the register[3]; or

(2) if default is made, or unnecessary delay takes place, in entering on the register the fact of any person having ceased to be a member[4].

On such an application the court may decide any question relating to the title of any person who is a party to the application to have his name entered in or omitted from the register, whether the question arises between members or alleged members, or between members or alleged members on the one hand and the company on the other hand; and generally may decide any question necessary or expedient to be decided for rectification of the register[5]. The court may either refuse the application, or may order rectification of the register and payment by the company of any damages sustained by any party aggrieved[6]. The company may be ordered to pay damages only when the register is ordered to be rectified[7]. If money has been paid on the shares, the amount will be ordered to be returned with interest at an appropriate rate[8], and the amount with costs is provable in a winding up[9].

In the case of a company required by the Companies Act 1985[10] to send a list of its members to the registrar of companies, the court, when making an order for rectification of the register, must by its order direct notice of the rectification to be given to the registrar[11].

1   For an example of an unmeritorious application by a member who was not affected see *Re Piccadilly Radio plc* [1989] BCLC 683 (cited in para 394 note 4 post).
2   Rectification of the share register is a matter for the court of the country of incorporation of the company: *International Credit and Investment Co (Overseas) Ltd v Adham* [1994] 1 BCLC 66 at 78 per Harman J. See also *Re Fagin's Bookshop plc* [1992] BCLC 118. As to custody of the register see para 389 ante.
3   The jurisdiction of the court under this provision is not limited to cases where a name has been entered improperly but extends to cases where a name stands on the register without sufficient cause: *Re Imperial Chemical Industries Ltd* [1936] 2 All ER 463. See *Re New Cedos Engineering Co Ltd* (1975) [1994] 1 BCLC 797; *Re Transatlantic Life Assurance Co Ltd* [1979] 3 All ER 352, [1980] 1 WLR 79. There is no necessity to show any wrongdoing by the company and any question of omission by error or entry by error can be raised. The phrase 'without sufficient cause' is a requirement that the court must be shown at the hearing that there is no sufficient cause for the omission or entry, as the case may be: *Re Diamond Rock Boring Co Ltd, ex p Shaw* (1877) 2 QBD 463 at 482, CA; *Re Fagin's Bookshop plc* [1992] BCLC 118 at 123. There is, however, no jurisdiction to rectify on the grounds of omission if there never was an entitlement to entry in the register in the first place: *Re BTR plc* (1988) 4 BCC 45; *Re Welsh Highland Railway Light Railway Co* [1993] BCLC 338. For a case where the register had been lost, and rectification of an entirely blank new register was ordered, see *Re Data Express Ltd* (1987) Times, 27 April.
4   Companies Act 1985 s 359(1). As to the power of the court to rectify the register when a company is being wound up see paras 396, 2486 et seq post.
5   Ibid s 359(3).
6   Ibid s 359(2).
7   *Re Ottos Kopje Diamond Mines Ltd* [1893] 1 Ch 618, CA. As to the measure of damages see *Re Ottos Kopje Diamond Mines Ltd* supra; *Skinner v City of London Marine Insurance Corpn* (1885) 14 QBD 882, CA.
8   *Karberg's Case* [1892] 3 Ch 1, CA; *Re Metropolitan Coal Consumers' Association, Wainwright's Case* (1889) 62 LT 30 (affd (1890) 63 LT 429, CA) (no fixed rate applicable); and see *Re Railway Time Tables Publishing Co, ex p Sandys* (1889) 42 ChD 98 at 108, CA.
9   *Re British Gold Fields of West Africa* [1899] 2 Ch 7, CA.
10   Ie by the Companies Act 1985 ss 363 (as amended), 364A(4) (as added): see paras 1062, 1064 post.
11   Ibid s 359(4).

394. Jurisdiction to rectify. The jurisdiction to rectify the register is discretionary[1]; and it is not limited by the provisions of the Companies Act 1985 to the cases mentioned above. Thus the court will rectify the register, apart from that Act, to enable the members of a company to have a fair and reasonable exercise of their rights[2].

When the court entertains the application, it is bound to go into all the circumstances of the case, and to consider what equity the applicant has to call for its interposition[3] and the purpose for which relief is sought[4].

The power to rectify has been exercised where there has been misrepresentation in the prospectus[5]; where it is expedient to have an order which will bind all the shareholders and effectually bar any subsequent application for restoration of a name struck out by the directors[6]; where shares have been illegally allotted at a discount[7]; where the application for shares has been made in the name of a person, as, for example, an underwriter, without his authority[8]; where there is no valid allotment of shares[9]; or the allotment is not made within a reasonable time[10], or is irregular[11]; where a transfer of shares has been improperly registered or registration has been refused[12]; where there are joint holders of shares who wish to divide the shares so held into two parts with their names entered in the register in respect of each part in a different order[13]; where the company puts on its register matters which are not required by the statute[14]; in order to set right allotments of shares which have been issued as fully paid without a proper contract being filed[15]; and where an oversea company was entered in the register without the permission of the Treasury, which was at the time required[16].

1 *Re Diamond Rock Boring Co Ltd, ex p Shaw* (1877) 2 QBD 463, CA; *Re Kimberley North Block Diamond Co, ex p Wernher* (1888) 59 LT 579, CA; cf *Ward and Henry's Case* (1867) 2 Ch App 431 at 441; *Re Tahiti Cotton Co, ex p Sargent* (1874) LR 17 Eq 273 at 276; *Re Piccadilly Radio plc* [1989] BCLC 683 at 697.

2 *Burns v Siemens Bros Dynamo Works Ltd* [1919] 1 Ch 225; cf *Re Welsh Highland Railway Light Railway Co* [1993] BCLC 338 at 351.

3 *Trevor v Whitworth* (1887) 12 App Cas 409 at 440, HL; *Re Joint Stock Discount Co, Sichell's Case* (1867) 3 Ch App 119; *Bellerby v Rowland and Marwood's SS Co Ltd* [1902] 2 Ch 14, CA; *Re Onward Building Society* [1891] 2 QB 463, CA; *Re Hannan's King (Browning) Gold Mining* (1898) 14 TLR 314, CA. In the corresponding provision in the Companies Act 1862 s 35 (repealed) the court might make an order for rectification 'if satisfied of the justice of the case'. The words last quoted have been omitted from the later Companies Acts, but, it seems, without affecting the law. See also para 322 note 2 ante.

4 *Re Piccadilly Radio plc* [1989] BCLC 683 (shares in a radio company were transferred without obtaining the consent of the broadcasting authority as required by the articles of association; rectification was refused; the applicants had no interest in the shares and were not seeking to have their own names restored to the register but were searching for a means to disenfranchise opposition to proposals to be put to the general meeting; the broadcasting authority had not complained; the transferor did not seek rectification and the company itself did not support the application). Cf *Dempsey v Celtic Football and Athletic Co Ltd* [1993] BCC 514, Ct of Sess.

5 See para 322 ante.

6 *Re Bank of Hindustan, China and Japan, ex p Martin* (1865) 2 Hem & M 669; *Re Bank of Hindustan, China and Japan, Higgs's Case* (1865) 2 Hem & M 657; *Re Bank of Hindustan, China and Japan, ex p Los* (1865) 6 New Rep 327.

7 See para 187 ante.

8 *Re Consort Deep Level Gold Mines Ltd, ex p Stark* [1897] 1 Ch 575, CA; cf *Re Henry Bentley & Co Ltd and Yorkshire Breweries, ex p Harrison* (1893) 69 LT 204, CA; *Hindley's Case* [1896] 2 Ch 121, CA; *Re Hannan's Empress Gold Mining and Development Co, Carmichael's Case* [1896] 2 Ch 643, CA.

9 *Re Homer District Consolidated Gold Mines, ex p Smith* (1888) 39 ChD 546 at 551; *Re Portuguese Consolidated Copper Mines Ltd* (1889) 42 ChD 160, CA. This arises eg where a director has, without his authority, been placed on the register in respect of qualification shares (*Re Printing, Telegraph and Construction Co of the Agence Havas, ex p Cammell* [1894] 2 Ch 392, CA) or where the allotment was made at an improperly constituted meeting of directors (*Re Sly, Spink & Co* [1911] 2 Ch 430).

10 *Re Bowron, Baily & Co, ex p Baily* (1868) 3 Ch App 592.

11 *Re Homer District Consolidated Gold Mines, ex p Smith* (1888) 39 ChD 546; *Re Cleveland Trust plc* [1991] BCC 33 (register rectified by deletion of bonus shares after bonus issue mistakenly made); *Re Thundercrest Ltd* [1995] 1 BCLC 117 (register rectified by cancellation of allotment to two members who were also directors when the third member of the company, to their knowledge, had not received a provisional letter of allotment of those shares to him, a letter which was in any event defective as it allowed insufficient time for acceptance).

12 *Pulbrook v Richmond Consolidated Mining Co* (1878) 9 ChD 610 at 615; *Re Bahia and San Francisco Rly Co* (1868) LR 3 QB 584 (forged transfer); *Re Stranton Iron and Steel Co* (1873) LR 16 Eq 559 (transfer to increase voting power); *Re Manchester and Oldham Bank* (1885) 54 LJ Ch 926; and see *Re Tahiti Cotton Co, ex p Sargent* (1874) LR 17 Eq 273, and *Re Diamond Rock Boring Co Ltd, ex p Shaw* (1877) 2 QBD 463, CA (disputes between transferor and transferee); *Re Stockton Malleable Iron Co* (1875) 2 ChD 101 (lien); *Re Ystalyfera Gas Co* (1887) 3 TLR 321; *Re Violet Consolidated Gold Mining Co* (1899) 68 LJ Ch 535; *Re Copal Varnish Co Ltd* [1917] 2 Ch 349; *Re Imperial Chemical Industries Ltd* [1936] 2 All ER 463 (entry of name proper, but name standing on register without good cause); *Welch v Bank of England* [1955] Ch 508, [1955] 1 All ER 811 (restoration of status quo after forged transfers); *International Credit and Investment Co (Overseas) Ltd v Adham* [1994] 1 BCLC 66 (restoration of status quo; no proper share transfers were executed, merely entries made in the share register purporting to deprive the true owner of entire holding); *Re New Cedos Engineering Co Ltd* (1975) [1994] 1 BCLC 797 (on their true construction right to be registered existed under the articles); *Stothers v William Steward (Holdings) Ltd* [1994] 2 BCLC 266, CA (directors purported to exercise their discretion to refuse registration, which power on the true construction of the articles they did not possess); and para 498 post.

13 *Burns v Siemens Bros Dynamo Works Ltd* [1919] 1 Ch 225.

14 *Re W Key & Son Ltd* [1902] 1 Ch 467; *Re T H Saunders & Co Ltd* [1908] 1 Ch 415.

15 *Re New Zealand Kapanga Gold Mining Co, ex p Thomas* (1873) LR 18 Eq 17n; *Re Denton Colliery Co, ex p Shaw* (1874) LR 18 Eq 16; *Re Broad Street Station Dwellings Co* [1887] WN 149; *Re Nottingham Brewery Ltd and Reduced* (1888) 4 TLR 429; *Re Maynards Ltd* [1898] 1 Ch 515; *Re Henry Lovibond & Sons (1900) Ltd* (1901) 17 TLR 315; *Re Darlington Forge Co* (1887) 34 ChD 522 (where the contract was oral).

16 *Re Transatlantic Life Assurance Co Ltd* [1979] 3 All ER 352, [1980] 1 WLR 79.

395. Procedure. The application for rectification may be made by the person aggrieved, by any member of the company, or by the company[1]. The application must be made to the court having jurisdiction to wind up the company[2]. It may be initiated by originating motion[3] or by an action commenced by writ. If by reason of its complexity or on the ground that there are matters requiring investigation or otherwise the court thinks that the case could more satisfactorily be dealt with by an action, it will decline to make an order on a motion, without prejudice to the right of the applicant to institute an action for rectification[4].

An action may be instituted for rectification of the register[5] without any direction by the court, a course which should be followed where there is much complexity, or where other relief is required. The court will not give substantive relief by way of rectification of the register on an interlocutory application in an action[6], nor will it rectify the register in the absence of third parties whose rights will be affected by the rectification[7]. The application to rectify must be made promptly[8].

The proper respondents to an application to rectify the register are the company and the registered holder or holders of the shares whose registration is in question, if not the applicant[9]. It is not necessary to join other shareholders who are registered in respect of shares other than those in respect of which rectification is sought[10]. Nor is it necessary to join the directors of the company where rectification is sought unless an order for costs is sought against them[11].

In cases in the High Court the jurisdiction is assigned to the Chancery Division[12]. The motion, and all affidavits, notices, and other documents in those proceedings must be entitled in the matter of the company and in the matter of the Companies Act 1985[13]. When the application is by the company to remove a number of names, it may be made ex parte[14].

1 See the Companies Act 1985 s 359(1) and para 393 ante. For instances of applications by the company see *Re Indo-China Steam Navigation Co* [1917] 2 Ch 100; *Re London Electrobus Co Ltd* (1906) 22 TLR 677; *Re Cleveland Trust plc* [1991] BCC 33.

2 Companies Act 1985 s 744. As to the courts having winding-up jurisdiction see paras 2004, 2196 et seq post.

3 RSC Ord 102 r 3(1)(g). The usual practice is for the application to be made by motion: *Duffin v Mexican Gold and Silver Ore Reduction Co* [1890] WN 116. Notice of motion must be served on the company at its registered office, not on its solicitor: *Re Denver United Breweries Ltd* (1890) 63 LT 96.

4 *Re National and Provincial Marine Insurance Co, ex p Parker* (1867) 2 Ch App 685; *Simpson's Case* (1869) LR 9 Eq 91; *Stewart's Case* (1866) 1 Ch App 574 at 585; *Re Gresham Life Assurance Society, ex p Penney* (1872) 8 Ch App 446 at 448; *Askew's Case* (1874) 9 Ch App 664; *Re Bagnall & Co, ex p Dick* (1875) 32 LT 536; *Re Greater Britain Insurance Corpn Ltd, ex p Brockdorff* (1920) 124 LT 194, CA; *Re Greater Britain Products Development Corpn Ltd* (1924) 40 TLR 488.

5 *Bloxam v Metropolitan Cab and Carriage Co* (1864) 4 New Rep 51; *Roots v Williamson* (1888) 38 ChD 485; *Moore v North Western Bank* [1891] 2 Ch 599; *Lynde v Anglo-Italian Hemp Spinning Co* [1896] 1 Ch 178; *McKeown v Boudard-Peveril Gear Co* (1896) 65 LJ Ch 735, CA.

6 *Siemens Bros & Co Ltd v Burns* [1918] 2 Ch 324 at 338.

7 *Re Greater Britain Insurance Corpn Ltd, ex p Brockdorff* (1920) 124 LT 194, CA.

8 *Sewells's Case* (1868) 3 Ch App 131 at 138.

9 *Morgan v Morgan Insurance Brokers Ltd* [1993] BCLC 676 at 678.

10 See *Morgan v Morgan Insurance Brokers Ltd* [1993] BCLC 676.

11 In *Morgan v Morgan Insurance Brokers Ltd* [1993] BCLC 676 it was held to be unjust to order the company to pay costs where rectification was sought by a shareholder owning three-quarters of the shares following a bona fide but improper refusal by the directors to register a transfer; but an order for costs was made against the directors personally. Cf *Re Keith Prowse & Co Ltd* [1918] 1 Ch 487; *Re Copal Varnish Co Ltd* [1917] 2 Ch 349 at 355. See also the Supreme Court Act 1981 s 51(1) (substituted by the Courts and Legal Services Act 1990 s 4(1)); *Re Fisher* [1894] 1 Ch 450, CA. As to costs generally see PRACTICE AND PROCEDURE vol 37 para 713.

12 RSC Ord 102 r 5(1).

13 RSC Ord 102 r 5(2).

14 *Re London Electrobus Co Ltd* (1906) 22 TLR 677 (where subscriptions for shares had been obtained by misrepresentation in a prospectus and the moneys subscribed were being returned to the subscribers).

396. Rectification after winding up. Notwithstanding that winding up has commenced, the court has power to rectify the register under the statutory power[1], on any of the grounds already mentioned; but a strong case must be made out[2]. When giving directions as to the distribution of surplus assets in a winding up, the court may treat as members those who would be entitled to have their names placed on the register without insisting on the formality of an application to rectify the register[3].

1 Ie the Companies Act 1985 s 359 (see para 393 ante), as applied in winding up by the Insolvency Act 1986 s 148(1): see *Re Joint Stock Discount Co, Sichell's Case* (1867) 3 Ch App 119 at 122 and para 2486 post.
2 *Re Onward Building Society* [1891] 2 QB 463, CA. See further para 2486 et seq post.
3 See *Re Baku Consolidated Oilfields Ltd* [1994] 1 BCLC 173 (liquidator sought directions under the Insolvency Act 1986 s 112 as to the distribution of funds to the members of a company, the assets of which had been seized by the Soviet government in 1920 and in respect of which compensation was paid by the Soviet authorities in 1990; the share register was necessarily incomplete, not having been maintained since 1920).

397. Order for rectification. In the case of a company required by the Companies Act 1985[1] to send a list of its members to the registrar of companies, the court must, in making an order for rectification, direct notice of the rectification to be given to him[2].

Where the court orders the register to be rectified by removing a name from it, the name should not be erased, but a line should be drawn through it, and an abstract of the order signed by the secretary of the company should be added[3].

Where a company does not rectify the register pursuant to an order of the court, the court may direct that the person by whom the order was obtained or some other person appointed by the court may do so[4].

1 Ie by the Companies Act 1985 ss 363, 364A(4) (as substituted): see paras 1062, 1064 post.
2 Ibid s 359(4).
3 *Re Iron Ship Building Co* (1865) 34 Beav 597.
4 RSC Ord 45 r 8. For orders made where the company by reason of resignations had no directors or secretary to carry out the original order of the court see *Re LL Syndicate Ltd* (1901) 17 TLR 711; *Re Manihot Rubber Plantations Ltd* (1919) 63 Sol Jo 827.

D. OVERSEAS BRANCH REGISTER AND REGISTERS IN FOREIGN COUNTRIES

398. Overseas branch register of members. A company having a share capital, whose objects comprise the transaction of business in Northern Ireland, any part of Her Majesty's dominions[1] outside the United Kingdom, the Channel Islands, the Isle of Man, or any of certain overseas countries and territories[2], may cause to be kept in any such country or territory in which it transacts business a branch register of members resident in that country or territory (an 'overseas branch register')[3]. Any company may[4], by its articles, make such provisions as it thinks fit respecting the keeping of overseas branch registers[5].

A company keeping an overseas branch register must give to the registrar of companies notice in the prescribed form[6] of the situation of the office where any overseas branch register is kept, and of any change in its situation, and, if it is discontinued, of its discontinuance[7]; and any such notice must be given within 14 days of the opening of the office or of the change or discontinuance, as the case may be[8]. If default is made in so giving notice, the company, and every officer of the company who is in default, is liable on summary conviction to a fine not exceeding one-fifth of the statutory maximum and, on conviction after continued contravention, to a daily default fine not exceeding one-fiftieth of the statutory maximum[9].

An overseas branch register is deemed to be part of the company's register of members ('the principal register')[10].

1   For the meaning of 'Her Majesty's dominions' see COMMONWEALTH vol 6 (Reissue) para 803.
2   Ie the countries and territories specified in the Companies Act 1985 s 362(1), Sch 14 Pt I. These are Bangladesh, Cyprus, Dominica, the Gambia, Ghana, Guyana, India, Kenya, Kiribati, Lesotho, Malawi, Malaysia, Malta, Nigeria, Pakistan, Republic of Ireland, Seychelles, Sierra Leone, Singapore, South Africa, Sri Lanka, Swaziland, Trinidad and Tobago, Uganda and Zimbabwe.
3   Ibid s 362(1), (2), Sch 14 Pt I. Under the Companies (Consolidation) Act 1908 s 34(1) (repealed), the corresponding provision in that Act, the register was called the colonial register. References to a colonial register occurring in articles registered before 1 November 1929 are to be read as referring to an overseas branch register: Companies Act 1985 s 362(2)(c). Under the Companies Act 1948 s 119 (repealed) such a register was called a dominion register. Any dominion register so kept is now to be known as an overseas branch register (Companies Act 1985 s 362(2)(a)); and, where any Act or instrument (including in particular a company's articles) refers to a company's dominion register, that reference is to be read, unless the context otherwise requires, as being to an overseas branch register kept under s 362 (s 362(2)(b)). As to the provisions applicable where the entries are recorded otherwise than in legible form see para 656 post.
4   Ie subject to the provisions of the Companies Act 1985.
5   Ibid s 362(3), Sch 14 Pt II para 7.
6   For the prescribed form of notice see the Companies (Forms) Regulations 1985, SI 1985/854, reg 4(1), Sch 3, Form 362 (amended by SI 1987/752).
7   Companies Act 1985 Sch 14 Pt II para 1(1).
8   Ibid Sch 14 Pt II para 1(2).
9   Ibid ss 362(3), 730, Sch 14 Pt II para 1(3), Sch 24. For the meaning of 'officer who is in default', 'the statutory maximum' and 'daily default fine' see para 1161 post.
10   Ibid Sch 14 Pt II para 2(1).

399. How overseas branch register kept. The overseas branch register must be kept in the same manner in which the principal register[1] is required to be kept, except that the advertisement before closing it[2] must be inserted in a newspaper circulating in the district where the overseas branch register is kept[3], and that any competent court in a country or territory where the register is kept may exercise the same jurisdiction to rectify it as is in respect of the principal register exercisable by the court in Great Britain[4], and that the offences of refusing inspection or copies of the register, and of authorising or permitting the refusal[5], may be prosecuted summarily before any tribunal having summary criminal jurisdiction[6]. However, this extension of jurisdiction applies only to those countries and territories where, immediately before 1 July 1985[7], provision to the same effect made under the corresponding provision of the Companies Act 1948[8], had effect as part of the local law[9].

Subject to the provisions mentioned below with respect to the duplicate register, the shares registered in an overseas branch register must be distinguished from the shares registered in the principal register; and no transaction with respect to any shares registered in an overseas branch register must, during the continuance of that registration, be registered in any other register[10].

The company must transmit to its registered office a copy of every entry in its overseas branch register as soon as may be after the entry is made, and must cause to be kept at the place where the company's principal register is kept[11], duly entered up from time to time, a duplicate of its overseas branch register, which duplicate is deemed to be part of the principal register[12]. If default is made in complying with this provision, the company, and every officer of the company who is in default, or, where the principal register is kept[13] at the office of some person other than the company, and non-compliance is due to any default of his, that person, is liable on summary conviction to a fine not exceeding one-fifth of the statutory maximum and, on conviction after continued contravention, to a daily default fine not exceeding one-fiftieth of the statutory maximum[14].

1 For the meaning of 'the principal register' see para 398 ante.
2 As to the advertisement of closing the register see para 390 ante.
3 Companies Act 1985 s 362(3), Sch 14 Pt II para 2(2).
4 As to rectification see para 393 et seq ante.
5 As to offences in relation to inspection and copies see paras 390, 391 ante.
6 Companies Act 1985 Sch 14 Pt II para 3(1). As to how far Acts of Parliament of the United Kingdom extend to dominions as part of their law otherwise than by consent see COMMONWEALTH vol 6 (Reissue) paras 803, 1099 et seq; and as to the application of these provisions to other countries see para 398 notes 1, 2 ante.
7 Ie the date of the coming into force of the Companies Act 1985: s 746.
8 Ie the Companies Act 1948 s 120(2) (repealed). Such a register was under that Act known as a dominion register: s 119(1) (repealed).
9 Companies Act 1985 Sch 14 Pt II para 3(2). The Companies Act 1948 ss 119–121 (repealed) applied in relation to the Republic of South Africa (see the South Africa Act 1962 s 2(1), Sch 2 para 4(1) (now substituted by SI 1986/1035)) and the whole of Malaysia (see the Federation of Malaya Independence Act 1957 s 2(3); Malaysia Act 1963 s 4(1); the Companies Registers (Malaysia) Order 1964, SI 1964/911) as if they were parts of Her Majesty's dominions and to Pakistan as if it had not withdrawn from the Commonwealth and as if the Pakistan (Consequential Provisions) Act 1956 had not been repealed (Pakistan Act 1973 s 4(1), Sch 3 para 3(1) (repealed by the Companies Consolidation (Consequential Provisions) Act 1985 s 29, Sch 1)).

These statutory provisions might also apply to Kenya, Malawi, Swaziland, Zanzibar and Tanzania (formerly Tanganyika). The first four named countries were the subject matter of an Order in Council dated 26 October 1931, SR & O 1931/931, which, if it was in force on 1 July 1948, was continued in force as if made under the Companies Act 1948: see s 459(2) (repealed). The provisions were applied to Tanganyika by the Tanganyika (Companies Dominion Register) Order in Council 1951, SI 1951/752. Both these orders were made under, or under provisions corresponding to, the Companies Act 1948 s 122 (repealed) (see para 402 post) and under the Foreign Jurisdiction Act 1890. The countries concerned all became part of the Commonwealth, and, when this happened, they were no longer such countries as are referred to in the Companies Act 1948 s 122 (repealed), more especially as they then became part of Her Majesty's dominions to which ss 119–121 (repealed) applied automatically. These orders would then presumably have lapsed, and would not automatically revive when these countries ceased to be part of Her Majesty's dominions and became independent under the Kenya Independence Act 1963, the Malawi Republic Act 1966, the Swaziland Independence Act 1968, the Zanzibar Act 1963 and the Tanganyika Independence Act 1961 respectively.

A further order made under provisions corresponding to the Companies Act 1948 s 122 (repealed), the Aden Protectorate (Application of Acts) Order 1938, SR & O 1938/1603, applied these provisions in relation to the Aden Protectorate. This order was not revoked, but has been overtaken by events.

The Companies Act 1948 s 122 (repealed) was applied to Pakistan: Pakistan Act 1973 s 4(1), Sch 3 para 3(1) (repealed: see supra).

Where a register of members of a company is kept in Bangladesh, it is not to be treated as improperly kept by reason only that, at any time after 3 February 1972 and before 1 September 1974, it includes members resident in Pakistan: Bangladesh Act 1973 s 1(3), Schedule para 10(1).
10 Companies Act 1985 Sch 14 Pt II para 5.
11 See para 389 ante.
12 Companies Act 1985 Sch 14 Pt II para 4(1). As to the provisions applicable where the entries are recorded otherwise than in legible form see para 656 post.
13 Ie by virtue of ibid s 353(1)(b): see para 389 ante.
14 Ibid ss 362(3), 730, Sch 14 Pt II paras 4(2), (3), Sch 24. For the meaning of 'officer who is in default', 'the statutory maximum' and 'daily default fine' see para 1161 post.

400. Ceasing to keep overseas branch register. A company may discontinue to keep an overseas branch register, and thereupon all entries in it must be transferred to some other overseas branch register kept by the company in the same country or territory, or to the principal register[1].

1 Companies Act 1985 s 362(3), Sch 14 Pt II para 6. For the meaning of 'the principal register' see para 398 ante. As to the giving of notice of discontinuance or change of situation of the register see para 398 ante; and as to the application of this provision to other countries see para 398 notes 1, 2 ante.

401. Transfers of shares. An instrument of transfer of a share registered in an overseas branch register (other than such a register kept in Northern Ireland) is deemed a transfer of property situated outside the United Kingdom[1].

1 Companies Act 1985 s 362(3), Sch 14 Pt II para 8 (amended by the Finance Act 1990 s 132, Sch 19 Pt VI).

402. Extension to foreign countries by Order in Council. The Foreign Jurisdiction Act 1890 has effect as if the statutory provisions relating to overseas branch registers[1] were included among the enactments which may be applied by Order in Council[2] to foreign countries in which for the time being Her Majesty has jurisdiction[3].

Her Majesty may, by Order in Council, direct that those statutory provisions relating to overseas branch registers shall extend, with such exceptions, modifications or adaptations, if any, as may be specified in the Order, to any territories under Her Majesty's protection to which those provisions cannot be extended under the Foreign Jurisdiction Act 1890[4].

1 Ie the Companies Act 1985 s 362(1), Sch 14 Pt II (paras 1–8) (as amended): see paras 398–401 ante.
2 Ie by virtue of the Foreign Jurisdiction Act 1890 s 5(1). Forthwith upon any such Order being made, the provisions operate to the extent of the jurisdiction of the Crown as if that country were a British possession, and as if the Crown in Council were the legislature of that possession: s 5(2).
3 Companies Act 1985 s 362(4). Corresponding provision was made for applying the Companies (Consolidation) Act 1908 ss 34–36, by the Foreign Jurisdiction Act 1913 s 1; by the Companies Act 1929 s 106, for applying ss 103–105 of that Act and by the Companies Act 1948 s 122 for applying ss 119–122 of that Act. Orders applying these earlier provisions which were in force on 1 July 1985 are continued in force as if made under the Companies Act 1985: see the Companies Consolidation (Consequential Provisions) Act 1985 s 31(2) and para 10 ante. As to the orders made under these provisions see para 399 note 9 ante.
4 Companies Act 1985 s 362(5).

(iv) Rights of Members

403. Rights of members generally. The rights of a member of a 'company', as that word is defined by the Companies Act 1985[1], are:

(1) statutory;
(2) given by the company's memorandum and articles;
(3) given by the general law, more particularly such rules as relate to contracts and members of corporations[2].

A shareholder seeking to enforce an individual right against the company is not entitled to an advance order for an indemnity as to costs[3].

1 For the meaning of 'company' see para 11 note 1 ante.
2 See generally CORPORATIONS.
3 *Re a Company (No 005136 of 1986)* [1987] BCLC 82. The principle of *Wallersteiner v Moir (No 2)* [1975] QB 373, [1975] 1 All ER 849, CA is confined to minority shareholders' actions: see para 1110 et seq post.

404. Statutory rights of individual members. The statutory rights of an individual member include: his right to have his name properly inserted in the company's register of members, to have an inspection and copies of the register, and to have it rectified when defective[1]; in the case of a public company, rights of pre-emption on the issue of further shares[2]; to inspect the company's registers of mortgages, charges and debentures[3]; to obtain a copy of the company's memorandum and articles of association on payment of the prescribed fee[4]; to recover compensation for misrepresentation, although not fraudulent, by directors or promoters[5]; to obtain repayment from the company of money paid in respect of shares which cannot legally be allotted[6]; to petition for a winding-up order[7]; to petition for relief when the affairs of the company are being conducted in a manner which is unfairly prejudicial to his interests[8]; to take proceedings for misfeasance against directors and officers of the company in a winding up[9]; to make application to the court in a voluntary winding up[10]; to require his interest to be purchased on a reconstruction of the company[11]; to be sent a copy of the company's annual accounts, together with a copy of the directors' report and of the auditors' report on those accounts[12]; to require the company to hold an annual general meeting in a year when it has elected not to do so[13]; except in the case of a company without a share capital, in any case where he has a right to attend and vote at a meeting of the company, the right to appoint a proxy[14] and demand or join in demanding a poll[15]; and, on payment, to have copies of resolutions and agreements of the company which are required to be delivered for registration[16].

1 See para 393 ante.
2 See para 457 et seq post.
3 See paras 1294, 1298 post.
4 See para 101 ante.
5 See paras 321, 338, 347, 350 ante.
6 See para 452 post.
7 See paras 2210, 2214 post.
8 See para 1405 post.
9 See para 2448 et seq post.
10 See para 2771 post.
11 See para 1480 post.
12 See para 823 post.
13 See para 658 post.
14 See para 674 post.
15 See para 672 post.
16 See para 692 post.

405. Statutory rights of members collectively. The members of a company collectively have statutory rights, some of which are exercisable by a bare majority, as, for example, an ordinary resolution[1], others by a particular majority, as in the case of a reconstruction[2], and others by a minority, as in the case of a requisition for a meeting of shareholders[3], or of an application to the Secretary of State to appoint an inspector to investigate the company's affairs[4].

Statutory rights cannot be taken away or modified by any provisions of the memorandum or articles[5].

1 See para 681 post.
2 See para 1483 post.
3 See para 662 post.
4 See para 1376 post.
5 See para 147 ante and para 537 post. A shareholders' agreement as to how to vote on a particular matter may effectively block the exercise of statutory rights: see paras 147, 149 ante and para 408 post.

406. Rights under memorandum of association. Rights may be conferred on the members of a company by its memorandum of association. Any alteration of class rights contained in the memorandum is subject to the provisions governing the variation of class rights[1]. In all other cases, if such conditions could lawfully have been contained in its articles of association, they may in general be altered by special resolution[2].

1 See para 182 ante
2 See para 99 ante.

407. Rights under articles. Rights may also be expressly conferred on the members by the articles of association[1], and some of the statutory rights of members may be exercised only if expressly authorised by the company's articles of association, such as the powers to alter capital by increasing or reducing it, consolidating or sub-dividing it, or by converting paid-up shares into stock, or reconverting the stock into paid-up shares[2]. In several cases the exercise of statutory rights requires confirmation in any case by the court, as, for example, where capital is reduced[3], and sometimes confirmation is required only if there are objectors, as, for example, where the objects of the company are altered[4].

The rights usually conferred on members by the express terms of the articles include those with regard to dividends, the transfer and transmission of shares, attending and voting at meetings of the company, appointment and removal of directors, appointment of auditors, and participation in a winding up in the surplus assets of the company[5].

1 As to the necessity of registration of particulars of newly created class rights see para 186 ante.
2 See para 201 et seq ante.
3 See para 241 ante.
4 See para 1184 post.
5 See the Companies (Tables A to F) Regulations 1985, SI 1985/805, Schedule, Table A (amended by SI 1985/1052) and para 529 et seq post.

408. Rights under the general law. The rights of a member under the general law include his right, where he has been induced to take shares by misrepresentation, to recover damages for misrepresentation if fraudulent or negligent[1], or to obtain a rescission of his contract to take shares, and rectification of the share register, together with a return of the money paid by him on the shares[2]; and to restrain directors from acting ultra vires the company or in excess of their own powers or acting unfairly to the members[3].

To supplement their rights under the articles[4] some or all of the shareholders may decide to enter into a shareholders' agreement, that is to say a separate contract apart from the articles[5]. Shareholders who are parties to such an agreement can enforce that agreement inter se in the same manner as any other contract.

1 See para 338 ante.
2 See para 321 et seq ante.
3 See paras 1104, 1110, 1111, 1405 et seq post.
4 See para 407 ante.
5 See para 149 ante.

(v) Liability of Members

409. Liability of members in general. Merely as such, members are not liable to anyone except to the extent and manner provided by the Companies Acts[1].

1 *Multinational Gas and Petrochemical Co v Multinational Gas and Petrochemical Services Ltd* [1983] Ch 258, [1983] 2 All ER 563, CA.

410. Where less than required number of members. If a company, other than a private company[1] limited by shares[2] or by guarantee[3], carries on business without having at least two members and does so for more than six months, a person who, for the whole or any part of the period that it so carries on business after those six months:

   (1) is a member of the company; and
   (2) knows that it is carrying on business with only one member,

is liable, jointly and severally with the company, for the payment of the company's debts contracted during the period or, as the case may be, that part of it[4].

The personal representatives of a deceased member or trustees of bankrupt members are not members within the meaning of this provision[5]. A member holding shares in a fiduciary capacity is counted in the number[6].

1 For the meaning of 'private company' see para 82 ante.
2 As to companies limited by shares see para 102 et seq ante.
3 As to companies limited by guarantee see para 108 et seq ante.
4 Companies Act 1985 s 24 (amended by the Companies (Single Member Private Limited Companies) Regulations 1992, SI 1992/1699, reg 2(1)(b), Schedule para 2). See also *Nisbet v Shepherd* [1994] 1 BCLC 300, CA (liquidator sought successfully to hold sole member liable under the Companies Act 1985 s 24 (as originally enacted)). As to single member private limited companies see para 81 ante.
5 *Re Bowling and Welby's Contract* [1895] 1 Ch 663, CA. They will not become 'members' until they take the appropriate steps to register: *Re Bowling and Welby's Contract* supra. The bankrupt remains a member as long as he is on the register notwithstanding that his trustee in bankruptcy may be able to secure registration of himself as the proprietor of the shares: *Morgan v Gray* [1953] Ch 83 at 87, 88, [1953] 1 All ER 213 at 217 per Danckwerts J. See further BANKRUPTCY vol 3(2) (Reissue) para 411.
6 *Salomon v A Salomon & Co Ltd* [1897] AC 22 at 30, HL per Lord Halsbury LC.

411. Unlimited company. Where the company is registered as an unlimited one, the liability of each past and present member extends to the whole amount of its debts and liabilities, and the expenses of its winding up[1], subject to a right of contribution from the other solvent members[2]. With regard to any policy of insurance or other contract, the liability of individual members may, however, by the terms of the policy or contract be restricted, or the funds of the company alone made liable[3]. If an unlimited company has a share capital, the liability on the shares is defined by its articles of association, which must state the amount of share capital with which it is registered[4]. The liability on the shares, if any, is the only liability which may be enforced by the company whilst it is carrying on business, although there is then an unlimited liability to creditors[5].

A past member is not liable to contribute if he has ceased to be a member for one year or more before the commencement of the winding up[6]; nor is he liable to contribute in respect of any debt or liability of the company contracted after he ceased to be a member[7]; nor unless it appears to the court that the existing members are unable to satisfy their required contributions[8].

1 See the Insolvency Act 1986 s 74(1) and para 2464 post; *Re Mayfair Property Co, Bartlett v Mayfair Property Co* [1898] 2 Ch 28 at 36, CA. This is a liability which neither the company nor its directors may dispose of to the prejudice of the creditors: *Re Mayfair Property Co* supra.
2 The right of contribution arises under the ordinary law of partnership, except so far as controlled by the memorandum or articles: *Robinson's Executor's Case* (1856) 6 De GM & G 572 at 588, CA.
3 See the Insolvency Act 1986 s 74(2)(e) and para 2476 post.
4 Companies Act 1985 s 7(2).
5 *Re Mayfair Property Co, Bartlett v Mayfair Property Co* [1898] 2 Ch 28, CA.
6 See the Insolvency Act 1986 s 74(2)(a) and para 2465 post.
7 See ibid s 74(2)(b) and para 2465 post.
8 See ibid s 74(2)(c) and para 2465 post. As to possible liability to contribute if the member has had shares which have been purchased or redeemed by the company see para 414 post.

412. Company limited by guarantee. The liability of a present or past member of a company limited by guarantee and without a share capital is limited to the amount which he undertakes by the memorandum of association to contribute to the assets of the company in the event of its being wound up[1]. If it has a share capital[2], he is liable in addition to the extent of any sums unpaid on any shares held by him[3]; and he may further under the articles of association, as regards his fellow members, incur an additional liability, which in the event of winding up must be enforced by action[4].

A past member is not liable to contribute if he has ceased to be a member for one year or more before the commencement of the winding up[5]; nor is he liable to contribute in respect of any debt or liability of the company contracted after he ceased to be a member[6]; nor unless it appears to the court that the existing members are unable to satisfy their required contributions[7].

1 See the Insolvency Act 1986 s 74(3) and para 2475 post. See also the Companies Act 1985 s 2(4) and para 108 ante.
2 With effect from 22 December 1980 a company cannot be formed as, or become, a company limited by guarantee with a share capital: ibid s 1(4).
3 See note 1 supra.
4 See para 2475 post.
5 See the Insolvency Act 1986 s 74(2)(a) and para 2465 post.
6 See ibid s 74(2)(b) and para 2465 post.
7 See ibid s 74(2)(c) and para 2465 post. As to possible liability to contribute if the member has had shares which have been purchased or redeemed by the company see para 414 post.

413. Company limited by shares. Save that a past member of an unlimited company which re-registers as limited[1] who was a member at the time of re-registration is liable to contribute to the assets of the company in respect of its debts and liabilities contracted before that time if a winding up commences within three years of such re-registration[2], the liability of a past or present member of a company limited by shares is limited to the amount, if any, unpaid on the shares in respect of which he is liable as a present or past member[3]. The articles may, however, impose a further liability on him in relation to other members[4]. Except where the articles otherwise provide, or by the terms of some special contract, there is no liability to pay for shares even in the case of signatories to the memorandum of association, except in pursuance of calls duly made in accordance with the articles[5], while the company is a going concern[6], or of calls duly made in the winding up of the company[7].

The liability of a past member can arise only if a winding up supervenes within 12 months of his ceasing to be a member[8], and he is not liable to contribute in respect of any debt or liability of the company contracted after he ceased to be a member[9]. Nor is he liable to contribute unless it appears to the court that the existing members are unable to satisfy the required contributions[10].

A person cannot become a member of a company in a representative capacity so as to be free from personal liability in respect of his shares[11]; but a trustee shareholder is entitled to be indemnified out of the trust estate if the shares are an investment authorised by the trust instrument or by statute[12], and he is entitled to be indemnified by a beneficial owner who is sui juris, whether such owner created the trust or accepted a transfer of the beneficial ownership[13].

1 Ie under the Companies Act 1985 s 51: see para 126 ante.
2 See the Insolvency Act 1986 s 77(2) and para 2466 post.
3 See ibid s 74(2)(d) and para 2464 post. Thus a shareholder in an English company carrying on business in a country where shareholders are liable for all the debts of the company cannot be made liable beyond the amount remaining payable on his shares unless he had assented to being made so liable: *Risdon Iron and Locomotive Works v Furness* [1906] 1 KB 49, CA.
4 See para 2475 post.
5 *Alexander v Automatic Telephone Co* [1900] 2 Ch 56, CA; *Nicol's Case, Tufnell and Ponsonby's Case* (1885) 29 ChD 421, CA.
6 See paras 417, 418 post.
7 See para 2493 et seq post.
8 See the Insolvency Act 1986 s 74(2)(a) and para 2465 post; *Re Premier Underwriting Association Ltd* [1913] 2 Ch 29.
9 See the Insolvency Act 1986 s 74(2)(b) and para 2465 post.
10 See ibid s 74(2)(c) and para 2465 post. As to possible liability to contribute if the member has had shares which have been purchased or redeemed by the company see para 414 post.
11 *Re Leeds Banking Co, Fearnside and Dean's Case, Dobson's Case* (1866) 1 Ch App 231; and see *Buchan's Case* (1879) 4 App Cas 549, HL (where the liability was unlimited) and para 518 post.
12 As to authorised investments and a trustee's implied indemnity see the Trustee Investments Act 1961 and TRUSTS vol 48 (Reissue) para 862 et seq.
13 *Hardoon v Belilios* [1901] AC 118, PC. See the cases cited in para 385 note 9 ante. The liability to indemnify the trustee will not be limited by the fact that the trustee is incapable of meeting the liability on the shares: *Liverpool Mortgage Insurance Co's Case* [1914] 2 Ch 617, CA; *British Union and National Insurance Co v Rawson* [1916] 2 Ch 476, CA.

414. Liability of persons whose shares have been redeemed or purchased by company. Where a company is being wound up and it has made a payment out of capital in respect of the redemption or purchase of any of its own shares[1] ('the relevant payment') and the aggregate amount of the company's assets and the amounts paid by way of contribution to its assets, apart from these provisions, are not sufficient for payment of its debts and liabilities, and the expenses of the winding up, and if the winding up commenced[2] within one year of the date on which the relevant payment was made, then:

(1) the person from whom the shares were redeemed or purchased; and
(2) the directors who signed the statutory declaration made[3] for purposes of the redemption or purchase, except a director who shows that he had reasonable grounds for forming the opinion set out in the declaration,

are, so as to enable that insufficiency to be met, liable to contribute to the following extent to the company's assets[4].

A person from whom any of the shares were so redeemed or purchased is liable to contribute an amount not exceeding so much of the relevant payment as was made by the company in respect of his shares; and the directors are jointly and severally liable with that person to contribute that amount[5]. A person who has contributed any amount to the assets in pursuance of these provisions may apply to the court for an order directing any other person jointly and severally liable in respect of that amount to pay him such amount as the court thinks just and equitable[6].

1 Ie under the Companies Act 1985 Pt V Ch VII (ss 159–181 (as amended): redeemable shares; purchase by a company of its own shares): see para 219 et seq ante.
2 As to the commencement of the winding up see para 2249 post.
3 Ie in accordance with the Companies Act 1985 s 173(3): see para 234 ante.
4 Insolvency Act 1986 s 76(1), (2).
5 Ibid s 76(3).
6 Ibid s 76(4). Section 74 (see para 2464 et seq post) and s 75 (see para 2477 post) do not apply in relation to liability accruing by virtue of s 76: s 76(5). Section 76 is deemed included in the Companies Act 1985 Pt V Ch VII (ss 159–181) (as amended) for the purposes of the Secretary of State's power to make regulations under s 179 (see para 240 ante): Insolvency Act 1986 s 76(6). As to contributories see para 2463 post.

415. Alterations in memorandum or articles as to members' liability. Notwithstanding anything in the memorandum or articles of a company, no member of the company is to be bound by an alteration made in the memorandum or articles after the date on which he became a member, if and so far as the alteration requires him to take or subscribe for more shares than the number held by him at the date on which the alteration is made, or in any way increases his liability as at that date to contribute to the company's share capital or otherwise to pay money to the company; but these provisions do not apply in any case where the member agrees in writing, either before or after the alteration is made, to be bound by the alteration[1].

1 Companies Act 1985 s 16(1), (2). See also para 537 post.

(vi) Calls

416. Meaning of 'call'. A call is a demand for payment of the amount or part of the amount which has not been paid or satisfied on a share, made by the company through its governing body upon its members prior to winding up, or by its liquidator when it is in course of winding up[1]. While the company is a going concern, or, in other words, prior to the time when its winding up commences, the liability of a member to calls is defined by its articles of association[2]. Even though the prospectus of a company relating to the issue of certain shares states that it is not intended to call up more than a specified amount per share, the company may call up the balance[3].

Where a limited company by special resolution[4] determines that any portion of its share capital which has not been already called up shall not be capable of being called up, except in the event of and for the purposes of the company being wound up, that portion of its share capital cannot be called up except in that event and for those purposes[5]; but the company may by special resolution alter the articles to give power to the directors to call up all the money unpaid on the shares[6].

1 As to calls in a winding up see para 2493 et seq post. Only calls prior to winding up are dealt with in this part of the title. A demand for payment of a sum due under terms of allotment is not a call: *Croskey v Bank of Wales* (1863) 4 Giff 314.
2 See the Companies (Tables A to F) Regulations 1985, SI 1985/805, Schedule, Table A arts 12–22. As to Table A generally see para 529 et seq post; and as to the manner of making calls see para 418 post.
3 *Alexander v Automatic Telephone Co* [1900] 2 Ch 56, CA; *Nicol's Case, Tufnell and Ponsonby's Case* (1885) 29 ChD 421, CA.

4 As to special resolutions see para 683 post.

5 Companies Act 1985 s 120. As to an unlimited company on its re-registration as a limited company providing that increase of uncalled share capital may only be called up in a winding up see para 128 ante.

6 *Accidental and Marine Insurance Corpn v Davis* (1866) 15 LT 182; *Malleson v National Insurance and Guarantee Corpn* [1894] 1 Ch 200.

417. Differences as to calls and advance payments. A company, if so authorised by its articles[1], may make arrangements on the issue of shares for a difference between the shareholders in the amounts and times of payment of calls on their shares[2]. Similarly, it may accept from any member the whole or a part of the amount remaining unpaid on any shares held by him, although no part of that amount has been called up[3]. The exercise of this latter power will be valid even though it confers a collateral benefit on the directors[4], but not if it is exercised solely for their benefit[5]. Capital cannot be paid up in advance by setting off an existing debt[6].

To the extent to which money is paid in advance of calls, the shareholder is a creditor of the company[7]; but he is not an ordinary creditor, for he cannot demand repayment of the money so paid, and the company cannot repay it unless the articles so provide[8].

1 Cf the Companies (Tables A to F) Regulations 1985, SI 1985/805, Schedule, Table A art 17. As to Table A generally see para 529 et seq post. In the absence of a provision in the articles, the directors' calls may not be made on some shareholders and not on others: *Galloway v Hallé Concerts Society* [1915] 2 Ch 233.

2 Companies Act 1985 s 119(a). As to the exercise of a power to differentiate between shareholders in the making of calls see para 420 post.

3 Ibid s 119(b). For purposes of sanctioning a scheme of arrangement, shareholders with uncalled moneys paid in advance on their shares were held to be a separate class from fully-paid shareholders: *Re United Provident Assurance Co Ltd* [1910] 2 Ch 477. As to the effect of such a payment in winding up see para 2595 post; and as to paying interest out of capital on such terms see para 271 ante.

4 *Poole, Jackson and Whyte's Case* (1878) 9 ChD 322, CA (where a debt was paid off for which the directors were liable); cf *Re South London Fish Market Co* (1888) 39 ChD 324, CA.

5 *Sykes' Case* (1872) LR 13 Eq 255 (where the money was used to pay the directors' fees); cf *Re Washington Diamond Mining Co* [1893] 3 Ch 95, CA.

6 *Kent's Case* (1888) 39 ChD 259, CA; cf *Ferrao's Case* (1874) 9 Ch App 355; and see *Re Liverpool and London Guarantee and Accident Insurance Co* (1882) 30 WR 378.

7 *Lock v Queensland Investment and Land Mortgage Co* [1896] 1 Ch 397 at 407, CA per Kay LJ; affd [1896] AC 461, HL.

8 *Lock v Queensland Investment and Land Mortgage Co* [1896] 1 Ch 397 at 407, CA (affd [1896] AC 461, HL); *Scottish Queensland Mortgage Co Ltd, Petitioners* (1908) 46 SLR 22 (where the court sanctioned a reduction of capital which included a ratification of repayments by the company to the shareholders of calls paid in advance); *London and Northern SS Co Ltd v Farmer* (1914) 111 LT 204.

418. Manner of making calls. Calls made prior to winding up are made, and payment of them is enforced, in pursuance of the power given by the company's articles of association and in the manner therein provided[1]. A power to make calls may be exercised only by a quorum of directors present at a meeting duly convened, unless the articles otherwise provide[2]; but a call made at an adjourned meeting is not bad because notice of the adjourned meeting was not given to each director[3].

A call made by a quorum may be bad if the total number of directors is less than the minimum number prescribed by the articles, but, if the direction as to the minimum number is not imperative, the call is good[4]; and a director who is one of the quorum may be estopped from denying the validity of the call[5].

Where by the articles a call is to be made by the directors, it must be made by directors properly appointed, acting as a duly constituted meeting of the board[6], and the power to make calls cannot be delegated except under an express power to delegate[7]. If a call is invalid by reason of any defect in the constitution of the board meeting, it may be confirmed by a duly convened and constituted board[8], and all acts of directors are valid notwithstanding any defect that may afterwards be discovered in their appointments or qualifications[9].

The resolution must comply with the provisions of the articles and must in any case state the amount of the call and the time at which it is to be paid; otherwise the call will be invalid[10].

1 There are no such provisions in the Companies Act 1985 but the Companies (Tables A to F) Regulations 1985, SI 1985/805, Schedule, Table A (amended by SI 1985/1052) (see para 529 et seq post) regulates the making of calls. Table A arts 12–22 contains provisions as to calls, and similar clauses more or less amplified or abbreviated are to be found in the articles of companies which exclude Table A, or adopt it with modification.
    See also Table A art 12 (general power to make calls), art 13 (time when calls deemed to be made), art 14 (liability of joint holders), art 15 (payment of interest), art 16 (sums payable on allotment or at fixed date deemed to be calls), art 17 (differentiation in amounts and times of calls).
    Under an article in like terms to those of art 12, it has been held that two calls payable at different times may be made at one meeting: *Universal Corpn Ltd v Hughes* 1909 SC 1434.
2 *Moore v Hammond* (1827) 6 B & C 456.
3 *Wills v Murray* (1850) 4 Exch 843.
4 *Bottomley's Case* (1880) 16 ChD 681; *Re British Empire Match Co, ex p Ross* (1888) 59 LT 291; *Faure Electric Accumulator Co v Phillipart* (1888) 58 LT 525; *Thames-Haven Dock and Rly Co v Rose* (1842) 4 Man & G 552.
5 See *Faure Electric Accumulator Co v Phillipart* (1888) 58 LT 525.
6 *Howbeach Coal Co Ltd v Teague* (1860) 5 H & N 151 (as to this case see *Re London and Southern Counties Freehold Land Co* (1885) 31 ChD 223); *Garden Gully United Quartz Mining Co v McLister* (1875) 1 App Cas 39, PC; *Tyne Mutual SS Insurance Association v Brown* (1896) 74 LT 283.
7 *Southampton Dock Co v Richards* (1840) 1 Man & G 448; *Howard's Case* (1866) 1 Ch App 561.
8 *Re Phosphate of Lime Co Ltd, Austin's Case* (1871) 24 LT 932.
9 See the Companies Act 1985 s 285 (cited in para 545 post) which does not cover a case where there has been a total absence of appointment or a fraudulent usurpation of authority: *Morris v Kanssen* [1946] AC 459, [1946] 1 All ER 586, HL.
10 *Johnson v Lyttle's Iron Agency* (1877) 5 ChD 687, CA; *Re Cawley & Co* (1889) 42 ChD 209, CA.

419. Conditions as to making calls.

Conditions precedent to the making of calls, such as those relating to time and amount[1], and all the requirements and formalities of the company's articles[2], must be strictly complied with[3]. A call may be made, although only a part of the capital is subscribed, unless by the regulations of the company[4] the subscription of the whole of the capital is a condition precedent to the exercise of the powers of the directors generally or their power to make calls[5].

1 *Baillie v Edinburgh Oil Gas Light Co* (1835) 3 Cl & Fin 639, HL; *Stratford and Moreton Rly Co v Stratton* (1831) 2 B & Ad 518; *Welland Rly Co v Berrie* (1861) 6 H & N 416.
2 As to the provisions of the Companies (Tables A to F) Regulations 1985, SI 1985/805, Schedule, Table A (amended by SI 1985/1052) see para 418 note 1 ante.
3 *Clubwa Tea Co of Assam v Barry* (1866) 15 LT 449.
4 *North Stafford Steel etc Co (Burslem) Ltd v Ward* (1868) LR 3 Exch 172.
5 *Ornamental Pyrographic Woodwork Co v Brown* (1863) 2 H & C 63, overruling a dictum in *Howbeach Coal Co v Teague* (1860) 5 H & N 151; and see *Re Great Cambrian Mining and Quarrying Co, Hawkins' Case* (1856) 2 K & J 253; *Elder v New Zealand Land Improvement Co Ltd* (1874) 30 LT 285.

420. Discretion as to making calls.

The discretion which directors possess as to making or abstaining from making calls is not reviewed by the court in the absence of bad faith[1]. The power to make calls is fiduciary as regards the shareholders, and, in making or abstaining from making calls, the directors must have regard to the interests of the company, and their powers must be exercised fairly as between different shareholders, and not with a view to giving themselves an unfair advantage[2]. Unless the directors have power to do so, prima facie they are not entitled to make a call on some members and not on others of the same class[3]; and, even if they have that power of differentiating between members, there must be a sufficient reason for its exercise[4]. The directors are not, however, trustees for the company's creditors[5].

1 *Odessa Tramways Co v Mendel* (1878) 8 ChD 235, CA; *Re Sankey Brook Coal Co* (1870) LR 9 Eq 721; *Re British Provident Life and Fire Assurance Society, Stanley's Case* (1864) 4 De GJ & Sm 407 at 415; *Tatham v Palace Restaurants Ltd* (1909) 53 Sol Jo 743; cf *Bailey v Birkenhead, Lancashire and Cheshire Junction Rly Co* (1850) 12 Beav 433.
2 *Gilbert's Case* (1870) 5 Ch App 559; *Alexander v Automatic Telephone Co* [1900] 2 Ch 56, CA; *Preston v Grand Collier Dock Co* (1840) 11 Sim 327. As to the fiduciary character of directors see further para 585 post.
3 As to the power to differentiate in making calls see para 417 ante.
4 *Galloway v Hallé Concerts Society* [1915] 2 Ch 233.
5 *Poole, Jackson and Whyte's Case* (1878) 9 ChD 322 at 328, CA; cf *Gaslight Improvement Co v Terrell* (1870) LT 10 Eq 168 at 175.

421. Notice of call. The notice of call must be served as directed by the articles of association; and, if addressed to a member at his registered address, as provided by the articles, it is good, notwithstanding his previous death, if the company has no notice of his death[1]. The call may be valid though the form of the notice is inaccurate[2], provided that it is clear notice of the call[3]. The fact that no notice has been sent to other shareholders[4] is immaterial.

1 *New Zealand Gold Extraction Co (Newbury-Vautin Process) v Peacock* [1894] 1 QB 622, CA.
2 *Shackleford, Ford & Co v Dangerfield* (1868) LR 3 CP 407 (where a company in course of changing its name used the new name).
3 *Chubwa Tea Co of Assam Ltd v Barry* (1866) 15 LT 449.
4 *Newry and Enniskillen Rly Co v Edmunds* (1848) 2 Exch 118.

422. Calls on directors' shares. A director may, before a call is made, transfer his shares to escape liability[1], and directors may pay the amount uncalled on their shares, and apply it in payment of a debt of the company in the ordinary course of business, even if the effect is to relieve them of their liability as guarantors of such debt[2].

1 *Re Cawley & Co* (1889) 42 ChD 209, CA.
2 *Poole, Jackson and Whyte's Case* (1878) 9 ChD 322, CA. As to payments in advance of calls on shares held by directors see para 271 ante; and *Re Exchange Banking Co, Ramwell's Case* (1881) 50 LJ Ch 827. Applying the advance in payment of the directors' fees may be a preference: see *Re Washington Diamond Mining Co* [1893] 3 Ch 95, CA.

423. Set-off against calls. A set-off purported to be made by a director within six months of a winding-up petition and with knowledge that the company is in a precarious condition, is a preference[1]. A debt presently due and owing by the company to a shareholder, but not one which is payable only at a future date, may be set off against a sum due from him upon calls while the company is a going concern[2]. An agreement to set off a present liability of the company against future calls is also good[3]. A call once made may be discharged by accord and satisfaction provided the consideration is not illusory[4]; but in general a company cannot contract that payment of future calls shall be accepted in goods or other money's worth[5].

1   *Re Washington Diamond Mining Co* [1893] 3 Ch 95, CA. See the Insolvency Act 1986 ss 239, 240(1)(b) and paras 2605, 2609 post. A director who, before winding up, gives a promissory note to secure a debt of the company cannot, after winding up, set off the amount against a call made before the winding up: *Re Norwich Equitable Fire Assurance Co, Brasnett's Case* (1884) 32 WR 1010; affd (1885) 53 LT 569, CA.

2   *Habershon's Case* (1868) LR 5 Eq 286; *Holden's Case* (1869) LR 8 Eq 444; *Adamson's Case* (1874) LR 18 Eq 670; and see *Re Norwich Equitable Fire Assurance Co, Brasnets's Case* (1885) 53 LT 569, CA. Cf *Sykes' Case* (1872) LR 13 Eq 255; *Christie v Taunton, Delmard, Lane & Co, Re Taunton, Delmard, Lane & Co* [1893] 2 Ch 175 (calls set off against debenture debt); *Rance's Case* (1870) 6 Ch App 104 at 115. As to set-off against calls in a winding up see para 2498 post.

3   *Re Jones, Lloyd & Co Ltd* (1889) 41 ChD 159.

4   *Re White Star Line Ltd* [1938] Ch 458, [1938] 1 All ER 607; *Re Wragg Ltd* [1897] 1 Ch 796.

5   *Black & Co's Case* (1872) 8 Ch App 254; *Pellatt's Case* (1867) 2 Ch App 527; *Elkington's Case* (1867) 2 Ch App 511; *Re London and Colonial Co, ex p Clark* (1869) LR 7 Eq 550; and see *Gardner v Iredale* [1912] 1 Ch 700 (where the principles laid down in *Pellatt's Case* (1867) 2 Ch App 527, were held not to be applicable to that case).

424. Interest on calls. The articles of the company usually provide for payment of interest on calls in arrear[1] and Table A contains a similar provision[2]. Even in the absence of any provision for interest, after notice to pay on a fixed day has been given, interest may be claimed from the date fixed until payment[3]. Interest on calls in arrear may be recovered after forfeiture for non-payment of the calls[4].

1   The provisions do not apply to calls made in a winding up: *Re Welsh Flannel and Tweed Co* (1875) LR 20 Eq 360.

2   See the Companies (Tables A to F) Regulations 1985, SI 1985/805, Schedule, Table A art 15. As to Table A generally see para 529 et seq post.

3   *Re Overend, Gurney & Co, ex p Lintott* (1867) LR 4 Eq 184; *Barrow's Case* (1868) 3 Ch App 784; *Stocken's Case* (1868) 3 Ch App 412. The rate then allowed was 5% per annum. As to the payment of interest generally, in the absence of a special provision, and the power of the court to award interest in proceedings for the recovery of a debt see the Supreme Court Act 1981 s 35A (added by the Administration of Justice Act 1982 s 15(1), Sch 1 Pt I) and MONEY vol 32 para 106 et seq.

4   *Faure Electric Accumulator Co Ltd v Phillipart* (1888) 58 LT 525.

425. Calls on transferred or forfeited shares. Where shares have been transferred, the transferor remains liable for calls already made[1].

Where shares are forfeited for non-payment of calls and then sold and the purchaser receives a certificate showing that the shares are not fully paid, but stating that the purchaser is to be deemed the holder of the 'said shares discharged from all calls due prior to the date hereof' the company may nevertheless make calls on the purchaser for the balance due on the shares, but the purchaser is not liable for interest on calls previously made[2]. On winding up the purchaser is, however, liable for calls only in respect of the balance owing on the shares after giving credit for any sums paid on the shares by the original holder, whether as a shareholder or as being a debtor under articles which render him liable after forfeiture[3].

1   *Re National Bank of Wales, Taylor, Phillips and Richard's Cases* [1897] 1 Ch 298 at 306, CA. Under an article in like terms to the Companies (Tables A to F) Regulations 1985, SI 1985/805, Schedule, Table A art 8 the company has a lien on shares for moneys called up in respect of them; and under art 24, or an article to the like effect, it may decline to register a transfer of shares on which it has a lien, the result being that the shareholders on the register when the call is made are those who are liable to pay the call: see *North American Colonial Association of Ireland v Bentley* (1850) 19 LJQB 427. As to Table A generally see para 529 et seq post.

2   *New Balkis Eersteling Ltd v Randt Gold Mining Co* [1904] AC 165, HL.

3   *Re Randt Gold Mining Co* [1904] 2 Ch 468. As to the power of forfeiture under the Companies (Tables A to F) Regulations 1985 Schedule, Table A see para 522 et seq post.

426. Recovery of calls. The procedure for recovery of a call is by action commenced by writ in which the company is plaintiff[1].

Calls made but not paid before winding up may be enforced by an action brought by the liquidator in the name of the company, although he has obtained a balance order[2]. Calls are specialty debts due from the members to the company[3].

1 As to obtaining summary judgment see RSC Ord 14 and PRACTICE AND PROCEDURE vol 37 para 410 et seq.
2 *Westmoreland Green and Blue Slate Co v Feilden* [1891] 3 Ch 15, CA. See paras 2496, 2763 post.
3 See para 140 ante. A call, which is a specialty debt, is not statute-barred until 12 years have expired after it became due: *Cork and Bandon Rly Co v Goode* (1853) 13 CB 826; Limitation Act 1980 s 8. As to satisfaction of the debt see para 423 ante.

427. Joint holders. Where there is no special clause as to several liability, two or more holders of the same share are only jointly liable[1].

1 *Re Maria Anna and Steinbank Coal and Coke Co, Maxwell's Case, Hill's Case* (1875) LR 20 Eq 585. Cf the Companies (Tables A to F) Regulations 1985, SI 1985/805, Schedule, Table A art 14 (joint and several liability in articles). As to Table A generally see para 529 et seq post.

428. Effect of bankruptcy. Calls which are unpaid at the date of the bankruptcy of a shareholder, and the estimated value of his liability in respect of any future calls, are provable in the bankruptcy[1]. If the dividend received is less than 100 pence in the pound on the amount of the proof, payment of the dividend does not make the shares fully-paid, so as to enable the bankrupt's estate to rank as a fully-paid shareholder in the distribution of surplus assets of the company[2]. Where shares have been forfeited and reissued, and the person against whom the forfeiture was exercised has become bankrupt, the company may prove in his bankruptcy only to the extent of its actual loss, that is the difference between the amount payable by the original holder in respect of the shares, including interest on calls, and the net amount received by the company in respect of the reissued shares[3]. Where any part of the property of a bankrupt consists of shares or stock constituting overseas property, his trustee in bankruptcy may disclaim them[4].

1 *Re Mercantile Mutual Marine Insurance Association* (1883) 25 ChD 415; *Re McMahon, Fuller v McMahon* [1900] 1 Ch 173; *Re Rowe, ex p West Coast Gold Fields Ltd* [1904] 2 KB 489 (where the company had a security by lien on the shares). Where a member who held both partly paid-up and fully paid-up shares became bankrupt and the company, after proving in respect of amounts due on the partly paid-up shares, altered its articles so as to give it a lien on fully paid-up shares, the company was not allowed to amend its proof or to substitute a fresh proof so as to set up its lien on the fully paid-up shares: *Re Rowe, ex p West Coast Gold Fields Ltd* supra. For the right of proof against the estate of a bankrupt contributory in a winding up see para 2469 post. As to a bankrupt's right to vote see para 670 post; and as to disclaimer of a contract to take shares by a trustee in bankruptcy and proof thereon see BANKRUPTCY.
2 *Re West Coast Gold Fields Ltd, Rowe's Trustee's Claim* [1905] 1 Ch 597; affd [1906] 1 Ch 1, CA.
3 *Re Bolton, ex p North British Artificial Silk Ltd* [1930] 2 Ch 48.
4 See the Insolvency Act 1986 s 315(1) and BANKRUPTCY vol 3(2) (Reissue) para 460. For the effect of disclaimer and rights of proof against the bankrupt's estate see para 2469 post.

429. Effect of death of shareholder. The estate of a deceased shareholder is liable for the payment of calls on shares standing in his name, whether the calls are made before or after his death, and his legal personal representatives are liable only in their representative character[1]. Personal representatives who distribute the estate amongst the beneficiaries without providing for the liability attaching to the estate in respect of shares not fully paid up, forming part of the estate, commit a devastavit, and are personally liable to pay calls on the shares up to the amount of the assets distributed[2]. If there is no legal personal representative, the court grants administration to the company's nominee as a creditor of the deceased person's estate[3]. If legal personal representatives unequivocally request that the shares should be transferred into their own names, they become personally liable, although on the register they are designated executors[4].

1 *Houldsworth v Evans* (1868) LR 3 HL 263 at 283; *Baird's Case* (1870) 5 Ch App 725; *New Zealand Gold Extraction Co (Newbury-Vautin Process) v Peacock* [1894] 1 QB 622, CA. It has been held in Ireland that an executor de son tort who takes the dividends on shares cannot be sued for calls de bonis propriis: *Blackstaff Flax Spinning and Weaving Co v Cameron* [1899] 1 IR 252.

2 *Taylor v Taylor* (1870) LR 10 Eq 477.

3 *Tomlinson v Gilby* (1885) 54 LJP 80.

4 *Buchan's Case* (1879) 4 App Cas 549, HL.

(vii) Lien on Shares

430. Company's lien on shares. Where there is an agreement to this effect, or the articles of association[1] so provide, a company may have a lien on a member's shares for money owing[2] by him to the company. Where fully-paid shares are, under the original articles, exempt from lien, the articles may be altered so as to subject the existing fully-paid shares to the lien with respect to existing debts[3]; but, if the company has already proved in the bankruptcy of the shareholder, it will not be allowed to set up a lien acquired subsequent to the bankruptcy[4].

1 *Re Kingstown Yacht Club* (1888) 21 LR Ir 199; *Allen v Gold Reefs of West Africa Ltd* [1900] 1 Ch 656, CA (where a lien was held good against executors). Where no express lien is conferred, but shares may be forfeited if money due in respect of them is not paid, the company has no lien: *Re Dunlop, Dunlop v Dunlop* (1882) 21 ChD 583, CA; *Re Kingstown Yacht Club* supra. The Companies Act 1862 Sch 1, Table A (repealed) did not give any express lien on shares, but art 10 (repealed) empowered the company to decline to register a transfer of shares to a person 'indebted to them', and 'indebted' meant on any account whatever, and either solely or jointly with other persons: *Ex p Stringer* (1882) 9 QBD 436; *Re Bentham Mills Spinning Co* (1879) 11 ChD 900, CA. Such a power does not create a lien and does not enable the company to obtain priority over an equitable charge created by the shareholder over his shares: *Bank of N T Butterfield & Son Ltd v Golinsky* [1926] AC 733, PC. Articles of association usually give a much more extensive lien actively enforceable by sale of the shares but, where a listing on the Stock Exchange is desired, the articles of association must provide that fully-paid shares are free from all lien: *Listing Rules* Ch 13 App 1 para 6; and see para 536 post. As to the *Listing Rules* generally see para 282 ante. The Companies (Tables A to F) Regulations 1985, SI 1985/805, Schedule, Table A art 8 gives the company a 'first and paramount lien on every share (not being a fully-paid share) for all moneys (whether presently payable or not) payable at a fixed time or called in respect of that share'. Articles 9–11 provide for enforcing the lien by sale of the shares. Such a power of sale does not of itself authorise the company to sell the shares otherwise than in accordance with the articles conferring a right of pre-emption on the other shareholders: *Champagne Perrier-Jouet SA v H H Finch Ltd* [1982] 3 All ER 713, [1982] 1 WLR 1359. As to Table A generally see para 529 et seq post.

2 The lien extends to moneys paid as directors' fees under a mistake of fact: *Re Bodega Co Ltd* [1904] 1 Ch 276.

3 *Allen v Gold Reefs of West Africa Ltd* [1900] 1 Ch 656, CA; cf *Liquidator of W and A McArthur Ltd v Gulf Line Ltd* 1909 SC 732. If such a provision empowers the company to forfeit shares which are subject to a lien for all debts for non-payment of these debts (which ex hypothesi are not in respect of calls), it is void: see para 523 text and note 2 post.

4 *Re Rowe, ex p West Coast Gold Fields Ltd* [1904] 2 KB 489. See also BANKRUPTCY.

431. Extent of lien. The lien extends to any moneys receivable by the shareholder in respect of the shares in a winding up[1]. The lien is a security within the meaning of an article which forbids the making of loans to shareholders without security[2].

If articles of association give a company a paramount lien on shares held by a group of people in respect of all moneys owing to the company by any of the holders, alone or jointly with any other persons, the company is entitled to a lien on shares held by trustees in respect of debts due to the company by a firm, of which one of such trustees is a member, paramount to the claims of the beneficiaries[3].

The company has no lien for debts due from beneficiaries who are not registered holders of shares[4], and cannot alter its register of shareholders by substituting their names for those of the trustees[5].

1 *Re General Exchange Bank, Re Lewis* (1871) 6 Ch App 818. A lien on the proceeds of sale of shares is a lien on the shares: *Deering and McQuestron v Hibernian Joint-Stock Banking Co* (1868) 16 WR 578.
2 *Re National Bank of Wales Ltd* [1899] 2 Ch 629 at 651, CA.
3 *New London and Brazilian Bank v Brocklebank* (1882) 21 ChD 302, CA.
4 *Re Perkins, ex p Mexican Santa Barbara Mining Co* (1890) 24 QBD 613, CA; *Paul's Trustee v Thomas Justice & Sons Ltd* 1912 SC 1303 (where the articles gave the lien against 'the holder'); *Mathieson v Gronow* (1929) 141 LT 553; *Re Collie, ex p Manchester and County Bank* (1876) 3 ChD 481, CA. As to registered holders see para 382 ante. See also TRUSTS.
5 *Re Ystalyfera Gas Co* [1887] WN 30.

432. Priority of lien. Where the company has by its articles a paramount lien on every share for all debts due from the holder to the company, it has no priority in respect of moneys which become due from the shareholder to the company after the company has received notice of a charge given to another person[1]. The lien continues to exist, however, although the shareholder has given the company unmatured bills for his debt; and it prevails over a charge given after the giving of the bills but before maturity[2].

1 *Bradford Banking Co Ltd v Briggs, Son & Co Ltd* (1886) 12 App Cas 29, HL, overruling on this point *Miles v New Zealand Alford Estate Co* (1886) 32 ChD 266, CA; *Rearden v Provincial Bank of Ireland* [1896] 1 IR 532; *Mackereth v Wigan Coal and Iron Co Ltd* [1916] 2 Ch 293.
2 *Re London, Birmingham and South Staffordshire Banking Co Ltd* (1865) 34 Beav 332.

433. Loss or discharge of lien. The company's lien is lost if it registers a transfer of the shares which are subject to the lien[1]; but a dividend declared after the execution but before registration of a transfer may be retained under the lien[2]. When a transfer is executed for value of certain shares forming part of a larger number on which the company has a lien and the company declines to register the transfer, the lien must, as between the transferor and transferee, be satisfied out of the remaining shares, if sufficient[3].

A lien on shares may be discharged by a new arrangement between the company and the shareholder, the terms of which are incompatible with retention of the lien, or which show an intention to waive it[4].

On payment of the debt in respect of which there is a lien, the debtor may require the company to assign the lien to his nominee[5].

1 *Higgs v Assam Tea Co* (1869) LR 4 Exch 387; *Re Northern Assam Tea Co, ex p Universal Life Assurance Co* (1870) LR 10 Eq 458. As to registration of transfers see para 498 post.
2 *Re M'Murdo, Penfold v M'Murdo* (1892) 8 TLR 507.
3 *Gray v Stone and Funnell* (1893) 69 LT 282.

4 *Bank of Africa v Salisbury Gold Mining Co* [1892] AC 281, PC; *Hunter v Stewart* (1861) 4 De GF & J 168.
5 *Everitt v Automatic Weighing Machine Co* [1892] 3 Ch 506.

(viii) Cessation of Membership

434. Cessation of membership. Membership ceases:
    (1) on death[1];
    (2) on the registration of a transfer of all the shares held by a member[2];
    (3) by a valid surrender or forfeiture of his shares[3];
    (4) on the registration as a member of a purchaser of shares under a sale to satisfy a lien[4]; or
    (5) on the dissolution of the company[5].

1 See para 504 post.
2 See para 517 post. As to his liability as a past member in winding up see para 2465 post.
3 See paras 520, 522 post.
4 See para 430 ante.
5 See para 2691 post.

435. Bankruptcy. A member who becomes bankrupt ceases to be a member when the trustee is registered as a member in his place, as he may be, if the articles permit it[1], or when the trustee's transferee is registered[2], or when the trustee disclaims the share and the name of the bankrupt is removed from the register[3]. Where a company is a member, its membership ceases when the transferee of the liquidator is registered or when the liquidator disclaims the shares[4].

1 *Re Bentham Mills Spinning Co* (1879) 11 ChD 900, CA; *Morgan v Gray* [1953] Ch 83 at 87, [1953] All ER 213 at 217; and see the Companies (Tables A to F) Regulations 1985, SI 1985/805, Schedule, Table A arts 30, 31. As to Table A generally see para 529 et seq post.
2 See BANKRUPTCY.
3 See BANKRUPTCY; *Wise v Lansdell* [1921] 1 Ch 420.
4 Ie under the Insolvency Act 1986 s 178: see para 2626 post.

(13) SHARES

(i) In general

436. Division of capital. The nominal capital of a company limited by shares or limited by guarantee and having a share capital must be divided into shares of a fixed pecuniary amount which must be stated in its memorandum of association[1]. In the case of an unlimited company having a share capital, the articles must state the amount of share capital[2], and it is usual in the articles of an unlimited company to state that the capital, if there is any, is divided into shares of a certain amount[3]. A provision in the memorandum or articles, or in any resolution of a company limited by guarantee registered on or after 1 January 1901[4], purporting to divide the company's undertaking into shares or interests, is to be treated as a provision for a share capital, although the nominal amount or number of the shares or interests is not thereby specified[5]. In the case of a company limited by guarantee not having a share capital and registered on or after 1 January 1901, every provision in the memorandum or articles or in any resolution of the company purporting to give any person a right to participate in the divisible profits of the company otherwise than as a member, is void[6]. With effect from 22 December 1980[7], a company cannot be formed as, or become, a company limited by guarantee with a share capital[8].

All the shares need not be of equal amount, nor need they be all of the same class; some may be preference shares and others ordinary, and there is no restriction on the number of classes of shares[9].

1 See the Companies Act 1985 s 2(5)(a) and paras 102, 108 ante.
2 Ibid s 7(2).
3 See the Companies (Tables A to F) Regulations 1985, SI 1985/805, Schedule, Table E art 3. As to Table E see para 116 note 3 ante and para 530 post.
4 Ie the date when the Companies Act 1900 (repealed) came into operation.
5 Companies Act 1985 s 15(2); Companies Consolidation (Consequential Provisions) Act 1985 s 10. See also para 109 ante. The object of this provision was to prevent further evasion of obligations as to paying capital duty etc: see *Malleson v General Mineral Patents Syndicate Ltd* [1894] 3 Ch 538.
6 Companies Act 1985 s 15(1); Companies Consolidation (Consequential Provisions) Act 1985 s 10. See also para 110 ante.
7 Ie the date when the Companies Act 1980 s 1 (repealed) came into operation.
8 Companies Act 1985 s 1(4).
9 See para 180 ante.

437. Attributes of shares. A share is a right to a specified amount of the share capital of a company[1], carrying with it certain rights and liabilities while the company is a going concern and in its winding up[2]. The shares or other interest of any member in a company are personal estate[3] transferable in the manner provided by its articles[4] but subject to the Stock Transfer Act 1963 (which enables securities of certain descriptions to be transferred by a simplified process)[5] and to regulations made under the Companies Act 1989 (which enable title to securities to be evidenced and transferred without a written instrument)[6] and are not in the nature of real estate[7].

1 A share cannot properly be likened to a sum of money, settled upon and subject to executory limitations to arise in the future; it is the interest of the holder in the company, measured, for the purposes of liability and dividend, by a sum of money: *Borland's Trustee v Steel Bros & Co Ltd* [1901] 1 Ch 279. In the Companies Act 1985, unless the context otherwise requires, 'share' includes stock, except where a distinction between stock and shares is expressed or implied: s 744(1). As used in s 2 it never means stock, for stock may be created only by conversion after shares have been issued and have been fully paid up: *Re Home and Foreign Investment and Agency Co Ltd* [1912] 1 Ch 72.
2 A share is often described as a 'bundle of rights': see *Re Banque des Marchands de Moscou (Koupetschesky)* [1958] Ch 182 at 220, [1957] 3 All ER 182 at 191. See also *Government of Mauritius v Union Flacq Sugar Estates Co Ltd* [1992] 1 WLR 903, PC (the property owned by a shareholder is his share and his right to vote in general meetings of the company is not property in its own right or an interest in or right over property but merely an incident of the ownership of a share).
3 Shares are 'goods' which may be ordered to be sold under RSC Ord 29 r 4: *Evans v Davies* [1893] 2 Ch 216. As to gifts of shares in a will and the words sufficient to include the same in a gift by will see WILLS vol 50 paras 479, 480. Shares transferable only by deed were choses in action within the meaning of the Bankruptcy Act 1914 s 38(c) (repealed): *Colonial Bank v Whinney* (1886) 11 App Cas 426, HL.
4 As to transfers see para 490 et seq post.
5 See para 506 et seq post.
6 Ie under the Companies Act 1989 s 207: see para 496 note 4 post and MONEY.
7 Companies Act 1985 s 182(1) (amended by the Uncertificated Securities Regulations 1995, SI 1995/3272, reg 40(1)).

438. Numbering of shares. Each share in a company having a share capital must be distinguished by its appropriate number[1], except that, if at any time all the issued shares in a company or all the issued shares in it of a particular class are fully paid up and rank pari passu for all purposes, none of those shares need thereafter have a distinguishing number so long as it remains fully paid up and ranks pari passu for all purposes with all shares of the same class for the time being issued and fully paid up[2]. This provision for numbering does not apply to a joint stock company whose shares are not numbered when registering[3] under the Companies Act 1985[4].

1 Companies Act 1985 s 182(2). The number referred to is usually called 'the denoting number'. The provision is merely directory, to enable the title of particular persons to be traced: *Ind's Case* (1872) 7 Ch App 485; cf *Wolverhampton New Waterworks Co v Hawksford* (1860) 7 CBNS 795 at 812, 813 (affd (1861) 11 CBNS 456); *East Gloucestershire Rly Co v Bartholomew* (1867) LR 3 Exch 15 at 21.
2 Companies Act 1985 s 182(2).
3 Ie under ibid Pt XXII Ch II (ss 680–690) (as amended).
4 See ibid s 689, Sch 21 para 6(3) and para 27 ante.

439. Shareholders. Where a company has a capital limited by shares, the shareholders are the only members[1].

1 See para 358 ante. As to share warrant bearers being members in accordance with provisions in articles see para 494 post.

440. Contracts to take shares. The principles applicable to a contract to take or subscribe[1] for shares in a company are identical with those which apply to other contracts[2]; and specific performance of an agreement to take and pay for shares may be obtained[3].

1 For the meaning of 'subscribe' see *Arnison v Smith* (1889) 41 ChD 348 at 357, CA (cited in para 194 note 2 ante); cf *Re London and Colonial Finance Corpn Ltd* (1897) 77 LT 146 at 147, CA ('subscribe' as used in a memorandum of association held to mean to take personally or to find someone else to take); *Whitwam v Watkin* (1898) 78 LT 188. See also para 1637 note 1 post.
2 See paras 370, 371 ante.
3 See para 376 ante.

441. Changes in shares. Shares may be consolidated into shares of larger amount[1] or sub-divided into shares of smaller amount[2], or, when fully paid up, may be converted into stock which may be reconverted into shares[3]. These operations may take place without application to the court[4]. After shares have been issued, they may be reduced in amount or as regards liability with the court's confirmation[5].

1 See para 205 ante.
2 See para 208 ante.
3 See para 209 ante.
4 See paras 205, 208, 209 ante.
5 See para 215 ante.

(ii) Allotment and Issue

A. APPLICATION AND ALLOTMENT

442. Application and allotment. In most cases the contract with the company is constituted by an application being made by the intending shareholder[1] to the company for an allotment[2] to him of so many shares, and by an allotment being made, and notified to him. The application is an offer by him to take a certain number of shares; and the allotment by the company is an acceptance of the offer. A binding contract is constituted to take, and issue, the shares when, and not before, the acceptance is notified to the applicant[3] or his agent for the purpose of receiving the notice[4]; until then the contract is not complete, even when the applicant's name is registered[5].

Only slight evidence is required as to the service of notice[6]; and, even where there is no formal notice, the receipt of notice of allotment may be implied from the conduct of the applicant[7].

If notice of allotment is sent by post, the acceptance is notified when the notice is posted[8], even though it never reaches the applicant[9]. In some cases, as, for example, on a reconstruction or amalgamation, the offer may, in effect, come from the company, and the application then operates as an acceptance[10].

Either the offer or the acceptance may be oral[11]. In general before notification of the acceptance is received[12], or if sent by post, posted[13], the offer may be withdrawn, and even if in writing, it may be withdrawn orally[14].

If there is unreasonable delay in accepting an application for shares, the applicant may repudiate them within a reasonable time after receiving notice of allotment[15], and before a winding up commences[16].

There is no contract where the offer to take shares in a company is made by a person who believes it to be a totally different company, and that belief is induced by those who represent the company[17].

1 As to persons who may not become shareholders see paras 362, 363 ante.

2 As to contracts to pay on allotment where the company is never registered see *Wheeler v Fradd* (1898) 14 TLR 302; and where the allotment is made but subsequently rescinded because the company cannot obtain a certificate to commence business see *Ellett v Sternberg* (1910) 27 TLR 127.

3 *Re Florence Land and Public Works Co, Nicol's Case, Tufnell and Ponsonby's Case* (1885) 29 ChD 421 at 426, CA; *Hebb's Case* (1867) LR 4 Eq 9. Acceptance is sufficiently communicated when a letter demanding payment for the shares is dispatched: *Forget v Cement Products Co of Canada* [1916] WN 259, PC.

4 *Harward's Case* (1871) LR 13 Eq 30; *Levita's Case* (1870) 5 Ch App 489; *Re Charles Laffite & Co Ltd, De Rosaz's Case* (1869) 21 LT 10, CA.

5 *Gunn's Case* (1867) 3 Ch App 40; *Sahlgreen and Carrall's Case* (1868) 3 Ch App 323; *Wallis's Case* (1868) 4 Ch App 325n; *Re Peruvian Railways Co, Crawley's Case, Robinson's Case* (1869) 4 Ch App 322; *Re Land Shipping Colliery Co, ex p Harwood, Gull, Geary and Stafford* (1869) 20 LT 736; *Ward's Case* (1870) LR 10 Eq 659; *Re Joseph Horner & Sons Ltd, Plimsoll's Case* (1871) 24 LT 653.

6 *Re National Funds Assurance Co, Sparling's Case* (1877) 26 WR 41.

7 *Richards v Home Assurance Association* (1871) LR 6 CP 591; *Re Valparaiso Water Works Co, Davies' Case* (1872) 41 LJ Ch 659; *Re Hampshire Co-operative Milk Co Ltd, Purcell's Case* (1880) 29 WR 170; *Re Saloon Steam Packet Co, ex p Fletcher* (1867) 37 LJ Ch 49; *Re Peruvian Railways Co, Crawley's Case, Robinson's Case* (1869) 3 Ch App 322; *Levita's Case* (1867) 3 Ch App 36 at 38; *Re United Ports and General Insurance Co, Brown's Case, Tucker's Case* (1871) 41 LJ Ch 157; *Re Imperial Land Credit Corpn Ltd, ex p Eve* (1868) 37 LJ Ch 844.

8 As to acceptance by post see CONTRACT vol 9 para 271 et seq; *Quenerduaine v Cole* (1883) 32 WR 185; *Household Fire Insurance Co v Grant* (1879) 4 ExD 216, CA (overruling *Re Constantinople and Alexandria Hotels Co, Finucane's Case* (1869) 17 WR 813; *Reidpath's Case* (1870) LR 11 Eq 86; and *British and American Telegraph Co Ltd v Colson* (1871) LR 6 Exch 108); *Re Cardiff and Caerphilly Iron Co Ltd, Gledhill's Case* (1861) 3 De GF & J 713; *Re Exhall Coal Mining Co Ltd, Miles' Case* (1864) 4 De GJ & Sm 471; *Re Natal Investment Co Ltd, Wilson's Case* (1869) 20 LT 962; *Re Metropolitan Fire Insurance Co, Wallace's Case* [1900] 2 Ch 671; *Re Whitley Partners Ltd, Steel's Case* (1879) 49 LJ Ch 176; *Re Scottish Petroleum Co, Maclagan's Case* (1882) 51 LJ Ch 841; *Wall's Case* (1872) LR 15 Eq 18; *Ritso's Case* (1877) 4 ChD 774, CA; *Truman's Case* [1894] 3 Ch 272; *Re General International Agency Co, Chapman's Case* (1866) LR 2 Eq 567. Cf *Re London and Northern Bank, ex p Jones* [1900] 1 Ch 220 (handing letter of allotment to postman does not constitute posting). As to contracts made by telex etc see CONTRACT vol 9 paras 272, 280.

9 *Jackson v Turquand* (1869) LR 4 HL 305 (offer by company of available shares pro rata to members; concluded contract in respect of shares so offered accepted by shareholders, but no contract in respect of application for surplus shares where no acceptance by company notified); *Household Fire Insurance Co v Grant* (1879) 4 ExD 216, CA.

10 *Adams' Case* (1872) LR 13 Eq 474; *Re United Ports and General Insurance Co, Brown's Case, Tucker's Case* (1871) 41 LJ Ch 157; cf *Wallace's Case* [1900] 2 Ch 671; *Re New Eberhardt Co, ex p Menzies* (1889) 43 ChD 118, CA.

11 *Re Electric Telegraph Co of Ireland, Cookney's Case* (1858) 3 De G & J 170 at 173; *Re New Theatre Co, Bloxam's Case* (1864) 33 LJ Ch 574; *Levita's Case* (1867) 3 Ch App 36.

12 *Ritso's Case* (1877) 4 ChD 774, CA; *Re London and Northern Bank, ex p Jones* [1900] 1 Ch 220; *Wallace's Case* [1900] 2 Ch 671; cf *Re Portuguese Consolidated Copper Mines Ltd, ex p Badman, ex p Bosanquet* (1890) 45 ChD 16, CA (where notification of an invalid allotment had been received); *Re Whitley Partners Ltd, Steel's Case* (1879) 49 LJ Ch 176; and as to notice of allotment see supra.

13 *Harris' Case* (1872) 7 Ch App 587; *Wall's Case* (1872) LR 15 Eq 18; *Re Natal Investment Co, Wilson's Case* (1869) 20 LT 962; *Truman's Case* [1894] 3 Ch 272.

14 *Ritso's Case* (1877) 4 ChD 774, CA.

15 *Ramsgate Victoria Hotel Co v Montefiore, Ramsgate Victoria Hotel Co v Goldsmid* (1866) LR 1 Exch 109; *Re Bowron, Baily & Co, ex p Baily* (1868) 3 Ch App 592; cf *Pentelow's Case* (1869) 4 Ch App 178; *Peek's Case* (1869) 4 Ch App 532.

16 *Re Land Loan Mortgage and General Trust Co of South Africa, Boyle's Case* (1885) 54 LJ Ch 550.

17 *Baillie's Case* [1898] 1 Ch 110; *Cundy v Lindsay* (1878) 3 App Cas 459, HL.

443. Conditional offer of allotment. In the case of a conditional offer to take shares, if the condition is a condition subsequent, there is a binding agreement to take the shares as soon as the company notifies its acceptance of the offer; but, where the condition is a condition precedent, there is no binding agreement to take the shares unless and until the condition is either fulfilled or waived[1]. If an acceptance introduces a new term, it will not constitute a contract unless the new term is accepted or acquiesced in[2].

An allotment may be made conditionally on the happening of some event, such as the allottee indicating his acceptance of the shares and paying certain money; in such a case he does not become a member until the condition is performed, even if his name is registered[3].

1 *Elkington's Case* (1867) 2 Ch App 511; *Pellatt's Case* (1867) 2 Ch App 527; *Bridger's Case* (1870) 5 Ch App 305; *Fisher's Case, Sherrington's Case* (1885) 31 ChD 120, CA; *Boyer Ltd v Edwardes* (1900) 17 TLR 16 (affd (1901) 18 TLR 3, CA); *Re Bultfontein Sun Diamond Mine, ex p Cox, Hughes and Norman* (1897) 75 LT 669, CA; *Shackleford's Case* (1866) 1 Ch App 567; *Roger's Case, Harrison's Case* (1868) 3 Ch App 633; *Wood's Case* (1873) LR 15 Eq 236.

2 *Addinell's Case* (1865) LR 1 Eq 225; *Beck's Case* (1874) 9 Ch App 392; cf *Howard's Case* (1866) 1 Ch App 561; *Jackson v Turquand* (1869) LR 4 HL 305; *Harris' Case* (1872) 7 Ch App 587.

3 *Spitzel v Chinese Corpn Ltd* (1899) 80 LT 347; cf *Pentelow's Case* (1869) 4 Ch App 178; cf *Hebb's Case* (1867) LR 4 Eq 9.

444. Meaning and effect of allotment. Allotment[1] is an appropriation to some person or corporation of a certain number of shares, but not necessarily of any specific shares. The legal effect of the appropriation depends on the circumstances; for it may be an offer of shares to the allottee or an acceptance of an application for shares by him[2]; of itself an allotment does not necessarily create the status of membership, even when the contract to take the shares is complete[3]; for the Companies Act 1985 makes the placing of the shareholder's name on the register, when he is not a signatory to the memorandum of association[4], a condition precedent to membership[5].

A contract is not constituted by an allotment of shares other than those applied for, as, for example, when the shares allotted are unpaid or partly paid instead of fully paid[6], or of larger nominal amount[7], or fewer in number, than those applied for[8]. If, however, the allottee accepts the shares and acts as shareholder, although under a mistake as to his liability, he is bound[9]. Where an allotment has been made on a binding contract to take shares, it cannot be cancelled by the company[10]. Allotments which were invalid as ultra vires[11] have, however, been rescinded, and an allotment may be rescinded which has been made, by mistake, of unpaid instead of fully-paid shares[12], or to the wrong persons[13], or when an allottee who has been induced to subscribe for shares by misrepresentation repudiates the contract[14] or where the allotment is made by directors in their own favour and in breach of the statutory pre-emption provisions[15].

Damages may be recovered against a company failing to allot shares under a binding agreement in addition to the grant of an order for specific performance[16].

Letters of allotment, and similar documents, may be made renounceable. Provided that the rights thereunder are made renounceable not later than six months after their issue, they will not attract stamp duty[17].

1 In an agreement providing for a repayment within a stated period of a company 'going to allotment', it was held that 'going to allotment' takes place as soon as the directors resolve to go to allotment and take the necessary steps to make their resolution effective, whatever the results may be: *Ellett v Sternberg* (1910) 27 TLR 127.

2 See paras 442, 443 ante.

3 *Spitzel v Chinese Corpn Ltd* (1899) 80 LT 347. Cf *Re Northern Electric Wire and Cable Manufacturing Co Ltd, ex p Hall* (1890) 63 LT 369.

4 See para 359 ante.

5 See paras 174, 361, 382 ante.

6 *Blake v Mowatt* (1856) 21 Beav 603 (revsd on other grounds sub nom *Mowatt v Blake* (1858) 31 LTOS 387, HL); *Amot's Case* (1887) 36 ChD 702, CA; *Re Almada and Tirito Co* (1888) 38 ChD 415, CA; *Re New Eberhardt Co, ex p Menzies* (1889) 43 ChD 118, CA; *Wynne's Case* (1873) 8 Ch App 1002; *Beck's Case* (1874) 9 Ch App 392.

7 *Gustard's Case* (1869) LR 8 Eq 438.

8 *Ex p Roberts* (1852) 1 Drew 204; *Re Oxford and Worcester Extension and Chester Junction Rly Co, ex p Barber* (1851) 20 LJ Ch 146. It is, however, usual for the prospectus to intimate that the number of shares allotted may be less than the number applied for, and for the applicant to offer to accept the number applied for, or any smaller number that may be allotted.

9 *Dent's Case, Forbes' Case* (1873) 8 Ch App 768; *Re Railway Time Tables Publishing Co, ex p Sandys* (1889) 42 ChD 98, CA; *Re James Pilkin & Co Ltd* (1916) 85 LJ Ch 318.

10 *Adams' Case* (1872) LR 13 Eq 474; *Duff's Executors' Case* (1886) 32 ChD 301, CA; *Re Saloon Steam Packet Co, ex p Fletcher* (1867) 37 LJ Ch 49; *Re Companies Guardian Society, Lord Wallscourt's Case* (1899) 7 Mans 235; cf *Hall's Case* (1870) 5 Ch App 707; *Re London and Provincial Consolidated Coal Co* (1877) 5 ChD 525 (where no allotment had been made).

11 *Barnett's Case* (1874) LR 18 Eq 507; *Tintin Exploration Syndicate Ltd v Sandys* (1947) 177 LT 412; *Bath's Case* (1878) 8 ChD 334, CA (where, however, the allottee was held liable as a past member); cf *Re British Provident Life and Fire Assurance Society, Coleman's Case* (1863) 1 De GJ & Sm 495. These cases must now be read in the light of the Companies Act 1985 s 35 (as substituted): see para 1107 post.

12 *Hartley's Case* (1875) 10 Ch App 157.

13 *Re Hoylake Rly Co, ex p Keightley* [1874] WN 18; affd [1874] WN 47, CA in Ch.

14 *Re London and Mediterranean Bank Ltd, Wright's Case* (1871) 7 Ch App 55; *Reese River Silver Mining Co v Smith* (1869) LR 4 HL 64 at 74; cf *Re Life Association of England, Blake's Case* (1865) 34 Beav 639. See also paras 324, 332 ante.

15 See *Re Thundercrest Ltd* [1995] 1 BCLC 117 and paras 447 note 2, 460 post.

16 *Sri Lanka Omnibus Co Ltd v Perera* [1952] AC 76, PC; and see further para 376 ante.

17 Ie neither under the heading 'Bearer Instrument' (see the Stamp Act 1891 s 1, Sch 1 exemption 3 (added by the Finance Act 1963 s 59(1); repealed from a day to be appointed by the Finance Act 1990 ss 107, 132, Sch 19 Pt VI))) nor under the heading 'Conveyance or Transfer on Sale' (see the Finance Act 1963 s 65(1) (repealed from a day to be appointed by the Finance Act 1990 Sch 19 Pt VI)). As to stamp duty reserve tax see para 514 post.

445. Meaning of 'allotment' and 'paid up'. For the purposes of the Companies Act 1985 in relation to an allotment of shares in a company, the shares are to be taken to be allotted when a person acquires the unconditional right to be included in the company's register of members in respect of those shares[1]. A share in a company is deemed paid up (as to its nominal value or any premium on it) in cash[2], or allotted for cash, if the consideration for the allotment or payment up is cash received by the company, or is a cheque received by it in good faith which the directors have no reason for suspecting will not be paid, or is a release of a liability of the company for a liquidated sum, or is an undertaking to pay cash to the company at a future date[3]. In relation to the allotment or payment up of any shares in a company, references in the Companies Act 1985[4] to consideration other than in cash and to the payment up of shares and premiums on shares otherwise than in cash include the payment of, or any undertaking to pay, cash to any person other than the company[5].

1 Companies Act 1985 s 738(1). As to the register of members see para 378 et seq ante.
2 For the purpose of determining whether a share is or is to be allotted for cash, or paid up in cash, 'cash' includes foreign currency: ibid s 738(4).
3 Ibid s 738(2). See also *System Control plc v Munro Corporate plc* [1990] BCLC 659 (an undertaking to pay cash means an undertaking given to the company in consideration of the allotment of the shares; it does not include the assignment of an earlier debt).
4 Ie except references in the Companies Act 1985 ss 89–94 (the pre-emption provisions): see paras 457–461 post.
5 Ibid s 738(3).

446. Issue of shares. The term 'issue' is also used in connection with shares[1]. The shares which are signed for by the signatories to the memorandum are issued when the company is registered[2]. As regards other shares, when a person who has agreed to take shares is entered on the register as a shareholder, the shares have been issued to him, although he has not obtained the share certificate[3]. A resolution to allot shares is not, however, necessarily the issue of them, and the term seems to mean allotment followed by registration or possibly by some other act, distinct from allotment, whereby the title of the allottee becomes complete[4].

The allotment creates an enforceable contract for the issue of shares[5]. The shares are issued when an application to the company has been followed by allotment and notification to the purchaser and completed by entry on the register of members[6].

Normally a company cannot issue shares in excess of the unissued amount of its authorised share capital; but, where it is proposing to redeem redeemable shares, it has power to issue shares up to the nominal value of the shares to be redeemed as if those shares had never been issued[7].

1 See eg the Companies Act 1985 s 185(1) and para 482 post.
2 *Dalton Time Lock Co v Dalton* (1892) 66 LT 704, CA.
3 *Blyth's Case* (1876) 4 ChD 140, CA; *A-G v Regent's Canal and Dock Co* [1904] 1 KB 263 at 270, CA. Cf *Bush's Case* (1874) 9 Ch App 554.
4 The statement in the text was approved in *National Westminster Bank plc v IRC, Barclays Bank plc v IRC* [1995] 1 AC 119 at 147, [1994] 3 All ER 1 at 26, HL per Lord Lloyd of Berwick. See also *Clarke's Case* (1878) 8 ChD 635, CA; *Spitzel v Chinese Corpn Ltd* (1899) 80 LT 347; *Pool's Case* (1887) 35 ChD 579. It would seem that the meaning of 'issue' depends on the context of the enactment in which the word occurs: see *Re Bank of Hindustan, China and Japan, Campbell's Case, Hippisley's Case, Alison's Case* (1873) 9 Ch App 1; *A-G v Anglo-Argentine Tramways Co Ltd* [1909] 1 KB 677; *Re Perth Electric Tramways Ltd, Lyons v Tramways Syndicate Ltd and Perth Electric Tramways Ltd* [1906] 2 Ch 216; *Oswald Tillotson Ltd v IRC* [1933] 1 KB 134; *National Westminster Bank plc v IRC, Barclays Bank plc v IRC* supra. The term is not a technical, but a mercantile, term: *Levy v Abercorris Slate and Slab Co* (1887) 37 ChD 260 at 264.
5 *National Westminster Bank plc v IRC, Barclays Bank plc v IRC* [1995] 1 AC 119 at 126, [1994] 3 All ER 1 at 6, HL.

6 *National Westminster Bank plc v IRC, Barclays Bank plc v IRC* [1995] 1 AC 119, [1994] 3 All ER 1, HL. See also para 174 ante.
7 See the Companies Act 1985 s 160(5) and para 220 ante.

B. RESTRICTIONS ON ALLOTMENT

447. Authority of company required for certain allotments. The directors of a company must not exercise any power of the company to allot relevant securities unless they are authorised[1] to do so by the company in general meeting, or by the company's articles[2]. For these purposes, 'relevant securities' means:

(1) shares in the company other than shares shown in the memorandum to have been taken by the subscribers to it[3] or shares allotted in pursuance of an employees' share scheme[4]; and

(2) any right to subscribe for, or to convert any security into, shares in the company (other than shares so allotted);

and a reference to the allotment of relevant securities includes the grant of such a right but not the allotment of shares pursuant to such a right[5].

Such authority may be given for a particular exercise of the power or for its exercise generally, and may be unconditional or subject to conditions[6]. The authority must state the maximum amount[7] of relevant securities that may be allotted under it and the date on which it will expire, which must be not more than five years from whichever is relevant of the following dates:

(a) in the case of an authority contained in the company's articles at the time of its original incorporation, the date of that incorporation; and

(b) in any other case, the date on which the resolution is passed by virtue of which the authority is given;

but such an authority (including an authority contained in the articles) may be previously revoked or varied by the company in general meeting[8].

The authority may be renewed or further renewed by the company in general meeting for a further period not exceeding five years; but the resolution must state (or restate) the amount of relevant securities which may be allotted under the authority or, as the case may be, the amount remaining to be allotted under it, and must specify the date on which the renewed authority will expire[9].

The directors may allot relevant securities, notwithstanding that authority under these provisions has expired, if they are allotted in pursuance of an offer or agreement made by the company before the authority expired and the authority allowed it to make an offer or agreement which would or might require relevant securities to be allotted after the authority expired[10]. A resolution of a company to give, vary, revoke or renew such an authority may, notwithstanding that it alters the company's articles, be an ordinary resolution[11].

A director who knowingly and wilfully contravenes, or permits or authorises a contravention of, these provisions, is liable on conviction on indictment to a fine, or on summary conviction to a fine not exceeding the statutory maximum[12].

Nothing in these provisions affects the validity of any allotment[13]. Nor do they apply to any allotment of relevant securities by a company, other than a public company[14] registered as such on its original incorporation, if it is made in pursuance of an offer or agreement made before the earlier of the following two dates:

(i) the date of the holding of the first general meeting of the company after its registration or re-registration as a public company; and

(ii) 22 June 1982[15];

but any resolution to give, vary or revoke an authority for the above purposes[16] has effect for those purposes if passed at any time after the end of April 1980[17].

1 Ie in accordance with the Companies Act 1985 s 80 (as amended) (see infra) or s 80A (as added) (see para 448 post).
2 Ibid s 80(1) (amended by the Companies Act 1989 s 115(1)). As to the exercise by directors of their power to allot see para 585 post. An abuse of their powers in this respect may be the subject of a petition alleging unfairly prejudicial conduct: see para 1405 post.
3 As to the subscribers' shares see para 102 ante.
4 For the meaning of 'employees' share scheme' see para 120 note 8 ante.
5 Companies Act 1985 s 80(2).
6 Ibid s 80(3).
7 For these purposes, references to the maximum amount of relevant securities that may be allotted under the authority are to the maximum amount of shares which may be allotted pursuant to the rights referred to: ibid s 80(6).
8 Ibid s 80(4).
9 Ibid s 80(5).
10 Ibid s 80(7).
11 Ibid s 80(8). Nevertheless a copy of the resolution must be forwarded to the registrar of companies within 15 days: see ss 80(8), 380 (as amended) and para 691 post. In general, a special resolution is required for the alteration of articles: see para 538 post.
12 Ibid ss 80(9), 730, Sch 24. For the meaning of 'the statutory maximum' see para 1161 post.
13 Ibid s 80(10).
14 For the meaning of 'public company' see para 82 ante.
15 Ie the date which is the end of the transitional period under the legislative predecessor of the Companies Act 1985 s 80 ie the Companies Act 1980 s 14: see ss 14(9), 87(1) and the Companies Act 1980 (Commencement No 2) Order 1980, SI 1980/1785.
16 Ie including the purposes of the Companies Act 1980 s 14 (repealed).
17 Companies Act 1985 s 80(11). The date of the passing of the Companies Act 1980 (repealed) was 1 May 1980.

448. Election by private company as to duration of authority. A private company[1] may elect, by elective resolution[2], that the following provisions shall apply[3] in relation to the giving or renewal, after the election, of any authority[4] for allotments[5]. The authority must state the maximum amount of relevant securities that may be allotted[6] under it and may be given for an indefinite period or for a fixed period, in which case it must state the date on which it will expire[7]. In either case an authority, including an authority contained in the articles, may be revoked or varied by the company in general meeting[8]. An authority given for a fixed period may be renewed or further renewed by the company in general meeting[9]. A resolution renewing an authority:

(1) must state, or restate, the amount of relevant securities which may be allotted under the authority or, as the case may be, the amount remaining to be allotted under it; and

(2) must state whether the authority is renewed for an indefinite period or for a fixed period, in which case it must state the date on which the renewed authority will expire[10].

If such an election ceases to have effect, an authority then in force which was given for an indefinite period or for a fixed period of more than five years:

(a) if given five years or more before the election ceases to have effect, expires forthwith; and

(b) otherwise, has effect as if it had been given for a fixed period of five years[11].

1 For the meaning of 'private company' see para 82 ante.
2 Ie in accordance with the Companies Act 1985 s 379A (as added): see para 686 post.

3 Ie instead of the provisions of ibid s 80(4), (5): see para 447 ante.
4 Ie an authority under ibid s 80 (as amended): see para 447 ante.
5 Ibid s 80A(1) (added by the Companies Act 1989 s 115(1)).
6 For these purposes, the references to the maximum amount of relevant securities that may be allotted are to be construed in accordance with the Companies Act 1985 s 80(6) (see para 447 note 7 ante): s 80A(6) (added by the Companies Act 1989 s 115(1)). For the meaning of 'relevant securities' see para 447 ante.
7 Companies Act 1985 s 80A(2) (added by the Companies Act 1989 s 115(1)).
8 Companies Act 1985 s 80A(3) (added by the Companies Act 1989 s 115(1)).
9 Companies Act 1985 s 80A(4) (added by the Companies Act 1989 s 115(1)).
10 Companies Act 1985 s 80A(5) (added by the Companies Act 1989 s 115(1)).
11 Companies Act 1985 s 80A(7) (added by the Companies Act 1989 s 115(1)).

449. Restrictions on powers of private company. A private limited company[1], other than a company limited by guarantee and not having a share capital, commits an offence if it:

(1) offers to the public, whether for cash or otherwise, any shares in or debentures of the company; or

(2) allots or agrees to allot, whether for cash or otherwise, any shares in or debentures of the company with a view to all or any of those shares or debentures being offered for sale to the public[2].

A company guilty of such an offence, and any officer of it who is in default, is liable on conviction on indictment to a fine or on summary conviction to a fine not exceeding the statutory maximum[3].

Nothing in the above provisions affects the validity of any allotment or sale of shares or debentures, or of any agreement to allot or sell shares or debentures[4].

1 For the meaning of 'private company' see para 82 ante.
2 Companies Act 1985 s 81(1). For these purposes, 'offer for sale to the public' has the meaning given by ss 58–60 (see para 105 note 2 ante): s 81(1). As to the extent of the repeal of ss 58–60, 81 by the Financial Services Act 1986 s 212(3), Sch 17 Pt I see para 105 note 2 ante.
     A private company may not apply for listing on the Stock Exchange: see the *Listing Rules* r 3.2. As to the *Listing Rules* see para 282 ante.
3 Companies Act 1985 ss 81(2), 730, Sch 24. See also note 2 supra. For the meaning of 'officer who is in default' and 'the statutory maximum' see para 1161 post.
4 Ibid s 81(3). See also note 2 supra.

450. Application for, and allotment of, shares and debentures. No allotment[1] may be made of a company's shares or debentures in pursuance of a prospectus issued generally[2], and no proceedings may be taken on applications made in pursuance of a prospectus so issued, until the beginning of the third day after that[3] on which the prospectus is first so issued[4] or such later time, if any, as may be specified in the prospectus[5]. The beginning of that third day, or that later time, is 'the time of the opening of the subscription lists'[6].

The validity of an allotment is not affected by any contravention of the above provisions[7]; but, in the event of contravention, the company, and every officer of it who is in default[8], is guilty of an offence and liable on conviction on indictment to a fine, or on summary conviction to a fine not exceeding the statutory maximum[9].

An application for shares in or debentures of a company which is made in pursuance of a prospectus issued generally is not revocable until after the expiration of the third day after the time of the opening of the subscription lists, or the giving before the expiration of that day of the appropriate public notice; and that notice is one given by some person responsible[10] for the prospectus and having the effect[10] of excluding or limiting the responsibility of the giver[11].

1 As applying to a prospectus offering shares or debentures for sale, the following provisions have effect as if for the references to allotment there were substituted references to sale: Companies Act 1985 s 82(6)(a).

2 For these purposes, 'a prospectus issued generally' means a prospectus issued to persons who are not existing members of the company or holders of its debentures: ibid s 744. For the meaning of 'prospectus' see para 105 note 2 ante. The definition of 'prospectus issued generally' is repealed by the Financial Services Act 1986 s 212(3), Sch 17 Pt I to the extent specified, that is to say in so far as it would apply in relation to any investment which is listed or the subject of listing under Pt IV (ss 142–156B (as amended): see para 281 et seq ante): Financial Services Act 1986 (Commencement No 3) Order 1986, SI 1986/2246, art 5, Sch 4.

3 In reckoning for this purpose the third day after another day: (1) any intervening day which is a Saturday or Sunday, or is a bank holiday in any part of Great Britain, is to be disregarded; and (2) if the third day (as so reckoned) is itself a Saturday or Sunday, or a bank holiday, there is to be substituted the first day after that which is none of them: Companies Act 1985 s 82(4). For the meaning of 'bank holiday' see para 71 note 9 ante.

4 For these purposes, the reference to the day on which the prospectus is first issued generally is to the day when it is first so issued as a newspaper advertisement; and, if it is not so issued as a newspaper advertisement before the third day after that on which it is first so issued in any other manner, the reference is to the day on which it is first so issued in any manner: ibid s 82(3).

5 Ibid s 82(1). Section 82, s 83 (see para 451 post), s 84(1) proviso (see para 452 post) and ss 86, 87 (see para 456 post) are repealed by the Financial Services Act 1986 Sch 17 Pt I to the following extent:
   (1) in so far as they apply in relation to any investment which is listed or the subject of an application for listing under Pt IV (ss 142–156B (as amended): see para 281 et seq post) (Financial Services Act 1986 (Commencement No 3) Order 1986, art 5, Sch 4);
   (2) in so far as they apply to a prospectus offering for subscription, or to any form of application for, units in a body corporate which is a recognised scheme (Financial Services Act 1986 (Commencement) (No 8) Order 1988, SI 1988/740, art 2, Schedule).

6 Companies Act 1985 s 82(2). See also note 5 supra.

7 Ie ibid s 82(1)–(4): see supra.

8 As applying to a prospectus offering shares or debentures for sale, these provisions have effect as if for the references to the company and every officer of it who is in default there were substituted a reference to any person by or through whom the offer is made and who knowingly and wilfully authorised or permits the contravention: ibid s 82(6)(b).

9 Ibid ss 82(5), 730, Sch 24. See also note 5 supra. For the meaning of 'officer who is in default' and 'the statutory maximum' see para 1161 post.

10 Ie under ibid ss 67–69 (sic). Sections 67–69 were, however, repealed without being retained for definitional purposes: see the Financial Services Act 1986 (Commencement) (No 13) Order 1995, SI 1995/1538, art 2(a).

11 Companies Act 1985 s 82(7). See also note 5 supra.

451. No allotment unless minimum subscription received. No allotment may be made of any share capital of a company offered to the public for subscription unless:
   (1) there has been subscribed the amount stated in the prospectus[1] as the minimum amount[2] which, in the opinion of the directors, must be raised by the issue of share capital in order to provide for the preliminary expenses, purchase of property, working capital etc[3]; and
   (2) the sum payable on application for the amount so stated has been paid to and received[4] by the company[5].

If the above conditions have not been complied with on the expiration of 40 days after the first issue of the prospectus, all money received from applicants for shares must be forthwith repaid to them without interest[6]. If any money is not repaid within 48 days after the issue of the prospectus, the directors of the company are jointly and severally liable to repay it with interest at the rate of 5% per annum from the expiration of the forty-eighth day, except that a director is not so liable if he proves that the default in the repayment of the money was not due to any misconduct or negligence on his part[7].

Any condition requiring or binding an applicant for shares to waive compliance with any requirement of the above provisions is void[8].

The above provisions do not apply to an allotment of shares subsequent to the first allotment of shares offered to the public for subscription[9].

1 For the meaning of 'prospectus' see para 105 note 2 ante.
2 The amount so stated in the prospectus is to be reckoned exclusively of any amount payable otherwise than in cash and is known as 'the minimum subscription': Companies Act 1985 s 83(3).
3 Ie the matters specified in ibid s 83(1), Sch 3 para 2. Where shares are offered to the public for subscription, the prospectus must give particulars as to:
   (1) the minimum amount which, in the opinion of the directors, must be raised by the issue of those shares in order to provide the sums (or, if any part of them is to be defrayed in any other manner, the balance of the sums) required to be provided in respect of each of the following:
     (a) the purchase price of any property purchased or to be purchased which is to be defrayed in whole or in part out of the proceeds of the issue;
     (b) any preliminary expenses payable by the company, and any commission so payable to any person in consideration of his agreeing to subscribe for, or of his procuring or agreeing to procure subscriptions for, any shares in the company;
     (c) the repayment of any money borrowed by the company in respect of any of the above matters;
     (d) working capital; and
   (2) the amounts to be provided in respect of the matters mentioned supra otherwise than out of the proceeds of the issue and the sources out of which those amounts are to be provided:
   Sch 3 para 2. Schedule 3 para 2 is repealed for all purposes by the Financial Services Act 1986 s 212(3), Sch 17 Pt I except in so far as it is necessary to retain it for the purposes of defining terms in the Companies Act 1985 s 83: see the Financial Services Act 1986 (Commencement) (No 13) Order 1985, SI 1985/1538, art 2(a)(ii).
4 For these purposes, a sum is deemed paid to the company, and received by it, if a cheque for that sum has been received in good faith by the company and the directors have no reason for suspecting that the cheque will not be paid: Companies Act 1985 s 83(2). See also note 5 infra.
5 Ibid s 83(1). As to the extent of the repeal of s 83 see para 450 note 5 ante.
6 Ibid s 83(4). See also note 5 supra.
7 Ibid s 83(5). See also note 5 supra.
8 Ibid s 83(6). See also note 5 supra.
9 Ibid s 83(7). See also note 5 supra.

452. Allotment where issue not fully subscribed. No allotment may be made of any share capital of a public company[1] offered for subscription unless:
   (1) that capital is subscribed[2] for in full; or
   (2) the offer states that, even if the capital is not subscribed for in full, the amount of that capital subscribed for may be allotted in any event or in the event of the conditions specified in the offer being satisfied;
and, where conditions are so specified, no allotment of the capital may be made by virtue of head (2) above unless those conditions are satisfied[3].

If shares are so prohibited from being allotted and 40 days have elapsed after the first issue of the prospectus[4], all money received from applicants for shares must be forthwith repaid to them without interest[5]. If any of the money is not repaid within 48 days after the issue of the prospectus, the directors of the company are jointly and severally liable to repay it with interest at the rate of 5% per annum from the expiration of the forty-eighth day; except that a director is not so liable if he proves that the default in repayment was not due to any misconduct or negligence on his part[6].

The above provisions apply in the case of shares offered as wholly or partly payable otherwise than in cash as they apply in the case of shares offered for subscription[7]. In the provisions relating to repayment[8] as they apply to the case of shares offered as wholly or partly payable otherwise than in cash, references to the repayment of money received from applicants for shares include the return of any other consideration so received (including, if the case so requires, the release of the applicant from any undertaking), or, if it is not reasonably practicable to return the consideration, the payment of money equal to its value at the time it was so received; and references to interest apply accordingly[9].

Any condition requiring or binding an applicant for shares to waive compliance with any of above requirements is void[10].

1 For the meaning of 'public company' see para 82 ante.
2 The Companies Act 1985 s 84 applies in the case of shares offered as wholly or partly payable otherwise than in cash as it applies in the case of shares offered for subscription, the word 'subscribed' in s 84(1) being construed accordingly: s 84(4).
3 Ibid s 84(1). Section 84(1) is without prejudice to s 83 (see para 451 ante): s 84(1) proviso. As to the extent of the repeal of ss 83, 84(1) proviso see para 450 note 5 ante.
4 For the meaning of 'prospectus' see para 105 note 2 ante.
5 Companies Act 1985 s 84(2).
6 Ibid s 84(3).
7 Ibid s 84(4). The word 'subscription' in s 84(1) (see supra) is to be construed accordingly: s 84(4).
8 Ie those contained in ibid s 84(2), (3): see supra.
9 Ibid s 84(5).
10 Ibid s 84(6).

453. Effect of irregular allotment. An allotment made by a company to an applicant in contravention of the above provisions[1] is voidable at the instance of the applicant within one month after the date of the allotment and not later, and is so voidable notwithstanding that the company is in the course of being wound up[2].

1 Ie the Companies Act 1985 s 83 (see para 451 ante) or s 84 (see para 452 ante). As to the extent of the repeal of s 83 see para 450 note 5 ante.
2 Ibid s 85(1).

454. Rescission and other relief. The applicant may within the month prescribed either:

(1) commence an action claiming relief, namely rescission of the allotment, rectification of the register, return of the moneys paid, and an injunction to restrain the company from parting or dealing with the moneys[1]; or
(2) give notice of avoidance (which need not specify the ground);
but the notice must be followed by prompt legal proceedings[2].

1 *Mears v Western Canada Pulp and Paper Co Ltd* [1905] 2 Ch 353, CA.
2 *Re National Motor Mail-Coach Co Ltd, Anstis' and McLean's Claims* [1908] 2 Ch 228.

455. Liability of director to compensate. If a director of a company knowingly contravenes[1], or permits or authorises the contravention of, any of the above provisions[2] with respect to allotment, he is liable to compensate the company and the allottee respectively for any loss, damages or costs which the company or the allottee may have sustained or incurred by the contravention; but proceedings to recover any such loss, damages or costs may not be commenced after the expiration of two years from the date of the allotment[3].

1 Ie contravenes with knowledge of the facts. A director cannot, however, escape liability by being ignorant of the law: *Burton v Bevan* [1908] 2 Ch 240.
2 Ie the Companies Act 1985 s 83 (see para 451 ante) or s 84 (see para 452 ante). As to the extent of the repeal of s 83 see para 450 note 5 ante.
3 Ibid s 85(2), (3). As to the liability of directors to repay application money see para 452 ante.

456. Allotment of shares to be dealt in on any stock exchange. The following provisions apply where a prospectus[1], whether issued generally[2] or not, states that application has been or will be made for permission for the shares of debentures offered by it to be listed on any stock exchange[3].

An allotment made on an application in pursuance of the prospectus is, whenever made, void if the permission has not been applied for before the third day after[4] the first issue of the prospectus or, if the permission has been refused[5] before the expiration of three weeks from the date of the closing of the subscription lists or such longer period, not exceeding six weeks, as may, within those three weeks, be notified to the applicant for permission by or on behalf of the stock exchange[6].

Where permission has not been applied for as above, or has been refused as above, the company must forthwith repay (without interest) all money received from applicants in pursuance of the prospectus[7]. If any of the money is not repaid within eight days after the company becomes liable to repay it, the directors of the company are jointly and severally liable to repay the money with interest at the rate of 5% per annum from the expiration of the eighth day, except that a director is not liable if he proves that the default in the repayment of the money was not due to any misconduct or negligence on his part[8].

All money received from applicants in pursuance of the prospectus must be kept in a separate bank account so long as the company may become liable to repay it[9]; and, if default is made in complying with this provision, the company, and every officer of it who is in default, is liable on conviction on indictment to a fine, or on summary conviction to a fine not exceeding the statutory maximum[10].

Any condition requiring or binding an applicant for shares or debentures to waive compliance with any requirement of the above provisions is void[11].

The above provisions have effect in relation to shares or debentures agreed to be taken by a person underwriting an offer of them by a prospectus as if he applied for them in pursuance of the prospectus[12].

1 For the meaning of 'prospectus' see para 105 note 2 ante.
2 For the meaning of 'prospectus issued generally' see para 450 note 2 ante.
3 Companies Act 1985 s 86(1). As regards the operation of s 86 in relation to a prospectus offering shares for sale, s 86(1) and s 86(2) (see infra) apply, but with the substitution for the reference in s 86(2) to allotment of a reference to sale: s 87(1), (2). As to the extent of the repeal of ss 86, 87 see para 450 note 5 ante.
4 In reckoning for this purpose the third day after another day: (1) any intervening day which is a Saturday or Sunday, or is a bank holiday in any part of Great Britain, is to be disregarded; and (2) if the third day (as so reckoned) is itself a Saturday or Sunday, or a bank holiday, there is to be substituted the first day after that which is none of them: ibid s 86(3). For the meaning of 'bank holiday' see para 71 note 9 ante.
5 For these purposes, permission is not deemed to be refused if it is intimated that the application for it, though not at present granted, will be given further consideration: ibid s 86(8). See also note 10 infra.
6 Ibid s 86(2). See also note 3 supra.
7 Ibid s 86(4). See also note 3 supra. As regards the operation of s 86 in relation to a prospectus offering shares for sale, s 86(4) and s 86(5) (see infra) do not apply but (1) if the permission referred to in s 86(2) (see supra) has not been applied for as there mentioned, or has been refused as there mentioned, the offeror of the shares must forthwith repay (without interest) all money received from applicants in

pursuance of the prospectus; and (2) if any such money is not repaid within eight days after the offeror becomes liable to repay it, he becomes liable to pay interest on the money due, at the rate of 5% per annum from the end of the eighth day: s 87(1), (3).

8 Ibid s 86(5). See also notes 3, 7 supra.
9 Ie under ibid s 86(4): see supra.
10 Ibid ss 86(6), 730, Sch 24. For the meaning of 'officer who is in default' and 'the statutory maximum' see para 1161 post. See also note 3 supra. As regards the operation of s 86 in relation to a prospectus offering shares for sale, s 86(6), s 86(7) (see infra), s 86(8) (see note 5 supra) and s 86(9) (see infra) apply, except that in s 86(6) for the first reference to the company there is to be substituted a reference to the offeror and for the reference to the company and every officer of the company who is in default there is to be substituted a reference to any person by or through whom the offer is made and who knowingly and wilfully authorises or permits the default: s 87(1), (4).
11 Ibid s 86(7). See also notes 3, 10 supra.
12 Ibid s 86(9). See also notes 3, 10 supra.

C. PRE-EMPTION RIGHTS

457. Offers to shareholders to be on pre-emptive basis. Subject to the following provisions[1], a company proposing to allot equity securities[2]:

(1)　must not allot any of them on any terms to a person unless it has made an offer to each person who holds relevant shares[3] or relevant employee shares[4] to allot to him on the same or more favourable terms a proportion of those securities which is as nearly as practicable equal to the proportion in nominal value held by him of the aggregate of relevant shares and relevant employee shares; and

(2)　must not allot any of those securities to a person unless the period during which any such offer may be accepted has expired or the company has received notice of the acceptance or refusal of every offer so made[5].

If, in accordance with any provision of a company's memorandum or articles which requires the company, when proposing to allot equity securities consisting of relevant shares of any particular class[6], not to allot those securities on any terms unless it has complied with the condition that it makes such an offer[7] to each person who holds relevant shares or relevant employee shares of that class:

(a)　a company makes an offer to allot securities to such a holder; and

(b)　he or anyone in whose favour he has renounced his right to their allotment accepts the offer,

the above restriction[8] does not apply to the allotment of those securities, and the company may allot them accordingly; but this is without prejudice to the application of that restriction in any other case[9].

The above restriction does not, however, apply to a particular allotment of equity securities if these are, or are to be, wholly or partly paid up otherwise than in cash; and securities which a company has offered to allot to a holder of relevant shares or relevant employee shares may be allotted to him, or anyone in whose favour he has renounced his right to their allotment, without contravening head (2) above[10]. Nor does that restriction apply to the allotment of securities which would, apart from a renunciation or assignment of the right to their allotment, be held under an employees' share scheme[11].

1 Ie provisions of the Companies Act 1985 ss 89–96: see infra and paras 458–463 post.
2 For these purposes, 'equity security', in relation to a company, means a relevant share in the company (other than a share shown in the memorandum to have been taken by a subscriber to the memorandum, or a bonus share) or a right to subscribe for, or to convert securities into, relevant shares in the company: ibid s 94(1), (2). For the meaning of 'relevant shares' see note 3 infra.

3 For these purposes, 'relevant shares', in relation to a company, means shares in the company other than (1) shares which as respects dividends and capital carry a right to participate only up to a specified amount in a distribution; and (2) shares which are held by a person who acquired them in pursuance of an employees' share scheme or, in the case of shares which have not been allotted, are to be allotted in pursuance of such a scheme: ibid s 94(1), (5). For the meaning of 'employees' share scheme' see para 120 note 8 ante.

4 For these purposes, 'relevant employee shares', in relation to a company, means shares of the company which would be relevant shares in it but for the fact that they are held by a person who acquired them in pursuance of an employees' share scheme: ibid s 94(1), (4).

5 Ibid s 89(1). A reference to the allotment of equity securities or of equity securities consisting of relevant shares of a particular class (see note 6 infra) includes the grant of a right to subscribe for, or to convert any securities into, relevant shares in the company, or (as the case may be) relevant shares of a particular class; but such a reference does not include the allotment of any relevant shares pursuant to such a right: s 94(1), (3). In relation to an offer to allot securities required by s 89(1) or by any provision to which s 89(3) (see infra) applies, a reference in ss 89–94, however expressed, to the holder of shares of any description is to whoever was at the close of business on a date, to be specified in the offer and to fall in the period of 28 days immediately before the date of the offer, the holder of shares of that description: s 94(1), (7). As to the position prior to 22 December 1980 when, by the Companies Act 1980 (Commencement No 2) Order 1980, SI 1980/1785, the Companies Act 1980 s 17 (repealed) was brought into operation see *Mutual Life Insurance Co of New York v Rank Organisation Ltd* [1985] BCLC 11. For the consequences of contravention see para 460 post.

6 For these purposes, a reference to a class of shares is to shares to which the same rights are attached as to voting and as to participation, both as respects dividend and as respects capital, in a distribution: Companies Act 1985 s 94(1), (6).

7 Ie such an offer as is described in ibid s 89(1): see supra.

8 Ie the prohibition contained in ibid s 89(1): see supra.

9 Ibid s 89(2), (3).

10 Ibid s 89(4).

11 Ibid s 89(5).

458. Communication of pre-emption offers to shareholders. The following provisions relate to the manner in which offers required by the above restriction[1], or by such a provision already referred to in a company's memorandum or articles of association[2], are to be made to holders[3] of a company's shares[4].

An offer must be in writing and must be made to a holder of shares either personally or by sending it by post (that is to say, prepaying and posting a letter containing the offer) to him or to his registered address or, if he has no registered address in the United Kingdom, to the address in the United Kingdom supplied by him to the company for the giving of notice to him[5]. Where shares are held by two or more persons jointly, the offer may be made to the joint holder first named in the register of members in respect of the shares[6].

In the case of a holder's death or bankruptcy, the offer may be made by sending it by post in a prepaid letter addressed to the persons claiming to be entitled to the shares in consequence of the death or bankruptcy by name, or by the title of representatives of the deceased, or trustee of the bankrupt, or by any like description, at the address in the United Kingdom supplied for the purpose by those so claiming, or (until such an address has been so supplied) by giving the notice in any manner in which it might have been given if the death or bankruptcy had not occurred[7].

If the holder has no registered address in the United Kingdom and has not given to the company an address in the United Kingdom for the service of notices on him, or is the holder of a share warrant, the offer may be made by causing it, or a notice specifying where a copy of it can be obtained or inspected, to be published in the Gazette[8]. The offer must state a period of not less than 21 days during which it may be accepted; and the offer must not be withdrawn before the end of that period[9].

The above requirements do not invalidate a provision of the nature previously considered[10] in a company's memorandum or articles because it requires or authorises an offer under it to be made in contravention of any of the above requirements; but, to the extent that the provision requires or authorises such an offer to be so made, it is of no effect[11].

1 Ie the Companies Act 1985 s 89(1): see para 457 ante.
2 Ie ibid s 89(3): see para 457 ante.
3 For the meaning of references to the holder of shares of any description see para 457 note 5 ante.
4 Companies Act 1985 s 90(1). For the consequences of contravention see para 460 post.
5 Ibid s 90(2). Section 90(2) is, however, subject to s 90(3)–(7) (see infra): s 90(2). As to the furnishing of such an address see para 1150 note 1 post. If sent by post, the offer is deemed to be made at the time at which the letter would be delivered in the ordinary course of post: s 90(2).
6 Ibid s 90(3).
7 Ibid s 90(4). As to notice by the company to its members in general see paras 1149, 1150 post.
8 Ibid s 90(5). For the meaning of 'the Gazette' see para 70 note 1 ante.
9 Ibid s 90(6).
10 Ie ibid s 89(3): see para 457 ante.
11 Ibid s 90(7).

459. Application to private companies. The requirement that offers to shareholders be made on a pre-emptive basis[1], and the provisions relating to communication of pre-emption offers[2], or the restriction relating to the period for the acceptance of the offer[3], may, as applying to allotments by a private company[4] of equity securities[5] or to such allotments of a particular description, be excluded by a provision contained in the memorandum or articles of that company[6]. A requirement or authority contained in the memorandum or articles of a private company, if it is inconsistent with any of the matters above referred to[7], has effect as a provision excluding that provision[8]; but a provision of a company's memorandum or articles which requires the company to make such an offer as is described above to each person who holds relevant shares or relevant employee shares of a particular class[9] is not to be treated as being inconsistent with the requirement that offers to shareholders be made on a pre-emptive basis[10].

1 Ie the Companies Act 1985 s 89(1): see para 457 ante.
2 Ie ibid s 90(1)–(5): see para 458 ante.
3 Ie ibid s 90(6): see para 458 ante.
4 For the meaning of 'private company' see para 82 ante.
5 For the meaning of 'equity security' see para 457 note 2 ante.
6 Companies Act 1985 s 91(1).
7 Ie ibid s 89(1), s 90(1)–(5) or s 90(6).
8 In *Re Thundercrest Ltd* [1995] 1 BCLC 117 the articles imported the statutory provisions except in so far as they were inconsistent. The articles failed to specify the period within which the pre-emption offer might be accepted and the statutory period of 21 days, therefore, applied: see the Companies Act 1985 s 90(6) and para 458 ante.
9 Ie ibid s 89(3): see para 457 ante.
10 Ibid s 91(2).

460. Consequences of contravention. If there is a contravention of the provision that equity securities[1] must be offered to shareholders on a pre-emptive basis[2], or of the provisions relating to the communication of pre-emptive offers[3], or of such a provision in the company's memorandum or articles of association as is referred to above[4], the company, and every officer of it who knowingly authorised or permitted the contravention, are jointly and severally liable to compensate any person to whom an offer should have been made under the provision contravened for any loss, damage, costs or expenses which the person has sustained or incurred by reason of the contravention[5]. No proceedings to recover any such loss, damage, costs or expenses may, however, be commenced after the expiration of two years from the delivery to the registrar of companies of the return of allotments in question or, where equity securities other than shares are granted, from the date of the grant[6].

1 For the meaning of 'equity security' see para 457 note 2 ante.
2 Ie the Companies Act 1985 s 89(1): see para 457 ante.
3 Ie ibid s 90(1)–(5) or s 90(6): see para 458 ante.
4 Ie a provision to which ibid s 89(3) applies: see para 457 ante.
5 Ibid s 92(1). No provision is made for improper allotments to be set aside; but see *Re Thundercrest Ltd* [1995] 1 BCLC 117 (where the court did set aside an allotment by directors in their own favour which was made in breach of the statutory requirements). See para 444 ante.
6 Companies Act 1985 s 92(2).

461. Saving for other restrictions as to offers. The statutory provisions relating to pre-emption rights[1] are without prejudice to any enactment by virtue of which a company is prohibited (whether generally or in specified circumstances) from offering or allotting equity securities[2] to any person[3]. Where a company cannot by virtue of such an enactment offer or allot equity securities to a holder[4] of relevant shares[5] or relevant employee shares[6], those provisions have effect as if the shares held by that holder were not relevant shares or relevant employee shares[7].

1 Ie the Companies Act 1985 ss 89–92: see paras 457–460 ante.
2 For the meaning of 'equity security' see para 457 note 2 ante.
3 Companies Act 1985 s 93(1).
4 For the meaning of references to the holder of shares see para 457 note 5 ante.
5 For the meaning of 'relevant shares' see para 457 note 3 ante.
6 For the meaning of 'relevant employee shares' see para 457 note 4 ante.
7 Companies Act 1985 s 93(2).

462. Disapplication of pre-emption rights. Where the directors of a company are generally authorised to allot relevant securities[1], they may be given power by the articles, or by a special resolution of the company, to allot equity securities[2] pursuant to that authority as if the pre-emptive basis of allotment[3] did not apply, or as if it applied to the allotment with such modifications as the directors may determine; and, where the directors make such an allotment, the above provisions[4] have effect accordingly[5].

Where the directors of a company are so authorised to allot relevant securities (whether generally or otherwise), the company may by special resolution resolve either that the pre-emptive basis shall not apply to a specified allotment of equity securities to be made pursuant to that authority, or that that basis shall apply to the allotment with such modifications as may be specified in the resolution; and, where such a resolution is passed, the above provisions have effect accordingly[6].

The power referred to above[7] ceases to have effect when the authority to which it relates is revoked or would (if not renewed) expire; but, if the authority is renewed, the power or (as the case may be) the resolution may also be renewed, for a period not longer than that for which the authority is renewed, by a special resolution of the company[8]. Notwithstanding that any such power or resolution has expired, the directors may allot equity securities in pursuance of an offer or agreement previously made by the company, if the power or resolution enabled the company to make an offer or agreement which would or might require equity securities to be allotted after it expired[9].

Such a special resolution providing that the pre-emptive basis shall not apply, or apply only with modifications, to a specified allotment[10], or a special resolution to renew such a resolution, may not be proposed unless it is recommended by the directors and there has been circulated, with the notice of the meeting at which the resolution is proposed, to the members entitled to have that notice a written statement by the directors setting out their reasons for making the recommendation, the amount to be paid to the company in respect of the equity securities to be allotted, and the directors' justification of that amount[11].

A person who knowingly or recklessly authorises or permits the inclusion in such a circulated statement of any matter which is misleading, false or deceptive in a material particular is liable on conviction on indictment to imprisonment for a term not exceeding two years or a fine, or to both, or on summary conviction to imprisonment for a term not exceeding six months or a fine not exceeding the statutory maximum, or to both[12].

1   Ie under the Companies Act 1985 s 80 (as amended): see para 447 ante. For the meaning of 'relevant securities' see para 447 ante.
2   For the meaning of 'equity security' see para 457 note 2 ante.
3   Ie that contained in the Companies Act 1985 s 89(1): see para 457 ante.
4   Ie ibid ss 89–94: see paras 457–461 ante.
5   Ibid s 95(1).
6   Ibid s 95(2). A written resolution is not effective if any of the requirements of s 381A(7), Sch 15A para 3 (as added) is not complied with: Sch 15A para 2(2) (added by the Companies Act 1989 s 114(1)). The following adaptations have effect in relation to a written resolution under the Companies Act 1985 s 95(2) or renewing a resolution thereunder: Sch 15A para 3(1) (added by the Companies Act 1989 s 114(1)). So much of the Companies Act 1985 s 95(5) (see infra) as requires the circulation of a written statement by the directors with a notice of meeting does not apply, but such a statement must be supplied to each relevant member at or before the time at which the resolution is supplied to him for signature: Sch 15A para 3(2) (added by the Companies Act 1989 s 114(1)). The Companies Act 1985 s 95(6) (see infra) applies in relation to the inclusion in any such statement of matter which is misleading, false or deceptive in a material particular: Sch 15A para 3(3) (added by the Companies Act 1989 s 114(1)). For the meaning of 'written resolution' and 'relevant member' see para 224 note 3 ante.
7   Ie that conferred by the Companies Act 1985 s 95(1) (see supra) or a special resolution under s 95(2) (see supra).
8   Ibid s 95(3).
9   Ibid s 95(4).
10 Ie a special resolution passed under ibid s 95(2): see supra.
11 Ibid s 95(5). See also note 6 supra.
12 Ibid ss 95(6), 730, Sch 24. For the meaning of 'the statutory maximum' see para 1161 post. See also note 6 supra.

463. Saving for company's pre-emption procedure operative before 1982.

Where a company which is re-registered[1] or registered as a public company[2] is or, but for the provisions of the Companies Act 1980[3] and the enactments replacing it, would be subject at the time of re-registration or (as the case may be) registration to a pre-1982 pre-emption requirement[4], the above provisions[5] do not apply to an allotment of the equity securities[6] which are subject to that requirement[7].

A requirement which is imposed on a private company (having been so imposed before the relevant date in 1982) otherwise than by the company's memorandum or articles, and which, if contained in the company's memorandum or articles, would have effect under the provisions entitling a private company to exclude the pre-emption provisions[8] to the exclusion of those provisions, has effect, so long as the company remains a private company, as if it were contained in the memorandum or articles[9]. If on the relevant date in 1982 a company, other than a public company registered as such on its original incorporation, was subject to a requirement obliging it, when proposing to allot equity securities consisting of relevant shares[10] of any particular class, not to allot those securities unless it had made a pre-emptive offer to its shareholders imposed otherwise than by the memorandum or articles[11], the requirement is to be treated for the purposes of the relevant provisions as if it were contained in the memorandum or articles[12].

1 As to re-registration as a public company see para 118 et seq ante.
2 As to registration as a public company see para 80 ante.
3 Pre-emption provisions were first introduced by the Companies Act 1980 ss 17–19 (repealed) and amended by the Companies Act 1981 s 119, Sch 3 para 40 (repealed).
4 For these purposes, 'a 'pre-1982 pre-emption requirement' is a requirement imposed, whether by the company's memorandum or articles, or otherwise, before the relevant date in 1982 by virtue of which the company must, when making an allotment of equity securities, make an offer to allot those securities or some of them in a manner which, otherwise than because involving a contravention of the Companies Act 1985 s 90(1)–(5) (see para 458 ante) or s 90(6) (see para 458 ante), is inconsistent with ss 89–94 (see paras 457–462 ante); and 'the relevant date in 1982' is (1) except in a case falling within head (2) infra, 22 June in that year; and (2) in the case of a company which was re-registered or registered as a public company on an application made before that date, the date on which the application was made: s 96(2).
5 Ie ibid ss 89–95: see paras 457–462 ante.
6 For the meaning of 'equity security' see para 457 note 2 ante.
7 Companies Act 1985 s 96(1).
8 Ie under ibid s 91: see para 459 ante.
9 Ibid s 96(3).
10 For the meaning of 'relevant shares' see para 457 note 3 ante.
11 Ie such a requirement as is mentioned in the Companies Act 1985 s 89(2): see para 457 ante.
12 Ibid s 96(4). As to the effect of this provision see para 457 ante.

D. AMOUNT AND MEANS OF PAYMENT

464. General rules as to payment for shares on allotment. Subject to the following provisions[1], shares allotted by a company, and any premium on them, may be paid up in money or money's worth, including goodwill and know-how[2]. A public company[3] must not accept at any time, in payment up of its shares or any premium on them, an undertaking given by any person that he or another should do work or perform services for the company or any other person[4]. If a public company accepts such an undertaking in payment up of its shares or any premium on them, the holder of the shares[5] when they or the premium are treated as paid up (in whole or in part) by the undertaking is liable:

(1) to pay the company in respect of those shares an amount equal to their nominal value, together with the whole of any premium or, if the case so requires, such proportion of that amount as is treated as paid up by the undertaking; and

(2) to pay interest at the appropriate rate[6] on the amount payable under head (1) above[7].

The above restriction does not prevent a company from allotting bonus shares[8] to its members or from paying up, with sums available for the purpose, any amounts for the time being unpaid on any of its shares, whether on account of the nominal value of the shares or by way of premium[9].

If a company contravenes any of the above provisions, the company, and any officer of it who is in default, is liable on conviction on indictment to a fine, or on summary conviction to a fine not exceeding the statutory maximum[10].

1 Ie subject to the Companies Act 1985 ss 99–116 (as amended): see infra and para 465 et seq post.
2 Ibid s 99(1).
3 For the meaning of 'public company' see para 82 ante. Except as provided by the Companies Consolidation (Consequential Provisions) Act 1985 s 9 (see para 139 ante), the Companies Act 1985 s 99 (see infra), ss 101–103 (as amended) (see paras 466–468 post), s 106 (see para 360 ante), s 108 (see para 471 post), s 110 (see para 473 post), s 111 (see para 474 post) and ss 112–115 (see paras 475–477 post) apply to a company which has passed and not revoked a resolution to be re-registered under s 43 (see para 118 ante) as a public company and to a joint stock company which has passed and not revoked a resolution that the company be a public company (see para 77 ante) as they apply to a public company: s 116 (amended by the Companies Act 1989 s 131(2)).
4 Companies Act 1985 s 99(2).
5 For these purposes, the reference to the holder of shares includes any person who has an unconditional right to be included in the company's register of members in respect of those shares, or to have an instrument of transfer of them executed in his favour: ibid s 99(5).
6 For the meaning of 'the appropriate rate' see para 187 note 3 ante.
7 Companies Act 1985 s 99(3).
8 For the meaning of 'bonus shares' see para 732 post.
9 Companies Act 1985 s 99(4).
10 Ibid ss 114, 730, Sch 24. For the meaning of 'officer who is in default' and 'the statutory maximum' see para 1161 post. As to the extended application of s 114 see note 3 supra.

465. Prohibition on allotment of shares at a discount. A company's shares must not be allotted at a discount[1]. If shares are allotted in contravention of this provision, the allottee is liable to pay the company an amount equal to the amount of the discount, with interest at the appropriate rate[2].

If a company contravenes this provision, the company, and any officer of it who is in default, is liable on conviction on indictment to a fine, or on summary conviction to a fine not exceeding the statutory maximum[3].

1 Companies Act 1985 s 100(1). See also para 187 ante.
2 Ibid s 100(2). For the meaning of 'the appropriate rate' see para 187 note 3 ante.
3 Ibid ss 114, 730, Sch 24. For the meaning of 'officer who is in default' and 'the statutory maximum' see para 1161 post.

466. Shares to be allotted as at least one-quarter paid up. A public company[1] must not allot a share, other than a share allotted in pursuance of an employees' share scheme[2], except as paid up at least as to one-quarter of its nominal value and the whole of any premium on it[3]. If a company allots a share in contravention of this provision, the share is to be treated as if one-quarter of its nominal value, together with the whole of any premium on it, had been received[4]; but the allottee is liable to pay the company the minimum amount which should have been so received in respect of the share (less the value of any consideration actually applied in payment up, to any extent, of the share and any premium on it), with interest at the appropriate rate[5].

If a company contravenes the above provisions, the company, and any officer of it who is in default, is liable on conviction on indictment to a fine, or on summary conviction to a fine not exceeding the statutory maximum[6].

1 For the meaning of 'public company' see para 82 ante. As to the extended application of the Companies Act 1985 s 101 see para 464 note 3 ante.
2 For the meaning of 'employees' share scheme' see para 120 note 8 ante.
3 Companies Act 1985 s 101(1), (2).
4 Ibid s 101(3). Section 101(3) and s 101(4) (see infra) do not apply to the allotment of bonus shares unless the allottee knew or ought to have known the shares were allotted in contravention of s 101(1) (see supra): s 101(5).
5 Ibid s 101(4). See also note 4 supra. For the meaning of 'the appropriate rate' see para 187 note 3 ante.
6 Ibid ss 114, 730, Sch 24. For the meaning of 'officer who is in default' and 'the statutory maximum' see para 1161 post. As to the extended application of s 114 see para 464 note 3 ante.

467. Restriction on payment by long-term undertaking. A public company[1] must not allot shares as fully or partly paid up (as to their nominal value or any premium on them) otherwise than in cash[2] if the consideration for the allotment is or includes an undertaking which is to be, or may be, performed more than five years after the date of the allotment[3]. If a company allots shares in contravention of this restriction, the allottee is liable to pay the company an amount equal to the aggregate of their nominal value and the whole of any premium (or, if the case so requires, so much of that aggregate as is treated as paid up by the undertaking), with interest at the appropriate rate[4].

Where a contract for the allotment of shares[5] does not contravene the above restriction, any variation of the contract which has the effect that the contract would have contravened this restriction, if the terms of the contract as varied had been its original terms, is void[6].

Where a public company allots shares for a consideration which consists of or includes an undertaking which is to be performed within five years of the allotment, but the undertaking is not performed within the period allowed by the contract for the allotment of the shares, the allottee is then liable to pay the company, at the end of the period so allowed, an amount equal to the aggregate of the nominal value of the shares and the whole of any premium (or, if the case so requires, so much of that aggregate as is treated as paid up by the undertaking), with interest at the appropriate rate[7].

If a company contravenes the above restriction, the company, and any officer of it who is in default, is liable on conviction on indictment to a fine, or on summary conviction to a fine not exceeding the statutory maximum[8].

1 For the meaning of 'public company' see para 82 ante. As to the extended application of the Companies Act 1985 s 102 see para 464 note 3 ante.
2 For the meaning of 'cash' see para 445 note 2 ante.
3 Companies Act 1985 s 102(1).
4 Ibid s 102(2). For the meaning of 'the appropriate rate' see para 187 note 3 ante.
5 For these purposes, a reference to a contract for the allotment of shares includes an ancillary contract relating to payment in respect of them: ibid s 102(7).
6 Ibid s 102(3). Section 102(3) applies also to the variation by a public company of the terms of a contract entered into before the company was re-registered as a public company: s 102(4).
7 Ibid s 102(5), (6).
8 Ibid ss 114, 730, Sch 24. For the meaning of 'officer who is in default' and 'the statutory maximum' see para 1161 post. As to the extended application of s 114 see para 464 note 3 ante.

468. Non-cash consideration to be valued before allotment. A public company[1] must not allot shares as fully or partly paid up (as to their nominal value or any premium on them) otherwise than in cash[2] unless:

(1) the consideration for the allotment has been independently valued[3]; and

(2) a report with respect to its value has been made to the company by a person appointed by the company[4] during the six months immediately preceding the allotment of the shares; and

(3) a copy of the report has been sent to the proposed allottee[5].

Where an amount standing to the credit of any of a company's reserve accounts, or of its profit and loss account, is applied in paying up (to any extent) any shares allotted to members of the company or any premiums on shares so allotted, the amount applied does not count as consideration for the allotment, and accordingly the above restriction does not apply in that case[6]. Nor does the restriction apply to the allotment of shares by a company in connection with an arrangement[7] providing for the allotment of shares in that company on terms that the whole or part of the consideration for the shares allotted is to be provided by the transfer to that company (or the cancellation) of all or some of the shares, or of all or some of the shares of a particular class, in another company, with or without the issue to that company of shares, or of shares of any particular class, in that other company[8]. However, it will nevertheless apply unless under the arrangement it is open to all the holders of the shares in the other company in question or, where the arrangement applies only to shares of a particular class, to all the holders of shares in that other company, being holders of shares of that class, to take part in the arrangement[9]. In determining whether that is the case, shares held by or by a nominee of the company proposing to allot the shares in connection with the arrangement, or by or by a nominee of a company which is that company's holding company[10] or subsidiary[11] or a company which is a subsidiary of its holding company must be disregarded[12]. The restriction on allotment of shares otherwise than in cash without a valuation[13] does not apply either to the allotment of shares by a company in connection with its proposed merger with another company, that is where one of the companies proposes to acquire all the assets and liabilities of the other in exchange for the issue of shares or other securities of that one to shareholders of the other, with or without any cash payment to shareholders[14].

If a company allots shares in contravention of the above restriction and either the allottee has not received the valuer's report required[15] to be sent to him, or there has been some other contravention of the above restriction or the provisions as to valuation[16] which the allottee knew or ought to have known amounted to a contravention, the allottee is liable[17] to pay the company an amount equal to the aggregate of the nominal value of the shares and the whole of any premium, or, if the case so requires, so much of that aggregate as is treated as paid up by the consideration, with interest at the appropriate rate[18].

If a company contravenes any of the above provisions, the company, and any officer of it who is in default, is liable on conviction on indictment to a fine, or on summary conviction to a fine not exceeding the statutory maximum[19].

1 For the meaning of 'public company' see para 82 ante. As to the extended application of the Companies Act 1985 s 103 (as amended) see para 464 note 3 ante.
2 For the meaning of 'cash' see para 445 note 2 ante.
3 Ie under the Companies Act 1985 s 108: see para 471 post.
4 Ie in accordance with the provisions of ibid s 108: see para 471 post.
5 Ibid s 103(1). See the cases cited in note 18 infra.
6 Ibid s 103(2).
7 For these purposes, 'arrangement' means any agreement, scheme or arrangement, including an arrangement sanctioned in accordance with ibid s 425 (as amended) (see para 1447 et seq post) or the Insolvency Act 1986 s 110 (see para 1480 post) (Companies Act 1985 s 103(7)(a) (amended by the Insolvency Act 1986 s 439(1), Sch 13 Pt I)); and any reference to a company, except where it is or is to be construed as a reference to a public company, includes any body corporate and any body to which letters patent have been issued under the Chartered Companies Act 1837 (repealed) (Companies Act 1985 s 103(7)(b)). As to the repeal of the Chartered Companies Act 1837 see para 14 ante.
8 Companies Act 1985 s 103(3).
9 Ibid s 103(4).
10 For the meaning of 'holding company' see para 827 post.
11 For the meaning of 'subsidiary' see para 827 post.
12 Companies Act 1985 s 103(4).
13 Ie the restriction contained in ibid s 103(1): see supra.
14 Ibid s 103(5).
15 Ie by ibid s 103(1): see supra.
16 Ie by ibid s 108: see para 471 post.
17 The effect is to create an immediate liability as if the allottee had agreed to take up the shares for cash: *Re Bradford Investments Ltd* [1991] BCLC 224 at 233.

18 Companies Act 1985 s 103(6). For the meaning of 'the appropriate rate' see para 187 note 3 ante. These penalties can be onerous (see *Re Ossory Estates plc* [1988] BCLC 213; *Re Bradford Investments plc (No 2)* [1991] BCLC 688) but can be mitigated by the court's powers under the Companies Act 1985 s 113 to give relief (see para 476 post). For the difficulties in applying s 103 in a case in which the contractual basis for payment of the consideration to the company has gone see *System Control plc v Munro Corporate plc* [1990] BCLC 659.

19 Companies Act 1985 ss 114, 730, Sch 24. For the meaning of 'officer who is in default' and 'the statutory maximum' see para 1161 post. As to the extended application of s 114 see para 464 note 3 ante.

469. Transfer to public company of non-cash asset in initial period.

A public company[1] formed as such must not, unless the following conditions have been complied with, enter into an agreement with a person for the transfer by him during the initial period of one or more non-cash assets[2] to the company or another, if that person is a subscriber to the company's memorandum, and the consideration for the transfer to be given by the company is equal in value at the time of the agreement to one-tenth or more of the company's nominal share capital issued at that time[3]. The 'initial period' for this purpose is two years beginning with the date of the company being issued with a certificate[4] that it was entitled to do business[5].

This restriction also applies to a company re-registered as a public company[6] but in that case there is substituted for the reference to a subscriber to the company's memorandum a reference to a person who is a member of the company on the date of registration or re-registration, and the initial period is then two years beginning with that date[7].

The conditions referred to above are:

(1) the consideration to be received by the company[8], and any consideration other than cash to be given by the company, must have been independently valued[9];

(2) a report with respect to the consideration to be so received and given must have been made to the company during the six months immediately preceding the date of the agreement;

(3) the terms of the agreement must have been approved by an ordinary resolution of the company; and

(4) not later than the giving of the notice of the meeting at which the resolution is proposed, copies of the resolution and report must have been circulated to the members of the company entitled to receive the notice and, if the person with whom the agreement in question is proposed to be made is not then a member of the company so entitled, to that person[10].

The above provisions do not apply in the case of the following agreements, namely:

(a) where it is part of the company's ordinary business to acquire, or arrange for other persons to acquire, assets of a particular description, an agreement entered into by the company in the ordinary course of its business for the transfer of an asset of that description to it or to such a person, as the case may be;

(b) an agreement entered into by the company under the supervision of the court, or of an officer authorised by the court for the purpose, for the transfer of an asset to the company or to another[11].

If a company contravenes any of the above provisions, the company, and any officer of it who is in default, is liable on conviction on indictment to a fine, or on summary conviction to a fine not exceeding the statutory maximum[12].

1 For the meaning of 'public company' see para 82 ante.

2 For these purposes, 'non-cash asset' means any property or interest in property other than cash; and 'cash' includes foreign currency: Companies Act 1985 s 739(1). A reference to the transfer of a non-cash asset includes the creation or extinction of an estate or interest in, or a right over, any property and also

the discharge of any person's liability, other than a liability for a liquidated sum: s 739(2). As to payments in cash see para 479 post.

3 Ibid s 104(1). For these purposes, the reference to consideration given for the transfer of an asset in s 104 or s 109 (see para 472 post) includes consideration given partly for its transfer: s 109(3). As to any necessary apportionment see s 109(3)(a), (b) and para 472 heads (i), (ii) post.

4 Ie under ibid s 117 or the previous corresponding provision.

5 Ibid s 104(2).

6 For these purposes, the reference to a company re-registered as a public company includes a private company so re-registered which was a public company before it was a private company, but excludes one re-registered under the Companies Act 1980 s 8 (repealed) or the Companies Consolidation (Consequential Provisions) Act 1985 s 2 (see para 133 ante) or under the Companies Act 1985 s 685 (see para 77 ante) or the previous corresponding provision: s 104(3).

7 Ibid s 104(3).

8 For these purposes, the reference to the consideration to be received by the company is a reference to the asset to be transferred to it, or the advantage to the company of the asset's transfer to another person; and the specified condition is without prejudice to any requirement to value consideration for the purposes of ibid s 103 (as amended) (see para 468 ante): s 104(5).

9 Ie under ibid s 109: see para 472 post.

10 Ibid s 104(4).

11 Ibid s 104(6).

12 Ibid ss 114, 730, Sch 24. For the meaning of 'officer who is in default' and 'the statutory maximum' see para 1161 post. As to the extended application of s 114 see para 464 note 3 ante.

470. Agreements contravening the restriction on transfer to public company of non-cash assets in initial period. The following provisions apply if a public company[1] enters into an agreement contravening the restriction on transfer of non-cash assets to the company in the initial period[2], the agreement being made with a subscriber to the company's memorandum or a person who was a member of the company at the date of registration or re-registration, as the case may be[3], and either that person has not received the valuer's report required for compliance with the conditions applicable to such restrictions[4] or there has been some other contravention of the statutory provisions[5] which he knew or ought to have known amounted to a contravention[6]. The company is then entitled to recover from that person any consideration given by it under the agreement, or an amount equal to the value of the consideration at the time of the agreement; and the agreement, so far as not carried out, is void[7]. If, however, the agreement is or includes an agreement for the allotment of shares in the company, then, whether or not the agreement also contravenes the provisions requiring a non-cash consideration to be valued before allotment takes place[8], the provision for recovery of the consideration given by the company[9] does not apply to it in so far as it is for the allotment of shares; and the allottee is liable to pay the company an amount equal to the aggregate of the nominal value of the shares and the whole of any premium, or, if the case so requires, so much of that aggregate as is treated as paid up by the consideration, with interest at the appropriate rate[10].

1 For the meaning of 'public company' see para 82 ante. Cf, however, the provisions of the Companies Act 1985 s 104(3): see para 469 ante.

2 Ie under ibid s 104: see para 469 ante.

3 Ie a person referred to in ibid s 104(1)(a) or s 104(3): see para 469 ante.

4 Ie required by ibid s 104(4): see para 469 ante.

5 Ie whether of those contained in ibid s 104 (see para 469 ante), s 108(1), (2) or (5) (see para 471 post) or s 109 (see para 472 post).

6 Ibid s 105(1).

7 Ibid s 105(2).

8 Ie those contained in ibid s 103(2): see para 468 ante.

9 Ie ibid s 105(2): see supra.

10 Ibid s 105(3). For the meaning of 'the appropriate rate' see para 187 note 3 ante.

471. Valuation and report; non-cash consideration. The valuation of a non-cash consideration[1] and the report required thereon[2] must be made by an independent person, that is to say a person qualified at the time of the report to be appointed, or continue to be, an auditor of the company[3]. Where, however, it appears to the independent person ('the valuer') to be reasonable for the valuation of the consideration, or part of it, to be made (or for him to accept such a valuation) by another person who appears to him to have the requisite knowledge and experience to value the consideration or that part of it, and is not an officer or servant[4] of the company or any other body corporate which is that company's subsidiary[5] or holding company[6] or a subsidiary of that company's holding company or a partner or employee of such an officer or servant, he may arrange for or accept such a valuation, together with a report which will enable him to make his own report under this provision and provide the note referred to below[7].

The valuer's report must state:

(1) the nominal value of the shares to be wholly or partly paid for by the consideration in question;

(2) the amount of any premium payable on the shares;

(3) the description of the consideration and, as respects so much of the consideration as he himself has valued, a description of that part of the consideration, the method used to value it and the date of the valuation;

(4) the extent to which the nominal value of the shares and any premium are to be treated as paid up by the consideration or in cash[8].

Where the consideration or part of it is valued by a person other than the valuer himself, the latter's report must state that fact and must also state the former's name and what knowledge and experience he has to carry out the valuation, and must describe so much of the consideration as was valued by the other person, and the method used to value it, and specify the date of the valuation[9].

The valuer's report must contain or be accompanied by a note by him:

(a) in the case of a valuation made by a person other than himself, that it appeared to himself reasonable to arrange for it to be so made or to accept a valuation so made;

(b) whoever made the valuation, that the method of valuation was reasonable in all the circumstances;

(c) that it appears to the valuer that there has been no material change in the value of the consideration in question since the valuation; and

(d) that on the basis of the valuation the value of the consideration, together with any cash by which the nominal value of the shares or any premium payable on them is to be paid up, is not less than so much of the aggregate of the nominal value and the whole of any such premium as is treated as paid up by the consideration and any such cash[10].

Where the consideration to be valued is accepted partly in payment up of the nominal value of the shares and any premium and partly for some other consideration given by the company, the relevant provisions[11] apply as if references to the consideration accepted by the company included the proportion of that consideration which is properly attributable to the payment up of that value and any premium; and the valuer must carry out, or arrange for, such other valuations as will enable him to determine that proportion; and his report must state what valuations have been made under this provision and also the reason for, and method and date of, any such valuation and any other matters which may be relevant to that determination[12].

1 For the meaning of 'cash' see para 469 note 2 ante.
2 Ie required by, where applicable, the Companies Act 1985 s 44 (as amended) (see para 119 ante) or s 103 (as amended) (see para 468 ante).
3 Ibid s 108(1). As to the extended application of s 108 see para 464 note 3 ante. See also *Re Ossory Estates plc* [1988] BCLC 213 at 215 where Harman J described the Companies Act 1985 s 108 as a curious and arcane provision.
4 For these purposes, the reference to 'officer or servant' does not include an auditor: ibid s 108(3). For the meaning of 'officer' see para 641 post.
5 For the meaning of 'subsidiary' see para 827 post.
6 For the meaning of 'holding company' see para 827 post.
7 Companies Act 1985 s 108(2). The note is required by s 108(6): see infra.
8 Ibid s 108(4).
9 Ibid s 108(5).
10 Ibid s 108(6).
11 Ie ibid s 44 (as amended) (where applicable), s 103 (as amended) and the provisions of s 108 (see supra).
12 Ibid s 108(7).

472. Valuation and report; non-cash assets. The statutory provisions relating to the maker of the valuation and report[1], the possibility of part of the consideration being valued by another person[2], and the contents of the valuer's report in such a case[3] apply also for the purpose of the provisions[4] relating to the valuation of a non-cash asset transferred to a public company in the initial period[5].

The valuer's report for those purposes must:

(1) state the consideration to be received by the company, describing the asset in question, specifying the amount to be received in cash[6], and the consideration to be given by the company, specifying the amount to be given in cash;

(2) state the method and date of valuation;

(3) contain or be accompanied by a note[7] by him:

    (a) in the case of a valuation made by a person other than himself, that it appeared to himself reasonable to arrange for it to be so made or to accept a valuation so made;

    (b) whoever made the valuation, that the method of valuation was reasonable in all the circumstances;

    (c) that it appears to the valuer that there has been no material change in the value of the consideration in question since the valuation; and

(4) contain or be accompanied by a note that on the basis of the valuation the value of the consideration to be received by the company is not less than the value of the consideration to be given by it[8].

A reference in the above provisions to consideration given for the transfer of an asset includes consideration given partly for its transfer; but:

    (i) the value of any consideration partly so given is to be taken as the proportion of the consideration properly attributable to its transfer;

    (ii) the valuer must carry out or arrange for such valuations of anything else as will enable him to determine that proportion; and

    (iii) his report[9] must state what valuation has been made under this provision and also the reason for and method and date of any such valuation and any other matters which may be relevant to that determination[10].

1 Ie those contained in the Companies Act 1985 s 108(1): see para 471 ante.
2 Ie under ibid s 108(2), (3): see para 471 ante.
3 Ie under ibid s 108(5): see para 471 ante.
4 Ie ibid s 104: see para 469 ante.
5 Ibid s 109(1).
6 For the meaning of 'cash' see para 469 note 2 ante.

7 Ie a note as to the matters mentioned in the Companies Act 1985 s 108(6)(a)–(c): see para 471 heads (a)–(c) ante.
8 Ibid s 109(2).
9 Ie his report for the purposes of ibid s 104: see para 469 ante.
10 Ibid s 109(3).

473. Entitlement of valuer to full disclosure. A person carrying out a valuation or making a report[1], with respect to any consideration proposed to be accepted or given by a company, is entitled to require from the officers[2] of the company such information and explanation as he thinks necessary to enable him to carry out the valuation[3] or make the report[4] and provide the required note[5].

A person who knowingly or recklessly makes a statement which is misleading, false or deceptive in a material particular, and is a statement made, whether orally or in writing, to a person carrying out such a valuation or making such a report[6], being a statement which conveys or purports to convey any information or explanation which that person requires, or is entitled[7] so to require, is guilty of an offence and liable on conviction on indictment to imprisonment for a term not exceeding two years or a fine, or to both, or on summary conviction to imprisonment for a term not exceeding six months or a fine not exceeding the statutory maximum, or to both[8].

1 Ie under either the Companies Act 1985 s 103 (as amended) (see para 468 ante) or s 104 (see para 469 ante).
2 For the meaning of 'officer' see para 641 post.
3 See note 1 supra.
4 Ie under the Companies Act 1985 s 108 (see para 471 ante) or s 109 (see para 472 ante).
5 Ibid s 110(1). The note will be provided under either s 108(6) (see para 471 ante) or s 109(2)(c) (see para 472 ante). As to the extended application of s 110 see para 464 note 3 ante.
6 See note 4 supra.
7 Ie under the Companies Act 1985 s 110(1): see supra.
8 Ibid ss 110(2), (3), 730, Sch 24. For the meaning of 'the statutory maximum' see para 1161 post.

474. Matters to be communicated to registrar. A company to which a report is made[1] as to the value of any consideration for which, or partly for which, it proposes to allot shares must deliver a copy of the report to the registrar of companies for registration at the same time that it files[2] the return of the allotments of those shares[3]. If default is made in complying with this obligation, every officer of the company who is in default is liable on conviction on indictment to a fine, or on summary conviction to a fine not exceeding the statutory maximum and, on conviction after continued contravention, to a daily default fine not exceeding one-tenth of the statutory maximum[4].

A company which has passed a resolution[5] with respect to the transfer of a non-cash asset in the initial period must, within 15 days of so doing, deliver to the registrar of companies a copy of the resolution together with the required valuer's report[6]. If a company fails to comply with this obligation, it, and every officer of it who is in default, is liable on summary conviction to a fine not exceeding one-fifth of the statutory maximum and, on conviction after continued contravention, to a daily default fine not exceeding one-fiftieth of the statutory maximum[7].

1 Ie under the Companies Act 1985 s 108: see para 471 ante.
2 Ie under ibid s 88: see para 478 post.
3 Ibid s 111(1). As to the extended application of s 111 see para 464 note 3 ante.
4 Ibid ss 111(3), 730, Sch 24. For the meaning of 'officer who is in default', 'the statutory maximum' and 'daily default fine' see para 1161 post. Section 111(3) is, however, subject to the same exception as is

made by s 88(6) (see para 480 post) in the case of default in complying with s 88 (see para 480 post): s 111(3).
5 Ie under ibid s 104: see para 469 ante.
6 Ibid s 111(2). The valuer's report is required by s 104: see para 469 ante.
7 Ibid ss 111(4), 730, Sch 24.

475. Liability of subsequent holders of shares allotted. If a person becomes a holder[1] of shares in respect of which there has been a contravention of a statutory provision[2] by virtue of which another is liable to pay any amount under the provision so contravened[3], that person is also liable to pay that amount (jointly and severally with any other person so liable), unless he is exempted from liability by the provision[4] set out below[5].

If a company enters into an agreement in contravention of the provisions relating to the transfer to a public company of a non-cash asset in the initial period[6] and:

(1) the agreement is or includes an agreement for the allotment of shares in the company; and

(2) a person becomes a holder of shares allotted under the agreement; and

(3) by virtue of the agreement and allotment under it, another person is statutorily[7] liable to pay any amount,

the person who becomes the holder of the shares is also liable to pay that amount (jointly and severally with any other person so liable), unless he is exempted from liability by the following provision[8]; and this applies whether or not the agreement also contravenes the provisions requiring a non-cash consideration to be valued before allotment[9].

A person otherwise liable under either of the above provisions is exempted from that liability if either he is a purchaser for value and, at the time of the purchase, he did not have actual notice of the contravention concerned[10]; or he derived title to the shares (directly or indirectly) from a person who became a holder of them after the contravention and was not liable under whichever of the relevant provisions above was applicable[11].

1 For these purposes, references to a holder, in relation to shares in a company, include any person who has an unconditional right to be included in the company's register of members in respect of those shares or to have an instrument of transfer of the shares executed in his favour: Companies Act 1985 s 112(4). See *System Control plc v Munro Corporate plc* [1990] BCLC 659 (a person in whose favour renounceable letters of allotment had been renounced had an unconditional right to be included in the company's register for these purposes).
2 Ie a contravention of the Companies Act 1985 s 99 (see para 464 ante), s 100 (see para 465 ante), s 101 (see para 466 ante) or s 103 (as amended) (see para 468 ante).
3 Ie by virtue of ibid s 99(3) (see para 464 ante), s 100(2) (see para 465 ante), s 101(4) (see para 466 ante) or s 103(6) (see para 468 ante).
4 Ie by ibid s 112(3): see infra.
5 Ibid s 112(1). As s 112(1) and s 112(3) (see infra) apply in relation to the contraventions there mentioned, they also apply (1) to a contravention of s 102 (see para 467 ante); and (2) to a failure to carry out a term of a contract as mentioned in s 102(5), (6): s 112(5). As to the extended application of s 112 see para 464 note 3 ante.
6 Ie those contained in ibid s 104: see para 469 ante.
7 Ie under ibid s 105(2), (3): see para 470 ante.
8 Ie by ibid s 112(2): see infra.
9 Ibid s 112(2). The valuation of a non-cash consideration is required by s 103 (as amended): see para 468 ante.
10 See *System Control plc v Munro Corporate plc* [1990] BCLC 659 (parties could not rely on this where it was clear that they had notice of the facts; it was not also necessary to show that the parties were aware of the terms of the statutory provision ie the Companies Act 1985 s 103).
11 Companies Act 1985 s 112(3). See also note 5 supra.

476. Relief in respect of certain liabilities. Where a person is liable to a company under any of the above provisions[1] in relation to payment in respect of any shares in the company, or is liable by virtue of an undertaking given to it in, or in connection with, payment for any such shares, the person so liable may make an application[2] to the court[3] to be exempted in whole or in part from the liability[4]. If such liability arises in relation to payment in respect of any shares, the court may, on such an application, exempt the applicant from the liability only:

(1) if and to the extent that it appears to the court just and equitable to do so having regard to the matters mentioned below[5];

(2) if and to the extent that it appears to the court just and equitable to do so in respect of any interest which he is liable to pay the company under any of the relevant provisions[6].

The matters to be taken into account by the court under head (1) above are:

(a) whether the applicant has paid, or is liable to pay, any amount in respect of any other liability arising in relation to those shares under any of the relevant provisions, or of any liability arising by virtue of any undertaking given in or in connection with payment for those shares;

(b) whether any person other than the applicant has paid or is likely to pay (whether in pursuance of an order of the court or otherwise) any such amount; and

(c) whether the applicant or any other person has performed, in whole or in part, or is likely so to perform any such undertaking, or has done or is likely to do any other thing in payment or part payment for the shares[7].

Where the liability arises by virtue of an undertaking given to the company in, or in connection with, payment for shares in it, the court may, on such an application, exempt the applicant from the liability only if and to the extent that it appears to the court just and equitable to do so having regard to whether the applicant has paid or is liable to pay any amount in respect of liability arising in relation to the shares under any of the statutory provisions and whether any person other than the applicant has paid or is likely to pay, whether in pursuance of an order of the court or otherwise, any such amount[8]. In determining whether it should exempt the applicant in whole or in part from any liability, the court must have regard to the following overriding principles[9], namely:

(i) that a company which has allotted shares should receive money or money's worth at least equal in value to the aggregate of the nominal value of those shares and the whole of any premium or, if the case so requires, so much of that aggregate as is treated as paid up[10]; and

(ii) subject to this, that, where such a company would, if the court did not grant the exemption, have more than one remedy against a particular person, it should be for the company to decide which remedy it should remain entitled to pursue[11].

If a person brings proceedings against another ('the contributor') for a contribution in respect of liability to a company arising under any of the relevant statutory provisions[12], and it appears to the court that the contributor is liable to make such a contribution, the court may exercise the following powers[13]. It may, if and to the extent that it appears to it, having regard to the respective culpability (in respect of the liability to the company) of the contributor and the person bringing the proceedings, that it is just and equitable to do so, exempt the contributor in whole or in part from his liability to make such a contribution or order the contributor to make a larger contribution than he would otherwise be liable to make[14].

Where a person is liable to a company as a result of the transfer to a public company of a non-cash asset in the initial period[15], the court may, on application, exempt him in whole or in part from that liability if and to the extent that it appears to the court just and equitable to do so having regard to any benefit accruing to the company by virtue of anything done by him towards the carrying out of the agreement for transfer[16].

1 Ie the Companies Act 1985 s 99 (see para 464 ante), s 102 (see para 467 ante), s 103 (as amended) (see para 468 ante), s 105 (see para 470 ante), s 112(1) by reference to a contravention of s 99 or s 103 (see para 475 ante) or s 112(2) or (5) (see para 475 ante).

2 The application in the High Court is by originating summons in the expedited form: RSC Ord 102 r 2(1), (2).

3 For the meaning of 'the court' see para 161 note 4 ante.

4 Companies Act 1985 s 113(1). As to the extended application of s 113 see para 464 note 3 ante. The burden is on the person applying for relief to satisfy the court that a case for relief under s 113 exists: *Re Bradford Investments plc (No 2)* [1991] BCLC 688. Quaere whether relief is available if in fact there is no subsisting contract for the allotment of shares in the first place: see *System Control plc v Munro Corporate plc* [1990] BCLC 659.

5 Ie in the Companies Act 1985 s 113(3): see infra. See also *Re Bradford Investments plc (No 2)* [1991] BCLC 688 at 693 (in the light of the Companies Act 1985 s 113(5) (see infra) these matters were not intended to be an exhaustive statement of the matters to which the court should or may have regard).

6 Companies Act 1985 s 113(2). See *Re Ossory Estates plc* [1988] BCLC 213; *System Control plc v Munro Corporate plc* [1990] BCLC 659; *Re Bradford Investments plc (No 2)* [1991] BCLC 688.

7 Companies Act 1985 s 113(3). See *Re Ossory Estates plc* [1988] BCLC 213.

8 Companies Act 1985 s 113(4).

9 See *Re Bradford Investments plc (No 2)* [1991] BCLC 688 at 694 (where Hoffmann J thought that the designation 'overriding principle' did not oblige the court to refuse relief unless the company had received at least the nominal value of the allotted shares and any premium; had that been the intention, the requirement would have been framed as a rule).

10 See *Re Ossory Estates plc* [1988] BCLC 213 (relief granted where the company had undoubtedly received at least money or money's worth equal in value, and probably exceeding in value, the aggregate of the nominal value of the shares and any premium); cf *System Control plc v Munro Corporate plc* [1990] BCLC 659 (no prospect of relief being granted when absolutely no evidence that the company had received the minimum amount); *Re Bradford Investments plc (No 2)* [1991] BCLC 688 (applicants failed to discharge the burden of showing that the company had received value for its shares).

11 Companies Act 1985 s 113(5).

12 Ie under ibid ss 99–105 (as amended) (see paras 464–470 ante) or s 112 (see para 475 ante).

13 Ibid s 113(6).

14 Ibid s 113(7).

15 The prohibition is contained in ibid s 104 (see para 469 ante) and the liability in consequence arises under s 105(2) (see para 470 ante).

16 Ibid s 113(8).

477. Undertakings to do work. Subject to the power of the court to grant relief[1], an undertaking given by any person, in or in connection with payment for shares in a company, to do work or perform services or to do any other thing, if it is enforceable by the company apart from the Companies Act 1985, is so enforceable notwithstanding that there has been a contravention in relation to it of a relevant statutory provision[2].

Where such an undertaking is given in contravention of the provisions relating to the transfer to a public company of a non-cash asset in the initial period[3] in respect of the allotment of shares, it is so enforceable notwithstanding the contravention[4].

1 Ie under the Companies Act 1985 s 113: see para 476 ante.

2 Ibid s 115(1). The relevant statutory provisions referred to are s 99 (see para 464 ante), s 102 (see para 467 ante) and s 103 (see para 468 ante). As to the extended application of s 115 see para 464 note 3 ante.

3 Ie ibid s 104: see para 469 ante.

4 Ibid s 115(2).

E. RETURN OF ALLOTMENTS AND REGISTRATION

478. Return of allotments to registrar. When a company limited by shares, or a company limited by guarantee and having a share capital, makes an allotment of its shares, it must within one month thereafter deliver to the registrar of companies for registration:

(1) a return of the allotments in the prescribed form[1] stating the number and nominal amount of the shares comprised in the allotment, the names and addresses of the allottees, and the amount, if any, paid or due and payable on each share whether on account of the nominal value of the share or by way of premium[2]; and

(2) in the case of shares allotted as fully or partly paid up otherwise than in cash, a contract[3] in writing constituting the title of the allottee to the allotment, together with any contract of sale, or for services or other consideration in respect of which that allotment was made, such contracts being duly stamped, and a return stating the number and nominal amount of shares so allotted, the extent to which they are to be treated as paid up, and the consideration for which they have been allotted[4].

Where such a contract is not reduced to writing, the company must within one month after the allotment deliver to the registrar of companies for registration the prescribed particulars[5] of the contract stamped with the same stamp duty as would have been payable if the contract had been reduced to writing[6]; and those particulars are deemed to be an instrument within the meaning of the Stamp Act 1891[7], and the registrar may require that the duty payable on them be adjudicated[8] as a condition of filing the particulars[9].

If default is made in complying with these provisions, every officer of the company who is in default is liable on conviction on indictment to a fine, or on summary conviction to a fine not exceeding the statutory maximum and, on conviction after continued contravention, to a daily default fine not exceeding one-tenth of the statutory maximum[10].

---

1 For the prescribed form of return of allotment see the Companies (Forms) (Amendment) Regulations 1988, SI 1988/1359, reg 2(1), Schedule, Form 88(2).

2 Companies Act 1985 s 88(1), (2)(a).

3 Where an option is granted to take fully paid shares as part of the consideration, it is not sufficient to deliver the agreement containing the option; a contract or memorandum of a contract exercising the option is also required: *Re Coolgardie Consolidated Gold Mines Ltd* (1898) 14 TLR 277.

4 Companies Act 1985 s 88(1), (2)(b). As to what is an adequate statement of the consideration see *Re Frost & Co Ltd* [1899] 2 Ch 207, CA; *Re Maynards Ltd* [1898] 1 Ch 515; cf *Re Robert Watson & Co Ltd* [1899] 2 Ch 509. As to the necessity of delivering a copy of any report under the Companies Act 1985 s 108 (see para 471 ante) to the registrar at the same time as the return of allotments see para 474 ante.

5 For the prescribed particulars see the Companies (Forms) Regulations 1985, SI 1985/854, reg 4(1), Sch 3, Form 88(3) (amended by SI 1987/752).

6 Companies Act 1985 s 88(3). As to the prospective exemption or reduction in stamp duty in relation to property other than land, an interest in the proceeds of sale of land held on trust for sale and a licence to occupy land see the Finance Act 1991 ss 110, 111 and STAMP DUTIES vol 44(1) (Reissue) para 1006.

7 'Instrument' includes every written document: Stamp Act 1891 s 122(1).

8 Ie under ibid s 12 (as amended): see STAMP DUTIES vol 44(1) (Reissue) para 1111.

9 Companies Act 1985 s 88(4).

10 Ibid ss 88(5), 730, Sch 24. For the meaning of 'officer who is in default', 'the statutory maximum' and 'daily default fine' see para 1161 post. As to relief which may be granted by the court see para 480 post.

479. Payment in cash. Any transaction in good faith between a company and a shareholder, which, if the company were to bring an action against him for calls, would support a plea of payment, constitutes payment in cash for the purposes of the provisions[1] previously stated[2]. Thus the cancellation of a debt for compensation due to a director[3] or, in a proper case, for money lent[4], or for consideration for property purchased[5], may constitute payment in cash; but the debt cancelled must have been a genuine debt presently due from the company[6].

1 Ie the Companies Act 1985 s 88(2)(b): see para 478 ante.
2 *Re Harmony and Montague Tin and Copper Mining Co, Spargo's Case* (1873) 8 Ch App 407; *Re Pen'Allt Silver Lead Mining Co, Fothergill's Case* (1873) 8 Ch App 270; *Re Limehouse Works Co, Coates' Case* (1873) LR 17 Eq 169 (set-off debt on sale of business to company against money due for shares); *Larocque v Beauchemin* [1897] AC 358, PC (set-off); *North Sydney Investment and Tramway Co v Higgins* [1899] AC 263, PC; and as to set-off cf *Tarrant v Roberts* (1930) 47 TLR 199 (set-off amounting to repayment of excess profits duty).
3 *Re Paraguassu Steam Tramway Co, Adamson's Case* (1874) LR 18 Eq 670; *Re Regent United Service Stores, ex p Bentley* (1879) 12 ChD 850.
4 See *Re Metropolitan Public Carriage and Repository Co, Cleland's Case* (1872) LR 14 Eq 387, where this was queried on principle, as there may be a debt presently payable for money lent, the cancellation of such a debt should be payment in cash: see the cases cited in para 480 note 6 post and *Re Barrow-in-Furness and Northern Counties' Land Investment Co* (1880) 14 ChD 400, CA.
5 *Re Barrow-in-Furness and Northern Counties' Land and Investment Co* (1880) 14 ChD 400, CA; *Re Limehouse Works Co, Coates' Case* (1873) LR 17 Eq 169; *Larocque v Beauchemin* [1897] AC 358, PC; but distinguish *Re Pen'Allt Silver Lead Mining Co, Fraser's Case* (1873) 42 LJ Ch 358, and *Re Rosherville Hotel Co, Robert's Case* (1890) 2 Meg 60 (where the transaction of cancellation was incomplete or no money was due); cf *Re Newport and South Wales Shipowners' Co Ltd, Rowland's Case* (1880) 42 LT 785, CA (where shares were allotted to a nominee, but at no moment of time was there a debt on one side which could be set off against a debt on the other side).
6 *Re Johannesburg Hotel Co, ex p Zoutpansberg Prospecting Co* [1891] 1 Ch 119, CA (actual demand for present payment necessary); *Re Church and Empire Fire Insurance Co, Pagin and Gill's Case* (1877) 6 ChD 681; *Re Church and Empire Fire Insurance Fund, Andress' Case* (1878) 8 ChD 126, CA; *Re Government Security Fire Insurance Co, White's Case* (1879) 12 ChD 511, CA (company not having become liable for debt); *Re Barangah Oil Refining Co, Arnot's Case* (1887) 36 ChD 702, CA; *Re Land Development Association, Kent's Case* (1888) 39 ChD 259, CA (agreement to write off at future time when cross-debts should become payable); *Re Eddystone Marine Insurance Co* [1893] 3 Ch 9, CA (contract in consideration of past services; ultra vires).

480. Power of court to extend time for registration. In the case of default in delivering for registration within due time any document required to be delivered[1], the company, or any officer liable for the default, may apply for relief to the court[2], which, if satisfied that the omission to deliver the document was accidental[3] or due to inadvertence[4], or that it is just and equitable to grant relief[5], may make extending the time for the delivery for such period as the court thinks proper[6]. The application is primarily in the interest of the company and its officers to obtain relief from the penalties. The shareholder is under no liability by reason of the omission to file the contract, and the omission does not prevent the shares from being fully or partly paid, as the case may be.

1 Ie any document required to be delivered within one month after the allotment by the Companies Act 1985 s 88: see para 478 ante.
2 For the meaning of 'the court' see para 161 note 4 ante.
3 'Accidental' means due to accident, and an accident is probably an unlooked for mishap or an untoward event which was not expected or designed: see *Fenton v J Thorley & Co Ltd* [1903] AC 443, HL; and see para 1314 post.
4 Inadvertence includes cases where there has been delay in adjudicating on the stamp duty (*Re Lucky Guss Ltd* (1898) 79 LT 722) or ignorance or forgetfulness of the law (*Re Jackson & Co Ltd* [1899] 1 Ch 348; *Re Tom-Tit Cycle Co* (1899) 43 Sol Jo 334; and see para 1314 post).

5 *Spiers and Bevan's Case* [1899] 1 Ch 210.
6 Companies Act 1985 s 88(6). As to the procedure see para 481 post. The statutory provisions apply whether any part or the whole of the consideration was other than cash (*Re Tom-Tit Cycle Co* (1899) 43 Sol Jo 334), and the court has a wide discretion. Relief has been granted under earlier Acts, when the filed contract was insufficiently or erroneously stated (*Re Mays' Metals Separating Syndicate Ltd, Smithson's Case* (1898) 68 LJ Ch 46; *Re Northern Creosoting and Sleeper Co Ltd* (1898) 79 LT 407; and see *Markham and Darter's Case* [1899] 2 Ch 480, CA); where there was no contract (*Re Jackson & Co Ltd* [1899] 1 Ch 348); and where the contract was only verbal (*Re Victoria Brick Works Co Ltd, Seaton's Case* (1898) 5 Mans 350). Where in a winding up relief is sought, the party seeking relief should give the liquidator the fullest information, otherwise he may be ordered to pay the costs of the liquidator on what is now the indemnity basis: *Re Farmer's United, Stephenson's Case* [1900] 2 Ch 442.

In *Re Anderson and Munro* 1924 SC 222, a company failed to file the required particulars. After the time for filing had expired the contract was reduced to writing, and the court gave leave to extend the time for filing the contract in writing.

481. Procedure. The application is made by originating motion[1] to the court having jurisdiction to wind up the company[2]. In cases in the High Court the jurisdiction is assigned to the Chancery Division[3].

The notice of motion and all affidavits, notices and other documents in the proceedings must be entitled in the matter of the company and in the matter of the Companies Act 1985[4].

The notice of motion must be supported by an affidavit, which should set out the reason for the failure to deliver the contract or the prescribed particulars of the contract, as the case may be, for registration[5].

1 RSC Ord 102 r 3(1)(a).
2 Companies Act 1985 s 744. As to the courts having winding-up jurisdiction see paras 2004, 2196 et seq post.
3 RSC Ord 102 r 5(1).
4 RSC Ord 102 r 5(2).
5 *Re Victoria Brick Works Co Ltd, Seaton's Case* (1898) 5 Mans 350.

(iii) Share Certificates

482. Time for issuing certificates. Unless the conditions of issue of the shares otherwise provide, every company must, within two months after the allotment of any of its shares, and within two months after the date on which a transfer[1] of any such shares is lodged with it, complete and have ready for delivery the certificates of all shares allotted or transferred[2]. Notwithstanding any enactment, instrument or rule of law, a participating issuer must not issue a certificate in relation to any uncertificated units of a participating security, save where uncertificated securities are being converted into certificated form[3].

This provision does not apply in the case of a transfer to any person where, by virtue of regulations under the Stock Transfer Act 1982[4], he is not entitled to a certificate or other document of or evidencing title in respect of the securities transferred; but, if in such a case he subsequently becomes entitled to such a certificate or other document by virtue of any provisions of those regulations and gives notice in writing of that fact to the company, the above provision has effect as if the reference to the date of the lodging of the transfer were a reference to the date of the notice[5].

A company of which shares are allotted to a recognised clearing house[6] or a nominee[7] of a recognised clearing house or of a recognised investment exchange, or with which a transfer is lodged for transferring any shares of the company to such a clearing house or nominee, is not required in consequence of the allotment or the lodging of the transfer to comply with the above provisions[8].

If default is made in complying with the above provisions, the company, and every officer of it who is in default, is liable on summary conviction to a fine not exceeding one-fifth of the statutory maximum and, on conviction after continued contravention, to a daily default fine not exceeding one-fiftieth of the statutory maximum[9].

Where a company obtains admission to the Official List, the share certificate must comply with specified requirements[10]; and in addition the company must arrange for transfers to be:

(1) certified against certificates or temporary documents of title and to be returned on the day of receipt or, should that not be a business day, on the first business day following their receipt, and to split and return renounceable documents within the same period;

(2) registered or rejected within two business days of their receipt[11].

The company must issue, without charge, certificates within one month of the date of expiration of any right of renunciation or within five business days of the lodgement of transfers[12].

1 For these purposes, the expression 'transfer' means a transfer duly stamped and otherwise valid, or an exempt transfer within the Stock Transfer Act 1982 (see STOCK EXCHANGE), and does not include such a transfer as the company is for any reason entitled to refuse to register and does not register: Companies Act 1985 s 185(2). As to notice of refusal see para 500 post.

2 Ibid s 185(1).

3 See the Uncertificated Securities Regulations 1995, SI 1995/3272, regs 26(2), 32(1) and MONEY. As to conversion of securities into certificated and uncertificated form see regs 26, 27; and as to the penalties for breach see regs 37, 38; and see generally MONEY.

4 Ie the Stock Transfer Act 1982 s 3: see para 1277 post. This relates to a computer-based system of transfer established by the Bank of England and the Stock Exchange for the transfer of 'specified securities' as defined in s 2. At present only the securities listed in Sch 1 (as amended) (securities traded in the gilt-edged market), the Stock Transfer (Specified Securities) Order 1988, SI 1988/231, art 2, Schedule and the Stock Transfer (Specified Securities) Order 1991, SI 1991/340, art 2, Schedule are so specified: see STOCK EXCHANGE.

5 Companies Act 1985 s 185(3).

6 For these purposes, 'recognised clearing house' means a recognised clearing house within the meaning of the Financial Services Act 1986 s 207(1) acting in relation to a recognised investment exchange: Companies Act 1985 s 185(4) (amended by the Financial Services Act 1986 s 194(5)(d)). For the meaning of 'recognised investment exchange' see para 223 note 1 ante. See further STOCK EXCHANGE.

7 No person is a nominee for this purpose unless he is a person designated for this purpose in the rules of the recognised investment exchange in question: Companies Act 1985 s 185(4) (amended by the Financial Services Act 1986 s 194(5)(c)). See STOCK EXCHANGE.

8 Companies Act 1985 s 185(4) (amended by the Financial Services Act 1986 s 194(5)). In the case of an unregistered company (see para 1765 et seq post) the Companies Act 1985 s 185(4) (as so amended) has effect as if for the words 'subsection (1)' there were substituted 'any provision of any instrument constituting or regulating the company': Companies (Unregistered Companies) Regulations 1985, SI 1985/680, reg 6(e).

9 Companies Act 1985 ss 185(5), 730, Sch 24. For the meaning of 'officer who is in default', 'the statutory maximum' and 'daily default fine' see para 1161 post.

10 Ie the requirements of the *Listing Rules* r 13.20. As to the *Listing Rules* see para 282 ante.

11 See the *Listing Rules* r 9.39.

12 See the *Listing Rules* r 9.40.

483. Enforcement of issue of certificate. If a company, on which a notice has been served requiring it to make good any default in complying with the above provision[1], fails to make good the default within ten days after the service of the notice, the court[2] may, on the application of the person entitled to have the certificate delivered to him, make an order directing the company and any officer of the company to make good the default within such time as may be specified in the order; and any such order may provide that all costs of and incidental to the application shall be borne by the company or by an officer of the company responsible for the default[3].

1 Ie the Companies Act 1985 s 185(1): see para 482 ante.
2 For the meaning of 'the court' see para 161 note 4 ante.
3 Companies Act 1985 s 185(6), (7).

484. Procedure. The application is made by originating summons in the expedited form[1] to the court having jurisdiction to wind up the company[2]. In cases in the High Court the jurisdiction is assigned to the Chancery Division[3]. The summons and all affidavits, notices, and other documents in the proceedings must be entitled in the matter of the company and in the matter of the Companies Act 1985[4].

1 RSC Ord 102 r 2(1), (2).
2 Companies Act 1985 s 744. As to the courts having winding-up jurisdiction see paras 2004, 2196 et seq post.
3 RSC Ord 102 r 5(1).
4 RSC Ord 102 r 5(2).

485. Split certificates. Whether a shareholder has the right to divide his shareholding and accordingly force the company to give him two or more certificates in respect of it depends entirely on the construction of the articles of the company[1].

1 *Sharpe v Tophams Ltd* [1939] Ch 373, [1939] 1 All ER 123, CA. In a company where there are no restrictions upon transfers the same result may be effected by transfers to nominees. As to members' rights to share certificates in the case of companies governed by the Companies (Tables A to F) Regulations 1985, SI 1985/805, Schedule, Table A see art 6. As to Table A generally see para 529 et seq post.

486. Clean certificates. A member is entitled to a 'clean' certificate, that is one which does not contain on it any statement derogatory to his title[1].

1 *Re W Key & Son Ltd* [1902] 1 Ch 467. As to the order in which the names of joint holders are to appear see para 383 ante.

487. Effect of share certificate. A certificate under the common seal[1] of the company specifying any shares[2] held by a member is prima facie evidence of his title to the shares[3]. This provision does not, however, apply to any document issued with respect to uncertificated shares; and a document issued by or on behalf of a participating issuer purportedly evidencing title to an uncertificated unit of a participating security is not evidence of title to the unit of the security[4].

The company has power[5] to issue a certificate certifying that the shareholder named in the certificate is the registered holder of the shares specified in it, the object being to give shareholders the opportunity of more easily dealing with their shares in the market and at once showing a marketable title[6]. The certificate is the only documentary evidence of title in the possession of a shareholder[7]. It is not a negotiable instrument or a warranty of title by the company issuing it[8]. It declares to all the world that the person who is named in it is the registered holder of certain shares in the company[9], and that the shares are paid up to the extent mentioned in it[10]; and it is given with the intention that it shall be used as such a declaration[11].

Share certificates are the proper subject of interpleader proceedings[12].

1   A company need no longer have a common seal: see the Companies Act 1985 s 36A(3) (as added) and para 1130 post. Accordingly, a share certificate may be issued under a company's common seal, if the company has one, or issued in accordance with s 36A(4) (as added) (execution otherwise than by affixing common seal: see para 1130 post) whether it has a common seal or not, or issued under s 40 (as amended) (official seal for share certificates etc: see para 1118 post). A share certificate is not a deed within the meaning of the word as used in the Law of Property Act 1925 s 74 relating to the execution of deeds by or on behalf of corporations: *South London Greyhound Racecourses Ltd v Wake* [1931] 1 Ch 496 at 503; and see *R v Morton* (1873) LR 2 CCR 22.

2   For the meaning of 'share' see para 209 note 2 ante.

3   Companies Act 1985 s 186(1) (substituted by the Companies Act 1989 s 130(7), Sch 17 para 5; amended by the Law Reform (Miscellaneous Provisions) (Scotland) Act 1990 s 74(1), (2), Sch 8 para 33(4), Sch 9; renumbered by the Requirements of Writing (Scotland) Act 1995 s 14(1), Sch 4 para 55). In the case of an unregistered company (see para 1765 et seq post) for the reference in the Companies Act 1985 s 186 (as so substituted) to the common seal of the company there must be substituted a reference to the common or other authorised seal of the company: Companies (Unregistered Companies) Regulations 1985, SI 1985/680, reg 6(d) (amended by SI 1990/1394). While membership of a company requires entry on the register of members, a liquidator may distribute surplus assets in a winding up to the possessors of share certificates without requiring them to perfect their title by registration where the liquidator is satisfied that they are beneficially entitled to the shares to which the certificate relates; but, where certificates have been purchased by collectors for their ornamental value, the holders of those certificates are not beneficially entitled to the shares to which the certificate relates: *Re Baku Consolidated Oilfields Ltd* [1994] 1 BCLC 173.

4   See the Uncertificated Securities Regulations 1995, SI 1995/3272, reg 32(3) and MONEY.

5   A person cannot insist on having a certificate of his title as a shareholder until he has done everything required to make him a shareholder: *Wilkinson v Anglo-Californian Gold Mining Co* (1852) 18 QB 728.

6   *Re Bahia and San Francisco Rly Co* (1868) LR 3 QB 584 at 595.

7   *Société Générale de Paris v Walker* (1885) 11 App Cas 20 at 29, HL. It applies only to the legal and not to the equitable title to the shares: *Shropshire Union Railways and Canal Co v R* (1875) LR 7 HL 496 at 509.

8   *Longman v Bath Electric Tramways Ltd* [1905] 1 Ch 646, CA.

9   *Re Bahia and San Francisco Rly Co* (1868) LR 3 QB 584; *Shropshire Union Railways and Canal Co v R* (1875) LR 7 HL 496.

10   *Bloomenthal v Ford* [1897] AC 156, HL; *Burkinshaw v Nicolls* (1878) 3 App Cas 1004, HL; *Barrow's Case* (1880) 14 ChD 432, CA; *Waterhouse v Jamieson* (1870) LR 2 Sc & Div 29 at 33, HL. Cf *Re A W Hall & Co* (1887) 37 ChD 712.

11   *Re Bahia and San Francisco Rly Co* (1868) LR 3 QB 584; *Webb v Herne Bay Comrs* (1870) LR 5 QB 642; *Balkis Consolidated Co v Tomkinson* [1893] AC 396, HL; *Dixon v Kennaway & Co* [1900] 1 Ch 833.

12   *Robinson v Jenkins* (1890) 24 QBD 275, CA; RSC Ord 17 r 1.

488. Estoppel. The company is estopped from disputing the truth of any statement in a share certificate as against any person not knowing that the statement is untrue, who has acted or refrained from acting on the faith of it, and has thereby suffered loss[1].

Where a person, who lends money to a company on the terms of having as security fully-paid shares, receives certificates of the shares as fully paid, and the shares are allotted, and he is registered accordingly, the company is estopped from asserting against him any liability in respect of them[2]. The company is also estopped where an allottee accepts a certificate for fully-paid shares in such circumstances that he may have reason to believe, when he accepts it, that the balance of the money due on the shares had been paid by another person[3].

The test is whether the shares were taken honestly on the faith of the certificate, and, if so, whether the holder afterwards honestly acted on the certificate or relied on it to his detriment[4]. If a person did not take the shares on the faith of the certificate, or ought to have known that the statements in it were untrue, there is no estoppel as against the company[5]. A company may be estopped although the certificate was signed by a director in favour of a firm of which he is the partner, provided that the director can prove that he did not at the time of signing know the true facts[6]. The company is, however, estopped or liable in respect of its share certificate only where it is issued by those who have authority or apparent authority to issue it; where the certificate is a forgery, as where the secretary forges the signatures of directors, the company is not estopped[7]. Payment of dividends on shares does not estop the company from denying the title of the payee to the shares[8].

If the company is estopped from denying that a share is fully paid as against a holder without notice, such a holder can give a good title to the share as fully paid even to a transferee who has notice that the shares are not fully paid[9].

A person who by reason of the issue of a certificate is entitled to shares by estoppel, and who acts on the certificate to his detriment, may recover from the company as damages the value of the shares at the time of the refusal of the company to recognise him as a shareholder, together with interest from that date[10]. Similarly, a person who as a consequence of relying on a certificate loses his power to get redress against a third party may recover damages from the company[11]. If, however, he has not altered his position on the faith of the certificate, he cannot recover damages[12].

1 *Balkis Consolidated Co v Tomkinson* [1893] AC 396, HL; *Bloomenthal v Ford* [1897] AC 156, HL; *Dixon v Kennaway & Co* [1900] 1 Ch 833; *Parbury's Case* [1896] 1 Ch 100; *Barrow's Case* (1880) 14 ChD 432, CA; *Burkinshaw v Nicolls* (1878) 3 App Cas 1004, HL; *Re Ottos Kopje Diamond Mines Ltd* [1893] 1 Ch 618, CA; *Shaw v Port Philip Gold Mining Co* (1884) 13 QBD 103; *Monarch Motor Car Co v Pease* (1903) 19 TLR 148; cf *Simm v Anglo-American Telegraph Co, Anglo-American Telegraph Co v Spurling* (1879) 5 QBD 188, CA; *Re Railway Time Tables Publishing Co, ex p Sandys* (1889) 42 ChD 98, CA; *Re London Celluloid Co* (1888) 39 ChD 190, CA; *Markham and Darter's Case* [1899] 1 Ch 414; *Re Newport and South Wales Shipowners' Co, Rowland's Case* (1880) 42 LT 785, CA; *Penang Foundry Co Ltd v Gardiner* 1913 SC 1203.
2 *Bloomenthal v Ford* [1897] AC 156, HL. This case, *Christchurch Gas Co v Kelly* (1887) 3 TLR 634, *Parbury's Case* [1896] 1 Ch 100, and *Penang Foundry Co Ltd v Gardiner* 1913 SC 1203 extend the doctrine of *Burkinshaw v Nicolls* (1878) 3 App Cas 1004, HL (a case of a transferee) to the case of an original allottee.
3 *Penang Foundry Co Ltd v Gardiner* 1913 SC 1203.
4 *Hart v Frontino and Bolivia South American Gold Mining Co Ltd* (1870) LR 5 Exch 111; *Dixon v Kennaway & Co* [1900] 1 Ch 833.
5 *Blyth's Case* (1876) 4 ChD 140 at 142, CA; *Simm v Anglo-American Telegraph Co, Anglo-American Telegraph Co v Spurling* (1879) 5 QBD 188, CA; *Re Vulcan Ironworks Co* [1885] WN 120. As to estoppel generally see ESTOPPEL vol 16 (Reissue) para 1085 et seq.
6 *Re Coasters Ltd* [1911] 1 Ch 86.
7 *Ruben v Great Fingall Consolidated* [1906] AC 439, HL; *Dixon v Kennaway & Co* [1900] 1 Ch 833; *South London Greyhound Racecourses Ltd v Wake* [1931] 1 Ch 496; cf *Shaw v Port Philip Gold Mining Co* (1884) 13 QBD 103.
8 *Foster v Tyne Pontoon and Dry Docks Co and Renwick* (1893) 63 LJQB 50.
9 *Barrow's Case* (1880) 14 ChD 432, CA; cf *Re London Celluloid Co* (1888) 39 ChD 190, CA.
10 *Re Bahia and San Francisco Rly Co* (1868) LR 3 QB 584; *Hart v Frontino and Bolivia South American Gold Mining Co Ltd* (1870) LR 5 Exch 111; *Re Ottos Kopje Diamond Mines Ltd* [1893] 1 Ch 618, CA; *Balkis Consolidated Co v Tomkinson* [1893] AC 396, HL.
11 *Dixon v Kennaway & Co* [1900] 1 Ch 833.
12 *Simm v Anglo-American Telegraph Co, Anglo-American Telegraph Co v Spurling* (1879) 5 QBD 188, CA (where the person claiming under estoppel had acted upon a forged transfer); *Platt v Rowe (Trading as Chapman and Rowe) and C M Mitchell & Co* (1909) 26 TLR 49 (transferee who paid for shares comprised in a transfer to him which were not registered in name of vendor recovered purchase price as on a total failure of consideration even though company had sent him a certificate).

489. Note on certificate. The usual note on a certificate, that without its production no transfer will be registered, is a mere warning to take care of it, and not a representation to or a contract with the holder of the certificate that a transfer will not be registered without its production[1].

1 *Rainford v James Keith and Blackman Co Ltd* [1905] 1 Ch 296 per Farwell J (revsd on another ground [1905] 2 Ch 147, CA); *Guy v Waterlow Bros and Layton Ltd* (1909) 25 TLR 515; cf *Société Générale de Paris v Walker* (1885) 11 App Cas 20, HL. As to the company's duties with regard to certificates deposited with it for the purpose of certification of transfers see para 512 post.

(iv) Transfer of Shares

490. Contract to sell shares. A contract for the sale of shares[1] may be made orally[2]. Specific performance may be ordered of a contract to sell shares[3], even though the company, pending the litigation, has gone into liquidation[4], and also of a contract to take a transfer of shares on which nothing has been paid[5].

1 See para 493 note 1 post.
2 *Humble v Mitchell* (1839) 11 Ad & El 205; *Watson v Spratley* (1854) 10 Exch 222; *Bowlby v Bell* (1846) 3 CB 284; *Bradley v Holdsworth* (1838) 3 M & W 422.
3 *Duncuft v Albrecht* (1841) 12 Sim 189; *Poole v Middleton* (1861) 4 LT 631; *Llewellin v Grossman* (1950) 83 Ll L Rep 462. See RSC Ord 86 and *Woodlands v Hind* [1955] 2 All ER 604, [1955] 1 WLR 688. See also *Langen and Wind Ltd v Bell* [1972] Ch 685, [1972] 1 All ER 296 (specific performance not granted where vendor's equitable lien for unpaid purchase money would not be safeguarded). As to damages for breach of contract see DAMAGES vol 12 para 1174 et seq.
4 *Paine v Hutchinson* (1868) 3 Ch App 388.
5 *Cheale v Kenward* (1858) 3 De G & J 27.

491. Vendor's obligation. Under an ordinary contract for sale of shares[1], made subject to the rules of the Stock Exchange, the vendor's only duty is to execute a valid transfer, hand it and the certificate to the purchaser, and do all that is necessary on his part to enable the purchaser to be registered, it being the purchaser's duty to obtain registration of the transfer[2]. Unless registration is refused because the transferor has no right to execute the transfer, the transferee must pay the consideration for the transfer, although registration is refused[3] in which case the transferor, so long as his name remains on the register, holds the shares in trust for the transferee[4] unless the transferor annuls the bargain[5]. Unless the transferor takes this course, the transferee becomes in equity the owner of the shares[6] and the transferor is bound not to prevent or delay the registration of the transferee as owner[7]. A vendor who contracts to sell registered shares is not entitled to complete the transaction by delivery of share warrants[8].

For breach of the vendor's obligations, an action for damages will lie at the suit of the purchaser[9]. Alternatively, unless the shares are freely available in the market, an action for specific performance will lie[10].

1 A sale may be subject to a special term eg 'with registration guaranteed': see *Cruse v Paine* (1869) 4 Ch App 441. As to stocks see para 493 note 1 post.
2 *Neilson v James* (1882) 9 QBD 546, CA; and see STOCK EXCHANGE vol 45 para 98.
3 *Stray v Russell* (1859) 1 E & E 888 (affd (1860) 1 E & E 916, Ex Ch); *Skinner v City of London Marine Insurance Corpn* (1885) 14 QBD 882, CA; *London Founders' Association v Clarke* (1888) 20 QBD 576, CA; *Ward and Henry's Case* (1867) 2 Ch App 431 at 438; and see *East Wheal Martha Mining Co* (1863) 33 Beav 119 at 121. For the vendor's obligation where he is not the transferor see *Hichens, Harrison, Woolston & Co v Jackson & Sons* [1943] AC 266, [1943] 1 All ER 128, HL.
4 *Stevenson v Wilson* 1907 SC 445.
5 *Lyle and Scott Ltd v Scott's Trustees* [1959] AC 763, [1959] 2 All ER 661, HL.
6 *Ward and Henry's Case* (1867) 2 Ch App 431 at 438; *Hawks v McArthur* [1951] 1 All ER 22.
7 *Hooper v Herts* [1906] 1 Ch 549, CA.
8 *Iredell v General Securites Corpn Ltd* (1916) 33 TLR 67, CA (where the contract provided that registration of transfers was to be carried out by the vendors free of charge; the company went into liquidation and the liquidator declined to register the transfer).

9 The measure of damages will be the market price at the contractual date for delivery less the contract price: *Shaw v Holland* (1846) 15 M & W 136; *Powell v Jessopp* (1856) 18 CB 336.
10 See SPECIFIC PERFORMANCE vol 44(1) (Reissue) paras 814, 826, 827.

492. Purchaser's obligation. On a sale of shares the purchaser is liable on an implied promise to indemnify the vendor, so long as he remains registered, against calls, whether made while the purchaser was beneficially entitled or after the purchaser sold them to a sub-purchaser[1].

For breach of the purchaser's obligations in all cases an action for damages will lie at the suit of the vendor[2]. Alternatively, unless the shares are freely disposable in the market, an action for specific performance will lie[3].

1 *Walker v Bartlett* (1856) 18 CB 845; *Kellock v Enthoven* (1873) LR 9 QB 241; *Spencer v Ashworth, Partington & Co* [1925] 1 KB 589, CA.
2 The measure of damages will be the contract price less the market price at the contractual date for completion: *Jamal v Moolla Dawood, Sons & Co* [1916] 1 AC 175, PC.
3 See SPECIFIC PERFORMANCE vol 44(1) (Reissue) paras 814, 826, 827.

493. Issue of share warrants. A company limited by shares, if so authorised by its articles, may, with respect to any fully paid-up shares[1], issue a warrant (a 'share warrant')[2] stating that the bearer[3] of the warrant is entitled to the shares specified in it[4]. A company which issues a share warrant, if so authorised by its articles, may provide (by coupons or otherwise) for the payment of the future dividends on the shares included in the warrant[5].

Where a company has obtained admission to the Official List of the Stock Exchange, the share warrant must comply with certain requirements[6].

A share warrant issued under the company's common seal[7] entitles the bearer to the shares specified in it; and the shares may be transferred by delivery of the warrant[8]. It is a negotiable instrument[9].

1 For the meaning of 'share' see para 209 note 2 ante. The fact that in the Companies Act 1985 s 355(1)(b) each share must, so long as the share has a number, be distinguished by that number in the statement to be inserted in the register of members on the issue of a warrant is not sufficient indication of an intention that the provisions of the Companies Act 1985 relating to share warrants do not apply to stock: *Pilkington v United Railways of the Havana and Regla Warehouses Ltd* [1930] 2 Ch 108.
2 As to the alterations to be made in the register see para 384 ante. Stamp duty is chargeable on a share warrant at the rate of three times the transfer duty, calculated on the market value of the shares: see the Stamp Act 1891 s 1, Sch 1, 'Bearer Instrument' (as amended; repealed from a day to be appointed by the Finance Act 1990 ss 107, 132, Sch 19 Pt VI) and STAMP DUTIES vol 44(1) (Reissue) para 1065 et seq. As to payment of the duty see the Finance Act 1963 s 60 (repealed from a day to be appointed by the Finance Act 1990 ss 107, 132, Sch 19 Pt VI) and STAMP DUTIES vol 44(1) (Reissue) para 1068.
3 As to how far the bearer of a share warrant is to be deemed to be a member of the company see para 494 post.
4 Companies Act 1985 s 188(1) (substituted by the Companies Act 1989 s 130(7), Sch 17 para 6).
5 Companies Act 1985 s 188(3) (substituted by the Companies Act 1989 Sch 17 para 6).
6 See the *Listing Rules* r 13.22. As to the *Listing Rules* see para 282 ante.
7 See para 487 note 1 ante.
8 Companies Act 1985 s 188(2) (substituted by the Companies Act 1989 Sch 17 para 6; amended by the Law Reform (Miscellaneous Provisions) (Scotland) Act 1990 s 74(1), (2), Sch 8 para 33(5), Sch 9; the Requirements of Writing (Scotland) Act 1995 s 14(1), Sch 4 para 56). The former criminal liability for impersonating the owner of a share warrant under the Companies Act 1948 s 84 (repealed) has been replaced by the more general provisions of the Theft Act 1968 ss 1–6: see CRIMINAL LAW vol 11(1) (Reissue) para 541 et seq.
9 *Webb, Hale & Co v Alexandria Water Co* (1905) 93 LT 339; cf *Stern v R* [1896] 1 QB 211; and see BILLS OF EXCHANGE vol 4(1) (Reissue) para 516.

494. Bearer of share warrant as member. If the articles of association so provide, the bearer of a share warrant may be deemed a member of the company within the meaning of the Companies Act 1985, either to the full extent or for any purposes defined in the articles[1]. For the purpose of any provision of the articles requiring a director or manager to hold any specified share qualification, the bearer of a share warrant is not deemed to be the holder of the shares specified in the warrant[2].

1   See the Companies Act 1985 s 355(5) and para 384 ante.
2   See ibid s 291(2) and para 556 post. Where the articles required directors to hold share warrants as a qualification, the validity of the provision was apparently not questioned: see *Pearson's Case* (1877) 5 ChD 336, CA.

495. Renounceable letters of allotment and other inland bearer instruments. Transfer may be effected by renouncing a renounceable letter of allotment in favour of, or delivering some other form of inland bearer instrument[1] to, the purchaser. All such documents as fall within the heading of 'inland bearer instrument' in the Stamp Act 1891[2] are liable to stamp duty accordingly[3]. However, a letter of allotment, letter of rights, or other similar instrument where the rights under the letter or instrument are renounceable not later than six months after the issue of the letter or instrument are exempt from such duty[4]; but, if the transfer is a transfer for consideration in money's worth, stamp duty reserve tax will be payable[5].

1   For these purposes, 'inland bearer instrument' means any of the following instruments issued by or on behalf of any company or body of persons corporate or unincorporate established in the United Kingdom: (1) any marketable security transferable by delivery; (2) any share warrant or stock certificate to bearer and any instrument to bearer (by whatever name called) having the like effect as such a warrant or certificate; (3) any deposit certificate to bearer; (4) any other instrument to bearer by means of which any stock can be transferred: Finance Act 1963 s 59(2)(a) (repealed from a day to be appointed by the Finance Act 1990 s 132, Sch 19 Pt VI).
2   Ie the Stamp Act 1891 s 1, Sch 1, 'Bearer Instrument' para (1) (amended by the Finance Act 1963 s 59(1); repealed from a day to be appointed by the Finance Act 1990 s 107, Sch 19 Pt VI): see STAMP DUTIES vol 44(1) (Reissue) para 1066.
3   See STAMP DUTIES vol 44(1) (Reissue) para 1066.
4   Stamp Act 1891 Sch 1, 'Bearer Instrument' exemption 3 (added by the Finance Act 1963 s 59(1), (4); repealed from a day to be appointed by the Finance Act 1990 Sch 19 Pt VI).
5   See para 514 post.

496. Methods of transfer of shares. Shares specified in a share warrant are transferable by the delivery of the warrant[1]. Other shares, and any other interests of a member in a company, are transferable in the manner provided by its articles of association[2], or by means of a stock transfer[3]. Where title to a unit of a security is evidenced otherwise than by a certificate by virtue of the Uncertificated Securities Regulations 1995, the transfer of title to such a unit of a security is subject to those Regulations[4]. An instrument of transfer must be executed[5]; but otherwise there are no restrictions on transfer except such as are imposed by the articles[6]. As a general rule, a director is just as free to deal with his shares as any other person, although he may, by parting with his qualification shares, cease to hold office as a director[7]. The mere fact that a transfer of shares is made in order to increase the voting power of the transferor, or in his interest, is no ground of objection to the transfer[8], nor is the fact that the transfer is made to avoid a prospective call[9]. If a transfer is real, in the sense that it was intended to effect an out-and-out assignment, and there is no covert agreement or understanding to the contrary, it is immaterial that the transferee is insolvent and unable to pay any future calls[10], but a colourable transfer, as to a clerk or other nominee of the transferor, will not discharge the transferor from liability[11], nor will a transfer in a case where some benefit is reserved to the transferor[12]. No transfer of shares made in contravention of the articles of the company may be registered and the board of directors is bound to refuse registration accordingly[13].

Where the directors have by the articles the right to refuse to register transfers, even an out-and-out transfer is of no avail if registration of it was obtained by misrepresentation as to the transferee's position or the consideration paid[14]. Whether a particular transfer is out-and-out is a question of fact, and the equities between the parties may be regarded to determine this question[15].

1 See para 493 ante.
2 Companies Act 1985 s 182(1)(b). A company registered under the Joint Stock Companies Acts (see para 11 ante) may cause its shares to be transferred in the manner in use or as the company may direct: see the Companies Act 1985 s 678(1) and para 12 ante. For restrictions on the transfer of securities by or on behalf of enemies, or to enemy subjects, see the Trading with the Enemy Act 1939 s 5 and WAR vol 49 para 148 et seq. In order that a company may obtain an official listing on the Stock Exchange, its articles must provide that it will register transfers without payment of any fee: see the *Listing Rules* Ch 13 App 1 para 5.
3 See para 506 post.
4 See the Uncertificated Securities Regulations 1995, SI 1995/3272, reg 2(2) and MONEY. The Secretary of State may make provision by regulations for enabling title to securities to be evidenced and transferred without a written instrument: Companies Act 1989 s 207(1). In exercise of the power so conferred the Secretary of State made the Uncertificated Securities Regulations 1995 which came into force on 19 December 1995 (see reg 1) and enable title to units of a security to be evidenced otherwise than by a certificate and transferred otherwise than by a written instrument in accordance with a computer-based system and procedures known as the 'relevant system' (see reg 2). See further MONEY.
5 Companies Act 1985 s 183(1) (amended by the Uncertificated Securities Regulations 1995 reg 40(2)(a)). See *Greene, Greene v Greene* [1949] Ch 333, [1949] 1 All ER 167 (articles providing for automatic transfer on death invalid) and para 142 ante. For the meaning of 'proper instrument of transfer' see para 505 text and note 3 post.
6 *Weston's Case* (1868) 4 Ch App 20 at 27; *Bargate v Shortridge* (1855) 5 HL Cas 297; *Re Stockton Malleable Iron Co* (1875) 2 ChD 101; *Gilbert's Case* (1870) 5 Ch App 559 at 565. A transfer of shares does not include the case of the renunciation in favour of a nominee of shares to which the person renouncing is entitled: *Re Pool Shipping Co Ltd* [1920] 1 Ch 251. For the meaning of a transfer 'in the usual form' see *Re Letheby and Christopher Ltd* [1904] 1 Ch 815. As to the power of the Secretary of State to impose restrictions on transfer in certain cases see para 1383 post.
7 *Gilbert's Case* (1870) 5 Ch App 559; *Re Cawley & Co* (1889) 42 ChD 209, CA; cf *Re South London Fish Market Co* (1888) 39 ChD 324, CA.
8 *Re Stranton Iron and Steel Co* (1873) LR 16 Eq 559; *Cannon v Trask* (1875) LR 20 Eq 669; *Pender v Lushington* (1877) 6 ChD 70; *Moffatt v Farquhar* (1878) 7 ChD 591.
9 *Re Cawley & Co* (1889) 42 ChD 209, CA; *Re Hafod Lead Mining Co, Slater's Case* (1866) 35 Beav 391. If the making of the call has been postponed on the faith of a representation that no transfer will be made, registration of the transfer may be refused: *Re National and Provincial Marine Insurance Co, ex p Parker* (1867) 2 Ch App 685; and see *Gilbert's Case* (1870) 5 Ch App 559.
10 *R v Lambourn Valley Rly Co* (1888) 22 QBD 463 at 465; *Re Hafod Lead Mining Co, Slater's Case* (1866) 35 Beav 391; *Masters' Case* (1872) 7 Ch App 292; *Re Mexican and South American Co, De Pass Case* (1859) 4 De G & J 544; *M'Lintock v Campbell* 1916 SC 966.
11 *Re Mexican and South American Co, Hyam's Case* (1859) 1 De GF & J 75; *Re Mexican and South American Co, Costello's Case* (1860) 2 De GF & J 302; cf *Re National and Provincial Marine Insurance Co, ex p Parker* (1867) 2 Ch App 685; *Re Bank of Hindustan, China and Japan, ex p Kintrea* (1869) 5 Ch App 95; *Re Imperial Mercantile Credit Association, Wilkinson's Case* [1869] WN 211.
12 *Re Athenaeum Life Assurance Society, Chinnocks's Case* (1860) John 714; cf *Re Esgair Mwyn Mining Co, Alexander's Case* (1861) 3 LT 883.
13 *Tett v Phoenix Property and Investment Co Ltd* [1986] BCLC 149, CA.
14 *Payne's Case* (1869) LR 9 Eq 223; *Williams' Case* (1869) LR 9 Eq 225n; *Re Imperial Mercantile Credit Association, Wilkinson's Case* [1869] WN 211; *Re Bank of Hindustan, China and Japan, Snow's Case* (1871) 25 LT 406.

15 *Re Electric Telegraph Co of Ireland, Budd's Case* (1861) 3 De GF & J 297, as explained in *Re Discoverers Finance Corpn Ltd, Lindlar's Case* [1910] 1 Ch 312 at 321, CA, overruling *Re Discoverers Finance Corpn Ltd* [1908] 1 Ch 141 (which was compromised on appeal [1908] 1 Ch 334, CA). As to registration of transfers in relation to liability in winding up see paras 2489–2491 post.

497. Restrictions on transfer. A participating issuer must register a transfer of title to uncertificated units of a security on a register of securities in accordance with an Operator-instruction unless:

(1) the transfer is prohibited by order of a court in the United Kingdom or by or under an enactment; or

(2) he has actual notice that the transfer is:

    (a) avoided by or under an enactment;

    (b) a transfer to a deceased person; or

    (c) where the participating issuer is constituted under the law of Scotland, prohibited by or under an arrestment; or

    (d) the prescribed circumstances[1] apply; or

    (e) he is entitled[2] to refuse to register the transfer[3].

A participating issuer may refuse to register a transfer of title to uncertificated units of a security in accordance with an Operator-instruction if the instruction requires a transfer of units:

    (i) to an entity which is not a natural or legal person;

    (ii) to a minor (which in relation to a participating issuer constituted under the law of Scotland means a person under 16 years of age);

    (iii) to be held jointly in the names of more persons than is permitted under the terms of the issue of the security; or

    (iv) where, in relation to the Operator-instruction, the participating issuer has actual notice from the Operator of any of the specified[4] matters[5].

A participating issuer must notify the Operator by issuer-instruction whether he has registered a transfer in response to an Operator-instruction to do so[6].

A participating issuer must not register a transfer of title to uncertificated units of a security on a register of securities unless he is required to do so by an Operator-instruction, an order of a court in the United Kingdom, by the relevant provision relating to minority shareholders[7], or by or under an enactment[8]; but this provision is not to be taken to prevent a participating issuer from entering a person on a register of securities to whom title to uncertificated units of a security has been transmitted by operation of law[9].

Any purported registration of a transfer of title to an uncertificated unit of a security other than in accordance with these provisions is of no effect[10].

The articles of many companies contain some restrictions on the right of transfer[11]. A restriction on the right to transfer shares is not repugnant to the absolute ownership of the shares, but is one of the original incidents of the shares attached to them by the contract contained in the articles[12]. Any condition precedent to transfer, such as obtaining the consent of the directors, must be observed[13], although the consent may be inferred from entries in the company's books[14], or from a constant disregard of the prescribed mode[15]. The rule against perpetuities has no application in such cases[16]. There is apparently no limit to the restriction on transfer which may be so imposed[17], although restrictive provisions are strictly construed[18] because shares, being personal property, are prima facie transferable[19]. Nevertheless if the intent and existence of the restrictions are sufficiently certain, they will not be rejected as being unworkable if a term can be implied which will give them business efficacy[20]. Articles restricting the transfer of a share are construed as restricting only a transfer of the legal title, and not as preventing the transfer of a beneficial interest therein[21]. Accordingly, a transfer for full consideration made in defiance of binding restrictive provisions will suffice to pass the equitable as distinct from the legal interest in the shares[22], although the transferor is entitled to annul the transaction if registration cannot be effected within a reasonable time[23].

Where the scheme and intent of the restrictions are to accord rights of pre-emption to the other members of the company, if there is no substantial compliance with the procedure laid down, the shareholder denied such rights is entitled to an appropriate injunction to protect his position[24].

Where shares have been issued to an officer of a company, and a provision, which prohibits the transfer of the shares for a period of years, has been inserted in the articles for the protection of the company, a valid transfer may be effected in spite of the prohibition, prior to the expiration of the period, if the consent of the company is obtained[25].

1 Ie the circumstances described in the Uncertificated Securities Regulations 1995, SI 1995/3272, reg 23(2). The circumstances so described are that the transfer is one of two or more transfers in respect of which the Operator has notified the participating issuer in accordance with reg 24(1), and that to those transfers reg 24(2) does not apply by virtue of reg 24(3): reg 23(2). See further MONEY.

2 Ie by virtue of ibid reg 23(3): see infra.

3 See ibid reg 23(1) and MONEY. The Companies Act 1985 s 183(5) (see para 500 post) applies in relation to a refusal by a participating issuer to register a transfer of securities in any of the circumstances specified in the Uncertificated Securities Regulations 1995 reg 23(1) as it applies in relation to a refusal by a company to register a transfer of shares or debentures; and in the Companies Act 1985 s 183(5) as it so applies the reference to the date on which the transfer was lodged with the company is to be taken to be a reference to the date on which the Operator-instruction was received by the participating issuer: Uncertificated Securities Regulations 1995 reg 23(8). Such sanctions as apply to a company and its officers in the event of a default in complying with the Companies Act 1985 s 183(5) apply to a participating issuer and his officers in the event of default in complying with s 183(5) as applied by the Uncertificated Securities Regulations 1995 reg 23(8): reg 23(9). As to the penalty for breach see regs 37, 38 and MONEY.

4 Ie any of the matters specified in ibid reg 29(5)(a)(i)–(iii): see MONEY.

5 See ibid reg 23(3) and MONEY.

6 See ibid reg 23(4) and MONEY.

7 Ie by ibid reg 35(2): see MONEY.

8 See ibid reg 23(5) and MONEY.

9 See ibid reg 23(6) and MONEY.

10 See ibid reg 23(7) and MONEY.

11 The Companies (Tables A to F) Regulations 1985, SI 1985/805, Schedule, Table A art 24 enables the directors to decline to register any transfers of shares (not being fully paid up) to a person of whom they do not approve, or any transfer of shares on which the company has a lien; and further restrictions are often contained in articles. As to Table A generally see para 529 et seq post. The discretion to refuse transfers of shares refers only to transfers and does not apply to a renunciation of a rights issue (*Re Pool Shipping Co* [1920] 1 Ch 251) or to an allotment of shares or a renunciation of an allotment (*System Control plc v Munro Corporate plc* [1990] BCLC 659 at 662, 663) or to a transmission of shares (*Re Bentham Mills Spinning Co* (1879) 11 ChD 900, CA; *Moodie v W and J Shepherd (Bookbinders) Ltd* [1949] 2 All ER 1044, HL). In some cases articles provide that no transfer shall be made without the consent of the directors; to comply with such an article it is not necessary to obtain their consent before executing the transfer; consent to the registration of the transfer is sufficient: *Re Copal Varnish Co Ltd* [1917] 2 Ch 349.

12 *Borland's Trustee v Steel Bros & Co Ltd* [1901] 1 Ch 279 at 289.

13 *Re Royal British Bank, Nicol's Case* (1859) 3 De G & J 387; *Roots v Williamson* (1888) 38 ChD 485; *Re Dublin North City Milling Co* [1909] 1 IR 179; *Hunter v Hunter* [1936] AC 222, HL; *Lyle and Scott Ltd v Scott's Trustees* [1959] AC 763, [1959] 2 All ER 661, HL ('desire to sell' covered situation where registration of transfer was to be delayed). The secretary has no authority to pass transfers: *Chida Mines Ltd v Anderson* (1905) 22 TLR 27. Consent of directors in an article means consent to the registration of transfer not consent to the execution of the transfer: see note 11 supra.

14 *Re Royal British Bank, ex p Walton, ex p Hue* (1857) 26 LJ Ch 545; *Re Branksea Island Co, ex p Bentinck (No 2)* (1888) 1 Meg 23, CA.
15 *Re Vale of Neath and South Wales Brewery Co, Walter's Case* (1850) 3 De G & Sm 149; affd 19 LJ Ch 501.
16 *Witham v Vane* (1883) Challis' Real Property (3rd Edn) App V, 440, HL; *Walsh v Secretary of State for India* (1863) 10 HL Cas 367; *Borland's Trustee v Steel Bros & Co Ltd* [1901] 1 Ch 279; *A-G for Ireland v Jameson* [1905] 2 IR 218.
17 See *Heron International Ltd v Grade and Associated Communications Corpn plc* [1983] BCLC 244, CA (where in order to transfer shares on sale a transfer notice had to be submitted which constituted the company the transferor's agent for sale at a price fixed in accordance with a formula; a contract by the directors controlling the company to transfer their shares at a different price, known by the proposing transferee to be in breach of the articles, was held unenforceable).
18 See *Re Bentham Mills Spinning Co* (1879) 11 ChD 900, CA (cited in para 502 note 2 post); *Delavenne v Broadhurst* [1931] 1 Ch 234; *Greenhalgh v Mallard* [1943] 2 All ER 234, CA (where the court refused to imply a prohibition on transfers to existing members of the company which was not expressed in terms); *Dean v Prince* [1954] Ch 409, [1954] 1 All ER 749, CA (transfer at price to be certified by auditors; certificate upheld on investigation). Cf *Re Cannock and Rugeley Colliery Co, ex p Harrison* (1885) 28 ChD 363, CA; and see *Chappell's Case* (1871) 6 Ch App 902; *Re Hobson, Houghton & Co Ltd* [1929] 1 Ch 300. As to the effect of informality on transfer see *Smellie's Trustees v Smellie* (1952) 103 LJo 139.
19 *Greenhalgh v Mallard* [1943] 2 All ER 234 at 237, CA per Lord Greene MR; *Re Smith and Fawcett Ltd* [1942] Ch 304 at 306, [1942] 1 All ER 542 at 543, CA.
20 *Tett v Phoenix Property and Investment Co Ltd* [1986] BCLC 149, CA (provision as to giving reasonable notice to persons entitled to take the benefit of the restrictive provisions implied; notice to be given to non-members, so entitled, being family of members, sufficiently satisfied if notice given to member himself).
21 See *Safeguard Industrial Investments Ltd v National Westminster Bank Ltd* [1982] 1 All ER 449, [1982] 1 WLR 589, CA; *Theakston v London Trust plc* [1984] BCLC 390.
22 *Hawks v McArthur* [1951] 1 All ER 22, distinguishing *Hunter v Hunter* [1936] AC 222, HL (mortgagee not authorised to sell beneficial apart from legal interest); and see *Re Hafner, Olhausen v Powderley* [1943] IR 264.
23 *Lyle and Scott Ltd v Scott's Trustees* [1959] AC 763, [1959] 2 All ER 661, HL.
24 *Curtis v J J Curtis & Co Ltd* [1984] 2 NZLR 267, NZ CA.
25 *London and Westminster Supply Association Ltd v Griffiths* (1883) Cab & El 15.

498. Exercise of power to refuse registration. The power of refusing to register a transfer may be conferred on the directors, and in such a case must be exercised by a resolution of the board of directors[1]. This power must be exercised, if no precise period is laid down by the articles, within a reasonable time[2], a reasonable time for these purposes being generally accepted to be within two months of the transfer being lodged with the company[3]. Thereafter the directors will no longer be able to exercise their discretion[4] and an application can be made to have the register rectified by the inclusion of the name of the transferee[5].

The power to refuse to register a transfer is a discretionary power and must be exercised reasonably and in good faith for the company's benefit, and not arbitrarily[6], although, in the absence of evidence to the contrary, the power will be presumed to have been properly exercised[7]. Where there are several grounds on which the power may be exercised, the directors are bound to state on which ground they act, unless excused from so doing by the articles[8] although they need not in any case give the reasons which influenced them in exercising their discretion on that ground[9], whether they do so under an absolute power[10] or under a power to refuse in specified events[11]. Where shares may be freely transferred to other members, registration of a transfer to another member may not be refused because that member has entered into equitable obligations with a non-member affecting such shares[12].

Where the directors' consent is required to a transfer, they must exercise their powers as trustees for the company and a consent given corruptly for their own benefit may be treated as a nullity[13]. Where their consent is necessary, they may refuse to consent to a transfer where the price payable is merely nominal, and the company is insolvent[14], but they may approve of an out-and-out transfer for a nominal consideration to the transferor's clerk if the transferor agrees to guarantee the payment of a call about to be made[15]. It is their duty to refuse to register a transfer giving a misleadingly false description of the transferee and falsely stating the consideration[16].

If the directors give their reasons, the court will examine them, but it will not overrule the decision of the directors because it disagrees with the conclusion they reached as to the advisability of refusing the transfer[17]. It will, however, do so if the directors have acted on a wrong principle[18].

The articles may provide for the suspension of the registration of transfers generally[19].

1 *Re Hackney Pavilion Ltd* [1924] 1 Ch 276. See also *Moodie v W and J Shepherd (Bookbinders) Ltd* [1949] 2 All ER 1044, 1950 SC (HL) 60, HL (right of refusal not exercised by failure to pass resolution approving transfer). See *Re Swaledale Cleaners Ltd* [1968] 3 All ER 619, [1968] 1 WLR 1710, CA (power lost by delay) and *Re New Cedos Engineering Co Ltd* (1976) [1994] 1 BCLC 797 (no properly appointed directors; power not exercisable).

2 *Re Swaledale Cleaners Ltd* [1968] 3 All ER 619, [1968] 1 WLR 1710, CA; and see *Re Zinotty Properties Ltd* [1984] 3 All ER 754, [1984] 1 WLR 1249.

3 This period is effectively dictated by the Companies Act 1985 s 183(5) (see para 500 post) which requires that notice of rejection be given within two months.

4 This is not required by ibid s 183(5) (see para 500 post) which simply imposes a fine for default (see s 183(6) and para 500 post); but it was accepted in *Re Swaledale Cleaners Ltd* [1968] 3 All ER 619, [1968] 1 WLR 1710, CA that this can be the only consequence of requiring the power to be exercised within a reasonable time.

5 Ie under the Companies Act 1985 s 359: see para 392 et seq ante.

6 *Re Coalport China Co* [1895] 2 Ch 404, CA; and see *Poole v Middleton* (1861) 29 Beav 646 at 651; *Slee v International Bank* (1868) 17 LT 425; *Shepherd's Case* (1866) 2 Ch App 16; *Re Yuruari* (1889) 6 TLR 119, CA; *Re South Yorkshire Wine, Spirit and Mineral Water Co* (1892) 8 TLR 413; *Re Hannan's King (Browning) Gold Mining Co Ltd* (1898) 14 TLR 314, CA; *Re Faure Electric Accumulator Co* (1888) 40 ChD 141; *Re Gresham Life Assurance Society, ex p Penney* (1872) 8 Ch App 446; *Re Bede Steam Shipping Co Ltd* [1917] 1 Ch 123, CA; *Kennedy v North British Wireless Schools Ltd* (1916) 53 SLR 543.

7 *Berry v Tottenham Hotspur Football and Athletic Co Ltd* [1936] 3 All ER 554 (where evidence as to systematic rejections of transfers of shares was held to be inadmissible); *Re Smith and Fawcett Ltd* [1942] Ch 304, [1942] 1 All ER 542. See, however, *Re Hafner, Olhausen v Powderley* [1943] IR 264 (evidence of improper motive in refusal; court entitled to draw an inference from the omission to state grounds of refusal, and to hold, in the absence of an explanation, that the refusal was not the result of a bona fide exercise of discretion); *Charles Forte Investments Ltd v Amanda* [1964] Ch 240, [1963] 2 All ER 940, CA (refusal to register does not normally give rise to a right to present a winding-up petition; other remedies are available if refusal wrongful). See also *Morgan v Morgan Insurance Brokers Ltd* [1993] BCLC 676 (where exceptionally directors were personally liable for the costs of an application to have the register of members rectified; rectification was sought by a shareholder owning three-quarters of the shares following a bona fide but improper refusal by the directors to register a transfer).

8 *Berry and Stewart v Tottenham Hotspur Football and Athletic Co Ltd* [1935] Ch 718.

9 *Duke of Sutherland v British Dominions Land Settlement Corpn* [1926] Ch 746; *Berry v Tottenham Hotspur Football and Athletic Co Ltd* [1936] 3 All ER 554.

10 *Re Gresham Life Assurance Society, ex p Penney* (1872) 8 Ch App 446.

11 *Re Coalport China Co* [1895] 2 Ch 404, CA.

12 *Theakston v London Trust plc* [1984] BCLC 390.

13 *Bennett's Case* (1854) 5 De GM & G 284; *Re Mitre Assurance Co, Eyre's Case* (1862) 31 Beav 177.

14 *Taft v Harrison* (1853) 10 Hare 489.

15 *Harrison's Case* (1871) 6 Ch App 286 at 292. A transfer is not invalidated by the fact that the directors would have refused to register it if they had known all the facts, unless they have been deliberately misled by the transferor: *Re Discoverers Finance Corpn Ltd* [1910] 1 Ch 312, CA.

16 *Payne's Case* (1869) LR 9 Eq 223; *William's Case* (1869) 9 LR Eq 225n. As to false description see further *Masters' Case* (1872) 7 Ch App 292; *Re Financial Insurance Co, Bishop's Case* (1869) 7 Ch App 296n; *Re Smith, Knight & Co, Battie's Case* (1870) 39 LJ Ch 391. See also the Companies Act 1985 s 352(2)

(occupation of the members of the company need not be stated on the register) and para 379 ante. As to approving the transfer of a director's shares see *Re Agriculturist Cattle Insurance Co, Bush's Case* (1870) 6 Ch App 246 (affd sub nom *Murray v Bush* (1873) LR 6 HL 37); *Re London and County Assurance Co, Jessopp's Case* (1858) 2 De G & J 638; *Re Kilbricken Mines Co, Libri's Case* (1857) 30 LTOS 185; *Re Cawley & Co* (1889) 42 ChD 209, CA; *Re South London Fish Market Co* (1888) 39 ChD 324, CA.

17   *Re Bell Bros Ltd, ex p Hodgson* (1891) 65 LT 245; *Re Bede Steam Shipping Co Ltd* [1917] 1 Ch 123, CA.

18   *Re Bede Steam Shipping Co Ltd* [1917] 1 Ch 123, CA; *Robinson v Chartered Bank of India* (1865) LR 1 Eq 32, explained in *Re Gresham Life Assurance Society, ex p Penney* (1872) 8 Ch App 446; *Moffatt v Farquhar* (1878) 7 ChD 591; *Re Stranton Iron and Steel Co* (1873) LR 16 Eq 559; *Tett v Phoenix Property and Investment Co Ltd* [1984] BCLC 599 (where in cross-examination the directors without objection disclosed their reasons); revsd on appeal [1986] BCLC 149, CA.

19   See the Companies (Tables A to F) Regulations 1985, SI 1985/805, Schedule, Table A art 26 which provides that the registration of transfers of shares or transfers of any class of shares may be suspended at such times and for such periods, not exceeding 30 days in any year, as the directors may determine. As to Table A generally see para 529 et seq post.

499. Provisions for compulsory transfer. Provisions made in good faith for the compulsory sale and transfer of shares at a fixed price, on the happening of a certain event, such as bankruptcy, are valid[1]. It is common for articles to grant pre-emption rights to existing members so that a member wishing to transfer may find himself obliged to offer his shares first to the existing members and at a price to be fixed by the company's auditors, although in appropriate circumstances a member may be able to prevent the company from exercising such powers by relying on statutory provisions protecting shareholders against inequitable or unfairly prejudicial conduct[2].

The articles often provide that such a pre-emption provision is triggered by a member 'wishing' or 'desiring' or 'intending' to transfer his shares and much will depend on whether, on a proper construction of the articles, and in the light of the conduct of the member, such an intention has been evidenced. A shareholder who has made a contract to sell his shares and has been paid the purchase price and is ready but not asked to execute an instrument of transfer, cannot say that he does not propose to, or is not desirous of, or does not wish to, sell his shares[3]. The mere fact that a shareholder is under a duty to transfer or sell when called upon to do so does not, however, mean that he desires or proposes to transfer[4]. A conditional agreement to sell shares subject to several events occurring (which were not within the control of either party to the agreement) did not constitute a present and unequivocal desire to transfer or dispose of the shares[5].

When the company has power to fix the purchase price not below a minimum stated in the articles, if it fixes the price at the minimum, which is in fact far less than the actual value of the shares, its action is not of itself fraudulent or oppressive[6]. When the value of the shares is to be ascertained by reference to the proportion of the value of the assets appearing in the books of the company to which the holders of the shares would be entitled in a winding up, deduction for depreciation of the assets is allowed[7].

Where the value of the shares is to be certified by the auditors, their bare certificate cannot be questioned in the absence of fraud[8], although an action will lie against them for making their valuation negligently[9]; but, if they disclose the basis of their valuation, or this figure is impossibly high or low, the court may inquire into its correctness, even though the certificate is expressed by the articles to be final[10].

Such provisions may constitute a contract of which the transferring shareholder is entitled to the benefit, so as to force the directors to purchase his shares where the articles designate the directors as the purchasers of shares of which the holder wishes to dispose[11].

1 *Borland's Trustee v Steel Bros & Co Ltd* [1901] 1 Ch 279. As to the alteration of articles by including provisions for the compulsory sale and transfer of shares see *Brown v British Abrasive Wheel Co* [1919] 1 Ch 290; *Sidebottom v Kershaw, Leese & Co Ltd* [1920] 1 Ch 154, CA; *Dafen Tinplate Co v Llanelly Steel Co (1907) Ltd* [1920] 2 Ch 124; and see *Greenhalgh v Arderne Cinemas Ltd* [1951] Ch 286, [1950] 2 All ER 1120, CA. As to the alteration of articles generally see paras 538–540 post.

2 See *Re Abbey Leisure Ltd, Virdi v Abbey Leisure Ltd* [1990] BCLC 342, CA (member entitled to seek winding up on the just and equitable ground under the Insolvency Act 1986 s 122(1)(g) (see para 2208 post) rather than submit to transfer and valuation procedures under the articles); *Re a company (No 00330 of 1991), ex p Holden* [1991] BCLC 597 (member entitled to relief under the Companies Act 1985 s 459 (as amended) (see para 1405 post) rather than submit to transfer and valuation procedures under the articles).

3 *Theakston v London Trust plc* [1984] BCLC 390 at 401; *Lyle and Scott Ltd v Scott's Trustees* [1959] AC 763, [1959] 2 All ER 661, HL. See also *Re Macro (Ipswich) Ltd, Re Earliba Finance Co Ltd, Macro v Thompson* [1994] 2 BCLC 354 at 401, 402.

4 *Safeguard Industrial Investments Ltd v National Westminster Bank Ltd* [1982] 1 All ER 449, [1982] 1 WLR 589; *Theakston v London Trust plc* [1984] BCLC 390.

5 *Re a company (No 005685 of 1988), ex p Schwarcz (No 2)* [1989] BCLC 427.

6 *Phillips v Manufacturers' Securities Ltd* (1917) 86 LJ Ch 305; reported on interlocutory application (1915) 31 TLR 451. This is now subject to the text to note 2 supra.

7 *Jacobsen v Jamaica Times Ltd* (1921) 90 LJPC 100. Where shares are required by the articles to be first offered for sale to the other shareholders, the offer must be accepted or rejected as a whole: *Ocean Coal Co Ltd v Powell Duffryn Steam Coal Co Ltd* [1932] 1 Ch 654.

8 See *Dean v Prince* [1954] Ch 409, [1954] 1 All ER 749, CA; and *Baber v Kenwood Manufacturing Co Ltd* [1978] 1 Lloyd's Rep 175, CA.

9 *Arenson v Casson Beckman, Rutley & Co* [1977] AC 405, [1975] 3 All ER 901, HL, applying *Sutcliffe v Thackrah* [1974] AC 727, [1974] 1 All ER 859, HL (negligent issue of interim certificate by architect).

10 *Dean v Prince* [1954] Ch 409, [1954] 1 All ER 749, CA; *Burgess v Purchase & Sons (Farms) Ltd* [1983] Ch 216, [1983] 2 All ER 4 (mistake by auditors in valuation of company's shares made honestly and in good faith, but speaking valuation on fundamentally wrong basis impeachable). As to valuation see *Re Howie and Crawford's arbitration* [1990] BCLC 686 (where an asset was a holding of shares in a private company, the market price of that asset would normally depend on the proportion of the shares of the company comprised in the holding and on any special rights or restrictions contained in the articles of association of the company as well as on the value of the net assets of the company and its profit and dividend record). The addition of the word 'fair' (as in 'fair market value') added nothing except to remind the valuer that the market price was to be ascertained on the assumption that no one was excluded from the bidding and to exclude the exceptional or freak price which might otherwise have had to be taken into account if an agreement as to valuation referred to the 'open market price': *Re Howie and Crawford's arbitration* supra.

11 *Rayfield v Hands* [1960] Ch 1, [1958] 2 All ER 194.

500. Notice of refusal to register. If a company refuses to register a transfer of any shares, it must send to the transferee notice of the refusal within two months after the date on which the transfer was lodged with the company[1]. If default is made in complying with the above provisions, the company, and every officer of the company who is in default, is liable on summary conviction to a fine not exceeding one-fifth of the statutory maximum and, on conviction after continued contravention, to a daily default fine not exceeding one-fiftieth of the statutory maximum[2].

1 Companies Act 1985 s 183(5); and see para 498 text to note 3 ante. See also the Companies (Tables A to F) Regulations 1985, SI 1985/805, Schedule, Table A arts 25, 28. As to Table A generally see para 529 et seq post. Before the Companies Act 1929 (repealed) a company was not bound to send notice to a transferee of its refusal to register a transfer: see *Gustard's Case* (1869) LR 8 Eq 438. Under the former law directors were entitled to a reasonable time in which to consider whether registration should be refused: see the cases cited in para 510 note 6 post.

2 Companies Act 1985 ss 183(6), 730, Sch 24. For the meaning of 'officer who is in default', 'the statutory maximum' and 'daily default fine' see para 1161 post.

501. Transfer where individual shareholding limited. Where a limited number of shares only may be held by a shareholder, a transfer to a person already holding the prescribed number by a transferor with notice of the fact is invalid. If the transferor is a director, he is deemed to have notice, and will remain a contributory[1].

1 *Re Newcastle-upon-Tyne Marine Insurance Co, ex p Brown* (1854) 19 Beav 97.

502. Transfer by a member indebted to the company. In the absence of express power to do so, directors cannot decline to register transfers of shares because calls on them are in arrear; but, if empowered to decline to register a transfer by a member who is indebted to the company, they may refuse to register a transfer made by a shareholder who is indebted to the company on any account whatever[1], and whether solely or jointly with others[2]. If directors with such a power register transfers, the transfers are valid, although the directors may be liable to make good any loss thereby caused to the company[3]. The power to decline to register for indebtedness is exercisable although the company holds unmatured bills of the shareholder in respect of the debt[4]. If a company delays registration of a transfer because of indebtedness where there is no indebtedness, nominal damages are recoverable by the transferor[5].

Where articles give a discretion to refuse registration of a transfer by a shareholder who is indebted to the company, the time for ascertaining whether he is so indebted is when the transfer is sent to the proper officer for registration, and not when it afterwards comes before a board meeting for registration[6].

1 *Ex p Stringer* (1882) 9 QBD 436.
2 *Re Bentham Mills Spinning Co* (1879) 11 ChD 900, CA. The term 'indebted' as used in the articles of a company was held in *Re Stockton Malleable Iron Co* (1875) 2 ChD 101 to mean owing a debt due and payable. Where an article provided that the company might refuse to register a transfer by a member who was indebted, and another article provided for the registration of persons becoming entitled to a share in consequence of bankruptcy, it was held that the company was not justified in refusing to register a member's trustee in bankruptcy: see *Re Bentham Mills Spinning Co* supra; *Re W Key & Son Ltd* [1902] 1 Ch 467 (trustee in bankruptcy entitled to a 'clean' registration). Cf *Re Cannock and Rugeley Colliery Co, ex p Harrison* (1885) 28 ChD 363, CA (trustee in bankruptcy not 'entitled' to the share by reason of a prior charge); but see the Companies (Tables A to F) Regulations 1985, SI 1985/805, Schedule, Table A arts 24, 30. Article 30 gives a person becoming entitled to a share in consequence of death or bankruptcy the right to be registered or to transfer the share. If he transfers the share, the articles relating to transfers will apply as if the transfer had been executed by the member and the death or bankruptcy had not occurred. As to the transmission of shares see para 518 post; and as to Table A generally see para 529 et seq post.
3 *Re Hoylake Rly Co, ex p Littledale* (1874) 9 Ch App 257; cf *Anderson's Case* (1869) LR 8 Eq 509 (where the registration of transfers, registered in ignorance that calls were in arrear, was cancelled).
4 *Re London, Birmingham and South Staffordshire Banking Co Ltd* (1865) 34 Beav 332; *Bank of Africa v Salisbury Gold Mining Co* [1892] AC 281, PC; cf *Holden's Case* (1869) LR 8 Eq 444.
5 *Skinner v City of London Marine Insurance Corpn* (1885) 14 QBD 882, CA.
6 *Re Cawley & Co* (1889) 42 ChD 209, CA; *R v Inns of Court Hotel Co, ex p Rudolf* (1863) 11 WR 806.

503. Transfer when company insolvent. Where the company has stopped payment or ceased to be a going concern, although no winding up has commenced, the directors may refuse registration of transfers executed for the purpose of avoiding liability[1]. The mere fact that the company is in difficulties is not, however, a ground for refusing registration[2].

1 *Nelson Mitchell v City of Glasgow Bank* (1879) 4 App Cas 624, HL: *Mitchell's Case* (1879) 4 App Cas 547 at 567, HL; cf *Chappell's Case* (1871) 6 Ch App 902; *Lankester's Case* (1870) 6 Ch App 905n; *Allin's Case* (1873) LR 16 Eq 449; *Dodds v Cosmopolitan Insurance Corpn Ltd* 1915 SC 992. As to transfers made after, or not registered before, a winding up see para 2461 post.

2 *Re Mexican and South American Co, De Pass's Case* (1859) 4 De G & J 544; *Re Smith, Knight & Co, Battie's Case* (1870) 39 LJ Ch 391; *Nation's Case* (1866) LR 3 Eq 77; *Re Taurine Co* (1883) 25 ChD 118, CA; cf *Re Mexican and South American Co, Hyam's Case* (1859) 1 De GF & J 75.

504. Persons who may transfer shares. The proper person to transfer shares is the registered holder or his attorney[1], or such other person as is by the articles or by statute empowered to transfer.

Although the legal representatives of a deceased member of the company do not become members unless themselves registered[2], a transfer of the share or other interest of a deceased member by his personal representative is as valid as if he were a member at the time of the execution of the transfer[3].

Shares or stock registered in the name of a person who, by reason of mental disorder, is incapable of managing his affairs may only be transferred under an order of the authority having jurisdiction under the Mental Health Act 1983[4]. Where he is a trustee, a vesting order of shares may be made by the court[5], and in certain cases where the authority has appointed a receiver, by the authority unless the trust is subject to an administrative order[6]. In such cases the jurisdiction of the court[7] is concurrent with that of the authority[8]. A transfer of shares by or to a minor is voidable during his minority or within a reasonable time after his attaining full age[9].

Shares held by a married woman as registered holder, or one of several registered joint holders, may be transferred without the concurrence of her husband[10].

Any shares or stock belonging to a bankrupt will vest automatically in his trustee in bankruptcy and may be transferred by him accordingly[11].

1 See *Chatenay v Brazilian Submarine Telegraph Co* (1890) 6 TLR 408; affd [1891] 1 QB 79, CA. A vesting declaration does not extend to shares or stock only transferable in the books of a company: see the Trustee Act 1925 s 40(4)(c) and TRUSTS vol 48 (Reissue) para 752. As to powers of attorney see AGENCY vol 1(2) (Reissue) para 32 et seq.
2 See para 429 ante.
3 Companies Act 1985 s 183(3); and see *Simpson v Molson's Bank* [1895] AC 270 at 279, PC. As to the transmission of shares see para 518 post.
4 Ie the Mental Health Act 1983 Pt VII (ss 93–113) (as amended): see MENTAL HEALTH vol 30 (Reissue) para 1432 et seq.
5 See the Trustee Act 1925 s 51 and TRUSTS vol 48 (Reissue) para 769 et seq.
6 See ibid s 54 (as substituted and amended) and MENTAL HEALTH vol 30 (Reissue) para 1480.
7 The court is the High Court or the county court where those courts respectively have jurisdiction: see the Trustee Act 1925 s 67(1) (as amended) and TRUSTS vol 48 (Reissue) para 531 note 3.
8 See ibid s 54 (as substituted and amended); MENTAL HEALTH vol 30 (Reissue) para 1480; and TRUSTS vol 48 (Reissue) para 736.
9 See para 374 ante. As to the attainment of majority at the age of 18 see the Family Law Reform Act 1969 s 1 and CHILDREN vol 5(2) (Reissue) para 601.
10 Law Reform (Married Women and Tortfeasors) Act 1935 s 1(a); and see *Re London, Bombay and Mediterranean Bank* (1881) 18 ChD 581; HUSBAND AND WIFE vol 22 para 1014.
11 See the Insolvency Act 1986 ss 306(1), 311(3) and BANKRUPTCY vol 3(2) (Reissue) paras 381, 386, 411. As to the voting rights of the bankrupt before transfer see para 670 post.

505. Form and execution of transfer. The instrument of transfer must either be in accordance with the articles of association and be executed in the manner thereby prescribed[1] or it must be a stock transfer, or in a common or usual form complying with the requirements as to execution and content which apply to a stock transfer[2]. Notwithstanding anything in the articles of a company, it is not lawful for a company to register a transfer of shares unless a proper instrument of transfer[3] has been delivered to the company or the transfer is an exempt transfer within the Stock Transfer Act 1982 or is in accordance with regulations made under the Companies Act 1989[4]. This does not, however, prejudice any power of the company to register as shareholder any person to whom the right to any shares of the company has been transmitted by operation of law[5].

Articles of association usually require that shares shall be transferred in a form set out or in any usual or common form[6]. Normally the transfer is required to be executed or signed by the transferor and, unless the share is fully paid, also by or on behalf of the transferee[7], and is not required to be by deed. When the articles require the common form, registration of a transfer cannot be refused because it omits particulars which would be found in the common form but are in the circumstances immaterial[8]. Irregularities in the form of transfer have been often condoned on such grounds as the usage of the company, lapse of time, and the acceptance of the transfer as valid[9].

Title to shares in a class which is permitted to be a participating security, which are recorded on a register of members (other than an overseas branch register) as being held in uncertificated form, may be transferred by means of the relevant system to which the permission relates[10].

1 See the Companies Act 1985 s 182 and para 437 ante.
2 See the Stock Transfer Act 1963 s 1(3) (as amended) and para 506 post.
3 This means an instrument which would attract stamp duty, not an instrument complying with every formality required by the articles: *Re Paradise Motor Co Ltd* [1968] 2 All ER 625, [1968] 1 WLR 1125, CA (transfer not signed by transferee); *Nisbet v Shepherd* [1994] 1 BCLC 300, CA (consideration omitted). It includes a stock transfer and a brokers transfer (Stock Transfer Act 1963 s 2(3)(a) (amended by the Companies Consolidation (Consequential Provisions) Act 1985 s 30, Sch 2)) and a court order under the Insurance Companies Act 1982 s 49, Sch 2C para 5(4) (substituted by the Insurance Companies (Third Insurance Directives) Regulations 1994, SI 1994/1696, reg 28(1)–(3), Sch 3) which operates to transfer property.
4 Companies Act 1985 s 183(1) (amended by the Uncertificated Securities Regulations 1995, SI 1995/3272, reg 40(2)(a)). See also *Re Greene, Greene v Greene* [1949] Ch 333, [1949] 1 All ER 167. As to the Secretary of State's power to make provision by regulations to enable title to securities to be evidenced and transferred without a written instrument see para 496 note 4 ante.
5 Companies Act 1985 s 183(2). As to transmission by operation of law see para 518 post.
6 See the Companies (Tables A to F) Regulations 1985, SI 1985/805, Schedule, Table A art 23. As to Table A generally see para 529 et seq post.
7 See ibid Table A art 23. Article 27 provides that no fee is to be charged for the registration of any instrument of transfer; and art 28 provides that the company is to be entitled to retain any instrument of transfer which is registered. The addition of a seal to the transfer is in such cases immaterial: *Ortigosa v Brown* (1878) 47 LJ Ch 168. As to execution by the donee of a power of attorney in connection with a stock exchange transaction see para 506 note 5 post. See further para 508 post.
8 *Re Letheby and Christopher Ltd* [1904] 1 Ch 815 (where the transferor's address and the denoting number of the share were omitted).
9 *Bargate v Shortridge* (1855) 5 HL Cas 297; *Straffon's Executors' Case* (1852) 1 De GM & G 576; *Burnes v Pennell* (1849) 2 HL Cas 497; *Barrow Mutual Ship Insurance Co v Ashburner* (1885) 54 LJQB 377, CA; *Ind's Case* (1872) 7 Ch App 485 (wrong denoting number); *Feiling's and Rimington's Case* (1867) 2 Ch App 714; *Murray v Bush* (1873) LR 6 HL 37; *Re General Floating Dock Co Ltd* (1867) 15 LT 526; *Re Taurine Co* (1883) 25 ChD 118, CA; *Smellie's Trustees v Smellie* (1952) 103 LJo 139. See also *Nisbet v Shepherd* [1994] 1 BCLC 300, CA (transfer relied on for more than seven years). Errors in the dates of transfers as entered on the register were held to be immaterial in *Weikersheim's Case* (1873) 8 Ch App 831.
10 See the Uncertificated Securities Regulations 1995 reg 14(1), (2) and MONEY. See also reg 23 (cited in para 497 ante).

506. Simplified transfer of securities. Certain specified[1] registered securities[2] may be transferred by means of an instrument under hand in the statutory form[3] known as a stock transfer[4]. The transfer is executed by the transferor only, but specifies the full name and address of the transferee[5]. Particulars of the consideration, of the description and number or amount of the securities and of the person by whom the transfer is made are also specified[6].

In the case of a transfer to a stock exchange nominee[7] neither particulars of the consideration nor the address of the transferee need be inserted[8]. A form used to transfer securities from a stock exchange nominee which is a body corporate need not be executed under hand but will be sufficiently executed if it bears a facsimile of the corporate seal of the transferor authenticated by the signature (whether actual or facsimile) of a director or the secretary of the transferor[9].

The execution of a stock transfer need not be attested[10]. Where a stock transfer has been executed for the purpose of a stock exchange transaction[11], the particulars of the consideration and of the transferee may either be inserted in that transfer or, as the case may require, supplied by means of separate instruments in the statutory form[12] known as brokers transfers[13]. A brokers transfer identifies the stock transfer and specifies the securities to which each instrument relates and the consideration paid for the securities[13].

The above provisions[14] have effect in relation to a transfer of specified securities notwithstanding anything to the contrary in any enactment or instrument relating to the transfer of those securities[15]. However, any right to refuse to register a person as the holder of any securities on any ground (other than the form in which the securities purport to be transferred to him) is unaffected[16]. Also unaffected is any enactment or rule of law regulating the execution of documents by companies or other bodies corporate, or any articles of association or other instrument regulating the execution of documents by any particular company or body corporate[17].

1 The securities which may be so transferred are fully paid-up registered securities of any description which are: (1) securities issued by any company within the meaning of the Companies Act 1985 except a company limited by guarantee or an unlimited company: (2) securities issued by any body (other than a company within the meaning of that Act) incorporated in Great Britain by or under any enactment or by royal charter except a building society within the meaning of the Building Societies Act 1986 or a society registered under the Industrial and Provident Societies Act 1965; (3) securities issued by the government of the United Kingdom, except stock or bonds in the National Savings Stock Register, and except national savings certificates; (4) securities issued by any local authority; (5) units of an authorised unit trust scheme or a recognised scheme within the meaning of the Financial Services Act 1986 (see MONEY): Stock Transfer Act 1963 s 1(4) (amended by the Finance Act 1964 ss 24, 26(7), Sch 8 para 10, Sch 9; the Post Office Act 1969 s 108(1)(f); the Companies Consolidation (Consequential Provisions) Act 1985 s 30, Sch 2; the Building Societies Act 1986 s 120(1), Sch 18 Pt I para 5; and the Financial Services Act 1986 s 212(2), Sch 16 para 4(a)). As to the application of this mode of transfer to Scotland see further the Stock Transfer Act 1963 s 2(4).

2 For these purposes, 'securities' means shares, stock, debentures, debenture stock, loan stock, bonds, units of a collective investment scheme within the meaning of the Financial Services Act 1986 (see MONEY), and other securities of any description: Stock Transfer Act 1963 s 4(1) (amended by the Financial Services Act 1986 Sch 16 para 4(b)). 'Registered securities' means transferable securities the holders of which are entered in a register (whether maintained in Great Britain or not): Stock Transfer Act 1963 s 4(1).

3 For the prescribed form of stock transfer see ibid Sch 1 (amended by the Stock Transfer (Amendment of Forms) Order 1974, SI 1974/1214, art 3(1)); and for the prescribed forms for use as alternatives where the transfer is to a stock exchange nominee or from a stock exchange nominee see the Stock Transfer Act 1963 Sch 1 (amended by the Stock Transfer (Amendment of Forms) Order 1974 art 2, Sch 2; the Stock Transfer (Substitution of Forms) Order 1990, SI 1990/18, art 2, Schedule). A form substantially corresponding to the prescribed form is permissible: Stock Transfer Act 1963 s 3(1). The Treasury may vary the form by order made by statutory instrument, which may itself be varied or revoked by a subsequent order: s 3(2), (4). Any such statutory instrument is subject to annulment in pursuance of a resolution of either House of Parliament: s 3(4). As to the possible contents of any such order see s 3(2), (3) and s 3(5) (added by the Stock Exchange (Completion of Bargains) Act 1976 s 6) and MONEY.

4 Stock Transfer Act 1963 s 1(1). Nothing in s 1 (as amended) is to be construed as affecting the validity of any instrument which would otherwise be effective to transfer securities: s 1(3). Any instrument purporting to be made in any form for which the form set out in the Stock Transfer (Substitution of Forms) Order 1990 Schedule, or in any other form otherwise authorised or required for that purpose, is sufficient, whether or not it is completed in accordance with the form, if it complies with the requirements as to execution and contents which apply to a stock transfer: Stock Transfer Act 1963 s 1(3) (amended by the Stock Transfer (Substitution of Forms) Order 1990 art 3(2)). In relation to the transfer of securities by means of a stock transfer and a brokers transfer (1) any reference in any enactment or instrument to the delivery or lodging of an instrument, or proper instrument, of transfer, is to be construed as a reference to the delivery or lodging of the stock transfer and the brokers transfer; and (2) any such reference to the date on which an instrument of transfer is delivered or lodged is to be construed as a reference to the date by which the later of those transfers to be delivered or lodged has been delivered or lodged: Stock Transfer Act 1963 s 2(3)(a), (b) (amended by the Companies Consolidation (Consequential Provisions) Act 1985 Sch 2). Subject thereto, the brokers transfer (and not the stock transfer) is, however, deemed to be the conveyance or transfer for stamp duty purposes: Stock Transfer Act 1963 s 2(3)(c) (repealed from a date to be appointed by the Finance Act 1990 s 132, Sch 19 Pt VI).

5 Stock Transfer Act 1963 s 1(1). Where the transfer is executed for the purpose of a stock exchange transaction by the donee of a power of attorney, it is conclusively to be presumed in favour of the transferee that the power had not been revoked at the date of the instrument if a statutory declaration to that effect is made by the donee of the power on or within three months after that date: Powers of Attorney Act 1971 s 6. For the meaning of 'stock exchange transaction' see note 11 infra.

6 Stock Transfer Act 1963 s 1(1). Section 1 (as amended) has effect (1) subject to the amendment that a sold transfer form, and a stock transfer form used to transfer securities to a stock exchange nominee, need not specify particulars of the consideration or the address of the transferee (Stock Transfer (Addition of Forms) Order 1979, SI 1979/277, art 3(1)); and (2) in relation to the form set out in the Stock Transfer (Substitution of Forms) Order 1990 Schedule, subject to the amendment that that form need not specify particulars of the consideration or the address of the transferee (art 4).

7 For these purposes, 'stock exchange nominee' means any person whom the Secretary of State designates by order made by statutory instrument as a nominee of the Stock Exchange for the purposes of the Stock Exchange (Completion of Bargains) Act 1976: s 7(2); Stock Transfer (Addition of Forms) Order 1979 art 4.

8 Ibid art 3(1).

9 Ibid art 3(2).

10 Stock Transfer Act 1963 s 1(2).

11 For these purposes, 'stock exchange transaction' means a sale and purchase of securities in which each of the parties is a member of a stock exchange acting in the ordinary course of his business as such or is acting through the agency of such a member: ibid s 4(1). 'Stock exchange' means the Stock Exchange London, and any other stock exchange (whether in Great Britain or not) which is declared by order of the Treasury to be a recognised stock exchange for the purposes of the Stock Transfer Act 1963: s 4(1). Any such order is made by statutory instrument, and may be varied or revoked by a subsequent order: s 4(2).

12 For the prescribed form of brokers transfer see ibid Sch 2 (amended by the Stock Transfer (Amendment of Forms) Order 1974 art 3(2)). A form substantially corresponding to the prescribed form is permissible: Stock Transfer Act 1963 s 3(1).

13 Ibid s 1(2). As to the prohibition of circulation of blank transfers see para 507 post.

14 Ie ibid s 1 (as amended): see supra.

15 Ibid s 2(1).

16 Ibid s 2(1)(a).

17 Ibid s 2(1)(b). Any enactment or instrument relating to the transfer of securities specified for the purposes of s 1 (as amended) applies with any necessary modifications to a transfer authorised by s 1 (as amended): s 2(2) (amended by the Companies Consolidation (Consequential Provisions) Act 1985 Sch 2).

507. Transfer in blank. Where shares are transferable only by deed, a blank transfer, although executed by the shareholder, gives no security to an equitable mortgagee, because the filling in of the transferee's name would be a material alteration in the deed rendering the instrument void unless made under an authority conferred by a deed[1]. The same principle is applied where blank spaces are left in the deed for the purchaser's name[2], the consideration and name of the transferee[3], and the names of the transferees and attesting witnesses[4]. Where, however, transfers are not required to be made by deed, an equitable mortgagee has an implied authority to complete the blank transfer for the purpose of protecting his security, and to procure it to be registered[5], although he cannot delegate such authority to another person to be used for a different purpose[6]. If the company refuses to register a transfer so completed, the court may direct an account of what is due, and, if the borrower declines to have the account taken within the time limited, may rectify[7] the register by substituting the name of the transferee[8]. The delivery by executors to a broker of a blank transfer signed by them with the certificates, so that the shares may be registered in their own names, does not estop them from setting up their title against persons who advance money to the broker on a deposit of the certificates, although in good faith and without notice of any fraud[9].

Where a transfer in blank relating to registered stock of any description has been delivered, pursuant to a sale or gift to or to the order of the purchaser or any person acting on his behalf, or to the donee, any person who in Great Britain parts with possession of that transfer, or who removes it or causes or permits it to be removed from Great Britain before it has been duly completed is liable to a fine[10].

1 *Société Générale de Paris v Walker* (1885) 11 App Cas 20, HL; *France v Clark* (1884) 26 ChD 257, CA; *Powell v London and Provincial Bank* [1893] 2 Ch 555, CA. Registration does not validate the transfer: *Hare v London and North Western Rly Co* (1860) John 722; cf *Tayler v Great Indian Peninsula Rly Co* (1859) 4 De G & J 559.

2 *Hibblewhite v M'Morine* (1840) 6 M & W 200.

3 *Tayler v Great Indian Peninsular Rly Co* (1859) 4 De G & J 559; *Société Générale de Paris v Walker* (1885) 11 App Cas 20, HL; *France v Clark* (1884) 26 ChD 257, CA; *Powell v London and Provincial Bank* [1893] 2 Ch 555, CA.

4 *Swan v North British Australasian Co* (1863) 2 H & C 175, Ex Ch. As to the signature of documents in blank see generally *Lloyds Bank v Cooke* [1907] 1 KB 794, CA; *Smith v Prosser* [1907] 2 KB 735, CA. See further DEEDS vol 12 para 1378.

5 *Re Tahiti Cotton Co, ex p Sargent* (1874) LR 17 Eq 273; *Re Tees Bottle Co, Davies' Case* (1876) 33 LT 834. As to filling in description and number of shares after execution see *Re Barned's Banking Co, ex p Contract Corpn* (1867) 3 Ch App 105; *Re Financial Insurance Co, Bishop's Case* (1869) 7 Ch App 296n; *Re Blakely Ordnance Co, Bailey's Case* [1869] WN 196. As to gaining priority over earlier equitable interests, of which a creditor had no notice when he advanced his money, by perfecting his security by registration even after he had notice of such prior interest see *Dodds v Hills* (1865) 2 Hem & M 424; *Macmillan Inc v Bishopsgate Investment Trust plc (No 3)* [1995] 3 All ER 747, [1995] 1 WLR 978 (affd on other grounds [1996] 1 All ER 585, CA).

6 Ie such as to secure a sub-mortgage: *France v Clark* (1884) 26 ChD 257, CA; cf *Fox v Martin* (1895) 64 LJ Ch 473; *Fry v Smellie* [1912] 3 KB 282, CA; and *Fuller v Glyn, Mills, Currie & Co* [1914] 2 KB 168.

7 Ie under the Companies Act 1985 s 359: see para 393 ante.

8 *Re Tees Bottle Co, Davies' Case* (1876) 33 LT 834.

9 *Colonial Bank v Cady and Williams* (1890) 15 App Cas 267, HL; *Colonial Bank v Hepworth* (1887) 36 ChD 36; *Fox v Martin* (1895) 64 LJ Ch 473; *Fry v Smellie* [1912] 3 KB 282, CA; *Fuller v Glyn, Mills, Currie & Co* [1914] 2 KB 168; *Hutchinson v Colorado United Mining Co and Hamill* (1886) 3 TLR 265, CA.

10 See the Finance Act 1963 s 67 (repealed from a day to be appointed by the Finance Act 1990 ss 109(3), 132, Sch 19 Pt VI) and STAMP DUTIES vol 44(1) (Reissue) para 1115.

508. Non-execution by transferee. When, as is usual, articles of association provide that the instrument of transfer shall be executed or signed both by the transferor and transferee[1], non-execution by the transferee only makes the transfer irregular and not a nullity; and, if it has been acted on for a long period, it cannot be impeached[2]. In the absence of such a provision, a transfer executed by the transferor only passes the property in the shares, subject to the transferee's right, on discovering any defect, to repudiate the shares[3]. If it is the practice of the company, the directors may decline to register a transfer where it has not been executed by the transferee[4], and it is their duty not to permit registration of a transfer of shares on which there is any liability except when satisfied that the consent of the transferee has been given. They may refuse to register a bona fide transfer to a minor because he is unable to accept it[5], but not a bona fide transfer to a pauper[6].

1 See the Companies (Table A to F) Regulations 1985, SI 1985/805, Schedule, Table A art 23 and para 505 ante. Cf the provisions for simplified transfer by a stock transfer: see para 506 ante. As to Table A generally see para 529 et seq post.
2 *Re Taurine Co* (1883) 25 ChD 118, CA; cf *Royal Bank of India's Case* (1869) 4 Ch App 252; *Cuninghame v City of Glasgow Bank* (1879) 4 App Cas 607, HL. Cf *Re Paradise Motor Co Ltd* [1968] 2 All ER 625, [1968] 1 WLR 1125, CA (transfer not signed by transferee). See also *Dempsey v Celtic Football and Athletic Co Ltd* [1993] BCC 514, Ct of Sess.
3 *Heritage's Case* (1869) LR 9 Eq 5; *Fitch Lovell Ltd v IRC* [1962] 3 All ER 685 at 694, [1962] 1 WLR 1325 at 1338, 1339; cf *Standing v Bowring* (1885) 31 ChD 282, CA.
4 *Marino's Case* (1867) 2 Ch App 596; cf para 506 ante.
5 *R v Midland Counties and Shannon Junction Rly Co* (1862) 15 ICLR 514; cf *Lumsden's Case* (1868) 4 Ch App 31; and see para 374 ante. As to the attainment of majority at the age of 18 see the Family Law Reform Act 1969 s 1 and CHILDREN vol 5(2) (Reissue) para 601.
6 *R v Midland Counties and Shannon Junction Rly Co* (1862) 15 ICLR 514; *Re Discoverers' Finance Corpn Ltd, Lindlar's Case* [1910] 1 Ch 312, CA.

509. Effect of registration of transfer. Until the instrument of transfer is registered, the transfer is not complete[1]; the transferor is the legal owner of the shares, and, if they are not fully paid, is liable to pay all the calls made on them, while his name remains on the register of members[2]. A transferee who has accepted the transfer, although he has not executed it, is, however, liable to indemnify the transferor as from its date[3].

1 See *Re Fry, Chase National Executors and Trustees Corpn v Fry* [1946] Ch 312, [1946] 2 All ER 106; cf *Re Rose, Rose v IRC* [1952] Ch 499, [1952] 1 All ER 1217, CA (gift complete even though delay in registration); and see generally GIFTS. An attempted transfer will not, prima facie, be validated as a declaration of trust (see CHOSES IN ACTION vol 6 (Reissue) para 27 note 2), but an assignment of a chose in action will be enforced, although voluntary, if everything required to be done by the donor has been done by him (see CHOSES IN ACTION vol 6 (Reissue) para 37).
2 *Sayles v Blane* (1849) 14 QB 205; cf *Symons' Case* (1870) 5 Ch App 298 at 300 per Giffard LJ. Even after the transfer is registered, he is, it is conceived, liable for calls already made: *Taylor, Phillips and Rickards' Cases* [1897] 1 Ch 298 at 306, CA per Lindley LJ: *Re Hoylake Rly Co, ex p Littledale* (1874) 9 Ch App 257 at 262; cf *Watson v Eales* (1857) 23 Beav 294. As to the effect of delay on the part of the company in registering see para 2490 post. He is also liable as a contributory in a winding up: see para 2463 et seq post.
3 *Loring v Davis* (1886) 32 ChD 625; *Levi v Ayers* (1878) 3 App Cas 842, PC; cf *Hardoon v Belilios* [1901] AC 118, PC. The transferor must hold as a trustee all the dividends declared on the shares from that date: *Stevenson v Wilson* 1907 SC 445.

510. Application for and registration of transfer. The transferee is the proper person to apply for registration[1]; but the transferor may also apply. On the application of the transferor of any share or interest in a company, the company must enter in its register of members the name of the transferee in the same manner and subject to the same conditions as if the application for the entry were made by the transferee[2]; but this does not affect the transferee's duty[3] to obtain registration[4]. The transferor may enforce the registration by obtaining an order for rectification of the register[5].

In order to ascertain whether a transfer is valid, and whether the transferee ought to be registered, the directors must have a reasonable time to consider the matter[6]; but this is subject to the obligation to notify the transferee within two months of the transfer being lodged[7]. Usually the directors notify the registered holder that a transfer has been lodged for registration[8]. If the registered holder does not reply to such a notification and a forged transfer is registered, he is not estopped from having the register rectified by substituting his name for that of the transferee[9].

The secretary has no implied authority from the directors or the company to register transfers[10].

1 See para 491 ante.
2 Companies Act 1985 s 183(4). Section 183(4) does not apply in relation to the transfer of uncertificated units of a security by means of a relevant system: Uncertificated Securities Regulations 1995, SI 1995/3272, reg 40(2)(b). See MONEY.
3 See para 492 ante.
4 *Skinner v City of London Marine Insurance Corpn* (1885) 14 QBD 882, CA.
5 *Re Stranton Iron and Steel Co* (1873) LR 16 Eq 559; and see para 393 ante.
6 *Société Générale de Paris v Walker* (1885) 11 App Cas 20, HL; *Re Ottos Kopje Diamond Mines Ltd* [1893] 1 Ch 618, CA; *Ireland v Hart* [1902] 1 Ch 522. They are not entitled to refuse to register a transfer on the assumption that the transfer is a breach of trust, but should give notice to any person objecting thereto that they will register the transfer unless proceedings to restrain its registration are taken within a reasonable time: see *Grundy v Briggs* [1910] 1 Ch 444.
7 See para 500 ante.
8 See *Tayler v Great Indian Peninsula Rly Co* (1859) 28 LJ Ch 285 at 288 (affd 28 LJ Ch 709); *Re North British Australasian Co Ltd, ex p Swan* (1860) 7 CBNS 400 at 438, 439; *Swan v North British Australasian Co* (1862) 7 H & N 603 at 631 (affd (1863) 2 H & C 175, Ex Ch); *Johnston v Renton* (1870) LR 9 Eq 181.
9 *Barton v London and North Western Rly Co* (1889) 24 QBD 77, CA.
10 See *Chida Mines v Anderson* (1905) 22 TLR 27; *Re Matlock Old Bath Hydropathic Co, Wheatcroft's Case* (1873) 42 LJ Ch 853.

511. Production of share certificate. Articles of association generally require a transfer of shares left for registration to be accompanied by the certificate of such shares[1]. The articles generally also provide for the granting of a new certificate on proof of the loss or destruction of the old certificate, or upon a satisfactory indemnity being given[2]. Where the articles provide that transfers shall be registered on presentation of the transfer accompanied by such evidence as the company may require of the transferor's title, the directors may refuse to register if the certificate is not so produced[3].

1 See the Companies (Tables A to F) Regulations 1985, SI 1985/805, Schedule, Table A art 24(a). Article 27 provides that no fee is to be charged for the registration of any instrument of transfer or other document relating to or affecting the title to any shares; and art 28 provides that the company is to be entitled to retain any instrument of transfer which is required. As to Table A generally see para 529 et seq post.
2 See ibid art 7. As to the splitting of certificates see para 485 ante.
3 *Re East Wheal Martha Mining Co* (1863) 33 Beav 119.

512. Certification of transfers. Where a shareholder sells some only of the shares comprised in one certificate, or sells some to one person and the rest to another, on the deposit of the transfer and certificate with the company, the secretary generally indorses a note on the transfer or transfers that the certificate has been lodged. This practice, called 'certification of transfers', arose from the difficulty felt by members of the Stock Exchange[1] in settling their accounts as buyers and sellers of shares where the seller's certificate does not accompany his transfer.

Certification by a company of any instrument of transfer of any shares in[2] the company is to be taken as a representation by the company to any person acting on the faith of the certification that there have been produced to the company such documents as on the face of them show a prima facie title to the shares in the transferor named in the instrument of transfer (which includes a brokers transfer[3]), but is not to be taken as a representation that the transferor has any title to the shares[4].

Where, however, any person acts on the faith of a false certification by a company made negligently, the company is under the same liability to him as if the certification had been made fraudulently[5]. For the purpose of the above provisions:

(1) an instrument of transfer is deemed to be certificated if it bears the words 'certificate lodged' or words to the like effect[6];

(2) the certification of an instrument of transfer is deemed to be made by a company if the person issuing the instrument is a person authorised to issue certificated instruments of transfer on the company's behalf and the certification is signed by a person authorised so to certificate transfers or by an officer or servant either of the company or of a body corporate so authorised[7]; and

(3) a certification is deemed to be signed by a person if it purports to be authenticated by his signature or initials, whether handwritten or not, and it is not shown that the signature or initials were placed there neither by himself nor by any person authorised to use the signature or initials for the purposes of certificating transfers on the company's behalf[8].

It will be appreciated that these provisions impose very serious liabilities upon a company, which, however, is not bound to certify transfers at all.

If the company by mistake returns the share certificate to the transferor, and the transferor is thereby enabled to obtain money on another transfer of the shares, the company is not liable to the second transferee, as it has no duty to the public with regard to the custody of the certificate[9].

1 Companies admitted to the Official List of the Stock Exchange must arrange for transfers to be certified against certificates or temporary documents of title and to be returned on the day of receipt or, should that not be a business day, on the first business day following their receipt and to split and return renounceable documents within the same period, and must arrange for transfers to be registered or rejected within two business days of their receipt:*Listing Rules* r 9.39. As to the *Listing Rules* see para 282 ante.

2 See para 496 et seq ante.

3 See the Stock Transfer Act 1963 s 2(2) and para 506 ante.

4 Companies Act 1985 s 184(1); and see *Bishop v Balkis Consolidated Co Ltd* (1890) 25 QBD 512 at 519, 520, CA.

5 Companies Act 1985 s 184(2) (which, together with s 184(3), negatives the effect of *George Whitechurch Ltd v Cavanagh* [1902] AC 117, HL and *Kleinwort, Sons & Co v Associated Automatic Machine Corpn Ltd* (1934) 151 LT 1, HL, in so far as they relate to fraudulent certifications made by an agent of the company but not for the company's benefit). Cf *McKay's Case* [1896] 2 Ch 757.

6 Companies Act 1985 s 184(3)(a).

7 Ibid s 184(3)(b).

8 Ibid s 184(3)(c).

9 *Longman v Bath Electric Tramways Ltd* [1905] 1 Ch 646, CA.

513. Stamp duty on transfers. Stamp duty is chargeable at the rate of 50 pence for every £100 or part of £100 of the consideration[1]. Directors may refuse to register a transfer which is not properly stamped, although the stamp it bears is in accordance with the consideration incorrectly stated in the transfer[2]; but, where a transfer with an insufficient stamp has been registered, the name of the transferee cannot be removed from the register after the proper stamp duty and penalty has been paid[3].

Where completion of the sale takes place, or may take place, without the necessity of bringing a stampable document of transfer into existence, stamp duty reserve tax may be payable[4].

1 See the Stamp Act 1891 s 1, Sch 1, 'Conveyance or Transfer on Sale' (as amended) and STAMP DUTIES vol 44(1) (Reissue) para 1029. As to the prospective abolition of stamp duty on transfers of securities see the Finance Act 1990 ss 108, 132, Sch 19 Pt VI and STAMP DUTIES vol 44(1) (Reissue) para 1005.
2 *Maynard v Consolidated Kent Collieries Corpn* [1903] 2 KB 121, CA; *Conybear v British Briquettes Ltd* [1937] 4 All ER 191.
3 *Re Indo-China Steam Navigation Co* [1917] 2 Ch 100.
4 See para 514 post and STAMP DUTIES vol 44(1) (Reissue) para 1118 et seq.

514. Stamp duty reserve tax. Stamp duty reserve tax is charged in respect of agreements to transfer certain securities for money or money's worth and in respect of arrangements involving depositary receipts and clearance services[1]. The principal charge in respect of agreements is deferred and will not arise if certain conditions are satisfied[2]; but there is also an immediate and unconditional charge in respect of agreements to transfer chargeable securities which are constituted by or transferable by means of certain renounceable instruments as soon as they are made, without regard to whether or not the agreement is implemented by an instrument of transfer[3]. In each case, tax is imposed at the rate of 50 pence for every £100 or part of £100 of the amount or value of the consideration[4]. A higher rate charge of £1.50 per £100 or part of £100 of the amount or value of the consideration is imposed in respect of certain transactions involving depositary receipts or clearance services which do not give rise to a transfer chargeable with ad valorem stamp duty in the same amount as the tax[5].

1 Stamp duty reserve tax was introduced by the Finance Act 1986 Pt IV (ss 86–99) (as amended): see s 86(1). As to stamp duty reserve tax generally see STAMP DUTIES vol 44(1) (Reissue) para 1118 et seq; as to exceptions and exemptions see STAMP DUTIES vol 44(1) (Reissue) para 1125 et seq; and as to the prospective abolition of stamp duty reserve tax see STAMP DUTIES vol 44(1) (Reissue) para 1110.
2 See STAMP DUTIES vol 44(1) (Reissue) para 1120.
3 See STAMP DUTIES vol 44(1) (Reissue) para 1121.
4 See STAMP DUTIES vol 44(1) (Reissue) paras 1120, 1121.
5 See STAMP DUTIES vol 44(1) (Reissue) paras 1122, 1123.

515. Forged transfers. The company owes a duty to each of its shareholders not to take his shares out of his name unless he has executed a valid transfer of them, and this duty involves the corresponding obligation not to give effect to a forged transfer[1]. If, however, the forged transfer is registered, the true owner of the shares may sue the company jointly with the transferee for rectification of the register of shareholders by striking out the name of the transferee and restoring his own[2]. Where this remedy is no longer possible (as in the case of the intervention of third party rights) he may sue the company alone for an order that the company shall purchase and register in his name the necessary shares[3]. The period of limitation[4] does not begin to run against him in favour of the company until the company resists his claim, as his cause of action is not the invalid transfer of his shares but the company's refusal, when the forgery is made known, to treat him as the shareholder[5]. Negligence on the part of the shareholder does not create an estoppel disentitling him to succeed, unless it is the proximate cause of what the company has done[6].

The mere registration of the transferee does not entitle him to compel the company to recognise him as the holder of the shares[7], since registration only gives effect to a prior valid transfer[8]. Nor is the company necessarily estopped from disputing, as against the transferee, the validity of the transfer[9]. The only duty which the company owes to the transferee is to consult the register[10]; but, even where such reference would have shown that the alleged transferor was not on the register, the company is not ipso facto liable by estoppel to the transferee[11].

However, the issue of a certificate for the shares in favour of the transferee can undoubtedly create an estoppel in favour of the transferee himself, or any third party, if he acts to his detriment on the faith of it[12].

A person who, innocently, and even without negligence, brings about the transfer is bound to indemnify the company against any liability to the owner of the shares who has been displaced by a forged transfer[13].

1 *Simm v Anglo-American Telegraph Co* (1879) 5 QBD 188 at 214, CA.
2 *Re Bahia and San Francisco Rly Co* (1868) LR 3 QB 584; *Barton v London North Western Rly Co* (1889) 24 QBD 77, CA; cf *Midland Rly Co v Taylor* (1862) 8 HL Cas 751 at 756.
3 *Barton v London and North Western Rly Co* (1888) 38 ChD 144 at 149, 152, CA; *Johnston v Renton* (1870) LR 9 Eq 181 at 188; *Welch v Bank of England* [1955] Ch 508, [1955] 1 All ER 811.
4 Ie under the Limitation Act 1980 s 2: cf LIMITATION OF ACTIONS vol 28 para 657.
5 *Barton v North Staffordshire Rly Co* (1888) 38 ChD 458 at 463; *Welch v Bank of England* [1955] Ch 508, [1955] 1 All ER 811.
6 *Mayor, Constables & Co of Merchants of the Staple of England v Governor & Co of Bank of England* (1887) 21 QBD 160 at 173, 174, CA; cf *Swan v North British Australasian Co* (1863) 2 H & C 175, Ex Ch. Failure to reply to an intimation by the company that the transfer is about to be made unless objected to is not negligence on the part of the shareholder: *Barton v London and North Western Rly Co* (1889) 24 QBD 77, CA; *Welch v Bank of England* [1955] Ch 508, [1955] 1 All ER 811.
7 *Simm v Anglo-American Telegraph Co* (1879) 5 QBD 188, CA.
8 *France v Clark* (1884) 26 ChD 257, CA; *Barton v London and North Western Rly Co* (1888) 38 ChD 144 at 149, CA.
9 *Waterhouse v London and South Western Rly Co* (1879) 41 LT 553; cf *Simm v Anglo-American Telegraph Co* (1879) 5 QBD 188, CA. See further para 488 ante and ESTOPPEL.
10 *Balkis Consolidated Co v Tomkinson* [1893] AC 396 at 412, 413, HL per Lord Field; *Dixon v Kennaway & Co* [1900] 1 Ch 833.
11 *Balkis Consolidated Co v Tomkinson* [1893] AC 396, HL; *Dixon v Kennaway & Co* [1900] 1 Ch 833, following *Knights v Wiffen* (1870) LR 5 QB 660; *Platt v Rowe (Trading as Chapman and Rowe) and C M Mitchell & Co* (1909) 26 TLR 49; cf *Foster v Tyne Pontoon and Dry Docks Co and Renwick* (1893) 63 LJQB 50 at 55 (where it was held that the fact that the fraudulent person had been insolvent from the first precluded the plaintiff from getting damages from the company).
12 See para 488 ante.
13 *Sheffield Corpn v Barclay* [1905] AC 392, HL. As to the liability of a stockbroker who, without fraud on his part, by acting on a forged transfer or by identification of a forger brings about a transfer, see *Starkey v Bank of England* [1903] AC 114, HL; *Bank of England v Cutler* [1908] 2 KB 208, CA; and as to costs of third parties see *Welch v Bank of England* [1955] Ch 508 at 548, [1955] 1 All ER 811 at 830.

516. Compensation for loss under forged transfer. A company may impose such reasonable restrictions on the transfer of its shares, stock or securities, or with respect to powers of attorney for the transfer of such, as it may consider requisite for guarding against losses arising from forgery[1]. Out of its funds it may grant compensation for losses caused by forged instruments or transfers under forged powers of attorney, and may, if it thinks fit, charge a fee at a rate not exceeding five pence on every £100, with a minimum charge equal to that for £25 transferred, to provide for such compensation, and may borrow on the security of its property to meet claims therefor[2]. Compensation may be paid whether the person receiving compensation or any person through whom he claims has or has not paid any fee or otherwise contributed to any fund out of which compensation is paid[3]. Where the company pays compensation, it is subrogated to the rights of the person compensated against the person liable for the loss[4].

1 Forged Transfers Act 1891 s 1(4). As to forgery generally see CRIMINAL LAW vol 11(1) (Reissue) para 605 et seq. The manner in which shares may be transferred is governed by the articles of the company and the general law: see para 505 et seq ante. The Companies (Tables A to F) Regulations 1985, SI 1985/805, Schedule, Table A art 24(b) provides that the directors may decline to recognise an

instrument of transfer in respect of more than one class of share. As to Table A generally see para 529 et seq post.

2 See the Forged Transfers Act 1891 s 1(1)–(3) (amended by the Forged Transfers Act 1892 ss 2, 3; the Decimal Currency Act 1969 s 11(1); the Stock Transfer Act 1982 s 3(3), Sch 2 para 1).

3 See the Forged Transfers Act 1891 s 1(1) (amended by the Forged Transfers Act 1892 s 2).

4 See the Forged Transfers Act 1891 s 1(5). These provisions apply to all companies incorporated by or in pursuance of any Act of Parliament or by royal charter or amalgamated with such a company: Forged Transfers Act 1891 s 2; Forged Transfers Act 1892 s 4.

517. Transferor's liability after registration. When a transfer has been duly registered, the transferor ceases to be a member of the company in respect of the shares transferred. Thereupon he becomes a 'past member' of the company, and in case of a winding up is liable to contribute towards the payment of its debts and liabilities and expenses of the winding up and for the adjustment of the rights of contributors among themselves, to the extent of the amount remaining unpaid on the shares, where it appears to the court that the existing members are unable to satisfy the contributions required to be made by them under the Insolvency Act 1986, unless the debt or liability was contracted after he has ceased to be a member, or unless he has ceased to be a member for a year or upwards before the commencement of the winding up[1].

Where a limited company is re-registered as unlimited[2], a person who, at the time when the application for it to be re-registered was lodged, was a past member of the company, and did not thereafter again become a member, does not have his liability increased[3].

Where an unlimited company is re-registered as limited[4], a past member of the company who was a member of it at the time of re-registration is, if the winding up commences within a period of three years from re-registration, liable to contribute to the assets of the company without limit in respect of debts and liabilities contracted before such re-registration[5]. Where no persons who were members of the company at that time are existing members of the company, a person who at such time was a present or past member of the company will (unless he has ceased to be a member for one year or upwards), if the winding up takes place within a period of three years from re-registration, be liable to contribute without limit notwithstanding that the existing members have satisfied the contributions required to be made by them under the Insolvency Act 1986[6].

1 See the Insolvency Act 1986 s 74(1), (2)(a)–(c) and paras 2464, 2465 post. As to his liability for calls already made see para 509 text and note 2 ante.

2 See paras 124, 125 ante.

3 See the Insolvency Act 1986 s 78 and para 2466 post.

4 See para 126 ante.

5 See the Insolvency Act 1986 s 77(1), (2), (4) and para 2466 post.

6 See ibid ss 74(2)(a), 77(3) and paras 2465, 2466 post.

(v) Transmission, Mortgage and Surrender of Shares

518. Transmission of shares on death etc. In Table A[1], and in articles of association generally, the word 'transmission' is used in contradistinction to the word 'transfer'; the former means transmission by operation of law, including devolution by death or bankruptcy[2], and the latter a transfer by the act of a member[3]. Unless the articles otherwise provide, the survivors or survivor of registered joint holders of shares are alone entitled to and liable upon such shares[4], even where one of the joint holders is a corporation[5].

Upon the death of the sole holder of shares, the title to his shares devolves upon his personal representatives[6], who, subject to any provisions in the articles of association, may transfer his shares without being registered as shareholders[7], or, in the absence of any right of veto conferred on the company by its articles, may have their names entered on the register[8]. Notwithstanding anything contained in the articles of a company, the production to a company of a document which is by law sufficient evidence of probate of the will or letters of administration of the estate or confirmation as executor of a deceased person having been granted to some person must be accepted by the company as sufficient evidence of the grant[9]. The personal representatives are liable for calls only in their representative capacity until they are registered as members with their consent; but after registration they become personally liable[10]. It is the duty of the representatives to give notice of the member's death as soon as possible[11]. Where executors are entitled to be registered as members, they are entitled to have their names inserted in such order as they please and the company cannot state on the register that they are executors[12]. On the death of a shareholder domiciled abroad the company may act only upon a grant of probate or administration in this country[13]. If, therefore, the company registers the name of or a transfer by any person who has not obtained such a grant or pays dividends to any such person, it becomes an executor de son tort, and is liable to penalties and to pay such duties as would have been payable on a grant of probate[14].

When new shares are offered to the members in proportion to their holdings while the name of a deceased member is on the register, the executors may claim their testator's proportion[15]. They must, however, be registered themselves as members in respect of the new shares, and become liable to the company as individuals[16], though as between them and the beneficiaries they hold the shares as part of the estate and have a right of indemnity against the estate[17].

On a registered member having a person appointed as trustee of his estate in bankruptcy, the right to transfer his shares will vest in the trustee in bankruptcy[18].

1 As to the Companies (Tables A to F) Regulations 1985, SI 1985/805, Schedule, Table A (amended by SI 1985/1052) see para 529 et seq post.
2 *Barton v London and North Western Rly Co* (1889) 24 QBD 77 at 88, CA.
3 See the Companies (Tables A to F) Regulations 1985 Schedule, Table A headings to arts 23–28, 29–31; *Re Bentham Mills Spinning Co* (1879) 11 ChD 900 at 904, CA; *Moodie v W and J Shepherd (Bookbinders) Ltd* [1949] 2 All ER 1044 at 1054, HL; *Stothers v William Steward (Holdings) Ltd* [1994] 2 BCLC 266 at 273, CA. The distinction between transfer and transmission is also recognised by the Companies Act 1985 s 183(2) which permits a company to register a person entitled by transmission as a shareholder without the delivery of a proper instrument of transfer: see para 505 ante.
4 *Re Maria Anna and Steinbank Coal and Coke Co, Maxwell's Case, Hill's Case* (1875) LR 20 Eq 585. It is usually so provided in the articles: see the Companies (Tables A to F) Regulations 1985 Schedule, Table A art 29, which provides further that nothing in the article shall release the estate of a dead joint holder from any liability in respect of any share which he had held jointly with others.
5 Bodies Corporate (Joint Tenancy) Act 1899 passed in consequence of *Law Guarantee and Trust Society Ltd and Hunter v Governor & Co of Bank of England* (1890) 24 QBD 406; and see *Re Thompson's Settlement Trusts, Thompson v Alexander* [1905] 1 Ch 229.
6 See *Re Greene, Greene v Greene* [1949] Ch 333, [1949] 1 All ER 167.
7 See the Companies Act 1985 s 183(3) and para 504 ante; and the Companies (Tables A to F) Regulations 1985 Schedule, Table A arts 29–31. See also *Stothers v William Steward (Holdings) Ltd* [1994] 2 BCLC 266, CA (articles properly construed permitted transfers by personal representatives to the same extent as transfers to privileged relations were permitted by members while alive; hence the personal representatives were able to transfer the shares of the deceased member to his widow (a privileged relation) without obtaining the consent of the directors to the transfer). As to voting by a person entitled by transmission see para 670 post.

8 *Scott v Frank F Scott (London) Ltd* [1940] Ch 794, [1940] 3 All ER 508, CA. Under the Companies (Tables A to F) Regulations 1985 Schedule, Table A art 30 there is also the right to nominate the person whose name is to be entered in respect of the shares.

9 Companies Act 1985 s 187.

10 *Duff's Executors' Case* (1886) 32 ChD 301, CA; *Buchan's Case* (1879) 4 App Cas 549, 583, HL. As to the personal representatives being put on the list of contributories see para 2471 post.

11 *New Zealand Gold Extraction Co (Newberg-Vautin Process) v Peacock* [1894] 1 QB 622 at 632, CA.

12 *Re T H Saunders & Co Ltd* [1908] 1 Ch 415; *Edwards v Ransomes and Rapier Ltd* (1930) 143 LT 594. As to the exclusion of trusts from the register see the Companies Act 1985 s 360 and para 385 ante.

13 See *Commercial Bank Corpn of India and the East, Fernandes' Executors' Case* (1870) 5 Ch App 314. As to the resealing of dominion and colonial grants see EXECUTORS vol 17 para 1032 et seq.

14 *New York Breweries Co v A-G* [1899] AC 62, HL. See also *Re Baku Consolidated Oilfields Ltd* [1994] 1 BCLC 173 at 176 (liquidator not bound to insist on an English grant being obtained if satisfied that the personal representatives would be so entitled and can distribute a deceased member's share of surplus assets without the formality of an English grant; he may seek a suitable indemnity to protect himself against liability as an executor de son tort).

15 *James v Buena Ventura Nitrate Grounds Syndicate Ltd* [1896] 1 Ch 456, CA.

16 *Re Leeds Banking Co, Fearnside and Dean's Case, Dobson's Case* (1866) 1 Ch App 231; *Duff's Executors' Case* (1886) 32 ChD 301, CA.

17 *Duff's Executors' Case* (1886) 32 ChD 301 at 309, 310, CA.

18 See the Insolvency Act 1986 ss 306, 311(3) and BANKRUPTCY vol 3(2) (Reissue) paras 381, 386, 411.

519. Mortgages of shares. A valid security may be given on shares either by a legal[1] or equitable[2] mortgage[3]. Where notice to the company is required, it must be given to the proper officers when conducting the business of the company[4].

1 See eg *Deverges v Sandeman, Clark & Co* [1902] 1 Ch 579, CA. On payment in full, the mortgagee will become a trustee of the shares and may not use the votes attached to them contrary to the interests of the mortgagor: *McGrattan v McGrattan* [1985] NI 28.

2 See eg *Harrold v Plenty* [1901] 2 Ch 314; cf *Hunter v Hunter* [1936] AC 222, HL.

3 As to the manner of effecting mortgages of stocks and shares, and as to the priority between equitable mortgages and the effect of notice to the company, see MORTGAGE vol 32 paras 526, 530, 531; and as to the right of an equitable claimant to stocks and shares to protect his claim by serving a stop notice see para 386 ante.

4 See CHOSES IN ACTION vol 6 (Reissue) para 57.

520. Surrender in case of company limited by shares. There are only minimal references to the surrender of shares in the Companies Act 1985[1]. Directors are, however, usually empowered by the articles of association to accept a surrender of shares. Where the company is limited by shares, such a power does not justify them either in accepting a surrender for any valuable consideration paid by the company out of its assets, as the transaction is a purchase by the company of its own shares[2], or in repaying to the member the amount paid on his shares[3]. Where a surrender of shares, whether fully paid up or not, amounts to a reduction of capital[4], it cannot be effected without confirmation by the court[5], except as a short cut to forfeiture where forfeiture would be justified[6] under the articles for failure to pay any sum payable in respect of the shares; and, perhaps, by way of compromise either of a genuine dispute as to whether the shares have been legally issued[7], or of a genuine claim for rectification of the register for misrepresentation[8].

It has been held that a surrender of fully paid shares in return for other shares of the same nominal amount does not amount to a reduction of capital and may be validly effected[9].

A transfer of shares to a nominee on behalf of the company is not a surrender, though the practical effect may be similar. Where some consideration moves from the company, such a transfer is invalid[10]; but, where no consideration moves from the company, it is valid[11] and may be made direct to the company itself.

1 Ie in the Companies Act 1985 s 143(3)(d) (see para 362 ante) and s 146(1)(a) (see para 366 ante).
2 Ie and prohibited by ibid s 143(1). See also *Trevor v Whitworth* (1887) 12 App Cas 409 at 438, HL; *Kirby v Wilkins* [1929] 2 Ch 444.
3 *Re Companies Guardian Society, Lord Wallscourt's Case* (1899) 7 Mans 235; *Re Walker and Hacking Ltd* (1887) 57 LT 763.
4 *Hope v International Financial Society* (1876) 4 ChD 327, CA; *Bellerby v Rowland and Marwood's SS Co Ltd* [1902] 2 Ch 14 at 32, CA. See the dictum of Cozens-Hardy LJ at 32, that every surrender involves reduction of capital, explained and modified in *Rowell v John Rowell & Sons Ltd* [1912] 2 Ch 609 at 620. See also *Hopkinson v Mortimer, Harley & Co Ltd* [1917] 1 Ch 646 at 653–655.
5 See para 241 et seq ante.
6 Ie under the Companies Act 1985 s 143(3)(d): see para 362 ante. See *Bellerby v Rowland and Marwood's SS Co Ltd* [1902] 2 Ch 14, CA. As to the powers of forfeiture see para 522 et seq post.
7 *Bath's Case* (1878) 8 ChD 334, CA; and see *Mother Lode Consolidated Gold Mines Ltd v Hill* (1903) 19 TLR 341.
8 *Re Life Association of England Ltd, Blake's Case* (1865) 34 Beav 639; *Fox's Case* (1868) LR 5 Eq 118; *Wright's Case* (1871) 7 Ch App 55; *Anderson's Case* (1881) 17 ChD 373; approved in *Re Scottish Petroleum Co* (1883) 23 ChD 413, CA; and see *Re MacDonald, Sons & Co* [1894] 1 Ch 89, CA. Cases depending on whether the articles purported to give power to accept surrenders, such as *Marshall v Glamorgan Iron and Coal Co* (1869) LR 7 Eq 129; *Snell's Case* (1869) 5 Ch App 22; *Hall's Case* (1870) 5 Ch App 707; *Re London and Provincial Consolidated Coal Co* (1877) 5 ChD 525, cannot be supported in the face of *Trevor v Whitworth* (1887) 12 App Cas 409, HL, and *Bellerby v Rowland and Marwood's SS Co Ltd* [1902] 2 Ch 14, CA; and see now the Companies Act 1985 s 143(1) and para 362 ante.
9 *Rowell v John Rowell & Sons Ltd* [1912] 2 Ch 609. Cf *Re St James' Court Estate Ltd* [1944] Ch 6 (where Simonds J refused to sanction a scheme for the surrender of preference shares in exchange for redeemable preference shares until proper resolution for reduction and increase of capital had been passed). Cf also *Re Ellenroad Ring Mill Ltd* (1942) 86 Sol Jo 235.
10 *Addison's Case* (1870) 5 Ch App 294; *Cree v Somervail* (1879) 4 App Cas 648, HL. It is otherwise where it is part of a purchase of its own shares permitted by the Companies Act 1985 s 162 et seq: see para 222 et seq ante.
11 See ibid s 143(3) and para 362 ante. Under the law prior to the Companies Act 1980 s 35(2) (repealed) the transfer had to be to a nominee: see *Kirby v Wilkins* [1929] 2 Ch 444 (the nominee had to vote as the company from time to time directed: at 453, 454) and *Re Castiglione's Will Trusts, Hunter v MacKenzie* [1958] Ch 549, [1958] 1 All ER 480 (company to whom shares bequeathed entitled to direct transfer to nominees for itself).

521. Surrender in case of unlimited company. An unlimited company which has power to do so under its articles may accept a surrender of shares on the terms of the member receiving back the amount paid up on them[1].

1 *Re Borough Commercial and Building Society* [1893] 2 Ch 242.

(vi) Forfeiture of Shares

522. Power given by articles. Until shares are reissued, their forfeiture causes in effect a reduction of the capital of the company; but the operation has statutory authority[1], and does not require the confirmation by the court required in most other cases of reduction[2]. Table A gives directors power by resolution to forfeit shares of a company limited by shares, after notice to the shareholder, for default in payment of a call, or instalment of a call, or a premium payable by the terms of issue; and it provides that forfeited shares may be sold or disposed of, that before sale or disposition the forfeiture may be cancelled, and that on forfeiture the holder of the shares ceases to be a member, but remains liable to pay money due on the shares at the time of forfeiture[3]. It further provides that the company may receive the consideration for the shares sold or disposed of and execute a transfer of them in favour of the person to whom they are sold or disposed of[3]. Similar provisions may be inserted in articles of association which exclude Table A[4], and the power may be given or extended by altering the articles[5].

1 See the Companies (Tables A to F) Regulations 1985, SI 1985/805, Schedule, Table A arts 18–22. As to Table A generally see para 529 et seq post.
2 See para 241 et seq ante.
3 See note 1 supra.
4 *Trevor v Whitworth* (1887) 12 App Cas 409, HL; *Bellerby v Rowland and Marwood's SS Co Ltd* [1902] 2 Ch 14, CA.
5 *Allen v Gold Reefs of West Africa Ltd* [1900] 1 Ch 656, CA.

523. Extent of power. The power to reduce capital by forfeiting shares is, however, confined to the case where calls on, or other amounts due in respect of, the shares are not paid[1]. Thus a power which in terms purports to empower the company to forfeit shares in order to enforce a lien for debts due from a member otherwise than in respect of calls is void[2]. If the ground of forfeiture is contrary to the policy of the law, the power is invalid; for example a purported power to forfeit the shares of a member who commences litigation against the company is void, although the article containing it also provides that the market value of the forfeited shares shall be paid to the shareholder[3].

1 *Hopkinson v Mortimer, Harley & Co Ltd* [1917] 1 Ch 646; *Re Dronfield Silkstone Coal Co* (1880) 17 ChD 76, CA; *Trevor v Whitworth* (1887) 12 App Cas 409, HL; *Clarke and Chapman v Hart* (1858) 6 HL Cas 633; *Re National Patent Steam Fuel Co, Barton's Case* (1859) 4 De G & J 46, CA. See also *Evans v Smallcombe* (1868) LR 3 HL 249; *Re Agriculturists' Insurance Co, Brotherhood's Case* (1862) 31 Beav 365 (affd 31 LJ Ch 861); *Lord Belhaven's Case* (1865) 3 De GJ & Sm 41; *Dixon v Evans* (1872) LR 5 HL 606; *Spackman v Evans* (1868) LR 3 HL 171; *Stanhope's Case* (1866) 1 Ch App 161; *Stewart's Case* (1866) 1 Ch App 511; *Houldsworth v Evans* (1868) LR 3 HL 263; *Re Midland Railway Carriage and Wagon Co* (1907) 23 TLR 661.
2 *Hopkinson v Mortimer, Harley & Co Ltd* [1917] 1 Ch 646. This decision proceeded on the basis that such a forfeiture involved a reduction of capital, and to the extent to which the power of forfeiture could be invoked to give effect to the company's lien for the debts, was a clog on the equity of redemption; and see *Re Bolton, ex p North British Artificial Silk Ltd* [1930] 2 Ch 48 at 56, 57 (where a power such as this was included, in addition to a power to forfeit for non-payment of calls, and it was held that the forfeiture was good as it was effected under the second of such powers).
3 *Hope v International Financial Society* (1876) 4 ChD 327, CA.

524. Exercise of power of forfeiture. A purported forfeiture of shares is invalid if it is not made for the company's benefit[1]. When by a provision of the articles the company may forfeit on default in payment of calls, the shareholder in default cannot insist on the provision being acted upon, even if he has received a notice that it would be[2].

Directors elected in a voluntary winding up may be authorised to exercise the forfeiture clauses in the articles[3]. The power to forfeit is not lost by the uncalled capital being charged in favour of debenture holders[4]. A valid forfeiture holds good against the liquidator[5].

1 *Harris v North Devon Rly Co* (1855) 20 Beav 384. Forfeiture is void when made to relieve a shareholder from liability: see *Re London and County Assurance Co, ex p Jones* (1858) 27 LJ Ch 666; *Re Esparto Trading Co* (1879) 12 ChD 191; *European Assurance Society, Manisty's Case* (1873) 17 Sol Jo 745; *Stanhope's Case* (1866) 1 Ch App 161 at 169. It has been held that forfeiture following a complaint that the contract to take the shares was induced by misrepresentation, but not followed by rectification of the register, did

not relieve the shareholder from unpaid calls: *Gowers' Case* (1868) LR 6 Eq 77. As to restraining forfeiture for non-payment of calls after proceedings for rescission have been commenced see para 330 ante.
2 *Bigg's Case* (1865) LR 1 Eq 309; cf *Harris v North Devon Rly Co* (1855) 20 Beav 384 (enforcement of contract to forfeit on terms).
3 *Ladd's Case* [1893] 3 Ch 450.
4 *Re Agency Land and Finance Co of Australia, Bosanquet v Agency Land and Finance Co of Australia* (1903) 20 TLR 41.
5 *Dawes's Case* (1868) LR 6 Eq 232; cf *Srimati Premila Devi v Peoples Bank of Northern India Ltd* [1938] 4 All ER 337, PC.

525. Observance of conditions as to forfeiture. In the forfeiture of shares, technicalities must be strictly observed[1]. Accordingly, as against the company the shareholder may resist forfeiture on the ground that the conditions precedent to forfeiture have not been strictly complied with[2]; but, if, as a director, he has been party to any informalities in connection with the forfeiture, he is estopped from relying on them[3]. A shareholder may rely on a forfeiture as against the company, although some formalities have not been complied with[4]. Laches on the part of the shareholder may bar the right to relief, even when the forfeiture is irregular[5], but not when it is wholly void[6]. Where the articles provide that notice of forfeiture shall be given to the shareholder, a forfeiture, when once complete, is not made invalid by the fact that no notice is sent[7]. Articles may provide that, if there has been irregularity in the forfeiture, the remedy of the member after the shares are disposed of is to be in damages only[8].

1 *Srimati Premila Devi v Peoples Bank of Northern India Ltd* [1938] 4 All ER 337, PC.
2 *Johnson v Lyttle's Iron Agency* (1877) 5 ChD 687, CA (time from which interest is demanded); *Stubbs v Lister* (1841) 1 Y & C Ch Cas 81 (undervalue when forfeiture was empowered to satisfy a lien); *Garden Gully United Quartz Mining Co v McLister* (1875) 1 App Cas 39, PC; *Bottomley's Case* (1880) 16 ChD 681 (invalid call); *Van Diemen's Land Co v Cockerell* (1857) 1 CBNS 732, Ex Ch; *Re New Chile Gold Mining Co* (1890) 45 ChD 598; *Watson v Eales* (1857) 23 Beav 294 (absence of, and irregularities in, or as regards service of, any notice required); and see *Goulton v London Architectural Brick and Tile Co* [1877] WN 141; cf *Graham v Van Diemen's Land Co* (1856) 1 H & N 541, Ex Ch (notices to a bankrupt shareholder); *Kelk's Case, Pahlen's Case* (1869) LR 9 Eq 107; *Sparks v Liverpool Waterworks Co* (1807) 13 Ves 428 (absence of giving or receiving notice). See also *Parkstone Ltd v Gulf Guarantee Bank plc* [1990] BCC 534 (notice posted to member whose registered address was outside the United Kingdom was effective and consistent with the articles; personal service was not required). As to tenders to prevent forfeiture see *Re New Quebrada Co, Clarke's Case* (1873) 27 LT 843; *Sweny v Smith* (1869) LR 7 Eq 324 (where the proceeding was on behalf of the plaintiff and all other shareholders). Where the power to forfeit is only the alternative to recovering calls by action, it cannot be exercised after action begun: *Giles v Hutt* (1848) 3 Exch 18.
3 *Jones v North Vancouver Land and Improvement Co* [1910] AC 317, PC.
4 *Knight's Case* (1867) 2 Ch App 321 (non-entry of resolution in books); *Re Phosphate of Lime Co, Austin's Case* (1871) 24 LT 932 (absence or insufficiency of notice); *Lyster's Case* (1867) LR 4 Eq 233; *Re Asiatic Banking Corpn, ex p Collum* (1869) LR 9 Eq 236; *Re Home Counties and General Life Assurance Co, Woollaston's Case* (1859) 4 De G & J 437; *Moore v Rawlins* (1859) 6 CBNS 289; *Re State Fire Insurance Co, Webster's Case* (1862) 32 LJ Ch 135 (non-rectification of the register); *King's Case* (1867) 2 Ch App 714 (after illegal conversion of shares). A prospective resolution for forfeiture if a notice is not complied with may be good: *Re Home Counties and General Life Assurance Co, Woollaston's Case* supra); *Painter v Ford* [1866] WN 77; *Knight's Case* (1867) 2 Ch App 321.
5 *Rule v Jewell* (1881) 18 ChD 660; *Prendergast v Turton* (1841) 1 Y & C Ch Cas 98; cf *Garden Gully United Quartz Mining Co v McLister* (1875) 1 App Cas 39, PC. Acquiescence by the company in an invalid forfeiture arranged between the directors and the shareholder may relieve the shareholder from liability: see *Spackman v Evans* (1868) LR 3 HL 171; *Re Agriculturists' Cattle Insurance Co, Brotherhood's Case* (1862) 31 Beav 365.
6 *Bellerby v Rowland and Marwood's SS Co Ltd* [1902] 2 Ch 14, CA.

7 *Knight's Case* (1867) 2 Ch App 321; *Re Home Counties and General Life Assurance Co, Woollaston's Case* (1859) 4 De G & J 437; *Re State Fire Insurance Co, Webster's Case* (1862) 32 LJ Ch 135; *Kelk's Case, Pahlen's Case* (1869) LR 9 Eq 107 at 117.
8 *Re New Chile Gold Mining Co* (1890) 45 ChD 598.

526. Liability for calls. Articles may provide that forfeiture is not to bar the company's right to recover calls then owing[1], in which case calls made before, but payable after, a forfeiture may be recovered[2]; but the company cannot prove in the bankruptcy of a person whose shares have been forfeited and reissued for more than the difference between the amount unpaid at the date of forfeiture and the amount received from subsequent holders of the shares[3]. The validity of a forfeiture cannot be disputed in the bankruptcy, but must be tried in a separate proceeding[4]. Forfeiture does not exempt the holder of shares from liability as a past member[5].

Where the due payment of calls has been guaranteed, the company, by forfeiting the shares for non-payment, releases the surety from his liability under the guarantee[6].

1 *Stocken's Case* (1868) 3 Ch App 412. As to interest on calls see *Stocken's Case* supra; *Ladies' Dress Association v Pulbrook* [1900] 2 QB 376, CA. Without express provision, there would probably be no liability for calls: *Stocken's Case* supra at 415 per Lord Cairns LJ. As to the liability of the purchaser of forfeited shares see para 528 post.
2 *Faure Electric Accumulator Co v Phillipart* (1888) 58 LT 525; *Re China SS and Labuan Coal Co, Dawes' Case* (1869) 38 LJ Ch 512.
3 *Re Bolton, ex p North British Artificial Silk Ltd* [1930] 2 Ch 48. Formerly, interest was not recoverable unless expressly provided for: *Stocken's Case* (1868) 3 Ch App 412; *Faure Electric Accumulator Co v Phillipart* (1888) 58 LT 525. As to the power of the court to award interest in proceedings for the recovery of a debt see the Supreme Court Act 1981 s 35A (added by the Administration of Justice Act 1982 s 15(1), Sch 1 Pt 1) and MONEY vol 32 para 106 et seq.
4 *Re Andrew, ex p Rippon* (1869) 4 Ch App 639; and see *Sweny v Smith* (1869) LR 7 Eq 324.
5 *Bridger's Case and Neill's Case* (1869) 4 Ch App 266; *Creyke's Case* (1869) 5 Ch App 63.
6 *Re Darwen and Pearce* [1927] 1 Ch 176.

527. Reinstatement. Where, as is usual, the articles empower directors to annul the forfeiture, the company cannot reinstate the former holder with the liabilities of a shareholder unless he consents[1].

1 *Larkworthy's Case* [1903] 1 Ch 711.

528. Re-allotting forfeited shares. Where shares have been forfeited by the company, on re-allotting them, it may give credit for money already received in respect of them. As re-allotment is not an issue of shares, this is not contrary to the principle that shares cannot be issued at a discount[1]. Where credit for the amount already paid is given, the new allottee becomes liable for the balance remaining unpaid on the shares[2].

1 *Morrison v Trustees, Executors, and Securities Insurance Corpn* (1898) 68 LJ Ch 11, CA; *Re Exchange Banking Co Ltd, Ramwell's Case* (1881) 50 LJ Ch 827. Forfeited shares have been treated as 'unissued' on a reduction of capital, where sums had already been received in respect of the shares: *Re Oceana Development Co Ltd* (1912) 56 Sol Jo 537; *Re Victoria (Malaya) Rubber Estates Ltd* (1914) 58 Sol Jo 706.
2 *New Balkis Eersteling Ltd v Randt Gold Mining Co* [1904] AC 165 at 168, HL; and see para 425 ante. The new allottee is not entitled to vote whilst calls are payable by the original holder of the shares, when the

articles provide that no member shall have a vote so long as any calls payable are unpaid: *Randt Gold Mining Co v Wainwright* [1901] 1 Ch 184.

(14) REGULATION AND MANAGEMENT

(i) In general

A. UNDER TABLE A

529. Table A. Table A[1] contains a model set of regulations for the management of a company limited by shares[2]; and in the case of such a company, if articles are not registered with the memorandum of association or, if articles are registered, in so far as the articles do not exclude or modify the regulations in Table A, those regulations are, so far as applicable and as in force at the date of the company's registration, the articles of the company in the same manner and to the same extent as if articles in that form had been duly registered[3].

Where a company is not formed under companies legislation but is authorised to register under the Companies Act 1985 and does so register[4], the regulations in Table A do not apply unless adopted by special resolution[5].

1   The expression 'Table A' in the Companies Act 1985 means that Table as prescribed by regulations made by the Secretary of State (s 8(1)) by statutory instrument subject to annulment in pursuance of a resolution of either House of Parliament (s 8(5)). The current Table A is that prescribed by the Companies (Tables A to F) Regulations 1985, SI 1985/805 (amended by SI 1985/1052) made under the powers contained in the Companies Act 1948 s 454(2) (repealed) and continued in force under the Companies Act 1985 s 8 by virtue of the Companies Consolidation (Consequential Provisions) Act 1985 s 31(2) (see para 10 ante). As to the continued application of the earlier statutory tables of articles to companies registered under the former Companies Acts see para 9 ante. For the meaning of 'the former Companies Acts' see para 11 note 2 ante.

2   Table A consists of articles which are grouped under the following headings, namely: interpretation (art 1); share capital (arts 2, 3, 4 (amended by SI 1985/1052), art 5); share certificates (arts 6, 7); lien (arts 8–11); calls on shares and forfeiture (arts 12–22); transfer of shares (arts 23–28); transmission of shares (arts 29–31); alteration of share capital (arts 32–34); purchase of own shares (art 35); general meetings (arts 36, 37); notice of general meetings (arts 38, 39); proceedings at general meetings (arts 40, 41 (amended by SI 1985/1052), arts 42–53); votes of members (arts 54–63); number of directors (art 64); alternate directors (arts 65–69); powers of directors (arts 70, 71); delegation of directors' powers (art 72); appointment and retirement of directors (arts 73–80); disqualification and removal of directors (art 81); remuneration of directors (art 82); directors' expenses (art 83); directors' appointments and interests (arts 84–86); directors' gratuities and pensions (art 87); proceedings of directors (arts 88–98); secretary (art 99); minutes (art 100); the seal (art 101); dividends (arts 102–108); accounts (art 109); capitalisation of profits (art 110); notices (arts 111–114, art 115 (amended by SI 1985/1052), art 116); winding up (art 117); and indemnity (art 118).

3   Companies Act 1985 s 8(2). For the meaning of 'articles' see para 140 note 2 ante. An article of Table A may be excluded by implication: see *R Paterson & Sons Ltd v Paterson* [1916] WN 352, HL; cf *Fisher v Black and White Publishing Co* [1901] 1 Ch 174, CA.

4   Ie under the Companies Act 1985 ss 680–690 (as amended): see para 75 et seq ante.

5   See ibid s 689, Sch 21 para 6(2) and para 27 ante.

530. Tables C, D and E. The form of the articles of association of a company limited by guarantee and not having a share capital must be in accordance with Table C prescribed by regulations made by the Secretary of State[1], or as near to that form as circumstances admit[2].

The form of the articles of association of a company limited by guarantee and having a share capital must be in accordance with Table D as so prescribed, or as near to that form as circumstances admit[3].

The form of the articles of association of an unlimited company having a share capital must be in accordance with Table E as so prescribed, or as near to that form as circumstances admit[4].

In all cases, most of the articles in these three Tables are those contained In Table A.

1 Companies Act 1985 s 8(4). Regulations so made are by statutory instrument subject to annulment in pursuance of a resolution of either House of Parliament: s 8(5). The current Tables C, D and E are those contained in the Companies (Tables A to F) Regulations 1985, SI 1985/805, Schedule made under the powers contained in the Companies Act 1948 s 454(2) (repealed) and continued in force under the Companies Act 1985 s 8 by virtue of the Companies Consolidation (Consequential Provisions) Act 1985 s 31(2) (see para 10 ante).

2 Companies Act 1985 s 8(4)(a). With effect from 22 December 1980, a company cannot be formed as, or become, a company limited by guarantee with a share capital: s 1(4). The Companies (Tables A to F) Regulations 1985 Schedule, Table C consists of 13 articles which are grouped under the following headings, namely: preliminary (art 1); interpretation (art 2); members (arts 3, 4); notice of general meetings (art 5); proceedings at general meetings (arts 6, 7); votes of members (art 8); directors' expenses (art 9); proceedings of directors (art 10); minutes (art 11); notices (arts 12, 13).

3 Companies Act 1985 s 8(4)(b). The Companies (Tables A to F) Regulations 1985 Schedule, Table D simply provides that the regulations of Table A are to constitute the articles of association of the company.

4 Companies Act 1985 s 8(4)(c). The Companies (Tables A to F) Regulations 1985 Schedule, Table E consists of four articles.

531. Table G. The Secretary of State may by regulations prescribe a Table G containing articles of association appropriate for a partnership company, that is, a company limited by shares whose shares are intended to be held to a substantial extent by or on behalf of its employees[1].

A company limited by shares may for its articles adopt the whole or any part of that Table[2].

If, in consequence of regulations so made Table G is altered, the alteration does not affect a company registered before the alteration takes effect, or repeal as respects that company any portion of the Table[3].

1 Companies Act 1985 s 8A(1) (added by the Companies Act 1989 s 128). The Companies Act 1989 s 128 comes into force on such day as the Secretary of State may appoint by order made by statutory instrument: s 215(2). At the date at which this volume states the law no such order had been made. Such regulations must be made by statutory instrument which is subject to annulment in pursuance of a resolution of either House of Parliament: Companies Act 1985 s 8A(4) (added by the Companies Act 1989 s 128). At the date at which this volume states the law no such regulations had been made.

2 Companies Act 1985 s 8A(2) (added by the Companies Act 1989 s 128). See also note 1 supra.

3 Companies Act 1985 s 8A(3) (added by the Companies Act 1989 s 128). See also note 1 supra.

532. Statutory authority of Table A. The Table A current from time to time has statutory authority, and provisions contained in it, or copied from it into special articles, are valid although not otherwise authorised by the provisions of the Act which gives it its status[1]; and its contents may be considered for the purpose of ascertaining the intentions of the legislature in that Act[2].

1 Ie the Companies Act 1985 s 8(1) ('Table A is as prescribed by regulations made by the Secretary of State'). See *Lock v Queensland Investment and Land Mortgage Co* [1896] AC 461, HL; *New Balkis Eersteling*

Ltd v Randt Gold Mining Co [1904] AC 165 at 167, HL per Lord Davey. See also *Trevor v Whitworth* (1887) 12 App Cas 409, HL.

2 *Re Barned's Banking Co, ex p Contract Corpn* (1867) 3 Ch App 105 at 113, 114 per Lord Cairns LJ; *Re Pyle Works* (1890) 44 ChD 534 at 571, CA.

533. Power to alter Table A. The Secretary of State may by regulations made by statutory instrument alter Table A[1]. Such a statutory instrument is, however, subject to annulment in pursuance of a resolution of either House of Parliament[2]. If, in consequence of regulations so made Table A is altered, the alteration does not affect a company registered before the alteration takes effect, or repeal as respects that company any portion of the Table[3].

1 Companies Act 1985 s 8(1), (5).
2 Ibid s 8(5).
3 Ibid s 8(3). As to the alteration of Table A under earlier enactments see para 9 ante.

B. UNDER SPECIAL ARTICLES

534. Special articles of association. Articles must in the case of a company limited by guarantee or unlimited, and may in the case of a company limited by shares, be registered with the memorandum of association, and any company may adopt all or any of the regulations contained in Table A[1].

In the case of an unlimited company having a share capital, the articles must state the amount of share capital with which the company proposes to be registered[2].

The adoption of Table A is unusual in the case of large companies, and such companies as a rule register special articles which contain many of the provisions of Table A supplemented by other provisions which are required to meet the particular circumstances of the company or are shown by experience to be useful or more convenient than the corresponding provisions of Table A[3].

1 Companies Act 1985 ss 7(1), 8(1). For the meaning of 'articles' see para 140 note 2 ante. As to the printing, division into paragraphs, stamping, signature, and registration of the articles see para 87 ante; and as to the supply of copies to members see para 101 ante. Where a company is limited by guarantee, or unlimited, having a share capital, the statutory forms adopt Table A, with the exclusion or modification if the company is limited by guarantee without a share capital or unlimited with a share capital of certain inapplicable articles: see para 529 ante.
2 Companies Act 1985 s 7(2).
3 Where the articles of a company adopt part of the then current Table A and supplement it by special articles, the Interpretation Act 1978 s 6, Sch 2 para 2 (see STATUTES vol 44(1) (Reissue) para 1388), which applies to the interpretation of the statutory articles adopted, also applies to the special articles used thereunder: *Fell v Derby Leather Co Ltd* [1931] 2 Ch 252; *Jarvis Motors (Harrow) Ltd v Carabott* [1964] 3 All ER 89, [1964] 1 WLR 1101 ('members' in pre-emption provisions read as including a member). As to the validity of articles which contain provisions similar to those contained in Table A see para 215 note 2 ante.

535. Contents. The contents of the articles depend to a great extent on the sort of company to which they apply, and many powers of the company are by statute required to be taken, if at all, by the articles as distinct from the memorandum of association. Examples include powers to increase or reduce capital, or to consolidate shares into shares of larger amount, or to issue redeemable preference shares[1].

1 See paras 181, 201, 205, 241 ante.

536. Requirements for Stock Exchange listing. If a company is to obtain admission to the Official List of the Stock Exchange, its articles of association must comply with the requirements of the Listing Rules[1]. If the articles comply with those requirements and have no unusual features, they do not need to be approved by the Stock Exchange but must be duly lodged[2].

1 *Listing Rules* r 13.8. Rule 13.8, Appendix 1 sets out the matters which must be provided for in the articles of association of a listed company: capital structure (para 1); non-voting shares (para 2); restricted voting shares (para 3); preference shares (para 4); transfer and registration (para 5); restriction on transfer (paras 6, 7); joint shareholders (para 8); the register (para 9); definitive certificates (para 10); bearer warrants (para 11); proxy forms (para 12); sanctions (para 13); untraceable members (paras 14, 15); dividends (para 16); forfeiture (para 17); notices (paras 18, 19); directors (para 20); casual vacancies (para 21); election of directors (para 22). Where the company is not subject to the Companies Act 1985, the *Listing Rules* Appendix 1 sets out the additional provisions which must be contained in the articles: variation of class rights (para 23(a)); class meetings (para 23(b)); redeemable shares (para 23(c)); removal of directors (para 23(d)). As to amendments to articles see r 13.9; and as to the *Listing Rules* generally see para 282 ante.
2 Ibid r 13.1(a). As to the lodging of documents with the Stock Exchange see r 13.2.

537. Invalid articles. Articles are not valid if they purport to restrict the rights of members as conferred by statute or to contravene the provisions of an Act of Parliament[1]. Although, if contemporaneous with the memorandum, articles may explain ambiguities in the memorandum, they cannot alter or extend it. Thus, a power to borrow contained in the memorandum cannot be enlarged by the articles into a power to issue irredeemable debenture stock[2]; and, if the memorandum defines the rights of the respective classes of shareholders, these cannot be altered by the articles[3]. The importance of this doctrine against the alteration of the memorandum by the articles has, however, been diminished by the statutory power to alter conditions which could have been contained in articles of association[4].

1 Eg an article restricting the right to alter the articles (*Malleson v National Insurance and Guarantee Corpn* [1894] 1 Ch 200; *Walker v London Tramways Co* (1879) 12 ChD 705; *Ayre v Skelsey's Adamant Cement Co Ltd* (1904) 20 TLR 587 (affd (1905) 21 TLR 464, CA)); excluding the power of the members to wind up voluntarily (see para 2698 post); restricting an individual shareholder's right to petition for the winding up of the company (*Re Peveril Gold Mines Ltd* [1898] 1 Ch 122, CA); or to take advantage of the Insolvency Act 1986 s 111 (see para 1480 et seq post) as a dissentient shareholder (*Baring-Gould v Sharpington Combined Pick and Shovel Syndicate* [1899] 2 Ch 80, CA; *Payne v Cork Co Ltd* [1900] 1 Ch 308; approved in *Bisgood v Henderson's Transvaal Estates Ltd* [1908] 1 Ch 743, CA; and see *Re Canning Jarrah Timber Co (Western Australia) Ltd* [1900] 1 Ch 708, CA); or to retain his properly-acquired shares (*Re Walker and Hacking Ltd* (1887) 57 LT 763); or to have full information about the reserve fund and other accounts (*Newton v Birmingham Small Arms Co Ltd* [1906] 2 Ch 378; but see further as to that case *Young v Brownlee & Co Ltd* 1911 SC 677 and para 729 note 5 post).
2 *Re Southern Brazilian Rio Grande do Sul Rly Co Ltd* [1905] 2 Ch 78.
3 *Ashbury v Watson* (1885) 30 ChD 376, CA; and see *Collins v Birmingham Breweries Ltd* (1899) 15 TLR 180, CA. The memorandum may itself provide for alterations. As to altering the memorandum generally see para 1184 post.
4 See paras 541, 542 post.

C. ALTERATION OF ARTICLES

538. How effected. A company may by special resolution[1] alter its articles[2], subject to the provisions of the Companies Act 1985 and any special conditions contained in its memorandum[3]; and any alterations so made are, subject to such provisions, as valid as if originally contained in the articles, and are subject in like manner to alteration by special resolution[4]. In the case of an unlimited company formed and registered under the Joint Stock Companies Acts[5], this power of altering the articles extends to altering any regulations relating to the amount of capital or to its distribution into shares, notwithstanding that those regulations are contained in the memorandum[6].

Such power of alteration, which is statutory, cannot be modified by the articles[7]. Nor can a company contract itself out of the power to alter its articles[8], even by the express terms of the articles[9]. The conferring of special voting rights on a particular class of shares, which would in effect make it impossible to alter the articles without the consent of a particular person, would not, however, be a provision depriving the company of the power to alter the series; it is otherwise if the provisions were merely that no alteration should be made without the consent of a particular person[10].

Directors cannot by resolution alter the articles[11]; but the words 'articles of association' as used in a contract may refer to provisions put forward by the company as its articles even if they have not been validly adopted[12].

1 As to special resolutions see para 683 post.
2 If an order of the court is in force requiring the company not to make any, or any specified, alteration in its articles (see para 1185 post), the leave of the court will be required to make an alteration in breach of that requirement: see the Companies Act 1985 s 5(6) and para 1185 post.
3 Ibid s 9(1). As to necessary alterations to the articles when a limited company re-registers as unlimited see para 125 ante.
4 Ibid s 9(2).
5 For the meaning of 'the Joint Stock Companies Acts' see para 11 note 2 ante.
6 Companies Act 1985 s 678(2).
7 *Ayre v Skelsey's Adamant Cement Co Ltd* (1904) 20 TLR 587; affd (1905) 21 TLR 464, CA.
8 *Malleson v National Insurance and Guarantee Corpn* [1894] 1 Ch 200; *Andrews v Gas Meter Co* [1897] 1 Ch 361, CA; and see para 540 text to note 6 post.
9 *Walker v London Tramways Co* (1879) 12 ChD 705. As to notification of alteration of articles see the Companies Act 1985 s 42(1)(b) and paras 71, 99 et seq ante.
10 *Bushell v Faith* [1970] AC 1099, [1970] 1 All ER 53, HL.
11 *De Ruvigne's Case* (1877) 5 ChD 306, CA.
12 *Muirhead v Forth and North Sea Steamboat Mutual Insurance Association* [1894] AC 72, HL; cf *Re Miller's Dale and Ashwood Dale Lime Co* (1885) 31 ChD 211, CA. Articles irregularly adopted may be treated as adopted by the company, if acted upon, amended and added to by the shareholders for many years without objection: *Ho Tung v Man On Insurance Co Ltd* [1902] AC 232, PC.

539. Rectification of mistake. A mistake in the articles may be rectified only by altering the articles by special resolution pursuant to the Companies Act 1985; the court will not rectify the mistake in an action[1]. A special resolution altering the articles may be followed immediately at the same meeting by a resolution operating under the articles as so altered[2]. Where, as in cases of reduction of capital[3], the Companies Act 1985 requires the articles to give the necessary power, the resolution purporting to exercise the power is of no avail unless the power is already in the articles or has been added by special resolution[4].

1 *Evans v Chapman* (1902) 86 LT 381; *Scott v Frank F Scott (London) Ltd* [1940] Ch 794, [1940] 3 All ER 508, CA.
2 Cf *Re Imperial Hydropathic Hotel Co, Blackpool v Hampson* (1882) 23 ChD 1, CA (decided on its own special facts); *Re Patent Invert Sugar Co* (1885) 31 ChD 166, CA (decided at a time when it was necessary that a special resolution should be passed and confirmed, and it was held that, until a special resolution altering the articles to empower the company to reduce its capital had been passed and confirmed, a special resolution for its reduction could not be proposed; but a special resolution need not now be confirmed).
3 See para 241 ante.
4 *James v Buena Ventura Nitrate Grounds Syndicate Ltd* [1896] 1 Ch 456 at 463, CA per Lord Herschell; *Harben v Phillips* (1883) 23 ChD 14, CA; *Boschoek Proprietary Co Ltd v Fuke* [1906] 1 Ch 148 at 163 per

Swinfen Eady J. This is not the case if the passing of the special resolution completes the transaction as far as is necessary for the company to act, the directors being able to do the rest under their general powers, as, for example, prior to the Companies Act 1929, to issue new capital (*Campbell's Case* (1873) 9 Ch App 1 at 7, 22 per Lord Selborne LC; followed in *Taylor v Pilsen Joel and General Electric Light Co* (1884) 27 ChD 268); or if sanction is given to what the company already has power to do (*Campbell's Case* (1873) 9 Ch App 1 at 22, 23 per Lord Selborne LC; *James v Buena Ventura Nitrate Grounds Syndicate Ltd* [1896] 1 Ch 456, CA). Cf *Re Metropolitan Cemetery Co* 1934 SC 65; and see para 201 note 10 ante. See further para 251 ante.

540. How far articles may be altered. Only such alterations are valid as would have been valid if originally contained in the articles[1]. Any alteration must be made in good faith for the benefit of the company as a whole[2], that is of the corporators as a general body[3]. Subject to this, articles may be freely altered. It is for the shareholders and not the court to determine whether or not the alteration is for the benefit of the company; and the court will not readily interfere with an alteration made in good faith unless it is of such a character that no reasonable person could have regarded it as made for the benefit of the company[4]. The alteration may affect the rights of a member as between himself and the company by retrospective operation, since the shares are held subject to the statutory power of altering the articles[5].

If a contract whether with a member or an outsider is so drawn as by its terms or implication to prohibit the company from altering its articles to the prejudice of the other contracting party, then, although the company cannot be precluded from altering its articles, thereby giving itself power to act upon the provisions of the altered articles, so to act may nevertheless be a breach of the contract[6].

The articles cannot be so altered as to increase the liability of a member to contribute to share capital or otherwise to pay money to the company without his consent[7]; and a special resolution altering articles may be impeached if its effect is to discriminate between the majority of shareholders and the minority shareholders so as to give the former an advantage of which the latter are deprived[8]. In a case where an order by the court by way of protection of a member of the company against unfair prejudice[9] requires the company not to make any, or any specified, alteration in its articles, the company has no power without leave of the court to make any such alteration[10].

1 Companies Act 1985 s 9(2). As to special resolutions see para 683 post.
2 *Allen v Gold Reefs of West Africa Ltd* [1901] 1 Ch 656 at 671, CA per Lindley MR; as explained by *Sidebottom v Kershaw, Leese & Co* [1920] 1 Ch 154, CA; and *Shuttleworth v Cox Bros & Co (Maidenhead) Ltd* [1927] 2 KB 9, CA; *Greenhalgh v Arderne Cinemas Ltd* [1951] Ch 286 at 291, [1950] 2 All ER 1120 at 1126, CA per Sir Raymond Evershed MR; cf *Brown v British Abrasive Wheel Co* [1919] 1 Ch 290; and *Dafen Tinplate Co v Llanelly Steel Co (1907) Ltd* [1920] 2 Ch 124. The court will not allow the majority of the shareholders to benefit qua shareholders at the expense of a minority: see para 1111 post. It is for the benefit of a company to alter articles for the purpose of clarifying the rights of the various classes of shareholders: *Caledonian Insurance Co v Scottish-American Investment Co Ltd* 1951 SLT 23; *Edinburgh Railway Access and Property Co v Scottish Metropolitan Assurance Co* 1932 SC 2 at 9.
3 *Greenhalgh v Arderne Cinemas Ltd* [1951] Ch 286 at 291, [1950] 2 All ER 1120 at 1126, CA per Sir Raymond Evershed MR.
4 *Shuttleworth v Cox Bros & Co (Maidenhead) Ltd* [1927] 2 KB 9, CA; disapproving dicta in *Dafen Tinplate Co v Llanelly Steel Co (1907) Ltd* [1920] 2 Ch 124.
5 *Allen v Gold Reefs of West Africa Ltd* [1900] 1 Ch 656, CA (where the fully-paid shares affected by the extension to them of the company's lien in respect of an existing debt were vendor's shares known by the company to be held by the shareholder as nominee for the vendor, and the alteration was intended to affect only this individual shareholder); and see *Last v Buller & Co Ltd* (1919) 36 TLR 35. Preference shares may be issued without a power in the memorandum: *Andrews v Gas Meter Co* [1897] 1 Ch 361, CA; cf *Pepe v City and Suburban Permanent Building Society* [1893] 2 Ch 311; *Botten v City and Suburban Permanent Building Society* [1895] 2 Ch 441; *James v Buena Ventura Nitrate Grounds Syndicate Ltd* [1896] 1 Ch 456, CA; *Swabey v Port Darwin Gold Mining Co* (1889) 1 Meg 385, CA. In *W and A M'Arthur Ltd*

(Liquidator) v Gulf Line Ltd 1909 SC 732, it was held that the rights of a transferee could not be prejudiced by an alteration in the articles made after the lodgment of the transfer, following the ratio decidendi in *Re Cawley & Co* (1889) 42 ChD 209 at 227, CA.

6 See *Southern Foundries (1926) Ltd v Shirlaw* [1940] AC 701 at 740, [1940] 2 All ER 445 at 469, HL per Lord Porter; *Re T N Farrer Ltd* [1937] Ch 352 at 356 per Simonds J; *Allen v Gold Reefs of West Africa Ltd* [1900] 1 Ch 656 at 673, 676; *Griffith v Paget* (1877) 5 ChD 894 (where the company had paid for property by preference shares and attempted to issue pre-preference shares). In *British Murac Syndicate Ltd v Alperton Rubber Co Ltd* [1915] 2 Ch 186, an injunction was granted to restrain an alteration of articles which would have involved a breach of contract. This was directly opposed to the decision in *Punt v Symons & Co Ltd* [1903] 2 Ch 506 (which was treated therein as being overruled by *Baily v British Equitable Assurance Co* [1904] 1 Ch 374, CA; revsd on other grounds sub nom *British Equitable Assurance Co Ltd v Baily* [1906] AC 35, HL), where it was held that a company could not contract itself out of its statutory powers of altering its articles as against an outside contractor (see *Re Barrow Haematite Steel Co* (1888) 39 ChD 582). *Punt v Symons & Co Ltd* supra was not, however, cited in the judgment in *Baily v British Equitable Assurance Co* [1904] 1 Ch 374, which seems only to restate the position that a company cannot justify a breach of contract by such alteration. It is implicit in both the majority and minority opinions in *Southern Foundries (1926) Ltd v Shirlaw* supra that *Punt v Symons & Co Ltd* supra was correct (see [1940] AC 701 at 713, 717, 722, 731, 739, 740, [1940] 2 All ER 445 at 452, 454, 458, 464, 468, 469), and that *British Murac Syndicate Ltd v Alperton Rubber Co Ltd* supra was wrongly decided (see [1940] AC 701 at 740, [1940] 2 All ER 445 at 469 per Lord Porter). Cf *Shuttleworth v Cox Bros & Co (Maidenhead) Ltd* [1927] 2 KB 9, CA.

7 See the Companies Act 1985 s 16(1)(b) and para 415 ante.

8 *Greenhalgh v Arderne Cinemas Ltd* [1951] Ch 286 at 291, [1950] 2 All ER 1120 at 1126, CA per Sir Raymond Evershed MR.

9 See para 1405 et seq post.

10 See the Companies Act 1985 s 461(3) and para 1414 post.

D. ALTERATION OF CONDITIONS OF MEMORANDUM WHICH COULD HAVE BEEN CONTAINED IN ARTICLES

541. Power of alteration. Subject to the statutory restriction on any alteration of the memorandum or articles increasing a member's liability to contribute additional share capital without his consent[1], and the statutory provisions relating to the protection of members against unfair prejudice[2], a condition contained in a company's memorandum which could lawfully have been contained in articles of association instead of the memorandum[3] may be altered by the company by special resolution[4]. If, however, an application[5] is made to the court for the alteration to be cancelled, it will not have effect except in so far as it is confirmed by the court[6].

The power does not apply where the memorandum itself provides for or prohibits the alteration of all or any of the conditions, nor does it authorise any variation or abrogation of the special rights of any class of members[7].

1 Ie the Companies Act 1985 s 16: see para 415 ante.

2 Ie ibid Pt XVII (ss 459–461) (as amended): see para 1405 et seq post.

3 As to the matters which must be contained in the memorandum see paras 84, 102 et seq ante.

4 Companies Act 1985 s 17(1), (2)(a). This power of alteration does not prevent any alteration of special rights under any other section eg s 425 (as amended) (see para 1447 et seq post): see *City Property Investment Trust Corpn Ltd, Petitioners* 1951 SC 570. If a company has a memorandum designating that which might otherwise be considered as a power as an object, it cannot rely upon this power of alteration: *Re Hampstead Garden Suburb Trust Ltd* [1962] Ch 806 at 825, [1962] 2 All ER 879 at 889. Regulations relating to the amount of capital for its distribution into shares contained in the memorandum of an unlimited company formed and registered under the Joint Stock Companies Acts may be altered in the same way as articles: see para 538 ante.

5 Ie an application by petition under RSC Ord 102 r 4(1)(b).

6 Companies Act 1985 s 17(1).

7 Ibid s 17(2)(b). As to the notification of alterations to a memorandum see s 42(1)(b) and paras 71, 100 et seq ante.

542. Application to cancel alteration. An application[1] to the court for the variation to be cancelled is governed by substantially the same provisions as in the case of an application for the cancellation of a variation of the objects of the company[2].

1 Ie an application by petition under RSC Ord 102 r 4(1)(b).
2 The provisions of the Companies Act 1985 s 5 (except s 5(2)(b), (8)) and s 6(1)–(3) apply to any alteration and application made under s 17 as they apply in relation to alterations and applications under ss 4–6 (as amended) (see paras 1184–1187 post): s 17(3).

(ii) Directors

A. APPOINTMENT

543. Requirement of directors. The affairs of a company are conducted by directors, either under that or some other name[1], such as 'trustees', 'members of the council', or 'governors', and every company must have at least one[2]. In the case of a company registered before 1 November 1929, it is not necessary to have more than one director[3]; but every company, other than a private company[4], registered on or after that date must have at least two directors[5]. Every private company, whenever registered, must have at least one director[6]. In cases where a company may have only one director, a limited company may be appointed to perform the duties and exercise the powers usually performed and exercised by individuals appointed as directors[7].

1 In the Companies Act 1985 'director' includes any person occupying the position of director, by whatever name called: s 741(1). In relation to a company, 'shadow director' means a person in accordance with whose directions or instructions the directors are accustomed to act: s 741(2). However, a person is not deemed a shadow director by reason only that the directors act on advice given by him in a professional capacity: s 741(2). For the purposes of s 309 (see para 582 post), s 319 (see para 563 post), ss 320–322 (as amended) (see paras 611, 612 post), s 322B (as added) (see para 597 post) and ss 330–346 (as amended) (see paras 598–607 post), being provisions under which shadow directors are treated as directors, a body corporate is not to be treated as a shadow director of any of its subsidiary companies by reason only that the directors of the subsidiary are accustomed to act in accordance with its directions or instructions: s 741(3) (amended by the Companies (Single Member Private Limited Companies) Regulations 1992, SI 1992/1699, reg 2(1)(b), Schedule para 3(2)). For the meaning of 'body corporate' see para 89 note 8 ante; and for the meaning of 'subsidiary' see para 827 post. As to the restrictions on classes of persons acting as directors see para 551 et seq post.
2 Companies Act 1985 s 282(1), (2). A company which has obtained admission to the Official List of the Stock Exchange must notify the Company Announcements Office without delay when a new director is appointed, the resignation or removal of a director takes effect or any important change in the functions of executive responsibilities of a director occurs: *Listing Rules* r 16.7. The notification so required must state the effective date of the change and, in the case of an appointment, whether the position is executive or non-executive and the nature of any specific function or responsibility: r 16.8. As to the *Listing Rules* generally see para 282 ante.
3 Companies Act 1985 s 282(2).
4 For the meaning of 'private company' see para 82 ante.
5 Companies Act 1985 s 282(1).
6 Ibid s 282(3).
7 *Re Bulawayo Market and Offices Co Ltd* [1907] 2 Ch 458; and see *Bank of Ireland v Cogry Spinning Co* [1900] 1 IR 219.

544. Appointment of first directors. The first directors of the company are those named in the statement which has to be delivered on the formation of the company, signed by or on behalf of the subscribers of the memorandum and containing a consent signed by each of the persons so named as directors to act in that capacity[1]. The first directors are often also named in the articles, which usually prescribe a maximum and minimum number of directors[2] but such an appointment is void, unless they are named as directors in the statement[3].

If for any reason, for example death, the persons so named do not assume office, it will be necessary for the subscribers of the memorandum (who will then be the only members) to convene a meeting for the appointment of directors. To the extent to which the articles do not make other provision in that behalf, two or more subscribers holding not less than one-tenth of the issued share capital, or, if the company does not have a share capital, not less than 5% in number of the members of the company may call the meeting[4]. Notice of the meeting must be served on every subscriber in the manner in which notices are required to be served by Table A as for the time being in force[5].

A meeting is not necessary if all the subscribers concur in the appointment[6].

1   See the Companies Act 1985 s 10(3) and para 88 ante.
2   The number may be fixed or left to be determined by the directors or shareholders. Under the Companies (Tables A to F) Regulations 1985, SI 1985/805, Schedule, Table A art 64, unless otherwise determined by ordinary resolution, the number of directors (other than alternate directors) is not subject to any maximum but must not be less than two. As to Table A generally see para 529 et seq ante.
3   See the Companies Act 1985 s 10(5) and para 88 ante.
4   See ibid s 370(3) and para 660 post.
5   See ibid s 370(2) and para 660 post.
6   *Re Great Northern Salt and Chemical Works, ex p Kennedy* (1890) 44 ChD 472.

545. Defect in appointment. If proper minutes of the company's meetings have been kept, then until the contrary is proved, all appointments of directors or managers are deemed to be valid[1]. Their acts are valid notwithstanding any defects[2] that may afterwards be discovered[3] in their appointment or qualification[4]. This presumption as to validity applies only to cases where there has been an appointment, albeit an invalid one[5]; it has no application to cases where in fact there has never been any appointment or where there has been a fraudulent usurpation of authority[6].

An article validating the acts of persons acting as directors, though it is afterwards discovered that there was a defect in their appointment or qualification[7], operates not only as between the company and outsiders, but also as between the company and its members[8], as where, for example, de facto directors make a call[9], summon meetings of the company[10], elect other directors[11], or allot shares[12]. A de facto director may be ordered to furnish a statement of affairs in a winding up[13]. Directors cannot take advantage of any informality in company proceedings in which they have themselves participated; they are estopped as between themselves and the company[14]; they are also estopped from saying they have been improperly appointed, if they have acted after their appointment[15]. Persons dealing with them who know of the invalidity are likewise estopped[16].

1   Companies Act 1985 s 382(4); and see para 694 post. A subsequent meeting may effectually ratify and confirm the acts of an irregularly constituted meeting (*Re Portuguese Consolidated Copper Mines Ltd, ex p Badman, ex p Bosanquet* (1890) 45 ChD 16, CA); but a person having notice that there is an irregularity or invalidity cannot avail himself of this provision (*Re Staffordshire Gas and Coke Co, ex p Nicholson* (1892) 66 LT 413; *Re Bridport Old Brewery Co* (1867) 2 Ch App 191; *Woolf v East Nigel Gold Mining Co Ltd* (1905) 21 TLR 660). A director need not be appointed at the company's office: *Smith v Paringa Mines Ltd* [1906] 2 Ch 193; cf *Barron v Potter* [1914] 1 Ch 895. An injunction may be obtained to restrain improperly appointed directors from acting: *Cheshire v Gordon Hotels* (1953) Times, 13 February.
2   Ie including the fact that the resolution to appoint is void pursuant to the Companies Act 1985 s 292(2) (appointments to be voted on individually: see para 546 post).

3 A defect that the person appointed had no share qualification was held to have been 'afterwards discovered' in *Albert Gardens (Manly) Pty Ltd v Mercantile Credits Ltd* (1973) 9 ALR 653 (Aust HC).

4 Companies Act 1985 s 285. Their liabilities are also as great as if they had been properly appointed: *Western Bank of Scotland v Bairds' Trustees* (1872) 11 M 96; and see *Briton Medical, General, and Life Association v Jones (2)* (1889) 61 LT 384; *Coventry and Dixon's Case* (1880) 14 ChD 660, CA; *Re Western Counties Steam Bakeries and Milling Co* [1897] 1 Ch 617, CA. A company which has put forward a resolution as being validly passed cannot, at any rate after lapse of considerable time, repudiate it as invalid: *Montreal and St Lawrence Light and Power Co v Robert* [1906] AC 196, PC.

5 *Albert Gardens (Manly) Pty Ltd v Mercantile Credits Ltd* (1973) 9 ALR 653 (Aust HC). If the holding of a share qualification is required, this is not a condition of the power of appointment. If it is not complied with, there will still be an appointment, although it will be defective.

6 *Morris v Kanssen* [1946] AC 459, [1946] 1 All ER 586, HL; *Tyne Mutual Steamship Insurance Association v Brown* (1896) 74 LT 283 at 285. A person acting as director but not in fact duly appointed to that office is not liable under a penal enactment as a director of the company: *Dean v Hiesler* [1942] 2 All ER 340, DC.

7 Under the Companies (Tables A to F) Regulations 1985, SI 1985/805, Schedule, Table A art 92 all acts done by any meeting of the directors or of a committee of directors, or by any person acting as a director, are, notwithstanding that it is afterwards discovered that there was a defect in the appointment of any such director, or that any of them were disqualified from holding office, or had vacated office, or were not entitled to vote, as valid as if every such person had been duly appointed and was qualified and had continued to be a director and had been entitled to vote. The words as to subsequent discovery of a defect mean a discovery that there is a defect, not a discovery of the facts which cause the defect: *British Asbestos Co Ltd v Boyd* [1903] 2 Ch 439 at 444; *Channel Collieries Trust Ltd v Dover, St Margaret's and Martin Mill Light Rly Co* [1914] 2 Ch 506, CA; *Albert Gardens (Manly) Pty Ltd v Mercantile Credit Ltd* (1973) 9 ALR 653 (Aust HC). As to the limitations upon the effectiveness of this article see also *Morris v Kanssen* [1946] AC 459, [1946] 1 All ER 586, HL. As to Table A generally see para 529 et seq ante.

8 *Dawson v African Consolidated Land and Trading Co* [1898] 1 Ch 6, CA, doubting *Howbeach Coal Co Ltd v Teague* (1860) 6 H & N 151; and see *Channel Collieries Trust Ltd v Dover, St Margaret's and Martin Mill Light Rly Co* [1914] 2 Ch 506, CA, following *Dawson v African Consolidated Land and Trading Co* supra.

9 *Dawson v African Consolidated Land and Trading Co* [1898] 1 Ch 6, CA; *Briton Medical, General, and Life Association v Jones (2)* (1889) 61 LT 384. As to calls see para 416 et seq ante.

10 *Southern Counties Deposit Bank v Rider and Kirkwood* (1895) 73 LT 374, CA. As to summoning of meetings see para 660 et seq post.

11 *British Asbestos Co Ltd v Boyd* [1903] 2 Ch 439; and see *Transport Ltd v Schonberg* (1905) 21 TLR 305.

12 *Channel Collieries Trust Ltd v Dover, St Margaret's and Martin Mill Light Rly Co* [1914] 2 Ch 506, CA; *Ellett v Sternberg* (1910) 27 TLR 127. As to allotment of shares see para 442 et seq ante.

13 *Re New Par Consols (No 1)* [1898] 1 QB 573. As to the criminal liability of de facto officers see para 354 et seq ante.

14 *Faure Electric Accumulator Co v Phillipart* (1888) 58 LT 525; *Murray v Bush* (1873) LR 6 HL 37; *Bank of Hindustan, China and Japan Ltd v Alison* (1871) LR 6 CP 222; cf *Re Miller's Dale and Ashwood Dale Lime Co* (1885) 31 ChD 211, CA; *Morris v Kanssen* [1946] AC 459, [1946] 1 All ER 586, HL.

15 *Tyne Mutual Steamship Insurance Association v Brown* (1896) 74 LT 283; *York Tramways Co v Willows* (1882) 8 QBD 685, CA, following *Harward's Case* (1871) LR 13 Eq 30, and *Fowler's Case* (1872) LR 14 Eq 316, and dissenting on this point from *Howbeach Coal Co Ltd v Teague* (1860) 5 H & N 151.

16 It is not sufficient to establish that they knew of the facts giving rise to the defect; it is necessary in addition to prove that they were aware that these facts gave rise to an invalidity: *Channel Collieries Trust Ltd v Dover, St Margaret's and Martin Mill Light Rly Co* [1914] 2 Ch 506 at 512, CA; *A M Spicer & Son Pty Ltd* (1931) 47 CLR 151 at 176 per Starke J (with whom Evatt J concurred) (Aust HC); *Albert Gardens (Manly) Pty Ltd v Mercantile Credits Ltd* (1973) 9 ALR 653 at 659 (Aust HC) per Gibbs J. See further paras 1137-1139 post.

546. Procedure for appointment. The power to appoint directors, other than first directors or directors to fill casual vacancies[1], is usually exercisable only by shareholders in general meeting[2]; and it is not competent for the directors to enter into contracts restricting the right of the company to appoint its own directors[3].

No motion for the appointment of two or more persons as directors of a public company by a single resolution may be made at a general meeting unless a resolution that it shall be so made has first been agreed to by the meeting without any vote being given against it[4]. For the purposes of this restriction, a motion to approve a person's appointment, or to nominate a person for appointment, is to be treated as a motion for his appointment[5]. A resolution moved in contravention of this restriction is void, whether or not it was objected to at the time[6], although the acts of any directors so appointed will be valid[7]. Further, if any such invalid resolution is moved and passed, no provision for the automatic reappointment of retiring directors in default of another appointment[8] will apply[9].

Sometimes provision is made for an outside body, for example debenture holders, to appoint a director; under such a provision the court will not enforce the appointment of a person who is objectionable to the company[10].

The company is not entitled to rely against other persons on any change among the company's directors if the change has not been officially notified at the material time and is not shown by the company to have been known at that time to the person concerned, or if the material time fell on or before the fifteenth day after the date of official notification or, where the fifteenth day was a non-business day, on or before the next day that was not, and it is shown that the person concerned was unavoidably prevented from knowing of the event at that time[11].

1 Ie vacancies occurring otherwise than by retirement in rotation: *Munster v Cammell Co* (1882) 21 ChD 183 at 187. As to appointment of first directors see para 544 ante.
2 See the Companies (Tables A to F) Regulations 1985, SI 1985/805, Schedule, Table A art 78. Article 75 provides that, if the company, at the meeting at which a director retires by rotation, does not fill the vacancy, the retiring director will, if willing to act, be deemed to have been reappointed unless at the meeting it is resolved not to fill the vacancy or unless a resolution for the reappointment of the director is put to the meeting and lost. Article 80 provides that a director who retires at an annual general meeting may, if willing to act, be reappointed. If he is not reappointed, he will remain in office until the meeting appoints someone in his place, or, if it does not do so, until the end of the meeting. Article 76 provides that no person other than a director retiring by rotation may be appointed or reappointed a director at any general meeting unless (1) he is recommended by the directors; or (2) not less than 14 nor more than 35 clear days before the date appointed for the meeting, notice executed by a member qualified to vote at the meeting has been given to the company of the intention to propose that person for appointment or reappointment stating the particulars which would, if he were so appointed or reappointed, be required to be included in the company's register of directors (see para 560 post) together with notice executed by that person of his willingness to be appointed or reappointed (see *Transport Ltd v Schonberg* (1905) 21 TLR 305). In such a case it was held that the date of the adjourned meeting, and not of the meeting at which it was proposed that he should be elected, was the date of election where he was not in fact elected until the adjourned meeting: *Catesby v Burnett* [1916] 2 Ch 325. Statutory provision is now made to like effect with respect to the date of resolutions at adjourned meetings: see the Companies Act 1985 s 381 and para 669 post. As to Table A generally see para 529 et seq ante.
3 *James v Eve* (1873) LR 6 HL 335; cf *Stace and Worth's Case* (1869) 4 Ch App 682.
4 Companies Act 1985 s 292(1).
5 Ibid s 292(3).
6 Ibid s 292(2).
7 See ibid s 285 and para 545 ante.
8 See para 634 note 5 post.
9 Companies Act 1985 s 292(2). Nothing in s 292 applies to a resolution altering the company's articles: s 292(4). The precise effect of this saving is, however, obscure.
10 *British Murac Syndicate Ltd v Alperton Rubber Co Ltd* [1915] 2 Ch 186; cf *Plantations Trust v Bila (Sumatra) Rubber Lands Ltd* (1916) 85 LJ Ch 801 (where the power was one of nomination and not appointment, and the court would not force the company to appoint the person nominated).
11 See the Companies Act 1985 s 42(1)(c) and para 71 ante.

547. Casual vacancies. The power to fill vacancies is usually vested in the continuing directors, with a proviso that the director so appointed is to hold office only during the natural term of office of the retiring director or until the next annual general meeting of the company[1]. If any such vacancy is not filled before a general meeting, it may be filled then, and if not, the power of filling the casual vacancy remains in the continuing directors[2]. If a qualified person must be appointed, he must hold the qualification shares at the time of appointment and cannot rely upon obtaining them within the two-month period allowed for directors[3].

1 See the Companies (Tables A to F) Regulations 1985, SI 1985/805, Schedule, Table A art 79. Where the articles provide that only qualified persons, ie persons with the requisite share qualification, may be appointed, a person is not qualified until he is registered as the holder of the necessary number of shares: *Channel Collieries Trust Ltd v Dover, St Margaret's and Martin Mill Light Rly Co* [1914] 2 Ch 506, CA; *Spencer v Kennedy* [1926] Ch 125; *Pollock v Garrett* 1957 SLT (Notes) 8. As to Table A generally see para 529 et seq ante.

2 *Munster v Cammell Co* (1882) 21 ChD 183 at 187; *Bennett Bros (Birmingham) v Lewis* (1903) 20 TLR 1, CA (where it was held that the power of filling a vacancy remaining to the continuing directors after a general meeting prevented the operation of an article providing that the number of directors was not to be less than a fixed number unless it should be determined at a general meeting to reduce the number).

If the number of directors is reduced below a quorum, the proper method is to summon a general meeting to elect fresh directors for the vacancies. The Companies Act 1985 s 285 (see para 545 ante) would not seem to apply: see *Morris v Kanssen* [1946] AC 459, [1946] 1 All ER 586, HL. Appointments may be validly made without duly complying with the formalities required by the articles: *Smith v Paringa Mines Ltd* [1906] 2 Ch 193; but cf *Barron v Potter* [1914] 1 Ch 895. Whether a person was appointed to fill a casual vacancy or as an additional director may depend on the determination of the question whether or not a vacancy was treated by the company as still subsisting at the time when the appointment was made: see *Zimmers Ltd v Zimmer* (1951) 95 Sol Jo 803. As to the requirement of official notification see para 546 ante.

3 Ie by the Companies Act 1985 s 291(1): *Pollock v Garrett* 1957 SLT (Notes) 8.

548. Additional directors. The directors are usually invested with the power of appointing additional directors[1]. In face of such a provision, a company cannot usurp the power entrusted to the directors[2], unless it is shown that the power could not be exercised by the directors owing to dissension or deadlock[3].

1 The Companies (Tables A to F) Regulations 1985, SI 1985/805, Schedule, Table A art 79 provides (inter alia) that the directors may appoint any person who is willing to act to be a director as an additional director, provided that the appointment does not cause the number of directors to exceed any number fixed by or in accordance with the articles as the maximum number of directors. As to the requirement of official notification see para 546 ante; and as to Table A generally see para 529 et seq ante.

2 *Blair Open Hearth Furnace Co v Reigart* (1913) 29 TLR 449. There may be a concurrent power: see *Isaacs v Chapman* (1916) 32 TLR 237, CA; *Worcester Corsetry Ltd v Witting* [1936] Ch 640, CA (where similar provisions to those in note 1 supra were held not to exclude the inherent power of the company in general meeting to appoint directors).

3 *Barron v Potter* [1914] 1 Ch 895.

549. Continuing directors after expiry of term. When the first board of directors or any subsequent board continues to act after the period for which the directors were appointed has expired, or where the directors are due to retire and no valid appointment of new directors has been made, the acting directors as a rule are qualified to act; but the articles may provide otherwise[1].

1 *Muir v Forman's Trustee* (1903) 5 F 546 at 566; cf *John Morley Building Co v Barras* [1891] 2 Ch 386 at 394; *Tyne Mutual Steamship Insurance Association v Brown* (1896) 74 LT 283; *Garden Gully United Quartz Mining Co v McLister* (1875) 1 App Cas 39, PC.

550. Restriction on assignment of office by a director. If, in the case of any company, provision is made by the articles or by any agreement entered into between any person and that company for empowering a director or manager to assign his office as such to another person, any assignment of office made in pursuance of the provision is of no effect unless and until it is approved by a special resolution[1] of the company, notwithstanding anything to the contrary contained in the provision[2].

1 As to special resolutions see para 683 post.
2 Companies Act 1985 s 308.

B. RESTRICTIONS ON APPOINTMENT

(A) *Automatic*

551. Secretary as director. No company may have as sole director either the secretary of the company[1], or a corporation the sole director of which is secretary to the company[2].

A provision requiring or authorising a thing to be done by or to a director and the secretary will not be satisfied by its being done by or to the same person acting both as director and as, or in place of, the secretary[3].

1 Companies Act 1985 s 283(2).
2 Ibid s 283(4)(b).
3 Ibid s 284.

552. Restriction on appointment over age limit. No person is capable of being appointed a director of a public company, or a private company which is a subsidiary[1] of a public company or of a body corporate registered under the law relating to companies for the time being in force in Northern Ireland as a public company, if at the time of his appointment he has attained the age of 70[2]. Nothing in these provisions, however, prevents the appointment of a director at any age, if his appointment is or was made or approved by the company in general meeting; but special notice[3] is required of any such resolution appointing or approving the appointment of a director for it to have effect under these provisions, and the notice of the resolution given to the company, and by the company to its members, must state, or have stated, the age of the person to whom it relates[4].

These provisions are also subject, in the case of a company first registered after the beginning of 1947, to the provisions of that company's articles, and, in the case of a company first registered before the beginning of that year:

(1) to any alterations of the company's articles made after the beginning of that year; and

(2) if at the beginning of that year the company's articles contained provision for retirement of directors under an age limit, or for preventing or restricting appointments of directors over a given age, the above restrictions will not apply to directors to whom that provision applies[5].

A person who is appointed, or to his knowledge proposed to be appointed director of a company to which these restrictions apply[6] at a time when he has attained any retiring age applicable to him as director, whether under the Companies Act 1985[7] or under the company's articles, is bound to give notice of his age to the company[8]. If he:

(a) fails to give such notice of his age; or

(b) acts as director under any appointment which is invalid by reason of his age, he is liable on summary conviction to a fine not exceeding one-fifth of the statutory maximum and, on conviction after continued contravention, to a daily default fine not exceeding one-fiftieth of the statutory maximum[9].

1 For the meaning of 'subsidiary' see para 827 post. See also note 2 infra.
2 Companies Act 1985 s 293(1), (2). A minor may, however, be a director: see *Copeman v William Flood & Sons Ltd* [1941] 1 KB 202 (disallowance of fees of director who is a minor for tax purposes). The Companies Act 1985 s 293 does not apply in relation to a director of a company if he had attained the age of 70 before the commencement of the Companies Act 1989 s 144(1) (ie 1 November 1990) (meaning of 'subsidiary' and 'holding company') and the company became a subsidiary of a public company by reason only of the commencement of s 144(1): s 144(4), Sch 18 para 34.
3 As to special notice see para 687 post.
4 Companies Act 1985 s 293(5).
5 Ibid s 293(7).
6 See para 637 post.
7 For these purposes, a company is deemed subject to the Companies Act 1985 s 293 notwithstanding that all or any of the provisions of s 293 are excluded or modified by the company's articles: s 294(2).
8 Ibid s 294(1). Section 294(1) does not apply in relation to a person's reappointment on the termination of a previous appointment as director of the company (s 294(3)), as in that case the director's age will be already known to the company, being one of the matters required to be inserted in the register of directors and secretaries (see paras 560, 649 post).
9 Ibid ss 294(4), 730, Sch 24. For the meaning of 'the statutory maximum' and 'daily default fine' see para 1161 post. For these purposes, a person who has acted as director under an appointment which is invalid is deemed to have continued so to act throughout the period from the invalid appointment until the last day on which he is shown to have acted thereunder: s 294(5).

553. Undischarged bankrupt acting as director. If a person, being an undischarged bankrupt, acts as director[1] of, or directly or indirectly takes part in or is concerned[2] in the promotion, formation or management of, a company[3], except with the leave of the court[4], he is liable on conviction on indictment to imprisonment for a term not exceeding two years or a fine, or to both, or on summary conviction to imprisonment for a term not exceeding six months or a fine not exceeding the statutory maximum, or to both[5]. The offence is one of strict liability[6].

In England and Wales, the leave of the court must not be so given unless notice of intention to apply for it has been served on the official receiver[7]; and it is the duty of the official receiver, if he is of the opinion that it is contrary to the public interest that such application should be granted, to attend on the hearing of the application and oppose it[8].

A person who acts in contravention of these provisions is also personally responsible for all the relevant debts of the company incurred whilst he was involved in its management[9].

1 For the meaning of 'director' see para 1417 note 2 post. For a provision in the articles that a director becoming bankrupt should vacate his office see para 634 text and note 13 post. As to the effect of bankruptcy where a director's qualification shares are required to be held in his own right see para 558 post.
2 'Concerned' may mean something different from 'interested': see *George Hill & Co v Hill* (1886) 55 LT 769 (a case on restraint of trade).
3 For these purposes, 'company' includes an unregistered company or a company incorporated outside Great Britain which has an established place of business in Great Britain: Company Directors Disqualification Act 1986 s 22(1), (2)(a).
4 For these purposes, 'the court' means the court by which the person was adjudged bankrupt: ibid s 11(2). As to the application for the leave of the court see the Insolvency Rules 1986, SI 1986/1925, Pt 6 Ch 20 (rr 6.203–6.205) and BANKRUPTCY vol 3(2) (Reissue) paras 689–691.
5 Company Directors Disqualification Act 1986 ss 11(1), 13. For the meaning of 'the statutory maximum' see para 1161 post.

6   *R v Brockley* [1994] 1 BCLC 606, CA.
7   References in the Company Directors Disqualification Act 1986 to the official receiver, in relation to the winding up of a company or the bankruptcy of an individual, are to any person who, by virtue of the Insolvency Act 1986 s 399 (see para 2263 post), is authorised to act as the official receiver in relation to that winding up or bankruptcy; and, in accordance with s 401(2) (see para 2267 post), references in the Company Directors Disqualification Act 1986 to an official receiver include a person appointed as his deputy: s 21(1).
8   See ibid s 11(3) and para 1423 post.
9   See ibid s 15(1)(a) and para 1445 post.

554. Clergymen. A clergyman who performs ecclesiastical duties may not act as director to any company formed to carry on trade or business for profit, but he may be a shareholder[1].

1   Pluralities Act 1838 ss 29, 31; Trading Partnerships Act 1841. See further ECCLESIASTICAL LAW vol 14 para 683 et seq.

(B) *Court Order*

555. Disqualification orders. In certain circumstances the court may, and in some circumstances must, make against a person a disqualification order[1], that is to say an order that he must not, without leave of the court:

(1)   be a director of a company; or
(2)   be a liquidator or administrator of a company; or
(3)   be a receiver or manager of a company's property; or
(4)   in any way, whether directly or indirectly, be concerned or take part in the promotion, formation or management of a company,

for a specified period beginning with the date of the order[2].

The court may make such an order:

(a)   where a person is convicted of certain indictable offences[3];
(b)   where a person has been persistently in default in relation to provisions of the companies legislation[4];
(c)   if, in the course of the winding up of a company, it appears that a person has been guilty of fraudulent trading, fraud or breach of duty[5];
(d)   where a person is convicted of certain summary offences[6];
(e)   where a person is unfit to be concerned in the management of a company[7];
(f)   where a person has participated in wrongful trading[8].

The court must make such an order in any case where it is satisfied:

(i)   that a person is or has been a director of a company which has at any time become insolvent, whether while he was a director or subsequently; and
(ii)   that his conduct as a director of that company, either taken alone or taken together with his conduct as a director of any other company or companies, makes him unfit to be concerned in the management of a company[9].

1   As to disqualification orders generally see para 1417 et seq post.
2   See the Company Directors Disqualification Act 1986 s 1(1) and para 1417 post.
3   See ibid s 2 (as amended) and para 1418 post.
4   See ibid s 3 and para 1419 post.
5   See ibid s 4 and para 1420 post.
6   See ibid s 5 and para 1421 post.
7   See ibid s 8 (as amended) and para 1431 post.

8 See ibid s 10 and para 1422 post.
9 See ibid s 6 and para 1425 post.

C. QUALIFICATION SHARES

556. Duty to hold a share qualification. Whether or not a director is required to possess any shareholding at all in the company depends on the provisions of the articles[1]. It is the duty of every director who is required by the articles of the company to hold a specified share qualification, and who is not already qualified, to obtain his qualification within two months after his appointment, or such shorter time as may be fixed by the articles[2]. For the purpose of any provision of the articles requiring a director or manager to hold any specified share qualification, the bearer of a share warrant is not deemed the holder of the shares specified in the warrant[3]. His office of director is vacated if he does not obtain his qualification within two months from the date of his appointment (or within such shorter time as may be fixed by the articles) or if after the expiration of that period or shorter time he ceases at any time to hold his qualification[4]. A person so vacating office is incapable of being reappointed a director until he has obtained his qualification[5]. If after the expiration of that period or shorter time any unqualified person acts as a director of the company, he is liable on summary conviction to a fine not exceeding one-fifth of the statutory maximum and, on conviction after continued contravention, to a daily default fine not exceeding one-fiftieth of the statutory maximum[6]; but the acts of a director or manager are valid if done before he is bound by law or the articles to acquire his qualification[7], or notwithstanding that a defect may afterwards be discovered in his qualification[8].

The holding of shares as one of several joint holders constitutes good qualification[9].

1 *De Ruvigne's Case* (1877) 5 ChD 306 at 321, 323, 326, CA. Under the Companies (Tables A to F) Regulations 1985, SI 1985/805, Schedule, Table A (amended by SI 1985/1052) no qualification is required. As to Table A generally see para 529 et seq ante.
2 Companies Act 1985 s 291(1). Time runs, when the election of directors is determined by a poll, only when the result of the poll is ascertained: *Holmes v Lord Keyes* [1959] 1 Ch 199, [1958] 2 All ER 129, CA.
3 Companies Act 1985 s 291(2). As to share warrants see paras 493, 494 ante.
4 Ibid s 291(3). Where the share qualification is increased, an existing director does not thereby cease to hold that larger qualification, but has a reasonable time in which to acquire it: *Molineaux v London, Birmingham and Manchester Insurance Co* [1902] 2 KB 589, CA.
5 Companies Act 1985 s 291(4).
6 Ibid ss 291(5), 730, Sch 24. For the meaning of 'the statutory maximum' and 'daily default fine' see para 1161 post. As to the power of the court to give relief against this penalty see para 624 post; *Re Barry and Staines Linoleum Ltd* [1934] Ch 227; *Re Gilt Edge Safety Glass Ltd* [1940] Ch 495, [1940] 2 All ER 237.
7 *Re International Cable Co, ex p Official Liquidator* (1892) 66 LT 253.
8 Companies Act 1985 s 285.
9 *Dunster's Case* [1894] 3 Ch 473 at 480, CA; *Grundy v Briggs* [1910] 1 Ch 444.

557. Liability for qualification shares. If a director resigns before the time fixed as the date after which, unless already qualified, he is under the articles to be deemed to have agreed to take his qualification shares from the company, he is not liable in respect of the shares to the company, although he acted as director without qualification[1]. If, however, he does not resign until after that date, he is liable, although he has never acted after accepting office[2].

A director who is bound by the articles to acquire a qualification, but who has not expressly agreed to take the shares from the company, is under no obligation to take the shares from the company[3], at any rate where it is possible for him to acquire his shares elsewhere[4], and where the time in which he is required to acquire them has not expired[5].

Where a director applies for his qualification shares, but no allotment is made and the company does not undertake the business for which it was incorporated, or any other business, within the period during which he is to qualify or else be deemed bound, he cannot be put on the list of contributories[6]. Again, if his appointment as director is void, and the only agreement to take shares as qualification shares consists in his acting as director and the registration of shares in his name, the acting director is not liable on them[7].

If shares sufficient to qualify a director are registered in his name before his resignation, even without his knowledge, he will be liable to pay for them unless he has acquired other shares before the time when he was bound to qualify; for as director he must be taken to know the contents of the register and therefore that the shares have been registered in his name[8].

A transfer of qualification shares with a view to avoid liability may be void for fraud[9].

1 *Re Pandora Theatre Co* (1884) 24 Sol Jo 238; *Karuth's Case* (1875) LR 20 Eq 506; *Green's Case* (1874) LR 18 Eq 428; *Re Self-Acting Sewing Machine Co* (1886) 54 LT 676 (where the conduct of the director was held equivalent to refusal to act or to resignation); *Austin's Case* (1866) LR 2 Eq 435; *Re Imperial Land Credit Corpn Ltd, ex p Eve* (1868) 37 LJ Ch 844; *Salisbury-Jones and Dale's Case* [1894] 3 Ch 356, CA.

2 *Re Hercynia Copper Co* [1894] 2 Ch 403, CA; *Isaacs' Case* [1892] 2 Ch 158, CA.

3 *Re Printing, Telegraph and Construction Co of the Agence Havas, ex p Cammell* [1894] 2 Ch 392, CA (where shares were allotted to a director without his knowledge before his resignation, and registered afterwards); *Re Wheal Buller Consols* (1888) 38 ChD 42, CA; *Brown's Case* (1873) 9 Ch App 102 at 105; *Green's Case* (1874) LR 18 Eq 428; *Austin's Case* (1866) LR 2 Eq 435; *Karuth's Case* (1875) LR 20 Eq 506 at 511; *Re Colombia Chemical Factory, Manure and Phosphate Works, Hewitt's Case, Brett's Case* (1883) 25 ChD 283, CA. See, however, *Harward's Case* (1871) LR 13 Eq 30; *Re Esparto Trading Co* (1879) 12 ChD 191. In *Re Bread Supply Association, Konrath's Case* (1893) 62 LJ Ch 376, Kekewich J held that the mere acting as director obliged him to qualify, and to do so by buying shares from the company, if he did not buy them elsewhere within a reasonable time, following, it was said, *Isaacs' Case* [1892] 2 Ch 158, CA, which case, however, is clearly distinguishable, as the clause ran 'he shall be deemed to have agreed to take his qualification shares from the company'. *Re Bread Supply Association, Konrath's Case* supra is apparently not consistent with *Re Medical Attendance Association, Onslow's Case* (1887) 57 LJ Ch 338n, CA, and *Re Wheal Buller Consols* (1888) 38 ChD 42, CA. As to the time within which qualification shares are required to be taken up see para 556 ante.

4 *Hamley's Case* (1877) 5 ChD 705. It may be different where he cannot obtain them elsewhere: *Hamley's Case* supra at 707.

5 See the Companies Act 1985 s 291(1) and para 556 ante.

6 *Re Youde's Billposting Ltd, Clayton's Case* (1902) 18 TLR 656, 731, CA; and see *General International Agency Co, Chapman's Case* (1866) LR 2 Eq 567 (where an allotment of a qualification was refused); *Tothill's Case* (1865) 1 Ch App 85 (where a smaller number was allotted); *Re Medical Attendance Association, Onslow's Case* (1887) 57 LJ Ch 338n, CA (where a smaller number of shares than the original qualification applied for was allotted, the company shortly afterwards reducing the required number to the same figure).

7 *Stace and Worth's Case* (1869) 4 Ch App 682; *Re Wheal Buller Consols* (1888) 38 ChD 42, CA; and see *Hamley's Case* (1877) 5 ChD 705 and the other cases cited in para 559 note 2 post. Acting as a director without qualification is not a misfeasance under the Insolvency Act 1986 s 212: see para 2448 et seq post and *Coventry and Dixon's Case* (1880) 14 ChD 660, CA.

8 *Re Portuguese Consolidated Copper Mines Ltd, ex p Lord Inchiquin* [1891] 3 Ch 28, CA; *Leeke's Case* (1871) 6 Ch App 469; *Molineaux v London, Birmingham and Manchester Insurance Co* [1902] 2 KB 589, CA; and see *Re Esparto Trading Co* (1879) 12 ChD 191 at 203 (where the shares were not registered, but the calls were debited and the director was held to have assented to the entries); *Harward's Case* (1871) LR 13 Eq 30 (where the allotment committee was said to be the agent of the director to make an allotment to him); and *Fowler's Case* (1872) LR 14 Eq 316 (where a director applied for further shares in ignorance that the qualifying number had been allotted to him). A director applying for shares as qualification in the place of other shares for which he had signed the memorandum, or when other shares had already been allotted to him, will not be held liable as a contributory in respect of those other shares: see *Duke's Case* (1876) 1 ChD 620, doubting *Fowler's Case* (1872) LR 14 Eq 316. Decisions relating to the question

what is a reasonable time within which a director must acquire his qualification shares are rendered nugatory by the Companies Act 1985 s 291 (see para 556 ante) but as to the acquisition of additional shares by existing directors, where the qualification is increased, see para 556 note 4 ante; and see the case cited in para 556 note 4 ante.

9 *Gilbert's Case* (1870) 5 Ch App 559; *Re South London Fish Market Co* (1888) 39 ChD 324 at 331, CA; and see para 496 ante.

558. Qualification shares held as trustee etc. A director who is bound to hold his qualification shares 'in his own right' is properly qualified if he holds in his name shares of which he is trustee[1]; and, if he is not bound to acquire his qualification shares from the company, is properly qualified if he holds shares which he receives as a present from the promoter by transfer or allotment[2]. In the latter case he may, however, be liable for misfeasance, and may be ordered to pay to the company the value of the shares[3].

Although a director fulfils the requirement of holding shares 'in his own right' if he holds shares as trustee, in spite of the beneficial interest being elsewhere, it is not sufficient if they are registered as held by the director in a representative capacity, as, for example, where he is registered as trustee in bankruptcy or as executor or as liquidator[4]; nor is it sufficient where he is bankrupt and his shares have, therefore, vested in his trustee, after which the company may no longer deal with the shares as the director's own[5]. No notice of any trust, expressed, implied or constructive must, however, be entered on the register[6] and the persons holding shares in a representative capacity are entitled to have a clean entry[7].

1 *Pulbrook v Richmond Consolidated Mining Co* (1878) 9 ChD 610; *Cooper v Griffin* [1892] 1 QB 740, CA; *Howard v Sadler* [1893] 1 QB 1; *Bainbridge v Smith* (1889) 41 ChD 462 at 475, CA; *Re Bainbridge, Reeves v Bainbridge* [1889] WN 228; *Sutton v English and Colonial Produce Co* [1902] 2 Ch 502.

2 *Brown's Case* (1873) 9 Ch App 102; *Carling, Hespeler and Walsh's Cases* (1875) 1 ChD 115, CA; and see *Miller's Case* (1877) 5 ChD 70, CA (where by the articles the qualification was to be provided by the company, and was forfeited on retirement, and the director was held not liable as shareholder). If shares are allotted and paid for out of money of the company fraudulently obtained by a promoter, they will be treated as unpaid although the director is innocent: *Leeke's Case* (1871) 6 Ch App 469; *Hay's Case* (1875) 10 Ch App 593; and see para 53 ante.

3 *De Ruvigne's Case* (1877) 5 ChD 306, CA; *Pearson's Case* (1877) 5 ChD 336, CA; *Re Great Northern and Midland Coal Co, Currie's Case* (1863) 3 De GJ & Sm 367; *Re London and South Western Canal Ltd* [1911] 1 Ch 346; and see para 42 ante and para 2448 et seq post.

4 *Boschoek Proprietary Co Ltd v Fuke* [1906] 1 Ch 148 (in which instances the company could not deal with the shares as those of the registered holder). The articles may, however, contemplate that a person may be a director in a representative capacity: *Grundy v Briggs* [1910] 1 Ch 444 at 451 per Eve J.

5 *Sutton v English and Colonial Produce Co* [1902] 2 Ch 502 (where registration of subsequently acquired shares was enforced, the trustee not objecting). As to the restriction on undischarged bankrupts acting as directors see para 553 ante and para 1423 post.

6 See the Companies Act 1985 s 360 and para 385 ante.

7 *Re T H Saunders & Co* [1908] 1 Ch 415; and see para 385 ante.

559. Condition precedent to holding office. If the holding of shares is a condition precedent to becoming a director, the director must actually be registered as the holder of qualification shares before he is appointed[1], otherwise his election is void[2]; but, where it is not a condition precedent, he may be appointed and act before he qualifies[3].

It is the duty of every director who is by the company's articles required to hold a specified share qualification, and who is not already qualified, to obtain his qualification within two months after his appointment, or such shorter time as may be fixed by the articles[4].

1   *Channel Collieries Trust Ltd v Dover, St Margaret's and Martin Mill Light Rly Co* [1914] 2 Ch 506, CA; *Spencer v Kennedy* [1926] Ch 125.

2   *Hamley's Case* (1877) 5 ChD 705; *Re Elham Valley Rly Co, Biron's Case* (1878) 26 WR 606; *Barber's Case* (1877) 5 ChD 963, CA; *Jenner's Case* (1877) 7 ChD 132, CA; cf *Stace and Worth's Case* (1869) 4 Ch App 682.

3   *Re International Cable Co Ltd* (1892) 66 LT 253; *Re Portuguese Consolidated Copper Mines Ltd* (1889) 42 ChD 160, CA.

4   See the Companies Act 1985 s 291(1) and para 556 ante.

D. REGISTER OF DIRECTORS ETC; PARTICULARS IN BUSINESS LETTERS; INSPECTION OF SERVICE CONTRACTS

560. Register of directors and secretaries. Every company must keep at its registered office a register of its directors and secretaries[1]. The register must contain the following particulars with respect to each director:

(1)   in the case of an individual, his present name[2], any former name[3], his usual residential address, his nationality, his business occupation (if any), particulars of any other directorships held by him or which have been held by him and the date of his birth; and

(2)   in the case of a corporation or Scottish firm, its corporate or firm name and registered or principal office[4].

It is not necessary, however, for the register to contain on any day particulars of a directorship:

(a)   which has not been held by a director at any time during the five years preceding that day;

(b)   which is held by a director in a company[5] which is dormant[6] or grouped[7] with the company keeping the register and, if he also held that directorship for any period during those five years, was for the whole of that period either dormant or so grouped;

(c)   which was held by a director for any period during those five years in a company which for the whole of that period was either dormant or grouped with the company keeping the register[8].

Within the period of 14 days from the occurrence of any change among its directors or any change in the particulars contained in the register, the company must send to the registrar of companies a notification in the prescribed form[9] of the change and of the date on which it occurred; and a notification of a person having become a director of the company must contain a consent, signed by that person, so to act[10].

The register must be open to the inspection of any member of the company without charge, and of any other person on payment of such fee as may be prescribed[11]. The company[12] must make the register available for such inspection for not less than two hours during the period between 9 am and 5 pm on each business day[13]; and it must permit a person inspecting the register to copy any information made available for inspection by means of the taking of notes or the transcription of the information[14].

If an inspection so required is refused, or, if default is made in so keeping the register[15] or in so sending to the registrar notification of any change among its directors or any change in the particulars contained in the register[16], the company, and every officer of it who is in default, is liable on summary conviction to a fine not exceeding the statutory maximum and, on conviction after continued contravention, to a daily default fine not exceeding one-tenth of the statutory maximum[17]. In the case of a refusal to allow inspection of the register, the court may by order compel an immediate inspection of the register[18].

The registrar of companies must cause to be published in the Gazette[19] notice of the receipt by him of any notification of a change among its directors; and he must state the name of the company, the description of the document and the date of its receipt[20].

1 Companies Act 1985 s 288(1). As to the provisions applicable where the entries are not recorded in legible form see para 656 post; and as to the contents of the register with regard to secretaries and notification of any change in a company's secretary see para 649 post.

2 For these purposes, 'name' means a person's Christian name (or other forename) and surname, except that in the case of a peer, or an individual usually known by a title, the title may be stated instead of his Christian name (or other forename) and surname, or in addition to either or both of them: ibid s 289(2)(a) (substituted by the Companies Act 1989 s 145, Sch 19 para 2(1), (4)).

3 For these purposes, the reference to a former name does not include (1) in the case of a peer, or an individual normally known by a British title, the name by which he was known previous to the adoption of or succession to the title; or (2) in the case of any person, a former name which was changed or disused before he attained the age of 18 years or which has been changed or disused for 20 years or more; or (3) in the case of a married woman, the name by which she was known previous to the marriage: Companies Act 1985 s 289(2)(b) (substituted by the Companies Act 1989 Sch 19 para 2(1),(4)).

4 Companies Act 1985 ss 288(1), 289(1) (amended by the Companies Act 1989 Sch 19 para 2(1)–(3)). For the purposes of the Companies Act 1985 ss 288, 289 (as amended), a shadow director of a company is deemed a director and officer of it: s 288(6). For the meaning of 'director' and 'shadow director' see para 543 note 1 ante. It seems that for these purposes 'director' does not include a de facto director: see *Re Lo-line Ltd* [1988] Ch 477 at 489, [1988] 2 All ER 692 at 699 obiter per Sir Nicholas Browne-Wilkinson.

5 For these purposes, 'company' includes any body corporate incorporated in Great Britain: Companies Act 1985 s 289(4). For the meaning of 'body corporate' see para 89 note 8 ante.

6 For these purposes, ibid s 250(3) (as substituted) (see para 1058 post) applies as regards whether and when a company is or has been dormant: s 289(4)(a) (amended by the Companies Act 1989 s 23, Sch 10 para 9).

7 For these purposes, a company is to be regarded as being, or having been, grouped with another at any time if at that time it was a company of which the other is or was a wholly-owned subsidiary, or if it is or was a wholly-owned subsidiary of the other or of another company of which that other is or was a wholly-owned subsidiary: Companies Act 1985 s 289(4)(b). For the meaning of 'subsidiary' see para 827 post.

8 Ibid s 289(3).

9 For the prescribed form of notification see the Companies (Forms) (Amendment) Regulations 1995, SI 1995/736, reg 3, Sch 2, Form 288a (appointment of director or secretary), Form 288b (resignation of director or secretary) and Form 288c (change of particulars for director or secretary). For the prescribed version of the form in Welsh see the Companies (Welsh Language Forms and Documents) (Amendment) Regulations 1995, SI 1995/734, reg 4, Schedule, Form 288aCYM (appointment of director or secretary), Form 288bCYM (resignation of director or secretary) and Form 288cCYM (change of particulars for director or secretary).

10 Companies Act 1985 s 288(2).

11 Ibid s 288(3) (amended by the Companies Act 1989 ss 143(6), 212, Sch 24). The fee so prescribed is £2.50 for each hour or part thereof during which the right of inspection is exercised: Companies (Inspection and Copying of Registers, Indices and Documents) Regulations 1991, SI 1991/1998, reg 5, Sch 2 para 1(b). As to the power to make regulations see para 230 ante.

12 For the meaning of 'company' see para 229 note 14 ante.

13 Companies (Inspection and Copying of Registers, Indices and Documents) Regulations 1991 reg 3(1), (2)(a). For the meaning of 'business day' see para 229 note 15 ante.

14 Ibid reg 3(1), (2)(b). Regulation 3(2)(b) is not, however, to be construed as obliging a company to provide any facilities additional to those provided for the purposes of facilitating inspection: reg 3(3).

15 Ie pursuant to the Companies Act 1985 s 288(1): see supra.

16 Ie pursuant to ibid s 288(2): see supra.

17 Ibid ss 288(4), 730, Sch 24. For the meaning of 'officer who is in default', 'the statutory maximum' and 'daily default fine' see para 1161 post.

18 Ibid s 288(5). The application is by originating summons in the expedited form: RSC Ord 102 r 2(1),(2). As to the procedure see para 390 note 10 ante.

19 For the meaning of 'the Gazette' see para 70 note 1 ante.
20 See the Companies Act 1985 s 711(1)(c) and paras 70, 71 ante.

561. Directors' names on company correspondence etc. No company registered under the Companies Act 1985 or under the former Companies Acts[1], unless it was registered before 23 November 1916[2], nor any company incorporated outside Great Britain which has an established place of business[3] within Great Britain, unless it had established such a place of business before that date, must state, in any form, the name of any of its directors[4] (otherwise than in the text or as a signatory) on any business letter[5] on which the company's name appears unless it states on the letter in legible characters the name[6] of every director of the company[7].

If a company makes default in complying with these provisions, every officer of the company who is in default is liable on summary conviction for each offence to a fine not exceeding one-fifth of the statutory maximum; and, for this purpose, where a corporation is an officer of the company, any officer of the corporation is deemed to be an officer of the company[8].

1 For the meaning of 'the former Companies Acts' see para 11 note 2 ante.
2 Ie the date from which the Registration of Business Names Act 1916 ss 18, 19 (repealed) were extended to companies by the Companies (Particulars as to Directors) Act 1917 ss 2(2), 3 (repealed).
3 For the meaning of 'place of business' see para 63 note 1 ante.
4 For these purposes, 'director' includes a shadow director and the reference in the Companies Act 1985 s 305(3) to an 'officer' is to be construed accordingly: Companies Act 1985 s 305(7) (substituted by the Companies Act 1989 s 145, Sch 19 para 4(1), (3)). For the meaning of 'director' and 'shadow director' see para 543 note 1 ante; and for the meaning of 'officer' see para 641 post.
5 As to other requirements in business letters see the Companies Act 1985 s 351 (as amended) and para 1135 post.
6 For the purposes of such obligation to state the name of every director of the company, a person's 'name' means (1) in the case of an individual, his Christian name (or other forename) and surname; and (2) in the case of a corporation or Scottish firm, its corporate or firm name: ibid s 305(4) (substituted by the Companies Act 1989 Sch 19 para 4(1), (3)). The initial or recognised abbreviation of a person's Christian name or other forename may be stated instead of the full Christian name or other forename: Companies Act 1985 s 305(5) (substituted by the Companies Act 1989 Sch 19 para 4(1), (3)). In the case of a peer, or an individual usually known by a title, the title may be stated instead of his Christian name (or other forename) and surname or in addition to either or both of them: Companies Act 1985 s 305(6) (substituted by the Companies Act 1989 Sch 19 para 4(1), (3)).
7 Companies Act 1985 s 305(1), (2) (amended by the Companies Act 1989 Sch 19 para 4(1), (2)).
8 Companies Act 1985 ss 305(3), 730, Sch 24. For the meaning of 'officer who is in default' and 'the statutory maximum' see para 1161 post.

562. Directors' service contracts. Every company must keep at an appropriate place[1]:

(1) in the case of each director[2] whose contract of service[3] with the company is in writing, a copy that contract;

(2) in the case of each director whose contract of service with the company is not in writing, a written memorandum setting out its terms;

(3) in the case of each director who is employed under a contract of service with a subsidiary of the company, a copy of that contract, or, if it is not in writing, a written memorandum setting out its terms[4];

and all copies and memoranda so kept by a company must be kept at the same place[5].

The above provisions do not apply to a director's contract of service with the company or with a subsidiary of it if that contract requires him to work wholly or mainly outside the United Kingdom; but the company must keep a memorandum:

(a) in the case of a contract of service with the company, giving the director's name and setting out the provisions of the contract relating to its duration; or

(b) in the case of a contract of service with a subsidiary, giving the director's name and the name and place of incorporation of the subsidiary, and setting out the provisions of the contract relating to its duration,

at the same place as copies and memoranda are kept[6] under the above provisions[7].

Every copy and memorandum required to be so kept must be open to the inspection, without charge, of any member of the company[8]. The company[9] must make those documents available for such inspection for not less than two hours during the period between 9 am and 5 pm on each business day[10]; and it must permit a person inspecting them to copy any information made available for inspection by means of the taking of notes or the transcription of the information[11].

Every company must send notice in the prescribed form[12] to the registrar of companies of the place where such copies and memoranda are so kept, and of any change in that place, save in a case in which they have at all times been kept at the company's registered office[13].

If default is made in keeping the requisite copies or memoranda[14], or an inspection[15] of them is refused, or default is made for 14 days in sending notice to the registrar[16], the company, and every officer of it who is in default, is liable on summary conviction to a fine not exceeding one-fifth of the statutory maximum and, on conviction after continued contravention, to a daily default fine not exceeding one-fiftieth of the statutory maximum[17], and, in the case of a refusal of an inspection, the court may by order compel an immediate inspection of such copies or memoranda[18].

The above provisions do not, however, require that there be kept a copy of, or memorandum setting out the terms of, a contract (or its variation) at a time when the unexpired portion of the term for which the contract is to be in force is less than 12 months, or at a time at which the contract can, within the next ensuing 12 months, be terminated by the company without payment of compensation[19].

1 The following are appropriate places for these purposes: (1) the company's registered office; (2) the place where its register of members is kept, if other than its registered office; or (3) its principal place of business, provided that is situated in that part of Great Britain in which the company is registered: Companies Act 1985 s 318(3). For the meaning of 'place of business' see para 63 note 1 ante.

2 For these purposes, a shadow director is treated as a director: ibid s 318(6). For the meaning of 'director' and 'shadow director' see para 543 note 1 ante.

3 For these purposes, 'contract of service' includes a variation of a director's contract of service: ibid s 318(10).

4 Ibid s 318(1).

5 Ibid s 318(2).

6 Ie in pursuance of ibid s 318(1): see supra.

7 Ibid s 318(5).

8 Ibid s 318(7) (amended by the Companies Act 1989 ss 143(7), 212, Sch 24).

9 For the meaning of 'company' see para 229 note 14 ante.

10 Companies (Inspection and Copying of Registers, Indices and Documents) Regulations 1991, SI 1991/1998, reg 3(1), (2)(a). For the meaning of 'business day' see para 229 note 15 ante. As to the power to make regulations see para 230 ante.

11 Ibid reg 3(1), (2)(b). Regulation 3(2)(b) is not, however, to be construed as obliging a company to provide any facilities additional to those provided for the purposes of facilitating inspection: reg 3(3).

12 For the prescribed form of notice see the Companies (Forms) (Amendment) Regulations 1995, SI 1995/736, reg 3, Sch 2, Form 318.

13 Companies Act 1985 s 318(4).

14 Ie default is made in complying with ibid s 318(1) or (5): see supra.

15 Ie an inspection required under ibid s 318(7) (as amended): see supra.

16 Ie default is made in complying with ibid s 318(4): see supra.

17 Ibid ss 318(8), 730, Sch 24. For the meaning of 'officer who is in default', 'the statutory maximum' and 'daily default fine' see para 1161 post.

18 Ibid s 318(9). The application is by originating summons in the expedited form: RSC Ord 102 r 2(1),(2).

19 Companies Act 1985 s 318(11).

563. Director's contract of employment for more than five years. The following provisions apply in respect of any term of an agreement whereby a director's[1] employment[2] with the company of which he is a director or, where he is the director of a holding company[3], his employment within the group[4], is to continue, or may be continued, otherwise than at the instance of the company, whether under the original agreement or under a new agreement entered into in pursuance of it, for a period of more than five years during which the employment cannot be terminated by the company by notice, or can be so terminated only in specified circumstances[5].

In any case where:

(1) a person is or is to be employed with a company under an agreement which cannot be terminated by the company by notice or can be so terminated only in specified circumstances; and

(2) more than six months before the expiration of the period for which he is or is to be so employed, the company enters into a further agreement, otherwise than in pursuance of a right conferred by or under the original agreement on the other party to it, under which he is to be employed with the company or, where he is a director of a holding company, within the group,

these provisions apply as if to the period for which he is to be employed under that further agreement there were added a further period equal to the unexpired period of the original agreement[6].

A company must not incorporate in an agreement such a term for the continuance of the employment as is mentioned above[7], unless the term is first approved by a resolution of the company in general meeting and, in the case of a director of a holding company, by a resolution of that company in general meeting[8]. No approval is required to be given under these provisions by any body corporate unless it is a company within the meaning of the Companies Act 1985[9], or was not formed under the companies legislation but is registered thereunder[10], or if it is a wholly-owned subsidiary of any body corporate, wherever incorporated[11]. A resolution of a company approving such a term[12] must not be passed at a general meeting of the company unless a written memorandum setting out the proposed agreement incorporating the term is available for inspection by members of the company both at the company's registered office for not less than 15 days ending with the date of the meeting, and at the meeting itself[13].

A term incorporated in an agreement in contravention of these provisions is, to the extent that it contravenes them, void; and that agreement and, in a case where the provisions applicable to entering into a further agreement apply[14], the original agreement, are deemed to contain a term entitling the company to terminate it at any time by the giving of reasonable notice[15].

It is immaterial whether the law which (apart from the Companies Act 1985) governs the agreement is the law of the United Kingdom, or of a part of it, or not[16].

1 For these purposes, a shadow director is treated as a director: Companies Act 1985 s 319(7). For the meaning of 'director' and 'shadow director' see para 543 note 1 ante.

2 For these purposes, 'employment' includes employment under a contract for services: ibid s 319(7)(a).

3 For the meaning of 'holding company' see para 827 post.

4 For these purposes, 'group', in relation to a director of a holding company, means the group which consists of that company and its subsidiaries: Companies Act 1985 s 319(7)(b). For the meaning of 'subsidiary' see para 827 post.
5 Ibid s 319(1). A written resolution is not effective if any of the requirements of s 381A(7), Sch 15A para 7 (as added) is not complied with: Sch 15A para 2(2) (added by the Companies Act 1989 s 114(1)). In relation to a written resolution approving any such term as is mentioned in the Companies Act 1985 s 319(1), s 319(5) (see infra) does not apply, but the documents referred to therein must be supplied to each relevant member at or before the time at which the resolution is supplied to him for signature: Sch 15A para 7 (added by the Companies Act 1989 s 114(1)). For the meaning of 'written resolution' and 'relevant member' see para 224 note 3 ante.
6 Companies Act 1985 s 319(2).
7 Ie in ibid s 319(1): see supra.
8 Ibid s 319(3).
9 See para 11 ante.
10 Ie pursuant to the Companies Act 1985 s 680: see para 23 et seq ante.
11 Ibid s 319(4).
12 Ie such a term as is mentioned in ibid s 319(1): see supra.
13 Ibid s 319(5). See also note 5 supra.
14 Ie ibid s 319(2): see supra.
15 Ibid s 319(6).
16 Ibid s 347.

E. DISCLOSURE OF DIRECTORS' SHAREHOLDINGS AND INTERESTS

(A) Obligation to notify Interests in Shares and Debentures

564. Notification of interests on appointment. A person who becomes a director[1] of a company and at the time when he does so is interested[2] in shares[3] in, or debentures of, the company or any other body corporate, being the company's subsidiary[4] or holding company[5] or a subsidiary of the company's holding company, is under obligation[6] to notify the company in writing:

(1) of the subsistence of his interests at that time[7]; and
(2) of the number of shares[8] of each class in, and the amount of debentures of each class of, the company or other such body corporate in which each interest of his subsists at that time[9].

Such an obligation is treated as not discharged unless the notice by means of which it purports to be discharged is expressed to be given in fulfilment of that obligation[10]. It is subject to any exceptions for which provision may be made by regulations made by the Secretary of State by statutory instrument[11]. Such information must be recorded in a register kept by the company for this purpose[12].

1 The Companies Act 1985 s 324 applies to shadow directors as to directors: s 324(6). For the meaning of 'director' and 'shadow director' see para 543 note 1 ante.
2 For the meaning of 'interested' see para 568 post.
3 Nothing in the Companies Act 1985 s 324 operates so as to impose an obligation with respect to shares in a body corporate which is the wholly-owned subsidiary of another body corporate: Companies Act 1985 s 324(6). For these purposes, a body corporate is deemed to be the wholly-owned subsidiary of another if it has no members except that other and that other's wholly-owned subsidiaries and its or their nominees: s 736(5)(b). For the meaning of 'body corporate' see para 89 note 8 ante.
4 For the meaning of 'subsidiary' see para 827 post.
5 For the meaning of 'holding company' see para 827 post.
6 An obligation so imposed on a person to notify an interest must be fulfilled, if he knows of the existence of the interest on the day on which he becomes a director, within five days beginning on the day following that day: Companies Act 1985 Sch 13 para 14(1). Otherwise the obligation must be fulfilled

before the expiration of the period of five days beginning with the day following that on which the existence of the interest came to his knowledge: Sch 13 para 14(2). For these purposes, in reckoning any period of days, a day that is a Saturday or Sunday or a bank holiday in any part of Great Britain is to be disregarded: Sch 13 para 16. For the meaning of 'bank holiday' see para 71 note 9 ante.

7 Ibid s 324(1)(a). Exceptions may be prescribed by the Secretary of State: see para 569 post.
8 For these purposes, 'number', in relation to shares, in contexts which admit of the references to shares being construed as including stock, includes 'amount': ibid s 744.
9 Ibid s 324(1)(b). As to penalties for offences relating to the obligation to notify see para 570 post.
10 Ibid s 324(5).
11 Ibid s 324(3). See further para 569 post.
12 See ibid s 325(1) and para 571 post.

565. Notification of changes in interests. A director[1] of a company is under obligation[2] to notify the company in writing of the occurrence, while he is a director, of any of the following events[3]:

(1) any event in consequence of whose occurrence he becomes, or ceases to be, interested[4] in shares in, or debentures of, the company or any other body corporate[5], being the company's subsidiary[6] or holding company[7] or a subsidiary of the company's holding company[8];

(2) the entering into by him of a contract to sell any such shares or debentures[9];

(3) the assignment by him of a right granted to him by the company to subscribe for shares in, or debentures of, the company[10]; and

(4) the grant to him by another body corporate, being the company's subsidiary or holding company or a subsidiary of the company's holding company, of a right to subscribe for shares in, or debentures of, that other body corporate, the exercise of such a right granted to him and the assignment by him of such a right so granted[11];

and notification to the company must state the number[12] or amount, and class, of shares or debentures involved[13].

Such an obligation to notify is treated as not discharged unless the notice by means of which it purports to be discharged is expressed to be given in fulfilment of that obligation[14]. It is subject to any exceptions for which provision may be made by regulations made by the Secretary of State by statutory instrument[15].

Such information must be recorded in a register kept by the company for this purpose[16].

Notification is not required of the occurrence of an event whose occurrence comes to the knowledge of a person after he has ceased to be a director[17].

1 The Companies Act 1985 s 324 applies to shadow directors as to directors: s 324(6). For the meaning of 'director' and 'shadow director' see para 543 note 1 ante. Nothing in s 324 operates so as to impose an obligation with respect to shares in a body corporate which is the wholly-owned subsidiary of another body corporate: see s 324(6) and para 564 note 3 ante.
2 If, at the time at which the event occurs, he knows of its occurrence and of the fact that its occurrence gives rise to the obligation, the obligation must be fulfilled before the expiration of the period of five days beginning with the day following that on which the event occurs: ibid s 324(3)(b), Sch 13 para 15(1). Otherwise the obligation must be fulfilled before the expiration of a period of five days beginning with the day following that on which the fact that the occurrence of the event gives rise to the obligation comes to his knowledge: Sch 13 para 15(2). In reckoning any period of days, a day that is a Saturday or Sunday, or a bank holiday in any part of Great Britain, is to be disregarded: Sch 13 para 16. For the meaning of 'bank holiday' see para 71 note 9 ante.
3 Ibid s 324(2).
4 For the meaning of 'interested' see para 568 post.
5 For the meaning of 'body corporate' see para 89 note 8 ante.
6 For the meaning of 'subsidiary' see para 827 post.
7 For the meaning of 'holding company' see para 827 post.

8 Companies Act 1985 s 324(2)(a). Where such an event consists of his entering into a contract for the purchase by him of shares or debentures, the obligation is not discharged unless the notice includes the price to be paid by him under the contract (which includes any consideration other than money): s 324(3)(c), Sch 13 paras 17(1), 20.

9 Ibid s 324(2)(b). The obligation is not discharged unless the notice includes the price to be received by him under the contract (which includes any consideration other than money): Sch 13 paras 17(2), 20.

10 Ibid s 324(2)(c). An obligation so imposed is not discharged unless the notice includes the consideration for the assignment (or, if there is no consideration, a statement to that effect): Sch 13 para 18(1).

11 Ibid s 324(2)(d). As to the extension of these provisions to the immediate family of a director see para 566 post. Where an event of whose occurrence a director is under obligation so to notify a company consists in the director's assigning a right, the obligation is not discharged unless the notice includes a statement of the consideration for the assignment (or, if there is no consideration, a statement to that effect): Sch 13 para 18(2). Where such an event consists in the grant to him of a right to subscribe for shares or debentures, the obligation is not discharged unless the notice includes the date on which the right was granted, the period during which or the time at which the right is exercisable, the consideration for the grant, or, if it be the case that there is no consideration, that fact, and the price (which includes any consideration other than money) to be paid for the shares or debentures: Sch 13 paras 19(1), 20. Where such an event consists in the exercise of a right granted to him to subscribe for shares or debentures, the obligation is not discharged in the absence of inclusion in the notice of a statement of the number of shares or amount of debentures in respect of which the right was exercised; and, if registered in his name, that fact; if not so registered, the name or names of the person or persons in whose name or names they were registered and, if registered in the names of two persons or more, the number or amount registered in the name of each of them: Sch 13 para 19(2).

12 For the meaning of 'number' in relation to shares see para 564 note 8 ante.

13 Companies Act 1985 s 324(2).

14 Ibid s 324(5).

15 Ibid s 324(3).

16 See ibid s 325(1) and para 571 post.

17 Ibid s 324(4).

566. Extension of notification of director's interests in shares etc to spouses and children. For the purposes of the statutory provisions relating to a director's duty to disclose shareholdings in his own company[1], an interest of the spouse of a director[2] of a company, not being herself or himself a director of it, in shares or debentures is to be treated as the director's interest, and the same applies to an interest of an infant[3] who is the son[4] or the daughter[5] of a director of a company, not being himself or herself a director of it, in shares or debentures[6]. For these purposes, a contract, assignment or right of subscription entered into, exercised or made by, or a grant made to, the spouse of a director of a company (not being herself or himself a director of it) is to be treated as having been entered into, exercised or made by, or, as the case may be, as having been made to, the director, and the same applies to a contract, assignment or right of subscription entered into, exercised or made by, or grant made to, an infant son or infant daughter of a director of a company, not being himself or herself a director of it[7]. A director of a company is under obligation to notify the company in writing of the occurrence, while he or she is a director, of either of the following events, namely:

(1) the grant to his or her spouse or to his or her infant son or infant daughter, by the company, of a right to subscribe for shares in, or debentures of, the company; and

(2) the exercise by his or her spouse or by his or her infant son or infant daughter of such a right granted by the company to the spouse, son or daughter[8].

Such information must be recorded in a register kept by the company for this purpose[9].

1 Ie the Companies Act 1985 s 324: see paras 564, 565 ante.

2 For the meaning of 'director' see para 564 note 1 ante.

3 As to the attainment of majority at the age of 18 see the Family Law Reform Act 1969 s 1 and CHILDREN vol 5(2) (Reissue) para 601.

4 For these purposes, 'son' includes stepson: Companies Act 1985 s 328(8).

5 For these purposes, 'daughter' includes stepdaughter: ibid s 328(8).

6 Ibid s 328(1).

7 Ibid s 328(2). The rules set out in Sch 13 Pt I (paras 1–13 (as amended): see para 568 post) have effect for the interpretation of, and otherwise in relation to, s 328(1), (2): s 328(7).

8 Ibid s 328(3). In a notice so given there must be stated: (1) in the case of the grant of a right, the like information as is required by s 324 to be stated by the director on the grant to him by another body corporate of a right to subscribe for shares in, or debentures of, that other body corporate; and (2) in the case of the exercise of a right, the like information as is required by s 324 to be stated by the director on the exercise of a right granted to him by another body corporate to subscribe for shares in, or debentures of, that other body corporate: s 328(4). An obligation imposed by s 328(3) on a director must be fulfilled before the end of five days beginning with the day following that on which the occurrence of the event giving rise to it comes to his knowledge; but in reckoning that period of days any Saturday or Sunday, and any day which is a bank holiday in any part of Great Britain, is to be disregarded: s 328(5). Section 324(5), (6), (8) (see para 564 ante and para 570 post), applies with any requisite modification for the purposes of these provisions: s 328(7). For the meaning of 'bank holiday' see para 71 note 9 ante.

9 See ibid s 325(1) and para 571 post.

567. Duty to notify investment exchange. Whenever a company whose shares or debentures are listed on a recognised investment exchange[1] other than an overseas investment exchange[2] is notified of any matter by a director in consequence of the fulfilment of a statutory obligation[3], and that matter relates to shares or debentures so listed, the company is under obligation to notify that investment exchange of that matter; and the investment exchange may publish, in such manner as it may determine, any information so received by it[4]. An obligation so imposed must be fulfilled before the end of the day next following that on which it arises; but, for this purpose, a day which is a Saturday or a Sunday, or a bank holiday[5] in any part of Great Britain, is disregarded[6]. If default is made in complying with this provision, the company, and every officer of it who is in default, is guilty of an offence and liable on summary conviction to a fine not exceeding one-fifth of the statutory maximum and, on conviction after continued contravention, to a daily default fine not exceeding one-fiftieth of the statutory maximum[7].

1 Ie within the meaning of the Financial Services Act 1986: see para 223 note 1 ante.

2 Ie within the meaning of the Financial Services Act 1986: see para 223 note 1 ante.

3 Ie one imposed by either the Companies Act 1985 s 324 (see paras 564, 565 ante) or s 328 (see para 566 ante).

4 Ibid s 329(1) (amended by the Financial Services Act 1986 s 212(2), Sch 16 para 20).

5 For the meaning of 'bank holiday' see para 71 note 9 ante.

6 Companies Act 1985 s 329(2).

7 Ibid ss 329(3), 730, Sch 24. For the meaning of 'officer who is in default', 'the statutory maximum' and 'daily default fine' see para 1161 post. Proceedings may not be instituted except by or with the consent of the Secretary of State or the Director of Public Prosecutions: see ss 329(3), 732(1), (2)(a) and para 1165 post.

568. Meaning of references to 'interests in shares or debentures'. A reference to a person's interest in shares in, or debentures[1] of, a company is to be read as including any interest of any kind whatsoever in shares or debentures[2]. Accordingly there are to be disregarded any restraints or restrictions to which the exercise of any right attached to the interest is or may be subject[3].

Where property is held on trust and any interest in shares or debentures is comprised in the property, any beneficiary of the trust who does not otherwise have any interest in the shares or debentures is to be taken as having such an interest[4].

A person is taken to have an interest in shares or debentures if:

(1) he enters into a contract for their purchase by him, whether for cash or other consideration; or

(2) not being the registered holder, he is entitled to exercise any right conferred by the holding of the shares or debentures, or is entitled to control the exercise of any such right[5].

For the purpose of head (2) above, a person is taken to be entitled to exercise or control the exercise of a right conferred by the holding of shares or debentures if he has a right, whether subject to conditions or not, the exercise of which would make him so entitled, or is under an obligation, whether or not so subject, the fulfilment of which would make him so entitled[6]. However, a person is not, by virtue of head (2) above, taken to be so interested by reason only that he has been appointed a proxy[7] to vote at a specified meeting of a company or of any class of its members and at any adjournment of that meeting, or has been appointed by a corporation to act as its representative[8] at any meeting of a company or of any class of its members[9].

A person is taken to be interested in shares or debentures if a body corporate[10] is interested in them and:

(a) that body corporate or its directors are accustomed to act in accordance with his directions or instructions; or

(b) he is entitled to exercise or control the exercise of one-third or more of the voting power at general meetings of that body corporate[11].

Where a person is entitled to exercise or control the exercise of one-third or more of the voting power at general meetings of a body corporate, and that body corporate is entitled to exercise or control the exercise of any of the voting power at general meetings of another body corporate ('the effective voting power') then, for the purposes of head (b) above, the effective voting power is taken to be exercisable by that person[12].

A person is taken to have an interest in shares or debentures if, otherwise than by virtue of having an interest under a trust, he has a right to call for delivery of the shares or debentures to himself or to his order, or he has a right to acquire an interest in shares or debentures or is under an obligation to take an interest in shares or debentures; whether in any case the right or obligation is conditional or absolute[13].

Persons having a joint interest are deemed each of them to have that interest[14].

So long as a person is entitled to receive, during the lifetime of himself or another, income from trust property comprising shares or debentures, an interest in the shares or debentures in reversion or remainder is to be disregarded[15].

A person is to be treated as uninterested in shares or debentures if, and so long as, he holds them as a bare trustee or as a custodian trustee[16].

An interest of a person subsisting by virtue of any authorised unit trust scheme[17], common investment schemes[18], local authority investment schemes[19] or the Church Funds Investment Scheme[20] is to be disregarded[21]. So also is any interest of the Church of Scotland General Trustees or of the Church of Scotland Trust in shares or debentures held by them, or of any other person in shares or debentures held by those Trustees or that Trust otherwise than as simple trustees[22].

1 It is immaterial that the shares or debentures in which a person has an interest are unidentifiable: Companies Act 1985 s 324(3)(a), Sch 13 para 8.

2 Ibid Sch 13 para 1(1).

3 Ibid Sch 13 para 1(2).

4 Ibid Sch 13 para 2. Schedule 13 para 2 is without prejudice to the provisions of Sch 13 paras 3–13 (as amended) (see infra): Sch 13 para 2.

5 Ibid Sch 13 para 3(1). Delivery to a person's order of shares or debentures in fulfilment of a contract for their purchase by him or in satisfaction of a right of his to call for their delivery, or failure to deliver shares or debentures in accordance with the terms of such a contract or on which such a right falls to be satisfied, is deemed to constitute an event in consequence of the occurrence of which he ceases to be interested in them; and so is the lapse of a person's right to call for the delivery of shares or debentures: Sch 13 para 13.

6 Ibid Sch 13 para 3(2).

7 As to the appointment of proxies see para 674 post.

8 As to the appointment of a representative by a corporation see para 678 post.

9 Companies Act 1985 Sch 13 para 3(3).

10 For the meaning of 'body corporate' see para 89 note 8 ante.

11 Companies Act 1985 Sch 13 para 4. As Sch 13 para 4 applies for the purposes of s 346(4), (5) (see para 607 post) 'more than one-half' is substituted for 'one-third or more': Sch 13 para 4.

12 Ibid Sch 13 para 5. As Sch 13 para 5 applies for the purposes of s 346(4), (5) (see para 607 post) 'more than one-half' is substituted for 'one-third or more': Sch 13 para 5.

13 Ibid Sch 13 para 6(1). Rights or obligations to subscribe for shares or debentures are not to be taken, for purposes of Sch 13 para 6(1), to be rights to acquire, or obligations to take, an interest in shares or debentures, but this is without prejudice to Sch 13 para 1 (see supra): Sch 13 para 6(2).

14 Ibid Sch 13 para 7.

15 Ibid Sch 13 para 9.

16 Ibid Sch 13 para 10.

17 Ie within the meaning of the Financial Services Act 1986: see STOCK EXCHANGE.

18 Ie made under the Charities Act 1993 s 24 or s 25 and the Administration of Justice Act 1982 s 42 (as amended): see CHARITIES vol 5(2) (Reissue) para 351, 352; and PRACTICE AND PROCEDURE.

19 Ie made under the Trustee Investments Act 1961 s 11 (as amended) (local authority investment schemes).

20 Ie set out in the Church Funds Investment Measure 1958 Schedule: see ECCLESIASTICAL LAW.

21 Companies Act 1985 Sch 13 para 11 (amended by the Financial Services Act 1986 s 212(2), Sch 16 para 25; the Charities Act 1992 s 78(1), Sch 6 para 11(b); and the Charities Act 1993 s 98(1), Sch 6 para 20(1),(3)); Interpretation Act 1978 s 17(2)(a).

22 Companies Act 1985 Sch 13 para 12. The 'Church of Scotland General Trustees' are the body incorporated by the order confirmed by the Church of Scotland (General Trustees) Order Confirmation Act 1921; and the 'Church of Scotland Trust' is the body incorporated by the order confirmed by the Church of Scotland Trust Order Confirmation Act 1932: Companies Act 1985 Sch 13 para 12.

569. Exceptions from liability to notify. The statutory provisions relating to a director's duty to disclose shareholdings in his own company[1] do not require notification of:

(1) interests in shares or debentures of any person in his capacity as trustee or personal representative of any trust or estate of which the Public Trustee is also a trustee (otherwise than as custodian trustee) or, as the case may be, a personal representative;

(2) interests in shares in, or debentures of, a society registered under the Industrial and Provident Societies Act 1965 or deemed to be so registered[2] under that Act;

(3) interests in shares or debentures of a person in his capacity as trustee of, or as beneficiary under, a trust relating exclusively to:

(a) any retirement benefits scheme which is an approved scheme[3] or a statutory scheme[4], and any retirement benefit scheme which is treated as being two or more separate retirement benefit schemes[5] where any of those separate schemes is an approved scheme or a statutory scheme; or

(b) a superannuation fund to which the Income and Corporation Taxes Act 1988[6] applies;

(4) any event occurring in relation to any person in any such capacity as is mentioned in heads (1) or (3) above or in relation to any such shares or debentures as are mentioned in head (2) above;

(5) interests in shares or debentures which a person is taken to have because he has control of a body corporate[7] where the body corporate in question is interested in those shares or debentures in its capacity as trustee of any such trust as is mentioned in head (3) above;

(6) any event occurring in relation to any person as a result of which he is taken to have any such interest as is mentioned in head (5) above;

(7) interests in shares in a body corporate which arise solely on account of any limitation imposed by the memorandum or articles of association of the body corporate on a person's right to dispose of a share[8].

Nor do those provisions require notification:

(i) to a company which is the wholly-owned subsidiary[9] of a body corporate incorporated outside Great Britain of interests in shares in, or debentures of, that body corporate or any other body corporate so incorporated, or of any event occurring in relation to any such shares or debentures;

(ii) to a company by a director of the company who is also the director of a body corporate of which the company is the wholly-owned subsidiary and which is itself statutorily required[10] to keep a register of interests in any shares or debentures or of any event occurring in relation to any shares or debentures[11].

1 Ie the Companies Act 1985 s 324(1), (2): see paras 564, 565 ante.
2 Ie by virtue of the Industrial and Provident Societies Act 1965 s 4: see INDUSTRIAL AND PROVIDENT SOCIETIES vol 24 (Reissue) para 3.
3 For the meaning of 'approved scheme' see SOCIAL SECURITY AND PENSIONS.
4 For the meaning of 'statutory scheme' see SOCIAL SECURITY AND PENSIONS.
5 Ie under the Income and Corporation Taxes Act 1988 s 611(3): see SOCIAL SECURITY AND PENSIONS.
6 Ie ibid s 608: see SOCIAL SECURITY AND PENSIONS.
7 Ie pursuant to the Companies Act 1985 s 324(3)(a), Sch 13 para 4: see para 568 ante.
8 Companies (Disclosure of Directors' Interests) (Exceptions) Regulations 1985, SI 1985/802, reg 2; Interpretation Act 1978 s 17(2)(b).
9 For these purposes, a company is deemed to be the wholly-owned subsidiary of another body corporate if it has no members but that other and that other's wholly-owned subsidiaries and its or their nominees: Companies (Disclosure of Directors' Interests) (Exceptions) Regulations 1985 reg 3(2).
10 Ie pursuant to the Companies Act 1985 s 352(1): see para 379 ante.
11 Companies (Disclosure of Directors' Interests) (Exceptions) Regulations 1985 reg 3(1).

570. Offences relating to notification. A person who fails to discharge, within the proper period, any obligation to notify the company[1], or who, in purported discharge of such an obligation, makes to a company a statement which he knows to be false, or recklessly makes to it a statement which is false, is guilty of an offence and liable on conviction on indictment to imprisonment for a term not exceeding two years or a fine, or to both, or on summary conviction to imprisonment for a term not exceeding six months, or a fine not exceeding the statutory maximum, or to both[2].

1 Ie an obligation to notify under the Companies Act 1985 s 324(1) or (2) (see paras 564, 565 ante) or, as the case may be, s 328(3) (see para 566 ante).
2 Ibid ss 324(7), 328(6), 730, Sch 24. For the meaning of 'the statutory maximum' see para 1161 post. Proceedings for these offences may not be instituted except by, or with the consent of, the Secretary of State or the Director of Public Prosecutions: see ibid ss 324(8), 328(7), 732(1), (2)(a) and para 1165 post. The Secretary of State may appoint inspectors to investigate circumstances which suggest contraventions of s 324 or s 328(3)–(5): see s 446(1) and para 1384 post.

(B) *Register of Directors' Interests*

571. Register of directors' interests. Every company must keep a register for the purpose of recording the information which a director[1] is under a statutory obligation[2] to notify to the company[3]. Whenever a company receives information from a director given in fulfilment of an obligation so imposed on him, it is under obligation to enter in the register, against the director's name, the information received and the date of the entry[4].

Whenever a company grants to a director a right to subscribe for shares in, or debentures of, the company, it is under obligation to enter in the register against his name:

(1) the date on which the right is granted;
(2) the period during which, or time at which, it is exercisable;
(3) the consideration for the grant, or, if there is no consideration, that fact; and
(4) the description of shares or debentures involved and the number[5] or amount of them, and the price to be paid for them or the consideration, if otherwise than in money[6].

Whenever such a right is exercised by a director, the company is under obligation to enter in the register against his name that fact, identifying the right, the number or amount of shares or debentures in respect of which it is exercised and, if they were registered in his name, that fact and, if not, the name or names of the person or persons in whose name or names they were registered, together, if they were registered in the names of two persons or more, with the number or amount of the shares or debentures registered in the name of each of them[7].

The company is not, by virtue of anything done for the purposes of the statutory provisions[8] relating to the register, affected with notice of, or put upon inquiry as to, the rights of any person in relation to any shares or debentures[9].

If default is made in complying with any of the above provisions, the company, and every officer of it who is in default, is liable on summary conviction to a fine not exceeding one-fifth of the statutory maximum and, on conviction after continued contravention, to a daily default fine not exceeding one-fiftieth of the statutory maximum[10].

1 For these purposes, a shadow director is deemed a director: Companies Act 1985 s 325(6). For the meaning of 'director' and 'shadow director' see para 543 note 1 ante.
2 Ie under ibid s 324: see para 564 et seq ante.
3 Ibid s 325(1). For these purposes, an obligation imposed on a director by s 325 is to be treated as if imposed by s 324 (see para 564 ante): s 328(9).
4 Ibid s 325(2). An obligation imposed by s 325(2) or s 325(4) (see infra) must be fulfilled before the expiration of the period of three days beginning with the day after that on which the obligation to make such entry in the register arises; but, in reckoning that period, a day which is a Saturday or Sunday or a bank holiday in any part of Great Britain is to be disregarded: s 325(5), Sch 13 para 22. If default is made in complying with Sch 13 para 22, the company, and every officer of it who is in default, is liable on summary conviction to a fine not exceeding one-fifth of the statutory maximum and, on conviction after continued contravention, to a daily default fine not exceeding one-fiftieth of the statutory maximum: ss 326(2)(b), 730, Sch 24. For the meaning of 'officer who is in default', 'the statutory maximum' and 'daily default fine' see para 1161 post; and for the meaning of 'bank holiday' see para 71 note 9 ante.
5 For the meaning of 'number' in relation to shares see para 564 note 8 ante.
6 Companies Act 1985 s 325(3).
7 Ibid s 325(4). See also note 4 supra.
8 Ie ibid s 325 or Sch 13 Pt IV (paras 21–29) (as amended).
9 Ibid s 325(5), Sch 13 para 24.
10 Ibid ss 326(1), (2)(a), Sch 24.

572. Form of register. The register[1] must be so made up that the entries in it against the several names appear in chronological order[2]. The nature and extent of an interest recorded in the register of a director in any shares or debentures must, if he so requires, be recorded in the register[3].

Unless the register is in such a form as to constitute in itself an index, the company must keep an index of the names inscribed in it; in respect of each name, the index must contain a sufficient indication to enable the information entered against it to be readily found and the index must be kept in the same place as the register[4]. The company must, within 14 days after the date on which a name is entered in the register, make any necessary alteration in the index[5].

If default is made in complying with the above provisions[6], the company, and every officer of it who is in default, is liable on summary conviction to a fine not exceeding one-fifth of the statutory maximum and, on conviction after continued contravention, to a daily default fine not exceeding one-fiftieth of the statutory maximum[7].

1 Ie the register required to be kept under the Companies Act 1985 s 325: see para 571 ante. As to the place where the register is kept see para 573 post.
2 Ibid s 325(5), Sch 13 para 21.
3 Ibid Sch 13 para 23.
4 Ibid Sch 13 para 28. As to the provisions applicable where the index is maintained otherwise than by recording the entries in legible form see para 684 post.
5 Ibid Sch 13 para 28.
6 Ie ibid Sch 13 paras 21 or 28: see supra.
7 Ibid ss 326(2)(b), 730, Sch 24. For the meaning of 'officer who is in default', 'the statutory maximum' and 'daily default fine' see para 1161 post.

573. Location of register. The register[1] must be kept at a company's registered office if the register of members is kept there[2]. If the register of members is not kept there, the register of directors' interests must be kept either at the registered office or at the place where the register of members is kept[3]. The company must send notice in the prescribed form[4] to the registrar of companies of the place where the register of directors' interests is kept and of any change in that place (save in a case in which it has at all times been kept at the registered office)[5].

If default is made for 14 days in complying with this obligation, the company, and every officer of it who is in default, is liable on summary conviction to a fine not exceeding one-fifth of the statutory maximum and, on conviction after continued contravention, to a daily default fine not exceeding one-fiftieth of the statutory maximum[6].

1 Ie the register required to be kept under the Companies Act 1985 s 325: see para 571 ante.
2 Ibid s 325(5), Sch 13 para 25(a). As to the location of the register of members see para 389 ante.
3 Ibid Sch 13 para 25(b).
4 For the prescribed form of notice see the Companies (Forms) (Amendment) Regulations 1995, SI 1995/736, reg 3, Sch 2, Form 325.
5 Companies Act 1985 Sch 13 para 27.
6 Ibid ss 326(1), (4), 730, Sch 24. For the meaning of 'officer who is in default', 'the statutory maximum' and 'daily default fine' see para 1161 post.

574. Inspection etc of register. The register[1] must be open to the inspection of any member of the company without charge and of any other person on payment of such fee as may be prescribed[2]. The company[3] must make the register available for such inspection for not less than two hours during the period between 9 am and 5 pm on each business day[4]; and it must permit a person inspecting the register to copy any information made available for inspection by means of the taking of notes or the transcription of the information[5]. If an inspection of the register is refused, the company, and every officer of it who is in default, is liable on summary conviction to a fine not exceeding one-fifth of the statutory maximum and, on conviction after continued contravention, to a daily default fine not exceeding one-fiftieth of the statutory maximum[6]. The register must also be produced at the commencement of the company's annual general meeting and remain open and accessible during the continuance of the meeting to any person attending the meeting[7]. If default is made in compliance, the company, and every officer of it who is in default, is liable on summary conviction to a fine not exceeding one-fifth of the statutory maximum[8]. In the case of a refusal of an inspection so required, the court may by order compel an immediate inspection of the register[9].

Any member of the company or other person may require a copy of the register, or any part of it, on payment of such fee as may be prescribed[10]. The company must cause any copy so required by a person to be sent to him within the period of ten days beginning with the day after that on which the requirement is received by the company[11]. If a copy so required is not sent within the proper period, the company, and every officer of it who is in default, is liable on summary conviction to a fine not exceeding one-fifth of the statutory maximum, and, on conviction after continued contravention, to a daily default fine not exceeding one-fiftieth of the statutory maximum[12]. In the case of failure to send within the proper period a copy so required, the court may by order direct that the copy required be sent to the person requiring it[13].

---

1 Ie the register required to be kept under the Companies Act 1985 s 325: see para 571 ante.
2 Ibid s 325(5), Sch 13 para 25 (amended by the Companies Act 1989 ss 143(10)(a), 212, Sch 24). The fee so prescribed is £2.50 for each hour or part thereof during which the right of inspection is exercised: Companies (Inspection and Copying of Registers, Indices and Documents) Regulations 1991, SI 1991/1998, reg 5, Sch 2 para 1(c). As to the power to make regulations see para 230 ante.
3 For the meaning of 'company' see para 229 note 14 ante.
4 Companies (Inspection and Copying of Registers, Indices and Documents) Regulations 1991 reg 3(1), (2)(a). For the meaning of 'business day' see para 229 note 15 ante.
5 Ibid reg 3(1), (2)(b). Regulation 3(2)(b) is not, however, to be construed as obliging a company to provide any facilities additional to those provided for the purposes of facilitating inspection: reg 3(3).
6 Companies Act 1985 ss 326(1), (3), 730, Sch 24. For the meaning of 'officer who is in default', 'the statutory maximum' and 'daily default fine' see para 1161 post.
7 Ibid Sch 13 para 29.
8 Ibid ss 326(1), (5), 730, Sch 24.
9 Ibid s 326(1), (6). Application to the court is by originating summons in the expedited form: RSC Ord 102 r 2(1), (2).
10 Companies Act 1985 Sch 13 para 26(1) (amended by the Companies Act 1989 s 143(10)(b)). The fee so prescribed is, for the first 100 entries or part thereof copied, £2.50; for the next 1,000 entries or part thereof copied, £20.00; and, for every subsequent 1,000 entries or part thereof copied, £15.00: Companies (Inspection and Copying of Registers, Indices and Documents) Regulations 1991 reg 5, Sch 2 para 2(c).
11 Companies Act 1985 Sch 13 para 26(2).
12 Ibid ss 326(1), (3), 730, Sch 24.
13 Ibid s 326(1), (6). Application to the court is by originating summons in the expedited form: RSC Ord 102 r 2(1), (2).

F. REMUNERATION OF DIRECTORS

575. Right to remuneration. In the absence of a clause in the memorandum or articles of association providing for their being paid for their services, directors are not entitled to be paid any remuneration[1], nor may they recover anything on a quantum meruit basis[2]. A person whose appointment as a director turns out to be a nullity may, however, recover on a quantum meruit for services rendered and accepted after the date of his purported appointment[3]. Where the articles provide that the remuneration of a managing director is to be determined by the board of directors, and no such determination is made, a managing director who claims remuneration on a quantum meruit basis will be unsuccessful[4]. The right to remuneration is based on an inference of law imposed on the parties where work has been done or goods have been delivered under what purports to be a binding contract, but is not so in fact[5]. Provided that there has been a genuine exercise of the company's power to award remuneration, the court will be reluctant to hold that the payments have been improper, but payments made where no services have in fact been rendered cannot properly be classified as remuneration[6]. Sums improperly received as remuneration may be recovered in an action, or, in a winding up, by misfeasance summons[7]. As the remuneration of a director is a payment for services rendered, the fact that a director holds his qualification shares as a trustee does not make him accountable for this remuneration to the beneficiary[8], unless the opportunity to gain that remuneration was gained as a result of a discretion vested in the director as a trustee[9]. Even if that opportunity was so gained, the terms of the trust instrument may render the trustees not accountable for their remuneration as directors[10].

The right to remuneration may be waived[11]; but a mere promise by the directors to forgo their remuneration, even if made in open meeting, is not enforceable[12]. Where there is an agreement not to claim remuneration which is supported by consideration, the agreement may be enforced by any party to it and would bar any claim by a director to remuneration[13].

1 *Dunston v Imperial Gas Light Co* (1831) 3 B & Ad 125; *Young v Naval, Military and Civil Service Co-operative Society of South Africa* [1905] 1 KB 687 (where travelling and hotel expenses were disallowed); *Re French Protestant Hospital* [1951] Ch 567, [1951] 1 All ER 938 (body corporate incorporated by royal charter; improper for directors to alter byelaws to enable payment to be made to them where constitution did not give right to remuneration); and see *York and North Midland Rly Co v Hudson* (1853) 16 Beav 485; but see *Marmor Ltd v Alexander* 1908 SC 78; *Re Whitehall Court Ltd* (1887) 3 TLR 402; *Re Liverpool Household Stores Association* (1890) 59 LJ Ch 616; and *Kerr v Marine Products Ltd* (1928) 44 TLR 292 (where the remuneration was under the articles to be determined by the company in general meeting, and no remuneration having been fixed, it was held that the directors were not entitled to pay a salary to a man appointed as overseas director under an article empowering the directors to appoint officers abroad and to fix their salary).

2 *Hutton v West Cork Rly Co* (1883) 23 ChD 654 at 671, CA; *Re George Newman & Co* [1895] 1 Ch 674, CA; *Re Bodega Co Ltd* [1904] 1 Ch 276 (where a director continued to act as such after his office was vacated); *Re Consolidated Nickel Mines Ltd* [1914] 1 Ch 883 (where directors failed to convene the annual meeting at which they would have vacated office and they were held not entitled to remuneration after the date on which it should have been convened).

3 *Craven-Ellis v Canons Ltd* [1936] 2 KB 403, [1936] 2 All ER 1066, CA; cf *Brown and Green Ltd v Hays* (1920) 36 TLR 330.

4 *Re Richmond Gate Property Co Ltd* [1964] 3 All ER 936, [1965] 1 WLR 335 (where there was a valid contract and no room for an implied contract or a contract imposed by law; and it appears from the judgment that there was an understanding that no remuneration should be paid to the managing director until the company got on its feet, which it never did), distinguishing *Craven-Ellis v Canons Ltd* [1936] 2 KB 403, [1936] 2 All ER 1066, CA.

5 *Craven-Ellis v Canons Ltd* [1936] 2 KB 403 at 410, [1936] 2 All ER 1066 at 1072, CA.

6 *Re Halt Garage (1964) Ltd* [1982] 3 All ER 1016.
7 *Re George Newman & Co* [1895] 1 Ch 674, CA; *Re Bodega Co Ltd* [1904] 1 Ch 276; *Re Oxford Benefit Building and Investment Society* (1886) 35 ChD 502; *Brown and Green Ltd v Hays* (1920) 36 TLR 330; *Re Halt Garage (1964) Ltd* [1982] 3 All ER 1016 (sums paid to wife of main shareholder who took no part in the business recoverable). They will be ordered jointly and severally to repay with 5% interest as on a breach of trust: *Re Oxford Benefit Building and Investment Society* supra; *Leeds Estate Building and Investment Co v Shepherd* (1887) 36 ChD 787 (where remuneration was payable only if a dividend had been paid); cf *Re Whitehall Court Ltd* (1887) 56 LT 280 at 281. As to misfeasance proceedings see para 2448 et seq post.
8 *Re Dover Coalfield Extension Ltd* [1908] 1 Ch 65, CA, explained, and dictum of Warrington J, in that case, as reported at first instance in [1907] 2 Ch 76 at 83, criticised in *Re Gee, Wood v Staples* [1948] Ch 284, [1948] 1 All ER 498. See also *Re Lewis, Lewis v Lewis* (1910) 103 LT 495.
9 *Re Macadam, Dallow and Moscrop v Codd* [1946] Ch 73, [1945] 2 All ER 664; and see *Williams v Barton* [1927] 2 Ch 9.
10 *Re Llewellin's Will Trusts, Griffiths v Wilcox* [1949] Ch 225, [1949] 1 All ER 487.
11 *Re Arigna Iron Mining Co* (1853) 1 Eq Rep 269.
12 *Lambert v Northern Railway of Buenos Ayres Co Ltd* (1869) 18 WR 180 (no evidence that shares had been purchased on the strength of the promise).
13 *West Yorkshire Darracq Agency v Coleridge* [1911] 2 KB 326 (agreement to which liquidator representing the company was party; consideration found in mutual forbearance to sue); *Re William Porter & Co Ltd* [1937] 2 All ER 361 (resolution of directors forgoing fees intended to be acted on by company).

576. How fixed. The remuneration of directors may be fixed by the articles[1] or the articles may provide that the remuneration is to be fixed by the company in general meeting[2] or in any other manner. If fixed by the articles, it is subject to alteration by special resolution[3]. If dependent on a resolution of the company, it may be altered and the company may by ordinary resolution discriminate between the directors as to the amount of their remuneration[4].

When a qualification is required, the date when remuneration commences depends on whether the director was empowered to act before acquiring the qualification[5]. When once fixed in general meeting, the remuneration runs from that time, unless the resolution is otherwise expressed; a reference in the subsequent balance sheet to a sum charged from an earlier date will not bind the company[6]. The fact that the duties of directors are diminished as the result of a sale of the undertaking and assets of the company does not disentitle them from receiving the same remuneration as before[7].

Where articles provide that the board of directors may fix the remuneration of the directors, and may in addition grant special remuneration to any director who serves on any committee or who devotes special attention to the business of the company or who otherwise performs special services, it is only the board as a whole which can fix or grant the remuneration; and this is so even where there is an article which defines the board as the directors of the company for the time being (or a quorum of such directors assembled at a meeting of directors duly convened) or any committee authorised by the board to act on its behalf[8].

1 The articles may be looked at to see the terms of the contract of service, though not forming the actual contract: *Re Peruvian Guano Co, ex p Kemp* [1894] 3 Ch 690 at 701; and see para 142 ante. As to share option schemes see para 1517 et seq post.
2 The Companies (Tables A to F) Regulations 1985, SI 1985/805, Schedule, Table A art 82 provides that the directors are entitled to such remuneration as the company by ordinary resolution determines; and, unless the resolution provides otherwise, the remuneration will be deemed to accrue from day to day. As to Table A generally see para 529 et seq ante. The company cannot refuse to pay on the ground that the fees stated in the articles are excessive: *Re Anglo-Greek Steam Co* (1866) LR 2 Eq 1. See also *Re George Newman & Co* [1895] 1 Ch 674, CA (where all the shareholders agreed, but not at a meeting). If the shareholders are asked to sanction any extra remuneration, the notice of the meeting must point out the matter very clearly to them: *Normandy v Ind, Coope & Co Ltd* [1908] 1 Ch 84. A statement in a balance sheet of remuneration paid is not sufficient ratification: *Re London Gigantic Wheel Co Ltd* (1908) 24 TLR 618, CA; and see *Baillie v Oriental Telephone and Electric Co Ltd* [1915] 1 Ch 503, CA. The absence of a

formal resolution for approval will not, however, be fatal, if the shareholders have applied their minds to the question: *Re Duomatic Ltd* [1969] 2 Ch 365, [1969] 1 All ER 161, applying *Parker and Cooper Ltd v Reading* [1926] Ch 975; and see para 696 post.

3 *Boschoek Proprietary Co Ltd v Fuke* [1906] 1 Ch 148.

4 *Foster v Foster* [1916] 1 Ch 532.

5 *Re International Cable Co Ltd, ex p Official Liquidator* (1892) 66 LT 253; *Salton v New Beeston Cycle Co* [1899] 1 Ch 775; *Ex p European Central Rly Co, Walford's Case* (1869) 20 LT 74.

6 *Re London Gigantic Wheel Co Ltd* (1908) 24 TLR 618, CA.

7 *Re Consolidated Nickel Mines Ltd* [1914] 1 Ch 883.

8 *Guinness plc v Saunders* [1990] 2 AC 663, [1990] 1 All ER 652, HL.

577. How payable. Unless otherwise stated, the remuneration is payable although no profits are made[1]. A fixed remuneration may be sued for, or proved for in a winding up, although there is no resolution of the board that it should be paid[2]. A statement in a balance sheet signed by the directors that a sum is due to those directors as remuneration is not a sufficient acknowledgment[3] as to prevent an action in respect of that remuneration being barred by lapse of time[4].

Whether the remuneration is apportionable, so that service for less than a whole year will entitle a director to a proportionate part, depends upon the construction of the contract or the articles as the case may be[5]. It is apportionable if the remuneration is payable 'at the rate of' a fixed sum per annum[6].

Directors who are remunerated by a percentage of the net profits[7] or by commission on the sum available for distribution[8] are entitled to compute their remuneration on the profits before corporation tax is deducted.

Where the remuneration of the directors is a lump sum to be divided as they think fit, no director may sue for remuneration until a division has taken place[9], unless it is in addition provided that in default of agreement the remuneration should be equally divided, and there has been no agreement[10]. A director cannot obtain a mandatory injunction to compel the remaining directors to fix his remuneration[11]. Where directors are given a discretion to determine the time for payment of a director's remuneration, no action will lie until they have so determined[12].

A special resolution of the company altering directors' remuneration cannot alter the contractual rights of the directors[13] as regards remuneration actually earned.

1 *Re Lundy Granite Co Ltd, Lewis's Case* (1872) 26 LT 673. There is no general presumption to the contrary: *Nell v Atlanta Gold and Silver Consolidated Mines* (1895) 11 TLR 407, CA.

2 *Re New British Iron Co, ex p Beckwith* [1898] 1 Ch 324; *Nell v Atlanta Gold and Silver Consolidated Mines* (1895) 11 TLR 407, CA. As to proof in winding up see paras 579, 2509 et seq post.

3 Ie within the meaning of the Limitation Act 1980 s 30.

4 *Re Coliseum (Barrow) Ltd* [1930] 2 Ch 44; *Re Transplanters (Holding Co) Ltd* [1958] 2 All ER 711, [1958] 1 WLR 822. As to the limitation period see the Limitation Act 1980 ss 5, 8 and LIMITATION OF ACTIONS vol 28 para 878 et seq.

5 Remuneration at a fixed sum per annum or for each year was held not to be apportionable in *McConnell's Claim* [1901] 1 Ch 728; *Inman v Ackroyd and Best Ltd* [1901] 1 KB 613, CA; and *Salton v New Beeston Cycle Co* [1899] 1 Ch 775. In *Moriarty v Regent's Garage Co* [1921] 1 KB 423, these decisions were strongly criticised and stated to be good law on the basis only that the payment to the directors in the two last-named cases was in the form of a lump sum, and that until a decision as to the division of the lump sum had been made no claim would lie, and it was held that the remuneration of a director was apportionable under the Apportionment Act 1870. *Moriarty v Regent's Garage Co* supra was overruled in the Court of Appeal [1921] 2 KB 766, but the appeal was not decided on the applicability of the Apportionment Act 1870, the court holding that this question could not then be raised as it had not been raised in the county court. Cf *Boschoek Proprietary Co Ltd v Fuke* [1906] 1 Ch 148; *Re Central De Kaap Gold Mines* (1899) 69 LJ Ch 18; *Kempf v Offin River Gold Estates Ltd* (1908) Times, 10 April; *Swabey v Port Darwin Gold Mining Co* (1889) 1 Meg 385, CA; *Re Shaws, Bryant & Co* (1901) 45 Sol Jo 580. A term that the remuneration is apportionable was implied in *Swabey v Port Darwin Gold Mining Co* supra,

but cf *Inman v Ackroyd and Best Ltd* [1901] 1 KB 613, CA, and *Moriarty v Regent's Garage Co* supra. Where it is provided that the directors are entitled to a share in profits by way of additional remuneration and that in default of agreement it should be divided equally, in the event of there being no agreement, a director who ceased to hold office during the year is entitled to a proportionate part: *Diamond v English Sewing Cotton Co Ltd* [1922] WN 237, CA.

6 *Gilman v Gülcher Electric Light Co* (1886) 3 TLR 133, CA; *Re A M Wood's Ships' Woodite Protection Co* (1890) 62 LT 760; *Swabey v Port Darwin Gold Mining Co* (1889) 1 Meg 385, CA; and see RENTCHARGES vol 39 para 1288.

7 *Johnston v Chestergate Hat Manufacturing Co Ltd* [1915] 2 Ch 338.

8 *Edwards v Saunton Hotel Co Ltd* [1943] 1 All ER 176.

9 *Morrell v Oxford Portland Cement Co Ltd* (1910) 26 TLR 682; *Joseph v Sonora (Mexico) Land and Timber Co Ltd* (1918) 34 TLR 220. Continuing directors with power to divide remuneration among the directors may thus entirely deprive a retiring director of remuneration: *Gilman v Gülcher Electric Light Co* (1886) 3 TLR 133, CA; and see *Moriarty v Regent's Garage Co* [1921] 1 KB 423 (on appeal [1921] 2 KB 766, CA).

10 *Diamond v English Sewing Cotton Co Ltd* [1922] WN 237, CA (where the remuneration sued for was additional remuneration by way of a share in profits at a fixed rate).

11 *Dashwood v Cornish* (1897) 13 TLR 337, CA.

12 *Caridad Copper Mining Co v Swallow* [1902] 2 KB 44, CA.

13 *Swabey v Port Darwin Gold Mining Co* (1889) 1 Meg 385, CA.

578. Prohibition of tax-free payments. It is not lawful for a company to pay a director remuneration (whether as director or otherwise) free of income tax, or otherwise calculated by reference to or varying with the amount of his income tax, or to or with any rate of income tax, except under a contract which was in force on 18 July 1945, providing expressly, and not by reference to the articles, for payment of such tax-free remuneration[1]. Any provision contained in a company's articles, or in any contract, except as mentioned above, or in any resolution of a company or a company's directors, for payment to a director of remuneration as mentioned above, has effect as if it provided for payment, as a gross sum subject to income tax, of the net sum for which it actually provides[2].

1 Companies Act 1985 s 311(1); Companies Consolidation (Consequential Provisions) Act 1985 s 15.
2 Companies Act 1985 s 311(2); Companies Consolidation (Consequential Provisions) Act 1985 s 15.

579. Proof in winding up; execution. The remuneration is not due to the director in his character of a member of the company. It may, therefore, be proved as a debt on winding up in competition with ordinary creditors[1]; and this will be in addition to remuneration earned in any other capacity, such as receiver and manager in a debenture holders' action[2].

Directors who are paid by a percentage of the amount paid by way of dividend may prove for this in the winding up after creditors have been paid, if it was not unreasonable at the time to propose such dividend[3]. If, however, they are paid by a percentage on 'net profits', this refers to the company as a going concern and does not entitle them to a proportion of its assets on a sale of the undertaking[4]; and similarly, where the only contract between the director and the company is contained in the articles, his employment ceases automatically upon the winding up of the company[5].

A receiver by way of equitable execution will not be appointed in respect of directors' fees[6].

1 *Re New British Iron Co, ex p Beckwith* [1898] 1 Ch 324; *Re Dale and Plant Ltd* (1889) 43 ChD 255; *Re Commercial and General Life Assurance etc Association, ex p Johnson* (1857) 27 LJ Ch 803; *Re Lundy Granite Co Ltd, Lewis's Case* (1872) 26 LT 673; *Re A1 Biscuit Co* (1899) 43 Sol Jo 657. *Re Leicester Club and County Racecourse Co, ex p Cannon* (1885) 30 ChD 629 cannot now be regarded as law; it was expressly disapproved in Northern Ireland in *Re Cinnamond Park & Co Ltd* [1930] NI 47. Remuneration which

has been waived by a director cannot be recovered if the company gave consideration (such as deciding to continue its business) for the waiver: *Re William Porter & Co Ltd* [1937] 2 All ER 361. As to proof of debts in winding up generally see para 2509 et seq post.

2 *Re South Western of Venezuela (Barquisimeto) Rly Co* [1902] 1 Ch 701.

3 *Re Peruvian Guano Co, ex p Kemp* [1894] 3 Ch 690; *Re Mercantile Trading Co, Stringer's Case* (1869) 4 Ch App 475.

4 *Frames v Bultfontein Mining Co* [1891] 1 Ch 140.

5 *Re T N Farrer Ltd* [1937] Ch 352, [1937] 2 All ER 505 (as employment conditional upon continued existence of company, no compensation for loss of office on winding up).

6 *Hamilton v Brogden* [1891] WN 36. Such an appointment would probably destroy the security. Past fees not paid may be attached: *Hamilton v Brogden* supra.

580. Special remuneration and expenses; pension.

Apart from special provision in the articles, directors are not entitled to claim travelling[1] or other[2] expenses; and, where they have power to pay a co-director for extra services, the latter must prove the services and the agreement to pay for them[3]. As a matter of account the payment must not be attributed to capital expenditure[4].

Where a power of altering remuneration is reserved to the company, it may not grant a 'pension' to a managing director who retires as manager but not as director[5]. It was formerly not competent for a company which had ceased to carry on business to vote gratuitous remuneration to its officers and employees[6], but there is now an express statutory power to do so[7].

The special provisions for taxation of expenses, allowances and benefits in kind in relation to directors are discussed elsewhere[8].

1 *Young v Naval, Military and Civil Service Co-operative Society of South Africa* [1905] 1 KB 687; *Marmor Ltd v Alexander* 1908 SC 78.

2 As to income tax on expenses allowances to directors and others see the Income and Corporation Taxes Act 1988 s 153 et seq (as amended) and INCOME TAXATION vol 23 (Reissue) para 727 et seq.

3 *Lockhart v Moldacot Pocket Sewing Machine Co Ltd* (1889) 5 TLR 307; and see *Boschoek Proprietary Co Ltd v Fuke* [1906] 1 Ch 148 at 163. Where a director's expense claims are made in a manner proper at the time and settled, it would be oppressive to make an order for account on the grounds that a subsequent retroactive memorandum requires such claims to be strictly documented: *Nelberg v Woking Shipping Co and Konnel SS Co Ltd* [1958] 2 Lloyd's Rep 560; *Guinness plc v Saunders* [1990] 2 AC 663, [1990] 1 All ER 652, HL.

4 *Ashton & Co Ltd v Honey* (1907) 23 TLR 253.

5 *Normandy v Ind, Coope & Co Ltd* [1908] 1 Ch 84. As to compensation for loss of office see para 608 et seq post.

6 *Stroud v Royal Aquarium and Summer and Winter Garden Society* (1903) 89 LT 243, following *Hutton v West Cork Rly Co* (1883) 23 ChD 654, CA; *Parke v Daily News Ltd* [1962] Ch 927, [1962] 2 All ER 929; cf *Cowan v Seymour (Inspector of Taxes)* [1920] 1 KB 500, CA (where the payments were made by the shareholders).

7 See the Companies Act 1985 s 719 and para 1101 post.

8 See the Income and Corporation Taxes Act 1988 s 153 et seq (as amended) and INCOME TAXATION vol 23 (Reissue) para 727 et seq.

581. Particulars of salaries etc to be given in accounts.

The following information must be given in notes to a company's annual accounts:

(1) the aggregate amount of directors' emoluments;

(2) details of the chairman's and directors' emoluments;

(3) emoluments waived;

(4) pensions of directors and past directors;

(5) compensation to directors for loss of office; and

(6) sums paid to third parties in respect of directors' services[1].

1 See the Companies Act 1985 s 232, Sch 6 Pt I (paras 1–14) (as substituted) and para 866 et seq post.

G. POWERS AND DUTIES OF DIRECTORS

582. Position of directors generally. The true position of directors is that of agents for the company[1]. As such they are clothed with the powers and duties of carrying on the whole of its business, subject, however, to the restrictions imposed by the articles and any statutory provisions[2]. The intention of the company may be established by its directors, even if acting informally, depending upon the nature of the matter under consideration, the relative positions of the directors in the company, and generally all the circumstances of the case[3].

Where a company gave an undertaking to the court to act in a way which required the consent of the company in general meeting, the court held that the directors were bound to convene a meeting and issue a circular inviting a favourable response, but that they had the same unrestricted right of voting at the meeting as they would have done if they were not directors[4].

The directors of a company owe a fiduciary duty to act in the interests of their company and to make full and honest disclosure to the shareholders before they vote on a resolution[5].

The matters to which the directors of a company must have regard in the performance of their functions include the interests of the company's employees in general, as well as the interests of its members[6]. Accordingly the duty so imposed is owed by them to the company (and the company alone) and it is enforceable in the same way as any other fiduciary duty owed to a company by its directors[7].

Where a petition to the court is made for an administration order[8], the court may make any order it thinks fit[9], and in particular without prejudice to this generality may, by interim order, restrict the exercise of any powers of the directors or of the company, whether by reference to the consent of the court, or of a person qualified to act as an insolvency practitioner[10] in relation to the company, or otherwise[11].

Articles of association generally give directors very large powers as to the control and management of the company and its affairs; the powers given by Table A[12] are sometimes amplified by special articles which enumerate the powers of the directors.

1　*Re Faure Electric Accumulator Co* (1888) 40 ChD 141. Directors are not ipso facto agents for the shareholders: *Gramophone and Typewriter Ltd v Stanley* [1908] 2 KB 89 at 106, CA; *Charitable Corpn v Sutton* (1742) 2 Atk 400 at 404; *Salmon v Quin & Axtens Ltd* [1909] 1 Ch 311 at 319, CA (affd [1909] AC 442, HL); *Re Olderfleet Shipbuilding and Engineering Co Ltd* [1922] 1 IR 26; cf *Briess v Woolley* [1954] AC 333, [1954] 1 All ER 909, HL (when there was an agency in fact). They have also been called 'servants' (*Smith v Anderson* (1880) 15 ChD 247 at 276, CA) and 'managing partners' (*Re Forest of Dean Coal Mining Co* (1878) 10 ChD 450 at 451; *York and North-Midland Rly Co v Hudson* (1853) 16 Beav 485 at 491; *London Financial Association v Kelk* (1884) 26 ChD 107 at 143; *Re Lands Allotment Co* [1894] 1 Ch 616 at 637, CA; *Automatic Self-Cleansing Filter Syndicate Co Ltd v Cunninghame* [1906] 2 Ch 34 at 45, CA); cf *Sputz v Broadway Engineering Co Ltd* (1944) 171 LT 50. Such expressions indicate useful points of view, but are not exhaustive: *Re Imperial Hydropathic Hotel Co, Blackpool v Hampson* (1882) 23 ChD 1 at 12, 13, CA. They have also been called 'the directing mind and will of the company': *H L Bolton (Engineering) Co Ltd v T J Graham & Sons Ltd* [1957] 1 QB 159 at 172, [1956] 3 All ER 624 at 630, CA per Denning LJ. Directors cannot in the absence of express contract be restrained from acting as directors of a competing company: *London and Mashonaland Exploration Co Ltd v New Mashonaland Exploration Co Ltd* [1891] WN 165. As to the liability of the company for the acts of its agents see para 1113 et seq post.
2　As to the powers of management conferred by the articles see para 589 post; and as to the powers of directors ceasing in a winding up see para 2250 post (compulsory winding up) and para 2756 post (voluntary winding up).
3　*H L Bolton (Engineering) Co Ltd v T J Graham and Sons Ltd* [1957] 1 QB 159, [1956] 3 All ER 624, CA (determination of company's intention for purposes of the Landlord and Tenant Act 1954 s 30: see LANDLORD AND TENANT vol 27(1) (Reissue) para 584 et seq). For a general consideration of the ascertainment of a company's intention see para 2208 post.

4 *Northern Counties Securities Ltd v Jackson and Steeple Ltd* [1974] 2 All ER 625, [1974] 1 WLR 1133.
5 *John Crowther Group plc v Carpets International plc* [1990] BCLC 460.
6 Companies Act 1985 s 309(1). Section 309 applies to shadow directors as it does to directors: s 309(3). For the meaning of 'shadow director' and 'director' see para 543 note 1 ante.
7 Ibid s 309(2). As to such enforcement see para 615 et seq post.
8 As to petitions for administration orders see para 2082 et seq post.
9 See the Insolvency Act 1986 s 9(4) and para 2088 post.
10 As to insolvency practitioners and their qualification see para 2007 et seq post.
11 See the Insolvency Act 1986 s 9(5) and para 2088 post.
12 See the Companies (Tables A to F) Regulations 1985, SI 1985/805, Schedule, Table A art 70 (cited in para 589 post). The directors may also, by power of attorney or otherwise, appoint any person to be the agent of the company for such purposes and on such conditions as they determine, including authority for the agent to delegate all or any of his powers: art 71. As to Table A generally see para 529 et seq ante.

583. Effect of lack of capacity of directors in favour of a person dealing in good faith. In favour of a person dealing with[1] a company in good faith, the power of the board of directors to bind the company, or authorise others to do so, is deemed to be free of any limitation under the company's constitution[2]. A person is not regarded as acting in bad faith by reason only of his knowing that an act is beyond the powers of the directors under the company's constitution; and a person is presumed to have acted in good faith unless the contrary is proved[3].

The doctrine of ultra vires, as it affects the directors[4] and the company[5], has, therefore, been abolished as regards a person dealing with the company in good faith. It remains, however, as between the directors and the company, and directors who exceed their actual powers, or who cause the company to enter into ultra vires contracts, will continue to remain liable in misfeasance for any damage suffered by the company[6]; and, in any event, the above provision has no application to the case of a constructive trust[7].

1 For these purposes, a person 'deals with' a company if he is a party to any transaction or other act to which the company is a party: Companies Act 1985 s 35A(2)(a) (substituted by the Companies Act 1985 s 108(1)).
2 See the Companies Act 1985 s 35A(1) (as substituted) and para 1108 post.
3 See ibid s 35A(2)(b), (c) (as substituted) and para 1108 post.
4 As to the position where the above provisions do not apply see para 584 et seq post.
5 See paras 1107-1109 post.
6 See para 615 et seq post.
7 *International Sales and Agencies Ltd v Marcus* [1982] 3 All ER 551, [1982] 2 CMLR 46.

584. Extent of powers. Directors may do whatever is fairly incidental to the exercise of their powers in carrying out the objects of the company[1].

Any power conferred on the company, or its officers, whether by the Companies Act 1985, or the Insolvency Act 1986, or by the memorandum or articles of association, which could be exercised in such a way as to interfere with the exercise by an administrator[2] of his powers is not exercisable except with the consent of the administrator, which may be given either generally or in relation to particular cases[3].

The question of the limitation of the powers of directors has often arisen in connection with powers of borrowing and mortgaging[4]. Where they have a power to mortgage, they may exercise it to secure a past debt[5], provided that this does not constitute a preference, or to secure sums owing upon a bill of exchange given by directors for a debt of the company[6], or to secure a guarantee or by way of indemnity[7].

They may issue debentures to satisfy the creditors of a purchased business or in payment of the vendor[8].

Where directors exercise their powers improperly, this may give rise to a claim by the company against them based on breach of duty[9]; but such an action will not lie at the suit of a creditor[10]. Further, if the other party to the transaction has notice that the powers of the directors are being improperly exercised, so that he cannot take advantage of the statutory protection for a person dealing with the company in good faith[11], he will be unable to enforce the transaction so far as executory, or to retain the benefits of it so far as it has been carried out[12]. Special rights may by suitable language be conferred on individual directors for their own personal benefits, in which case they may be used as they think fit[13].

1 *Hutton v West Cork Rly Co* (1883) 23 ChD 654, CA; *Re Horsley and Weight Ltd* [1982] Ch 442 at 448, [1982] 3 All ER 1045 at 1050, CA per Buckley LJ. They may bring an action in the name of the company (*Compagnie de Mayville v Whitley* [1896] 1 Ch 788 at 803, CA); petition in bankruptcy (*Re JG Tomkins & Co* [1901] 1 KB 476, CA); give gratuities to the employees (*Hampson v Price's Patent Candle Co* (1876) 45 LJ Ch 437); without interference by a meeting of the company itself, issue negotiable instruments, if the company has that power (*Peruvian Rlys Co v Thames and Mersey Marine Insurance Co, Re Peruvian Rlys Co* (1867) 2 Ch App 617); if they are directors of an insurance company, they may pay losses beyond those insured against (*Taunton v Royal Insurance Co* (1864) 2 Hem & M 135); they may grant pensions to the family of a manager (*Henderson v Bank of Australasia* (1888) 40 ChD 170 (but cf *Re Lee, Behrens & Co Ltd* [1932] 2 Ch 46 (where a grant of a pension to the widow of a managing director was held ultra vires) and *Re W & M Roith Ltd* [1967] 1 All ER 427, [1967] 1 WLR 432 (where a service agreement providing for a similar pension to a widow was held invalid as not having been entered into bona fide for the benefit of and to promote the property of the company); but as to the authority of these cases see further para 1102 post); or to old retired employees or officers (*Cyclists' Touring Club v Hopkinson* [1910] 1 Ch 179); may borrow and give security (*Gibbs and West's Case* (1870) LR 10 Eq 312; *Re Pyle Works (No 2)* [1891] 1 Ch 173 at 186; *General Auction Estate and Monetary Co v Smith* [1891] 3 Ch 432); issue debentures at a discount (*Re Anglo-Danubian Steam Navigation and Colliery Co* (1875) LR 20 Eq 339 at 341); and without special authorisation, and subject to any reservation contained in the articles, directors may make calls (*Ambergate, Nottingham and Boston and Eastern Junction Rly Co v Mitchell* (1849) 4 Exch 540); or enter into a compromise (*Bath's Case* (1878) 8 ChD 334, CA). Directors may pay reasonable brokerage on the issue of shares: *Metropolitan Coal Consumers' Association v Scrimgeour* [1895] 2 QB 604, CA. As to paying promotion expenses see para 51 ante. Directors with very extensive powers were held justified in acquiring an estate for another company to build the Alexandra Palace and in promoting a subsidiary company (*London Financial Association v Kelk* (1884) 26 ChD 107), and in advancing on speculative building etc (*Sheffield and South Yorkshire Permanent Building Society v Aizlewood* (1889) 44 ChD 412; and see *Butler v Northern Territories Mines of Australia Ltd* (1906) 96 LT 41). However, in *Parke v Daily News Ltd* [1962] Ch 927, [1962] 2 All ER 929 it was held that directors were not entitled to treat dismissed employees generously beyond all entitlement; but see now the Companies Act 1985 s 719 and para 1101 post.

2 As to the administrator of a company see para 2092 et seq post.

3 See the Insolvency Act 1986 s 14(4) and para 2097 post.

4 The delegation of borrowing powers to the directors does not restrict the general power of the company to borrow, and it may exercise this power through agents so long as this is not prohibited by the memorandum or articles: *Mercantile Bank of India Ltd v Chartered Bank of India, Australia and China and Strauss & Co Ltd* [1937] 1 All ER 231.

5 *Shears v Jacob* (1866) LR 1 CP 513; *Re Inns of Court Hotel Co* (1868) LR 6 Eq 82; *Re Patent File Co, ex p Birmingham Banking Co* (1870) 6 Ch App 83; *Australian Auxiliary Steam Clipper Co v Mounsey* (1858) 4 K & J 733.

6 *Scott v Colburn* (1858) 26 Beav 276.

7 *Re Pyle Works (No 2)* [1891] 1 Ch 173 at 186.

8 *Salomon v A Salomon & Co Ltd* [1897] AC 22 at 39, HL.

9 The director is under no obligation to disclose the fact that he intends to commit such a breach: *Horcal Ltd v Gatland* [1984] BCLC 549, CA.

10 *Western Finance Co Ltd v Tasker Enterprises Ltd* (1979) 106 DLR (3d) 81 (Man CA).

11 Ie the Companies Act 1985 s 35A (as substituted): see para 583 ante and 1108 post.

12 *Sinclair v Brougham* [1914] AC 398, HL; *Re Jon Beauforte (London) Ltd* [1953] Ch 131, [1953] 1 All ER 634; *Re Introductions Ltd, Introductions Ltd v National Provincial Bank Ltd* [1970] Ch 199, [1969] 1 All ER

887, CA: *Rolled Steel Products (Holdings) Ltd v British Steel Corpn* [1986] Ch 246, [1985] 3 All ER 52, CA; although whether the true explanation of these cases is that the transaction is ultra vires, or that the other party cannot rely upon the rule in *Royal British Bank Ltd v Turquand* (see paras 1137-1139 post), remains undecided: see para 1102 post. In *Charterbridge Corpn Ltd v Lloyds Bank Ltd* [1970] Ch 62, [1969] 2 All ER 1185 it was held that no exercise of an express power could be bad because of the state of mind of the directors concerned; sed quaere if this is known to the other party to the transaction.

13   *Bersel Manufacturing Co Ltd v Berry* [1968] 2 All ER 552, HL (power in life directors to remove other directors).

585. Fiduciary position of directors in exercising their powers. Directors in the exercise of their powers are fiduciary agents[1] for the company[2] and they owe a duty to the company to exercise an independent judgment accordingly[3]. Their powers of making calls and forfeiting shares etc must not be used to favour themselves above other shareholders[4], or to favour particular classes of shareholders[5].

Save in relation to the special case of providing for employees on cessation or transfer of business[6], directors cannot in any case lawfully use their powers except for the benefit, or intended benefit, of the company[7]. It is unconstitutional for directors to enter into a management agreement which would frustrate the powers of management by directors at a time when, to the directors' knowledge, shareholders intend to appoint new directors, even though the directors so acting believe this to be in the best interests of the company[8].

On the same principle that the powers of the directors are fiduciary, they must not fetter their powers by contracts with or promises to other persons[9]. If, nevertheless, they exercise any of their intra vires powers improperly, their acts may be ratified by an ordinary resolution after full and frank disclosure by the directors to the shareholders[10].

The exercise by the directors of discretionary powers will not be interfered with unless it is proved that they have acted from some improper motive or arbitrarily and capriciously[11]. Nor will the court be ready to grant an injunction at the suit of a minority of the directors to control the activities of the majority[12].

Where powers are delegated by the company to the directors, and the directors owing to dissensions and quarrels between them are unwilling or unable to act, the powers may be exercised by the company in general meeting[13]. If, owing to disputes amongst the directors, they are unable to act and the affairs of the company cannot be carried on, the court will interfere by injunction and by the appointment of a receiver and manager of the undertaking and assets of the company until the management of the company is restored to a proper footing[14]. Similarly, where a petition had been presented for protection of a member of the company against unfair prejudice[15], the shareholdings in the company being equal and there being evidence that the shareholder with a casting vote was not managing the affairs of the company in the interests of all the members, a receiver was appointed to preserve the status quo pending the resolution of the disputes[16].

In a case of alleged conduct prejudicial to a minority shareholder in a company which is in substance a partnership, the court will in a proper case on prima facie proof of the allegations appoint a receiver on the same principles as apply in partnership cases to preserve the status quo pending determination of the petition[16].

1   See para 1115 post.
2   They are trustees of the property of the company in their hands or under their control: see para 591 post.
3   See para 620 post. As to their responsibilities in a take-over situation see para 1193 et seq post. See also *Dawson International plc v Coats Patons plc* 1988 SLT 854, Ct of Sess (where directors were held not in general to be under a fiduciary duty to shareholders, particularly current shareholders, in the context of a take-over, as distinct from their duty to consider the interests of shareholders in their fiduciary duty to the company; sed quaere).

The provisions of the Supply of Goods and Services Act 1982 s 13 (implied term that suppliers of service will use reasonable care and skill) do not apply to services rendered to a company by a director in his capacity as such: Supply of Services (Exclusion of Implied Terms) Order 1982, SI 1982/1771, art 2(2).

4 *Alexander v Automatic Telephone Co* [1900] 2 Ch 56, CA; *Harris v North Devon Rly Co* (1855) 20 Beav 384 (forfeiture); *Bennett's Case* (1854) 5 De GM & G 284 at 297 (where shareholders surrendered shares to nominees of the company and paid a considerable sum to the company out of which a debt due to a director was liquidated); *Gilbert's Case* (1870) 5 Ch App 559 (where a call was deferred to enable a director to transfer his shares). The onus is on the party who impeaches a call to show improper motive: *Odessa Tramways Co v Mendel* (1878) 8 ChD 235, CA.

5 *Kerry v Maori Dream Gold Mines Ltd* (1898) 14 TLR 402, CA; *Howard Smith Ltd v Ampol Petroleum Ltd* [1974] AC 821, [1974] 1 All ER 1126, PC (power to issue and allot shares improperly exercised where sole object was to dilute the voting power of the majority shareholders so as to enable the minority shareholders to sell their shares more advantageously).

6 See para 1102 post.

7 They may not approve transfers in order to compromise proceedings against themselves (*Bennett's Case* (1854) 5 De GM & G 284; *Re Mitre Assurance Co, Eyre's Case* (1862) 31 Beav 177), nor postpone a call for that purpose, nor cancel shares to release a shareholder from liability (*Richmond's Case, Painter's Case* (1858) 4 K & J 305), nor arrange with an applicant that he shall pay for shares only out of his emoluments as an officer of the company (*National House Property Investment Co v Watson* 1908 SC 888, following *Pellatt's Case* (1867) 2 Ch App 527; cf *Power v Hoey* (1871) 19 WR 916); they may not issue shares for an indirect purpose, such as to create votes (*Fraser v Whalley* (1864) 2 Hem & M 10; *Punt v Symons & Co Ltd* [1903] 2 Ch 506; *Piercy v Mills & Co* [1920] 1 Ch 77; *Hogg v Cramphorn Ltd* [1967] Ch 254, [1966] 3 All ER 420; cf *Abbotsford Hotel Co Ltd and Bell v Kingham and Mann* (1910) 102 LT 118, CA; *Teck Corpn v Millar* (1972) 33 DLR (3d) 288 (BC SC); or draw bills for other purposes (*Balfour v Ernest* (1859) 5 CBNS 601); or summon a company meeting at such a date as to prevent shareholders voting (*Cannon v Trask* (1875) LR 20 Eq 669), or on a misleading notice (*Alexander v Simpson* (1889) 43 ChD 139, CA; *Jackson v Munster Bank* (1884) 13 LR Ir 118); or prevent a properly elected director acting (*Pulbrook v Richmond Consolidated Mining Co* (1878) 9 ChD 610; *Munster v Cammell Co* (1882) 21 ChD 183; *Kyshe v Alturas Gold Co* (1888) 36 WR 496; *Harben v Phillips* (1883) 23 ChD 14, CA; *Grimwade v BPS Syndicate Ltd* (1915) 31 TLR 531).

8 *Lee Panavision Ltd v Lee Lighting Ltd* [1992] BCLC 22, CA.

9 *Clark v Workman* [1920] 1 IR 107; and see *Horn v Henry Faulder & Co Ltd* (1908) 99 LT 524 (agreement giving manager exclusive powers in department contrary to article giving the directors supreme control in management of company held ultra vires the articles).

10 *Bamford v Bamford* [1970] Ch 212, [1969] 1 All ER 969, CA (issue of shares) applying dicta of Lord Russell of Killowen in *Regal (Hastings) Ltd v Gulliver* [1967] 2 AC 134n at 150, [1942] 1 All ER 378 at 380, HL, and of Sir Richard Baggallay in *North-West Transportation Co Ltd and Beatty v Beatty* (1887) 12 App Cas 589 at 593, 594, PC.

11 *Cannon v Trask* (1875) LR 20 Eq 669; *Robinson v Chartered Bank of India* (1865) LR 1 Eq 32. Even in such a case the order will not be made at the instance of some only of the members of the company: *Pergamon Press Ltd v Maxwell* [1970] 2 All ER 809, [1970] 1 WLR 1167 (see further para 1110 post). In the absence of evidence to the contrary the court will take it for granted that the directors have acted reasonably and in good faith: *Re Gresham Life Assurance Society, ex p Penney* (1872) 8 Ch App 446; *Gaiman v National Association for Mental Health* [1971] Ch 317, [1970] 2 All ER 362 (power of expulsion of members); *Mutual Life Insurance Co of New York v Rank Organisation Ltd* [1985] BCLC 11 (for good reasons, directors discriminated between shareholders when allotting shares to be offered for sale; since the power was exercised in good faith for the benefit of the company, and was exercised fairly as between the different shareholders, which did not require identical treatment, the exercise was valid; and see now the Companies Act 1985 s 89 et seq and para 457 et seq ante). As to the exercise by directors of their discretion with regard to transfers of shares see para 498 ante.

12 *Lord Duncan Sandys v House of Fraser plc* 1985 SLT 200.

13 *Barron v Potter* [1914] 1 Ch 895 (appointment of additional directors); *Foster v Foster* [1916] 1 Ch 532 (appointment of a managing director).

14 *Featherstone v Cooke* (1873) LR 16 Eq 298; *Trade Auxiliary Co v Vickers* (1873) LR 16 Eq 303; *Stanfield v Gibbons* [1925] WN 11.

15 See para 1405 et seq post.

16 *Re a Company (No 00596 of 1986)* [1987] BCLC 133.

586. Exercise of powers in case of insolvent company. Directors of an insolvent company cannot use their powers to benefit themselves in view of an impending winding up[1].

A director to whom a debt is owing by the company is not in such a good position as an outside creditor; thus, where he is aware that the company is insolvent, he cannot by pressure obtain a valid security for his debt[2].

1 *Sykes' Case* (1872) LR 13 Eq 255; and see *Gibson's Executor v Gibson* 1980 SLT 2.
2 *Gaslight Improvement Co v Terrell* (1870) LR 10 Eq 168. As to transactions at an undervalue and preferences in a winding up see para 2602 et seq post.

587. Delegation of powers. Without express authority to do so, directors cannot delegate their duties or powers[1].

Articles of association, however, generally confer authority on the directors to delegate their powers to committees or local boards[2] or managing directors[3]. Where they have sufficient powers of delegation, the directors may delegate any of their powers to committees, or even to a single director[4].

Where any specific powers are properly delegated, the directors are absolved from liability for the exercise of those powers by the delegates[5]; but the directors cannot delegate the whole of their responsibilities, and must continue to exercise a proper supervision[6]. Powers of delegation must be used bona fide and directors cannot form a committee to deal with the affairs of the company in order to exclude one or more of their number from acting[7].

Where powers are delegated to a committee and there is no provision for a quorum, the whole of a committee must meet and then act by a majority, and the committee has no power to add to its number or fill a vacancy[8]. An excessive exercise of the committee's powers may be ratified by the directors[9], who do not by delegation divest themselves of their powers[10], or, if need be, by the company. Business informally transacted may, generally speaking, be ratified by a subsequent formal meeting[11].

A private company need not have more than one director[12], in which case the whole of the directors' powers will be vested in him.

1 *Howard's Case* (1866) 1 Ch App 561 (allotment of shares); *Southampton Dock Co v Richards* (1840) 1 Man & G 448 (making call); and see *Hom v Henry Faulder & Co* (1908) 99 LT 524 (delegation of control to departmental manager). As to the extent to which a stranger contracting with the company is protected where there is a power but it has not been properly exercised see paras 1137-1139 post.
2 The Companies (Tables A to F) Regulations 1985, SI 1985/805, Schedule, Table A art 72 provides that the directors may delegate any of their powers to any committee consisting of one or more directors. They may also delegate to any managing director or any director holding any other executive office such of their powers as they consider desirable to be exercised by him. Any such delegation may be made subject to any conditions the directors may impose, and either collaterally with or to the exclusion of their own powers and may be revoked or altered. Subject to any such conditions, the proceedings of a committee with two or more members must be governed by the articles regulating the proceedings of directors so far as they are capable of applying. As to Table A generally see para 529 et seq ante.
3 For articles authorising the appointment of managing directors see para 588 note 3 post.
4 *Re Fireproof Doors Ltd* [1916] 2 Ch 142; *Re Taurine Co* (1883) 25 ChD 118, CA; *Re Scottish Petroleum Co, Maclagan's Case* (1882) 51 LJ Ch 841; *Harris' Case* (1872) 7 Ch App 587 (committee for allotment).
5 *Weir v Bell* (1878) 3 ExD 238, CA.
6 *Re City Equitable Fire Insurance Co Ltd* [1925] Ch 407.
7 *Kyshe v Alturas Gold Co* (1888) 4 TLR 331; *Bray v Smith* (1908) 124 LT Jo 293.
8 *Re Liverpool Household Stores Association* (1890) 59 LJ Ch 616.
9 *Bolton Partners v Lambert* (1889) 41 ChD 295, CA; *Re Portuguese Consolidated Copper Mines Ltd, ex p Badman, ex p Bosanquet* (1890) 45 ChD 16; *Hooper v Kerr, Stuart & Co Ltd* (1900) 83 LT 729; *Re City Equitable Fire Insurance Co Ltd* [1925] Ch 407.

10 *Huth v Clarke* (1890) 25 QBD 391.
11 *Re Phosphate of Lime Co, Austin's Case* (1871) 24 LT 932.
12 See the Companies Act 1985 s 282(3) and para 543 ante.

588. Managing directors. A managing director may be either merely a director with additional functions and additional remuneration[1], or else he may be a person holding two distinct positions, that of a director and that of a manager[2]. The directors have no general right to appoint a managing director[3], nor, it seems, to remunerate him under a power to remunerate employees[4], nor to delegate to him powers which they themselves would not possess unless expressly given to them[5]. Where such a power of appointment is conferred upon the directors by the articles, the company cannot take it away by means of an ordinary resolution[6]; but, if, owing to internal dissensions, the directors cannot make the appointment, the company may do so[7].

The appointment of a director as managing director without any specified time limit does not entitle him to hold office as managing director so long as he remains a director, nor does an article which forbids a director from voting on a contract in which he is interested prevent him from voting for his own appointment as managing director, if the appointment carries no special remuneration; but it is otherwise if it does[7]. The appointment will usually terminate if for any reason the managing director ceases to be a director[8]. If, however, he ceases to be a director before the period for which he was appointed has expired as the result of the exercise of a power introduced into the articles after his appointment, he will be entitled to damages for breach of contract[9]; but he will not be so entitled if the power existed in the articles at the date of his appointment[10].

If invalidly appointed, he may sue for services rendered upon a quantum meruit basis[11].

1 *Re Newspaper Proprietary Syndicate Ltd, Hopkinson v Newspaper Proprietary Syndicate Ltd* [1900] 2 Ch 349 at 350. It is obviously beyond the powers of the directors to purport to appoint a non-director to this position: see *Craven-Ellis v Canons Ltd* [1936] 2 KB 403, [1936] 2 All ER 1066, CA. His duties may be strictly controlled by contract: *Harold Holdsworth & Co (Wakefield) Ltd v Caddies* [1955] 1 All ER 725, [1955] 1 WLR 352, HL.
2 *Goodwin v Brewster (Inspector of Taxes)* (1951) 32 TC 80, CA. The statement in the text was approved in *Harold Holdsworth & Co (Wakefield) Ltd v Caddies* [1955] 1 All ER 725 at 729, [1955] 1 WLR 352 at 357, HL per Viscount Kilmuir LC. As to presuming delegation see para 1138 et seq post; and as to the duty of a managing director to exploit every opening for the company's business even if it involves an alteration of the objects see *Fine Industrial Commodities Ltd v Powling* (1954) 71 RPC 253 at 258.
3 *Boschoek Proprietary Co Ltd v Fuke* [1906] 1 Ch 148 at 159. The Companies (Tables A to F) Regulations 1985, SI 1985/805, Schedule, Table A art 84 provides that, subject to the provisions of the Companies Act 1985, the directors may appoint one or more of their number to the office of managing director or to any other executive office under the company and may enter into an agreement or arrangement with any director for his employment by the company or for the provision by him of any services outside the scope of the ordinary duties of a director. Any such appointment, agreement or arrangement may be made upon such terms as the directors determine and they may remunerate any such director for his services as they think fit. Any appointment of a director to an executive office will terminate if he ceases to be a director but without prejudice to any claim to damages for breach of the contract of service between the director and the company. A managing director and a director holding any other executive office are not to be subject to retirement by rotation: cf *Read v Astoria Garage (Streatham) Ltd* [1952] Ch 637, [1952] 2 All ER 292, CA. See also *Harben v Phillips* (1883) 23 ChD 14 at 39, CA; cf *Bainbridge v Smith* (1889) 41 ChD 462 at 474, CA; *Horn v Henry Faulder & Co Ltd* (1908) 99 LT 524. As to Table A generally see para 529 et seq ante.
4 *Normandy v Ind, Coope & Co Ltd* [1908] 1 Ch 84; *Re Lee, Behrens & Co Ltd* [1932] 2 Ch 46 (as to the status of this case see para 1102 post); *Kerr v Walker* 1933 SC 458; and see *Sputz v Broadway Engineering Co Ltd* (1944) 171 LT 50. In *Anderson v James Sutherland (Peterhead) Ltd* 1941 SC 230 it was, however, stated that the functions of a managing director and a director were not the same, and that in the former capacity he

was within the category of members of the company 'employed by the company in any capacity'. As to payment by a percentage of profits see paras 577, 579 ante.

5 *Cartmell's Case* (1874) 9 Ch App 691; cf *Gibson v Barton* (1875) LR 10 QB 329 at 336.

6 *Thomas Logan Ltd v Davis* (1911) 104 LT 914; affd 105 LT 419, CA.

7 *Foster v Foster* [1916] 1 Ch 532.

8 *Bluett v Stutchbury's Ltd* (1908) 24 TLR 469, CA; *Re Alexander's Timber Co* (1901) 70 LJ Ch 767.

9 *Nelson v James Nelson & Sons Ltd* [1914] 2 KB 770, CA; *Southern Foundries (1926) Ltd v Shirlaw* [1940] AC 701, [1940] 2 All ER 445, HL.

10 *Read v Astoria Garage (Streatham) Ltd* [1952] Ch 637, [1952] 2 All ER 292, CA. Cf *Shindler v Northern Raincoat Co Ltd* [1960] 2 All ER 239, [1960] 1 WLR 1038 where *Read v Astoria Garage (Streatham) Ltd* supra was not followed because the terms of the managing director's contract were inconsistent with powers in the articles which were held to be restricted by the contract, whereas there was no such inconsistency in *Read v Astoria Garage (Streatham) Ltd* supra.

11 *Craven-Ellis v Canons Ltd* [1936] 2 KB 403, [1936] 2 All ER 1066, CA; and see para 575 ante.

589. How far controllable by members. If, as is usual, the management of the company's affairs is entrusted to the directors by the articles of association[1], a numerical majority of the shareholders insufficient to alter the articles cannot, in the absence of any provision in the articles reserving appropriate power, impose its will on the directors as regards matters so entrusted to them[2]. If the articles provide that regulations may be made by extraordinary resolution, an ordinary resolution is not sufficient to make a regulation which will control the directors[3]. If no power is reserved to the company to control the directors when acting within the powers conferred on them by the articles, the articles must be altered by special resolution, if it is desired to give the company such power[4]. Where, under the articles, the business of the company is to be managed by the directors and the articles confer on them the full powers of the company subject to such regulations, not inconsistent with the articles, as may be prescribed by the company in general meeting, the shareholders are not enabled by resolution passed at a general meeting without altering the articles, to give effective directions to the directors as to how the company's affairs are to be managed, nor are they able to overrule any decision reached by the directors in the conduct of company business[5]. An agreement made by the company which is inconsistent with the powers of management of the directors under the articles, as, for example, an agreement purporting to confer authority upon the manager of a department to act without interference by the directors, is ultra vires[6].

1 See eg the Companies (Tables A to F) Regulations 1985, SI 1985/805, Schedule, Table A art 70 which provides that, subject to the provisions of the Companies Act 1985, the memorandum and the articles, and to any directions given by special resolution, the business of the company will be managed by the directors who may exercise all the powers of the company. No alteration of the memorandum or articles and no such direction will invalidate any prior act of the directors which would have been valid if that alteration had not been made or that direction had not been given. The powers so given will not be limited by any special power given to the directors by the articles and a meeting of directors at which a quorum is present may exercise all powers exercisable by the directors. Under art 70 the entire management of the company, including its financial direction, rests solely in the hands of the directors, and accordingly resolutions by the company in general meeting purporting to interfere with this management are invalid: see *Scott v Scott* [1943] 1 All ER 582 (resolutions to make advance payments to shareholders pending declaration of dividends). As to Table A generally see para 529 et seq ante.

2 See *Gramophone and Typewriter Ltd v Stanley* [1908] 2 KB 89 at 105, 106, CA per Buckley LJ; *Grundt v Great Boulder Proprietary Gold Mines Ltd* [1948] Ch 145 at 157, [1948] 1 All ER 21 at 29, CA per Cohen LJ. The power of a majority to remove the directors under the Companies Act 1985 s 303 must be borne in mind: see para 639 post.

3 *Automatic Self-Cleansing Filter Syndicate Co Ltd v Cuninghame* [1906] 2 Ch 34, CA; *Thomas Logan Ltd v Davis* (1911) 104 LT 914 (affd 105 LT 419, CA). See also *Re Olderfleet Shipbuilding and Engineering Co Ltd* [1922] 1 IR 26.

4 *Quin & Axtens Ltd v Salmon* [1909] AC 442, HL.

5 See *John Shaw & Sons (Salford) Ltd v Shaw* [1935] 2 KB 113 at 134, CA per Greer LJ; *Scott v Scott* [1943] 1 All ER 582; and see the cases cited in notes 2, 3 supra. Cf *Marshall's Valve Gear Co Ltd v Manning, Wardle & Co Ltd* [1909] 1 Ch 267.

6 *Horn v Henry Faulder & Co Ltd* (1908) 99 LT 524.

590. Acts beyond the directors' powers; acts ultra vires the company. In favour of a person dealing with a company in good faith, the power of the board of directors to bind the company, or authorise others to do so, is deemed to be free of any limitation under the company's constitution[1]; nevertheless, as regards the directors and the company any acts done by either which are beyond the constitution will be ultra vires and therefore invalid[2]. Any act of the directors which is not ultra vires the company may be ratified by the company in general meeting[3], or at an informal meeting of all the shareholders[4], or by the acquiescence of all the shareholders without a meeting[5]. Though an ordinary resolution will suffice for this purpose, a special resolution is necessary to confer authority to enter into future transactions of the like nature[6]. A representative action cannot be brought by a shareholder against directors for an act which, though beyond the powers of the directors, may be ratified by the company at any time[7].

Apart from ratification, the company will be answerable for any property which has come into its possession through the unauthorised acts of the directors[8].

1 See the Companies Act 1985 s 35A(1) (as substituted), para 583 ante and para 1108 post.
2 See *Spokes v Grosvenor Hotel Co* [1897] 2 QB 124; *Hoole v Great Western Rly Co* (1867) 3 Ch App 262; and para 1086 et seq post.
3 See *Bamford v Bamford* [1970] Ch 212, [1969] 1 All ER 969, CA.
4 *Re Oxted Motor Co* [1921] 3 KB 32; *Re Express Engineering Works Ltd* [1920] 1 Ch 466, CA.
5 *Parker and Cooper Ltd v Reading* [1926] Ch 975. See further para 696 post.
6 *Re Phosphate of Lime Co, Austin's Case* (1871) 24 LT 932; *Irvine v Union Bank of Australia* (1877) 2 App Cas 366, PC; *Grant v United Kingdom Switchback Railways Co* (1888) 40 ChD 135, CA; *Boschoek Proprietary Co Ltd v Fuke* [1906] 1 Ch 148; *Re Olderfleet Shipbuilding Co* [1922] 1 IR 26; cf *Kent v Jackson* (1852) 2 De GM & G 49; *Re Piercy, Whitwham v Piercy* [1907] 1 Ch 289; and see para 1125 post.
7 See para 1110 post.
8 *Re Royal British Bank, Nicol's Case* (1859) 3 De G & J 387 at 423; *British and American Telegraph Co v Albion Bank* (1872) LR 7 Exch 119 at 122.

591. Directors as trustees of the company's property. Directors are trustees of the property of the company in their hands or under their control[1]; but they are not trustees for individual shareholders[2] or the creditors[3] of the company, nor are they in the same position as trustees of a will or settlement[4]. Unless so directed by the articles, they are not bound to invest the funds, such as, for example, reserve funds of the company, only in securities which a trustee may invest in, but they may purchase such securities as they consider to be most beneficial for the company[5]. They may invest in the name of a sole trustee[5], and lend on securities of a speculative nature[6], but they are liable in respect of an investment made contrary to a resolution of the company effectively[7] directing a different investment[8]. Except in so far as they have properly delegated the duty of investing the funds of the company, and attending to the securities in which they are invested, directors are bound to see that the funds are in a proper state of investment[9]; and in order to ascertain the financial position of the company with a view to paying a dividend the directors should at least have before them a list of the investments[9].

1 *Re Faure Electric Accumulator Co* (1888) 40 ChD 141; *Flitcroft's Case* (1882) 21 ChD 519, CA; *Re Sharpe, Re Bennett, Masonic and General Life Assurance Co v Sharpe* [1892] 1 Ch 154, CA; *Re Oxford Benefit*

Building and Investment Society (1886) 35 ChD 502 at 509; *Great Eastern Rly Co v Turner* (1872) 8 Ch App 149 at 152; *Lindgren v L & P Estates Ltd* [1968] Ch 572, [1968] 1 All ER 917, CA (specific performance of contract ordered); *Selangor United Rubber Estates Ltd v Cradock (a bankrupt) (No 3)* [1968] 2 All ER 1073, [1968] 1 WLR 1555 (money in company's bank account); *International Sales and Agencies Ltd v Marcus* [1982] 3 All ER 551. See also *Regal (Hastings) Ltd v Gulliver* [1967] 2 AC 134n, [1941] 1 All ER 378; cf *Boardman v Phipps* [1967] 2 AC 46, [1966] 3 All ER 721, HL; *Canadian Aero Service Ltd v O'Malley* (1973) 40 DLR (3d) 371 (Can SC); *Weber Feeds Ltd v Weber* (1979) 24 OR (2d) 754 (Ont CA); *Belmont Finance Corpn Ltd v Williams Furniture Ltd (No 2)* [1980] 1 All ER 393, CA; *Rolled Steel Products (Holdings) Ltd v British Steel Corpn* [1986] Ch 246, [1985] 3 All ER 52, CA. Consequently a change in the shareholders will not diminish their obligation to account: *Abbey Glen Property Corpn v Stumborg* (1978) 85 DLR (3d) 35 (Alta SC). As to the general fiduciary position of directors see para 585 ante. By the Companies Act 1985 s 313(2), a director is deemed to be trustee for the company of illegal payments made to him by way of compensation etc: see paras 608–614 post. As to joint and several liability see para 617 post.

2 They may, therefore, purchase shares in the company without disclosing to the vendors advantageous prospects of the company: *Percival v Wright* [1902] 2 Ch 421; cf *Allen v Hyatt* [1914] 30 TLR 444, PC. For an example of a director being deemed to be trustee for individual shareholders or ex-shareholders see the Companies Act 1985 s 315(1) and para 609 post.

3 *Redekop v Robco Construction Ltd* (1978) 89 DLR (3d) 507 (BC SC). See further para 616 post.

4 *Owen and Ashworth's Claim, Whitworth's Claim* [1901] 1 Ch 115, CA (where a director took a transfer of a security irregularly issued to a creditor who had no notice of the irregularity).

5 *Burland v Earle* [1902] AC 83 at 97, PC.

6 Cf *Sheffield and South Yorkshire Permanent Building Society v Aizlewood* (1889) 44 ChD 412.

7 As to the extent to which shareholders can control directors' powers see para 589 ante.

8 *Re British Guardian Life Assurance Co* (1880) 14 ChD 335.

9 *Re City Equitable Fire Insurance Co Ltd* [1925] Ch 407 at 501, CA. A finance committee is not entitled to leave even temporary investment of the company's funds under the entire control of one member: *Re City Equitable Fire Insurance Co Ltd* supra.

592. Accountability of directors. A director must account to the company for all of the company's property in his control[1]. He is liable also to account to the company for any unauthorised profits made by him by virtue of his office[2]. This rule is absolute and independent of any question of fraud or absence of good faith[3], and it matters not that the company itself could not have made the profits which the director made[4]. If, however, the company, with full knowledge of all the circumstances, renounces its interest in a particular venture, which is then taken up by the director concerned, he will no longer be liable to account[5]. If directors use their position as directors to obtain for themselves the property of the company, as, for example, by means of a beneficial contract, they cannot by using their voting power as shareholders in general meeting prevent the company from claiming the benefit of it[6]. A director's fiduciary duty does not necessarily come to an end when he ceases to be a director, especially if he ceases by resignation with a view to taking advantage of current business opportunities available to the company[7].

Directors who make what they believe to be a beneficial contract for the company are not chargeable with breach of trust merely because in promoting the interests of the company they were promoting their own interests by enabling themselves to sell their shares at a profit[8].

1 *Cramer v Bird* (1868) LR 6 Eq 143 (defunct company; surplus assets); *Re Forest of Dean Coal Mining Co* (1878) 10 ChD 450 (omission to get in a debt; not liable for non-feasance in absence of fraud or dishonesty); *Re Lands Allotment Co* [1894] 1 Ch 616 at 631, CA; *Selangor United Rubber Estates Ltd v Cradock (a bankrupt) (No 3)* [1968] 2 All ER 1073, [1968] 1 WLR 1555 (directors accountable for money of the company); *Canadian Aero Service Ltd v O'Malley* (1973) 40 DLR (3d) 371 (Can SC) (president and executive vice-president appropriating contract they had been negotiating on behalf of the company). As to relief against breach of trust or negligence see para 624 post. Thus a de facto director who improperly receives the company's property will become an express trustee of it, and consequently will not be protected by any period of limitation for its recovery: see the Limitation Act 1980 s 21 and *Tintin*

Exploration Syndicate Ltd v Sandys (1947) 177 LT 412. As to the general principle see AGENCY vol 1(2) (Reissue) para 104 et seq.

2 *Parker v McKenna* (1874) 10 Ch App 96 (where directors had to account for profits made in dealings with new capital); *Cockburn v Newbridge Sanitary Steam Laundry Co Ltd and Llewellyn* [1915] 1 IR 237, CA. This applies to a person who has agreed to become a director (*Henderson v Huntington Copper and Sulphur Co* (1877) 5 R 1, HL; *Albion Steel and Wire Co v Martin* (1875) 1 ChD 580), and to persons entering into contracts on behalf of an intended company (*Phosphate Sewage Co v Hartmont* (1877) 5 ChD 394, CA), and to a de facto director; and see *Re Imperial Land Co of Marseilles, ex p Larking* (1877) 4 ChD 566, CA (where the directors were not allowed to make a profit out of a fraudulent transaction). See further text infra and para 593 post.

3 *Regal (Hastings) Ltd v Gulliver* [1967] 2 AC 134n, [1942] 1 All ER 378. See also *Boardman v Phipps* [1967] 2 AC 46, [1966] 3 All ER 721, HL; *Industrial Development Consultants Ltd v Cooley* [1972] 2 All ER 162, [1972] 1 WLR 443 (where there was an element of bad faith). In Canada this has been held to apply to the profits of business obtained by a former director who had started a competing business from direct solicitation of former clients of the company: *W J Christie & Co Ltd v Greer* [1981] 4 WWR 34 (Man CA).

4 *Weber Feeds Ltd v Weber* (1979) 24 OR (2d) 754 (Ont CA).

5 *Queensland Mines Ltd v Hudson* (1978) 52 ALJR 399, PC.

6 *Cook v Deeks* [1916] 1 AC 554, PC; cf *EBM Co Ltd v Dominion Bank* [1937] 3 All ER 555, PC (transaction unenforceable where company purported to apply its property for the benefit of certain directors).

7 *Island Export Finance Ltd v Umunna* [1986] BCLC 460.

8 *Hirsche v Sims* [1894] AC 654 at 660, PC. The court has power to sanction a sale by a trustee in bankruptcy to a company of which he and the committee of inspection are to be directors: see *Re Spink, ex p Slater* (1913) 108 LT 572; and see BANKRUPTCY vol 3(2) (Reissue) para 328.

593. Bribes. Whenever a director becomes entitled to a sum of money[1] by way of a bribe from a vendor to the company, the company may recover, from the person giving the bribe, a sum equal to the amount of the bribe, on the basis that the person who gave it, the vendor, received from the company more than he was entitled to, measured by the amount of the bribe, the excess being money received by the vendor to the company's use[2]. If property representing the bribe increases in value or if a cash bribe is invested advantageously, the false fiduciary is accountable not only for the original amount or value of the bribe but also for the increased value of the property representing the bribe[3]. The fact that the director has agreed subsequently with the person giving the bribe to accept a smaller sum in prompt settlement and that this has been recovered from the director in full satisfaction of all claims against him is no defence to the person giving the bribe in an action by the company for the balance[3]. The company may also recover against the person who gives the bribe damages for any loss sustained through entering a disadvantageous contract[4], or it may rescind the contract[5]. A contract may be enforced by the company against the director if he has contracted as principal, deducting the amount of any secret profit which might accrue to him[6].

The director is liable as debtor only, and the company cannot follow the profit or bribe as trust property[7].

1 As to an offer of employment alleged to be in the nature of a bribe, but which did not lead to any conflict of interest, see *Amalgamated Industrials Ltd v Johnson & Firth Brown Ltd* (1981) Times, 15 April.

2 *Grant v Gold Exploration and Development Syndicate* [1900] 1 QB 233 at 249, CA. The principle that a person in a fiduciary position must not make secret profits is not based on actual fraud, but on motives of public policy: see *Bray v Ford* [1896] AC 44 at 51, HL; *Harrington v Victoria Graving Dock Co* (1878) 3 QBD 549 (where it was held that, although the person to whom the bribe is payable has not in fact been perverted, he cannot recover the bribe in an action). Cf *Kregor v Hollins* (1913) 109 LT 225, CA. As to bribery of agents generally see AGENCY vol 1(2) (Reissue) para 105 et seq.

3 *A-G for Hong Kong v Reid* [1994] 1 AC 324 at 331, [1994] 1 All ER 1 at 5, PC.
4 *Salford Corpn v Lever* [1891] 1 QB 168, CA; and see *Grant v Gold Exploration and Development Syndicate* [1900] 1 QB 233 at 244, CA.
5 *Panama and South Pacific Telegraph Co v India Rubber, Gutta Percha and Telegraph Works Co* (1875) 10 Ch App 515.
6 *Whaley Bridge Calico Printing Co v Green* (1880) 5 QBD 109.
7 *Re Thorpe, Vipont v Radcliffe* [1891] 2 Ch 360; *Lister & Co v Stubbs* (1890) 45 ChD 1, CA (doubted in *A-G for Hong Kong v Reid* [1994] 1 AC 324, [1994] 1 All ER 1, PC). As to the joint and several nature of the liability where more than one director is concerned, see para 617 text to note 9 post.

594. Statutory duty to declare interest in contracts. It is the duty of a director of a company who is in any way, whether directly or indirectly, interested in a contract or proposed contract with the company to declare the nature of his interest at a meeting of the directors of the company[1]. In the case of a proposed contract, the declaration must be made at the meeting of the directors at which the question of entering into the contract is first taken into consideration, or, if the director was not at the date of that meeting interested in the proposed contract, at the next meeting of the directors held after he became so interested; and, in a case where the director becomes interested in a contract after it is made, the declaration must be made at the first meeting of the directors held after the director becomes so interested[2].

For these purposes, a general notice given to the directors of a company by a director to the effect that:

(1) he is a member of a specified company or firm and is to be regarded as interested in any contract which may, after the date of the notice, be made with that company or firm; or

(2) he is to be regarded as interested in any contract which may after the date of the notice be made with a specified person who is connected[3] with him,

is deemed a sufficient declaration of interest in relation to any such contract[4].

However, no such notice is of effect unless either it is given at a meeting of the directors, or the director takes reasonable steps to secure that it is brought up and read at the next meeting of the directors after it is given[5].

The above provisions apply to any transaction or arrangement made or entered into on or after 22 December 1980, whether or not the same constitutes a contract[6]. For these purposes, a transaction or arrangement of a nature prohibited by the general restriction on the company's right to make loans and give other forms of financial assistance to directors[7] made by a company for a director of the company, or a person connected with such a director, is treated (if it would not otherwise be so treated, and whether or not so prohibited) as a transaction or arrangement in which that director is interested[8].

These provisions apply to a shadow director[9] as they apply to a director, except that a shadow director must declare his interest, not at a meeting of the directors, but by a notice in writing to the directors which is either:

(a) a specific notice given before the date of the meeting at which, if he had been a director, the declaration required from a director would have had to be made; or

(b) a general notice which under the above provisions falls to be treated as a sufficient declaration of that interest or would fall to be treated as a sufficient declaration of that interest, apart from any question of its being read at the next meeting of directors[10].

Failure to comply with these obligations does not render the contract void or unenforceable, but only voidable at the instance of the company, so that, if it is no longer possible to restore the parties to their former position, rescission is impossible[11].

A director who fails to comply with these provisions is liable on conviction on indictment to a fine, or on summary conviction to a fine not exceeding the statutory maximum[12].

Nothing in these provisions requiring disclosure of interest prejudices the operation of any rule of law restricting directors of a company from having any interest in contracts with the company[13].

1 Companies Act 1985 s 317(1). See *Lee Panavision Ltd v Lee Lighting Ltd* [1992] BCLC 22, CA (where the court hesitated to find that the failure formally to declare at a board meeting an interest common to all members and ex hypothesi already known to all of the members of the board, was a breach of the Companies Act 1985 s 317). For provisions in the articles and in the Companies (Tables A to F) Regulations 1985, SI 1985/805, Schedule, Table A as to disclosure of interest by directors see para 635 post. Prior to statutory provision it was held that a company might by apt words in its articles waive its right to full disclosure: *Imperial Mercantile Credit Association v Coleman* (1871) 6 Ch App 558 (revsd without affecting this point (1873) LR 6 HL 189); *Costa Rica Rly Co Ltd v Forwood* [1901] 1 Ch 746 at 760, CA. Since the enactment of this provision, it would appear that a company cannot so waive its right as to sanction a contravention of such right.
   As to contracts with sole members who are directors see para 597 post.
2 Companies Act 1985 s 317(2).
3 For the meaning of 'connected' see para 607 post.
4 Companies Act 1985 s 317(3).
5 Ibid s 317(4).
6 Ibid s 317(5).
7 Ie under ibid s 330: see para 598 post.
8 Ibid s 317(6).
9 For the meaning of 'shadow director' see para 543 note 1 ante.
10 Companies Act 1985 s 317(8).
11 *Hely-Hutchinson v Brayhead Ltd* [1968] 1 QB 549 at 585, [1967] 3 All ER 98 at 103, CA per Lord Denning MR; *Guinness plc v Saunders* [1990] 2 AC 663, [1990] 1 All ER 652, HL. In the latter case the director had rendered services to the company and had been paid. If there was a contract, which it was held there was not, it would not have been possible to restore the director to the status quo ante, so that rescission would appear to be impossible: *Erlanger v New Sombrero Phosphate Co* (1878) 3 App Cas 1218, HL. In *Guinness plc v Saunders* supra at 698 and at 665 obiter Lord Goff of Chieveley suggested that the appellant could no doubt be placed in the status quo ante by a court of equity making a just allowance for the services he had rendered.
12 Companies Act 1985 ss 317(7), 730, Sch 24. For the meaning of 'the statutory maximum' see para 1161 post.
13 Ibid s 317(9). As to the effect of directors having an interest in contracts made with the company see para 596 post.

595. Disclosure on sales to the company. Apart from the statutory penalty[1], where a director sells property to his company, without disclosing his interest, the company may, on discovery, either rescind the sale, if that is still practicable, or affirm the sale and sue for damages[2], in which case it must prove a breach of duty by the director amounting to negligence or misfeasance and resulting in pecuniary loss to the company[3]. If the director, while employed as a director to purchase property, buys on his own account and sells to the company without disclosure, he must account for the profit made by him[4]; but, if he acquired his interest in the property before he became a director, failure to disclose the fact that he is interested, and the amount of the profit which he is making, though it is a breach of duty enabling the company to rescind the contract, will not in itself entitle the company to recover the difference between the market value and the price paid by the company[5].

1 Ie under the Companies Act 1985 s 317: see para 594 ante.
2 *Benson v Heathorn* (1842) 1 Y & C Ch Cas 326; *Jacobus Marler Estates Ltd v Marler* (1913) 85 LJPC 167n; and see *Cavendish Bentinck v Fenn* (1887) 12 App Cas 652 at 658, HL; *Ladywell Mining Co v Brookes* (1887) 35 ChD 400, CA; *Re VGM Holdings Ltd* [1942] Ch 235, [1942] 1 All ER 224, CA.

3 *Cavendish Bentinck v Fenn* (1887) 12 App Cas 652 at 662, HL.
4 *Cavendish Bentinck v Fenn* (1887) 12 App Cas 652, HL.
5 *Re Lady Forrest (Murchison) Gold Mine Ltd* [1901] 1 Ch 582; *Re Cape Breton Co* (1885) 29 ChD 795, CA
   (affd on other grounds sub nom *Cavendish Bentinck v Fenn* (1887) 12 App Cas 652, HL); *Ladywell Mining
   Co v Brookes* (1887) 35 ChD 400, CA; and see paras 45, 46 ante.

596. Director a party to or interested in contract with company. A contract
between a company and a director or his firm[1], or a company in which he is interested
as a director or shareholder even though only a trustee of the shares[2], is valid at
common law, but in equity the other contracting party would (unless relieved of the
obligation by compliance with the relevant article or statutory provision) be liable to
account for any profit made, by reason of the fiduciary position of the director[3].
Further, in most cases the fiduciary position of the director would also render the
contract voidable at the instance of the company[4]. If the articles or statutory provisions
are not complied with, the contract, being voidable and not void, may be affirmed by
the company when in possession of full information[5].

In order that the director may retain a profit which he has made on a contract with
the company, it is not enough that he should reveal the existence of his interest without
specifying exactly what it is. No ratification may take place in the absence of full
disclosure[6]; but, if full disclosure is contained in the notice convening the meeting, the
company may by ordinary resolution confirm the contract[7]. It is unnecessary to hold a
meeting if all the shareholders acquiesce[8].

If the articles are not complied with and the company objects, it is immaterial that
the terms are advantageous to it[9], or that as between the interested director and his
co-directors the whole matter was above board[10]. Such a contract will not be
specifically enforced[11], and the director cannot retain the profits[12], but this rule does
not apply to contracts made before the company was formed with persons whose
business is acquired by the company on formation[12].

A company owning shares in a second company, which are transferred to one of its
own directors in order to qualify him as director of the second company to represent
the interests of the first company, is not entitled to claim from the director his
remuneration as director of the second company[13].

Although a director may be precluded by the articles from voting as a director in
respect of his contract with the company, he may vote as a shareholder at a general
meeting[14].

1 *Flanagan v Great Western Rly Co* (1868) LR 7 Eq 116. The restriction applies to all contracts in which a
   director is interested and which are made in the execution of the company's business, such as
   appointment of a managing director at a salary (*Foster v Foster* [1916] 1 Ch 532); the allotment of
   debentures (*Cox v Dublin City Distillery (No 2)* [1915] 1 IR 345, CA; *Re North Eastern Insurance Co* [1919]
   1 Ch 198); issue of debentures as security for an overdraft guaranteed by the directors (*Victors Ltd v
   Lingard* [1927] 1 Ch 323); allotment of shares (*Quinn v Robb* (1916) 141 LT Jo 6; *Neal v Quinn* [1916]
   WN 223); a contract entered into with a business of which the director is a mortgagee in possession (*Star
   Steam Laundry Co v Dukas* (1913) 108 LT 367); and see *Holden v Southwark Corpn* [1921] 1 Ch 550; *Lapish
   v Braithwaite* [1926] AC 275, HL. The bankers of the company may still be its directors (*Sheffield,
   Ashton-under-Lyne and Manchester Rly Co v Woodcock* (1841) 7 M & W 574 at 582); and a director may
   lend money to his company at a profit (*Bluck v Mallalue* (1859) 27 Beav 398; *Re Cardiff Preserved Coal and
   Coke Co Ltd, Hill's Case* (1862) 32 LJ Ch 154), if it is without an unusual profit, such as a bonus.
2 *Transvaal Lands Co v New Belgium (Transvaal) Land and Development Co* [1914] 2 Ch 488, CA (rescission
   ordered after completion; other company had notice of the irregularity; rescission possible); cf *Regal
   (Hastings) Ltd v Gulliver* (1942) [1967] 2 AC 134n at 152n, [1942] 1 All ER 378 at 390, 391, HL.
3 *Costa Rica Rly Co Ltd v Forwood* [1900] 1 Ch 756 (affd [1901] 1 Ch 746, CA); *Albion Steel and Wire Co v
   Martin* (1875) 1 ChD 580; *Redekop v Robco Construction Ltd* (1978) 89 DLR (3d) 507 (BC SC); cf *Re
   Republic of Bolivia Exploration Syndicate Ltd* [1914] 1 Ch 139. See generally *Hely-Hutchinson v Brayhead*

Ltd [1968] 1 QB 549 at 571, [1967] 2 All ER 14 at 28 per Roskill J; affd [1968] 1 QB 573, [1967] 3 All ER 98, CA.

4   *Aberdeen Rly Co v Blaikie Bros* (1854) 2 Eq Rep 1281, HL; *Ernest v Nicholls* (1857) 6 HL Cas 401; *Ridley v Plymouth Grinding and Baking Co* (1848) 2 Exch 711; *Albion Steel and Wire Co v Martin* (1875) 1 ChD 580. A contract is made with a director if made with a person who is elected an honorary director until completion and an ordinary director afterwards: *Stears v South Essex Gas-Light and Coke Co* (1860) 9 CBNS 180. When the articles provide that the interest of a director must be disclosed in the minutes, the contract is invalid unless the entry is made within a reasonable time: *Toms v Cinema Trust Co Ltd* [1915] WN 29; and see *Re British America Corpn* (1903) 19 TLR 662; *Exploring Land and Minerals Co Ltd v Kolckmann* (1905) 94 LT 234, CA. As to the statutory duty of a director to disclose his interest see para 594 ante.

5   *North-West Transportation Co Ltd and Beatty v Beatty* (1887) 12 App Cas 589, PC; *Grant v United Kingdom Switchback Rlys Co* (1888) 40 ChD 135, CA; *Murray's Executors' Case* (1854) 5 De GM & G 746. See also *Cook v Deeks* [1916] 1 AC 554, PC; *Jacobus Marler Estates Ltd v Jacobus Marler* (1913) 85 LJPC 167n.

6   *Imperial Mercantile Credit Association (Liquidators) v Coleman* (1873) LR 6 HL 189 (where the articles required the director to vacate his seat if he did not 'declare his interest' in any contract); and see *Dunne v English* (1874) LR 18 Eq 524.

7   See *Kaye v Croydon Tramways Co* [1898] 1 Ch 358, CA; *Bamford v Bamford* [1970] Ch 212, [1969] 1 All ER 969, CA; and para 594 ante.

8   *Parker and Cooper Ltd v Reading* [1926] Ch 975.

9   *Aberdeen Rly Co v Blaikie Bros* (1854) 2 Eq Rep 1281, HL.

10   *Albion Steel and Wire Co v Martin* (1875) 1 ChD 580; cf *Bray v Ford* [1896] AC 44, HL.

11   *Flanagan v Great Western Rly Co* (1868) LR 7 Eq 116; *Imperial Mercantile Credit Association (Liquidators) v Coleman* (1873) LR 6 HL 189.

12   See note 3 supra.

13   *Re Dover Coalfield Extension Ltd* [1908] 1 Ch 65, CA. Cf *Re Macadam, Dallow v Codd* [1946] Ch 73, [1945] 2 All ER 664; and see para 575 ante.

14   See the cases cited in para 670 note 2 post.

597. Contracts with sole member who is also a director. Where a private company[1] limited by shares or by guarantee having only one member enters into a contract with the sole member[2] of the company and the sole member is also a director of the company, the company must, unless the contract is in writing, ensure that the terms of the contract are either set out in a written memorandum or are recorded in the minutes of the first meeting of the directors of the company following the making of the contract[3]. This provision does not, however, apply to contracts entered into in the ordinary course of the company's business[4]. If a company fails to comply with the above provisions, the company, and every officer of it who is in default, is guilty of an offence and liable on summary conviction to a fine not exceeding level 5 on the standard scale[5].

Nothing in the above provisions is to be construed as excluding the operation of any other enactment or rule of law applying to contracts between a company and a director of that company[6]. Failure to comply with the above provisions with respect to a contract does not, however, affect the validity of that contract[7].

1   For the meaning of 'private company' see para 82 ante.

2   For these purposes, a sole member who is a shadow director is treated as a director: Companies Act 1985 s 322B(3) (added by the Companies (Single Member Private Limited Companies) Regulations 1992, SI 1992/1699, reg 2(1)(b), Schedule para 3(1)). For the meaning of 'shadow director' and 'director' see para 543 note 1 ante.

3   Companies Act 1985 s 322B(1) (added by the Companies (Single Member Private Limited Companies) Regulations 1992 Schedule para 3(1)).

4   Companies Act 1985 s 322B(2) (added by the Companies (Single Member Private Limited Companies) Regulations 1992 Schedule para 3(1)).

5   Companies Act 1985 s 322B(4) (added by the Companies (Single Member Private Limited Companies) Regulations 1992 Schedule para 3(1)); Companies Act 1985 s 730, Sch 24 (amended by the Companies

(Single Member Private Limited Companies) Regulations 1992 Schedule para 3(3)). For the meaning of 'the standard scale' see CRIMINAL LAW vol 11(2) (Reissue) para 808.

6 Companies Act 1985 s 322B(5) (added by the Companies (Single Member Private Limited Companies) Regulations 1992 Schedule para 3(1)).

7 Companies Act 1985 s 322B(6) (added by the Companies (Single Member Private Limited Companies) Regulations 1992 Schedule para 3(1)).

H. PROHIBITIONS AND RESTRICTIONS

(A) *Restrictions on a Company's Power to make Loans to and confer Other Financial Benefits on Directors and Persons connected with them*

598. Prohibition of loans to directors. Subject to certain exceptions[1], a company must not make a loan to any person who is its director[2], or a director of its holding company[3], or enter into any guarantee[4] or provide any security in connection with a loan made by any person to such a director[5].

A relevant company[6] must not make a quasi-loan[7] to a director of the company or of its holding company, or make a loan or a quasi-loan to a person connected[8] with such a director, or enter into a guarantee or provide any security in connection with a loan or quasi-loan made by any other person for[9] such a director or a person so connected[10].

A relevant company must not enter into a credit transaction[11] as creditor for such a director or a person so connected, or enter into any guarantee or provide any security in connection with a credit transaction made by any other person for[12] such a director or a person so connected[13].

A company must not arrange for the assignment to it, or the assumption by it, of any rights, obligations or liabilities under a transaction which, if it had been entered into by the company, would have contravened any of the above provisions, but, for the purposes of the relevant statutory provisions[14], the transaction is to be treated as having been entered into on the date of the arrangement[15].

A company must not take part in any arrangement whereby another person enters into a transaction which, if it had been entered into by the company, would have contravened any of the above provisions and that other person, in pursuance of the arrangement, has obtained, or is to obtain, any benefit from the company or its holding company or a subsidiary of the company or its holding company[16].

For all the above purposes, it is immaterial whether the law which, apart from the Companies Act 1985, governs any arrangement or transaction is the law of the United Kingdom, or a part of it, or not[17].

1 Ie subject to the exceptions in the Companies Act 1985 ss 332–338 (as amended): see paras 599–601 post. As to the taxation consequences of a beneficial loan arrangement see the Income and Corporation Taxes Act 1988 s 160(1) (as amended) and INCOME TAXATION vol 23 (Reissue) para 740 et seq.

2 For these purposes, a shadow director is treated as a director: s 330(5). For the meaning of 'shadow director' and 'director' see para 543 note 1 ante.

3 For the meaning of 'holding company' see para 827 post.

4 For these purposes, 'guarantee' includes indemnity, and cognate expressions are to be construed accordingly: Companies Act 1985 s 331(1), (2).

5 Ibid s 330(1), (2).

6 For these purposes, 'relevant company' means a company which (1) is a public company; or (2) is a subsidiary of a public company; or (3) is a subsidiary of a company which has as another subsidiary a public company; or (4) has a subsidiary which is a public company: ibid s 331(1), (6). For the meaning of 'public company' see para 82 ante; and for the meaning of 'subsidiary' see para 827 post.

7 For these purposes, a quasi-loan is a transaction under which one party ('the creditor') agrees to pay, or pays otherwise than in pursuance of an agreement, a sum for another ('the borrower') or agrees to

reimburse, or reimburses otherwise than in pursuance of an agreement, expenditure incurred by another party for another ('the borrower'): (1) on terms that the borrower (or a person on his behalf) will reimburse the creditor; or (2) in circumstances giving rise to a liability on the borrower to reimburse the creditor: ibid s 331(1), (3). Any reference to the person to whom a quasi-loan is made is a reference to the borrower; and the liabilities of a borrower under a quasi-loan include the liabilities of any person who has agreed to reimburse the creditor on behalf of the borrower: s 331(1), (4).

8 For the meaning of 'connected' see para 607 post.

9 For these purposes, a loan or quasi-loan is made 'for' a person if it is made to him: Companies Act 1985 s 331(1), (9)(a). A transaction or arrangement is made 'for' a person if, in the case of a guarantee or security, it is entered into or provided in connection with a loan or quasi-loan made to him or a credit transaction made for him (s 331(1), (9)(c)); and in the case of any other transaction or arrangement for the supply or transfer of, or of any interest in, goods, land or services, if he is the person to whom the goods, land or services (or the interest) are supplied or transferred (s 331(1), (9)(e)). For the meaning of 'credit transaction' see note 11 infra; and as to the circumstances in which a credit transaction is made 'for' a person see note 12 infra.

10 Ibid s 330(3).

11 For these purposes, a credit transaction is a transaction under which one party ('the creditor'): (1) supplies any goods or sells any land under a hire-purchase agreement or a conditional sale agreement; (2) leases or hires any land or goods in return for periodical payments; (3) otherwise disposes of land or supplies goods or services on the understanding that payment, whether in a lump sum or instalments or by way of periodical payments or otherwise, is to be deferred: ibid s 331(1), (7). 'Services' means anything other than goods or land: s 331(1), (8). 'Conditional sale agreement' bears the same meaning as in the Consumer Credit Act 1974 s 189(1) (see HIRE PURCHASE vol 22 para 37): Companies Act 1985 s 331(10). For the meaning of 'hire-purchase agreement' see para 214 note 4 ante.

12 For these purposes, a credit transaction is made 'for' a person if he is the person to whom goods or services are supplied, or land is sold or otherwise disposed of, under the transaction: ibid s 331(1), (9)(b).

13 Ibid s 330(4).

14 Ie ibid ss 330–347 (as amended): see paras 599–607 post.

15 Ibid s 330(6).

16 Ibid s 330(7).

17 Ibid s 347.

599. General exceptions. Notwithstanding the general prohibition[1], a company may make a quasi-loan[2] to one of its directors or to a director[3] of its holding company[4] if the quasi-loan contains a term requiring the director or a person on his behalf to reimburse the company his expenditure within two months of its being incurred, and the aggregate of the amount of that quasi-loan and of the amount outstanding under each relevant quasi-loan does not exceed £5,000[5]. A quasi-loan is relevant for this purpose if it was made to the director by virtue of this provision by the company or its subsidiary[6], or, where the director is a director of the company's holding company, any other subsidiary of that company; and 'the amount outstanding' is the amount of the outstanding liabilities of the person to whom the quasi-loan was made[7].

In the case of a relevant company which is a member of a group of companies (meaning a holding company and its subsidiaries) the above provisions[8] prohibiting loans or quasi-loans by a relevant company[9] do not prohibit the company from making a loan or quasi-loan to another member of that group, or entering into a guarantee[10] or providing any security in connection with a loan or quasi-loan made by any other person to another member of the group, by reason only that a director of one member of the group is associated with another[11].

A company is not, however, prohibited[12] from making a loan to a director of the company or its holding company if the aggregate of the relevant amounts does not exceed £5,000[13].

The provisions relating to a relevant company not entering into a credit transaction or guarantee[14] do not prohibit a company from entering into a transaction for[15] a person if the aggregate of the relevant amounts does not exceed £10,000[16]. Nor do they prohibit a company from entering into a transaction if it is entered into by the company in the ordinary course of its business, and the value of the transaction is not greater, and the terms on which it is entered into are no more favourable, in respect of the person for whom the transaction is made, than that or those which it is reasonable to expect the company to have offered to or in respect of a person of the same financial standing but unconnected with the company[17].

Nothing in any of the prohibitions referred to above[18] prohibits:

(1) a loan or quasi-loan by a company to its holding company or a company entering into a guarantee or providing any security in connection with a loan or quasi-loan made by any person to its holding company;

(2) a company entering into a credit transaction as creditor for its holding company or entering into a guarantee or providing any security in connection with a credit transaction made by any other person for its holding company[19].

For all the above purposes, it is immaterial whether the law which, apart from the Companies Act 1985, governs any arrangement or transaction is the law of the United Kingdom, or a part of it, or not[20].

1 Ie the Companies Act 1985 s 330(3): see para 598 ante.
2 For the meaning of 'quasi-loan' see para 598 note 7 ante.
3 For these purposes, a shadow director is treated as a director: Companies Act 1985 s 330(5). For the meaning of 'shadow director' and 'director' see para 543 note 1 ante.
4 For the meaning of 'holding company' see para 827 post.
5 Companies Act 1985 s 332(1) (amended by the Companies Act 1989 s 138(a)). The Secretary of State may by order in a statutory instrument substitute for any sum of money specified in the Companies Act 1985 Pt X (ss 311–347) (as amended) a larger sum specified in the order (s 345(1)); and any such order is subject to annulment in pursuance of a resolution of either House of Parliament (s 345(2)). Such an order does not have effect in relation to anything done or not done before its coming into force; and accordingly proceedings in respect of any liability, whether civil or criminal, incurred before that time may be continued or instituted as if the order had not been made: s 345(3). In exercise of the power so conferred the Secretary of State made the Companies (Fair Dealing by Directors) (Increase in Financial Limits) Order 1990, SI 1990/1393, which came into force on 31 July 1990: art 1.
6 For the meaning of 'subsidiary' see para 827 post.
7 Companies Act 1985 s 332(2).
8 Ie ibid s 330(3)(b), (c): see para 598 ante.
9 For the meaning of 'relevant company' see para 598 note 6 ante.
10 For the meaning of 'guarantee' see para 598 note 4 ante.
11 Companies Act 1985 s 333. For the meaning of 'associated with' see para 607 post.
12 Ie by ibid s 330(2)(a): see para 599 ante.
13 Ibid s 334 (amended by the Companies Act 1989 s 138(b)). The Companies Act 1985 s 334 (as so amended) is without prejudice to any other provisions of ss 332–338 (as amended): s 334 (as so amended). For the meaning of 'the relevant amounts' see para 602 post. See also note 5 supra.
14 Ie ibid s 330(4): see para 598 ante.
15 As to the circumstances in which a transaction is made 'for' a person see para 598 notes 9, 12 ante.
16 Companies Act 1985 s 335(1) (amended by the Companies (Fair Dealing by Directors) (Increase in Financial Limits) Order 1990 art 2(b)). See also note 5 supra.
17 Companies Act 1985 s 335(2).
18 Ie ibid s 330: see para 598 ante.
19 Ibid s 336.
20 Ibid s 347.

600. Funding of director's expenditure on duty to company. A company is not prohibited[1] from doing anything to provide a director[2] with funds to meet expenditure incurred or to be incurred by him for the purposes of the company or for the purpose of enabling him properly to perform his duties as an officer of the company[3]. Nor is the company prohibited from doing anything to enable a director to avoid incurring such expenditure[4].

The above provisions apply, however, only if one of the following conditions is satisfied:

(1) the thing in question is done with prior approval of the company given at a general meeting at which all the following matters are disclosed:

    (a) the purpose of the expenditure incurred or to be incurred, or which would otherwise be incurred by the director;

    (b) the amount of the funds to be provided by the company; and

    (c) the extent of the company's liability under any transaction which is or is connected with the thing in question;

(2) that thing is done on condition that, if the approval of the company is not so given at or before the next annual general meeting, the loan is to be repaid, or any other liability arising under any such transaction discharged, within six months from the conclusion of that meeting[5].

Nevertheless, a relevant company[6] is not authorised to enter into any such transaction if the aggregate of the relevant amounts exceeds £20,000[7].

For the above purposes, it is immaterial whether the law which, apart from the Companies Act 1985, governs any arrangement or transaction is the law of the United Kingdom, or a part of it, or not[8].

1 Ie by the Companies Act 1985 s 330: see para 598 ante.
2 For these purposes, a shadow director is treated as a director: ibid s 330(5). For the meaning of 'shadow director' and 'director' see para 543 note 1 ante.
3 Ibid s 337(1).
4 Ibid s 337(2).
5 Ibid s 337(3) (amended by the Companies (Fair Dealing by Directors) (Increase in Financial Limits) Order 1990, SI 1990/1393, art 2(c)); Companies Act 1985 s 337(4). See also para 599 note 5 ante. A written resolution is not effective if any of the requirements of s 381A(7), Sch 15A para 8 (as added) is not complied with: Sch 15A para 2(2) (added by the Companies Act 1989 s 114(1)). In relation to a written resolution giving approval under the Companies Act 1985 s 337(3)(a) (see text head (1) supra), the requirement thereof that certain matters be disclosed at the meeting at which the resolution is passed does not apply, but those matters must be disclosed to each relevant member at or before the time at which the resolution is supplied to him for signature: Sch 15A para 8 (added by the Companies Act 1989 s 114(1)). For the meaning of 'written resolution' and 'relevant member' see para 224 note 3 ante.
6 For the meaning of 'relevant company' see para 598 note 6 ante.
7 Companies Act 1985 s 337(3) (as amended: see note 5 supra).
8 Ibid s 347.

601. Loan or quasi-loan by money-lending company. There is excepted from the general prohibitions[1] a loan or quasi-loan[2] made by a money-lending company[3] to any person, or a money-lending company entering into a guarantee in connection with any other loan or quasi-loan[4]. This exception applies only if both the following conditions are satisfied:

(1) the loan or quasi-loan in question is made by the company, or it enters into the guarantee, in the ordinary course of the company's business; and

(2) the amount of the loan or quasi-loan, or the amount guaranteed, is not greater, and the terms of the loan, quasi-loan or guarantee are not more favourable, in the case of the person to whom the loan or quasi-loan is made or in respect of whom the guarantee is entered into, than that or those which it is reasonable to expect that company to have offered to or in respect of a person of the same financial standing but unconnected with the company[5].

The exception does not, however, authorise a relevant company[6], unless it is a banking company[7], to enter into any transaction if the aggregate of the relevant amounts[8] exceeds £100,000[9].

The condition specified in head (2) above does not of itself prevent a company from making a loan to one of its directors[10] or a director of its holding company[11]:

(a) for the purpose of facilitating the purchase, for use as that director's only or main residence, of the whole or part of any dwelling house together with any land to be occupied and enjoyed with it;

(b) for the purpose of improving a dwelling house or part of a dwelling house so used or any land occupied and enjoyed with it;

(c) in substitution for any loan made by any person and falling within heads (a) or (b) above,

if loans of that description are ordinarily made by the company to its employees and on terms no less favourable than those on which the transaction in question is made, and the aggregate of the relevant amounts does not exceed £100,000[12].

For the above purposes, it is immaterial whether the law which, apart from the Companies Act 1985, governs any arrangement or transaction is the law of the United Kingdom, or a part of it, or not[13].

1 Ie those contained in the Companies Act 1985 s 330: see para 598 ante.
2 For the meaning of 'quasi-loan' see para 598 note 7 ante.
3 For these purposes, 'money-lending company' means a company whose ordinary business includes the making of loans or quasi-loans, or the giving of guarantees in connection with loans or quasi-loans: Companies Act 1985 s 338(2). For the meaning of 'guarantee' see para 598 note 4 ante.
4 Ibid s 338(1).
5 Ibid s 338(3).
6 For the meaning of 'relevant company' see para 598 note 6 ante.
7 For the meaning of 'banking company' see para 117 note 8 ante.
8 For the meaning of 'the relevant amounts' see para 602 post. In determining that aggregate, a company which a director does not control is deemed not to be connected with him: Companies Act 1985 s 338(5). See further para 602 text to note 3 post.
9 Ibid s 338(4) (amended by the Companies Act 1989 ss 23, 138(c), Sch 10 para 10). See also para 599 note 5 ante.
10 For these purposes, a shadow director is treated as a director: Companies Act 1985 s 330(5). For the meaning of 'shadow director' and 'director' see para 543 note 1 ante.
11 For the meaning of 'holding company' see para 827 post.
12 Companies Act 1985 s 338(6) (amended by the Companies Act 1989 s 138(c)). See also para 599 note 5 ante.
13 Companies Act 1985 s 347.

602. Meaning of 'relevant amounts'. The following provisions have effect for defining the 'relevant amounts' to be aggregated under the above exceptions[1]; and, in relation to any proposed transaction or arrangement and the question whether it falls within one or other of the statutory exceptions, 'the relevant exception' is that exception; but, where the relevant exception is in relation to loans of small amount[2], references to a person connected with a director are to be disregarded[3]. Subject to the following provisions, the relevant amounts in relation to a proposed transaction or arrangement are:

(1) the value of the proposed transaction or arrangement;

(2) the value of any existing arrangement which:

(a) provides for the assignment to or the assumption by the company of rights, obligations or liabilities under a transaction which, if it had been entered into by the company, would have contravened the statutory prohibitions[4]; or whereby another person enters into a transaction which, if it had been entered into by the company, would have contravened any of those prohibitions and that other person, in pursuance of the arrangement, has obtained or is to obtain any benefit from the company or its holding company[5] or a subsidiary[6] of the company or its holding company[7]; and

(b) also falls within the statutory provisions below[8]; and

(c) was entered into by virtue of the relevant exception by the company or by a subsidiary of the company or, where the proposed transaction or arrangement is to be made for[9] a director of its holding company or a person connected with such a director, by that holding company or any of its subsidiaries;

(3) the amount outstanding under any other transaction:

(a) falling within the statutory provisions below[10]; and

(b) made by virtue of the relevant exception; and

(c) made by the company or by a subsidiary of the company or, where the proposed transaction or arrangement is to be made for a director of its holding company or a person connected with such a director, by that holding company or any of its subsidiaries[11].

A transaction falls within these provisions if it was made for the director for whom the proposed transaction or arrangement is to be made, or for any person connected with that director; or, where the proposed transaction or arrangement is to be made for a person connected with a director of a company, for that director or any person connected with him; and an arrangement also falls within these provisions if it relates to a transaction which does so[12]. Where, however, the proposed transaction falls within the exception relating to money-lending companies[13] and is one which a banking company[14] proposes to enter into by way of loan for the purchase or improvement of a dwelling house or in substitution for a loan made for such a purpose[15], any other transaction or arrangement which would otherwise fall within these provisions does not do so unless it was entered into in pursuance of such a loan[16]. A transaction entered into by a company which is, at the time of that transaction being entered into, a subsidiary of the company which is to make the proposed transaction, or is a subsidiary of that company's holding company, does not fall within these provisions if at the time when the question arises, that is to say, the question whether the proposed transaction or arrangement falls within any relevant exception, it no longer is such a subsidiary[17].

For the above purposes, it is immaterial whether the law which, apart from the Companies Act 1985, governs any arrangement or transaction is the law of the United Kingdom, or a part of it, or not[18].

1 Ie those under the Companies Act 1985 s 334 (as amended) (see para 599 ante), s 335(1) (as amended) (see para 599 ante), s 337(3) (as amended) (see para 600 ante) and s 338(4) (as amended) (see para 601 ante).

2 Ie under ibid s 334: see para 599 ante.

3 Ibid s 339(1). For these purposes, a shadow director is treated as a director: ibid s 330(5). For the meaning of 'shadow director' and 'director' see para 543 note 1 ante. For the meaning of 'connected' see para 607 post.

4 Ie those contained in ibid s 330(2), (3), (4): see para 598 ante.

5 For the meaning of 'holding company' see para 827 post.

6 For the meaning of 'subsidiary' see para 827 post.

7 Ie an arrangement falling within the Companies Act 1985 s 330(7): see para 598 ante.

8 Ie ibid s 339(3): see infra.

9 As to the circumstances in which a transaction or arrangement is made 'for' a person see para 598 notes 9, 12 ante.

10 See note 8 supra.

11 Companies Act 1985 s 339(2). Values for the purposes of s 339(2) are to be determined in accordance with s 340 (as amended) (see para 603 post); and 'the amount outstanding' for the purposes of s 339(2)(c) (see text head (3) supra) is the value of the transaction less any amount by which that value has been reduced: s 339(6).

12 Ibid s 339(3).
13 Ie ibid s 338 (as amended): see para 601 ante.
14 For the meaning of 'banking company' see para 117 note 8 ante.
15 Ie under the Companies Act 1985 s 338(6): see para 601 ante.
16 Ibid s 339(4) (amended by the Companies Act 1989 s 23, Sch 10 para 10).
17 Companies Act 1985 s 339(5).
18 Ibid s 347.

603. Value of transactions and arrangements. The following provisions have effect for determining the value of a transaction or arrangement for the purposes of restrictions[1] on a company's power to make loans to and confer financial benefits on directors and persons connected with them[2].

The value of a loan is the amount of its principal[3].

The value of a quasi-loan[4] is the amount, or maximum amount, which the person to whom the quasi-loan is made is liable to reimburse the creditor[5].

The value of a guarantee[6] or security is the amount guaranteed or secured[7].

The value of an arrangement[8]:

(1) which provides for the assignment to or the assumption by the company of rights, obligations or liabilities under a transaction which, if it had been entered into by the company, would have contravened the statutory prohibitions; or

(2) whereby another person enters into a transaction which, if it had been entered into by the company would have contravened any of those prohibitions and that other person, in pursuance of the arrangement, has obtained or is to obtain any benefit from the company or its holding company[9] or a subsidiary[10] of the company or its holding company,

is the value of the transaction to which the arrangement relates less any amount by which the liabilities under the arrangement or transaction of the person for whom the transaction was made have been reduced[11].

The value of a transaction or arrangement not falling within the above provisions is the price which it is reasonable to expect could be obtained for the goods, land or services[12] to which the transaction or arrangement relates if they had been supplied, at the time the transaction or arrangement is entered into, in the ordinary course of business and on the same terms, apart from price, as they have been supplied, or are to be supplied, under the transaction or arrangement in question[13].

For the above purposes:

(a) the value of a transaction or arrangement which is not capable of being expressed as a specific sum of money, because the amount of any liability arising under the transaction or arrangement is unascertainable, or for any other reason, whether or not any liability under the transaction or arrangement has been reduced, is deemed to exceed £100,000[14]; and

(b) it is immaterial whether the law which, apart from the Companies Act 1985, governs any arrangement or transaction is the law of the United Kingdom, or a part of it, or not[15].

1 Ie the Companies Act 1985 ss 330–339 (as amended): see paras 598–602 ante.
2 Ibid s 340(1).
3 Ibid s 340(2).
4 For the meaning of 'quasi-loan' see para 598 note 7 ante.
5 Companies Act 1985 s 340(3).
6 For the meaning of 'guarantee' see para 598 note 4 ante.
7 Companies Act 1985 s 340(4).
8 Ie an arrangement to which ibid s 330(6) or (7) applies: see para 598 ante.

9 For the meaning of 'holding company' see para 827 post.
10 For the meaning of 'subsidiary' see para 827 post.
11 Companies Act 1985 s 340(5). As to the circumstances in which a transaction or arrangement is made 'for' a person see para 598 notes 9, 12 ante.
12 For the meaning of 'services' see para 598 note 11 ante.
13 Companies Act 1985 s 340(6).
14 Ibid s 340(7) (amended by the Companies (Fair Dealing by Directors) (Increase in Financial Limits) Order 1990, SI 1990/1393, art 2(d)). See also para 599 note 5 ante.
15 Companies Act 1985 s 347.

604. Civil remedies for breach of prohibition on loans to directors. If a company enters into a transaction or arrangement in contravention of the prohibition on loans and similar benefits to directors[1], the transaction or arrangement is voidable at the instance of the company unless:

(1) restitution of any money or any other asset which is the subject matter of the arrangement or transaction is no longer possible, or the company has been indemnified in pursuance of head (b) below for the loss or damage suffered by it; or

(2) any rights acquired bona fide for value and without actual notice of the contravention by a person other than the person for[2] whom the transaction or arrangement was made would be affected by its avoidance[3].

Where an arrangement or transaction is made by a company for a director[4] of the company or its holding company[5] or a person connected[6] with such a director in contravention of such prohibition, that director and the person so connected and any other director of the company who authorised the transaction or arrangement (whether or not it has been avoided in pursuance of heads (1) or (2) above) is liable:

(a) to account to the company for any gain which he has made directly or indirectly by the arrangement or transaction; and

(b) jointly and severally with any other person liable under this provision, to indemnify the company for any loss or damage resulting from the arrangement or transaction[7].

This is without prejudice to any liability imposed otherwise than by this provision, but is subject to the exceptions set out below[8].

Where an arrangement or transaction is entered into by a company and a person connected with a director of the company or its holding company in contravention of such prohibition, that director is not liable under heads (a) or (b) above if he shows that he took all reasonable steps to secure the company's compliance with that provision[9]. In any case, a person so connected and any such other director as is therein mentioned is not so liable if he shows that, at the time the arrangement or transaction was entered into, he did not know the relevant circumstances constituting the contravention[10].

For the above purposes, it is immaterial whether the law which, apart from the Companies Act 1985, governs any arrangement or transaction is the law of the United Kingdom, or a part of it, or not[11].

1 Ie the Companies Act 1985 s 330: see para 598 ante.
2 As to the circumstances in which a transaction or arrangement is made 'for' a person see para 598 notes 9, 12 ante.
3 Companies Act 1985 s 341(1).
4 For these purposes, a shadow director is treated as a director: ibid s 330(5). For the meaning of 'shadow director' and 'director' see para 543 note 1 ante.
5 For the meaning of 'holding company' see para 827 post.
6 For the meaning of 'connected' see para 607 post.
7 Companies Act 1985 s 341(2).

8 Ibid s 341(3).
9 Ibid s 341(4).
10 Ibid s 341(5).
11 Ibid s 347.

605. Criminal penalties for breach of prohibition on loans to directors. A director[1] of a relevant company[2] who authorises or permits the company to enter into a transaction or arrangement knowing or having reasonable cause to believe that the company was thereby contravening the prohibition on loans and similar benefits to directors[3] is guilty of an offence[4].

A relevant company which enters into a transaction or arrangement for[5] one of its directors or for a director of its holding company[6] in contravention of such prohibition is guilty of an offence[7] unless it shows that, at the time the transaction or arrangement was entered into, it did not know the relevant circumstances[8].

A person who procures a relevant company to enter into a transaction or arrangement knowing or having reasonable cause to believe that the company was thereby contravening such prohibition is guilty of an offence[9].

A person guilty of an offence under these provisions is liable on conviction on indictment to imprisonment for a term not exceeding two years or to a fine, or to both, or, on summary conviction, to imprisonment for a term not exceeding six months or a fine not exceeding the statutory maximum, or to both[10].

For the above purposes, it is immaterial whether the law which, apart from the Companies Act 1985, governs any arrangement or transaction is the law of the United Kingdom, or a part of it, or not[11].

1 For these purposes, a shadow director is treated as a director: Companies Act 1985 s 330(5). For the meaning of 'shadow director' and 'director' see para 543 note 1 ante.
2 For the meaning of 'relevant company' see para 598 note 6 ante.
3 Ie the Companies Act 1985 s 330: see para 598 ante.
4 Ibid s 342(1).
5 As to the circumstances in which a transaction or arrangement is made 'for' a person see para 598 notes 9, 12 ante.
6 For the meaning of 'holding company' see para 827 post.
7 Companies Act 1985 s 342(2).
8 Ibid s 342(5).
9 Ibid s 342(3).
10 Ibid ss 342(4), 730, Sch 24. For the meaning of 'the statutory maximum' see para 1161 post.
11 Ibid s 347.

606. Record of transactions not disclosed in company accounts. A company which is a banking company[1] or is the holding company[2] of a credit institution must[3], where it takes advantage of the exemption from disclosure in relation to a financial year[4], keep a register containing a copy of every transaction, arrangement or agreement of which particulars would, but for that exemption, be required to be disclosed in the company's accounts or group accounts for that financial year and for each financial year in the preceding ten in relation to which the company has taken advantage of that exemption[5]. In the case of a transaction, arrangement or agreement which is not in writing, a written memorandum setting out its terms must be contained in the register[6].

Where such a company takes advantage of the exemption from disclosure in relation to the last complete financial year preceding its annual general meeting, that company must before that meeting make available at its registered office for not less than 15 days ending with the date of the meeting a statement containing the particulars of transactions, arrangements and agreements which the company would, but for that exemption, be required to disclose in its accounts or group accounts for that financial year[7]. The statement must be so made available for inspection by members of the company; and such a statement must also be made available for their inspection at the annual general meeting[8]. It is the duty of the company's auditors to examine the statement before it is made available to members of the company and to make a report to the members on it; and the report must be annexed to the statement before it is made so available[9]. The auditors' report must state whether in their opinion the statement contains the required particulars[10]; and, where their opinion is that it does not, they must include in the report, so far as they are reasonably able to do so, a statement giving the required particulars[11].

If a company fails to comply with any of the above provisions[12], every person who at the time of the failure is a director[13] of it is guilty of an offence and liable on conviction on indictment to a fine, or on summary conviction to a fine not exceeding the statutory maximum[14]. It is, however, a defence in proceedings against a person for this offence to prove that he took all reasonable steps for securing compliance with the provision concerned; and a person is not guilty of the offence by virtue only of being a shadow director of the company[15].

For purposes of the application of the above provisions to loans and quasi-loans[16] made by a company to persons connected with[17] a person who at any time is a director of the company or of its holding company, a company which a person does not control is not connected with him[18].

The above provisions do not apply in relation to transactions or arrangements made or subsisting during a financial year by a company or by a subsidiary[19] of a company for[20] a person who was at any time during that year a director of the company or of its holding company, or was connected with such a director, or an agreement made or subsisting during that year to enter into such a transaction or arrangement, if the aggregate of the values[21] of each transaction or arrangement made for that person, and of each agreement for such a transaction or arrangement, less the amount, if any, by which the value of those transactions, arrangements and agreements has been reduced, did not exceed £2,000 at any time during the financial year[22].

1 For the meaning of 'banking company' see para 117 note 8 ante.
2 For the meaning of 'holding company' see para 827 post.
3 Ie subject to the Companies Act 1985 s 344 (as amended): see infra.
4 Ie the provisions of ibid Sch 9 Pt IV para 2 (as substituted).
5 Ibid s 343(1) (amended by the Companies Act 1989 s 23, Sch 10 para 10); Companies Act 1985 s 343(2) (substituted by the Companies Act 1985 (Bank Accounts) Regulations 1994, SI 1994/233, reg 6(1)–(3)). For the purposes of the Companies Act 1985 s 343 (as amended), it is immaterial whether the law which, apart from the Companies Act 1985, governs any arrangement or transaction is the law of the United Kingdom, or of a part of it, or not: s 347.
6 Ibid s 343(3).
7 Ibid s 343(4) (substituted by the Companies Act 1985 (Bank Accounts) Regulations 1994 reg 6(1), (4)). The Companies Act 1985 s 343(4) (as so substituted) and s 343(5) (see infra) do not, however, apply to a banking company which is the wholly-owned subsidiary of a company incorporated in the United Kingdom: s 344(2) (amended by the Companies Act 1989 Sch 10 para 10). For the meaning of 'wholly-owned subsidiary' see para 827 post.
8 Companies Act 1985 s 343(5). See also note 7 supra.
9 Ibid s 343(6).
10 Ie the particulars required by ibid s 343(4) (as substituted): see supra.
11 Ibid s 343(7).
12 Ie any provision of ibid s 343(2)–(5) (as amended): see supra.

13 For these purposes, a shadow director is treated as a director: ibid s 330(5). For the meaning of 'shadow director' and 'director' see para 543 note 1 ante.
14 Ibid ss 343(8), 730, Sch 24. For the meaning of 'the statutory maximum' see para 1161 post.
15 Ibid s 343(8)(a), (b).
16 For the meaning of 'quasi-loan' see para 598 note 7 ante.
17 For the meaning of 'connected' see para 607 post.
18 Companies Act 1985 s 343(9).
19 For the meaning of 'subsidiary' see para 827 post.
20 As to the circumstances in which a transaction or arrangement is made 'for' a person see para 598 notes 9, 12 ante.
21 For these purposes, values are to be determined as under the Companies Act 1985 s 340 (as amended) (see para 603 ante): s 344(1).
22 Ibid s 344(1) (amended by the Companies (Fair Dealing by Directors) (Increase in Financial Limits) Order 1990, SI 1990/1393, art 2(e)). See also para 599 note 5 ante.

607. Meaning of 'connected persons' etc. The following provisions have effect with respect to references in Part X of the Companies Act 1985[1] to a person being 'connected' with a director[2] of a company, and to a director being 'associated with' or 'controlling' a body corporate[3].

A person is connected with a director of a company if, but only if, he, not being himself a director of it, is:

(1) that director's spouse, child or stepchild; or
(2) except where the context otherwise requires, a body corporate with which the director is associated; or
(3) a person acting in his capacity as trustee of any trust the beneficiaries of which include:
  (a) the director, his spouse or any children or stepchildren of his; or
  (b) a body corporate with which he is associated,
  or of a trust whose terms confer a power on the trustees that may be exercised for the benefit of the director, his spouse, or any children or stepchildren of his, or any such body corporate; or
(4) a person acting in his capacity as partner of that director or of any person who, by virtue of heads (1), (2) or (3) above is connected with that director; or
(5) a Scottish firm in which that director is a partner, a partner is a person who, by virtue of heads (1), (2) or (3) above, is connected with that director, or a partner is a Scottish firm in which that director is a partner or in which there is a partner who, by virtue of heads (1), (2) or (3) above is connected with that director[4].

In the above provisions, a reference to the child or stepchild of any person includes an illegitimate child of his, but does not include any person who has attained the age of 18, and head (3) above does not apply to a person acting in his capacity as trustee under an employees' share scheme[5], or a pension scheme[6].

A director of a company is associated with a body corporate if, but only if, he and the persons connected with him, together, are interested in shares comprised in the equity share capital[7] of that body corporate of a nominal value equal to at least one-fifth of that share capital, or are entitled to exercise or control the exercise of more than one-fifth of the voting power at any general meeting of that body[8].

A director of a company is deemed to control a body corporate if, but only if, he, or any person connected with him is interested in any part of the equity share capital of that body or is entitled to exercise or control the exercise of any part of the voting power at any general meeting of that body, and that director, the persons connected with him and the other directors of that company, together, are interested in more than one-half of that share capital or are entitled to exercise or control the exercise of more than one-half of that voting power[9].

For these purposes, a body corporate with which a director is associated is not to be treated as connected with that director unless it is also connected with him by virtue of head (3) or (4) above[10]; and a trustee of a trust the beneficiaries of which include, or may include, a body corporate with which a director is associated is not to be treated as connected with a director by reason only of that fact[11].

References to voting power the exercise of which is controlled by a director include[12] voting power whose exercise is controlled by a body corporate controlled by him[13].

There are also further statutory rules[14] for the interpretation of the above provisions[15].

1 Ie the Companies Act 1985 Pt X (ss 311–347) (as amended): see paras 560–567, 570, 571, 573, 574, 578, 594, 598 et seq ante and paras 608–610 post.
2 For these purposes, a shadow director is treated as a director: ibid s 330(5). For the meaning of 'shadow director' and 'director' see para 543 note 1 ante.
3 Ibid s 346(1).
4 Ibid s 346(2).
5 For the meaning of 'employees' share scheme' see para 120 note 8 ante.
6 Companies Act 1985 s 346(3).
7 For these purposes, 'equity share capital' means the company's issued share capital excluding any part of that capital which, neither as respects dividends nor as respects capital, carries any right to participate beyond a specified amount in a distribution: ibid s 744.
8 Ibid s 346(4).
9 Ibid s 346(5).
10 Ibid s 346(6)(a).
11 Ibid s 346(6)(b).
12 Ie without prejudice to other provisions of ibid s 346(4), (5): see supra.
13 Ibid s 346(8).
14 Ie the rules set out in ibid Sch 13 Pt I (paras 1–13) (as amended): see para 568 ante.
15 Ibid s 346(7).

(B) *Restrictions on a Company's Power to pay Compensation for Loss of Office*

608. Prohibition of payment of compensation to director for loss of office without disclosure. It is not lawful for a company to make to a director any payment by way of compensation for loss of office, or as consideration for or in connection with his retirement from office, without particulars of the proposed payment, including its amount, being disclosed to members of the company and the proposal being approved by the company[1]. If the proposal is not so approved, the directors responsible for authorising the payment are guilty of misfeasance[2]. For these purposes[3], references to payments made to a director by way of compensation for loss of office or as consideration for or in connection with his retirement from office do not include any bona fide payment by way of damages[4] for breach of contract or by way of pension[5] in respect of past services[6]. Nor do the provisions apply to contractual payments due under service agreements, as, for example, between the company and its managing director[7].

Where the sum paid as compensation is payable under the terms of the service agreement upon the company electing to terminate it in accordance with its terms, the sum is a profit from the employment and taxable as such[8]. Compensation paid in consideration of the abrogation of the agreement is taxable under a special code[9].

1 Companies Act 1985 s 312.
2 *Re Duomatic Ltd* [1969] 2 Ch 365, [1969] 1 All ER 161. As to the power of the court to grant relief from liability in certain cases see para 624 post.
3 Ie and for the purposes of the Companies Act 1985 ss 313–315: see para 609 post.
4 If the director's service agreement contains inflation-proofing of his salary, this may be taken into account in arriving at any damages: *Re Crowther & Nicholson Ltd* (1981) 125 Sol Jo 529.
5 For these purposes, 'pension' includes any superannuation allowance, superannuation gratuity or similar payment: Companies Act 1985 s 316(3).
6 Ibid s 316(3). As to the assessment of damages for the wrongful dismissal of a director see *Beach v Reed Corrugated Cases Ltd* [1956] 2 All ER 652, [1956] 1 WLR 807; *Re Houghton Main Colliery Co Ltd* [1956] 3 All ER 300, [1956] 1 WLR 1219.
7 *Taupo Totara Timber Co Ltd v Rowe* [1978] AC 537, [1977] 3 All ER 123, PC (sum contractually payable on retirement).
8 *Dale v De Soissons* [1950] 2 All ER 460, CA.
9 See the Income and Corporation Taxes Act 1988 ss 148, 188 (as amended) and INCOME TAXATION vol 23 (Reissue) para 719 et seq.

609. Prohibition of payment of compensation for loss of office through transfer of undertaking or shares without disclosure. It is not lawful, in connection with the transfer of the whole or any part of the undertaking or property of a company, for any payment to be made to a director of the company by way of compensation for loss of office[1], or as consideration for or in connection with his retirement from office[2], unless particulars of the proposed payment, including its amount, have been disclosed to members of the company and the proposal approved by the company[3]. Where a payment unlawful under these provisions is made to a director of the company, the amount received is deemed to have been received by him in trust for the company[4].

Where, in connection with the transfer to any persons of all or any of the shares in a company, being a transfer resulting from:

(1)   an offer made to the general body of shareholders[5]; or
(2)   an offer made by or on behalf of some other body corporate with a view to the company becoming its subsidiary or a subsidiary of its holding company[6]; or
(3)   an offer made by or on behalf of an individual with a view to his obtaining the right to exercise or control the exercise of not less than one-third of the voting power at any general meeting of the company[7]; or
(4)   any other offer which is conditional on acceptance to a given extent[8],

a payment is to be made to a director by way of compensation for loss of office, or as consideration for or in connection with his retirement from office[9], then in those circumstances it is the director's duty to take all reasonable steps to secure that particulars of the proposed payment, including its amount, are included in or sent with any notice of the offer made for their shares which is given to any shareholders[10].

If the director fails to take such steps, or if any person who has been properly required by any such director to include those particulars in or send them with any such notice fails to do so, he is liable on summary conviction to a fine not exceeding one-fifth of the statutory maximum[11].

If in the case of any such payment to a director[12] his duty under the above provisions[13] is not complied with or the making of the proposed payment is not, before the transfer of any shares in pursuance of the offer, approved by a meeting, summoned for the purpose, of the holders of the shares to which the offer relates and of other holders of shares of the same class as any of those shares[14], any sum received by the director on account of the payment is deemed to have been received by him in trust for persons who have sold their shares as a result of the offer made; and the expenses incurred by him in distributing that sum among those persons are to be borne by him and not retained out of that sum[15].

1   For the meaning of references to payments made to a director by way of compensation for loss of office see the Companies Act 1985 s 316(3) and para 608 ante.
2   As to proposed payments not requiring to be disclosed and approved, and payments deemed to be within the application of ibid s 313, see para 610 post.
3   Ibid s 313(1). As to the saving for the operation of rules of law relating to disclosure see para 610 post.
4   Ibid s 313(2). Section 313(2) gives effect to and somewhat expands a principle of law already well recognised: see *Southall v British Mutual Life Assurance Society* (1871) 6 Ch App 614; *Gaskell v Chambers* (1858) 28 LJ Ch 385; *Kaye v Croydon Tramways Co* [1898] 1 Ch 358, CA; *Tiessen v Henderson* [1899] 1 Ch 861. See also paras 1192, 1482 post. See also *Clarkson v Davies* [1923] AC 100, PC. In an action to recover sums improperly paid to a director by way of compensation on the transfer of a business from one company to another, the transferor company is a necessary party: *Clarkson v Davies* supra. As to the fiduciary position of directors in respect of company property under their control see paras 585, 591 ante.
5   Companies Act 1985 s 314(1)(a).
6   Ibid s 314(1)(b). For the meaning of 'subsidiary' and 'holding company' see para 827 post.
7   Ibid s 314(1)(c).
8   Ibid s 314(1)(d).
9   For the meaning of references to payments made to a director by way of compensation for or in connection with retirement from office see ibid s 316(3) and para 608 ante.
10   Ibid s 314(1), (2).
11   Ibid s 314(3), 730, Sch 24. For the meaning of 'the statutory maximum' see para 1161 post.
12   Ie any such payment as is mentioned in ibid s 314(1): see supra.
13   Ie under ibid s 314: see supra.
14   Where such shareholders are not all the members of the company, and no provision is made by the articles for summoning or regulating such a meeting, the provisions of the Companies Act 1985, and of the company's articles relating to general meetings of the company apply, for this purpose, to the meeting either without modification or with such modifications as the Secretary of State on the application of any person concerned may direct for the purpose of adapting them to the circumstances of the meeting: s 315(2). If at a meeting summoned to approve such a proposed payment a quorum is not present, and, after the meeting has been adjourned to a later date, a quorum is again not present, the payment is deemed to have been approved: s 315(3).
15   Ibid s 315(1).

610. Supplemental provisions. Bona fide payments by way of damages for breach of contract or by way of pension, including superannuation allowance or gratuity or similar payment[1], made to a director in respect of past services are not payments by way of compensation for loss of office, or as consideration for or in connection with his retirement from office for the above[2] purposes[3]. Where in proceedings for the recovery of any payment as having been received by any person in trust[4], it is shown that:

(1) the payment was made in pursuance of any arrangement entered into as part of the agreement for the transfer in question, or within one year before or two years after that agreement or the offer leading to it; and

(2) the company or any person to whom the transfer was made was privy to that arrangement,

the payment is deemed to be one to which the above provisions apply, except in so far as the contrary is shown[5].

If, in connection with any such transfer[6]:

(a) the price to be paid to a director of the company, whose office is to be abolished or who is to retire from office, for any shares in the company held by him is in excess of the price which could at the time have been obtained by other holders of the like shares; or

(b) any valuable consideration is given to any such director, the excess or the money value of the consideration, as the case may be, is, for such purposes, deemed to have been a payment made to him by way of compensation for loss of office or as consideration for or in connection with his retirement from office[7].

Nothing in the above provisions[8] prejudices the operation of any rule of law requiring disclosure to be made with respect to any such payments, or with respect to any other like payments made or to be made to the directors of a company[9].

1 This does not cover a lump sum payment made by directors who have no other power to pay pensions on the eve of liquidation: *Gibson's Executor v Gibson* 1980 SLT 2.
2 Ie for the purposes of the Companies Act 1985 ss 312–315: see paras 608, 609 ante.
3 Ibid s 316(3). Cf the Companies (Tables A to F) Regulations 1985, SI 1985/805, Schedule, Table A art 87. As to Table A generally see para 529 et seq ante.
4 Ie by virtue of the Companies Act 1985 s 313(2) or s 315(1): see para 609 ante.
5 Ibid s 316(1).
6 Ie mentioned in ibid ss 313–315: see para 609 ante.
7 Ibid s 316(2).
8 Ie ibid ss 312–315.
9 Ibid s 316(4).

(C) *Restrictions on a Company's Power to enter into Substantial Property Transactions involving Directors*

611. Substantial property transactions involving directors. A company must not enter into an arrangement[1] whereby:

(1) a director[2] of the company or its holding company[3], or a person connected with[4] such a director, acquires or is to acquire one or more non-cash assets[5] of the requisite value from the company; or

(2) the company acquires or is to acquire one or more non-cash assets of the requisite value from such a director or a person so connected,

unless the arrangement is first approved by a resolution of the company in general meeting and, if the director or connected person is a director of its holding company or a person connected with such a director, by a resolution in general meeting of the holding company[6].

For this purpose, a non-cash asset is of the requisite value if at the time the arrangement in question is entered into its value is not less than £2,000 but (subject to that) exceeds £100,000 or 10% of the company's asset value, that is:

(a) except in a case falling within head (b) below, the value of the company's net assets determined by reference to the accounts prepared and laid[7] in respect of the last preceding financial year in respect of which such accounts were so laid; and

(b) where no accounts have been so prepared and laid before that time, the amount of the company's called-up share capital[8].

No such approval is required to be given by any body corporate unless it is a company within the meaning of the Companies Act 1985[9] or was not formed under the companies legislation but is registered thereunder[10] or, if it is a wholly-owned subsidiary[11] of any body corporate, wherever incorporated[12]. Nor do the above provisions apply to an arrangement for the acquisition of a non-cash asset if:

(i) the asset is to be acquired by a holding company from any of its wholly-owned subsidiaries or from a holding company by any of its wholly-owned subsidiaries, or by one wholly-owned subsidiary of a holding company from another wholly-owned subsidiary of that same holding company; or

(ii) the arrangement is entered into by a company which is being wound up, unless the winding up is a members' voluntary winding up[13];

and head (a) above does not apply to an arrangement whereby a person is to acquire an asset from a company of which he is a member, if the arrangement is made with that person in his character as a member[14].

Nor do the above provisions apply to a transaction on a recognised[15] investment exchange which is effected by a director or a person connected with him, through the agency of a person who in relation to the transaction acts as an independent broker[16].

For all the above purposes, it is immaterial whether the law which, apart from the Companies Act 1985, governs any arrangement or transaction is the law of the United Kingdom, or a part of it, or not[17].

1 Ie subject to the Companies Act 1985 s 321 (as amended): see para 612 post.
2 For these purposes, a shadow director is treated as a director: ibid s 320(3). For the meaning of 'shadow director' and 'director' see para 543 note 1 ante.
3 For the meaning of 'holding company' see para 827 post.
4 For the meaning of 'connected' see para 607 ante.
5 For the meaning of 'non-cash asset' see para 469 note 2 ante.
6 Companies Act 1985 s 320(1).
7 Ie under ibid Pt VII (ss 221–262A) (as amended): see para 801 et seq post.
8 Ibid s 320(2) (amended by the Companies (Fair Dealing by Directors) (Increase in Financial Limits) Order 1990, SI 1990/1393, art 2(a)). See also para 599 note 5 ante.
9 See para 11 ante.
10 Ie pursuant to the Companies Act 1985 s 680 (as amended): see para 24 ante.
11 For the meaning of 'subsidiary' see para 827 post.
12 Companies Act 1985 s 321(1).
13 Ibid s 321(2).
14 Ibid s 321(3).
15 For these purposes, 'recognised', in relation to an investment exchange, means recognised under the Financial Services Act 1986 (see MONEY): Companies Act 1985 s 321(4) (added by the Companies Act 1989 s 145, Sch 19 para 8).
16 Companies Act 1985 s 321(4) (as added: see note 15 supra). For these purposes, 'independent broker' means (1) in relation to a transaction on behalf of a director, a person who independently of the director selects the person with whom the transaction is to be effected; and (2) in relation to a transaction on behalf of a person connected with a director, a person who independently of that person or the director selects the person with whom the transaction is to be effected: s 321(4) (as so added).
17 Ibid s 347.

612. Liabilities arising from contravention of restrictions on property transactions. An arrangement entered into by a company in contravention of the above provision[1], and any transaction entered into in pursuance of the arrangement, whether by the company or any other person, is voidable at the instance of the company unless one or more of the following conditions is satisfied[2]. Those conditions are that:

(1) restitution of any money or other asset which is the subject matter of the arrangement or transaction is no longer possible or the company has been indemnified in pursuance of these provisions by any other person for the loss or damage suffered by it; or

(2) any rights acquired bona fide for value and without actual notice of the contravention by any person who is not a party to the arrangement or transaction would be affected by its avoidance; or

(3) the arrangement is, within a reasonable period, affirmed by the company in general meeting and, if it is an arrangement for the transfer of an asset to or by a director[3] of its holding company[4] or a person who is connected with[5] such a

director, is so affirmed with the approval of the holding company given by a resolution in general meeting[6].

If an arrangement is entered into with a company by a director of the company or its holding company or a person connected with him in contravention of the above provision[7], that director and the person so connected, and any other director of the company who authorised the arrangement or any transaction entered into in pursuance of such an arrangement, is liable to account to the company for any gain which he has made directly or indirectly by the arrangement or transaction, and, jointly and severally with any other person so liable, to indemnify the company for any loss or damage resulting from the arrangement or transaction[8]. This is without prejudice to any liability imposed otherwise than by this provision, and is subject to the following two exceptions[9]; but such liability[10] arises whether or not the arrangement or transaction entered into has been avoided[11]. If an arrangement is entered into by a company and a person connected with a director of the company or its holding company in contravention of the above provision, that director is not liable[12] if he shows that he took all reasonable steps to secure the company's compliance with that provision[13]. In any case, a person so connected and any other director who authorised the arrangement is not so liable if he shows that, at the time the arrangement was entered into, he did not know the relevant circumstances constituting the contravention[14].

For all the above purposes, it is immaterial whether the law which, apart from the Companies Act 1985, governs any arrangement or transaction is the law of the United Kingdom, or of a part of it, or not[15].

1 Ie the Companies Act 1985 s 320: see para 611 ante.
2 Ibid s 322(1).
3 For these purposes, a shadow director is treated as a director: ibid s 320(3). For the meaning of 'shadow director' and 'director' see para 543 note 1 ante.
4 For the meaning of 'holding company' see para 827 post.
5 For the meaning of 'connected' see para 607 ante.
6 Companies Act 1985 s 322(2).
7 See note 1 supra.
8 Companies Act 1985 s 322(3).
9 Ie ibid s 322(5), (6): see infra.
10 Ie under ibid s 322(3): see supra.
11 Ibid s 322(4).
12 See note 10 supra.
13 Companies Act 1985 s 322(5).
14 Ibid s 322(6).
15 Ibid s 347.

613. Invalidity of certain transactions involving directors etc. The following provisions apply where a company enters into a transaction[1] to which the parties include:

(1) a director of the company or of its holding company[2]; or
(2) a person connected[3] with such a director or a company with which such a director is associated[4],

and the board of directors, in connection with the transaction, exceeds any limitation on their powers under the company's constitution[5].

The transaction is voidable at the instance of the company[6]. Whether or not it is avoided, any such party to the transaction as is mentioned in heads (1) or (2) above, and any director of the company who authorised the transaction is liable to account to the company for any gain which he has made directly or indirectly by the transaction and to indemnify the company for any loss or damage resulting from the transaction[7]. A person other than a director of the company is, however, not so liable if he shows that at the time the transaction was entered into he did not know that the directors were exceeding their powers[8].

Nothing in the above provisions is to be construed as excluding the operation of any other enactment or rule of law by virtue of which the transaction may be called into question or any liability to the company may arise[9].

The transaction ceases to be voidable if:

(a) restitution of any money or other asset which was the subject matter of the transaction is no longer possible; or

(b) the company is indemnified for any loss or damage resulting from the transaction; or

(c) rights acquired bona fide for value and without actual notice of the directors' exceeding their powers by a person who is not a party to the transaction would be affected by the avoidance; or

(d) the transaction is ratified by the company in general meeting, by ordinary[10] or special[11] resolution or otherwise as the case may require[12].

These provisions do not affect the operation of the statutory provisions relating to the powers of the directors to bind the company[13] in relation to any party to the transaction not within heads (1) or (2) above[14].

1 For these purposes, 'transaction' includes an act: Companies Act 1985 s 322A(8) (added by the Companies Act 1989 s 109(1)).
2 For the meaning of 'holding company' see para 827 post.
3 For the meaning of 'connected' see para 607 ante.
4 For the meaning of 'associated with' see para 607 ante.
5 Companies Act 1985 s 322A(1) (added by the Companies Act 1989 s 109(1)). For these purposes, the reference to limitations under the company's constitution includes limitations deriving (1) from a resolution of the company in general meeting or a meeting of any class of shareholders; or (2) from any agreement between members of the company or of any class of shareholders: Companies Act 1985 s 322A(8) (as added: see note 1 supra).
6 Ibid s 322A(2) (added by the Companies Act 1989 s 109(1)).
7 Companies Act 1985 s 322A(3) (added by the Companies Act 1989 s 109(1)).
8 Companies Act 1985 s 322A(6) (added by the Companies Act 1989 s 109(1)).
9 Companies Act 1985 s 322A(4) (added by the Companies Act 1989 s 109(1)).
10 As to ordinary resolutions see para 681 post
11 As to special resolutions see para 683 post.
12 Companies Act 1985 s 322A(5) (added by the Companies Act 1989 s 109(1)).
13 Ie the Companies Act 1985 s 35A (as substituted): see para 1108 post.
14 Companies Act 1985 s 322A(7) (added by the Companies Act 1989 s 109(1)). Where, however, a transaction is voidable by virtue of the Companies Act 1985 s 322A (as added) and valid by virtue of s 35A (as substituted) in favour of such a person, the court may, on the application of that person or of the company, make such order affirming, severing or setting aside the transaction, on such terms, as appear to the court to be just: s 322A(7) (as so added).

(D) *Restrictions on Dealings by Directors and their Families in Options on Shares and Debentures*

614. Prohibition on directors and their families dealing in share options. It is an offence for a director[1] of a company to buy:

(1) a right to call for delivery at a specified price[2] and within a specified time of a specified number[3] of relevant shares[4] or a specified amount of relevant debentures[5]; or

(2) a right to make delivery at a specified price and within a specified time of a specified number of relevant shares or a specified amount of relevant debentures[6]; or

(3) a right (as he may elect) to call for delivery at a specified price and within a specified time or to make delivery at a specified price and within a specified time of a specified number of relevant shares or a specified amount of relevant debentures[7].

A person guilty of such an offence is liable on conviction on indictment to imprisonment for a term not exceeding two years or a fine, or to both, or on summary conviction to imprisonment for a term not exceeding six months or a fine not exceeding the statutory maximum, or to both[8].

The above provisions apply to the spouse of a director[9] of a company, not being himself or herself a director of it, and to an infant[10] who is the son[11] or the daughter[12] of a director of a company, not being himself or herself a director of it, as they apply to the director himself or herself; but it is a defence for a person charged with such an offence to prove that he or she had no reason to believe that his or her spouse, or, as the case may be, parent[13], was a director of the company in question[14].

The above provisions are not to be taken as penalising a person who buys a right to subscribe for shares in, or debentures of, a body corporate or buys debentures of a body corporate that confer upon the holder of them a right to subscribe for, or to convert the debentures (in whole or in part) into, shares of that body[15].

1 The Companies Act 1985 s 323 applies to a shadow director as to a director: s 323(4). For the meaning of 'shadow director' and 'director' see para 543 note 1 ante.
2 For these purposes, 'price' includes any consideration other than money: ibid s 323(3)(c).
3 For the meaning of 'number' see para 564 note 8 ante.
4 For these purposes, 'relevant shares', in relation to a director of a company, means shares in the company or in any other body corporate, being the company's subsidiary or holding company, or a subsidiary of the company's holding company, being shares as respects which there has been granted a listing on a stock exchange, whether in Great Britain or elsewhere: Companies Act 1985 s 323(3)(a). For the meaning of 'body corporate' see para 89 note 8 ante; and for the meaning of 'subsidiary' and 'holding company' see para 827 post.
5 Ibid s 323(1)(a). For these purposes, 'relevant debentures', in relation to a director of a company, means debentures of the company or of any other body corporate, being the company's subsidiary or holding company, or a subsidiary of the company's holding company, being debentures as respects which there has similarly been granted such a listing on a stock exchange, whether in Great Britain or elsewhere: s 323(3)(b).
6 Ibid s 323(1)(b).
7 Ibid s 323(1)(c).
8 Ibid ss 323(1), (2), 730, Sch 24. For the meaning of 'the statutory maximum' see para 1161 post.
9 For these purposes, a shadow director of a company is deemed a director of it: ibid s 327(2)(c)
10 As to the attainment of majority at the age of 18 see the Family Law Reform Act 1969 s 1 and CHILDREN vol 5(2) (Reissue) para 601.
11 For these purposes, 'son' includes stepson: Companies Act 1985 s 327(2)(a).
12 For these purposes, 'daughter' includes stepdaughter: ibid s 327(2)(a).
13 For these purposes, 'parent' is to be construed in the light of the statutory definitions of 'son' and 'daughter' (see notes 11, 12 supra): ibid s 327(2)(a).
14 Ibid s 327(1).
15 Ibid s 323(5).

I. LIABILITY OF DIRECTORS

615. Liability to company. Directors acting as such within their powers and within the powers of the company and without negligence or breach of fiduciary duty incur no personal liability[1]. Where, however, they expend the property of the company in a manner which is ultra vires the company, as, for example, in paying a dividend out of capital[2], or returning capital without legal reduction of capital[3], or in purchasing property which the company had no power to purchase[4], there is a liability on them to recoup any loss, and, if they occasion damage to the company by negligence, they may be liable to the extent of the damage caused[5]. A director who signed various stock transfers whereby shares held by the company as trustee for a number of pension funds were transferred to another company of which he was also a director, without the authority of the board of directors, and as a result of the transfer the company suffered loss, was in breach of duty and liable to the company for the loss as he was exercising his powers for an improper purpose[6]. If a company is the victim of a conspiracy by its directors who force it to do something illegal, it is not to be regarded as a party thereto by reason of the directors' knowledge, but may sue them in conspiracy for any loss it suffers[7]. The action should be brought by the company, but, where the acts of the directors are ultra vires the company or fraudulent and the persons against whom the relief is sought hold and control the majority of the shares and will not allow an action to be brought in the company's name, any shareholder may take action[8]. In the case of negligence, the company may, if there is no fraud, ratify or condone the act or omission and thereby become estopped from claiming damages against the directors[9].

Proceedings may be taken in the winding up of a company against the directors for negligence, default, breach of duty, and breach of trust[10].

The liability of a director is extinguished by the dissolution of the company, unless the dissolution is set aside by the court[11].

1 They are not liable for the company's torts unless they have expressly authorised the acts complained of: *Rainham Chemical Works v Belvedere Fish Guano Co* [1921] 2 AC 465 at 475, 476, HL per Lord Buckmaster; *Performing Right Society Ltd v Ciryl Theatrical Syndicate Ltd* [1924] 1 KB 1, CA; *British Thomson-Houston Co Ltd v Sterling Accessories Ltd* [1924] 2 Ch 33; *Mancetter Developments Ltd v Garmanson Ltd* [1986] QB 1212, [1986] 1 All ER 449, CA. As to criminal liability see para 1159 post. Like other agents, directors may be liable for their own torts: see paras 1115, 1120, 1124 post.

2 *Re Sharpe, Re Bennett, Masonic and General Life Assurance Co v Sharpe* [1892] 1 Ch 154, at 165, 166, CA per Lindley LJ; and see para 701 post.

3 See *Moxham v Grant* [1900] 1 QB 88, CA (claim for repayment enforceable against directors or shareholders; directors entitled to indemnity); *Holmes v Newcastle-upon-Tyne Freehold Abattoir Co* (1875) 1 ChD 682 (all shareholders and persons who took part in the transaction being before the court, repayment ordered). The doing of ultra vires acts may also be restrained: *Smith v Duke of Manchester* (1883) 24 ChD 611.

4 *Re Claridge's Patent Asphalte Co Ltd* [1921] 1 Ch 543 (where the directors who acted on the opinion of counsel were granted relief under the Companies (Consolidation) Act 1908 s 279 (repealed: see now the Companies Act 1985 s 727 and para 624 post)).

5 A director is bound to show only reasonable diligence, and would not be liable for an improper payment sanctioned by him in good faith on the report of a finance committee that it was proper: see *Re Railway and General Light Improvement Co, Marzetti's Case* (1880) 42 LT 206, CA; *Re Faure Electric Accumulator Co* (1888) 40 ChD 141.

6 *Bishopsgate Investment Management Ltd (in liquidation) v Maxwell (No 2)* [1994] 1 All ER 261 at 265, CA.

7 *Belmont Finance Corpn Ltd v Williams Furniture Ltd* [1979] Ch 250, [1979] 1 All ER 118, CA (financial aid by company for purchase of its own shares).

8 See paras 1110, 1111 post.

9 *Western Bank of Scotland v Bairds' Trustees* (1872) 11 M 96; *Ammonia Soda Co v Chamberlain* [1918] 1 Ch 266 at 278, CA per Peterson J; *Re Horsley & Weight Ltd* [1982] Ch 442, [1982] 3 All ER 1045, CA; sed quaere whether this is possible in a case of misfeasance, or where the interests of creditors would be

affected: see *Re Horsley & Weight Ltd* supra at 455, 456, and at 1055, 1056 per Cumming-Bruce, Templeman LJJ; and see para 1125 post.

10 See para 2448 et seq post.

11 *Re Pinto Silver Mining Co* (1878) 8 ChD 273, CA; *Re London and Caledonian Marine Insurance Co* (1879) 11 ChD 140, CA; *Coxon v Gorst* [1891] 2 Ch 73; and see para 2696 post.

616. Not liable to creditors. Directors are not trustees for the creditors, present[1] or future[2], of the company, even as regards one to whom the company stands in a fiduciary relationship[3]. The creditors, therefore, except as holders of security on any property of the company, and for the purpose of realising their security, have no right of interference with the company or its affairs, and have no remedy against a director for negligence in the conduct of its business[4] or for breach of contract by the company[5] except in the very rare case of those companies in which by the memorandum the liability of directors is unlimited[6]. A creditor cannot obtain an injunction against either the company or its directors in respect of ultra vires acts[7]. However, the rule making the directors liable for acts ultra vires the company operates to preserve the capital of the company and make it available for payment of creditors[8].

Directors may, however, be liable to third persons for breach of warranty of authority to act on behalf of the company[9]; and they are also jointly and severally liable, if a public company of which they are directors enters into transactions before the company has been issued by the registrar with a certificate that it may do business and exercise borrowing powers[10] and then fails to comply with its obligations in that connection within 21 days from being called upon to do so, to indemnify the other party to the transaction in respect of any loss or damage suffered by him by reason of such failure by the company[11].

Directors are not liable in negligence to the company's creditors unless particular circumstances exist, for example, by way of agreement or a contractual guarantee[12].

1 *Poole, Jackson and Whyte's Case* (1878) 9 ChD 322, CA (where directors paid up their shares in full, whereby a creditor was preferred in obtaining payment and they themselves were relieved from liability as guarantors); *Re A M Wood's Ships' Woodite Protection Co Ltd* (1890) 62 LT 760 (where directors, in good faith, paid themselves remuneration in advance which they applied in payment of amounts unpaid on their shares).

2 *Multinational Gas and Petrochemical Co v Multinational Gas and Petrochemical Services Ltd* [1983] Ch 258 at 288, [1983] 2 All ER 563 at 585, CA per Dillon LJ.

3 *Bath v Standard Land Co Ltd* [1911] 1 Ch 618, CA.

4 *Wilson v Lord Bury* (1880) 5 QBD 518, CA.

5 *Ferguson v Wilson* (1866) 2 Ch App 77 (where an action was founded on a resolution of the board to allot shares to plaintiff).

6 See para 103 ante and para 627 post.

7 *Mills v Northern Rly of Buenos Ayres Co* (1870) 5 Ch App 621; and see *Lawrence v West Somerset Mineral Rly Co* [1918] 2 Ch 250 at 256, 257 per Eve J.

8 See para 2448 post.

9 *Firbank's Executors v Humphreys* (1886) 18 QBD 54, CA; *Elkington & Co v Hurter* [1892] 2 Ch 452; *West London Commercial Bank v Kitson* (1884) 13 QBD 360, CA (acceptance of bills); and see para 1123 post. If the misrepresentation is as to law, they will not be liable: *Rashdall v Ford* (1866) LR 2 Eq 750; *Beattie v Lord Ebury* (1874) LR 7 HL 102; and see AGENCY vol 1(2) (Reissue) paras 172, 173.

10 See the Companies Act 1985 s 117(1) and para 652 post.

11 See ibid s 117(8) and para 653 post.

12 See *Nordic Oil Services Ltd v Berman* 1993 SLT 1164.

617. Breach of trust. A director who has misapplied, or retained, or become liable or accountable for any money or property of the company, or who has been guilty of any breach of trust in relation to the company, must make restitution or compensate the company for the loss[1]. Where the money of the company has been applied for purposes which the company cannot sanction, the directors must replace it, however honestly they may have acted[2].

A director is liable for the acts of his co-directors, if, knowing that they intend to commit a breach of trust, he does not, by applying for an injunction or otherwise[3], take steps to prevent it. A managing director is equally responsible although required 'to act under the orders and directions of the board'[4], but a director is not so liable where he does not know of the breach of trust before or at its occurrence, for example, by his absence from a board meeting, and does not expressly or tacitly concur in its continuance[5]. If he is in fact acting on the instructions of a third party, he will be fixed with that person's knowledge of the transaction[6]. Merely attending a director's meeting which confirms the illegal acts of a past meeting is not necessarily sufficient to fix responsibility[7]. A director, while not bound to attend all board meetings, should attend whenever he is reasonably able to do so[8].

The liability of directors participating in breaches of trust and in respect of secret profits is joint and several[9].

The estate of a deceased director has always been liable for his breaches of trust[10]; and since 25 July 1934[11], all causes of action subsisting against a deceased person at his death survive against his estate[12].

1 *Land Credit Co of Ireland v Lord Fermoy* (1870) 5 Ch App 763 (company's money used for purchasing its shares); *Joint Stock Discount Co v Brown* (1869) LR 8 Eq 381 (buying shares in another company); *Imperial Mercantile Credit Association v Chapman* (1871) 19 WR 379 (loans to brokers for losses incurred in 'bulling' the market); *Selangor United Rubber Estates Ltd v Cradock (a bankrupt) (No 3)* [1968] 2 All ER 1073, [1968] 1 WLR 1555 (company's money utilised for acquisition of its own shares). Proceedings are generally taken in the winding up of the company: see para 2448 post.

2 *Re Sharpe, Re Bennett, Masonic and General Life Assurance Co v Sharpe* [1892] 1 Ch 154 at 165, 166, CA per Lindley LJ; *Cullerne v London and Suburban General Permanent Building Society* (1890) 25 QBD 485 at 490, CA per Lindley LJ, overruling *Pickering v Stephenson* (1872) LR 14 Eq 322; and see *Peel v London and North Western Rly Co* [1907] 1 Ch 5 at 20, CA per Buckley LJ; *London Trust Co Ltd v Mackenzie* (1893) 62 LJ Ch 870; contra *Re Kingston Cotton Mill Co (No 2)* [1896] 1 Ch 331 at 346 per Vaughan Williams J (revsd on one point [1896] 2 Ch 279, CA). Where money paid to a company for a particular purpose has been misapplied by the sole shareholders and directors, they may be personally liable to account for the company's breach of trust to the persons paying the money: *Brenes & Co v Downie* 1914 SC 97.

3 *Re Lands Allotment Co* [1894] 1 Ch 616, CA; cf *J & P Coats Ltd v Crossland* (1904) 20 TLR 800. A protest is not sufficient (*Jackson v Munster Bank* (1885) 15 LR Ir 356; *Joint Stock Discount Co v Brown* (1869), LR 8 Eq 381); and see *Ramskill v Edwards* (1885) 31 ChD 100 at 111 per Pearson J; *Land Credit Co of Ireland v Lord Fermoy* (1870) 5 Ch App 763; *London Trust Co Ltd v Mackenzie* (1893) 62 LJ Ch 870. Acquiescence is not to be too readily inferred: *Ashhurst v Mason* (1875) LR 20 Eq 225. As to ratification by acquiescence see AGENCY vol 1(2) (Reissue) para 83.

4 *Ramskill v Edwards* (1885) 31 ChD 100.

5 *Cargill v Bower* (1878) 10 ChD 502; *Caledonian Heritable Security Co (Liquidator) v Curror's Trustee* (1882) 9 R 1115 (loan without security); *Re Denham & Co* (1883) 25 ChD 752 (dividends paid out of capital); *Marquis of Bute's Case* [1892] 2 Ch 100.

6 *Selangor United Rubber Estates Ltd v Cradock (No 3)* [1968] 2 All ER 1073, [1968] 1 WLR 1555.

7 *Re Montrotier Asphalte Co, Perry's Case* (1876) 34 LT 716; *Ashhurst v Mason* (1875) LR 20 Eq 225.

8 *Re City Equitable Fire Insurance Co Ltd* [1925] Ch 407, CA.

9 *Re Carriage Co-operative Supply Association* (1884) 27 ChD 322; *Re Englefield Colliery Co* (1878) 8 ChD 388, CA; *Re Oxford Benefit Building and Investment Society* (1886) 35 ChD 502; *Leeds Estate Building and Investment Co v Shepherd* (1887) 36 ChD 787; *Re Faure Electric Accumulator Co* (1888) 40 ChD 141 at 158 per Kay J; cf *General Exchange Bank v Homer* (1870) LR 9 Eq 480; *Gluckstein v Barnes* [1900] AC 240 at 255, HL per Lord Macnaghten; *Benson v Heathorn* (1842) 1 Y & C Ch Cas 326.

10 *Re Sharpe, Re Bennett, Masonic and General Life Assurance Co v Sharpe* [1892] 1 Ch 154, CA; *Joint Stock Discount Co v Brown* (1869) LR 8 Eq 381 at 407; *Ramskill v Edwards* (1885) 31 ChD 100; cf *Shepheard v Bray* [1906] 2 Ch 235 (revsd by consent, and doubted [1907] 2 Ch 571, CA).

11 Ie the date of the coming into force of the Law Reform (Miscellaneous Provisions) Act 1934.

12 Ibid s 1. There are certain immaterial exceptions: s 1(1). See further EXECUTORS vol 17 (Reissue) para 1563.

618. Persons sharing in breach of trust. All persons dealing with a director, knowing that he is committing a breach of trust in the transaction, must repay the loss to the company with interest[1].

A director who is in partnership is liable as regards his separate estate for the property of a company which has come into the hands of his firm and which is misappropriated by his firm with his concurrence[2].

1 *Gray v Lewis* (1869) LR 8 Eq 526 at 544 per Sir R Malins V-C (revsd on the facts (1873) 8 Ch App 1035); cf *Lund v Blanshard* (1844) 4 Hare 9; *Bryson v Warwick and Birmingham Canal Co* (1853) 4 De GM & G 711. As to the rate of interest for breach of trust see TRUSTS vol 48 (Reissue) para 966.
2 *Re Macfadyen, ex p Vizianagaram Mining Co Ltd* [1908] 2 KB 817, CA. The proof is for a debt and not for damages: *Re Macfadyen, ex p Vizianagaram Mining Co Ltd* supra; *Re Collie, ex p Adamson* (1878) 8 ChD 807 at 819, CA, per James and Baggallay LJJ.

619. Termination of liability. An order of discharge in bankruptcy releases a director from any liability for a breach of trust, unless it is a fraudulent breach of trust[1].

A director who is charged with breach of trust may plead the Limitation Act 1980 except where the claim is founded upon any fraud or fraudulent breach of trust to which he was a party or privy, or is to recover trust property or the proceeds thereof still, at the time of the action brought[2], retained by him or previously received by him and converted to his use[3].

If money wrongfully paid has been replaced before litigation either specifically or by contra accounts, the directors cannot be made liable in misfeasance proceedings[4].

1 See BANKRUPTCY.
2 *Thorne v Heard and Marsh* [1894] 1 Ch 599, CA.
3 Limitation Act 1980 s 21; *Re Lands Allotment Co* [1894] 1 Ch 616, CA; *Re Sharpe, Re Bennett, Masonic and General Life Assurance Co v Sharpe* [1892] 1 Ch 154, CA; and see LIMITATION OF ACTIONS vol 28 paras 833, 834. As to actions in respect of the statutory liability with regard to offer documents see paras 347, 350 ante.
4 *Re David Ireland & Co* [1905] 1 IR 133, CA.

620. Negligence. A director is liable for negligence if he fails to exercise such degree of care as a reasonable person might be expected to take in the circumstances on his own behalf, and the company in consequence suffers loss[1]. A director may, however, rely on fellow directors or other responsible officers for some acts and is entitled to do so in the absence of grounds for suspicion[2].

Directors who act in a matter which is within their powers and discretion, but neglect to exercise their discretion and judgment as directors, are liable for the resulting loss[3]. If they act in accordance with the wishes of a third party, they will be fixed with his knowledge of all the relevant facts[4].

They are not guilty of negligence if they fail to supervise acts of co-directors whom they have no reason to distrust[5] or act in reliance on the officers of the company whom they are entitled to trust and whose reports and statements have misled them[6]; nor are they bound to know the contents of the company's books[7].

A director is not liable for the misapplication of a cheque properly drawn[8], but, before a director signs a cheque, he should satisfy himself that a resolution of the directors or of a committee of the directors has authorised the payment[9]. A director is not liable for omitting to claim a debt to the company, or to enforce a liability incurred before he joined the board[10].

Facts which may show imprudence in the exercise of powers clearly conferred upon directors will not subject them to personal responsibility unless the imprudence amounts to negligence, which must be distinctly charged[11]. If they act within their powers, they are not liable for loss to the company occasioned by mere imprudence or error of judgment[12], and, in making investments, they are only bound to act in the same manner as business persons of ordinary prudence[13].

1 *Re Denham & Co* (1883) 25 ChD 752 (director had done nothing but simply left matters to his co-directors); *Re City Equitable Fire Insurance Co Ltd* [1925] Ch 407 at 429 per Romer J; *Norman v Theodore Goddard (a firm), (Quirk, third party)* [1991] BCLC 1028.

2 *Re City Equitable Fire Insurance Co Ltd* [1925] Ch 407 at 501, CA; *Merchants' Fire Office v Armstrong* (1901) 17 TLR 709, CA (where directors paid a de facto director for alleged services rendered in floating the company greatly in excess of the actual expenditure and without any inquiry).

3 *Re New Mashonaland Exploration Co* [1892] 3 Ch 577; cf *Re Englefield Colliery Co* (1878) 8 ChD 388, CA; *Re Faure Electric Accumulator Co* (1888) 40 ChD 141.

4 *Selangor United Rubber Estates Ltd v Cradock (a bankrupt) (No 3)* [1968] 2 All ER 1073, [1968] 1 WLR 1555. Cf *Lindgren v L & P Estates Ltd* [1968] Ch 572, [1968] 1 All ER 917, CA (where the directors concerned applied their own minds to the transaction).

5 *Huckerby v Elliott* [1970] 1 All ER 189, DC (director failed to make specific inquiry whether a gaming licence had been obtained by a co-director).

6 *Dovey v Cory* [1901] AC 477, HL (affg *Re National Bank of Wales Ltd* [1899] 2 Ch 629, CA); *Prefontaine v Grenier* [1907] AC 101, PC; *Re City Equitable Fire Insurance Co Ltd* [1925] Ch 407, CA; *Ammonia Soda Co v Chamberlain* [1918] 1 Ch 266, CA.

7 *Hallmark's Case* (1878) 9 ChD 329, CA (where there was no obligation on the director to take shares, and knowledge that his name was on the share register was not imputed to him); *Re Printing Telegraph and Construction Co of the Agence Havas, ex p Cammell* [1894] 1 Ch 528; affd [1894] 2 Ch 392, CA (where the director retired upon being asked to apply for shares); *Dovey v Cory* [1901] AC 477 at 492, HL per Lord Davey (knowledge of the financial state of the company and reliance on statement of officers), following *Re Denham & Co* (1883) 25 ChD 752; *Cartmell's Case* (1874) 9 Ch App 691 (knowledge of the contents of the share register and entries in other books showing purchase of company's shares); and see *Turquand v Marshall* (1869) 4 Ch App 376; *Re British Provident Life and Fire Assurance Society, Lane's Case* (1863) 1 De GJ & Sm 504; *Re City Equitable Fire Insurance Co Ltd* [1925] Ch 407 at 501, CA. As to liability for failing to take reasonable steps to secure that proper accounts are kept see para 801 post.

8 *Re Montrotier Asphalte Co, Perry's Case* (1876) 34 LT 716.

9 *Re City Equitable Fire Insurance Co Ltd* [1925] Ch 407 (in which is also discussed at 460 how far precautions should be taken when the resolution which is acted on is one for payment of cheques up to an aggregate amount); *Joint Stock Discount v Brown* (1869) LR 8 Eq 381 at 404 per Sir W M James V-C; cf *Ramskill v Edwards* (1885) 31 ChD 100.

10 *Re Forest of Dean Coal Mining Co* (1878) 10 ChD 450.

11 *Overend, Gurney & Co v Gibb and Gibb* (1872) LR 5 HL 480 at 487, 495 per Lord Hatherley LC; *Lagunas Nitrate Co v Lagunas Syndicate* [1899] 2 Ch 392 at 435, CA per Lindley MR; *Re National Bank of Wales Ltd* [1899] 2 Ch 629, CA. In *Re City Equitable Fire Insurance Co Ltd* [1925] Ch 407 at 428, Romer J discusses the difference between gross negligence which renders a director liable and ordinary negligence, and stated that the difference really lay in the duty of care imposed in both cases; the fact that a director is liable only for gross negligence shows that he is only bound to exercise such care as a reasonable person would exercise; he does not owe a duty to take all possible care; and see, on this point, *Re Brazilian Rubber Plantations and Estates Ltd* [1911] 1 Ch 425. Cf para 585 note 3 ante.

12 Eg by making loans to customers or others on insufficient security (*Dovey v Cory* [1901] AC 477, HL; *Re New Mashonaland Exploration Co* [1892] 3 Ch 577; *Rainford v James Keith and Blackman Co Ltd* [1905] 2 Ch 147, CA; *Turquand v Marshall* (1869) 4 Ch App 376; *Grimwade v Mutual Society* (1884) 52 LT 409); approving transfer of partly paid shares (*Re Faure Electric Accumulator Co* (1888) 40 ChD 141; but see *Re Hoylake Rly Co, ex p Littledale* (1874) 9 Ch App 257, where calls were due); including bad debts as good in balance sheet (*Re Railway and General Light Improvement Co, Marzetti's Case* (1880) 42 LT 206, CA); or allowing calls to remain unpaid (*Re Liverpool Household Stores Association* (1890) 59 LJ Ch 616 at 625 per Kekewich J); or not suing for a debt (*Re Forest of Dean Coal Mining Co* (1878) 10 ChD 450; and see *London Financial Association v Kelk* (1884) 26 ChD 107. As to improper payment of dividends see paras 721, 722 post.

13 *Sheffield and South Yorkshire Permanent Building Society v Aizlewood* (1889) 44 ChD 412 at 454, 459 per
Stirling J.

621. Torts. The mere fact that its directors are the sole directors and shareholders
will not automatically render them liable for torts committed by the company[1]. Nor is
a governing or managing director automatically so liable[2]. If, however, the commission of the tortious act by the company is expressly procured or directed by a
director, he may become personally liable for the tort and the damage flowing
therefrom[3]. Such liability is not automatic; if the tort involved required some particular
state of mind or knowledge on the part of the tortfeasor, the director could not be made
liable without proof that he himself had that state of mind or knowledge[4]. However,
the suggestion that he must, to be liable, in every case act deliberately or recklessly is
not justified[5]. Actions against the company in respect of a tort in which a director or
directors are joined as additional defendants are not to be encouraged, especially where
the joinder is a mere tactical move. In such cases an application to strike out may well
be justified[6].

1 *British Thomson-Houston Co Ltd v Sterling Accessories Ltd* [1924] 2 Ch 33.
2 *Performing Right Society Ltd v Ciryl Theatrical Syndicate Ltd* [1924] 1 KB 1 at 14, 15, CA per Atkin LJ.
3 *Wah Tat Bank Ltd v Chan Cheng Kum* [1975] AC 507, [1975] 2 All ER 257, PC; *C Evans & Sons Ltd v
Spritebrand Ltd* [1985] 2 All ER 415, [1985] 1 WLR 317, CA.
4 *C Evans & Sons Ltd v Spritebrand Ltd* [1985] 2 All ER 415 at 424, [1985] 1 WLR 317 at 329, CA per Slade
LJ.
5 *C Evans & Sons Ltd v Spritebrand Ltd* [1985] 2 All ER 415, [1985] 1 WLR 317, CA, disapproving *White
Horse Distillers Ltd v Gregson Associates Ltd* [1984] RPC 61 and dictum of Whitford J in *Hoover plc v George
Hulme (Stockport) Ltd* [1982] FSR 565 at 595–597 and doubting *Mentmore Manufacturing Co Ltd v
National Merchandising Manufacturing Co Inc* (1978) 89 DLR (3d) 195.
6 *C Evans & Sons Ltd v Spritebrand Ltd* [1985] 2 All ER 415 at 424, [1985] 1 WLR 317 at 329, CA per Slade
LJ.

622. False statements. Directors may incur liability to persons who subscribe for
shares or debentures of the company in reliance on offer documents which contain
material misrepresentations of fact[1].

They may also incur liability by reason of false reports made by them to the company
with the intention of attracting investors, and acted on by a subsequent investor to his
damage[2].

A director is not liable for untrue representations made to the shareholders in the
balance sheets of the company if he honestly believed the representations to be true,
and acted without negligence[3]. Where a company is formed to take over an existing
business which turns out to be ruinous, the directors will not be responsible for making
the purchase unless the ruinous nature of the business must have been obvious to any
person acting with an ordinary degree of prudence, on the same principle that protects
an agent purchasing by authority of his principal[4]. Shareholders will be liable in
damages to persons to whom they have sold their shares on the faith of fraudulent
statements made on their behalf by a director authorised to negotiate on their behalf[5].

A director who has in fact retired is not liable for subsequent statements or acts,
although he may know that his name is appearing on a report which is impugned[6].

1 See para 332 et seq ante. As to criminal liability for false statements see paras 1069, 1159 post.
2 *Scott v Dixon* (1859) 29 LJ Ex 62n. See further para 338 text and notes 5, 6 ante.
3 *Dovey v Cory* [1901] AC 477, HL.
4 *Overend, Gurney & Co v Gibb and Gibb* (1872) LR 5 HL 480 at 487, 495 per Lord Hatherley LC. See
AGENCY vol 1(2) (Reissue) para 88 et seq.

5 *Briess v Woolley* [1954] AC 333, [1954] 1 All ER 909, HL.
6 *Re National Bank of Wales Ltd* [1899] 2 Ch 629, CA; affd on other grounds sub nom *Dovey v Cory* [1901] AC 477, HL.

623. Avoidance of exemptions from liability. Any provision, whether contained in the articles of a company or in any contract with the company or otherwise, for exempting any officer of the company or any person (whether an officer of the company or not) employed by the company as auditor from, or indemnifying him against, any liability which by virtue of any rule of law would otherwise attach to him in respect of any negligence, default, breach of duty or breach of trust of which he may be guilty in relation to the company is void[1].

The above provisions do not, however, prevent a company:

(1) from purchasing and maintaining for any such officer or auditor insurance against any such liability;

(2) from indemnifying any such officer or auditor against any liability incurred by him in defending any proceedings, whether civil[2] or criminal, in which judgment is given in his favour or he is acquitted, or in connection with any application for relief under the provisions relating to the acquisition of shares by a company's nominee[3] or relating to a director's conduct not being dishonest or unreasonable[4] in which relief is granted to him by the court[5].

1 Companies Act 1985 s 310(1), (2).
2 The article may be so framed as to cover proceedings for liability for ultra vires acts: *Viscount of the Royal Court of Jersey v Shelton* [1986] 1 WLR 985, PC disapproving dictum in *Cullerne v London and Suburban General Permanent Building Society* (1890) 25 QBD 485 at 488, CA and applying *Re Claridge's Patent Asphalte Co Ltd* [1921] 1 Ch 543.
3 Ie the Companies Act 1985 s 144: see para 365 ante.
4 Ie ibid s 727: see para 624 post.
5 Ibid s 310(3) (substituted by the Companies Act 1989 s 137(1)). A director's expenses of defending himself against an allegation that he did something which he did not in fact do and which it was not his duty to do are not incurred by him as such and are therefore not recoverable under an indemnity covering 'any act done by him as director', or under the general law: *Tomlinson v Scottish Amalgamated Silks Ltd (Liquidators)* 1935 SC (HL) 1.

624. Power of court to give relief against liability. If in any proceedings for negligence, default, breach of duty or breach of trust against an officer[1] of a company or a person employed by the company as auditor (whether or not he is an officer of the company), it appears to the court hearing the case that that officer or person is or may be liable in respect of the negligence, default, breach of duty or breach of trust, but that he has acted honestly and reasonably[2], and that having regard to all the circumstances of the case[3], including those connected with his appointment, he ought fairly to be excused for the negligence, default, breach of duty or breach of trust, that court may relieve him, either wholly or partly, from his liability on such terms as the court thinks fit[4]. The power to grant relief applies to personal breaches of duty only; it does not extend to claims by third parties[5].

Where such a case is being tried by a judge with a jury, the judge, after hearing the evidence, may, if he is satisfied that the defendant ought to be relieved either in whole or in part from the liability sought to be enforced against him, withdraw the case in whole or in part from the jury and forthwith direct judgment to be entered for the defendant on such terms as to costs or otherwise as the judge may think proper[6].

If any such officer or person has reason to apprehend that any claim will or might be made against him in respect of any negligence, default, breach of duty or breach of trust, he may apply to the court for relief; and the court on any such application has the same power to relieve him as it would have had if it had been a court before which proceedings against that person for negligence, default, breach of duty or breach of trust had been brought[7].

The application to the court is made by way of petition[8]. The application is made to the court having jurisdiction to wind up the company[9]. In cases in the High Court of Justice the proceedings are assigned to the Chancery Division[10]. The petition and all affidavits, notices and other documents in the proceedings under it must be entitled in the matter of the company and in the matter of the Companies Act 1985[11].

Under the above provisions a director may be relieved against liability in respect of a transaction wholly ultra vires the company[12], or against the penalties imposed by the Act[13] where he has acted without obtaining[14] or after ceasing to hold[15] his qualification shares.

1 For the meaning of 'officer' see para 641 post. As an officer of the company an administrator could be protected under the Companies Act 1985 s 727: *Re Home Treat Ltd* [1991] BCLC 705 (court protected the administrators by an order relieving them of any future claim against them).

2 Failure to seek legal advice was held to be acting unreasonably in *Re Duomatic Ltd* [1969] 2 Ch 365, [1969] 1 All ER 161; as was the making of a payment which the directors had no power to make in *Gibson's Executor v Gibson* 1980 SLT 2. Questions of reasonableness may depend to some extent on past practice of the company: *Re Duomatic Ltd* supra at 375 and 170 per Buckley J.

3 See *Re J Franklin & Son Ltd* [1937] 4 All ER 43 (relief refused); *Selangor Rubber Estates Ltd v Cradock (a bankrupt) (No 3)* [1968] 2 All ER 1073, [1968] 1 WLR 1555 (relief refused where directors acted blindly at behest of third party). In general, the wishes of the members (or, if the company is insolvent, its creditors) must be taken into account: *Re Barry and Staines Linoleum Ltd* [1934] Ch 227.

4 Companies Act 1985 s 727(1). Relief under s 727(1) may be granted only by the court in which the pending proceedings are taken (*Re Gilt Edge Safety Glass Ltd* [1940] Ch 495, [1940] 2 All ER 237); but relief under the Companies Act 1985 s 727 is not available to a director against whom a liquidator has sought a contribution in the insolvent liquidation of the company under the Insolvency Act 1986 s 214 (see para 2673 post) (*Halls v David* (1989) Times, 18 February). This provision for relief was originally taken from the Judicial Trustees Act 1896 s 3 (repealed: see now the Trustee Act 1925 s 61); and, although the power of relief extends to proceedings for negligence, default and breach of duty under the Companies Act 1985, regard should be had to the cases decided on the above provisions: see TRUSTS vol 48 (Reissue) para 980. Where, as is usually the case, a director is paid for his services, the court is less disposed to give him relief than it would be to give it to a person acting gratuitously: *National Trustees Co of Australasia v General Finance Co of Australasia* [1905] AC 373 at 381, PC. See also *Re Welfab Engineers Ltd* [1990] BCLC 833 (directors who were alleged to have breached their duty by selling company's assets at an undervalue were held not to have acted in breach of that duty and, even if they had, it was a case where, having acted honestly and reasonably, they ought to be excused under the Companies Act 1985 s 727).

5 *Customs and Excise Comrs v Hedon Alpha Ltd* [1981] QB 818, [1981] 2 All ER 697, CA.

6 Companies Act 1985 s 727(3). The Companies Act 1985 s 727 need not be pleaded: *Singlehurst v Tapscott SS Co Ltd* [1899] WN 133, CA; *Re Kirbys Coaches Ltd* [1991] BCLC 414. If, however, it is pleaded, no particulars of the plea can be ordered, since the plea could, with leave, be deleted and such leave would, on a proper exercise of discretion, be given; but the right to claim relief would continue, even if the plea were deleted: *Re Kirbys Coaches Ltd* supra.

7 Companies Act 1985 s 727(2). Section 727(2) is directed only to future proceedings and does not apply to proceedings which have been commenced and are pending before another court: *Re Gilt Edge Safety Glass Ltd* [1940] Ch 495, [1940] 2 All ER 237.

8 RSC Ord 102 r 4(1)(i). In a winding up the application is by originating application where there are no pending proceedings before the court, or by ordinary application in any other case: see the Insolvency Rules 1986, SI 1986/1925, rr 7.2, 7.3 and paras 2815, 2816 post.

9 Companies Act 1985 s 744. As to the jurisdiction of the High Court see para 2197 post; and as to the jurisdiction of county courts see para 2198 post.

10 RSC Ord 102 r 5(1).

11 RSC Ord 102 r 5(2). A summons for directions must be taken out: RSC Ord 102 r 6(1).

12 *Re Claridge's Patent Asphalte Co Ltd* [1921] 1 Ch 543.

13 Ie by the Companies Act 1985 s 291(5): see para 556 ante and para 1158 et seq post.

14 *Re Barry and Staines Linoleum Ltd* [1934] Ch 227.
15 *Re Gilt Edge Safety Glass Ltd* [1940] Ch 495, [1940] 2 All ER 237.

625. Right to indemnity. Directors are entitled to be indemnified by the company for all debts, expenses, and liabilities incurred in the ordinary course of business, and for money borrowed and applied for those purposes[1], together, in the case of an actual expenditure, with simple interest[2]. If they guarantee a secured loan, they have, on paying off the loan, the usual right of a surety to subrogation[3].

The right to indemnity is limited to expenditure which has been incurred or an obligation adopted by directors on behalf of the company and in subjection to the special purposes of the company in accordance with its constitution[4]. Accordingly, directors may not use the funds of the company in payment of their own costs of legal proceedings, although these would not have been incurred if they had not been directors, unless incurred on behalf of the company or for its benefit[5].

In the absence of special provision to the contrary, the directors are not entitled to their expenses in travelling to and from board meetings[6].

If directors are holders on behalf of the company of unpaid shares which it has power to hold, they are entitled to be indemnified[7]. If, however, there is no such power, as where, for example, the shares are in the same company, they are liable for calls without any right of indemnity, even when all the shareholders have consented to the purchase[8]; but they are not liable in a winding up as contributories in respect of the amounts unpaid on shares transferred to them as trustees by way of security on the terms that the transfer is to be registered only with their consent, and they have given no consent to its registration[9].

If, although acting in the ordinary course of business, the directors exceed their borrowing powers, they cannot claim an indemnity from the company unless the borrowing is within the powers of the company and is ratified[10].

1   As eg in respect of holding as lessees (*Re Pooley Hall Colliery Co* (1869) 21 LT 690); or as shareholders in other companies (see text infra); or in respect of contracts for the benefit of the company (*Gleadow v Hull Glass Co* (1849) 19 LJ Ch 44; *Poole, Jackson and Whyte's Case* (1878) 9 ChD 322, CA; *Gray v Seckham* (1872) 7 Ch App 680); or money advanced (*Re International Life Assurance Society, ex p Certain Directors* (1870) 39 LJ Ch 271; *Re Court Grange Silver-Lead Mining Co, ex p Sedgwick* (1856) 2 Jur NS 949; *Lowndes v Garnett and Moseley Gold Mining Co of America Ltd* (1864) 33 LJ Ch 418; *Baker's Case* (1860) 1 Drew & Sm 55); and see *Re German Mining Co, ex p Chippendale* (1853) 4 De GM & G 19; *Re Norwich Yarn Co, ex p Bignold* (1856) 22 Beav 143; *Troup's Case* (1860) 29 Beav 353; *Re Electric Telegraph Co of Ireland, Hoare's Case* (1861) 30 Beav 225. As to dividends paid out of capital with the knowledge of the shareholders and the directors' right of indemnity against them in such a case see para 722 post; and as to the right of a person appointed with unlimited liability as a director of a limited company without the statutory statement or notice being added or given to recover for damage sustained thereby see para 627 post.
2   *Re Norwich Yarn Co, ex p Bignold* (1856) 22 Beav 143. The rate then allowed was 5% per annum. See generally MONEY vol 32 para 106 et seq.
3   *Gibbs and West's Case* (1870) LR 10 Eq 312; cf *Owen and Ashworth's Claim, Whitworth's Claim* [1901] 1 Ch 115, CA. It is a proper proceeding to give a charge on future calls in order to indemnify directors: *Re Pyle Works (No 2)* [1891] 1 Ch 173. As to subrogation see generally GUARANTEE vol 20 (Reissue) para 228.
4   *Pickering v Stephenson* (1872) LR 14 Eq 322 at 340 per Sir John Wickens V-C.
5   *Pickering v Stephenson* (1872) LR 14 Eq 322 (costs of prosecution for libel on themselves); *Studdert v Grosvenor* (1886) 33 ChD 528; cf *Tomlinson v Scottish Amalgamated Silks Ltd (Liquidators)* 1935 SC (HL) 1. These costs they must repay (*Cullerne v London and Suburban General Permanent Building Society* (1890) 25 QBD 485 at 490, CA per Lindley LJ, effectively overruling *Pickering v Stephenson* supra on this point; *Re Liverpool Household Stores Association* (1890) 59 LJ Ch 616); but costs of a prosecution for libel on the company itself, if properly incurred, must be paid by the company (*Studdert v Grosvenor* (1886) 33 ChD 538; but see *Kernaghan v Williams* (1868) LR 6 Eq 228). Directors cannot charge the company with the costs of an unsuccessful petition to wind up, presented by themselves, or of an unsuccessful appeal

(*Smith v Duke of Manchester* (1883) 24 ChD 611) although authorised by the articles to take proceedings etc. Cf the Companies (Tables A to F) Regulations 1985, SI 1985/805, Schedule, Table A art 118. See also *Re Crossmore Electrical and Civil Engineering Ltd* [1989] BCLC 137; *Re a company (No 004502 of 1988), ex p Johnson* [1992] BCLC 701.

6 *Young v Naval, Military and Civil Service Co-operative Society of South Africa* [1905] 1 KB 687; *Marmor Ltd v Alexander* 1908 SC 78; *Steel v Northern Co-operative Society Ltd* 1962 SLT 50. Cf the Companies (Tables A to F) Regulations 1985 Schedule, Table A art 83 which makes provision for the payment of such expenses. As to Table A generally see para 529 et seq ante.

7 *Re Financial Corpn, Goodson's Claim* (1880) 28 WR 760; and see *Re Waterloo Life etc Assurance Co, Saunders' Case* (1864) 2 De GJ & Sm 101 (where the shares were held as qualification shares); and see para 385 ante.

8 *Cree v Somervail* (1879) 4 App Cas 648, HL.

9 *Gray's Case* (1876) 1 ChD 664.

10 *Re Worcester Corn Exchange Co* (1853) 3 De GM & G 180; *Re German Mining Co, ex p Chippendale* (1853) 4 De GM & G 19. The ratification may be in general meeting (*Irvine v Union Bank of Australia* (1877) 2 App Cas 366, PC), without special resolution (*Grant v United Kingdom Switchback Rlys Co* (1888) 40 ChD 135, CA); or it may be inferred (*Re Magdalena Steam Navigation Co* (1860) John 690); and see para 1238 post.

626. Right to contribution. A director is entitled to contribution from such of his co-directors as have concurred in a transaction ultra vires the company in respect of which money has been recovered from him[1]. This is an equitable right quite apart from contract[2], and is available against the estate of a deceased director who was liable to contribute[2].

Shareholders who receive illegal payments knowingly, being constructive trustees for the company, must indemnify directors who are called upon to repay, or must themselves repay, if sued directly[3]. A director who has had the sole benefit of the breach of trust may not claim contribution against his co-directors[4].

In an action for contribution the defendant is not estopped from disputing the validity of the judgment in the action against the plaintiff[5].

Directors who have concurred in the cancellation of the shares of a co-director in pursuance of an agreement ultra vires the company, although they may be liable to the company, are not liable to their co-director for contribution towards his liability for costs[6].

1 *Ashhurst v Mason* (1875) LR 20 Eq 225 (where he was transferee of unpaid shares to relieve an ex-director); *Ramskill v Edwards* (1885) 31 ChD 100 (where he had afterwards concurred in an unauthorised loan).

2 *Jackson v Dickinson* [1903] 1 Ch 947; *Ramskill v Edwards* (1885) 31 ChD 100 (where the defendant died after action brought); *Shepheard v Bray* [1906] 2 Ch 235 (compromised on appeal [1907] 2 Ch 571, CA); *Wolmershausen v Gullick* [1893] 2 Ch 514. As to contribution in respect of statutory liability with regard to offer documents see para 341 ante.

3 *Moxham v Grant* [1900] 1 QB 88, CA; *Re National Funds Assurance Co* (1878) 10 ChD 118 at 129 per Jessel MR (cases of dividends paid out of capital).

4 *Walsh v Bardsley* (1931) 47 TLR 564.

5 See *Parker v Lewis* (1873) 8 Ch App 1056; *Shepheard v Bray* [1906] 2 Ch 235 (compromised on appeal [1907] 2 Ch 571, CA); cf *Printing, Telegraph and Construction Co of the Agence Havas v Drucker* [1894] 2 QB 801, CA; *Furness, Withy & Co Ltd v Pickering* [1908] 2 Ch 224; *Wye Valley Rly Co v Hawes* (1880) 16 ChD 489, CA.

6 *Walkers' Case* (1856) 8 De GM & G 607.

627. Unlimited liability of directors. In the case of a limited company the liability of the directors or managers, or of the managing director, may, if so provided by the memorandum of association, be unlimited[1]. Such a company, if so authorised by its articles, may, by special resolution, alter its memorandum so as to render unlimited the liability of its directors, or managers, or of any managing director[2]. When such a special resolution is passed, its provisions are as valid as if they had been originally contained in the memorandum[3]. In the case of a limited company in which the liability of a director or manager is unlimited, the directors and any managers of the company, and the member who proposes any person for election or appointment to the office of director or manager, must add to that proposal a statement that the liability of the person holding that office will be unlimited[4]. Before the person accepts the office or acts in it, notice in writing that his liability will be unlimited must be given to him by the following (or one of the following) persons, namely the promoters, directors, any managers and secretary of the company[5].

If a director, manager or proposer makes default in adding such a statement or if a promoter, director, manager or secretary makes default in giving the notice, then he is liable on conviction on indictment to a fine, or on summary conviction to a fine not exceeding the statutory maximum[6]. He is also liable for any damage which the person so elected or appointed may sustain from the default; but the liability of the person elected or appointed is not affected by the default[7].

1 Companies Act 1985 s 306(1). Cf *Milton Butler Priest & Co Ltd (in liquidation) v Ross* (1976) Times, 22 December (no unlimited liability because of Stock Exchange Rules and Regulations).
2 Companies Act 1985 s 307(1).
3 Ibid s 307(2). As to the requirement of official notification of a change in the memorandum of association see paras 71, 99 ante.
4 Ibid s 306(2).
5 Ibid s 306(3).
6 Ibid ss 306(4)(a), 730, Sch 24. For the meaning of 'the statutory maximum' see para 1161 post.
7 Ibid s 306(4)(b).

J. MEETINGS OF DIRECTORS

628. Meetings of directors. Articles of association generally contain elaborate provisions as to meetings of directors[1], and they include provisions concerning the election of a chairman[2] and regarding committees[3]. Directors may validly act only when assembled at a board meeting[4], unless the articles otherwise provide[5], except as regards strangers who contract with the company without notice of this defect[6].

A meeting of directors is not duly convened unless due notice has been given to all the directors entitled to receive it[7], and the business put through at a meeting not duly convened is invalid[8]. Whether or not there was a regular board meeting is immaterial for purposes of binding the company if all the shareholders consent to what is done[9]. It is not necessary to give notice of an adjourned meeting[10]. If no fixed notice is required, the notice must be fair and reasonable[11].

Where the only two directors of a company meet casually, one director cannot treat the meeting as a board meeting against the wishes of the other[12].

1 See the Companies (Tables A to F) Regulations 1985, SI 1985/805, Schedule, Table A arts 88–89. Article 88 provides that, subject to the provisions of the articles, the directors may regulate their proceedings as they think fit. A director may, and the secretary at the request of a director must, call a meeting of the directors. It will not be necessary to give notice of a meeting to a director who is absent from the United Kingdom. Questions arising at a meeting must be decided by a majority of votes. In the case of an equality of votes, the chairman will have a second or casting vote. A director who is also an alternate director will be entitled, in the absence of his appointor, to a separate vote on behalf of his appointee in addition to his own vote. The validity of acts of the meeting notwithstanding a defect in appointment or disqualification is provided for by art 92; cf the Companies Act 1985 s 285 and para 545 ante. As to Table A generally see para 529 et seq ante.

2 The Companies (Tables A to F) Regulations 1985 Schedule, Table A art 91 provides that the directors may appoint one of their number to be the chairman of the board of directors and may at any time remove him from that office. Unless he is unwilling to do so, the director so appointed will preside at every meeting of directors at which he is present; but, if there is no director holding that office, or if the director holding it is unwilling to preside or is not present within five minutes after the time appointed for the meeting, the directors present may appoint one of their number to be chairman of the meeting. Where a chairman is elected for an unspecified period, he is not entitled to remain chairman so long as he is a director: see *Foster v Foster* [1916] 1 Ch 532. Where a director is appointed chairman irregularly, it has been held that acquiescence for a long period does not regularise his appointment: see *Clark v Workman* [1920] 1 IR 107.

3 Delegation to committee is governed by the Companies (Tables A to F) Regulations 1985 Schedule, Table A art 72 (cited in para 587 note 2 ante); and in regard to companies to which Table A applies, proceedings of a committee with two or more members are governed by the articles relating to the proceedings of directors so far as they are capable of applying (art 72); and the validity of acts notwithstanding defects in appointment is regulated by art 92 (cited in para 545 note 7 ante).

4 *Re Athenaeum Life Assurance Society, ex p Eagle Insurance Co* (1858) 4 K & J 549 at 558, 559; *D'Arcy v Tamar, Kit Hill and Callington Rly Co* (1867) LR 2 Exch 158; *Bosanquet v Shortridge* (1850) 4 Exch 699; *Re Haycraft Gold Reduction and Mining Co* [1900] 2 Ch 230; and see para 629 post. Cf *Re Liverpool Household Stores Association Ltd* (1890) 59 LJ Ch 616.

5 See the Companies (Tables A to F) Regulations 1985 Schedule, Table A art 93 which provides that a resolution in writing signed by all the directors entitled to receive notice of a meeting of directors or of a committee of directors will be as valid and effectual as if it has been passed at a meeting of directors or (as the case may be) a committee of directors duly convened and held and may consist of several documents in the like form each signed by one or more directors; but a resolution signed by an alternate director need not also be signed by his appointor and, if it is signed by a director who has appointed an alternate director, it need not be signed by the alternate director in that capacity.

6 *Re Bonelli's Telegraph Co, Collie's Claim* (1871) LR 12 Eq 246. See also para 583 ante.

7 *Young v Ladies' Imperial Club* [1920] 2 KB 523, CA; *Re Portuguese Consolidated Copper Mines Ltd* (1889) 42 ChD 160, CA; *Moore v Hammond* (1827) 6 B & C 456; cf *Smyth v Darley* (1849) 2 HL Cas 789. The question whether a meeting has been duly convened if notice is dispatched to a director but not received, where the articles are silent on the point, is undecided: *Leary v National Union of Vehicle Builders* [1971] Ch 34 at 53, [1970] 2 All ER 713 at 723, 724 per Megarry J. In the absence of special circumstances, every director who is within reach ought to have notice; residence abroad may amount to special circumstances; a director who is travelling about with no known address may be out of reach: see *Halifax Sugar Refining Co v Francklyn* (1890) 59 LJ Ch 591. Cf the Companies (Tables A to F) Regulations 1985 Schedule, Table A art 88 (cited in note 1 supra).

8 See para 629 post.

9 *Re Express Engineering Works Ltd* [1920] 1 Ch 466, CA.

10 *Wills v Murray* (1850) 4 Exch 843.

11 *Re Homer District Consolidated Gold Mines, ex p Smith* (1888) 39 ChD 546; cf *Browne v La Trinidad* (1887) 37 ChD 1, CA.

12 *Barron v Potter* [1914] 1 Ch 895.

629. Business at meetings. At their properly convened meetings directors may transact all business within their powers though no notice has been given to the members of the board that any special business is to be transacted[1]. They may take the items of business in such order as they think proper, and not necessarily in the order on the agenda paper[2].

Unless the articles otherwise provide[3], business may be properly conducted by the directors only at a meeting which is duly convened[4] and held, and at which there is the prescribed quorum[5]. If a power is given to directors by an article of association, the decision of the directors to exercise it should, it seems, be unanimous unless on the true construction of the article of association a majority decision is enough[6]. A subsequent meeting may ratify the business done at an informal meeting[7], and may ratify an unauthorised act of an agent of the company[8].

1 *Compagnie de Mayville v Whitley* [1896] 1 Ch 788, CA; *A-G v Davy* (1741) 2 Atk 212.

2 *Re Cawley & Co* (1889) 42 ChD 209, CA.

3 See para 628 note 5 ante.

4 *Moore v Hammond* (1827) 6 B & C 456.

5 See, however, *Re Peruvian Rlys Co, ex p International Contract Co* (1868) 19 LT 803 at 805 (on appeal (1869) 4 Ch App 322) and *Southern Counties Deposit Bank Ltd v Rider and Kirkwood* (1895) 73 LT 374, CA (where the court refused to declare a resolution invalid, which was passed at a meeting of the company called by less than a quorum of directors, the number having been the acting quorum for six years); *Boschoek Proprietary Co Ltd v Fuke* [1906] 1 Ch 148 at 162 (where a meeting called by de facto directors was held to be well called and the confirmation there passed was sufficient). An informal meeting may not be sufficient to bind members (*Bottomley's Case* (1880) 16 ChD 681; *Re Scottish Petroleum Co* (1883) 23 ChD 413, CA) apart from such an articles as the Companies (Tables A to F) Regulations 1985, SI 1985/805, Schedule, Table A art 93. As to Table A generally see para 529 et seq ante. See also para 628 note 5 ante.

6 *Perrott and Perrott Ltd v Stephenson* [1934] Ch 171 (where Bennett J considered that the rule of corporation law that, when a duty is delegated to a body of persons, those persons may act by a majority, has no application to companies incorporated under the Companies Acts, but applies to cases where a corporation is entrusted with a duty of a public nature; cf the Companies (Tables A to F) Regulations 1985 Schedule, Table A art 88 (cited in para 628 note 1 ante) which provides for majority decisions).

7 *Re Portuguese Consolidated Copper Mines Ltd, ex p Badman, ex p Bosanquet* (1890) 45 ChD 16, CA (allotment); *Re Phosphate of Lime Co, Austin's Case* (1871) 24 LT 932; cf *Briton Medical, General and Life Association v Jones* (2) (1889) 61 LT 384; *Hooper v Kerr, Stuart & Co Ltd* (1900) 83 LT 729; *Re Kinward Holdings* (1962) Guardian, 28 February (resolution to present petition for winding up of debtor company).

8 *Molineaux v London, Birmingham and Manchester Insurance Co Ltd* [1902] 2 KB 589, CA.

630. Date of a resolution of directors. Where a resolution is passed at an adjourned meeting of the directors of a company, the resolution is to be treated for all purposes as having been passed on the date on which it was in fact passed and is not to be deemed to have been passed on any earlier date[1].

1 Companies Act 1985 s 381(c); and see para 669 note 9 post.

631. Invalidity of appointment and irregularity. In the absence of provisions in the articles[1], directors invalidly appointed cannot bind the shareholders[2] unless the defect is unknown at the time[3]. In the case of irregularity or informality, where a shareholder has changed his position in reliance upon the acts of the directors being regular, the company cannot set up the irregularity of the proceedings to his detriment[4]; nor may it rely on the absence of a required authority given by general meeting[5]. Persons dealing with the company are, however, protected from the consequences of any internal irregularities if they have acted without notice[6].

1 See the Companies (Tables A to F) Regulations 1985, SI 1985/805, Schedule, Table A art 92 (cited in para 545 note 7 ante). As to Table A generally see para 529 et seq ante.

2 *Garden Gulley United Quartz Mining Co v McLister* (1875) 1 App Cas 39, PC (making a call and forfeiting shares).

3 Companies Act 1985 s 285; and see para 545 ante.

4 *Bargate v Shortridge* (1855) 5 HL Cas 297. Cf *Morris v Kanssen* [1946] AC 459, [1946] 1 All ER 586, HL (where this doctrine did not assist the invalidly appointed director himself).

5 *Re British Provident Life and Fire Assurance Society, Grady's Case* (1863) 1 De GJ & Sm 488 (where shares had been transferred and registered).

6 See para 1137 post.

632. Quorum. A quorum means the minimum number of directors who are authorised to act as a board at a duly convened board meeting[1]. Each director of the quorum must be qualified to act, and, if by the withdrawal of those directors who are disqualified from voting on the ground of interest or otherwise there would be no quorum, no business may be transacted[2]. Where some of the directors are interested in a contract and not by the articles permitted to vote[3], a reduction in the quorum for the purpose of authorising the contract is invalid[4]; and, where a transaction is really one transaction, the necessary quorum cannot be obtained by dividing the transaction into two[4]. The articles may provide that, in the case of certain contracts or arrangements, a director may be permitted to vote and be included in the quorum present notwith-standing the fact that otherwise he would have been disqualified on grounds of interest[5]. Where no quorum is specified in the articles, the number who usually act will constitute a quorum[6]. Although one director cannot constitute a 'meeting'[7], the articles may permit one director to constitute a quorum[8]. Unless so provided by the articles, there cannot be a quorum competent to act where the number of directors is not filled up to the minimum number[9].

Even though a quorum is specified in the articles, the court may refuse to declare illegal resolutions passed by a number of directors less than that required to constitute the quorum, if that lesser number has been acting as a quorum for a number of years[10].

1 The Companies (Tables A to F) Regulations 1985, SI 1985/805, Schedule, Table A art 89 provides that the quorum necessary for the transaction of the business of the directors may be fixed by the directors and, unless so fixed at any other number, will be two. A person who holds office only as an alternate director is, if his appointor is not present, to be counted in the quorum. By art 90 the continuing directors or a sole continuing director may act notwithstanding any vacancies in their number, but, if the number of directors is less than the number fixed as the quorum, the continuing director or directors may act only for the purpose of filling vacancies or of calling a general meeting. As to Table A generally see para 529 et seq ante.

2 *Re Greymouth-Point Elizabeth Rly and Coal Co Ltd, Yuill v Greymouth-Point Elizabeth Rly and Coal Co Ltd* [1904] 1 Ch 32; *Cox v Dublin City Distillery (No 2)* [1915] 1 IR 345, CA; *Re Olderfleet Shipbuilding and Engineering Co Ltd* [1922] 1 IR 26. The court will, however, rectify the register of a company by registering a transferee of shares if one of two directors refuses to attend a board meeting to pass the transfer and so prevents it being effected: *Re Copal Varnish Co Ltd* [1917] 2 Ch 349; cf *Lubin v Draeger* [1918] 144 LT Jo 274.

3 For a case where a director was entitled to vote if he declared his interest but failed to do so and so was not entitled to vote see *Rolled Steel Products (Holdings) Ltd v British Steel Corpn* [1986] Ch 246, [1985] 3 All ER 52, CA. As to directors' interests in contracts generally see para 594 et seq ante and para 635 post.

4 *Re North Eastern Insurance Co* [1919] 1 Ch 198.

5 See the Companies (Tables A to F) Regulations 1985 Schedule, Table A art 94.

6 *Lyster's Case* (1867) LR 4 Eq 233 (where a forfeiture was good although ordered by a meeting of two out of six directors); and see *Re English etc Rolling Stock Co, Lyon's Case* (1866) 35 Beav 646 (allotment); *Re Regent's Canal Iron Co* [1867] WN 79; *Re Portuguese Consolidated Copper Mines Ltd* (1889) 42 ChD 160, CA; *York Tramways Co v Willows* (1882) 8 QBD 685 at 698, CA.

7 Cf *Sharp v Dawes* (1876) 2 QBD 26, CA and *Re London Flats Ltd* [1969] 2 All ER 744, [1969] 1 WLR 711; but see *Re Fireproof Doors Ltd* [1916] 2 Ch 142.

8 *Re Fireproof Doors Ltd* [1916] 2 Ch 142. See para 667 note 4 post.

9 *Re Scottish Petroleum Co* (1883) 23 ChD 413 at 431, CA; *Re Sly, Spink & Co Ltd* [1911] 2 Ch 430; *Faure Electric Accumulator Co v Phillipart* (1888) 58 LT 525; *Bottomley's Case* (1880) 16 ChD 681; *Kirk v Bell* (1851) 16 QB 290; but see *Thames-Haven Dock and Rly Co v Rose* (1842) 4 Man & G 552; cf *Owen and Ashworth's Claim, Whitworth's Claim* [1901] 1 Ch 115, CA.

10 See the cases cited in note 6 supra. As to the refusal of the court to interfere with the internal management of companies on the ground of irregularities see further paras 664, 1110 post.

633. Minutes of directors' meetings. Every company must cause minutes of all proceedings at meetings of its directors and, where there are managers, all proceedings at meetings of its managers to be entered in books[1] kept for that purpose[2]. If the company fails to comply with this provision, the company, and every officer of the company who is in default, is liable on summary conviction to a fine not exceeding one-fifth of the statutory maximum and, on conviction after continued contravention, to a daily default fine not exceeding one-fiftieth of the statutory maximum[3]. Any such minute, if purporting to be signed by the chairman of the meeting at which the proceedings were had, or by the chairman of the next succeeding meeting, is evidence of the proceedings[4]. Where minutes have been so made, then, until the contrary is proved, the meeting is deemed to have been duly held and convened, and all proceedings had at the meeting to have been duly had; and all appointments of directors, managers or liquidators are deemed valid[5].

Where a shadow director[6] by means of a notice[7] declares an interest in a contract or proposed contract, the making of that declaration is deemed to form part of the proceedings at a particular meeting[8]. If it is a specific notice, the declaration is deemed to have been made at the meeting of the directors at which the question of entering into the contract was first taken into consideration, or, if he was not then interested in the proposed contract, at the next meeting of the directors held after he became so interested[9]; otherwise, as if the declaration had been made at the meeting of the directors next following the giving of the notice[10].

The signature by the chairman of an entry in the minute book of a resolution accepting an agreement is a sufficient signature for the purposes of a memorandum required by the Statute of Frauds[11]. It is not necessary to prove that the person signing as chairman was in fact the chairman[12]. An entry of an allotment of shares to a director then present, who signed the minutes at the next meeting, is sufficient evidence of his agreement to take shares[13], but not where he was not present at either meeting and denies all knowledge[14].

In the absence of a minute other evidence may be given[15]; and, if the books of a company show a record of a transaction, as, for example, the forfeiture of shares, which would not be valid without a resolution of the directors, the court will, in the absence of other evidence, presume that such a resolution has been passed[16].

1   A collection of loose leaves fastened together between two covers but readily detachable is not a 'book' within the meaning of this provision (see *Hearts of Oak Assurance Co Ltd v James Flower & Sons* [1936] Ch 76), but may presumably be another method of recording the necessary information permitted by the Companies Act 1985 s 722(1) (see para 378 note 2 ante).

2   Ibid s 382(1).

3   Ibid ss 382(5), 730, Sch 24. For the meaning of 'officer who is in default', 'the statutory maximum' and 'daily default fine' see para 1161 post. Where under the articles a contract can stand only if a minute of the directors approving it is entered in the books, the entry must be made within a reasonable time: *Toms v Cinema Trust Ltd* [1915] WN 29.

     The Companies (Tables A to F) Regulations 1985, SI 1985/805, Schedule, Table A art 100 provides that the directors must cause minutes to be made in books kept for the purpose: (1) of all appointments of officers made by the directors; and (2) of all proceedings at meetings of the company, of the holders of any class of shares in the company, and of the directors, and of committees of directors, including the names of the directors present at each such meeting. The right of the beneficiaries of trust shares held by directors on their behalf to inspect a company's documents is not greater than the right conferred on shareholders by statute or the articles: see *Butt v Kelson* [1952] Ch 197, sub nom *Re Butt, Butt v Kelson* [1952] 1 All ER 167, CA; and TRUSTS. As to Table A generally see para 529 et seq ante.

4   Companies Act 1985 s 382(2). It is only prima facie evidence: *Re Indian Zoedone Co* (1884) 26 ChD 70, CA; *Re Pyle Works (No 2)* [1891] 1 Ch 173 at 184; *Re Leicester Mortgage Co Ltd* (1894) 38 Sol Jo 531, 564.

5   Companies Act 1985 s 382(4); and see the Companies (Tables A to F) Regulations 1985 Schedule, Table A art 88 (cited in para 628 note 1 ante).

6   For the meaning of 'shadow director' see para 543 note 1 ante.

7   Ie by Companies Act 1985 s 317(8): see para 594 ante.

8   Ibid s 382(3).

9   Ibid ss 317(8)(a), (2), 382(3)(a).

10   Ibid ss 317(8), 382(3)(b).

11 Ie the Statute of Frauds (1677) s 4 (amended by the Law of Property Act 1925 s 207, Sch 7; the Law Reform (Enforcement of Contracts) Act 1954 s 1). See *Jones v Victoria Graving Dock Co* (1877) 2 QBD 314, CA.

12 *Sheffield, Ashton-under-Lyne and Manchester Rly Co v Woodcock* (1841) 7 M & W 574.

13 *Re Llanharry Hematite Iron Ore Co Ltd, Roney's Case, Stock's Case* (1864) 4 De GJ & Sm 426.

14 *Tothill's Case* (1865) 1 Ch App 85.

15 *Re Pyle Works (No 2)* [1891] 1 Ch 173.

16 *Knight's Case* (1867) 2 Ch App 321; *Re Fireproof Doors Ltd* [1916] 2 Ch 142.

K. RETIREMENT AND REMOVAL OF DIRECTORS

634. Provision in articles. Articles of association usually contain full provisions as to the retirement and removal of directors[1]. Thus provision may be made for the retirement of a proportion of the directors annually[2], for determining which directors shall retire in any year[3], for enabling retiring directors to be re-elected[4], for filling at the meeting the office of a director vacated at that meeting by retirement[5], for the election of new directors[6], for increasing or reducing the number of directors[7], for filling casual vacancies other than in annual meeting[8], and for the removal of a director from office[9], and to appoint another director in his place[10].

Provision is also usually made for vacation of office by a director in all or some of the following cases[11], that is to say if he:

(1) fails to acquire or ceases to hold his qualification[12]; or

(2) becomes bankrupt[13] or insolvent[14]; or

(3) becomes of unsound mind; or

(4) is concerned or participates in the profits of any contract with the company[15]; or

(5) continually absents himself for more than the prescribed period from the meetings of the board without leave[16]; or

(6) is convicted of an indictable offence[17]; or

(7) resigns his office; or

(8) reaches an age limit[18].

The articles may also provide for vacation of office by any director who holds any other office of profit under the company except that of managing director or manager[19].

The wording of the articles is usually such that the office is automatically vacated by any of the acts specified, and the board of directors cannot waive the vacation[20]; but each case depends upon the true construction of the articles.

If the articles provide for the director to vacate office if he is so requested by all his co-directors, although the power of removal is fiduciary, the office will be vacated immediately if the director receives a notice in writing signed by all the other directors, even if one or more of them had acted for ulterior reasons[21].

If, as the result of the operation of any such articles, there are no directors of the company, no valid decisions may be taken which are required by the articles to be taken by the directors[22].

1 As to the retirement and removal of directors see the Companies (Tables A to F) Regulations 1985, SI 1985/805, Schedule, Table A arts 73–81; and as to Table A generally see para 529 et seq ante.

2 Ibid Schedule, Table A art 73 provides that at the first annual general meeting of the company all the directors must retire from office, and at every subsequent annual general meeting one-third of the directors who are subject to retirement by rotation or, if their number is not three or a multiple of three, the number nearest to one-third, must retire from office; but, if there is only one director who is subject to retirement by rotation, he must retire. Article 73 does not apply to an extraordinary meeting (*Lord Claud Hamilton's Case* (1873) 8 Ch App 548), or to signatories of the memorandum (*John Morley Building*

Co v Barras [1891] 2 Ch 386). As to the Companies (Tables A to F) Regulations 1985 Schedule, Table A art 73 see also *Walker v Kenns Ltd* [1937] 1 All ER 566, CA (effect of vacation of office on service agreement providing for ipso facto determination), and *Re David Moseley & Sons Ltd* [1939] Ch 719, [1939] 2 All ER 791 (article providing number 'nearest to but not exceeding one-third' inapplicable when only two directors). Under a special Act it was held that directors had no power to retire until the first ordinary meeting: see *Re South London Fish Market Co* (1888) 39 ChD 324, CA.

3 The Companies (Tables A to F) Regulations 1985 Schedule, Table A art 74 provides that, subject to the provisions of the Companies Act 1985, the directors to retire by rotation are those who have been longest in office since their last appointment or reappointment, but as between persons who became or were last reappointed directors on the same day those to retire must (unless they otherwise agree among themselves) be determined by lot. If the article uses instead of 'by lot' the term 'by ballot', which may mean either by lot or by secret vote, the exact meaning must be determined by the construction of the articles as a whole: *Eyre v Milton Proprietary Ltd* [1936] Ch 244, CA.

4 See the Companies (Tables A to F) Regulations 1985 Schedule, Table A art 80.

5 Ibid Schedule, Table A art 75 provides that, if the company, at the meeting at which a director retires by rotation, does not fill the vacancy, the retiring director must, if willing to act, be deemed to have been reappointed, unless at the meeting it is resolved not to fill the vacancy or unless a resolution for the reappointment of the director is put to the meeting and lost. This last proviso was designed to avoid the position arising in *Grundt v Great Boulder Proprietary Gold Mines Ltd* [1948] Ch 145, [1948] 1 All ER 21 (approving *Holt v Catterall* (1931) 47 TLR 332, and disapproving *Robert Batcheller & Sons Ltd v Batcheller* [1945] Ch 169, [1945] 1 All ER 522), where provisions for automatic re-election were held to apply even though the director had in fact been refused such re-election. See also *Re Great Northern Salt and Chemical Works, ex p Kennedy* (1890) 44 ChD 472. The article does not apply if at an adjourned meeting the place is filled: *Spencer v Kennedy* [1926] Ch 125. The article does not apply to signatories of the memorandum: *Jon Morley Building Co v Barras* [1891] 2 Ch 386; and see *Bennett Bros (Birmingham) Ltd v Lewis* (1903) 20 TLR 1, CA.

6 See the Companies (Tables A to F) Regulations 1985 Schedule, Table A art 76 which provides that no person other than a director retiring by rotation may be appointed or reappointed a director at any general meeting unless (1) he is recommended by the directors; or (2) not less than 14 nor more than 35 clear days before the date appointed for the meeting, notice executed by a member qualified to vote at the meeting has been given to the company of the intention to propose that person for appointment or reappointment stating the particulars which would, if he were so appointed or reappointed, be required to be included in the company's register of directors, together with notice executed by that person of his willingness to be appointed or reappointed.

7 See ibid Schedule, Table A art 64.

8 See para 638 post.

9 Cf the Companies Act 1985 s 303: see para 639 post. Where the statutes of a company provide for the removal of directors for reasonable cause, the criterion of reasonableness is that which is reasonable in the eyes of a meeting of the company: *Inderwick v Snell* (1850) 2 Mac & G 216. Where a company in regular meeting has resolved on the removal of directors, the court will not, in the absence of fraud, review the considerations which might have affected the passing of the resolution: *Inderwick v Snell* supra. For a case where the validity of a non-fiduciary power vested in life directors to remove other directors was upheld see *Bersel Manufacturing Co Ltd v Berry* [1968] 2 All ER 552, HL.

10 As to the obligation of a company which has obtained admission to the Official List of the Stock Exchange to notify the Company Announcements Office of board changes see para 543 note 2 ante.

11 The Companies (Tables A to F) Regulations 1985 Schedule, Table A art 81 provides that the office of a director must be vacated if (1) he ceases to be a director by virtue of any provision of the Companies Act 1985 eg s 291 (failure to obtain qualification shares: see para 556 ante); and s 293 (age limit: see para 637 post) or he becomes prohibited by law from being a director eg under the Company Directors Disqualification Act 1986 (see para 1417 et seq post); or (2) he becomes bankrupt or makes any arrangement or composition with his creditors generally; or (3) he is, or may be, suffering from mental disorder and either (a) he is admitted to hospital in pursuance of an application for admission for treatment under the Mental Health Act 1983, or in Scotland, an application for admission under the Mental Health (Scotland) Act 1960; or (b) an order is made by a court having jurisdiction (whether in the United Kingdom or elsewhere) in matters concerning mental disorder for his detention or for the appointment of a receiver, curator bonis, or other person to exercise powers with respect to his property or affairs; or (4) he resigns his office by notice to the company; or (5) he is absent for more than six consecutive months without permission of the directors from meetings of directors held during that period and the directors resolve that his office be vacated.

12 Where a specified qualification is required by the articles, the duty to obtain and continue to hold the qualification is imposed by statute: see para 556 ante. Where the article declared the office of director

vacated 'if he cease to hold the due qualification', it was held that the article did not apply to a case in which the qualification had never been held (*Salton v New Beeston Cycle Co* [1899] 1 Ch 775; *Dent's Case, Forbes's Case* (1873) 8 Ch App 768 at 775); but it was otherwise if the words were 'if he does not acquire etc'. Where the amount of qualification is increased, an existing director does not thereby cease to hold the requisite qualification, but must obtain the larger qualification within a reasonable time: *Molineaux v London, Birmingham and Manchester Insurance Co Ltd* [1902] 2 KB 589, CA.

13 Being already a bankrupt is not becoming bankrupt: *Dawson v African Consolidated Land and Trading Co* [1898] 1 Ch 6, CA. As to undischarged bankrupts acting as directors see para 553 ante.

14 A director is 'insolvent' where his creditors pass a resolution accepting a composition of their claims (*Harold Sissons & Co Ltd v Sissons* (1910) 54 Sol Jo 802), or where he makes offers of a composition to them (*James v Rockwood Colliery Co* (1912) 106 LT 128), or where there are a number of bankruptcy petitions which are withdrawn in order to give the director time to pay (*London and Counties Assets Co Ltd v Brighton Grand Concert Hall and Picture Palace Ltd* [1915] 2 KB 493, CA).

15 *Star Steam Laundry Co v Dukas* (1913) 108 LT 367. Cf the Companies (Tables A to F) Regulations 1985 Schedule, Table A art 94. See further para 635 post.

16 For the meaning of 'absents himself' see *McConnell's Claim* [1901] 1 Ch 728; *Re London and Northern Bank, Mack's Claim* [1900] WN 114 (both these cases showing that the absence must be voluntary and not accidental). See also *Willsmore v Willsmore and Tibbenham Ltd* (1965) 109 Sol Jo 699 (injunction granted on balance of convenience to restrain directors from treating plaintiff as having vacated office, it being alleged that the absences of the plaintiff, who owned half the shares, were in part involuntary and in part with the informal consent of the other directors). The absence dates from the first meeting which the director fails to attend: *McConnell's Claim* supra; *Re London and Northern Bank, Mack's Claim* supra.

17 'Indictable offence' in such an article means an offence which is capable of being dealt with on indictment: *Hastings and Folkestone Glassworks Ltd v Kalson* [1949] 1 KB 214, [1948] 2 All ER 1013, CA.

18 This requirement is obligatory in relation to all public companies: see further the Companies Act 1985 s 293 and para 637 post. For the meaning of 'public company' see para 82 ante.

19 This provision is not included in the Companies (Tables A to F) Regulations 1985 Schedule, Table A arts 84–86. The holding of the office of unpaid secretary is not holding another office of profit (*Iron Ship Coating Co v Blunt* (1868) LR 3 CP 484); but the paid trusteeship of a debenture trust deed is a place of profit, although it is not, strictly speaking, held under the company (*Astley v New Tivoli Ltd* [1899] 1 Ch 151). A solicitor does not hold an office of profit (*Re Harper's Ticket Issuing and Recording Benefit Machine Ltd* [1912] WN 263), unless he has a fixed salary and certain obligations (*Re Liberator Permanent Benefit Building Society* (1894) 71 LT 406, DC). As to the secretary and other officers see para 641 et seq post.

20 *Re Bodega Co Ltd* [1904] 1 Ch 276. As to the effect of an article validating any act by any person acting as director notwithstanding disqualification or defect in appointment see para 545 ante.

21 *Samuel Tak Lee v Chou Wen Hsien* [1984] 1 WLR 1202, PC.

22 *Re Zinotty Properties Ltd* [1984] 3 All ER 754, [1984] 1 WLR 1249.

635. Director interested in contract. If the articles provide for a director being disqualified by being in any way interested in a bargain or contract with the company, his office is vacated by his being a shareholder in another company with which the contract is made[1]; and, if it provides for the vacation of his seat if he enters into a contract with the company without declaring his interest, it is not sufficient for him to intimate that he has an interest without declaring its specific nature[2].

1 *Todd v Robinson* (1884) 14 QBD 739, CA. The Companies (Tables A to F) Regulations 1985, SI 1985/805, Schedule, Table A arts 85, 94 assume full disclosure of the director's interest in accordance with the Companies Act 1985 s 317 (see para 594 ante); with some exceptions they forbid him to vote in respect of such contract, but provide no further sanction. As to the statutory duty to disclose an interest see para 594 ante; and as to the avoidance of contracts see paras 595, 596 ante. As to Table A generally see para 529 et seq ante.

2 *Imperial Mercantile Credit Association (Liquidators) v Coleman* (1873) LR 6 HL 189; cf *Trundle v West Riding Athletic Club Leeds Ltd* (1894) 70 LT 92. In the absence of an agreement the court will not restrain the chairman and director of one company from joining the board of another competing company: *London and Mashonaland Exploration Co Ltd v New Mashonaland Exploration Co Ltd* [1891] WN 165; cf *Wilson v London, Midland and Scottish Rly Co* [1940] Ch 393, [1940] 2 All ER 92; and see para 596 ante and para 670 text and note 2 post.

636. Resignation. Where by the articles a director has power to resign at any time[1], his resignation takes effect independently of acceptance by the other directors or the company[2]. Where the articles of association of a company provide that the office of a director is to be vacated ipso facto if by notice in writing to the company a director resigns office, an oral resignation, if accepted by the company, is valid[3].

1 Ie as under the Companies (Tables A to F) Regulations 1985, SI 1985/805, Schedule, Table A art 81(d).
2 *Glossop v Glossop* [1907] 2 Ch 370; *Transport Ltd v Schonberg* (1905) 21 TLR 305 (where it was also held that the other directors accepted the resignation); *Re Montrotier Asphalte Co, Perry's Case* (1876) 34 LT 716; cf *Municipal Freehold Land Co v Pollington* (1890) 59 LJ Ch 734. Where the resignation of a director has been concealed from the shareholders, the director is not liable for statements made in the report with his name on it if he has not taken part in the concealment: see *Re National Bank of Wales Ltd* [1899] 2 Ch 629 at 667, CA.
3 *Latchford Premier Cinema Ltd v Ennion* [1931] 2 Ch 409.

637. Retirement under age limit. A director of a public company, or a private company which is a subsidiary[1] of a public company or of a body corporate registered under the law relating to companies for the time being in force in Northern Ireland as a public company, must vacate his office at the conclusion of the annual general meeting commencing next after he attains the age of 70[2] but subject, in the case of a company first registered after the beginning of 1947, to the provisions of that company's articles, and in the case of a company first registered before the beginning of that year, to any subsequent alterations of that company's articles[3]. Also, in the latter case, if at the beginning of that year the company's articles contained provision for retirement of directors under an age limit, or for preventing or restricting appointments of directors over a given age, the above statutory retiring age will not apply to directors to whom that provision applies[3].

Acts done by a person as director are valid notwithstanding that it is afterwards discovered that his appointment had terminated by virtue of the above provisions on attaining the age of 70[4]; but, if he acts as a director under any appointment which has terminated by reason of his age, he is liable on summary conviction to a fine not exceeding one-fifth of the statutory maximum and, on conviction after continued contravention, to a daily default fine not exceeding one-fiftieth of the statutory maximum[5].

Where a person retires on reaching the statutory age limit, no provision for the automatic reappointment of retiring directors in default of another appointment applies; and, if at the meeting at which he retires the vacancy is not filled, it may be filled as a casual vacancy[6].

Nothing in the above provisions requires a director to retire at any time, if his appointment is or was made or approved by the company in general meeting; but special notice[7] is required of any resolution appointing or approving the appointment of a director for this purpose and the notice given to the company and by the company to its members must state or must have stated the age of the person to whom it relates[8]. A person who is so reappointed director on retiring on reaching the statutory age limit, or appointed in place of a director so retiring, is to be treated, for the purpose of determining the time at which he or any other director is to retire[9], as if he had become director on the day on which the retiring director was last appointed before his retirement; but, subject to that, the retirement of a director out of turn under the statutory age limit is to be disregarded in determining when any other directors are to retire[10].

1 For the meaning of 'subsidiary' see para 827 post.
2 Companies Act 1985 s 293(1), (3). In the case of all companies the register of directors and secretaries must contain the date of the director's birth: see s 289(1)(a)(vii) (as substituted) and para 560 ante.
3 Ibid s 293(7).
4 Ibid s 293(3).
5 Ibid ss 294(4)(b), 730, Sch 24. For the meaning of 'the statutory maximum' and 'daily default fine' see para 1161 post. For these purposes, a person who has acted as director under an appointment which has terminated is deemed to have continued so to act throughout the period from the date on which the appointment terminated until the last day on which he is shown to have acted thereunder: s 294(5). For the purposes of s 294, a company is deemed to be subject to s 293 notwithstanding that all or any of the provisions of s 293 are excluded or modified by the company's articles: s 294(2).
6 Ibid s 293(4).
7 As to special notice see para 687 post.
8 Companies Act 1985 s 293(5).
9 See para 634 ante.
10 Companies Act 1985 s 293(6).

638. Casual vacancies. Articles usually provide for a casual vacancy on the board of directors to be filled by the directors, and that the person so appointed is to hold office until the next ordinary general meeting, or that he is to be subject to retirement as if he had become a director when the director whom he replaces was last elected[1]. A casual vacancy is any vacancy that does not occur through retirement by rotation[2].

1 The Companies (Tables A to F) Regulations 1985, SI 1985/805, Schedule, Table A art 79 provides that the directors may appoint a person who is willing to act to be a director, either to fill a vacancy or as an additional director, provided that the appointment does not cause the number of directors to exceed any number fixed by or in accordance with the articles as the maximum number of directors. A director so appointed will hold office only until the next following annual general meeting and will not be taken into account in determining the directors who are to retire by rotation at the meeting. If not reappointed at such annual general meeting, he must vacate office at the conclusion of that meeting. As to this article see *Eyre v Milton Proprietary Ltd* [1936] Ch 244, CA and para 547 ante. As to Table A generally see para 529 et seq ante.
2 A casual vacancy may be thus filled although a general meeting has subsequently been held: *Munster v Cammell Co* (1882) 21 ChD 183; and see *Bennett Bros (Birmingham) Ltd v Lewis* (1903) 20 TLR 1, CA.

639. Removal from office. A company may by ordinary resolution remove a director before the expiration of his period of office, notwithstanding anything in its articles or in any agreement between it and him[1], except in the case of a director of a private company who was holding office for life on 18 July 1945, whether or not subject to retirement under an age limit by virtue of the articles or otherwise[2]. Special notice[3] is required of such a resolution to remove him, or to appoint somebody instead of a director so removed at the meeting at which he is removed[4]. On receipt of notice of an intended resolution so to remove a director, the company must forthwith send a copy of it to the director concerned; and the director (whether or not he is a member of the company[5]) is entitled to be heard on the resolution at the meeting[6]. Where notice of any such intended resolution has been given, and the director concerned makes representations in writing not exceeding a reasonable length[7] to the company with respect to it and requests their notification to members of the company, the company must, unless the representations are received by it too late for it to do so:

(1) state the fact that such representations have been made in any notice of the resolution given to its members[8]; and

(2) send a copy of such representations to every member of the company to whom notice of the meeting is sent (whether before or after receipt of the representations by the company)[9];

and, if a copy of the representations is not sent in accordance with these provisions because it was received too late, or because of the company's default, the director may (without prejudice to his right to be heard orally) require that the representations shall be read out at the meeting[10].

Copies of the representations need not be sent out, however, nor need the representations be read out at the meeting if, on the application either of the company or of any other person who claims to be aggrieved, the court is satisfied that these rights are being abused to secure needless publicity for defamatory matter[11]. The court may order the company's costs on such an application to be paid in whole or in part by the director, notwithstanding that he is not a party to the application[12].

Where directors attempt to avoid removal under these provisions by failing to call a meeting and then omitting to attend a requisitioned general meeting, so as to avoid the presence of a quorum, the court will convene a meeting in exercise of its statutory powers[13].

A vacancy created by the removal of a director under the above powers, if not filled at the meeting at which he is removed, may be filled as a casual vacancy[14]; and a person appointed director in his place is treated, for the purpose of determining the time at which he or any other director is to retire, as if he had become director on the day on which the person in whose place he is appointed was last appointed a director[15].

The above provisions are not to be taken as depriving a person removed under them of compensation or damages payable to him in respect of the termination of his appointment as director or of any appointment terminating with that as director, or as derogating from any power to remove a director which may exist apart from such powers[16].

The administrator[17] of a company has power to remove any director of the company and to appoint any person to be a director of it, whether to fill a vacancy or otherwise[18].

1 Companies Act 1985 s 303(1). Section 381A (as added) (written resolutions of private companies: see para 697 post) does not apply to a resolution under s 303 removing a director before the expiration of his period of office: s 381A(7), Sch 15A para 1(a) (added by the Companies Act 1989 s 114(1)).

By a suitable loading of voting rights in favour of a director threatened with removal, these provisions may be effectively nullified: *Bushell v Faith* [1970] AC 1099, [1970] 1 All ER 53, HL. Before 1948 it was impossible to remove directors who had been appointed for a definite period, unless the original articles, or the articles as altered by special resolution, gave power to do so *(Re Imperial Hydropathic Hotel Co, Blackpool v Hampson* (1882) 23 ChD 1, CA), nor could they resign *(Re South London Fish Market Co* (1888) 39 ChD 324, CA); but an alteration of the articles made in good faith for the benefit of the company which enabled a permanent director to be removed was (and still would be) valid *(Shuttleworth v Cox Bros & Co (Maidenhead) Ltd* [1927] 2 KB 9, CA; and see *Southern Foundries (1926) Ltd v Shirlaw* [1940] AC 701, [1940] 2 All ER 445, HL). The court would not have enforced an agreement that a director should be irremovable; and, if the company had in general meeting resolved that a director must retire, the court would not have compelled it to allow him to act *(Bainbridge v Smith* (1889) 41 ChD 462, CA; *Harben v Phillips* (1883) 23 ChD 14, CA; *Browne v La Trinidad* (1887) 37 ChD 1, CA), even if there had been irregularities of procedure, provided that the final result was not in doubt *(Bentley-Stevens v Jones* [1974] 2 All ER 653, [1974] 1 WLR 638; cf *Hall v British Essence Co Ltd* (1946) 62 TLR 542). See also note 16 infra.

2 Companies Consolidation (Consequential Provisions) Act 1985 s 14.

3 As to special notice see para 687 post.

4 Companies Act 1985 s 303(2).

5 There is no necessity for a director to be a shareholder. The Companies (Tables A to F) Regulations 1985, SI 1985/805, Schedule, Table A (amended by SI 1985/1052) contains no such requirement, but art 44 provides that a director is, notwithstanding that he is not a member, entitled to attend and speak at any general meeting and at any separate meeting of the holders of any class of shares in the company. See para 556 ante. As to Table A generally see para 529 et seq ante.

6 Companies Act 1985 s 304(1).

7 Presumably 1,000 words would be reasonable in a normal case: cf ibid s 376(1)(b) (cited in para 688 post).

8 Ibid s 304(2)(a).

9 Ibid s 304(2)(b).

10 Ibid s 304(3).

11 Ibid s 304(4).

12 Ibid s 304(5). The application to the court is made by way of originating summons in the expedited form: see RSC Ord 102 r 2(1), (2). In cases in the High Court all proceedings are assigned to the Chancery Division: RSC Ord 102 r 5(1). The summons must be entitled in the matter of the company and in the matter of the Companies Act 1985: RSC Ord 102 r 5(2).

13 *Re El Sombrero Ltd* [1958] Ch 900, [1958] 3 All ER 1. As to the court's power to convene meetings see para 661 post.

14 Companies Act 1985 s 303(3); and see para 638 ante.

15 Ibid s 303(4).

16 Ibid s 303(5). A director appointed for a fixed term who was removed from office before the termination of his period of office under a power introduced by a change of the articles after his appointment was held in *Southern Foundries (1926) Ltd v Shirlaw* [1940] AC 701, [1940] 2 All ER 445, HL to be entitled to damages for breach of contract. Exactly similar principles would be applicable to removal under the above power. Conditions of appointment of a director may, however, authorise his removal without the giving of reasonable notice: see *Read v Astoria Garage (Streatham) Ltd* [1952] Ch 637, [1952] 2 All ER 292, CA and para 588 note 3 ante.

In addition to the above statutory right of removal see the Companies (Tables A to F) Regulations 1985 Schedule, Table A art 81 (cited in para 634 note 11 ante).

17 As to administrators see para 2092 et seq post.

18 See the Insolvency Act 1986 s 14(2)(a) and para 2097 post.

640. Alternate directors. The articles of the company may permit the appointment of alternate directors[1]. Such an alternate may be another director, or a third person, depending upon the provisions of the articles. Normally such a person represents for all purposes the director to whom he is an alternate during the absence of such director from meetings of the board. His appointment cannot outlast the directorship of the person to whom he is an alternate, but may be made to continue notwithstanding such person's retirement by rotation and reappointment. Whilst the alternate is acting as a director, he stands in a fiduciary position in relation to the company, and accordingly owes the company all the same non-statutory duties as are owed by a director. Having regard to the statutory definition of 'director' in the Companies Act 1985, as including any person occupying the position of a director, by whatever name called[2], it would appear that he also is subject to the statutory obligations which are imposed on directors[3].

1 See the Companies (Tables A to F) Regulations 1985, SI 1985/805, Schedule, Table A arts 65–69. As to Table A generally see para 529 et seq ante.

2 Companies Act 1985 s 741(1) (cited in para 543 note 1 ante).

3 The Companies (Tables A to F) Regulations 1985 Schedule, Table A art 69 expressly provides that 'an alternate director shall be deemed for all purposes to be a director'. There are thus obvious advantages in appointing a person who is already a director as an alternate.

(iii) Secretary and other Officers

641. Officers of the company. Any persons who are regularly employed as part of their business or occupation in conducting the affairs of the company may be 'officers' of the company. The term is defined by the Companies Act 1985 as including any director[1], manager or secretary[2]. 'Manager' means, in everyday language, a person who has the management of the whole affairs of the company[3]. It connotes a person holding, whether de jure or de facto, a position in or with the company of a nature charging him with the duty of managing the affairs of the company for the company's benefit[4]. It does not include a local manager[5].

The following have been held to be officers of the company under the corresponding provisions of previous Companies Acts, which prior to the Companies Act 1948 contained no definition of 'officer': its secretary[6]; its auditors[7], except a person casually employed by the directors to prepare a balance sheet[8]; a solicitor when remunerated by fixed salary, but not when employed in the ordinary way[9]; persons whose duty it is to invest the company's money and hold the investments[10]; and a liquidator[11]. The following have been held not to be officers: trustees of the company[12]; trustees of a debenture trust deed[13]; bankers[14]; experts employed to investigate and report on the management of the company[15]; and the editor or chief reporter of a newspaper[16].

1 For the meaning of 'director' see para 543 note 1 ante.
2 Companies Act 1985 s 744.
3 *Gibson v Barton* (1875) LR 10 QB 329 at 336.
4 *Re B Johnson & Co (Builders) Ltd* [1955] Ch 634 at 661, [1955] 2 All ER 775 at 790.
5 *Registrar of Restrictive Trading Agreements v W H Smith & Son Ltd* [1969] 3 All ER 1065 at 1069, CA.
6 *McKay's Case* (1875) 2 ChD 1, CA; *Re Stapleford Colliery Co, Barrow's Case (No 2)* (1880) 42 LT 12; *Re Mutual Aid Permanent Benefit Building Society, ex p James* (1883) 49 LT 530. See also paras 647, 648 post.
7 *Re London and General Bank* [1895] 2 Ch 166, CA; *Leeds Estate Building and Investment Co v Shepherd* (1887) 36 ChD 787; *Re Kingston Cotton Mill Co* [1896] 1 Ch 6 at 14, CA; *Re Republic of Bolivia Exploration Syndicate Ltd* [1914] 1 Ch 139; *Re City Equitable Fire Insurance Co Ltd* [1925] Ch 407, CA; *R v Shacter* [1960] 2 QB 252, [1960] 1 All ER 61, CCA.
8 *Re Western Counties Steam Bakeries and Milling Co* [1897] 1 Ch 617, CA.
9 See para 651 post.
10 *Re British Guardian Life Assurance Co* as reported in [1880] WN 63.
11 See para 2726 post. See also para 645 note 1 post.
12 *Cornell v Hay* (1873) LR 8 CP 328.
13 *Astley v New Tivoli Ltd* [1899] 1 Ch 151 at 154. As to the liability of such trustees under the Companies Act 1985 s 192 see para 1253 post.
14 *Re Imperial Land Co of Marseilles, Re National Bank* (1870) LR 10 Eq 298; *Re General Provident Assurance Co, ex p National Bank* (1872) LR 14 Eq 507; *Re Kingston Cotton Mill Co* [1896] 1 Ch 6 at 14, CA per Vaughan Williams J.
15 *Openshaw v Fletcher* (1916) 32 TLR 372, CA.
16 *Murray v 'The Northern Whig' Ltd* (1911) 46 ILT 77.

642. Appointment and qualifications. The secretary and other officers are usually appointed by the directors[1].

It is the duty of the directors of a public company to take all reasonable steps to secure that the secretary (or each joint secretary) of the company is a person who appears to them to have the requisite knowledge and experience to discharge the functions of secretary of the company and who:

(1) on 22 December 1980 held the office of secretary or assistant or deputy secretary of the company; or

(2) for at least three of the five years immediately preceding his appointment as secretary held the office of secretary of a company other than a private company; or

(3) is a member of a specified body[2]; or

(4) is a barrister, advocate or solicitor called or admitted in any part of the United Kingdom; or

(5) is a person who, by virtue of his holding or having held any other position or his being a member of any other body, appears to the directors to be capable of discharging those functions[3].

1 See the Companies (Tables A to F) Regulations 1985, SI 1985/805, Schedule, Table A art 99. As to Table A generally see para 529 et seq ante; and as to contracts being provisional in the case of certain companies until they are entitled to commence business see para 1128 post.
2 The bodies so specified are (1) the Institute of Chartered Accountants in England and Wales; (2) the Institute of Chartered Accountants of Scotland; (3) the Chartered Association of Certified Account-ants; (4) the Institute of Chartered Accountants in Ireland; (5) the Institute of Chartered Secretaries and Administrators; (6) the Institute of Cost and Management Accountants; (7) the Chartered Institute of Public Finance and Accountancy: Companies Act 1985 s 286(2).
3 Ibid s 286(1). For the meaning of 'public company' see para 82 ante.

643. Remuneration and lien. A provision that the remuneration of an officer (other than a director[1]) is to be determined only in general meeting does not prevent him from bringing an action for a quantum meruit[2]. He has no lien on the books or any other property of the company for money due to him[3].

1 See para 575 et seq ante.
2 *Bill v Darenth Valley Rly Co* (1856) 1 H & N 305 (secretary). Cf *Craven-Ellis v Canons Ltd* [1936] 2 KB 403, [1936] 2 All ER 1066 (remuneration to director for services as estate agent), explained in *Re Richmond Gate Property Co Ltd* [1964] 3 All ER 936, [1965] 1 WLR 335; and see para 575 ante. See further EMPLOYMENT vol 16 (Reissue) para 19.
3 *Barnton Hotel Co Ltd v Cook* (1899) 1 F 1190.

644. Dismissal by appointment of receiver or winding up. The appointment of a receiver and manager by the court operates as a dismissal of the employees of the company[1], and so does the making of a compulsory winding-up order[2]. A resolution to wind up voluntarily also operates as a notice of dismissal, if it involves a termination of the employees' employment by the company[3]. However, the appointment of a receiver out of court does not so operate[4].

The continuance of employment by the liquidator during arrangements for recon-struction does not make a fresh contract of service with the company if the business carried on is not carried on on its behalf[5]; such a contract must be clearly proved[6]. Employees of the company do not automatically become employees of a receiver or manager[7]; but fresh employment may diminish the damages for wrongful dismissal or reduce them to nominal damages[8].

1 *Reid v Explosives Co Ltd* (1887) 19 QBD 264, CA. See para 1359 post.
2 *Chapman's Case* (1866) LR 1 Eq 346; *MacDowall's Case* (1886) 32 ChD 366, distinguishing *Re English Joint Stock Bank, ex p Harding* (1867) LR 3 Eq 341. See para 2250 post. As to proof in the winding up for damages for breach of contract in such cases see para 2512 post and *Re T N Farrer Ltd* [1937] Ch 352, [1937] 2 All ER 505 (cited in para 579 note 5 ante).
3 *Midland Counties District Bank Ltd v Attwood* [1905] 1 Ch 357 (where the employee left the service of the company before his employment had de facto been determined); distinguishing *Shirreff's Case* (1872) LR 14 Eq 417; *Reigate v Union Manufacturing Co (Ramsbottom) Ltd and Elton Cop Dyeing Co Ltd* [1918] 1 KB 592, CA; *Re Gramophone Records Ltd* [1930] WN 42; and see *Re Forster & Co, ex p Schumann* (1887) 19 LR Ir 240; *Re Etic Ltd* [1928] Ch 861 at 862; *Fowler v Commercial Timber Co Ltd* [1930] 2 KB 1, CA.
4 *Re Mack Trucks (Britain) Ltd* [1967] 1 All ER 977, [1967] 1 WLR 780; *Re Foster Clark Ltd's Indenture Trusts, Loveland v Horscroft* [1966] 1 All ER 43 at 49, [1966] 1 WLR 125 at 132 per Plowman J; *Griffiths v Secretary of State for Social Services* [1974] QB 468, [1973] 3 All ER 1184; *Re Peek, Winch & Tod Ltd* (1979) 130 NLJ 116, CA. See also para 1359 post.
5 *MacDowall's Case* (1886) 32 ChD 366.
6 *Re English Joint Stock Bank, ex p Harding* (1867) LR 3 Eq 341.
7 *Re Marriage, Neave & Co, North of England Trustee, Debenture and Assets Corpn v Marriage, Neave & Co* [1896] 2 Ch 663, CA; but as to the adoption of contracts of employment see the Insolvency Act 1986 s 37(1)(a) (cited in para 1330 post) and s 44(1)(b) (as amended) (cited in para 2160 post).
8 *Reid v Explosives Co Ltd* (1887) 19 QBD 264, CA. The whole of this paragraph was cited with approval by Kilner-Brown J in *Fox Bros (Clothes) Ltd (in Liquidation) v Bryant* [1979] ICR 64 at 66.

645. Misfeasance proceedings, indemnity and relief. Managers and other officers[1] are in the same position as directors as regards liability to misfeasance proceedings[2] in a winding up, as regards the extent to which they may be indemnified by clauses in the articles[3], and as regards the power of the court to grant them relief where proceedings are taken against them, or where they apprehend that any claim will or may be made against them, in respect of any negligence, default, breach of duty or breach of trust[4].

1 It was not argued in *Re Windsor Steam Coal Co (1901) Ltd* [1929] 1 Ch 151, CA that a liquidator was not an officer within this provision.
2 See para 2448 et seq post.
3 See the Companies Act 1985 s 310 and para 623 ante.
4 See ibid s 727 and para 624 ante.

646. Appointment of secretary. Every company must have a secretary[1]; but anything required or authorised to be done by or to the secretary[2], may, if the office is vacant or if there is for any other reason no secretary capable of acting, be done by or to any assistant or deputy secretary or, if there is no assistant or deputy secretary capable of acting, by or to any officer of the company authorised generally or specially in that behalf by the directors[3].

The secretary should always be appointed by the company under a written agreement specifying the general conditions of service, including the term of office and the period of notice for its termination. Apart from any written agreement, he holds his office on such conditions of service as may be implied from the articles of association or the practice of the company[4] or of other like companies and subject to reasonable notice on either side[5].

No person may be appointed as secretary of the company who is:

(1) the sole director of the company[6]; or

(2) a corporation, the sole director of which is the sole director of the company[7].

A provision requiring or authorising a thing to be done by or to a director and the secretary is not satisfied by its being done by or to the same person acting both as director and as, or in place of, the secretary[8].

1 Companies Act 1985 s 283(1). As to the necessary qualifications of the secretary of a public company see para 642 ante. For the meaning of 'public company' see para 82 ante.
2 As to his statutory duties see para 648 post.
3 Companies Act 1985 s 283(3). As to the avoidance of acts done by a person in dual capacity as director and secretary see, however, infra.
4 *Burland v Earle* [1902] AC 83 at 101, PC. If the terms of a written agreement are clear, the articles cannot vary or modify the agreed conditions of service: *Re Alexander's Timber Co* (1901) 70 LJ Ch 767 at 769.
5 *Creen v Wright* (1876) 1 CPD 591; *James v Thomas H Kent & Co Ltd* [1951] 1 KB 551, [1950] 2 All ER 1099, CA.
6 Companies Act 1985 s 283(2).
7 Ibid s 283(4)(a).
8 Ibid s 284.

647. Nature of employment of secretary. The secretary, being an agent only, is in the same position as any other agent of a company[1]. If his dealings are such that his company is not bound by them, he may himself be liable, either as principal or on the ground of breach of warranty of authority[2]. Whereas it has formerly been held that he had no authority by virtue of his position to make representations to induce persons to contract with the company, his functions being ministerial only[3], his status has now greatly increased[4]. The secretary regularly makes representations on behalf of the company and enters into contracts on its behalf which come within the day-to-day running of the company's business; he signs contracts connected with the administrative side of a company's affairs; and all these matters are now within his ostensible authority[5]. However, he is not, whilst merely performing the duties appropriate to his office, a party to the carrying on of the business of the company, so as to make him responsible without more for fraudulent trading[6].

He has no power, without the resolution of the directors, to call a meeting of the company[7] or to commence proceedings on behalf of the company[8]; nor may he alter the register of members[9]; but any such act may be ratified by the directors[10].

A secretary may not make a secret profit in connection with the affairs of the company[11].

A secretary is normally an employee so as to be entitled to preferential payment in a winding up[12].

1 See para 1113 et seq post. A secretary is liable to the company for the acts of a sub-agent employed by him and not by the company: *Re Mutual Aid Permanent Benefit Building Society, ex p James* (1883) 49 LT 530.

2 See para 1123 post and AGENCY vol 1(2) (Reissue) para 172.

3 *Barnett v South London Tramways Co* (1887) 18 QBD 815 at 817, CA; *Chapleo v Brunswick Permanent Benefit Building Society* (1881) 6 QBD 696, CA; *Williams v Chester and Holyhead Rly Co* (1851) 15 Jur 828; *Newlands v National Employers' Accident Association Ltd* (1885) 54 LJQB 428, CA. As to the certification of transfers see para 512 ante.

4 Before the Companies Act 1948 (see s 177(1) (repealed)) it was not even obligatory for a company to have a secretary at all.

5 *Panorama Developments (Guildford) Ltd v Fidelis Furnishing Fabrics Ltd* [1971] 2 QB 711, [1971] 3 All ER 16, CA.

6 *Re Maidstone Building Provisions Ltd* [1971] 3 All ER 363, [1971] 1 WLR 1085. As to fraudulent trading see para 2670 post.

7 *Re Haycraft Gold Reduction and Mining Co* [1900] 2 Ch 230; *Re State of Wyoming Syndicate* [1901] 2 Ch 431.

8 *Daimler Co Ltd v Continental Tyre and Rubber Co (Great Britain) Ltd* [1916] 2 AC 307, HL.

9 *Chida Mines v Anderson* (1905) 22 TLR 27; *Re Matlock Old Bath Hydropathic Co, Wheatcroft's Case* (1873) 42 LJ Ch 853 at 857.

10 *Molineaux v London, Birmingham and Manchester Insurance Co Ltd* [1902] 2 KB 589 at 596, CA.

11 *Re Morvah Consols Tin Mining Co, McKay's Case* (1875) 2 ChD 1. A secretary who before the formation of a company aids the promoter in forming the company (and so is himself a promoter), and is paid by him for his services, does not receive this money to the use of the company or as trustee: *Re Sale Hotel and Botanical Gardens, ex p Hesketh* (1898) 78 LT 368, CA. Cf generally AGENCY vol 1(2) (Reissue) paras 98, 99.

12 See para 2523 et seq post.

648. Statutory duties of secretary. Among the statutory duties which must be, can be or usually are, discharged by a secretary are: signing the annual return[1]; delivering for registration returns of allotments, and contracts for the allotments of shares paid up otherwise than in cash[2]; making the statutory declaration as to a public company's share capital being not less than the authorised minimum[3]; giving notice to any proposed director that his liability is to be unlimited[4]; issuing certificates of shares, debentures and debenture stock[5]; delivering particulars of mortgages or charges for registration[6], when these duties have not already been performed by some other officer; allowing inspection of the debenture register to debenture holders[7]; giving notice to the registrar of an increase of share capital[8]; allowing inspection of, and sending copies of, the register of members[9]; allowing inspection of the register of directors and secretaries[10]; and, in the case of winding up by the court, assisting in making out the statement of the affairs of the company[11].

He may also make statutory declarations verifying that all requirements under the Companies Act 1985 in respect of registration and of matters precedent to and incidental to it have been complied with[12], that a company satisfies the conditions for exemption from the requirement to use the word 'limited' as part of its name[13], and that the conditions for re-registration of a private company as a public company[14], or a limited company as unlimited[15], are satisfied.

1 See the Companies Act 1985 s 363(2)(c) (as substituted) and para 1062 post.
2 See ibid s 88 and para 478 ante.
3 See ibid s 117(3) and para 652 post.
4 See ibid s 306(3) and para 627 ante.
5 See ibid s 185 (as amended) and para 482 ante and para 1282 post.
6 See ibid ss 399, 400 and paras 1308, 1309 respectively post.
7 See ibid s 191 (as amended) and para 1294 post.
8 See ibid s 123 and para 203 ante.
9 See ibid s 356 (as amended) and paras 390, 391 ante.
10 See ibid s 288 (as amended) and para 560 ante. In case of non-compliance by a company with many of the provisions of the Companies Act 1985, the secretary may be liable as an 'officer who is in default': see further para 1161 post.
11 See para 2279 et seq post.
12 See the Companies Act 1985 s 12(3)(b) and para 88 ante.
13 See ibid s 30(5) and para 112 ante.
14 See ibid s 43(3)(e) and para 118 ante.
15 See ibid s 49 and para 124 ante.

649. Register of directors and secretaries. The register of directors and secretaries[1] must contain the following particulars with respect to the secretary or, where there are joint secretaries, with respect to each of them:

(1) in the case of an individual, his present name[2], any former name[3] and his usual residential address; and

(2) in the case of a corporation or a Scottish firm, its corporate or firm name and registered or principal office[4].

Where, however, all partners in a firm are joint secretaries, the name and principal office of the firm may be stated instead of the particulars specified above[5].

Within the period of 14 days from the occurrence of any change in its secretary or any change in the particulars contained in the register, the company must send to the registrar of companies a notification in the prescribed form[6] of the change and of the date on which it occurred; and a notification of a person having become a secretary or one of joint secretaries must contain a consent, signed by that person, so to act[7].

1 Ie the register to be kept under the Companies Act 1985 s 289 (as amended): see para 560 ante. As to the general provisions regarding the register of directors and secretaries, inspection of the register and the penalties for failure to permit such inspection see para 560 ante.
2 For these purposes, ibid s 289(2)(a) (as substituted) (meaning of 'name': see para 560 note 2 ante) applies for the purposes of the obligation to state the name of an individual: s 290(3) (substituted by the Companies Act 1989 s 145, Sch 19 para 3(1),(3)).
3 For these purposes, the Companies Act 1985 s 289(2)(b) (as substituted) (meaning of references to a former name: see para 560 note 3 ante) applies for the purposes of the obligation to state the former name of an individual: s 290(3) (as substituted: see note 2 supra).
4 Ibid s 290(1) (amended by the Companies Act 1989 Sch 19 para 3(1),(2)).
5 Companies Act 1985 s 290(2).
6 For the prescribed form of notification see the Companies (Forms) (Amendment) Regulations 1995, SI 1995/736, reg 3, Sch 2, Form 288a (appointment of director or secretary), Form 288b (resignation of director or secretary) and Form 288c (change of particulars for director or secretary). For the prescribed version of the form in Welsh see the Companies (Welsh Language Forms and Documents) (Amendment) Regulations 1995, SI 1995/734, reg 4, Schedule, Form 288aCYM (appointment of director or

secretary), Form 288bCYM (resignation of director or secretary) and Form 288cCYM (change of particulars for director or secretary).

7 Companies Act 1985 s 288(2).

650. Manager. If a manager[1] commits such a breach of his duty as to cause a loss to the company, he is liable in damages[2]; and a de facto manager is also liable to penalties wherever the 'manager' is made liable by the Companies Act 1985[3]. A manager who takes a secret commission may be dismissed[4]. A secretary who has in fact acted as manager is liable for negligence in preparing balance sheets and accounts whereby he has caused dividends to be paid out of capital[5].

1 For the meaning of 'manager' see para 641 text and notes 3-5 ante.

2 *Leeds Estate Building and Investment Co v Shepherd* (1887) 36 ChD 787 (where owing to his fraudulent accounts the directors paid a dividend).

3 See *Gibson v Barton* (1875) LR 10 QB 329; *Coventry and Dixon's Case* (1880) 14 ChD 660, CA; *Re Western Counties Steam Bakeries and Milling Co* [1897] 1 Ch 617, CA; *R v Lawson* [1905] 1 KB 541. The authority of a manager to 'take entire charge of the interest of a company' in South America does not extend to an unusual transaction, such as a promise to pay a guarantor of the company whose fund has been forfeited: *Re Cunningham & Co Ltd, Simpson's Claim* (1887) 36 ChD 532; cf *Cartmell's Case* (1874) 9 Ch App 691.

4 *Boston Deep Sea Fishing and Ice Co v Ansell* (1888) 39 ChD 339, CA (where the manager was dismissed on other grounds which could not be substantiated, and the taking of a commission was not discovered until a later date). See also EMPLOYMENT vol 16 (Reissue) para 300.

5 *Municipal Freehold Land Co Ltd v Pollington* (1890) 59 LJ Ch 734.

651. Solicitor. A solicitor is not ordinarily an officer of a company[1]; but, if he is paid by way of salary and has certain duties to perform, he may be an officer[2]. It is not within the province of the company's solicitor to make any representations to possible investors as to the financial state of the company[3].

In the case of the bringing out of a particular company, a solicitor is not the agent of the company in bringing it out, but the agent of the promoter, to whom he must look for payment[4]. The company cannot become liable to the solicitor by ratifying his acts, as it cannot ratify acts done before it was incorporated[5]; but it may become liable if the contract is novated[6]. If a solicitor charges the company for his professional services in the formation of the company, he cannot also charge the vendors on the sale of the business to the company[7]. An agreement made before the company is formed does not give him any right to employment[8]. The appointment of a solicitor is sometimes provided for in the articles, but the articles themselves do not constitute a contract with him[9].

A company's solicitor cannot set off an unliquidated claim for his costs against calls made in respect of shares held by him in the company[10].

He has no lien on the registers or books of the company, which must be kept at the company's office or otherwise under the control of the company[11], but he may have a lien on documents which the company does not need for the conduct of its business. A winding up will not displace this lien[12]. He cannot, however, assert such a lien as would prejudice the conduct of the winding up[13]; nor has he a lien for costs incurred in business that he knows to be ultra vires[14]; nor may he assert a lien against a third party[15].

1 *Re Great Wheal Polgooth Co Ltd* (1883) 53 LJ Ch 42; *Re Great Western Forest of Dean Coal Consumers' Co Ltd, Carter's Case* (1886) 31 ChD 496; *Re Kingston Cotton Mill Co* [1896] 1 Ch 6 at 14, CA; *Re Harper's Ticket Issuing and Recording Machine Ltd* (1912) 29 TLR 63.

2 *Re Liberator Permanent Benefit Building Society* (1894) 71 LT 406, DC.

3 *Burnes v Pennell* (1849) 2 HL Cas 497.

4 *Re Rotherham Alum and Chemical Co* (1883) 25 ChD 103, CA; *Re English and Colonial Produce Co Ltd* [1906] 2 Ch 435, CA; *Re National Motor Mail-Coach Co Ltd, Clinton's Claim* [1908] 2 Ch 515 at 521, CA. Hence he is not a promoter: *Re Great Wheal Polgooth Co Ltd* (1883) 32 WR 107.

5 See para 1127 post.

6 *Re Hereford and South Wales Waggon and Engineering Co* (1876) 2 ChD 621, CA; *Nichols v Regent's Canal Co* (1894) 63 LJQB 641; revsd on other grounds sub nom *Nichols v North Metropolitan Rly and Canal Co* (1894) 71 LT 836, CA; decision of Court of Appeal affd (1896) 74 LT 744, HL; and see *Howard v Patent Ivory Manufacturing Co, Re Patent Ivory Manufacturing Co* (1888) 38 ChD 156. See further para 1127 post.

7 *Welsh v Forbes* (1906) 8 F 453.

8 Cf *Re Dale and Plant Ltd* (1889) 61 LT 206.

9 *Eley v Positive Government Security Life Assurance Co* (1876) 1 ExD 88, CA.

10 *Johnson v Lyttle's Iron Agency* (1877) 5 ChD 687, CA.

11 *Re Anglo-Maltese Hydraulic Dock Co Ltd* (1885) 54 LJ Ch 730.

12 *Re Rapid Road Transit Co* [1909] 1 Ch 96; *Re Ardtully Copper Mines Ltd* (1915) 50 ILT 95; and see para 2567 post.

13 *Re Capital Fire Insurance Association* (1883) 24 ChD 408, CA; *Re Anglo-Maltese Hydraulic Dock Co* (1885) 54 LJ Ch 730; *Graham (Liquidator of Donaldson & Co) v White and Park* 1908 SC 309; *Re Hawkes* [1898] 2 Ch 1, CA; *Rorie v Stevenson* 1908 SC 559; *Re South Essex Estuary and Reclamation Co, ex p Paine and Layton* (1869) 4 Ch App 215; *Re Union Cement and Brick Co, ex p Pulbrook* (1869) 4 Ch App 627. As to the priority of the lien of a solicitor over a floating charge see para 1262 post.

14 *Re Phoenix Life Assurance Co, Howard and Dollman's Case* (1863) 1 Hem & M 433.

15 See *Re Aveling Barford Ltd* [1988] 3 All ER 1019, [1989] 1 WLR 360, following *Re South Essex Estuary and Reclamation Co, ex p Paine and Layton* (1869) 4 Ch App 215.

(iv) Commencement of Business; Company Records

652. Restrictions on commencement of business. A company registered as a public company on its original incorporation[1] must not do business or exercise any borrowing powers unless the registrar of companies has issued it with a certificate under the following provisions, or the company is re-registered[2] as a private company[3]. The registrar must issue a company with such a certificate if, on an application made to him by the company in the prescribed form[4], he is satisfied that the nominal value of the company's allotted share capital[5] is not less than the authorised minimum[6] and there is delivered to him a statutory declaration in the prescribed form signed by a director or secretary of the company[7]. The statutory declaration must:

(1) state that the nominal value of the company's allotted share capital is not less than the authorised minimum;

(2) specify the amount paid up, at the time of the application, on the allotted share capital of the company;

(3) specify the amount, or estimated amount, of the company's preliminary expenses and the persons by whom any of those expenses have been paid or are payable; and

(4) specify any amount or benefit paid or given or intended to be paid or given, to any promoter[8] of the company, and the consideration for the payment or benefit[9].

The registrar may accept a statutory declaration delivered to him under these provisions as sufficient evidence of the matters stated in it[10]. A certificate so issued in respect of a company is conclusive evidence that the company is entitled to do business and exercise any borrowing powers[11]. Evidence cannot be received to show that the facts did not warrant the issuing of the certificate[12].

If a company does business, or exercises borrowing powers in contravention of these provisions, the company, and any officer of it who is in default, is liable on indictment to a fine, or on summary conviction to a fine not exceeding the statutory maximum[13].

1 See para 80 et seq ante.
2 See para 129 et seq ante.
3 Companies Act 1985 s 117(1). As to the conclusiveness of the registrar's certificate see *Re Yolland, Husson and Birkett Ltd, Leicester v Yolland, Husson and Birkett Ltd* [1908] 1 Ch 152, CA.
4 For the prescribed form of application see the Companies (Forms) (Amendment) Regulations 1995, SI 1995/736, reg 3, Sch 2, Form 117.
5 For these purposes, a share allotted in pursuance of an employees' share scheme may not be taken into account in determining the nominal value of the company's allotted share capital, unless it is paid up at least as to one-quarter of the nominal value of the share and the whole of any premium on the share: Companies Act 1985 s 117(4). For the meaning of 'employees' share scheme' see para 120 note 8 ante.
6 For these purposes, 'authorised minimum' means £50,000 or such other sum as the Secretary of State may by order, made by statutory instrument, specify instead: ibid s 118(1). No such order may be made unless a draft of it has been laid before Parliament and approved by resolution of each House: s 118(3). Any order increasing the authorised minimum may (1) require any public company having an allotted share capital of which the nominal value is less than the amount specified in the order as the authorised minimum to increase that value to not less than that amount or make application to be re-registered as a private company; (2) make, in connection with any such requirement, provision for any of the matters for which provision is made by the Companies Act 1985 relating to a company's registration, re-registration or change of name, to payment for any share comprised in a company's capital and to offers of shares in, or debentures of, a company to the public, including provision as to the consequences (whether in criminal law or otherwise) of a failure to comply with any requirement of the order; and (3) contain such supplemental and transitional provisions as the Secretary of State thinks appropriate, make different provision for different cases and, in particular, provide for any provision of the order to come into operation on different days for different purposes: s 118(2). Since the authorised minimum is expressed in pounds sterling, the company must have allotted share capital of this amount in pounds sterling, whatever other capital it may have in whatever currency (see para 84 text to notes 12-14 ante): *Re Scandinavian Bank Group plc* [1988] Ch 87 at 104, [1987] 2 All ER 70 at 77 per Harman J.
7 Companies Act 1985 s 117(2),(3).
8 As to promoters see para 37 et seq ante.
9 Companies Act 1985 s 117(3).
10 Ibid s 117(5).
11 Ibid s 117(6).
12 *Re Yolland, Husson & Birkitt Ltd, Leicester v Yolland, Husson & Birkitt Ltd* [1908] 1 Ch 152, CA.
13 Companies Act 1985 ss 117(7), 730, Sch 24. For the meaning of 'officer who is in default' and 'the statutory maximum' see para 1161 post.

653. Transactions entered into before company entitled to commence business. The restrictions on commencement of business[1] do not in any way affect the validity of any transaction entered into by a company; but, if a company enters into a transaction in contravention of those restrictions and fails to comply with its obligations in that connection within 21 days from being called upon to do so, the directors of the company are jointly and severally liable to indemnify the other party to the transaction in respect of any loss or damage suffered by him by reason of the company's failure to comply with those obligations[2].

1 See para 652 ante.
2 Companies Act 1985 s 117(8).

654. Form of company records. Any register[1], index[2], minute book[3] or accounting records[4] required by the Companies Acts[5] to be kept by a company may be kept either by making entries in bound books or by recording the matters in question in any other manner[6]. Where any such register, index, minute book or accounting record is not kept by making entries in a bound book, but by some other means, adequate precautions must be taken for guarding against falsification and facilitating its discovery[7]. If default is made in complying with this last requirement, the company, and every officer of it who is in default, is liable on summary conviction to a fine not exceeding one-fifth of the statutory maximum and, on conviction after continued contravention, to a daily default fine not exceeding one-fiftieth of the statutory maximum[8].

1   See para 378 ante (register of members); para 398 ante (duplicate of overseas branch register); paras 560, 649 ante (register of directors and secretaries); para 571 ante (register of directors' interests); para 747 post (register of notifiable interests in shares); para 1293 post (register of debenture holders); and para 1297 post (register of charges).
2   See para 381 ante (index of members' names); para 572 ante (index of directors' interests in shares of the company); paras 747, 749 post (index of notifiable interests in shares).
3   As to minutes of meetings of directors see para 633 ante; and as to minutes of general meetings of the company see para 694 post.
4   As to accounting records see para 801 post.
5   For the meaning of 'the Companies Acts' see para 60 note 1 ante.
6   Companies Act 1985 s 722(1).
7   Ibid s 722(2).
8   Ibid ss 722(3), 730, Sch 24. For the meaning of 'officer who is in default', 'the statutory maximum' and 'daily default fine' see para 1161 post.

655. Use of computers for company records. The power conferred on a company[1] to keep a register or other record by recording the matters in question otherwise than by making entries in bound books includes power to keep the register or other record by recording those matters otherwise than in a legible form, so long as the recording is capable of being reproduced in a legible form[2]. Any provision of an instrument made by a company before 12 February 1979 which requires a register of holders of the company's debentures[3] to be kept in a legible form is to be read as requiring the register to be kept in a legible or non-legible form[4].

If any such register or other record of a company, or a register of holders of a company's debentures, is kept by the company by recording the matters in question otherwise than in a legible form, any duty imposed on the company by the Companies Act 1985[5] to allow inspection of, or to furnish a copy of, the register or other record or any part of it is to be treated as a duty to allow inspection of, or to furnish, a reproduction of the recording or of the relevant part of it in a legible form[6]. The Secretary of State may by regulations in a statutory instrument make such additional provision as he considers appropriate in connection with such registers or other records as are mentioned above, and are kept as so mentioned; and the regulations may make modifications of provisions of the Companies Act 1985 relating to such registers or other records[7].

1   Ie by the Companies Act 1985 s 722(1): see paras 378, 654 ante.
2   Ibid s 723(1).
3   As to the register of debenture holders see paras 1293, 1294 post.
4   Companies Act 1985 s 723(2).
5   See eg paras 378-381 ante (register of members and index of members' names); para 398 ante (duplicate of overseas branch register); paras 560, 649 ante (register of directors and secretaries); para 571 ante (register of directors' interests); para 747 post (register of notifiable interests in shares); para 1297 post (register of charges).
6   Companies Act 1985 s 723(3).
7   Ibid s 723(4). A statutory instrument under s 723(4) is subject to annulment in pursuance of a resolution of either House of Parliament: s 723(5). In exercise of the power so conferred the Secretary of State made the Companies (Registers and other Records) Regulations 1985, SI 1985/724 (see paras 656, 1295 post) which came into operation on 1 July 1985: reg 1(1).

656. Registers kept otherwise than in a legible form. The following provisions apply with respect to certain registers[1] which are kept by a company by recording the matters in question otherwise than in a legible form[2].

The company must in such cases perform the duty to allow inspection of such registers at a specified[3] place[4]. In the case of any such register the company is not required:

(1) to keep it in any place where it is required to be kept under the Companies Act 1985;

(2) to give any notice to the registrar of companies required to be given under the 1985 Act of the place where the register is kept, or of any change in that place; or

(3) to include in its annual return any statement required to be given under the 1985 Act of the address of the place where the register is kept[5].

Where provision is made in the 1985 Act with respect to default in complying with any requirement of that Act regarding the place where such a register is to be kept, that provision has effect in relation to any such register as if there were substituted for the reference in it to such default, a reference to default in complying with the requirement to allow inspection at a specified place[6].

Where a company keeps certain[7] registers by recording the matters in question otherwise than in a legible form, the company must send to the registrar of companies notice in the prescribed form[8] of the place for inspection of that register and of any change in that place[9]. The company is not, however, obliged to give such notice:

(a) where the company changes from keeping a register in a legible form to keeping it otherwise than in a legible form and the place for inspection of the register immediately following the change is the same as the place where the register was kept in a legible form immediately prior to the change; or

(b) in the case of the register of members or the register of directors' interests where, since the register first came into existence, it has been kept by recording the matters in question otherwise than in a legible form, and the place for inspection has been the registered office of the company[10].

Where the register of members of a company is kept by recording the matters in question otherwise than in a legible form and the place for inspection of that register is elsewhere than at the registered office, the company must include in its annual return a statement of the address of the place for inspection of that register[11].

Where a register is kept by recording the matters in question otherwise than in a legible form, any reference to such register in any provision of the Companies Act 1985 relating to the place where a duplicate of such register, another register or duplicate of another register is required to be kept, is to be construed as a reference to the place for inspection of the first-mentioned register[12].

Where the place for inspection of the register of members is the office of some person other than the company and by reason of any default of that person the company fails to comply with the above duty[13] to allow inspection of the index of the register of members, or the above provisions[14] relating to the register of members, such person is liable to the same penalties as if he were an officer of the company who was in default[15], and the power of the court in the case of such refusal or default to compel an immediate inspection of the register or direct that the copies required be sent to the persons requiring them[16] extends to the making of orders against such person and his officers and servants[17].

Where an overseas branch register is kept by a company by recording the matters in question otherwise than in a legible form, the statutory provisions relating to the keeping of the register[18], and the authority of a competent court[19] have effect as if, for the references to the country or territory where that register is kept, there were substituted references to the country or territory where the place for inspection of the register is situated[20].

Where the register of directors' interests is kept by a company by recording the matters in question otherwise than in a legible form, the statutory obligation to produce and make available the same at an annual general meeting[21] has effect as if, for the reference to that register, there were substituted a reference to a reproduction of the recording of that register in a legible form[22].

Where the accounting records of a company are kept otherwise than in a legible form and the place for inspection of such records is outside Great Britain, the statutory requirement to transmit accounts and returns to a place in Great Britain where inspection is to be afforded[23] will have effect as if, for the references to the accounting records being kept at a place outside Great Britain, there were substituted references to the place for inspection of such records being at a place outside Great Britain[24].

1   The registers within the scope of these provisions, the statutory provision under which they fall to be kept, and the place for the performance of the duty to allow inspection of registers kept otherwise than in a legible form are as follows:

STATUTORY PROVISION	REGISTER	PLACE
COMPANIES ACT 1985		
Section 211(8)	Register and any associated index of interests in voting shares	(a) Where the register of directors' interests is kept otherwise than in a legible form, the place for inspection of that register. (b) Where the register of directors' interests is kept in a legible form, the place where it is so kept.
Section 222(1)	Accounting records	The registered office of the company or such other place as the directors of the company think fit.
Section 288(1)	Register of directors and secretaries	The registered office of the company.
Section 353(1)	Register of members	The registered office of the company provided that— (a) if the work of ensuring that the requirements of the Act with regard to entries in the register are complied with is done at another office of the company, the place for inspection may be that other office and (b) if the company arranges with some other person for the carrying out of the work referred to in (a) supra to be undertaken on behalf of the company by that other person, the place for inspection may be the office of that other person at which the work is done; so however that the place for inspection must not, in the case of a company registered in England and Wales, be at a place outside England and Wales and, in the case of a company registered in Scotland, be at a place outside Scotland.

STATUTORY PROVISION	REGISTER	PLACE
COMPANIES ACT 1985		
Section 354(3)	Index of the register of members	(a) Where the register of members is kept otherwise than in a legible form, the place for inspection of that register. (b) Where the register of members is kept in a legible form, the place where it is so kept.
Section 362(1)	Overseas branch register	Any place where, but for the Companies (Registers and other Records) Regulations 1985 the register would be permitted to be kept under section 362(1) of the Act.
Section 407(1)	Register of charges	The registered office of the company.
Schedule 13 para 25	Register of directors' interests	(a) Where the register of members is kept otherwise than in a legible form: (i) if the place for inspection of that register is the registered office of the company, that office, and (ii) if not, the place for inspection of that register or the registered office of the company. (b) Where the register of members is kept in a legible form: (i) if that register is kept at the registered office of the company, that office, and (ii) if that register is not so kept, the place where that register is kept or the registered office of the company.
Schedule 13 para 28	Index of the register of directors' interests	(a) Where the register of directors' interests is kept otherwise than in a legible form, the place for inspection of that register. (b) Where the register of directors' interests is kept in a legible form, the place where it is so kept.
Schedule 14 para 4(1)	Duplicate of overseas branch register	(a) Where the register of members is kept otherwise than in a legible form, the place for inspection of that register. (b) Where the register of members is kept in a legible form, the place where it is so kept.

See the Companies (Registers and other Records) Regulations 1985, SI 1985/724, reg 2(1), Sch 1.
2 Ibid reg 2(1).
3 Ie a place specified in ibid Sch 1 col 3: see note 1 supra.
4 Ibid reg 2(2).
5 Ibid reg 2(3).
6 Ibid reg 2(4).
7 The registers in question are (1) the register of members (see para 378 ante); (2) an overseas branch register (see para 398 ante); and (3) the register of directors' interests (see para 571 ante): ibid reg 3(2).
8 For the prescribed forms see ibid Sch 2 Pt 1, Forms 325a, 353a, 362a.
9 Ibid reg 3(1). If a company makes default for 14 days in complying with this requirement, the company, and every officer of it who is in default, is liable on summary conviction to a fine not exceeding one-fifth of the statutory maximum and, on conviction after continued contravention,

to a daily default fine not exceeding one-fiftieth of the statutory maximum: Companies Act 1985 ss 353(4), 730, Sch 24 (applied by the Companies (Registers and other Records) Regulations 1985 reg 3(5)). For the meaning of 'officer who is in default', 'the statutory maximum' and 'daily default fine' see para 1161 post.
10 Ibid reg 3(3).
11 Ibid reg 3(4). If a company fails to comply with this requirement, the company, and every officer of it who is in default, is liable on summary conviction to a fine not exceeding the statutory maximum and, on conviction after continued contravention, to a daily default fine not exceeding one-tenth of the statutory maximum: Companies Act 1985 ss 363(7), 730, Sch 24 (applied by the Companies (Registers and other Records) Regulations 1985 reg 3(5)).
12 Ibid reg 6(1).
13 Ie imposed by ibid reg 2: see supra.
14 Ie contained in ibid reg 3: see supra.
15 As to such penalties see the Companies Act 1985 s 356(5) (see para 390 ante) and notes 9, 11 supra.
16 Ie under ibid s 357: see para 381 ante.
17 Ibid s 357 (applied by the Companies (Registers and other Records) Regulations 1985 reg 3(5)).
18 Ie the Companies Act 1985 s 326(1), Sch 14 para 2(2): see para 399 ante.
19 Ie ibid Sch 14 para 3(1): see para 399 ante.
20 Companies (Registers and other Records) Regulations 1985 reg 6(3).
21 Ie the Companies Act 1985 s 325(5), Sch 13 para 29: see para 574 ante.
22 Companies (Registers and other Records) Regulations 1985 reg 6(4).
23 Ie the Companies Act 1985 s 222 (as substituted): see para 802 post.
24 Companies (Registers and other Records) Regulations 1985 reg 6(5).

(v) Meetings of Members

A. KINDS OF MEETINGS

657. Different kinds of meetings. The general meetings of the company's members are either ordinary or extraordinary. An ordinary meeting is any meeting which by statute or the articles of the company must be held periodically, and generally means the annual general meeting of the company[1]. An extraordinary meeting is any meeting which is not an ordinary meeting and not the annual general meeting[2].

Articles of association always contain provisions as to the meetings of the company[3]. The members, as a body, may act only through a general meeting unless all the shareholders assent[4].

1 See the Companies Act 1985 s 366 and para 658 post.
2 See the Companies (Tables A to F) Regulations 1985, SI 1985/805, Schedule, Table A art 36 (cited in note 3 infra). As to Table A generally see para 529 et seq ante.
3 Ibid Schedule, Table A art 38 provides that an annual general meeting and an extraordinary general meeting called for the passing of a special resolution or a resolution appointing a person as a director must be called by at least 21 clear days' notice. All other extraordinary general meetings must be called by at least 14 days' notice but a general meeting may be called by shorter notice if it is so agreed (1) in the case of an annual general meeting, by all the members entitled to attend and vote thereat; and (2) in the case of any other meeting, by a majority in number of the members having a right to attend and vote being a majority together holding not less than 95% in nominal value of the shares giving that right. The notice must specify the time and place of the meeting and the general nature of the business to be transacted and, in the case of an annual general meeting, must specify the meeting as such. Subject to the provisions of the articles and to any restrictions imposed on any shares, the notice must be given to all the members, to all persons entitled to a share in consequence of the death or bankruptcy of a member and to the directors and auditors.
   In the absence of fraud, the place of meeting is entirely at the discretion of the directors: *Martin v Walker* (1918) 145 LT Jo 377.
   The Companies (Tables A to F) Regulations 1985 Schedule, Table A art 36 provides that all general meetings other than annual general meetings are to be called extraordinary general meetings. Apart from any special provision, directors cannot postpone an ordinary meeting: *Smith v Paringa Mines Ltd* [1906] 2 Ch 193. The Companies (Tables A to F) Regulations 1985 Schedule, Table A art 37 provides that the directors may call general meetings and, on the requisition of members pursuant to the

provisions of the Companies Act 1985 (see para 662 post), must forthwith proceed to convene an extraordinary general meeting for a date not later than eight weeks after receipt of the requisition; and, if there are not within the United Kingdom sufficient directors to call a general meeting, any director or any member of the company may call a general meeting. See *Hooper v Kerr, Stuart & Co Ltd* (1900) 83 LT 729 (a meeting summoned by a notice issued without authority of the directors after receipt of a requisition is validly summoned on ratification of notice by directors).

Where the net assets of a public company are half or less of its called-up share capital, the directors must, not later than 28 days from the earliest day on which that fact is known to a director of the company, duly convene an extraordinary general meeting of the company for a date not later than 56 days from that day for the purpose of considering whether any, and if so what, steps should be taken to deal with the situation: see the Companies Act 1985 s 142(1) and para 213 ante.

4 See para 696 post.

658. Annual general meeting; in general. Every company must in each year[1] hold a general meeting as its annual general meeting in addition to any other meetings in that year, and must specify the meeting as such in the notices calling it[2]; and not more than 15 months must elapse between the date of one annual general meeting of a company and that of the next[3]. However, so long as a company holds its first annual general meeting within 18 months of its incorporation, it need not hold it in the year of its incorporation or in the following year[4].

If default is made in so holding a meeting of the company, the Secretary of State may, on the application of any member of the company, call, or direct the calling of, a general meeting of the company and give such ancillary or consequential directions as he thinks expedient, including directions modifying or supplementing, in relation to the calling, holding and conduct of the meeting, the operation of the company's articles[5]; and the directions which he may give include a direction that one member of the company present in person or by proxy shall be deemed to constitute a meeting[6]. A general meeting so held is deemed, subject to any directions of the Secretary of State, to be an annual general meeting of the company; but, where a meeting so held is not held in the year in which the default in holding the company's annual general meeting occurred, the meeting so held is not to be treated as the annual general meeting for the year in which it is held, unless at that meeting the company resolves that it shall be so treated[7]. Where a company resolves that it shall be so treated, a copy of the resolution must, within 15 days after its passing, be forwarded to the registrar of companies and recorded by him[8]. If default is made in holding the annual general meeting in accordance with the above provisions[9] or in complying with any directions given by the Secretary of State under the powers referred to above, the company, and every officer of it who is in default, is liable on conviction on indictment to a fine, or on summary conviction to a fine not exceeding the statutory maximum[10]; and, if default is made in forwarding such resolution to the registrar, the company, and every officer of it who is in default, is liable on summary conviction to a fine not exceeding one-fifth of the statutory maximum and, on conviction after continued contravention, to a daily default fine not exceeding one-fiftieth of the statutory maximum[11].

1 Ie the period of time commencing on 1 January and ending on 31 December: *Gibson v Barton* (1875) LR 10 QB 329.
2 Companies Act 1985 s 366(1). As to elections by private companies to dispense with annual general meetings see para 659 post.
3 Ibid s 366(3).
4 Ibid s 366(2). So far as the business which may be transacted at this meeting is concerned, the articles generally state what is usual business, and that all other is special, and sufficient notice of special business must be given to the shareholders. As to the effect of insufficient notice see para 664 post.
5 Ibid s 367(1).
6 Ibid s 367(2).

7 Ibid s 367(4).
8 Ibid s 367(5).
9 These provisions create two separate offences: that of not holding the meeting in the calendar year; and that of not holding it within 15 months after the last meeting: *Smedley v Companies' Registrar* [1919] 1 KB 97.
10 Companies Act 1985 ss 366(4) (failure to hold), 367(3) (failure to comply with directions), 730, Sch 24. For the meaning of 'officer who is in default' and 'the statutory maximum' see para 1161 post.
11 Ibid ss 367(5), 730, Sch 24. For the meaning of 'daily default fine' see para 1161 post.

659. Election by private company to dispense with annual general meeting. A private company[1] may elect by elective resolution[2] to dispense with the holding of annual general meetings[3]. An election has effect for the year in which it is made and subsequent years, but does not affect any liability already incurred by reason of default in holding an annual general meeting[4].

In any year in which an annual general meeting would be required to be held but for the election, and in which no such meeting has been held, any member of the company may, by notice to the company not later than three months before the end of the year, require the holding of an annual general meeting in that year[5].

If the election ceases to have effect, the company is not obliged to hold an annual general meeting in that year if, when the election ceases to have effect, less than three months of the year remain[6].

1 For the meaning of 'private company' see para 82 ante.
2 Ie in accordance with the Companies Act 1985 s 379A (as added): see para 686 post.
3 Ibid s 366A(1) (added by the Companies Act 1989 s 115(2)).
4 Companies Act 1985 s 366A(2) (added by the Companies Act 1989 s 115(2)).
5 Companies Act 1985 s 366A(3) (added by the Companies Act 1989 s 115(2)). If such a notice is given, the provisions of the Companies Act 1985 s 366(1),(4) (see para 658 ante) apply with respect to the calling of the meeting and the consequences of default: s 366A(4) (added by the Companies Act 1989 s 115(2)).
6 Companies Act 1985 s 366A(5) (added by the Companies Act 1989 s 115(2)). This does not affect any obligation of the company to hold an annual general meeting in that year in pursuance of a notice given under the Companies Act 1985 s 366A(3) (as added) (see supra): s 366A(5) (as so added).

B. CONVENING OF MEETINGS

660. Notice. A meeting is convened by notice to the members, which notice must comply with the articles[1] and the requirements of the Companies Act 1985[2]. A provision of the articles which provides for the calling of a meeting of the company (other than an adjourned meeting) by a shorter notice than:

(1) in the case of the annual general meeting[3], 21 days' notice[4] in writing[5]; and
(2) in the case of a meeting other than an annual general meeting or a meeting for the passing of a special resolution[6], 14 days' notice in writing in the case of a company other than an unlimited company and seven days' notice in writing in the case of an unlimited company[7],

is void[8].

Save in so far as the articles of a company make other provision in that behalf, not being a provision avoided by the above restrictions, a meeting of the company, other than an adjourned meeting, may be called:

(a) in the case of the annual general meeting, by 21 days' notice in writing[9]; and
(b) in the case of a meeting other than an annual general meeting or a meeting for the passing of a special resolution, by 14 days' notice in writing in the case of a

company other than an unlimited company and by seven days' notice in writing in the case of an unlimited company[10].

In so far as the articles of the company do not make other provision in that behalf, notice of the meeting must be served on every member of the company in the manner in which notices are required to be served by Table A as for the time being in force[11]; and two or more members holding not less than one-tenth of the issued share capital, or if the company does not have a share capital, not less than 5% in number of the members of the company, may call a meeting[12].

1 *Woolf v East Nigel Gold Mining Co Ltd* (1905) 21 TLR 660. The Companies (Tables A to F) Regulations 1985, SI 1985/805, Schedule, Table A arts 38, 39 (see *Re West Canadian Collieries Ltd* [1962] Ch 370, [1962] 1 All ER 26) govern the giving of notice of meetings; and the method of giving notice is governed by the Companies (Tables A to F) Regulations 1985 Schedule, Table A arts 111–116 (amended by SI 1985/1052). As to Table A generally see para 529 et seq ante. See also *Bradman v Trinity Estates plc* [1989] BCLC 757 (notices not timeously served because of postal strike; injunction granted restraining the holding of the meeting until a later date).

   In *Dickson v Halesowen Steel Co* [1928] WN 33, a company's articles provided that, if a member had no registered address in the United Kingdom and had not supplied the company with an address in the United Kingdom for the giving of notices to him, a notice in a newspaper was to be deemed notice duly given to him. The combined effect of that article and an article corresponding to the Companies (Tables A to F) Regulations 1985 Schedule, Table A art 112 was that no notice need be served on a member abroad, who leaves no registered address in the United Kingdom and no address for the service of notices in the United Kingdom, in order to render the meeting valid: *Dickson v Halesowen Steel Co* supra.

2 As to the necessity for the notice to call attention to the right of appointing a proxy see para 664 post.
3 As to the annual general meeting see para 658 ante.
4 This means 21 clear days between the day on which the member would receive the notice in ordinary course of post in England and the day of the meeting: *Re Railway Sleepers Supply Co* (1885) 29 ChD 204; cf *Papillon v Brunton* (1860) 29 LJ Ex 265; *Gresham House Estate Co v Rossa Grande Gold Mining Co* [1870] WN 119; and see *Re Hector Whaling Ltd* [1936] Ch 208; *Re Pavilion, Newcastle-upon-Tyne Ltd and Reduced* [1911] WN 235 (where there was an inconsistency in the articles as to notice). As to the position in Scotland see *Neil McLeod & Sons Ltd, Petitioners* 1967 SLT 46. This is a matter which concerns the company and shareholders only: *Re Miller's Dale and Ashwood Dale Lime Co* (1885) 31 ChD 211. Where notice is to be by advertisement in a newspaper, the clear days count from the day after the issue of the newspaper: *Sneath v Valley Gold Ltd* [1893] 1 Ch 477, CA.
5 Companies Act 1985 s 369(1)(a).
6 See para 683 post.
7 Companies Act 1985 s 369(1)(b).
8 Ibid s 369(1).
9 Ibid s 369(2)(a).
10 Ibid s 369(2)(b).
11 Ibid s 370(1),(2). See generally paras 1149, 1150 post; and see note 1 supra. As to the statutory authority of Table A see para 532 ante.
12 Companies Act 1985 s 370(1),(3). This applies (inter alia) where there are regulations, but no board of directors to carry them out: *Re Brick and Stone Co* [1878] WN 140.

661. Meeting convened by court. If for any reason it is impracticable to call a meeting of a company in any manner in which meetings of that company may be called[1], or to conduct the meeting in manner prescribed by the articles or the Companies Act 1985[2], the court may, either of its own motion or on the application of any director of the company or of any member of the company who would be entitled to vote at the meeting, order a meeting of the company to be called, held and conducted in any manner the court thinks fit[3]. Where such an order is made, the court may give such ancillary or consequential directions as it thinks expedient; and these may include a direction that one member of the company present in person or by proxy be deemed to constitute a meeting[4]. A meeting called, held and conducted in accordance with any such order is for all purposes deemed to be a meeting of the company duly called, held and conducted[5].

1 See para 660 ante.
2 See para 667 et seq post.
3 Companies Act 1985 s 371(1). The application to the court is made by originating summons in the expedited form: RSC Ord 102 r 2(1),(2). As to procedure on the originating summons see para 390 note 10 ante.
    As to the exercise of the court's discretion see further *Re El Sombrero Ltd* [1958] Ch 900, [1958] 3 All ER 1; *Re Opera Photographic Ltd* [1989] 1 WLR 634; *Re Sticky Fingers Restaurant Ltd* [1992] BCLC 84; *Harman v BML Group Ltd* [1994] 1 WLR 893, CA, distinguishing *Re El Sombrero Ltd* supra.
4 Companies Act 1985 s 371(2). See further *Re Edinburgh Workmen's Houses Improvement Co* 1935 SC 56; *Re El Sombrero Ltd* [1958] Ch 900, [1958] 3 All ER 1; *Re H R Paul & Son Ltd* (1973) 118 Sol Jo 166.
5 Companies Act 1985 s 371(3).

662. Requisition for meeting. Notwithstanding anything in the articles of a company, its directors must, on the requisition of members of the company holding at the date of the deposit of such requisition not less than one-tenth of such of the paid-up capital of the company as at that date carries the right of voting at general meetings of the company, or, in the case of a company not having a share capital, members of it representing not less than one-tenth of the total voting rights of all the members[1] having at the date of deposit of such requisition a right to vote at general meetings, forthwith proceed duly to convene an extraordinary general meeting of the company[2]. The requisition must state the objects of the meeting, and must be signed by the requisitionists and deposited at the registered office of the company[3]. It may consist of several documents in like form[4], each signed by one or more requisitionists[5].

If the directors do not within 21 days from the date of the deposit of the requisition proceed duly to convene a meeting[6], the requisitionists, or any of them representing more than one-half of the total voting rights of all of them, may themselves convene a meeting[7]. The notice convening the meeting need not state the statutory authority under which it is convened, nor is it necessary for the notice to be signed by all the requisitionists provided that documents accompanying the notice clearly indicate that the meeting is in fact being called by all of them[8]; but any meeting so convened must not be held after the expiration of three months from the date of deposit of the requisition[9].

A meeting so convened by requisitionists must be convened in the same manner, as nearly as possible, as that in which meetings are to be convened by directors[10]. Any reasonable expenses incurred by the requisitionists by reason of the failure of the directors duly to convene a meeting must be repaid to the requisitionists by the company; and any sum so repaid must be retained out of any sums due or to become due from the company by way of fees or other remuneration in respect of their services to such of the directors as were in default[11].

In the case of a meeting at which a resolution is to be proposed as a special resolution, the directors are deemed not to have duly convened the meeting if they do not give the notice required[12] for a special resolution[13].

A meeting convened on requisition cannot transact any business other than that covered by the terms of the requisition[14].

The directors are deemed not to have duly convened a meeting if they convene a meeting for a date more than 28 days after the date of the notice convening the meeting[15].

1 See note 10 infra.
2 Companies Act 1985 s 368(1),(2).
3 Ibid s 368(3).
4 See *Fruit and Vegetable Growers' Association Ltd v Kekewich* [1912] 2 Ch 52.
5 Companies Act 1985 s 368(3).
6 The meeting must be duly convened but not necessarily held within the 21-day period: *Re Windward Islands (Enterprises) UK Ltd* [1983] BCLC 293.
7 Companies Act 1985 s 368(4).
8 *Dalex Mines Ltd (NPL) v Schmidt* (1974) 38 DLR (3d) 17, BC.
9 Companies Act 1985 s 368(4).
10 Ibid s 368(5). This provision was first introduced by the Companies Act 1929 and differs considerably from the former law. Directors, upon being properly requested, as above, should include in the notice convening the meeting all the matters which the requisitionists require to be dealt with, so far as they can lawfully be dealt with at the meeting and, if they do not, the requisitionists may themselves convene a meeting: *Isle of Wight Rly Co v Tahourdin* (1883) 25 ChD 320, CA. If the shareholders can do so, an order will not be made to compel the directors to summon a meeting: *MacDougall v Gardiner* (1875) 10 Ch App 606. If the requisitionists are joint holders of shares, it is necessary that each joint holder should sign the requisition: *Patent Wood Keg Syndicate Ltd v Pearse* [1906] WN 164. A meeting cannot be validly convened within the 21 days by the secretary acting without the authority of the board: *Re State of Wyoming Syndicate* [1901] 2 Ch 431.
11 Companies Act 1985 s 368(6).
12 Ie by ibid s 378(2): see para 683 post.
13 Ibid s 368(7).
14 *Patent Wood Keg Syndicate Ltd v Pearse* [1906] WN 164; *Ball v Metal Industries Ltd* 1957 SC 315.
15 Companies Act 1985 s 368(8) (added by the Companies Act 1989 s 145, Sch 19 para 9).

663. Necessity for authorisation. Normally, the authority of the board is required for the convening of a meeting. A meeting of the company called by a secretary without a resolution duly passed at a directors' meeting cannot pass effectual resolutions[1]; but the directors may, before the meeting, ratify the secretary's act[2]. A meeting of the company called by a de facto director and adopted by the other directors[3], or one called by an acting quorum[4], is good under Table A[5]. Directors may by valid resolutions ratify any irregularity in the convening of a meeting committed by a de facto director[6].

An administrator[7] has power to call any meeting of the members[8].

1 *Re Haycraft Gold Reduction and Mining Co* [1900] 2 Ch 230; *Re State of Wyoming Syndicate* [1901] 2 Ch 431 (where a resolution to wind up was passed).
2 *Hooper v Kerr Stuart & Co Ltd* (1900) 83 LT 729 (requisitioned meeting).
3 *Transport Ltd v Schonberg* (1905) 21 TLR 305, following *British Asbestos Co Ltd v Boyd* [1903] 2 Ch 439; *Southern Counties Deposit Bank Ltd v Rider and Kirkwood* (1895) 73 LT 374, CA.
4 *Re Peruvian Rlys Co, ex p International Contract Co* (1868) 19 LT 803 at 805; on appeal (1869) 4 Ch App 322.
5 Ie under the Companies (Tables A to F) Regulations 1985, SI 1985/805, Schedule, Table A art 92. As to Table A generally see para 529 et seq ante.
6 *Boschoek Proprietary Co Ltd v Fuke* [1906] 1 Ch 148 (the matter being one of internal arrangement, with which the court would not interfere); and see *Browne v La Trinidad* (1887) 37 ChD 1, CA; *Southern Counties Deposit Bank Ltd v Rider and Kirkwood* (1895) 73 LT 374, CA; *British Asbestos Co Ltd v Boyd* [1903] 2 Ch 439; *Grant v United Kingdom Switchback Rlys Co* (1888) 40 ChD 135, CA; *Bentley-Stevens v Jones* [1974] 2 All ER 653, [1974] 1 WLR 638. Directors may ratify a notice given without authority: *Hooper v Kerr Stuart & Co Ltd* (1900) 83 LT 729.
7 As to administrators see para 2092 et seq post.
8 See the Insolvency Act 1986 s 14(2)(b) and para 2097 post.

664. Insufficient notice. Notwithstanding that it is called by shorter notice than is necessary, whether by statute or in the articles, as the case may be, a meeting is deemed to have been duly called if it is so agreed:

(1) in the case of a meeting called as the annual general meeting, by all the members entitled to attend and vote at it[1]; and

(2) in the case of any other meeting, by a majority in number of the members having a right to attend and vote at the meeting, being a majority together holding not less than 95% in nominal value of the shares giving a right to attend and vote at the meeting, or, in the case of a company not having a share capital, together representing not less than 95% of the total voting rights at that meeting of all the members[2].

A private company[3] may elect by elective resolution[4] that the above provisions shall have effect in relation to the company as if for the reference to 95% there were substituted references to such lesser percentage, but not less than 90%, as may be specified in the resolution or subsequently determined by the company in general meeting[5].

Provisions in the articles requiring special business to be specially notified and any other directions in the articles must be followed[6]. If the notice is misleading, the court will restrain the holding of the meeting[7], or restrain the directors from acting on resolutions passed on insufficient notice, until confirmed by the company at a meeting properly notified[8]. The transaction of business which has not been sufficiently notified or which is substantially different from that notified is invalid[9], but want of notice of some of the business does not invalidate such business as has been properly notified[10]. Amendments fairly arising on a proposed resolution may be passed[11]; thus a meeting summoned to pass a special resolution to wind up may appoint a different liquidator from the one named in the notice convening the meeting[12].

A notice of a meeting to pass a resolution 'with such amendments and alterations as shall be determined at the meeting' enables substantial alteration to be made, although the business is special business, the general nature of which is required by the articles to be notified[13].

In every notice calling a meeting of a company having a share capital there must appear with reasonable prominence a statement that a member entitled to attend and vote is entitled to appoint a proxy or, where that is allowed, one or more proxies to attend and vote instead of him, and that a proxy need not also be a member[14]. If, however, default is made in complying with this provision as respects any meeting, every officer of the company who is in default is liable on summary conviction to a fine not exceeding one-fifth of the statutory maximum[15].

1 Companies Act 1985 s 369(3)(a). See also note 2 infra. As to the annual general meeting see para 658 ante; and as to notice see para 660 ante.
2 Ibid s 369(3)(b),(4) (amended by the Companies Act 1989 s 115(3)). But for the Companies Act 1985 s 369(3), no business could be transacted in such a case in the absence of a special provision in the articles: *Garden Gully United Quartz Mining Co v McLister* (1875) 1 App Cas 39, PC; *Lawe's Case* (1852) 1 De GM & G 421; *Tiessen v Henderson* (1899) 1 Ch 861.
3 For the meaning of 'private company' see para 82 ante.
4 Ie in accordance with the Companies Act 1985 s 379A (as added): see para 686 post.
5 Ibid s 369(4) (as amended: see note 2 supra).
6 See the Companies (Tables A to F) Regulations 1985, SI 1985/805, Schedule, Table A art 38; para 660 ante; *Graham v Van Diemen's Land Co* (1856) 1 H & N 541, Ex Ch; *Normandy v Ind, Coope & Co Ltd* [1908] 1 Ch 84. A notice specifying the business as 'to elect directors' was held to have sufficiently specified the general nature of the business to elect directors up to the number permitted by the articles in *Choppington Collieries Ltd v Johnson* [1944] 1 All ER 762, CA. In *Robert Batcheller & Sons Ltd v Batcheller* [1945] Ch 169, [1945] 1 All ER 522 (overruled on another point by *Grundt v Great Boulder Proprietary Gold Mines Ltd* [1948] Ch 145, [1948] 1 All ER 21, CA), a reminder of a poll was held insufficient notice of a meeting. See also *Carruth v Imperial Chemical Industries Ltd* [1937] AC 707, [1937] 2 All ER 422, HL. As to specifying the intention to pass a resolution as an extraordinary or special resolution see paras 682, 683 post. It is doubtful whether it is necessary that the notice of a resolution to substitute new articles for

the present articles should be accompanied by a circular explaining the alterations or alternatively a copy of the proposed new articles: see *Young v South African and Australian Exploration and Development Syndicate* [1896] 2 Ch 268; *Normandy v Ind, Coope & Co Ltd* supra at 97; *Re North of Scotland and Orkney and Shetland Steam Navigation Co Ltd* 1920 SC 94. A director's report accompanying a notice may supplement it: *Boschoek Proprietary Co Ltd v Fuke* [1906] 1 Ch 148. The notice may be looked at to see if the proceedings are regular: *Betts & Co Ltd v Macnaghten* [1910] 1 Ch 430.

7 *Jackson v Munster Bank* (1884) 13 LR Ir 118.

8 *Kaye v Croydon Tramways Co* [1898] 1 Ch 358, CA; *Baillie v Oriental Telephone and Electric Co Ltd* [1915] 1 Ch 503, CA; *Pacific Coast Coal Mines Ltd v Arbuthnot* [1917] AC 607, PC. Cf *Bentley-Stevens v Jones* [1974] 2 All ER 653, [1974] 1 WLR 638 (injunction refused as no doubt about ultimate result and any invalidity was curable).

9 *Re Bridport Old Brewery Co* (1867) 2 Ch App 191; *Imperial Bank of China, India and Japan v Bank of Hindustan, China and Japan* (1868) LR 6 Eq 91; *Re Teede and Bishop Ltd* (1901) 70 LJ Ch 409; cf *Henderson v Bank of Australasia* (1890) 45 ChD 330, CA.

10 *Re British Sugar Refining Co* (1857) 3 K & J 408; *Re London and Mediterranean Bank Ltd, Wright's Case* (1871) 7 Ch App 55; cf *Cleve v Financial Corpn* (1873) LR 16 Eq 363.

11 See para 690 post.

12 *Re Trench Tubeless Tyre Co, Bethell v Trench Tubeless Tyre Co* [1900] 1 Ch 408, CA. This case was decided under the law existing before the Companies Act 1929, which required a special resolution to be passed and confirmed at separate meetings, but the principles laid down in that case would appear to apply equally where there is only one meeting. It was further decided under the old law requiring two meetings that the resolution at the first meeting need not follow the exact terms of the notice: *Torbock v Lord Westbury* [1902] 2 Ch 871.

13 *Betts & Co Ltd v Macnaghten* [1910] 1 Ch 430 (where the notice proposed that three directors only should be re-elected, but other directors, not previously named, were at the meeting proposed and elected). Cf *Choppington Collieries Ltd v Johnson* [1944] 1 All ER 762, CA (cited in note 3 supra).

14 Companies Act 1985 s 372(3).

15 Ibid ss 372(4), 730, Sch 24. For the meaning of 'officer who is in default' and 'the statutory maximum' see para 1161 post.

665. Notice when director to gain advantage. Unequivocal notice must be given of a resolution involving the pecuniary advantage of a director[1]. A notice not stating the particulars of the advantage is insufficient and the consequent resolutions are void[2].

1 *Hutton v West Cork Rly Co* (1883) 23 ChD 654, CA; and see para 594 et seq ante.

2 *Normandy v Ind, Coope & Co Ltd* [1908] 1 Ch 84; *Tiessen v Henderson* [1899] 1 Ch 861 (resolution giving an option on shares to a director); and see *Kaye v Croydon Tramways Co* [1898] 1 Ch 358, CA; *Baillie v Oriental Telephone and Electric Co Ltd* [1915] 1 Ch 503, CA; and distinguish *Young v South African and Australian Exploration and Development Syndicate* [1896] 2 Ch 268 at 276. As to when an action will lie at the suit of an individual shareholder see para 1111 post.

666. Ratification of acts beyond the directors' powers. A notice stating that the meeting will be asked to ratify an act of the directors, which while beyond the powers of the directors is intra vires the company, is sufficient[1], although it does not say why such ratification is required[2].

1 *Boschoek Proprietary Co Ltd v Fuke* [1906] 1 Ch 148 at 164, applying *Irvine v Union Bank of Australia* (1877) 2 App Cas 366 at 375, PC. See also *Hogg v Cramphorn Ltd* [1967] Ch 254, [1966] 3 All ER 420.

2 *Grant v United Kingdom Switchback Rlys Co* (1888) 40 ChD 135, CA.

C. PROCEEDINGS AT MEETINGS

667. Quorum at meeting. Articles of association usually prescribe the number of members who must be present in order that a valid general meeting may be held[1]. If there is no provision in the articles relating to a quorum, in the case of any company two members personally present are a quorum². If the quorum is not present within the prescribed time after the time appointed for the meeting, no business may be transacted, except as provided by the regulations of the company³. Where the number of shareholders is less than the requisite quorum, or where there is only one member of the class, the consent of all the members or the only member must be obtained⁴. A representative of a corporation which is a shareholder may be counted as one of the quorum⁵, but special provision must be made by the articles if a proxy or attorney acting on behalf of a member is to be counted⁶.

Notwithstanding any provision to the contrary in the articles of a private company⁷ limited by shares or by guarantee having only one member, one member present in person or by proxy is a quorum⁸.

1 See the Companies (Tables A to F) Regulations 1985, SI 1985/805, Schedule, Table A arts 40, 41 (amended by SI 1985/1052). Under Table A art 41, if during a meeting the quorum ceases to be present, the meeting must be adjourned. Cf *Re Hartley Baird Ltd* [1955] Ch 143, [1954] 3 All ER 695 (in default of such a provision, quorum must be present when meeting proceeds to business but not necessarily when a vote is taken). As to conduct of a meeting generally see *Carruth v Imperial Chemical Industries Ltd* [1937] AC 707, [1937] 2 All ER 422, HL.
2 Companies Act 1985 s 370(1),(4). See also para 669 note 9 post.
3 A resolution passed at a meeting at which there is no quorum is void: *Re Cambrian Peat, Fuel and Charcoal Co Ltd, De la Mott's Case and Turner's Case* (1875) 31 LT 773; *Re Romford Canal Co, Pocock's Claim, Trickett's Claim, Carew's Claim* (1883) 24 ChD 85. The question whether a member present only by proxy may be counted in a quorum was, as a matter of construction of the relevant articles, treated as doubtful in *Re Cambrian Peat, Fuel and Charcoal Co Ltd* supra, as was the question whether members not entitled to vote may be entitled to form a quorum in *Young v South African and Australian Exploration and Development Syndicate* [1896] 2 Ch 268 at 277. In *Re M J Shanley Contracting (in voluntary liquidation)* (1979) 124 Sol Jo 239 it was held (distinguishing *Neil McLeod & Sons Ltd, Petitioners* 1967 SLT 46) that one shareholder could not constitute a meeting. In the latter case (doubted by Oliver J in the former) there were two persons actually present, one of whom also held a proxy; it was held that the necessary quorum of three was present.
4 See para 696 post. Strictly speaking, one shareholder cannot form a meeting: *Sharp v Dawes* (1876) 2 QBD 26, CA (followed in *Re Prain & Sons Ltd* 1947 SC 325 and *Re London Flats Ltd* [1969] 2 All ER 744, [1969] 1 WLR 711); *Re Sanitary Carbon Co* [1877] WN 223; but see *East v Bennett Bros Ltd* [1911] 1 Ch 163 (where there was only one preference shareholder, and it was held that a provision in the memorandum requiring the sanction of a meeting of the holders of preference shares should not be construed strictly, and written consent was enough).
5 See the Companies Act 1985 s 375(2) and para 678 post.
6 *M Harris Ltd, Petitioners* 1956 SC 207.
7 For the meaning of 'private company' see para 82 ante.
8 Companies Act 1985 s 370A (added by the Companies (Single Member Private Limited Companies) Regulations 1992, SI 1992/1699, reg 2(1)(b), Schedule para 5). As to single member private limited companies see para 81 ante.

668. Chairman. Provision is usually made in the articles for the chairman of the board of directors to preside as chairman of general meetings of the company, and for the members or directors to choose a chairman in his place if he is not present within a specified time¹. In default of any provision in this behalf in the articles, any member elected by the members present at a meeting may be chairman².

1 See the Companies (Tables A to F) Regulations 1985, SI 1985/805, Schedule, Table A arts 42, 43.
2 Companies Act 1985 s 370(1),(5).

669. Adjournment of meeting. Except where empowered by the regulations of the company, the chairman¹ cannot adjourn the meeting, nor dissolve it, while any of the business for which it was called remains untransacted²; and, if he refuses to act, the meeting may elect another chairman. If he has the right, with the meeting's consent, to adjourn it, the majority of the members present at the meeting cannot compel him to do so[3]. He cannot, however, adjourn or dissolve the meeting against the wish of the majority[4], but he has prima facie authority to decide all incidental questions which arise and necessarily require decision at the time[5]. Where, however, there is a meeting at which the views of the majority cannot be validly ascertained, the chairman has a residual common law power to adjourn the meeting without its consent in order to give all persons entitled a reasonable opportunity of voting and speaking at the meeting[6].

Where the business of a meeting has been completed with the exception of the taking of a poll, the subsequent taking of the poll is part of the same meeting for the purposes of determining the validity of proxies[7]. Similarly, if a meeting is reconstituted subsequent to the taking of a poll on a motion for adjournment which is lost, the reconstituted meeting is the same meeting[8].

For the purposes of considering what business may be transacted at an adjourned meeting, the adjourned meeting must be considered as the original meeting[9]; but, where a resolution is passed at an adjourned meeting of a company or of the holders of any class of shares, the resolution is treated as having been passed on the date on which it was in fact passed, and is not deemed passed on any earlier date[10]. A meeting of shareholders cannot by a majority refuse to hear the views of the minority, but, after a reasonable opportunity has been afforded for the expression of their views, it is competent for the chairman, with the meeting's consent, to declare the discussion closed and put the motion to the vote[11].

1 Such a power is conferred by the Companies (Tables A to F) Regulations 1985, SI 1985/805, Schedule, Table A art 45.
2 *National Dwellings Society v Sykes* [1894] 3 Ch 159. In the absence of special powers the directors cannot postpone a meeting properly convened: *Smith v Paringa Mines Ltd* [1906] 2 Ch 193. Cf *John v Rees* [1970] Ch 345 at 381, 382, [1969] 2 All ER 274 at 292 (where Megarry J suggested that a chairman has an inherent power to adjourn for serious disorder).
3 *Salisbury Gold Mining Co v Hathorn* [1897] AC 268, PC.
4 *National Dwellings Society v Sykes* [1894] 3 Ch 159; cf *Henderson v Bank of Australasia* (1890) 45 ChD 330, CA.
5 *Re Indian Zoedone Co* (1884) 26 ChD 70, CA.
6 *Byng v London Life Association Ltd* [1990] Ch 170, [1989] 1 All ER 560, CA.
7 *Shaw v Tati Concessions Ltd* [1913] 1 Ch 292; *Spiller v Mayo (Rhodesia) Development Co (1908) Ltd* [1926] WN 78. As to the lodging of and the revocation of proxies see paras 675, 677 post.
8 *Jackson v Hamlyn* [1953] Ch 577, [1953] 1 All ER 887.
9 *Scadding v Lorant* (1851) 3 HL Cas 418; *McLaren v Thomson* [1917] 2 Ch 261 at 264, CA. An adjourned ordinary meeting cannot be an extraordinary meeting: *Wills v Murray* (1850) 4 Exch 843. It is sometimes provided that the members present at the adjourned meeting shall form a quorum but such a provision does not apply to a meeting of a special class of shareholders: *Hemans v Hotchkiss Ordnance Co* [1899] 1 Ch 115, CA.
10 Companies Act 1985 s 381(a), (b). This provision removed some of the difficulties caused by the decision in *Neuschild v British Equatorial Oil Co* [1925] 1 Ch 346.
11 *Wall v London and Northern Assets Corpn* [1898] 2 Ch 469, CA.

670. Voting. The articles usually contain provisions as to voting at meetings[1]. Unless otherwise provided by the articles, a shareholder, even if a director, is not debarred from using his voting power to carry a resolution by reason of his having a particular interest in the subject matter of the vote[2]; but, if members holding a majority of the voting power use their votes for a corrupt purpose, such as obtaining an unfair advantage for themselves or another company in which they are shareholders, the resolutions will be set aside[3]. An agreement by a shareholder, although in a representative capacity, with the purchaser or the mortgagee of some of his shares that he will vote as the purchaser directs is good and will be enforced by a mandatory injunction[4]. Directors may legitimately use their influence with the shareholders as to the way in which they should vote[5].

It is usual to provide that every member present in person has one vote on a show of hands and on a poll one vote for each share of which he is the holder[6]. If there is no provision in that behalf contained in the articles, in the case of a company originally having a share capital, every member has one vote in respect of each share or each £10 of stock held by him, and in any other case every member has one vote[7].

It is not unusual to provide that a resolution signed by all members entitled to vote at the general meeting at which it would otherwise have been proposed is as valid as if it has been passed at such a meeting[8].

It is sometimes provided that a person entitled by transmission may vote in respect of the shares to which he is so entitled, although not registered, if he satisfies the directors that he is so entitled[9]. It is doubtful whether, in the absence of any provision specifically giving the right to vote, a person entitled by transmission and not registered as a member is entitled to vote[10].

Under the general law an unpaid vendor of shares has the right to vote the shares which remain registered in his name and is free from any obligation to comply with the directions of the purchaser[11].

Subject to any regulations in the articles, a bankrupt is entitled to vote so long as the shares remain registered in his name, but he must exercise his votes in accordance with the directions of the persons beneficially entitled to his shares[12].

During a state of war the right of an alien enemy to vote is suspended and cannot be exercised by him[13].

Every registered holder is entitled to vote subject to any regulations in the articles[14], as where the member must have been registered for a fixed term before voting[15], or where a member is only allowed to vote in respect of preference shares held by him in certain cases[16]. Where under the articles there is no right to vote while any sum is due in respect of the shares, a purchaser of a forfeited share cannot vote while calls, for which the former holder alone is liable, are unpaid[17].

Where a company gave an undertaking to the court which involved the company in general meeting passing a resolution for the issue and allotment of shares, it was held that a shareholder voting against that resolution would not be in contempt of court[18].

It is not unusual in private companies for the shareholders to enter into an agreement outside the articles relating to voting their shares[19].

1 See the Companies (Tables A to F) Regulations 1985, SI 1985/805, Schedule, Table A arts 46–63. Article 46 provides that a resolution put to the vote of a meeting is to be decided on a show of hands unless before, or on the declaration of the result of, the show of hands a poll is duly demanded and that a demand by a person as proxy for a member is the same as a demand by a member; art 49 for the poll being taken as the chairman directs (see para 672 post); art 50 for the event of equality of votes, whether on a show of hands or on a poll; art 51 for the time of taking a poll demanded; art 54 for the number of votes each member has on a poll and a show of hands; art 55 for the voting of joint holders; art 56 for voting by a member suffering from mental disorder; art 57 for the requirement that all calls must be paid before a member may vote; art 58 for the raising of objections to the qualifications of voters; art 59 for giving votes on a poll either personally or by proxy; art 60 for the instrument appointing a proxy to be in writing; arts 60, 61 for the forms of proxy; art 62 for the depositing of the instrument appointing a proxy at the registered office of the company; and art 63 for the validity of votes given by proxy before notice of termination of authority reaches the company.

   For orders imposing restrictions on the voting rights in respect of any shares see para 1395 post.
2 *North-West Transportation Co Ltd and Beatty v Beatty* (1887) 12 App Cas 589, PC; *Ving v Robertson and Woodcock Ltd* (1912) 56 Sol Jo 412; *Burland v Earle* [1902] AC 83 at 94, PC; *Pender v Lushington* (1877) 6

ChD 70; *East Pant Du United Lead Mining Co Ltd v Merryweather* (1864) 2 Hem & M 254; *Baird v J Baird & Co (Falkirk) Ltd* 1949 SLT 368; cf *Mason v Harris* (1879) 11 ChD 97, CA. As to a director using his vote to appropriate the company's property see, however, *Cook v Deeks* [1916] 1 AC 554, PC and para 592 text and note 6 ante.

3 *Menier v Hooper's Telegraph Works* (1874) 9 Ch App 350; *Re Consolidated South Rand Mines Deep Ltd* [1909] 1 Ch 491; *Brown v British Abrasive Wheel Co* [1919] 1 Ch 290; *Clemens v Clemens Bros Ltd* [1976] 2 All ER 268 and see para 1110 et seq post.

4 *Greenwell v Porter* [1902] 1 Ch 530; *Puddephatt v Leith* [1916] 1 Ch 200. See, however, *Greenhalgh v Mallard* [1943] 2 All ER 234 (where it was held that such restrictions would not be binding upon third parties into whose hands the shares might come). An unpaid vendor of shares who remains the registered holder of them after the contract for sale retains vis-à-vis the purchaser the prima facie right to vote in respect of those shares: *Musselwhite v C H Musselwhite & Son Ltd* [1962] Ch 964, [1962] 1 All ER 201.

5 *Campbell v Australian Mutual Provident Society* (1908) 77 LJPC 117.

6 See the Companies (Tables A to F) Regulations 1985 Schedule, Table A art 54 and paras 671, 672 post.

7 Companies Act 1985 s 370(1),(6). Since the articles form a contract between the company and its members, there is no reason why the articles should not provide for different voting rights for different categories or classes of shares; private companies often have different classes of shares which either have different voting rights or rights which differ according to the resolution proposed. See further *Holt v Holt* [1990] 1 WLR 1250, PC ('A' shares carried 10,000 votes and 'B' shares one vote each); *Bushell v Faith* [1970] AC 1099, [1970] 1 All ER 53 (articles provided that, in the event of a resolution being proposed at any general meeting of the company for the removal from office of any director any shares held by that director should on a poll in respect of such a resolution carry the right to three votes per share).

8 See the Companies (Tables A to F) Regulations 1985 Schedule, Table A art 53.

9 *Marks v Financial News Ltd* (1919) 35 TLR 681.

10 See the Companies (Tables A to F) Regulations 1985 Schedule, Table A art 30; *Llewellyn v Kasintoe Rubber Estates Ltd* [1914] 2 Ch 670, CA; contra *Collins v Donald* (1895) 3 SLT 57. As to the continuance of the rights of a deceased member in his personal representative see *James v Buena Ventura Nitrate Grounds Syndicate Ltd* [1896] 1 Ch 456, CA; *New Zealand Gold Extraction Co (Newbury-Vautin Process) v Peacock* [1894] 1 QB 622, CA; *Howling's Trustees v Smith* (1905) 7 F 390; *Allen v Gold Reefs of West Africa Ltd* [1900] 1 Ch 656.

It is not clear how such a person could have an effective vote for an extraordinary or special resolution which requires a specific majority of the members who vote. Until he is registered, he is not a member. As to extraordinary resolutions see para 682 post; and as to special resolutions see para 683 post.

11 *JRRT (Investments) Ltd v Haycraft, Haycraft v JRRT (Investments) Ltd* [1993] BCLC 401.

12 *Wise v Lansdell* [1921] 1 Ch 420; *Morgan v Gray* [1953] Ch 83, [1953] 1 All ER 213.

13 *Robson v Premier Oil and Pipe Line Co Ltd* [1915] 2 Ch 124, CA. In most cases his right to receive notices of meetings will also be suspended, as all communications are normally prohibited: see *Re Anglo-International Bank Ltd* [1943] Ch 233, [1943] 2 All ER 88. See further *Re Pharaon et Fils* [1916] 1 Ch 1, CA; and see WAR vol 49 para 148 et seq. As to the Department of Trade and Industry's power by order to vest any securities, or the right to transfer them in the Custodian of Enemy Property see the Trading with the Enemy Act 1939 s 7(1)(b),(c) and WAR vol 49 para 157.

14 See *Pender v Lushington* (1877) 6 ChD 70 at 80 (where shares had been transferred to increase voting power) and para 496 ante.

15 *Pender v Lushington* (1877) 6 ChD 70.

16 *Coulson v Austin Motor Co Ltd* (1927) 43 TLR 493.

17 *Randt Gold Mining Co Ltd v Wainwright* [1901] 1 Ch 184.

18 *Northern Counties Securities Ltd v Jackson & Steeple Ltd* [1974] 2 All ER 625, [1976] 1 WLR 1133.

19 As to such agreements see para 149 ante.

671. Show of hands. Unless a poll is demanded, voting is by show of hands and each member personally present and voting is counted as one, proxies and the votes conferred by the shares represented being ignored[1]. The chairman's declaration as to the result of the voting by show of hands may, by the articles, be either sufficient or conclusive[2]. When it is only to be sufficient, evidence may be given to disprove it[3]. Even when it is to be conclusive, it may be disputed where it is inaccurate on the face of it[4], or where fraud is shown[5]; otherwise it cannot be disputed[6]. The chairman's ruling that a resolution has been passed by show of hands cannot be challenged if not challenged at the time[7]. If his decision is challenged, it is his duty to take steps to ascertain the true numbers[8]. If there is only a mistake and no fraud, the proper course is to call another meeting[8]. If votes are improperly excluded, the court will intervene on proper evidence[9].

Where there are two resolutions before a meeting of shareholders, the chairman may, it seems[10], put the resolutions to the meeting en bloc if no shareholder requires them to be put separately and there is a right to a poll[11], but at a general meeting of a public company a motion for the appointment of two or more persons as directors is not, in general, to be made[12].

1 *Ernest v Loma Gold Mines Ltd* [1897] 1 Ch 1 at 5, CA overruling *Re Bidwell Bros* [1893] 1 Ch 603; and see *Re Caloric Engine and Siren Fog Signals Co Ltd* (1885) 52 LT 846; *Re Horbury Bridge Coal, Iron and Waggon Co* (1879) 11 ChD 109, CA; the Companies Act 1985 s 372(2)(c) and para 674 post.
2 The Companies (Tables A to F) Regulations 1985, SI 1985/805, Schedule, Table A art 47 makes the chairman's declaration together with an entry to that effect in the minutes conclusive. As to the effect of the chairman's declaration in case of an extraordinary or special resolution see para 684 post.
3 *Re Indian Zoedone Co* (1884) 26 ChD 70, CA; *Re Horbury Bridge Coal, Iron and Waggon Co* (1879) 11 ChD 109, CA; *Wandsworth and Putney Gas Light and Coke Co v Wright* (1870) 22 LT 404.
4 *Re Caratal (New) Mines Ltd* [1902] 2 Ch 498 (where the declaration showed that the requisite majority had not been obtained); *Re Clark & Co Ltd* 1911 SC 243.
5 *Wall v London and Northern Assets Corpn* [1899] 1 Ch 550 (approved in *Wall v Exchange Investment Corpn* [1926] Ch 143, CA); *Arnot v United African Lands Ltd* [1901] 1 Ch 518, CA; *Allison v Johnson* (1902) 46 Sol Jo 686.
6 *Arnot v United African Lands Ltd* [1901] 1 Ch 518, CA; *Colonial Gold Reef Ltd v Free State Rand Ltd* [1914] 1 Ch 382; *Oppert v Brownhill Great Southern Ltd* (1898) 14 TLR 249, CA; *Re Hadleigh Castle Gold Mines Ltd* [1900] 2 Ch 419, distinguishing *Young v South African and Australian Exploration and Development Syndicate* [1896] 2 Ch 268; and see *Wandsworth and Putney Gas Light and Coke Co v Wright* (1870) 22 LT 404; *Re Graham's Morocco Co* 1932 SC 269.
7 *Arnot v United African Lands Ltd* [1901] 1 Ch 518, CA.
8 *R v St Pancras (Vestrymen)* (1839) 11 Ad & El 15.
9 *Pender v Lushington* (1877) 6 ChD 70; *Young v South African and Australian Exploration and Development Syndicate* [1896] 2 Ch 268; *Re Indian Zoedone Co* (1884) 26 ChD 70, CA.
10 Cf, however, para 672 post.
11 See *Re R E Jones Ltd* (1933) 50 TLR 31 (reduction of capital and conversion of preference into ordinary shares; show of hands, and poll).
12 See the Companies Act 1985 s 292 and para 546 ante.

672. Poll. At common law a person entitled to vote at a meeting has a right to demand a poll[1], and a provision contained in a company's articles[2] limiting this right is void in so far as it would have the effect either:

(1) of excluding the right to demand a poll at a general meeting on any question other than the election of the chairman of the meeting or the adjournment of the meeting; or

(2) of making ineffective a demand for a poll on any such question which is made either:

    (a) by not less than five members having the right to vote at the meeting; or

    (b) by a member or members representing not less than one-tenth of the total voting rights of all the members having the right to vote at the meeting; or

    (c) by a member or members holding[3] shares in the company conferring a right to vote at the meeting, being shares on which an aggregate sum has been paid up equal to not less than one-tenth of the total sum paid up on all the shares conferring that right[4].

For these purposes a proxy has the same right to demand or join in demanding a poll as the member he represents[5] as also has the representative of a corporation which is a member of the company[6]. Any such right should be exercised immediately after the declaration of the chairman on the result of the show of hands[7]; where the articles provide that a resolution is to be decided on a show of hands unless a poll is demanded 'before or on the declaration' of the result of the show of hands[8], a poll may be validly demanded without going through the formality of a show of hands[9]. The demand may be made privately to the chairman and by him communicated to the meeting[10]. If the chairman refuses a poll on a motion for adjournment which he has declared carried, the court will not interfere[11]. Unless the articles state the place and time for taking the poll[12], the chairman may direct the manner of taking it[13]; but, where a poll is required to be taken 'immediately at the meeting', the poll must be taken as soon as practicable in all the circumstances[14]. If the articles contemplate voting on the poll in person, the chairman cannot direct the votes to be taken by means of voting papers[15].

Where two resolutions before a meeting have been separately voted upon and a poll has been demanded, each must be put to the poll separately[16]; but resolutions may be put en bloc if there is a right to demand a poll and no member objects[17]. If after a rightful demand for a poll the poll is not taken, the resolution is void[18]. A poll is part of the meeting, and, for the purpose of taking it, the meeting continues until the poll is closed[19].

In a poll of members of a company present at a meeting there is no confidentiality which prevents the company from knowing how votes are cast[20].

1 *R v Wimbledon Local Board* (1882) 8 QBD 459, CA; *Campbell v Maund* (1836) 5 Ad & El 865. As to the demand for a poll in the case of extraordinary or special resolutions see para 685 post; and as to the adjournment of a meeting for the taking of a poll see para 669 ante.

2 See the Companies (Tables A to F) Regulations 1985, SI 1985/805, Schedule, Table A art 46. As to the statutory right of a single member of a private company to demand a poll on a resolution to sanction payment out of its capital for the purchase of its own shares see the Companies Act 1985 s 174(3); paras 235, 670 note 1 ante.

3 This will include joint holders of the specified number: *Siemens Bros & Co Ltd v Burns* [1918] 2 Ch 324, CA.

4 Companies Act 1985 s 373(1). The articles may extend the right to demand a poll (see the Companies (Tables A to F) Regulations 1985 Schedule, Table A art 46 (cited in para 670 note 1 ante)); and, where such a power is given to the chairman of the meeting, it is not a personal right to be exercised according to his wishes, but one to be exercised so as to ascertain the real sense of the meeting (*Second Consolidated Trust Ltd v Ceylon Amalgamated Tea and Rubber Estates Ltd* [1943] 2 All ER 567).

5 See the Companies Act 1985 s 373(2) and para 674 post.

6 See ibid s 375(2) and para 678 post.

7 *Campbell v Maund* (1836) 5 Ad & El 865 at 881, Exch.

8 Ie as in the Companies (Tables A to F) Regulations 1985 Schedule, Table A art 46.

9 *Holmes v Lord Keyes* [1959] Ch 199, [1958] 2 All ER 129, CA.

10 *Re Phoenix Electric Light and Power Co* (1883) 31 WR 398.

11 *MacDougall v Gardiner* (1875) 1 ChD 13, CA; *Foss v Harbottle* (1843) 2 Hare 461.

12 *Re British Flax Producers' Co Ltd* (1889) 60 LT 215.

13 *Re Chillington Iron Co* (1885) 29 ChD 159.

14 *Jackson v Hamlyn* [1953] Ch 577, [1953] 1 All ER 887.

15 *McMillan v Le Roi Mining Co Ltd* [1906] 1 Ch 331.

16 *Blair Open Hearth Furnace Co Ltd v Reigart* (1913) 29 TLR 449; cf *Patent Wood Keg Syndicate Ltd v Pearse* [1906] WN 164.

17 *Re R E Jones Ltd* (1933) 50 TLR 31. This is subject to the qualification mentioned in para 671 text to note 12 ante.

18 *R v Cooper* (1870) LR 5 QB 457.

19 *Shaw v Tati Concessions Ltd* [1913] 1 Ch 292; *Spiller v Mayo (Rhodesia) Development Co (1908) Ltd* [1926] WN 78; *Jackson v Hamlyn* [1953] Ch 577, [1953] 1 All ER 887; *Holmes v Lord Keyes* [1959] Ch 199, [1958] 2 All ER 129, CA.

20 *Haarhaus & Co GmbH v Law Debenture Trust Corpn plc* [1988] BCLC 640.

673. Voting by members entitled to a number of votes. On a poll taken at a meeting of a company, or a meeting of any class of members of a company[1], a member entitled to more than one vote need not, if he votes, use all his votes or cast all the votes he uses in the same way[2].

1 See para 1451 post.
2 Companies Act 1985 s 374. This is an important right for shareholders who may, as trustees or otherwise, hold shares for different persons, some of whom may wish their shares to be voted one way and some another way (or not at all).

674. Voting by proxy. There is no common law right on the part of a member to vote by proxy[1], but, by statute, any member of a company entitled to attend and vote at a meeting of it, including a meeting of any class of members[2], is entitled to appoint another person, whether a member or not, as his proxy to attend and vote instead of him[3]; and a proxy appointed to attend and vote instead of a member of a private company also has the same right as the member to speak at the meeting[4]. Unless the articles provide to the contrary, however, this provision does not apply in the case of a company not having a share capital, nor may a member of a private company appoint more than one proxy to attend on the same occasion[5].

Unless the articles otherwise provide, proxies are not entitled to vote except on a poll[6]. The instrument appointing a proxy to vote at a meeting is, however, deemed to confer authority to demand, or join in demanding, a poll, and, so far as the statutory rights are concerned[7], a demand by a person as proxy for a member is the same as a demand by the member[8]. A vote by a proxy holder 'for self and proxies' is good for all the votes he represents[9].

The form of proxy is generally given in the articles[10]. When attestation is required, a proxy holder cannot be the attesting witness to his own proxy form[11]. Where the article setting out the form of proxy is merely directory, the fact that the form refers to a particular meeting does not prevent the execution of a general form of proxy[12]. The proxy form, when signed by the member, may have blanks for the date of execution and the day of the meeting provided that some person duly authorised by him fills in the blanks[13].

Where the articles require that the instrument of proxy of a corporation must be under its common seal, this requirement only applies to such corporations as have a common seal[14].

In cases where the articles may and do provide that a proxy must be a member, a proxy paper directed to any member of a named firm is good, although at the date of the proxy the person who eventually used the proxy was not a member of the firm or of the company[15].

1 *Harben v Phillips* (1883) 23 ChD 14 at 35, CA.
2 Companies Act 1985 s 372(7).
3 This right is to be notified in the notice convening the meeting: see para 664 ante.
4 Companies Act 1985 s 372(1).
5 Ibid s 372(2)(a), (b).
6 Ibid s 372(2)(c).
7 See para 672 ante.
8 Companies Act 1985 s 373(2).
9 *Foerster v Newlands (West Griqualand) Diamond Mines Ltd* (1902) 18 TLR 497.
10 See the Companies (Tables A to F) Regulations 1985, SI 1985/805, Schedule, Table A arts 60, 61; and para 670 note 1 ante; and see *Re Waxed Papers Ltd* [1937] 2 All ER 481, CA (where the form of proxy

enabled the holder to vote as and when he chose); *Oliver v Dalgleish* [1963] 3 All ER 330, [1963] 1 WLR 1274 (proxy not invalidated by misprint or palpable mistake on face of instrument of proxy). As to the obligations of a company which has obtained admission to the Official List of the Stock Exchange in respect of proxies see the *Listing Rules* rr 9.26, 13.28, 13.29. As to the *Listing Rules* generally see para 282 ante.

11 *Re Parrott, ex p Cullen* [1891] 2 QB 151.
12 *Isaacs v Chapman* (1915) 32 TLR 183.
13 *Sadgrove v Bryden* [1907] 1 Ch 318, following *Ernest v Loma Gold Mines Ltd* [1896] 2 Ch 572 (affd [1897] 1 Ch 1, CA); and see *Re Lancaster, ex p Lancaster* (1877) 5 ChD 911, CA.
14 *Colonial Gold Reef Ltd v Free State Rand Ltd* [1914] 1 Ch 382. A company need no longer have a common seal: see the Companies Act 1985 s 36A(3) (as added) and para 1130 post.
15 *Bombay-Burmah Trading Corpn v Dorabji Cursetji Shroff* [1905] AC 213, PC.

675. Lodging proxies. It is usual to provide in the articles that a proxy should be lodged a specified time before the meeting or adjourned meeting[1] at which it is proposed to be used[2]. A provision contained in the articles is void in so far as it would have the effect of requiring the instrument appointing a proxy, or any other document necessary to show the validity of or otherwise relating to the appointment of a proxy, to be received by the company or any other person more than 48 hours before a meeting or adjourned meeting in order that the appointment may be effective[3].

1 As to what are not adjourned meetings for the purposes of determining the validity of proxies see the cases cited in para 669 notes 6–8 ante.
2 Cf the Companies (Tables A to F) Regulations 1985, SI 1985/805, Schedule, Table A art 62: see para 670 note 1 ante.
3 Companies Act 1985 s 372(5). This provision negatives the effect of the decision in *McLaren v Thomson* [1917] 2 Ch 261, CA. See, however, *Jackson v Hamlyn* [1953] Ch 577, [1953] 1 All ER 887 (as to a resumed meeting).

676. Issue of proxies at company's expense. The directors may pay out of the company's funds the cost of printing and stamping proxy papers and of posting them to the members, if, in so doing, they are acting in good faith in the interests of the company[1]. If for the purpose of any meeting of a company invitations to appoint as proxy a person or one of a number of persons specified in the invitations are issued at the company's expense to some only of the members entitled to be sent a notice of the meeting and to vote at it by proxy, every officer of the company who knowingly and wilfully authorises or permits their issue in that manner is liable on summary conviction to a fine not exceeding one-fifth of the statutory maximum; but an officer is not so liable by reason only of the issue to a member at his request in writing of a form of appointment naming the proxy, or of a list of persons willing to act as proxy, if the form or list is available on request in writing to every member entitled to vote at the meeting by proxy[2].

1 *Peel v London and North Western Rly Co* [1907] 1 Ch 5, CA (a case relating to a statutory company, where the proxies were for one particular meeting only and would not now require a stamp), overruling on this point *Studdert v Grosvenor* (1886) 33 ChD 528. See para 679 post.
2 Companies Act 1985 s 372(6), 730, Sch 24. For the meaning of 'the statutory maximum' see para 1161 post. As to the obligations of a company which has obtained admission to the Official List of the Stock Exchange in respect of proxies see the *Listing Rules* rr 9.26, 13.28, 13.29. As to the *Listing Rules* generally see para 282 ante.

677. Revocation of proxy. Ordinarily a proxy may be revoked at any time before it is used, and, if two are given, the later one revokes the earlier one. The articles of a company usually provide, however, that a proxy is valid notwithstanding its revocation unless notice of the revocation is received before the meeting at which it is used[1]. Under such a provision, where the meeting is adjourned for the purpose solely of taking a poll, notice of the revocation must be given before the original meeting[2]. A shareholder by attending in person at such an adjourned meeting and voting thereat revokes a proxy given by him[3].

1 See the Companies (Tables A to F) Regulations 1985, SI 1985/805, Schedule, Table A art 63.
2 *Spiller v Mayo (Rhodesia) Development Co (1908) Ltd* [1926] WN 78. This decision proceeded on the ground that, where there is a continuation of a meeting at a subsequent date for the purpose of taking a poll, it is all one meeting (*Cousins v International Brick Co Ltd* [1931] 2 Ch 90 at 99, CA per Lord Hanworth MR); but it may be otherwise if the meeting is adjourned for other purposes. As to adjourned meetings see para 696 ante.
3 *Cousins v International Brick Co Ltd* [1931] 2 Ch 90, CA.

678. Corporation representatives. A corporation, whether or not a company within the meaning of the Companies Act 1985[1], may:

(1) if it is a member of another corporation, being such a company, by resolution of its directors or other governing body[2], authorise such person as it thinks fit to act as its representative at any meeting of the company or at any meeting of any class of members of the company[3];

(2) if it is a creditor, including a holder of debentures, of another corporation, being such a company, by resolution of its directors or other governing body authorise such person as it thinks fit to act as its representative at any meeting of creditors of the company held in pursuance of the 1985 Act or of rules made under it, or in pursuance of the provisions contained in any debenture or trust deed, as the case may be[4].

A person so authorised is entitled to exercise the same powers on behalf of the corporation which he represents as that corporation could exercise if it were an individual shareholder, creditor or debenture holder of the other company[5].

The right to vote in such a case depends on whether the resolution was properly passed and not on the sufficiency of the evidence of its passing tendered at the meeting[6].

1 The extension of the provision to cover foreign companies negatives the effect of the decision in *Blair Open Hearth Furnace Ltd v Reigart* (1913) 108 LT 665.
2 A liquidator may be the 'governing body' of a company at the appropriate time: see *Hillman v Crystal Bowl Amusements Ltd* [1973] 1 All ER 379, [1973] 1 WLR 162, CA.
3 Companies Act 1985 s 375(1)(a).
4 Ibid s 375(1)(b). For this purpose, the Companies Act 1985 is to be read as including certain provisions of the Insolvency Act 1986, and the Company Directors Disqualification Act 1986: see para 20 text to note 12 and note 12 ante.
5 Companies Act 1985 s 375(2).
6 *Colonial Gold Reef Ltd v Free State Rand Ltd* [1914] 1 Ch 382.

679. Stamp duty. An ordinary proxy paper or a power of attorney to vote at one or more meetings or any adjournment of them is not liable to stamp duty[1].

1 Finance Act 1985 s 85(1), Sch 24 para (g).

D. RESOLUTIONS

680. Kinds of resolutions. Resolutions[1] are of four kinds: ordinary resolutions[2]; extraordinary resolutions[3]; special resolutions[4]; and elective resolutions[5]. In addition certain resolutions require special notice[6].

Where a poll is held, the date of the resolution is that on which the result of the poll is announced[7].

1 A company which has obtained admission to the Official List of the Stock Exchange must forward to the Company Announcements Office six copies of all resolutions passed by the company, other than resolutions concerning ordinary business at an annual general meeting, without delay after the relevant general meeting: *Listing Rules* r 9.31(b). As to the *Listing Rules* generally see para 282 ante.
2 See para 681 post.
3 See para 682 post.
4 See para 683 post.
5 See para 686 post.
6 See para 687 post.
7 *Holmes v Lord Keyes* [1959] Ch 199, [1958] 2 All ER 129, CA.

681. Ordinary resolutions. An ordinary resolution is one which is passed when a bare majority of votes is sufficient. An ordinary resolution is sufficient to effect any transaction which is within the powers of the company and is not required, either by the articles or the Companies Act 1985, to be effected in some other manner.

682. Extraordinary resolutions. A resolution is an extraordinary resolution when it has been passed by a majority of not less than three-fourths of such members as, being entitled to do so, vote in person or, where proxies are allowed, by proxy, at a general meeting of which notice specifying the intention to propose the resolution as an extraordinary resolution has been duly given[1].

1 Companies Act 1985 s 378(1). For these purposes, notice of a meeting is deemed to be duly given and the meeting to be duly held when the notice is given and the meeting held in the manner provided by the 1985 Act or the company's articles: s 378(6). It is apprehended that an article which requires a larger majority than that required by s 378(1) is not valid, at any rate as regards matters required by the Companies Act 1985 to be effected by special resolution: see *Ayre v Skelsey's Adamant Cement Co Ltd* (1904) 20 TLR 587; affd on other grounds (1905) 21 TLR 464, CA.

Where an extraordinary resolution is proposed to be passed, notice of the intention to propose it as an extraordinary resolution must be given: see *McConnell v E Prill & Co Ltd* [1916] 2 Ch 57. It was held under the Companies (Consolidation) Act 1908 s 69 (repealed) that, in the case of a special as opposed to an extraordinary resolution, the notice need not specify that the resolution was a special resolution: see *Re Penarth Pontoon Shipway and Ship Repairing Co Ltd* (1911) 56 Sol Jo 124; see further *Re North of Scotland and Orkney and Shetland Steam Navigation Co Ltd* 1920 SC 94. The provisions of the Companies Act 1985 s 378 (as amended) require specification of the actual nature of the resolution to be made in the notice in both cases; but it would seem that such notice may still be dispensed with under exceptional circumstances: see *Re Oxted Motor Co Ltd* [1921] 3 KB 32.

It has been held that a notice of a meeting to pass an extraordinary winding-up resolution should expressly state the substance of the resolution: see para 2702 post.

683. Special resolutions. A resolution is a special resolution when it has been passed by such a majority as is required for the passing of an extraordinary resolution at a general meeting of which not less than 21 days' notice[1] specifying the intention to propose the resolution as a special resolution[2] has been duly given[3]. If, however, it is so agreed by a majority in number of the members having the right to attend and vote at any such meeting, being a majority together holding not less than 95% in nominal value of the shares giving that right, or, in the case of a company not having a share capital, together representing not less than 95% of the total voting rights at that meeting of all the members, a resolution may be proposed and passed as a special resolution at a meeting of which less than 21 days' notice has been given[4].

A private company[5] may elect by elective resolution[6] that the above provisions shall have effect in relation to the company as if for the references to 95% there were substituted references to such lesser percentage, but not less than 90%, as may be specified in the resolution or subsequently determined by the company in general meeting[7].

To be valid, the resolution passed at the meeting must be the same as that specified in the notice convening it, both in form and in substance[8].

1 The days must be clear days exclusive of the day of service, or the day deemed by the articles to be the day of service, and the day on which the meeting is to be held; the articles cannot alter the statutory period: *Re Hector Whaling Ltd* [1936] Ch 208. See also the cases cited in para 660 note 1 ante.
2 As to the notice specifying the intention see para 682 note 1 ante.
3 Companies Act 1985 s 378(2). As to the term 'duly' see para 682 note 1 ante. For examples of powers exercisable only by special resolution see para 1091 post.
4 Ibid s 378(3) (amended by the Companies Act 1989 s 115(3)). The persons who agree to a resolution being passed on short notice must appreciate that it is being passed on short notice and agree to its being so passed with that consideration in their minds: *Re Pearce, Duff & Co Ltd* [1960] 3 All ER 222, [1960] 1 WLR 1014.
5 For the meaning of 'private company' see para 82 ante.
6 Ie in accordance with the Companies Act 1985 s 379A (as added): see para 686 post.
7 Ibid s 378(3) (as amended: see note 4 supra).
8 *Re Moorgate Mercantile Holdings Ltd* [1980] 1 All ER 40, [1980] 1 WLR 227.

684. Chairman's declaration that resolution is carried. At any meeting at which an extraordinary resolution or a special resolution is submitted to be passed, a declaration by the chairman that the resolution is carried is, unless a poll is demanded, conclusive evidence of the fact without proof of the number or proportion of the votes recorded in favour of or against the resolution[1], but any formalities, such as the showing of hands, must be complied with, even on an unopposed motion[2].

1 Companies Act 1985 s 378(4). See also para 671 ante.
2 *Re Citizens' Theatre* 1946 SC 14.

685. Poll to pass special or extraordinary resolution. A poll[1] is effectively demanded if demanded by such number of members for the time being entitled under the articles to vote at the meeting as may be specified in the articles[2]. In computing the majority on a poll demanded on the question that such a resolution be passed, reference must be had to the number of votes cast for and against the resolution[3].

1 It would seem that in cases where the Companies Act 1985 demands the passing of a special resolution, the provisions of it are sufficiently complied with if a special resolution is passed on a show of hands even though by the articles it is provided that such resolution must be passed as the result of a poll: *Etheridge v Central Uruguay Northern Extension Rly Co* [1913] 1 Ch 425.
2 For the statutory provisions see para 672 ante.
3 Companies Act 1985 s 378(5).

686. Elective resolutions of private company. An election by a private company[1] for the purposes of:

(1) the duration of an authority to allot shares[2];

(2) dispensing with laying accounts and reports before a general meeting[3];

(3) dispensing with the holding of annual general meetings[4];

(4) the majority required to authorise short notice of a meeting[5]; or

(5) dispensing with the appointment of auditors annually[6],

must be made by resolution (an 'elective resolution') of the company in general meeting in accordance with the following provisions[7].

An elective resolution is not effective unless:

(a) at least 21 days' notice in writing is given of the meeting, stating that an elective resolution is to be proposed and stating the terms of the resolution; and

(b) the resolution is agreed to at the meeting, in person or by proxy, by all the members entitled to attend and vote at the meeting[8].

The company may revoke an elective resolution by passing an ordinary resolution[9] to that effect[10].

An elective resolution ceases to have effect if the company is re-registered as a public company[11].

An elective resolution may be passed or revoked in accordance with the above provisions, and the above provisions[12] have effect, notwithstanding any contrary provision in the company's articles of association[13].

The Secretary of State may by regulations make provision enabling private companies to elect by elective resolution[14] to dispense with compliance with such requirements of the Companies Act 1985 as may be specified in the regulations, being requirements which appear to the Secretary of State to relate primarily to the internal administration and procedure of companies[15]. The regulations may:

(i) add to, amend or repeal provisions of that Act and may provide for any such provision to have effect, where an election is made, subject to such adaptations and modifications as appear to the Secretary of State to be appropriate[16];

(ii) make different provision for different cases and may contain such supplementary, incidental and transitional provisions as appear to the Secretary of State to be appropriate[17].

1 For the meaning of 'private company' see para 82 ante.

2 Ie for the purposes of the Companies Act 1985 s 80A (as added): see para 448 ante.

3 Ie for the purposes of ibid 252 (as substituted): see para 923 post.

4 Ie for the purposes of ibid s 366A (as added): see para 659 ante.

5 Ie for the purposes of ibid s 369(4) (as amended) (see para 664 ante) or s 378(3) (as amended) (see para 683 ante).

6 Ie for the purposes of ibid s 386 (as substituted): see para 1030 post.

7 Ibid s 379A(1) (added by the Companies Act 1989 s 116(1),(2)).

8 Companies Act 1985 s 379A(2) (added by the Companies Act 1989 s 116(1),(2)).

9 As to ordinary resolutions see para 681 ante.

10 Companies Act 1985 s 379A(3) (added by the Companies Act 1989 s 116(1),(2)).

11 Companies Act 1985 s 379A(4) (added by the Companies Act 1989 s 116(1),(2)).

12 Ie the Companies Act 1985 s 379A(1) (as added): see supra.

13 Ibid s 379A(5) (added by the Companies Act 1989 s 116(1),(2)).

14 Ie in accordance with the Companies Act 1985 s 379A (as added): see supra.

15 Companies Act 1989 s 117(1). Any such regulations must be made by statutory instrument (s 117(4)); and no regulations may be so made unless a draft of the instrument containing the regulations has been laid before Parliament and approved by a resolution of each House (s 117(5)). At the date at which this volume states the law no such regulations had been made.

16 Ibid s 117(2).

17 Ibid s 117(3).

687. Resolutions requiring special notice. Where, by any provision of the Companies Act 1985, special notice of a resolution is required, the resolution is not effective unless notice of the intention to move it has been given to the company at least 28 days before the meeting at which it is moved[1]; and the company must give its members notice of any such resolution at the same time and in the same manner as it gives notice of the meeting or, if that is not practicable, must give them notice either by advertisement in a newspaper having an appropriate circulation or in any other mode allowed by the company's articles, at least 21 days before the meeting[2]. This provision does not confer upon an individual member the right to compel inclusion of an item in the agenda; it merely deals with the question of notice to the members[3]. If, after notice of the intention to move such a resolution has been given to the company, a meeting is called for a date 28 days or less after the notice has been given, the notice is deemed properly given, though not given within the time required[4].

1 Companies Act 1985 s 379(1).
2 Ibid s 379(2). For examples of resolutions requiring special notice see s 388 (as substituted) (filling casual vacancies in the office of auditor: para 1032 post), s 303 (removal of directors: para 639 ante), s 293 (reappointment of over-age director: para 552 ante).
3 *Pedley v Inland Revenue Waterways Association Ltd* [1977] 1 All ER 209.
4 Companies Act 1985 s 379(3). See *Fenning v Fenning Environmental Products Ltd* [1982] LS Gaz R 803.

688. Circulation of members' resolutions. On the requisition in writing of such number of members of the company as is specified below and, unless the company otherwise resolves, at the expense of the requisitionists, it is the duty of a company:
(1) to give to members entitled to receive notice of the next annual general meeting notice of any resolution which may properly be moved and is intended to be moved at that meeting[1];
(2) to circulate to members entitled to have notice of any general meeting sent to them any statement of not more than 1,000 words with respect to the matter referred to in any proposed resolution or the business to be dealt with at that meeting[2].
The number of members necessary for such a requisition is:
(a) any number of members representing not less than one-twentieth of the total voting rights of all the members having at the date of the requisition a right to vote at the meeting to which the requisition relates[3]; or
(b) not less than 100 members holding shares in the company on which there has been paid up an average sum, per member, of not less than £100[4].
Notice of any such resolution must be given, and any such statement must be circulated, to members of the company entitled to have notice of the meeting sent to them, by serving a copy of the resolution or statement on each such member in any manner permitted for service of notice of the meeting[5]; and notice of any such resolution must be given to any other member by giving notice of the general effect of the resolution in any manner permitted for giving him notice of meetings of the company[6]. For compliance with the above provisions, the copy must be served, or notice of the effect of the resolution given, as the case may be, in the same manner and, so far as practicable, at the same time as notice of the meeting; and, where it is not practicable for it to be served or given at the same time, it must be served or given as soon as practicable thereafter[7].
A company is not, however, bound to give notice of any resolution or to circulate any statement under the above provisions unless:

(i) a copy of the requisition signed by the requisitionists[8] (or two or more copies which between them contain the signatures of all the requisitionists) is deposited at the registered office of the company either, in the case of a requisition requiring notice of a resolution, not less than six weeks before the meeting, or, in the case of any other requisition, not less than one week before the meeting[9]; and

(ii) there is deposited or tendered with the requisition a sum reasonably sufficient to meet the company's expenses in giving effect to it[10].

Similarly, the company is not bound to circulate any statement if, on the application[11] either of the company or of any other person who claims to be aggrieved, the court is satisfied that these rights are being abused to secure needless publicity for defamatory matter; and the court may order the company's costs on such an application to be paid in whole or in part by the requisitionists, notwithstanding that they are not parties to the application[12].

Notwithstanding anything in the company's articles, the business which may be dealt with at an annual general meeting includes any resolution of which notice has been given in accordance with the above provisions; and, for this purpose, notice is deemed to have been so given, notwithstanding the accidental omission, in giving it, of one or more members[13].

In the event of default in complying with the above provisions, every officer of the company who is in default is liable on conviction on indictment to a fine or on summary conviction to a fine not exceeding the statutory maximum[14].

1 Companies Act 1985 s 376(1)(a).
2 Ibid s 376(1)(b).
3 Ibid s 376(2)(a).
4 Ibid s 376(2)(b). In the case of shares denominated in a currency other than pounds sterling, the court must find the appropriate date on which to effect the necessary conversion into pounds sterling: *Re Scandinavian Bank Group plc* [1988] Ch 87 at 102-104, [1987] 2 All ER 70 at 76, 77 per Harman J.
5 Companies Act 1985 s 376(3). See also para 660 ante.
6 Ibid s 376(4).
7 Ibid s 376(5).
8 In the case of joint shareholders, all must sign the requisition: *Patent Wood Keg Syndicate Ltd v Pearse* [1906] WN 164.
9 Companies Act 1985 s 377(1)(a). If, however, after a copy of a requisition requiring notice of a resolution has been deposited at the registered office of the company, an annual general meeting is called for a date six weeks or less after the copy has been deposited, the copy (though not deposited within the time required by s 377(1)) is deemed to have been properly deposited for the purposes of s 377(1): s 377(2).
10 Ibid s 377(1)(b).
11 The application is made by originating summons in the expedited form: RSC Ord 102 r 2(1),(2).
12 Companies Act 1985 s 377(3).
13 Ibid s 376(6).
14 Ibid ss 376(7), 730, Sch 24. For the meaning of 'officer who is in default' and 'the statutory maximum' see para 1161 post.

689. Valid and invalid resolutions passed together. If an ultra vires or invalid resolution is combined, as part of the same transaction, with a resolution otherwise valid, the whole transaction is void[1]; but, where the two resolutions are separate and distinct, the invalidity of one will not affect the validity of the other[2].

1 *Re Imperial Bank of China, India and Japan* (1866) 1 Ch App 339 at 347.
2 Ie as in *Thomson v Henderson's Transvaal Estates Ltd* [1908] 1 Ch 765, CA (where a special reconstruction scheme was bad, but the resolution to wind up was good), following *Cleve v Financial Corpn* (1873) LR 16 Eq 363 at 378, and *Re Irrigation Co of France, ex p Fox* (1871) 6 Ch App 176.

690. Amendments to resolutions. Any amendment fairly arising on a resolution which is specified in the notice of meeting and within the scope of the notice may be proposed and passed at the meeting, and a chairman has no right to refuse to put such an amendment[1].

It is usual for a resolution or an amended resolution to be moved by one voter and seconded by another; but, if the chairman chooses, he may put it to the vote without these formalities[2].

1   *Torbock v Lord Westbury* [1902] 2 Ch 871; *Betts & Co Ltd v Macnaghten* [1910] 1 Ch 430; *Henderson v Bank of Australasia* (1890) 45 ChD 330, CA (where the chairman refused to put the amendment and the resolution was set aside).

     As regards extraordinary and special resolutions, having regard to the terms of the Companies Act 1985 s 378(1),(2) (see paras 682, 683 ante), the terms of the resolution have to be specified in the notice calling the meeting, so that there must be complete identity between the substance of such a resolution as passed and as notified: *Re Moorgate Mercantile Holdings Ltd* [1980] 1 All ER 40, [1980] 1 WLR 227.

2   *Re Horbury Bridge Coal, Iron and Waggon Co* (1879) 11 ChD 109 at 117, CA.

691. Registration of copies of certain resolutions and agreements. Within 15 days after any of the following resolutions or agreements is passed or made, a copy thereof, either printed or in some other form approved by the registrar, must be forwarded to the registrar of companies and recorded by him[1]:

(1) special resolutions;

(2) extraordinary resolutions;

(3) an elective resolution or a resolution revoking such a resolution;

(4) resolutions or agreements which have been agreed to by all the members of a company but which, if not so agreed to, would not have been effective for their purpose unless, as the case may be, they had been passed as special resolutions or as extraordinary resolutions;

(5) resolutions or agreements which have been agreed to by all the members of some class of shareholders but which, if not so agreed to, would not have been effective for their purpose unless they had been passed by some particular majority or otherwise in some particular manner, and all resolutions or agreements which effectively bind all the members of any class of shareholders though not agreed to by all those members;

(6) a resolution passed by the directors of a company in compliance with a direction[2] by the Secretary of State to change its name;

(7) a resolution[3] of a company to give, vary, revoke or renew an authority to the directors to allot relevant securities;

(8) a resolution[4] of the directors to alter the company's memorandum on the company ceasing to be a public company following acquisition of its own shares;

(9) a resolution[5] conferring, varying, revoking or renewing authority to a company to make market purchases of its own shares;

(10) a resolution[6] for voluntary winding up passed when the period, if any, fixed for the duration of the company by the articles expires, or the event, if any, occurs on the occurrence of which the articles provide that the company is to be dissolved;

(11) a resolution[7] passed by the directors of an old public company that it should be re-registered as a public company;

(12) a resolution[8] of the directors that title to shares of a class issued or to be issued by the company may be evidenced and transferred without a written instrument; and

(13) a resolution[9] of a company preventing or reversing a resolution of the directors that title to shares of a class issued or to be issued by the company may be evidenced and transferred without a written instrument[10].

If a company fails to comply with the above provisions, the company, and every officer of it who is in default, is liable on summary conviction to a fine not exceeding one-fifth of the statutory maximum and, on conviction after continued contravention, to a daily default fine not exceeding one-fiftieth of the statutory maximum[11]. For these purposes, a liquidator is deemed to be an officer of the company[12].

1 Companies Act 1985 s 380(1).
2 Ie under ibid s 31(2): see para 114 ante.
3 Ie pursuant to ibid s 80 (as amended): see para 447 ante.
4 Ie pursuant to ibid s 147(2): see para 366 ante.
5 Ie pursuant to ibid s 166: see para 226 ante.
6 Ie under the Insolvency Act 1986 s 84(1)(a): see para 2702 post.
7 Ie pursuant to the Companies Consolidation (Consequential Provisions) Act 1985 s 2(1): see para 133 ante.
8 Ie a resolution passed by virtue of the Uncertificated Securities Regulations 1995, SI 1995/3272, reg 16(2): see MONEY.
9 Ie a resolution passed by virtue of ibid reg 16(6): see MONEY.
10 Companies Act 1985 s 380(4) (amended by the Insolvency Act 1986 s 439(1), Sch 13 Pt I; the Companies Act 1989 s 116(1),(3); the Uncertificated Securities Regulations 1995 reg 40(3))); Insolvency Act 1986 s 84(3) (cited in para 2698 post). It seems that text head (4) supra gives recognition to the principle laid down in *Parker and Cooper Ltd v Reading* [1926] Ch 975, that, where all the corporators assent, the formalities required for the passing of a resolution need not be complied with. See further para 696 post.
11 Companies Act 1985 ss 380(5), 730, Sch 24. For the meaning of 'officer who is in default', 'the statutory maximum' and 'daily default fine' see para 1161 post.
12 Ibid s 380(7).

692. Copies to be annexed to articles and sent to shareholders. Where articles have been registered, a copy of every such resolution or agreement[1] for the time being in force must be embodied in or annexed to every copy of the articles issued after the passing of the resolution or the making of the agreement[2]; and, where articles have not been registered, a printed copy of every such resolution or agreement must be forwarded to any member at his request on payment of five pence or such less sum as the company may direct[3].

If a company fails to comply with the above provisions, the company, and every officer of it who is in default, is liable on summary conviction to a fine not exceeding one-fifth of the statutory maximum on each occasion when copies are issued, or, as the case may be, requested[4]. For these purposes, a liquidator is deemed to be an officer of the company[5].

1 Ie every resolution or agreement to which the Companies Act 1985 s 380(1) applies: see para 691 ante.
2 Ibid s 380(2).
3 Ibid s 380(3).
4 Ibid ss 380(6), 730, Sch 24. For the meaning of 'officer who is in default' and 'the statutory maximum' see para 1161 post.
5 Ibid s 380(7).

693. Privilege for newspaper reports of meetings. A fair and accurate newspaper report of the proceedings at a general meeting of any company, not being a private company, is privileged for the purpose of proceedings for defamation unless the publication is proved to have been made with malice[1].

1　See the Defamation Act 1952 s 7(1), Schedule para 11; para 1155 post; and LIBEL vol 28 para 130.

E. EVIDENCE AS TO MEETINGS

694. Minutes of general meetings. Every company must cause minutes of all proceedings of general meetings to be entered in books kept for that purpose[1]. If the company fails to comply with this provision, the company, and every officer of it who is in default, is liable on summary conviction to a fine not exceeding one-fifth of the statutory maximum and, on conviction after continued contravention, to a daily default fine not exceeding one-fiftieth of the statutory maximum[2]. If purporting to be signed by the chairman of the meeting at which the proceedings were had, or by the chairman of the next succeeding meeting, any such minute is evidence[3] of the proceedings[4]. Where minutes have been so made of the proceedings at any general meeting of the company, then, until the contrary is proved, the meeting is deemed duly held and convened, and all proceedings had at the meeting to have been duly had, and all appointments of directors, managers or liquidators are deemed valid[5]. The chairman's signature need not be written at the meeting[6].

Where a shadow director[7] declares an interest in a contract or proposed contract pursuant to the provisions in that behalf[8], these provisions apply, if it is a specific notice, as if the declaration had been made at the meeting at which, had he been a director, he would have had to make it, and otherwise as if it had been made at the meeting of the directors next following the giving of the notice; and the making of the declaration is in either case deemed to form part of the proceedings at that meeting[9].

1　Companies Act 1985 s 382(1). A collection of loose leaves fastened together between two covers, but readily detachable, is not a 'book' within the meaning of this provision (*Hearts of Oak Assurance Co Ltd v James Flower & Sons* [1936] Ch 76), but may be another method of recording the information in a manner permitted by the Companies Act 1985 s 722(1): see para 378 note 2 ante.
2　Ibid ss 382(5), 730, Sch 24. For the meaning of 'officer who is in default', 'the statutory maximum' and 'daily default fine' see para 1161 post.
3　Ie prima facie evidence: see *Re Indian Zoedone Co* (1884) 26 ChD 70, CA; *Re Llanharry Hematite Iron Oil Co Ltd, Roney's Case, Stock's Case* (1864) 4 De GJ & Sm 426.
4　Companies Act 1985 s 382(2).
5　Ibid s 382(4); and see the Companies (Tables A to F) Regulations 1985, SI 1985/805, Schedule, Table A art 47 which provides that minutes are conclusive evidence of the carrying or losing of a resolution. Where articles provided that the minutes of any meeting, if purporting to be signed by the chairman, 'shall be conclusive evidence without any further proof of the facts therein stated', it was held that (in the absence of fraud) such evidence could not be displaced and was conclusive as between any parties bound by the minutes: see *Kerr v John Mottram Ltd* [1940] Ch 657, [1940] 2 All ER 629.
6　*Re Llanharry Hematite Iron Oil Co Ltd, Roney's Case, Stock's Case* (1864) 4 De GJ & Sm 426 at 432. The minute book may be transcribed or made from rough minutes taken at the time of the meeting: see *Re Jennings* (1851) 1 I Ch R 236; on appeal without touching this point, 1 I Ch R 654.
7　For the meaning of 'shadow director' see para 543 note 1 ante.
8　Ie under the Companies Act 1985 s 317(8): see para 594 ante.
9　Ibid s 382(3).

695. Inspection of minute books. The books containing the minutes of proceedings of any general meeting of a company held on or after 1 November 1929 must be kept at the company's registered office, and must be open to the inspection of any member without charge[1]. The company[2] must make the minute books available for such inspection for not less than two hours during the period between 9 am and 5 pm on each business day[3]; and it must permit a person inspecting the books to copy any information made available for inspection by means of the taking of notes or the transcription of the information[4].

Any member is entitled to be furnished, within seven days after he has made a request in that behalf to the company, with a copy of any such minutes on payment of such fee as may be prescribed[5].

If an inspection so required is refused, or if a copy so required is not sent within the proper time, the company, and every officer of it who is in default, is liable in respect of each offence on summary conviction to a fine not exceeding one-fifth of the statutory maximum[6].

In the case of any such refusal or default, the court may by order compel an immediate inspection of the books in respect of all proceedings of general meetings, or direct that the copies required must be sent to the persons requiring them[7].

1 Companies Act 1985 s 383(1) (amended by the Companies Act 1989 ss 143(9)(a), 212, Sch 24).
2 For the meaning of 'company' see para 229 note 14 ante.
3 Companies (Inspection and Copying of Registers, Indices and Documents) Regulations 1991, SI 1991/1998, reg 3(1),(2)(a). For the meaning of 'business day' see para 229 note 15 ante. As to the power to make regulations see para 230 ante.
4 Ibid reg 3(1),(2)(b). Regulation 3(2)(b) is not, however, to be construed as obliging a company to provide any facilities additional to those provided for the purposes of facilitating inspection: reg 3(3).
5 Companies Act 1985 s 383(3) (amended by the Companies Act 1989 s 143(9)(b), Sch 24). The fee so prescribed is ten pence per 100 words, or part thereof, copied: Companies (Inspection and Copying of Registers, Indices and Documents) Regulations 1991 reg 5, Sch 2 para 3(b).
6 Companies Act 1985 ss 383(4), 730, Sch 24. For the meaning of 'officer who is in default' and 'the statutory maximum' see para 1161 post.
7 Ibid s 383(5). The application is made by way of originating summons in the expedited form: RSC Ord 102 r 2(1),(2). As to the procedure on a summons under RSC Ord 102 see para 390 note 10 ante.

F. DECISIONS REACHED WITHOUT MEETINGS

696. Decisions reached without meetings. The members of a company, as a body, may in general act only through a general meeting[1]. Where each and every shareholder assents to or sanctions an act which is intra vires the company, that will constitute an effective act by the company[2]. It is not necessary for the members to meet together or to give their assent simultaneously[3]. Assent can be oral, in writing or, it seems, by conduct[4]. Further, where it is shown that all members who have a right to attend and vote at a general meeting of the company assent to any matter which a general meeting of the company could carry into effect, that assent is as binding as a resolution in general meeting would be[5]. A similar position obtains in the case of resolutions by classes of members[6].

1 See *Re George Newman & Co Ltd* [1895] 1 Ch 674, CA. As to the various types of resolutions see para 680 et seq ante.
2 *Re Express Engineering Works Ltd* [1920] 1 Ch 466, CA (meeting styled a directors' meeting; all five shareholders present and they could have turned it into a general meeting and transacted the same business; business transacted valid); *Re Oxted Motor Co Ltd* [1921] 3 KB 32 (it was held competent for all the shareholders of the company acting together to waive the statutory formalities required as to notice of intention to propose a resolution as an extraordinary resolution). Quaere whether, in the case of joint holders, the assent of the first-named joint holder is sufficient or whether a second joint holder might challenge such a decision.
   See also the Companies Act 1985 s 380(4)(c),(d),(4) (registration of resolutions or agreements) and para 691 ante. As to written resolutions of private companies see para 697 post; and as to decisions by a sole member see para 700 post.

3 *Parker and Cooper Ltd v Reading* [1926] Ch 975 at 984. See also *Salomon v A Salomon & Co Ltd* [1897] AC 22 at 57 per Lord Davey HL; *Barthels Shewan & Co Ltd v Winnipeg Cigar Co* (1909) 10 WLR 263; *Mid-West Collieries Ltd v McEwen* [1925] SCR 326 (Can SC); *Re Pearce Duff & Co Ltd* [1960] 3 All ER 222, [1960] 1 WLR 1014 (the consent of all ordinary shareholders having been obtained to a special resolution for reduction of capital being treated as valid, and the petition being prosecuted on that footing, the court ought not to hear any such shareholder to say that the resolution was invalid), doubted in *Cane v Jones* [1981] 1 All ER 533, [1980] 1 WLR 1451 (all the corporators of a company acting together can do anything which is intra vires the company); *Roman Hotels Ltd v Desrochers Hotels Ltd* (1977) 69 DLR (3d) 126 (Sask CA).

4 See *Re Bailey, Hay & Co Ltd* [1971] 3 All ER 693, [1971] 1 WLR 1357 (the three corporators who did not vote in favour of the resolution allowed it to be passed with knowledge of their power to stop it and by their subsequent conduct were to be deemed to have assented to it).

5 *Re Duomatic Ltd* [1969] 2 Ch 365, [1969] 1 All ER 161; and see *Re M J Shanley Contracting Ltd (in voluntary liquidation)* (1979) 124 Sol Jo 239.

6 *East v Bennett Bros Ltd* [1911] 1 Ch 163 (there being nothing in the constitution of the company to prevent the whole of the original preference shares being held by one shareholder, the word 'meeting' in the memorandum and articles had to be taken to have been used not in its strict sense but as applicable to the case of a single shareholder; there had been a sufficient compliance with the requirements of the memorandum and articles and the new preference shares had been validly issued).

G. WRITTEN RESOLUTIONS OF PRIVATE COMPANIES

697. In general. Notwithstanding any provision of the company's memorandum and articles, anything which in the case of a private company[1] may be done by resolution of the company in general meeting or by resolution of a meeting of any class of members of the company, may be done, without a meeting and without any previous notice being required, by resolution in writing signed by or on behalf of all the members of the company who at the date of the resolution[2] would be entitled to attend and vote at such meeting[3]. The signatures need not be on a single document provided that each is on a document which accurately states the terms of the resolution[4].

A resolution agreed to in accordance with these provisions has effect as if passed by the company in general meeting or by a meeting of the relevant class of members of the company, as the case may be[5].

A resolution may be agreed to in accordance with these provisions which would otherwise be required to be passed as a special[6], extraordinary[7] or elective[8] resolution[9].

1 For the meaning of 'private company' see para 82 ante.

2 For these purposes, the date of the resolution means when the resolution is signed by or on behalf of the last member to sign: Companies Act 1985 s 381A(3) (added by the Companies Act 1989 s 113(1),(2)). Any reference in any enactment to the date of passing of a resolution is, in relation to a resolution agreed to in accordance with the Companies Act 1985 s 381A (as added), a reference to the date of the resolution, unless s 381B(4) (as added) (see para 698 post) applies, in which case it is to be construed as a reference to the date from which the resolution has effect: s 381A(5) (added by the Companies Act 1989 s 113(1),(2)).

3 Companies Act 1985 ss 381A(1), 381C(1) (added by the Companies Act 1989 s 113(1),(2)). The Companies Act 1985 s 381A (as added) has effect subject to the exceptions specified in s 381A(7), Sch 15A Pt I (para 1) (as added) (see para 639 note 1 ante and para 1047 note 2 post); and, in relation to certain descriptions of resolution under s 381A (as added), the procedural requirements of the Companies Act 1985 have effect with the adaptations specified in Sch 15A Pt II (paras 2-8) (as added) (see paras 224 note 3, 234 note 3, 276 note 13, 462 note 6, 563 note 5, 600 note 5 ante): s 381A(7) (added by the Companies Act 1989 s 113(1),(2)).

Nothing in the Companies Act 1985 s 381A (as added) affects any enactment or rule of law as to (1) things done otherwise than by passing a resolution; or (2) cases in which a resolution is treated as having been passed, or a person is precluded from alleging that a resolution has not been duly passed: s 381C(2) (added by the Companies Act 1989 s 113(1),(2)).

As to the recording of written resolutions see para 699 post.

4 Companies Act 1985 s 381A(2) (added by the Companies Act 1989 s 113(1),(2)).
5 Companies Act 1985 s 381A(4) (added by the Companies Act 1989 s 113(1),(2)). Any reference in any enactment to a meeting at which a resolution is passed or to members voting in favour of a resolution is to be construed accordingly: Companies Act 1985 s 381A(4) (as so added).
6 As to special resolutions see para 683 ante.
7 As to extraordinary resolutions see para 682 ante.
8 As to elective resolutions see para 686 ante.
9 Companies Act 1985 s 381A(6) (added by the Companies Act 1989 s 113(1),(2)).

698. Rights of auditors in relation to written resolution. Notwithstanding any provision of the company's memorandum and articles, a copy of any written resolution proposed to be agreed by the members of a private company[1] must be sent to the company's auditors[2]. If the resolution concerns the auditors as auditors, they may, within seven days from the day on which they receive the copy, give notice to the company stating their opinion that the resolution should be considered by the company in general meeting or, as the case may be, by a meeting of the relevant class of members of the company[3].

A written resolution does not have effect unless:

(1) the auditors notify the company that in their opinion the resolution does not concern them as auditors or does so concern them but need not be considered by the company in general meeting or, as the case may be, by a meeting of the relevant class of members of the company; or

(2) the period for giving a notice[4] expires without any notice having been duly[5] given[6].

A written resolution previously agreed to[7] does not have effect until that notification is given or, as the case may be, that period expires[8].

1 Ie in accordance with the Companies Act 1985 s 381A (as added): see para 697 ante.
2 Ibid ss 381B(1), 381C(1) (added by the Companies Act 1989 s 113(1),(2)). Nothing in the Companies Act 1985 s 381B (as added) affects any enactment or rule of law as to (1) things done otherwise than by passing a resolution; or (2) cases in which a resolution is treated as having been passed, or a person is precluded from alleging that a resolution has not been duly passed: s 381C(2) (added by the Companies Act 1989 s 113(1),(2))
3 Companies Act 1985 s 381B(2) (added by the Companies Act 1989 s 113(1),(2)).
4 Ie under the Companies Act 1985 s 381B(2) (as added): see supra.
5 Ie in accordance with ibid s 381B(2) (as added).
6 Ibid s 381B(3) (added by the Companies Act 1989 s 113(1),(2)).
7 See note 1 supra.
8 Companies Act 1985 s 381B(4) (added by the Companies Act 1989 s 113(1),(2)).

699. Recording of written resolutions. Where a written resolution is agreed to[1] which has effect as if agreed by the company in general meeting, the company must cause a record of the resolution, and of the signatures, to be entered in a book in the same way as minutes of proceedings of a general meeting of the company[2].

Any such record, if purporting to be signed by a director of the company or by the company secretary, is evidence of the proceedings in agreeing to the resolution; and, where a record is so made, then, until the contrary is proved, the requirements of the Companies Act 1985 with respect to those proceedings are deemed to be complied with[3].

1 Ie in accordance with the Companies Act 1985 s 381A (as added): see para 697 ante.
2 Ibid s 382A(1) (added by the Companies Act 1989 s 113(1),(3)). The Companies Act 1985 s 382(5) (see para 694 ante) applies in relation to a failure to comply with s 382A(1) (as so added); and s 383 (as

amended) (see para 695 ante) applies in relation to a record made in accordance with s 382A (as added) as it applies in relation to the minutes of a general meeting: s 382A(3) (added by the Companies Act 1989 s 113(1),(3)). As to minutes of proceedings of a general meeting see para 694 ante.
3 Companies Act 1985 s 382A(2) (added by the Companies Act 1989 s 113(i),(3)).

H. DECISIONS BY SOLE MEMBER

700. Recording of decisions by the sole member. Where a private company[1] limited by shares or by guarantee has only one member and he takes any decision which may be taken by the company in general meeting and which has effect as if agreed by the company in general meeting, he must, unless that decision is taken by way of a written resolution, provide the company with a written record of that decision[2].

If the sole member fails to comply with the above provisions, he is liable on summary conviction to a fine not exceeding level 2 on the standard scale[3].

Failure by the sole member to comply with the above provisions does not affect the validity of any such decision[4].

1 For the meaning of 'private company' see para 82 ante.
2 Companies Act 1985 s 382B(1) (added by the Companies (Single Member Private Limited Companies) Regulations 1992, SI 1992/1699, reg 6(1)). As to single member private limited companies see para 81 ante.
3 Companies Act 1985 s 382B(2) (added by the Companies (Single Member Private Limited Companies) Regulations 1992 reg 6(1)); Companies Act 1985 s 730, Sch 24 (amended by the Companies (Single Member Private Limited Companies) Regulations 1992 reg 6(2)). For the meaning of 'the standard scale' see CRIMINAL LAW vol 11(2) (Reissue) para 808.
4 Companies Act 1985 s 382B(3) (added by the Companies (Single Member Private Limited Companies) Regulations 1992 reg 6(1)).

(vi) Distribution of Profits and Assets

A. LIMITS OF COMPANY'S POWER OF DISTRIBUTION

701. Distributions by company. A company must not make a distribution except out of profits[1] available for the purpose[2]. 'Distribution' means[3] every description of distribution of a company's assets to its members, whether in cash or otherwise, except distribution by way of:

(1) an issue of shares as fully or partly paid bonus shares[4];
(2) the redemption or purchase of any of the company's own shares out of capital (including the proceeds of any fresh issue of shares) or out of unrealised profits[5];
(3) the reduction of share capital by extinguishing or reducing the liability of any of the members on any of the company's shares in respect of share capital not paid up, or by paying off paid up share capital[6]; and
(4) a distribution of assets to members of the company on its winding up[7].

For these purposes a company's profits available for distribution are its accumulated, realised profits, so far as not previously utilised by distribution or capitalisation[8], less its accumulated, realised losses, so far as not previously written off in a reduction or reorganisation of capital duly made, subject to special provisions[9] for investment and other companies[10].

A company must not apply an unrealised profit in paying up debentures, or any amounts unpaid on its issued shares[11].

Where the directors of a company are, after making all reasonable inquiries, unable to determine whether a particular profit made before 22 December 1980[12] is realised or unrealised, they may treat the profit as realised; and, where, after making such inquiries, they are unable to determine whether a particular loss so made is realised or unrealised, they may treat the loss as unrealised[13].

1 For these purposes, references to profits and losses of any description are, respectively, to profits and losses of that description made at any time and, except where the context otherwise requires, are, respectively, to revenue and capital profits and revenue and capital losses: Companies Act 1985 s 280(1),(3).
2 Ibid s 263(1).
3 Ie for the purposes of ibid Pt VIII (ss 263–281) (as amended): see infra and para 702 et seq post. The provisions of Pt VIII (ss 263–281) (as amended) are without prejudice to any enactment or rule of law, or any provision of a company's memorandum or articles, restricting the sums out of which, or the cases in which, a distribution may be made: s 281.
4 As to the issue of bonus shares see para 732 post.
5 Ie in accordance with the Companies Act 1985 Pt V Ch VII (ss 159–181) (as amended): see para 219 et seq ante.
6 As to reduction of capital see para 215 et seq ante.
7 Companies Act 1985 s 263(2). As to distribution in a winding up see para 2563 et seq post.
8 For these purposes, 'capitalisation', in relation to a company's profits, means any of the following operations (whenever carried out): (1) applying the profits in wholly or partly paying up unissued shares in the company to be allotted to members of the company as fully or partly paid bonus shares; or (2) transferring the profits to capital redemption reserve: ibid s 280(1), (2).
9 Ie ibid ss 265, 266 (as amended): see para 703 post.
10 Ibid s 263(3).
11 Ibid s 263(4).
12 Ie the day appointed for the commencement of the Companies Act 1980 Pt III (ss 39–45) (repealed) by the Companies Act 1980 (Commencement No 2) Order 1980, SI 1980/1785.
13 Companies Act 1985 s 263(5).

702. Restriction on distribution of assets. A public company[1] may only make a distribution[2] at any time:

(1) if at that time the amount of its net assets[3] is not less than the aggregate of its called-up share capital[4] and undistributable reserves[5]; and

(2) if, and to the extent that, the distribution does not reduce the amount of those assets to less than that aggregate[6].

These requirements are subject to special provisions[7] for investment and other companies[8].

A public company must not include any uncalled share capital as an asset in any accounts relevant for these provisions[9].

1 For the meaning of 'public company' see para 82 ante.
2 For the meaning of 'distribution' see para 701 ante.
3 For these purposes, 'net assets' means the aggregate of the company's assets less the aggregate of its liabilities; and 'liabilities' includes any provision for liabilities or charges within the Companies Act 1985 s 226(3) (as substituted), Sch 4 para 89 (see para 832 note 24 post): s 264(2). For modifications where a company has prepared accounts in accordance with the special provisions of Pt VII (ss 221–262A) (as amended) relating to banking companies (see para 716 post) see s 279, Sch 11 paras 1, 2 (substituted by the Companies Act 1985 (Bank Account) Regulations 1991, SI 1991/2705, regs 7, 9, Sch 3 para 1); and for modifications where a company has prepared accounts in accordance with the special provisions of the Companies Act 1985 Pt VII (ss 221–262A) (as amended) relating to insurance companies (see para 716 post), see Sch 11 para 7 (substituted by the Companies Act 1985 (Miscellaneous Accounting Amendments) Regulations 1996, SI 1996/189, reg 14(8), Sch 6 paras 1, 2).
4 For the meaning of 'called-up share capital' see para 174 ante.
5 For these purposes, a company's undistributable reserves are (1) the share premium account (see para 188 ante); (2) the capital redemption reserve (see para 231 ante); (3) the amount by which the

company's accumulated, unrealised profits, so far as not previously utilised by capitalisation of a description to which this head (3) applies, exceed its accumulated, unrealised losses, so far as not previously written off in a reduction or reorganisation of capital duly made; and (4) any other reserve which the company is prohibited from distributing by any enactment, other than one contained in the Companies Act 1985 Pt VIII (ss 263–281) (as amended), or by its memorandum or articles: s 264(3). Head (3) supra applies to every description of capitalisation except a transfer of profits of the company to its capital redemption reserve on or after 22 December 1980: s 264(3). As to the significance of that date see para 701 note 12 ante.

6 Ibid s 264(1). No reserve apparently thrown up by any alteration in the accounts due to fluctuations in the rate of exchange required to convert share capital expressed in any currency other than the currency in which the accounts are drawn is a reserve capable of distribution or capitalisation: *Re Scandinavian Bank Group plc* [1988] Ch 87 at 107, [1987] 2 All ER 70 at 79 per Harman J.

7 Ie the Companies Act 1985 ss 265, 266 (as amended): see para 703 post.

8 Ibid s 264(1).

9 Ibid s 264(4).

703. Other distributions by investment companies. Subject to the following provisions, an investment company may, in addition to distributions normally permitted[1], make a distribution at any time out of its accumulated, realised revenue profits so far as not previously utilised by a distribution or capitalisation[2], less its accumulated revenue losses (whether realised or unrealised), so far as not previously written off in a reduction or reorganisation of capital duly made if at that time the amount of its assets is at least equal to one and a half times the aggregate of its liabilities[3], and if, and to the extent that, the distribution does not reduce that amount to less than one and a half times that aggregate[4]. The company must not include any uncalled share capital[5] as an asset in any accounts relevant for these purposes[6].

An investment company may not so make a distribution unless:

(1) its shares are listed on a recognised investment exchange[7] other than an overseas investment exchange[8] and during the relevant period[9] it has not:

    (a) distributed any of its capital profits; or

    (b) applied any unrealised profits or any capital profits (realised or unrealised) in paying up debentures or amounts unpaid on its issued shares[10]; and

(2) it gave to the registrar of companies the requisite notice[11] of the company's intention to carry on business as an investment company before the beginning of the relevant period or, in the case of a company incorporated on or after 22 December 1980[12], as soon as may have been reasonably practicable after the date of its incorporation[13].

For these purposes, 'investment company' means a public company[14] which has given notice in the prescribed form[15] (which has not been revoked) to the registrar of companies of its intention to carry on business as an investment company, and has since the date of that notice complied with the following requirements[16]:

(i) that the business of the company consists of investing its funds mainly in securities, with the aim of spreading investment risk and giving members of the company the benefit of the results of the management of its funds[17];

(ii) that none of the company's holdings in companies, other than those which are for the time being investment companies, represents more than 15% by value of the investing company's investments[18];

(iii) that distribution of the company's capital profits is prohibited by its memorandum or articles of association[19];

(iv) that the company has not retained, otherwise than in compliance with the relevant statutory provisions[20], in respect of any accounting reference period more than 15% of the income it derives from securities[21].

Such notice to the registrar of companies may be revoked at any time by the company on giving notice in the prescribed form[22] to the registrar that it no longer wishes to be an investment company within the meaning of the above provisions; and, on giving such notice, the company ceases to be such a company[23].

1 Ie by the Companies Act 1985 ss 263, 264: see paras 701, 702 ante.
2 For the meaning of 'capitalisation' see para 701 note 8 ante.
3 For these purposes, 'liabilities' includes any provision for liabilities or charges within the meaning of the Companies Act 1985 s 226(3) (as substituted), Sch 4 para 89 (see para 832 note 24 post): s 265(2).
4 Ibid s 265(1).
5 For the meaning of 'uncalled share capital' see para 174 note 14 ante.
6 Companies Act 1985 s 265(3).
7 For the meaning of 'recognised investment exchange' see para 223 note 1 ante.
8 For the meaning of 'overseas investment exchange' see para 223 note 1 ante.
9 For these purposes, the 'relevant period' is the period beginning with the first day of the accounting reference period immediately preceding that in which the proposed distribution is to be made, or where the distribution is to be made in the company's first accounting reference period, the first day of that period, and ending with the date of the distribution: Companies Act 1985 s 265(5). For the meaning of 'accounting reference period' see para 807 post.
10 Ibid s 265(4) (amended by the Financial Services Act 1986 s 212(2), Sch 16 para 19).
11 Ie notice under the Companies Act 1985 s 266(1): see infra.
12 As to the significance of that date see para 701 note 12 ante.
13 Companies Act 1985 s 265(6).
14 For the meaning of 'public company' see para 82 ante.
15 For the prescribed form of notice see the Companies (Forms) (Amendment) Regulations 1995, SI 1995/736, reg 3, Sch 2, Form 266(1).
16 Companies Act 1985 s 266(1).
17 Ibid s 266(2)(a).
18 Ibid s 266(2)(b). The Income and Corporation Taxes Act 1988 s 842(1A)–(3) (as amended) (see INCOME TAXATION vol 23 (Reissue) para 1420) applies for the purposes of the Companies Act 1985 s 266(2)(b) as for those of the Income and Corporation Taxes Act 1988 s 842(1)(b) (limiting the scope of '15% by value' in certain circumstances: see INCOME TAXATION vol 23 (Reissue) para 1420): Companies Act 1985 s 266(4) (substituted by the Finance Act 1988 s 117(3), (4)).
19 Companies Act 1985 s 266(2)(c).
20 Ie ibid Pt VIII (ss 263–281) (as amended): see paras 701, 702 ante and paras 704–716 post.
21 Ibid s 266(2)(d).
22 For the prescribed form of notice see the Companies (Forms) (Amendment) Regulations 1995 Sch 2, Form 266(3).
23 Companies Act 1985 s 266(3).

704. Extension of relaxations to certain other companies. The Secretary of State may by regulations in a statutory instrument extend the provisions of the above relaxations[1] (with or without modifications) to companies whose principal business consists of investing their funds in securities, land or other assets with the aim of spreading investment risk and giving their members the benefit of the results of the management of the assets[2].

1 Ie those contained in the Companies Act 1985 ss 265, 266 (as amended): see para 703 ante.
2 Ibid s 267(1). Such regulations may make different provision for different classes of companies and may contain such transitional and supplemental provisions as the Secretary of State considers necessary, and must not be made unless a draft of the statutory instrument containing them has been laid before Parliament and approved by a resolution of each House: s 267(2)(a), (b). At the date at which this volume states the law no such regulations had been made.

705. Realised profits of insurance company with long term business. Where an insurance company[1] carries on long term business[2]:

(1) any amount included in the relevant part of the balance sheet[3] of the company which represents a surplus[4] in the fund or funds maintained by it in respect of that business and which has not been allocated to policy holders[5] or carried forward unappropriated[6]; and

(2) any deficit[7] in that fund or those funds,

are to be respectively treated, for purposes of these provisions[8], as a realised profit[9] and a realised loss[9]; and, subject to this, any profit or loss arising in that business is to be left out of account for those purposes[10].

1 Ie an insurance company to which the Insurance Companies Act 1982 Pt II (ss 15–71) (as amended) applies: see INSURANCE vol 25 (Reissue) para 803.

2 For these purposes, 'long term business' has the same meaning as in ibid s 1(1), Sch 1 (see INSURANCE vol 25 (Reissue) para 18): Companies Act 1985 s 268(3)(b).

3 For these purposes, the reference to the relevant part of the balance sheet is to that part of the balance sheet which represents Liabilities item A.V (profit and loss account) in the balance sheet format set out in ibid Sch 9A Pt I Ch I Section B (as added): s 268(2)(aa) (added by the Companies Act 1985 (Miscellaneous Accounting Amendments) Regulations 1996, SI 1996/189, reg 13(1), (3)).

4 For these purposes, the reference to a surplus in any fund or funds of an insurance company is to an excess of the assets representing the fund or those funds over the liabilities of the company attributable to its long term business, as shown by an actuarial investigation; and the reference to a deficit in any such fund or funds is to the excess of those liabilities over those assets, as so shown: Companies Act 1985 s 268(2). 'Actuarial investigation' means an investigation to which the Insurance Companies Act 1982 s 18 (see INSURANCE vol 25 (Reissue) para 823) applies or which is made in pursuance of a requirement imposed by s 42 (see INSURANCE vol 25 (Reissue) para 824): Companies Act 1985 s 268(3)(a).

5 Ie under the Insurance Companies Act 1982 s 30(1): see INSURANCE vol 25 (Reissue) para 820.

6 Ie as mentioned in ibid s 30(7): see INSURANCE vol 25 (Reissue) para 820.

7 For the meaning of 'deficit' see note 4 supra.

8 Ie the Companies Act 1985 Pt VIII (ss 263–281) (as amended): see paras 701–704 ante and paras 706–716 post.

9 For the meaning of references to profits and losses see para 701 note 1 ante.

10 Companies Act 1985 s 268(1) (amended by the Companies Act 1985 (Miscellaneous Accounting Amendments) Regulations 1996 reg 13(1), (2)).

706. Treatment of development costs. Subject to the following provisions, where development costs are shown as an asset in a company's accounts, any amount shown in respect of those costs is to be treated:

(1) in relation to universally permitted distributions[1] as a realised loss[2]; and

(2) in relation to other distributions by an investment company[3] as a realised revenue loss[4].

This does not, however, apply to any part of that amount representing an unrealised profit made on revaluation of those costs; nor does it apply if there are special circumstances in the company's case justifying the directors in deciding that the amount there mentioned is not to be treated as required by the above provisions and the requisite note to the accounts giving the reasons for showing development costs as an asset[5] states that the amount is not to be so treated and explains the circumstances relied upon to justify the decision of the directors to that effect[6].

1 Ie under the Companies Act 1985 s 263: see para 701 ante.

2 For the meaning of references to profits and losses see para 701 note 1 ante.

3 Ie under the Companies Act 1985 s 265 (as amended): see para 703 ante.

4 Ibid s 269(1). For modifications where a company has prepared accounts in accordance with the special provisions of Pt VII (ss 221–262A) (as amended) relating to banking companies (see para 716 post) see s 279, Sch 11 paras 1, 3 (substituted by the Companies Act 1985 (Bank Account) Regulations 1991, SI

1991/2705, regs 7, 9, Sch 3 para 1); and for modifications where a company has prepared accounts in accordance with the special provisions of the Companies Act 1985 Pt VII (ss 221–262A) (as amended) relating to insurance companies (see para 716 post) see Sch 11 paras 1, 8 (substituted by the Companies Act 1985 (Insurance Companies Accounts) Regulations 1993, SI 1993/3246, regs 5(1), 7, Sch 2 para 8).

5 Ie as required by the Companies Act 1985 s 226(3) (as substituted), Sch 4 para 20: see para 811 post.
6 Ibid s 269(2). See also note 4 supra.

B. RELEVANT ACCOUNTS

707. Distribution to be justified by reference to company's accounts. These and the following provisions[1] are for determining the question whether a distribution may be made by a company without contravening the above limitations[2].

The amount of a distribution which may be made is determined by reference to the following items as stated in the company's accounts:

(1) profits[3], losses[3], assets and liabilities;
(2) provisions[4] of any of the kinds requiring disclosure in the company's accounts (depreciation, diminution in value of assets, retentions to meet liabilities etc); and
(3) share capital and reserves (including undistributable reserves)[5].

Except in a case falling within the next provision, the company's accounts which are relevant for this purpose are its last annual accounts[6].

In the following two cases:

(a) where the distribution would be found to contravene the relevant statutory provision if reference were made only to the company's last annual accounts; or
(b) where the distribution is proposed to be declared during the company's first accounting reference period, or before any accounts are laid in respect of that period,

the relevant accounts[7] (called 'interim accounts' in the first case, and 'initial accounts' in the second) are those necessary to enable a reasonable judgment to be made as to the amounts of the items mentioned in heads (1), (2) and (3) above[8].

The relevant statutory provision is treated as contravened in the case of a distribution unless the statutory requirements[9] about the relevant accounts are complied with in relation to that distribution[10].

1 Ie the Companies Act 1985 ss 271–276: see infra and paras 708–713 post.
2 Ibid s 270(1). The limitations referred to are ss 263, 264 or 265 (as amended) (see paras 701, 702, 703 respectively ante): s 270(1).
3 For the meaning of references to profits and losses see para 701 note 1 ante.
4 Ie provisions of any of the kinds mentioned in the Companies Act 1985 s 226(3) (as substituted), Sch 4 paras 88, 89: see paras 810 note 4, 832 note 24 respectively post.
5 Ibid s 270(2). For modifications where a company has prepared accounts in accordance with the special provisions of Pt VII (ss 221–262A) (as amended) relating to banking companies (see para 716 post) see s 279, Sch 11 paras 1, 4 (substituted by the Companies Act 1985 (Bank Account) Regulations 1991, SI 1991/2705, regs 7, 9, Sch 3 para 1); and for modifications where a company has prepared accounts in accordance with the special provisions of the Companies Act 1985 Pt VII (ss 221–262A) (as amended) relating to insurance companies (see para 716 post) see Sch 11 para 9 (substituted by the Companies Act 1985 (Miscellaneous Accounting Amendments) Regulations 1996, SI 1996/189, reg 14(8), Sch 6 paras 1, 3).
6 Companies Act 1985 s 270(3). For these purposes, the last annual accounts are those prepared under Pt VII (ss 221–262) (as amended) which were laid in respect of the last preceding accounting reference period in respect of which accounts so prepared were laid; and for this purpose accounts are laid if s 241(1) (as substituted) (see para 817 post) has been complied with in relation to them: s 270(3).
7 Ie relevant under ibid s 270.
8 Ibid s 270(4).

9 Ie ibid ss 270–273 (as amended): see supra and paras 708–710 post.
10 Ibid s 270(5).

708. Requirements for last annual accounts. If the company's last annual accounts constitute the only accounts relevant for justifying the distribution[1], the accounts must have been properly prepared in accordance with the Companies Act 1985[2], or have been so prepared subject only to matters which are not material for determining[3] whether the distribution would contravene the relevant statutory provision; and, without prejudice to the above provisions, so much of the accounts as consists of a balance sheet must give a true and fair view of the state of the company's affairs as at the balance sheet date, and so much of the accounts as consists of a profit and loss account must give a true and fair view of the company's profit[4] or loss[4] for the period in respect of which the accounts were prepared[5].

The auditors must have made their report[6] on the accounts; and, if the report is a qualified report, that is to say, it is not a report without qualification to the effect that in the auditors' opinion the accounts have been properly prepared in accordance with the Companies Act 1985, the auditors must in that case also have stated in writing (either at the time of their report or subsequently[7]) whether, in their opinion, the matter in respect of which their report is qualified is material for determining[8] whether the distribution would contravene the relevant statutory provision; and a copy of the statement must have been laid before the company in general meeting[9]. Such a statement suffices for purposes of a particular distribution not only if it relates to a distribution which has been proposed but also if it relates to distributions of any description which includes that particular distribution, notwithstanding that at the time of the statement it has not been proposed[10].

1 Ie under the Companies Act 1985 s 270: see para 707 ante.
2 See para 825 et seq post.
3 Ie by reference to the items mentioned in the Companies Act 1985 s 270(2): see para 707 ante.
4 For the meaning of references to profits and losses see para 701 note 1 ante.
5 Companies Act 1985 s 271(1), (2).
6 Ie under ibid s 235 (as substituted): see paras 1059 post.
7 Ie but before the distribution is made: *Precision Dippings Ltd v Precision Dippings Marketing Ltd* [1986] Ch 447, [1985] 3 WLR 812, CA. This is not a merely procedural matter which may be waived by the unanimous consent of all members: *Precision Dippings Ltd v Precision Dippings Marketing Ltd* supra.
8 Ie by reference to the Companies Act 1985 s 270(2): see note 3 supra.
9 Ibid s 271(3), (4) (amended by the Companies Act 1989 s 23, Sch 10 para 4).
10 Companies Act 1985 s 271(5).

709. Requirements for interim accounts. The following provisions are the statutory requirements in respect of interim accounts prepared for a proposed distribution by a public company[1]. The accounts must have been properly prepared[2], or have been so prepared subject only to matters which are not material for determining[3] whether the proposed distribution would contravene the relevant provision[4]. Without prejudice to the above provisions, so much of the accounts as consists of a balance sheet must give a true and fair view of the state of the company's affairs as at the balance sheet date, and so much of the accounts as consists of a profit and loss account must give a true and fair view of the company's profit[5] or loss[5] for the period in respect of which the accounts were prepared[6]. A copy of the accounts must have been delivered to the registrar of companies[7].

If the accounts are in a language other than English and the normal statutory requirement as to a translation[8] does not apply, a translation into English of the accounts, certified in the prescribed manner[9] to be a correct translation, must also have been delivered[10] to the registrar[11].

1   Companies Act 1985 s 272(1). For the meaning of 'public company' see para 82 ante. For modifications where a company has prepared accounts in accordance with the special provisions of Pt VII (ss 221–262A) (as amended) relating to banking companies (see para 716 post) see s 279, Sch 11 paras 1, 5 (substituted by the Companies Act 1985 (Bank Account) Regulations 1991, SI 1991/2705, regs 7, 9, Sch 3 para 1); and for modifications where a company has prepared accounts in accordance with the special provisions of the Companies Act 1985 Pt VII (ss 221–262A) (as amended) relating to insurance companies (see para 716 post) see Sch 11 paras 1, 10 (substituted by the Companies Act 1985 (Insurance Companies Accounts) Regulations 1993, SI 1993/3246, regs 5(1), 7, Sch 2 para 8).

2   For these purposes, 'properly prepared' means that the accounts must comply with the Companies Act 1985 s 226 (as substituted) (applying s 226 (as substituted), Sch 4 (as amended) (see para 809 et seq post) with such modifications as are necessary because the accounts are prepared otherwise than in respect of an accounting reference period) and any balance sheet comprised in the accounts must have been signed in accordance with s 233 (as substituted) (see para 937 post): s 272(3) (amended by the Companies Act 1989 s 23, Sch 10 para 5(a), (b)). See also note 1 supra.

3   Ie by reference to items mentioned in the Companies Act 1985 s 270(2): see para 707 ante.

4   Ibid s 272(2).

5   For the meaning of references to profits and losses see para 701 note 1 ante.

6   Companies Act 1985 s 272(3)(a), (b).

7   Ibid s 272(4).

8   Ie ibid s 242(1), second sentence (as substituted): see para 818 post.

9   For the prescribed manner of certification see para 303 note 6 ante.

10   Ie subject to the Companies Act 1985 s 710B(6) (as added): see para 90 ante.

11   Ibid s 272(5) (amended by the Companies Act 1989 Sch 10 para 6; the Welsh Language Act 1993 s 30(4)(b)).

710. Requirements for initial accounts. The following are the statutory requirements in respect of initial accounts prepared for a proposed distribution by a public company[1]. The accounts must have been properly prepared[2], or they must have been so prepared subject only to matters which are not material for determining[3] whether the proposed distribution would contravene the relevant statutory provision[4].

The company's auditors must have made a report stating in their opinion the accounts have been properly prepared; and, if their report is a qualified report, that is to say it is not a report without qualification to the effect that in the auditors' opinion the accounts have been so prepared, the auditors must in that case also have stated in writing whether, in their opinion, the matter in respect of which their report is qualified is material for determining[5] whether the distribution would contravene the relevant statutory provision[6]. A copy of the accounts, of the auditors' report and of the auditors' statement, if any, must have been delivered to the registrar of companies[7]. If the accounts are, or the auditors' report or their statement, if any, is in a language other than English and the normal statutory requirement as to a translation does not apply[8], a translation into English of the accounts, the report or the statement (as the case may be), certified in the prescribed manner[9] to be a correct translation, must also have been delivered[10] to the registrar[11].

1   Companies Act 1985 s 273(1). For the meaning of 'public company' see para 82 ante. For modifications where a company has prepared accounts in accordance with the special provisions of Pt VII (ss 221–262A) (as amended) relating to banking companies (see para 716 post) see s 279, Sch 11 paras 1, 5 (substituted by the Companies Act 1985 (Bank Account) Regulations 1991, SI 1991/2705, regs 7, 9, Sch 3 para 1); and for modifications where a company has prepared accounts in accordance with the special provisions of the Companies Act 1985 Pt VII (ss 221–262A) (as amended) relating to insurance companies (see para 716 post) see Sch 11 paras 1, 10 (substituted by the Companies Act 1985 (Insurance Companies Accounts) Regulations 1993, SI 1993/3246, regs 5(1), 7, Sch 2 para 8).

2   The Companies Act 1985 s 272(3) (see para 709 note 2 ante) applies as respects the meaning of 'properly prepared': s 273(3).

3 Ie by reference to items in ibid s 270(2): see para 707 ante.
4 Ibid s 273(2).
5 See note 3 supra.
6 Companies Act 1985 s 273(4), (5).
7 Ibid s 273(6).
8 Ie ibid s 242(1), second sentence (as substituted): see para 818 post.
9 For the prescribed manner of certification see para 303 note 6 ante.
10 Ie subject to the Companies Act 1985 s 710B(6) (as added): see para 90 ante.
11 Ibid s 273(7) (amended by the Companies Act 1989 s 23, Sch 10 para 6; the Welsh Language Act 1993 s 30(4)(b)).

711. Method of applying justification by relevant accounts to successive distributions. For the purpose of determining by reference to particular accounts whether a proposed distribution may be made by a company, the statutory provisions[1] relating to justification by reference to relevant accounts have effect, in a case where one or more distributions have already been made in pursuance of determinations made by reference to those same accounts, as if the amount of the proposed distribution was increased by the amount of the distribution so made[2]. The above provisions apply, if they would not otherwise do so, to:

(1) financial assistance[3] lawfully given by a public company out of its distributable profits[4] in a case where the assistance is required[5] to be so given by statute[6];

(2) financial assistance lawfully given by a private company out of its distributable profits in a case where the assistance is required[7] to be so given by statute[8];

(3) financial assistance given by a company in contravention of the general statutory prohibition[9], in a case where the giving of that assistance reduces the company's net assets[10] or increases its net liabilities[11];

(4) a payment made by a company in respect of the purchase by it of shares in the company[12], except a payment lawfully made otherwise than out of distributable profits[13]; and

(5) a payment[14] of any description (apart from purchase price) to be made out of distributable profits[15],

being financial assistance given or payment made since the relevant accounts were prepared, as if any such financial assistance or payment were a distribution already made in pursuance of a determination made by reference to those accounts[16].

1 Ie the Companies Act 1985 s 270: see para 707 ante.
2 Ibid s 274(1).
3 For these purposes, 'financial assistance' means the same as in ibid Pt V Ch VI (ss 151–158 (as amended): see para 241 ante): s 274(3)(a).
4 For the meaning of references to profits and losses see para 701 note 1 ante.
5 Ie by the Companies Act 1985 s 154: see para 275 ante.
6 Ibid s 274(2)(a). For the meaning of 'public company' see para 82 ante. Section 274(2) and s 274(3) (see note 11 infra) are deemed to be included in Pt V Ch VII (ss 159–181) (as amended) for the purposes of the Secretary of State's power to make regulations under s 179 (see para 240 ante): s 274(4).
7 Ie by ibid s 155(2): see para 276 ante.
8 Ibid s 274(2)(b). For the meaning of 'private company' see para 82 ante.
9 Ie ibid s 151: see para 273 ante.
10 For these purposes, 'net assets' has the meaning given by ibid s 154(2)(a) (see para 275 ante): s 275(3).
11 Ibid s 274(2)(c). For these purposes, 'net liabilities', in relation to the giving of financial assistance by a company, means the amount by which the aggregate amount of the company's liabilities (within the meaning of s 154(2)(b): see para 275 ante) exceeds the aggregate amount of its assets, taking the amount of the assets and liabilities to be as stated in the company's accounting records immediately before the financial assistance is given: s 274(3). See also note 6 supra.
12 See ibid Pt V Ch VII (ss 159–181) (as amended) and para 219 et seq ante.
13 Ibid s 274(2)(d).

14 Ie of the descriptions mentioned in ibid s 168: see para 228 ante.
15 Ibid s 274(2)(e).
16 Ibid s 274(2).

712. Treatment of assets in the relevant accounts. For the purposes of the prohibitions and restrictions in relation to distributions[1], a provision of any kind which falls to be disclosed in the accounts[2], other than one in respect of a diminution in value of a fixed asset appearing on a revaluation of all the fixed assets of the company, or of all of its fixed assets other than goodwill, is treated as a realised loss[3]. If, on the revaluation of a fixed asset, an unrealised profit is shown to have been made and, on or after the revaluation, a sum is written off or retained for depreciation of that asset over a period, then an amount equal to the amount by which that sum exceeds the sum which would have been so written off or retained for the depreciation of that asset over that period, if that profit had not been made, is treated for the purposes of such prohibitions and restrictions as a realised profit made over that period[4].

Where there is no record of the original cost of an asset, or a record cannot be obtained without unreasonable expense or delay, then for the purpose of determining whether the company has made a profit or loss in respect of that asset, its cost is taken to be the value ascribed to it in the earliest available record of its value made on or after its acquisition by the company[5].

Subject to the qualification below, any consideration by the directors of the value at a particular time of a fixed asset is treated as a revaluation of the asset for the purposes of determining whether any such revaluation of the company's fixed assets as is required for purposes of the above exception has taken place at that time[6]. Where, however, any such assets which have not actually been revalued are treated as so revalued for those purposes, that exception applies only if the directors are satisfied that their aggregate value at the time in question is not less than the aggregate amount at which they are for the time being stated in the company's accounts[7].

Where the accounts have been properly prepared[8], the above provisions[9] do not apply for the purpose of determining whether a revaluation of the company's fixed assets affecting the amount of the relevant items[10] as stated in those accounts has taken place, unless it is stated in a note to the accounts:

(1) that the directors have considered the value at any time of any fixed assets of the company, without actually revaluing those assets;

(2) that they are satisfied that the aggregate value of those assets at the time in question is or was not less than the aggregate amount at which they are or were for the time being stated in the company's accounts; and

(3) that the relevant items in question are accordingly stated in the relevant accounts on the basis that a revaluation of the company's fixed assets which by virtue of the above provisions[11] included the assets in question took place at that time[12].

1 Ie the Companies Act 1985 ss 263, 264: see paras 701, 702 ante.
2 Ie pursuant to ibid s 226(3) (as substituted), Sch 4 paras 88, 89: see paras 810 note 5, 832 note 24 respectively post.
3 Ibid s 275(1). For the meaning of references to profits and losses see para 701 note 1 ante. For modifications where a company has prepared accounts in accordance with the special provisions of Pt VII (ss 221–262A) (as amended) relating to banking companies (see para 716 post) see s 279, Sch 11 paras 1, 4 (substituted by the Companies Act 1985 (Bank Account) Regulations 1991, SI 1991/2705, regs 7, 9, Sch 3 para 1); and for modifications where a company has prepared accounts in accordance with the special provisions of the Companies Act 1985 Pt VII (ss 221–262A) (as amended) relating to insurance companies (see para 716 post) see Sch 11 para 9 (substituted by the Companies Act 1985 (Miscellaneous Accounting Amendments) Regulations 1996, SI 1996/189, reg 14(8), Sch 6 paras 1, 3).

4 Companies Act 1985 s 275(2).
5 Ibid s 275(3).
6 Ibid s 275(4).
7 Ibid s 275(5).
8 Ie under ibid s 271(2) (see para 708 ante) or s 272(2) (see para 709 ante) or s 273(2) (see para 710 ante).
9 Ie ibid s 275(4), (5): see supra.
10 Ie the items mentioned in ibid s 270(2): see para 707 ante.
11 See note 9 supra.
12 Companies Act 1985 s 275(6).

713. Distributions in kind. Where a company makes a distribution of or including a non-cash asset[1], and any part of the amount at which that asset is stated in the accounts relevant for the purposes of the distribution in accordance with the statutory provisions[2] represents an unrealised profit, that profit[3] is to be treated as a realised profit for the purposes of:

(1) determining the lawfulness of the distribution[4] (whether before or after the distribution takes place); and

(2) the application of the statutory provisions[5] (whereby only realised profits are to be included in or transferred to the profit and loss account) in relation to anything done with a view to or in connection with the making of that distribution[6].

1 For the meaning of 'non-cash asset' see para 469 note 2 ante.
2 Ie the Companies Act 1985 ss 270–275 (as amended): see paras 707–712 ante.
3 For the meaning of references to profits and losses see para 701 note 1 ante.
4 Ie in accordance with the Companies Act 1985 Pt VIII (ss 263–281) (as amended): see paras 707–712 ante and paras 714–716 post.
5 Ie ibid s 226(3) (as substituted), Sch 4 paras 12(a), 34(3)(a) (as substituted): see paras 809, 813, 825 post.
6 Ibid s 276 (amended by the Companies Act 1989 s 23, Sch 10 para 7). For modifications where a company has prepared accounts in accordance with the special provisions of the Companies Act 1985 Pt VII (ss 221–262A) (as amended) relating to banking companies (see para 716 post) see s 279, Sch 11 paras 1, 6 (substituted by the Companies Act 1985 (Bank Account) Regulations 1991, SI 1991/2705, regs 7, 9, Sch 3 para 1); and for modifications where a company has prepared accounts in accordance with the special provisions of the Companies Act 1985 Pt VII (ss 221–262A) (as amended) relating to insurance companies (see para 716 post) see Sch 11 paras 1, 11 (substituted by the Companies Act 1985 (Insurance Companies Accounts) Regulations 1993, SI 1993/3246, regs 5(1), 7, Sch 2 para 8).

C. SUPPLEMENTARY PROVISIONS

714. Consequences of unlawful distribution. Where a distribution, or part of one, made by a company to one of its members is made in contravention of the statutory provisions[1] and, at the time of the distribution, he knows or has reasonable grounds for believing that it is so made, he is liable to repay it (or that part of it, as the case may be) to the company or (in the case of a distribution made otherwise than in cash) to pay the company a sum equal to the value of the distribution (or part) at that time[2]. The above requirement is without prejudice to any obligation imposed apart from this provision on a member of a company to repay a distribution unlawfully made to him; but this provision does not apply in relation to financial assistance given by a company in contravention of the statutory prohibition[3] or any payment made by a company in respect of the redemption or purchase by the company of shares in itself[4].

1 Ie the Companies Act 1985 Pt VIII (ss 263–281) (as amended): see paras 701–713 ante and paras 715, 716 post.

2 Ibid s 277(1).

3 Ie ibid s 151: see para 273 ante.

4 Ibid s 277(2). Section 277(2) is deemed included in Pt V Ch VII (ss 159–181) (as amended) for the purposes of the Secretary of State's power to make regulations under s 179 (see para 240 ante): s 277(3).

715. Saving for provision in articles operative before the Companies Act 1980. Where immediately before 22 December 1980[1] a company was authorised by a provision of its articles to apply its unrealised profits in paying up in full or in part unissued shares to be allotted to members of the company as fully or partly paid bonus shares, that provision continues, subject to any alteration of the articles, as authority for those profits to be so applied after that date[2].

1 For the significance of this date see para 701 note 12 ante.

2 Companies Act 1985 s 278. Since an issue of shares as fully paid or partly paid bonus shares is specifically excluded from the scope of 'distribution' by s 263(2)(a) (see para 701 ante) and so excluded from the restrictions and prohibitions contained in ss 263, 264 (see paras 701, 702 ante), the purpose of this provision is somewhat obscure. For cases decided before 22 December 1980 see *IRC v Thornton, Kelley & Co Ltd* [1957] 1 All ER 650, [1957] 1 WLR 482; *Westburn Sugar Refineries Ltd v IRC* [1960] TR 105; *Dimbula Valley (Ceylon) Tea Co Ltd v Laurie* [1961] Ch 353, [1961] 1 All ER 769. As to capitalisation of profits see also the Companies (Tables A to F) Regulations 1985, SI 1985/805, Schedule, Table A art 110.

716. Distribution by banking and insurance companies. Where a company's accounts relevant for the purposes of the statutory provisions relating to distribution of profits and assets[1] are prepared in accordance with the special provisions relating to banking or insurance companies[2], these provisions[3] apply subject to certain modifications[4].

1 Ie the Companies Act 1985 Pt VIII (ss 263–281) (as amended): see paras 701–715 ante.

2 Ie the special provisions of ibid Pt VII (ss 221–262A) (as amended): see paras 926–928 post.

3 Ie ibid ss 265–275 (as amended): see paras 703–712 ante.

4 Ibid s 279 (substituted by the Companies Act 1989 s 23, Sch 10 para 8). For the modifications see the Companies Act 1985 s 279, Sch 11 paras 1–6 (substituted by the Companies Act 1985 (Bank Account) Regulations 1991, SI 1991/2705, regs 7, 9, Sch 3 para 1) (banking companies); and the Companies Act 1985 Sch 11 paras 7–11 (substituted by the Companies Act 1985 (Insurance Companies Accounts) Regulations 1993, SI 1993/3246, regs 5(1), Sch 2 para 8; amended by the Companies Act 1985 (Miscellaneous Accounting Amendments) Regulations 1996, SI 1996/189, reg 14(8), Sch 6 paras 1–3) (insurance companies).

D. DECLARATION AND PAYMENT OF DIVIDENDS

717. Meaning of 'dividend'. The ordinary meaning of 'dividend' is a share of profits, whether at a fixed rate or otherwise, allocated to the holders of shares in a company[1]. The term is generally used with reference to trading or other companies[2], and to payments made to members of a company as such and not by way of remuneration for services[3]. Although it usually implies a share of profits periodically payable, it may also refer to such shares of profits as are divided only occasionally and are usually called 'bonuses' or 'bonus dividends'[4]. The terms 'preference dividend', 'preferential dividend', and 'cumulative preferential dividend' refer to shares having preferential rights[5]. An 'interim dividend' is a dividend declared at some date between the ordinary general meetings[6].

A voucher or written authority for payment to a shareholder of the amount of a dividend on his shares is usually described as a dividend warrant[7].

1   *Henry v Great Northern Rly Co* (1857) 1 De G & J 606; *Chelsea Water Works Co v Metropolitan Water Board*
    [1904] 2 KB 77, CA; *Bond v Barrow Haematite Steel Co* [1902] 1 Ch 353 at 363; cf *Lamplough v Kent*
    Waterworks (Company of Proprietors) [1903] 1 Ch 575 at 580, 581, CA (on appeal sub nom *Kent*
    Waterworks (Company of Proprietors) v Lamplough without taking this point [1904] AC 27, HL).
2   *Jones v Ogle* (1872) 8 Ch App 192 at 197, CA (decided under the Apportionment Act 1870).
3   *Royal College of Music v Vestry of St Margaret's and St John's, Westminster* [1898] 1 QB 809 at 819, CA.
4   *Re Griffith, Carr v Griffith* (1879) 12 ChD 655.
5   See para 180 ante. Even as regards preference shares, 'interest' is not an apt word to express the return by
    way of share of profits to which a shareholder is entitled in respect of shares paid up in due course and
    not by way of advance, although it may be used as an inaccurate mode of expressing the measure of the
    share of profits: *Bond v Barrow Haematite Steel Co* [1902] 1 Ch 353. It is a fundamental misconception to
    argue that the receipt of dividends is merely a distribution of assets belonging to the shareholder: see
    Hood-Barrs v IRC [1946] 2 All ER 768, CA.
6   See further para 723 post.
7   As to the recipient's right to request a written statement showing the amount or value of a qualifying
    distribution and whether or not he is entitled to a tax credit see INCOME TAXATION vol 23 (Reissue)
    para 910; and as to bankers' duties and liabilities with regard to dividend warrants as cheques see
    BANKING vol 3(1) (Reissue) para 231.

718. Right to dividends. The general rights of shareholders with reference to
dividends, especially as regards the rate per cent and priorities, are sometimes stated in
the memorandum of association, with a view to making the rights, as far as may be,
unalterable[1], sometimes in the articles, and occasionally in both of those instruments,
but the manner in which they are to be declared and paid is usually stated in the
articles[2].

1   As to the extent to which the contents of the memorandum may be altered see para 541 ante.
2   The Companies (Tables A to F) Regulations 1985, SI 1985/805, Schedule, Table A arts 102–108 relate
    to dividends; in particular they give power to declare dividends, including interim dividends (see
    para 723 post) and prohibit the payment of dividends otherwise than out of profits available for
    distribution (see para 701 et seq ante); and they provide for the payment of dividends according to
    amounts paid or credited as paid on shares (see para 719 post); for the payment of dividends by
    distribution of assets (see para 732 post), and for the payment and method of payment of dividends in
    cash and interest free (see paras 724–726 post). As to restrictions imposed by the Secretary of State on the
    payment of dividends on any shares see para 1383 post.

719. Dividends on shares not fully paid up. If under the articles dividends are
payable on shares, without qualifying words, this means without regard to the amount
paid up on them[1], and it is not competent for a company to pay a dividend to
shareholders in proportion to the amount paid up on the shares held by them[2]. If so
authorised by its articles, a company may, however, pay dividend in proportion to the
amount paid up on each share where a larger amount is paid up on some shares than on
others[3].

1   *Oakbank Oil Co v Crum* (1882) 8 App Cas 65, HL; *Wilkinson v Cummins* (1853) 11 Hare 337; cf *Birch v*
    Cropper, Re Bridgewater Navigation Co Ltd (1889) 14 App Cas 525, HL; *Re Wakefield Rolling Stock Co*
    [1892] 3 Ch 165 at 172.
2   *Oakbank Oil Co v Crum* (1882) 8 App Cas 65, HL; *Morgan v Great Eastern Rly Co (No 2)* (1863) 1 Hem &
    M 560.
3   Companies Act 1985 s 119(c). Cf the Companies (Tables A to F) Regulations 1985, SI 1985/805,
    Schedule, Table A art 104 which provides that, except as otherwise provided by the rights attached to
    shares, all dividends must be declared and paid according to the amounts paid up on the shares on which
    the dividend is paid. All dividends must be apportioned and paid proportionately to the amounts paid
    up on the shares during any portion or portions of the period in respect of which the dividend is paid;
    but, if any share is issued on terms providing that it shall rank for dividend as from a particular date, that
    share will rank for dividend accordingly.

720. Guarantee by vendor of business. A guarantee given by the vendor on the sale of a business to a company guaranteeing the payment of dividends on its shares during a certain period is valid and enforceable[1]. In such a case there is no implied contract on the company's part to carry on business during the whole of the period, so as to disentitle it to enforce the guarantee if it discontinues; and, if there are several businesses, the discontinuance of one does not release the vendor[2]. In a proper case such a guarantee may be released by the company[3]. In a bona fide case payments under such a guarantee are not assets of the company which may be claimed by the creditors[4], although it will be otherwise in the case of a guarantee fund furnished out of the purchase money payable to the vendor[5]. A guarantor of the dividends on preference shares is entitled to be subrogated to the rights of the preference shareholders, but is not entitled to claim against the company as a creditor for sums paid under such a guarantee, and any provision to this effect in the guarantee is ultra vires the company[6].

1 *Re South Llanharran Colliery Co, ex p Jegon* (1879) 12 ChD 503, CA (where the amount payable under the guarantee was repayable out of future profits); and see *Addison v Ness* (1839) 9 TLR 607, HL.
2 *Brown & Co v Brown* (1877) 36 LT 272, CA.
3 *Sheffield Nickel Co v Unwin* (1877) 2 QBD 214.
4 *Re South Llanharran Colliery Co, ex p Jegon* (1879) 12 ChD 503; *Re Gelly Deg Colliery Co* (1878) 38 LT 440; *Richardson v English Spelter Co Ltd* (1885) 1 TLR 249.
5 *Re Stuart's Trusts* (1876) 4 ChD 213; *Re Menell et Cie Ltd* [1915] 1 Ch 759 (where the money deposited pursuant to the guarantee was held to be available for the creditors of the purchaser company).
6 *Re Walters' Deed of Guarantee, Walters Palm Toffee Ltd v Walters* [1933] Ch 321.

721. Court's interference as to dividends. If the directors have fairly come to a conclusion as to what proportion of the profits available for distribution should be distributed as dividend, then prima facie the court will not interfere[1]. The court will not compel directors to declare a dividend against their judgment[2], but, at the instance of an individual shareholder, it will restrain the payment of an improper dividend[3]. Thus, payment of a dividend may be restrained if proper provision has not been made for expenses, which ought to be paid out of income[4], or if the dividend is proposed to be paid out of any moneys not available for that purpose[5].

Where, after properly investigating the company's financial position, the directors make an estimate of the available profits and declare a dividend on that basis, the court will not review the decision on the ground that their estimates were erroneous, if the view taken was one which reasonable persons might take[6]. Where, however, directors act without proper investigation or professional assistance, the burden lies on them to show that the payment was fairly made out of profits available for that purpose[7]. Therefore, if it would be evident on proper accounts that there were no profits available for distribution, the shareholders have no power to declare and pay it, and their receipt of the dividend does not protect the directors; for they cannot bind the company by an act which is ultra vires[8]. The court will not interfere at the instance of an unsecured creditor[9], or at the instance of a holder of debenture stock unless his security is presently enforceable[10].

1 *Stewart v Sashalite Ltd* [1936] 2 All ER 1481 at 1485.
2 *Lambert v Neuchatel Asphalte Co Ltd* (1882) 51 LJ Ch 882; *Yool v Great Western Rly Co* (1869) 20 LT 74; *Bond v Barrow Haematite Steel Co* [1902] 1 Ch 353. The directors have a discretion as to reserve funds: see para 728 post.
3 *Hoole v Great Western Rly Co* (1867) 3 Ch App 262; *Bloxam v Metropolitan Rly Co* (1868) 3 Ch App 337.
4 *Re Mercantile Trading Co, Stringer's Case* (1869) 4 Ch App 475; *Davison v Gillies* (1879) cited 16 ChD 347n; *City of Glasgow Bank (Liquidators) v Mackinnon* (1882) 9 R 535; *Lee v Neuchatel Asphalte Co* (1889) 41 ChD 1, CA.

5 *Guinness v Land Corpn of Ireland* (1882) 22 ChD 349, CA; and see *Famatina Development Corpn Ltd v Bury* [1910] AC 439, HL.
6 *Re Peruvian Guano Co, ex p Kemp* [1894] 3 Ch 690; *Re Kingston Cotton Mill Co (No 2)* [1896] 1 Ch 331 (revsd [1896] 2 Ch 279, CA); *Re City Equitable Fire Insurance Co Ltd* [1925] Ch 407 at 477. The court will not hold directors liable for erroneous estimates after they have been laid before and approved by the company: *Ammonia Soda Co Ltd v Chamberlain* [1918] 1 Ch 266 at 272, CA.
7 *Rance's Case* (1870) 6 Ch App 104.
8 *Flitcroft's Case* (1882) 21 ChD 519, CA; *Re City Equitable Fire Insurance Co Ltd* [1925] Ch 407 at 477. The onus of proving that a payment of dividend is ultra vires is on the person so alleging: *Re City Equitable Fire Insurance Co Ltd* supra at 477. A case comparable to *Re National Bank of Wales Ltd* [1899] 2 Ch 629, CA, where revenue items were improperly charged to capital in order to swell revenue profits, could not now arise in view of the Companies Act 1985 s 280(3): see para 701 note 1 ante.
9 *Mills v Northern Rly of Buenos Ayres Co* (1870) 5 Ch App 621.
10 *Lawrence v West Somerset Mineral Rly Co* [1918] 2 Ch 250; *Cross v Imperial Continental Gas Association* [1923] 2 Ch 553.

722. Liability of directors, auditors and shareholders where improper dividend is paid. Directors[1] and auditors[2] who are parties to the payment of an improper dividend are liable to proceedings by action, or, in the case of winding up, by misfeasance summons[3]; and the amount improperly paid may be recovered from them with interest, and without any allowance for income tax[4].

Where directors have paid improper dividends, shareholders who have received the dividend with knowledge that it was improper are bound to indemnify the directors against their liability in respect of the payment[5]. A shareholder who knows all the relevant facts and who has been paid an improper dividend cannot maintain an action against the company and its directors to make the directors liable for paying such a dividend unless he has first returned the dividend to the company, although he may be ordered to repay that dividend on a counterclaim by the company[6]. Improper dividends which are innocently received by shareholders, even if directors, cannot be recovered, at any rate where there is no winding up[7].

1 See *Denham & Co* (1883) 25 ChD 752; *Municipal Freehold Land Co Ltd v Pollington* (1890) 59 LJ Ch 734; *Prefontaine v Grenier* [1907] AC 101, PC; and *Turquand v Marshall* (1869) 4 Ch App 376 (bad debts); *Re Mercantile Trading Co, Stringer's Case* (1869) 4 Ch App 475; and see para 2448 et seq post. As to the consequences of an unlawful distribution see para 714 ante.
2 See *Re London and General Bank* [1895] 2 Ch 166, CA; *Re London and General Bank (No 2)* [1895] 2 Ch 673, CA (auditors appointed as such in pursuance of statute and articles of association); *Re Thomas Garrard & Son Ltd* [1968] Ch 455, [1967] 2 All ER 525.
3 See para 2448 et seq post.
4 *Re National Bank of Wales Ltd* [1899] 2 Ch 629, CA; affd without affecting the decision on this point sub nom *Dovey v Cory* [1901] AC 477, HL (where the rate of interest allowed was 5% per annum).
5 *Moxham v Grant* [1900] 1 QB 88, CA; *Re National Funds Assurance Co* (1878) 10 ChD 118; *Re Alexandra Palace Co* (1882) 21 ChD 149.
6 *Towers v African Tug Co* [1904] 1 Ch 558, CA.
7 *Towers v African Tug Co* [1904] 1 Ch 558, CA; *Lucas v Fitzgerald* (1903) 20 TLR 16; and see *James v Eve* (1873) LR 6 HL 335.

723. Declaration of dividends. Before any dividend is declared, there must be profits in an amount necessary to sustain the dividend in existence in the company itself[1]. A power to pay interim dividends[2] is usually vested by the articles in the directors[3]. The directors may pay an interim dividend, if, after making proper inquiries, they estimate that the profits available for distribution will be sufficient[4]. In such a case the court will not interfere with the directors' discretion at the instance of a shareholder[5]. A directors' declaration of an interim dividend may be rescinded before payment has been made[6].

As a rule a final dividend may be sanctioned only at the annual general meeting, when the accounts are presented to it[7], and the articles usually contain a specific provision to this effect, and also provide that no dividend shall exceed the amount recommended by the directors[8].

1 *Industrial Equity Ltd v Blackburn* (1977) 17 ALR 575 (Aust HC).
2 An interim dividend is one payable at some date between the ordinary general meetings. An interim dividend is not apportionable under the Apportionment Act 1870 unless it is declared in respect of a definite period: *Re Jowitt, Jowitt v Keeling* [1922] 2 Ch 442 at 447.
3 See eg the Companies (Tables A to F) Regulations 1985, SI 1985/805, Schedule, Table A art 102. Under such an article the payment of an interim dividend is in the sole hands of the directors, and cannot be usurped by the company: *Scott v Scott* [1943] 1 All ER 582.
4 *Lucas v Fitzgerald* (1903) 20 TLR 16; and see *Towers v African Tug Co* [1904] 1 Ch 558, CA.
5 *Lever v Land Securities Co Ltd* (1891) 8 TLR 94 (where a reserve fund of past profits was resorted to).
6 *Lagunas Nitrate Co Ltd v Schroeder & Co and Schmidt* (1901) 85 LT 22 (where an interim dividend account had been opened at a bank); *Potel v IRC* [1971] 2 All ER 504.
7 See *Nicholson v Rhodesia Trading Co* [1897] 1 Ch 434.
8 Cf the Companies (Tables A to F) Regulations 1985 Schedule, Table A art 102 which provides that, subject to the provisions of the Companies Act 1985, the company may by ordinary resolution declare dividends in accordance with the respective rights of the members, but no dividend must exceed the amount recommended by the directors.
  As to the obligations of a company which has obtained admission to the Official List of the Stock Exchange with regard to dividends see the *Listing Rules* rr 9.34, 9.35, 12.40. As to the *Listing Rules* generally see para 282 ante.

724. When dividend recoverable. Upon the declaration of a dividend for the payment of which no time is stipulated, the sums due for dividend become debts immediately due from the company to the shareholders[1], and the shareholders may sue the company for the dividend. Nevertheless, the relation of trustee and beneficiary is not created, and time immediately begins to run[2] under the Limitation Act 1980, the period of limitation being six years[3]. If, however, the articles contain the usual power of the directors to manage the company's business[4], they normally specify, when recommending a final dividend, the date on which the dividend is to be paid[5]. In this case a shareholder has no right to enforce payment until the due date for payment arrives[6].

The articles sometimes provide that amounts due from any member in respect of calls may be deducted from any dividends payable to him; but, even in the absence of such a provision, calls and dividends may be set off[7] before a winding up commences[8].

In the absence of special provision to the contrary[9], dividends must be paid in money[10] and not in shares or securities[11]. The articles usually provide that dividends shall not bear interest against the company[12].

1 *Bond v Barrow Haematite Steel Co* [1902] 1 Ch 353; *Re Accrington Corpn Steam Tramways Co* [1909] 2 Ch 40; and see *Godfrey Phillips Ltd v Investment Trust Corpn Ltd* [1953] Ch 449, [1953] 1 All ER 7. In the case of a fixed preference dividend, the declaration of a dividend is not always essential: *Evling v Israel and Oppenheimer Ltd* [1918] 1 Ch 101; but see *Re Catalinas Warehouses and Mole Co Ltd* [1947] 1 All ER 51; cf *Re Buenos Ayres Great Southern Rly Co Ltd, Buenos Ayres Great Southern Rly Co v Preston* [1947] Ch 384, [1947] 1 All ER 729.
2 *Re Severn and Wye and Severn Bridge Rly Co* [1896] 1 Ch 559; *Dalton v Midland Counties Rly Co* (1853) 13 CB 474 at 478 per Jervis CJ.
3 Limitation Act 1980 s 5; *Re Compania De Electricidad de la Provincia de Buenos Aires Ltd* [1980] Ch 146, [1978] 3 All ER 668, not following *Re Artisans' Land and Mortgage Corpn* [1904] 1 Ch 796 and *Re Drogheda SS Co* [1903] 1 IR 512; cf *Smith v Cork and Bandon Rly Co* (1870) IR 5 Eq 65, CA. Cf the Companies (Tables A to F) Regulations 1985, SI 1985/805, Schedule, Table A art 108 which provides that any dividend which has remained unclaimed for 12 years from the date when it became due for payment, will, if the directors so resolve, be forfeited and cease to remain owing by the company.

4 See eg ibid Schedule, Table A art 70 (cited in para 589 note 1 ante).
5 *Thairlwall v Great Northern Rly Co* [1910] 2 KB 509; *Potel v IRC* [1971] 2 All ER 504.
6 *Re Kidner, Kidner v Kidner* [1929] 2 Ch 121; *Potel v IRC* [1971] 2 All ER 504.
7 Lindley's Law of Companies (6th Edn) 610; cf *Christie v Taunton, Delmard, Lane & Co, Re Taunton, Delmard, Lane & Co* [1893] 2 Ch 175 (calls and debentures); and see RSC Ord 18 r 17.
8 As to set-off in winding up see para 2498 post.
9 See para 732 post.
10 There is usually a provision regarding the method of payment in the articles: see eg the Companies (Tables A to F) Regulations 1985 Schedule, Table A art 106 which provides that any dividend or other moneys payable in respect of shares may be paid by cheque sent by post to the registered address of the person entitled, and makes provision for payment of dividends to joint holders. In the absence of a provision such as this in the articles, a shareholder may impliedly agree to payment by cheque sent through the post: see *Thairlwall v Great Northern Rly Co* [1910] 2 KB 509.
11 *Hoole v Great Western Rly Co* (1867) 3 Ch App 262; *Wood v Odessa Waterworks Co* (1889) 42 ChD 636.
12 See eg the Companies (Tables A to F) Regulations 1985 Schedule, Table A art 107.

725. Dividends on preference shares. The question whether preference share-holders are entitled to be paid their arrears of dividends in priority to the holders of other shares out of any profit distributed by the company, or merely to rank in priority in respect of any profits distributed in the current year, depends on whether their dividends are cumulative or non-cumulative[1]. Where cumulative preference shares of the same class have been issued at different times and the arrears of dividend due on them are of varying amounts, the fund available for dividend must be distributed pro rata among the holders of those shares according to the respective amounts of the arrears on the shares held by them[2]. Holders of preference shares may obtain an injunction to restrain a proposed payment of an interim dividend in excess of that authorised by the articles[3] or of any ordinary dividend in prejudice of their rights[4]. Where business is carried on abroad, they are entitled, in the absence of express stipulation, to their full dividend without deducting any income tax payable there[5].

1 As to the priority of preference shares as regards dividend and the circumstances in which the dividend is cumulative see para 180 ante; and as to the rights of preference shareholders in a winding up to payments in respect of past dividends see para 2592 post.
2 *First Garden City Ltd v Bonham-Carter* [1928] Ch 53.
3 *Durlacher v Hotchkiss Ordnance Co Ltd* (1887) 3 TLR 807.
4 *Henry v Great Northern Rly Co* (1857) 1 De G & J 606; *Sturge v Eastern Union Rly Co* (1855) 7 De GM & G 158, CA; *Matthews v Great Northern Rly Co* (1859) 28 LJ Ch 375; *Webb v Earle* (1875) LR 20 Eq 556; *Foster v Coles and M B Foster & Sons Ltd* (1906) 22 TLR 555; *Godfrey Phillips Ltd v Investment Trust Corpn Ltd* [1953] Ch 449, [1953] 1 All ER 7.
5 *Spiller v Turner* [1897] 1 Ch 911, followed in *Indian and General Investment Trust Ltd v Borax Consolidated Ltd* [1920] 1 KB 539; and *London and South American Investment Trust Ltd v British Tobacco Co (Australia) Ltd* [1927] 1 Ch 107. As to the taxation of company distributions see paras 733, 734 post.

726. Calculation of dividends tax free up to a certain limit. Where dividends are payable tax free up to a specified rate in the pound sterling, the deduction in respect of the excess rate of income tax over the specified figure must be calculated on the amount of the stated dividend, and not on the amount of that dividend grossed up at the tax-free figure[1].

1 *Friends Provident and Century Life Office v Investment Trust Corpn Ltd* [1951] 2 All ER 632, HL; *Austin Motor Co Ltd v British SS Investment Trust Ltd* [1950] 1 All ER 632, CA.

727. Forfeiture of unclaimed dividends. The articles sometimes provide that a dividend, unclaimed within a specified period from its declaration, may be forfeited by a resolution of the directors[1]; such an article will only be enforced, if at all, on its being strictly complied with[2].

1 See eg the Companies (Tables A to F) Regulations 1985, SI 1985/805, Schedule, Table A art 108 (cited in para 724 note 3 ante).
2 *Ward v Dublin North City Milling Co Ltd* [1919] 1 IR 5. This case is not a binding authority for the proposition that such an article will be enforced.

728. Discretion as to reserve fund. If the directors have power, as is usual, to set aside out of the profits a sum for or towards a reserve fund, their discretion cannot be questioned on the ground that it reduces the amount available for dividend, whether on ordinary or preference shares[1]. If they have no such express power, the company has an implied power to the same effect; for there is no principle which compels a company while a going concern to divide the whole of its profits among the shareholders[2]. The power may, however, be negatived by the articles[3]. Subject to any provisions in the articles, the questions what portion of the profits available for distribution should be divided and what portion retained, are questions of internal management which the shareholders must decide for themselves. The court cannot control or review their decision, and it makes no difference whether the undivided balance is retained to the credit of the profit and loss account, or carried to the credit of a reserve fund, or appropriated to any other use of the company, though a power to invest would not justify speculating in stocks and shares. The company[4] may invest the undivided money on such securities as the directors, subject to the control of a general meeting, may select[5]. As a rule a reserve fund formed out of profits retains its character of profits, and is capable of future division as such[6]. If the formation of a reserve fund is forbidden, the articles may be altered to authorise it[7].

1 *Long Acre Press Ltd v Odhams Press Ltd* [1930] 2 Ch 196; *Fisher v Black and White Publishing Co* [1901] 1 Ch 174, CA; *Re Buenos Ayres Great Southern Rly Co Ltd, Buenos Ayres Great Southern Rly Co Ltd v Preston* [1947] Ch 384, [1947] 1 All ER 729; and see *Burland v Earle* [1902] AC 83, PC; *Wemyss Collieries Trust Ltd v Melville* (1905) 8 F 143. Similarly, where an outside contractor agrees to take a share in the profits available for dividend, his right to share in them is subject to any provisions which may be made for reserves: *Bagot Pneumatic Tyre Co v Clipper Pneumatic Tyre Co* [1902] 1 Ch 146, CA; *Stewart v Sashalite Ltd* [1936] 2 All ER 1481.
2 *Burland v Earle* [1902] AC 83, PC.
3 *Evling v Israel and Oppenheimer Ltd* [1918] 1 Ch 101; *R Paterson & Sons Ltd v Paterson* [1916] WN 352, HL.
4 *Burland v Earle* [1902] AC 83 at 95, PC.
5 *Burland v Earle* [1902] AC 83 at 96, PC.
6 *Lever v Land Securities Co Ltd* (1891) 8 TLR 94; *Re Hoare & Co Ltd and Reduced* [1904] 2 Ch 208, CA. Cf *Drown v Gaumont-British Picture Corpn Ltd* [1937] Ch 402, [1937] 2 All ER 609 (the actual decision in which is overridden by the Companies Act 1985 s 130: see paras 188, 189 ante).
7 *British Equitable Assurance Co Ltd v Baily* [1906] AC 35, HL; *Allen v Gold Reefs of West Africa Ltd* [1900] 1 Ch 656, CA.

729. Secret reserve. Provision is made for the basis upon which a company's fixed assets are to be valued[1], and the amount of such a valuation may be less than the market value.

To this extent there may be a reserve of values which might be described as a secret reserve; but the balance sheet must contain a statement of the aggregate amounts of reserves[2] and provisions[3] under separate headings[4], and the articles must not preclude the auditors from fulfilling their statutory duties to the shareholders[5].

1 See the Companies Act 1985 s 226(3), Sch 4 Pt II paras 17–23, 29–32 and para 810 et seq post.
2 See ibid Sch 4, Balance Sheet Formats 1, 2 (as amended) and paras 832, 833 post.
3 For the meaning of 'provisions' see ibid Sch 4 paras 88, 89 and paras 810 note 4, 832 note 24 respectively post. As to the statutory balance sheet formats see paras 832, 833 post.
4 Ibid s 226(3), Sch 4 Pt I, Balance Sheet Formats 1, 2 (as amended),.
5 *Newton v Birmingham Small Arms Co Ltd* [1906] 2 Ch 378. So far as they might be considered as approving the practice of maintaining secret reserves the dicta of Buckley J at 387 must be treated as modified by the Companies Act 1985 Sch 4 (as amended), which should be read in conjunction with the report required from the auditors by s 235 (as substituted) (see para 1059 post). See also *Young v Brownlee & Co* 1911 SC 677.

730. Participation in dividend. As between the company and its members, and subject to the articles[1], only those members who are on the register when the dividend is declared are entitled to participate in it[2]. As between the vendor and the purchaser of shares, where the contract for sale is silent as to dividends, the purchaser is, however, entitled to dividends declared on the shares after the date of the contract, even where the dividend is declared in respect of a period before that date[3]. It is otherwise where the dividend is declared prior to the date of the contract, even where it is payable by instalments, some of which are unpaid at that date[4].

In the case of securities sold on the Stock Exchange, in the absence of special bargains, sales are made 'cum dividend' or 'ex dividend' according to the Official List quotation, which varies with different classes of securities. If they are not so quoted, the dealers by means of special bargains fix the dates at which the securities become 'ex dividend'. The same practice applies in the case of 'rights' in respect of existing holdings. The right to future dividends may be sold, and such a contract, if carried out by a broker for a client, will be enforced against the client[5].

1 See the Companies (Tables A to F) Regulations 1985, SI 1985/805, Schedule, Table A art 31, under which persons to whom shares are transmitted by reason of the holder's death or bankruptcy are entitled to dividends even though not registered.
2 *Re Wakley, Wakley v Vachell* [1920] 2 Ch 205, CA; *Godfrey Phillips Ltd v Investment Trust Corpn Ltd* [1953] Ch 449, [1953] 1 All ER 7 (payment of arrears of underpayments on preference shares).
3 *Black v Homersham* (1878) 4 ExD 24; *Re Wimbush, Richards v Wimbush* [1940] Ch 92, [1940] 1 All ER 229. Similarly, the purchaser may claim all rights accrued due to the vendor in respect of the shares after the date of purchase, such as the right to an allotment of further shares in the company: see *Stewart v Lupton* (1874) 22 WR 855; *Rooney v Stanton* (1900) 17 TLR 28, CA; cf *Re Morgan, ex p Phillips, ex p Marnham* (1860) 2 De GF & J 634.
4 *Re Kidner, Kidner v Kidner* [1929] 2 Ch 121.
5 *Marten v Gibbon* (1875) 33 LT 561, CA.

731. Dividends on settled shares. Where a person who holds shares as trustee for another person is registered as a shareholder, he is the only person recognised by the company as entitled to payment of a dividend[1], and the company is not concerned with the interests of the beneficiaries or the apportionment or distribution of profits between capital and income[2].

1 See the Companies Act 1985 s 360 and para 385 ante.
2 See ibid s 360; the Companies (Tables A to F) Regulations 1985, SI 1985/805, Schedule, Table A art 29. As to the division of dividends on settled shares between the tenant for life and remainderman see eg *Re Kleinwort's Settlements, Westminster Bank Ltd v Bennett* [1951] Ch 860, [1951] 2 All ER 328 and SETTLEMENTS vol 42 para 956.

732. Dividends in specie and capitalisation of profits. Articles of association usually provide that any meeting of the company declaring a dividend may resolve that the dividend be paid wholly or partly by the distribution of specific assets such as paid-up shares or debentures in that or any other company[1]. Further, they usually provide[2] that any undivided profits available for dividend[3] may be capitalised and distributed among the shareholders on the footing that they become entitled to the profits as capital, and that any undivided profits distributed may be applied in paying up in full unissued shares or debentures[4] of the company or towards payment of the amount unpaid on any issued shares or debentures. In the absence of such express authority dividends may not be paid otherwise than in cash[5]; and, although profits may to some extent be capitalised without any such provisions in the articles[6], the provisions in question enable the company definitely to determine whether the fund distributed is to be regarded as capital or income[7].

1 See eg the Companies (Tables A to F) Regulations 1985, SI 1985/805, Schedule, Table A art 105. For an example of such a distribution see *Pool v Guardian Investment Trust Co* [1922] 1 KB 347. In the case of a company which has obtained admission to the Official List of the Stock Exchange, in a capitalisation issue, other than one in lieu of dividend, if a shareholder's entitlement includes a fraction of a security, that fraction must be sold for the benefit of the holder, save that, if its value (net of expenses) does not exceed £3.00, it may be sold for the company's benefit; sales of fractions may be made before listing is granted: *Listing Rules* r 4.32. As to the *Listing Rules* generally see para 282 ante.

2 See eg the Companies (Tables A to F) Regulations 1985 Schedule, Table A art 110.

3 As to profits available for distribution see para 702 ante.

4 See *IRC v Fisher's Executors* [1926] AC 395, HL.

5 *Wood v Odessa Waterworks Co* [1889] 42 ChD 636; *Hoole v Great Western Rly* (1867) 3 Ch App 262. See also para 724 note 10 ante.

6 *Bouch v Sproule* (1887) 12 App Cas 385, HL (where accumulated profits were in substance credited to shareholders as payment on new shares allotted to them; the shareholders could individually have refused to accept the new shares).

7 *Bouch v Sproule* (1887) 12 App Cas 385, HL; *IRC v Blott* [1921] 2 AC 171 at 182, HL; *Re Outen's Will Trusts, Starling v Outen* [1963] Ch 291, [1962] 3 All ER 478. As to the payment of income tax on capitalised profits see INCOME TAXATION vol 23 (Reissue) para 934 et seq; and as to restrictions on the issue of bonus shares in connection with the restrictions on shares by the Secretary of State on the investigation of ownership of a company see para 1383 post.

E. TAXATION OF COMPANY DISTRIBUTIONS

733. United Kingdom company distributions not generally liable to corporation tax. Except as otherwise provided by the Corporation Tax Acts, corporation tax is not chargeable on dividends and other distributions of a company resident in the United Kingdom; nor are any such dividends or distributions to be taken into account in computing income for corporation tax[1].

1 See the Income and Corporation Taxes Act 1988 s 208 and INCOME TAXATION vol 23 (Reissue) para 875. As to the taxation of company distributions generally see INCOME TAXATION vol 23 (Reissue) para 875 et seq.

734. Charge to tax. Income tax is charged on the recipients of distributions by companies under Schedule F[1]. Income tax under Schedule F is chargeable for any year of assessment in respect of all dividends and other distributions in that year of a company resident in the United Kingdom which are not specially excluded from income tax; and for the purposes of income tax all such distributions are to be regarded as income however they fall to be dealt with in the hands of the recipient[2]. For the purposes of Schedule F and all other purposes of the Tax Acts, any such distribution in respect of which a person is entitled to a tax credit[3] is to be treated as representing income equal to the aggregate of the amount or value of that distribution and the amount of that credit; and income tax under Schedule F is accordingly charged on that aggregate[4].

Except in the case of underwriters, no distribution chargeable under Schedule F is chargeable under any other provision of the Income Tax Acts[5].

1 See the Income and Corporation Taxes Act 1988 s 20(1), Schedule F (as amended) and INCOME TAXATION vol 23 (Reissue) para 878. As to the taxation of company distributions generally see INCOME TAXATION vol 23 (Reissue) para 875 et seq.
2 See ibid Schedule F para 1 and INCOME TAXATION vol 23 (Reissue) para 878.
3 As to tax credits see INCOME TAXATION vol 23 (Reissue) para 907 et seq.
4 See the Income and Corporation Taxes Act 1988 Schedule F para 2 and INCOME TAXATION vol 23 (Reissue) para 878.
5 See ibid s 20(2) (as amended) and INCOME TAXATION vol 23 (Reissue) para 878.

(15) DISCLOSURE OF INTERESTS IN SHARES

(i) Individual and Group Acquisitions

735. Obligation of disclosure. Where a person either:
(1) to his knowledge acquires an interest in shares comprised in a public company's relevant share capital[1], or ceases to be interested in shares so comprised (whether or not retaining an interest in other shares so comprised); or
(2) becomes aware that he has acquired an interest in shares so comprised or that he has ceased to be interested in shares so comprised in which he was previously interested,

then in certain circumstances he comes under an obligation ('the obligation of disclosure') to make notification to the company with respect to his interests, if any, in its shares[2].

Where, otherwise than in the above circumstances, a person:
(a) is aware at the time when it occurs of any change of circumstances affecting facts relevant to the application of the statutory provisions[3] to an existing interest of his in shares comprised in a company's share capital of any description; or
(b) otherwise becomes aware of any such facts, whether or not arising from any such change of circumstances,

then in certain circumstances he comes under the obligation of disclosure[4].

The existence of the obligation in a particular case depends, in part, on circumstances obtaining before and after whatever is in that case the relevant time, that is to say:
(i) in a case within heads (1) or (a) above, the time of the event or change of circumstances there mentioned; and
(ii) in a case within heads (2) or (b) above, the time at which the person became aware of the facts in question[5].

1 In relation to a public company, 'relevant share capital' means the company's issued share capital of a class carrying rights to vote in all circumstances at general meetings of the company; and for the avoidance of doubt it is declared that (1) where a company's share capital is divided into different classes of shares, references in the Companies Act 1985 Pt VI (ss 198–220 (as amended): see infra and para 736 et seq post) to a percentage of the nominal value of its relevant share capital are to a percentage of the nominal value of the issued shares comprised in each of the classes taken separately; and (2) the temporary suspension of voting rights in respect of shares comprised in issued share capital of a company of any such class does not affect the application of Pt VI (ss 198–220) (as amended) in relation to interests

in those or any other shares comprised in that class: ss 198(2), 220(1) (substituted by the Disclosure of Interests in Shares (Amendment) Regulations 1993, SI 1993/1819, regs 2, 9). As to the Secretary of State's power by regulations to amend the Companies Act 1985 s 198(2) see para 746 post. For the meaning of 'public company' see para 82 ante.

2 Ibid s 198(1) (amended by the Disclosure of Interests in Shares (Amendment) Regulations 1993 regs 2, 3).

3 Ie the Companies Act 1985 s 199 (as amended): see para 736 post.

4 Ibid s 198(3).

5 Ibid s 198(4).

736. Interests to be disclosed. For the purposes of the obligation of disclosure[1], the interests to be taken into account are those in relevant share capital[2] of the company concerned[3]. Where a person is interested in shares comprised in relevant share capital, then:

(1) if in some or all of those shares he has interests which are material interests[4], he has a notifiable interest at any time when the aggregate nominal value of the shares in which those material interests subsist is equal to or more than 3% of the nominal value of that share capital;

(2) he has a notifiable interest at any time when, not having such an interest by virtue of head (1) above, the aggregate nominal value of the shares in which he has interests, whether or not including material interests, is equal to or more than 10% of the nominal value of the relevant share capital[5].

All facts relevant to determining whether a person has a notifiable interest at any time (or the percentage level of his interest) are taken to be what he knows the facts to be at that time[6].

The obligation of disclosure arises[7] where the person has a notifiable interest immediately after the relevant time[8], but did not have such an interest immediately before that time[9]. The obligation also arises[10] where:

(a) the person had a notifiable interest immediately before the relevant time, but does not have such an interest immediately after it; or

(b) he had a notifiable interest immediately before that time, and has such an interest immediately after it, but the percentage levels of his interest[11] immediately before and immediately after that time are not the same[12].

1 For the meaning of 'the obligation of disclosure' see para 735 ante.

2 For the meaning of 'relevant share capital' see para 735 note 1 ante.

3 Companies Act 1985 s 199(1).

4 For these purposes, a material interest is any interest other than (1) an interest which a person authorised to manage investments belonging to another has by virtue of having the management of such investments under an agreement in or evidenced in writing; (2) an interest which a person has by virtue of being the operator of an authorised unit trust scheme, a recognised scheme or a UCITS; (3) an interest in shares in a listed company which, if that company were not listed, would fall to be disregarded by virtue of ibid s 209(10) (as substituted) (see para 744 post); or (4) an interest of another which a person is taken to have by virtue of the application of s 203 (as amended) (see para 738 post) or s 205 (see para 740 post), where the interest of that other person falls within heads (1), (2) or (3) supra: s 199(2A) (substituted by the Disclosure of Interests in Shares (Amendment) Regulations 1993, SI 1993/1819, regs 2, 4(1)); Companies Act 1985 s 220(1) (substituted by the Disclosure of Interests in Shares (Amendment) Regulations 1993 regs 2, 4(1)). 'UCITS' means a collective investment scheme which (a) is constituted in a member State other than the United Kingdom; and (b) complies with the conditions necessary for it to enjoy the rights conferred by EC Council Directive 85/611 (OJ L375, 31.12.85, p 3) co-ordinating the laws, regulations and administrative provisions relating to undertakings for collective investment in transferable securities; and the Financial Services Act 1986 s 86(8) (meaning of 'constituted in a member State': see MONEY) applies for the purposes of head (a) supra as it applies for the purposes of s 86: Companies Act 1985 s 199(8) (added by the Disclosure of Interests in Shares (Amendment) Regulations 1993 regs 2, 4(3)); Companies Act 1985 s 220(1) (as so substituted). A person

is authorised to manage investments belonging to another if (i) he is an authorised person under the Financial Services Act 1986 Pt I Ch III (ss 7–34 (as amended): see MONEY) and may manage that other's investments without contravening any specified prohibition; or (ii) it is an authorised credit institution which may manage that other's investments without being in breach of its authorisation: Companies Act 1985 s 199(6) (added by the Disclosure of Interests in Shares (Amendment) Regulations 1993 regs 2, 4(3)). The prohibitions so specified are: (A) any prohibition contained in rules which make provision of a description in the Financial Services Act 1986 s 48(2)(a), (b) (see MONEY) and which are made by the Secretary of State, the Treasury, a designated agency, a recognised professional body or a recognised self-regulating organisation; and (B) any prohibition imposed under s 65 (see MONEY): Companies Act 1985 s 199(7) (added by the Disclosure of Interests in Shares (Amendment) Regulations 1993 regs 2, 4(3)). 'Authorised unit trust scheme' has the same meaning as in the Financial Services Act 1986 Pt I Ch VIII (ss 75–95 (as amended): see MONEY): Companies Act 1985 s 220(1) (as so substituted). 'Authorised credit institution' means a credit institution as defined in EC Council Directive 77/780 (OJ L322, 17.12.77, p 30) art 1 which is authorised to carry on the business of a credit institution by a competent authority of a member State other than the United Kingdom: Companies Act 1985 s 220(1) (as so substituted). 'Designated agency', 'recognised scheme', 'recognised professional body' and 'recognised self-regulating organisation' have the same meaning as in the Financial Services Act 1986 (see MONEY): Companies Act 1985 s 220(1) (as so substituted). 'Listed company' means a company any of the shares in which are officially listed on a relevant stock exchange; and 'listed' is to be construed accordingly: Companies Act 1985 s 220(1) (as so substituted). 'Relevant stock exchange' means a stock exchange situated or operating in a member State: Companies Act 1985 s 220(1) (as so substituted).

5 Ibid s 199(2) (substituted by the Disclosure of Interests in Shares (Amendment) Regulations 1993 regs 2, 4(1)). As to the Secretary of State's power by regulations to amend the percentage giving rise to a 'notifiable interest' see para 746 post.

6 Companies Act 1985 s 199(3).

7 Ie under ibid s 198(1) (as amended) (see para 735 ante) or s 198(3) (see para 735 ante).

8 For the meaning of 'relevant time' see para 735 ante.

9 Companies Act 1985 s 199(4).

10 See note 7 supra.

11 For these purposes, 'percentage level' means the percentage figure found by expressing the aggregate nominal value of all the shares comprised in the share capital concerned in which the person has material interests immediately before or, as the case may be, immediately after the relevant time as a percentage of the nominal value of that share capital and rounding that figure down, if it is not a whole number, to the next whole number: Companies Act 1985 s 200(1) (substituted by the Disclosure of Interests in Shares (Amendment) Regulations 1993 regs 2, 5). In relation to a notifiable interest which a person has when the aggregate nominal value of the shares in which he is interested is equal to more than 10% of the nominal value of that relevant share capital, the Companies Act 1985 s 200(1) (as so substituted) has effect as if for the words 'has material interests' there were substituted 'is interested': s 200(2) (substituted by the Disclosure of Interests in Shares (Amendment) Regulations 1993 regs 2, 5). Where the nominal value of the share capital is greater immediately after the relevant time than it was immediately before, the percentage level of the person's interest immediately before, as well as immediately after, that time is determined by reference to the larger amount: Companies Act 1985 s 200(3) (substituted by the Disclosure of Interests in Shares (Amendment) Regulations 1993 regs 2, 5).

12 Companies Act 1985 s 199(5) (amended by the Disclosure of Interests in Shares (Amendment) Regulations 1993 regs 2, 4(2)).

737. Particulars to be contained in notification. Where notification with respect to a person's interest, if any, in shares comprised in relevant share capital[1] of a public company is required[2], the obligation to make the notification must be performed within the period of two days[3] next following the day on which that obligation arises; and the notification must be in writing to the company[4]. The notification must specify the share capital to which it relates, and must also:

(1) state[5] the number of shares comprised in that share capital in which the person making the notification knows he had material interests immediately after the time when the obligation arose; or

(2) in a case where the person no longer has a notifiable interest[6] in shares comprised in that share capital, state that he no longer has that interest[7].

A notification, other than one stating that a person no longer has a notifiable interest, must include the following particulars, so far as known to the person making the notification at the date when it is made:

(a) the identity of each registered holder of shares to which the notification relates and the number of such shares held by each of them; and

(b) the number of such shares in which the interest of the person giving the notification is a specified[8] interest[9].

A person who has an interest in shares comprised in a company's relevant share capital, that interest being notifiable, is under obligation to notify the company in writing of any such particulars[10] in relation to those shares and of any change in those particulars, of which in either case he becomes aware at any time after any interest notification date[11] and before the first occasion following that date on which he comes under any further obligation of disclosure with respect to his interest in shares comprised in that share capital[12]. A person who at any time has an interest in shares which is so notifiable is to be regarded for this purpose as continuing to have a notifiable interest in them unless and until he comes under obligation to make a notification stating that he no longer has such an interest in those shares[13].

An obligation arising under the above provisions must be performed within the period of two days[14] next following the day on which it arises[15].

1 For the meaning of 'relevant share capital' see para 735 note 1 ante.

2 Ie by the Companies Act 1985 s 198 (as amended): see para 735 ante.

3 For these purposes, where the period allowed by any provision of ibid Pt VI (ss 198–220 (as amended): see paras 735, 736 ante; infra; and para 738 et seq post) for fulfilling an obligation is expressed as a number of days, any day that is a Saturday or Sunday or a bank holiday in any part of Great Britain is to be disregarded in reckoning that period: s 220(2). For the meaning of 'bank holiday' see para 71 note 9 ante.

4 Ibid s 202(1) (amended by the Companies Act 1989 ss 134(1), (3), 212, Sch 24). As to the Secretary of State's power by regulations to amend the Companies Act 1985 s 202(1) (as so amended) see para 746 post.

5 Ie subject to ibid s 202(2A), (2B) (as added). Where, immediately after the relevant time, the aggregate nominal value of the shares in which the person making the notification is interested is equal to or more than 10% of the nominal value of that relevant share capital, s 202(2)(a) (as substituted) (see text head (1) supra) has effect as if for the words 'had material interests' there were substituted 'was interested': s 202(2A) (added by the Disclosure of Interests in Shares (Amendment) Regulations 1993, SI 1993/1819, regs 2, 6(2)). Nothing in the Companies Act 1985 s 202(2) or (2A) (as respectively amended and added) requires a notification to state, in relation to any shares, whether the interest of the person making the notification is, or is not, a material interest: s 202(2B) (added by the Disclosure of Interests in Shares (Amendment) Regulations 1993 regs 2, 6(2)). For the meaning of 'relevant time' see para 735 ante; and for the meaning of 'material interest' see para 736 note 4 ante.

6 For the meaning of 'notifiable interest' see para 736 ante.

7 Companies Act 1985 s 202(2) (amended by the Disclosure of Interests in Shares (Amendment) Regulations 1993 regs 2, 6(2)).

8 Ie an interest such as is mentioned in the Companies Act 1985 s 208(5): see para 743 post.

9 Ibid s 202(3) (substituted by the Companies Act 1989 s 134(1), (4)).

10 Ie the particulars specified in the Companies Act 1985 s 202(3) (as substituted): see supra.

11 For these purposes, the reference to an interest notification date, in relation to a person's interest in shares comprised in a public company's relevant share capital, is to either of the following: (1) the date of any notification made by him with respect to his interest under ibid Pt VI (ss 198–220) (as amended); and (2) where he has failed to make a notification, the date on which the period allowed for making it came to an end: s 202(5).

12 Ibid s 202(4).

13 Ibid s 202(6).

14 See note 3 supra.

15 Companies Act 1985 s 202(4) (amended by the Companies Act 1989 s 134(1), (3)). As to the Secretary of State's power by regulations to amend the Companies Act 1985 s 202(4) (as so amended) see para 746 post.

738. Notification of family and corporate interests. For purposes of the above provisions[1], a person is taken to be interested in any shares in which his spouse or any infant[2] child or stepchild of his is interested[3]. For those purposes also, a person is taken to be interested in shares if a body corporate[4] is interested in them and:

(1) that body or its directors are accustomed to act in accordance with his directions or instructions; or

(2) he is entitled to exercise or control the exercise[5] of one-third or more of the voting power at general meetings of that body corporate[6].

Where a person is entitled to exercise or control the exercise of one-third or more of the voting power at general meetings of a body corporate and that body corporate is entitled to exercise or control the exercise of any of the voting power at general meetings of another body corporate ('the effective voting power') then, for the purposes of head (2) above, the effective voting power is taken as exercisable by that person[7].

1 Ie the Companies Act 1985 ss 198–202 (as amended): see paras 735–737 ante.
2 As to the attainment of majority at the age of 18 see the Family Law Reform Act 1969 s 1 and CHILDREN vol 5(2) (Reissue) para 601.
3 Companies Act 1985 s 203(1).
4 For the meaning of 'body corporate' see para 89 note 8 ante.
5 For these purposes, a person is entitled to exercise or control the exercise of voting power if he has a right (whether subject to conditions or not) the exercise of which would make him so entitled, or he is under an obligation (whether or not so subject) the fulfilment of which would make him so entitled: Companies Act 1985 s 203(4).
6 Ibid s 203(2).
7 Ibid s 203(3).

739. Agreement to acquire interests in a particular public company. In certain circumstances the obligation of disclosure[1] may arise from an agreement[2] between two or more persons which includes provision for the acquisition by any one or more of them of interests in shares of a particular public company ('the target company'), being shares comprised in the relevant share capital[3] of that company[4]. These provisions apply to such an agreement if:

(1) the agreement also includes provisions imposing obligations or restrictions on any one or more of the parties to it with respect to their use[5], retention or disposal of their interests in that company's shares acquired in pursuance of the agreement (whether or not together with any other interests of theirs in the company's shares to which the agreement relates); and

(2) any interest in the company's shares is in fact acquired by any of the parties in pursuance of the agreement,

and, in relation to such an agreement, references below[6] to the target company are to the company which is[7] the target company for that agreement[8].

Once any interest in shares in the target company has been acquired in pursuance of such an agreement as is mentioned above, these provisions continue to apply to that agreement irrespective of:

(a) whether or not any further acquisitions of interests in the company's shares take place in pursuance of the agreement; and

(b) any change in the persons who are for the time being parties to it; and

(c) any variation of the agreement,

so long as the agreement continues to include provisions of any description mentioned in head (1) above[9].

These provisions do not, however, apply to any agreement which is not legally binding unless it involves mutuality in the undertakings, expectations or understandings of the parties to it; nor do they apply to an agreement to underwrite or sub-underwrite any offer of shares in a company, provided the agreement is confined to that purpose and any matters incidental to it[10].

1 For the meaning of 'the obligation of disclosure' see para 735 ante.
2 For these purposes, 'agreement' includes any agreement or arrangement; and references to provisions of an agreement (1) accordingly include undertakings, expectations or understandings operative under any arrangement; and (2) without prejudice to head (1) supra also include any provisions, whether express or implied and whether absolute or not: Companies Act 1985 s 204(5).
3 For the meaning of 'relevant share capital' see para 735 note 1 ante.
4 Companies Act 1985 s 204(1). For the meaning of 'public company' see para 82 ante.
5 For these purposes, the reference to the use of interests in shares in the target company is to the exercise of any rights of any control or influence arising from those interests (including the right to enter into any agreement for the exercise, or for control of the exercise, of any of those rights by another person): ibid s 204(3).
6 Ie in ibid ss 204–206 (as amended): see infra and paras 740, 741 post.
7 Ie in accordance with ibid s 204(1), (2).
8 Ibid s 204(2).
9 Ibid s 204(4). For these purposes, references to the agreement include any agreement having effect (whether directly or indirectly) in substitution for the original agreement: s 204(4).
10 Ibid s 204(6).

740. Obligation of disclosure arising under an agreement to acquire an interest in a particular public company. In the case of an agreement to acquire an interest in a particular public company[1], each party to the agreement is taken, for purposes of the obligation of disclosure[2], to be interested in all shares in the target company[3] in which any other party to it is interested apart from the agreement, whether or not the interest of the other party in question was acquired, or includes any interest which was acquired, in pursuance of the agreement[4]. For these purposes, an interest of a party to such an agreement in shares in the target company is an interest apart from the agreement if he is interested in those shares otherwise than by virtue of the application of the relevant statutory provisions[5] in relation to the agreement[6]. Accordingly, any such interest of the person, apart from the agreement, includes for those purposes any interest treated as his[7] in relation to any other agreement with respect to shares in the target company to which he is a party[8].

A notification with respect to his interest in shares in the target company made to that company under these provisions[9] by a person who is for the time being a party to an agreement to acquire an interest in a particular company must:

(1) state that the person making the notification is a party to such an agreement;
(2) include the names and (so far as known to him) the addresses of the other parties to the agreement, identifying them as such; and
(3) state whether or not any of the shares to which the notification relates are shares in which he is interested by virtue of the relevant statutory provisions[10] and, if so, the number of those shares[11].

Where a person makes a notification to a company under these provisions in consequence of ceasing to be interested in any shares of that company by virtue of the fact that he or any other person has ceased to be a party to an agreement to acquire an interest in a particular public company, the notification must include a statement that he or that other person has ceased to be a party to the agreement, as the case may require, and also (in the latter case) the name and, if known to him, the address of that other[12].

1 As to such agreements see para 739 ante. For the meaning of 'agreement' see para 739 note 2 ante.
2 For the meaning of 'the obligation of disclosure' see para 735 ante.
3 For the meaning of 'target company' see para 739 ante.
4 Companies Act 1985 s 205(1). For the meaning of 'public company' see para 82 ante.
5 Ie ibid ss 204, 205: see infra and para 739 ante.
6 Ibid s 205(2).
7 Ie under ibid ss 203–205: see infra and paras 738, 739 ante.
8 Ibid s 205(3).
9 Ie those contained in ibid Pt VI (ss 198–220) (as amended).
10 See note 5 supra.
11 Companies Act 1985 s 205(4).
12 Ibid s 205(5).

741. Obligation of persons acting together to keep each other informed. A person who is a party to an agreement to acquire an interest in a particular company[1] is subject to the following requirements at any time when:

(1) the target company[2] is a public company[3], and he knows it to be so; and

(2) the shares in that company to which the agreement relates consist of or include shares comprised in relevant share capital[4] of the company, and he knows that to be the case; and

(3) he knows the facts which make the agreement such an agreement[5].

Such a person is under obligation to notify every other party to the agreement, in writing, of the relevant particulars[6] of his interest (if any) apart from the agreement in shares comprised in relevant share capital of the target company on his first becoming subject to these requirements, and, on each occurrence after that time while he is still subject to these requirements, of any event or circumstances within the obligation of disclosure[7] (as it applies to his case otherwise than by reference to interests treated as his by virtue of the provisions previously mentioned[8] as applying to that agreement)[9].

The relevant particulars to be so notified are:

(a) the number of shares, if any, comprised in the target company's relevant share capital in which the person giving the notice would be required to state his interest if he were under the wide obligation of disclosure[10] with respect to that interest, apart from the agreement, immediately after the time when the obligation to give such notice arose; and

(b) the relevant particulars with respect to the registered ownership of those shares, so far as known to him at the date of the notice; and

(c) except where the aggregate nominal value of the shares comprised in relevant share capital is equal to or more than 10% of the nominal value of the relevant share capital, the number of shares, if any, out of the number given under head (a) above in which he knows that, immediately after the time when the obligation to give the notice arose, he had interests, apart from the agreement, which were not material interests[11].

A person who is for the time being subject to these requirements is also under obligation to notify every other party to the agreement, in writing, of any relevant particulars with respect to the registered ownership of any shares comprised in relevant share capital of the target company in which he is interested apart from the agreement, and of any change in those particulars, of which in either case he becomes aware at any time after any interest notification date[12] and before the first occasion following that date on which he becomes subject to any further obligation to give notice[13] with respect to his interest in shares comprised in that share capital[14].

A person who is a party to an agreement to acquire an interest in a particular company is under an obligation to notify each other party to the agreement, in writing, of his current address on his first becoming subject to the requirements of these provisions, and on any change in his address occurring after that time and while he is still subject to these requirements[15].

A person's obligation to give any notice required by these provisions to any other person must be performed within the period of two days[16] next following the day on which that obligation arose[17].

1 As to such agreements to see para 739 ante.
2 For the meaning of 'target company' see para 739 ante.
3 For the meaning of 'public company' see para 82 ante.
4 For the meaning of 'relevant share capital' see para 735 note 1 ante.
5 Companies Act 1985 s 206(1).
6 For these purposes, a reference to the relevant particulars with respect to the registered ownership of shares is to such particulars in relation to those shares as are mentioned in ibid s 202(3)(a) or (b) (as substituted) (see para 737 heads (a), (b) ante): s 206(7).
7 Ie ibid s 198(1) (as amended): see para 735 ante.
8 Ie ibid s 205: see para 740 ante.
9 Ibid s 206(2).
10 For these purposes, 'the wide obligation of disclosure' means the obligation to disclose the number of shares in which the person concerned has any interest, material or otherwise: ibid s 206(3B) (added by the Disclosure of Interests in Shares (Amendment) Regulations 1993, SI 1993/1819, regs 2, 7(2)). For the meaning of 'material interest' see para 736 note 4 ante.
11 Companies Act 1985 s 206(3) (amended by the Disclosure of Interests in Shares (Amendment) Regulations 1993 regs 2, 7(1)); Companies Act 1985 s 206(3A) (added by the Disclosure of Interests in Shares (Amendment) Regulations 1993 regs 2, 7(2)).
12 For these purposes, the reference to an interest notification date, in relation to a person's interest in shares comprised in the target company's relevant share capital, is to either of the following: (1) the date of any notice given by him with respect to his interest under the Companies Act 1985 s 206(2) (see supra); and (2) where he has failed to give that notice, the date on which the period allowed for giving the notice came to an end: s 206(5).
13 Ie under ibid s 206(2): see supra.
14 Ibid s 206(4).
15 Ibid s 206(6).
16 As to the calculation of such period see para 737 note 3 ante.
17 Companies Act 1985 s 206(8) (amended by the Companies Act 1989 s 134(1), (3)). As to the Secretary of State's power by regulations to amend the Companies Act 1985 s 206(8) (as so amended) see para 746 post.

742. Interests in shares by attribution. Where the provisions relating to the obligation of disclosure[1] and the interests to be disclosed[2] refer to a person acquiring an interest in shares or ceasing to be interested in shares, that reference in certain cases includes his becoming or ceasing to be interested in those shares by virtue of another person's interest[3]. Such is the case where he becomes or ceases to be interested by virtue of the provisions relating to family and corporate interests[4], or agreements to acquire an interest in a particular public company[5] whether:

(1) by virtue of the fact that the person who is interested in the shares becomes or ceases to be a person whose interests (if any) fall by virtue of either provision to be treated as his; or

(2) in consequence of the fact that such a person has become or ceased to be interested in the shares; or

(3) in consequence of the fact that he himself becomes or ceases to be a party to such an agreement to acquire an interest in a particular company[6] to which the person interested in the shares is for the time being a party; or

(4) in consequence of the fact that an agreement to which both he and that person are parties becomes or ceases to be an agreement to acquire an interest in a particular company[7].

The person is then to be treated as knowing he has acquired an interest in the shares or (as the case may be) that he has ceased to be interested in them, if and when he knows both:

(a) the relevant facts with respect to the other person's interest in the shares; and

(b) the relevant facts by virtue of which he himself has become or ceased to be[8] so interested in them[9].

He has the knowledge referred to in head (a) above if he knows (whether contemporaneously or not) either of the subsistence of the other person's interest at any material time[10] or of the fact that the other has become or ceased to be interested in the shares at any such time[11]. A person is to be regarded as knowing of the subsistence of another's interest in shares or, as the case may be, that another has become or ceased to be interested in shares if he has been notified[12] of facts with respect to the other's interest which indicate that he is or has become or ceased to be interested in the shares, whether on his own account or by virtue of a third party's interest in them[13].

1 Ie the Companies Act 1985 s 198 (as amended): see para 735 ante.
2 Ie ibid s 199 (as amended): see para 736 ante.
3 Ibid s 207(1).
4 Ie ibid s 203 (as amended): see para 738 ante.
5 Ie ibid s 205: see para 740 ante. For the meaning of 'public company' see para 82 ante.
6 As to such agreements see para 739 ante.
7 Companies Act 1985 s 207(2).
8 Ie in accordance with ibid s 203 (as amended) or s 205.
9 Ibid s 207(3).
10 For these purposes, 'material time' means any time at which the other's interests, if any, fall or fell to be treated as his under ibid s 203 (as amended) or s 205: s 207(4).
11 Ibid s 207(4).
12 Ie under ibid s 206 (as amended): see para 741 ante.
13 Ibid s 207(5).

743. Interests in shares which are to be notified. Subject to the interests to be disregarded[1], the following provisions apply in determining for purposes of the provisions relating to the obligation of disclosure[2], the interests to be disclosed[3], and ancillary provisions[4], whether a person has a notifiable interest in shares[5].

A reference to an interest in shares is to be read as including an interest of any kind whatsoever in the shares; and accordingly there are to be disregarded any restraints or restrictions to which the exercise of any right attached to the interest is or may be subject[6]. Where property is held on trust and an interest in shares is comprised in the property, a beneficiary of the trust who apart from this provision does not have an interest in the shares is to be taken as having such an interest[7].

A person is taken to have an interest in shares if:

(1) he enters into a contract for their purchase by him (whether for cash or other consideration); or

(2) not being the registered holder, he is entitled to exercise any right[8] conferred by the holding of the shares or is entitled to control the exercise of any such right[9].

A person is also taken to have an interest in shares if, otherwise than by virtue of having an interest under a trust, he has a right to call for delivery of the shares to himself or to his order, or he has a right to acquire an interest in shares or is under an obligation to take an interest in shares, whether in any case the right or obligation is conditional or absolute[10].

Persons having a joint interest are taken each of them to have that interest[11]. It is immaterial that shares in which a person has an interest are unidentifiable[12].

1 Ie under the Companies Act 1985 s 209 (as substituted): see para 744 post.
2 Ie ibid s 198 (as amended): see para 735 ante.
3 Ie ibid s 199 (as amended): see para 736 ante.
4 Ie ibid ss 200–202 (as amended): see paras 736, 737 ante.
5 Ibid s 208(1). As to notifiable interests in shares see para 736 ante; and as to the interests in shares to be disregarded see para 744 post. As to the Secretary of State's power by regulations to amend s 208 see para 746 post.
6 Ibid s 208(2). See also note 5 supra.
7 Ibid s 208(3). See also note 5 supra.
8 For these purposes, a person is entitled to exercise or control the exercise of any right conferred by the holding of shares if he has a right, whether subject to conditions or not, the exercise of which would make him so entitled, or is under an obligation, whether so subject or not, the fulfilment of which would make him so entitled: ibid s 208(6).
9 Ibid s 208(4). See also note 5 supra.
10 Ibid s 208(5). See also note 5 supra.
11 Ibid s 208(7). See also note 5 supra.
12 Ibid s 208(8). See also note 5 supra.

744. Interests to be disregarded. The following interests in shares are to be disregarded[1]:

(1) where property is held on trust and an interest in shares is comprised in that property, an interest of a person, being a discretionary interest or an interest in reversion or remainder or any interest of a bare trustee[2];

(2) an interest which a person has by virtue of holding units in an authorised unit trust scheme[3], a recognised scheme[4] or a UCITS[5];

(3) an interest of a person which is an exempt security interest[6];

(4) an interest which a person has by virtue of being a beneficiary[7] under a retirement benefits scheme[8];

(5) an interest which a person has in shares as a result of the acceptance of a take-over offer[9] made by him, either alone or jointly with one or more other persons, for shares where the offer is subject to a threshold acceptance condition[10] and the threshold acceptance condition is not fulfilled[11];

(6) an interest of a person which is an exempt custodian interest[12];

(7) an interest which a person has by virtue of his being a personal representative of any estate[13];

(8) an interest which a person has by virtue of his being a trustee of an authorised unit trust scheme or, in relation to a recognised scheme or a UCITS, by virtue of his being entrusted with the custody of the property in question, whether or not under a trust[14].

An interest in shares of a company is also to be so disregarded if it is held by a market maker in securities or derivatives[15] for the purposes of his business but only in so far as it is not used by him for the purpose of intervening in the management of the company[16].

The following interests in shares in a public company which is not listed[17] are also to be so disregarded:

(a) an interest which subsists by virtue of a scheme made under the Charities Act 1993[18], the Charities Act (Northern Ireland) 1964[19], the Trustee Investments Act 1961[20] or the Administration of Justice Act 1982[21] or the scheme[22] set out in the Church Funds Investment Measure 1958[23];

(b) an interest of the Church of Scotland General Trustees or of the Church of Scotland Trust in shares held by them or of any other person in shares held by those Trustees or that Trust otherwise than as simple trustees[24];

(c) an interest for the life of himself or another of a person under a settlement in the case of which the property comprised in the settlement consists of or includes shares, and the specified conditions[25] are satisfied[26];

(d) an interest of the Accountant General of the Supreme Court in shares held by him[27];

(e) an interest of the Public Trustee[28];

(f) an interest of the Probate Judge subsisting[29] by virtue of the Administration of Estates Act (Northern Ireland) 1955[30].

1   Ie for the purposes of the Companies Act 1985 ss 198–202 (as amended): see para 735 et seq ante. An interest referred to in any of s 209(1)(a)–(h) (as substituted) (see text heads (1)–(8) infra), other than s 209(1)(c) (as substituted) (see text head (3) infra) is disregarded only if the person referred to therein or in s 209(4) (as substituted) (see note 12 infra) is not entitled to exercise or control the exercise of voting rights in respect of the shares concerned; and, for this purpose, he is not so entitled if he is bound, whether by contract or otherwise, not to exercise the voting rights, or not to exercise them otherwise than in accordance with the instructions of another: s 209(5) (substituted by the Disclosure of Interests in Shares (Amendment) Regulations 1993, SI 1993/1819, regs 2, 8). In the case of an interest referred to in the Companies Act 1985 s 209(1)(c) (as substituted), an interest of a person referred to in s 209(2) (as substituted) (see note 6 infra) is disregarded only if that person (1) is not entitled, within the meaning of s 209(5) (as so substituted) to exercise or control the exercise of voting rights in respect of the shares concerned; or (2) is so entitled, but has not evidenced any intention to exercise them or control their exercise nor taken any step to do so: s 209(6) (substituted by the Disclosure of Interests in Shares (Amendment) Regulations 1993 regs 2, 8). For the purposes of the Companies Act 1985 s 209(5), (6) (as so substituted), voting rights which a person is entitled to exercise or of which he is entitled to control the exercise only in certain circumstances are to be taken into account only when the circumstances have arisen and for so long as they continue to obtain: s 209(7) (substituted by the Disclosure of Interests in Shares (Amendment) Regulations 1993 regs 2, 8).

2   Companies Act 1985 s 209(1)(a) (substituted by the Disclosure of Interests in Shares (Amendment) Regulations 1993 regs 2, 8). As to the Secretary of State's power by regulations to amend the Companies Act 1985 s 209 (as substituted) see para 746 post.

3   For the meaning of 'authorised unit trust scheme' see para 736 note 4 ante.

4   For the meaning of 'recognised scheme' see para 736 note 4 ante.

5   Companies Act 1985 s 209(1)(b) (substituted by the Disclosure of Interests in Shares (Amendment) Regulations 1993 regs 2, 8). For the meaning of 'UCITS' see para 736 note 4 ante.

6   Companies Act 1985 s 209(1)(c) (substituted by the Disclosure of Interests in Shares (Amendment) Regulations 1993 regs 2, 8). For these purposes, an interest in shares is an exempt security interest (1) if it is held by a person who is (a) a person authorised under the Banking Act 1987 Pt I (ss 1–49 (as amended): see BANKING vol 3(1) (Reissue) para 17 et seq), an authorised credit institution, a person authorised under the law of a member State other than the United Kingdom to accept deposits who would, if he were to accept such deposits in the United Kingdom, require authorisation under Pt I (ss 1–49) (as amended), or an authorised insurance undertaking; or (b) a person authorised under the law of a member State to deal in securities or derivatives, who deals in securities or derivatives on a relevant stock exchange or on a relevant investment exchange, whether as a member or otherwise; or (c) a relevant stock exchange, a relevant investment exchange or a recognised clearing house; or (2) if it is held by the Bank of England or by the central bank of a member State other than the United Kingdom; and it is held by way of security only for the purposes of a transaction entered into in the ordinary course of his or its business as such a person: Companies Act 1985 s 209(2) (substituted by the Disclosure of Interests in Shares (Amendment) Regulations 1993 regs 2, 8; amended by the Disclosure of Interests in Shares (Amendment) (No 2) Regulations 1993, SI 1993/2689, regs 2, 3). For the meaning of 'authorised credit institution' see para 736 note 4 ante. 'Authorised insurance undertaking' means an insurance undertaking which has been authorised in accordance with EC Council Directive 73/239 (OJ L228, 16.8.73, p 3) arts 6 or 23 or EC Council Directive 79/267 (OJ L63, 13.3.79, p 1) arts 6 or 27 or is authorised under the law of a member State to carry on insurance business restricted to reinsurance: Companies Act 1985 s 220(1) (substituted by the Disclosure of Interests in Shares (Amendment) Regulations 1993 regs 2, 9). 'Relevant investment exchange' means an exchange situated or operating in a member State on which derivatives are traded: Companies Act 1985 s 220(1) (as so substituted).

'Derivatives' means (i) options to acquire or dispose of shares; and (ii) rights under a contract falling within the Financial Services Act 1986 Sch 1 para 8 (see STOCK EXCHANGE), where the property in question is shares: Companies Act 1985 s 220(1) (as so substituted). For the meaning of 'relevant stock exchange' see para 736 note 4 ante.

7 Ie a beneficiary under a retirements benefit scheme as defined in the Income and Corporation Taxes Act 1988 s 611: see SOCIAL SECURITY AND PENSIONS.

8 Companies Act 1985 s 209(1)(d) (substituted by the Disclosure of Interests in Shares (Amendment) Regulations 1993 regs 2, 8).

9 For these purposes, 'take-over offer' has the same meaning as in the Companies Act 1985 Pt XIIIA (ss 428–430F (as amended): see para 1202 post): s 209(3)(a) (substituted by the Disclosure of Interests in Shares (Amendment) Regulations 1993 regs 2, 8).

10 For these purposes, 'a threshold acceptance condition' means a condition that acceptances are received in respect of such proportion of the shares for which the take-over offer is made as is specified in or determined in accordance with the terms of the take-over offer: Companies Act 1985 s 209(3)(b) (substituted by the Disclosure of Interests in Shares (Amendment) Regulations 1993 regs 2, 8).

11 Companies Act 1985 s 209(1)(e) (substituted by the Disclosure of Interests in Shares (Amendment) Regulations 1993 regs 2, 8).

12 Companies Act 1985 s 209(1)(f) (substituted by the Disclosure of Interests in Shares (Amendment) Regulations 1993 regs 2, 8). For these purposes, an interest of a person is an exempt custodian interest if it is held by him (1) as a custodian, whether under a trust or by a contract; or (2) under an arrangement pursuant to which he has issued, or is to issue, depositary receipts in respect of the shares concerned: Companies Act 1985 s 209(4) (substituted by the Disclosure of Interests in Shares (Amendment) Regulations 1993 regs 2, 8). A person is not, by virtue of the Companies Act 1985 s 208(4)(b) (see para 743 head (2) ante), taken to be interested in shares by reason only that he has been appointed a proxy to vote at a specified meeting of a company or of any class of its members and at any adjournment of that meeting, or has been appointed by a corporation to act as its representative at any meeting of a company or of any class of its members: s 209(12) (substituted by the Disclosure of Interests in Shares (Amendment) Regulations 1993 regs 2, 8). 'Depositary receipt' means a certificate or other record, whether or not in the form of a document: (a) which is issued by or on behalf of a person who holds shares or who holds evidence of the right to receive shares, or has an interest in shares, in a particular company; and (b) which evidences or acknowledges that another person is entitled to rights in relation to those shares or shares of the same kind, which includes the right to receive such shares, or evidence of the right to receive such shares, from the person mentioned in head (a) supra: Companies Act 1985 s 220(1) (as substituted: see note 6 supra).

13 Ibid s 209(1)(g) (substituted by the Disclosure of Interests in Shares (Amendment) Regulations 1993 regs 2, 8).

14 Companies Act 1985 s 209(1)(h) (substituted by the Disclosure of Interests in Shares (Amendment) Regulations 1993 regs 2, 8).

15 For these purposes, a person is a market maker in securities or derivatives if (1) he is authorised under the law of a member State to deal in securities or derivatives and so deals on a relevant stock exchange or a relevant investment exchange, whether as a member or otherwise; and (2) he holds himself out at all normal times as willing to acquire and dispose of securities or derivatives at prices specified by him and, in so doing, is subject to the rules of that exchange; and he holds an interest for the purposes of his business if he holds it for the purposes of a business carried on by him as a market maker in a member State: Companies Act 1985 s 209(9) (substituted by the Disclosure of Interests in Shares (Amendment) Regulations 1993 regs 2, 8).

16 Companies Act 1985 s 209(8) (substituted by the Disclosure of Interests in Shares (Amendment) Regulations 1993 regs 2, 8).

17 For the meaning of 'listed' see para 736 note 4 ante.

18 Ie under the Charities Act 1993 s 24 or s 25: see CHARITIES vol 5(2) (Reissue) para 352.

19 Ie the Charities Act (Northern Ireland) 1964 s 25.

20 Ie under the Trustee Investments Act 1961 s 11 (as amended) (local authority investment schemes).

21 Ie under the Administration of Justice Act 1982 s 42 (as amended) (common investment schemes).

22 Ie the scheme set out in the Church Funds Investment Measure 1958 Schedule: see ECCLESIASTICAL LAW vol 14 para 1250.

23 Companies Act 1985 s 209(10)(a) (substituted by the Disclosure of Interests in Shares (Amendment) Regulations 1993 regs 2, 8).

24 Companies Act 1985 s 209(10)(b) (substituted by the Disclosure of Interests in Shares (Amendment) Regulations 1993 regs 2, 8).

25 The conditions so specified are, in relation to a settlement (1) that it is irrevocable; and (2) that the settlor, within the meaning of the Income and Corporation Taxes Act 1988 s 670 (see INCOME

TAXATION vol 23 (Reissue) para 1504), has no interest in any income arising under, or property comprised in, the settlement: Companies Act 1985 s 209(11) (substituted by the Disclosure of Interests in Shares (Amendment) Regulations 1993 regs 2, 8).

26   Companies Act 1985 s 209(10)(c) (substituted by the Disclosure of Interests in Shares (Amendment) Regulations 1993 regs 2, 8).

27   Companies Act 1985 s 209(10)(e) (substituted by the Disclosure of Interests in Shares (Amendment) Regulations 1993 regs 2, 8).

28   Companies Act 1985 s 209(10)(f) (substituted by the Disclosure of Interests in Shares (Amendment) Regulations 1993 regs 2, 8).

29   Ie by virtue of the Administration of Estates Act (Northern Ireland) 1955 s 3.

30   Companies Act 1985 s 209(10)(g) (substituted by the Disclosure of Interests in Shares (Amendment) Regulations 1993 regs 2, 8).

745. Other provisions about notification. Where a person authorises another ('the agent') to acquire or dispose of, on his behalf, interests in shares comprised in relevant share capital[1] of a public company[2], he must secure that the agent notifies him immediately of acquisitions or disposals effected by the agent which will or may give rise to any obligation of disclosure imposed on him by these provisions[3] with respect to his interest in that share capital[4].

An obligation of disclosure so imposed[5] on a person is treated as not being fulfilled unless the notice by means of which it purports to be fulfilled identifies him and gives his address and, in a case where he is a director of the company, is expressed to be given in fulfilment of that obligation[6].

A person who:

(1)   fails to fulfil, within the proper period, an obligation of disclosure imposed on him by these provisions; or

(2)   in purported fulfilment of any such obligation makes to a company a statement which he knows to be false, or recklessly makes to a company a statement which is false; or

(3)   fails to fulfil, within the proper period, an obligation to give another person a notice as thereby required[7] by the statutory provisions; or

(4)   fails without reasonable excuse to secure that he is notified by his agent as required above,

is guilty of an offence and liable on conviction on indictment to imprisonment for a term not exceeding two years or a fine, or to both, or on summary conviction to imprisonment for a term not exceeding six months or a fine not exceeding the statutory maximum, or to both[8].

It is a defence for a person charged with an offence under head (3) above to prove that it was not possible for him to give the required notice[9] to the other person within the proper period, and either that it has not since become possible for him to give the notice so required, or that he gave the notice as soon after the end of that period as it became possible for him to do so[10].

Where a person is convicted of an offence under these provisions (other than an offence relating to his ceasing to be interested in a company's shares), the Secretary of State may by order direct that the shares in relation to which the offence was committed shall, until further order, be subject to the restrictions of the Companies Act 1985[11]; and such an order may be made notwithstanding any power in the company's memorandum or articles enabling the company to impose similar restrictions on those shares[12]. If the Secretary of State is satisfied that such an order may unfairly affect the rights of third parties in respect of shares, then the Secretary of State, for the purpose of protecting such rights and subject to such terms as he thinks fit, may direct that such acts by such persons or descriptions of persons and for such purposes as may be set out in the order, shall not constitute a breach of the statutory provisions[13] relating to orders imposing restrictions on shares[14].

1 For the meaning of 'relevant share capital' see para 735 note 1 ante.
2 For the meaning of 'public company' see para 82 ante.
3 Ie the Companies Act 1985 Pt VI (ss 198–220) (as amended): see para 735 et seq ante.
4 Ibid s 210(1).
5 Ie by any provision of ibid ss 198–202 (as amended): see paras 735–737 ante.
6 Ibid s 210(2). As to the other obligations of directors with regard to the notification of share interests see para 564 et seq ante.
7 Ie by ibid s 206 (as amended): see para 741 ante.
8 Ibid ss 210(3), 730, Sch 24. For the meaning of 'the statutory maximum' see para 1161 post. Section 732 (restriction on prosecution: see para 1165 post) and s 733(2), (3) (as amended) (liability of directors etc: see para 1162 post) apply to offences under s 210: s 210(6).
9 See note 7 supra.
10 Companies Act 1985 s 210(4).
11 Ie ibid Pt XV (ss 454–457) (as amended): see paras 1395–1397 post.
12 Ibid s 210(5).
13 See note 11 supra.
14 Companies Act 1985 s 210(5A) (added by the Companies (Disclosure of Interests in Shares) (Orders imposing restrictions on shares) Regulations 1991, SI 1991/1646, regs 2, 3).

746. Secretary of State's power to make further provision. The Secretary of State may by regulations amend:
   (1) the definition of 'relevant share capital'[1];
   (2) the percentage giving rise to a 'notifiable interest'[2];
   (3) the periods within which an obligation of disclosure must be fulfilled or a notice be given[3];
   (4) the provisions as to what is taken to be an interest in shares[4] and what interests are to be disregarded[5]; and
   (5) the provisions as to company investigations[6];
and the regulations may amend, replace or repeal the provisions referred to above and make such other consequential amendments or repeals[7] as appear to the Secretary of State to be appropriate[8].

The regulations may in any case make different provision for different descriptions of company; and regulations under heads (2), (3) or (4) above may make different provision for different descriptions of person, interest or share capital[9]. The regulations may contain such transitional and other supplementary and incidental provisions as appear to the Secretary of State to be appropriate, and may in particular make provision as to the obligations of a person whose interest in a company's shares becomes or ceases to be notifiable by virtue of the regulations[10].

Any such regulations must be made by statutory instrument[11]; and no such regulations may be made unless a draft of the regulations has been laid before and approved by a resolution of each House of Parliament[12].

1 Ie the Companies Act 1985 s 198(2): see para 735 note 1 ante.
2 Ie ibid s 199(2) (as substituted): see para 736 ante.
3 Ie ibid s 202(1), (4) (as amended) (see para 737 ante) and s 206(8) (as amended) (see para 741 ante).
4 Ie ibid s 208: see para 743 ante.
5 Ie ibid s 209 (as substituted): see para 744 ante.
6 Ie ibid s 212: see para 748 post.
7 Ie of provisions of ibid Pt VI (ss 198–220) (as amended): see para 735 et seq ante and para 747 et seq post.
8 Ibid s 210A(1) (added by the Companies Act 1989 s 134(1), (5)).

9 Companies Act 1985 s 210A(2) (added by the Companies Act 1989 s 134(1), (5)). In exercise of the power so conferred the Secretary of State made the Disclosure of Interests in Shares (Amendment) Regulations 1993, SI 1993/1819, which came into force on 18 September 1993 (reg 1) and the Disclosure of Interests in Shares (Amendment) (No 2) Regulations 1993, SI 1993/2689, which came into force on 29 October 1993 (reg 1).

10 Companies Act 1985 s 210A(3) (added by the Companies Act 1989 s 134(1), (5)).

11 Companies Act 1985 s 210A(4) (added by the Companies Act 1989 s 134(1), (5)).

12 Companies Act 1985 s 210A(5) (added by the Companies Act 1989 s 134(1), (5)).

(ii) Registration and Investigation of Share Acquisitions and Disposals

747. Register of interests in shares. Every public company[1] must keep a register for purposes of the provisions[2] relating to disclosures of interests in shares and, whenever the company receives information from a person in consequence of the fulfilment of an obligation imposed on him by any of those provisions, it is under obligation to inscribe in the register, against that person's name, that information and the date of the inscription[3]. Without prejudice to this obligation, where a company receives a notification under those provisions[4] which includes a statement that the person making the notification, or any other person, has ceased to be a party to an agreement to acquire an interest in a particular company[5], the company is under obligation to record that information against the name of that person in every place where his name appears in the register as a party to that agreement, including any entry relating to him made against another person's name[6]. An obligation imposed by the above provisions must be fulfilled within the period of three days[7] next following the day on which it arises[8].

The company is not, by virtue of anything done for the purposes of these provisions, affected with notice of, or put upon inquiry as to, the rights of any person in relation to any shares[9].

The register must be so made up that the entries against the several names entered in it appear in chronological order[10]. Unless the register is in such form as to constitute in itself an index, the company must keep an index of the names entered in the register which must in respect of each name contain a sufficient indication to enable the information entered against it to be readily found; and the company must, within ten days after the date on which a name is entered in the register, make any necessary alteration in the index[11].

If the company ceases to be a public company, it must continue to keep the register and any associated index[12] until the end of the period of six years beginning with the day next following that on which it ceases to be such a company[13].

The register and any associated index must be kept at the place at which the register of directors' interests is kept[14], and, subject to the following provisions, must be available for inspection in accordance with the relevant statutory provisions[15].

Neither the register nor any associated index need be available for inspection in accordance with those provisions[16] in so far as it contains information with respect to a company for the time being entitled to avail itself of the benefit conferred by the exceptions from the miscellaneous matters required to be disclosed in its accounts[17] afforded in respect of such disclosures which would be harmful to the company's business[18].

If default is made in complying with any of the above provisions[19], the company, and every officer of it who is in default, is liable on summary conviction to a fine not exceeding one-fifth of the statutory maximum and, on conviction after continued contravention, to a daily default fine not exceeding one-fiftieth of the statutory maximum[20].

1 For the meaning of 'public company' see para 82 ante.
2 Ie the Companies Act 1985 ss 199–202 (as amended): see paras 736, 737 ante.
3 Ibid s 211(1). Any register kept by a company under the Companies Act 1967 s 34 (repealed) (provisions for securing that information furnished by persons obliged to notify acquisition etc of shares in company carrying unrestricted voting rights was recorded and made available) immediately before 15 June 1982 (the day when the corresponding provisions of the Companies Act 1981 came into force: Companies Act 1981 (Commencement No 4) Order 1982, SI 1982/672, art 2(2)) must continue to be kept by the company under and for the purposes of the Companies Act 1985 s 211 (as amended): s 211(11). As to the provisions applicable to a register maintained otherwise than by recording the entries in legible form see para 656 ante.
4 Ie ibid Pt VI (ss 198–220) (as amended): see para 735 et seq ante.
5 Ie an agreement to which ibid s 204 applies: see para 739 ante.
6 Ibid s 211(2).
7 As to the calculation of such period see para 737 note 3 ante.
8 Companies Act 1985 s 211(3).
9 Ibid s 211(4). As to the notice to the company of trusts and equitable interests generally see para 385 ante.
10 Ibid s 211(5).
11 Ibid s 211(6).
12 For these purposes, 'associated index', in relation to a register, means the index kept in relation to that register in pursuance of ibid s 211(6): s 220(1) (substituted by the Disclosure of Interests in Shares (Amendment) Regulations 1993, SI 1993/1819, regs 2, 9).
13 Companies Act 1985 s 211(7).
14 Ie under ibid s 325: see para 571 ante.
15 Ibid s 211(8). The relevant statutory provisions are contained in s 219 (as amended) (see para 755 post): s 211(8).
16 Ie ibid s 219 (as amended).
17 Ie by ibid s 231(3) (as substituted): see para 853 post.
18 Ibid s 211(9) (amended by the Companies Act 1989 s 23, Sch 10 para 3).
19 Ie the Companies Act 1985 s 211(1) or (2) or any of s 211(5)–(7): see supra.
20 Ibid ss 211(10), 730, Sch 24. For the meaning of 'officer who is in default', 'the statutory maximum' and 'daily default fine' see para 1161 post.

748. Investigations by company itself. A public company[1] may by notice in writing require a person[2] whom the company knows or has reasonable cause to believe to be or, at any time during the three years immediately preceding the date on which the notice is issued, to have been interested in shares[3] comprised in the company's relevant share capital[4], to confirm that fact or, as the case may be, to indicate whether or not it is the case, and, where he holds or has during that time held an interest in shares so comprised, to give such further information as may be required in accordance with the following provisions[5].

Such a notice may require the person to whom it is addressed:

(1) to give particulars of his own past or present interest in shares comprised in relevant share capital of the company, held by him at any time during such three-year period;

(2) where the interest is a present interest and any other interest in the shares subsists or, in any case, where another interest in the shares subsisted during that three-year period at any time when his own interest subsisted, to give, so far as lies within his knowledge, such particulars with respect to that other interest as may be required by the notice;

(3) where his interest is a past interest, to give, so far as lies within his knowledge, particulars of the identity of the person who held that interest immediately upon his ceasing to hold it[6].

The particulars referred to in heads (1) and (2) above include particulars of the identity of persons interested in the shares in question and of whether persons interested in the same shares are or were parties to any agreement to acquire an interest in a particular company[7], or to any agreement or arrangement relating to the exercise of any rights conferred by the holding of the shares[8].

Such a notice must require any information given in response to the notice to be given in writing within such reasonable time as may be specified in the notice[9].

These provisions apply in relation to a person who has or previously had, or is or was entitled to acquire, a right to subscribe for shares in a public company which would on issue be comprised in relevant share capital of that company as they apply in relation to a person who is or was interested in shares so comprised; and references in the above provisions to an interest in shares so comprised and to shares so comprised are to be read accordingly in any such case as including respectively any such right and shares which would on issue be so comprised[10].

1 For the meaning of 'public company' see para 82 ante.
2 'Person' includes a foreigner: *Re F H Lloyd Holdings plc* [1985] BCLC 293 (foreign corporation which could not and did not carry on business in the United Kingdom and had no presence of any kind there, or an individual having an equivalent status).
3 For the purpose of construing references in the Companies Act 1985 s 212 to persons interested in shares and to interests in shares respectively, ss 203–205 (as amended) (see paras 738–740 ante) and s 208 (see para 743 ante) apply as they apply in relation to ss 198–201 (as amended) (see paras 735, 736 ante), but with the omission of any reference to s 209 (as substituted) (see para 744 ante): s 212(5).
4 For the meaning of 'relevant share capital' see para 735 note 1 ante.
5 Companies Act 1985 s 212(1). As to the Secretary of State's power by regulations to amend s 212 see para 746 ante. The answers to a notice under s 212 must be given to the best of the knowledge of the recipient of the notice at the date when the reply is given, but the interests must be described as they stood at the date stated in the notice: *Re Ricardo Group plc (No 2)* [1989] BCLC 766 at 767.
6 Companies Act 1985 s 212(2). See also note 5 supra.
7 Ie any agreement to which ibid s 204 applies: see para 739 ante.
8 Ibid s 212(3). See also note 5 supra.
9 Ibid s 212(4). See also note 5 supra. In determining what is a reasonable period of notice, regard should be had to the urgency with which such information is currently needed, and the length of time needed by the recipient of the notice to seek advice and collect the information: *Re Lonrho plc (No 2)* [1989] BCLC 309.
10 Companies Act 1985 s 212(6). See also note 5 supra.

749. Registration of interests found on company's investigations. Whenever, in pursuance of a requirement imposed on a person by the statutory provisions relating to company investigations[1], a company receives information which relates to the present interests held by any persons in shares comprised in relevant share capital[2] of the company in question, it is under obligation to enter against the name of the registered holder of those shares, in a separate part of its register of interests in shares[3] the fact that the requirement was imposed and the date on which it was imposed, and any information to which these provisions apply received in pursuance of the requirement[4].

1 See para 748 ante.
2 For the meaning of 'relevant share capital' see para 735 note 1 ante.
3 For these purposes, 'register of interests in shares' means the statutory register of interests in shares kept in pursuance of the Companies Act 1985 s 211 (as amended) (see para 747 ante) including, except where the context otherwise requires, that part of the register kept in pursuance of s 213 (see infra): s 220(1)

(substituted by the Disclosure of Interests in Shares (Amendment) Regulations 1993, SI 1993/1819, regs 2, 9).

4 Companies Act 1985 s 213(1), (2). Section 211(3)–(10) (as amended) (see para 747 ante) applies in relation to any part of the register maintained in accordance with s 213(1) as it applies in relation to the remainder of the register, reading references to s 211(1) to include s 213(1): s 213(3).

In the case of a register kept by a company immediately before 15 June 1982 (the day when the corresponding provisions of the Companies Act 1981 came into force: Companies Act 1981 (Commencement No 4) Order 1982, SI 1982/672, art 2(2)) under the Companies Act 1967 s 34 (repealed) (provisions for securing that information furnished by persons obliged to notify acquisition etc of shares in company carrying unrestricted voting rights was recorded and made available), any part of the register so kept for the purposes of the Companies Act 1976 s 27 (repealed) (duty of company to record disclosures of beneficial interests in its voting shares which it had required to be so disclosed) must continue to be kept by the company under and for the purposes of the Companies Act 1985 s 213: s 213(4).

750. Investigation by company on requisition by members. A company may be required to exercise its powers of investigation[1] on the requisition of members of the company holding at the date of the deposit of the requisition not less than one-tenth of such of the paid-up capital of the company as carries at that date the right of voting at general meetings of the company[2]. The requisition must:

(1) state that the requisitionists are requiring the company to exercise its powers of investigation;

(2) specify the manner in which they require those powers to be exercised; and

(3) give reasonable grounds for requiring the company to exercise those powers in the manner specified,

and must be signed by the requisitionists and deposited at the company's registered office[3].

The requisition may consist of several documents in like form each signed by one or more requisitionists[4].

On the deposit of a requisition complying with the above requirements it is the company's duty to exercise its powers in the manner specified in the requisition[5]. If default is made in complying with this provision, the company, and every officer of it who is in default, is liable on conviction on indictment to a fine, or on summary conviction to a fine not exceeding the statutory maximum[6].

1 Ie under the Companies Act 1985 s 212: see para 748 ante.
2 Ibid s 214(1).
3 Ibid s 214(2).
4 Ibid s 214(3).
5 Ibid s 214(4).
6 Ibid ss 214(5), 730, Sch 24. For the meaning of 'officer who is in default' and 'the statutory maximum' see para 1161 post.

751. Report by company to members. On the conclusion of an investigation carried out by a company in pursuance of a requisition by members[1], it is the company's duty to cause a report of the information received in pursuance of that investigation to be prepared, and the report must be made available at the company's registered office within a reasonable period after the conclusion of that investigation[2]. Where a company undertakes an investigation in pursuance of such a requisition, and the investigation is not concluded before the end of three months beginning with the date immediately following the date of the deposit of the requisition, it is the duty of the company to cause to be prepared, in respect of that period and each successive period of three months ending before the conclusion of the investigation, an interim report of the information received during that period in pursuance of the investigation; and each such report must be made available at the company's registered office within a reasonable period after the end of the period to which it relates[3]. The period for making any such report so available must not exceed 15 days[4].

Such a report need not include any information with respect to a company entitled to avail itself of the benefit conferred by the exceptions from the miscellaneous matters required to be disclosed in its accounts[5] afforded in respect of such disclosures which would be harmful to the company's business; but, where any such information is omitted, that fact must be stated in the report[6]. The company must, within three days[7] of making any report prepared under these provisions available at its registered office, notify the requisitionists that the report is so available[8].

An investigation carried out by a company in pursuance of such a requisition is regarded for these purposes as concluded when the company has made all such inquiries as are necessary or expedient for the purposes of the requisition and, in the case of each such inquiry, either a response has been received by the company or the time allowed for a response has elapsed[9].

A report prepared under the above provisions must be kept at the company's registered office from the day on which it is first available there in accordance with the above provisions until the expiration of six years beginning with the day next following that day[10]. It must be available for inspection in accordance with the statutory provisions in that behalf[11] so long as it is so kept[12].

If default is made in complying with the above provisions[13], the company, and every officer of it who is in default, is liable on conviction on indictment to a fine, or on summary conviction to a fine not exceeding the statutory maximum[14].

1 Ie pursuant to the Companies Act 1985 s 214: see para 750 ante.
2 Ibid s 215(1).
3 Ibid s 215(2).
4 Ibid s 215(3). As to the calculation of such period see para 737 note 3 ante.
5 Ie ibid s 231(3) (as substituted): see para 853 post.
6 Ibid s 215(4) (amended by the Companies Act 1989 s 23, Sch 10 para 3).
7 See note 4 supra.
8 Companies Act 1985 s 215(5).
9 Ibid s 215(6).
10 Ibid s 215(7)(a).
11 Ie ibid s 219 (as amended): see para 755 post.
12 Ibid s 215(7)(b).
13 Ie ibid s 215(1), (2), (5) or (7)(a): see supra.
14 Ibid ss 215(8), 730, Sch 24. For the meaning of 'officer who is in default' and 'the statutory maximum' see para 1161 post.

752. Penalty for failure to provide information. Where notice is served by a company requiring information from a person believed to be interested in shares comprised in its relevant share capital[1], on a person[2] who is or was interested in shares of the company and that person fails to give the company any information required by the notice within the time specified in it, the company may apply to the court[3] for an order[4] directing that the shares in question be subject to the restrictions[5] of the Companies Act 1985[6]. On such an application the court may make an interim order and any such order may be made unconditionally or on such terms as the court thinks fit[7]. If the court is satisfied that such an order[8] may unfairly affect the rights of third parties in respect of shares, then the court, for the purpose of protecting such rights and subject to such terms as it thinks fit, may direct that such acts by such persons or descriptions of persons and for such purposes as may be set out in the order, shall not constitute a breach of the restrictions[9] of the Companies Act 1985[10]. Any such order[11] may be made by the court notwithstanding any power contained in the applicant company's memorandum or articles enabling the company itself to impose similar restrictions on the shares in question[12].

Subject to the following provisions, a person[13] who fails so to comply with a notice or who, in purported compliance with such a notice, makes any statement which he knows to be false in a material particular or recklessly makes any statement which is false in a material particular is guilty of an offence and liable on conviction on indictment to imprisonment for a term not exceeding two years or a fine, or to both, or on summary conviction to imprisonment for a term not exceeding six months or a fine not exceeding the statutory maximum, or to both[14].

A person is not guilty of such an offence by virtue of failing to comply with such a notice if he proves that the requirement to give the information was frivolous or vexatious[15].

A person is not obliged to comply with such a notice if he is for the time being exempted by the Secretary of State from the operation of the relevant statutory provisions[16]; but the Secretary of State must not grant any such exemption unless he has consulted with the Governor of the Bank of England and he (the Secretary of State) is satisfied that, having regard to any undertaking given by the person in question with respect to any interest held or to be held by him in any shares, there are special reasons why that person should not be subject to the obligations imposed by those provisions[17].

1 Ie under the Companies Act 1985 s 212: see para 750 ante.
2 For the meaning of 'person' see para 748 note 2 ante.
3 For the meaning of 'the court' see para 161 note 4 ante.
4 Application for such an order is by way of originating summons in the general form: RSC Ord 102 r 2(1), (2)(d).
5 Ie the restrictions contained in the Companies Act 1985 Pt XV (ss 454–457) (as amended): see paras 1395–1397 post.
6 Ibid s 216(1). As to the basis on which the court will impose or continue such a restriction see *Re Ricardo Group plc (No 2)* [1989] BCLC 766; *Re Ricardo Group plc (No 3)* [1989] BCLC 771 (although a company has a prima facie right to know who owns its shares, the statutory provisions make it a matter for the discretion of the court whether or not a freezing order should be imposed or continued).
7 Companies Act 1985 s 216(1A) (added by the Companies (Disclosure of Interests in Shares) (Orders imposing restrictions on shares) Regulations 1991, SI 1991/1646, regs 2, 4(a)).
8 Ie an order under the Companies Act 1985 s 216(1): see supra.
9 See note 5 supra.
10 Companies Act 1985 s 216(1B) (added by the Companies (Disclosure of Interests in Shares) (Orders imposing restrictions on shares) Regulations 1991 regs 2, 4(a)).
11 Ie an order under the Companies Act 1985 s 216 (as amended).
12 Ibid s 216(2) (amended by the Companies (Disclosure of Interests in Shares) (Orders imposing restrictions on shares) Regulations 1991 regs 2, 4(b)).
13 For these purposes, 'person' may exclude a foreigner: see *Re F H Lloyd Holdings plc* [1985] BCLC 293 at 300 per Nourse J.
14 Companies Act 1985 ss 216(3), 730, Sch 24. For the meaning of 'the statutory maximum' see para 1161 post. Section 733(2), (3) (as amended) (liability of individuals for corporate default: see para 1162 post) applies to offences under s 210: s 210(6).
15 Ibid s 216(4).
16 Ie ibid s 212: see para 748 ante.
17 Ibid s 216(5).

753. Removal of entries from register. A company may remove an entry against a person's name from its register of interests in shares[1] if more than six years have elapsed since the date of the entry being made, and either:

(1) that entry recorded the fact that the person in question had ceased to have a notifiable interest[2] in relevant share capital of the company; or

(2) it has been superseded by a later entry[3] against the same person's name;

and in a case within head (1) above the company may also remove that person's name from the register[4].

If a person in pursuance of an obligation imposed[5] on him gives to a company the name and address of another person as being interested in shares in the company, the company must, within 15 days[6] of the date on which it was given that information, notify the other person that he has been so named and must include in that notification:

(a) particulars of any entry relating to him made, in consequence of its being given that information, by the company in its register of interests in shares; and

(b) a statement informing him of his right to apply to have the entry removed in accordance with the following provisions[7].

A person who has been so notified that an entry relating to him has been made in the company's register of interests in shares may apply in writing to the company for the removal of that entry from the register; and the company must remove the entry if satisfied that the information in pursuance of which the entry was made was incorrect[8].

If a person who is identified in a company's register of interests in shares as being a party to an agreement to acquire an interest in a particular company[9], whether by an entry against his own name or by an entry relating to him made against another person's name[10], ceases to be a party to that agreement, he may apply in writing to the company for the inclusion of that information in the register; and, if the company is satisfied that he has ceased to be a party to the agreement, it must record that information, if not already recorded, in every place where his name appears as a party to that agreement in the register[11].

If an application[12] is refused (in a case within the latter provision[13], otherwise than on the ground that the information has already been recorded), the applicant may apply[14] to the court[15] for an order directing the company to remove the entry in question from the register or, as the case may be, to include the information in question in the register; and the court may, if it thinks fit, make such an order[16].

Where a name is removed from a company's register of interests in shares in pursuance of the above provisions whether by the company or an order of the court, the company must within 14 days of the date of that removal make any necessary alteration in any associated index[17].

If default is made in complying with the above provisions[18], the company, and every officer of it who is in default, is liable on summary conviction to a fine not exceeding one-fifth of the statutory maximum and, on conviction after continued contravention, to a daily default fine not exceeding one-fiftieth of the statutory maximum[19].

1 See the Companies Act 1985 s 211 (as amended) and s 213 and paras 747, 749 respectively ante. For the meaning of 'register of interests in shares' see para 749 note 3 ante.

2 Ie under ibid Pt VI (ss 198–220) (as amended): see para 735 et seq ante.

3 Ie made under ibid s 211 (as amended): see para 747 ante.

4 Ibid s 217(1).

5 Ie by any provisions of ibid Pt VI (ss 198–220) (as amended): see para 735 et seq ante.

6 As to the calculation of such period see para 737 note 3 ante.

7 Companies Act 1985 s 217(2).

8 Ibid s 217(3).

9 Ie an agreement to which ibid s 204 applies: see para 739 ante.

10 Ie as mentioned in ibid s 217(2)(a): see text head (a) supra.

11 Ibid s 217(4).

12 Ie under ibid s 217(3) or (4): see supra.

13 Ie ibid s 217(4).

14 The application is by way of originating motion: RSC Ord 102 r 3(1)(h).
15 For the meaning of 'the court' see para 161 note 4 ante.
16 Companies Act 1985 s 217(5).
17 Ibid s 217(6). For the meaning of 'associated index' see para 747 note 12 ante.
18 Ie ibid s 217(2) or (6): see supra.
19 Ibid ss 217(7), 730, Sch 24. For the meaning of 'officer who is in default', 'the statutory maximum' and 'daily default fine' see para 1161 post.

754. Otherwise, entries not to be removed. Entries in a company's register of interests in shares[1] must not be deleted except in accordance[2] with the statutory provisions[3]. If an entry is deleted from a company's register of interests in shares in contravention of the statutory provisions, the company must restore that entry to the register as soon as is reasonably practicable[4].

If default is made in complying with either of the above provisions[5], the company, and every officer of it who is in default, is liable on summary conviction to a fine not exceeding one-fifth of the statutory maximum and, on conviction after continued contravention of the latter provision[6], to a daily default fine not exceeding one-fiftieth of the statutory maximum[7].

1 For the meaning of 'register of interests in shares' see para 749 note 3 ante.
2 Ie in accordance with the Companies Act 1985 s 217: see para 753 ante.
3 Ibid s 218(1).
4 Ibid s 218(2).
5 Ie ibid s 218(1) or (2): see supra.
6 Ie ibid s 218(2): see supra.
7 Ibid ss 218(3), 730, Sch 24. For the meaning of 'officer who is in default', 'the statutory maximum' and 'daily default fine' see para 1161 post.

755–800. Inspection of register and reports. Any register of interests in shares[1] and any report made in pursuance of a requisition by members[2] that the company exercise its powers of investigation[3] which is required to be available for inspection[4] must be open to the inspection of any member of the company or of any other person without charge[5]. The company[6] must make those documents available for such inspection for not less than two hours during the period between 9 am and 5 pm on each business day[7]; and it must permit a person inspecting them to copy any information made available for inspection by means of the taking of notes or the transcription of the information[8].

Any such member or other person may require a copy of any such register or report, or any part of it, on payment of such fee as may be prescribed[9]; and the company must cause any copy so required by a person to be sent to him before the expiration of the period of ten days[10] beginning with the day next following that on which the requirement is received by the company[11].

If an inspection so required is refused or a copy so required is not sent within the proper period, the company, and every officer of it who is in default, is liable on summary conviction to a fine not exceeding one-fifth of the statutory maximum and, on conviction after continued contravention, to a daily default fine not exceeding one-fiftieth of the statutory maximum[12].

In the case of a refusal of an inspection required under these provisions of any register or report, the court[13] may by order compel an immediate inspection of it; and in the case of failure to send a copy so required, the court may by order direct that the copy required shall be sent to the person requiring it[14].

1 For the meaning of 'register of interests in shares' see para 749 note 3 ante.
2 Ie under the Companies Act 1985 s 214: see para 750 ante.
3 Ie under ibid s 212: see para 748 ante.
4 Ie in accordance with ibid s 215(7): see para 751 ante.
5 Ibid s 219(1) (amended by the Companies Act 1989 ss 143(5)(a), 212, Sch 24).
6 For the meaning of 'company' see para 229 note 14 ante.
7 Companies (Inspection and Copying of Registers, Indices and Documents) Regulations 1991, SI 1991/1998, reg 3(1), (2)(a). For the meaning of 'business day' see para 229 note 15 ante. As to the power to make regulations see para 230 ante.
8 Ibid reg 3(1), (2)(b). Regulation 3(2)(b) is not, however, to be construed as obliging a company to provide any facilities additional to those provided for the purposes of facilitating inspection: reg 3(3).
9 The fee so prescribed is, for the first 100 entries or part thereof copied, £2.50; for the next 1,000 entries or part thereof copied, £20.00; and, for every subsequent 1,000 entries or part thereof copied, £15.00: ibid reg 5, Sch 2 para 2(b).
10 As to the calculation of such period see para 737 note 3 ante.
11 Companies Act 1985 s 219(2) (amended by the Companies Act 1989 s 143(5)(b)).
12 Companies Act 1985 ss 219(3), 730, Sch 24. For the meaning of 'officer who is in default', 'the statutory maximum' and 'daily default fine' see para 1161 post.
13 For the meaning of 'the court' see para 161 note 4 ante.
14 Companies Act 1985 s 219(4). Applications under these provisions are by way of originating summons in the expedited form: RSC Ord 102 r 2(1), (2).

INDEX

Companies

This Index relates only to entries appearing in Volume 7(1). A consolidated Index for Volumes 7(1) and 7(2) appears in Volume 7(2); and a consolidated Index for Volumes 7(1), 7(2) and 7(3) appears in Volume 7(3).

ARTICLES OF ASSOCIATION—*continued*
  statutory construction and restrictions, 148
  statutory requirements, 87
  sub-division of shares, 207
  surrender of shares, 520, 521
  suspension of registration of share transfers, 498n[19]
  Table A. *See* TABLE A
  Table B, continuance of former provisions, 9
  Table C, 530
  Table D, 530
  Table E, 530
  Table G, 531
  transfer of shares, restricting, 497
  unlimited company, 116, 530
  unlimited company having share capital, 87
  unlimited liability of directors, 627
  unregistered company, application of legislation, 100n[1]
  vacation of office of director, 634
  void provisions, 147, 148
  voting at members' meetings, 670
  Welsh, in, 90n[7]
ASSENT
  limited company re-registering as unlimited, to, 124n[12]
ASSETS
  company distributions. *See* COMPANY DISTRIBUTION; DIVIDEND
ASSIGNMENT
  office of director or manager, of, 550
AUDITOR
  improper dividend, liability, 722
  written resolutions, rights as to, 698
AUDITORS' REPORT
  initial accounts, 710
  last annual accounts, 708
  prospectus, in, 312
  redemption or purchase of own shares by private company, 236
BANKING COMPANY
  meaning, 117n[8]
  loans to directors, 601
  record of loans to directors, 606
BANKRUPTCY
  calls on shares, effect on, 428
  director of company, restriction, 553
  membership of company, cessation of, 435
  qualification shares, 558
  transmission of shares on, 518
BOARD MEETING
  company directors. *See* DIRECTOR OF COMPANY (meetings)
BREACH OF DUTY
  manager of company, by, liability, 650
BREACH OF TRUST
  director's liability, 617, 618
  persons sharing in, liability, 618
BRIBERY
  director of company, 593

BUSINESS NAME
  application of legislation, 166
  approval of Secretary of State, requiring, 168
  business: meaning, 166n[1]
  civil remedies for breach of disclosure requirements, 170
  corporate offences, 172
  disclosure requirements, 169, 170
  government or local authority, implying connection with, 167
  lawful: meaning, 167n[7]
  offences, 172
  permitted additions, 166
  persons subject to Business Names Act 1985 . . 166
  prohibition of certain names, 167
  regulations, 171
  relevant bodies for approval, 168n[4]
  stationery requirements, 169
  summary proceedings, 172n[2]
  words requiring approval, 168n[3, 4]
CALL ON SHARES
  meaning, 416
  advance payment distinguished, 417
  articles, according to, 418
  bankruptcy, effect of, 428
  conditions precedent, 419
  death of shareholder, 429
  directors, by, 418
  directors' shares, on, 422
  discretion as to, 420
  forfeited shares, 425, 526
  interest on, 424
  joint holders, 427
  manner of making, 418
  misrepresentation in offer document, defence of, 323
  notice of, 421
  recovery of, 426
  set-off against, 423
  special resolution limiting, 416
  transferred shares, on, 425
CAPITAL
  company, of. *See* SHARE CAPITAL
  redemption reserve. *See* CAPITAL REDEMPTION RESERVE
CAPITAL DUTY
  abolition, 280
  transitional provisions, 280n[2]
CAPITAL GAINS TAX
  reduction of capital, on, 215n[1]
CAPITAL REDEMPTION RESERVE
  meaning, 231
  application of Companies Act 1985 . . 231
  construction of references, 221
  redemption or purchase of shares wholly out of profits, 231
CERTIFICATE
  list of creditors on reduction of capital, as to, 262
  re-registration, of. *See under* REREGISTRATION
  share certificate. *See* SHARE CERTIFICATE

References are to paragraph numbers; superior figures refer to notes

DEBENTURE HOLDER
directors, appointment of, 546
promoter, remedies against, 47
register to be kept at registered office, 153

DECEIPT
misrepresentation in offer document. *See under* MISREPRESENTATION IN OFFER DOCU-MENT

DEFAMATION
newspaper reports of company meetings, privilege, 693

DEFENCE (PLEADING)
misrepresentation in offer document as, 323
misstatement in offer document, as to, 340

DELEGATION
directors' powers, 587

DIRECTOR OF COMPANY
meaning, 543n[1]
accountability, 592
additional, power to appointment, 548
administrator, removal by, 639
age limit, 552, 637
agent of company, as, 582
alternate directors, 640
appointment—
 additional directors, 548
 alternate directors, 640
 automatic restrictions, 551–554
 casual vacancies, 547
 debenture holders, by, 546
 defective, 545
 directors continuing on expiry of term, 549
 disclosure of interests, 564
 first directors, 544
 invalid, power to bind company, 631
 managing director, 588
 procedure, 546
 reappointment of retiring director, 546n[2], 634
 requirement for, 543
 restrictions—
  age limit, 552
  bankrupt, 553
  clergymen, 554
  disqualification order, 555
  secretary, 551
 Table A, 546n[2]
assignment of office, restriction, 550
authority for convening members' meetings, 663
board meeting. *See* meetings *below*
breach of duty by improper exercise of powers, 584
breach of trust, liability, 617, 618
breach of warranty of authority, liability, 616
bribes, 593
calls on shares by, 418
calls on shares of, 422
casual vacancies, 547, 638
chairman of board, 628n[2]
change of, entry on register, 560
clergyman, restriction, 554
committee meetings, 628n[3]

DIRECTOR OF COMPANY—*continued*
compensation for loss of office—
 disclosure requirements, 608, 609
 excluded payments, 610
 payments deemed to be, 610
 supplemental provisions, 610
 transfer of undertaking or shares, 609
consent to transfer of shares, 498
continuing after expiry of term, 549
contracts with company, 596
contribution, right to, 626
control by members, 589
credit transactions with company, 598, 599
declaration of interests in contracts, 594, 635
defect in appointment, 545
delegation of powers, 587
disclosure of interests—
 appointment, on, 564
 changes in interests, 565
 exceptions, 569
 interests in shares or debentures: meaning, 568
 investment exchange, notice to, 567
 offences, 570
 register. *See* REGISTER OF DIRECTORS' INTERESTS
 spouses and children, 566
 time limit, 564n[6], 565n[2]
disqualification order, 555
employment for more than 5 years, contract provisions, 563
exemption from liability, void provisions, 623
expenditure on duty to company, 600
expenses, 580
false and misleading statements, criminal liability, 354
fiduciary position in exercise of powers, 585
first—
 meaning, 544
 appointment, 544
fraudulent statements, 354
gift from promoter, 53
improper exercise of powers, 584
indemnity by company, right to, 625
indemnity insurance, 623
interests in contracts, declaration of, 594
lack of capacity, effect on person dealing in good faith, 583
liability—
 allotment restrictions, as to, 455
 avoidance of exemption, 623
 breach of trust, 617, 618
 breach of warranty of authority, 616
 company, to, 615
 contribution, right to, 626
 court's power to give relief, 624
 creditors, to, 616
 dissolution of company, on, 615
 exemption from, void provisions, 623
 false statements, 622
 improper dividend, 722
 indemnity, right to, 625

References are to paragraph numbers; superior figures refer to notes

References are to paragraph numbers; superior figures refer to notes

MISREPRESENTATION IN OFFER DOCU-
MENT—*continued*
director's liability, 622
false and misleading statements, criminal liability, 355
joinder of causes, 331
misstatement—
Financial Services Act 1986, under. *See* statutory compensation *below*
negligent, 338
negligent misrepresentation or negligent misstatement, 338
rectification of register, 322
remedies, 321
rescission—
cause of action, 324
compromise by surrender of shares, 329
forfeiture of shares, restraining, 330
grounds, 324
joinder of causes, 331
loss of right, 328
materiality, 327
misrepresentation of fact, 326
sub-underwriters, 325
specific performance, defence to, 323
statutory compensation—
contribution, right to, 341
costs, 342
defence pleading reasonable belief, 340
liability generally, 339
limitation period, 343
listed securities—
exemption from liability, 348
false or misleading particulars or prospectus,
347
liability, 345
persons responsible, 346
survival of actions, 344
unlisted securities—
application of statutory provisions, 353
exemption from liability, 351
false or misleading prospectus, 350
loss by contravention of provisions, 352
persons responsible, 349
MISSTATEMENT
offer document, in. *See under* MISREPRESEN-
TATION IN OFFER DOCUMENT
MORTGAGE
shares, of, 519
NAME
business. *See* BUSINESS NAME
company, of. *See under* COMPANY
NATIONALITY
company, of, 94
NEGLIGENCE
director's liability, 620
secretary of company, of, 650
NEWSPAPER
reports of company meetings, privilege, 693
NOTICE
change of registered office, of, 150
memorandum and articles, of, 145

NOTICE OF HEARING
confirmation of reduction of capital, as to, 263
NOTICE OF MEETING
amendments to resolutions, and, 690
directors' meetings, 628n[7]
elective resolution, as to, 686
insufficient notice of members' meeting, 664
members' meetings, 660
pecuniary advantage of director, resolution as to,
665
proxy statement, 664
requisition, convened on, 662
special resolution, as to, 683
ultra vires acts of directors, to ratify, 666
OBJECTION
creditors', by, to reduction of capital, 255
redemption or purchase of own shares by private
company, to, 237
OFFER (LISTED SECURITIES)
meaning, 286, 287
admission to list, 285
applications for listing, 284
approval of advertisements etc, 294, 295
conditions for offer to public in UK, 287
discontinuance and suspension of listing, 288
documents requiring approval, 295
European documents, recognition, 299
exemptions from disclosure, 291
general duty of disclosure, 289
issuer: meaning, 284n[4]
listing rules, 282
mini-prospectus, approval of, 295
misrepresentation and misstatement. *See* MIS-
REPRESENTATION IN OFFER DOCUMENT
mutual recognition of listing particulars and
prospectuses, 299
obligations of issuers, 293
offer notice—
meaning, 295n[4]
approval, 295
official listing of securities, 281
prospectus—
approval where no listing application, 297
publication, 298
statutory provisions, application of, 296
public in UK, to: meaning, 287
registration of listing particulars, 292
securities: meaning, 283
supplementary listing particulars, 290
OFFER (UNLISTED SECURITIES)
meaning, 304, 305
advertisements etc, restriction, 319
contraventions, 320
EEA market, investment advertisements
required by, 319
investments within scope of provisions, 301
misrepresentation and misstatement. *See* MIS-
REPRESENTATION IN OFFER DOCUMENT
mutual recognition of prospectuses, 303

References are to paragraph numbers; superior figures refer to notes

References are to paragraph numbers; superior figures refer to notes

SHARE IN COMPANY—*continued*
preference. *See* PREFERENCE SHARE
private company, supplementary provisions, 367
public company—
  charges on own shares, 214
  disclosure of interests. *See* disclosure of interests *above*
  held by or for, 366
purchase of own shares by company. *See* PURCHASE OF OWN SHARES
qualification shares. *See* QUALIFICATION SHARES
redeemable. *See* REDEEMABLE SHARES
register of acquisitions and disposals—
  company's investigations, interests found on, 749
  contents and form, 747
  deletions, restrictions, 754
  inspection, 747, 755
  removal of entries, 753
  statutory provisions, 747
repudiation of, 442
restrictions on, power of Secretary of State to impose, 745
settled, payment of dividend, 731
share premium account, 188
stop notice, 386
sub-division—
  notice to registrar, 208
  powers, 207
subscription or purchase, offers for. *See* OFFER (LISTED SECURITIES); OFFER (UNLISTED SECURITIES)
sub-underwriting, 199, 325
surrender—
  company limited by shares, 520
  transfer to nominee distinguished, 520
  unlimited company, 521
transfer. *See* SHARE TRANSFER
transferred, calls on, 425
transmission on death etc, 518
underwriting—
  meaning, 194
  allotment at discount, commission for, 197
  commission, 194
  option to take shares at par, 195
  reconstruction, 196
  statutory requirements, 194
  sub-underwriting, 199, 325
  underwriting letters, 198
unissued, cancellation of, 218
warrant. *See* SHARE WARRANT
SHARE ISSUE
meaning, 174, 446
allotment, on, 446
merger relief, 189
premium, at—
  extension or restriction of relief, 193
  group reconstructions, relief, 190
  merger relief, 189
  minimum premium value, 190

SHARE ISSUE—*continued*
premium, at—*continued*
  redemption of shares, 220
  retrospective relief, 191
  share premium account, 188
  supplementary provisions, 192
restriction on allotment where not fully subscribed, 452
time of, 446
Treasury consent to, 357
underwriting. *See under* SHARE IN COMPANY
SHARE OPTION
dealing by directors and families, prohibition, 614
provisions generally, 377
relevant debentures, 614n[5]
relevant shares, 614n[4]
SHARE TRANSFER
application for registration, 510
blank, in, 507
brokers transfer, application of provisions, 506n[4]
certification of, 512
compulsory, 499
conditions precedent, observance of, 497
consent of directors to, 498
contract for sale of shares, 490
contravention of articles, in, 496
effect of registration, 509
execution of, 505
exercise of power to refuse to register, 498
false certification, liability, 512
forged—
  compensation for loss, 516
  liability and remedies, 515
  rectification of register, 510
form of, 505
individual shareholding limited, where, 501
inland bearer instruments, 495
insolvent company, 503
joint stock companies, 496n[2]
married women, by, 504
member indebted to company, by, 502
mentally disordered persons, 504
methods, 496
minor, to, 504
non-execution by transferee, 508
note on share certificate as to, 489
notice of refusal to register, 500
overseas branch register, 401
personal representative, by, 504
persons able to transfer, 504
pre-emption provisions, 499
proper instrument of: meaning, 505n[3]
purchaser's obligation, 492
rectification of register, 510
refusal to register, 496, 498, 500
registration—
  application for, 510
  effect, 509
  notice of refusal, 500
  procedure, 510
  production of share certificate, 511
  rectification, 510

References are to paragraph numbers; superior figures refer to notes

References are to paragraph numbers; superior figures refer to notes

Words and Phrases

These Words and Phrases relate only to entries appearing in Volume 7(1). A consolidated Words and Phrases for Volumes 7(1) and 7(2) appears in Volume 7(2); and a consolidated Words and Phrases for Volumes 7(1), 7(2) and 7(3) appears in Volume 7(3).

Words in parentheses indicate the context in which the word or phrase is used

References are to paragraph numbers; superior figures refer to notes

References are to paragraph numbers; superior figures refer to notes